Special Edition Using

Microsoft® Windows® 2000 Server

Roger Jennings

201 W. 103rd Street
Indianapolis, Indiana 46290

Contents

Part I: ...

1. Windows 2000 Server for NT 4.0 Users—What's New 19
2. Understanding IP, DNS Namespaces, and TCP/IP 63
3. Introducing the Active Directory and LDAP 93
4. Optimizing Your Active Directory Topology 147
5. Choosing and Testing Migration Strategies 193
6. Preparing NT 4.0 for Windows 2000 Server Migration 259
7. Specifying Server and Data Storage Hardware 297

Part II: Deploying Windows 2000 Server 339

8. Deploying Windows 2000 Production Servers 341
9. Installing RAID and Removable Media Systems 413
10. Working with the Windows 2000 Registry 453
11. Setting Up Key- and Certificate-Based Security 485
12. Interoperating with NetWare Servers 519
13. Integrating UNIX and Linux Networks 545

Part III: Delivering Network Resources to Clients 583

14. Providing Clients with DHCP and WINS 585
15. Establishing Group Policies, User Accounts, and Logons 617
16. Managing Server Shares and the Distributed File System 675
17. Installing Network Printers 723
18. Connecting Windows 2000, NT, and 9x Clients 757
19. Serving Macintosh, Windows 3.11, and DOS Clients 791
20. Supplying IntelliMirror and Application Installation Services 827
21. Using Remote Installation Services 857
22. Monitoring and Tuning Your Network 889
23. Optimizing, Backing Up, and Restoring Your Servers 919

Part IV: Wide-Area Networking, Intranets, and the Internet 981

24. Communicating with Remote Sites and Domains 983
25. Managing Remote Access and Routing Services 1023
26. Setting Up a Virtual Private Network 1075
27. Administering Internet Information Server 5.0 1105

Part V: Advanced Management and Enterprise Systems 1137

28. Managing Transaction and Messaging Services 1139
29. Deploying Windows Terminal Services 1195
30. Clustering with Windows 2000 Advanced Server 1227

Part VI: Appendixes 1253

A. Installing and Using the ADS125 Active Directory Application 1255
B. Glossary 1287
CD Streaming with Windows Media Technologies 4 CD1
Index 1317

Special Edition Using Microsoft® Windows® 2000 Server

Copyright© 2000 by Que Corporation

All rights reserved. No part of this book shall be reproduced, stored in a retrieval system, or transmitted by any means, electronic, mechanical, photocopying, recording, or otherwise, without written permission from the publisher. No patent liability is assumed with respect to the use of the information contained herein. Although every precaution has been taken in the preparation of this book, the publisher and authors assume no responsibility for errors or omissions. Nor is any liability assumed for damages resulting from the use of the information contained herein.

International Standard Book Number: 0-7897-2122-8

Library of Congress Catalog Card Number: 99-65445

Printed in the United States of America

First Printing: October 2000

02 01 00   4 3 2 1

Trademarks

All terms mentioned in this book that are known to be trademarks or service marks have been appropriately capitalized. Que Corporation cannot attest to the accuracy of this information. Use of a term in this book should not be regarded as affecting the validity of any trademark or service mark. FireWire is a registered trademark of Apple Computer, Inc.

Warning and Disclaimer

Every effort has been made to make this book as complete and as accurate as possible, but no warranty or fitness is implied. The information provided is on an "as is" basis. The authors and the publisher shall have neither liability nor responsibility to any person or entity with respect to any loss or damages arising from the information contained in this book or from the use of the CD or programs accompanying it.

Associate Publisher
Dean Miller

Senior Acquisitions Editor
Jenny L. Watson

Development Editors
Lorna Gentry
Jill Hayden
Rick Kughen

Managing Editor
Thomas F. Hayes

Senior Editor
Susan Ross Moore

Copy Editors
Nancy Albright
Maryann Steinhart

Indexer
Aamir Burki

Proofreaders
Jeanne Clark
Juli Cook
Bob LaRoche
Kaylene Riemen

Technical Editors
David Bixler
Wayne Gardner
Doug Mitchell
Greg Newman
Ariel Silverstone
John Wiley
Daniel F. Wygant

Team Coordinator
Vicki Harding

Media Developers
Craig Atkins
Jay Payne

Interior Designer
Ruth Lewis

Cover Designers
Dan Armstrong
Ruth Lewis

Production
Gloria Schurick

Contents

Introduction 1

An Operating System for the Millennium 2

Who Should Read This Book? 4

How This Book Is Organized 5
    Part I: Planning Your Microsoft Windows 2000 Server Installation 5
    Part II: Deploying Windows 2000 Server 6
    Part III: Delivering Network Resources to Clients 7
    Part IV: Wide-Area Networking, Intranets, and the Internet 8
    Part V: Advanced Management and Enterprise Systems 8
    Part VI: Appendixes 9
    The Accompanying CD-ROM 9

How This Book Is Designed 10

Bibliography 11
    Que Books About Windows 2000 Server and Related Topics 11
    Que Books About Windows 2000 Professional 12
    Periodicals That Emphasize Windows 2000 Topics 13
    Online Windows 2000 Resources 14

I Planning Your Microsoft Windows 2000 Server Installation 17

1 Windows 2000 Server for NT 4.0 Users—What's New 19

The Long Road from Cairo 20
    Upgrade Incentives 20
    Upgrade Uncertainties 21

Server Versions 21

Active Directory 23
    Active Directory Schema 23
    Windows 2000 Domain Architecture 24
    Domain Namespaces and DNS 25
    Group and User Hierarchies 28
    The Active Directory Upgrade Process 30
    The Active Directory Migration Tool 30
    Active Directory Administration 33

Security Services 36
    Security Principals 38
    Kerberos Authentication 38
    Smart Card Logon 39

Networking and Internet Services 40
    IP and TCP/IP 40
    ATM 43
    Internet Information Server 5.0 44
    Interoperability 46

Storage, File, and Print Services 46
    Storage Management 47
    Distributed File System 50
    Print Services 51

Remote Communication Services 52

Streaming Media Services 53

Application Services 56

Terminal Services 57

Kernel Architecture Upgrades 58

Integration with Microsoft Exchange 2000 59

MCSE Corner: An Introduction 60

2 Understanding IP, DNS Namespaces, and TCP/IP 63

Decoding and Assigning IP Addresses 64
    IP Address Notation 65

IP Address Restrictions 65
IP Address Allocation 66
IP Subnets and Routers 67
IP Next-Generation Protocol 72

Understanding IP Datagrams 73
IP Datagram Structure 73
Testing for Datagram Errors 75

Matching IP and NIC Addresses with ARP 76

Resolving Names with the Domain Name System 77
DNS Namespaces 77
DNS Components 79
DNS Zones 80
Assignment of Internet Domain Names 81

Taking Advantage of Windows 2000 Server's DNS Service 82
Dynamic DNS 82
Initial DDNS Configuration with Active Directory 83
DDNS Management 85

Communicating Reliably with TCP/IP 86
TCP Ports and Processes 87
TCP Headers 88

Taking Chances with UDP Delivery 89

Troubleshooting 90

MCSE Corner: Understanding IP, DNS Namespaces, and TCP/IP 91
70-216 Implementing and Administering a Microsoft Windows 2000 Network Infrastructure 91
70-221 Designing a Microsoft Windows 2000 Network Infrastructure 91

3 Introducing the Active Directory and LDAP 93

Understanding the Role of Directory Services 94

Learning Active Directory Terminology 95

Installing Active Directory 96

Administering Active Directory 105
Administering Domains and Trusts 105
Viewing Sites and Services 113
Working with Groups, Users, and Computers 114

Getting Acquainted with LDAP 121
Entries and Attributes 123
Namespaces and Naming Conventions 123
Operations 124

Using the Active Directory Schema Manager 124
Installing Schema Manager 125
Viewing the AD Namespace 126
Viewing and Adding AD Class Properties 128
Assigning Optional Attribute Values to AD Objects 129

Taking Advantage of LDAP OUs 132
Creating Domain OUs 132
Moving Objects Into and Between OUs 133

Searching for AD Objects with LDAP 135
Using the AD Query Feature 136
Applying LDAP Filters 138

Programming Directory-Enabled Applications with ADSI 139
ADSI 2.5 and Visual Basic 140
The ADSI25 Visual Basic Application 141

Troubleshooting   143

MCSE Corner: Introducing the Active Directory and LDAP   144
    70-217   Implementing and Administering a Microsoft Windows 2000 Directory Services Infrastructure   144
    70-219   Designing a Microsoft Windows 2000 Directory Services Infrastructure   145

4 Optimizing Your Active Directory Topology   147

Starting the Domain Planning Process   148
    Elements of Domain Topology   149
    Single-Master Operations   150
    Email Directory Integration   151
    User Attributes and Active Directory Database Size   153
    Integration with Other Directories   153

Designing Single-Tree Directories   154
    The OakLeaf University Network Topology Example   154
    The Single-Domain Model   155
    The Parent-Child Model   158

Adding a Sample Child Domain   160
    Creating a Child Domain with Dcpromo   160
    Setting Up DNS Zones for the Child Domain   166
    Changing Child Domain Attributes   170
    Administering Other Domains from a Child DC   172

Administering a Child Domain   172
    Adding OUs, Groups, and Users to a Child Domain   172
    Moving OUs, Groups, and Users Within a Domain   173
    Moving a Child Domain to a New Site   176

Establishing Security Policies for a Child Domain   181
    Using the Domain Security Policy Console   182
    Viewing All Group Policies for the Domain   185

Working with Enterprise-Scale Directories   187

Changing Your Domain Model   187

Administering Domains with Windows 2000 Professional   188

Troubleshooting   190

MCSE Corner: Optimizing Your Active Directory Topology   191
    70-217   Implementing and Administering a Microsoft Windows 2000 Directory Services Infrastructure   191
    70-219   Designing a Windows 2000 Directory Services Infrastructure   191

5 Choosing and Testing Migration Strategies   193

Developing a Windows 2000 Migration Plan   194
    An Historical Perspective on Windows NT Upgrades   194
    The Migration Timeline   195

Setting Up a Migration Test Facility   195
    Equipment Requirements   195
    Basic Upgrade Emulation Steps   197

Migrating a Single-Domain Configuration   198
    Creating an Upgradeable PDC from a BDC in an Existing Domain   198
    Installing a New PDC and Adding Accounts with ADSI25   200
    Upgrading the Test PDC to Windows 2000   204
    Configuring AD on the Test Domain Controller   206

Verifying the AD Upgrade 208
Confirming Client Connectivity 211

Moving Accounts from the Users Container to OUs 211
Using Custom Filters to Classify Users by Group Membership 212
Classifying Users by Account Description 216

Reorganizing Migrated Security Groups 220
Changing the DC to Native Mode 220
Creating and Nesting Global Security Groups 221

Delegating Administrative Responsibilities for OUs 223
Using the Delegation of Control Wizard 223
Testing Delegation of Control 228

Testing Migration of Multiple Domains 230

Emulating Domain Migration with the Active Directory Migration Tool 231
Installing ADMT on a Windows 2000 Domain Controller 233
Running a Groups and Users Migration Test 237
Migrating an Entire Group Structure 245
Preparing Migration Reports 246
Migrating Windows NT Computer Accounts 248
Updating Service Accounts 253
Exploring Other ADMT Features 255

Troubleshooting 255

MCSE Corner: Choosing and Testing Migration Strategies 257
70-215 Installing, Configuring, and Administering Microsoft Windows 2000 Server 258
70-222 Upgrading from Microsoft Windows NT 4.0 to Microsoft Windows 2000 258

6 Preparing NT 4.0 for Windows 2000 Server Migration 259

Getting Ready for Windows 2000 Server 260

Moving from NetBEUI to TCP/IP 261
Choosing Internal IP Addresses 262
Adding the TCP/IP Protocol and Related Services to a NetBEUI-Only Server 263
Upgrading BDCs and Testing IP Connectivity 266

Automating Client TCP/IP Settings with DHCP 267
Creating a DHCP Scope 268
Setting DHCP Options and Attributes 269
Adding a Backup DHCP Server 271

Enabling NetBIOS Name Resolution with WINS 272

Providing DNS Name Resolution 275
Creating a Primary Zone with DNS Manager 276
Enabling WINS Lookup 279
Testing DNS 280
Adding a Secondary DNS Server 281

Adding Fixed DNS and WINS Addresses to Servers 282

Migrating Client PCs to DHCP, WINS, and DNS 284
Installing TCP/IP 284
Verifying DHCP, WINS, and DNS Operation 285
Eliminating Client Reliance on NetBEUI 287

Cleaning Up User and Group
Accounts   287
   Listing and Scavenging User
Accounts   288
   Creating Group Membership
Files   291

Troubleshooting   293

MCSE Corner: Preparing NT 4.0 for
Windows 2000 Server Migration   295
   70-215   Installing, Configuring, and
Administering Microsoft Windows
2000 Server   295
   70-222   Upgrading from Microsoft
Windows NT 4.0 to Microsoft
Windows 2000   295

7 Specifying Server and Data Storage Hardware   297

Setting Server Objectives   298
   Maximizing Availability   298
   Improving Performance   302
   Delivering Scalability   304

Creating a Secure, Controlled Server
Environment   307
   Physical Security   307
   Power Supply and Conditioning
Systems   308
   Ambient Temperature Control   310

Getting the Most from Your New Server
Expenditures   311

Upgrading Existing Servers for Windows
2000   313

Taking Advantage of Windows 2000
Hardware Management   315
   Using Device Manager   316
   Deciding on Windows 2000 Driver
Signing   323

Choosing the Optimum RAID
System   325
   SCSI Drives for RAID Systems   325
   Common RAID Classifications   329

   Software-Based RAID   329
   Hardware RAID Controllers and
Subsystems   330
   Fibre Channel Subsystems and
Adapters   331

Troubleshooting   333

MCSE Corner: An Overview of the
Exams   334
   70-215   Installing, Configuring, and
Administering Microsoft Windows
2000 Server   334
   70-216   Implementing and
Administering a Microsoft Windows
2000 Network Infrastructure   335
   70-217   Implementing and
Administering a Microsoft Windows
2000 Directory Services
Infrastructure   335
   70-219   Designing a Microsoft
Windows 2000 Directory Services
Infrastructure   335
   70-220   Designing Security for a
Microsoft Windows 2000
Network   336
   70-221   Designing a Microsoft
Windows 2000 Network
Infrastructure   336
   70-222   Upgrading from Microsoft
Windows NT 4.0 to Microsoft
Windows 2000   337
   70-240   Microsoft Windows 2000
Accelerated Exam for MCPs Certified
on Microsoft Windows NT 4.0   337

II Deploying Windows 2000 Server   339

8 Deploying Windows 2000 Production Servers   341

Planning Migration Tactics   342

Performing Domain Upgrades   343
   Sequencing Multiple-Domain
Upgrades   343

Upgrading a Single Domain   345
Recovering from an Upgrade Disaster   347

Restructuring Domains   348

Optimizing Drive Partitioning   350

Upgrading a Windows NT 4.0 Production Server   352
Starting the Operating System Upgrade   354
Enduring the Unattended Setup Cycle   356
Testing the Upgrade to Windows 2000   357
Verifying DNS, WINS, and DHCP Upgrades   359

Adding Other Services, Programs, and Tools to the DC   361

Promoting the PDC to Active Directory   363

Verifying the Active Directory Upgrade   367
Testing Primary DC Operations and Authorizing Zone Transfers   367
Checking Trusts from Windows NT Domains   373
Testing Client DHCP, WINS, and DNS Services   375

Upgrading and Testing BDCs   376
Upgrading the BDC   377
Testing the Domain's Second DC   379
Adding Backup Services   379

Adding and Removing DCs in a Windows 2000 Domain   380
Adding a Windows 2000 DC at a Remote Site   380
Creating an Additional Global Catalog Server   381
Establishing Secondary DNS Zones   381
Adding a New Windows NT BDC to an Existing Domain   382

Removing a DC from a Domain with More Than One DC   383
Performing Post-Upgrade Operations   383

Installing Windows 2000 on a New Server   384
Running Windows 2000 Server Setup   385
Installing the DC for the First Domain   388
Verifying Operability of the New Domain   389

Upgrading Resource Domains   392
Upgrading the Resource Domain's PDC   394
Recovering from a Failed Child Domain Promotion   396

Throwing the Native-Mode Switch   397

Using ADMT to Restructure Windows NT Domains   398

Setting Security Policies for Domains and Domain Controllers   400

Recovering from a Disabled System   403
Preparing for Recovery   404
Backing Up System State   405
Running in Safe Mode   405
Using the Recovery Console   407

Seizing the FSMO Roles of a Failed DC   408

Troubleshooting   409

MCSE Corner: Deploying Windows 2000 Production Servers   410
70-215   Installing, Configuring and Administering Windows 2000 Server   410
70-217   Implementing and Administering a Microsoft Windows 2000 Directory Services Infrastructure   411

70-222 Upgrading from Microsoft Windows NT 4.0 to Microsoft Windows 2000 411

9 Installing RAID and Removable Media Systems 413

Enhancing Storage Management with Windows 2000 414

Understanding Windows 2000 Storage Concepts 416
   Dynamic Disks, Basic Disks, and Volumes 416
   Logical Disk Manager 418

Using the Disk Management Snap-In 418
   Implementing Dynamic Disks 418
   Creating a Simple Volume 419
   Extending the Volume Size 421
   Creating a Spanned Volume 422
   Deleting a Volume 423

Reviewing Fundamental Concepts of NTFS 424
   NTFS 5 Clusters 424
   Master File Table 425
   NTFS Security 426
   Sparse File Support 426
   NTFS Change Journals 426
   Reparse Points and File System Filters 427
   Volume Mount Points 427
   NTFS Data Streams 428
   Unicode Support 428
   Implementing NTFS Compression 428
   Additional NTFS Features 430

Working with RAID Implementations 430
   Understanding RAID Levels 431
   RAID 0 432
   RAID 1 433
   Stacked RAID—RAID 0/1 434
   RAID 5 435

RAID Recovery 437
   Creating a RAID-5 Stripe Set 437
   Recovering from Disk Failure with RAID 5 438
   Creating a Mirror (RAID 1) Volume 439
   Breaking the Mirror 440
   Recovering from System Disk Failure with RAID 1 440

Using Removable Storage and Media Pools 442
   Removable Storage Management Snap-In 442
   Media Pools 443
   Physical Locations 445
   Work Queue 446
   Operator Requests 447

Using Windows 2000 Disk Management Tools 448
   Disk Defragmenter 448
   Chkdsk 450
   Disk Cleanup 450

Troubleshooting 451

MCSE Corner: Installing RAID, Backup, and Removable Media Systems 452

10 Working with the Windows 2000 Registry 453

What's New in Windows 2000 Server's Registry 454

Tracking Configuration Settings in the Registry 454
   Types of Registry Information 455
   Registry-Based Configuration Management 455
   Registry Organization 456
   The Danger of Changing Registry Values 457
   How the Windows 2000 and Windows 9x Registries Vary 459

Viewing the Registry's Organization 459
  Registry Editor Root Keys 460
  Registry Files and Hives 461
  Value Entries 464

Understanding Important Root Keys, Keys, and Subkeys 466
  The HKEY_LOCAL_MACHINE Root Key 466
  HKEY_CURRENT_CONFIG and Hardware Profiles 471
  HKEY_CLASSES_ROOT and File Associations 472
  HKEY_CURRENT_USER and User Profiles 473
  HKEY_USERS for Local Logons 474

Using the Windows 2000 System Information Tool 474

Backing Up the Registry 476

Inspecting Another Computer's Registry 478

Maintaining Server Registry Security 479

Troubleshooting 481

MCSE Corner: Exam Types 482

11 Setting Up Key- and Certificate-Based Security 485

Enhancing File and Network Security 486

Understanding Public Key Encryption 486
  Cryptography and Key-Based Encryption 486
  Certificate Authorities and PKI 487
  Windows 2000 Encrypting File System (EFS) 488
  IP Security (IPSec) in Windows 2000 489
  Windows 2000 Certificate Services 489

Encrypting and Decrypting Files 489
  Understanding the Encrypting File System 490
  Encrypting File System Architecture 491
  Encrypting Folders and Files in Windows Explorer 492
  Encrypting Folders and Files with the Cipher Command 494

Configuring Servers for Encryption 495
  Distributed EFS—Understanding the Trusted for Delegation Option 495
  Providing Encrypted Data Transmission with IPSec 497
  Configuring IPSec 498
  Understanding IP Security Policies 499
  Implementing IP Security Policies 500

Providing Encrypted File Recovery 501
  Implementing Data Recovery Agents 502
  Securing the DRA Private Key 504

Establishing and Managing Certificate Authority Servers 506
  Choosing a Certificate Authority Type 506
  Choosing Advanced Options 507
  Entering CA Identifying Information and Choosing a Data Storage Location 508
  Installing Certificate Services 508
  Using the Certification Authority MMC Snap-In 510
  Viewing Certificate Information Using the MMC Snap-In 511
  Revoking Certificates Using the MMC Snap-In 512

Working with User Certificates 512
  Configuring the Certificates Snap-In 513
  Requesting a Certificate 513

Troubleshooting   515

MCSE Corner: Setting Up Key- and Certificate-Based Security   516
   70-215   Installing, Configuring, and Administering Microsoft Windows 2000 Server   516
   70-216   Implementing and Administering a Microsoft Windows 2000 Network Infrastructure   516
   70-220   Designing Security for a Microsoft Windows 2000 Network   517

12 Interoperating with NetWare Servers   519

Introducing NetWare   520

Comparison of Protocols   521

Comparing NetWare and Windows 2000   522

Integrating Windows 2000 Server into a Predominantly NetWare Environment   524
   Installing IPX   524
   Sharing Windows 2000 Files and Printers   526
   File and Print Services for NetWare   528

Integrating NetWare Server into a Predominantly Windows Environment   529
   Installing Gateway Services for NetWare (GSNW)   529
   Using Gateway Services for NetWare   530

Directory Synchronization   534
   Installing Microsoft Directory Synchronization Services   535
   Creating a Synchronization Session   536
   Performing the Synchronization   539

Troubleshooting   542

MCSE Corner: Interoperating with NetWare Servers   544

13 Integrating UNIX and Linux Networks   545

Introducing UNIX Integration Methods   546

Using Telnet   546
   The Telnet Client Program   546
   The Telnet Server Program   547
   The Telnet Protocol   547
   Windows 2000 Telnet Client Support   547
   HyperTerminal's Telnet Client   550
   Telnet Advantages   552
   Telnet Disadvantages   553
   Configuring Windows 2000 for Telnet Server Operation   553

Taking Advantage of X Window   556
   X Window History   557
   X Window Servers for Windows 2000   557

Integrating Windows and UNIX Printers   558
   Providing Print Services to UNIX Clients   558
   Accessing Printers on UNIX Servers for Windows 2000 Clients   560

Using the File Transfer Protocol   561
   The FTP Command-Line Client   561
   FTP Support in Internet Explorer 5.0+   562

Running Microsoft Services for UNIX   563
   SFU 2.0 Contents   564
   SFU 2.0 Installation   565
   Configuring the Mapping Server   566
   Configuring the Windows 2000 NFS Server   569

Sharing a Windows 2000 Folder with NFS Clients   571
Configuring the Windows 2000 NFS Client   572
Connecting to a UNIX NFS Server   575
Integrating UNIX and Windows Directories   577

Troubleshooting   580

MCSE Corner: Question Types, Part 1   581
Multiple Choice   581
Choose All That Apply   581
Select and Place   582

III Delivering Network Resources to Clients   583

14 Providing Clients with DHCP and WINS   585

Assigning IP Addresses and Resolving NetBIOS Names   586

Understanding the Dynamic Host Configuration Protocol   586
DHCP Client and Server Communication   587
New Features of Windows 2000 DHCP   588

Installing the DHCP Service   589

Configuring DHCP with the DHCP Snap-In   590
Creating a DHCP Scope with the New Scope Wizard   591
Specifying DHCP Options   593
Activating and Testing the New DHCP Scope   597
Viewing DHCP Statistics and Properties   600

Using the DHCP Relay Agent   601

Understanding the Windows Internet Naming Service   604

Installing and Configuring WINS   606
Managing Local and Remote WINS Servers   606
Designating Replication Partners   610

Troubleshooting   613

MCSE Corner: Providing Clients with DHCP and WINS   615
70-216   Implementing and Administering a Microsoft Windows 2000 Network Infrastructure   615
70-221   Designing a Microsoft Windows 2000 Network Infrastructure   616

15 Establishing Group Policies, User Accounts, and Logons   617

Understanding Windows 2000's Group Policies   618
Client Computer and User Settings   618
Group Policy Hierarchy and Inheritance   620
Security Group Filtering   620
AD Structures for Group Policy Optimization   621

Using the Group Policy Snap-In to Edit Group Policy Objects   622
Navigating the Default Domain Policy   623
Enforcing Computer Security Policies   625
Understanding Administrative Templates   628
Exploring User Configuration   631

Creating New Group Policy Objects   632
Importing Workstation Security Settings Policies   635

Linking Group Policies Across Domains   638
Establishing Group Policies for OUs   640

Designing and Populating Security Group Structures   643
Creating a New Global Group Structure   644
Adding Computer Accounts to New Security Groups   648
Reorganizing Existing Groups   649

Filtering GPOs with Security Groups   650
Exempting Administrators from GPO Application   650
Exempting Other Groups from GPO Application   652
Delegating Administrative Control of GPO Linkage   653

Working with User Accounts   654
Adding New User Accounts   654
Adding Optional Attribute Values   655

Specifying User Profiles for Downlevel Clients   658
Understanding User Profiles   658
Establishing Mandatory User Profiles   660

Implementing Downlevel System Policies   663
Applying System Policies to User Accounts   665
Working with Computer System Policies   668

Setting Up User Home Folders   670
Common Versus Individual Home Folder Shares   670
Logon Scripts for Mapping Home Folders   671

Troubleshooting   672

MCSE Corner: Establishing Group Policies, User Accounts, and Logons   673

16 Managing Server Shares and the Distributed File System   675

Understanding the Principles of File Sharing   676
Default Shares and Their Properties   676
File Sharing Security   678
High-Level Folder and File Permissions   680
Low-Level Folder and File Permissions   682

Creating New Shared Folders   683
Using the ADSI25 Application to Generate a Folder Hierarchy   683
Assigning Hierarchical Share and Folder Permissions   686
Creating Second-Tier Faculty$, Staff$, and Students$ Shares with Read Permission   688
Creating Third-Tier Faculty$ Shares with Write and Modify Permissions   691
Creating Third-Tier Students$ Shares with Multiple Group Permissions   693

Mapping Shares to Drives with Windows 2000 Logon Scripts   694

Sharing Folders on Your Intranet   697

Publishing Shares in Active Directory   701

Indexing File Contents   703
Configuring Index Service Prior to Startup   704
Starting and Testing the Indexing Service   706

Taking Advantage of the Distributed File System   707
   Understanding Dfs Terminology   708
   Creating Dfs Roots   710
   Populating Dfs Roots by Linking Shares   712
   Testing Dfs Shares with Windows 2000 and Downlevel Clients   715

Using the File Replication Service with Dfs   716
   Creating a Fault-Tolerant Share Replica Set   716
   Viewing FRS Entries in Active Directory   718

Troubleshooting   719

MCSE Corner: Managing Server Shares and the Distributed File System   720

17 Installing Network Printers   723

What's New in Windows 2000 Network Printing   724
   Changes to Printer Setup   724
   Administration Improvements   724
   User Benefits   725

Understanding the Printing Process with a Shared Printer   725

Installing the Three Types of Shared Printers   726
   Installing with Plug and Play   727
   Installing a Network-Attached Printer   727
   Configuring a Network-Attached Printer   728
   Configuring a Server-Connected or Workstation-Owned Printer   732

Configuring a Shared Printer After Installation   734

Configuring Print Server Properties   739

Connecting Clients to Shared Printers   742
   Installing the Directory Service Client on Downlevel Computers   742
   Publishing Printers Shared by Downlevel Servers or Workstations   743
   Finding and Installing Shared Printers Published in Active Directory   745
   Installing Unpublished Printers   747

Taking Advantage of Internet Printing   748
   How Internet Printing Works   749
   Installing Internet Printing   749
   Managing a Printer over the Internet or an Intranet   750

Establishing Group Policies for Printing   752

Troubleshooting   754

MCSE Corner: Installing Network Printers   756

18 Connecting Windows 2000, NT, and 9x Clients   757

Assessing the Networking Requirements of 32-Bit Windows Clients   758

Preparing for Windows 2000 Client Upgrades   759
   Upgrades Versus Clean Installations   760
   Network Interface Card Issues   761

Creating Windows 2000 Client Computer Accounts   762

Delegating Authority for Computer Account Creation   764

Setting Up Windows 2000 Client Networking   765
   Performing a Standard Installation of Windows 2000 Professional   766

Exploring Network Adapter Device Properties 767
Setting Local Area Connection Properties 770
Specifying Fixed IP Addresses for Clients 772
Changing Network Adapters 774

Connecting Windows NT 4.0 Clients 775
Setting Up a New Windows NT 4.0 Client 776
Altering the Networking Properties of Windows NT Clients 777

Accommodating Windows 9x Clients 780
Setting Up a New Windows 98 Client for Networking 780
Adding a Network Printer 783
Setting Network and NIC Properties 784

Installing and Testing the Directory Services Client for Windows 9x 786

Troubleshooting 788

MCSE Corner: Connecting Windows 2000, NT, and 9x Clients 789
70-064 Implementing and Supporting Microsoft Windows 95, 70-073 Implementing and Supporting Microsoft Windows NT Workstation 4.0, 70-098 Implementing and Supporting Microsoft Windows 98, and 70-210 Installing, Configuring, and Administering Microsoft Windows 2000 Professional 790
70-215 Installing, Configuring, and Administering Microsoft Windows 2000 Server 790
70-217 Implementing and Administering a Microsoft Windows 2000 Directory Services Infrastructure 790
Troubleshooting 790

19 Serving Macintosh, Windows 3.11, and DOS Clients 791

Integrating Other Clients with Windows 2000 792

Understanding the Macintosh Networking System 792
Understanding the AppleTalk Protocol Layers 793
The AppleTalk Numbering and Zone Systems 794
AppleTalk Routing 795

Integrating a Macintosh Client into the Network 795
Installing the AppleTalk Protocol 796
Configuring AppleTalk Routing 796

Adding Print Services for Macintosh 799
Connecting Windows 2000 Server to AppleTalk Printers 799
Connecting Macintoshes to Windows 2000 Printers 802
Sharing a Printer 803
Connecting a Macintosh Client to a Windows 2000 Macintosh Printer 803

Installing, Configuring, and Using File Services for Macintosh 803
Installing File Services for Macintosh 804
Setting System-Wide File Server Parameters 804
Enabling Microsoft Authentication on Macintosh Clients 806
Enabling Macintosh User Accounts to Interact with Windows 2000 Accounts 807
Sharing Volumes with Macintosh Clients 808
Setting Volume Properties 811
Working with the Macintosh File Structure 812

Setting File and Creator Types on Shared Files   812
Monitoring Macintosh Sessions   814
Using Remote Access to Support Macintosh Dial-in Clients   815

Upgrading Windows for Workgroups 3.11 Clients to TCP/IP   815
Obtaining the TCP/IP-32 Setup Files   816
Installing TCP/IP-32   816
Testing WfW 3.11 TCP/IP Clients   819

Adding TCP/IP to the Network Client v3.0 for MS-DOS and Windows   820
Creating Client Installation Disks   821
Adding TCP/IP to the Client for DOS   821

Troubleshooting   823

MCSE Corner: Serving DOS, Windows 3.11, and Macintosh Clients   825

20 Supplying IntelliMirror and Application Installation Services   827

Defining IntelliMirror   828

Managing User Settings   829
Group Policies   829
Roaming User Profiles   833

Providing User Data Management   835
Offline Files   836
Synchronization Manager   841
Disk Quotas   844

Using the Application Installation Service   846
Requirements of Application Installation Service   847

Setting Up a Typical Software Installation   848
Viewing and Changing Package Properties   849
Completing and Testing the Software Installation   851

Redirecting Folders   852

Troubleshooting   854

MCSE Corner: Supplying IntelliMirror and Application Installation Services   855
70-215   Installing, Configuring, and Administering Microsoft Windows 2000 Server   855
70-217   Implementing and Administering a Microsoft Windows 2000 Directory Services Infrastructure   855
70-219   Designing a Microsoft Windows 2000 Directory Services Infrastructure   856

21 Using Remote Installation Services   857

Simplifying Standardized Installations with Remote Installation Services   858

Preparing for Installation: RIS Components Checklist   860
Client Requirements for RIS   862
Server Requirements to Support RIS   864

Installing and Configuring RIS   865
Installing RIS   865
Configuring an RIS Share for Testing   866
Configuring RIS Server Properties   868

Creating and Testing a Remote Installation Boot Disk   872
Performing a Test of Automatic OS Installation   872
Adding the Domain User Account to a Local Group   876
Reviewing the New Client Computer Account Properties   876
Editing the SIF File   877

Setting Group Policy for RIS Installation   879

Using RIPrep to Create a Corporate-Standard Installation Image   882
   Using the Remote Installation Preparation Wizard   883
   Testing the SYSPREP Image   885

Troubleshooting   886

MCSE Corner: Using Remote Installation Services   888
   70-217   Implementing and Administering a Windows 2000 Directory Services Infrastructure   888
   70-220   Designing Security for a Microsoft Windows 2000 Network   888

22 Monitoring and Tuning Your Network   889

Staying Ahead of Network Problems   890

Using Performance Monitor's Network Counters   890
   Installing the Network Monitor Driver   892
   Starting PerfMon and Adding Basic Network Counters to SysMon   892
   Altering the Scale and Appearance of the Graph   893
   Saving and Reusing a Custom PerfMon Configuration   896

Simulating Network Traffic Load for Performance Testing   896
   Adding Baseline Network Traffic with the NetTraffic Application   897
   Measuring Simulated Network Traffic with SysMon   898
   Using Effective Network Performance Data   901

Recording Network Traffic Data with Counter Logs   902
   Configuring Counter Logs   902
   Enabling the Performance Logs and Alerts Service to Connect to Remote Servers   905

Logging and Viewing Counter Data   906

Setting Alerts on Out-of-Bounds Counter Values   907

Monitoring Network Activity with NetMon   911
   Setting Up NetMon   911
   Displaying and Analyzing Captured Frame Data   912

Understanding the Browsing Process   914

Troubleshooting   916

MCSE Corner: Monitoring and Tuning Your Network   917
   70-215   Installing, Configuring, and Administering Microsoft Windows 2000 Server   917
   70-216   Implementing and Administering a Microsoft Windows 2000 Network Infrastructure   918

23 Optimizing, Backing Up, and Restoring Your Servers   919

Adapting to the Optimization and Backup Routine   920

Server Optimization—Sizing and Tuning   920
   Server Tuning Tools   921

Tuning Fixed-Disk Drives and RAID Arrays   926
   Altering the Default Cluster Size   926
   Organizing Drives and RAID Sets by Read- and Write-Mostly Operation   932
   Defragmenting Files   934
   Spreading the Drive Workload   936
   Setting Drive Properties   937
   Analyzing Disk Caching   938

Optimizing Memory Management   940
   Sizing Paging Files   941
   Setting a Low-Virtual-Memory Alert   945
   Improving Paging File Performance   947

Understanding the Backup Process   948
   The Archive Bit   948
   Normal Backups   949
   Copy Backups   950
   Incremental Backups   951
   Differential Backups   952
   Daily Copy Backups   953
   System State and System Volume Information   953
   Choosing Among the Backup Types   954

Developing a Backup Strategy   956
   Organizing Disk Storage   956
   Ensuring Backup Integrity   957
   Dealing with Open Files and Windows 2000 Backup   958
   Matching Backup Media Capacity to Disk Size   959

Organizing Backup Tape Rotation Methods   959
   Weekly Normal Backup with Daily Differential Backup (Four-Tape Method)   960
   Weekly Normal Backup with Daily Incremental Backup (10-Tape Method)   961
   Daily Full Backups with Two Set Rotation (an Alternate 10-Tape Method)   962
   Grandfather-Father-Son Rotation (21-Tape Method)   963
   Tower of Hanoi Rotation (TOH)   964

Using the Windows 2000 Backup Application   965
   Running an Initial Full Backup   965
   Backing Up Remote Servers   970

Restoring from Windows 2000 Backups   971
   Restoring Member Servers   971
   Restoring Files and System State on Domain Controllers   975

Automating Backup Operations with the Task Scheduler   976

Troubleshooting   978

MCSE Corner: Optimizing, Backing Up, and Restoring Your Servers   979

IV Wide-Area Networking, Intranets, and the Internet   981

24 Communicating with Remote Sites and Domains   983

Analyzing Intersite Replication Requirements and Administration   984
   Site Requirements   984
   Site Administration   985
   Synchronous Intersite Operations   986

Choosing an Intersite Communication Method   987

Setting Up a Test to Estimate Replication Traffic   990
   Designing an Intersite Replication Test Network   990
   Configuring Active Directory Sites and Services   992
   Setting Up Network Monitor   997

Performing the AD Replication Traffic Tests   1000
   Setting Up ADSI25 for the Test   1000
   Running the Add-Users Test   1001
   Testing Global Catalog Traffic   1003
   Testing Domain Restructuring Traffic   1005

Analyzing NetMon Replication Capture Files 1005
   Viewing the Frame List and Frame Content Detail 1006
   Applying a Frame Type Filter 1008

Using the Active Directory Replication Monitor Support Tool 1011
   Setting Up Replication Monitor 1011
   Monitoring Replication 1014

Troubleshooting 1020

MCSE Corner: Communicating with Remote Sites and Domains 1022
   70-217 Implementing and Administering a Microsoft Windows 2000 Directory Services Infrastructure 1022
   70-219 Designing a Microsoft Windows 2000 Directory Services Infrastructure 1022

25 Managing Remote Access and Routing Services 1023

Getting Acquainted with Windows 2000's Remote Access Features 1024

Providing Basic Dial-In Network Access to Remote Clients 1025
   RAS Hardware and Telephone Requirements 1025
   Installing Windows 2000 RRAS 1027
   Using the Phone and Modem Tool to Verify Modem Property Values 1027
   Setting Up Routing and Remote Access Services for DUN 1029
   Testing the RAS Server with a Windows 2000 DUN Client 1032

Configuring a Production RAS Server 1037
   Setting Local RAS Server Policies 1038
   Setting DUN User Profiles 1041
   Using RADIUS Authentication and Accounting 1044

Establishing Group Policies for DUN Clients 1048

Integrating Windows NT 4.0 RAS Servers 1050

Configuring Downlevel DUN Clients 1051
   Windows NT 4.0 Workstation Clients 1051
   Windows 9x Clients 1054

Taking Advantage of Network Address Translation (NAT) 1056
   Understanding NAT Port Translation 1057
   Configuring NAT for Connecting Clients to the Internet 1058
   Setting Up NAT for a Demand-Dial Modem Connection 1059
   Adding Route Hints to the Clients' DNS Server 1063
   Adding the NAT Server as a Gateway for Clients 1064
   Testing Client Connections to the Internet 1065
   Fine-Tuning Demand-Dial Properties 1065
   Configuring NAT with a DSL or Cable Modem Connection 1067
   Configuring Clients for DSL-Based NAT 1070

Troubleshooting 1071

MCSE Corner: Managing Remote Access and Routing Services 1072
   70-215 Installing, Configuring, and Administering Microsoft Windows 2000 Server 1072
   70-216 Implementing and Administering a Microsoft 2000 Network Infrastructure 1072
   70-220 Designing Security for a Microsoft Windows 2000 Network 1073
   70-221 Designing a Microsoft Windows 2000 Network Infrastructure 1073

26 Setting Up a Virtual Private Network 1075

Securing Wide Area Communication over the Internet 1076
    Windows 2000 VPN Protocols 1076
    Understanding the Tunneling Process 1078

Setting Up a PPTP VPN Server 1079

Configuring Windows 2000 Dial-In PPTP Clients 1082
    Configuring the ISP Dial-Up Connection 1083
    Setting Up and Testing the Windows 2000 VPN Connection 1085
    Testing Domain Logon with the VPN Connection 1087

Setting Up Windows 9x VPN Clients 1088
    Configuring a Windows 98 PPTP Tunnel Client 1089
    Testing the Windows 98 PPTP Connection 1090

Enabling Windows NT 4.0 PPTP Clients 1092
    Adding the PPTP Protocol 1092
    Adding and Testing the Phonebook Entry for the First VPN 1093

Securing the Internet Connection with PPTP Filters and Policies 1094

Configuring an L2TP VPN Server 1097
    Providing Servers and Clients with Computer Certificates 1097
    Verifying Certificate Enrollment 1100
    Testing a Windows 2000 VPN Client 1101

Troubleshooting 1101

MCSE Corner: Setting Up a Virtual Private Network 1103
    70-215 Installing, Configuring, and Administering Microsoft Windows 2000 Server 1103
    70-216 Implementing and Administering a Microsoft Windows 2000 Network Infrastructure 1103
    70-220 Designing Security for a Microsoft Windows 2000 Network 1103
    70-221 Designing a Microsoft Windows 2000 Network Infrastructure 1104

27 Administering Internet Information Server 5.0 1105

Assessing the Role of Internet Information Server 5.0 1106

Upgrading to or Installing IIS 5.0 1106
    Installing or Modifying the Installation of IIS 5.0 1107
    Reviewing the Default IIS 5.0 Installation 1108
    Setting Master IIS Properties 1110
    Connecting to IIS 5.0 from Client Browsers 1114

Adding a Test Web Site as a Virtual Directory 1115

Assigning a Conventional URL to the Default Web Site 1118

Adding a New Virtual Site with a Host Header Record 1119

Reading Web Server Log Files 1123

Setting Up the Default FTP Site 1125

Adding a Newsgroup to the Default NNTP Virtual Server 1128
    Setting the Properties of the Default NNTP Virtual Server 1128
    Adding the First Newsgroup 1130
    Establishing a Newsgroup Account and Adding Messages 1131

Configuring the Default SMTP Virtual Server 1133

Troubleshooting   1134

MCSE Corner: Administering Internet Information Server 5.0   1136

V   Advanced Management and Enterprise Systems   1137

28   Managing Transaction and Messaging Services   1139

Understanding the Role of Windows 2000 Application Servers   1140
  Purpose-Built Application Servers   1140
  Three-Tier Component Architecture   1141

Bonding Components with COM and Its Derivatives   1145

Brokering Objects and Processing Transactions   1147

Exploring the Windows 2000 Component Services Tool   1150

Understanding COM+'s Role-Based Security   1153
  Adding Groups to the Administrators Role   1154
  Adding and Deleting Roles   1156

Installing COM+ Applications   1156
  Understanding COM+ Properties   1156
  Installing and Testing the Tic-Tac-Toe MTS 2.0 Sample Application   1158
  Inspecting Application and Component Properties   1162
  Installing the Tic-Tac-Toe Client on Remote Workstations   1166
  Setting Client DCOM Properties   1168

Installing the Sample Bank Application and Creating a File DSN   1171
  Installing the Sample Bank Components   1172
  Creating a File DSN   1173
  Testing the Components and File DSN with the Sample Bank Client   1176
  Exporting Sample Bank Client and Server Installer Packages   1177

Administering the Distributed Transaction Coordinator   1178

Upgrading or Installing Message Queuing Services   1180
  Upgrading from MSMQ 1.0 to 2.0   1180
  Installing an MSMQ 2.0 Server   1183
  Installing an MSMQ 2.0 Client for Windows 2000 Professional   1185
  Installing MSMQ 2.0 on Member Servers   1187

Managing Message Queuing Services   1187

Troubleshooting   1192

MCSE Corner: Exam Question Types Part II   1193
  Case Study   1193
  Scenario   1193
  Simulation   1194

29   Deploying Windows Terminal Services   1195

Understanding Windows NT 4.0, Terminal Server Edition   1196
  Terminology   1196
  Windows NT 4.0 Server Versus Windows NT 4.0, Terminal Server Edition   1196
  Remote Desktop Protocol (RDP)   1197

Comparing Windows 2000 Terminal Services with Windows NT 4.0, Terminal Server Edition 1198

Installing Windows 2000 Terminal Services Server 1199
   Installation Considerations 1200
   Performing the Installation 1201
   Upgrading from Windows NT 4.0, Terminal Server Edition 1203
   Installing Applications 1204

Using Terminal Services' Configuration Snap-In 1205
   Adding a New Terminal Services Connection 1206
   Modifying Connection Properties 1206
   Using the Server Settings Folder 1210

Using Terminal Services Manager 1211

Licensing Terminal Services 1214
   Installing Terminal Services License Server 1215

Installing and Deploying the Terminal Services Client 1217
   What's New in the Terminal Services Client? 1217
   Hardware Requirements 1218
   Installing the Terminal Services Client 1218
   Deploying the Terminal Services Client 1219
   Setting Up Terminal Services Connections 1221
   Setting Up a Default Connection 1223
   Hot-Key Combinations for Client Sessions 1224

Troubleshooting 1224

MCSE Corner: Deploying Windows Terminal Services 1225
   70-215 Installing, Configuring, and Administering Microsoft Windows 2000 Server 1226
   70-220 Designing Security for a Microsoft Windows 2000 Network 1226

30 Clustering with Windows 2000 Advanced Server 1227

Introducing Cluster Technology and Terminology 1228

Using Clustering to Improve Service Availability 1229

Understanding the Elements of Cluster Services 1231
   Cluster Servers 1231
   The Shared-Disk Subsystem 1231
   The Heartbeat Connection 1232
   The LAN Connection 1233
   Cluster Resources 1233

Installing and Configuring the Cluster Service 1234
   Preinstallation Checklist 1234
   Installing Cluster Service 1235

Installing Applications in a Cluster Environment 1238
   Setting Up a Virtual Server for Shared Folders 1239

Using Cluster Administrator 1243
   Working with Resource Groups 1243
   Assigning Resources 1245
   Working with Cluster Nodes 1248
   Resource Group Failover and Failback 1249
   Setting Advanced Properties of Resources 1250

Troubleshooting 1251

MCSE Corner: Registering for an
Exam, What to Expect, and Testing
Innovations   1252
    Registering for an Exam   1252
    What to Expect   1252
    Testing Innovations   1252

VI   Appendixes   1253

A   Installing and Using the ADSI25 Active Directory Application   1255

ADSI25 Application Description   1255
    Feature Set   1256
    Data Source   1257

Installation Prerequisites   1258
    Creating Test Shares   1258
    Installation on a Windows 2000 DC or Workstation   1259
    Installation on a Windows NT 4.0 Workstation or Server   1260

Running the ADSI25 Setup Program   1262
    ADSI25.msi for Windows 2000   1262
    Setup.exe for Windows NT 4.0   1263
    Files Added by Setup   1264

Running ADSI25   1265
    Running ADSI25 Under Windows 2000   1265
    Running ADSI25 Under Windows NT   1275

Adding Students to a Different Domain   1279
    Adding Student Accounts to a Windows 2000 Child Domain   1280
    Adding Student Accounts to a Second Windows NT Domain   1283

Removing ADSI25 from Your System   1285

User License   1285

Troubleshooting   1286

B   Glossary   1287

Index   1388

About the Authors

Roger Jennings is a consultant and author specializing in Windows 2000 network design and deployment, Active Directory programming, and *n*-tier database systems. His books for Macmillan USA have sold more than one million copies and have been translated into more than 20 languages.

Roger is the author of Que's *Special Edition Using Windows NT Server 4* (two editions); *Special Edition Using Access 1.0, 1.1, 2.0, 95, 97* (two editions) and *2000*; *Platinum Edition Using Access 97*; *Unveiling Windows 95*; and *Discover Windows 3.1 Multimedia*. For Macmillan USA's Sams imprint, he's written two editions of *Access Developer's Guide* and three editions of *Database Developer's Guide for Visual Basic* (versions 3.0, 4.0, and 6.0) and is series editor for the *Roger Jennings' Database Workshop* titles. Roger also is a contributing editor for Fawcette Technical Publications' *Visual Basic Programmer's Journal*; his feature articles and "Database Design" columns appear regularly in *VBPJ* (http://www.vbpj.com/). The ADSI25 for Active Directory application—used to create many of the examples for this book and included on the accompanying CD-ROM—was the subject of *VBPJ*'s December 1999 cover article, "Automate the Active Directory."

Roger was a member of the Microsoft technical beta testing team for Windows NT 3.5, 3.51, 4.0, and 2000 Server; Windows 3.1, 95, and 98; SQL Server 4.21a, 6.0, 6.5, and 2000; Visual Basic 3.0, 4.0, 5.0, and 6.0; and every version of Microsoft Access. He's also the co-author of articles for *Microsoft Developer Network News* and content for the Microsoft Developer Network CD-ROM.

Roger has more than 25 years of computer-related experience ranging from the Wang 700 desktop calculator/computer to IBM and Hitachi mainframes. His full biography is at http://www.mcp.com/publishers/que/authors/roger_jennings/. He's the Webmaster and writer/producer for OakLeaf Music (http://www.oakmusic.com/). You can contact Roger at Roger_Jennings@compuserve.com.

Richard Cardona (Chapter 17, "Installing Network Printers") is a network engineer at the Annenberg School for Communication of the University of Pennsylvania. Rich specializes in LAN/WAN environments and management and holds an MCP. He's worked with Windows 2000 since its Beta 2 release and continues to implement creative solutions in networking across multiplatform operating systems. Rich earned his B.A. from the University of Pennsylvania in 1997. He lives in Philadelphia with his wife, Maureen. Rich can be reached at richcardona@asc.upenn.edu.

Kyle Cassidy (Chapter 17, "Installing Network Printers") holds MCSE and MCP+Internet certifications and is a network engineer at the University of Pennsylvania's prestigious Annenberg School for Communication. He has a degree in English literature from Rowan University and has been writing about computers and technology since 1986. Kyle lives in Philadelphia with his wife, Linda Harris, and her huge cat, Thunderbelly. When he's not up on a ladder dragging cables through the drop ceiling, he's writing pithy blurbs about himself in the third person. Contact Kyle at kylecassidy@asc.upenn.edu.

Mark Darnell (Chapter 13, "Integrating UNIX and Linux Networks," and Chapter 19, "Serving Macintosh, Windows 3.11, and DOS Clients") is president and founder of PRU Consulting, a consulting firm providing system design and integration services to a wide array of corporations. Past clients and projects span a diverse range from satellite and ground-control systems for NASA to very-large-scale COM-based ERP applications. Mark has been working with Microsoft products since the early 1980s, but took a several-year hiatus to spend time on Unix and Macintosh platforms. He has since returned to the Microsoft fold, the primary impetus being the release of Windows NT 3.1 Beta in 1993. Mark earned his Bachelor's and Master's degrees in electrical and computer engineering from the University of Colorado at Boulder, where he still resides. You can reach Mark at `mdarnell@pruconsulting.com`.

Tim Darnell (Chapter 30, "Clustering with Windows 2000 Advanced Server") has been working for the last three years as a Network Engineer for the Internet Development branch of a Fortune 500 civil engineering firm. He has spent the last year contributing to design and implementation of secure high-availability network infrastructures for project collaboration applications on the Internet. His main areas of focus lay in the physical layer technologies such as firewalls and routing, as well as Internet security. Contact Tim at `tim.darnell@pbid.com`.

Brian Gallagher (Chapter 30, "Clustering with Windows 2000 Advanced Server") has been writing about the Internet, systems, and networking for more than six years. He is an author, columnist, and MCSE. Brian manages a high-availability Web server farm and an innovative Web services IT team. He can be reached at `briang@spintheweb.com`.

Michael Helstrom (Chapter 9, "Installing RAID and Removable Media Systems," and Chapter 11, "Setting Up Key- and Certificate-Based Security") is a Senior Consultant with Xpedior, an international consulting firm providing innovative, comprehensive eBusiness solutions for Global 2000 companies, government, and emerging digital businesses. Mike specializes in the architecture of distributed application/network services and holds an MCSE+I, MCSD, and MCT. He's worked with Windows 2000 since its Beta 1 release and continues to implement creative and innovative solutions on the Windows platform. Mike earned his Bachelor's degree in computer science from Saint Anselm College in Manchester, New Hampshire. You can reach Mike via email at `michael.helstrom@xpedior.com`. For more information about Xpedior, visit `http://www.xpedior.com`.

David Mackey (Chapter 12, "Interoperating with NetWare Servers," and Chapter 29, "Deploying Windows Terminal Services") is a software development project manager for a Fortune 500 computer company. In his free time, he is a systems consultant, Webmaster, and writer. He has a broad base of experience with Windows and NetWare platforms and holds the Microsoft Certified Systems Engineer and Certified NetWare Administrator credentials. David also co-created the popular Windows troubleshooting site, `http://www.fixwindows.com`, to offer free troubleshooting information and help weary Windows users. You can reach David via email at `dmackey@fixwindows.com`.

Blair Rampling ("MSCE Corners") holds an MCSE and is a full-time Systems Administrator with a streaming-media and e-commerce provider working with the Windows platform in a high-traffic Internet server configuration. He also administrates Sun Solaris and Linux platforms that provide application and database services. Blair has experience in all sizes of networks, from 20 to 6,500 clients and from 1 to 150 sites. Blair's specialty is working with heterogeneous networks that run Windows, Solaris, Linux, OpenVMS and BSD UNIX.

Mark Randol (Chapter 20, "Supplying IntelliMirror and Application Installation Services," and Chapter 30, "Clustering with Windows 2000 Advanced Server") has been working as a Windows NT administrator and architecture designer on high-volume, high-availability networks for more than five years. He specializes in systems integration and Windows NT security. Currently, most of Mark's work is developing high-availability Internet clusters. Contact Mark at `mark.randol@pbid.com`.

Dedication

This book is dedicated to Aaron Weule, IT director of a major West Coast Web site that runs under Windows NT and 2000. Aaron's operating system and hardware expertise are reflected in the content of several chapters of this book.

Acknowledgments

Jenny Watson, acquisitions editor, recruited contributing authors and technical editors, and made sure I didn't fall too far behind the manuscript submission and author review schedule. Development editors **Jill Hayden**, **Lorna Gentry**, and **Rick Kughen** aided in the overall organization of the book and made sure that the manuscript adhered to Que's author guidelines. **Nancy Albright** and **Maryann Steinhart**, copy editors, corrected my grammatical and spelling errors. Senior Editor **Susan Moore** worked hard to assure that all of the components of this edition flowed through the copy editing process and got to their final destinations on time. **Greg Newman**, **Ariel Silverstone**, **David Bixler**, and members of the Huntsville NT Users Group [www.HUNTUG.org], **Daniel F. Wygant** (Founder, 1st Chairman, Review Editor), **John (Coyote) Wiley** (Secretary), **Wayne Gardner** (1st President), and **Doug Mitchell** (Newsletter Editor) handled the technical editing chores. The responsibility for any errors or omissions, however, rests solely on my shoulders.

Tell Us What You Think!

As the reader of this book, *you* are our most important critic and commentator. We value your opinion and want to know what we're doing right, what we could do better, what areas you'd like to see us publish in, and any other words of wisdom you're willing to pass our way.

As an Associate Publisher for Que Corporation, I welcome your comments. You can fax, email, or write me directly to let me know what you did or didn't like about this book—as well as what we can do to make our books stronger.

Please note that I cannot help you with technical problems related to the topic of this book, and that due to the high volume of mail I receive, I might not be able to reply to every message.

When you write, please be sure to include this book's title and author as well as your name and phone or fax number. I will carefully review your comments and share them with the author and editors who worked on the book.

Fax: 317-581-4666

Email: opsys@mcp.com

Mail: Dean Miller
Associate Publisher
Que Corporation
201 West 103rd Street
Indianapolis, IN 46290 USA

INTRODUCTION

In this introduction

    An Operating System for the Millennium   2

    Who Should Read This Book?   4

    How This Book Is Organized   5

    How This Book Is Designed   10

    Bibliography   11

An Operating System for the Millennium

Microsoft changed the name of the long-delayed successor to Windows NT 4.0 from Windows NT 5.0 to Windows 2000 in October 1998. Originally scheduled for release in the second half of 1997, Microsoft finally set February 17, 2000, as the retail availability date of Windows 2000. The breadth and depth of Windows 2000 Server's feature set and the size of its underlying source code base clearly qualifies the product as the "Operating System of the Millennium."

Industry pundits offer varying projections of when customers will migrate to Windows 2000 Server. The consensus of computer journalists appears to be that IT managers and network administrators are loathe to replace the mature Windows NT 4.0 operating system, which has six—going on seven—service packs under its belt. Conservative IT executives within large organizations probably will wait for the first three or four Windows 2000 service packs to appear before trusting their network to the new operating system in 2001. More impulsive system administrators in small- to medium-sized firms might take the plunge after Service Pack 1, which was in the development process when Windows 2000 "went gold" in December 1999 and was released in August 2000. There's no question, however, that Internet Information Server (IIS) 5.0 running under Windows 2000 Server is ready for deployment out of the box. Just two months after its official release, Microsoft claimed more than 65,000 Web sites were running IIS 5.0.

Regardless of your Windows 2000 Server deployment schedule, now's the time to start planning and testing your migration strategy to Microsoft's mammoth new operating system. The most radical change from Windows NT 4.0 to Windows 2000 is Active Directory, which overcomes the serious limitations of Windows NT's domain architecture. Microsoft emphasizes the role of Active Directory in distributed enterprise-scale networks, but Active Directory also aids the administration of small- to medium-size networks.

The major challenge facing Windows 2000 Server administrators is gaining a full understanding of Active Directory's architecture and its management techniques. Much of the content of this book is a hands-on guide to implementing, testing, and managing Active Directory in new installations and Windows NT upgrade scenarios. Unlike other books in its category, *Special Edition Using Microsoft Windows 2000 Server* includes on the accompanying CD-ROM a custom-written application—ADSI25 for Active Directory—that generates Active Directory objects for you. Most of the examples in this book take advantage of ADSI25.exe to eliminate manually adding large numbers of Active Directory objects. ADSI25 will save you many hours of laborious typing when you reconfigure your test domains with the Active Directory Installation Wizard.

When you run ADSI25.exe under Windows 2000, the program creates a set of 43 nested Organizational Units (OUs) and Security Groups, and generates and publishes 41 server shares in Active Directory. You can quickly add up to a maximum of about 27,500 user accounts to the various OUs and, optionally, generate a corresponding number of computer accounts. Figure I.1 shows ADSI25's main window displaying the first few Security Groups and OUs (upper left), membership for the Anthropology department group (lower left), some of the user accounts (upper right), and the first eight Active Directory attributes of a selected user account (lower right).

→ For a brief description of the sample OakLeaf University organization used by the ADSI25 application, see "The Accompanying CD-ROM," p. 9.

Figure I.1
The ADSI25.exe application automatically adds Security Groups, OUs, and user and computer accounts to Active Directory.

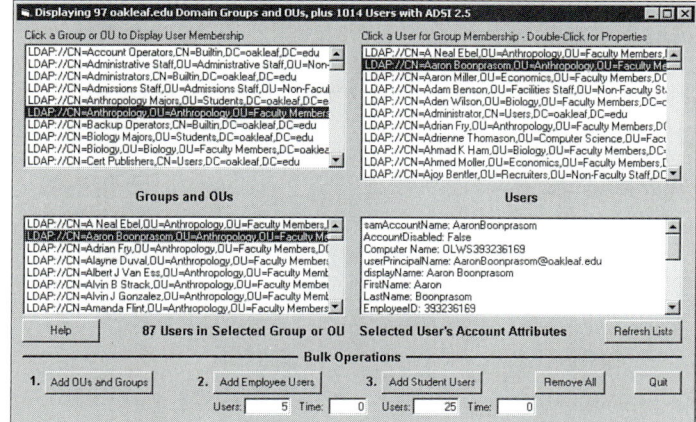

Running ADSI25.exe under Windows NT lets you generate groups and user and computer accounts for testing the Windows NT Server 4.0 in-place upgrade process, migrating Windows NT domains to Windows 2000 and Active Directory, or both. If you have an Exchange Server 5.5 (SP 3+) test installation, running ADSI25.exe under Windows NT 4.0 SP 4+ lets you add Exchange mailboxes for each user, complete with a full set of the most common Exchange account attributes. This feature lets you test upgrading a large number of mailboxes from Exchange 5.5 running under Windows NT 4.0 to Exchange 2000.

Note
If you're interested in Active Directory programming with Visual Basic 6.0 or VBScript, the CD-ROM includes the complete source code of the ADSI25 for Active Directory application.

Active Directory and related topics receive the emphasis in this book, but *Special Edition Using Microsoft Windows 2000 Server* also provides detailed coverage of the other new networking features of Windows 2000 Server. You don't have to be a Windows NT expert to get full value from this book; with the exception of Chapter 5, "Choosing and Testing Migration Strategies," and Chapter 6, "Preparing NT 4.0 for Windows 2000 Server Migration," no prior experience with Windows NT 4.0 is needed. Chapters devoted to integration with NetWare—including directory synchronization with Novell Directory Services (NDS)—and UNIX explain Windows 2000 Server's internetworking features. When you complete this book and its hands-on examples, you'll be well prepared to install and manage an enterprise-scale Windows 2000 network.

Who Should Read This Book?

Special Edition Using Microsoft Windows 2000 Server is intended for an eclectic audience, from junior networking administrators to network designers and administrators responsible for setting up and maintaining large, distributed networks using Windows 2000 Server and Active Directory, either alone or with other network operating systems. This book isn't an introduction to Windows 2000—it covers only those elements of Windows 2000 Professional that relate to networking with Windows 2000 Server.

→ If you need to learn more about the basic features, functions, and navigation of Windows 2000, **see** "Que Books about Windows 2000 Professional," **p. 12**.

Folks for whom *Special Edition Using Microsoft Windows 2000 Server* offers the most usefulness fall into the following general categories:

- Network architects and system administrators designing local-area or wide-area networks that incorporate Windows 2000 Servers and Active Directory, either in a Microsoft-only or in a heterogeneous networking environment

- Network administrators handling the day-to-day chores necessary to ensure network and directory availability, security, and reliability

- Educational institutions and training firms needing an advanced-level text on Windows 2000 networking for their students and a Windows 2000 application—ADSI25 for Active Directory on the accompanying CD-ROM—to aid in learning enterprise-scale Active Directory management techniques

- Network support personnel keeping Windows Networking clients online and helping users gain the maximum benefit from the Windows 2000 domain(s) to which they connect and the Active Directory resources they use

- NetWare system administrators integrating or replacing NewWare 3.x, 4.x, or 5.x and Novell Directory Services (NDS) infrastructures with Windows 2000 Server and Active Directory

- Users of various UNIX flavors who find Windows 2000 Server encroaching on the sacred ground of their erstwhile "open system"

- Information systems managers responsible for planning and administering downsizing or upsizing corporate data distribution systems

- Human resources directors responsible for overseeing remote-access telecommuting services for their firms' employees

- Database administrators seeking to provide networked users with expedited access to relational database management systems and corporate "information warehouses"

- Microsoft Solution Providers who provide network management and database consulting services

- Value-added resellers (VARs) of complete networking solutions, which include Windows 2000 Servers

- Line management personnel who are members of re-engineering committees charged with integrating information management into the re-engineering process

- Educators, members of corporate training departments, and television broadcast/cable personnel involved in evaluating and/or deploying streaming media services for the Internet or intranets

The preceding list includes only the most obvious classifications of the potential audience for this book. Even if you're just curious about Microsoft's completely revamped operating system and new Internet, client-server, and *n*-tier application strategies, you'll find this book useful.

How This Book Is Organized

Special Edition Using Microsoft Windows 2000 Server consists of 30 chapters divided into five parts; a bonus chapter, "Streaming with Windows Media Technologies 4," on the CD-ROM; plus an appendix and glossary. The organization follows the process of establishing a new Windows 2000 network—beginning with the planning process, and continuing with production server installation, delivering network resources to client PCs, and working in wide-area network and Internet/intranet environments. The chapters at the end of the book deal with advanced Windows 2000 Server and Advanced Server management topics.

Part I: Planning Your Microsoft Windows 2000 Server Installation

Planning plays an extremely important role in successfully rolling out Windows 2000 Server networks, whether you're starting from ground zero or upgrading existing Windows NT or NetWare installations. The chapters of Part I concentrate on Windows 2000's Dynamic DNS, TCP/IP, and Active Directory features, including the Lightweight Directory Access Protocol (LDAP).

- Chapter 1, "Windows 2000 Server for NT 4.0 Users—What's New," briefly describes the important new features of Windows 2000 Server, Advanced Server, AppCenter Server, and Datacenter Server.
- Chapter 2, "Understanding IP, DNS Namespaces, and TCP/IP," is intended for readers new to the Internet Protocol, Domain Naming System, and the Transmission Control Protocol/Internet Protocol. A thorough knowledge of IP, DNS, and TCP/IP is required for understanding Windows 2000 networking and Active Directory (AD).
- Chapter 3, "Introducing the Active Directory and LDAP," gets you started with the basics of AD, including installing AD on a test server, creating Organizational Units (OUs) and Security Groups within a single domain, adding user and computer accounts, and related topics. The chapter uses the ADSI25 for Active Directory application and the Active Directory Users and Computers administrative tool to teach you the basics of AD administration and how to use LDAP filters to search for AD objects.
- Chapter 4, "Optimizing Your Active Directory Topology," expands your horizons to AD's child domains, multiple sites, moving Domain Controllers (DCs) between domains and sites, and remotely administering AD with Windows 2000 Professional.

- Chapter 5, "Choosing and Testing Migration Strategies," describes the planning and evaluation process for upgrading your Windows NT 4.0 network to Windows 2000 Server. The chapter describes several migration methods, including use of the Active Directory Migration Tool (ADMT) developed for Microsoft by Mission Critical Software.

- Chapter 6, "Preparing NT 4.0 for Windows 2000 Server Migration," deals primarily with optimizing your Windows NT 4.0 servers and networking clients to ease the move to Windows 2000. The chapter covers setting up Windows Internet Naming Service (WINS), Dynamic Host Configuration Protocol (DHCP), and DNS on the Windows NT 4.0 Primary Domain Controllers (PDCs) that you intend to upgrade to Windows 2000 Domain Controllers (DCs).

- Chapter 7, "Specifying Server and Data Storage Hardware," gives you the guidance you need to purchase servers and Redundant Arrays of Inexpensive Disks (RAID) subsystems that deliver the best performance/cost ratio with Windows 2000. Chapter 7 also covers upgrading your current servers to meet Windows 2000 hardware requirements.

PART II: DEPLOYING WINDOWS 2000 SERVER

After you've completed your domain planning and AD migration tests, and purchased or upgraded your server hardware for Windows 2000, it's time to put Windows 2000 Server in production. The chapters of Part II provide the knowledge you need to become an expert Windows 2000 system administrator in a Windows-only or heterogeneous network environment.

- Chapter 8, "Deploying Windows 2000 Production Servers," details the steps involved in safely upgrading Windows NT PDCs to Windows 2000 DCs, or setting up new Windows 2000 DCs within existing Windows NT domains. Chapter 8 also provides instructions on how to recover from a disabled system with Safe Mode, the Recovery Console, and Automated System Recovery backups.

- Chapter 9, "Installing RAID and Removable Media Systems," covers the use of Windows 2000's software RAID implementations, adding backup tape and CD-ROM drives, and taking advantage of Windows 2000's remote and hierarchical storage management features.

- Chapter 10, "Working with the Windows 2000 Registry," explains the structure of the Windows 2000 Registry and shows you how to use the two Registry editors—RegEdit.exe and RegEdt32.exe—to repair or alter the contents of the Registry.

- Chapter 11, "Setting Up Key- and Certificate-Based Security," describes Windows 2000's public-key security features for the new Encrypting File System (EFS), and how users can take advantage of EFS for total file security. The chapter also covers setting up and managing certificate servers and administering user certificates.

- Chapter 12, "Interoperating with NetWare Servers," shows you how to set up the IPX/SPX protocol, use File and Print Services for NetWare (FPNW), install Gateway Services for NetWare (GSNW), and run the Directory Services Migration Tool. Chapter 12 also shows you how to set up and administer the Directory Synchronization (DirSync) tool in a mixed NetWare and Windows 2000 environment.
- Chapter 13, "Integrating UNIX and Linux Networks," discusses interaction with UNIX hosts as clients and servers. Topics include Telnet, FTP, Client for NFS, Server for NFS, Gateway Services for NFS, and NIS integration with AD.

PART III: DELIVERING NETWORK RESOURCES TO CLIENTS

The primary objective of Windows 2000 Server is to provide network resources to clients. The chapters of Part III concentrate on the new network management features of Windows 2000 Server that reduce the Total Cost of Ownership (TCO) of client PCs.

- Chapter 14, "Providing Clients with DHCP and WINS," shows you how to assign Windows 2000, NT, and 9x clients IP address leases with DHCP, and how to use WINS with downlevel (Windows NT and 9x) clients to locate network servers.
- Chapter 15, "Establishing Group Policies, User Accounts, and Logons," explains how to take full advantage of Windows 2000's new Group Policies for domains and OUs, and techniques for managing user and computer accounts, logon scripts, and roaming user profiles.
- Chapter 16, "Managing Server Shares and the Distributed File System," describes how to administer user home folders, publish shares in AD, and set up the Distributed File System (Dfs). Chapter 16 also shows you how to take advantage of Remote Storage Services (RSS), Hierarchical Storage Management (HSM), and Index Services for locating shared files by attribute or content.
- Chapter 17, "Installing Network Printers," covers setting up server-connected and network-attached printers, publishing printer resources in AD, and using the new Internet Publishing Protocol (IPP) to specify a network printer by its URL.
- Chapter 18, "Connecting Windows 2000, NT, and 9x Clients," describes how to optimize 32-bit Windows client connectivity with Windows 2000 server, and use the AD client add-in to enable Windows 9x clients to find resources published in AD.
- Chapter 19, "Serving Macintosh, Windows 3.11, and DOS Clients," shows you how to set up Windows 2000's Services for Macintosh (SfM), which provides support for AppleTalk networking; set up file and print services for Mac clients; and share Mac printers on the Windows 2000 network. Chapter 19 also covers installation and use of the Network Client for MS-DOS and Windows 3.1x.
- Chapter 20, "Supplying IntelliMirror and Application Installation Services," explains Windows 2000's new IntelliMirror feature that lets users store working files on the server, synchronize server files with offline revisions, and automatically receive new or upgraded applications. This chapter also shows you how to apply user desktop settings management to lock down client configurations.

- Chapter 21, "Using Remote Installation Services," describes how to set up and manage Remote Installation Services (RIS) to install Windows 2000 Professional automatically on client PCs having network adapters with DHCP PXE-enabled remote-boot ROMs or by using the remote installation boot disk.
- Chapter 22, "Monitoring and Tuning Your Network," introduces you to the Network Monitor and Performance Monitor administrative tools and shows you how to use these tools to discover network bottlenecks and troubleshoot network failures.
- Chapter 23, "Optimizing, Backing Up, and Restoring Your Servers," describes the ongoing processes of maintaining server performance with increasing workloads, and using the new Windows 2000 Backup application to enable recovery in the event of a disk or system failure. This chapter emphasizes use of Performance Monitor to uncover and solve memory usage and allocation problems.

PART IV: WIDE-AREA NETWORKING, INTRANETS, AND THE INTERNET

Wide-area networks (WANs) present bandwidth and reliability issues that don't ordinarily occur within local-area networks (LANs). The chapters of Part IV are devoted primarily to providing connectivity between Windows 2000 Servers in remote sites, and between dial-up clients and servers—regardless of the method by which they connect and the level of security you require.

- Chapter 24, "Communicating with Remote Sites and Domains," shows you how to use the Active Directory Sites and Services administrative tool to manage WAN connections between servers, and illustrates techniques for estimating and monitoring intersite traffic with the Network and Replication Monitors.
- Chapter 25, "Managing Remote Access and Routing Services," introduces you to the successor to Windows NT's Routing and Remote Access Services (RRAS). The chapter covers setting up RAS with the Configure Your Server Wizard, establishing RAS policies, and creating client accounts with the Remote Access Dial-Up User Service (RADIUS). Chapter 25 also covers Network Address Translation (NAT) routing and Dial-on-Demand services for remote office clients and servers.
- Chapter 26, "Setting Up a Virtual Private Network," covers Windows 2000's implementation of PPTP and L2TP for VPN support, setting up standard configurations for a VPN server, connecting Windows 9x and NT clients with PPTP, and configuring Windows 2000 Professional clients for L2TP over IPSec.
- Chapter 27, "Administering Internet Information Server 5.0," guides you through the initial installation and setup or upgrade procedures for Internet Information Server (IIS) 5.0, File Transfer Protocol (FTP), Internet News (NNTP), and Mail (SMTP).

PART V: ADVANCED MANAGEMENT AND ENTERPRISE SYSTEMS

The final chapters of *Special Edition Using Microsoft Windows 2000 Server* concentrate on advanced topics—setting up and managing application servers for COM+ and messaging services, Terminal Services, and Advanced Server clustering extensions.

How This Book Is Organized

- Chapter 28, "Managing Transaction and Messaging Services," describes the basic function of application servers that support the middle tier(s) of *n*-tier componentized applications. The chapter delivers the details of upgrading Microsoft Transaction Server (MTS) 2.0 components to Windows 2000's COM+ and using the Component Manager administrative tools to upgrade and test the MTS 2.0 Sample Bank application. Chapter 28 also shows you how to install and manage Microsoft Message Queue Services 2.0 (MSMQ).

- Chapter 29, "Deploying Windows Terminal Services," compares Windows 2000 Server's built-in Terminal Services with Windows NT 4.0 Terminal Services Edition, and then goes on to show you how to install and administer Terminal Services and Terminal Services Licensing. The chapter also covers deploying Terminal Services clients and setting up connections.

- Chapter 30, "Clustering with Windows 2000 Advanced Server," covers two-node failover clustering capabilities to ensure availability of cluster-aware applications, such as IIS 5.0, and the Enterprise versions of SQL Server 7+ and Exchange Server 5.5+.

PART VI: APPENDIXES

- Appendix A, "Installing and Using the ADSI25 Active Directory Application," provides detailed instructions for setting up and using the ADSI25.exe Visual Basic program that's described at the beginning of this introduction and in the next section.

- Appendix B, "Glossary," supplies definitions of many of the terms used in this book that might be unfamiliar to readers without substantial experience with 32-bit Windows operating systems or Microsoft Windows Networking.

THE ACCOMPANYING CD-ROM

The accompanying CD-ROM includes the following added-value elements:

- The ADSI25 for Active Directory application, located in the \Seuw2ks\ADSI25 folder, is a full-featured application for automating the creation of OUs, Security Groups, user and computer accounts, and publishing file shares for OakLeaf University. OakLeaf U is a mythical Texas institution having about 2,500 employees—including faculty members and non-teaching staff—and 25,000 students. You also can create Windows NT 4.0 accounts and groups for bulk migration to Windows 2000. Most of the AD examples of this book take advantage of the ADSI25 application to eliminate the drudgery of manually creating AD objects. The full Visual Basic 6.0 source code—about 5,000 lines—is included. You must have Visual Basic 6.0 Standard Edition or higher with Service Pack 3 to run the source code from the VB 6.0 Integrated Development Environment (IDE). The Microsoft Installer version (ADSI25.msi) is for Windows 2000; the Visual Studio 6.0 Setup.exe installs ADSI25.exe under Windows NT 4.0.

- The NetTraffic (NetTraf.exe) application (installed from \Seuw2ks\NetTraf\NetTraf.msi) is a simple Visual Basic 6.0 application that you can use to generate various levels of network traffic for file server performance and tuning purposes. Chapter 22, "Monitoring and Tuning Your Network," uses NetTraf.exe in its examples.
- "Streaming with Windows Media Technologies 4," a bonus chapter in printable PDF format (\Seuw2ks\BonusChp\Stream32.pdf), delivers extensive coverage of setting up and administering Windows Media Services for delivering audio/visual content by unicasting or broadcasting over your intranet and the Internet. The chapter also shows you how to use Microsoft's client-side tools to create audio and video content in Active Streaming Format (.asf) files.

How This Book Is Designed

The following special features are included in this book to assist you as you read:

- The *New Feature of Windows 2000 Server* icon appears next to sections that describe features in Windows 2000 Server that weren't implemented in Windows NT 4.0. Chapters devoted entirely to new Windows 2000 Server features—such as Active Directory—don't use the New Feature icon.

- The *On the Accompanying CD-ROM* icon points out content that relies on the ADSI25 for Active Directory application and other materials on the CD-ROM attached to the inside back cover of this book.

- *Cross-references* include the names of sections elsewhere in this book that contain information related to the associated text and the page on which you'll find the sections. Cross-references look like these:

→ To review this subject, **see** "Name of Section Earlier in the Book," **p. xxx**.

→ To skip ahead to this subject, **see** "Name of Section Later in the Book," **p. xxx**.

Note

Notes offer suggestions and comments related to the text that precedes the note. Some notes provide references to Web sites that provide content related to the subject matter of the preceding text.

Tip from
RJ

Tips describe shortcuts and alternative approaches to gaining an objective. Many of these tips are based on the experience the authors gained during months of testing successive beta and release-candidate versions of Windows 2000 Server.

Caution

Cautions appear where an action might lead to an unexpected or unpredictable result, including possible loss of data or other serious consequence. The text provides an explanation of how you can avoid such a result.

This book uses the following typographic conventions to make reading easier:

- Active Directory object and attribute names and values, Internet Protocol (IP) addresses, and Domain Name System (DNS) names (including Web site addresses), appear in `monospace` font. Examples of Visual Basic Script (VBScript) and other code also appear in `monospace`.
- Replaceable elements of DNS and other names use *`italic monospace`*, as in *`servername.domainname`*`.com`.
- The **bold** attribute is used for the text you type at the command prompt or into text boxes.
- The *italic* attribute is used for text definitions (instead of double quotation marks) and to set off initial items in bulleted lists, where appropriate. The *italic* attribute also is used for emphasis.

BIBLIOGRAPHY

Publishing limitations preclude a full bibliography for Windows 2000 and applications—such as SQL Server and Exchange Server—designed for running under Windows 2000 Server. The following sections describe selected print and online resources to further your Windows 2000 education.

QUE BOOKS ABOUT WINDOWS 2000 SERVER AND RELATED TOPICS

Que is an imprint of Macmillan USA, the world's largest computer book publisher. Following is a list of Que books related to Windows 2000 Server that were published or scheduled for publication when this book was written:

- *The Active Directory: Administration and Security* by Banyan Systems, Inc. and Roger Abell (Que, ISBN 0-7897-2210-0) supplements Chapters 3 through 6 of this book by supplying additional insights on AD user management, file security, auditing access, planning services, replication, performance optimization, deployment, and upgrading and migrating from earlier Windows NT versions and Novell NDS.
- *Microsoft Windows 2000 Registry Handbook* by Jerry Honeycutt (Que, ISBN 0-7897-1674-7) extends the scope of Chapter 10 with detailed guidance for administering and securing the Registry, customizing Windows 2000, scripting Registry changes, troubleshooting, and diagnosing common Registry errors.
- *Microsoft Windows 2000 Security Handbook* by Jeff Schmidt (Que, ISBN 0-7897-1999-1) provides extensive coverage of NTFS fault tolerance, Kerberos authentication, Windows 2000 intruder detection, and writing secure applications for Windows 2000.

- *Deploying and Supporting Internetworking Services in Windows 2000* by James Ramsey (Que, ISBN 0-7897-2230-5) shows you how to successfully deploy and support internetworking services in a Windows 2000 environment, and provides vital information on topics such as VPN, DHCP, DNS, WINS, NetWare, UNIX, Linux, and other internetworking subjects.

- *Implementing Remote Access Services with Microsoft Windows 2000* by Marcus Goncalves (Que, ISBN 0-7897-2138-4) provides an in-depth discussion about remote access systems through a variety of network technologies, including broadband, information services digital networks (ISDN), public service telephone networks (PSTN), digital subscriber line (DSL), asymmetric digital subscriber line (ADSL), virtual private networks (VPN), and the Internet.

- *Special Edition Using Samba* by Richard Sharpe (Que, ISBN 0-7897-2319-0) shows you how to obtain, install, and configure Samba, with examples and protocol traces where necessary; the various sections of the smb.conf file; and automation via macros. Detailed information on accessing Samba from the various clients is provided, including Windows 2000, OS2, and the UNIX clients, smbclient and rpcclient.

- *Special Edition Using Microsoft Exchange Server 2000* by Kent Joshi (Que, ISBN 0-7897-2278-X) emphasizes integrating Exchange with the Internet, as well as extending its functionality into the area of collaboration.

- *Planning and Deploying Microsoft Exchange Server 2000* by Kent Joshi (Que, ISBN 0-7897-2798) is a companion to *Special Edition Using Microsoft Exchange Server 2000* that delivers real-world solutions and useful tips for advanced Exchange 2000 administrators.

- *Special Edition Using Microsoft SQL Server 7.0* by Stephen Wynkoop (Que, ISBN 0-7897-1523-6) walks you through installing, operating, administering, and developing databases and database applications with SQL Server 7.0.

- *SQL Server 2000 Database Development from Scratch* by Rob Hawthorne (Que, ISBN 0-7897-2447-2) is a road map to creating and maintaining spy tracker database applications while learning SQL Server 2000.

- *Advanced Messaging Applications with MSMQ and MQSeries* by Rhys Lewis (Que, ISBN 0-7897-2023-X) complements Chapter 28 by focusing on the internal programming procedures and concepts associated with Microsoft's Message Queuing Server. The book provides an in-depth look at the MSMQ architecture, programming techniques, securing and configuring MSMQ, and interoperability and programming issues associated with connecting to IBM's message queuing middleware, MQSeries.

QUE BOOKS ABOUT WINDOWS 2000 PROFESSIONAL

Supporting Windows 2000 Professional users requires a thorough knowledge of the features and functions of Windows 2000 Professional. Following are Que books that cover the client side of the network equation:

- *Special Edition Using Microsoft Windows 2000 Professional* by Robert Cowart (Que, ISBN 0-7897-2125-2) covers upgrading from Windows 9x and Windows NT 4.0, working with the enhanced Windows 2000 interface, setting up Internet connections, configuring network security, working remotely, and internetworking with Windows 2000 Server, Windows 9x, Linux, Novell, and Macintosh.
- *Microsoft Windows 2000 Professional User Manual* by Jim Boyce (Que, ISBN 0-7897-2140-6) describes all the user-oriented features in Windows 2000 Professional, as well as those administrative topics applicable to the average user, without requiring you to wade through an excessive amount of descriptive text to find the function, command, or other feature you need.
- *Practical Microsoft Windows 2000 Professional* by Ed Bott (Que, ISBN 0-7897-2124-4) provides coverage for the Windows 2000 Professional user who doesn't want to read extraneous material. Topics include customizing the Windows 2000 desktop, taskbar, and Start menu; installing and uninstalling programs; sharing files, folders, and printers over a network; preventing unauthorized access to sensitive data; connecting to the Internet; and browsing the Web. Additional topics are foolproof Internet security settings, using Windows 2000 on a notebook, troubleshooting hardware problems, and recovering from data disasters.
- *Microsoft Windows 2000 Professional Installation and Configuration Handbook* by Jim Boyce (Que, ISBN 0-7897-2133-3) delivers the knowledge you need to install and configure your operating system for optimum performance and flexibility, and provides tips and techniques to boost productivity. Topics include installing Windows 2000 Professional, adding and modifying hardware, administering Windows 2000 Professional, administrative tools, installing and configuring communication, Internet and networking, managing and tuning critical subsystems, and mass installation with disk duplication utilities.

You can find additional information on Que's entire series of books about Windows 2000 Professional, Server, and related topics at `http://www.mcp.com/que/`.

Periodicals That Emphasize Windows 2000 Topics

Following is a short list of popular monthly and bimonthly magazines devoted to or including substantial coverage of Windows 2000 topics:

- *Windows 2000 Magazine* (formerly *Windows NT Magazine*), is a monthly publication of Duke Communications International, Inc. that's designed to help power users and network administrators get the most out of Windows 2000. For subscription information, check `http://www.win2000mag.net/`, or call (800) 621-1544 or (970) 663-4700.
- *Enterprise Development*, published by Fawcette Technical Publications, Inc., is a controlled-circulation magazine targeted at IS managers looking for help with gluing together the platforms, tiers, components, languages, ERP systems, front ends, and back ends of enterprise-scale applications, including those built on Windows 2000.

You can subscribe from Fawcette's Development Exchange Web site, `http://www.devx.com/`, or by calling (800) 848-5523 or (650) 833-7100.

- *XML Magazine* is a new bimonthly Fawcette publication devoted to providing hands-on, how-to information about the architecture and structure of XML, as well as case studies and technical instruction for incorporating XML into Windows, Java, e-commerce and Web environments. Subscribe to *XML Magazine* at `http://www.devx.com/`, or by calling one of the preceding numbers.

- *Exchange & Outlook* magazine is the latest Fawcette bimonthly periodical intended to support developers and IT professionals with the technical information, programming methodology, and new product information needed to master administration of Microsoft Exchange 2000 and take advantage of its myriad new features.

ONLINE WINDOWS 2000 RESOURCES

A complete list of online resources that offer Windows 2000-related content would fill several pages. Following are a few of the most useful links for Windows 2000 system administrators:

- The primary Microsoft starting point for "official" information on Windows 2000 is `http://www.microsoft.com/Windows2000`. This location offers product overviews, technical white papers, and news, interspersed with a substantial amount of Windows 2000 Professional and Server propaganda.

- The Microsoft BackOffice home page at `http://www.microsoft.com/backofficeserver/` leads to sources of information on the components of BackOffice 4.5+. The `http://www.microsoft.com/backofficeserver/prodinfo/win2000sps.htm` page lists the service packs you must install to upgrade BackOffice components to Windows 2000 Server.

- Windows Media Technologies has its own headquarters at `http://www.microsoft.com/windows/windowsmedia/en/default.asp`. You can download the latest add-ons and updates to Windows Media Technologies 7+ at `http://www.microsoft.com/windows/windowsmedia/en/download/default.asp`.

- The System Internals Web site at `http://www.sysinternals.com/` delivers utilities—such as Diskmon and Filemon—for Windows 2000 that you can't find anywhere else.

- *Windows 2000 Magazine*'s Professional Support Forums for Windows NT and 2000 are located at `http://www.win2000mag.net/forums/`.

- InformIT (`www.informit.com`) offers reference content from all computer-related imprints of Macmillan USA and selected imprints of Pearson plc. Excerpts from books on Windows 2000 and articles by Macmillan USA authors of interest to Windows 2000 administrators appear regularly on the site.

- CMP, publisher of *Information Week* and other IT-related magazines, offers a Windows 2000 section in its PlanetIT Technology Centers at `http://www.planetit.com/techcenters/windows_2000`.

- Developer's Exchange, Fawcette Technical Publications' Web site for Windows developers at `http://www.devx.com/`, offers a wide range of news, features, and product reviews of interest to Windows 2000 Server administrators and programmers.
- Sunbelt Software's site at `http://www.sunbelt-software.com/` provides an online catalog of Windows 2000 and NT utilities for network administrators and software developers. You also can subscribe to *Win2KNews*, which Sunbelt calls the "world's largest Windows 2000 weekly newsletter."
- *Windows Magazine*'s Windows 2000/NT Watcher page at `http://www.winmag.com/windows/win2knt.htm` has links to Windows 2000 news, reviews, and workshops.

PART I

PLANNING YOUR MICROSOFT WINDOWS 2000 SERVER INSTALLATION

1 Windows 2000 Server for NT 4.0 Users—What's New   19

2 Understanding IP, DNS Namespaces, and TCP/IP   63

3 Introducing the Active Directory and LDAP   93

4 Optimizing Your Active Directory Topology   147

5 Choosing and Testing Migration Strategies   193

6 Preparing NT 4.0 for Windows 2000 Server Migration   259

7 Specifying Server and Data Storage Hardware   297

CHAPTER 1

WINDOWS 2000 SERVER FOR NT 4.0 USERS—WHAT'S NEW

In this chapter

The Long Road from Cairo   20

Server Versions   21

Active Directory   23

Security Services   36

Networking and Internet Services   40

Storage, File, and Print Services   46

Remote Communication Services   52

Streaming Media Services   53

Application Services   56

Terminal Services   57

Kernel Architecture Upgrades   58

Integration with Microsoft Exchange 2000   59

MCSE Corner: An Introduction   60

The Long Road from Cairo

Windows 2000 is Microsoft's most prodigious software development project to date—35 million lines of source code, according to industry estimates. Windows 2000 undoubtedly sets a new computer industry record for development expenditures to upgrade an operating system, but it also sets a new Microsoft record for delayed delivery—more than two years behind the original schedule for the release of "Cairo." Cairo was the original code name for the successor to Windows NT 4.0, which was scheduled for release in the second half of 1997 as Windows NT 5.0. The last mention of Cairo in a Microsoft press release was in June 1996, and Microsoft changed the official name from Windows 5.0 to Windows 2000 in late October 1998.

There are many reasons for Windows 2000's extended gestation period, but the primary culprit is a plethora of new features, many of which—such as laptop power management and support for the five-button wheel mouse—benefit only users of the Workstation version. This chapter summarizes the most important new features of Windows 2000 Server, Advanced Server, and Datacenter Server for Windows NT Server 4.0 administrators. The chapter also briefly discusses Windows 2000 AppCenter Server, which Microsoft announced in September 1999 and has scheduled for release in mid-2000. Windows 2000 Professional features receive coverage only when they relate to interaction with servers.

Tip from
RJ

> If you don't have prior experience with Windows NT Server 4.0, skim this chapter and continue with the next three chapters of Part I, "Planning Your Microsoft Windows 2000 Server Installation," which describe the foundation of Windows 2000 Server networking and directory services. To give Windows 2000 Server a quick test drive on an isolated network, skip the network design and planning chapters in Part I and go directly to Chapter 8, "Deploying Windows 2000 Production Servers."

Upgrade Incentives

Upgrading from Windows NT version 3.1 to 3.5 and from 3.51 to 4.0 Server was a no-brainer. These upgrades were evolutionary, straightforward, and—for most network administrators—uneventful. Windows NT Server 4.0 with Service Pack 4+ has proven itself to be an acceptably stable, reliable, and predictable operating system for networks of modest scope. Windows NT Server 4.0 captured the "sweet spot" of the server market—networks with 25 or fewer servers and less than 500 clients, often called *departmental networks*. According to International Data Corp. (IDC), a computer-industry market research firm, Microsoft sold 1.56 million Windows NT Server 4.0 licenses in 1998—close to 50% more licenses than for Novell NetWare and more than twice the sales of all versions of UNIX. Microsoft designed Windows 2000 Server to garner the high-end of the server market—*enterprise networks* that run UNIX. Windows NT hasn't made serious inroads into the enterprise market segment because of actual or perceived scalability and manageability issues. These issues arise primarily from Windows NT's ungainly domain trust architecture and lack of an enterprise-class directory system comparable to Novell's NetWare Directory

Services (NDS). Windows 2000's Active Directory, described in the "Active Directory" section that follows shortly, offers the potential to overcome these serious limitations of Windows NT 4.0 Server and its predecessors.

Upgrade Uncertainties

Moving from Windows NT Server 4.0 to one of the three Windows 2000 server versions is a major undertaking, especially in larger, distributed networks. Taking full advantage of Active Directory can become a Herculean task—a total, top-down restructuring of your existing Windows NT domain architecture, groups, and group membership assignment. According to the Gartner Group, Inc., another well-respected computer market research organization, "The benefits of Windows 2000 Release 1 will generally not be compelling enough to justify a large-scale and risky upgrade from NT v.4.0, especially for servers." Gartner went on to state, "Microsoft is making positive claims about the quality of Windows 2000. In reality, uptime will be better, but product reliability—unpredictable downtime—will be an issue."

To allay the fear, uncertainty, and doubt (FUD) raised by the computer press and industry pundits, Microsoft unofficially released Windows 2000 on April 29, 1999, by shipping 670,000 CD-ROM sets of the Beta 3 version.

A $59.95 membership in the Corporate Preview Program (CPP) delivered a five-license Windows 2000 Server, two licenses for Windows 2000 Professional, and a two-CD Windows 2000 Evaluation and Deployment kit. For an additional $20, Microsoft added the Advanced Server version that supports network load balancing, server clustering, and other enhancements to Windows NT Server 4.0 Enterprise Edition (EE). The CPP licenses expire in 445 days after installation; if you installed Beta 3 in May 1999, your licenses expire in July or August 2000. Based on the Gartner Group's findings, it's a good bet that most current users of Windows NT Server 4.0 won't be ready to put Windows 2000 Server into production until well after the CPP license expiration date. Conservative network administrators undoubtedly will delay production deployment until Windows 2000 Server receives at least its first Service Pack (SP) or two.

Server Versions

Windows 2000 is or will be available in the following four Server versions:

- *Server* is the counterpart of Windows NT 4.0 Server and includes most of the server features described in this chapter. Windows 2000 Server serves the needs of about 90% of the server market. This book devotes all but one of its chapters to the Server version.
- *Advanced Server* corresponds to Windows NT 4.0 Server Enterprise Edition. Advanced Server adds load balancing and clustering features to the server version. Advanced Server is best suited for database applications and Web site hosting where high availability—the ratio of uptime to total in-use time—and performance are primary objectives. Advanced Server enables you to install up to 64GB of RAM in servers using the forthcoming 64-bit Intel Itanium CPUs, originally code-named Merced.

- *Datacenter Server* scales up the symmetrical multiprocessing (SMP) and clustering features of Advanced Server. Microsoft hadn't released Datacenter Server when this book was written. The Datacenter version is intended primarily for use by commercial Internet service providers (ISPs) and organizations running very large databases (VLDBs). VLDBs usually have a size of 1TB (one terabyte) or more. Datacenter server uses Microsoft's Advanced Windowing Extensions (AWE) and Intel's Physical Address Extensions (PAE) to support up to 64GB of RAM with Pentium Xeon processors.

- *AppCenter Server* is intended for deploying and managing Web server farms, which consist of banks of multiple Windows 2000 servers running Internet Information Server (IIS) 5.0 and COM+ components. AppCenter Server provides Web administrator with a set of tools to automatically replicate Web pages, applications, and configuration settings across multiple Web servers. Component Load Balancing (CLB)—which Microsoft removed from the Advanced and Datacenter versions in September 1999—plus monitoring, analysis, and load testing/capacity tools round out the promised AppCenter version.

Table 1.1 compares the feature sets, multiprocessing limits, and maximum installed RAM of each Windows 2000 Server version. Advanced, Datacenter and AppCenter Servers' 4GB tuning (4GT) for Intel-compatible (*x*86) CPUs is identical to that of Windows NT 4.0 Enterprise edition. If you have 4GB of RAM installed in your server, 4GT enables you to assign 3GB of RAM to applications and services—such as SQL Server, Exchange Server, or Internet Information Server—instead of the standard 2GB allocation.

TABLE 1.1   PRIMARY FEATURES, MAXIMUM NUMBER OF CPUS PER SERVER, AND MAXIMUM RAM PER SERVER FOR THE THREE VERSIONS OF WINDOWS 2000 SERVER

Version	Primary Features	CPUs per Server	Maximum RAM per Server
Server	Active Directory Kerberos/public-key security Windows Terminal Services COM+ component services Internet Information Server 5	Up to 4	4GB
Advanced Server	All Server features 4GB tuning for *x*86 CPUs Fail-over, two-node clustering High-performance sorting Network load balancing	Up to 8	64GB with Intel Itanium CPUs
Datacenter Server	All Advanced Server features Four-node clustering Advanced clustering features	Up to 32	64GB with Intel Itanium CPUs
AppCenter Server	All Advanced Server features Component Load Balancing Single-application image and other features for Web server farms	Up to 8	64GB with Intel Itanium CPUs

Active Directory

Active Directory (AD), called OLE Directory Services in the Cairo era, is the single most important new feature of Windows 2000 Server. AD is a hierarchical, distributed database—derived from the Microsoft Exchange Server database—that contains information on all enterprise resources, regardless of the domain in which they're located. *Resources* consist of physical entities, such as computers, printers, and users, and logical entities, including Windows 2000 services, user policies, and file folders. AD refers to resources and all other entities about which information is stored in AD as *objects*.

AD also includes the service components required to implement create, read, update, and delete (CRUD) operations on instances of object classes.

→ For definitions of common AD terms, **see** "Learning Active Directory Terminology," **p. 95**.

Active Directory uses *multimaster replication* to synchronize the content of AD databases between domain controllers (DCs) within a site and at remote locations. *Multimaster* means that updates to an AD database copy on any computer ultimately propagate to all DCs, which eliminates the distinction between Windows NT 4.0 primary domain controllers (PDCs) and backup domain controllers (BDCs). The replication process is similar to that for Exchange Server's directory. Replication isn't immediate, especially over WAN links, so Microsoft describes AD database copies as having "loose consistency." Network connections permitting, all copies of the AD database ultimately become identical—a process called *convergence*. If you're familiar with Exchange Server replication, you're at least halfway to understanding how AD replication works. Chapter 3, "Introducing the Active Directory and LDAP," explains replication in more detail.

> **Note**
> Active Directory consists of database and log files stored in the \Winnt\Ntds folder and a shared system volume whose default location is \Winnt\Sysvol. Sysvol contains folders that store enterprisewide and domain-level group policy objects and scripts. You must install Sysvol on a drive formatted with NTFS 5.0. If you don't have an NTFS 5.0 volume, you can't install AD, either in a standalone installation or when upgrading Windows NT Server 4.0.

Active Directory Schema

The Schema object contains a full description of each AD object class, including a list of the object's properties (called *attributes*) and the location of the class in the AD hierarchy. The common term for a collection of descriptions of database objects, the schema, is *metadata*—data about data.

The AD Schema is *extensible*; that is, you can define your own object classes and add the definitions to the Schema. Windows 2000 designates a single DC as holding the Schema Master Role; only users designated as Schema Administrators can modify the Schema object. After you add a new object class, you can't remove it, so be judicious when extending the schema.

> **Note**
>
> Only the DC holding the Schema Master Role can modify the schema. Thus, schema replication is single-master, not multimaster. Schema replication is one of several directory functions that Microsoft calls flexible single-master operations (FSMOs, pronounced "fizmos").

Active Directory also provides the *Class Store* to specify the location of networked application components. The Class Store doesn't extend the AD schema with additional object classes. Class Store is an additional AD namespace that stores pointers to custom-programmed COM and COM+ objects.

→ "Application Services," **p. 56**, describes COM+ and explains how Class Store aids developers of multitier applications.

Windows 2000 Domain Architecture

Windows 2000 Server retains the domain-based structure of Windows NT Server 4.0 and its forebears, but adds to the AD hierarchy two new objects—*forests* and *trees*—above domains, and *sites* within or spanning domains. Forests and trees provide the foundation for AD's *spanning tree of transitive trusts*, which overcomes the burdensome limitations of Windows NT's nontransitive (one-way) trusts between domains. Domains support a hierarchy of subdomains in parent-child relationships. Sites are groups of server and client computers connected by a high-speed—10Mbps or faster—network.

Figure 1.1 illustrates possible relationships of members of AD's physical resource hierarchy. Most AD diagrams use triangles to represent trees and domains, lines with large arrows at each end for transitive trusts, and circles to represent sites.

Figure 1.1
This forest of three domain trees contains domain hierarchies of varying depth.

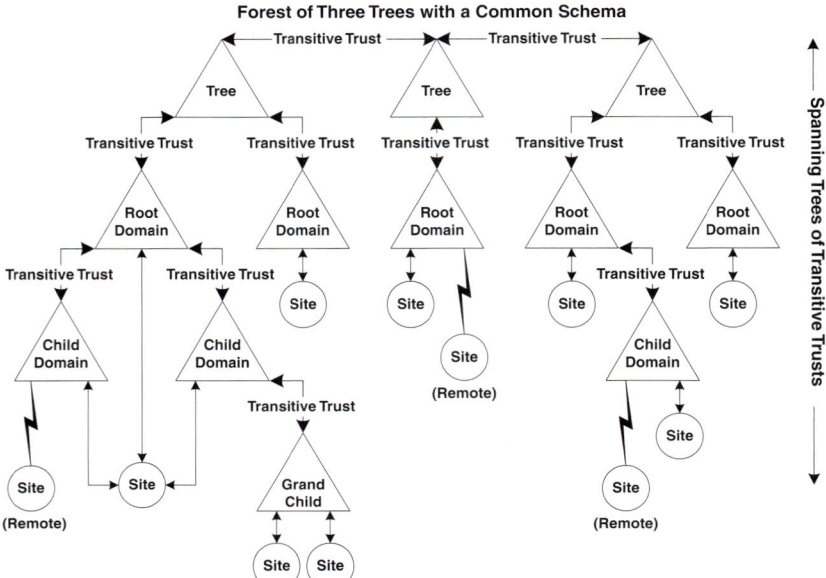

Technically, sites aren't elements of domains and aren't included in your domain namespace(s). Sites have geographic, not functional, boundaries; sites can span multiple domains and domains can have multiple sites. Figure 1.1 illustrates domains with multiple sites and three domains sharing one site. Sites define AD replication boundaries and enable users to log in to the closest DC. When you install the first Windows 2000 DC, setup creates a single default site named `Default-First-Site-Name`.

> **Note**
> You use the Active Directory Sites and Services Manager, described in the "Active Directory Administration" section later in the chapter, to rename, create, and delete sites, and assign specific computers to sites. The Active Directory Domains and Trusts snap-in, described in the same section, manages domains in forests and trusts between domains.

The domain structure of Figure 1.1 illustrates a deeply nested domain structure that's more complex than necessary for most organizations. Regardless of the depth of the hierarchy, each domain within a forest of domain trees maintains a complete trust relationship with all other domains in the forest. Setting up the equivalent trust relationships in Windows NT would require you to create 9 * (9 – 1), or 72, one-way trusts. AD automatically creates the 11 transitive trusts shown in Figure 1.1 as you add domains to the forests and trees. You can specify one-way (nontransitive) explicit trusts between forests to implement custom security policies for particular domain trees.

AD includes an additional component called the *global catalog* (GC). The GC, which you create when adding the first Windows 2000 domain, spans all forests and provides a means for locating any resource or user on the network. To minimize replication traffic, the GC contains only a partial replica of domain objects. Chapter 3 describes how the GC fits into the AD hierarchy.

Domain Namespaces and DNS

Windows NT uses NetBIOS computer names in a flat namespace; AD requires a hierarchical namespace to support parent-child domain relationships. A *namespace* defines a set of rules for assigning consistent names to objects. The domain name system (DNS), a set of Internet standards, provides a well-accepted namespace for computers within a hierarchically structured domain. This book's examples use `oakleaf.edu` as the primary domain name; `oakmusic.com` and `oakstudents.edu` appear in multidomain examples. Chapter 2, "Understanding IP, DNS Namespaces, and TCP/IP," provides a detailed description of Internet addresses and DNS name resolution for friendly names (`oakmusic.com`) and public IP addresses (`209.249.8.35`). The internal IP addresses for the `oakmusic.com` and `oakleaf.edu` domains are in the `10.7.1.1` to `10.7.254.254` range. Translation between internal and public IP addresses is one of the subjects of the "Remote Communication Services" section later in the chapter.

You must use DNS to identify computers within Windows 2000 domains, whether you're upgrading existing Windows NT domains or creating a network from scratch. Domains represent *security boundaries* within domain trees, and each domain has at least one copy of the AD database. One of the primary justifications for creating multiple domains is to establish different security policies—such as password length, uniqueness, and duration—for domain resources. You also can establish specific administration, replication, and group policies for each domain. By default, child domains inherit policies from their parent domain to simplify group policy administration.

Following are the basic rules for creating and naming Windows 2000 domain trees and forests:

- A domain must have at least one Windows 2000 domain controller. Every Windows 2000 DC has its own AD copy, so Windows 2000 doesn't distinguish between primary and backup domain controllers (PDCs and BDCs).
- The first Windows 2000 DC you create—either in a new network or by upgrading a Windows NT PDC—becomes the *initial root domain* of the forest. The initial root domain contains the configuration and schema for the entire forest, and, by default, handles all FSMO roles. Even if your network has only one domain, it has a forest with an initial root domain.

> **Caution**
> The name of AD's first domain becomes the forest name. You can't delete, rename, or change the role of the initial root domain of a forest. Unlike Windows NT, you can rename other Windows 2000 domains and change the name of servers within all domains. Microsoft promises that future versions of Windows 2000 will permit renaming, dividing, and merging forests.

- All computers within a domain tree must share a *contiguous namespace*. A contiguous namespace requires that the rightmost two components of the DNS name (`domainname.ext`) must be identical.
- You add child domain names and computer (host) names to the left of the base DNS name of the tree (`childdomain.domainname.ext` or `computername.domainname.ext`).

> **Note**
> It's a common practice to add Windows NT resource domains as child domains of their account (master) domain.
>
> Unlike Windows NT, you can duplicate computer names in different domains, including child domains. Duplicating computer names, however, isn't a recommended practice in any network.

Figure 1.2 illustrates a typical DNS namespace for the leftmost domain tree of Figure 1.1. The first domain added to the tree, `oakleaf.edu`, becomes the initial root domain of the forest. As you add child domains, you prepend the child domain name (`research`) to the parent domain name (`oakleaf.edu`) to form the child domain name (`research.oakleaf.edu`). You prepend server and client names to the parent or child domain name, as in `oakleaf1.oakleaf.edu` or `rescli7.research.oakleaf.edu`. Only computers (hosts) have IP addresses. The right-to-left hierarchy of domain and host names forms the foundation of DNS lookup of IP addresses from friendly names, and vice versa. Windows 2000 Server upgrades Windows NT's DNS Manager to Dynamic DNS (DDNS), a proposed Internet standard that defines the method for automating updates to the DNS database. DDNS takes the drudgery out of keeping DNS records up to date; as you add or remove hosts, DDNS automatically creates or deletes host records.

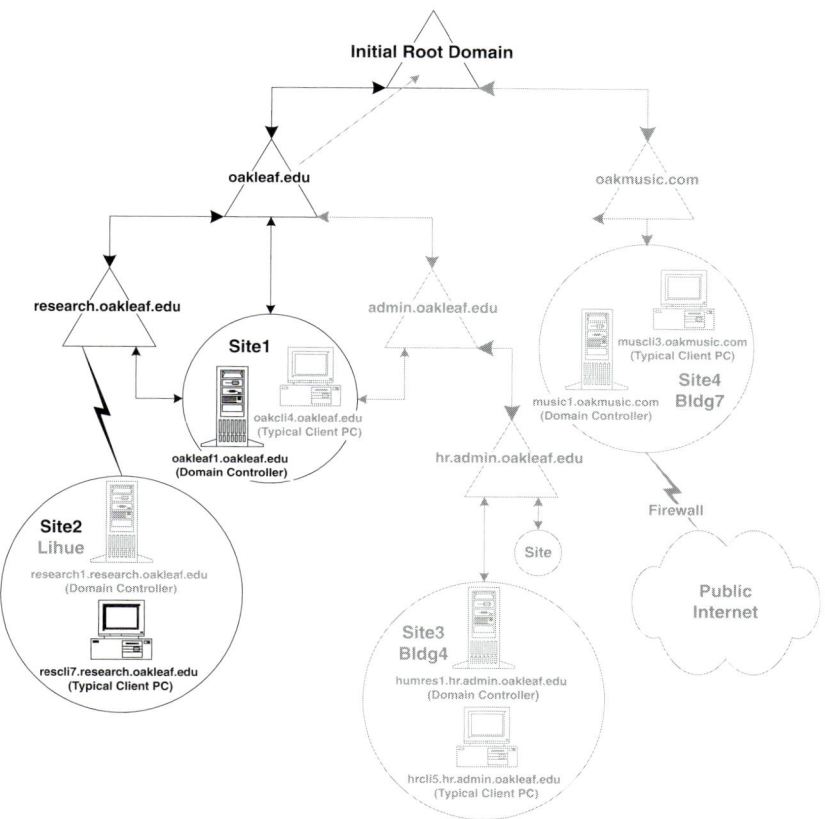

Figure 1.2
In this example of a DNS namespace for a forest of two domains, `oakleaf.edu` has child and grandchild domains.

Tip from RJ	Prepare your Windows NT domains for upgrading to AD with the Windows NT 4.0's DNS Manager, if you haven't already implemented DNS. Integrate your DNS servers with the Windows Internet Naming Service (WINS) to support clients that rely on NetBIOS names to locate DCs. Implementing DNS for your Windows NT domain(s) enables you to become familiar with DNS before you upgrade to Windows 2000. Chapter 6, "Preparing NT 4.0 for Windows 2000 Server Migration," describes how to optimize your existing Windows NT domain infrastructure for AD and ease the pain of the upgrade process.

Group and User Hierarchies

Windows NT permits only single-level nesting of security groups, such as the nesting of the global Domain Users group within the local Users group. Local groups can contain global groups, but global groups can't contain local groups, nor can global groups contain other global groups. Windows 2000's AD permits unlimited nesting of its equivalent to groups, called organizational units (OUs).

Organizational Units

Exchange Server uses Organizations (Os) and OUs to create a hierarchy of Exchange users based on the Lightweight Directory Access Protocol (LDAP version 3.0), another Internet standard derived from the X.500 directory protocol of the International Telecommunication Union (ITU). AD uses an extended version of LDAP 3.0 for publishing the availability of and locating resources within forests and finding users within domains. Domain OUs also form the basis for setting resource security and delegating administrative rights within a domain. Once again, an understanding of Exchange aids you in learning AD's hierarchical structure.

OUs are particularly useful when you establish child domains based on geography, rather than business functionality. For instance, if you organize your sales department into child domains by country, you can duplicate the OU structure for each country's sales domain. Figure 1.3 illustrates this OU structure for two countries and adds the *full LDAP path* to the lowest OUs in the hierarchy, plus a simpler path to the `admins` OU of the top domain in the tree. Each element of the path is prefixed with its class abbreviation and an equals sign—`ou=` for OUs and `dc=` for domain components. The full LDAP path to a particular object is called the object's *distinguished name (DN)*.

Figure 1.3
This figure shows how the Organizational Units (OUs) are duplicated for each sales domain to make administration easier. It also shows the full LDAP path for each OU.

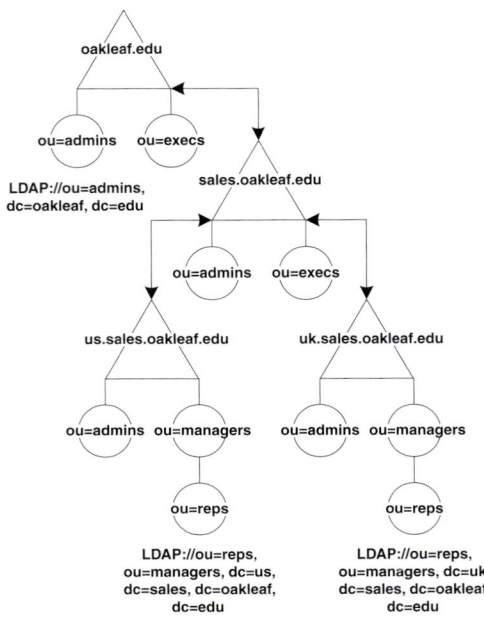

Active Directory   29

> **Note**
>
> LDAP DNs are far too lengthy and complex for most users to remember or type correctly. You assign a user principal name (UPN) having the email address format (*username*@*primarydomainname*.com) as a DN substitute. UPNs must be unique within the users' domain tree, and the UPN remains constant when a user moves from one OU to another. It's a common practice for administrators of organizations running Exchange to assign each user his or her Internet email address as the UPN. When you upgrade a Windows NT domain, Windows 2000 creates the UPN for each user from his or her logon ID and the new DNS domain name you specify during the upgrade process.

PART
I

CH
1

AD's full LDAP path is similar to that for Microsoft Exchange objects, such as the Recipients container for which the LDAP path is LDAP://*servername*/CN=Recipients/OU=*exchangesite*, O=*exchangeorg*. Fortunately, you needn't be concerned with full LDAP paths unless you develop directory-enabled applications with the Active Directory Service Interfaces (ADSI) version 2.5 that's included with Windows 2000 Server. The ADSI25 application, included in the \Seua2ks\Adsi25 folder of the accompanying CD-ROM, is a Visual Basic 6.0 project that enables you to view existing Windows NT or 2000 users and groups. ADSI25 also enables you to add 28 groups and a large number (up to about 27,500) of users to simulate real-life upgrade to Windows 2000 of a moderately large Windows NT domain.

➜ To give ADSI25 a try in a Windows NT upgrade test environment, **see** "The ADSI25 Visual Basic Application," **p. 141**.

> **Tip from**
> *RJ*
>
> Keep your OU hierarchy simple. You can nest OUs as deeply as you want to emulate a highly structured, bureaucratic organization, such as a government agency. An objective of business process reengineering (BPR)—one of the buzz-terms of the late 1990s—is to flatten organizational structures, which reengineering advocates contend increases efficiency. Regardless of your opinion of BPR, a flattened OU structure aids networking efficiency.

SECURITY GROUPS

Windows NT has predefined (BuiltIn) and user-defined security groups with two classes of scope—global and local. Windows 2000 defines the following three hierarchical classes of security groups:

- *Universal* groups can contain members (groups, users, or both) of any domain in a forest. To minimize replication traffic between domains, Microsoft recommends that Universal groups contain only other groups. There is no Windows NT equivalent of Universal groups.

- *Global* groups are the analog of Windows NT's global groups, such as Domain Administrators and Domain Users. Replication of a Global group is limited to the domain in which you create the group. Unlike Windows NT, you can nest Global groups; nested Global groups enable you to keep group size to a reasonable number of users. Microsoft recommends limiting individual Global group membership to a "few thousand" users.

- *Domain Local* groups are similar to Windows NT's local groups, but members of Domain Local groups are valid only within the domain in which you add them. Like Windows NT's local groups, you can add Global groups to Domain Local groups, but Windows 2000 also enables you to add Universal groups and Global groups from trusted domains to Domain Local groups. If you decide to create Domain Local groups, take advantage of the ability to import other groups to keep Domain Local membership small.

The "Security Services" section, later in this chapter, provides a brief overview of the new security features of Windows 2000. Chapter 4, "Optimizing Your Active Directory Topology," provides in-depth coverage of the ramifications of nesting groups and assignment of users to Universal, Global, or Domain Local groups.

THE ACTIVE DIRECTORY UPGRADE PROCESS

After you've added a Windows 2000 DC to your network by upgrading a Windows NT PDC, you can continue to connect to servers and resources within other trusting Windows NT domains. Domains with one or more Windows 2000 DCs and at least one Windows NT 4.0 BDC are called *mixed mode*. In mixed mode, trusts to other Windows NT domains remain one-way (nontransitive), and you can't create Universal groups.

AD provides a *PDC emulator* to service Windows NT BDCs and downlevel clients. Microsoft calls *downlevel* any computer or application that hasn't been upgraded to the company's latest and greatest release.

After you upgrade all BDCs in the domain to Windows 2000 Server, you "throw the switch" in the Active Directory Domains and Trusts tool and change to *native mode*. Native mode enables all AD features for domain servers, such as the ability to nest Global groups within other Global groups and create Universal groups.

Moving to native mode also enables AD-enabled clients to take advantage of AD features. Windows 2000 is AD-enabled, of course, but you must install the ADClient package on Windows 9x workstations. Running Dsclient.exe, which is located in the \Clients\Win9x folder of the Windows 2000 Server distribution CD-ROM, installs ADClient on Windows 9x machines. Microsoft stated in October 1999 that an ADClient package for Windows NT Workstation was "possible" in Service Pack 7.

→ For additional implications of moving from mixed to native mode, **see** "Throwing the Native-Mode Switch," **p. 397**.

THE ACTIVE DIRECTORY MIGRATION TOOL

Incremental migration of user and computer accounts is a more conservative approach to upgrading from Windows NT to Windows 2000 Server and AD. Incremental migration, which Microsoft calls *domain restructuring*, involves duplicating (cloning) Windows NT groups and user and computer accounts in a newly created native-mode domain, called a *pristine forest*. The advantage of incremental migration is that you can move users—either in bulk or a few at a time—to newly created Windows 2000 accounts. If problems occur during migration, you can instruct users to return to their original logon ID and password in the Windows NT domain.

Cloned objects receive a new security ID (SID) in their Windows 2000 domain but retain a copy of their original SIDs that are valid for the Windows NT domain. The copies of Windows NT SIDs, stored in the object's sIDHistory attribute, enables the cloned accounts to continue to access existing Windows NT resources. The sIDHistory attribute is the key element in the incremental migration process.

The Windows 2000 Server Support Tools include a set of Visual Basic Scripting Edition (VBScript) files for cloning Windows NT local groups (Clonelg.vbs), global groups (Clonegg.vbs), individual users (Clonepr.vbs), and all global groups and users together (Cloneggu.vbs). These scripts take advantage of a COM dynamic link library (DLL) called ClonePrincipal (Clonepr.dll). Running the ClonePrincipal scripts requires several premigration modifications to the Windows NT source PDC and the Windows 2000 destination DC. In addition, you need experience with the command-line scripting host (Cscript.exe) and VBScript programming to migrate groups and users with the ClonePrincipal scripts.

To simplify the incremental migration process, Microsoft licensed Mission Critical Software's Domain Migrator technology in June 1999. Mission Critical Software (http://www.missioncritical.com/) publishes the OnePoint suite of directory-enabled domain management products for Windows NT and 2000, of which Domain Migrator is a member. The end result of the Microsoft–Mission Critical collaboration is the Active Directory Migration Tool (ADMT), a collection of Wizards for automating ClonePrincipal and several other operations required to clone Windows NT objects as full-fledged AD security principals.

ADMT isn't included on the Windows 2000 Server distribution CD-ROM; you install ADMT on a Windows 2000 server from Microsoft's Windows Update site, http://windowsupdate.microsoft.com. Alternatively, you can download Admt.exe from http://microsoft.com/windows2000/downloads/deployment/admt/. Installing ADMT adds an Active Directory Migration Tool choice to your Administrative Tools menu. Launching ADMT opens a deceptively sparse Microsoft Management Console (MMC) window. Right-clicking the Active Directory Migration Tool node displays a menu that enables you to choose one of 11 migration-related wizards (see Figure 1.4). Most wizards offer the ability to run in test mode to create reports detailing prospective group and account migration.

Figure 1.4
Choose one of 11 Active Directory Migration Tool wizards.

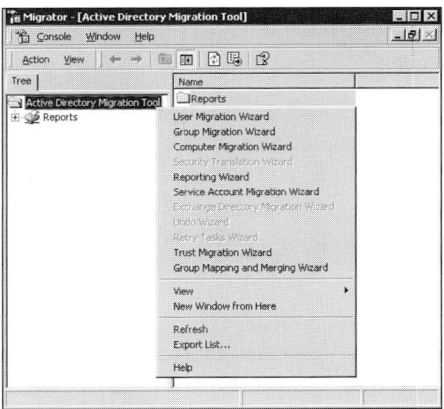

Following are brief descriptions of the basic ADMT wizards:

- The User Migration Wizard clones or moves individual or a collection of user accounts, together with their group membership data, to a single OU. This Wizard is useful when destination OUs for users don't correspond to their global group membership.
- The Group Migration Wizard enables you to create clones of one or more local and global groups and, optionally, their members within a single existing OU you specify. The Group Migration Wizard is especially effective when user OU membership corresponds to global group membership.
- The Computer Migration Wizard clones selected Windows NT computer accounts into a specified OU. Placing computer accounts in appropriate OUs, rather than in the default Computers container, simplifies account management.
- The Reporting Wizard dispatches agents to gather migration data from servers you specify and creates an HTML table with a row for each cloned object. Figure 1.5 illustrates the first few rows of the Migrated Accounts (MigrAcct.htm) report for Windows NT accounts cloned from the OAKLEAF domain to the Anthropology department's OU of `oakleaf.edu`.

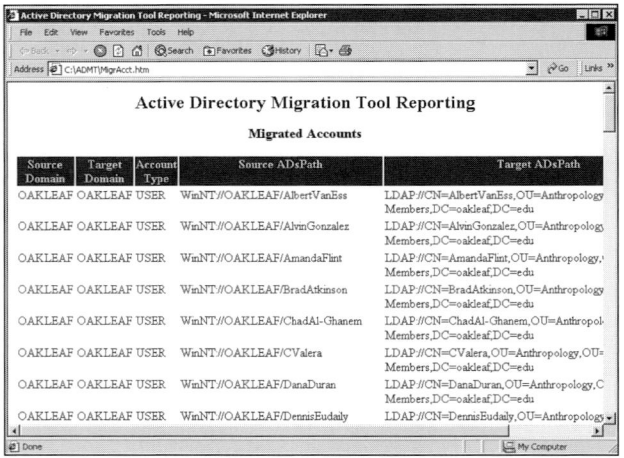

Figure 1.5
The Active Directory Migration Tool Report shows the source location and destination of each account being closed from the Windows NT 4.0 Domain called OAKLEAF to the specified LDAP paths in the Active Directory of Windows 2000.

Most ADMT wizards generate .log files with entries appended for each operation on every object cloned. Log files are especially important for troubleshooting problems with individual accounts or specific operations on all accounts, such as adding sIDHistory attribute values. Figure 1.6 shows entries at the start of a Migration.log file generated by the Group Migration Wizard. Setting each user's temporary Windows 2000 password, sIDHistory attribute, and group membership generates additional log entries that indicate success or failure of each operation.

Figure 1.6
The Migration.log file for the Active Directory Migration Tool shows which options were specified for the migration and each account that was created with a time and date stamp.

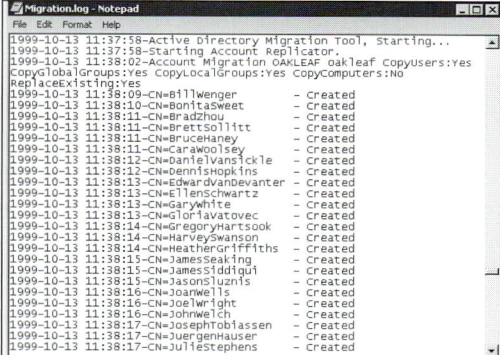

Active Directory Administration

Almost all Windows 2000 Server administrative tools are MMC 1.2 snap-ins. Snap-ins are .msc files that define the user interface and available actions for sets of AD object classes. You open the most administrative snap-ins from the Start, Programs, Administrative Tools menu. You also can launch most snap-ins by typing *Filename*.msc in the Run dialog's Open text box.

Use the following snap-ins to administer users, groups, computers, policies, domains, forests, sites, and the AD Schema:

- Active Directory Users and Computers (Dsa.msc), which replaces Windows NT's User Manager, is the primary user interface for administering AD objects. AD publishes computers, DCs, groups (OUs), users, and other directory objects to this snap-in. Right-clicking an object or container and choosing Properties displays its Properties dialog. Figure 1.7 shows Dsa.msc displaying published objects for the oakleaf.edu domain and the Account properties page for a member of the Anthropology OU.

Figure 1.7
The Active Directory Users and Computers snap-in is open in this figure, showing some of the accounts created during the migration process. The properties for the selected account are shown in the foreground dialog, while the background window shows the Organizational Units under the domain in the left pane, and the list of users in the selected container (Anthropology) in the right pane.

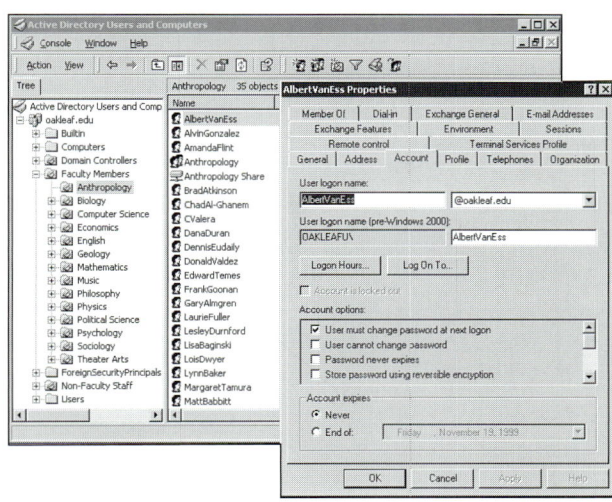

→ To learn more about the Active Directory Users and Computers snap-in, **see** "Working with Groups, Users, and Computers," **p. 114**.

- Active Directory Domains and Trusts (Domain.msc) enables you to specify explicit trusts between domains and change the domain mode from mixed to native mode. Right-clicking the `oakleaf.edu` node, choosing Properties, and clicking the Trusts tab displays the Trusts for the domain. Figure 1.8 illustrates nontransitive trusts to Windows NT domains and transitive trusts between parent and child domains.

Figure 1.8
The Active Directory Domains and Trusts snap-in shows a two-way nontransitive trust between the Windows 2000 do-main `oakleaf.edu` and the Windows NT 4.0 domain OAKLEAF. It also shows transitive two way trusts between `oakleaf.edu` and its child domains `resource.oakleaf.edu` and `student.oakleaf.edu`.

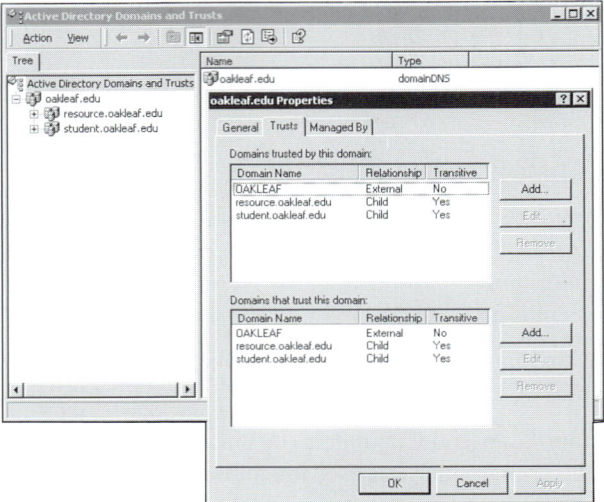

→ For additional information on the Domain.msc snap-in, **see** "Administering Domains and Trusts," **p. 105**.

- Group Policy (Gpedit.msc) is a snap-in that replaces Windows NT 4.0's Group Policy Editor. You can apply specific configuration, security, and software policies to sites, domains, domain controllers, and organizational units, in sequence. Group Policy isn't an Administrative Tools menu choice; you launch Gpedit.msc by right-clicking an AD container or site, choosing Properties, clicking the Group Policy tab, and clicking Edit. Figure 1.9 shows the default Group Policy for the `oakleaf.edu` domain. Chapter 15, "Establishing Group Policies, User Accounts, and Logons," shows you how to set up and maintain Group Policies for Windows 2000 clients.

You establish security policies within the AD hierarchy with the Security Policy Editor (Secpol.msc). The Domain Security Policy, Domain Controller Security Policy, and Local Security Policy choices of the Administrative Tools menu launch Secpol.msc with the chosen security scope.

Figure 1.9
The Group Policies page of the `oakleaf.edu` properties window shows the Default Domain Policy applied to that domain.

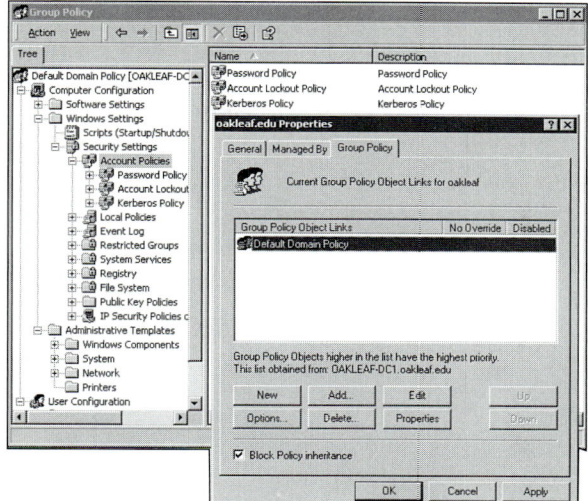

→ For an example of the use of Group Policies and Secpol.msc, **see** "Setting Security Policies for Domains and Domain Controllers," **p. 400**.

- Active Directory Sites and Services (Dssite.msc) handles site-related administration. This snap-in enables you to configure an existing site; delegate site control; add, move, and remove the site's servers (including DCs); and set up replication topology between sites. Figure 1.10 shows Dssite.msc displaying properties for the default Internet Protocol (IP) replication (`DEFAULTIPSITELINK`) between two sites with relatively high-speed (T3) connectivity.

Figure 1.10
The General page of the properties window for `DEFAULT-IPSITELINK` within the Active Directory Sites and Services snap-in allows the configuration of the sites joined by this link, as well as the link cost and replication frequency.

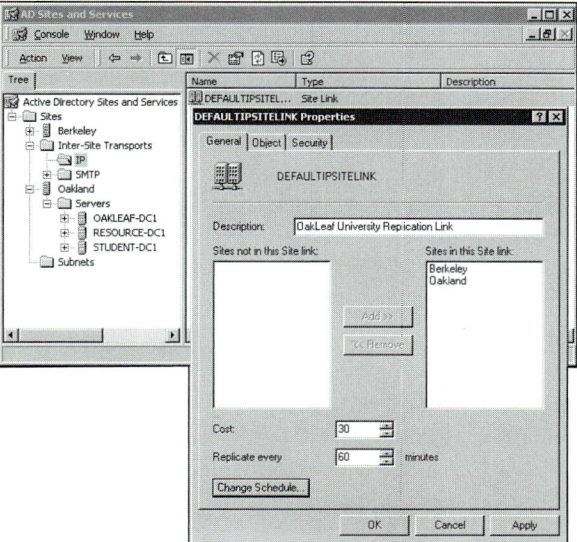

→ To learn how to use Dssite.msc, **see** "Viewing Sites and Services," **p. 113**.

- Active Directory Schema Manager (Schmmgmt.msc) manages changes to the AD Schema. Modifying the AD schema isn't for novices, and Microsoft requires that you install the Schmmgmt.msc snap-in manually and alter the Registry before you can make schema changes. Like Group Policy, Schema Manager isn't an Administrative Tools menu choice, so you must open Schmmgmt.msc manually after you install it. You must be a member of the Schema Administrators group to use Schmmgmt.msc. Windows 2000 automatically adds the Administrator of the initial root domain DC to the Schema Managers and Enterprise Admins groups. Figure 1.11 shows Schema Manager displaying the first 16 of the more than 200 optional and mandatory attributes of the user object.

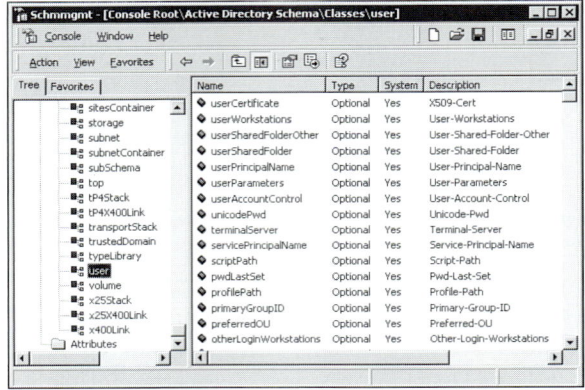

Figure 1.11
The Active Directory Schema Manager shows the available attributes and their properties for the user object in the Active Directory schema.

→ For instructions on installing and working with Schmmgmt.msc, **see** "Using the Active Directory Schema Manager," **p. 124**.

Security Services

Windows NT 4.0 has had more than its fair share of hackers who attempt to breach network security barriers, usually through an unauthorized remote connection. The NetBus Trojan horse, a cousin of the Cult of the Dead Cow's BackOrifice for Windows 9x, and L0phtcrack 2.5 from the L0ft group are just two examples of programs that have successfully compromised Windows NT 4.0 security. Windows 2000's enhanced security features offer the potential to make your local and wide area networks much more resistant—but not immune—to network intrusion and data interception by hackers or disgruntled employees.

Windows 2000 provides the following new security features:

- Kerberos version 5 provides network logon authentication and AD transitive trust authentication between Windows 2000 domains. Windows 2000 continues to support Windows NT LAN Manager (NTLM) authentication for downlevel computers. The "Kerberos Authentication" section that follows briefly describes the Kerberos protocol.

- Smart Card logon is an extension to Kerberos v5 to support the use of client and server Smart Card readers for user authentication. The user inserts his or her Smart Card in the reader and types a personal identification number (PIN) to log on to the network directly or via Remote Access Service (RAS). The "Smart Card Logon" section that follows describes the use of Smart Cards with Windows 2000 and Windows 98.

- Public Key Infrastructure (PKI) provides secure communication over wide area networks (WANs) by means of public- and private-key encryption. PKI relies on certificates issued by a trusted certificate authority (CA), such as VeriSign. Alternatively, you can generate your own certificates when you install the Windows 2000 Certification Authority snap-in, Certsrv.msc (see Figure 1.12). After you install Enterprise Root Certificate Services on a DC, you can't change the DC's domain.

Chapter 11, "Setting Up Key- and Certificate-Based Security," provides a complete description of Windows 2000's PKI implementation and how to take best advantage of Microsoft Certificate Services.

Figure 1.12
The Certification Authority snap-in is shown with the properties dialog open for the Oakleaf University enterprise root certificate showing its General properties page.

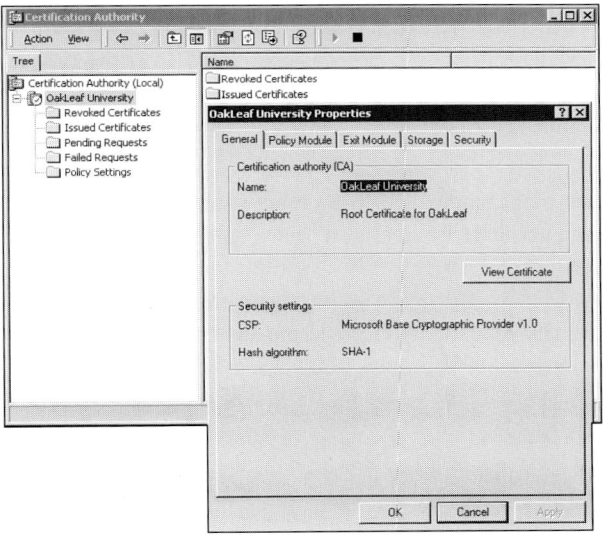

- Encrypting File System (EFS) offers enhanced security for NTFS volumes or folders containing sensitive information. EFS uses PKI encryption based on an EFS Users certificate that Windows 2000 generates automatically. By default, the domain Administrator account is the designated recovery agent and possesses EFS Recovery certificates to decrypt files whose EFS Users certificate has been lost or corrupted. One of the primary uses for EFS is protecting file contents in lost or stolen laptop computers.

> **Note**
>
> You must upgrade Windows NT 4.0 NTFS volumes to the new Windows 2000 NTFS 5.0 format to take advantage of EFS. If you're running a dual-boot server, you can't access encrypted folders or files with Windows NT Server 4.0.

- Group security policy, a subset of AD's Group Policy feature, simplifies management of group and user security settings. Windows 2000 enables you to delegate management of group security policy for specific OUs to other administrators.
- Internet Protocol Security (IPSec) provides secure authentication and communication encryption for TCP/IP networks, including the Internet, and one option for creating virtual private networks (VPNs). IPSec is one of the subjects of Chapter 26, "Setting Up a Virtual Private Network."

SECURITY PRINCIPALS

Windows 2000 defines a *security principal* as any object that can initiate an action. The most common security principals are users, computers, and operating system services. Each security principal has credentials from a *security authority (SA)*. If the Local Security Authority (LSA) of the machine on which the action is to take place trusts the SA, the security principal is authenticated and is permitted to execute its task. Windows 2000's LSA trusts Kerberos, Smart Card, and NTLM SAs.

The visibility to security principals of AD objects, such as shared folders and files, is determined by their credentials. If a user doesn't have credentials for a particular server share, it doesn't appear in the Active Directory Users and Computers management tool. Even if the share is visible, the user might not be able to open the share or specific files if these files have additional security restrictions. Like Windows NT, Access Control Lists (ACLs, pronounced "ackels") determine Windows 2000 object permissions.

KERBEROS AUTHENTICATION

The Kerberos authentication protocol, developed at the Massachusetts Institute of Technology, uses *shared-secret (symmetrical)* encryption, not the PKI infrastructure. Kerberos is an Internet standard—Request for Comments (RFC) 1510—that uses a Key Distribution Center (KDC) database to store account information of security principals in its realm; the KDC shares the secret keys. A *Kerberos realm* is the equivalent of a Windows 2000 domain. The database stores a cryptographic key (secret) for each security principal; the key—initially derived from a user's password and called a *long-term key*—is known only to the security principal and the KDC. Users obtain their keys during the first logon to the network; a server obtains its key when it's added to the domain.

When a client requests a connection to a server—either for logon or for access to server resources—the client sends a request to the KDC, which creates a unique session key called a *Kerberos ticket* for the client and server connection. The server's copy of the ticket is encrypted with the server's key and embedded in the client's ticket copy, which is encrypted with a new client key that replaces the long-term key. The KDC sends both ticket copies to the client in the session key, along with a Ticket Granting Ticket (TGT). The client stores the session key in RAM (not on disk), and uses it for server connections until the key expires—usually eight hours after issuance. The client expedites successive requests for tickets by sending its TGT to the KDC. TGTs are valid across domain (realm) boundaries having transitive trusts. Kerberos encrypts all communications between the client, server, and KDC.

Kerberos is a remarkably efficient protocol that is substantially more secure than the NTLM protocol of Windows NT 4.0 and its predecessors. Upgrading Windows 9x and Windows NT 4.0 workstations with Dsclient.exe adds a Kerberos logon option.

Tip from
RJ

Disable NTLM logon after you throw the native-mode switch on your Windows 2000 network and upgrade all clients (including mobile computers) with `Dsclient.exe`.

Making Kerberos your sole logon protocol provides a substantial improvement in network security.

Maintain production DCs in a secure (locked) location. The KDC database holds persistent (disk-based) key data, which makes location security even more important when you implement Kerberos security.

Smart Card Logon

Smart Cards are credit-card–size plastic cards having an embedded microprocessor that's powered and read by a Smart Card reader. Smart Card readers that qualify for the Windows 2000 Logo support Plug and Play, so installing readers on Windows 9x and 2000 clients and Windows 2000 servers is a relatively simple process. You can obtain a list of tested Smart Card readers at `http://microsoft.com/hwtest/hcl/`.

Smart Cards use a Kerberos extension to support their nonsymmetrical PKI encryption system. The Smart Card stores the user's public and private keys and shares the public key with any requester, including the KDC. Instead of pressing Ctrl+Alt+Delete at logon, the user inserts the Smart Card in the reader and types his or her PIN. The LSA uses the pin to extract on the client the user's X.509 v3 certificate (which contains the public key) and the private key and sends the certificate to the KDC. The KDC encrypts the initial session key and TGT with the user's public key for authentication. The client decrypts the session key with the Smart Card's private key and uses the TGT key after initial authentication.

Smart Card authentication provides the highest degree of network security, because Smart Cards don't depend on a typed password that is subject to inadvertent disclosure or interception. A user must possess the Smart Card and know the PIN to use it. Three or more successive PIN errors disable the Smart Card, making unauthorized use of a found or stolen card very unlikely.

> **Tip from**
> *RJ*
>
> Implement Smart Card authentication for every server and for every client used by Windows 2000 administrators. Smart Card readers certified for Windows NT 4.0 are very likely to be certified for Windows 2000. Many firms use Smart Cards for access to secure facilities, as well as to clients and servers. You gain a higher level of security by using a Smart Card lock on your server closet and a second Smart Card to log on to the network as an administrator. Ordinary users can use the same Smart Card to gain access to other secure building areas and the network.

NETWORKING AND INTERNET SERVICES

A significant change to Windows NT 4.0's networking services is abandoning the NetBEUI protocol in favor of TCP/IP. Windows 2000 continues to support NetWare's IPX/SPX protocol for downlevel networks, but most NetWare administrators have already migrated or plan to migrate from Novell's proprietary IPX/SPX protocol to TCP/IP. NetBEUI isn't a routable protocol, so it's suitable only for very small networks that don't interact with the Internet. Most small organizations running single-office NetBEUI networks migrated to TCP/IP when upgrading to Windows NT 4.0 or shortly thereafter.

> **Note**
>
> NetBEUI is an optional network protocol that you can add when you install Windows 2000 Server. The primary purpose of NetBEUI in a Windows 2000 network environment is supporting dial-up users who don't have TCP/IP installed on their PCs. In the very unlikely event you must support such users, install NetBEUI; otherwise, accept the default installation of the TCP/IP protocol only.

IP AND TCP/IP

Basic features of Windows 2000's TCP/IP network configuration dialog don't differ substantially from those of Windows NT. The route to the Internet Protocol (TCP/IP) Properties sheet, however, is circuitous. You right-click the My Network Places icon on the Desktop, choose Properties to open the Network and Dial-up Connections window, right-click the Local Area Connection item, choose Properties again to open the Local Area Connection Properties dialog, select the Internet Protocol (TCP/IP) item, and click Properties to finally open the General page of the Internet Protocol (TCP/IP) Properties sheet (see Figure 1.13). If you have more than one network adapter in your server, Windows 2000 assigns additional adapters to Local Area Connection 2 and higher. Dial-up connections, if present, also appear in the connection list.

Figure 1.13
Open the Internet Protocol (TCP/IP) Properties dialog from the Desktop's My Network Places icon.

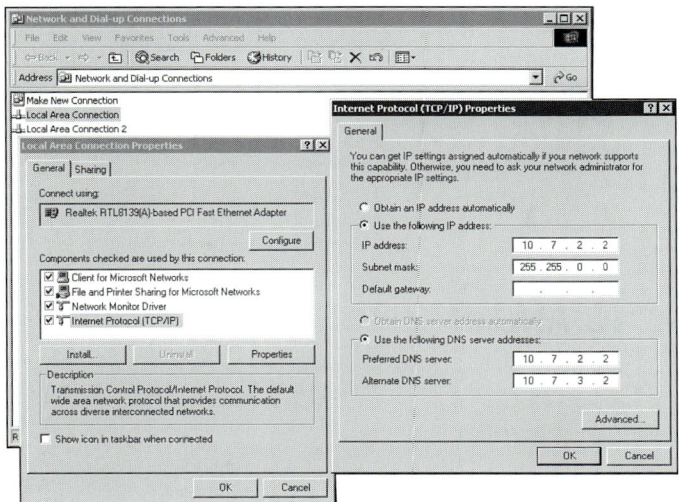

Tip from
RJ

Alternatively, you can open Control Panel and then open the Dial-up and Network Connections window. Neither approach is an expeditious method of reaching the Internet Protocol (TCP/IP) Properties dialog.

Windows 2000's IP support services and updated TCP/IP stack add the following new networking features:

- High-speed network support (RFC 1323) and Selective Acknowledgments (SACK) to improve performance of Internet connections and wireless networks.

- Quality of Service (QoS) components, including Differential Quality of Service (Diffserv), Admission Control Service (ACS), IEEE 802.1p prioritized LANs, and Resource Reservation Protocol (RSVP)—QoS provides dedicated bandwidth for time-sensitive applications, such as streaming audio/video content and teleconferencing. AD provides administration services for ACS.

- Internet Group Membership Protocol (IGMP) version 2, an Internet standard (RFC 1112) for IP multicasting over the Internet's multicast backbone (MBONE)—Multicasting enables you to send a single stream of packets, such as streaming audio from a live musical performance, to multiple listeners. Unfortunately, relatively few ISPs support MBONE.

- Dynamic DNS (DDNS) to automate updates to the Windows 2000 DNS servers required to support AD, as discussed in the "Domain Namespaces and DNS" section earlier in this chapter (see Figure 1.14)—Dynamic Host Configuration Protocol (DHCP) (see Figure 1.15) and Windows Internet Naming Service (WINS) (see Figure 1.16) integrate with DDNS. You need WINS to provide NetBIOS name resolution service until you upgrade all clients to AD. Windows 2000 provides Administrative Tools menu choices to open snap-ins for managing DNS, DHCP, and WINS.

Figure 1.14
The DNS manager snap-in (Dnsmgmt.msc) is open displaying an Active Directory-integrated DDNS forward lookup zone (oakleaf.edu), two secondary zones (resource.oakleaf.edu and student.oakleaf.edu), and an integrated reverse lookup zone for the 10.7.x.x Subnet, all seen in the left pane. Contents of the oakleaf.edu zone are shown in the right pane.

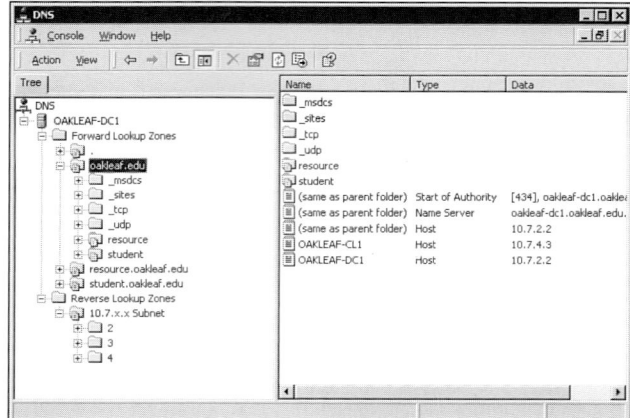

Figure 1.15
The DHCP Manager snap-in (Dhcpmgmt.msc) shows the currently allocated IP address leases including address and computer name in the right pane when the Address Leases node is selected in the left pane.

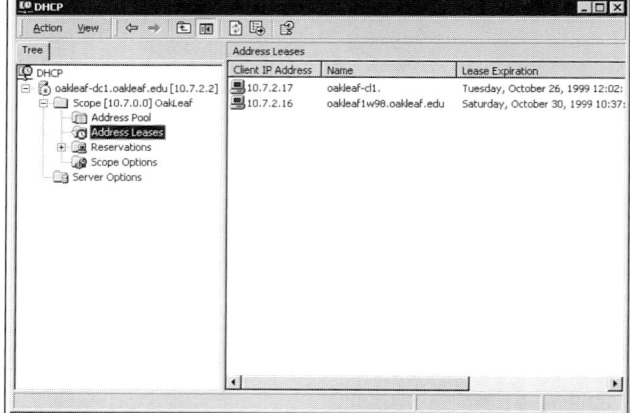

- Multicast DHCP, which provides a wizard to assign client multicast addresses—The "Streaming Media Services" section later in the chapter describes applications for multicast services.
- Plug and Play for network interface card (NIC) management—Plug and Play features are of more significance to Windows 2000 Professional users, because you rarely change NICs in network servers.

Figure 1.16
When the Active Registrations node is selected in the left pane of the WINS manager snap-in (Winsmgmt.msc) it shows WINS database records for clients in the 10.7.2.0 subnet including the system WINS name, computer type, IP address, and the state of the WINS mapping, all in the right pane.

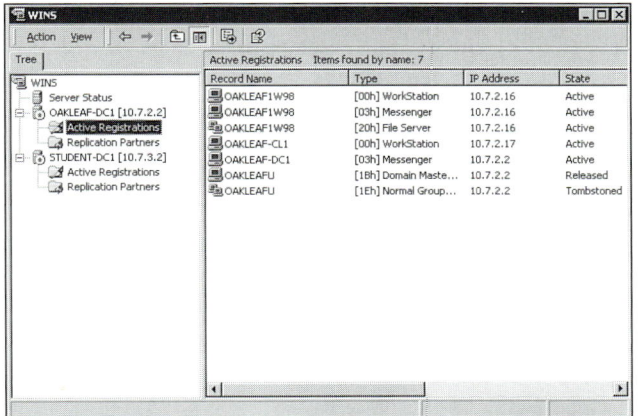

> **Note**
> Windows NT administrators are justifiably suspicious of Plug and Play features for servers. Microsoft implemented Plug and Play to bring Windows 2000 Professional into hardware-upgrade parity with Windows 9x. Plug and Play primarily is intended to simplify the addition or exchange of sound, video capture, network, and other adapters for consumer-grade PCs. During the course of writing this book, tests conducted with many different network adapters and other common server peripherals indicates that Windows's 2000 Plug and Play features are well-suited to the server environment.

ATM

Windows 2000 now supports Asynchronous Transfer Mode (ATM) networking natively. The primary markets for ATM, which offers speeds of 1.5, 25, 100, 155, 622, and 2,488Mbps, currently are telecommunications and campus-area network backbones that run at 155Mbps or faster. *Network backbones* provide high-speed switched interconnections between buildings—usually within a radius of a mile or two—and between floors of large buildings. ATM uses fixed-length (53-byte) packets—called *cells*—instead of the variable-length packets delivered over Ethernet and Token-Ring transports. Using fixed-length packets greatly increases switching efficiency, because ATM switches don't need to find the end of the variable-length packet frame.

Windows 2000 provides LAN Emulation (LANE) for interconnecting clients and servers on switched ATM networks. LANE breaks up variable-length Ethernet and Token-Ring packets into ATM cells. 155Mbps ATM NICs are much more costly than 100BASE-T NICs, and ATM switches for LANs are very expensive, compared with 100BASE-T hubs and routers. Windows 2000's IP over ATM (RFC 1577) feature creates a logical IP subnet over an ATM network.

A primary selling point of ATM has been its QoS features, which enable you to specify a Constant Bit Rate (CBR) mode for video and voice-over-IP services. Windows 2000's QoS for TCP/IP, described in the preceding section, serves the same purpose. Very few firms have adopted ATM as a LAN transport, and ATM currently is losing ground to Gigabit Ethernet transport for network backbones. Gigabit Ethernet switches and other network infrastructure components are much less costly than their ATM counterparts. It remains to be seen whether Windows 2000's ATM implementation, which is intended to support Microsoft's investment in and ultimate entry into the telecommunications networking market, will gain a significant number of users in other industry segments.

Internet Information Server 5.0

Internet Information Server (IIS) 4.0, included in the Windows NT 4.0 Option pack, proved to be a versatile and reliable Web server for private intranets and the public Internet. Windows 2000 Server's IIS 5.0 is an incremental upgrade to IIS 4.0 that adds the following primary services:

- Web Distributed Authoring and Versioning (WebDAV) is a set of extensions to the HTTP protocol that enable multiple users to collaborate in the editing and management of documents stored on local or remote Web servers. WebDAV adds conventional file system behavior to HTML documents; you can move, copy, and edit Web documents in the same way you handle word processing files. WebDAV is the product of an official Internet Engineering Task Force (IETF) working group (http://www.ics.uci.edu/pub/ietf/webdav/). WebDAV offers features similar to Office 2000's Office Server Extensions (OSE) that enable users to collaborate in the editing of XML-encoded Word, Excel, and other Office documents.

- Web Folders present a common namespace and user interface for Web server content, local file folders, and network shares. Web Folders is a proprietary Microsoft extension to WebDAV.

- Internet mail and newsgroup protocols—Simple Mail Transport Protocol (SMTP) and Network News Transport Protocol (NNTP)—are fully integrated with IIS 5.0.

- Multiple site support with a single IP address uses host headers to create more than one Web site on a single IP address.

- Support for Distributed File System (Dfs) as the root for Web sites enables you to change the physical location of Web content folders without altering their HTML links. Dfs is described in the "Distributed File System" section that follows shortly.

- File Transfer Protocol (FTP) Restart resumes file transfer from the point at which an interruption in the connection occurs, instead of requiring a complete resend of the file.

- Kerberos authentication for Web servers provides users a single logon to a secure Web site.

- Certificate Wizard, which replaces the Key Manager utility of IIS 4.0 and earlier, eases the process of creating user or CA certificates to implement Secure Sockets Layer (SSL) on your Web site. SSL currently is the most common method of authenticating servers and encrypting e-commerce traffic.

- Network load balancing—provided by the Advanced and Datacenter server versions—distributes client TCP/IP connections over multiple Web, proxy, and FTP servers.
- Component load balancing, included in AppCenter Server, enables groups of middle-tier servers to run multiple instances of COM+ business-object components to handle e-commerce and other data-intensive Web-based applications.
- Processor Quotas implement processor throttling for multiple virtual Web servers to prevent a single Web server from consuming all available CPU cycles and preventing other servers from delivering pages.
- Process accounting enables administrators to monitor the processor time devoted to individual Web pages or an entire virtual Web site. Many ASP applications, especially multitier systems having multiple database connections, are very CPU-intensive. One of the primary objectives of processor accounting is to enable bill-back for supporting individual departmental Web sites. ISPs can use process accounting to bill customers by actual CPU resources consumed, rather than for peak bandwidth or similar conventional measures of Web site activity.
- eXtensible Markup Language (XML) integration with ActiveX Data Objects (ADO) 2.5 simplifies database access for Active Server Pages (ASP) in two-tier and three-tier configurations. All versions of Windows 2000 include the supporting components for OLE DB and ADO 2.5.

Figure 1.17 shows the Internet Information Services Manager (iis.msc) console and the Web Site page of the OakMusic (IIS 5.0) Properties dialog for the intranet version of the `oakmusic.com` Web site. Chapter 27, "Installing Internet Information Server 5.0," covers new Web server setup and upgrading from IIS 4.0.

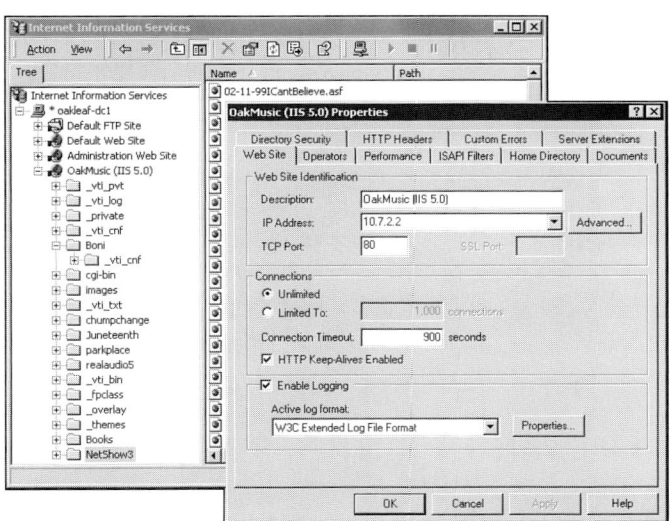

Figure 1.17
The IIS 5.0 Administration snap-in is open and showing the Web Site page of the properties window for the OakMusic Web site. The list of installed IIS sites is shown in the left pane of the background window with the OakMusic site expanded.

> **Note** The first wide-scale production deployment of Windows 2000 Server and Advanced Server probably will be as Web servers. Web servers run as member (resource) servers and don't require AD installation and management. The benefits of new IIS 5.0 features clearly outweigh the relatively minor risks associated with adopting Windows 2000 as a Web-server operating system.

Interoperability

Not much has changed on the interoperability front in Windows 2000 Server. Windows 2000 Server includes Windows NT's Gateway Services for NetWare (GSNW) and Print Services for UNIX, but File and Print Services for NetWare (FPNW) and Services for UNIX remain separate, extra-charge option packs. Chapter 12, "Interoperating with NetWare Services," covers GSNW and FPNW; Chapter 13, "Integrating UNIX and Linux Networks," shows you how to use Services for UNIX's NFS client and server for file sharing, and third-party applications, such as Samba (a freeware service), for Windows networking on UNIX boxes.

Windows 2000 Server doesn't include Windows NT's Directory Services Migration Tool for Netware. The replacement, Microsoft Directory Synchronization Services (MSDSS), is a component of Microsoft Services for Netware, which also includes FPNW versions 4.0 and 5.0, plus Directory Service Manager for Netware for Windows NT. MSDSS takes advantage of ADSI 2.5 to provide two-way synchronization with Novell Directory Services (NDS), migration from NDS to AD, and synchronization with NetWare 2.x, 3.x, and 4.x Binderies.

Like its predecessors, Windows 2000 Server provides interoperability with the aging AppleTalk networking protocol, File Server for Macintosh (MacFile), and Print Server for Macintosh (MacPrint).

> **Note** Microsoft announced at its May 1999 Tech*Ed conference a suite of interoperability components, code-named Babylon, for Windows 2000. Availability of Babylon and an upgraded Services for UNIX 2.0 are scheduled well after the retail release of Windows 2000. Babylon, an add-on to Microsoft SNA Server, translates XML messages into what Microsoft calls "legacy" formats—IBM's MQSeries, DB2, and CICS, among others. Babylon also interacts with BizTalk, a Microsoft-sponsored framework for the use of XML to enable e-commerce between businesses. You can learn more about the nascent BizTalk standards at http://www.biztalk.org/.

Storage, File, and Print Services

Many of the most significant additions to Windows 2000 Server fall in the storage management and file services categories. Windows NT 4.0's print services receive only a relatively minor update in Windows 2000, but Microsoft has increased dramatically the number of printers supported by drivers installed from the distribution CD-ROM.

Storage Management

The most evident change to storage management is Windows 2000's new disk management snap-in (Diskmgmt.msc) for the Computer Management console (see Figure 1.18).

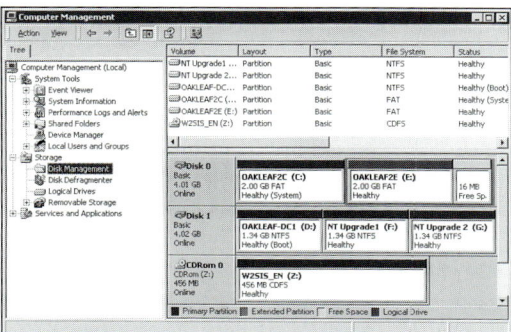

Figure 1.18
In this figure showing the Computer Management snap-in with the Disk Management tool open, logical drives are shown in list form at the top of the right pane, and in graphical form at the bottom of the right pane.

Following are the most important of the new Windows 2000 storage management features, most of which rely on NTFS 5.0:

- Dynamic volume management enables you to increase or decrease volume size without rebooting the server. Increasing volume size, of course, depends on your having—or making—free space available on an accessible drive. Unlike Windows NT, you can administer dynamic volumes remotely. You can't directly access FAT or NTSF 5.0 dynamic volumes if you dual-boot your server into Windows NT 4.0 or other Windows versions, whose file systems Microsoft calls basic storage.

- Disk defragmentation improves server performance by physically relocating file clusters in their logical sequence. Microsoft originally claimed that NTFS files didn't fragment, but a thriving market in third-party disk defragmentation tools belied Microsoft's contention. Like Windows 9x, Windows 2000 now includes a defragmentation utility (see Figure 1.19).

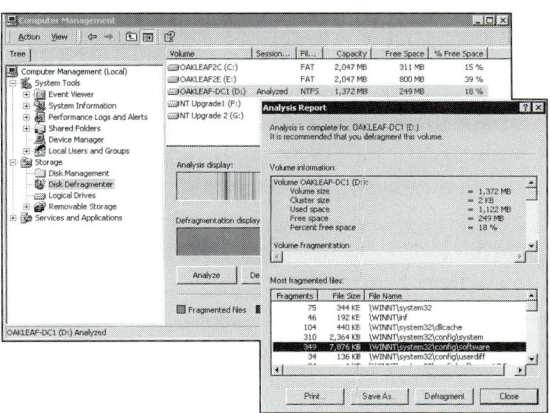

Figure 1.19
The Computer Management snap-in is shown here with the Disk Defragmenter snap-in and a disk analysis report window open in the foreground. This Analysis Report shows the recommendation of the defragmenter snap-in.

- Hierarchical Storage Management (HSM) enables you to automatically or manually move seldom-used files and folders from fixed-disk to tape or other low-cost storage media. Folder and file pointers remain on the fixed-disk drive for redirection to the offline location when users open a moved file. Index Server, included with Windows 2000 Server, optionally incorporates HSM content in full-text searches.

- Backup and Recovery Tools substitutes a "lite" version of Seagate Backup Exec for the developmentally challenged NT Backup utility of Windows NT (see Figure 1.20). You open the Backup and Recover Tools application, which isn't an MMC snap-in, from the Programs, Accessories, System Tools, Backup menu. The Backup utility handles live backup of AD, File Replication Service, and Certificate Server on DCs. Like the majority of Windows NT Server administrators, most Windows 2000 administrators choose to upgrade to the full version of Backup Exec or upgrade their current third-party backup application to Windows 2000.

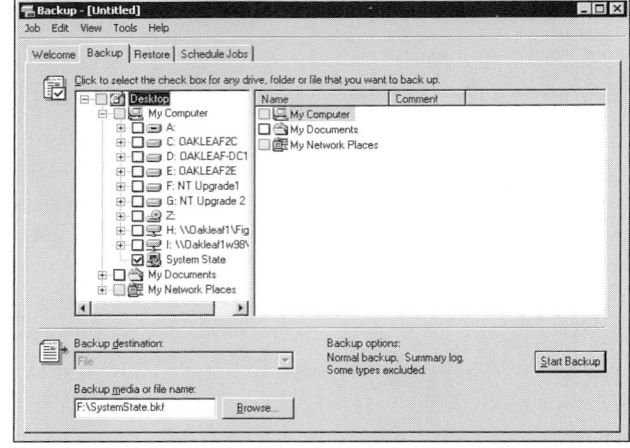

Figure 1.20
The Backup and Recovery Tools application is open to the Backup page and is ready to begin backing up the system state of a Domain Controller to a file on disk. Note that the System State box is checked in the left pane and the backup file is specified below that.

- Removable Storage Management (RSM) supports robotic tape changers and jukeboxes for CD-ROM, DVD-ROM, magneto-optical (MO), and other disc-based media. RSM enables you to create *media pools* of related storage types, such as backup tapes or MO discs that store scanned document images (see Figure 1.21). RSM categorizes media as Unrecognized (not cataloged), Free (cataloged blank media), or Import (cataloged media with data). You can automate backup operations with RSM-enabled applications.

Figure 1.21
This is the Computer Management snap-in open to the Removable Storage tool, and the Create a New Media Pool Properties dialog is open. The information specified in this dialog will create a pool of 6mm tapes when OK is clicked.

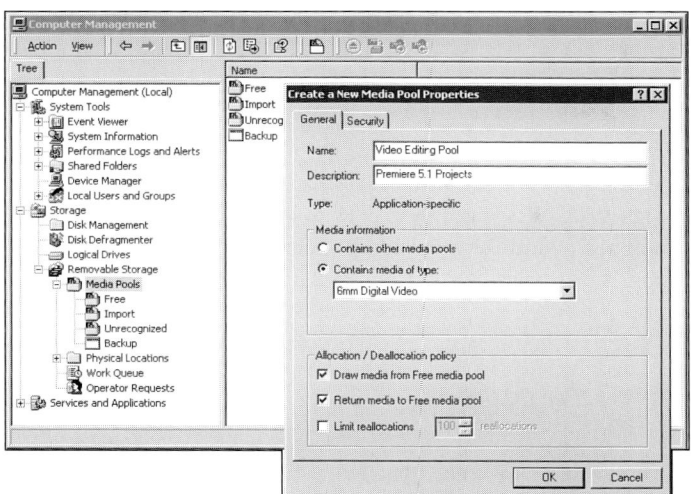

- Disk quotas permit administrators to use Group Policies to limit allocation of server disk space on NTFS volumes to Windows 2000 clients. You enforce disk quotas for Windows 2000 domain members by altering values in Group Policy's Computer Configuration, Administrative Templates, System, Disk Quotas Properties dialogs (see Figure 1.22.) You must enable and enforce disk quotas to make quota limits and warning levels effective. Windows NT required third-party add-ins to establish and manage disk quotas.

Figure 1.22
The Group Policy administration snap-in is open; an OU and a Default Quota Limit and Warning Level are being set in the foreground dialog. The quota limit specifies the maximum amount of disk space users are entitled to.

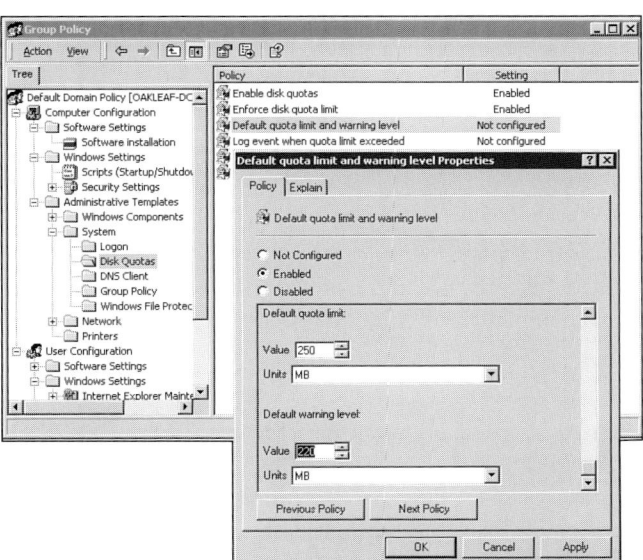

- Remote Storage Services (RSS) monitor each Windows 2000 Professional user's free fixed-disk space. When free space drops below an assigned limit, RSS deletes local files after confirming that a server share holds current copies.

- Sparse files enable developers to create very large files that consume comparatively small amounts of disk space until needed. Sparse files are similar conceptually to Excel's sparse matrices; only cells with content occupy disk space.

- Multiple data streams in a single file enable NTFS 5.0 to store individual components of compound documents in separate data streams. Applications extract an individual data stream by appending a colon and the stream name to the filename.

- Distributed link tracking solves problems associated with moving files to which clients have previously established links. Link tracking assigns an object identifier (Object ID or OID) to each file. AD maintains the relationship between the location of the file and its OID. Only Windows 2000 clients support distributed link tracking.

- IntelliMirror takes advantage of Windows 2000's AD, Group Policies, Synchronization Manager, and disk quotas to provide Windows 2000 Professional users with a dedicated server share for the contents of their My Documents and, optionally, My Pictures folders. Maintaining all user documents on a server assures regular data backups and enables users to access their files from any client PC. Roaming user profiles, also stored in the user's share, presents the user's standard or custom desktop, regardless of client location. IntelliMirror also provides automated software setup and maintenance features specified by group policies.

Chapter 9, "Installing RAID and Removable Media Systems," covers dynamic volume management, disk defragmentation, RSM, and backup management. Disk quotas, distributed link tracking, and RSS are subjects of Chapter 16, "Managing Server Shares and the Distributed File System." Chapter 20, "Supplying IntelliMirror and Application Installation Services," shows you how to set up IntelliMirror features.

Distributed File System

Technically, Dfs isn't a new feature; Dfs 1.0 Windows NT 4.0 appeared in late 1996, and Microsoft posted version 4.1 in July 1997 at http://www.microsoft.com/NTServer/all/downloads.asp. Relatively few Windows NT Server administrators downloaded the free Dfs upgrade, possibly because Windows 95 clients need an update to connect to Dfs shares. Dfs now is an integral component of Windows 2000 Server, assuring its widespread adoption in 2000 and beyond.

File systems provide a uniform naming convention and access method for a collection of physical disk sectors. Dfs delivers the same services for server shares, but Dfs provides additional features that most file systems don't include. Microsoft calls Dfs a "logical view of physical storage." Figure 1.23 illustrates creating a link to an existing share with the Distributed File System snap-in (Dfsgui.msc). Windows 2000 Server includes a Wizard to establish the Dfs root share. The Wizard has an option to create a single AD-integrated or conventional Dfs root share on each server.

Figure 1.23
The Distributed File System snap-in and the Create a New Dfs Link dialog are open to establish a link to a first-level Dfs share.

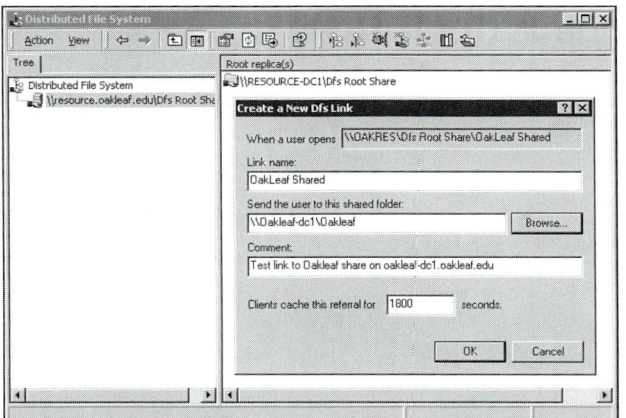

The most important benefits of implementing Dfs are

- Custom hierarchical network shares enable administrators to define a share name and a simple folder tree that enables users to access folders resident on multiple servers as if they were subfolders of a single network share.
- Improved data availability comes with copies of read-only data having the same Dfs root name, but stored on multiple volumes. If one Dfs root share is inaccessible or becomes corrupted, Dfs automatically switches users to a Dfs copy.
- File load balancing uses copies of read-only data stored on multiple servers to maintain high performance during peak file-reading periods.

Chapter 16 guides you through the process of setting up and managing Dfs.

PRINT SERVICES

Windows NT 4.0 print services have proven adequate for most networks, so print services receive only the following facelift features in Windows 2000:

- Internet Print Protocol support, which enables clients to use Internet URLs to access remote printers via intranets and the Internet
- Printer search by AD attributes, which enables searching for a network printer by physical location and capabilities, such as two-sided or color printing
- Better color print accuracy with the Image Color Management (ICM) 2.0 API

UniDrive5, the basic Windows 2000 printer driver, makes it relatively easy for developers to enable custom printer features. Microsoft claims that Windows 2000 supports more than 2,500 printers. Chapter 17, "Installing Network Printers," covers printer installation and support under Windows 2000.

Remote Communication Services

Virtual Private Networks can greatly reduce telecommunications charges to large organizations having many mobile and telecommuting workers and multiple branch offices. Thus, most of the new remote communication features of Windows 2000 Server, described in the following list, concentrate on easing VPN setup and administration:

- Internet Authentication Service (IAS) uses Remote Authentication Dialup User Service (RADIUS) for user authentication over Internet and VPN connections.
- Increased RAS security comes from added secure protocols—IPSec and Layer-2 Tunneling Protocol (L2TP)—for Internet and VPN connections. L2TP is a multiprotocol relative of the Point-to-Point Tunneling Protocol (PPTP).
- Network Address Translation (NAT) provides a simple proxy to transfer packets between your internal network and the public Internet. The advantage of NAT is that you can map multiple internal network addresses to the single IP address or group of IP addresses assigned to your organization by your ISP. All network users can connect to the Internet through a single dial-up, ISDN, xDSL, or T-1 connection. Windows 98 Second Edition supplies a related connection sharing feature for peer-to-peer home networks. Windows NT 4.0 requires purchase of a license for and installation of Microsoft Proxy Server to provide connection sharing.

Note Use private IP host addresses in the range of 10.1.1.1 to 10.254.254.254, 172.16.1.1 to 172.32.254.254, or 192.168.1.1 to 192.168.254.254 for your internal network to implement NAT. Addresses outside this range, other than IP addresses assigned to multicasting (224.1.1.1 through 239.254.254.254), are allocated already (or will be allocated) to organizations and individuals by the Internet Assigned Numbers Authority (IANA).

- Connection Manager Administration Kit (CMAK) enables administrators to tailor group or individual RAS clients for your available RAS services.
- Phone Book Administrator provides a central source of RAS and VPN phone numbers.
- Connection Point Services combine Phone Book Administrator and CMAK functions to distribute access number updates automatically to clients.

The Routing and Remote Access (RRAS) components for Windows 2000 Server, which extend the features included in Windows NT 4.0's RRAS add-in, supplies most of the new communications elements of Windows 2000 server. You administer RRAS with the Routing and Remote Access MMC snap-in (Rrasmgmt.msc). Figure 1.24 illustrates the RRAS console's Port Status dialog for a VPN using the L2TP protocol. Chapter 25, "Managing Remote Access and Routing Services," and Chapter 26 cover Windows 2000's remote communication services.

Figure 1.24
The Routing and Remote Access snap-in is open and displaying the properties for an L2TP VPN port which is currently inactive in the foreground window. The right pane of the background window lists all installed ports.

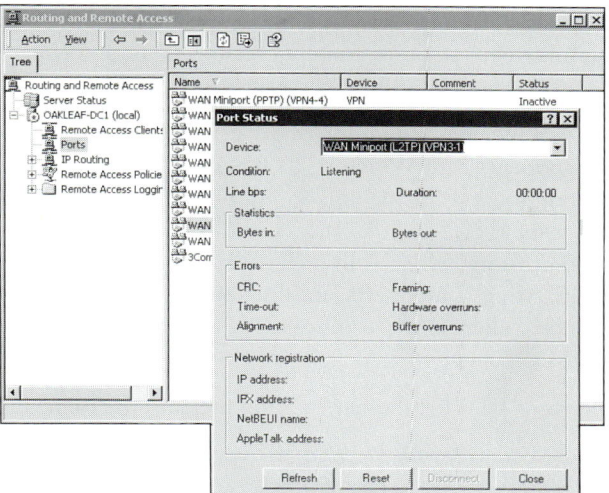

Note
Microsoft, Cisco, Ascend, IBM, and 3COM jointly developed the L2TP protocol. L2 derives from Cisco's Layer-2 Forwarding protocol (L2F). Unlike PPTP, which requires a Point-to-Point Protocol (PPP) connection, L2TP runs over X.25, frame relay, and ATM transports. L2TP also supports upgraded Multilink PPP (MPPP) that lets clients aggregate the bandwidth of two Internet VPN dialup connections without requiring the ISP to support MPPP. The Windows 2000 Server connected—presumably by a T-1 or faster line—to the ISP reassembles the traffic from the two client connections.

Streaming Media Services

Microsoft has a history of being the multimedia runner-up. Apple computers and its QuickTime multimedia file system and operating environment gained an early lead among artistically inclined developers—graphic designers, musicians, videographers, and animators. Only recently has the Windows platform gained grudging respect among media professionals, due at least in part to the reversal of Apple's fortunes under former CEO Gil Amelio. Despite Apple Computer's revival under Steve Jobs' stewardship, by mid-1999, most high-end audio/video hardware and software producers were dedicating their products—or at least initial release of products—to 32-bit Windows.

Microsoft is again faced with playing catch-up in the streaming media market with its Windows Media Technologies (WMT). RealNetworks' RealAudio and RealMedia formats continue to dominate Internet-based streaming audio and video content delivery. RealNetworks claims users have downloaded 80 million copies of its RealPlayers, and more than 85% of Web pages that deliver streaming media use RealSystem software. As of August 1999, Microsoft claimed 40 million downloads of Windows Media Player. The primary source of RealNetworks revenue is media server licenses, the cost of which increases with the number of simultaneous streams, content creation tools, and enhanced versions of RealPlayer.

In contrast, Microsoft includes Windows Media Player with all Windows 2000 versions and most WMT 4 components with Windows 2000 Server. You can download WMT content authoring and editing tools, available only for Windows 9x and Windows NT when this book was written, from `http://www.microsoft.com/windows/windowsmedia/`. WMT 4 supports on-demand unicasting, which delivers a dedicated stream for each connected client, and broadcast multicasting, a more efficient distribution method that supplies a single stream to all connected clients. Microsoft released a beta version of Windows Media Technologies 7 in May 2000.

Windows 2000 Server's WMT 4 implementation includes the following enhancements:

- Microsoft Audio coder/decoder (codec) delivers improved sound and image quality compared with the Voxware codec of NetShow 3.0 and its predecessors, and offers a multiple bit-rate delivery (called Intelligent Streaming) option. Microsoft claims that the new audio codec has the same audio quality at half the bit rate as downloadable MPEG-1 Layer 3 (MP3) files.

> **Note** MPEG is the acronym for the Moving Pictures Experts Group, an international organization devoted to developing digital audio/video (a/v) encoding standards. MPEG-1—designed for original CD-ROM data rates in the 1.5Mbps range—was the group's first a/v codec. MPEG-2 underlies high-power digital broadcast satellite (DBS) transmissions of DirecTV and EchoStar. MPEG-2 also is the foundation of the digital television (DTV), formerly advanced television (ATV) and high-definition television (HDTV), broadcast standards adopted in North America and Japan. MPEG-4 version 1—the standard for multimedia applications—was approved in October 1998; MPEG-4 version 2 was added as a standard in March 2000. You can read the official MPEG standards at `http://drogo.cselt.stet.it/mpeg/`.

- MPEG-4 version 3 video codec provides better image quality than NetShow 3.0's version 2 at comparable bit rates and also has an Intelligent Streaming option. MPEG-4 version 3 isn't an official standard.

- Multiple bit-rate video incorporates up to six video streams and a single audio stream within an individual `.asf` (Active Streaming Format) file. The server determines the bandwidth of the client connection and then delivers the video content at a bit rate commensurate with the available network bandwidth.

- Windows Media Rights Manager adds copyright protection for audio and video content. A Pay-Per-View Wizard enables you to charge for watching video content or listening to live or recorded industry conferences. Pay-per-view (PPV) events require an SQL Server database for user registration and billing and a Web server dedicated to PPV pages. You can download Windows Media Rights Manager 1.0 from `http://www.microsoft.com/windows/windowsmedia/en/download/default.asp`.

STREAMING MEDIA SERVICES | 55

Note

You don't have to upgrade your NetShow 3.0 server to use the new WMT 4 codecs, but downlevel clients must upgrade to the new Windows Media Player. You must upgrade your server if you want to implement Intelligent Streaming and other new features offered by Windows 2000's implementation of Windows Media Services.

Windows 2000 Server Setup doesn't install Windows Media Server by default, but you can specify its inclusion during the setup process or use the Add/Remove Windows Components feature of Control Panel's Add/Remove Programs tool to add Media Services. If you want to take advantage of high-performance User Datagram Protocol (UDP) streaming, you must devote a Web server to delivering content. Unlike other Windows 2000 administrative tools, the Windows Media Administrator, shown in Figure 1.25, isn't an MMC snap-in. Installing Windows Media Server sets up a default folder, ASFRoot, to contain .asf audio and video files.

→ To learn more about UDP, **see** "Taking Chances with UDP Delivery," **p. 89**.

Figure 1.25
This is the Windows Media Administrator Unicast Publishing Points page showing the default location for streaming .asf content.

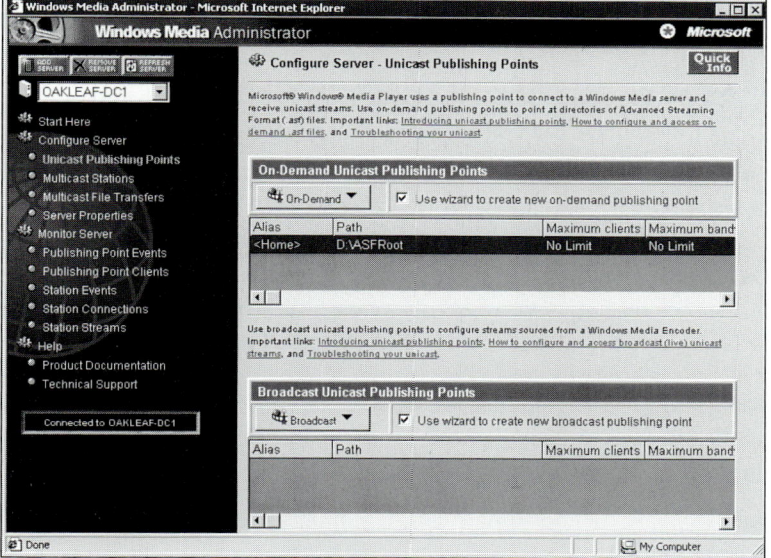

You can install WMT 4 under Windows NT Server 4.0 SP4; upgrading to Windows 2000 doesn't alter your WMT 4 installation. If you're currently running NetShow 3.0, WMT 4's predecessor, the upgrade to WMT 4 is optional (but highly recommended).

The "Streaming with Windows Media Technologies 4" bonus chapter on the CD-ROM describes how to set up WMT 4 and demonstrates how to create and deliver audio and video content via unicasting to the Internet and by multicasting for intranets.

Application Services

Windows 2000 Server's application services center on COM+, which integrates Microsoft Transaction Server (MTS) 2.0 and Microsoft Message Queue Server (MSMQ) with Windows 2000 Server. Microsoft's Component Object Model (COM) is an outgrowth of Microsoft's OLE technology for creating compound documents with Office applications. COM provides the underpinnings of Microsoft's ActiveX and other Active technologies. COM+ provides the foundation for Bill Gates' vision of Windows Distributed interNet Architecture (Windows DNA). You can learn more about Windows DNA at http://www.microsoft.com/windowsdna/.

The Windows NT 4.0 Option Pack added MTS and MSMQ to Windows NT Server 4.0; MTS and MSMQ now are elements of the Windows 2000 operating system. When you upgrade Windows NT Server 4.0's MTS 2.0 and MSMQ 1.0 with Windows 2000, existing components automatically become COM+ components. Developers must rewrite some of the components' code to take full advantage of Windows 2000's application services.

COM+ includes several new features to simplify implementing and deploying multitier (also called *n-tier*) applications. A *multitier application* is divided into the following three layers:

- *Presentation services* provide the client user interface—typically an Active Server Pages (ASP) Web page or a Visual Basic front end. One of the goals of multitier architecture is to minimize the amount of code at the presentation services layer.

- *Application services* (also called *business services*, rules, or logic) are custom-programmed components that manage business-related operations, such as e-commerce transaction processing. Developers write middle-tier components with Visual Basic, C++, or Java.

- *Data services* are back-end databases that provide persistent storage for the results of successful transactions. Data services also include database connectivity components, such as OLE DB and ActiveX Database Objects (ADO).

Application services and data services commonly run on separate, dedicated servers. Application services supplement—and sometimes replace—database stored procedures for transaction processing operations.

Following are the most important new application services supplied by Windows 2000 Server's COM+:

- Queued components take advantage of MSMQ features to assure completion of transactions, even if a network connection to one of the participants in the transaction isn't immediately available. A typical application for queued components is third-party credit-card validation and debiting for e-commerce. Queued components greatly reduce the programming code needed to take advantage of MSMQ's messaging features.

- Object pooling enables developers to precreate multiple instances of business service objects that clients can share a process called *just-in-time* activation. Object pooling improves overall performance, because creating new instances of middle-tier objects consumes a substantial amount of server resources. MTS 2.0 advertised—but didn't implement—object pooling.

- Dynamic component load balancing enables administrators to put copies of middle-tier objects on multiple servers. Load balancing routes client requests for object instances to the least-loaded server. Component load balancing is a feature of the AppCenter and Datacenter Server versions.

- Active Directory Object Store is a component of IntelliMirror that provides clients with a pointer to the server that stores required application services. Clients automatically download an application proxy for the component class. You deploy COM+ application services with the Microsoft Installer (MSI).

- Component event services provide a publish-and-subscribe model for intercomponent notification of "interesting" events. Microsoft refers to the publish-and-subscribe model as providing "loosely coupled" events—a concept similar to AD's loosely consistent replication model.

Tradition associates applications services with developers. The integration of COM+ into Windows 2000 Server and new features, such as the Object Store and component load balancing, require network administrators to become component deployment experts. Chapter 28, "Managing Transaction and Messaging Services," covers application services in the context of Windows 2000 Server administration. Chapter 20 shows you how to deploy applications and application services to users.

Terminal Services

Windows 2000 Server merges the features of Windows NT Server 4.0, Terminal Server Edition—originally code-named Hydra—with the basic operating system. You no longer need to purchase the Terminal Server Edition and purchase separate Terminal Services client licenses. The Standard Windows 2000 Server license and Client Access Licenses (CALs) are valid for both conventional and Terminal Server clients. Microsoft supplies Terminal Services clients for Windows 3.1x, 9x, and 2000; third parties offer support for DOS, Macintosh, and UNIX clients.

Terminal Services let underpowered (thin) or incompatible clients run Windows applications on a Windows 2000 server. Only keystrokes, mouse actions, and screen changes move between the client and server, which is similar to the operation of remote access software, such as PCAnywhere. Remote applications run in a single interactive session dedicated to a particular client; thus, you need substantial server horsepower—multiple CPUs and large amounts of RAM—and usually multiple servers to handle more than a few clients simultaneously. Adding multiple isolated sessions (processes) to Windows NT's conventional single-user console required Microsoft to make major-scale alterations to the kernel's Win32 subsystem.

Installing Windows 2000 Server's Terminal Services features is optional; Chapter 29, "Deploying Windows Terminal Services," covers installation of Terminal Services on servers and compatible clients.

Kernel Architecture Upgrades

Microsoft makes evolutionary—not revolutionary—additions to the Windows NT kernel in each successive release. One of the major changes to Windows NT 4.0's kernel was moving most graphics operations from Gdi32.exe to Kernel32.exe with the objective of improving video adapter performance. Server administrators were justifiably suspicious of kernel modifications that many believed sacrificed server stability for improved PC game display on workstations. As it turned out, running graphics drivers in the kernel wasn't a significant cause of "blue screens of death" (BSODs).

Kernel upgrades from Windows NT 4.0 to Windows 2000 are more conservative. Following are brief descriptions of the new kernel features of Windows 2000 Server:

- Windows Driver Model (WDM) unifies 32-bit Windows 98 and Windows 2000 hardware device drivers. WDM also enables Windows Management Instrumentation (WMI) for monitoring hardware problems and configuring devices remotely. Windows 2000 will force many manufacturers of specialty hardware devices—especially high-end audio and video processing cards—to accelerate movement from obsolete virtual device drivers (VxDs) to WDM. Specialty adapters, however, are of interest primarily to Windows 2000 Professional users, not Server administrators.

- Enterprise Memory Architecture (EMA) enables Windows 2000 Advanced and Datacenter Servers to support up to 32GB of memory with Itanium CPUs. Very Large Memory (VLM) applications, such as relational database management systems (RDBMSs), must be specifically coded and compiled to support VLM.

- High-performance sorting, available in the Advanced and Datacenter versions, moves database query sorting operations to the kernel for increased speed. Like EMA, RDBMSs must be customized to take advantage of high-performance sorting; SQL Server 7.0 is the first RDBMS to implement this feature.

- Scatter/gather I/O primarily enhances the performance of application servers running RDBMSs by gathering scattered memory blocks into contiguous disk clusters. Service Pack 3 added scatter/gather I/O to Windows NT 4.0 to support SQL Server 7.0.

- Intelligent I/O Architecture (I2O) is another SP 3 add-on to Windows NT 4.0 that's become a native operating system feature in Windows 2000. Intel developed the I2O specification, which defines the architecture of device drivers that operate independently of the host PC. I2O offloads much of the overhead for I/O processing to a dedicated microprocessor, most commonly a customized I/O version of Intel's i960 reduced instruction set computer (RISC) chip. You can learn more about I2O at http://www.intel.com/design/iio/i2osig.htm.

- Spin count doesn't keep track of the number of press releases prepared by Waggener Edstrom to describe this week's description of the benefits of the latest flavor Windows DNA. Spin count helps multiprocessor systems deal with contention issues, such as deadlock in RDBMSs. If one CPU's process is attempting to write to a table row that the other CPU's process has locked, spin count keeps track of the failed write attempts. If the number of blocked write attempts exceeds a specified threshold, the writing query waits until the other CPU's process releases the lock.

Chapter 7, "Specifying Server and Data Storage Hardware," has individual sections that cover WDM, I2O, and EMA.

INTEGRATION WITH MICROSOFT EXCHANGE 2000

Microsoft Exchange 2000, formerly code-named Platinum, is a major revision of Exchange Server 5.5. Exchange 2000, which runs only under Windows 2000 Server, moves its directory store to AD and offers a compelling set of new features that simplify management of user accounts, improve message store backup and recovery, and separate front-end management from back-end database operations. Exchange 2000 promises to provide the impetus for many large organizations to migrate their messaging systems from Windows NT to Windows 2000 Server.

The Active Data Connector—which you install as a separate Windows 2000 Server component from the \Valueadd\Msft\Mgmt\Adc folder of the distribution CD-ROM—delivers two-way synchronization between the Exchange 5.5 SP3+ directory and AD. You can connect to Exchange 5.5 running under Window NT or Windows 2000 Server, and replicate Exchange containers into AD or vice versa. The Exchange 2000 administrative tools, however, aren't fully compatible with Exchange 5.5, so you must continue to administer Exchange 5.5 with its own Administrator application. ADMT includes a wizard to migrate Exchange 5.5 accounts to Exchange 2000.

Installing Exchange 2000 adds a second version of Active Directory Users and Computers to the Programs, Microsoft Exchange menu, and adds new Action menu choices to both Users and Computers versions for adding, deleting, and administering mailboxes. Exchange 2000 optionally supports voicemail and instant messaging. Figure 1.26 shows Exchange 2000's Users and Computers snap-in with added E-Mail Address and Exchange Alias columns. Selecting multiple user accounts and choosing Add Exchange Mailbox from the context menu automatically sets up email addresses and mailboxes for the users. When you create a mailbox, the *Username* Properties dialog opened from Exchange's Users and Computers tool gains three new Exchange pages—Exchange General, E-mail Addresses, and Exchange Features (see Figure 1.27).

Figure 1.26
The Active Directory Users and Computers administration snap-in on a Windows 2000 PC with Exchange 2000 installed shows the integration of Exchange with Active Directory. The email addresses and aliases are displayed in the same location as other user properties.

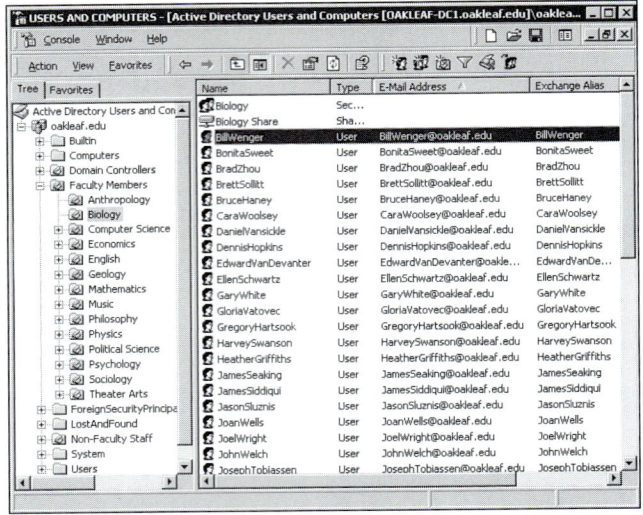

Figure 1.27
Once Exchange 2000 is installed on a Windows 2000 Server in an Active Directory environment, extra tabs are added to the standard user properties page for configuring Exchange settings. The Exchange General page is shown here.

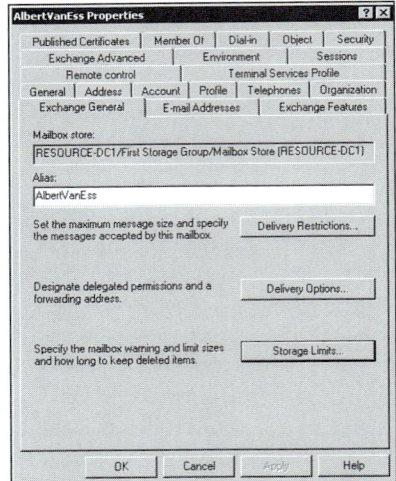

Microsoft plans to release the final version of Exchange 2000 Server in mid-2000; Figures 1.26 and 1.27 are from the Beta 3 version that Microsoft made available in late 1999 on CD-ROM or by downloading from http://www.microsoft.com/exchange/.

MCSE Corner: An Introduction

The MCSE Corner is a section at the end of each chapter of this book that provide you insight on the Microsoft Certified Professional (MCP) exams relating to Windows 2000 Server.

The MCSE Corner tells you what topics covered in the chapter you just read are tested on the exams. It also explains what concepts are most important to understand in order to do well on the exam and gives you hints and tips for the test.

The exams pertaining to Windows 2000 Server are listed in detail in the MCSE Corner at the end of Chapter 7, but the base exam for Windows 2000 Server is 70-215, "Installing, Configuring, and Administering Windows 2000 Server." Check the following `http://www.microsoft.com/mcp/examinfo/exams.htm`, for detailed information about what is covered on each exam.

The topics in this book relate to Exam 70-215 more than any other. Keep in mind while reading the MCSE Corners that not all the topics tested by the exams are covered in this book. This book is a guide to setting up and administering Windows 2000 Server and not an exam preparation guide, so it cannot cover everything on the exam.

Not every chapter in the book covers topics that are tested on the MCP exams, so there are some MCSE Corners that cover general topics about the exams. Chapter 7 contains a detailed listing of the exams and their contents. Chapter 10 explains the two exam types and covers the Computer Adaptive Test (CAT) in detail. The types of questions are listed and explained in Chapters 13 and 27.

CHAPTER 2

UNDERSTANDING IP, DNS NAMESPACES, AND TCP/IP

In this chapter

Decoding and Assigning IP Addresses   64

Understanding IP Datagrams   73

Matching IP and NIC Addresses with ARP   76

Resolving Names with the Domain Name System   77

Taking Advantage of Windows 2000 Server's DNS Service   82

Communicating Reliably with TCP/IP   86

Taking Chances with UDP Delivery   89

Troubleshooting   90

MCSE Corner: Understanding IP, DNS Namespaces, and TCP/IP   91

Decoding and Assigning IP Addresses

The public Internet and private intranets require every host to have a unique 32-bit Internet Protocol (IP) address that identifies both its network—a particular collection of hosts—and the host computer or router itself. In theory, 32-bit addresses can accommodate a total of 4,294,967,296 (2^{32}) hosts on a single network or, for example, 256 (2^8) different networks with 16,777,216 (2^{24}) hosts. The basic restriction is that the product of the total number of networks and hosts not exceed 2^{32}.

The early architects of the Internet couldn't agree on the number of networks that might be interconnected or how many hosts each network might need to support. In its formative period, the Internet had only a few networks, but the visionaries foresaw the requirement for a very large number of individual networks. As a compromise, the designers came up with an addressing scheme that accommodates networks of varying sizes, designated by class.

Following are the five classes of IP addresses:

- *Class A addresses* provide relatively few networks with many hosts. The network address starts with a 0 bit, followed by 7 address bits *(netid)* and 24 host address *(hostid)* bits. In theory, there can be 128 (2^7) Class A networks on the Internet, each with 16,777,216 (2^{24}) hosts. Some addresses are restricted, so the actual number of Class A netids is 125, each with 16,777,214 hostids.
- *Class B addresses* begin with bits 1 and 0, followed by a 14-bit netid and a 16-bit hostid. The Class B address space can accommodate 16,384 netids and 65,534 hosts per network.
- *Class C addresses* begin with two 1 bits, a 0, a 21-bit netid, and an 8-bit hostid, which provide 2,097,152 netids supporting 254 hosts per network.
- *Class D addresses* begin with 1110 and are restricted to multicast transmissions.
- *Class E addresses*, which begin with 11110, are designated for experimental purposes.

Figure 2.1 illustrates the bit patterns of the five address classes. By convention, you read address bit patterns from the most-significant bit (MSB) on the left to the least-significant bit (LSB) on the right. The LSB is bit 0 and the MSB is bit 31 for a 32-bit double-word *(dword)*, also called a *quadlet*.

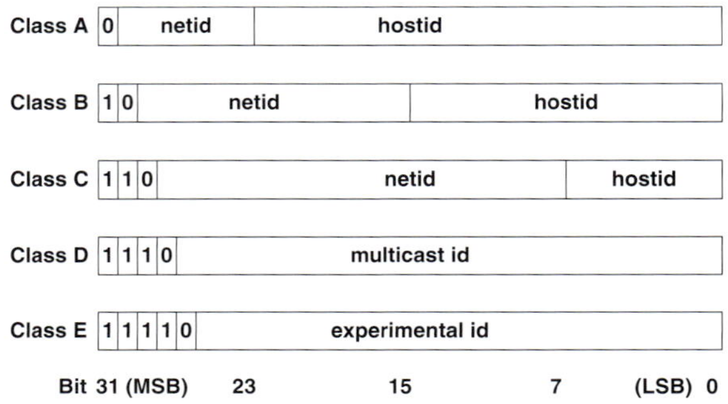

Figure 2.1
This diagram shows the bit patterns for the five predetermined IP address classes. A Class A address starts with a 0 bit, a class B with 10, and so on.

Class A	0 netid	hostid
Class B	1 0 netid	hostid
Class C	1 1 0 netid	hostid
Class D	1 1 1 0	multicast id
Class E	1 1 1 1 0	experimental id

Bit 31 (MSB)   23   15   7   (LSB) 0

> **Note**
>
> Class A, B, and C addresses support unicast mode. *Unicasting* is the conventional IP mode, which specifies that packets flow from one host to a single specified host. Multicasting enables a host to transmit packets to multiple hosts, which intercept packets within the Class D address range as a multicast stream. Receiving hosts must know in advance the address assigned to a multicast stream. The "Streaming with Windows Media Technologies 4" bonus chapter on the CD-ROM describes the use of multicasting for audio and video content.

IP Address Notation

Bit patterns (a string of 32 1s or 0s) aren't easy for nonprogrammers to fathom, so IP addresses commonly use *dotted-decimal word notation* for easier readability. Dots separate the decimal values of the four 8-bit bytes that make up the full IP address. Bytes in networking terminology are called *octets*.

For example, the IP address of oakmusic.com, one of the Internet domain names used in the examples of this book, is 209.249.8.35. This address is 11010001111110010001000000100011 in binary format.

The first three bits (110) of the binary address indicate that oakmusic.com has been assigned a single host ID within a Class C address. The first eight bits (11010001) of the first octet represent $128 + 64 + 0 + 16 + 0 + 0 + 0 + 1 = 209$.

> **Tip from**
> *RJ*
>
> Use Windows 2000's Calculator in scientific mode to convert between binary and decimal values. To change from the default Standard mode, choose View, Scientific.

> **Note**
>
> The founding fathers of the Internet—which didn't include Vice President Gore—understandably didn't envision the day when IP addresses would become scarce and thus a valuable commodity. Ford Motor, Eli Lilly, Hewlett-Packard, Mercedes Benz, and many government agencies hold Class A addresses. Mercedes Benz' IP address for its domain name (mercedesbenz.com) is 12.6.111.11 and Eli Lilly's is 40.33.1.27. Initial word values of 127 (0111111) or less indicate a Class A address. Mercedes Benz obtained its Class A address based on a desire to assign each of its vehicles an IP address. In contrast, the Peoples Republic of China is reported to have received an assignment of only 16 Class B addresses, supporting about 1.04 million hosts.

IP Address Restrictions

The following netids and hostids are reserved for special purposes:

- Netids with a value of 0 specify the host's local network, called *this network*. An IP address of 10.10.0.0 specifies the network with the netid 10.10. Thus, hostids can't have 0 values for the last octet.

- Netid 127 is assigned as the loopback address for network testing. Messages sent to 127.1.1.1 through 127.255.255.255 aren't sent to the network; instead, they return to the sending host.

- Hostid 255 creates a broadcast message to all hosts on the network. For example, every host on the 10.10.0.0 network receives messages sent on IP address 10.10.255.255.
- The Class A netid 10 is reserved for internal networks; no public Internet addresses begin with 10.
- IP addresses in the range of 224.1.1.1 through 224.254.254.254 are allocated to low-level multicasting services. Multicast addresses don't have hostids. Few, if any, hosts transmit on this special address range.
- IP Addresses 225.1.1.1 through 239.254.254.254 are reserved for conventional multicasting over the Internet multicast backbone (MBONE).

IP Address Allocation

The Internet Assigned Numbers Authority (IANA, http://www.iana.org/), founded by the late Dr. Jonathan B. Postel and initially sponsored by the U.S. Department of Commerce, is entrusted with the difficult task of allocating and assigning the remaining blocks of IP addresses. Assignment of IP addresses and domain names became a political "hot potato" as the demand for both grew exponentially in the mid-1990s. In October 1998, the Commerce Department "privatized" IANA by making it a component of the not-for-profit Internet Corporation for Assigned Names and Numbers (ICANN, http://www.icann.org/), headed by Internet guru and newsletter editor Esther Dyson. ICANN has been in political hot water since it was founded; much of the controversy surrounds how and by whom the group's organizational meetings have been run.

ICANN has retained IANA's three Regional Internet Registries (RIRs)—American Registry for Internet Numbers (ARIN, http://www.arin.net/), Réseaux IP Européens (RIPE, http://www.ripe.net/), and Asia Pacific Network Information Center (APNIC, http://www.apnic.net/) to assign IP addresses in their respective parts of the globe. ARIN wholesales blocks of IP addresses to Internet service providers (ISPs); ARIN doesn't deal with individual end-user address allocation. The minimum size block available from ARIN is 4,096 host addresses (called a /20 block) and costs $2,500 per year, plus a $1,000 per-year membership fee.

Note Assignment of IP addresses and domain names isn't handled by a single organization. You must have an assigned IP address or block of addresses, usually acquired from your ISP, before you can obtain a domain name. Allocation of names in the .com, .org, and .net domains is the subject of the "Resolving Names with the Domain Name System" section later in the chapter. Individual countries assign domain names identified by their ISO-3166 two-letter country codes, such as .us, .ca, .jp, and .uk. Tonga (.to) and Tuvulu (.tv) have established a lucrative business selling domain names.

Blocks of IP addresses have become a valuable commodity, and smaller ISPs usually purchase addresses from other holders (called *upstream providers*) in order to support a growing clientele. Large ISPs, such as America Online and CompuServe in the U.S., own giant blocks of IP addresses to service the fraction of their membership that's online at any given time.

Dynamic Host Configuration Protocol (DHCP) is the standard method of assigning temporary IP addresses to subscribers. Cable modem and Asymmetric Digital Subscriber Line (ADSL) connections are always on, so customers using AT&T's @Home network and Pacific Bell's FasTrak DSL, as examples, need at least a semipermanent IP address. As mentioned in the preceding note, if you want your own domain name, you must first acquire a permanent IP address from the ISP that you want to host your Web site, not a DHCP-assigned or semipermanent IP address.

IP SUBNETS AND ROUTERS

Subnets are groups of hosts that connect to other hosts through routers. Grouping hosts in subnets greatly improves local area network (LAN) efficiency, especially for LANs with hundreds or thousands of hosts, by isolating traffic between the subnet's hosts from other subnets.

Subnets also enable administrators to segment networks into individual LANs that connect through wide area networks (WANs). Subnets, which have high-speed connectivity between hosts, define Active Directory (AD) sites. AD sites are discussed in more detail in Chapter 4, "Optimizing Your Active Directory Topology."

→ For a brief description of how sites fit into AD domains, **see** "Windows 2000 Domain Architecture," **p. 24**.

A *router* is a network device having two or more network connections that isolate intranetwork (subnet) traffic from internetwork traffic.

Routers can connect networks with different physical transport media, such as Ethernet to Asynchronous Transfer Mode (ATM) for WANs or Ethernet to Token Ring in heterogeneous LANs. The more common term for a router that connects dissimilar networks is *gateway*. Another name for any type of router is *multihomed host*, but this term usually refers to a host with two network adapters assigned to individual subnets.

Conventional routers have a pair of IP gateway addresses that hosts use to communicate through the router; each gateway address subtracts from the number of computer hosts available to the subnet. The Internet depends on a very large number of high-performance routers to deliver billions of packets per second between millions of hosts.

Routers most commonly are standalone hardware devices, but Windows 2000 Server's Routing and RAS (RRAS) service provides moderate-performance software routing by servers with multiple network interface cards (NICs).

Network Address Translation (NAT) routes traffic from one or more public IP addresses to an internal (private) IP network, usually with the Class A netid 10. Chapter 25, "Managing Remote Access and Routing Services," shows you how to set up RRAS and NAT.

If you adopt the private Class A netid 10 for your internal network, you start with a single network having the potential to attach 16,777,214 hosts. There is no way, however, that even a small fraction of 16 million hosts can communicate over a single LAN because of network congestion. The maximum number of computers on a subnet depends on network transport speed and server locations. It's relatively uncommon to have more than 254 computers (the maximum number of hostids for a Class C address) on a single subnet.

The IETF developed in 1985 the IP subnetting system (RFC 950, "Internet Standard Subnetting Procedure," http://www.ietf.org/rfc/rfc0950.txt) to enable network administrators to divide their bank of hostids into arbitrary combinations of subnetids and hostids. The total number of bits in the subnetid and hostid fields equals the number of bits in the original hostid field, 24 for Class A or 16 for Class B.

You specify the total number of netid plus subnetid bits with a subnet mask, which identifies the host's subnet. A *subnet mask* is a 32-bit binary value that uses the dotted-decimal format, but requires that you work with the binary representation. The bits remaining after you specify the netid and subnetid bits are available for assigning hostids. 1s in the binary string represent netid and subnet bits, and 0s specify hostid bits.

If you take advantage of subnetting anywhere in your network, you must specify subnet masks for all IP addresses. Microsoft's TCP/IP implementation requires you to specify a subnet mask for each IP address you assign to host. Table 2.1 lists the default subnet masks for Class A, B, and C addresses; the default masks don't have a subnetid component.

TABLE 2.1 DECIMAL VALUES AND BINARY REPRESENTATIONS OF DEFAULT SUBNET MASKS FOR IP CLASS A, B, AND C ADDRESSES

IP Class	Decimal Value	Binary Representation
A	255.0.0.0	11111111 00000000 00000000 00000000
B	255.255.0.0	11111111 11111111 00000000 00000000
C	255.255.255.0	11111111 11111111 11111111 00000000

Subnet masks almost always consist of a contiguous series of 1s followed by a series of 0s. RFC 950 permits noncontiguous subnet masks, but few administrators take advantage of this dubious option.

Table 2.2 lists the decimal values of contiguous subnet masks that you can use for a Class B address with Windows hosts. Bold type indicates subnetids in the Binary Representation column. The first row of Table 2.2 is the default subnet mask for a Class B address, and the last row represents the subnet mask for a Class C address. Choose the subnet mask from Table 2.2 that delivers a sufficient number of hostids to accommodate the number of computers on a particular subnet and allows for reasonable future growth.

TABLE 2.2 NUMBER OF HOSTIDS, DECIMAL VALUES, AND BINARY REPRESENTATIONS OF CONTIGUOUS SUBNET MASKS FOR A CLASS B ADDRESS

Hostids	Decimal Value	Binary Representation
32,766	255.255.128.0	11111111 11111111 **1**0000000 00000000
16,382	255.255.192.0	11111111 11111111 **11**000000 00000000
8,190	255.255.224.0	11111111 11111111 **111**00000 00000000
4,094	255.255.240.0	11111111 11111111 **1111**0000 00000000

Hostids	Decimal Value	Binary Representation
2,046	255.255.248.0	11111111 11111111 **11111000** 00000000
1,022	255.255.252.0	11111111 11111111 **11111100** 00000000
510	255.255.248.0	11111111 11111111 **11111110** 00000000
254	255.255.255.0	11111111 11111111 **11111111** 00000000

> **Note**
>
> You often see references to IP addresses followed by /17 or /23. The number following the virgule—more commonly called a slash—is the number of 1 bits in the subnet mask. The shortage of IP addresses caused InterNIC to discontinue assignment of A, B, and C addresses and substitute Classless Internet Domain Routing (CIDR) assignments. CIDR enables the address authority to issue smaller groups of addresses—such as a half, a quarter, or an eighth of a Class B address—called *slash network* types. The first entry of Table 2.2 corresponds to a slash 17 network type, and the last entry is a slash 24, which is equivalent to a Class C address group.

It's possible to subnet an assigned Class C address, but you lose at least 31 IP addresses be-cause the subnetid value of a conventional subnet mask can't be 0, and each router consumes two subnet addresses. Table 2.3 lists the subnet address (equivalent to a nonsubnetted network address) and the decimal values for a network with a Class C address of 209.249.8.0 and a subnet mask of 255.255.255.224 (11111111 11111111 11111111**11100000**).

> **Note**
>
> Subnet masks consisting of all 0s caused problems with early router versions, and all 1s in a subnet mask conflicts with the address for all-subnets broadcasts. Windows NT and Windows 2000 support all-0 or all-1 subnet masks, but some routers and hosts don't.

TABLE 2.3 STANDARD SUBNETIDS AND AVAILABLE IP ADDRESS RANGES FOR THE CLASS C ADDRESS 209.249.8.0 WITH A SUBNET MASK OF 255.255.255.224

Subnetid	First Hostid	Last Hostid
209.249.8.32	209.249.8.33	209.249.8.62
209.249.8.64	209.249.8.65	209.249.8.94
209.249.8.96	209.249.8.97	209.249.8.126
209.249.8.128	209.249.8.129	209.249.8.158
209.249.8.160	209.249.8.161	209.249.8.190
209.249.8.192	209.249.8.193	209.249.8.222

The subnet mask divides the network into six subnets, each of which has 30 hostids, for a total of 180. The last address of the subnet—209.249.8.0, for example—is reserved for broadcasts. Five routers—usually assigned the first hostid—are required to interconnect the subnets, and one router connects to the Internet, so you lose an additional 11 hostids for servers and clients.

You end up with 169 out of the 254 available hostids of a nonsubnetted Class C address; only 67% of your precious IP addresses remain for host computers with conventional routing restrictions. Figure 2.2 illustrates three of the six subnets specified in Table 2.3.

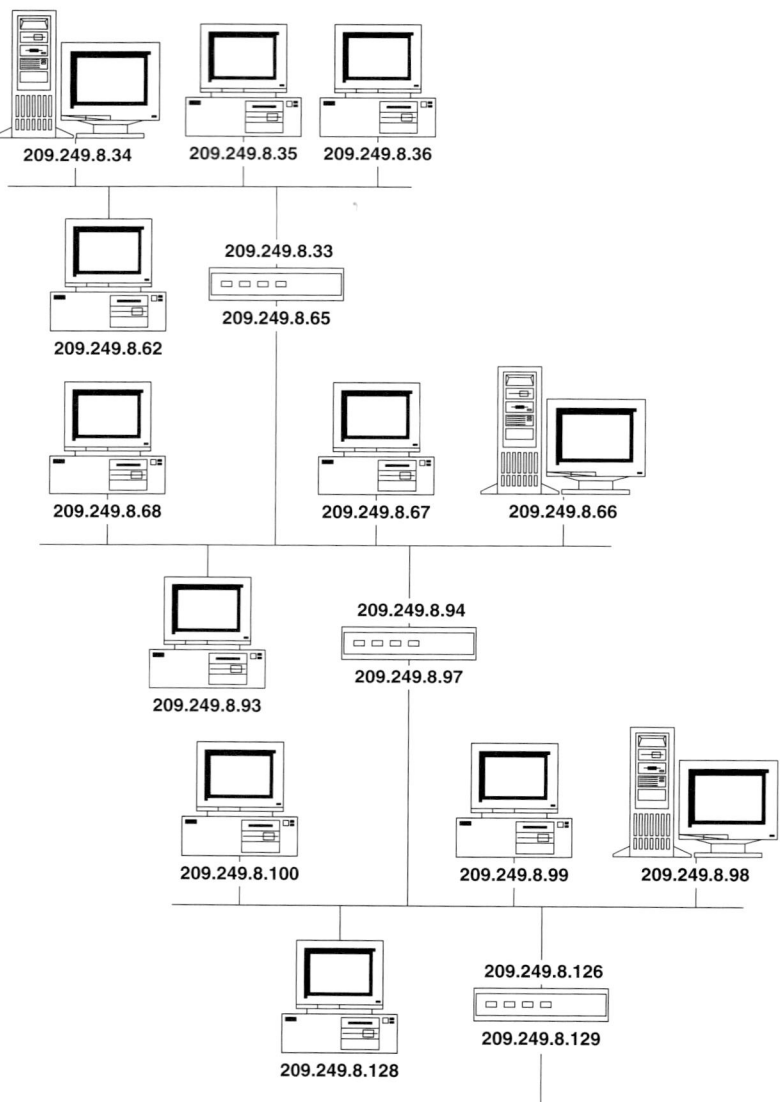

Figure 2.2
A network diagram for the first three of the six standard subnets for a Class C address with a `255.255.255.224` subnet mask illustrates assignment of router and host IP addresses.

You specify a host IP address and subnet mask in Windows 2000's Internet Protocol (TCP/IP) Properties dialog during initial server setup. Chapter 8, "Deploying Windows 2000 Production Servers," shows you how to upgrade Windows NT 4.0 servers to Windows 2000 Server or perform a new installation that enables you to migrate user and computer accounts from your existing Windows NT network.

DECODING AND ASSIGNING IP ADDRESSES | 71

> **Note**
>
> The step-by-step examples in this chapter assume that you've installed Windows 2000 Server "out of the box" with default setup options on an isolated test network or without an active network connection. These examples are intended to illustrate Windows 2000 Server features in an early evaluation setting, not in a production environment.

To change the IP address of your server after installation, do the following:

1. Launch Control Panel's Network and Dial-up Connections Tool.
2. Right-click Local Area Connection and choose Properties to open the Local Area Connection Properties dialog.
3. Select Internet Protocol (TCP/IP) in the list box and click Properties to open the Internet Protocol (TCP/IP) Properties dialog.
4. Select the Use the Following IP Address option, if you installed Windows 2000 Server with the default DHCP option.
5. Type the IP address, subnet mask, and the address of the default gateway (the address of the subnet's router). You specify a default gateway only if your server is on a subnet.
6. Leave the Preferred DNS Server and Alternate DNS Server addresses empty, unless you want to specify existing Domain Name System (DNS) servers (see Figure 2.3). DNS is the subject of the "Resolving Names with the Domain Name System" section that follows shortly.
7. Click OK twice to close the two dialogs.

Figure 2.3
Set server hostid, subnet mask, default gateway, and DNS server addresses in Windows 2000's Internet Protocol (TCP/IP) Properties dialog.

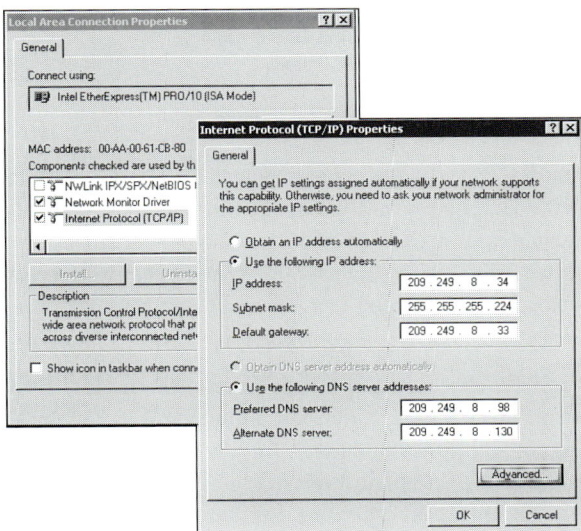

Tip from
RJ

If you're setting up the first Windows 2000 Server on a network and intend to create the initial AD domain, be sure to leave both the Preferred DNS Server and Alternate DNS Server addresses empty. Installing AD sets the Preferred DNS Server to the loopback address—`127.0.0.1`. An advantage of using the loopback address is that you can change the IP address of the server without having to change its DNS address.

If you're adding another DC to an existing Windows 2000 domain or creating a new domain, however, set the Alternate DNS Server address to that of the first DC—the initial root domain server—so that the Active Directory Setup Wizard can find the first DC by resolving its FQDN to an IP address.

Unlike Windows NT, you don't need to reboot your server (or workstation) when changing Windows 2000's IP addresses. Although you probably won't make frequent changes to server IP addresses, eliminating a server reboot for IP address reassignment is a convenient new Windows 2000 feature.

Tip from
RJ

Assign fixed IP addresses to all Windows 2000 servers. Microsoft offers DHCP as an option during the Windows 2000 Server setup process and as the default option in the Windows NT 4.0 Server setup process. Windows 2000 Setup displays a message suggesting you assign a fixed IP address to your server. DHCP IP addresses are only semipermanent. DHCP leases addresses to hosts; if your server's lease expires, it's likely to receive a different IP address when obtaining a new lease.

You must assign a fixed (permanent) IP address to Windows 2000 domain controllers that implement Windows Internet Naming Service (WINS), DNS, or both. Only member servers, the Windows 2000 counterpart of Windows NT servers in resource domains, can—but never should—use DHCP for IP address assignment.

IP Next-Generation Protocol

The current IP version (IPv4) is running out of available IP addresses at a rapid rate. All Class A addresses were assigned several years ago, and about two-thirds of all Class B addresses had been allocated by the end of 1995. Class C addresses, especially in more desirable contiguous groups, now are in short supply. One of the primary sources of the IP address shortage is hoarding of unused Class A and Class B netids by early acquirers, such as Mercedes Benz.

To alleviate the IP address shortage and streamline the IP, the IETF adopted in 1994 Request for Comments (RFC) 1752, "The Recommendations for the IP Next Generation Protocol," which became a Draft Standard in August 1998. The formal abbreviation is *IPv6*, but you also see references to *IP(v6)* and *IPng*. You can download "A Practical Guide to IPV6" from `http://www.ipv6.com`.

> **Note**
>
> One of the primary motives for adopting IPv6 is the need for a vastly increased number of IP addresses to support low-cost portable Internet appliances, high-priced interactive digital television (DTV) sets and set-top boxes, and other devices needing a unique, publicly known network address. The consumer electronics industry ships more than 15 million television sets into the U.S. market every year. If every set came with its own IP address, each year's shipments would consume almost all the hostids for an IPv4 Class A netid.

IPv6 promises the following improvements to IPv4:

- Increasing the IP address size from 32 to 128 bits—The additional address bits provide—using the most pessimistic calculation—1,564 addresses per square meter of the earth's surface. Optimistic estimates range in the quadrillions of addresses per square meter.
- Adding a scope field to multicast addresses, which increases multicast scalability.
- Providing a new anycast address type for additional control of traffic paths.
- Simplifying the IP header format by dropping or making optional some IP header fields—The next section, "Understanding IP Datagrams," describes IPv4 header fields.
- Adding Quality-of-Service (QoS) features to support real-time packet transmission, primarily for streaming audio and video transport.
- Improving security by supporting packet encryption with Encapsulated Security—Payload (ESP) and proving the identity of the packets' sender with Authentication Header (AH).

The designers of IPv6 intend the new addressing scheme to interoperate with IPv4. Early adopters have created an IPv6 virtual overlay network on the Internet called *6bone*, and hardware vendors, such as Cisco Systems and 3Com, are adding IPv6 capabilities to their routers. IPv6 requires major changes to the Internet's infrastructure; most observers expect that the transition from IPv4 to IPv6 will take 10 years.

Understanding IP Datagrams

You need to know the basics of IP datagrams to understand the relationship between TCP, User Datagram Protocol (UDP), and IP, as well as to fathom the workings of IP security for e-commerce transactions and virtual private networks (VPNs).

IP Datagram Structure

IP datagrams are the basic method by which IP routes information over a network. IP considers each datagram to be an independent message, so datagrams are considered connectionless. The IP datagram service is said to be unreliable, because it doesn't guarantee data delivery. Higher-level protocols, such as TCP/IP, are responsible for constructing complete messages from multiple IP datagrams and requesting retransmission of missing or garbled datagrams.

IP datagrams are variable-length packets with a maximum size of 65,535 octets (bytes), the maximum number of octets that a 16-bit number can specify. Datagrams consist of a variable-length header with a minimum size of 20 octets followed by data (often called *payload*). Figure 2.4 illustrates the structure of the standard IP datagram header. Unlike IP addresses, illustrations of header structures show the LSB on the left and MSB to the right.

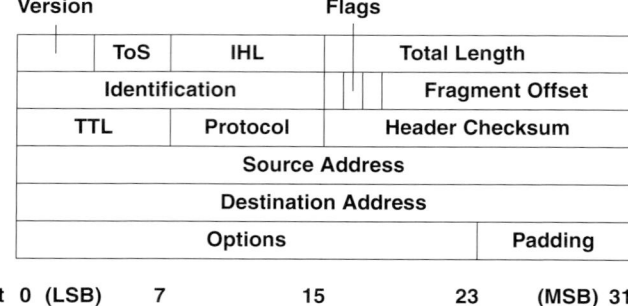

Figure 2.4
This diagram shows the layout of a typical IP datagram header with a single options field with a length less than one quadlet and padding to increase the header size to 20 full octets.

Following is a brief explanation of each of the elements of the IP datagram header:

- *Version* is a 4-bit field having a value of 0x4 for IPv4.
- *Type-of-Service (ToS)* is an octet for requesting available QoS options.
- *Internet Header Length (IHL)* is a 4-bit field that specifies the length of the header in 4-octet units and thus the beginning position (offset) of packet data. The minimum value is 0x5 (20 octets), and the maximum is 0xF (60 octets).
- *Length* is a 2-octet field that specifies the total packet length, including the header length.
- *Identification* is a 2-octet field that identifies datagram fragments. If the datagram's Length value is greater than the length of a network transport's frame, gateways divide the datagram into fragments. All fragments of a single datagram have a common value.
- *Flags* is a 3-bit field with a More Fragments flag (bit) as the last bit. The gateway sets the flag (to 1) when it receives the first long packet and resets it (to 0) when delivering the last fragment.
- *Offset* is a 12-bit field that specifies the sequence of the fragment based on the original position of the data in the IP datagram.
- *Time-to-Live (TTL)* is an 8-bit counter that's set to the maximum number of passes through routers a packet can make before the packet is considered to be looping. Each time the packet traverses a router, the router decrements the counter. When the counter reaches 0, the next router discards the packet. TTL is especially important in multicast mode.
- *Protocol* is an octet that identifies the nature of the payload. There are about 100 types of protocols identified in RFC 1700 ("Assigned Number," October 1996, http://www.ietf.org/rfc/rfc1700.txt) Internet Standard. ICMP (1), TCP (6), and UDP (17) are the most common IP protocol types for payload.

- *Checksum* is a 16-bit field whose value the destination host tests against its own calculated checksum of the header contents. Checksum provides packet error detection, but not error correction. The source host resends packets that fail the destination host's test.
- *Source Address* is the 4-octet IP address of the sending host.
- *Destination Address* is the 4-octet IP address of the recipient host.
- *Options* is a variable-length field that contains a list of datagram options.
- *Padding* is a variable-length field that fills the datagram to a 4-octet boundary, when necessary. If there are no options specified, Padding is 4 octets long.

Testing for Datagram Errors

Hosts, routers, and gateways use the Internet Control Message Protocol (ICMP) to report datagram errors. The UNIX `ping` utility, which Microsoft includes with all 32-bit Windows versions, sends ICMP echo request messages to specified hosts. The `ping` program tests whether the network is alive and all intervening routers and gateways are functioning correctly.

> **Note**
> Many popular Internet hosts, such as microsoft.com, block `ping` requests with firewalls because hackers use destructive variations of `ping` and other ICMP protocols to initiate denial-of-service attacks on Web sites. Some denial-of-service attacks flood the site with bogus ICMP requests, which can shut down the entire Web site.

To use Windows 2000's `ping` program, open the Command window and type `ping`, a space, and the IP address you want to test in dotted-decimal format. When you press Enter, `ping` reports the results of an attempt to send four packets with 32 bytes of data to the designated host. The upper part of Figure 2.5 shows the result of pinging a host on a LAN. The Windows 2000 version of `ping` offers several command-line parameters that extend the program's utility; to get a list of the parameters and their actions, type `ping`—without the IP address—and press Enter (see Figure 2.5, bottom).

Figure 2.5
Comparing results of pinging a LAN host (top) and running `ping` without an IP address or host name (bottom) shows `ping` parameters when the IP address is missing.

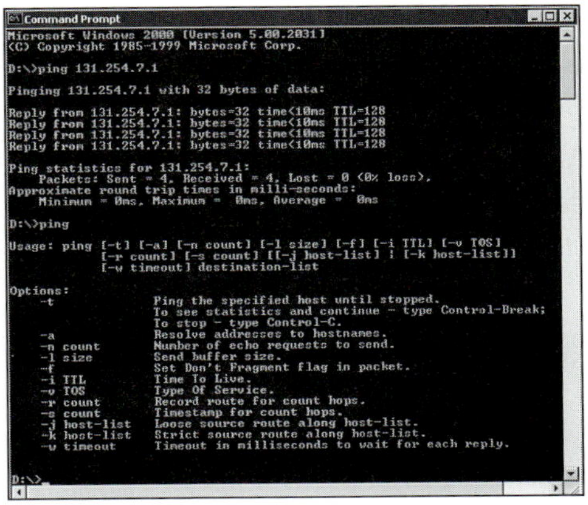

Tip from
RJ

> Use `ping` to check host connectivity whenever you encounter an unexpected network error. You can test the health of the TCP/IP stack on the local host by pinging the IP address of the server from the console. Inability to ping hosts on your subnet usually is the fault of a bad hub or switch, or a break in a network cable. If you can't ping a remote host on another subnet, an intervening router probably is dead.

Matching IP and NIC Addresses with ARP

Sending packets between IP hosts on an Ethernet (IEEE 802.3) or Token Ring (IEEE 802.5) LAN requires the ability to identify the NIC installed in a particular host by a physical address.

The Institute of Electrical and Electronic Engineers (IEEE) is the standards body that maintains the Ethernet and Token-Ring specifications. Each NIC has a 6-octet Medium Access Control (MAC) address that uniquely identifies the manufacturer and every NIC made by the manufacturer. MAC addresses are similar to Active Directory (AD) Object ID (OID) values, which also have a unique code for the organization that defines the object. Each NIC has a small read-only memory chip or similar device that stores the MAC address. The MAC address of the Intel NIC that appears in the Local Area Connection Properties dialog of Figure 2.3 is 00-AA-00-61-CB-80.

MAC addresses differ from IP addresses in structure and length; within subnets, IP searches for the MAC address of the destination NIC to which to send packets.

IP calls the Address Resolution Protocol (ARP) with the IP address of the host; ARP returns the MAC address and caches the value in RAM for future reference. IETF RFC 826, "An Ethernet Address Resolution Protocol," (http://www.ietf.org/rfc/rfc0826.txt) is the current Internet standard for Ethernet ARP.

IP and ARP take the following steps to obtain a host MAC address:

1. If IP can't find the MAC address in the cache, it calls ARP and hands off the destination and source IP addresses.
2. ARP broadcasts an ARP request frame over the LAN. The Ethernet address of a request frame is FF-FF-FF-FF-FF-FF. All NICs listen to the broadcast frame.
3. If a host recognizes the destination IP address as its own, it puts its MAC address in a field of the ARP request frame.
4. The destination host sends the filled-in request frame to the source host, which returns the MAC address to IP and stores the IP and MAC addresses in a RAM cache table.

The cache table is an important ARP feature; if ARP didn't provide a local cache table, the network would be congested—and probably overwhelmed—by constant ARP request-frame traffic.

> **Note**
>
> The Reverse Address Resolution Protocol (RARP, IETF 903, http://www.ietf.org/rfc/rfc0903.txt) is the complement of ARP; RARP lets a source host locate the IP address of a destination host from its MAC address. Use of RARP is relatively uncommon compared with ARP.

Resolving Names with the Domain Name System

Substituting readable names, such as oakmusic.com, for numerical addresses on the Internet is critical to its ease of use and thus its commercial success. It's highly unlikely that Super Bowl viewers would remember even one advertised Web site address if it appeared in dotted-decimal notation.

The system that ties the names to IP addresses is the Internet's DNS, a hierarchical naming system used for Internet navigation and within many organizations that use TCP/IP. Like WINS, DNS maps friendly (readable) names to numeric IP addresses—209.249.8.35 for oakmusic.com. Windows 2000 uses friendly DNS names for trees of AD domains; you can't take advantage of AD if you don't implement DNS on your server(s).

→ For more information on the interaction beween DNS and WINS, **see** "Installing and Configuring WINS," **p. 606**.

DNS Namespaces

The Internet started as a simple network of a few systems. Each system was responsible for maintaining a hosts file, which mapped every system's friendly name to its IP address. Following are the first few records in a simple hosts file for the first subnet defined in Table 2.3:

```
127.0.0.1       localhost
209.249.8.33    router
209.249.8.34    oakserv1.subnet1.oakmusic.com  s1serv1
209.249.8.35    oakcli1.subnet1.oakmusic.com   s1cli1
209.249.8.36    oakcli2.subnet1.oakmusic.com   s1cli2
...
```

One or more spaces separates the fields of host file records. The last field designates abbreviated alias names for the host names. Host name values are case-sensitive in UNIX but not in Windows.

The drawback of maintaining a static hosts text database becomes apparent when you consider a network of more than a few dozen hosts. Registering a host requires manual addition of a line of text to the hosts file; if a host's IP address changes, administrators must alter every computer's host file that includes a reference to the altered host. DNS was developed to eliminate the need for manual maintenance of very large hosts files and to provide dynamic name resolution services as the Internet grew and evolved. Although the original designers of DNS didn't envision the Internet growing to tens of millions of hosts, the DNS system has, with a few enhancements along the way, scaled quite well.

> **Note**
> DNS is based on a pair of 1987 Internet standards—RFC 1034, "Domain Names—Concepts and Facilities," and RFC 1035, "Domain Names—Implementation and Specification." You can read the text of these and all other IETF standards at http://www.ietf.org/rfc/.

> **Note**
> The Windows equivalent of UNIX's hosts file is lmhosts (LAN Manager hosts). Windows 9x and Windows NT 4.0 included a sample lmhosts file (lmhosts.sam) in the \Windows and \Winnt\System32\Drivers\Etc folder. (UNIX stores hosts files in the /etc directory.) The lmhosts file has many enhancements over the standard UNIX hosts file. Windows 2000 Server doesn't install a sample lmhosts file.

The DNS namespace is a tree; the root of the tree has no name (called a *null* value). Domain names are nodes (branches), and hosts are leaves on the tree (see Figure 2.6). A *fully qualified domain name (FQDN)* is constructed by concatenating the domain names to the system name from left to right as you climb the tree. FQDNs play a very important role in DNS administration and AD domain design.

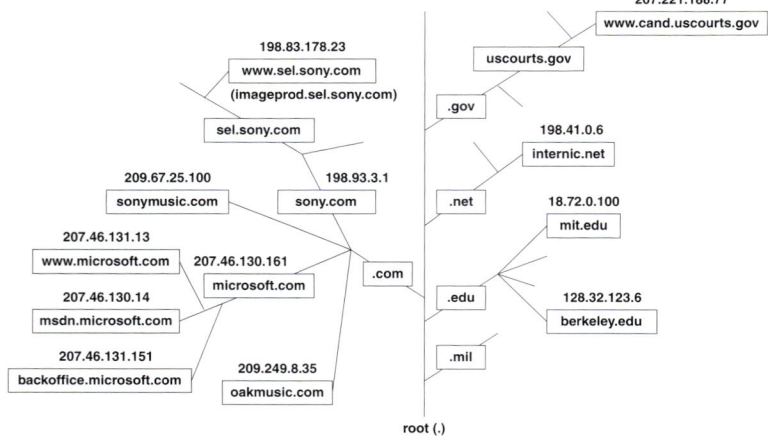

Figure 2.6
A hierarchical view of the Internet domain naming system illustrates the root and higher-level domains.

Each component of the name is separated by a dot, and names can include only letters, numbers, dashes, and dots. The first level above the root domain is .com for most Web sites, although .org (organization), .net (network), .edu (four-year colleges and universities), .gov (U.S. government), and country codes (.ca for Canada and .uk for the United Kingdom, for example) also are common. First-level domain names commonly are called top-level domains.

> **Note**
> Windows NT allows independent naming and structuring of computer domains and DNS domains; Windows 2000 doesn't. Your Windows 2000 domain names and structures are defined by DNS—or vice versa. Thus, it's very important that you fully understand how DNS works *before* you migrate from Windows NT to Windows 2000 or create a new Windows 2000 network.

The organization name (microsoft, sony, and oakmusic) in Figure 2.6 is prepended to the root domain—as in microsoft.com, sony.com—and oakmusic.com, forming an FQDN that corresponds to a particular IP address. Association of a domain name with an IP address is called *name resolution*.

Second- and third-level domain names shown without IP addresses in Figure 2.6 can't be resolved directly, because these domain names don't have registered IP public addresses.

Finally a service prefix, typically www (World Wide Web), ftp (File Transfer Protocol), or news (for Internet newsgroups) is added, as in www.microsoft.com.

Some firms, such as Sony, interpose a subdomain name between the service prefix and the domain name, as in www.sel.sony.com for Sony Electronics. AD refers to subdomains as child domains; in this example, sel.sony.com is the child domain of the sony.com parent domain.

The IP address of sony.com is 198.93.3.1; www.sel.sony.com is 198.83.178.23. You receive an "Unknown host" reply if you try to ping sel.sony.com, because the Sony Electronics subdomain actually is the imageprod.sel.sony.com sub-subdomain.

> **Note**
> You can infer from the IP addresses of microsoft.com third-level domain names that Microsoft has a Class B address allocation. All microsoft.com subdomains shown in Figure 2.6 start with 207.46.

The http:// protocol prefix used by Web browsers (http://www.microsoft.com) identifies the hypertext transport protocol for HTML. There are a variety of other protocol prefixes in use, such as msbd:// (Microsoft broadcast datagram) for transporting Windows Media files to a Windows Media server and mms:// (Microsoft media server) for receiving Windows Media files from the server. For email, the service prefix typically is the person's email alias, separated from the domain name with an ampersand, as in roger@oakmusic.com. Windows 2000 uses the equivalent of email addresses for user logon to AD domains.

DNS Components

DNS uses the following components for name resolution:

- *DNS servers* run a DNS server program to resolve local and client queries for IP addresses of named domains. Windows 2000 Server preferentially uses its own DNS program, described in the next section. You can substitute any other DNS server program, such as the current BIND release, that supports the DNS UPDATE command.

- *DNS resolvers* programs execute DNS queries against DNS servers. Most queries seek the IP address for a domain name; *reverse lookup* returns the domain name for a specified IP address. The Windows TCP/IP implementation (called a *TCP/IP stack*) includes a DNS resolver utility.
- *Resource records*, which correspond to host file records, are stored in the DNS database. Resource records map IP addresses to domain names and vice versa.
- *Zone files* contain resource records for the DNS zones for which the server is authoritative. Only one DNS server, plus its alternate, is authoritative for a domain. Changes to resource records of the authoritative DNS server ultimately propagate through the DNS server hierarchy.

Windows 2000's preferred DNS implementation uses AD to store the equivalent of resource records and doesn't use zone files. AD's replicated resource records are authoritative for all AD-compliant hosts within an entire enterprise.

> **Note** Windows 2000's *DDNS* uses zone files for forward and reverse lookups if you don't implement AD. There's little justification to upgrade your network to Windows 2000 if you don't take advantage of AD's features.

DNS Zones

Administering a single DNS server for the entire Internet would be an impossible task, so the DNS namespace is divided into zones. DNS zones are administrative subsets of the DNS namespace, in the same way that OUs can be administrative subsets of other OUs. Each DNS zone requires a *primary master name server* that stores resource records for all the hosts within the zone. *Secondary master name server(s)* receive updates from the primary master name server for the zone by a replication process called *zone transfers*. By default, master name servers are responsible for all subdomains in their namespace subset.

> **Note** AD handles zone transfers by multimaster replication, so Windows 2000 DDNS retains primary and secondary designations only for conformance with the IETF DNS standard. Like Windows 2000 DCs, which take the place of Windows NT primary and backup DCs, primary and secondary (backup) master name servers are equals in contents.

DNS servers can be authoritative for multiple zones that aren't on the same branch of the DNS namespace tree. It's possible for a primary master to be a secondary name server for other zone(s), and vice versa. By making name servers handle primary and secondary duties for different zones, you can minimize the number of name servers required to provide name server backup.

Assignment of Internet Domain Names

If your network isn't connected directly to the Internet, you can choose any domain name(s) you like for your Windows 2000 installation. Choosing a local domain name that's registered by someone else, however, isn't a recommended practice. If you ultimately decide to connect your network to the Internet, you can't use your existing domain name for your Web site and Internet email. Thus, you should register your domain name, if the name is available.

Domain Name Registrars

Until mid-1999, InterNIC was the sole registrar of second-level Internet domain names for the three primary nongovernmental top-level domains: .com, .net, and .org. The U.S. Department of Commerce contracted in 1993 with Network Solutions, Inc. (NSI) to run InterNIC (http://www.internic.net) as a government-authorized monopoly. InterNIC also had the sole authority to establish new top-level domains.

> **Tip from**
> *RJ*
>
> You can use ping as a preliminary test to determine if the domain name you want (*yourcompany*.com or *you*.com) is registered by someone else. Only NSI's InterNIC DNS databases, however, currently are authoritative for registering second-level domain names in the three primary top-level domains. The InterNIC databases also contain in-process and contested domain names that probably won't appear in response to a ping.
>
> The register.com Web site (http://www.register.com) offers a no-frills search service for .com, .net, and .org, plus a variety of other top-level domains, including .md (Moldavia) for physicians.

NSI's administration of InterNIC as a monopoly generated a great deal of controversy among members of the Internet community. Simultaneously with transfer of IP address assignment to ICANN, discussed in the "IP Address Allocation" section earlier in this chapter, the Commerce Department privatized assignment of domain names by authorizing ICANN to create a Shared Registration System. ICANN decided to give a select group of five initial registrars, called Testbed Participants, the right to allocate second-level domain names in the .com, .net, and .org domains. ICANN appointed in April 1999 America Online (U.S.), CORE Council of Internet Registrars (global), France Telecom/Olean (France), Melbourne IT (Australia), and register.com (U.S.) as testbed registrars.

ICANN grandfathered NSI (http://www.networksolutions.com) as an Internet registrar, and NSI claims ownership of the Internet's DNS database. When this book was written, NSI intended to charge other registrars a fee for adding new domain names to the database. ICANN's and NSI's activities in the post-monopoly era are the subject of much tumult and shouting in the trade press and Internet newsgroups.

Domain Names and ISPs

Regardless of your opinion of the proper role of the government and ICANN in the Internet's DNS namespace, you must contract with one of the six registrars to register your domain name. As mentioned earlier in the chapter, you must have an IP address prior to name registration. The registration process also requires that you provide the registrar with the IP address of primary and alternate DNS servers that are *authoritative* for your domain. In this case, authoritative means that the DNS servers are the initial source for other DNS servers that need to look up the IP address of your domain.

Most organizations and all individuals rely on commercial ISPs to obtain IP address(es) and provide DNS servers for Internet name resolution. Commercial ISPs, not online service providers such as AOL and CompuServe, perform the IP address acquisition and name registration duties for small- to medium-size firms and individuals. The primary activity of online service providers is supplying dial-up, cable modem, and other types of Internet connectivity to individuals and organizations. Some ISPs that specialize in hosting Web sites also act as online service providers. Most online service providers offer their clients limited Web site hosting services accessible through the service provider's IP addresses.

You can have more than one domain name that points to the same IP address. ISPs also provide the Internet DNS servers that hold your IP address and domain name(s), and supply Post Office Protocol 3 (POP3) or, less frequently, Internet Message Access Protocol (IMAP) mailboxes for designated recipients. If you want to run your own Internet mail system with Microsoft Exchange or a similar service, you ordinarily use a direct—not a dialup—connection to the Internet through your ISP.

After you or your ISP complete the registration process and pay about $70 for the first two years, your DNS record percolates through the hierarchical Internet DNS structure. It usually takes a day or two before you can successfully ping your new domain name.

Taking Advantage of Windows 2000 Server's DNS Service

Windows NT Server 4.0 introduced a native DNS service with a graphical user interface. For earlier Windows NT servers, you had to buy third-party DNS packages, or, more likely, a UNIX server provided DNS services. The Berkeley Internet Name Domain (BIND) is the most popular UNIX DNS implementation; the Windows NT 4.0 Resource Kit includes a Windows port of BIND. Regardless of the DNS server you used, updating resource records remained a manual, static process; DNS's major role was eliminating the need to maintain hosts files.

Dynamic DNS

Windows 2000 Server improves on its predecessor's DNS implementation by offering Dynamic DNS (DDNS) implemented by dynamic updates, a pending IETF standard (RFC

2136, "Dynamic Updates in the Domain Name System," `http://www.ietf.org/rfc/rfc2136.txt`). Windows 2000's DDNS requires each domain controller (DC) to run the DNS Server service. With DDNS, changes to a resource record in one DNS server's database or IP address assignments by DHCP automatically propagate to other DNS servers. AD replication between sites keeps all DDNS servers in sync.

You seldom change the name or IP address of servers, but DHCP clients routinely and frequently come and go. It's not an uncommon practice to make bulk changes that affect DNS, such as converting fixed client IP addresses to DHCP-assigned addresses or moving groups of clients from one subnet to another. DDNS automatically handles the changes to resource records for you. Even if you don't use DHCP, DDNS minimizes administrative duties for your Windows 2000 domain(s).

WINS continues to play an important role in Windows 2000 mixed-mode domains. As noted in Chapter 1, "Windows 2000 Server for NT 4.0 Users—What's New," mixed-mode domains consist of Windows 2000 Server DCs and Windows NT 4.0 backup domain controllers (BDCs) and standalone servers. Downlevel (non-Windows 2000) clients and servers continue to rely on WINS for NetBIOS name resolution. When you upgrade all your servers to Windows 2000 and upgrade or AD-enable your client PCs, you no longer need to support WINS.

Initial DDNS Configuration with Active Directory

After you make a new installation of Windows 2000 Server, upgrading to AD with Configure Your Server's Active Directory choice or running Dcpromo.exe automatically installs and configures DDNS. The Active Directory Installation Wizard establishes a pair of Active Directory–integrated DNS forward lookup zones for the FQDN you specify. Installing AD, however, doesn't establish a reverse lookup zone for the domain.

> **Note**
> You can install conventional—not Dynamic—DNS Server service on a workgroup or domain member server without installing AD. If you don't install AD, you must configure DNS manually.

→ For the detailed, step-by-step Windows 2000 server installation process, **see** "Installing Windows 2000 on a New Server," **p. 384**.

To review the auto-configured DNS server and add a reverse lookup zone after installing AD, do the following:

1. Choose Administrative Tools, DNS to open the DNS snap-in.
2. Expand the nodes in the tree pane to display the hierarchy of DNS entries (see Figure 2.7).

Figure 2.7
The DNS snap-in displays entries for the initial root domain DC having two child domains, student and resource.

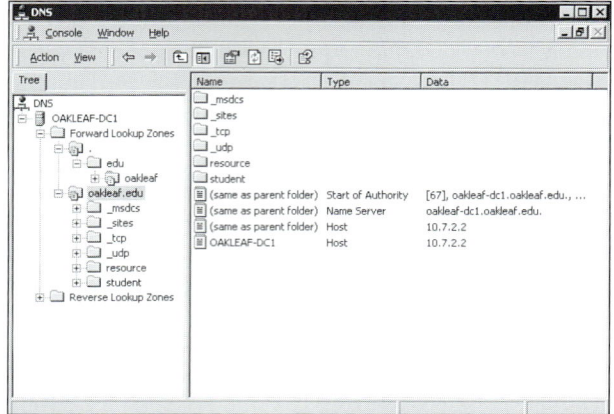

The root node (.) is present only in the first DNS server you install for a domain. If your domain has child domains—student.oakleaf.edu and resource.oakleaf.edu in the example domain of Figure 2.7—additional nodes appear for the child domains. Node names beginning with an underscore—such as _msdcs—are called *service locator (SRV)* resource records. SRV records provide AD-specific references to DCs, sites, and Kerberos authentication services.

> **Note**
> If you don't see a forward lookup zone node with your domain name when you expand the DNS tree view, see the "Missing Forward Lookup Zones" topic of the "Troubleshooting" section at the end of the chapter.

3. Right-click the Reverse Lookup Zones node and choose Add Zone to start the New Zone Wizard. Click Next.
4. In the New Zone Wizard dialog, select the Active Directory-integrated option (see Figure 2.8) and click Next.

Figure 2.8
Selecting the type of reverse lookup zone to add.

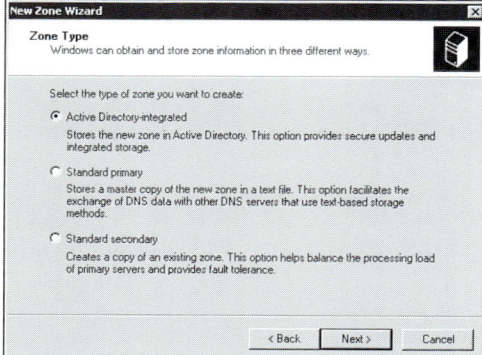

5. In the Reverse Lookup Zone dialog, accept the default Network ID option and type the IP address octets corresponding to the subnet mask of your server's network ID. For a Class B subnet (255.255.0.0), type the first 2 octets (see Figure 2.9); for a Class C subnet (255.255.255.0), type the first 3 octets.

The Name text box appends .in-addr.arpa to the IP address with the sequence of IP netid octets reversed, the address format required for reverse lookups (see Figure 2.9). The maximum number of IP octets you can enter is 3. Click Next and Finish.

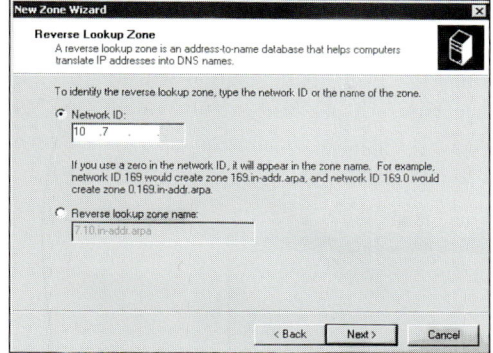

Figure 2.9
The Reverse Lookup Zone dialog requires you to specify the partial IP address of the subnet for which to add the reverse lookup zone. Only enter the network ID section of an IP address here.

The new Reverse Lookup Zones node contains a single entry for the subnet address you typed in step 5, but in the normal order of the subnet's IP address (see Figure 2.10).

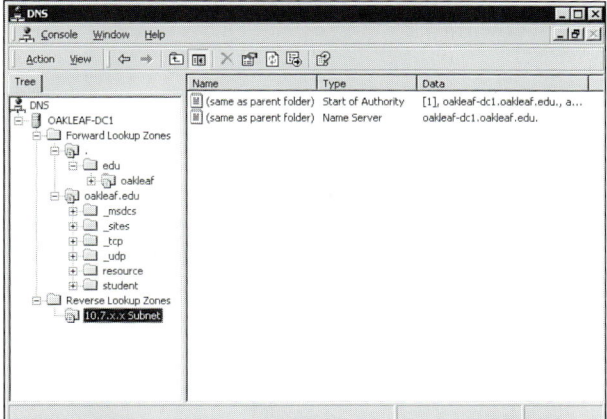

Figure 2.10
The DNS Management snap-in displays entries for forward and reverse lookup zones.

DDNS Management

After you or Windows 2000 Server setup has configured DDNS, choose Administrative Tools, DNS to launch MMC with the Dnsmgmt.msc snap-in. Following is a list of the most important changes you can make to forward and reverse lookup zones with the DNS Management MMC tool:

- To add another forward lookup zone, right-click the Forward Lookup Zones node and choose New Zone, which starts the Create a New Zone Wizard with the Select a Zone Type dialog active. Follow the Wizard's instructions. Adding secondary forward lookup zones that receive updates from other DNS servers improves lookup performance by load balancing and provides a backup in case the primary (authoritative) server fails.
- To add another reverse lookup zone, right-click the Reverse Lookup Zones node, choose New Zone, and do the same as for Forward Lookup zones.
- To change the properties of a lookup zone, right-click the individual zone entry and choose Properties to open the tabbed *zonename.com* Properties dialog. The General page enables you to pause the service, change the zone type, and enable dynamic update. The Start of Authority (SOA) page enables you to alter administrative and replication properties (see Figure 2.11). You can add or remove Name Server records, specify whether to use WINS for name resolution, and enable or disable Zone Transfers in the other three pages.

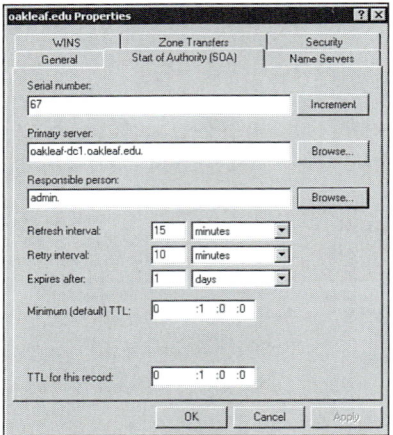

Figure 2.11
The Start of Authority (SOA) tab of the properties window of a forward lookup DNS zone allows you to configure administrative and replication parameters.

Communicating Reliably with TCP/IP

Up to this point, the chapter has concentrated on IP addresses and domain names, which are the foundation of the TCP/IP protocol. TCP is a 1981 Internet standard (RFC 793, http://www.ietf.org/rfc/rfc0793.txt) for host-to-host communication within an IP infrastructure. DARPA funded development of TCP at the Information Sciences Institute (ISI) of the University of Southern California; the objective was to improve the reliability of data transmission over the early Internet.

ISI's research and engineering staff, in which Jon Postel played a leading role, clearly achieved its objective. TCP/IP handles almost all communications between hosts on the Internet and within the majority of today's private LANs and WANs. The remainder of the IP traffic uses an unreliable transport, called the User Datagram Protocol (UDP).

→ For more information on UDP, **see** "Taking Chances with UDP Delivery," **p. 89**.

> **Note**
>
> Windows 2000 supports TCP/IP, Novell NetWare IPX/SPX protocols, and the nonroutable NetBEUI protocol that dates from the early PC era. IPX/SPX is a proprietary protocol intended primarily for file and printer sharing. The protocol is in widespread use because of NetWare's very large user base and continuing success as Microsoft's primary competitor in the networking market.
>
> Despite the fact that TCP/IP predates IPX/SPX—Novell was founded in 1983—most industry observers consider IPX/SPX to be a legacy protocol. Most sites running Novell 4+ probably will make TCP/IP their primary network protocol by the end of 2000. Windows 2000 only uses NetBEUI to handle remote access dial-in by PCs that don't support TCP/IP or IPX/SPX.

TCP Ports and Processes

TCP concerns itself with transmitting data to and from host processes. A process can be a Windows NT service, such as DNS or the routing feature of RRAS, or be spawned from an application, such as Explorer or a File Transfer Protocol (FTP) client. Numbered *ports* define the interface between a process and TCP. RFC 1700 defines *well-known ports* for a variety of IP services, in addition to IP payload protocol types. For example, FTP data runs on port 20 and FTP control uses port 21; port 80 is assigned to HTTP for the Web. IANA manages assignment of well-known IP ports. Port numbers 1024 through 65,535 are *registered ports* for what the standard calls "ordinary user processes or programs executed by ordinary users." Microsoft SQL Server, for instance, uses port 1433, and SQL Server Agent uses port 1434.

Port numbers and IP addresses combine to form a *socket*, which is unique on the network. The sending and receiving sockets create a *full-duplex* (bidirectional) connection between each host's process. Full-duplex connections can transmit and receive packets simultaneously.

The BSD Sockets application programming interface (API)—the most popular UNIX implementation of sockets—is the foundation for the Windows Sockets (WinSock) API of Windows 9x, NT, and 2000.

TCP uses *windowing*—which has nothing to do with Microsoft Windows—to manage the flow of data between hosts, a process called *flow control*. TCP depends on the host to specify the window size—the amount of data (number of octets) the host is prepared to receive in one chunk, commonly called a data *segment*. The size of the segment usually depends on the recipient's buffer size. A *buffer* is a block of RAM that's accessible both to TCP and the process.

The sending host continues to send data while waiting for an acknowledgment (ACK) from the recipient of the last segment received and processed. Each segment is an IP datagram and has an assigned sequence number. If the recipient doesn't acknowledge a segment within a calculated round-trip time (RTT), the sender retransmits the missing or corrupt segment in the stream of new segments; the recipient reassembles the segment in the correct order. ACK and retransmission are the backbone of TCP reliability.

> **Note** TCP automatically adapts to network congestion by reducing the size of the send window to slow the transmission rate. Overloaded routers that begin discarding packets indicate the onset of congestion. As congestion reduces and bandwidth increases, TCP slowly tries to return the window to the maximum size accepted by the recipient. TCP uses a *congestion control window* to constantly adjust window size when necessary. Thus, TCP is called a *sliding windows protocol*.

TCP Headers

The TCP header follows the IP header in the IP datagram, and the data payload follows the TCP header. Figure 2.12 shows the TCP header structure, which, like the IP header, is organized by quadlets.

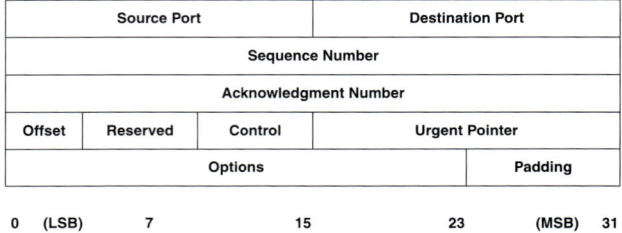

Figure 2.12
A TCP header consists of nine data fields, plus padding if the total header length is less than 20 quadlets.

Following is a brief description of each field of the TCP header:

- *Source port* is the 16-bit port number of the process running on the sending host.
- *Destination port* is the 16-bit port number of the process running on the sending host, which in almost all cases is the same as the source port.
- *Sequence number* is a 32-bit counter incremented by the sender for each segment sent and acknowledged.
- *Acknowledgment number* is a 32-bit value returned by the recipient that represents the next sequence number the recipient expects.
- *Data offset* is a 4-bit value that specifies the number of 32-bit quadlets in the header.
- *Reserved* is a 6-bit field that currently must contain all zeroes.
- *Control bits* are status flags—URG (urgent), ACK, PSH (push function), RST (reset connection), SYN (synchronize counters), and FIN (finished, close the connection).
- *Window* is a 16-bit value that specifies the maximum number of bytes the recipient can accept in a single segment.
- *Checksum* is an error control value calculated over the TCP header, pseudoheader, and data.
- *Urgent pointer* is a 16-bit field that identifies the sequence number offset of urgent data.
- *Options* is a variable-length field that can contain a list of values, such as maximum segment size.

- *Padding* appends empty octets to the packet so that the last options item final bit falls on 32-bit boundary.

A 96-bit TCP pseudoheader, illustrated by Figure 2.13, follows the TCP header and contains the following fields:

- *Source address* is the 32-bit IP address of the sender.
- *Destination address* is the 32-bit IP address of the recipient.
- *Reserved* is 8 0 bits.
- *Protocol* is an 8-bit field that duplicates the TCP value (6) in the protocol field of the IP header.
- *TCP length* is a 16-bit field that specifies the number of bytes of TCP data that follows the pseudoheader.

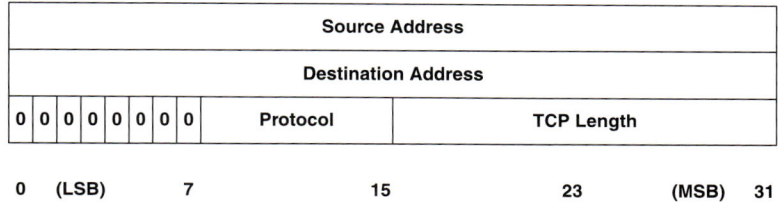

Figure 2.13
The TCP pseudoheader structure defines the source and destination addresses and the number of bytes of TCP data in the packet.

The purpose of the pseudoheader is to ensure that the segment reaches its intended destination identified by the destination address field value.

Taking Chances with UDP Delivery

The combination of the IP and TCP headers creates a substantial amount of overhead in each packet transmitted. *Overhead* is the ratio of header octets to total octets for a packet, expressed as a percentage. The IP header is a minimum of 24 octets, and the TCP header and pseudoheader add at least another 36 octets. A TCP packet containing 240 bytes of data has a minimum size of 300 bytes; the 60 bytes of header information represent 20% overhead.

Many types of data don't require reliable transmission, which guarantees that the recipient ultimately receives every data octet intended for it. Internet audio and video streams are examples of real-time data types that benefit from UDP's best-efforts attempt to deliver packets. If network congestion delays packets, resending them is a waste of time and effort. You suffer a brief interruption in sound or a frozen video frame until packets can resume their trip through the network. Several other UNIX-based applications, such as the Network File System (NFS) and Simple Network Management Protocol (SNMP), benefit from substituting UDP for TCP. NFS implements its own reliability features, and SNMP-enabled devices repeat their status update messages periodically.

UDP has a simple, 8-octet header and a 12-octet pseudoheader, for a fixed total of 20 bytes, compared with TCP's minimum of 60 bytes. The UDP header consists of 16-bit source port, destination port, data length, and checksum fields. The 12-octet pseudoheader is identical to TCP's pseudoheader, shown in Figure 2.13, except for the value stored in the protocol field—17 for UDP.

Windows Media, RealAudio, RealVideo, and all other popular Internet-based streaming media formats use UDP for delivery. Windows Media (formerly NetShow) falls back to TCP if UDP transmission fails, and to HTTP if TCP packets can't get through a firewall on the client side.

TROUBLESHOOTING

MISSING FORWARD LOOKUP ZONES

After installing Active Directory with Configure Your Server or Dcpromo.exe, the DNS snap-in doesn't show the domain's forward lookup zone.

When you run the Active Directory Installation Wizard the first time on your test network, the Wizard attempts to locate an active DNS server. If the Wizard doesn't find an active DNS server, a message box gives you the option of installing DNS as part of the AD upgrade process. If you don't accept the offer, the zone isn't created. If the Wizard finds an active DNS server, the assumption is that the DNS server found is authoritative for the domain and the message box with the DNS option doesn't appear.

In either case, you can use the DNS snap-in to add an Active Directory-integrated forward lookup zone by following these steps:

1. Right-click the Forward Lookup Zone node and choose New Zone to launch the New Zone Wizard. Click Next to bypass the Welcome dialog.
2. In the Zone Type dialog, select the Active Directory Integrated option and click Next.
3. In the Zone Name dialog, type the name of your domain—`oakleaf.edu` for the examples in this chapter. Click Next and then Finish to dismiss the Wizard and add the new forward lookup zone.

If there's another AD-integrated DNS server on your network, the root (.) node doesn't appear under the server name node. The root node appears in the first DNS server you create.

Demoting a DC to a member server by running Dcpromo.exe a second time removes AD-integrated—but not primary and secondary—forward or reverse lookup zones from the computer's DNS server. The DNS Service runs independently of AD, but AD-integrated DNS zones rely on the computer's local AD database, `Ntds.dit`. Without AD installed, the Active Directory Integrated option in step 2 is disabled.

MCSE Corner: Understanding IP, DNS Namespaces, and TCP/IP

This chapter provides an introduction to TCP/IP and DNS. TCP/IP is tested in all the new Microsoft Certification exams, because it is widely implemented in both the Internet and many private networks.

DNS has become an integral part of Windows 2000, as has TCP/IP. You should know DNS and TCP/IP thoroughly, especially many of the specific components of Windows 2000 Server, such as directory services and messaging. The topics covered in this chapter are important both for specific exam topics, as listed below, and for other exam topics that may be based on TCP/IP or DNS.

DNS is tested in several Windows 2000 exams. Exams 70-217, "Implementing and Administering a Microsoft Windows 2000 Directory Services Infrastructure," and 70-219, "Designing a Microsoft Windows 2000 Directory Services Infrastructure," test your knowledge of DNS and how it applies to the Active Directory service. Exam 70-220, "Designing Security for a Microsoft Windows 2000 Network," tests your ability to work with DNS security.

The topics in Chapter 2 are tested heavily in Exams 70-216, "Implementing and Administering a Microsoft Windows 2000 Network Infrastructure," and 70-221, "Designing a Microsoft Windows 2000 Network Infrastructure."

70-216   Implementing and Administering a Microsoft Windows 2000 Network Infrastructure

This exam probably contains several IP-related questions about installing and configuring the TCP/IP protocol. It is not likely that your knowledge of IP packet structure and subnetting will be tested, but there is extensive testing of the installation and configuration of the Windows 2000 DNS service. You should know how to install the service and configure root name servers and zones. You should also be familiar with managing DNS.

The exam might contain simulation-type questions, in which you are required to install or configure the DNS service, and multiple-choice and fill-in-the-blank questions testing your knowledge of the principles behind the operation of DNS with Windows 2000.

70-221   Designing a Microsoft Windows 2000 Network Infrastructure

This exam tests your ability to analyze the requirements of an organization and make recommendations based on those requirements. You must be able to determine the optimum IP addressing and subnetting for a given environment. You should also be able to design a DNS implementation for a given environment, so be familiar with DNS naming, security, and availability (that is, multiple DNS servers).

CHAPTER 3

INTRODUCING THE ACTIVE DIRECTORY AND LDAP

In this chapter

Understanding the Role of Directory Services   94

Learning Active Directory Terminology   95

Installing Active Directory   96

Administering Active Directory   105

Getting Acquainted with LDAP   121

Using the Active Directory Schema Manager   124

Taking Advantage of LDAP OUs   132

Searching for AD Objects with LDAP   135

Programming Directory-Enabled Applications with ADSI   139

Troubleshooting   143

MCSE Corner: Introducing the Active Directory and LDAP   144

Understanding the Role of Directory Services

Active Directory (AD) is Microsoft's critical component of Windows 2000 Server. AD is a directory service, and as such is analogous to Novell's NetWare Directory Services (NDS) and Sun Microsystems' Sun Directory Service (SDS). *Directory service* describes a combination of a directory and the application(s) to make the directory information available to users and other applications. Windows Explorer and one or more file systems combine to create a simple directory service. Technically, AD is a directory service; DS is a common alternative abbreviation for directory service.

Directory services have the following primary objectives:

- Creating a single, enterprise-wide view of every network element and its characteristics, regardless of the element's physical or logical location.
- Providing single-point management of the entire network, together with the ability to delegate to individual admins management of particular parts of the network.
- Enabling admins and users to easily and quickly find a particular network element—such as a file, printer, or coworker—by specifying a set of properties for the element sought.

Directory services deliver their greatest benefit to moderate- to large-size organizations that must manage hundreds or thousands of servers and 20 times or more client computers and users. Directory services also provide the backbone for Internet e-commerce by supporting "white pages" directories of individuals and "yellow pages" for locating organizations. Directory services can replace relational databases for handling user membership tasks at free and subscription Web sites.

Although they are similar technologies, Microsoft's AD and Novell's NDS accomplish their objectives with different architectures. AD takes advantage of the Internet-standard Lightweight Directory Access Protocol *(LDAP)* as its native method for querying, reading, and updating the directory. NDS uses a proprietary protocol for directory operations; Novell's LDAP implementation is an NDS add-on and requires translation of LDAP queries to and from NDS formats. AD takes advantage of a high-performance hierarchical database, while NDS uses a set of flat files to store records that represent directory objects. Microsoft bases its namespace on the Internet's Domain Name System (DNS), while Novell retains its traditional naming conventions.

Note

In its competition with Novell, Microsoft is counting on its more sophisticated, standards-based AD architecture—plus its marketing prowess—to make up for the late arrival of Windows 2000 Server. When this book was written, NDS for NetWare 5.0 was at version 8.

You can read biased comparisons of AD and NDS on the Microsoft Web site (`http://www.microsoft.com/windows/server/Eval/comparisons/ADandNDScomp.asp`) and on the Novell site (`http://www.novell.com/advantage/nds/ndsactive.html`). The war of words between these two competitors and their respective allies undoubtedly will extend well past the millennium.

Microsoft and Novell compete with Sun Microsystems' Sun Directory Service (SDS) for the Solaris UNIX flavor. SDS primarily is an e-mail directory service; SDS doesn't integrate e-mail (Sun Internet Mail Server, SIMS) and Solaris user accounts. SDS 3.1 isn't as fully integrated with the network as NDS nor is it an integral part of the operating system as is AD. An objective comparison of AD, NDS, and SDS from *Computerworld* is at `http://www.computerworld.com/home/print.nsf/all/981214835E`.

> **Note**
> Microsoft intends to merge the Exchange directory with AD in Exchange 2000, which runs only under Windows 2000 Server and its siblings. Microsoft has scheduled Exchange 2000 for distribution a few months after the official Windows 2000 release date.

LEARNING ACTIVE DIRECTORY TERMINOLOGY

To gain a basic understanding of AD, you need to know the definitions of the following terms:

- *Directory* means a source of information about a particular set of entities, which AD calls *objects*. Telephone books and association membership lists are examples of paper-based directories of person objects. FAT16, FAT32, and NTFS file systems have built-in directories of logical folder and file objects.

- *Directory database(s)* are the directory's information store. AD's directory database is Ntds.dit; the *Extensible Storage Engine (ESE)*—related to the "blue" version of the Jet database engine—provides the communication link to individual objects.

- *Objects* are abstractions of categories of real-world network objects, such as files, printers, and individual users.

- *Containers* establish the AD hierarchy. Containers hold groups of similar objects and, optionally, other containers. You can nest object containers to any depth you want. Some of the Windows 2000 default containers created during AD installation don't permit nesting.

- *Organizational units (OUs)* are named containers of users and other objects. OUs provide the mechanism for dividing Windows 2000 domains into logical administrative groups. OUs are containers, but not all AD containers are OUs.

- *Attributes* are properties of objects, such as name, address, city, state, ZIP Code, and telephone number for individuals or companies, or name, size, and date for files. Directories that use databases store attribute values in individual *fields*.

- *Schema* store information about types of objects (called *classes*), their mandatory and optional attributes, and the possible parent(s) of the object class. Technically, individual objects are *instances* of their class. AD's schema are extensible—that is, you can define your own AD classes.

- *Global catalog (GC)* is a hierarchical database containing entries for all objects in enterprise domains. To minimize database size and speed searches, GC stores only those object attributes needed to locate the desired object.

- *Active Directory Service Interface (ADSI)* version 2.5 provides programmatic access to AD by supplying a set of methods to read and write attribute values with LDAP version 3 (extended). ADSI also provides connectivity to the Exchange directory, NetWare Directory Services (NDS), Windows NT 4.0, and NetWare 3. Developers can use ADSI with C++, Visual Basic, Java, and other programming languages that support Microsoft's Component Object Model (COM). ADSI 2.5 runs under Windows 9x, Windows NT 4.0, and Windows 2000.

- *Downlevel (clients, servers, domains,* and so forth*)* Microsoft calls Windows 9x and NT *downlevel* operating systems; any object or operation associated with those systems is also referred to as *downlevel*.

- *Distributed directory* means a directory with partial or complete copies on multiple networked computers. Like Windows NT primary and backup domain controllers (PDCs and BDCs), Windows 2000 domain controllers maintain copies of group and user data. Windows 2000 peer-to-peer AD doesn't distinguish between PDCs and BDCs, and stores many more types of objects and attributes than Windows NT's SAM (Security Account Manager) database.

- *Replication* is the process by which distributed directories synchronize their contents. AD replication is similar to that of Exchange server—after creating a directory copy on a remote computer, only changes replicate between the computers. Replication isn't instantaneous, especially over slow WAN links, so the contents of AD database copies differ until replication completes. Microsoft calls this replication model *multi-master loose consistency with convergence*.

- *Sites* are groups of computers having high-speed (10Mbps or greater) network connectivity, and usually are defined as Internet Protocol (IP) subnets. Sites define replication boundaries and can include computers in one or more domains. Replication within sites occurs approximately every five minutes. Replication between sites, which is assumed to involve a WAN link, is much less frequent; the default schedule is every three hours. A Windows 2000 site is analogous to an Exchange Server site.

→ To learn definitions of terms associated specifically with AD's use of LDAP as its access protocol, **see** "Getting Acquainted with LDAP," **p. 121**.

Installing Active Directory

The step-by-step examples in this chapter require installation of AD on a server with a network card configured for TCP/IP during the setup process. It's a common practice to install Windows 2000 Server initially on a test or evaluation server that's not connected to a production network. Specifying a workgroup name, rather than a domain name, during setup creates a standalone server and doesn't start the Active Directory service. If your server is running in standalone mode, you must configure the Active Directory service. AD requires DNS; setting up AD also installs and configures DNS, if the DNS service isn't already running.

→ For detailed installation instructions for Windows 2000 Server, **see** "Installing Windows 2000 on a New Server," **p. 384**.

Installing Active Directory

Tip from
RJ

Click the Active Directory link of the Configure Your Server dialog to determine if AD is installed. To open this dialog, choose Start, Programs, Administrative Tools, Configure Your Server. If the Active Directory page states, "Active Directory is already installed on your server," skip to the next section.

If you want to change the domain name you picked when you first installed Windows 2000, you can do so by following the instructions in this section for removing AD and starting over. You can't change your domain name after installing AD.

Caution

You must have a partition formatted with NTFS on which to install the Shared System Volume (Sysvol) that contains the AD replication files. If you installed Windows 2000 Server in a partition formatted with FAT16 or FAT32, you must reformat the partition to NTFS 5.0 or create a new NTFS 5.0 partition for Sysvol. You can create the new partition from free space or by formatting as NTFS another FAT partition on a drive. Windows NT 4.0 NTFS partitions don't support Sysvol.

Reformatting to NTFS doesn't result in loss of data, but you won't be able to access the data in the NTFS partition from Windows 9x in a dual-boot configuration. Windows NT 4.0 with Service Pack (SP) 4+ can read and write NTFS partitions formatted as basic NTFS volumes, but only can read data from NTFS volumes you convert to dynamic storage. Basic storage is the format operation's default. Chapter 8, "Deploying Windows 2000 Production Servers," and Chapter 9, "Installing RAID and Removable Media Systems," describe partition formatting options.

You can use the Configure Your Server tool to promote your standalone server to a domain controller (DC), but most administrators prefer to use the Active Directory Installation Wizard (Dcpromo.exe) to promote or demote servers.

Tip from
RJ

Make sure you have a basic understanding of AD domains, trees, and forests before promoting (or demoting) a server. Chapter 1, "Windows 2000 Server for NT 4.0 Users—What's New," provides a brief introduction to AD domain structure. Chapter 4, "Optimizing Your Active Directory Topology," shows you how to design the AD structure that's best for your organization.

 To understand the significance of the first DC you install, **see** "Domain Namespaces and DNS," **p. 25**.

To install AD, optionally removing AD to permit a new installation, do the following:

1. Choose Start, Run, type **dcpromo** in the Open text box, and press Enter to start the Active Directory Installation Wizard. If this is your initial installation of AD, move to step 3.

2. If AD is running, the first dialog of the Wizard lets you remove AD and start over. To re-create your initial domain, click Next and complete the Wizard's removal steps,

which demotes your DC to a standalone server. You must provide the Directory Service Restore Mode password you used when you created the domain to demote the DC. The demotion process takes only a few minutes. After you reboot and log on to the local computer, run Dcpromo.exe again.

Don't demote your DC if it is the first controller you installed and you have other Windows 2000 DCs in the forest and domain(s). The first DC is the initial root domain of the forest, maintains the GC, and is the domain master controller in the default mixed-mode domain.

Demoting the only DC of a domain to a standalone server re-creates the Administrator account. You lose all custom desktop shortcuts and personalization features you added while your computer was a DC. If you have a second DC for the domain on the test network, your demoted DC becomes a member server, and your Administrator account and personalization features aren't affected.

 If you have problems demoting a DC, see "Problems Removing Orphaned Domain Controllers" in the "Troubleshooting" section near the end of this chapter.

3. In the Welcome dialog, click Next to open the Domain Controller Type dialog.

4. Accept the default Domain Controller for a New Domain option (see Figure 3.1), and click Next to open the Create Tree or Child Domain dialog.

Figure 3.1
The Domain Controller Type dialog allows you to specify whether the system is the first domain controller in a new domain (shown here) or a domain controller in an existing domain.

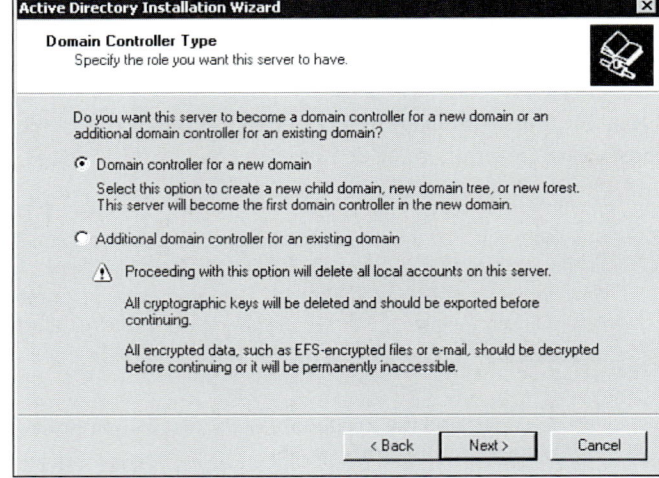

5. Accept the default Create a New Domain Tree option (see Figure 3.2). The new domain tree will have the same name as the domain name you choose in step 7. Click Next to open the Create or Join Forest dialog.

6. Accept the default Create a New Forest of Domain Trees option to specify that your DC is the initial root domain of a new forest (see Figure 3.3). Click Next to open the New Domain Name dialog.

Installing Active Directory   99

Figure 3.2
The Create Tree or Child Domain dialog allows you to specify whether the domain is the first domain in a tree (shown here) or a child of an existing domain.

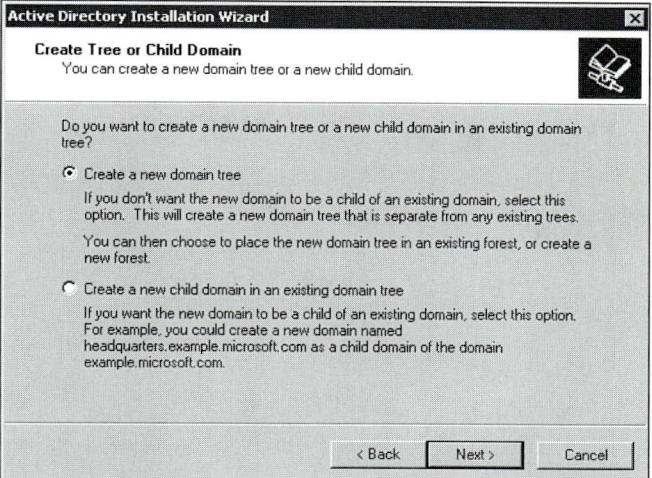

Figure 3.3
The Create or Join Forest dialog specifies whether the new domain should be the first domain in a new forest or a member of an existing forest.

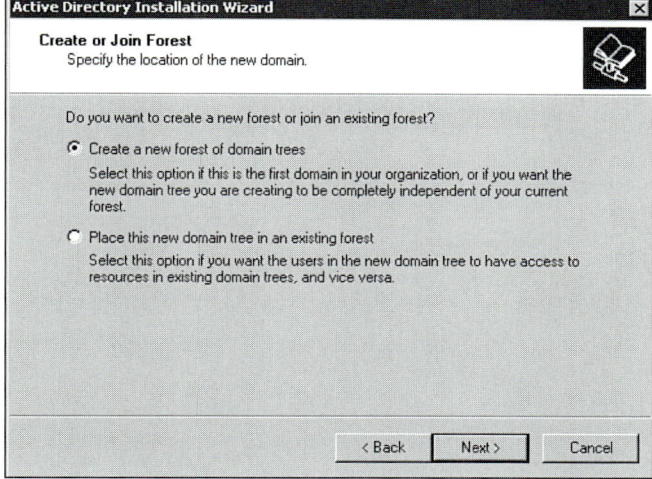

7. Type your domain name, **oakleaf.edu** for this and most of the other examples in this book, in the text box (see Figure 3.4), and click Next. After a delay of a minute or two, the NetBIOS Domain Name dialog opens.

> **Note**
> If your test server is connected to an operating network, don't use a current Windows NT 4.0 domain name as the Windows 2000 domain name. You must upgrade a Windows NT primary domain controller (PDC) to Windows 2000 Server to create an operable mixed-mode (Windows NT and 2000) domain.

Figure 3.4
The New Domain Name dialog is where you enter the name for the domain you are creating. It will become the initial root domain name.

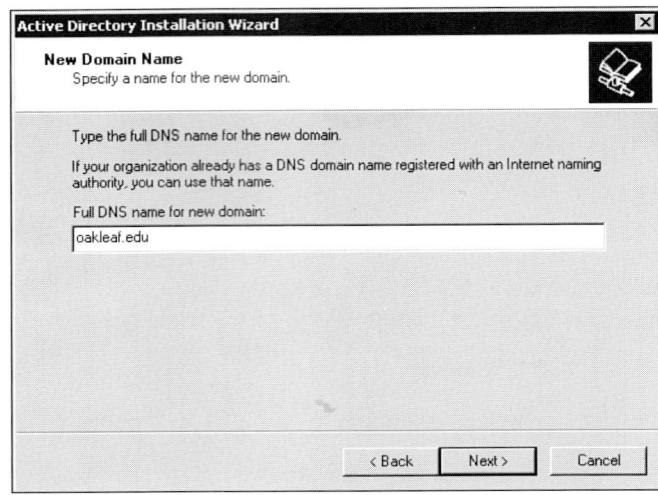

8. Unless you have a good reason to do otherwise, accept the default NetBIOS name, which is created from the second-level domain name you chose in the preceding step. A Windows NT OAKLEAF domain controller sometimes connects to the test network, so OAKLEAFU is the downlevel domain name for this and other examples (see Figure 3.5). Click Next to open the Database and Log Locations dialog.

Figure 3.5
The NetBIOS Domain Name dialog allows you to specify the domain name that will be used by downlevel systems, such as Windows NT and Windows 9x. A default name is created for you.

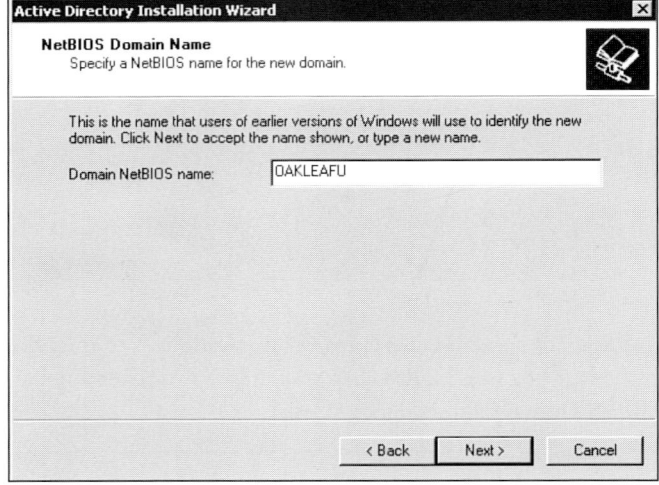

INSTALLING ACTIVE DIRECTORY | 101

> **Note**
> Downlevel servers and clients continue to log on with the NetBIOS domain name until you upgrade them to Windows 2000 or install Dsclient.exe. Windows 2000 and its applications often use NetBIOS names (OAKLEAFU or \\OAKLEAF-DC1) instead of DNS names (oak-leaf.edu or oakleaf-dc1.oakleaf.edu).

→ To directory-enable Windows 9x clients with Dsclient.exe, **see** "Connecting Windows NT 4.0 Clients," **p. 775** and "Accommodating Windows 9x Clients," **p. 780**.

9. The default location for the AD database (Ntds.dit) and transaction log files (edb.log and others) is *d*:\Winnt\NTDS, where *d* is the drive on which you installed Windows 2000 Server (see Figure 3.6). Click next to accept the default location and open the Shared System Volume dialog.

Figure 3.6
The next step is to specify the locations for the Active Directory database and log files. You can change the default locations to any drive with enough space. It is recommended to store the database and logs on different physical drives.

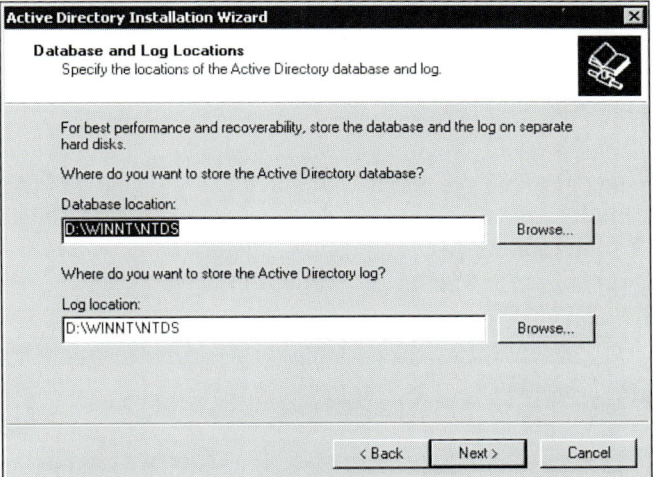

> **Note**
> The database and log files need not be located in an NTFS partition of a test installation, but both files should be stored in NTFS partitions on a production server. To protect your database against a drive malfunction, install the Ntds.log in an NTFS partition of a separate drive.

10. If your Winnt folder is formatted for NTFS, accept the default location for Sysvol, *d*:\Winnt\Sysvol (see Figure 3.7). Otherwise, specify a folder named ...\Sysvol in the NTFS 5.0 partition. Click Next.

PART
I
CH
3

Figure 3.7
The Shared System Volume dialog is where you specify the location for system files that are shared amongst domain controllers. These files must be stored on an NTFS 5.0 volume.

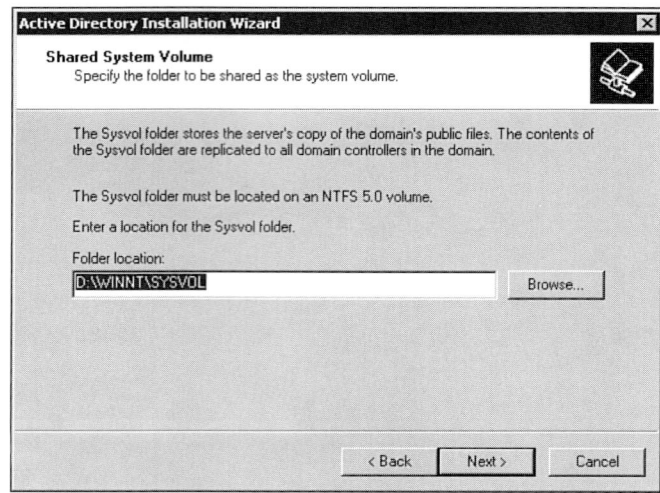

11. After another delay of a minute or two, you receive a "Can't contact the DNS server" message if you haven't previously configured DNS for the standalone or a prior DC server with the same domain name. Click OK to open the Configure DNS dialog (see Figure 3.8). Accept the Yes, Install and Configure DNS on This Computer option, and click Next to open the Windows NT 4.0 RAS Servers dialog.

Figure 3.8
Accept the default option to install and configure AD-integrated (dynamic) DNS automatically on the server.

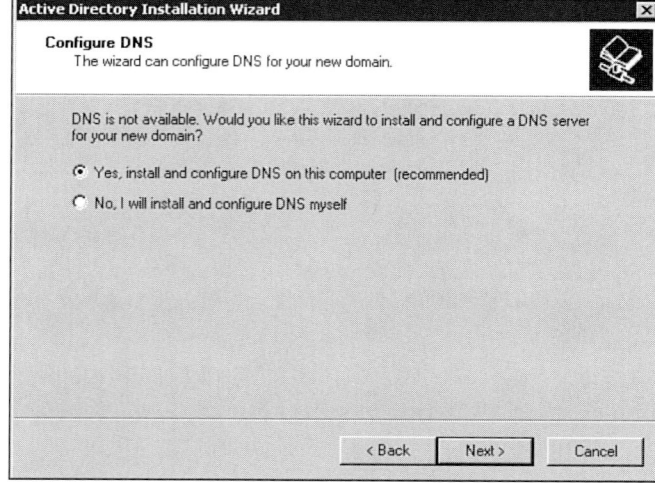

12. The test server isn't intended to connect to production Windows NT servers, so choose the most secure option (see Figure 3.9), and click Next to display the Directory Services Restore Mode Administrator Password dialog.

INSTALLING ACTIVE DIRECTORY | 103

Figure 3.9
The Permissions dialog allows you to specify whether there are systems that use anonymous access such as server programs that run on non-Windows 2000 servers in the domain. The setting shown is the most secure, but all server programs in the domain must be running on Windows 2000 servers.

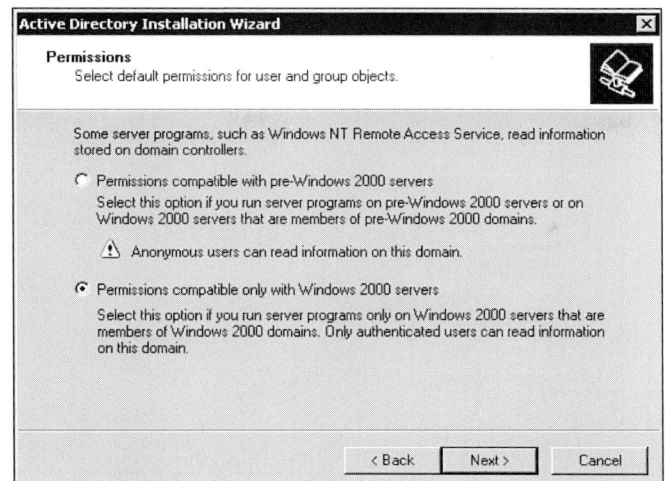

PART
I
CH
3

13. Type and confirm a password that you use to start the DC in Directory Services Restore Mode or when you run Dcpromo.exe again to demote the DC (see Figure 3.10). Make sure that you remember this password. Click Next to open the Wizard's Summary dialog.

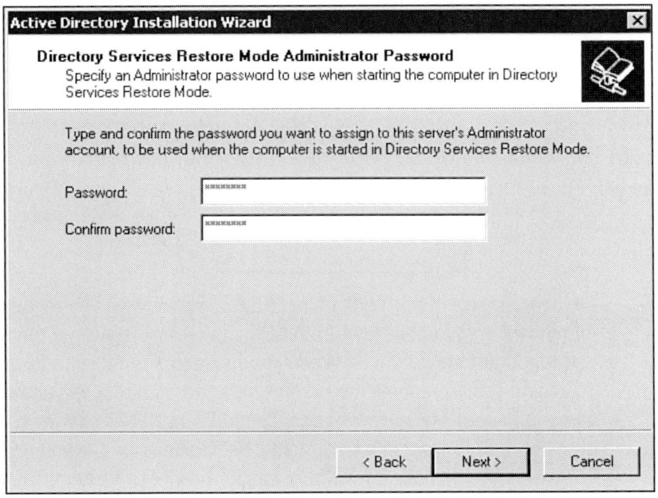

Figure 3.10
This dialog allows you to set the Directory Services Restore Mode Administrator password that is used to remove Active Directory from a server or to start Active Directory in restore mode.

14. Review the choices you made in the preceding steps (see Figure 3.11). Click Back as often as is necessary to return to any of the dialogs that contain settings you want to alter. Change those settings and click Next to return to the Summary dialog. When you're satisfied with your AD choices, click Next to configure and start the Active Directory service.

Figure 3.11
The Summary page shows all of the choices you made in the previous dialogs for review before Active Directory is installed.

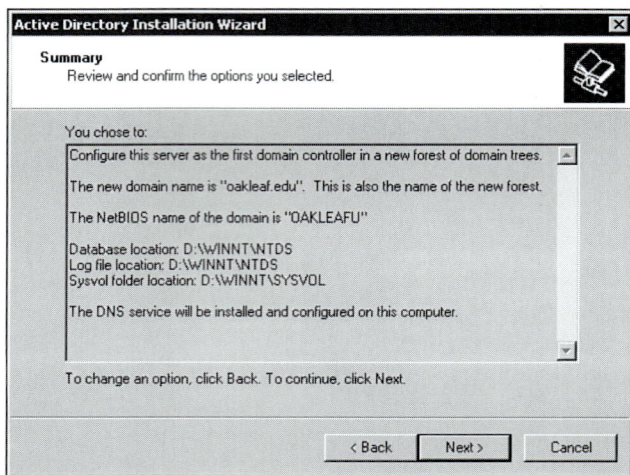

15. The Configuring Active Directory dialog displays messages describing the task in progress. After a few minutes, you see the Completing the Active Directory Installation dialog. Click Finish and reboot your computer when instructed.

After you install AD, the Preparing Network Connections and Applying Computer Settings tasks take considerably longer to complete than in standalone server mode. When the Log On to Windows dialog finally appears, it sports a new Log On To list with the NetBIOS name of your new domain as the default Log On To item and your conventional username (**Administrator** in this case) as the default logon name. Logging on with Windows 2000's format, Administrator@*domain*.com (this is the Administrator's user principal name), disables the Log On To list, because you've entered a fully qualified username. Dhcphelp.exe runs for a few seconds in a command window the first time you log on after promoting a server to a DC.

Tip from
RJ

All the examples in this book make the assumption that you're logged on as Administrator@*domainname*.com. Using the Administrator account doesn't pose security issues in a test environment. When you move to a production installation of Windows 2000, you should rename the Administrator account to a less common and more secure name to increase security. You also should change your password to include a combination of upper- and lowercase letters, numerals, hyphens, and even an ampersand (&). Passwords should have a minimum length of eight characters. These characters are illegal in passwords: "/\[]:;|=,+*?<>.

> **Caution**
>
> Don't perform non-administrative operations with the renamed Administrator account; you might accidentally walk away from your computer, leaving it open for others to perform unauthorized and possibly malicious operations. You also expose your Internet-connected computer to Trojan Horse attacks if you log on as a member of the Administrators or Domain Admins group. Create a new account for yourself in the Users or Power Users group to use when performing non-administrative functions.
>
> When you need Administrators privileges, log on to the computer or network as a user, and take advantage of the runas command to open applications or run programs from the command prompt. Using runas lets you specify your Administrators group credentials as a command-line argument and is much more secure than logging on as a member of the Administrators or Domain Admins group. For more information on using the runas command and syntax examples, search Windows 2000 online help index for "Run as."

ADMINISTERING ACTIVE DIRECTORY

Microsoft Management Console (MMC) snap-ins (.msc files) provide the user interface (UI) for all AD administrative chores. Following are the AD administrative tools that the AD installation process adds to the Programs, Administrative Tools menu:

- Active Directory Domains and Trusts (Domain.msc)
- Active Directory Sites and Services (Dssite.msc)
- Active Directory Users and Computers (Ads.msc)

The following three sections describe how to use these tools within a test or evaluation environment.

> **Note**
>
> Upgrading a Windows NT 4.0 PDC to a Windows 2000 DC automatically sets up initial domains, sites, groups, and users based on your existing server installation. Before you upgrade a production network, however, it's a good practice to become familiar with the tools that you use for basic network administration. You also use the basic AD tools to reorganize the topology of your network after the initial migration process.

ADMINISTERING DOMAINS AND TRUSTS

Windows 2000 *domains* are DNS namespaces that define network security and administrative boundaries. A *namespace* is a region with a consistent naming convention that lets you translate readable names into references (pointers) to particular objects. *Trusts* define security relationships between domains, domain trees, and forests of domain trees. Unlike Windows NT 4.0, Windows 2000 creates two-way, transitive trusts between AD domains, forests, and trees automatically. You manually establish pairs of one-way, non-transitive trusts between independent Windows NT 4.0 and Windows 2000 domains.

→ For a review of the differences between AD and Windows NT 4.0 domains and trusts, **see** "Windows 2000 Domain Architecture," **p. 24**.

> **Note**
>
> *Transitive trusts* span related trust relationships. If domain A trusts domain B and domain C trusts domain A, then domain C also trusts domain B. Windows NT 4.0's *non-transitive trusts* require explicit trusts between domain C and domain A and between domain C and domain B. Non-transitive trusts lead to very complex and difficult-to-administer trust relationships between Windows NT 4.0 servers. Upgrading large networks to Windows 2000 Server eliminates most of the administrative burden of managing and repairing non-transitive trusts.

Your first DC is the only member of your domain at this point. To view your simple domain structure, choose Programs, Administrative Tools, Active Directory Domains and Trusts to launch MMC with the Domain.msc snap-in active. Right-click the domain name node and choose Properties to open the default General page of the Domain Name Properties dialog (see Figure 3.12). You can add a description of your domain, if you want, and change the domain from the default mixed mode to native mode. You also can delegate administrative responsibility for the domain by completing entries in the Managed By page.

> **Caution**
>
> Don't change your test domain from mixed to native mode at this point. Native mode disables the ability of Windows NT 4.0 BDCs to synchronize with AD. Native mode requires that all servers in the domain run Windows 2000.

Figure 3.12
This figure shows the Active Directory Domains and Trusts snap-in with the General page of the Properties dialog open for the newly created domain.

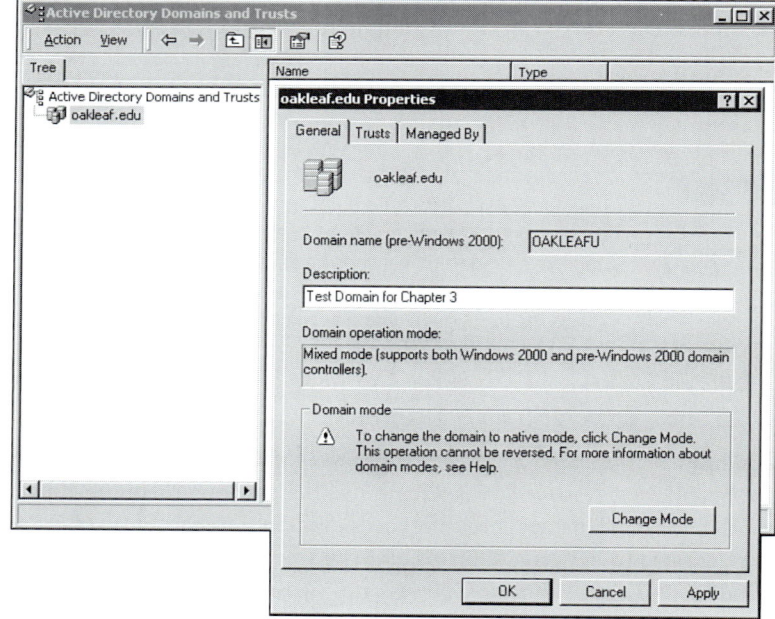

Establishing Non-Transitive Trusts with Windows NT 4.0 Domains

If your test network connects to a Windows NT domain, you can create downlevel, non-transitive, two-way trusts between your Windows 2000 and Windows NT domains. Creating trusts with an existing Windows NT domain makes visible computers and shares on PCs running NetBIOS. The trusts let you use your test server as a conventional workstation having access to all resources in the trusting Windows NT domain. The following example assumes that you have at least Domain Admins privileges in both domains. When you promote a standalone or member server to a DC, your Administrator account automatically becomes a member of the Enterprise Admins and Domain Admins groups.

> **Note**
> The interdomain trust relationships you create in this section don't set up a connection between Windows NT PDCs or BDCs and Windows 2000 DCs. The trust only supports interdomain authentication for resource access. Changes you make to objects in the Windows NT 4.0 domain don't propagate to the Windows 2000 domain and vice versa. To synchronize Windows NT and Windows 2000 domains, you must upgrade the Windows NT PDC to Windows 2000 to create a true mixed-mode domain.

To add a two-way, non-transitive trust with a Windows NT domain, do the following:

1. Launch MMC with the Domain.msc snap-in active, if it isn't running.
2. Expand the Active Directory and Trust node to display your newly added domain.
3. Right-click the domain node and choose Properties to open the Domain Name Properties dialog.
4. Click the Trusts tab, then click the upper Add button to open the Add Trusted Domain dialog.
5. Type the NetBIOS name of the Windows NT domain to trust in the Trusted Domain text box.
6. Type a password—usually your Administrator account password— in the Initial Password and Confirm Password text boxes (see Figure 3.13).
7. Click OK to establish the first trust direction, and close the Add Trusted Domain dialog. Dismiss the warning about password problems with the reverse-direction trust.
8. Repeat steps 4 through 7 for the trusting (lower) domain, and don't attempt to verify the trust at this point.
9. Select the trust in either list and click Edit to open the NetBIOSDomain Properties dialog, OAKLEAF for this example (see Figure 3.14).

Figure 3.13
Specify the name and password for a down-level trusted domain, OAKLEAF.

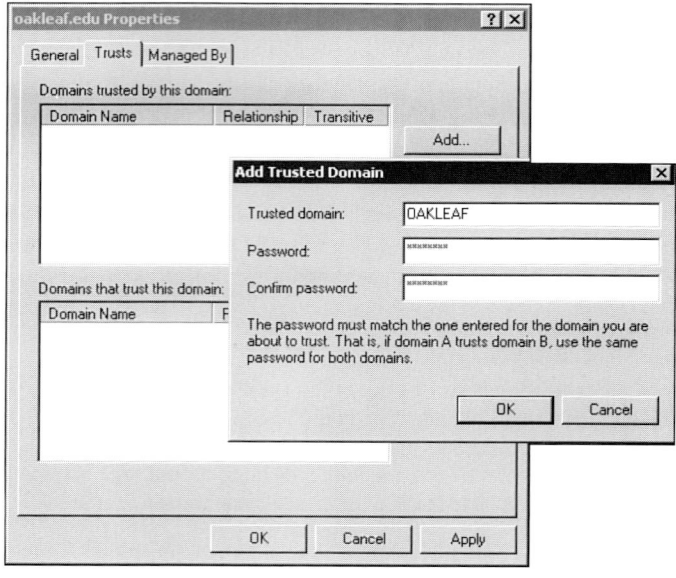

Figure 3.14
The OAKLEAF properties dialog shows the properties of the trust including the fact that it is a two way, non-transitive trust between oakleaf.edu, a Windows 2000 domain, and OAK-LEAF, a downlevel domain.

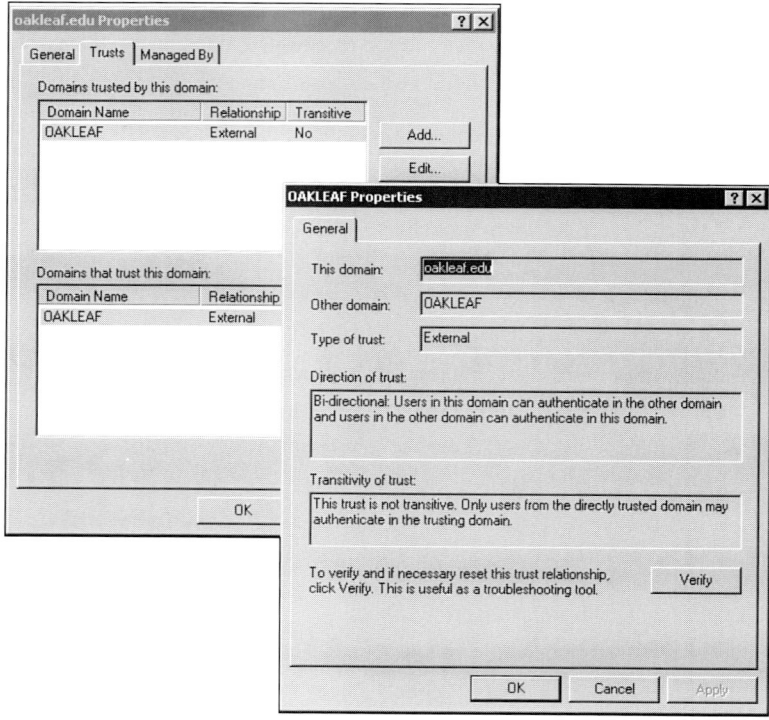

10. Click OK twice to close both Properties dialogs.
11. Run User Manager for Domains on the Windows NT 4.0 PDC or BDC, and choose Policies, Trust Relationships to open the Trust Relationships dialog.
12. Click the Add button for Trusted Domains to open the Add Trusted Domain dialog. Type the name of the trusted domain (**OAKLEAFU**) and the password you used in step 6 (see Figure 3.15), and click OK. After a few seconds, a message box confirms creation of the trust.

Figure 3.15
The User Manager tool in Windows NT 4.0 is being used to add the OAKLEAFU domain to its list of trusted domains.

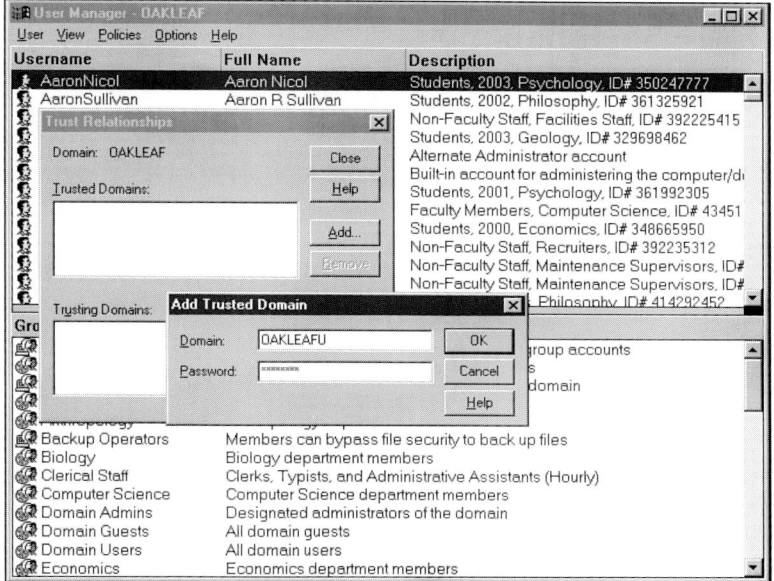

13. Repeat step 12 for the Trusting Domains entry. You must type and confirm the password to establish a trusting domain. Clicking OK creates the trust immediately. Click OK to close the Trust Relationships dialog.
14. To verify the trust, double-click the Administrators group in User Manager for Domains' lower pane to open the Add Users and Groups dialog. Select OAKLEAFU in the List Names From list; after a few seconds, the default Security Groups and user accounts in the Windows 2000 domain appear in the Names list.
15. Select the Administrator account in the Names list, and click Add to make your Windows 2000 Administrator account a member of the Windows NT domain's Administrators group. Optionally, add the OAKLEAFU Domain Admins group to the local Administrators group (see Figure 3.16). Click OK twice to close the two dialogs.
16. Choose User, Select Domain to open the Select Domain dialog, and double-click OAKLEAFU in the Select Domain list. User Manager displays the default users and groups created when you promoted the Windows 2000 server to a DC (see Figure 3.17).

Figure 3.16
The User Manager tool in Windows NT 4.0 is being used to add administrative accounts from the Windows 2000 domain OAKLEAFU to the Administrators group on the Windows NT 4.0 domain, OAKLEAF.

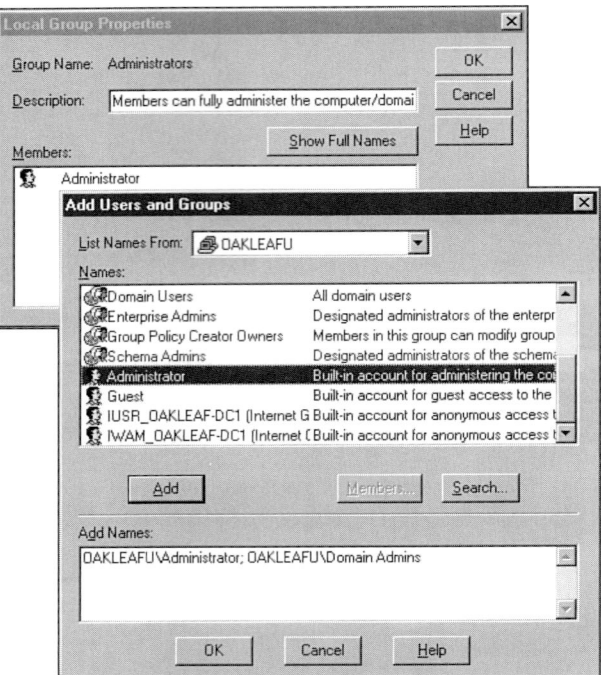

Figure 3.17
The User Manager tool in Windows NT 4.0 is showing the user accounts and groups in the Windows 2000 domain OAKLEAFU.

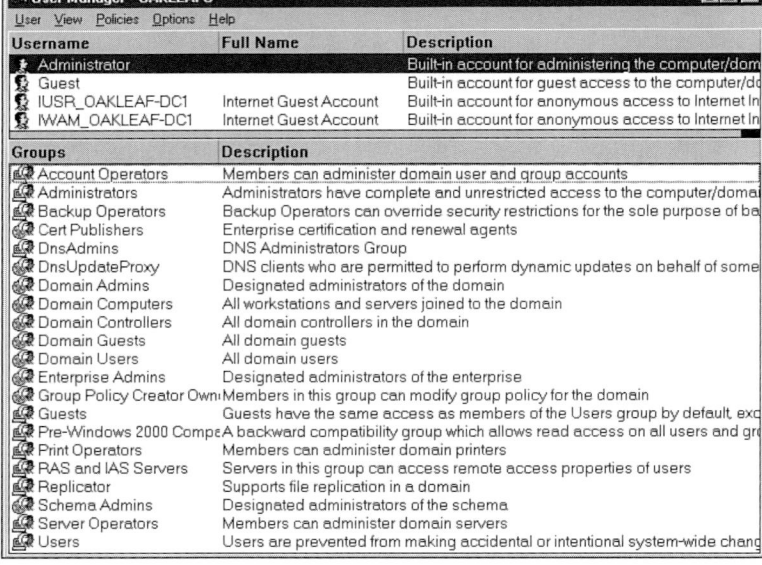

17. Launch My Network Places, double-click Entire Network, and double-click Microsoft Windows Network to display Windows NT domain(s) that trust your Windows 2000 domain, and peer workgroup(s). Double-clicking domain and workgroup icons shows the individual computers, and doubling-clicking a computer icon displays Windows NT server shares (see Figure 3.18).

Figure 3.18
My Network Places is being used to access shares on the Oakleaf1 computer in the OAKLEAF domain after configuring the trust relationship.

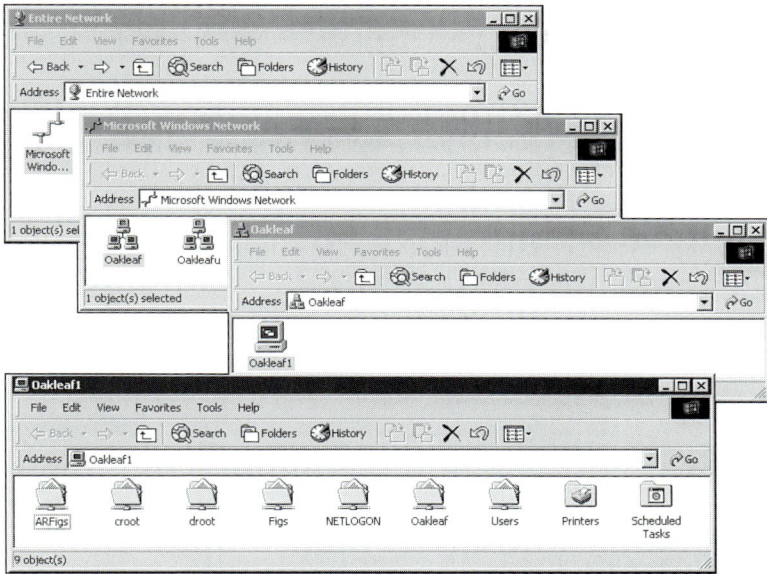

ADMINISTERING WINDOWS NT 4.0 DOMAINS FROM WINDOWS 2000

You can't administer Windows NT 4.0 domains from Windows 2000 servers using the standard administrative tools installed when you promote a server to a DC. However, you can run the Windows NT 4.0 administrative tools under Windows 2000 Server or Professional, if you have Administrators privileges in the trusting Windows NT 4.0 domain. The most common Windows NT tools you might want to install are User Manager for Domains (Usrmgr.exe) and Server Manager (Srvmgr.exe).

> **Note**
> The Setup.bat program in the Windows NT Server 4.0 distribution CD-ROM's \Clients\Srvtools\Winnt folder throws errors when you attempt to run it under Windows 2000 Server or Professional. Thus, you must manually install the specific tools you want to use.

To install User Manager and Server Manager for Windows NT 4.0 under Windows 2000, do the following:

1. Log on to Windows 2000 Server or Professional with an account having Administrators privileges in the Windows 2000 and Windows NT domains.
2. Create a new folder, such as \Program Files\WinNT Tools for the tool files on your Windows 2000 computer.
3. Insert the Windows NT 4.0 Server CD-ROM, and navigate to the *d*:\Clients\Srvtools\Winnt\I386 folder.
4. Copy Usrmgr.exe, Srvmgr.exe, and, optionally, Usrmgr.hlp and Srvmgr.hlp, to the folder you created in step 1. Create desktop shortcuts to the executable files if you plan to use the tools routinely.
5. Run User Manager for Domains, choose User, Select Domain, and double-click the Windows NT domain in the Select Domain list. Verify that you can add and delete user accounts in the Windows NT domain.
6. Run Server Manager and verify that you can add and delete computer accounts in the Windows NT domain (see Figure 3.19).

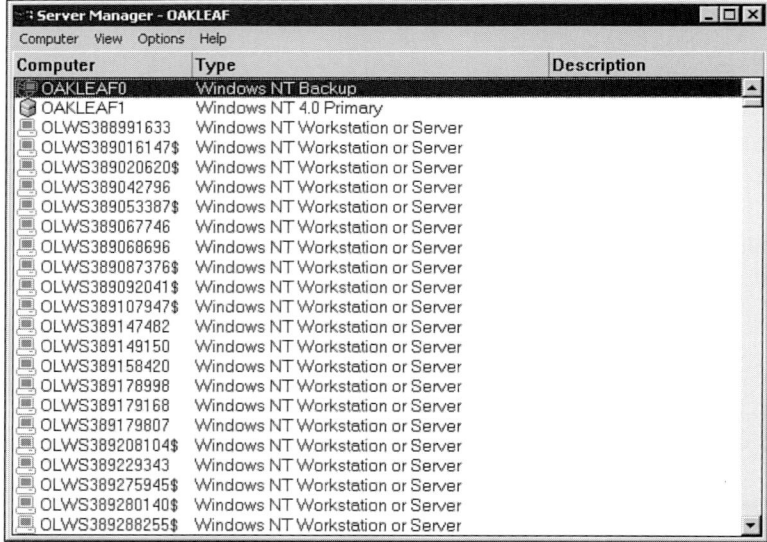

Figure 3.19
This figure shows the Windows NT 4.0 Server Manager tool running on a Windows 2000 server, and showing computer accounts in the Windows NT 4.0 domain OAKLEAF.

You can select the Windows 2000 domain in User Manager or Server Manager, and add or delete users or groups. It's not a good practice, however, to use Windows NT Server tools to manage AD objects in Windows 2000 domains. You use Active Directory Users and Computers to manage Security Groups, and user and computer accounts.

Viewing Sites and Services

Choose Programs, Administrative Tools, Active Directory Sites and Services to launch MMC with the Dssites.msc snap-in installed, choose View, Show Services Node, and expand the nodes to display the objects and containers shown in Figure 3.20. Windows 2000 creates a Default-First-Site-Name entry for you. Select the Default-First-Site-Name node and press F2 to rename it to a geographically oriented name that describes your LAN—Oakland for this example.

Figure 3.20
The Active Directory Sites and Services snap-in is open and showing the default nodes and objects for the Oakland site containing one server.

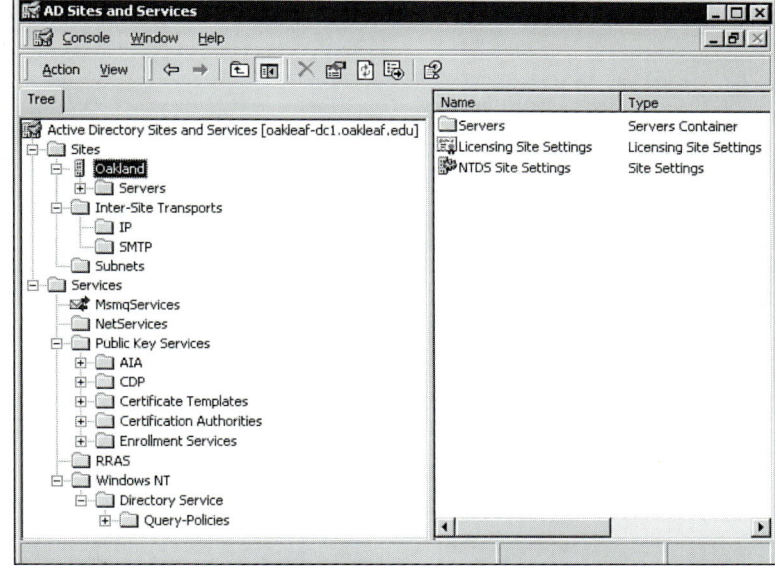

Following are brief descriptions of other nodes displayed by the Dssites.msc snap-in:

- *Servers* lists each server in a site and lets you move servers between sites. One of the most important features of the Servers element is the ability to designate additional servers to store the GC for backup purposes.

- *NTDS Settings* lets you specify replication connections and schedules between servers within the site.

- *Intersite Transports* (IP and SMTP, Simple Mail Transport Protocol) lets you alter replication mechanisms and schedules between sites. IP is the default and most efficient replication transport. Mail-based SMTP replication for remote sites isn't available in the Beta 3 version of Windows 2000.

- *Subnets* lets you assign specific IP address ranges to a site.

- *Services* lets you alter the site-related properties of specific Windows 2000 services, such as Microsoft Message Queue Server (MsmqServices) and Routing and Remote Access Services (RRAS). MSMQ is the subject of Chapter 28, "Managing Transaction and Messaging Services," and Chapter 25, "Managing Remote Access and Routing Services."

Most nodes have property dialogs that you open by right-clicking the node and choosing Properties. Figure 3.21 shows the Security page of the Oakland Properties dialog for the renamed site. Only members of the Enterprise Admins group have Full Control permissions for site objects, because sites can span multiple domains. Disabled (grayed) check boxes indicate that you can't change site permissions for Enterprise Admins.

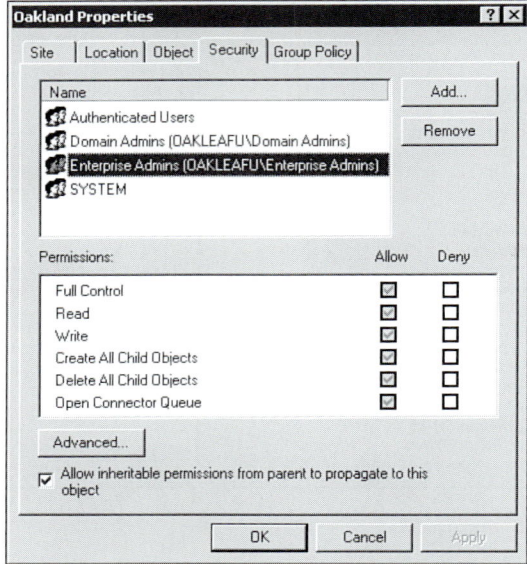

Figure 3.21
The Security page of the Properties dialog for the Oakland site is open and displaying permanent permissions for the Enterprise Admins security group.

Installing Windows 2000 Server as a DC or running Dcpromo.exe on a standalone server automatically creates the initial site and sets default property values for all site objects. In the ordinary course of server administration, you use Dssites.msc primarily to alter site topology and tune your distributed network for improved performance.

→ To learn more about working with AD sites in a WAN environment, **see** "Configuring Active Directory Sites and Services," **p. 992**.

WORKING WITH GROUPS, USERS, AND COMPUTERS

Installing Windows 2000 Server as a DC or running Dcpromo.exe creates a default set of predefined Security Groups that includes the local and domain-level user groups of Windows NT 4.0, a new set of groups specific to Windows 2000, and groups of computers categorized by function. The default set of groups and any other groups you add at this point are LDAP Organizational Units (OUs) in a flat OU namespace. A *flat namespace* is one in which objects aren't nested; the default OUs are at the top level of the OU hierarchy.

→ For a brief description of the hierarchy and scope of Windows 2000 groups, **see** "Group and User Hierarchies," **p. 28**.

→ To learn how to manipulate universal, global, and domain local groups to achieve a security hierarchy, **see** "Moving OUs, Groups, and Users Within a Domain," **p. 173**.

Choose Programs, Administrative Tools, Active Directory Users and Computers to launch MMC with Dsa.msc active. Figure 3.22 shows the Users node displaying default security groups and user accounts for a new Windows 2000 DC.

Figure 3.22
In this listing of the default Domain Local and Global user groups and default users for a new Windows 2000 domain, the Guest and krbtg accounts are disabled, as designated by the "X" that appears over their icons.

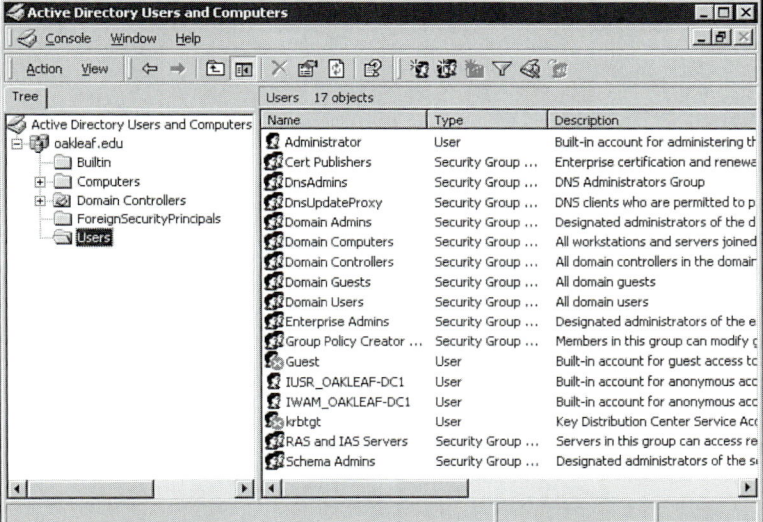

Following are brief descriptions of the five default nodes in the left pane of Dsa.msc:

- *Builtin* is a container for a set of predefined Domain Local security groups for local accounts. Builtin groups are the subject of the next section.

- *Computers* is the default container that holds computer accounts created during an upgrade from Windows NT.

- *Domain Controllers* is an OU containing Windows 2000 DC accounts within the domain.

- *ForeignSecurityPrincipals* is a container for security identifiers (SIDs) of upgraded Windows NT objects that don't correspond to the object categories of the other four nodes. You can't add or remove objects from this container with Active Directory Users and Computers.

- *Users* is the default container for Domain User accounts created during a Windows NT upgrade. Although Microsoft documentation calls the Users container an OU, you can't nest other OUs within Users.

Windows 2000 sets up the default Administrator, Guest, Internet Information Server (IIS) 5.0 anonymous (IUSR_*ServerName* and IWAM_*ServerName*, and the Kerberos ticket-granting ticket (krbtgt) users for Certificate Server. By default, the Guest user account is disabled; if you haven't set up Certificate Services, the krbtgt account also is disabled.

Windows calls individual members of security groups, including computers, *security principals*.

→ For a discussion of security principals and the Windows 2000 security system, **see** "Security Principals," **p. 38**.

BUILTIN GROUPS

DCs can't contain Local groups; Local groups are valid only for member servers or computers that aren't members of a domain, such as a standalone PC running Windows 2000 Professional or Server. Windows 2000 creates a special set of Builtin Local groups to accommodate upgrading Windows NT 4.0 local groups, such as Account Operators and Print Operators (see Figure 3.23). Builtin Local groups don't show in the list that appears when you double-click the Users node.

Figure 3.23
The Builtin local security groups shown here do not appear in the Users nodes list.

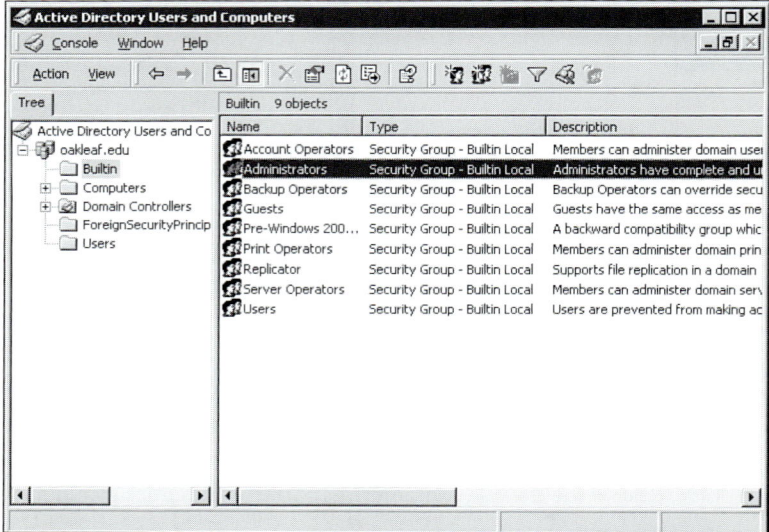

You can't place Builtin Local groups within any other Windows 2000 groups, but you can place Global groups within Builtin Local groups to assign Global group privileges in the domain. For example, the Domain Users group is a default member of the Users Builtin Local group; Domain Admins and Enterprise Admins are default members of the Administrators Builtin Local group, which also includes the Administrator account. In the Builtin list, right-click the Users or Administrators node, choose Properties, and click the Members tab to display group (and account) members. Figure 3.24 shows default membership of the Administrators Builtin Local group.

Figure 3.24
The properties dialog for the builtin Administrators local group shows the default member users and groups.

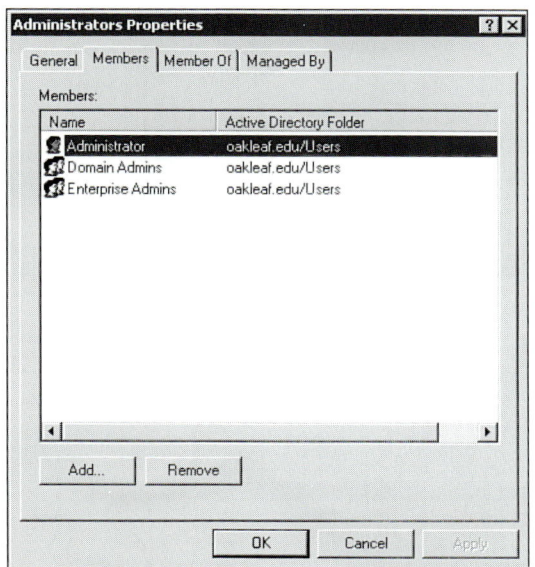

> **Note**
>
> Upgrading a Windows NT 4.0 PDC to a **Windows 2000 DC** migrates all existing domain groups and users to AD and makes no changes to group membership. Initially, only the Administrator account has membership in user security groups that aren't present in Windows NT 4.0, such as Enterprise Admins and Schema Admins.

SYSTEM GROUPS

All computers running Windows 2000 have a set of predefined System groups that don't appear in Dsa.msc, but you can assign resource permissions, such as for shared folders or printers, to these groups. Windows 2000 manages System group membership. AD calls System groups *WellKnown Security Principals*; they appear in the Select Users, Computers or Groups list that opens when you click the Add button of the resource's Property dialog to grant permissions for the resource (see Figure 3.25). The most commonly used members are Everyone (the default), Authenticated Users, and DIALUP.

→ To learn more about folder and file security issues, **see** "Managing Server Shares and the Distributed File System," **p. 675**.

> **Tip from**
> *RJ*
>
> Granting permissions to the Everyone group invites breaches of security by not requiring Kerberos authentication to access resources. If you want to assign widespread permissions for a resource, specify the Authenticated Users group.

Figure 3.25
This figure shows some of the default security groups created by Windows 2000 which you can use to grant access to resources such as files and folders, printers and file and Dfs shares like the droot share in this example.

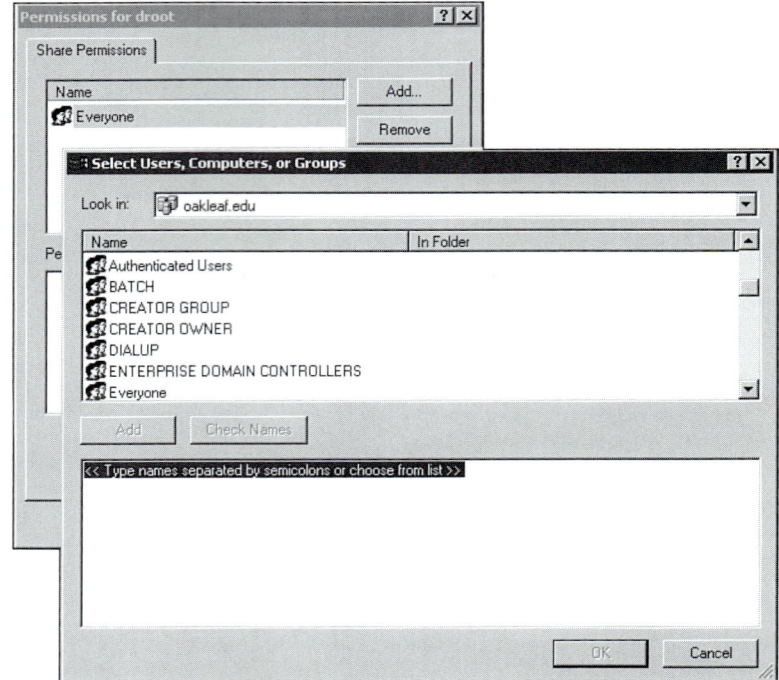

ADDING GROUPS AND USERS

You can add new Security Groups to AD, but it's a better practice to wait until you design your domain OU structure before adding new groups and a substantial number of users to your domain. Creating an OU hierarchy and moving users from groups to OUs is the subject of the "Taking Advantage of LDAP OUs" section later in the chapter.

To add a temporary Global Security Group named Authors and add a new user to the Authors group do the following:

1. Right-click the Users node, and select New, Group to open the Create New Object - Group dialog.

2. Type the name of the group, **Authors** for this example, in the Group Name text box, which also fills the Group Name (Pre-Windows 2000) text box.

3. Accept the default Group Scope option (Global) and the default Group Type option (Security), as shown in Figure 3.26. Click OK to close the dialog and create the new group. The Authors group appears in the Users list.

4. Right-click the Users node, and select New, User, to open the Create New Object (User) dialog. You can't add a new user to the Authors group directly.

5. Type the user's given name and surname in the First Name and Last Name text boxes, which completes the Full Name entry. You must enter at least a first or a last name.

Figure 3.26
The New Object – Group dialog allows you to create a new security or distribution group and specify the scope of the new group.

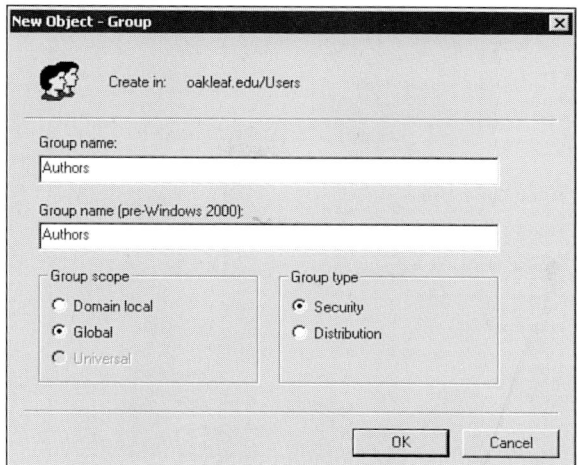

6. In the User Logon Name text box, type a valid logon ID for the user, which also fills the Downlevel Logon Name text box (see Figure 3.27). Logon IDs can consist only of letters, numbers, and hyphens; spaces and other punctuation symbols aren't permitted. User logon IDs are mandatory and must be unique for each user in the domain. The Next button isn't enabled until you type a name and logon ID. Click Next.

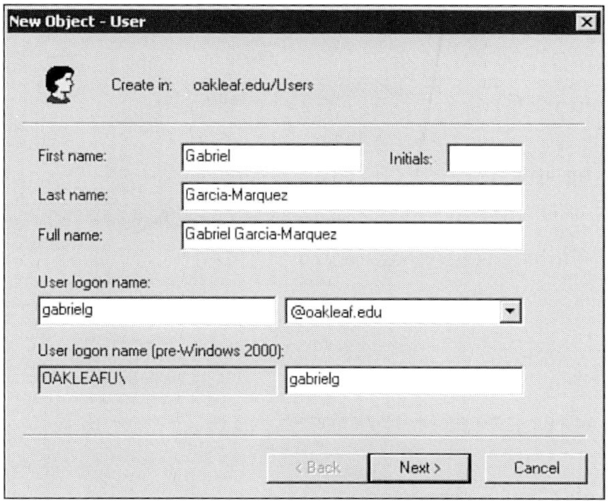

Figure 3.27
The first dialog of the New Object – User dialog is used to specify full name and logon name when creating a new user account.

7. Type **password** or an alternative, such as the user's logon ID, in the Password text box and again in the Confirm Password text box.

8. Mark the User Must Change Password at Next Logon check box (see Figure 3.28), and click Next.

Figure 3.28
The next dialog of the New Object – User window is used to set the initial password for the account and set the account password properties.

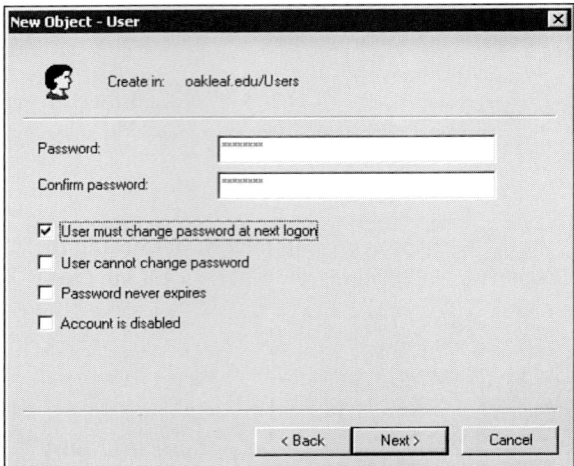

9. Review the initial user properties you set. Click Finish to close the dialog box and add the new user to the Domain Users group.
10. Right-click the Authors group in the Users node, choose Properties to open the Authors Property dialog, and click the Members tab.
11. Click Add to open the Select Users, Contacts, or Computers dialog.
12. Select the author's name in the upper list, and click Add to add the user to the lower list (see Figure 30.29).

Figure 3.29
The Members page of the Authors Security Group properties dialog is being used to add the newly created user account to the group.

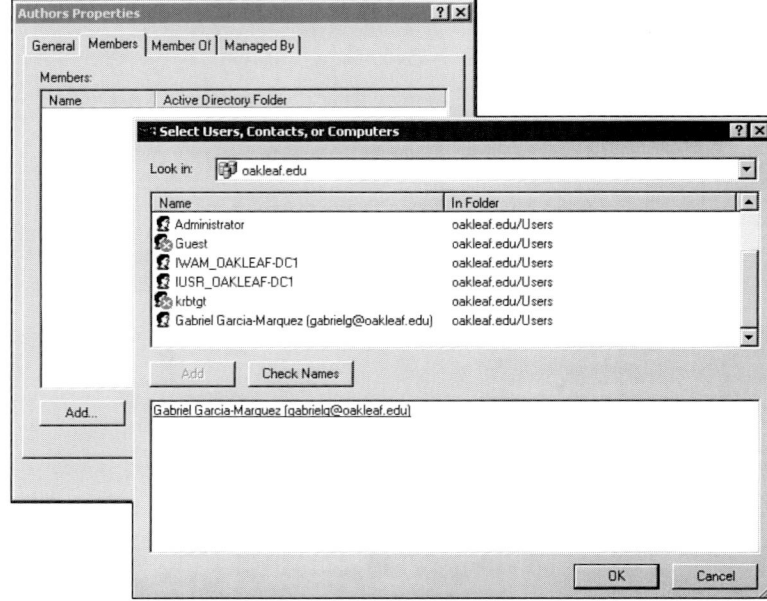

13. Click OK to close the dialog, then click OK again to close the properties dialog and add the new user to the Authors group.

An alternative method of adding a user to a group is to open the *Username* Properties dialog, click the Member Of tab, and add the user to group(s) you select. The advantage of adding users from the *GroupName* Properties dialog is that you can add many users to the group at once.

You can verify the new user's group membership by right-clicking the user in the Users node list, choosing Properties, and clicking the Member Of tab (see Figure 30.30). The *Username* Properties dialog has several other pages, most of which let you enter optional LDAP entry attribute values for the user. Several of the pages set user properties for Terminal Services; these pages appear regardless of whether you've installed Windows 2000's Terminal Services.

→ To learn more about LDAP attribute values, **see** "Entries and Attributes," **p. 123**, and "Using the Active Directory Schema Manager," **p. 124**.

Figure 3.30
The Member Of page of the user account properties dialog is being used to verify that the user account has been successfully added to the Authors group.

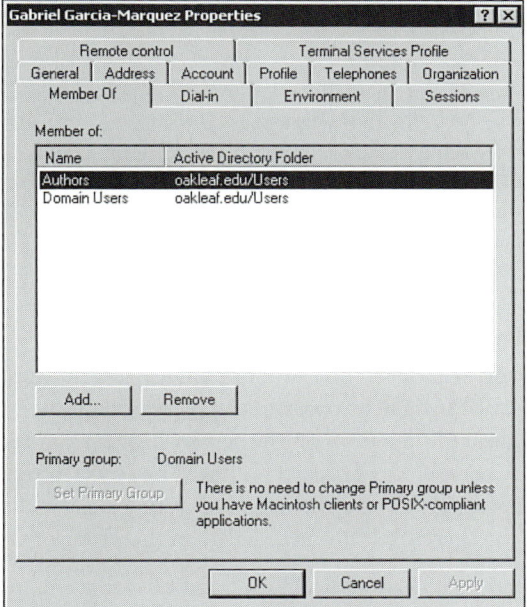

GETTING ACQUAINTED WITH LDAP

The Lightweight Directory Access Protocol (LDAP) is an Internet protocol that enables users to access and search directory databases through a Web browser. LDAP began life as a lightweight front end for International Telecommunications Union (ITU) X.500 directories, which are based on the International Standards Organization (ISO) Open Standards

Interconnection (OSI) networking model. X.500 has a complex structure that's not well adapted to the Internet and consumes an excessive amount of computer resources for PC-based directory operations. X.500 directories—most of which run on mainframes—and the heavyweight *Directory Access Protocol (DAP)* for directory searches (queries) are better suited for use by large telecommunications carriers than for use by small- to moderate-size organizations.

> **Note**
>
> Windows 2000 Server implements LDAP version 3 (LDAP v3) with extensions to accommodate AD. The Internet Engineering Task Force (IETF) is responsible for the LDAP v3 proposed standard, RFC 2251 (http://www.ietf.org/rfc/rfc2251.txt).
>
> ITU-T Rec(ommendation) X.500, "The Directory: Overview of Concepts, Models, and Service," 1993 is the official reference to the X.500 standard in IETF documents.

LDAP runs on TCP/IP, which eliminates the session and presentation overhead of the OSI networking model. LDAP delivers most of the capabilities of X.500, but consumes less than 10% of the resources required to support the heavyweight protocol. LDAP is the sole means of reading and writing AD objects.

> **Note**
>
> X.500 provides the management for X.509 digital certificates that define the Public Key Infrastructure (PKI). GTE Internetworking, for example, uses an X.500 directory and X.509 certificates for authentication in its Virtual Private Network (VPN) Advantage offering. IETF RFC 2559, "Internet X.509 Public Key Infrastructure Operational Protocols - LDAPv2 (http://www.ietf.org/rfc/rfc2559.txt) is the proposed standard for using LDAP to retrieve and manage PKI information. Chapter 11, "Setting Up Key- and Certificate-Based Security," covers Windows 2000's use of X.509 version 3 certificates for authentication of VPN users.

LDAP employs a client/server model—one or more LDAP servers store a *Directory Information Tree (DIT)*. An LDAP client transmits a protocol request, commonly called a *query*, that describes the desired operation on the server. A query can request information about an object or modify the object's property values. The server processes the query and returns an asynchronous response to the client. LDAP requires each client request to receive a response from the server, but not necessarily in the order of the client's requests.

One of the principal differences between LDAP v2 and v3 is that the newer version can return to the client a referral to another server for the requested information. AD's GC issues referrals to the appropriate domain database if the GC can't fully satisfy a client's request. The GC is a partial replica of all entries in the domain and only includes the most commonly searched attribute values. Using a partial replica minimizes network traffic when replicating GCs between domains.

Entries and Attributes

An LDAP entry holds information about a particular instance of an object class—usually a real-world entity. An entry consists of one or more named attributes, and each attribute has a type and one or more values. The attribute type has a syntax that specifies the storage format of values. For example, the standard common name, or CN, attribute has the syntax `caseIgnoreString`, which specifies a case-insensitive character value. The `telephoneNumber` attribute syntax searches only on digits, ignoring spaces, hyphens, and parentheses in query comparison tests. Attributes also can have constraints, such as digits-only, single-value data, or maximum attribute size. Maximum attribute size is useful, for example, if you want to limit the number of bytes used to store an employee's digitized photograph. Replicating graphic images between DCs creates a substantial amount of network traffic.

> **Note**
> Microsoft's LDAP implementation includes a set of standard LDAP attributes, such as `telephoneNumber`, that derive from the X.500 specification. Microsoft Exchange also uses many of these standard attributes. Microsoft's extensions to LDAPv3 are proprietary, AD-specific attributes, which are permitted by the LDAP specification. The Schema Manager MMC snap-in, described in the "Using the Active Directory Schema Manager" section later in the chapter, has a node that lists all default AD attribute names.

Contents rules define the mandatory and optional attributes for a specific object class. For example, given name, surname, common name, logon ID (user principal name), and password (even if empty) are mandatory attributes for AD User entries. You can't add a new user account without filling in all text boxes in the first Create New Object (User) dialog in step 6 of the example of the preceding "Adding Groups and Users" section.

Namespaces and Naming Conventions

Every LDAP object has a distinguished name (DN) that's unique within the scope of the directory. AD requires that DNs be unique within an enterprise. DNs constitute the namespace of the directory.

> **Note**
> IETF RFC 1779, "A String Representation of Distinguished Names," (http://www.ietf.org/rfc/rfc1779.txt) defines the formal grammar of LDAP DNs.

A conventional LDAP white pages entry for an X.500 style directory creates a DN from a series of relative distinguished name (RDN) components, such as

`cn=Gabriel Garcia-Marquez, ou=Authors, o=OakLeaf Music, l=California, co=US`

where `cn=` is the common name, `ou=` is an organizational unit, `o=` is the organization name, `l=` is locality (state in the U.S.), and `co=` is an ISO 3166 country code.

→ For a few other examples of ISO 3166 country codes, **see** "IP Address Allocation," **p. 66**.

The RDN for the parent container of the user's CN is `cn=Users`.

DNs are arranged in a least- to most-significant order, as opposed to other hierarchical naming models, such as UNIX, DOS, and Windows folders and files, which begin with the most-significant element—the drive letter.

AD DNs differ from the conventional LDAP white pages format by substituting domain components (DCs) for geographically based organization, locality, and country RDN components. IETF added `dc=` to the LDAP specification to make LDAP DNS-compliant. The AD DN for the preceding example is

`cn=Gabriel Garcia-Marquez, ou=Authors, dc=oakmusic, dc=com`

where the first `dc=` is the second-level domain name and the second `dc=` is the first-level domain name of the domain of which the user is a member.

Fortunately, Windows 2000 administrative tools handle the creation of DN strings for you in most cases. You only need to work with DN strings when creating directory-enabled applications with ADSI. The "Programming Directory-Enabled Applications with ADSI" section near the end of the chapter describes ADSI's capabilities.

OPERATIONS

LDAP defines the following three basic operations, called *functions*:

- *Interrogation* lets you search for LDAP attributes and compare attribute values. ADSI provides an arcane query language for AD searches. The "Searching for AD Objects with LDAP" section later in the chapter shows you how to use AD's built-in query processor.

- *Update* lets you add (insert) a new entry, delete an existing entry, modify an existing attribute or its value, and change the name of an attribute. You used the update function when you added a new user in the earlier "Adding Groups and Users" section.

- *Authentication* identifies your user account as valid to read and, if you have Domain Admins permissions, add, update, and delete AD entries. Only members of the Schema Admins group can add new AD attributes. The official term for connecting to AD is *binding*. The AD administrative tools handle LDAP binding automatically.

AD administrative applications, such as Dsa.msc, use ADSI 2.5 to perform LDAP functions.

USING THE ACTIVE DIRECTORY SCHEMA MANAGER

You can gain a better perspective on AD's use of LDAP by running MMC with the Schema Manager snap-in. Active Directory Schema Manager doesn't appear as an Administrative Tools menu choice, nor is Schmmgmt.msc, the required MMC snap-in, available in the usual snap-in folder—\Winnt\System32.

Installing Schema Manager

To register and install Schema Manager, do the following:

1. Choose Start, Run and type `regsvr32 schmmgmt.dll` in the Open text box.
2. Press Enter to register Schmmgmt.dll as a standalone snap-in. Click OK to close the message box that advises successful registration of Schmmgmt.dll.
3. Choose Start, Run, and type `mmc` in the Open text box.
4. Press Enter to launch MMC without an active snap-in.
5. Choose Console, Add/Remove Snapin to open the Add/Remove Snapin dialog with the Standalone page active, click Add to open the Add Standalone Snapin dialog, and select the Active Directory Schema in the Available Standalone Snap-Ins list (see Figure 3.31).

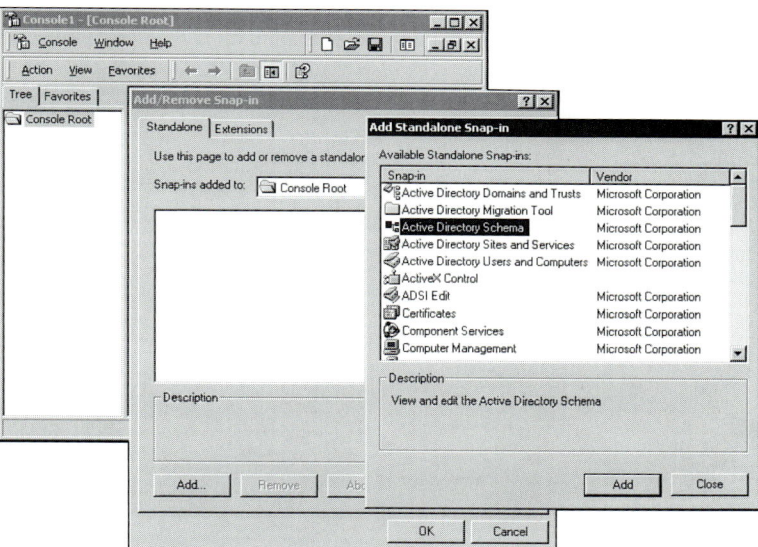

Figure 3.31
Add Schmmgmt.dll as an MMC standalone snap-in to permit viewing and altering the AD schema.

6. Click Add and then Close to add the snap-in to Standalone list, and click OK to close the Add/Remove Snap-In dialog. The Active Directory Schema node appears under the Console Root node.
7. Choose Console, Save As to open the Save As dialog, type `Schema Manager` in the File Name text box, and click Save to save the Active Directory Schema Manager console in the default \Programs\Administrative Tools folder.

To launch MMC with the Schmmgmt.msc snap-in active, choose Programs, Administrative Tools, Schema Manager.

Viewing the AD Namespace

The AD namespace consists of all LDAP entries in the Schema. With the Schmmgmt.msc snap-in active, do the following to explore AD's default set of classes and attribute entries:

1. Expand the Schema Manager's Active Directory and Classes nodes, scroll to the Computer class, and double-click the Computer node to list the Name, Type, System value, and Description for the attributes of the computer class, as shown in Figure 3.32.

2. Scroll to the bottom of the attribute list to display most of the standard set of mandatory attributes required of all AD objects—objectClass, objectCategory, nTSecurityDescriptor, and instanceType. Other mandatory attributes for the computers class are sAMAccountName and objectSID, which appear earlier in the list.

   The cn attribute also is mandatory for all objects, despite the Optional Type value for the cn entry shown in the list; another cn attribute earlier in the list has a Mandatory Type value. Class attribute names appear in no discernable list order.

Figure 3.32
The mandatory *objectClass*, *objectCategory*, *nTSecurityDescriptor*, and *instanceType* attributes appear at the bottom of the right-pane list.

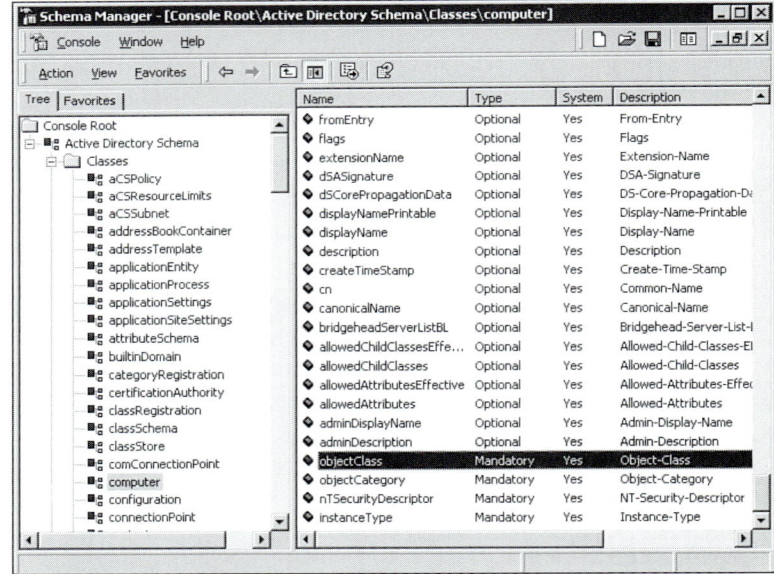

3. Expand the Attributes node to list all object attributes with Name, Syntax, and Description values (see Figure 3.33). The list is alphabetized by the name of the entry.

The most common syntax for LDAP attribute values is Unicode String (telephoneNumber in Figure 3.33). Unicode uses two bytes to represent a character in languages that previously required the double-byte character set (DBCS)—primarily Asian pictographic characters. Graphic images (thumbnailLogo and thumbnailPhoto) use the Octet String syntax, which is a variable length binary string of eight-bit bytes.

Figure 3.33
The right pane of the Schema Manager snap-in shows part of the list of all defined Active Directory attributes in alphabetical order.

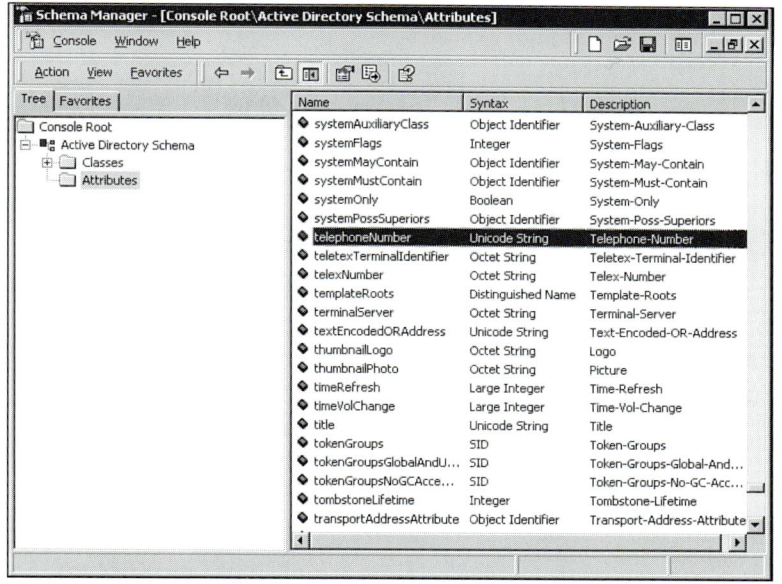

The convention for X.500-style LDAP attribute names uses lower-case letters for the first element of compound names, with remaining elements initial-letter-capitalized. This convention results in the oddly-formatted nTSecurityDescriptor name you saw earlier. Attribute names are case-sensitive in UNIX LDAP implementations, but not in Windows.

To enable modifications to the AD Schema, you must be logged on as Administrator or have assigned Schema Admins rights. The Administrator account is a default member of Schema Admins, and Enterprise Admins members also have Schema Admins rights. Right-click the Active Directory Schema node and choose Change Operations Master to open the Change Operations Master properties dialog. You must mark The Schema May Be Modified on This Server check box to enable attribute changes and additions, and changes to permissions.

Tip from
RJ
> Don't modify the Schema unless you have a very good reason to do so and know exactly what you intend to do. Experimenting with Schema modifications can cause the AD database to become corrupt and prevent Windows 2000 Server from booting or prevent you from logging on as Administrator to fix the problem you created.

You also use the Change Operations Master properties dialog to move the Schema Operations Master to another server. You must move the Operations Master to another DC before you remove AD from a DC that serves as the current Operations Master.

VIEWING AND ADDING AD CLASS PROPERTIES

Each class has a properties dialog that displays attribute values of the class. If you've enabled Schema modifications, you can alter some of these values and add new optional attributes to the class.

Right-click the user class in the Classes list to open the user Properties dialog. The General page (see the left side of Figure 3.34) has the following fields:

- *Description* is intended as a more readable version of the common name of the class. The default Description value is the common name; you can modify the description without affecting Schema operation.
- *Common Name* is the cn attribute of the class, which you can't change.
- *X.500 OID* is a fixed Object ID that's unique for every class in an LDAP directory. In the U.S., you register with American National Standards Institute (ANSI) to obtain a root ID, which comprises the first four elements (1.2.840.113556, assigned to Microsoft) of dotted-decimal representation of the OID.
- *Class Type* is Structural for the default classes that form the AD structure.
- *Category* is the name you use to perform LDAP operations—such as querying—on the class.

Marking the Show Objects of This Class While Browsing check box makes the class visible in AD browse operations. AD-enabled clients can browse AD to find specific objects and resources.

Marking the Deactivate This Class check box removes the class from AD, but doesn't delete the class; don't mark this check box.

> **Tip from**
> *RJ*
>
> You display a brief description of the purpose of each field in the *className* Properties dialog by placing the mouse pointer in the field and pressing F1.

The Relationship page of the user Properties dialog (see the right side of Figure 3.34) shows the relationship of the class with other classes in the AD hierarchy. Following are the fields of the Relationship page:

- *Parent Class* is immediately above the selected class in the AD hierarchy. The user class is a child of the LDAP-standard organizationalPerson class.
- *Auxiliary Classes* are classes to which members of the class also are added when you create a new instance of the class—a new user. A new user automatically becomes a Windows 2000 securityPrincipal and a mailRecipient object, even if you don't have Microsoft Exchange installed. You add auxiliary classes by clicking Add and selecting attribute(s) from the current Attributes list.
- *Possible Superior* is a list of other classes to which class members belong. For instance, users usually belong to an organizationalUnit (OU).

USING THE ACTIVE DIRECTORY SCHEMA MANAGER | 129

Figure 3.34
You can describe the class on the General (left) page of the user Properties dialog. The Relationship page is on the right.

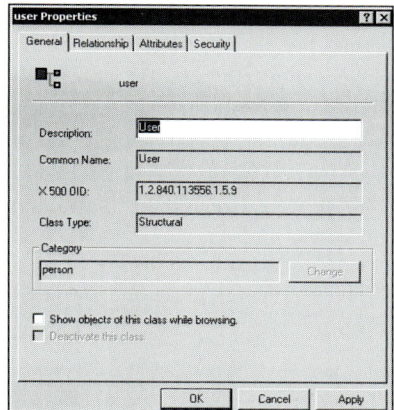 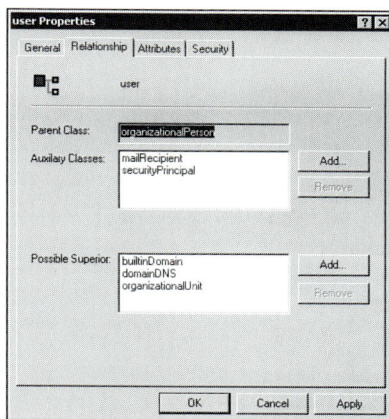

> **Note**
>
> The `mailRecipient` auxiliary class prepares AD for integration with Microsoft Exchange. Installing Exchange 2000 makes extensive additions and changes to the AD schema.

The Attributes page (see the left side of Figure 3.35) has lists for Mandatory and Optional attributes but only the default set of Optional AD attributes for the class appears. You can click the Add button to add Optional attributes for the class from the Attributes list.

The options in the Security page (see the right side of Figure 3.35) set the security parameters for the class. You can add or remove security groups from the upper list, and set permissions for objects of the user class in the Permissions list. Removing a security group from the list prevents users from reading AD entries. The only default permission for the Everyone group is Change Password.

> **Tip from**
> *RJ*
>
> The most important attribute value on the Security page is the Allow Inheritable Permissions from Parent to Propagate to This Object check box. Unless you have a very good reason to inhibit permissions inheritance, leave this check box marked.

ASSIGNING OPTIONAL ATTRIBUTE VALUES TO AD OBJECTS

High-level AD objects, such as members of the Users, Computers, and Domain Controllers containers, have standard sets of optional attributes whose values you set with AD's administrative tools. As an example, the General page of the *UserName* Properties dialog for User objects has optional fields (text boxes) for Description, Office, Telephone, E-Mail, and Home Page. All fields of the Address page are optional, as are those of the Organization page. Figure 3.36 shows a completed General page (left) and Address page (right) for the example Gabriel Garcia-Marquez user account. Most of the optional fields have counterparts in Exchange Server mailbox attributes.

Two fields of the General page—Telephone Number and Web Page—have Other buttons that let you add additional, multiple values for an attribute. Multi-value attributes appear in AD's lists as *Attribute Name* (Other). Optional attribute entries are useful for LDAP searches against address components, department names, and other object properties. Setting some attribute values, such as Manager Name in the Organization page, requires you to click a Change button, which opens the Select User or Contact dialog (see Figure 3.37). *Contacts* are user-like objects in OUs that don't have user accounts in the domain.

> **Note**
>
> Adding a Manager Name attribute value causes the user's name to appear in the manager's Organization page's Direct Reports list. You can't add Direct Reports entries directly to the list.

Figure 3.35
The Attributes page of the properties dialog for the user AD object is shown on the left; all attributes associated with the object are shown here, in either the mandatory or optional boxes. The Security page of the same properties dialog is shown on the right, displaying the permissions for the Everyone group.

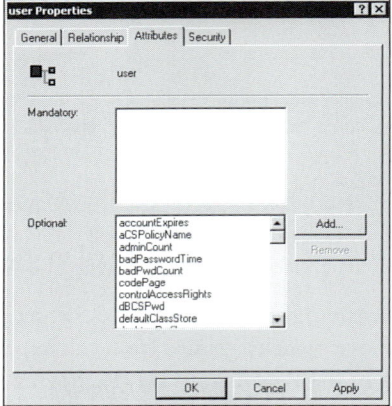
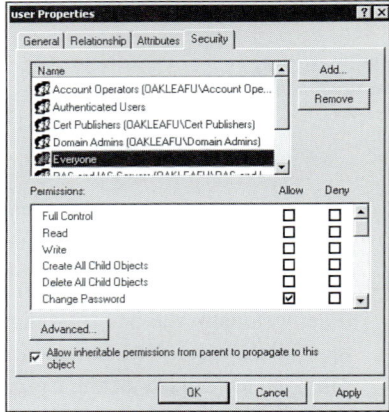

Figure 3.36
The General page of the properties dialog for a user is shown on the left and the Address tab is on the right. The newly added attributes are shown in these dialogs.

USING THE ACTIVE DIRECTORY SCHEMA MANAGER | 131

Figure 3.37
Use the Select User or Contact dialog for adding an attribute value, such as Manager Name, from a list of AD entries.

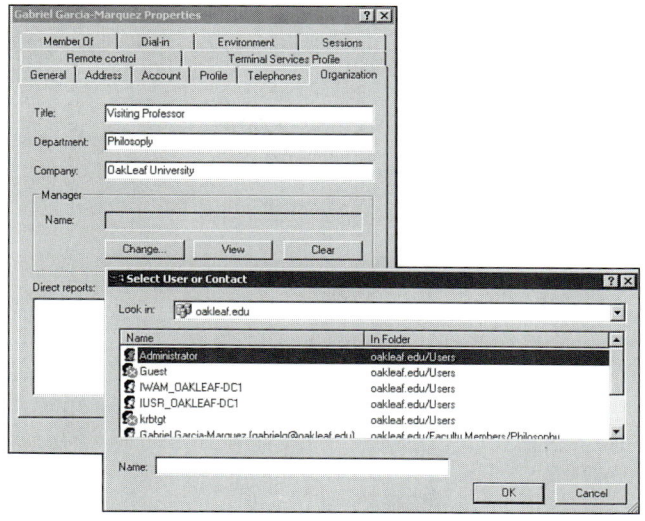

Most of the captions of the *UserName* Properties dialog pages translate readily to attribute names in the Name column of Schema Manager's list for the User node. Table 3.1 lists each of the field captions for the three dialog pages shown in the preceding two figures and the corresponding LDAP attribute name for the field. You need to know the names of commonly used attributes to write directory-enabled ADSI applications and to perform many types of LDAP queries.

TABLE 3.1   FIELD CAPTIONS AND ATTRIBUTE NAMES FOR THREE *USERNAME* PROPERTIES DIALOG PAGES

	General Page		Address Page		Organization Page
Caption	**Attribute Name**	**Caption**	**Attribute Name**	**Caption**	**Attribute Name**
First Name	GivenName	Street	streetAddress	Title	title
Last Name	Sn	P.O. Box	postOfficeBox	Department	department
Display Name	Cn	City	l	Company	company
Description	Description	State/Province	st	Manager	manager
Office	PhysicalDeliver-OfficeName	ZIP/Postal Code	postalCode	Direct Reports	directReports
Telephone Number	TelephoneNumber	Country/Region	c		
E-Mail	Mail				
Web Page	WWWHomePage				

PART
I
CH
3

Taking Advantage of LDAP OUs

Security groups offer limited nesting ability; you must obey the Windows NT groups nesting rules in a mixed-mode domain. OUs permit more flexibility in organizing groups, including unlimited nesting, and offer the advantage of default inherited permissions and Group Policies throughout an OU hierarchy. Inherited permissions and Group Policies, which you can override, simplify management of lower-level members of the hierarchy.

→ For an in-depth discussion of Group Policies, **see** "Understanding Windows 2000's Group Policies," **p. 618**.

Creating Domain OUs

The Active Directory Computers and Users tool lets you quickly and easily create or modify an OU hierarchy for your domain. An example OU structure used in this book is for a fictional OakLeaf University that has a 25,000-member student body, 1,648 faculty members, and 627 non-teaching salaried employees in 11 staff categories. OakLeaf U offers 1,755 sections of 645 courses in 16 departments. Each department has a dean and department chairperson. The examples in this and the remaining chapters of this book use the `oakleaf.edu` (OAKLEAFU) test domain. The OAKLEAF Windows NT domain remains the production domain for OakLeaf U until upgrading OAKLEAF's PDC to Windows 2000 in Chapter 8.

Note

A 5MB Jet 4.0 database (Oakleaf.mdb) contains the data used to create the groups, user and computer accounts, and Microsoft Exchange 5.5 mailboxes in the OAKLEAF domain, and similar objects, plus OUs in the `oakleaf.edu` domain. Most of the optional attributes of the User class are Exchange mailbox attributes. Oakleaf.mdb is included in the \Seuw2ks\ADSI25 folder of the accompanying CD-ROM, which also contains the executable and source code files for the ADSI25 for Active Directory application discussed at the end of this chapter.

Oakleaf.mdb is derived from the Beckwith.mdb Jet 3.5 database created by Steven Gray and Rick Lievano for *Roger Jennings' Database Workshop: Microsoft Transaction Server 2.0* (Sams Publishing, ISBN 0-672-31130-5), and incorporated in *Database Developers Guide with Visual Basic 6* (Sams Publishing, ISBN 0-672-31063-5) and *Special Edition Using Access 2000* (Que Corporation, ISBN 0-7897-1606-2).

This example uses the domain you specified when you installed Windows 2000 Server or that you created in the "Installing Active Directory" section near the beginning of this chapter.

Do the following to create a top-level OU:

1. Right-click the domain name node, and choose Add, Organizational Unit to open the Create New Object (Organization Unit) dialog.
2. Type the name of the OU in the text box.
3. Click OK to close the dialog and add the new OU to the domain.

You can add as many top-level OUs as you want; this example for OakLeaf U has Faculty Members, Staff, and Students as the three top-level OUs.

You add second-level OUs with the preceding process, except that you right-click the top-level OU node to add the second-level OU. You also can use the context menu to create new computer accounts; add groups, users, and contacts; and publish (make available) printers and server shares at any level in the OU hierarchy. Figure 3.38 illustrates the two-level OU hierarchy of faculty members and departments. The OU also contains a Faculty Members Domain Local Security Group.

Figure 3.38
The Active Directory Users and Computers snap-in is open to the Faculty Members Organizational Unit showing a number of child OUs and the Faculty Members Security Group as OU members.

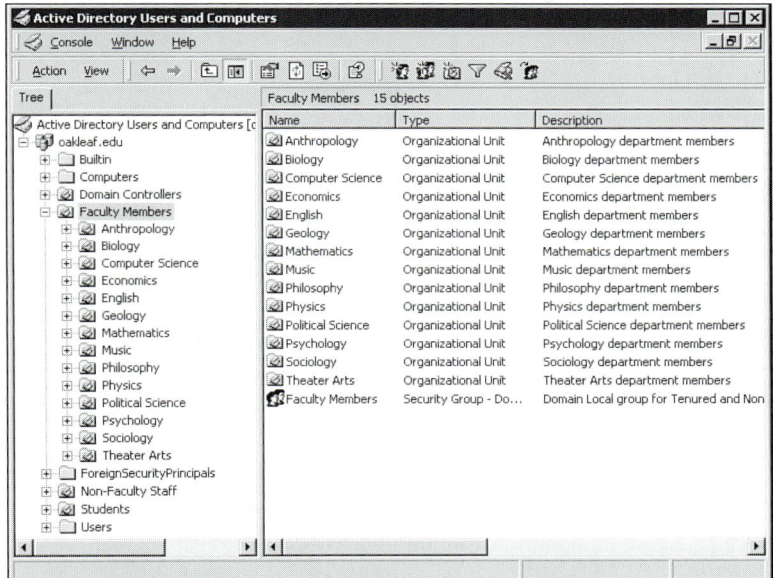

Moving Objects Into and Between OUs

You can move an AD object from its original (default) location to an OU, and move objects between OUs. For example, you can move the user you added in the earlier "Adding Groups and Users" section from the Users group to one of the second-level OUs of the Faculty OU. You can select a contiguous collection of users by clicking the first member of a collection in the right pane, then Shift+clicking the last member. For a non-contiguous collection, Ctrl+click the individual users in the right pane. Version 1.2 of MMC (the version included with Windows 2000 Server) doesn't have drag-and-drop capability.

Tip from
RJ

To enable full expansion of nodes in the left MMC pane, choose View, Users Groups and Computers as Containers. You can select and move a single object with a left-pane selection, but you can't multi-select objects.

With the object(s) you want to move selected, do the following:

1. Right-click a selected object and choose Move to open the Move dialog.

2. Expand the nodes as necessary, and select the OU to which to move the object(s) (see Figure 3.39).
3. Click OK to close the Move dialog and send the object(s) to their new OU (see Figure 3.40).

Figure 3.39
The object Move window (foreground) shows a move of the user objects selected in the Active Directory Users and Computers snap-in in the background to the Philosophy OU which is a child of the Faculty Members OU.

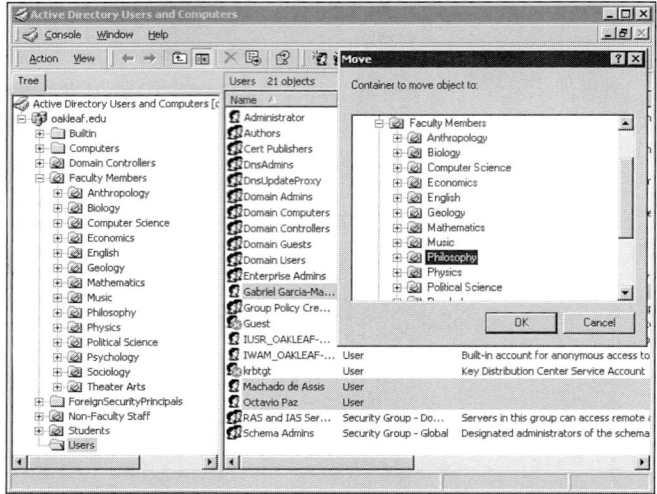

Objects you move from the Users group no longer appear in the Users node's list, but retain their membership in the Domain Users group to which all ordinary users belong. Moving a user to an OU or between OUs doesn't affect security group membership, nor does it alter the location of the user's directory container, `DomainName.com/Users`.

Figure 3.40
The Active Directory Users and Computers snap-in is showing the moved users in the target OU. This OU also contains a share and a Global Security Group.

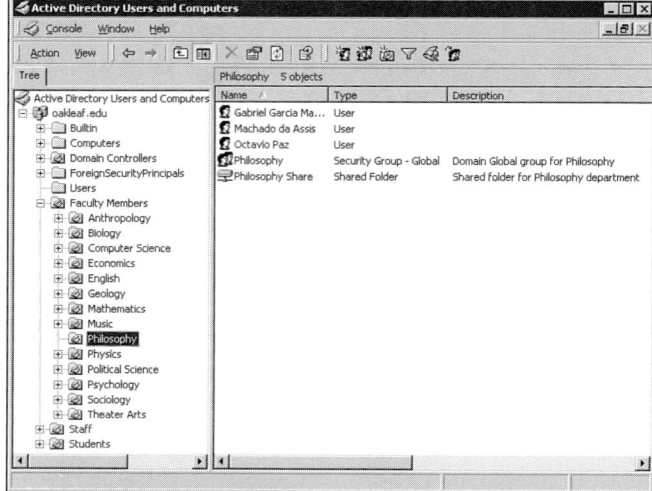

The user's new OU appears in the Object page of the *UserName* Properties dialog (see Figure 3.41). The Fully Qualified Domain Name of Object text box uses UNIX-style virgules (/) as path separators, similar to Web paths, for the OU hierarchy. The general display syntax for the LDAP path is `DomainName.com/OU1Name[/OU2Name/OU3Name...]/UserName`. The equivalent reverse-reading X.500-style syntax is `cn=UserName[..., ou=OU3Name[, ou=OU2Name]], dc=DomainName, dc = com`.

Unique Sequence Number (USN) is an attribute of the NTFS 5.0 Change Journal that provides a log of all changes to a file on an NTFS 5.0 volume. The AD replication process uses the USN Created and USN Modified values shown in Figure 3.41 to determine which attribute values replicate to other DCs. Each DC stores a `HighestCommittedUSN` value, which contains the maximum USN value in its AD database. If the USN value for a new or modified object exceeds the `HighestCommittedUSN` value, the AD's database is updated. The replication process uses the corresponding timestamp values (Created and Modified) to resolve conflicts between updates by two admins. The update with the latest timestamp wins.

Figure 3.41
The Object page of the *UserName* Properties dialog displays the user's location in the OU hierarchy. The Object and Published Certificates pages appear only if you choose View, Advanced.

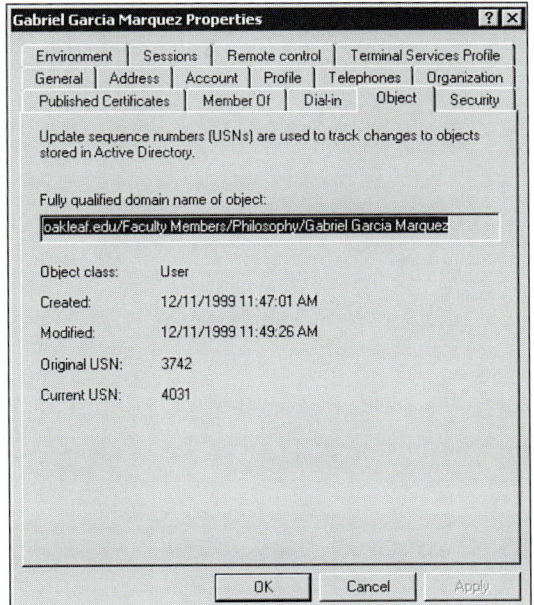

SEARCHING FOR AD OBJECTS WITH LDAP

The primary function of LDAP is to provide a means for querying the directory to determine the location of objects. Like queries against relational databases, LDAP queries use attribute values as criteria. You can search for objects by their common name or any other attribute value of the object.

The SQL equivalent of an LDAP search criteria for a value with Unicode String syntax is a `WHERE attribute-name LIKE '%attribute-value%'`. The % symbols are wildcards, which permit searching on a substring value—such as `Jones`—in the `cn` attribute, which usually includes first and last names.

USING THE AD QUERY FEATURE

The Active Directory Users and Computers tool provides a Find function for LDAP queries. To find a user, do the following:

1. In the left pane, select the node at which you want to begin the search. To search the entire domain, select the domain name.
2. Choose View, Find, or right-click the selected node and choose Find to open the default Find Users, Contacts, and Groups dialog.
3. In the In list, select the scope of your search. You can override the search scope selection you made in step 1.
4. In the Name text box, type the first few characters of the common name of the user you want to find. Alternatively, you can search for a match in the Description field.
5. Click Find Now to execute the LDAP query. The query result set appears in a list box at the bottom of the dialog (see Figure 3.42).

Figure 3.42
The Find Users, Contacts, and Groups dialog has been used to search the Faculty Members OU for a name containing Garcia. The results are in the lower part of the window.

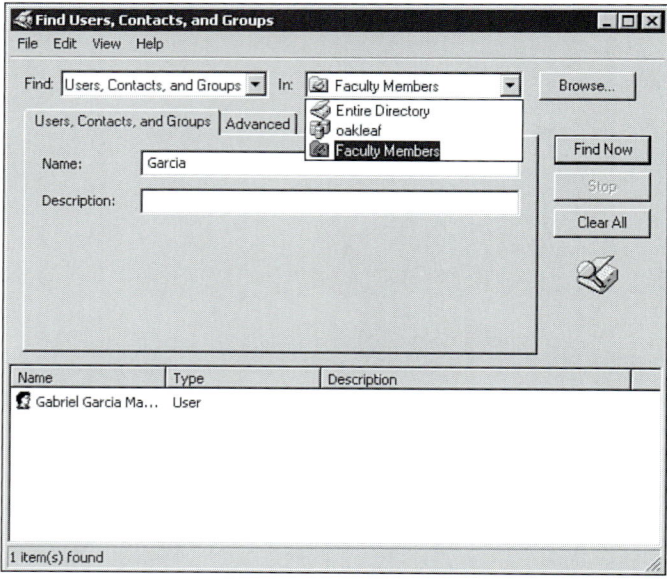

The default query syntax finds any occurrence of the characters you type in the Name text box within the user's common name; for this example, the query uses the equivalent of a `WHERE cn LIKE '%Garcia%'` SQL criterion.

Searching for AD Objects with LDAP

The Find list lets you select other classes of objects to locate—Computers, Printers, Shared Folders, Organization Units, or MSMQ Queues (if you've installed the Message Queue Service). You also can select Custom Search from the Find list to enable Field list selection from a longer list of object classes in which to search. The second Field menu level lets you choose an attribute name from those associated with the chosen object class (see Figure 3.43). After you choose the attribute to search, accept the Starts With Condition, type the first few characters of the name in the Value text box, and click Find Now to conduct the search.

Clicking the Advanced tab of the Find Users, Contacts, and Groups dialog lets you choose a User, Group, or Contact search. Choosing User presents you with the attribute choice listing shown in Figure 3.44. The scrollable menu offers more than 50 attribute names on which you can base a search of users.

Figure 3.43
The Find Custom Search page is open, showing the selection of a specific AD Object Class (Organizational Unit) and Attribute (Name) from the field selection drop-down box.

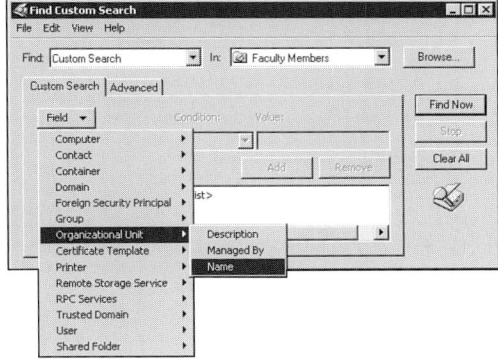

Figure 3.44
The Advanced page of the Find Users, Contacts, and Groups window is open and the first 33 possible Attributes for the Users object class are shown. You can base a search on any of these attributes.

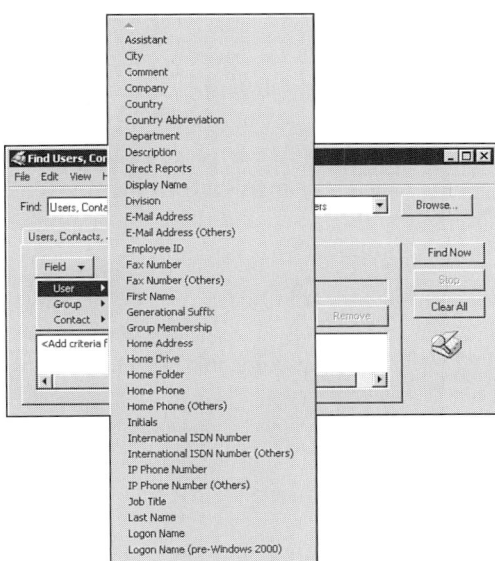

To perform a typical advanced user search, do this:

1. Select the attribute name for the search from the scrolling menu.
2. Open the Condition list to specify the search logic. The default is Starts With. Table 3.2 lists the Condition values and their equivalent SQL WHERE clause syntax.
3. Type the characters for the search in the Value text box.
4. Click the Add button to add the criterion to the list.

   You can specify multiple criteria to narrow the search by repeating steps 1 through 4. The equivalent of the SQL AND operator concatenates multiple search criteria.

5. Click the Find Now button to return the result set to the lower list box.

TABLE 3.2   ADVANCED FIND SEARCH CONDITIONS AND EQUIVALENT SQL WHERE CLAUSE CRITERIA

Search Condition	Equivalent SQL WHERE Clause
Starts with	WHERE *attribute-name* LIKE '%*attribute-value*'
Ends with	WHERE *attribute-name* LIKE '*attribute-value*%'
Is (exactly)	WHERE *attribute-name* = '*attribute-value*'
Is not	WHERE *attribute-name* != '*attribute-value*'
Present	WHERE *attribute-name* IS NOT NULL
Not Present	WHERE *attribute-name* IS NULL

Advanced find doesn't offer the equivalent of the default find operation's WHERE *attribute-name* LIKE '%*attribute-value*%' syntax.

APPLYING LDAP FILTERS

You can apply an LDAP filter to the query result set by clicking the Set Filtering Options toolbar button or choosing View, Filter Options to display the Filter Options dialog. Filters are helpful when searching a class that contains a large number of entries for multiple object subclasses. You also use filters for selecting many users or other objects by a common attribute value. You select the entire filtered set, and then, for example, use the Move command to move a group of users from one OU to another.

The default filter criterion is none—Show All Objects. Select the Show Only the Following Types of Objects option, as shown in Figure 3.45, to alter the object classes to display in Active Directory Users and Computers' right pane and in LDAP query result sets.

Figure 3.45
The Filter Options dialog is used to define which object types are shown in the results of a search.

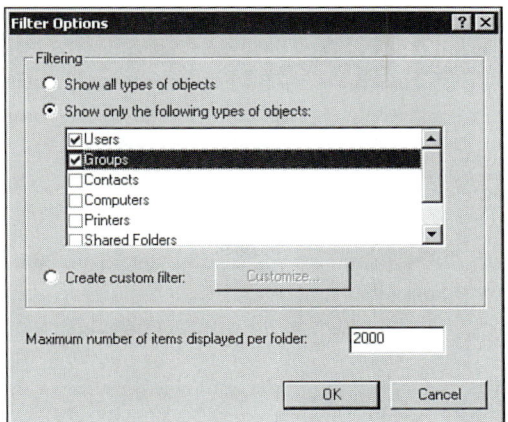

The SQL equivalent of a two-object-class filter is `SELECT cn FROM directory-scope WHERE object-class = 'Users' OR object-class = 'Groups'`.

Selecting the Create Custom Filter option and clicking the Customize button in the Filter Options dialog opens the Find Custom Search dialog discussed in the preceding section. If you've chosen View, Advanced Features, the Advanced page lets you type a search expression in the Enter LDAP Query text box. LDAP search expressions use an arcane syntax. Unfortunately, Microsoft doesn't explain the LDAP query dialect in the online help for Active Directory Users and Computers or elsewhere. You must download the help file for the ADSI 2.5 from `http://www.microsoft.com/windows/server/Technical/directory/adsilinks.asp`, and open the "Search Filter Syntax" topic to obtain an introduction to the LDAP query dialect. Fortunately, the Find Custom Search dialog is adequate for most searches, so you seldom need to write your own LDAP query.

Tip from	Be sure to remove the filter you applied after you finish using it. Otherwise, you encounter
RJ	unexpected results, such as no users appearing in the Users container or OUs. To remove a filter, click the Set Filtering Options button, and select the Show All Types of Objects option in the Filter Options dialog. The last custom query you created is saved for reuse.

 If some types of filters don't return the result you expect, see "Solving Custom Filter Problems" in the "Troubleshooting" section near the end of this chapter.

Programming Directory-Enabled Applications with ADSI

ADSI is Microsoft's Component Object Model (COM) interface to LDAP-based and other directory structures. ADSI lets developers write directory-enabled applications to perform create, read, update, and delete operations on directory objects and their attributes. All Windows 2000 versions install ADSI 2.5 during setup. You must download The ADSI 2.5 Software Development Kit (SDK) from http://www.microsoft.com/windows/server/Technical/directory/adsilinks.asp or install a commercial Windows 2000 directory-enabled application to add ADSI 2.5 components to Windows NT and 9x computers. The ADSI 2.5 SDK includes the previously mentioned ADSI documentation in HTML Help format and offers sample applications written in Visual Basic and Visual C++.

Mission Critical Software (http://www.missioncritical.com/) publishes the OnePoint suite of directory-enabled domain management products for Windows NT and 2000. Microsoft announced on June 16, 1999, that Windows 2000 would include Mission Critical's Active Directory Migration Tool (ADMT), which is based on the OnePoint technology. ADMT uses ADSI 2.5 to migrate Windows NT 4.0 and Exchange directory objects to Windows 2000. ADMT is available for download from Microsoft's Windows Upgrade Web site for Windows 2000 Server.

→ For detailed information on ADMT, **see** "Emulating Domain Migration with the Active Directory Migration Tool," **p. 231**.

ADSI 2.5 AND VISUAL BASIC

ADSI 2.5 includes an automation wrapper (type library) for the ADSI COM objects to make them accessible to Visual Basic for Applications (VBA) and Visual Basic Script (VBScript) programmers. The two type libraries required for secure connectivity to directory services are Active DS Type Library (Activeds.tlb) and ADsSecurity 2.5 Type Library (Adssecurity.dll). The Active DS Type Library's objects connect to the directory service with any of the following four ADSI providers:

- LDAP:// for Windows 2000's AD and the Exchange 5.5 directory
- WinNT:// for Windows NT 4.0's Security Account Manager (SAM)
- NDS:// for NetWare Directory Services
- NWCOMPAT:// for NetWare 3.x's bindery

The :// following the provider ID in the preceding list designates the first element of the ADsPath to the object. The ADsPath specifies the container or object to which the program connects. Each provider uses its own syntax to create the ADsPath to a particular container or object.

ADSI also lets you create ActiveX Data Objects (ADO) Recordset objects (ADODB.Recordset) whose rows list objects within containers. A Recordset is an in-memory representation of a relational or hierarchical database table. In most cases, you can use familiar SQL-style SELECT statements, instead of LDAP query dialect, to define the Recordset. The ability to use your database programming skills with AD objects is one of the principal benefits of ADSI.

THE ADSI25 VISUAL BASIC APPLICATION

The ability to use multiple ADSI providers in a single Visual Basic application or script lets developers write custom directory applications that, for example, simultaneously connect to the Windows NT SAM, Windows 2000 AD, and the Exchange directory. The ADSI25 for Active Directory Visual Basic 6.0 application, included in the \Seuw2ks\ADSI25 folder of the accompanying CD-ROM, uses the WinNT and LDAP providers to create Windows NT 4.0 user accounts and Exchange 5.5 mailboxes from data stored in the Oakleaf.mdb Jet 4.0 database. The earlier "Creating Domain OUs" section describes the contents of Oakleaf.mdb. ADSI25 runs under Windows NT 4.0 (SP4+) or Windows 2000, but not under Win9x; Win95 doesn't support the security features required by ADSI25 to create Exchange mailboxes.

Generating a large number of Windows NT 4.0 accounts with ADSI25 lets you emulate a real-world upgrade of one or more production domains without the risk of migrating a production PDC.

→ To install the ADSI25.exe application under Windows NT, **see** "Setup.exe for Windows NT 4.0," **p. 1263**.

→ For an in-depth discussion of how to upgrade a Windows NT 4.0 domain with accounts created by ADSI25, **see** "Promoting the PDC to Active Directory," **p. 363**.

Figure 3.46 shows the opening dialog of Adsi25.exe running under Windows NT 4.0, in which you specify the directory type (WinNT or LDAP) and downlevel domain name(s) for employee and student accounts. If you mark the Check to Add New-User Exchange 5.5+ Mailboxes check box, you can add mailboxes when you add Windows NT user accounts for upgrade testing.

Figure 3.46
This figure shows the opening dialog of the directory-enabled ADSI25 Visual Basic application running on a Windows NT 4.0 system.

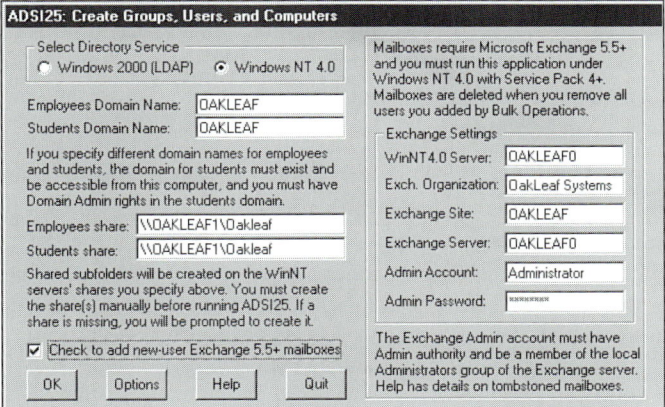

Clicking OK opens ADSI25's main form that initially displays lists of groups and users. Clicking an item in the Groups list displays the group's user membership. Similarly, clicking an item in the Users list displays the groups of which the user is a member (see Figure 3.47).

Students are assigned to department groups according to their major subject. The lists display the full ADsPath value for each item. The (Type: 2) suffixes aren't part of the ADsPath; domain-level groups are Type 2; local groups are Type 4. You also can add and delete groups and users, and remove a user from a group.

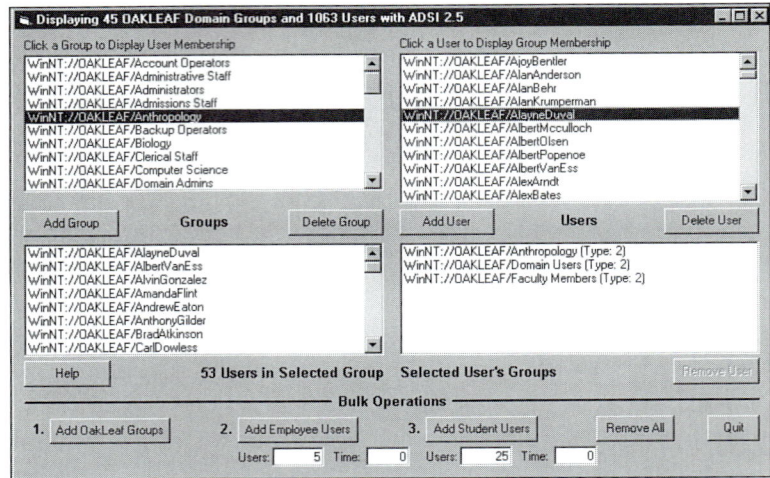

Figure 3.47
This is the main window of the ADSI25 program showing the members of the Anthropology group and the groups of which the selected user is a member.

The Bulk Operations section of the form enables adding large numbers of sample employee and student accounts to the domain(s). If you marked the Check to Add New-User Exchange 5.5+ Mailboxes check box in ADSI25's opening dialog (refer to Figure 3.46), employees and students get an Exchange mailbox during account creation. After you upgrade the Windows NT 4.0 PDC that stores the test accounts, you can write code similar to that in ADSI25 to copy the Exchange attribute values to the same or related attributes of the user's AD account.

When you run ADSI25 under Windows 2000, the ADsPath prefix changes to LDAP://, and is followed by the distinguished name of the directory object, as shown in Figure 3.48. Displaying DNs for objects is helpful when you must specify the exact DN string in a search or filter. The Select User's Account Attributes list displays values added by ADSI25 for each of the common attribute values for the User object that you double-click in the user list above. Under Windows 2000, ADSI25 adds OUs and places user accounts and Global Security Groups in the appropriate OU container.

→ To install the ADSI25 application under Windows 2000, **see** "ADSI25.msi for Windows 2000," **p. 1262**.

Figure 3.48
This is the main window of the ADSI25 program running on a Windows 2000 system showing the distinguished names of Security Groups and Users, and the Active Directory attributes for a selected user.

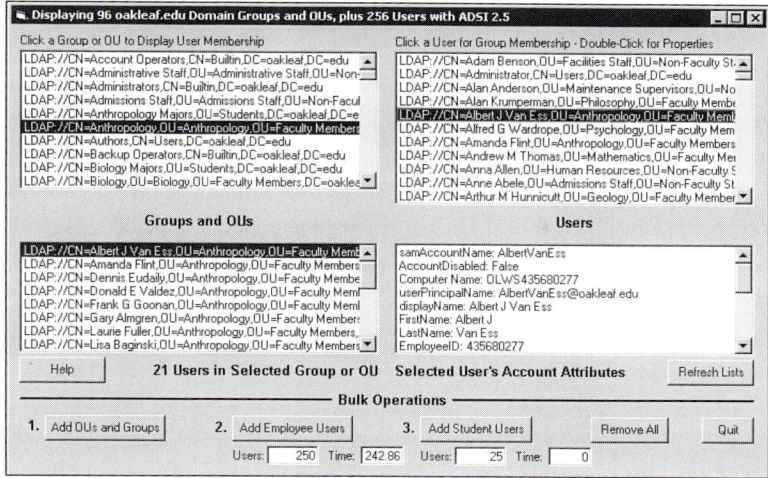

ADSI programming is beyond the scope of this book, but if you have Visual Basic 6.0 with SP3 installed, you can review the application's VBA code to gain insight on LDAP programming techniques. Most subprocedures in the `frmGroupsUsers` form contain both `WinNT://` and `LDAP://` examples; the `AddUserMailbox` subprocedure illustrates how to add Exchange mailboxes and the use of security objects defined by the ADsSecurity 2.5 Type Library.

Troubleshooting

Problems Removing Orphaned Domain Controllers

Attempts to remove AD from a second DC in a domain or the primary DC of a child domain fail with "Unable to connect to domain controller" messages.

If you have two or more domain controllers in your test configuration, the first (initial root) domain controller plays the schema master, configuration master, and other flexible single-master (FSMO) roles. Demoting another DC in the domain or a dependent child domain requires replicating changes to and modifying the schema of the initial root DC. If you remove AD from the domain controller performing the FSMO roles without transferring these roles to another DC, the other DC(s) no longer can replicate their changes. The same problem occurs if a second DC loses network connectivity to the initial root DC; in this case restoring the connection solves the problem.

On a second DC in the domain, you can use the Ntdsutil.exe command-line program to seize the FSMO roles for the domain. You also can use Ntdsutil's Metadata Cleanup feature to remove references to nonexistent domains. In a test configuration, however, it's often quicker to reformat the system partition, and reinstall Windows 2000 Server than to attempt repair of the orphaned DC.

→ For details on the use of Ntdsutil.exe, **see** "Seizing the FSMO Roles of a Failed DC," **p. 408**.

Solving Custom Filter Problems

Using the `Group Membership` *attribute of the* `User` *object class and specifying a known-good group name fails.*

The most common filters use string or substring matches on text-based attributes, such as Last Name or Title. Some attributes of User and other object classes require a reference to an object in the Value text box. In this case, you must specify the full distinguished name of the object, not just its common name. For instance, if you add a filter (or perform a search) with Group Membership Starts With Anthro or Group Membership Is (Exactly) Anthropology, all entries disappear from the Anthropology OU user list.

Group Membership is an example of attributes that require a DN as the Value in the Find Custom Search dialog. To return the desired result, you must specify the complete DN of the group, such as `cn=Anthropology,ou=Anthropology,ou=Faculty Members,dc=oakleaf,dc=edu` for the Anthropology Security Group of the `oakleaf.edu` domain.

MCSE Corner: Introducing the Active Directory and LDAP

Chapter 3 gives you an introductory view of the Windows 2000 Active Directory service. Active Directory is covered in several exams. It is possible that there will be some questions on Active Directory on the base Windows 2000 Server exam (70-215), but it will not be covered in detail.

Active Directory is tested thoroughly in the two exams 70-217, "Implementing and Administering a Microsoft Windows 2000 Directory Services Infrastructure," and 70-219, "Designing a Microsoft Windows 2000 Directory Services Infrastructure." This chapter gives you an idea of the role that Active Directory plays in a complete Windows 2000 Server–based network. You should be familiar with that role and how Active Directory integrates with the rest of the network for these exams.

70-217 Implementing and Administering a Microsoft Windows 2000 Directory Services Infrastructure

This exam tests your ability to work with the Windows 2000 Active Directory service in a medium-to-large-sized distributed environment. You must be able to install, configure, and troubleshoot the Active Directory service. You should be familiar with creating sites and organizational units (OUs).

More specifically, you should be familiar with the sections on administering domains and trusts, viewing sites and services, and working with groups, users, and computers. Working with LDAP and the Active Directory schema is unlikely to be tested. Programming directory-enabled applications are definitely not covered on this exam.

It is very likely that this exam has several simulation-type questions, where you are required to perform given operations with respect to installing and configuring Active Directory. You may be required to perform an installation or configure a new site. It is also likely that the exam contains several other types of questions, such as multiple choice, requiring knowledge of how to administer Active Directory, and a background on how Active Directory works.

70-219   Designing a Microsoft Windows 2000 Directory Services Infrastructure

For the exam covering the design aspects of Windows 2000 directory services, you should be able to analyze the requirements of an organization and design an implementation of Active Directory to fit those requirements. You should be familiar with the use of Active Directory Sites and Servers. You should also be able to design a schema modification policy. Another specific topic to be familiar with for this exam is the creation and use of organizational units (OUs). You should be able to design and plan the structure of OUs.

CHAPTER 4

OPTIMIZING YOUR ACTIVE DIRECTORY TOPOLOGY

In this chapter

Starting the Domain Planning Process   148

Designing Single-Tree Directories   154

Adding a Sample Child Domain   160

Administering a Child Domain   172

Establishing Security Policies for a Child Domain   181

Working with Enterprise-Scale Directories   187

Changing Your Domain Model   187

Administering Domains with Windows 2000 Professional   188

Troubleshooting   190

MCSE Corner: Optimizing Your Active Directory Topology   191

STARTING THE DOMAIN PLANNING PROCESS

The most perplexing issue facing prospective Windows 2000 Server administrators is domain architecture. Active Directory's versatility is a two-edged sword—you have virtually unlimited options for creating domain and organizational unit (OU) hierarchies, but an overly structured design leads to administrative migraine. You must fit the Active Directory (AD) topology to your organization's current business practices and administrative hierarchy. Your AD design also must accommodate the organization's growth to minimize periodic domain and OU restructuring. Restructuring domains and OUs is a traumatic experience for users and administrators alike. AD makes the process of moving users and resources between domains relatively easy. The trauma is the result of a torrent of help-desk calls from network users unaccustomed to the new domain structure and nomenclature.

Planning is the key to achieving an efficient, manageable domain and OU structure, even for small organizations. Planning is such an important element of Windows 2000 Server implementation that this and the following three chapters of Part I, "Planning Your Microsoft 2000 Server Installation," are devoted to the network planning process. Before you even *think* about making a production Windows 2000 Server installation or upgrading your Windows NT primary domain controllers (PDCs), plan for—and experiment with—your future domain and OU structures.

Tip from
RJ

> Windows 2000 Server's HTML Help files have an "Active Directory" component (Adconcepts.chm), which was mentioned in Chapter 3, "Introducing the Active Directory and LDAP." The "Planning for Active Directory" topic of Adconcepts.chm contains basic domain planning concepts.
>
> Windows 2000's Support Tools include a Deployment Planning Guide, Deploy.chm, which has a more detailed "Designing the Active Directory Structure" section. Install the Support Tools files into your \Program Files\Support Tools folder by running Setup.exe or double-clicking W2krkst.msi in the \Support\Tools folder of the distribution CD-ROM; installation consumes about 20MB of disk space.

Planning your domain architecture requires that you have a basic understanding of the capabilities and limitations of AD to restructure your initial design. Whether you start with a domain structure inherited from upgrading one or more Windows NT PDCs or a fresh Windows 2000 Server installation, there's a good chance that you'll decide to alter the initial topology. For instance, you might want to take advantage of child domains to segregate user and computer accounts that have different security requirements. If you must accommodate more than one second-level Domain Name System (DNS) name, you must create multiple domain trees. Thus, this chapter includes step-by-step instructions for creating child domains and new domain trees.

The ADSI25 Visual Basic application, described in Appendix A, "Installing and Using the ADSI25 Active Directory," populates the sample domains of this chapter with organization units (OUs), Security Groups, and user and computer accounts. ADSI25 lets you emulate an

AD test installation having up to about 27,500 users in one or two domains. The ability to add a large number of users to test domains lets you determine performance issues that relate to directory size and structure.

→ **See** "The ADSI25 Visual Basic Application," **p. 141** and "ADSI25 Application Description," **p. 1255**.

ELEMENTS OF DOMAIN TOPOLOGY

Planning your domain topology requires you to take into account the structure and location of the following AD containers:

- *Domains* to establish autonomous administrative units with specific security policies. Windows NT treats domains as a combined security and administrative boundary. Windows 2000 sets security policies at the domain level and lets you delegate administrative functions with OUs. AD permits merging multiple Windows NT resource domains into a single domain. Elimination of the need for Windows NT resource domains and their network of non-transitive trusts is one of the most important advantages of Windows 2000.

- *Organization units (OUs)* to create a hierarchy of containers and objects within a domain. OUs enable dividing a large number of user and computer accounts within a single domain into groups of manageable size.

→ **See** "Taking Advantage of LDAP OUs," **p. 132**.

- *Resources* to provide user access to printers, folder shares, and other network elements. You publish links (pointers) to resources in the domain container or within OUs. User permissions for the resource's OU is the primary determinant of access to published resources.

- *Security Groups* to assign resource permissions for users. You can place Security Groups in domain or OU containers, and nest groups within other groups to establish inherited permissions. Users also inherit resource permissions through the OU hierarchy. Unlike OUs, Security Groups can contain users, computers, and shared resources from multiple domains in a forest. In a mixed-mode environment, group nesting is limited to the Windows NT model—Global groups contained within Domain Local groups. Moving to native mode gives you greater Security Group nesting flexibility and permits creating Universal groups.

→ For a discussion of native mode, **see** "Administering Domains and Trusts," **p. 105**.

> **Note**
> Sites aren't included in the preceding list, because sites represent replication boundaries, not containers. A site can include clients and servers assigned to multiple domains.

Tip from
RJ

> The "Managing Users" and "Managing Groups" topics of the HTML Help file for the Microsoft Active Directory 2.5 Software Development Kit (SDK), Adsi25.chm, offer more comprehensive information about user accounts and group membership than the Windows 2000 help files. Adsi25.chm is intended for programmers, but the introductory topics make useful reading for Windows 2000 admins. You can download Adsi25.chm, independently of the other components of Active Directory Service Interfaces (ADSI) 2.5 from http://www.microsoft.com/windows/server/Technical/directory/adsilinks.asp.

SINGLE-MASTER OPERATIONS

Windows 2000 Domain Controllers (DCs) are equals, but some DCs are more equal than others. For example, the first DC you create in an AD forest becomes the forest's initial root domain. You can't delete or rename the initial root domain DC, unless you use Dcpromo.exe to remove AD from all other DCs, remove AD from the first DC, and reconstruct your entire directory structure from scratch. The first DC in an AD forest is an AD *operations master*. Operations masters perform roles that aren't suited to multi-master replication, such as arbitrating new domain names, which must initiate on and propagate from a single DC. Microsoft calls these activities *flexible single-master operations (FSMOs)*.

Following are AD's five FSMOs:

- *Schema master* is a forest-wide role for handling updates and changes to the forest's schema. There can only be one schema master in the entire forest. The DC holding the schema master role must be online to permit schema modifications.

- *Domain naming master* is a forest-wide role for adding and removing domains from the forest. The DC holding the domain naming master role—usually the DC holding the schema master role—must be online to add or delete domains.

- *Relative ID (RID) master* is a domain-wide role for creating RIDs for conventional security IDs (SIDs) in the domain. RIDs are necessary to permit moving objects between domains without having to change their SIDs. To move objects between domains in a single domain tree, you must run the Movetree.exe Support Tools application (MoveTree) on the RID master. The "Changing Your Domain Model" section later in the chapter discusses MoveTree.

- *Infrastructure master* is a domain-wide role for establishing and maintaining relationships between users and groups. The infrastructure master arbitrates all changes to group membership for the entire domain.

- *PDC emulator* is a domain-wide role that serves as a Windows NT PDC in both mixed- and native-mode domains. The PDC emulator handles logons for downlevel (Windows 9x and NT) clients and, in mixed mode only, propagates password and other user account changes to Windows NT Backup Domain Controllers (BDCs).

You can reassign the three domain-wide roles—RID master, infrastructure master, and PDC emulator—to another DC in the same domain. You also can change the DC that acts as the schema or domain naming master to another DC in the forest.

The most common reason to reassign domain-level FSMO roles is to improve performance in domains that service a large number of users having downlevel client computers. Assigning the PDC emulator role to a DC in the site that isn't handling other domain-level roles improves logon performance. Similarly, if you make large-scale changes or additions to group membership, reassigning the infrastructure master to another DC in the site helps balance the FSMO load.

> **Tip from**
> *RJ*
>
> Verify that domain-level FSMOs are the source of performance problems before you assign roles to another DC. All three domain-level FSMO roles must be operational for the domain to function properly. Spreading the roles over multiple DCs increases the probability that the domain will become non-operational as the result of hardware or software failure of one of the DCs.

Reassigning FSMO roles requires that the DC performing the role be online and functional. You transfer all but the schema master role with the Active Directory Domains and Trust snap-in (Domain.msc). Use the Active Directory Schema snap-in (Schmmgmt.msc) to reassign the schema master role. Reassign the schema master and domain naming master only in the event of an unrecoverable hardware failure.

→ To set up the Schmmgmt.msc snap-in, **see** "Installing Schema Manager," **p. 125**.

If an FSMO DC fails and can't be restored to service within a reasonable period of time, you must seize the failed DC's FSMO role on another DC. You must use the Support Tools' Ntdsutil.exe command-line application with the fsmo maintenance option to seize the role.

→ For the steps involved in seizing FSMO operations, **see** "Seizing the FSMO Roles of a Failed DC," **p. 408**.

> **Caution**
>
> Seizing an FSMO role is a drastic step; you can't return to the network a DC whose role has been seized by another DC. After you repair the failed DC, you must use Dcpromo.exe with the computer offline to remove AD—if it exists after the repair—or reinstall Windows 2000 Server.

→ To use Dcpromo.exe to remove and re-create AD, **see** "Installing Active Directory," **p. 96**.

EMAIL DIRECTORY INTEGRATION

Larger organizations also must consider how the new domain and OU structure meshes with existing directory-based applications, such as email services. If you're running Microsoft Exchange Server, you probably have set up company-wide and departmental distribution lists. A well-designed email distribution list structure often can serve as the initial model for your OU hierarchy. Exchange Server's replication methodology is very similar to AD's, so your current Exchange Server site structure is likely to be applicable to your AD site configuration.

> **Note**
>
> Active Directory includes *Distribution Group* and *Contact* objects. Distribution Groups are intended primarily for email purposes and don't grant members access to resources. Contact objects are similar to User objects, except that Contact objects aren't security principals with logon rights. You use Contacts to add entries that refer to persons or organizations that don't have accounts in the domain. A typical application for Distribution Groups and Contacts is providing references to vendors or consultants that manage elements of your information technology infrastructure (called IT outsourcing).

Email accounts commonly contain personal attribute values—office location, title, department, division, direct reports, and the like—that have corresponding User object attributes in AD. The type of information commonly incorporated in Exchange Server's directory is equally or more useful to users and administrators when stored in AD. Figure 4.1 illustrates attribute values for an Exchange recipient, and Figure 4.2 shows corresponding User attribute values in Active Directory Users and Computers.

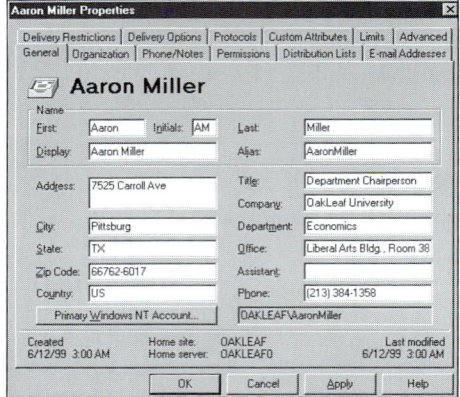

Figure 4.1
The General page of the properties dialog for a specified user in the Exchange Administrator program is showing the personal attributes associated with the user.

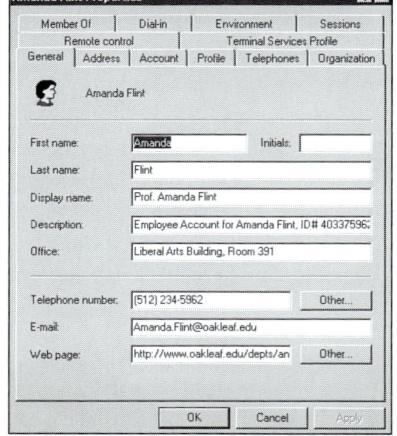
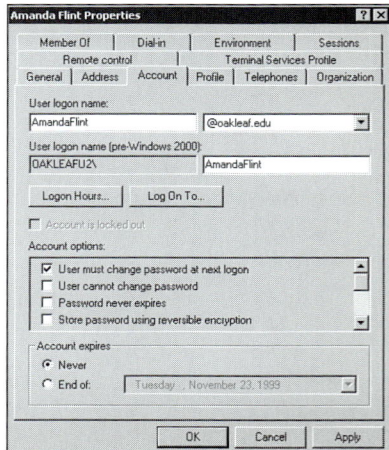

Figure 4.2
The General page (left) and Account page (right) of the properties dialog for a specified user in the Active Directory Users and Computers snap-in are used to display and edit the properties of a selected user account.

Tip from

> Exchange Server 2000—formerly code-named Platinum—is tightly integrated with Windows 2000's AD. As an example, AD security groups and OUs can substitute for Exchange distribution lists. If you're running Exchange Server 5.5, consider delaying your final domain, OU, and security group topology decision until you've evaluated a late beta or the release version of Exchange 2000. Microsoft's and third-party vendors' approaches to migrating Exchange users to AD might have a major influence on your domain and OU structure. Information on Exchange 2000 is available at http://www.microsoft.com/exchange/prodinfo/2000/default.htm.

USER ATTRIBUTES AND ACTIVE DIRECTORY DATABASE SIZE

In a large organization, user and computer accounts represent the vast majority of objects and consume most of the space in the AD database, Ntds.dit. Microsoft's database size estimates are based on User objects having only mandatory attribute values, which results in a value of about 3,650 bytes per user account. Taking full advantage of AD and its search features requires adding many optional attribute values for users and several attribute values for computers.

Tests with the ADSI25 application used to create the examples in this chapter show that the combination of a user and computer account with a full set of useful attributes consumes about 16KB of disk space. The AD files for the domain of about 25,000 users that are described in this chapter consume about 400MB of disk space. The 25,000 users and 25,000 computer accounts exceed Microsoft's recommended limit of 40,000 objects in a mixed-mode domain.

Tip from

> You must use available drive free space to determine the size of the AD database and log files. In normal operation, Ntds.dit always is open; thus, the file's size isn't updated as you add AD entries. When you install AD, record the Free Space value of the drive. Subtract the new Free Space value from the recorded value to obtain the amount of space used by the current AD database and log files.

INTEGRATION WITH OTHER DIRECTORIES

If your organization has other directory services in use, take into account the structure of these directories when designing your domain and OU topology. If you plan to continue use of non-Microsoft directory services, you're likely to need a *meta-directory*. A meta-directory describes relationships between directories and is an analog of metadata—data about data—that database management applications commonly store in a repository database. Meta-directories catalog attribute names and syntaxes—such as those for usernames and passwords—for storing common values in each supported directory.

Microsoft announced in July 1999 the acquisition of ZOOMIT Corp., a developer of meta-directory applications that are destined for integration with AD in 2000. ZOOMIT's Via integrates multiple directory systems to provide enterprise-wide *identity management*, also called "single-sign-on" or "hire/fire" systems. Identity management provides a single source of information for users and unifies entries in such diverse directory services as Lotus Domino's address book, Exchange Server's directory, Netscape Directory Server, Novell Directory Services (NDS), and IBM's Resource Access Control Facility (RACF) for mainframes.

Hire/fire systems are common applications for meta-directories. When a firm hires a new employee, administrators add attribute values in a single meta-directory application, which distributes appropriate subsets of the employee information to all directories used by the firm. Similarly, when the employee quits or is terminated, a single administrative action takes care of updating every directory containing an entry for the individual.

Extensible Markup Language (XML) is the next step in directory integration. In July 1999, Microsoft, Novell, and other directory vendors joined the Directory Service Markup Language (DSML) working group (`http://www.dsml.org/`) started by Bowstreet Software. The primary objective of the working group is to provide Web-based directory interoperability for business-to-business e-commerce applications. The DSML participants intend to develop a standard XML schema for LDAP and other directory structures.

Designing Single-Tree Directories

Organizations with 100 or fewer users and a few servers in one or two Windows NT domains don't face large-scale planning issues or the need for meta-directories. If you're presently using Windows NT 4.0 Server, upgrading your PDC, BDCs, and standalone or resource domain servers—if any—to Windows 2000 is a reasonably quick and easy process. Once you have your Windows 2000 servers and their applications running, you can decide whether grouping users and subdividing administrative duties into OUs is a worthwhile project.

Note When you upgrade Windows NT domain(s), the migration process automatically establishes your initial domain structure. If you've implemented Windows NT resource domains, the resource domains migrate intact. Fortunately, AD lets you move resource objects—such as file, printer, and application servers, and printers—between domains and into OUs. Moving resource domains into OUs eliminates the need for interdomain trusts and simplifies administration. The process of moving objects between domains is called *pruning* (cutting) from the existing domain and *grafting* (pasting) to the new domain. Pruning and grafting aren't easy with the first iteration of the AD support tools. Thus, it's more common to migrate Windows NT resource domains to AD child domains.

The OakLeaf University Network Topology Example

OakLeaf University, as noted in the prior chapters, is the organization used for the example domains of this book. OakLeaf U is a fictional four-year institution with a single Texas campus. OakLeaf U has a Gigabit Ethernet fiber-optic campus backbone between the Administration and combined classroom/office buildings. The backbone connects to the

Internet via a 155.52Mbps OC-3 fiber-optic cable. Classrooms and labs have a switched 10BaseT connection at each student seat; Professors and executive staff members have switched 100BaseT connections. Lecturers, teaching assistants, and other staff members connect to standard 10BaseT hubs. The Administration and Computer Science buildings house OakLeaf U's network administrators.

A telephone company (telco) T3 (44.736Mbps) leased line connects each off-campus dormitory to the backbone. Campus buildings and dormitories are separate sites, despite the relatively high-speed intersite connectivity. Making each building a separate site lets site administrators control AD replication frequency.

Every dormitory resident has a 10BaseT connection to the network; off-campus students have a subsidized dial-up Internet connection and can log on through a virtual private network (VPN). Students carry their laptop PCs from dormitories or off-campus residences to classes.

Active Directory lets students log on to the network when connected to any campus network port. Making each location a site with multiple domain controllers (DCs) lets all users log on to a local DC, which minimizes intersite network traffic. Faculty members running Windows 2000 Professional gain the advantage of IntelliMirror and other Windows 2000-only features regardless of where or how they connect to the network. The prospect of several thousand students attempting to simultaneously log on to IntelliMirror shares at the beginning of each class period caused OakLeaf U's administrators to decide against providing IntelliMirror services to the student body.

THE SINGLE-DOMAIN MODEL

Active Directory eliminates most of the constraints imposed by Windows NT's Security Account Manager (SAM) database and the ensuing requirement for large organizations to establish multiple domains and trusts. AD lets you delegate administrative responsibilities for object classes through OUs rather than domains. The ability to independently manage OUs makes the single-domain model practical, even for large organizations.

Tip from *RJ*	If possible—even remotely possible—start with a single domain for a small organization. At its simplest, a single domain requires only two DCs that independently perform the roles of a Windows NT PDC and BDC. You need two servers running as DCs to provide AD redundancy in case one DC fails. As your organization grows, you can add child domains to accommodate member servers, special classes of users, or both.

As an example for the single-domain model, OakLeaf University registers `oakleaf.edu` as its domain name and, because of its alumni's political clout, obtains a Class B IP address. The Class B address, which supports 65,534 hosts, easily accommodates the number of students (50,000) and staff (5,000) envisioned by OakLeaf U's 10-year plan. DHCP assigns IP addresses to employee and student computers, each of which is required to run Windows 9x, NT 4.0 Workstation, or 2000 Professional. OakLeaf U has an Office 2000 Professional educational license for every employee and student.

Figure 4.3 shows the site topology and the initial design for the top-level OUs of the oak-leaf.edu domain. Currently, OakLeaf U has the following employee classifications and count:

- Non-Faculty Staff—625 employees in one of 10 classifications, housed in the 25-story Administration Building. Administrators are responsible for faculty computer accounts, and registrars assign student computer accounts.
- Deans and Department Chairpersons—28 with offices in the Liberal Arts, Science, Music, or Computer Science buildings. Department chairpersons are full professors who report to the dean of the department. Deans and department chairpersons jointly administer user accounts and resource permissions for department faculty members, except teaching assistants (TAs).
- Professors—1047, of which 700 have offices in the Liberal Arts, Science, Music, or Computer Science buildings. The 347 and adjunct and emeritus professors don't have campus offices. Professors report to the department chairperson and administer teaching assistant user accounts.
- Lecturers—255 with offices in the Liberal Arts, Science, Music, or Computer Science buildings. Lecturers report to their department chairperson.
- Teaching Assistants—346 without assigned offices. TAs report to professors.

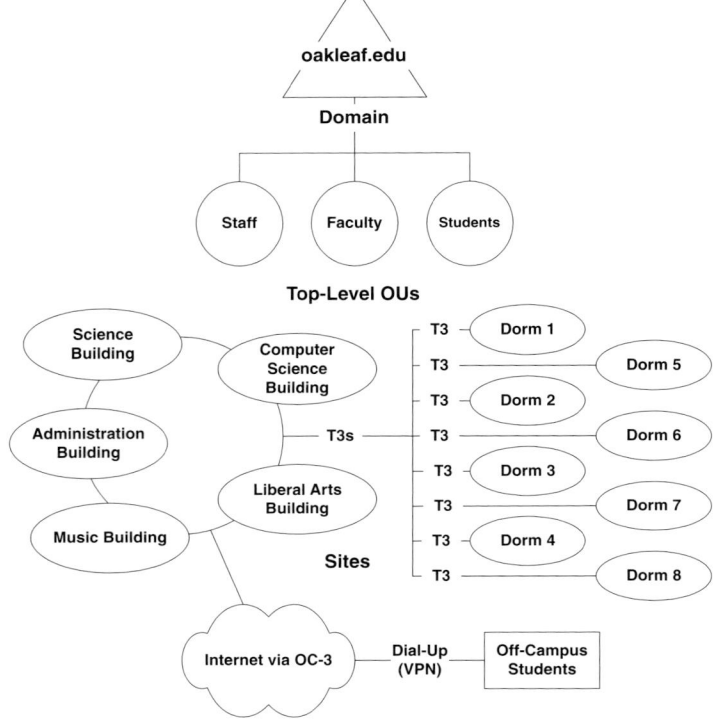

Figure 4.3
This figure shows the domain and top-level organizational units for the Oakleaf organization in the upper portion, and the site topology in the lower section.

Designing Single-Tree Directories | 157

You assign second-level OUs by staff function—administrators, registrars, and so on—and by faculty department—such as Computer Science or Economics. In most cases, the OU hierarchy mimics the top two or three levels of the organization chart of a firm or institution. Minimizing the depth of the OU hierarchy simplifies domain administration.

To ease the administrative burden by delegation, OakLeaf U classifies its 25,344 students by school year—freshmen (6,222), sophomores (6,386), juniors (6,447), and seniors (6,289)—in second-level OUs. (OakLeaf U has a very low student drop-out rate.) At the end of each school year, administrators move graduating senior account data to an alumni database and delete the corresponding user and computer accounts. First-, second-, and third-year students who've accumulated sufficient course credits advance by one year in the Students OUs. Registrars add accounts for matriculating students to the Students/Freshmen OU.

Further classification of students by major subject provides for assignment of a faculty advisor from the appropriate department, and gives students limited permissions for department-level resources—such as read-only permission for shared department files—and connection to specialized videoconferences and streaming media multicasts. Figure 4.4 is a diagram of the two-level OU hierarchy for the single-domain example.

Figure 4.4
This is a detailed structural diagram of how Organizational Units would be used in the Oakleaf.edu domain using a single domain model.

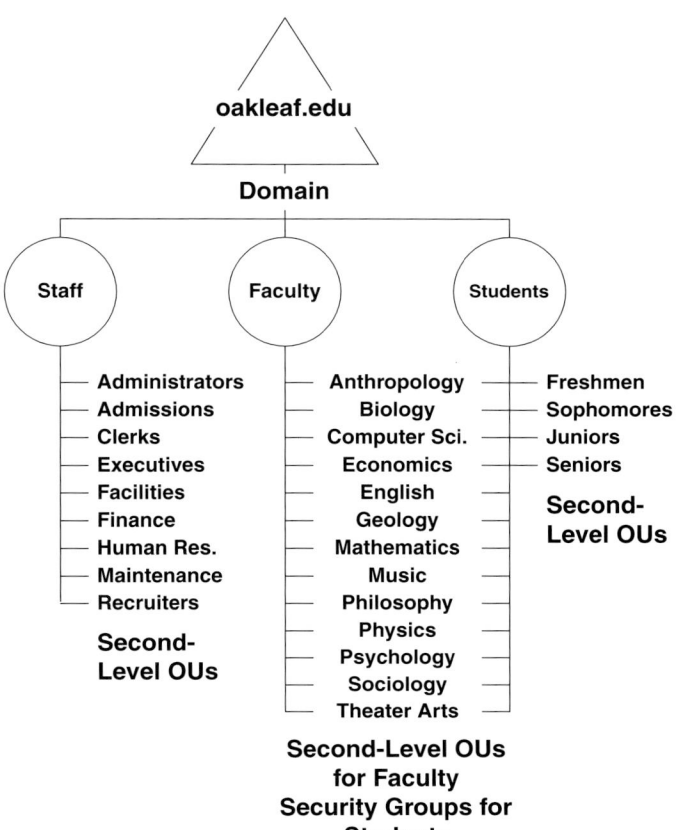

PART
I
CH
4

Tip from
RJ

> Use Security Groups, not further OU subdivisions, to grant specialized permissions for users at the second or lower level of the OU hierarchy. Adding a third OU layer to classify students by year and major department (or vice versa) multiplies the number of OUs by 14.
>
> You must choose the proper group type if there's a possibility that you might want to move an OU, such as Students, to its own child domain or to another domain in a new forest. The later "Changing Your Domain Model" section discusses MoveTree's restrictions on the type of groups that you can move between domains.

Note

> Microsoft recommends that you limit group membership "to a maximum of a few thousand users" to minimize replication traffic. Keeping OU and group membership within a reasonable size also improves the performance of the Active Directory Users and Computers tool (dsa.msc snap-in).

THE PARENT-CHILD MODEL

It's uncomfortable for most administrators to mix student, faculty, and employee accounts and resources in the same domain. Faculty members and employees undoubtedly share the same reservation, regardless of the bulletproof security group structure you devise to prevent students from hacking the system. Adding a new domain to the tree requires a minimum of two more DCs to provide redundancy, plus member servers and other resources, such as shared folders and printers.

The single-tree, parent-child model adds child domains within a contiguous DNS namespace. When you create a child domain, AD automatically creates a two-way, transitive trust to the parent domain and any additional child domains you add. If you add more than one child domain, the transitive trusts between the parent and child domains automatically provide trusts between the child domains.

Creating child domains is an alternative to establishing OUs for grouping users. Child domain DCs and member servers can be located in the same site as the parent domain or assigned to a separate site.

Note

> One of the primary advantages of creating child domains is the ability to operate the parent domain in mixed mode to accommodate Windows NT BDCs, and run the child domain(s) that don't include Windows NT servers in native mode. This mixed/native-mode configuration lets you use Movetree.exe to migrate OUs and local groups from the parent to the child domain.

For the single-tree example, the students domain is student.oakleaf.edu, a child of the oakleaf.edu parent domain of the preceding section. Figure 4.5 illustrates the relationship between the parent and child domains. In this example, the student.oakleaf.edu child domain is the organizational equivalent of the Students OU in the single-domain model that was illustrated by Figure 4.3. There's no need for a Students OU in the child domain, unless you need another OU for non-students—such as faculty advisors. Thus, the second-level Student OUs—Freshmen, Sophomores, and so on—of the single-domain model can become first-level OUs in the child domain. Adding the Students Domain Local or Global group shown in Figure 4.5 is optional, because you can set permissions for all members of the Students domain in the default properties dialog for the Domain Users group.

Figure 4.5

If a multiple domain model using parent and child domains were used, the structure of the Organization would look like this.

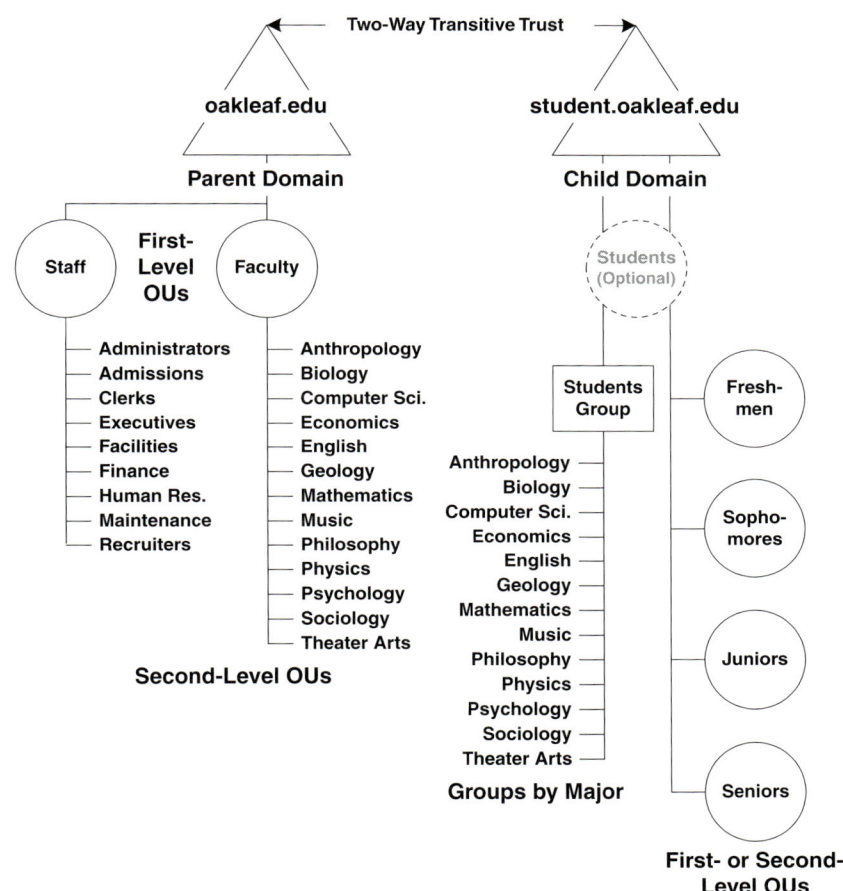

| Tip from RJ | Make sure not to create naming conflicts between child domains and first-level OUs in the parent domain. You can't have two objects in AD with the same distinguished name (DN). For example, you can't create a `students.oakleaf.edu` child domain if you have a first level `Students` OU object in the `oakleaf.edu` parent domain. AD considers both objects to have the same distinguished name. |

Adding a Sample Child Domain

The examples in the preceding chapters of this book assume that you're using a single Windows 2000 Server DC in a test network. Creating a sample child domain requires an operating DC for the parent domain, plus a second networked PC with Windows 2000 Server installed to serve as the child DC. Chapter 3 has instructions for creating the parent domain with Dcpromo.exe. Both DCs should have a minimum of 128MB of RAM to achieve reasonable performance; you'll find a 64MB DC to be quite sluggish.

→ For detailed instructions on setting up an initial test DC, see "Installing Active Directory," p. 96.

Adding a child domain to an existing parent domain involves the following steps, each of which is discussed in the sections following this one:

1. Use Dcpromo.exe to create the new domain.
2. Change the child domain to native mode if the child domain doesn't need to support Windows NT BDCs.
3. Set up an AD-integrated DNS zone for the child domain.
4. Add OUs, groups, and users to the domain.
5. Optionally, create a new site for the domain, and move the domain and its contents to the new site.

Tip from
RJ

Before you add another DC to a test or production network, synchronize the computer's clock with the parent DC. DCs use timestamps based on the computer's system clock for replication operations and to resolve conflicts between AD entries for the same object(s) performed on different DCs. The first DC you install provides the master clock for all DCs you add. Windows 2000 uses the Network Time Protocol (NTP) service to synchronize system time of all DCs and, optionally, Windows 2000 clients, on the network. NTP uses multicasting to transmit timeclock information to all subscribing servers on IP address `224.0.1.1`.

To synchronize the system time before upgrading to AD, at the command prompt of each DC, type `net time //dcname /set`, where *dcname* is the NetBIOS name of your initial root domain DC. In this and preceding chapters, the NetBIOS name of the initial root domain's DC is OAKLEAF-DC1. Make sure you receive a "The command completed successfully" message when you press Enter. If you don't synchronize the server you're upgrading, you might encounter an error when you attempt to add a new child domain or start another domain tree.

 If the addition of a new domain tree or child domain generates "insufficient memory" errors in the AD Event Log, see "Active Directory Installation Problems," located in the "Troubleshooting" section near the end of this chapter.

Creating a Child Domain with Dcpromo

Do the following to add a new child domain to a Windows 2000 DC or member server:

ADDING A SAMPLE CHILD DOMAIN | 161

1. In the Internet Protocol (TCP/IP) Properties dialog for the server to upgrade, verify that the Preferred DNS Server IP address is set to the server's address, and set the Alternate DNS Server IP address to that of the parent DC. For this example, the child domain server address is 10.7.3.2 and the parent domain DC's address is 10.7.2.2. You can't connect to the DC of the parent domain to create the child domain if you don't add the parent DC's DNS address.

   To add the Alternate DNS Server address, right-click My Network Places, choose Properties to open the Network and Dial-up Connections window. Right-click Local Area Connection, and choose Properties to open the Local Area Connection Properties dialog. Select Internet Protocol (TCP/IP) and click Properties to open the eponymous Properties dialog. Type the parent domain DC's address in the Alternate IP Address text box (see Figure 4.6). Click OK twice to close the dialogs.

Figure 4.6
The TCP/IP properties page is being used to add the DNS server of the parent domain as a secondary DNS lookup server to facilitate DNS lookups between the parent and child domains.

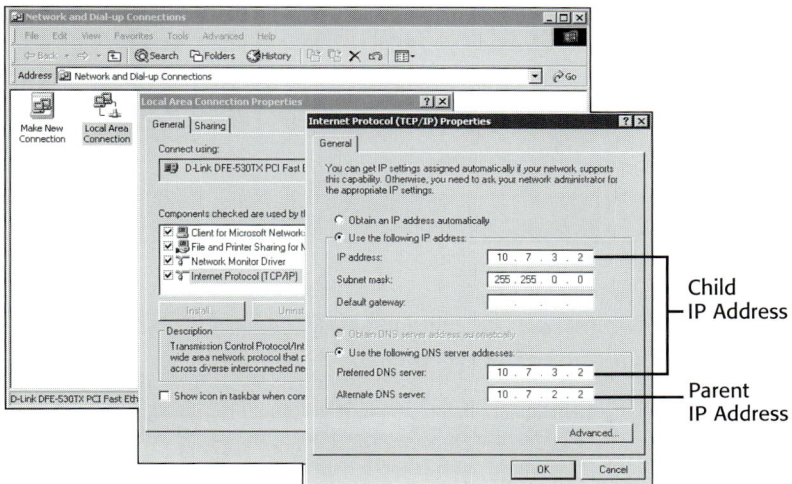

2. Choose Start, Run to open the Run dialog, type **dcpromo** in the Open text box, and click OK to launch the Active Directory Installation Wizard.

 If the Active Directory Installation Wizard fails prematurely with an "Active Directory is busy" error, see "Active Directory Installation Problems" in the "Troubleshooting" section near the end of this chapter.

3. Click Next to bypass the Welcome… dialog.

4. If AD is installed on the computer you intend to use as the DC for the new child domain, click Next to remove AD, reboot your computer at the end of the AD removal process, and repeat steps 2 and 3. Be prepared for a substantial wait while the Wizard demotes your DC to a member server of the parent domain.

PART
I
CH
4

Caution
When demoting a server, the Wizard's second dialog has a This Server is the Last Domain Controller in the Domain check box. Marking this check box and continuing with the Wizard removes the domain from the Global Catalog. Don't remove AD from the DC serving as the initial root domain or a DC that plays an FSMO role. If you do so, your parent domain probably will become inoperable.

5. In the Domain Controller Type dialog, select the Domain Controller for a New Domain option (see Figure 4.7), and click Next.

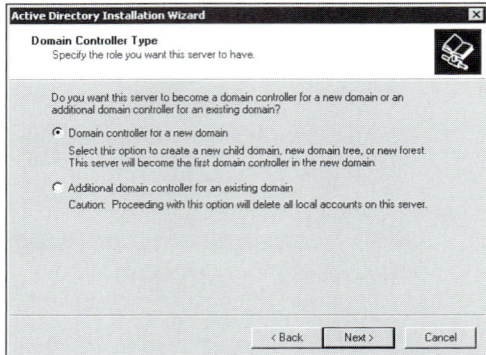

Figure 4.7
The Domain Controller Type dialog allows you to create a new domain and make this system the first domain controller (selected here), or add this system as a domain controller to an existing domain.

6. In the Create Tree or Child Domain dialog, select the Create a New Child Domain in an Existing Domain Tree option (see Figure 4.8), and click Next.

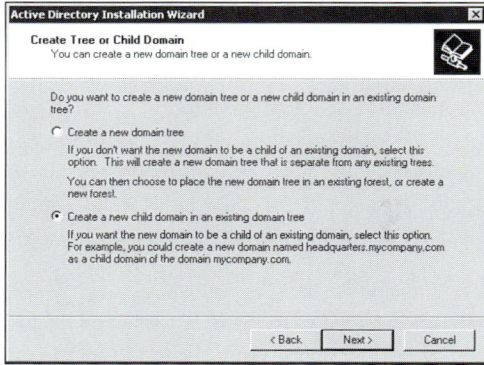

Figure 4.8
When you create a new domain (as shown in Figure 4.7), the Active Directory Installation Wizard allows you to select whether the domain will be in a new tree, or an existing tree with the Create Tree or Child Domain dialog.

7. Type your Enterprise Admins username (or a Domain Admins username in the parent domain), password, and the name of the parent domain in the three text boxes of the Network Credentials dialog (see Figure 4.9), and click Next.

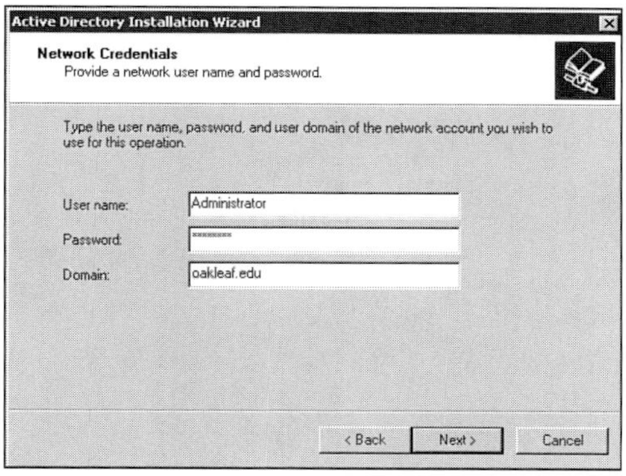

Figure 4.9
You must supply administrative credentials valid in the specified parent domain in the Network Credentials dialog to be able to create a child domain.

8. Type the name of the parent domain and the prefix of the child domain in the two text boxes of the Child Domain Installation dialog. As you type the domain names, the Complete DNS Name of New Domain text box fills with your entry (see Figure 4.10). Click Next.

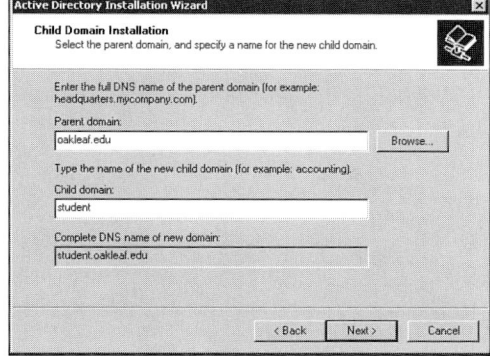

Figure 4.10
From this dialog in the Active Directory Installation Wizard, you enter the full name of the parent domain in the tree, and the name of the new child domain. The full name of the child domain is generated from this information, and displayed in the bottom text box.

9. In the Domain NetBIOS Name dialog, accept or change the default downlevel domain name, and click Next.
10. In the Database and Log Locations dialog, accept the default locations for the AD database and log, unless you have a good reason to do otherwise, and click Next.
11. In the Shared System Volume dialog, accept the default location for the Sysvol folder, which must be located in an NTFS 5.0 partition, and click Next.
12. In the Permissions dialog, accept the default Permissions Compatible with Pre-Windows 2000 Servers, and click Next.
13. In the Directory Services Restore Mode Administrator Password dialog, type and confirm the password to use when you want to run Windows 2000 Server in Safe Mode without opening the AD database and log files (see Figure 4.11). It's a good practice to use your Administrator account password, because you're likely to remember it. Click Next.

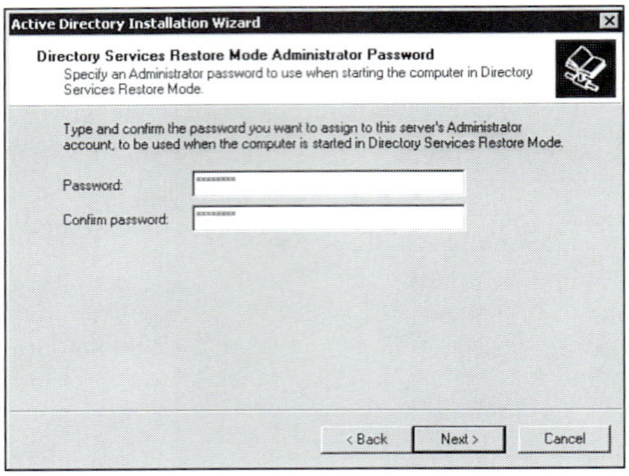

Figure 4.11
The Directory Services Restore Mode Administrator Password dialog is where you specify a password that you use to put the system in Directory Services Restore Mode, if there is ever a problem with the directory, or to demote a domain controller.

Tip from
RJ

If you practice safe password policies for your Administrator account—using a complex password and changing it periodically—make sure to save in a safe place a note with your Restore password. You can't demote a DC controller with Dcpromo.exe or repair the AD database in Safe Mode if you forget this password.

14. In the Summary dialog, review the configuration of your child domain (see Figure 4.12). Click the Back button if you need to change an option; otherwise, click Next to create the new child domain.

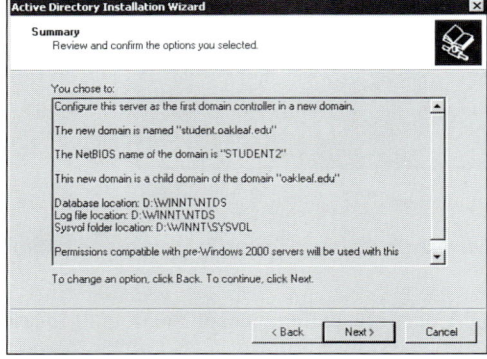

Figure 4.12
The summary dialog shows all of the options chosen in the Active Directory Installation Wizard. You can review the options before Active Directory is installed.

A series of Configuring Active Directory progress dialogs display the actions the Wizard executes to create the new domain, including replication of schema and configuration objects, and securing folders on your local drive. Completing the configuration process takes a few minutes.

15. When the Completing the Active Directory Installation Wizard dialog appears (see Figure 4.13), note if the text box reports errors. By default, the Wizard places the new child domain in the parent domain's site. Click Finish to close the Wizard.

ADDING A SAMPLE CHILD DOMAIN | 165

Figure 4.13
The final summary window of the Active Directory Installation Wizard displays the results of the installation, in this case the name of the new domain and new site.

16. Click Restart Now to reboot the computer as the DC for the new child domain. The startup process takes longer than usual, with a few minutes' wait for AD replication to occur in the Preparing Network Connections stage.

17. Log on to the computer with your Administrator credentials in the new child domain—**Administrator@student.oakleaf.edu** for this example.

If the Wizard reports errors in step 15, launch Event Viewer and double-click the Directory Service node. During a normal AD installation, the only warning you should receive is that shown in Figure 4.14, and no errors should appear in Event Viewer.

Figure 4.14
A Warning message in the Event Viewer shows that Write Caching has been disabled by the system for the volume on which Active Directory is installed to avoid data loss caused by power failures while there is still data in the write cache.

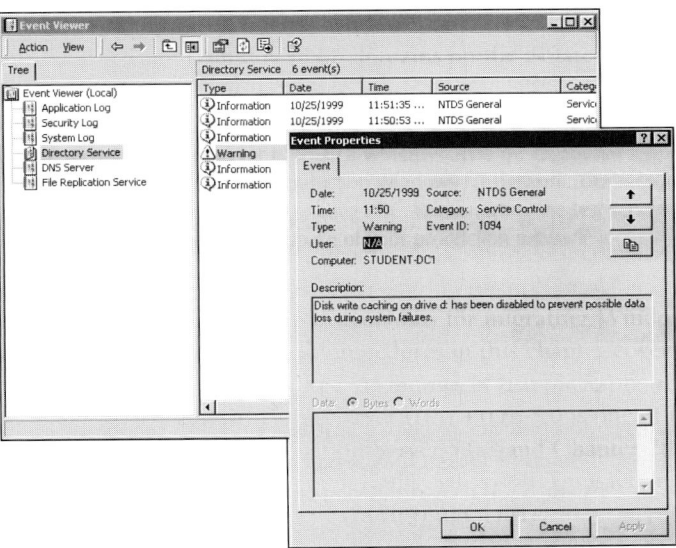

PART
I
CH
4

> **Tip from**
> *RJ*
>
> It isn't uncommon to receive a "One or more services failed to start" message during the first reboot of a new child domain DC, especially if your test server has less than 128MB of memory. A symptom of initial boot problems is a delay of up to several minutes after you log on to the server and before desktop icons appear. If your event logs list many errors, reboot the computer, recheck, and then clear the logs. A second reboot usually resolves the logon problems.

 To resolve common problems with creating child domains, see "Child Domain Creation Problems" in the "Troubleshooting" section near the end of this chapter.

Installing AD disables write caching on the volume you specify in preceding steps 10 and 11. The purpose of disabling write caching is to assure than AD updates aren't held in a write buffer whose contents would be lost in the event of a power failure or other hardware problem.

> **Tip from**
> *RJ*
>
> Set up a separate NTFS 5.0 volume to hold AD's database, logs, and Sysvol folder for production servers. Using a volume dedicated to AD lets you maintain write caching on the volume in which you've installed Windows 2000 Server and other applications. Write caching greatly improves performance of applications that perform frequent disk write operations.
>
> In a production installation, use a RAID5 (or better) volume to hold the AD files and folders to further improve performance and reliability.

 For information on specifying RAID systems, **see** "Choosing the Optimum RAID System," **p. 325**.

SETTING UP DNS ZONES FOR THE CHILD DOMAIN

The next operation you perform after adding a new child domain is setting up DNS zones for the domain. DCs offer the option of integrating DNS with AD to provide automatic zone updates with DDNS. When you promote a computer to a parent domain DC, AD installs the DDNS server, but the Active Director Installation Wizard doesn't prompt you to set up DNS when creating a child domain. The DNS prompt doesn't appear because you specified the parent domain's DNS server at the beginning of the earlier "Creating a Child Domain with Dcpromo" section.

 For an explanation of Windows 2000 Server's DDNS implementation, **see** "Taking Advantage of Windows 2000 Server's DNS Service," **p. 82**.

It's a recommended practice to set up at least one DNS server for each domain, including child domains. The child DC's DNS server then backs up the parent's DNS server for the child domain. To add a DDNS zone for your child domain, do the following:

1. Choose Administrative Tools, DNS to launch MMC with the DNS manager snap-in (dnsmgmt.msc).

2. Right-click the computer name node for your DC, STUDENT-DC1 for this example, and choose New Zone to launch the New Zone Wizard. Click Next to bypass the Welcome… dialog.
3. Select the Active Directory Integrated option in the Zone Type dialog (see Figure 4.15). Standard Primary is the default option, even with AD running. Click Next to open the Forward or Reverse Lookup Zone dialog.

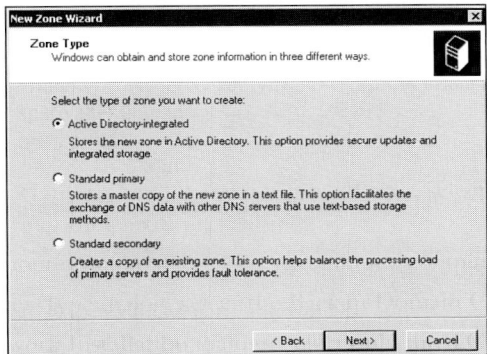

Figure 4.15
The New Zone Wizard prompts for the type of DNS zone to create; the Active Directory Integrated option is selected here.

4. Accept the default Forward Lookup Zone option (see Figure 4.16), and click Next to open the Zone Name dialog.

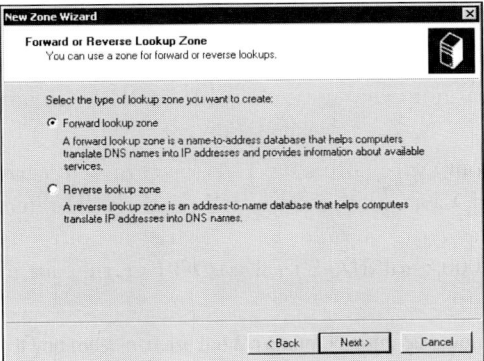

Figure 4.16
From this dialog in the New Zone Wizard you can select whether to configure the new zone as a forward lookup zone (shown here) or a reverse lookup zone.

5. Type the name of the zone in the text box, `students.oakleaf.edu` for this example (see Figure 4.17). The zone name can differ from the child domain name, but should be related to the domain name for identification. Click Next to open the Competing the Zone Wizard dialog.

Figure 4.17
The zone name is specified in this part of the New Zone Wizard.

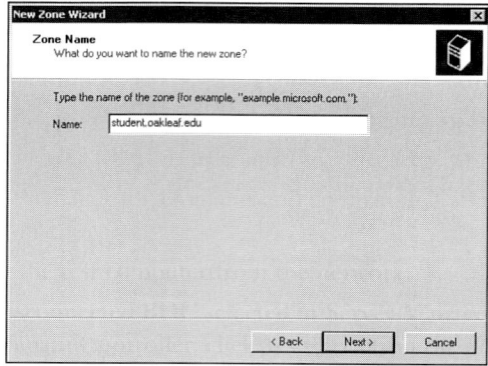

6. Review the proposed zone name and click Finish to add the forward lookup zone and dismiss the Wizard.
7. Repeat steps 1, 2, and 3.
8. Select the Reverse Lookup Zone option, and click Next to open the Zone Name dialog.
9. Type the IP octets for your child domain's subnet, without trailing zeroes. For a Class B subnet, type the first two octets (see Figure 4.18); for a Class C subnet, type the first three octets.

Figure 4.18
In this example, a reverse lookup zone is being created for the 10.7.0.0 network, and is called 7.10.in-addr.arpa according to the DNS standard. A reverse lookup zone allows DNS names to be located when only the IP address is known.

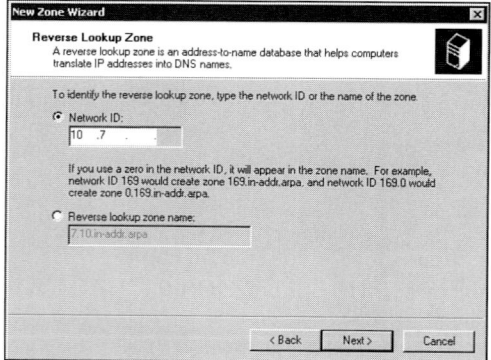

10. Review the proposed zone name and click Finish to add the reverse lookup zone and dismiss the Wizard. Dnsmgmt.msc displays the new forward and reverse lookup zones (see Figure 4.19).

Figure 4.19
The DNS snap-in shows the newly created forward and reverse lookup zones for the STUDENT-DC1 domain controller of student.oakleaf.edu in the left pane. The nodes contained in the zone are shown in the right window.

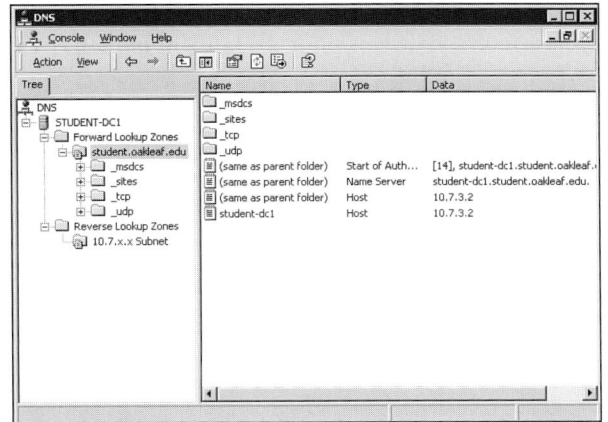

11. Log off the child DC as Administrator of the child domain, and log on with your Enterprise or Domain Admins credentials in the parent domain.
12. Right-click the DNS node and choose Connect to Computer to open the Select Target Computer dialog.
13. Select The Following Computer option and type the name of the DC for the parent domain, **OAKLEAF-DC1** for this chapter's examples (see Figure 4.20). Specify the computer running the DC for the initial root domain if you have more than one DC in the parent domain. Click OK to close the dialog.

Figure 4.20
From the DNS snap-in you can select the parent domain's Domain Controller to add to the snap-in. This way you can view the lookup zones of the parent domain from this system.

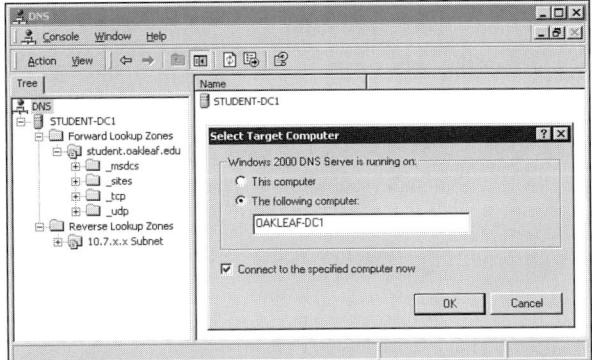

14. Expand the first- and second-level nodes for the parent domain DC to verify that the student child domain node appears in the tree (see Figure 4.21), and then close DNS manager.

Figure 4.21
This figure shows the DNS snap-in with the lookup zones of both the parent domain, oakleaf.edu and the child domain, student.oakleaf.edu in the left pane. This way, administration can be performed on both domains.

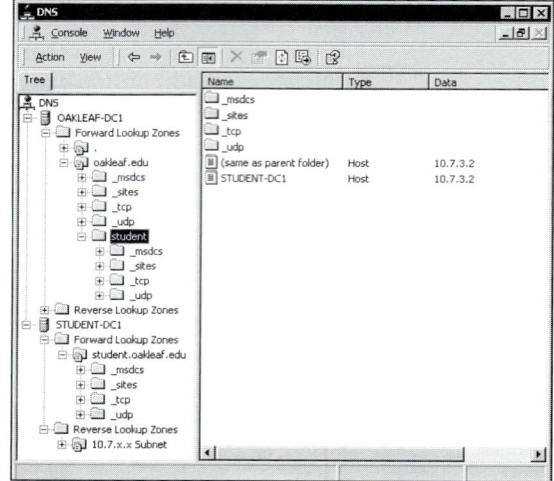

Registration of the child domain with the domain controller's DDNS server is independent of the zone creation process of preceding steps 1 through 11. When you specify the Active Directory Integrated option for DNS in step 3, AD automatically adds to the parent domain the forward lookup zone for the child domain.

CHANGING CHILD DOMAIN ATTRIBUTES

Entries in the *DomainName* Properties sheet for the child domain are similar to those of the parent domain. If your child domain doesn't need to interoperate with Windows NT domain controllers, you can convert the child domain to native mode and set the Managed By attribute value by doing the following:

1. Launch the Active Directory Domains and Trusts tool (Domain.msc).
2. Expand the nodes to display your child domain, right-click the child domain node, and select properties to open the *DomainName* Properties dialog.
3. In the General page, type a description of the domain in the Description text box (see the left side of Figure 4.22).
4. Click the Change Mode button to make the nonreversible conversion to native mode. After a few seconds, the *DomainName* Properties dialog reflects the change (shown on the right side of Figure 4.22).

ADDING A SAMPLE CHILD DOMAIN | 171

Figure 4.22
The General page of the Properties dialog for the domain is shown before a change to native mode on the left, and after the change to native mode on the right. The Domain Operation Mode box shows Native Mode and the Change Mode box disappears after the change. Now native mode-only features such as Universal Groups are enabled.

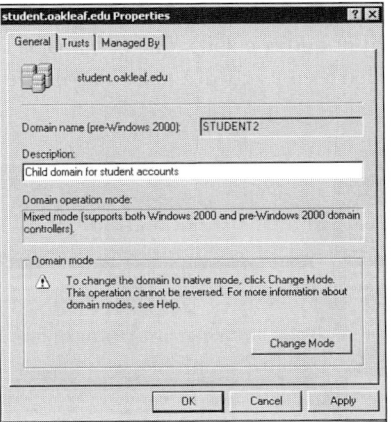 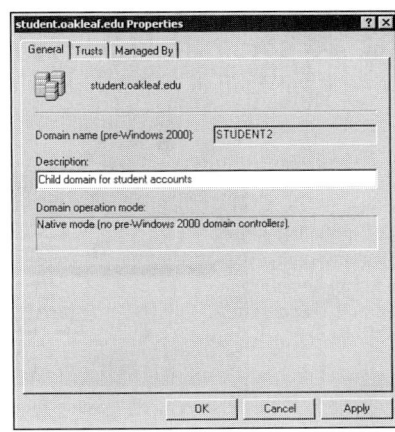

5. Verify the trust between the parent and child domains by clicking the Trusts page (see the left side of Figure 4.23).

6. Optionally, click the Managed By tab, click the Change button, and double-click the Administrator account in the Select User or Contact list to specify Administrator as the manager of the child domain (see the right side of Figure 4.23).

Figure 4.23
The Trusts page of the domain properties dialog for the child domain is shown on the left, from which you can verify a transitive trust between the parent and child domains. On the right is the Managed By page of the same window where you can specify the manager of the domain, the parent domain administrator in this case.

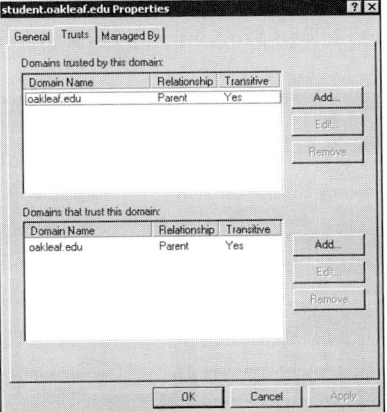

PART
I
CH
4

Administering Other Domains from a Child DC

Your Administrator account in the child domain includes membership in the default Domain Admins, Domain Users, and Group Policy Creators Global groups, and the Administrators Domain Local group. As a member of the Domain Admins group for the child domain, you have read access to objects in other domains in the tree, in this case the parent domain, but you don't have write access. You must be a member of the Domain Admins group of the parent domain to administer all domains in a tree and have membership in Enterprise Admins group to manage objects in other domain trees.

The easiest way to gain write access to the parent domain from a DC in the child domain is to log on with the Administrator credentials for the parent domain, which usually is the initial root domain. The Administrator account of the initial root domain automatically becomes a member of the Enterprise Admins group, so you can administer all domains in the parent tree and other trees in any forest.

The alternative method of administering all domains from a child domain DC is to add the local Administrator account to the Enterprise Admins group. Both the parent and child domains must run in native mode to enable the Enterprise Admins group addition. If all domains aren't running in native mode, add the Administrator account of the child domain to the Domain Admins group of all other domains.

Administering a Child Domain

Child domains and OUs are administrative entities, but establishing a child domain instead of an OU simplifies some administrative tasks, such as setting Group Policies for a particular class of users. For example, you can specify a default Domain Group Policy for a child domain that's independent of the Domain Group Policy of the parent domain.

Adding OUs, Groups, and Users to a Child Domain

The default set of groups and users for child domains is the same as those for all other domains. You add OUs, Security Groups, and users to a child domain by the same process as for the parent domain. Launch AD Users and Computers (dsa.msc), and right-click the domain node—student.oakleaf.edu for this example—choose New, and select the object type you want to add from the submenu.

→ For a brief description of how to add common objects to a test domain, **see** "Administering Active Directory," **p. 105**.

Figure 4.24 shows the four OUs, and 15 Global security groups and shared folders added by the ADSI25 application to the student.oakleaf.edu domain. ADSI25 also adds user and computer accounts to the child domain. Figure 4.25 shows the General (left) and Member Of (right) property pages for a typical student account added by ADSI25 to the child domain.

→ For instructions on how to use ADSI25 with a child domain, **see** "Adding Students to a Different Domain," **p. 1279**.

Figure 4.24
The Active Directory Users and Computers snap-in shows the OUs, security groups, and folder shares added to the `student.oakleaf.edu` domain by the ADSI25 application.

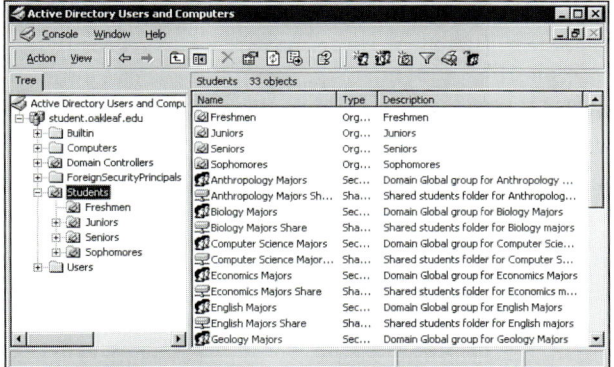

Figure 4.25
On the left is the General page and on the right the Member Of page for a typical example of a student account in the child domain.

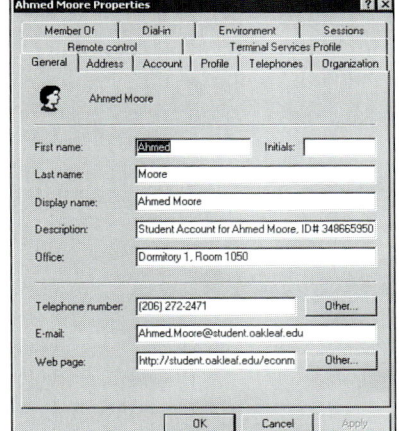
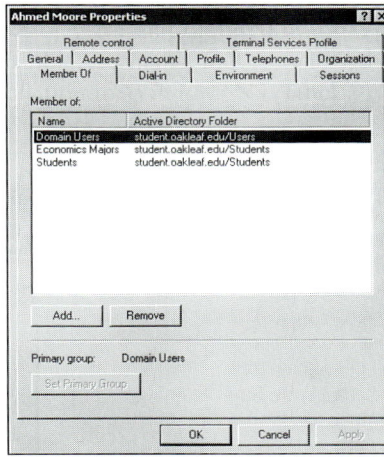

Moving OUs, Groups, and Users Within a Domain

Moving directory objects to new locations within domains is a simple process; moving objects between domains is not. The Move choice of the context menu for a directory object in AD Users and Computers lets you move an OU, Security Group, user, or computer account to a different location in the domain. You must use the MoveTree command-line application, described in the later "Changing Your Domain Model" section, to move objects between domains.

> **Note**
> This section uses in its examples the standard OUs and security groups created by ADSI25. The procedures described for moving objects, however, apply to most multilevel OU and security group structures.

The Students OU is superfluous in a child domain that contains only student accounts and OUs to segregate students by school year. One of the basic rules of domain organization is to avoid unnecessary nesting of OUs. If you use ADSI25 to create the student child domain, you can conform the OU structure of the domain to the single level that was shown in Figure 4.5 by following these steps:

1. In AD Users and Computers, double-click the Students OU node to display its OUs and security groups.
2. Select the Freshmen OU, and then Shift+click the Sophomores OU to select the four OUs.
3. Right-click your multiple selection and choose Move to open the Move dialog.
4. Accept the default student node in the tree (see Figure 4.26) and click OK to move the four OUs to the root of the domain.

After the move completes, which takes only a few seconds, the Students OU appears as shown in Figure 4.27. The Freshmen, Sophomores, Juniors, and Seniors OUs have moved to the root of the child domain.

Figure 4.26
The Move dialog of the Active Directory Users and Computers snap-in is shown ready to move the four OUs selected in the right pane of the background window to the domain root, selected in the foreground window.

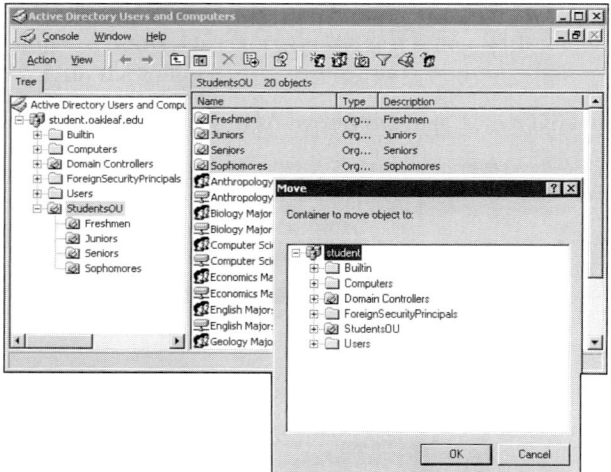

Figure 4.27
The right pane of the Active Directory Users and Computers tool shows the security groups remaining in the Students OU after the four OUs were moved out in Figure 4.26.

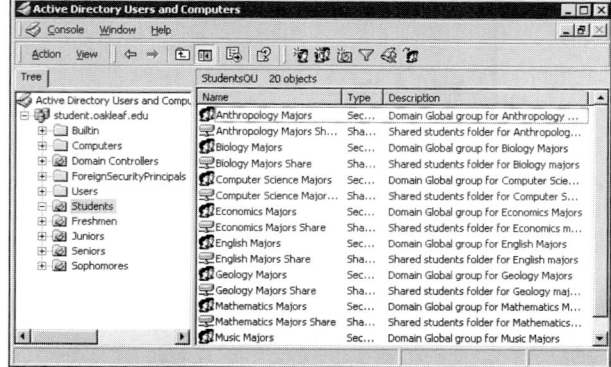

Eliminating the Students OU requires that you move the Students Domain Local group and the Global major subject Security Groups to the child domain root. As mentioned in the earlier "The Parent-Child Model" section, you can't duplicate DNs in a domain. Thus, you must change the name of the Students OU before you can move all the groups to the root of the domain.

To move the security groups and folder shares from the Students OU to the child domain root, do the following:

1. Select the Students OU in the Tree, press F2, and rename Students to **StudentsOU**.
2. Double-click **StudentsOU** to display the security groups and folder shares in the right pane.
3. Select the first security group (Anthropology) and Shift+click the last share (Theater Arts) to select all the groups.
4. Right-click the multiple selection, choose Move, accept the default students domain, and click OK to move the security groups.
5. Select the empty **StudentsOU** node and press Delete to remove the OU. Click Yes to dismiss the confirmation message.
6. Double-click student.oakleaf.edu to display the relocated OUs and security groups (see Figure 4.28). The structure of the domain now corresponds to what was illustrated in Figure 4.5.

Figure 4.28
The groups and OUs in the root of the domain selected in the left pane are shown in the right pane of the Active Directory Users and Computers tool. These are the groups and OUs after they have been moved from the Students OU.

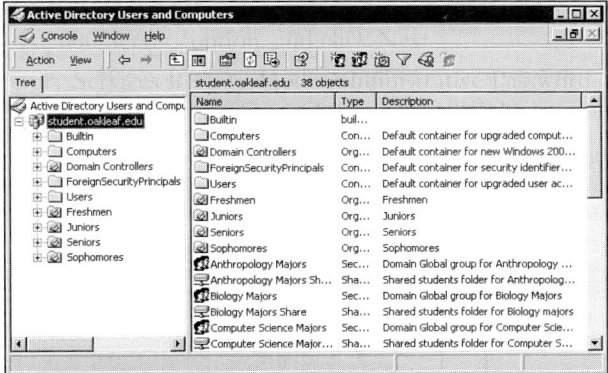

7. Verify that the changes of OU and Security Group location you made in the preceding steps have propagated to user accounts by double-clicking one of the Global Security Groups, such as Anthropology Majors, to open the *GroupName* Properties dialog.
8. Click the Members tab to display the group's user membership (see Figure 4.29). OUs appear at the domain root level.
9. Click the Member Of tab to show the group's membership (see Figure 4.29). The group is a member of the Domain Local Students group, which is at the domain root level.

Figure 4.29
From the Members (left) and Member Of (right) pages of the Properties dialog for a Security Group, you can verify the propagation of location changes after the move.

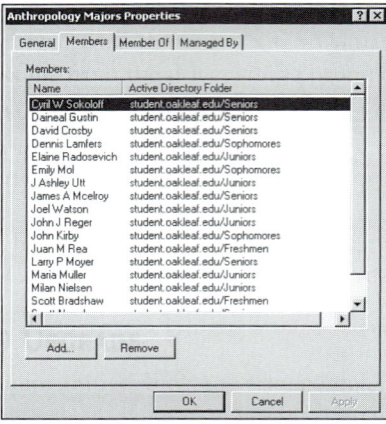 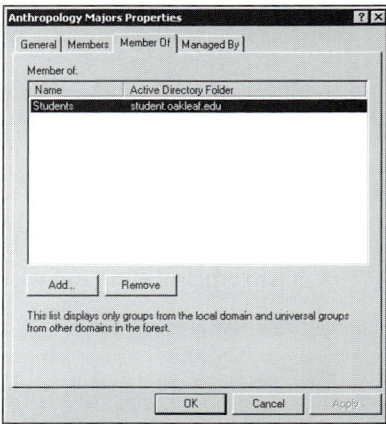

Tip from
RJ

Re-create the Students OU and return the second-level (school year) OUs and all security groups to their original location in the Students first-level OU if you're using ADSI25 to add student accounts to the child domain. Attempting to add new accounts to a different OU structure throws an ADSI25 runtime error.

Use **StudentsOU** as the name for the re-created first-level OU, move the other OUs and the security groups into StudentsOU, and then rename StudentsOU to **Students**.

Moving a Child Domain to a New Site

Child domains join the site of the parent domain by default. Oakland is the default site for the sample parent domain you created in Chapter 3. If the DCs, member servers, and computer accounts of the child domain need to be located in a different site, you can use the AD Sites and Services tool (Dssites.msc) to create a new site, move the child domain's DC and all AD objects to the new site, and set the replication frequency.

→ To review creation of the Oakland site, **see** "Viewing Sites and Services," **p. 113**.

Creating a new site for a child domain, or any other domain(s), requires you to perform the following operations, which are covered in detail in the sections that follow:

1. Create the new site.
2. Move or add a DC for the site.
3. Set up the replication schedule.
4. Specify the subnets of the original and new sites.

The examples in the following four sections apply to creating new sites in general, not just to the present context of creating a site for a child domain. Sites can include multiple domains and domains can span multiple sites.

CREATING A NEW SITE

The following steps create a new site named Berkeley, and move the STUDENT-DC1 server, the DC for the `student.oakleaf.edu` domain, to the Berkeley site:

1. Log in as Administrator of the `oakleaf.edu` parent domain at the parent or child domain DC.

    Adding a new site requires membership in the Enterprise Admins group.

2. Launch AD Sites and Services, right-click the Sites node, and choose New Site to open the New Object - Site dialog.

3. Type the name of the site, **Berkeley** for this example, and select the DEFAULTIP-SITELINK entry in the Link Name list (see Figure 4.30). The Example SMTP Site Link was added as a sample link for the Simple Mail Transport Protocol, which Microsoft Exchange 2000 uses for message replication. IP is the preferred protocol for AD replication.

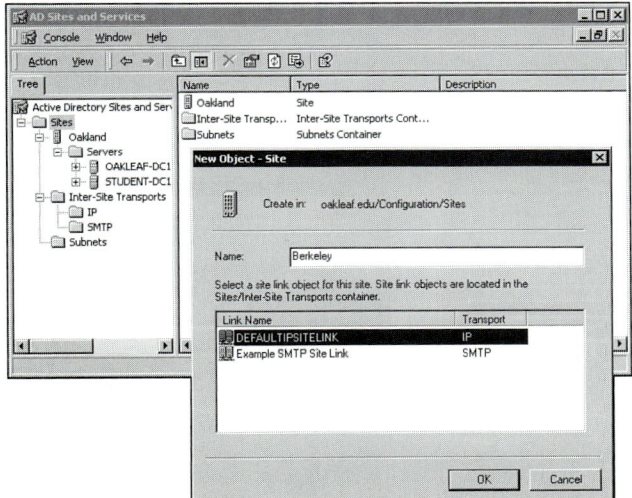

Figure 4.30
The New Object – Site dialog is shown in the Active Directory Sites and Services snap-in being used to add a new site for the child domain.

4. Click OK to create the new link. Click OK after reviewing the advisory message shown in Figure 4.31.

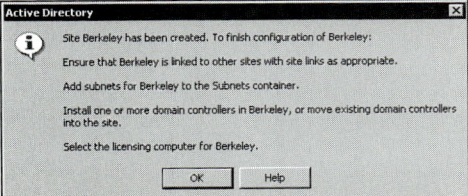

Figure 4.31
This message tells you the remaining steps for adding a site after the site creation performed in Figure 4.30.

> **Note**
>
> Adding a new site requires several steps, so it's logical to expect a "New Site Wizard" to appear on choosing New Site. Unfortunately, Windows 2000 Server doesn't include this wizard.

Moving the Child Domain Controller to the New Site

When you create a new site without a DC, the existing DC temporarily covers for the missing DC. Follow these steps to move the DC to the new Berkeley site:

1. Expand the original site node (Oakland for this example), right-click the name of the DC for the child domain (STUDENT-DC1), and choose Move to open the Move Server dialog.

2. Select the new site (Berkeley) in the Site Name list (see Figure 4.32), and click OK to move the DC.

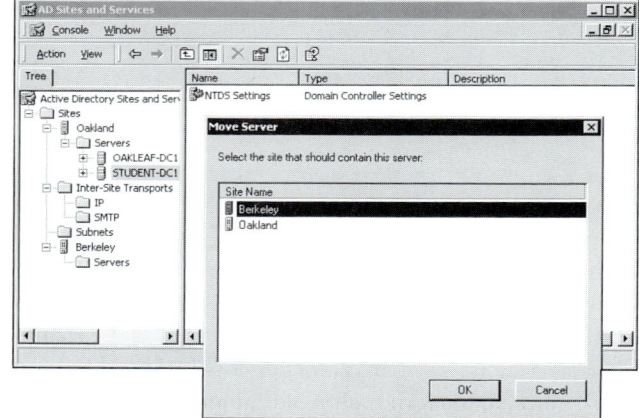

Figure 4.32
The Move Server dialog is shown moving the Domain Controller for the child domain, selected in the left pane of the background window to the new site, selected in the foreground dialog.

3. Expand the Berkeley site node to verify that the child domain DC moved to the new site (see Figure 4.33).

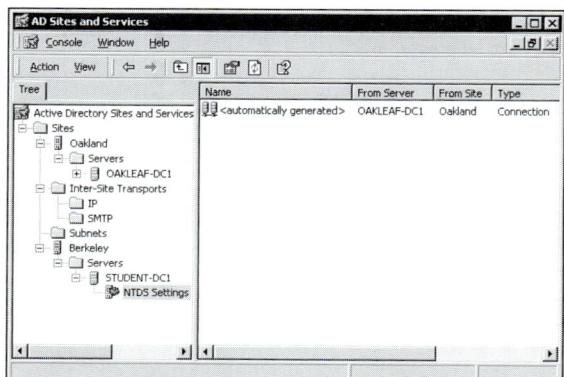

Figure 4.33
The Active Directory Sites and Services snap-in is shown confirming the move performed in Figure 4.32. The Domain Controller for the child domain is now under the new site, shown in the left pane.

> **Note**
>
> You can verify temporary coverage by the original site's DC by launching Event Viewer, double-clicking System Log, and checking Netlogon events. When you create the Site, you receive a lengthy event message describing the coverage. After you move the DC to the new site, another event message notifies you that the original DC no longer covers the new site.

SETTING THE REPLICATION SCHEDULE

By default, intersite replication occurs at 15-minute intervals. To change the replication frequency, do the following:

1. Click the IP node of the Intersite Transports Node, then double-click in the right pane the DEFAULTIPSITELIK item to open its properties dialog.

   By default, the Sites in This Link list includes all sites for the forest. You can exclude sites by selecting a site and clicking the Remove button.

2. In the General page, type a name for the link in the Description text box and click Change Schedule to open the Schedule for DEFAULTIPSITELINK dialog.

3. Type the replication frequency in minutes in the Replicate Every spin box (see Figure 4.34). If you want to restrict the days of the week or hours of the day during which replication occurs, click the Change Schedule button and mark or clear the appropriate time-of-day blocks.

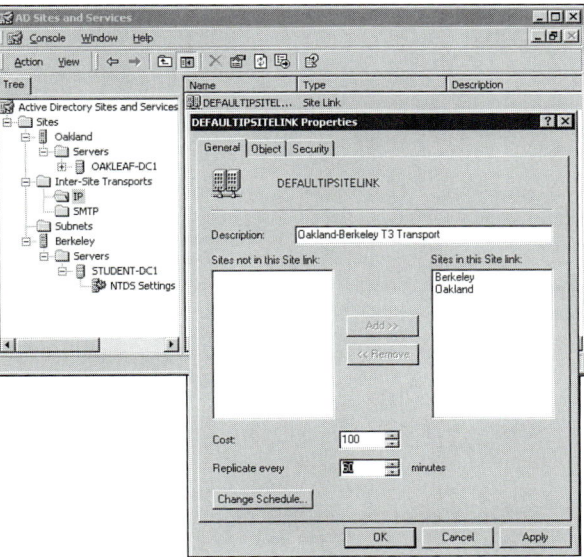

Figure 4.34
From the General page of the SiteLink Properties page you can specify the replication schedule and frequency.

4. Click OK to save the replication frequency changes and return to AD Sites and Services.

Specifying Site Subnets

When you add a new site, you must specify subnets for both the original and the new site. The sites of this example, like most of the other examples in this book, are on the same `10.7.0.0` Class B subnet. AD won't let you specify the same subnet for two sites, because sites ordinarily consist of a single subnet. The example that follows is based on separate Oakland (`10.7.2.0`) and Berkeley (`10.7.3.0`) Class C subnets.

The following steps serve only as an example for setting site subnets:

1. Right-click the Subnets node and choose New Subnet to open the New Object - Subnet dialog.
2. Type the parent DC's network address and subnet mask in the Address and Mask text boxes, and select the site to which the subnet applies in the Site Name list (see Figure 4.35).

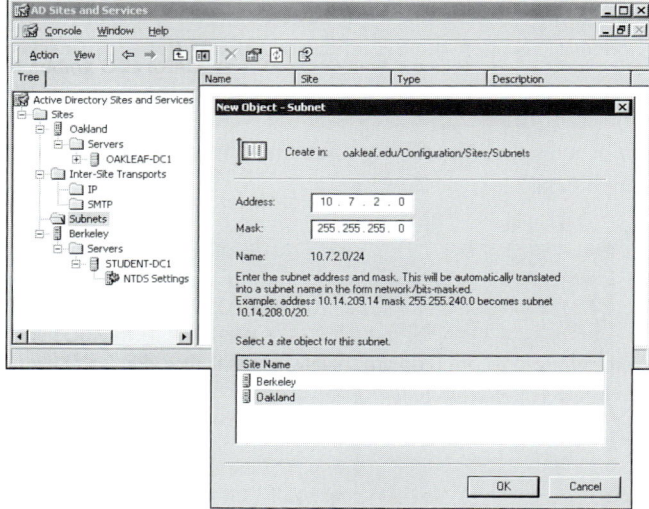

Figure 4.35
The New Object – Subnet window is shown which allows you to set the subnet properties for the parent domain, and remove the child domain.

3. Click OK to add the subnet for the parent site.
4. Repeats steps 1 through 3, but type the child DC's IP address and subnet mask in the text boxes.

The two subnets appear in AD Sites and Services as shown in Figure 4.36.

Figure 4.36
The Subnets node of the Active Directory Sites and Services tool is selected in the left pane, and the defined subnets are shown in the right pane.

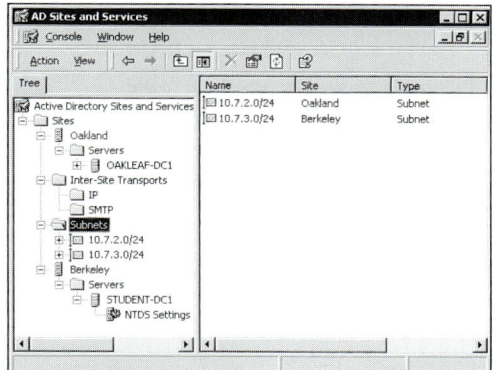

Tip from
RJ

Don't create multiple sites unless you need them to control replication across wide-area networks (WANs) in a production environment. Move the child domain's DC back to the parent DC's site, delete the two subnet items, and then delete the site you added in the preceding four sections. Replication between DCs within a single site is more efficient than between sites.

Establishing Security Policies for a Child Domain

As noted in the earlier "Elements of Domain Topology" section, one of the primary advantages of establishing a child domain is the ability to set domain security policies for a particular class of users. For example, you might want to set a higher level of logon security for students than for faculty members and administrative staff. You set the security policies for the domain by choosing Administrative Tools, Domain Security Policy. Alternatively, you can specify domain and OU security policies from within Active Directory Users and Computers. In either case, AD uses Group Policy Objects (GPOs) to set domain-wide and OU security policies.

Students have their own laptop or desktop computers, or both, so GPOs that enforce policies applicable to employees—such as desktop lockdown or automatic software installation—aren't applicable. Many of the GPO values apply only to Windows 2000 users. The important basic security settings for students relate to passwords, account lockout after failed logon attempts, boilerplate to advise students of their user rights—or lack thereof—in the domain user has access to, and access rights to the domain based on group membership. GPOs apply only to computers running Windows 2000; you must use Windows NT 4.0 Policy Editor (Poledit.exe) to establish security policies for Windows NT and Windows 9x clients. Windows 2000 Server installs Poledit.exe during the administrative tools setup process.

182 Chapter 4 Optimizing Your Active Directory Topology

→ For more information on GPOs and their support by Windows 2000, **see** "Understanding Windows 2000's Group Policies," **p. 618**.

You set individual Group Policies for Computer and User objects. The Netlogon process sets Computer Configuration Group Policies from the domain that contains the computer account during the Establishing Network Connections phase of the boot process. User Configuration Group policies are set after the user logs on, when the Applying Security Settings message appears.

Using the Domain Security Policy Console

To establish GPOs that apply to all Windows 2000 users who log on to the student.oakleaf.edu domain, do the following:

1. Choose Administrative Tools, Domain Security Policy to open the Domain Security Policy snap-in (Secpol.msc).

2. Expand the Account Policies and Local Policies nodes, then click the Password Policy node to display the list of available password policies in the right pane. The Computer Settings column displays default values.

3. Double-click the policy you want to establish or change to open the Security Policy Setting dialog. The type of dialog controls—check boxes, spin boxes, text boxes, list boxes, or dropdown lists—depend on the policy being set. Figure 18.37 illustrates changing the Enforce Password History policy to prevent reuse of users' preceding three passwords. You must mark the Define This Policy Setting check box to enable the Keep Password History spin box.

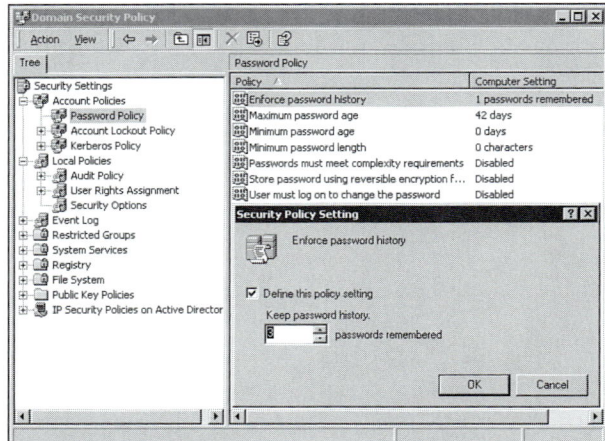

Figure 4.37
From the Domain Security Policy snap-in you can set the Enforce Password History policy to remember a number of old passwords and force users to choose a new password that is unique.

4. Repeat step 3 for each policy setting you want to change. For instance, you might want to set the Maximum Password Age for students to 30 days and the Minimum Password Length to eight characters, and require complex passwords.

ESTABLISHING SECURITY POLICIES FOR A CHILD DOMAIN | 183

5. Click the Account Lockout Policy node, double-click the Account Lockout Policy item, and mark the Define This Policy Setting check box in the Security Policy Setting Dialog. When you set the Lockout Duration value to a reasonable value—such as 60 minutes—and click OK, a Suggested Values dialog opens to set required related policies (see Figure 4.38). Click OK twice to close the dialogs. You can change the related Computer Settings values, if you want, at this point.

Figure 4.38
The Suggested Value Changes dialog appears to help you change policy objects which are related to the change you are currently making.

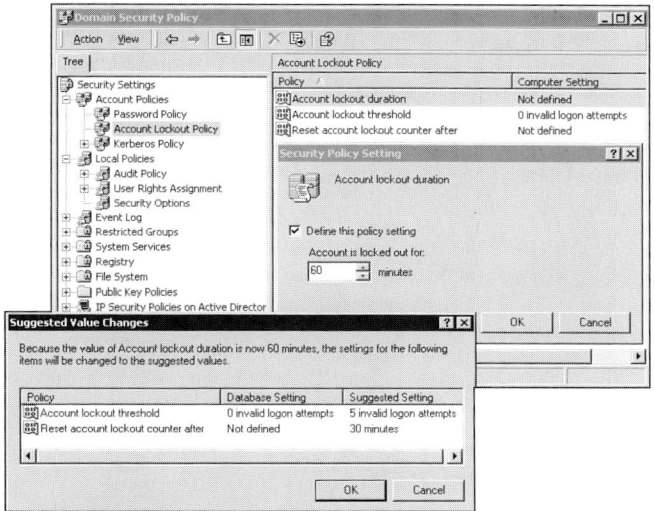

6. Click the Security Options node and scroll to the Message Title for Users Attempting to Log On policy, double-click the item to open the Security Policy Dialog, and mark the Define This Policy Setting check box. Type the title for the text box that student users see after pressing Ctrl+Alt+Del to log on (see Figure 4.39).

Figure 4.39
The Message Title for Users Attempting to Log on policy allows you to set the title of a message box displayed to all users after pressing Ctrl+Alt+Del but before logging on, sometimes referred to as the Legal Notice.

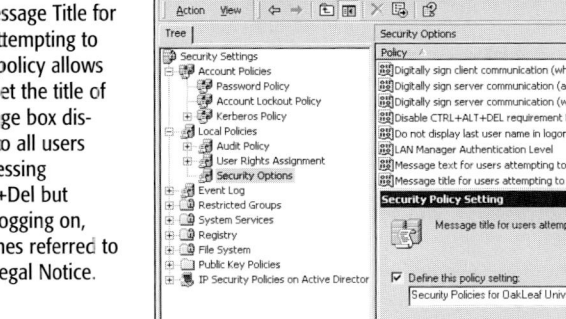

PART
I
CH
4

7. Repeat step 6 for the Message Text for Users Attempting to Log On policy, and type the body of the message in the text box.

Tip from
RJ

Logon titles and messages for users—which Windows NT calls logon banners—are useful for presenting users with important information or satisfying your legal department's recommendations or requirements. For instance, you might want to notify users periodically that company email policies are being enforced, and Big Brother is scanning everyone's email for infractions. You can create the Message Text for Users Attempting to Log On value in Notepad, but carriage-return/linefeed pairs added by pressing Enter terminate the message, so you're limited to a message with a single text paragraph.

8. Click the Audit Policies node and double-click the Audit Logon Events. Mark the Define These Policy Settings and Failure check boxes (see Figure 4.40) to add an event to the Security event log for each failed logon attempt.

Figure 4.40
The Audit Account Logon Events Audit Policy dialog is shown, configured to audit all failed logons and log them to the Security Event Log.

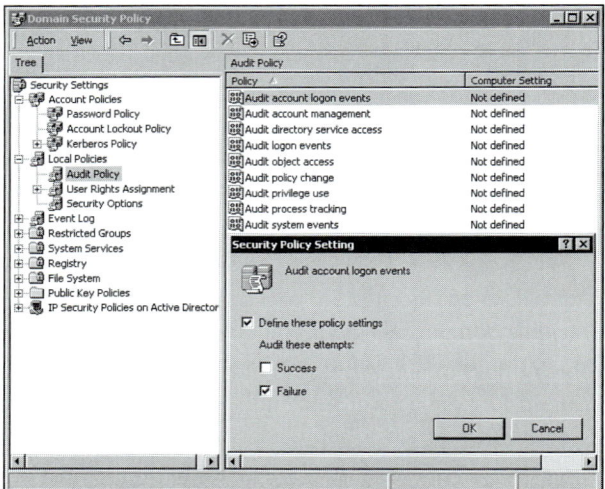

9. Close Secpol.msc after you've set all GPO values you want to apply to the child domain.

Changes to group policies don't take effect immediately due to replication latency with the DC that holds the PDC Emulator FSMO role, so reboot the DC on which you added or altered the GPOs to force replication to the PDC emulator during the Netlogon process.

Tip from
RJ

Test the Domain Security Policies you set by rebooting the DC and verifying that the policies you added work. For instance, if you set logon titles and message text for users, the message should appear during the next reboot, assuming that you've waited long enough for the policy changes to replicate to the DC with the PDC Emulator FSMO role.

ESTABLISHING SECURITY POLICIES FOR A CHILD DOMAIN | 185

> To verify that Domain Security Policies propagate to domain computers, reboot a Windows 2000 client having a computer account in the domain. If the policies don't appear to take effect, verify in the client's Network Identification page of its System Properties dialog that the client is a member of the appropriate domain.

→ To join a new or different domain from a client, **see** "Administering Domains with Windows 2000 Professional," **p. 188**.

VIEWING ALL GROUP POLICIES FOR THE DOMAIN

The Domain Security Policy console displays only security-related GPOs for the domain. You can view all available Group Policies for the domain by doing the following:

1. Launch Active Directory Users and Computers, right-click the domain node, and choose Properties to open the *DomainName* Properties dialog.

2. Click the Group Policy tab, and double-click the Default Domain Policy in the list to open the Group Policies console.

3. Expand the nodes to display Administrative Templates under the Computer and Users nodes, which set policy-related Registry key values of domain computers during the Netlogon and user logon process.

→ To learn more about Registry-based operations, **see** "Registry-Based Configuration Management," **p. 455**.

4. Expand the Computer Configuration, Administrative Templates, System node and click Group Policy to list Registry-based policies that apply to the security policies you applied in the preceding section (see Figure 4.41).

Figure 4.41
The Registry-based policies that affect Computer Configuration settings, shown here, are applied during the Netlogon process.

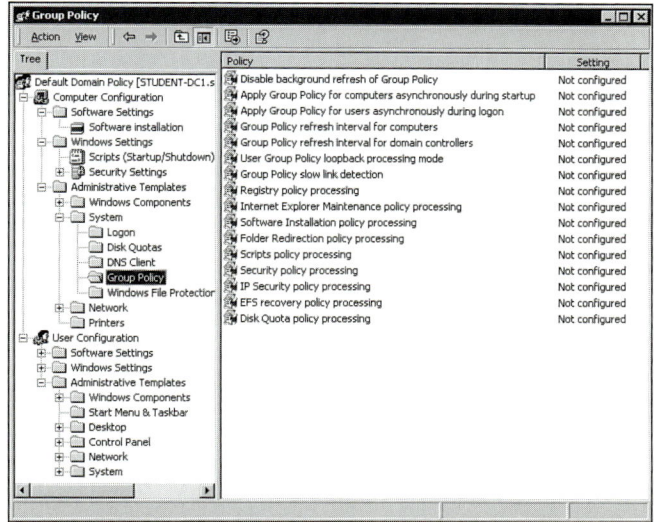

5. Policies you set with Administrative Templates add an Explain page, which describes the effect of applying the policy, to their properties dialogs (see Figure 4.42). It's unfortunate that Microsoft didn't add Explain pages for all policy items.

Figure 4.42
The Explain page of a typical Administrative Template Policy tells you the results and any caveats of enabling the policy as well as related policies.

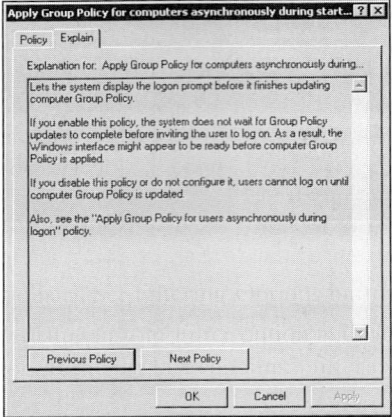

The Group Policy console for Default Domain Policies lets you change the DC that replicates Group Policies to other DCs. Right-click the Default Domain Policy node, and choose View, DC Options to open the Options for Domain Controller Settings dialog. Select The One Used by the Active Directory Snap-Ins option to specify the current DC as the originator of replicated GPOs for the domain (see Figure 4.43). This setting eliminates the replication latency between the originating DC and the DC with the PDC Emulator role.

Figure 4.43
The Options for Domain Controller Selection dialog shows the option selected to specify the Domain Controller on which you're setting group policies as the originating Domain Controller for the policies.

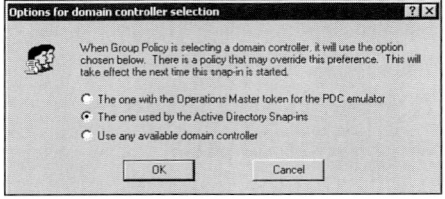

The preceding two sections deal only with security policies appropriate to users—such as students or vendors—who have more client-side independence than might be granted to employees. Chapter 15, "Establishing Group Policies, User Accounts, and Logons," covers the application of Group Policies to computers and users over which your organization has administrative control.

Working with Enterprise-Scale Directories

Large organizations—especially multinational corporations—must deal with unique issues, such as AD replication between divisions or subsidiaries in multiple countries, local political considerations, and governmental regulations. You might find it necessary to establish many domain trees, because local divisions or subsidiaries have noncontiguous namespaces. For example, the domain name for Yamaha Corp.'s Japanese main headquarters is yamaha.co.jp, the European headquarters is yamaha.co.uk, Yamaha Kemble (U.K.) is yamahauk.com, Yamaha Music Canada Ltd. is yamaha.ca, Yamaha de Mexico is yamaha.com.mx, and the U.S. subsidiary is yamaha.com. Yamaha Corp.'s 10 world-wide subsidiaries potentially require 10 trees in one or more forests.

Multinational corporations often require multiple forests to accommodate different schemas and configurations, or limit the scope of trusts between domains. All domains in a forest trust one another, which might not be appropriate for a headquarters-subsidiary business relationship. Thus, yamaha.co.jp might elect to have its own forest, and create a second forest for overseas subsidiaries.

The long-forthcoming 64-bit version of Windows 2000 will deliver a major upgrade to AD for large enterprises with Intel Itanium servers. Scheduled for release when Intel delivers the Itanium chips, this upgrade to Windows 2000 Datacenter Server is expected to include the ability to merge forests from non-Microsoft directories into AD.

The ability to segment a large corporation's directory into multiple forests of trees with an unlimited number of child, grandchild, and great-grandchild domains can generate an astronomical number of domain design permutations. A full discussion of the ramifications of single- versus multiple-forest designs is beyond the scope of this book. The general rule for directory architecture, however, prevails in all business environments—Simpler is Better.

Changing Your Domain Model

The Movetree.exe Support Tool is a command-line utility for moving collections of objects—users, OUs, and groups—between domains within the same forest. You use MoveTree, for example, when consolidating upgraded Windows NT resource domains in OUs of a single Windows 2000 domain.

MoveTree's command-line syntax is less than elegant. For example, following is the command-line statement for testing a move of the Students OU and its members from the oakleaf.edu parent to the student.oakleaf.edu child domain:

```
MOVETREE /check /s oakleaf3.oakleaf.edu /d oakleaf2.student.oakleaf.edu
/sdn OU=Students,DC=oakleaf,DC=edu /ddn DC=student,DC=oakleaf,DC=edu
```

The entire statement must be typed on a single line, so most administrators write MoveTree instructions in Notepad, copy the text to the clipboard, and paste it into Command Prompt. Replacing the /check argument with /start moves the objects. The /s and /d arguments specify the source and destination (target) domain controllers, respectively. /sdn and /ddn determine the source and destination DN of a single user, OU, or group, respectively. If a DN contains spaces, you must enclose the DN in double quotes.

MoveTree doesn't support moving users who are members of Global groups, nor does it move Domain Local or Global groups that contain users, or computer accounts. The source domain can run in mixed or native mode, but the destination domain must run in native mode. MoveTree does handle movement of Universal groups. If both the source and destination domains run in native mode, you can temporarily change your Global groups to Universal groups to move them, then change the Universal groups back to Global groups.

You use the AD-enabled version of Windows NT 4.0's Netdom.exe (NetDom) Support Tools utility to move computer accounts between domains. The command-line statement you execute on a DC in the oakleaf.edu domain for moving a student's computer account from oakleaf.edu to student.oakleaf.edu is

`NETDOM MOVE d:/student.oakleaf.edu STUC319978818`

where the last argument is the workstation's computer name. Unlike MoveTree, NetDom only moves one computer account at a time. You must write a script or application to move multiple computer accounts in a batch operation.

> **Note** You can use the Active Directory Migration Tool (ADMT) to move objects between domain trees that are in separate forests. Moving objects between forests eliminates the restrictions on group population, and lets you move User and Computer objects in bulk. To use ADMT, you must add a new DC, install AD in a new forest, and then move the objects to the pristine forest.

Administering Domains with Windows 2000 Professional

The examples in this chapter assume that you're working at a DC of a parent or child domain. In a production environment, administrators most commonly use Windows 2000 Professional for domain administration. The Professional version doesn't include the AD administrative tool, which you must install from the Windows 2000 Server, Advanced Server, or Datacenter Server version's distribution CD-ROM.

To install the AD administrative tools for Windows 2000 Professional, do the following:

1. Navigate to the \i386 folder of the Server distribution CD-ROM, and double-click Adminpak.msi to start Windows Installer.
2. Click Next in the Windows 2000 Administration Tools Setup Wizard's first dialog to start the installation process.
3. Click Finish to dismiss the Wizard.

Adminpak.msi installs the full set of AD and other administrative tools, including Terminal Services Client and Cluster Administrator, even if you don't have Terminal Services or Windows 2000 Advanced Server installed on your servers. To use the newly installed tools, log on to the domain with an account having at least Domain Admins privileges for the domain you intend to administer.

To set up Windows 2000 Professional workstation computer and user account for domain administration, do the following:

1. Create a Domain Computers account for the workstation, if you haven't already done so.

   To create a computer account in Active Directory Users and Computers, right-click any node in the domain, choose New, Computer to open the New Object - Computer dialog. Type the workstation name in the Computer Name text box, and click OK.

2. At the workstation, right-click My Computer and choose Properties to open the System Properties dialog.

3. Click the Network Identification tab and the Network ID button to start the Network Identification Wizard. Click Next to bypass the Welcome dialog.

4. In the Connecting to the Network dialog, accept the default This Computer Is Part of a Business Network option, and click Next.

5. Accept the default My Company Uses a Network with a Domain option, and click Next. Click Next again to bypass the Network Information dialog.

6. In the User Account and Domain Information dialog, type your Domain Admins account name, password, and the downlevel domain name. Click Next.

7. Click Yes when the "An account for this computer has been found in the domain 'DomainName'" message appears.

8. In the Access Level dialog, select the Other option and choose Administrators from the list. Click Next and then click Finish to dismiss the Wizard.

9. Click OK to acknowledge the reboot message, click OK to close the System Properties dialog, and click Yes to reboot the workstation.

10. Log on to the workstation with your Domain Admins credentials.

11. Verify Domain Admins access to the domain controller by launching Active Directory Users and Computers.

Tip from
RJ

Administer remote DCs from a workstation running Windows 2000 Professional, not a DC or member server. Performance of AD tools is somewhat better under the Professional than the Server version, especially on workstations with limited RAM or slower processors. For example, tool performance under Professional is adequate with 64MB of RAM but barely acceptable when running Server on the same machine. Further, the license cost for Professional is significantly less than for the Server versions.

Troubleshooting

Active Directory Installation Problems

The Active Directory Installation Wizard fails prematurely with an "Active Directory is busy" error.

The most common source of this unrecoverable error is a child domain naming conflict. Verify that the domain name or child domain prefix isn't used in an existing domain. For example, attempting to add a child domain with the same prefix as the name of a first-level OU in the parent domain throws an "Active Directory is busy" or similar error.

Addition of a new domain tree or child domain generates "insufficient memory" errors in the AD Event Log.

If you have 128MB or more RAM, this message probably is the result of a memory leak, most likely in a Windows 2000 service. With 64MB of RAM, "insufficient memory" errors are especially common when running the full complement of Windows 2000 Server services. If the errors don't reoccur when you reboot the computer and log on to the new domain, you can ignore them.

If "insufficient memory" errors occur each time you restart your DC, disable unneeded services with the Services snap-in (Services.msc) that you access from the Program Files, Administrative Tools menu. Alternatively, try increasing the size of the virtual memory paging file or, if your computer has less than 128MB, add RAM.

Child Domain Creation Problems

The Active Directory Installation Wizard fails with an "Unable to Connect to Parent Domain" or similar message from a dialog or early in the AD installation process.

DNS was unable to resolve the parent domain's IP address from its domain name. The most common cause of this problem is failure to specify the parent domain's IP address as the Preferred or Alternate DNS Server in the Internet Protocol (TCP/IP) Properties dialog. Make sure the IP address of the parent domain is correct.

If the parent domain's IP address is correct, check the status of the parent DC's DNS server with the DNS administrative tool. Check that the parent DC uses Active Directory-integrated DNS (DDNS) and that all required entries are present by expanding the Forward Lookup Zone node. If the parent DC's DNS server indicates problems, it's usually quicker and easier to delete and re-create the Forward Lookup Zone than to troubleshoot the server.

Once you've corrected the IP address or DNS server problem, cancel and restart the Active Directory Installation Wizard on the child domain server.

MCSE Corner: Optimizing Your Active Directory Topology

In Chapter 4, you learned about creating a new site and configuring site replication. These topics are covered on exam 70-217, "Implementing and Administering a Microsoft Windows 2000 Directory Services Infrastructure." This exam also covers topics such as security policies and troubleshooting.

This chapter covers the design of Active Directory and Domain Topology. It is a good primer for the topics covered in exam 70-219, "Designing a Microsoft Windows 2000 Directory Services Infrastructure." For this exam, you must be able to determine from a set of parameters the optimum layout for the Active Directory.

70-217   Implementing and Administering a Microsoft Windows 2000 Directory Services Infrastructure

This exam tests your ability to install, administer, and troubleshoot the Active Directory service. Chapter 3 covered installation and basic administration, and this chapter covers advanced administration and troubleshooting. Advanced administration topics that you should be familiar with are setting up DNS zones and working with child domains and sites, including specifying site subnets. You should also be able to configure replication between sites.

This exam also requires you to be able to configure and troubleshoot security with Active Directory, which is covered in the sections on using the Domain Security policy console and viewing the Group Policies for a domain. You should also be familiar with troubleshooting Active Directory installation problems.

This exam requires an ability to implement and maintain (including troubleshoot) a fully integrated directory services system. This includes the ability to integrate Active Directory with other services, such as name resolution with DNS.

70-219   Designing a Windows 2000 Directory Services Infrastructure

Topics from this chapter that are tested on the exam include determining the optimum domain topology, given a description of the environment. Also tested on the exam are designing site boundaries and site replication strategies.

You should be able to assess the technical and business needs of an organization, including the existing network layout and the physical locations of main and branch offices. Other factors to take into account are systems management and technical support structures, company process flow, performance requirements, projected growth, and resource distribution. From all these factors, you should be able to specify a domain model, resource distributions, and Active Directory sites. This ability will be covered extensively on the exam, mainly through case study and scenario-type questions.

The goal of this exam is to test your ability to provide a client or an employer with a tightly integrated directory services model with the lowest possible total cost of ownership (TCO), including implementation and ongoing support costs.

CHAPTER 5

CHOOSING AND TESTING MIGRATION STRATEGIES

In this chapter

Developing a Windows 2000 Migration Plan   194

Setting Up a Migration Test Facility   195

Migrating a Single-Domain Configuration   198

Moving Accounts from the Users Container to OUs   211

Reorganizing Migrated Security Groups   220

Delegating Administrative Responsibilities for OUs   223

Testing Migration of Multiple Domains   230

Emulating Domain Migration with the Active Directory Migration Tool   231

Troubleshooting   255

MCSE Corner: Choosing and Testing Migration Strategies   257

Developing a Windows 2000 Migration Plan

Once you've decided on an Active Directory (AD) topology, you must design and test a migration plan to deploy Windows 2000 Server on your production hardware. This chapter assumes that you intend to upgrade an existing Windows NT 4.0 single- or multiple-domain network to Windows NT 2000 Server. If you're starting a Windows 2000 network from scratch, skip ahead to Chapter 7, "Specifying Server and Data Storage Hardware."

Integrate your Windows 2000 Professional rollout plan in conjunction with that for your servers, assuming your client PCs have the necessary RAM and compatible hardware. Desktop and mobile users can't take advantage of many of Windows 2000's new features without installing Windows 2000 Professional. Many large organizations avoided the upgrade from Windows 95 to 98 in anticipation of moving to Windows 2000 during early 1999. Others made the transition from Windows 3.1x or 95 desktops to Windows NT 4.0 Workstation. Aside from additional license fees, the primary deterrent to client upgrades is insufficient RAM and lack of available fixed-disk space. Even if you don't anticipate a wholesale upgrade to Windows 2000 Professional, however, it's important to consider the client side of the migration equation in your plans.

> **Note**
>
> Windows 2000 Professional incorporates power management, full support for the Universal Serial Bus (USB) and PCMCIA cards, Virtual Private Network (VPN) enhancements, and other features badly needed by mobile users. Unfortunately, most existing laptop and notebook PCs have 32MB or less of RAM and fixed disks with capacities less than 1GB. BIOS and display driver problems preclude upgrading many older laptops, and many recent models may even require BIOS and driver updates.

An Historical Perspective on Windows NT Upgrades

Upgrading Windows NT Server from version 3.1 (called Advanced Server) to 3.5 and from 3.5 to 3.51 was an uneventful, evolutionary process. Version 3.5 production upgrades and the 3.51 update required little advance planning by network administrators, and usually took less than an hour per server.

Windows NT 4.0 Server, which added Internet Information Server (IIS) and a plethora of new and improved TCP/IP-related features, complicated the upgrade path. The Windows 4.0 upgrade process was straightforward; preplanning efforts centered primarily on implementing or taking the kinks out of TCP/IP networks.

The primary problem with Windows NT 4.0 Server was that the software didn't reach what most administrators considered production quality until SP3, which accompanied the Windows NT 4.0 Option Pack. When this book was written, SP5 was in common use, and SP6A had been released. Adding new servers to the network became a nightmare of running Windows NT 4.0 Server SP1 Setup, adding SP3, installing the Option Pack, and then updating to the latest SP. It wouldn't surprise most administrators to receive CD-ROMs of Windows NT 4.0 SP15+ in 2001 or 2002, when Microsoft intends to cease supporting version 4.0.

The Migration Timeline

Experience with prior versions of Windows NT demonstrates that it takes at least a couple of SPs before Microsoft's new server software reaches full production quality. This observation is even more applicable to a product as complex as Windows 2000 Server and AD. Microsoft released SP1 for Windows 2000 in the summer of 2000, and you can expect release of Windows 2000 SPs at more frequent intervals than for Windows NT 4.0.

It's up to you and your organization's management to decide when Windows 2000 Server reaches the state of stability, predictability, and reliability necessary to meet your network usability and uptime objectives. In the meantime, invest in a migration test program to ready your organization for an orderly and uneventful transition to Windows 2000.

> **Tip from**
> *RJ*
>
> For an early review of the Microsoft and Intel PC design specification that's scheduled to apply to hardware that's delivered in the last half of 2001 and beyond, download the current draft of the *PC 2001 System Design Guide* from `http://www.pcdesguide.org/pc2001/`.

Setting Up a Migration Test Facility

The objective of a migration test facility is to provide network administrators the ability to emulate upgrading a production Windows NT 4.0 network to Windows 2000. There's no substitute for testing the upgrade process with the full complement of user and computer accounts, security groups, and other objects that duplicate your production environment.

> **Note**
>
> The Windows 2000 Resource Kit Deployment Planning Guide (Deploy.chm) has a "Building a Windows 2000 Test Lab" section. Choose Programs, Windows 2000 Support Tools, Deployment Planning Guide to review the online help file.

Upgrading a Windows NT 4.0 primary domain controller (PDC) to a Windows 2000 domain controller (DC) is a one-way process, so you must be prepared to make multiple test installations of Windows NT Server to evaluate different upgrade scenarios. Migration testing can consume an appreciable amount of time, but the payoff is a high probability of a successful upgrade to the production network on the first attempt.

Equipment Requirements

The minimum testing facility for emulating migration from Windows NT 4.0 to 2000 Server has the following components:

- Pentium-class server computer(s) with a minimum of 128MB of RAM and 1.5GB of free disk space running Windows NT 4.0 server to serve as the primary domain controller (PDC) for each domain you plan to upgrade, including resource domains. 16X or faster CD-ROM drives accelerate the installation process.

- Client PC(s) running each operating system you intend to support. If client PCs are in short supply, you can multiboot clients with Windows 9x, NT Workstation, and 2000 Professional. Clients running Windows 2000 Professional need a minimum of 64MB of RAM.

- An independent network that's separable from your production network. The easiest way to create a separable network is to attach or detach the uplink port of a four- or eight-port 10/100-BaseT hub for the test network to a production network hub or switch.

It isn't necessary to purchase the latest and fastest hardware for migration testing, but the server you use to administer the upgraded network—usually the first PDC you upgrade—should have 128MB or more RAM and an Ultra DMA/33 IDE or better fixed-disk drive.

Note

128MB RAM is the minimum for servers to meet the requirements of the "Windows NT Server Design Guide, Version 2.0", available at http://www.microsoft.com/hwdev/serverdg.htm. Windows 2000's Administrative Tools perform sluggishly on PCs with 64MB RAM; the "Design Guide" states that 64MB, the minimum originally specified in version 1.0, "will not provide an enhanced end-user experience."

Tip from
RJ

Verify whether your test servers appear in the System/Server Uniprocessor or System/Server Multiprocessor categories of the Windows 2000 Hardware Compatibility List (HCL). The \Support folder of the Windows 2000 Server distribution CD-ROM includes a text (Hcl.txt) and HTML (Hcl.chm) version of the HCL, but Microsoft's HCL Web site—http://www.microsoft.com/hcl/default.asp—is more up-to-date. Chapter 7 provides added information about the Windows 2000 HCL.

If your server computers haven't been tested with Windows 2000 Server, indicated by a check mark in the Windows 2000 x86 column of the Web-based list, verify that each significant component has been tested. The older the computer, the more important the HCL check becomes.

 For an unforeseen hardware issue that can cause serious downstream problems, see the "Hardware Faults During Upgrade" topic of the "Troubleshooting" section near the end of this chapter.

Comparing the performance of Windows 2000 Server and AD with that of your existing network requires test hardware that's similar—preferably identical—to that used in production. Multiprocessor Pentium III Xeon servers with high-performance RAID drives and processor-based input/output (I/O) subsystems, such as Intel's I2O, deliver a dramatic improvement in AD performance on 100BaseT subnets. You also experience much better response from the AD administrative tools when dealing with a large number of user accounts.

It's also necessary to simulate your current and projected average and peak network traffic on local subnets and over wide-area networks (WANs) connecting multiple AD sites. AD intersite replication traffic can consume a significant percentage of WAN bandwidth. WANs represent the primary bottleneck of intersite replication; increasing server performance has only a minor effect on WAN-based replication.

→ For a replication traffic test scenario, **see** "Setting Up a Test to Estimate Replication Traffic," **p. 990**.

BASIC UPGRADE EMULATION STEPS

With the testing facility equipment in place, you're ready to test the server migration. To do so, follow these steps:

1. Attach the upgrade test server(s) to the production network through the separable hub.
2. Install Windows NT 4.0 Server on the test computers(s) as a backup domain controller (BDC) for each domain to be upgraded, and then apply SP4 or higher.
3. Increase the Registry quota to accommodate the size of the SAM database, if necessary. 16MB of Registry space accommodates 5,000 user and computer accounts.

   To increase the Registry quota, right-click My Computer, choose Properties, click the Performance tab, click the Change button, and type the new value in the Maximum Registry Size text box. You must reboot the server to make the new Registry size value effective.
4. Synchronize each BDC with its PDC (primary domain controller), and then disconnect the test hub from the production hub or switch.
5. Promote each BDC to a PDC for its domain.
6. Remove trusts with Windows NT domains that won't have PDCs in the isolated network.
7. Upgrade the first PDC to Windows 2000 Server, and perform client connectivity tests to the upgraded and trusting Windows NT domains on the isolated network.

> **Caution**
>
> Never reconnect a test server running a Windows 2000 DC created by the method described in this section to your production Windows NT network. The accounts on the test server duplicate those of the originating PDC. Reconnecting the test server might cause serious problems with the SAM database of your production network.

The following sections provide step-by-step instructions for migrating Windows NT 4.0 domains to Windows 2000. The upgrade test procedures in this chapter cover only domain migration. Later chapters cover upgrading other Windows NT applications and services. For example, upgrading Internet Information Server (IIS) 4.0 to 5.0 is one of the subjects of Chapter 27, "Administering Internet Information Server 5.0," and Chapter 28, "Managing Transaction and Messaging Services," covers migrating Microsoft Transaction Server 2.0 (MTS) and Microsoft Message Queue Server (MSMQ) to COM+.

Tip from
RJ

If you have sufficient fixed-disk space, create multiple partitions to multiboot several upgraded Windows NT 4.0 Server configurations for comparison. Windows NT and 2000 require installation on a primary system partition.

You can create up to four upgradeable primary partitions on a single drive with 6GB or greater capacity, but the boot partition (drive C:) must remain formatted with FAT16 (not FAT32) if you want to multiboot other operating systems.

MIGRATING A SINGLE-DOMAIN CONFIGURATION

Emulating a single-domain migration gives you a preview of the Windows 2000 domain upgrade process, which Chapter 8, "Deploying Windows 2000 Production Servers," describes in detail. Performing a simple test upgrade also gives you insight into the many issues you must deal with when upgrading your production domains.

This chapter's migration examples use the production OAKLEAF Windows NT 4.0 domain with 5,000 user and computer accounts added by the ADSI25 Visual Basic application. ADSI25 is described in preceding chapters and Appendix A, "Installing and Using the ADSI25 Active Directory Application." ADSI25, which is included in the \Seuw2ks\ADSI25 folder of the accompanying CD-ROM, also creates and populates 29 global groups with OakLeaf University employee and student accounts.

→ For examples of AD domains created with ADSI25, **see** "The ADSI25 Visual Basic Application," **p. 141**, and "Adding a Sample Child Domain," **p. 160**.

CREATING AN UPGRADEABLE PDC FROM A BDC IN AN EXISTING DOMAIN

This section assumes that you're running a production Windows NT 4.0 domain having a substantial number of user and computer accounts, and a full complement of local and global groups. If you don't have network access to a production domain, skip to the next section, "Installing a New PDC and Adding Accounts with ADSI25," which describes how to create a new PDC populated by the ADSI25 application.

Tip from
RJ

Windows NT user accounts you create with ADSI25 have Description attribute values specifically designed for assigning group members to a hierarchical Organizational Unit (OU) structure. If you want to test movement of a large number of users into OUs, and try other ADSI25-specific operations in this chapter, run a second Windows 2000 upgrade of the standalone PDC described in the next section. Alternatively, run the ADSI25-based upgrade examples, and then upgrade a copy of your production domain.

To create the BDC and upgrade it to a PDC in the isolated domain, do the following:

1. With the test server connected to your existing Windows NT network, install Windows NT 4.0 Server SP1 from the distribution CD-ROM in unpartitioned disk space (proceed with steps 2, 3, and 4) or a previously formatted FAT16 partition at least 1.35GB in size (skip to step 5).

2. If you want to install Windows NT 4.0 Server in unpartitioned space, and New (Unformatted) appears in the partition list of the setup screen, press D to delete the partition, and then press L to confirm the deletion.

3. Select Unpartitioned Space and press C to create a new partition. Specify a size of about 1,500MB to accommodate a maximum of about 10,000 user and computer accounts. Using 1,350MB per partition lets you create three active partitions on a 4.3GB drive for 5,000 or fewer users.

> **Note**
> You need a minimum of about 1GB of free space after installing Windows NT to upgrade to Windows 2000 Server with AD. AD refuses to install if you have less than 250MB of free space after upgrading.

4. Select New (Unformatted) partition, press Enter, select Format with NTFS, and press Enter to format the partition.

5. In the Computer Name dialog specify a unique computer name for the test.

6. In the Server Type dialog, select the Backup Domain Controller option.

7. In the Network Installation dialogs, select only the TCP/IP protocol and accept the four default network services—RPC Configuration, NetBIOS Interface, Workstation, and Server—for the initial test.

    You don't need to install DHCP, DNS, and WINS at this point; setting up and testing migration of these three services are subjects of Chapter 6, "Preparing NT 4.0 for Windows 2000 Server Migration."

8. If your PDC has a large number of user and computer accounts, click Cancel to temporarily halt replication of the PC's SAM database. Complete the setup process.

9. Log on to the new BDC. SAM replication operations continue in the background, if you canceled them in the previous step.

10. If you receive a System Process - Low on Registry Quota message, launch Control Panel's System tool, click the Performance tab, click Change to open the Virtual Memory dialog, and increase the Maximum Registry Size to a value equal to or greater than that for the current PDC (at least 24MB for 5,000 user and computer accounts).

> **Note**
> If you must increase the Maximum Registry Size, you have the opportunity to increase the paging file size in the Virtual Memory dialog. Windows 2000 Server sets the default minimum paging file size to 1.5 times the amount of RAM installed, so type this value in the Initial Size text box, and type two times the amount of RAM in the Maximum Size text box. Increasing the paging file size at this point reduces potential fragmentation when you upgrade to Windows 2000 Server.

11. If you changed the Maximum Registry Size or paging file size values, click OK and Close to dismiss the System tool and reboot your computer to make the new virtual memory settings effective.

12. Launch Server Manager, select the computer whose name you assigned in step 5, choose Computer, Synchronize with Primary Domain Controller, and click Yes and then OK to close the two Server Manager message boxes and resynchronize the BDC.

    Wait a minute or two at this point to ensure synchronization completes.
13. Confirm in Server Manager that all computer accounts are present and enabled.
14. Open User Manager for Domains and confirm that all user accounts and groups are present.
15. Disconnect the test computer from the network.
16. With the disconnected BDC selected in Server Manager, choose Computer, Promote to Primary Domain Controller, click Yes to confirm the pending change, and click OK when you receive a "Cannot Find Primary for *DOMAIN*" message.

    If Server Manager hangs or displays no computer entries, close and reopen it. Promotion from BDC to PDC usually takes only a minute or two.
17. Install device drivers for graphics adapters or other hardware that aren't included on the Windows NT 4.0 Server distribution CD-ROM.
18. In User Manager for Domains, choose Policies, Trust Relationships, and delete trusts to domains not present on your isolated network.
19. Apply SP4 or later.
20. Reboot, and log on to the isolated PDC.

When you promote an isolated BDC to a PDC, Server Manager's entry for the original PDC appears as a BDC and is disabled. Disconnecting from the original domain also disables Server Manager entries for other PDCs and BDCs. The only active entry at this point should be the name of the newly promoted PDC you assigned in step 5.

INSTALLING A NEW PDC AND ADDING ACCOUNTS WITH ADSI25

If you're evaluating Windows 2000 server with only a single server PC, or if you want to take advantage of ADSI25's pre-preparation for moving user accounts to OUs, you can install a new Windows NT 4.0 PDC and use ADSI25 to add users, computers, and groups.

> **Note**
>
> In most scenarios, you can run ADSI25 from any Windows NT workstation in a domain. For this example, you must install and run ADSI25 and its supporting files on the Windows NT PDC you intend to upgrade. Running ADSI25 on the PDC permits upgrading with only a single computer.

To install an isolated Windows NT 4.0 PDC and ADSI25, do the following:

1. On a server disconnected from the network, but with a network interface card (NIC) installed, follow steps 1 through 5 of the preceding section to start installation of Windows NT 4.0 Server SP1.

2. In the Computer Name dialog, type any computer name you want for the PDC; **OAKTEST1** is used in this and the following single-domain examples.

3. In the Server Type dialog, select the Primary Domain Controller option. Use **OAKTEST** as the name for the new domain. The domain name you enter here becomes the downlevel (Windows NT and 9x) name of the Windows 2000 domain.

4. In the Network Installation dialogs, select only the TCP/IP protocol and the four default network services for the initial upgrade test.

5. Complete the SP1 installation and apply SP4 or later.

6. Launch Control Panel's System tool, click the Performance tab, click Change to open the Virtual Memory dialog, and increase the Maximum Registry Size to 24MB.

7. Change the Initial Size of the paging file to Windows 2000 Server's default size—1.5 times the amount of RAM installed on your computer. Change the Maximum Size to twice the amount of RAM.

8. Click OK and Close to dismiss the System tool, and reboot your computer to make the new virtual memory settings effective.

9. Run Ads_nt.exe from the \Seuw2ks\ADSI25 folder of the accompanying CD-ROM. Ads_nt.exe installs the required ADSI 2.5 distributable files in \Winnt\System32.

> **Note**
> You must successfully install the ADSI 2.5 support files before running ADSI25's Setup program. If you don't run Ads_nt.exe before running Setup, your ADSI25 installation fails.

10. Run Setup.exe in the \Seuw2ks\ADSI25 folder of the accompanying CD-ROM to install the ADSI25 application.

    Setup first installs the Microsoft Data Access Components (MDAC) 2.1, and then the files required for ADSI25.

→ For detailed ADSI25 installation instructions, **see** "Installation on a Windows NT 4.0 Workstation or Server," **p. 1260**.

> **Note**
> If you encounter a Setup message stating that some of the system files are out-of-date on your computer, click OK to update the system files, click OK to reboot your server, and run ADSI25's Setup.exe again.

11. Choose Start, Run, type **regsvr32 adssecurity.dll** in the Open text box, and click OK to register Adssecurity.dll.

> **Note**
> Setup copies Adssecurity.dll to your \Winnt\System32 folder. If you don't register Adssecurity.dll before running the ADSI25 application for the first time, you encounter a runtime error when adding computer accounts or creating Exchange mailboxes.

12. Create two new folders named Employees and Students on the server drive. Share the folders as Employees and Students, respectively, with default permissions for the Everyone group. ADSI automatically adds folders and test files to these shares.
13. Choose Start, Program Files, ADSI25 for Active Directory to open the ADSI25: Create Groups, Users, and Computers dialog and select the Windows NT 4.0 option. Click Help to open a help dialog that offers installation information.
14. Change the default domain names (OAKLEAF) to **OAKTEST** and the share names to **\\OAKTEST1\Employees** and **\\OAKTEST1\Students**, for this example, in the Employees Share and Students Share text boxes (see Figure 5.1). Click OK to close the dialog and display ADSI25's main window. Click Help to open a help dialog that explains ADSI25's feature set.

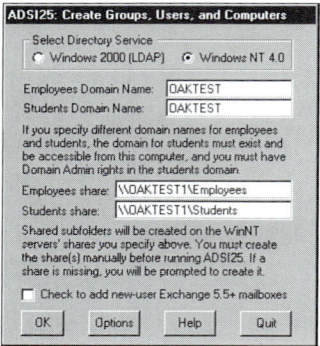

Figure 5.1
Specify the Windows NT domain names and server shares for employees and students in ADSI25's opening dialog.

15. Click Add OakLeaf Groups to add the 29 global groups to the built-in groups and add subfolders and sample files to the shares.
16. Click Add Employee Users with the default 5 users, then click Add Student Users to add 25 more user and computer accounts as an initial test.

→ For additional information on adding OakLeaf accounts, **see** "Using Windows NT 4.0 Mode," **p. 1275**.

17. You can add up to 2,275 employee and about 25,000 student accounts based on records in the OakLeaf.mdb database. Type the number of accounts to add in the Users text boxes and click the appropriate Add… buttons.
18. Click Quit and Yes to exit ADSI25 when you've added at least 500 employee and 500 student accounts. You can add more accounts, if you want, after upgrading to Windows 2000.

It takes between 0.3 and 0.7 second to add a user account, depending on the speed of your computer and disk drive. You can add a large number of users in unattended mode, but adding employee and student users are separate operations.

MIGRATING A SINGLE-DOMAIN CONFIGURATION | 203

Figure 5.2 shows ADSI25's main window after adding 1,000 user and computer accounts. To see the users in a selected group, click a group in the Click a Group list; the users appear in the bottom-left list. To see what Groups a user belongs to, click that user in the Click a User list, and the memberships are displayed in the lower-right pane of the window.

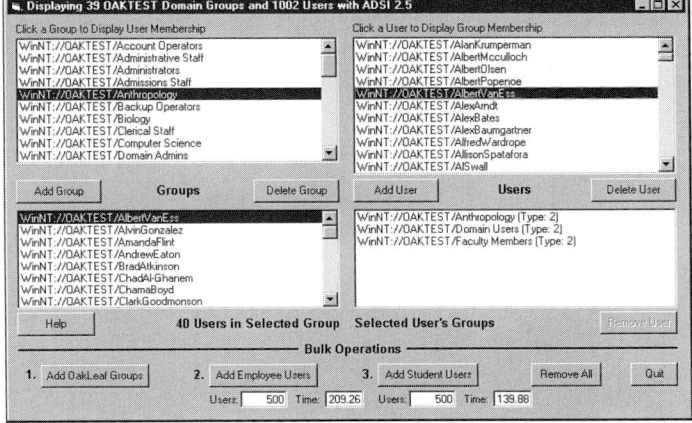

Figure 5.2
ADSI25's main window displays the 28 groups and 1,000 user accounts added to the new PDC.

Choose Programs, Administrative Tools, User Manager for Domains to verify creation of user and group accounts (see Figure 5.3). The comma-separated list in User Manager's Description column provides searchable group membership information; you use this information to assign employees and students to the new OUs you create in the later "Moving Accounts from the Users Container to OUs" section.

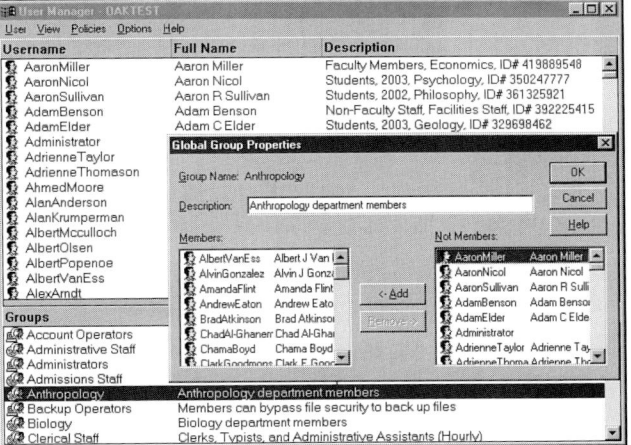

Figure 5.3
User Manager for Domains shows added user accounts and faculty membership of the Anthropology department group.

PART
I
CH
5

Choose Programs, Administrative Tools, Server Manager to display a list of the computer accounts added for employees (OLWS prefix) and students (STUC prefix) in Server Manager. The nine-digit number following the prefix corresponds to the employee or student ID number shown at the right of User Manager's Description column in Figure 5.3.

UPGRADING THE TEST PDC TO WINDOWS 2000

Upgrading a server from Windows NT 4.0 to Windows 2000 takes considerably longer than upgrading to Windows NT 4.0 Server from earlier NT versions. Fortunately, Microsoft has automated the Windows 2000 Server upgrade process so the most time-consuming elements of the upgrade run unattended. In addition, there are fewer reboots during the upgrade process, and the reboots proceed without user intervention.

Do the following to initiate the upgrade to your isolated Windows NT 4.0 PDC:

1. Insert the Windows 2000 Server CD-ROM in the drive, and click Yes when the "Would You like to upgrade to Windows 2000" message appears to start the Windows 2000 Setup Wizard.

    If AutoStart doesn't display this message, run Winnt32.exe from the \i386 folder of the CD-ROM to start the Windows 2000 Setup Wizard.

2. Select the Upgrade to Windows 2000 option in the first dialog of the Windows 2000 Setup Wizard (see Figure 5.4). Click Next.

Figure 5.4
Confirm the Windows 2000 Server upgrade to your Windows NT 4.0 PDC.

3. Select the I Accept this Agreement option in the License Agreement Dialog, and click Next.

4. If requested, type the 25-charcter product key in the Your Product Key dialog (see Figure 5.5). Click Next.

MIGRATING A SINGLE-DOMAIN CONFIGURATION | 205

Figure 5.5
Enter your unique 25-character product key for your Windows 2000 Server license, if the Your Product Key dialog opens. Some versions of the distribution CD-ROM—such as the Microsoft Developer Network (MSDN) version—don't request a product key.

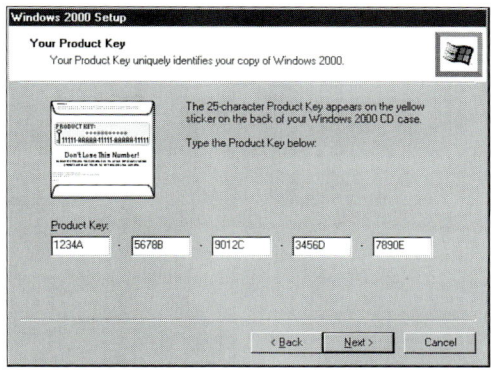

5. Review items in the Report System Compatibility dialog (see Figure 5.6). Select an item and click Details to learn why the program is incompatible with, not required by, or replaced in Windows 2000 Server. Saving the incompatible executable files is useless, because you can't revert a Windows 2000 Server installation to Windows NT. Click Next to begin the upgrade process.

Figure 5.6
The Report System Compatibility dialog shows a typical graphics adapter application installed under Windows NT 4.0 that fails the Windows 2000 compatibility test.

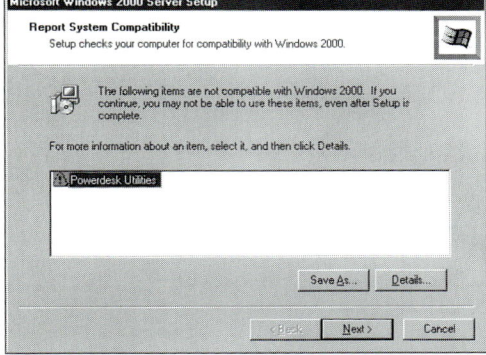

Windows 2000 Setup installs many files, reboots automatically to Setup's standard blue screen, copies files from the CD-ROM to the Windows NT 4.0 partition, and—after about 20 to 30 minutes—reboots into Windows 2000, which displays a Please Wait message for several more minutes of intense CD-ROM and fixed-disk activity.

Tip from
RJ

This is a good spot in the upgrade process to have lunch, go to the gym for a workout, or read the rest of this chapter. The reported estimated elapsed times to upgrade the PDC are for a 300MHz Pentium II PC with 128MB of RAM and a 16X CD-ROM drive. PCs with faster processors and CD-ROM drives can expect a marginal—but not dramatic—improvement in upgrade speed.

PART
I
CH
5

The Windows 2000 Server Upgrade's Installing Devices dialog detects your hardware and substitutes Win32 Driver Model (WDM) drivers for supported hardware; setting up device drivers takes about 20 to 30 minutes for an average server.

The Networking settings dialog consumes about five minutes, and Installing Components drags on for another 10 minutes or so. Performing Final Tasks has three steps that require about 20 minutes. Fortunately, the entire Windows 2000 Server upgrade process usually runs unattended until the initial Active Directory Installation Wizard dialog appears.

Configuring AD on the Test Domain Controller

Configuring AD on an upgraded server is somewhat simpler than installing AD on new Windows 2000 Server installation. With the exception of the DNS domain name, oaktest.edu for this example, you can accept the Active Directory Installation Wizard's default values. As mentioned earlier, the Windows NT domain name, OAKTEST, becomes the downlevel domain name. You can't change the downlevel name of an upgraded server, and you can't alter the DNS domain name after you've installed AD.

→ To review how using Dcpromo.exe to create a new AD installation differs from the upgrade process, **see** "Installing Active Directory," **p. 96**.

To install and configure Active Directory on the test server with the Active Directory Installation Wizard, do the following:

1. Run Dcpromo.exe and click Next to bypass the first Active Directory Installation Wizard dialog.

2. In the Create Tree or Child Domain dialog, accept the default Create a New Domain Tree option (see Figure 5.7), and click Next.

Figure 5.7
Create a new domain tree for the oaktest.edu domain.

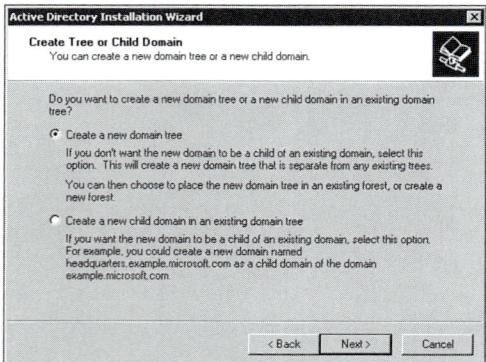

3. In the Create or Join Forest dialog, accept the default Create a New Forest of Domain Trees option (see Figure 5.8), and click Next.

Figure 5.8
Create a new forest of domain trees to contain the first Windows 2000 `oaktest.edu` domain on your network. If you have another DC on the network, you can select the Place This Domain Tree in an Existing Forest option.

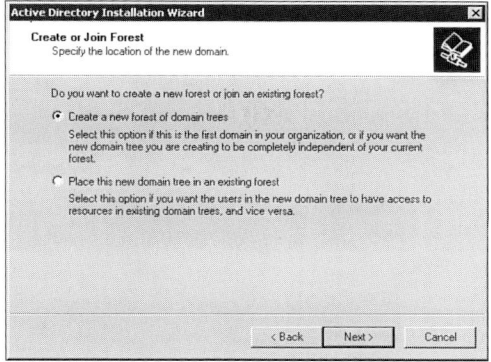

4. In the New Domain Name dialog, type the name for your test domain, **oaktest.edu** for this example, in the text box, and click Next.
5. In the Database and Log Locations dialog, accept the default locations, and click Next.
6. In the Shared System Volume dialog, accept the default location and click Next.
7. When warned that the Wizard can't contact a DNS server, click OK.
8. In the Configure DNS dialog, accept the default Yes, Install and Configure DNS on This Computer option. Click Next.
9. In the Windows NT 4.0 RAS Servers dialog, select the Permissions Compatible with Pre-Windows 2000 Servers option, and click Next.
10. In the Directory Services Restore Mode Administrative Password dialog, type your Administrator password in the two text boxes, and Click Next.
11. Review your selections and entries in the Summary dialog (see Figure 5.9), and click Next to set up AD with DNS and a new forest and domain tree.

Figure 5.9
Review the proposed AD configuration, and if you need to correct an entry, click the Back button repeatedly to move to the appropriate dialog, then click Next as many times as necessary to return to the Summary dialog.

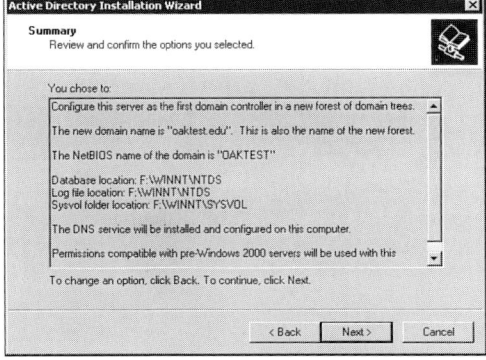

Installing AD takes about 10 to 15 minutes, depending on the number of user and computer accounts in your Windows NT SAM database. If you've removed the Windows 2000 CD-ROM from the drive, you're prompted to insert it.

12. When the Wizard's final dialog appears, click Finish to dismiss the dialog, and then click the Restart Now option to reboot the server with AD operational and AD Administrative Tools installed.

After the first reboot, which takes a few minutes, the Windows 2000 Configure Your Server dialog appears. Clear the Show This Screen on Startup check box and close the dialog.

VERIFYING THE AD UPGRADE

Use the AD Administrative Tools to verify completeness of the upgrade process before making changes to the AD structure. The Active Directory Users and Computers tool takes over most of the functions of Windows NT 4.0's User Manager for Domains and Server Manager. Active Directory Domains and Trusts handles transitive AD trusts and downlevel Windows NT non-transitive trusts.

Tip from
RJ

> Delete inoperable non-transitive trusts with other Windows NT domains at this point, if you didn't remove them in step 18 of the preceding "Creating an Upgradeable PDC from a BDC in an Existing Domain" section. (This tip doesn't apply if you created a new PDC and added accounts with ADSI25.)
>
> Choose Programs, Administrative Tools, Active Directory Domains and Trusts to launch the Active Directory Domains and Trusts tool. Right-click the domain name node, and choose Properties to open the *DomainName* Properties dialog, click the Trusts tab, select the trust to delete in either list, click Remove, and confirm the deletion in the message boxes.

Choose Programs, Administrative Tools, to open Active Directory Users and Computers. Upgraded SAM database objects from the Windows NT 4.0 PDC appear in the following AD containers:

- *Domain User* accounts move to the default Users container (node), as expected (see Figure 5.10). The number of users appears in a caption above the user list in the right pane. Double-click a user item to display the *UserName* Properties dialog. The General page displays the Description and FullName (Display Name) attributes from the Windows NT account (see Figure 5.11, left). The Member Of page demonstrates that user group membership propagates from the SAM database (see Figure 5.11, right).

MIGRATING A SINGLE-DOMAIN CONFIGURATION | 209

Figure 5.10
The Active Directory Users and Computers' Users container lists AD user accounts and security groups upgraded from Windows NT 4.0.

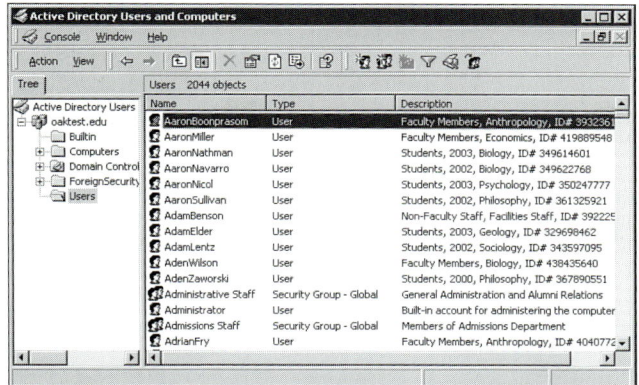

Note

The Description column of the Users list shown in Figure 5.10 contains group membership information added to the Description attribute of the Windows NT user account. Adding group membership data to the Description attribute is an alternative to filtering users by group membership for movement to corresponding OUs, the subject of the later "Moving Accounts from the Users Container to OUs" section.

Figure 5.11
The General (left) and Member Of (right) pages of an upgraded user account show migrated user account attributes and group membership, respectively.

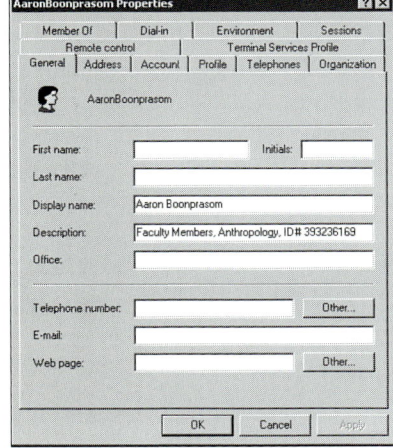 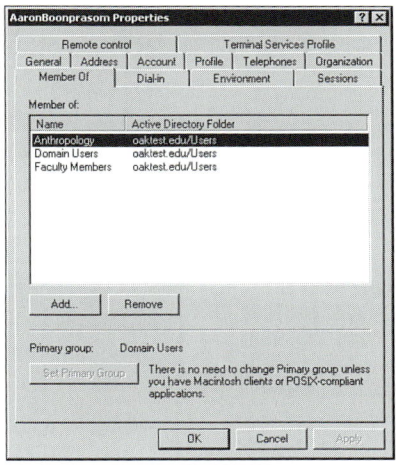

- *Groups*, other than Windows NT's standard set of local groups, also move to the Users container, as illustrated by the Administrative Staff Global group in Figure 5.10. Promoting to AD automatically adds the Builtin container, which accommodates Windows NT's standard local groups. Apply a Custom Filter to display only Group objects in AD Users and Computers' list. Double-click a group item to display the *GroupName* Properties dialog. The General page displays the group name, description, and group scope and type (see Figure 5.12, left). You can't change the group scope or type. The Members page shows group membership (see Figure 5.12, right). Double-clicking a member displays the user's Properties dialog.

→ To review use of AD Users and Computers' Custom Filter feature, **see** "Searching for AD Objects with LDAP," **p. 135**.

Figure 5.12
The General (left) and Members (right) pages of an upgraded global group show group properties and membership, respectively.

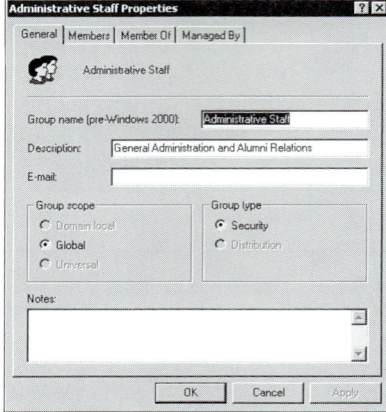 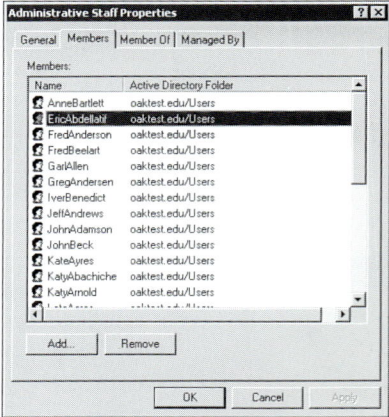

- *Computer* accounts move to the Computers container. AD treats Computer objects as a subclass of the User object, but AD Users and Computers filters the objects into separate containers. Figure 5.13 shows the first few migrated computer accounts and the General page of the *ComputerName* Properties dialog. When a computer logs on to the domain, its DNS address (OLWS388991633.oaktest.com for this example) appears in the DNS Name text box. The logon operation also adds operating system name, version, and current service pack, if applicable, values to the Operating System page.

Figure 5.13
Upgraded computer accounts appear in Active Directory Users and Computers' Computers container, and the General page of the *ComputerName* Properties dialog shows two read-only property values for each computer account.

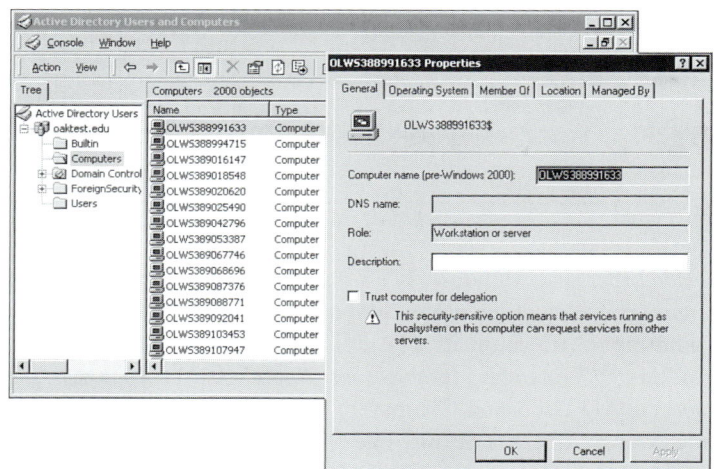

| Tip from | If you have more than 2,000 User or Computer objects, you receive a message that you |
| RJ | must click the Filter button or choose View, Filter Options and set the Maximum Number of Items Displayed per Folder to a larger value. As noted in previous chapters, there is a default limit of 2,000 objects in AD Users and Computers' lists. |

CONFIRMING CLIENT CONNECTIVITY

It's important to verify that Windows NT 4.0 computer accounts successfully upgrade to AD computer accounts. The following two sections assume that you have a Windows NT or 2000 client PC with a network connection to the isolated DC. Testing with a Windows 9x client confirms connectivity, but doesn't test account migration.

| Tip from | If you don't have a spare hub available, use a crossover cable between the DC's and client's |
| RJ | NICs. |

Create a test share of a drive or folder on the isolated DC, and then do one of the following to test client logon to and browsing of the new DC:

- For a DC upgraded from a production PDC, connect a client with a computer account in the domain. Log on with your Administrator credentials in the original Windows NT domain.

- For a DC upgraded from a simulated production PDC, set your client's NetBIOS computer name to one of the added computer accounts, such as OLWS388991633, and log on as Administrator in the OAKLEAF domain.

In both cases, you might need to wait up to five minutes before client browsing is enabled by a periodic refresh of the random password for the computer account. Alternatively, right-click the client's computer account in the Computer container, and choose Refresh to force an immediate update of the computer password.

 If you encounter a problem changing the computer name or domain name of a Windows 2000 Professional client that's already a member of another domain, see the "Clients Are Unable to Log on to an Existing Computer Account" topic of the "Troubleshooting" section near the end of the chapter.

MOVING ACCOUNTS FROM THE USERS CONTAINER TO OUs

One of the primary objectives of migration to Windows 2000 Server is AD's ability to segregate user accounts and Security Groups into OUs. A Users container with several thousand accounts is unmanageable; dividing user accounts into OUs lets you delegate account and group management to other administrators. Another benefit of dividing user accounts into OUs is a significant speedup of AD Users and Computers' performance. Moving Security Groups into OUs offers you the opportunity to take advantage of inherited permissions to simplify group management. You also can apply a specific set of Group Policies to individual OUs.

In most cases, you move all user accounts into the lowest level of the OU hierarchy. You can, however, distribute related user accounts into two or more OU levels. For example, the `oaktest.edu` domains' second-level Faculty Members, *Department Name* OUs might contain a third-level OU for teaching assistants. You can restrict the teaching assistants' access to department-level resources by disabling particular inherited security group permissions.

Using Custom Filters to Classify Users by Group Membership

If your current Windows NT group structure mirrors your OU structure, you can use custom LDAP filters to generate a list of group members that you can move to the corresponding OU you establish with the AD Users and Computers tool. Altering Windows NT group structure and membership to correspond with your proposed OU hierarchy is one of the subjects of the next chapter.

Following are the generalized steps to move user accounts from the Users container into OUs based on group membership:

1. In AD Users and Computers, create your OU hierarchy.

→ For instructions on adding OUs to AD, **see** "Creating Domain OUs," **p. 132**.

2. Create a Users, Group Membership Custom Filter with the Is (Exactly) condition, and specify the fully qualified distinguished name (FQDN) of the group for the OU as the value. The generalized FQDN of an upgraded Global group is `cn=GroupName,cn=Users,cn=domain2,cn=domain1`. For example, the FQDN of the upgraded Windows NT Anthropology group is `cn=Anthropology,cn=Users,dc=oaktest,dc=edu`.

> **Note**
>
> Online help for Active Directory Users and Computers doesn't disclose that you need to use the FQDN when specifying an AD object or container as a Custom Filter value. Filter help topics deal only with character values as criteria for filtering on name or description attributes. Using the common name of the group (Anthropology) as the Value doesn't work; no users appear in the Users list after you apply the filter.

→ For related Custom Filter examples, **see** "Applying LDAP Filters," **p. 138**.

→ To review LDAP FQDN syntax, **see** "Namespaces and Naming Conventions," **p. 123**.

3. Apply the filter, expand the Users node, and select all the entries in the Users list.
4. Move the selected users to the OU, and then move the specified Security Group to the OU.
5. Repeat steps 2 through 4 for each Security Group/OU pair.

Moving Accounts from the Users Container to OUs

Tip from
RJ

Run the ADSI25 for Active Directory application to display the full LDAP path for upgraded groups. The full LDAP path consists of the prefix `LDAP://`, followed by the distinguished name (DN) of the object. When you first run ADSI25 under Windows 2000, you must again change the default domain names and server shares to OAKTEST (refer to Figure 5.1). Figure 5.14 shows ADSI25's main window displaying the LDAP paths for some of the upgraded groups, such as Administrative Staff, Admissions Staff, Anthropology, and Biology. Don't click the bulk operations buttons; using ADSI25 to add AD objects at this point results in a fatal runtime error.

Figure 5.14
ADSI25's main window displays the full LDAP path of Builtin (Account Operators) groups, upgraded Windows NT global groups (Anthropology), and added AD groups (Cert Publishers).

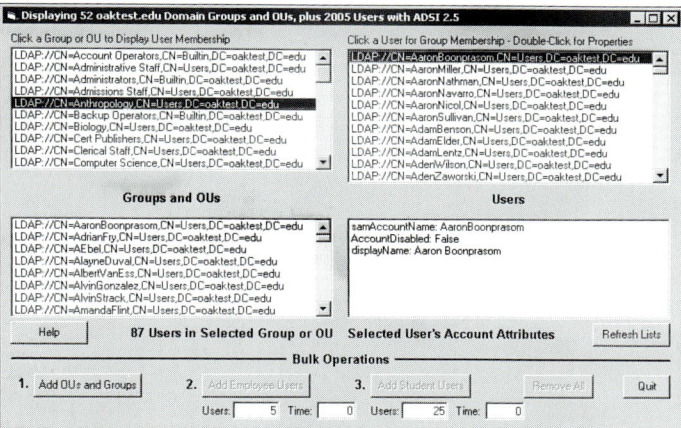

To create an example OU—Faculty Members, Anthropology—and move members of the Anthropology Global group into the new OU, do the following:

1. Right-click the oaktest.edu node, and choose New, Organizational Unit to open the New Object - Organizational Unit dialog. Type **Faculty Members** in the Name text box, and click OK to create the OU.

2. Right-click the Faculty Members OU node, choose New, Organizational Unit, type **Anthropology** in the Name text box, and click OK.

3. Click the Set Filtering Options toolbar button (with the funnel icon; refer to Figure 5.16) to open the Set Filter Options dialog. Select the Create Custom Filter option, and click Customize to open the Find Custom Search dialog.

4. Click Field, and choose User, Group Membership from the context menu.

5. Select Is (Exactly) in the Condition list.

6. Type **cn=Anthropology,cn=Users,dc=oaktest,dc=edu** in the Value text box. Values aren't case-sensitive.

7. Click Add to add your filter expression to the text box (see Figure 5.15). Click OK twice to close the dialogs.

Figure 5.15
Add the DN (LDAP path without the LDAP:// prefix) of the Anthropology Global group as the filter value.

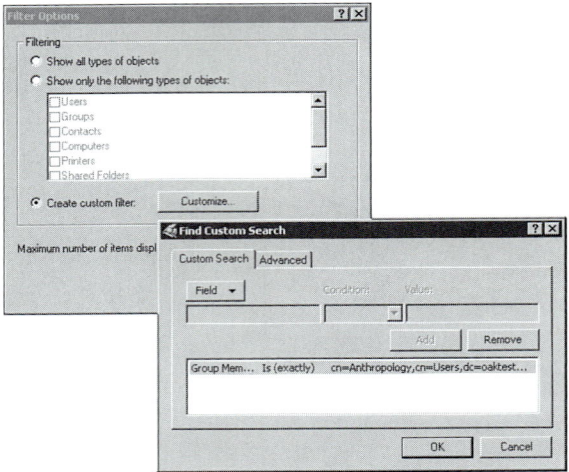

8. Click the Users node to display the members of the Anthropology Global group. Figure 5.16 shows 87 group members from a total of 1,000 employee accounts. Depending on the number of users in the container, it might take a minute or two for the filtered list to appear.

Figure 5.16
Entries for the 87 members of the Anthropology group appear in the filtered Users container.

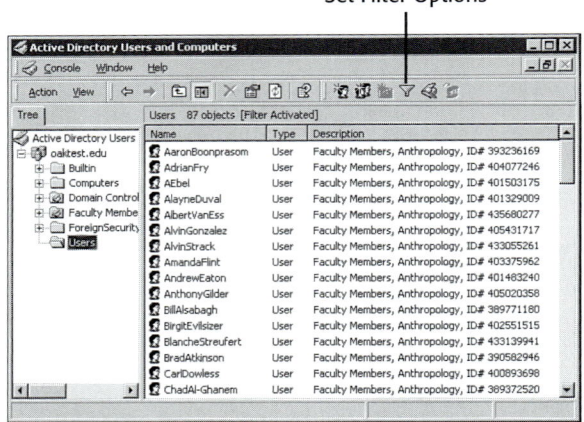

Tip from
RJ

If no user entries appear in the list, you made a typing error in step 6. No error message appears if your FQDN doesn't correspond to an existing AD object or container.

9. Click the first entry in the list, scroll to and Shift+click the last entry to select all filtered users.

10. Right-click anywhere in the highlighted user list, and choose Move to open the Move dialog. Expand the Faculty Members OU to display the Anthropology node (see Figure 5.17).

Figure 5.17
In the Move dialog, select the OU to which to move the 87 members of the Anthropology group.

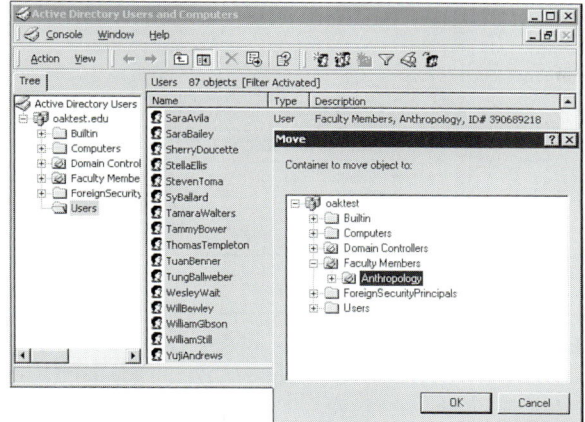

11. Click OK to close the Move dialog and move the selected users to the Faculty Members, Anthropology OU.

Tip from
RJ

> If you're moving members of several groups in the Users container to OUs, you can shortcut writing a complete FQDN for each group. Open the Find Custom Search dialog and double-click the entry in the text box to repopulate the Field, Condition, and Value controls with your prior entries. Edit the first cn= entry, and click Add to use the edited criterion in the next move operation.

12. Click the Set Filtering Options button, select the Show Only the Following Types of Objects option in the Filter Options dialog, mark the Groups check box, and click OK to display only groups in the Users container.
13. Right-click the Anthropology group in the Users container, choose Move, and move the group to the Faculty Members, Anthropology OU.
14. Click the Set Filtering Options button, select the Show All Types of Objects option in the Filter Options dialog, and click OK to display all objects in the Users container.
15. Verify movement of the group and users by expanding the Faculty Members node and clicking the Anthropology node. The Anthropology group and 87 users appear in the Anthropology OU list (see Figure 5.18).

Figure 5.18
The 87 users and one group moved from the Users container to the Faculty Members, Anthropology OU.

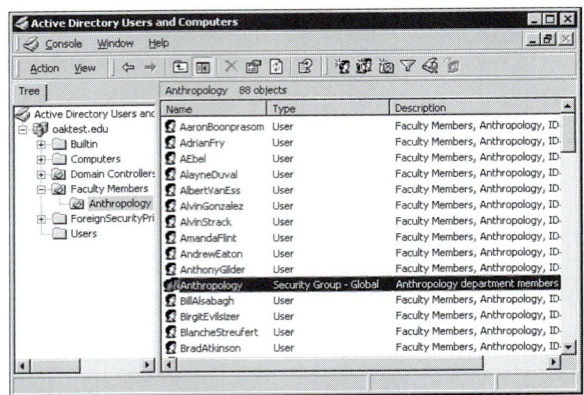

> **Tip from**
> *RJ*
>
> Make sure to select the Show All Types of Objects option in the Filter Options dialog when you complete the movement of groups and users. If you forget to do this, you see only the last set of groups and users you added.

Classifying Users by Account Description

If your Windows NT group structure differs significantly from your proposed OU hierarchy, or you don't have a group that corresponds to the OU membership you want, you're faced with these three options:

- Manually move each user account into the appropriate OU. This tedious process requires reference to a list of users and their OU membership(s).

- Manually add a special Description property value to each Windows NT user account prior to upgrading. The Description value must consist of the names of OUs or equivalent searchable values in left-to-right order of the OU hierarchy. Values in the Description column of preceding Figure 5.10, generated by the ADSI25 application, satisfy this requirement.

> **Note**
>
> Description values must be in left-to-right order of the OU hierarchy because Microsoft didn't include a Contains or similar operator in the Condition list of the Find Custom Search dialog. Contains would be the equivalent of `*value*` in an advanced LDAP filter query or an SQL `WHERE Description LIKE '%value%'` clause. The reason for the omission of a Contains operator probably is due to poor search performance with indexed attributes.

- Write a script or Visual Basic application to add the Description value to the Windows NT User object based on OU assignments stored in a database table, Excel worksheet, or suitably formatted text file. ADSI25 generates the Description value from the data in related Jet 4.0 (Access 2000) tables of Oakleaf.mdb.

→ **For a complete description of AD's search capabilities, see** "Searching for AD Objects with LDAP," **p. 135**.

Administrators faced with assigning thousands of upgraded user accounts to their appropriate OU probably won't like any of the preceding options. Manual entry of OU names, even if abbreviated, as Description values requires exogenous data and incurs the risk of typographical errors. Automated OU assignment is a much better choice. To accomplish this, you need a script to add Description values from an existing data source to Windows NT or upgraded user accounts. If you're an accomplished Windows Scripting Host (WSH) or Visual Basic programmer and are familiar with ADSI 2.5 and ActiveX Data Objects (ADO) 2.x, you can write and test such a script in about an hour.

Tip from
RJ

The cmdAddBulkEmpls and cmdAddBulkStuds subprocedures of ADSI25's frmGroupsUsers form illustrate the VBA code required to add Description values to newly created or existing Windows NT or 2000 User objects. Changing the value of the Description property of a Windows NT user account isn't a hazardous operation in a production environment.

Moving user accounts into OUs based on elements of the Description property is a routine process. The following OU assignment procedure applies to the oaktest.edu domain upgraded from the Windows NT OAKTEST domain. This example assumes that you added at least a few hundred student accounts in accordance with the instructions in the "Installing a New PDC and Adding Accounts with ADSI25" section near the beginning of the chapter. ADSI25 doesn't add global school-year groups, so you must do this manually.

Note

For students, the graduation year values—2000, 2001, 2002, and 2003—in the description column correspond to the Seniors, Juniors, Sophomores, and Freshmen OUs, respectively, through June 30, 2000. ADSI25 automatically alters the graduation year values for each student every year at the end of June. For example, when you run ADSI25 during July 1, 2000 through June 30, 2001, graduation year values are 2001, 2002, 2003, and 2004.

To move student user accounts into the appropriate school-year OUs, follow these steps:

1. In AD Users and Computers, right-click the domain name node, select New, Organizational Unit, type **Students** in the New Object dialog, and click OK to create the first-level Students OU.

2. Add the four second-level OUs—Freshmen, Sophomores, Juniors, and Seniors—to the Students OU (see Figure 5.19).

Figure 5.19
Add four school-year OUs under the Students OU for classifying student accounts by graduation year.

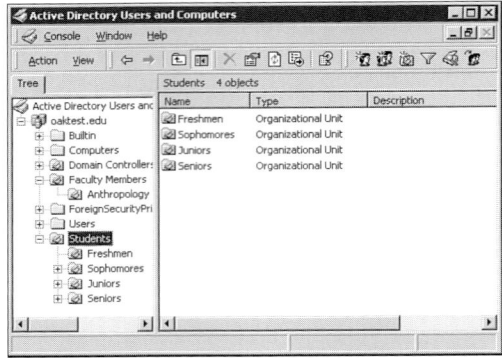

3. Click the toolbar's Set Filtering Options button to open the Filter options dialog.
4. Select the Create Custom Filter option and click Customize to open the Find Custom Search dialog. If the list box contains a filter expression, select it and click the Remove button.
5. Click Field and select User, Description from the menus. Accept the default Starts With value in the Condition list.
6. Type the names of the first two OU levels, separated by a space and comma—**Students, 2000,** for this example—in the Value text box (see Figure 5.20), and click Add to add the filter expression to the list box.

Figure 5.20
Apply the custom LDAP filter for senior student user accounts identified by Students, 2000 at the beginning of the account's Description value.

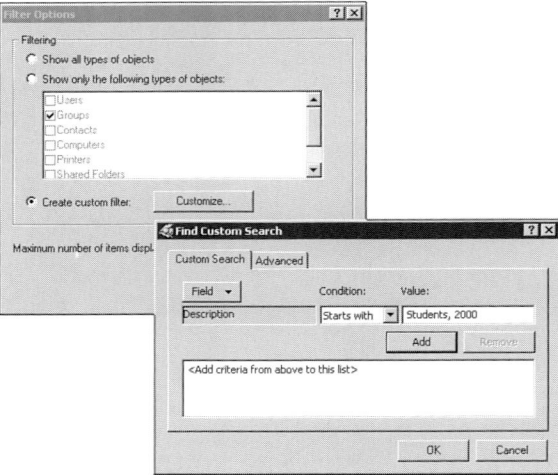

7. Click OK twice to close the filter dialogs and apply the filter to the Users container. Wait for the search to complete, which may require up to a minute or two if you have a large number of users, limited RAM, or a slow PC.

Moving Accounts from the Users Container to OUs

8. Scroll to the bottom of the Users list to verify that all matching users are added, and then click the last list item.
9. Scroll to the top of the Users list, and Shift+click the first list item to multi-select all the matching users.
10. Right-click the selection, choose Move to open the Move dialog, and select the container to which to move the users, in this case Students, Seniors (see Figure 5.21).

Figure 5.21
Use the Move dialog to move the selected set of senior students to the Students, Seniors OU.

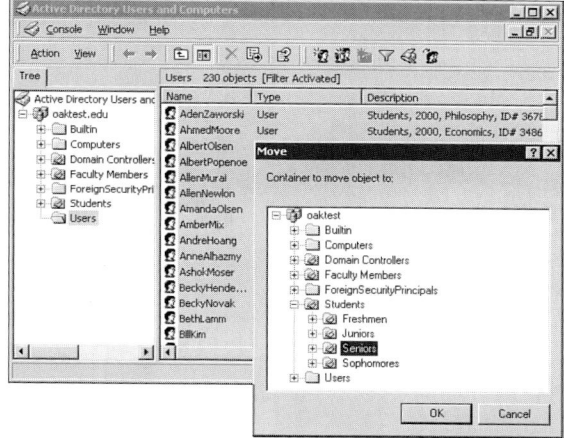

11. Click OK to move the users. A progress dialog opens and then closes when the move is complete.
12. In the tree pane of the AD Users and Computers window, select the node of the OU to which you moved the users to verify the move (see Figure 5.22).

Figure 5.22
Verifying senior student membership in the new Students, Seniors OU.

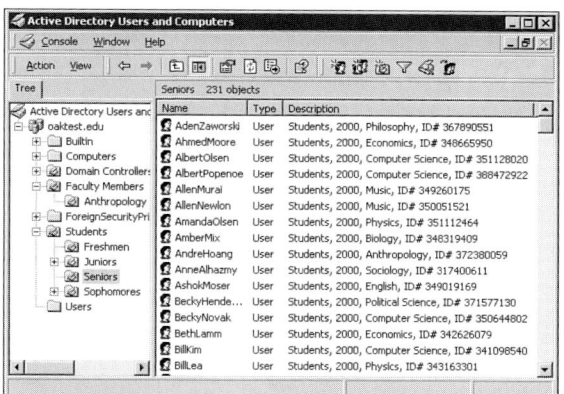

13. Repeat steps 3 through 12 for the 2001, 2002, and 2003 second-level OUs you added to the three first-level OUs. Double-click the filter expression in the list to repopulate the Field, Condition, and Value controls; edit the last digit of the year; and click Add to create the new expression quickly.

14. When you complete moving users into OUs, remove the filter criterion for the last operation in the Find Custom Search dialog, and select the Show All Types of Objects option in the Filter Options dialog.

15. Right-click the Students Security Group - Global entry in the Users list, choose Move, and move the group to the Students OU.

> **Tip from**
> *RJ*
>
> Use the Ends With condition and the nine-digit ID of the `User.Description` column in the Find Custom Search dialog to find the user account associated with a computer account. Computer accounts consist of a four-letter prefix—OLWS for employees or STUC for students—followed by the employee or student ID number.

Reorganizing Migrated Security Groups

After you complete moving all user accounts to OUs, the only objects remaining in the Users container are upgraded Global security groups that you didn't move in the preceding sections. To permit delegation of full administrative responsibility for individual OUs, you also must move the corresponding security group to the OU.

Moving to native mode lets you create Universal groups and removes the Windows NT global group nesting restrictions. In native mode you can nest Windows 2000 Global groups in one another or in Domain Local or Global groups.

You also can add new, special-purpose security groups and add collections of users meeting specific criteria to these groups.

Changing the DC to Native Mode

Up to this point, your isolated DC is running in mixed mode, which lets the DC synchronize with downlevel Windows NT BDCs. When upgrading a production domain, you don't change DCs to native mode until you've upgraded *all* Windows NT PDCs and BDCs in your network to Windows 2000. Windows NT member (standalone) servers are unaffected by the change to native mode. There are no Windows NT BDCs in this migration test scenario, so you can safely make the one-way change to native mode. Changing one DC to native mode propagates the change to all other DCs in the DC's domain. Changing a domain to native mode has no effect on the mode of other domains.

Do the following to change your test DC to native mode:

1. Launch Active Directory Domains and Trusts.

2. Right-click the domain name node and choose Properties to open the default General page of the *DomainName* Properties dialog.
3. Click Change Mode, and confirm the change in the warning message box.
4. Close the *DomainName* Properties dialog, and close Active Directory Domains and Trusts.

CREATING AND NESTING GLOBAL SECURITY GROUPS

The ability to nest Global security groups simplifies creating hierarchical security structures and minimizes group membership. Maintaining group membership at a reasonable number of users—a couple of thousand or less—improves AD's performance. Global group nesting also permits lower-level groups to inherit permissions in groups above them, which simplifies administration of group permissions. You nest security groups by adding higher-level groups in the *GroupName* Properties dialog's Member Of page.

In most real-world cases, you establish a hierarchical group structure within your OU structure as follows:

1. Create new lower-level groups within the appropriate OUs. Your set of OUs should contain all user accounts in the higher-level group.
2. Populate the lower-level groups from membership in the OU with the Add Users to Group menu choice. Adding all members of an OU to a corresponding security group is easy and fast.
3. After you've added all users in the set of OUs to a lower-level group, remove all the users from the higher-level group.
4. Nest each lower-level group within the higher-level group.
5. Set Group Policies on higher-level groups, which the lower-level nested groups inherit. Set additional or override inherited Group Policies, if necessary, on the lower group.

> **Tip from**
> *RJ*
>
> Before deleting a Global security group of an upgraded production domain, make sure to document its Domain Local group memberships and group policy assignments so you can reconstruct access to resources and group policies when you re-create the group.

The upgraded Students group added by ADSI25 includes every student user account, because Windows NT doesn't permit nesting global groups. In native mode, you can nest global groups to emulate your OU structure, so inclusion of user accounts in the Students group is redundant after you move the users to school-year OUs and add the users to school-year Global groups contained in the OUs.

To create the new Global school-year groups, populate group membership, and nest the new groups within a depopulated Global Students group, do the following:

1. In Active Directory Users and Computers, right-click the Students, Freshmen OU node, and choose New, Group to open the New Object - Group dialog.

2. Type **Freshmen** in the Name text box, accept the default Global scope and Security group type options, and click OK to create the new group.

3. Right-click the Freshmen node, and choose Add Members to A Group to open the Select Group dialog. Scroll to and select the newly added Freshmen group (see Figure 5.23), and click OK to close the dialog. Click Yes to All when asked if you want to add all members to the group.

Figure 5.23
Select the Freshmen group for addition of all users in the Students, Freshmen OU.

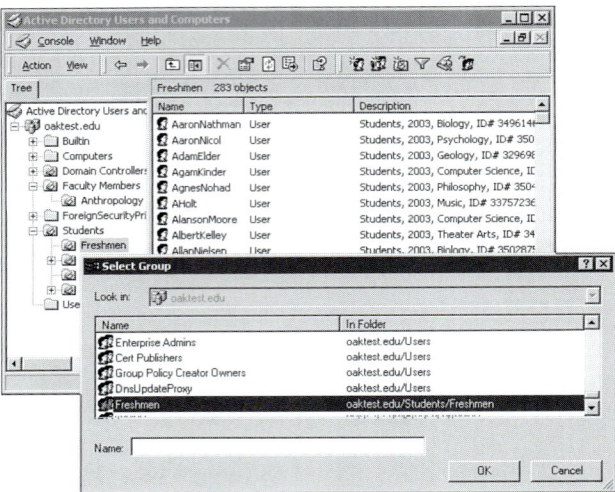

> **Note**
> There's no user feedback, such as an hourglass cursor, to indicate that addition of users to the group is taking place. Wait for the Add to Group Operation Was Successfully Completed message to appear before proceeding to the next step.

4. Double-click the Freshmen group entry in the OU to open the Freshmen Properties dialog, and click the Members tab to confirm that the preceding step worked as advertised.

5. Repeat steps 1 through 4 to create and populate Sophomores, Juniors, and Seniors groups within the corresponding OU.

6. Click the Students node and double-click the Students Security Group - Global entry to open the Members page of the group's properties dialog. Select all users, click Remove, confirm the removal, and close the dialog.

7. Return to the Freshmen OU, double-click the Freshmen group entry, and click the Properties dialog's Member Of page. Click Add to open the Select Groups dialog, select Students in the list, and click Add to add the Students group to the lower text box (see Figure 5.24). Click OK twice to close the two dialogs and nest the Freshmen group in the Students group.

Figure 5.24
In the Member Of page of the Freshmen Properties dialog, select the Students group in the Select Groups dialog to nest the Freshmen group within the Students group.

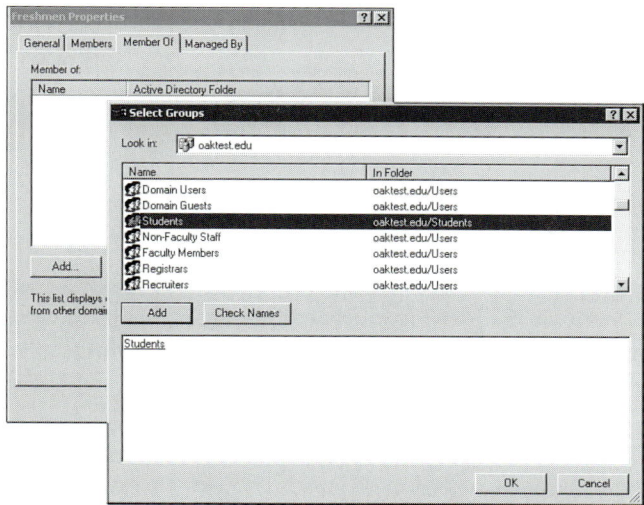

8. Repeat step 7 for the other three school-year groups.
9. Return to the Students node, double-click the Students group entry, and click the Members tab to confirm membership of the four school-year groups.

For time-based OU and group membership, you must manually change OU and group membership at the end of the interval—graduation day for this example. The school's Registrar commonly is responsible for maintaining student accounts and handling OU and group changes resulting from matriculation.

Delegating Administrative Responsibilities for OUs

Several preceding sections mention delegation of OU administrative responsibility as a primary incentive for establishing the OU structures described in this and earlier chapters. Delegation of administrative control by OU is the AD feature that lets you coalesce multiple Windows NT domains into a single domain or add them as child domains to a tree. Here's your opportunity to actually delegate control of an OU to one or more other users and test the result.

Using the Delegation of Control Wizard

Windows 2000 offers the Delegation of Control Wizard to lead you through what's basically a two-step process of selecting the user(s) or group to which to delegate control, and then specifying the tasks to assign to the delegate administrators. This section uses `oaktest.edu`'s Anthropology OU as an example, but the method described applies to delegation of control of any OU and its contained objects.

To delegate control of user accounts and group membership of the Anthropology OU, follow these steps:

1. Select the Anthropology OU node under Faculty Members, and click Action, Delegate Control to start the Delegation of Control Wizard.
2. Click Next to bypass the Welcome dialog.
3. In the Users or Groups dialog, click Add to open the Select Users, Computers, or Groups dialog.
4. Users in the Name list aren't sorted in any discernable order, so select the default entry in the list and type the user logon name of the individual(s) to whom you want to grant control. For this example, **GregAllen** is dean and **GaryAlmgren** is chairman of the Anthropology department. Separate multiple name entries by semicolons.

    The sort-order mystery is compounded by the appearance of computer accounts at the bottom of the list. It's highly improbable that anyone would want to delegate control of an OU to a Computer object.

5. Click Check Names to verify the user account name(s) you typed are correct. If correct, the full downlevel logon IDs of the user(s) appear (see Figure 5.25). Otherwise, you receive an error message reporting that the name you typed isn't found in the directory.

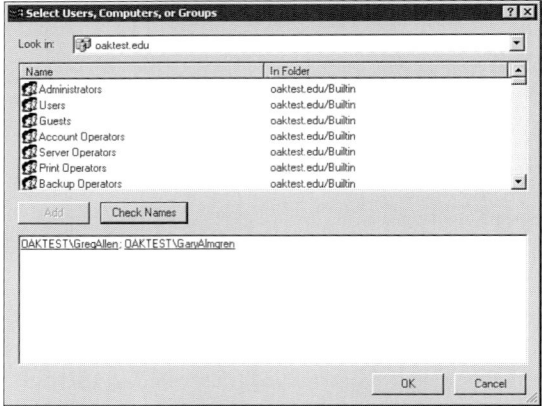

Figure 5.25
The lower pane shows the downlevel logon IDs of two users, Greg Allen and Gary Almgren, to be delegated control of the Anthropology OU.

6. Click OK to close the Users, Computers, or Groups dialog and display the logon IDs in the Wizard's Users or Groups dialog (see Figure 5.26).

Figure 5.26
The two user delegates are added to the User or Groups dialog's list.

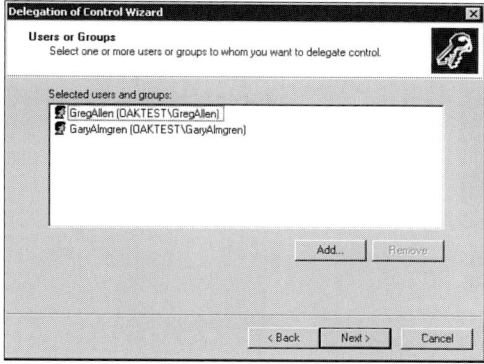

7. Click Next to display the Tasks to Delegate dialog. Mark the tasks associated with managing the OU (see Figure 5.27). Unless you have a reason to exclude a particular task, such as Manage Group Policy Links, mark all the common tasks to enable full management of user and group membership in the OU.

Figure 5.27
Specify the user- and group-related tasks to delegate to the new administrators. Delegate all tasks, unless you want to reserve the Manage Group Policy Links task for Domain Admins.

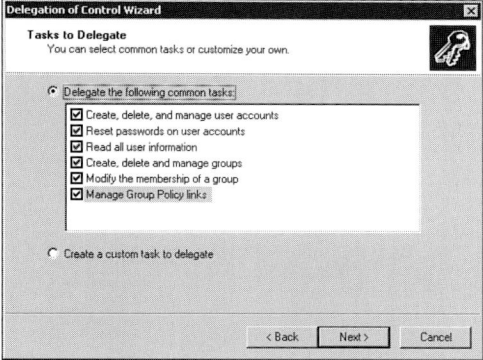

8. Click Next to move to the Completing the Delegation of Control Wizard screen that provides an *ex post facto* confirmation of your choices (see Figure 5.28). Scroll the text box to view the task list, and then click Finish to dispense with the wizard.

Figure 5.28
The wizard confirms the delegation of control of the Anthropology OU to Greg Allen and Gary Almgren.

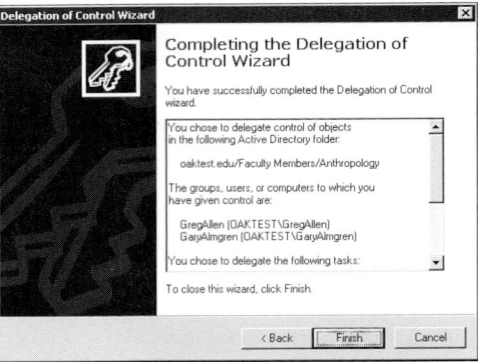

9. Right-click the Anthropology OU, choose Properties, and click the Managed By tab of the Anthropology Properties dialog. Delegating OU management with the wizard doesn't add either manager to the Managed By page, which can have only a single manager entry.

10. Click Change to open the Select User or Contact dialog, type **GaryAlmgren** in the Name text box, and click OK to add the fully qualified path to the manager's user account to the page's Name text box. If the user account has additional attributes, these values appear in the corresponding text boxes (see Figure 5.29).

Figure 5.29
Click Change to open the Select User or Contact dialog that enables you to specify the primary manager of the OU in the Properties dialog's Managed By page.

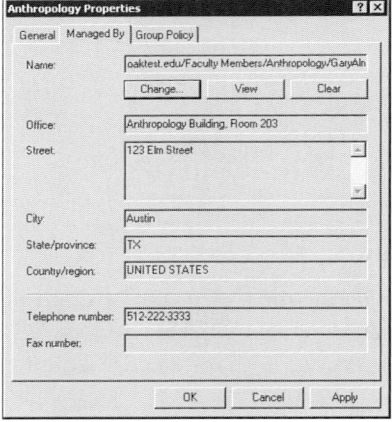

In some circumstances, you might want to delegate control of multiple OUs to a single user or group. For example, members of the Registrars group can assume responsibility for all student accounts by delegation of control of the Students OU. Lower-level OUs inherit the delegation of control properties of their top-level OU. You also can limit tasks permitted specific groups or users, such as enabling the Admissions Staff group to add—but not modify or delete—student accounts. In this case, you must create a custom task to delegate.

To create a custom task for the Admissions Group, do the following:

1. Select the OU, Students for this example, click Action, Delegate Control, and bypass the first Wizard dialog.
2. Click Add in the Users or Groups dialog, type **Admissions** in the Select Users, Computers or Groups text box, click Check Names, and click OK to add Admissions Staff to the Users or Groups dialog's list. Click Next.
3. In the Tasks to Delegate dialog, select the Create a Custom Task to Delegate option (refer to Figure 5.27), and click Next.
4. In the Active Directory Object Type dialog, select the Only the Following Objects in the Folder option, and mark the User Objects check box in the list (see Figure 5.30). This restricts members of the Admissions Staff group to administering User objects only. Click Next.

Figure 5.30
Create a custom task to restrict a delegated group to administration of a single object class (User).

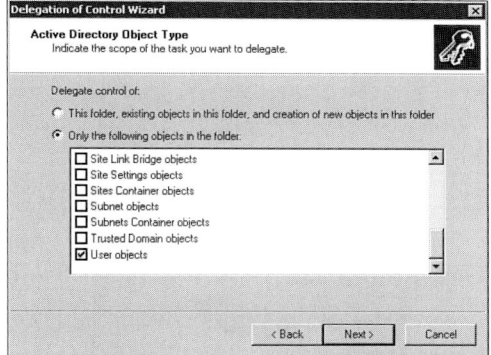

5. In the Permissions dialog, mark the General, Property-Specific, and Creation/Deletion of Specific Child Objects options to create a full list of all permissions for the User object.
6. Mark Read to allow reading of all User object attributes, which automatically marks the Read All Properties and many other check boxes, and mark Create All Child Objects to allow adding new User objects in the Students OUs (see Figure 5.31). Granting Write permission would allow delegates to modify existing accounts, and granting Full Control would allow deleting accounts.

Figure 5.31
You can use a custom task to delegate permissions to read properties for all users, and add new user accounts to the child OUs—Freshmen, Sophomores, Juniors, and Seniors for this example.

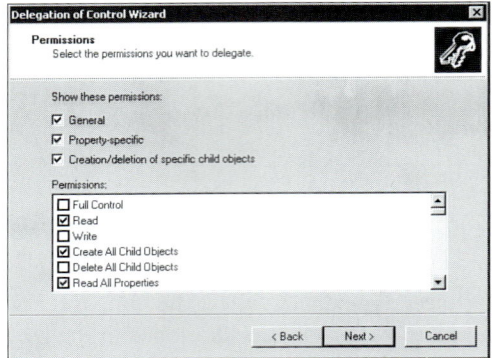

7. Click Next and Finish to delegate limited management of the parent and child OUs.

There's no limitation on the number of groups or users to which you can delegate control of permissions on particular objects within an OU.

Testing Delegation of Control

To verify that the user(s) or group(s) to whom you delegated control can execute the tasks you assigned in the preceding section, you must log on with the user's account and test the ability to add and delete user accounts and group membership in the assigned OU. You also must verify that the user's or group's delegation doesn't propagate to other OUs.

The quickest way to confirm proper delegation of an OU's administrative privileges is to do the following:

1. Add the delegate user(s) or group(s) to test to the Builtin Backup Operators group of the upgraded DC. This step is required to let the user you're testing log on locally to the DC.

2. Log off as Administrator and log on as the delegate user or a member of the delegate group. If you're testing the oaktest.edu domain, log on as **GaryAlmgren** with **password** as the default user password assigned by ADSI25.

3. Launch AD Users and Computers, and double-click the OU to test—Anthropology for this example—to display its user membership.

4. Select a user account, press delete, and confirm the deletion.

5. Right-click the corresponding security group, choose Properties, click the Members tab to verify deletion of the user account from the group, and close the Properties dialog.

6. Select another OU (Students, Freshmen, for example), and attempt to delete a user account. You receive a "Cannot delete object UserName because: Insufficient access rights to perform the operation" message.

   A similar message appears if you attempt to delete a member from the selected security group.

DELEGATING ADMINISTRATIVE RESPONSIBILITIES FOR OUs | 229

7. Right-click the original OU (for this example, Anthropology) and choose New, User to open the New Object - User dialog. Only User and Group appear as New menu choices, because the delegated manager only has permissions to manage user and group accounts.

8. Complete the account information in the first New Object - User dialog (see Figure 5.32), and click Next to open the second New Object - User dialog.

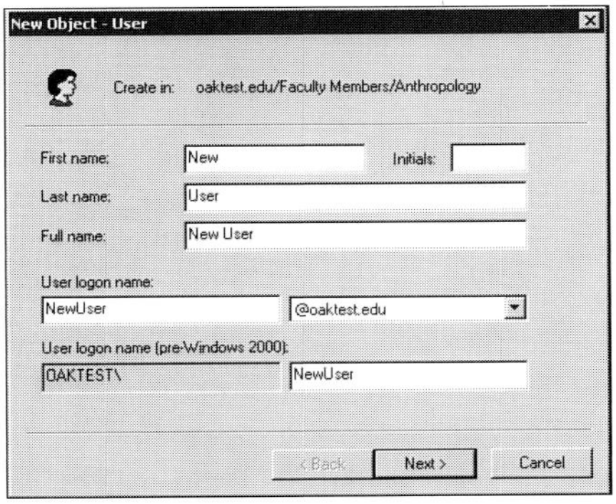

Figure 5.32
Logging on as the delegated manager of an OU and adding a new user account prove that delegation succeeded.

9. Add and confirm a temporary password for the user, and mark the Must Change Password on Next Logon check box (see Figure 5.33).

Figure 5.33
Add a temporary user password and set password attributes for the new user.

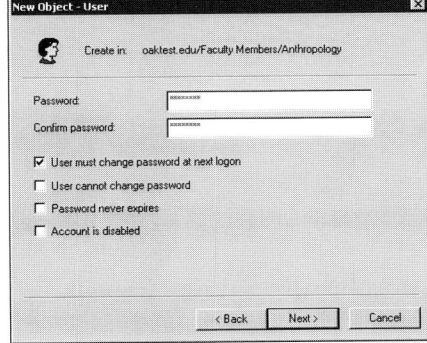

10. Click Next and Finish to complete the addition process.
11. Click the toolbar's Refresh button; in the right pane, select the user account you added; and click the Adds the Selected Objects to a Group You Specify button to open the Select Group dialog.
12. Scroll to the corresponding security group in the list, select the group, and click OK. Click OK again to dismiss the confirmation message.
13. Repeat steps 11 and 12, but choose another security group, such as Biology. You receive an "Insufficient access rights" message.

PART
I
CH
5

If your test client runs Windows 2000 Professional and has the AD administrative tools installed, you can emulate users' ability to administer an OU from their workstations.

→ To install the AD administrative tools on a workstation, **see** "Administering Domains with Windows 2000 Professional," **p. 188**.

TESTING MIGRATION OF MULTIPLE DOMAINS

The test scenario for migrating more than one Windows NT domain to Windows 2000 requires installing a new Windows NT BDC, disconnecting and promoting the BDC to a PDC, and upgrading a PDC for each domain. You must have one test server for each domain and a client PC, which preferably multiboots Windows 9x, NT 4.0, and 2000 Professional, to verify client connectivity to objects in the upgraded domain(s). You also might need additional test servers to emulate upgrading resource domains.

The process of emulating the migration of multiple production domains is similar to the processes described in the earlier "Creating an Upgradeable PDC from a BDC in an Existing Domain," "Upgrading the Test PDC to Windows 2000," and "Configuring AD on the Test Domain Controller" sections. The only significant difference between upgrading one domain and upgrading multiple domains is that the latter usually involves configuration of one or more secondary DCs as child domains when installing AD.

Following are the basic steps to emulate upgrading multiple production domains:

1. Install on a server for each domain Windows NT 4.0 SP1 as a BDC, and then upgrade the BDC to SP4.
2. Manually synchronize each BDC with its PDC.
3. Disconnect all test BDCs from the production network by removing the connection to their dedicated hub or switch.
4. Change server IP addresses and subnet masks, if necessary, so the test servers and clients run on the same subnet.
5. Promote each BDC to a PDC.
6. Reestablish and verify trusts between the PDCs of each domain in the test network.
7. Assign the Administrator account of the primary domain to the local Administrators group of all other domains to permit single-logon domain administration.
8. Upgrade the primary PDC to Windows 2000 and install AD. The primary DC serves as AD's initial root domain, so you create a new forest and domain tree.
9. Verify with Active Directory Domains and Trusts downlevel, non-transitive trusts between the upgraded DC and the Windows NT PDCs and member servers.
10. Upgrade the other PDCs and member servers, if any, to Windows 2000 and install AD on the upgraded PDCs. Designate the secondary domains as children of the primary domain, unless you must create a new domain tree to accommodate a noncontiguous DNS namespace for a secondary domain.

→ To review how to configure a child domain with the Active Directory Installation Wizard, **see** "Adding a Sample Child Domain," **p. 160**.

 If you encounter errors when attempting to add a child domain to the domain tree, see the "Child Domain Creation Problems" topic of the "Troubleshooting" section at the end of the chapter.

Emulating Domain Migration with the Active Directory Migration Tool

Microsoft recommends that you upgrade your production PDCs to Windows 2000 Server by the methods described in the preceding sections of this chapter. The primary advantage of taking the in-place upgrade approach is that the upgrade is totally transparent to your users and to administrators of resource domains. In mixed mode, the SAM databases of the upgraded domain's BDCs synchronize with the changes you make with AD administrative tools. Upgrading retains security identifiers (SIDs) for all objects, so users maintain their group membership(s) and access to all domain resources for which they have permissions.

The primary disadvantage of the in-place upgrade is that the process is basically irreversible. You can recover from a failed upgrade by removing the PDC, reconnecting your backup BDC, and promoting the backup BDC to the PDC for the domain. The backup BDC must be a mirror image of the PDC and be capable of delivering all services and resources of the PDC it's called upon to replace. You lose all changes to the downed PDC after you remove the backup BDC from the network. Recovery from a failed in-place upgrade is chancy, at best.

It takes substantial courage for a network administrator to "bite the bullet" and perform an in-place upgrade of a fully functioning Windows NT production domain to Windows 2000 Server. This is especially true prior to the first few SPs that address problems not discovered or fixes that Microsoft deferred in order to release Windows 2000 to production on December 15, 1999.

Microsoft calls the alternative to an in-place upgrade "domain restructure." Domain restructure involves re-creating existing security principal objects in a new, native-mode domain, and then migrating users, either singly or in batches, to a Windows 2000 clone of the Windows 2000 domain. Re-creating a complex domain structure by manual addition of user and computer accounts, groups, and resource permissions is a formidable and thankless task.

Windows 2000 Server's Support Tools include a Clone Principal dynamic link library (Clonepr.dll) that, together with Visual Basic scripts, automates creation of AD duplicates (clones) of Windows NT security principals—users and groups—with new SIDs. To preserve group and user permissions for domain resources, Clone Principal generates *SID histories* for security principals. SID histories are copies of the original SIDs that match those in the existing Access Control List (ACL) of resources. Like in-place upgrades, running Clonepr.dll from command-line scripts isn't for the faint of heart.

Fortunately, Microsoft and Mission Critical Software joined to provide an easier-to-use alternative to Clone Principal called the Active Directory Migration Tool (ADMT). ADMT packages all the features of Clone Principal into a graphical MMC console, and eliminates the need to write scripts to copy security principals to a new Windows 2000 domain. ADMT offers many additional features, including the ability to migrate roaming profiles, and create and enable Windows NT client computer accounts in the new domain. ADMT dispatches an agent to prepare Windows NT client PCs for logon to the new domain; the agent automatically reboots each computer you migrate after the initial computer account migration process completes. ADMT offers a complete solution for incremental transition of simple or complex domains from Windows NT 4.0 to Windows 2000 Server.

The prerequisites for using ADMT are as follows:

- A DC running in native mode with sufficient disk space to accommodate the AD objects you intend to clone. ADMT runs only under Windows 2000 with AD in native mode. To clone a few large domains, you should have at least 1GB of free space. For a trial with only a couple of thousand users, 200MB is adequate. 128MB of server RAM is satisfactory, but the accompanying documentation recommends 256MB of RAM for migrating a large number (30,000 or more) of accounts.
- A network connection to the Windows NT 4.0 SP4+ test or production domain's PDC to clone. Running ADMT against a test Windows NT 4.0 domain before cloning the production PDC is definitely recommended. When you run ADMT25 for the first time, adding a special Registry key requires rebooting the Windows NT server.
- Domain Admins privileges in the Windows NT (source) and Windows 2000 (destination or target) domain.
- Non-transitive trusts between the destination domain and the source domain, and trusts with all domains trusted by the source domain. A complete set of trusts is required to migrate accounts in local groups of domains trusted by the Windows NT source domain.
- Administrator rights for all computers that the agent alters after the computer account migration process completes.
- Success/failure auditing of group and user account operations for both the source PDC and the destination DC.

> **Note** To translate security for Exchange 5.5 mailboxes, you must install the Microsoft Exchange Administrator application on the DC and have at least Permissions Admins privileges for Exchange Server. Translating Exchange mailbox security is beyond the scope of this book, but you can use mailboxes you create with ADSI25 in Windows NT 4.0 mode to test mailbox security migration.

The sections that follow describe the basic processes for cloning security principals and computer accounts. The examples of these sections use Windows NT 4.0 objects created by ADSI25 in the OAKLEAF Windows NT 4.0 domain, but the methods demonstrated apply to any simple Windows NT 4.0 domain structure.

Installing ADMT on a Windows 2000 Domain Controller

The final version of ADMT didn't make the December 15, 1999, deadline for release on the Windows 2000 Server distribution CD-ROM, so you must download it as Admt.exe from `http://www.microsoft.com/windows2000/downloads/deployment/admt/default.asp`. Admt.exe is a wrapper for a Microsoft Installer (.msi) file that installs ADMT.

Once you've downloaded the ADMT files, do the following to prepare for and install ADMT:

1. If your DC is running AD, remove AD with Dcpromo.exe, and reinstall AD. Specify a DC for a new domain in a new tree and, if this is your only DC or you want complete isolation from any existing test domains, select a new forest of domain trees. The DC for this example is `oaktest1.oaktest.edu`, the same name as that used in the earlier sections.

> **Note**
>
> It's possible to use an existing DC as the destination domain controller, but doing so requires that you manually remove any objects whose names might conflict with migrated objects. Demoting and promoting the DC eliminates any conflicts or settings that might interfere with operation of ADMT.

2. Launch Active Directory Domains and Trusts, right-click the domain node, choose Properties, click Change Mode, and confirm the change to native mode. ADMT only runs on native-mode DCs.

→ For detailed instructions on throwing the native-mode switch, **see** "Changing the DC to Native Mode," **p. 220**.

3. In Active Directory Domains and Trusts, create one-way trusts between the destination and source domains. On the Trusts tab of the oakleaf.edu Properties sheet, click the upper Add button to open the Add Trusted Domain dialog, type the name of the source domain (**OAKLEAF** for this example), and type and confirm the password for the trust (see Figure 5.34). Click OK to close the dialog, and click OK to acknowledge the message that the trust can't be confirmed.

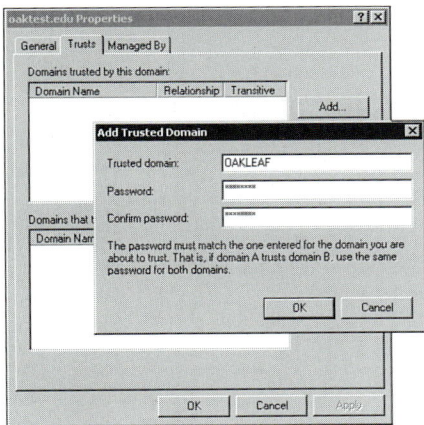

Figure 5.34
Establish a one-way transitive trust to the Windows NT source domain in Active Directory Domains and Trusts' Properties dialog for the `oaktest.edu` domain.

4. Repeat step 3, but click the lower Add button to open the Add Trusting Domain dialog, and enter the domain name, trust password, and password confirmation. Click OK, and then click No when asked if you want to verify the trust. The trusts with the example OAKLEAF domain appear as shown in Figure 5.35. Click OK to close Active Directory Domains and Trusts.

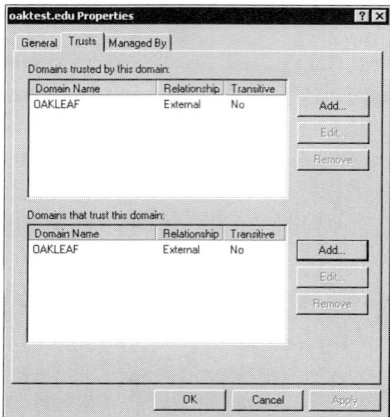

Figure 5.35
Active Directory Domains and Trusts's oaktest.edu's Properties dialog displays the pair of one-way trusts created, but not verified, on the Windows 2000 destination DC.

5. Enable account management auditing on the destination DC by choosing Programs, Administrative Tools, Domain Controller Security Policy to open the Group Policy Editor. Navigate to the Security Settings, Local Policies, Audit Policy node, and double-click the Audit Account Management item to open the Security Policy Setting dialog (see Figure 5.36). Mark the Success and Failure check boxes, click OK, and exit the Group Policy Editor console.

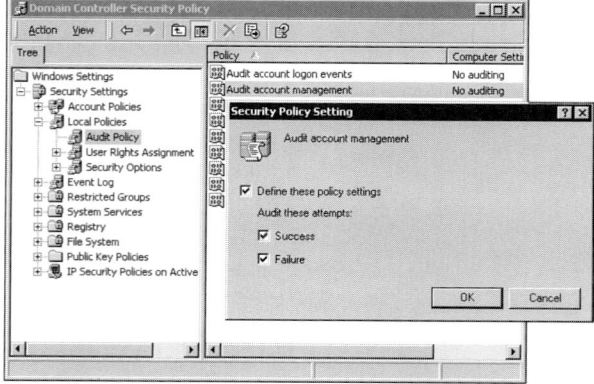

Figure 5.36
Enable auditing of success or failure of account management operations on the destination DC. ADMT fails if you don't enable Audit Account Management for success and failure.

EMULATING DOMAIN MIGRATION WITH THE ACTIVE DIRECTORY MIGRATION TOOL | 235

6. On the Windows NT source PDC, choose Programs, Administrative Tools, User Manager for Domains to open User Manager, and choose Policies, Trust Relationships to open the Trust Relationships dialog. Click the upper Add button to open the Add Trusted Domain dialog, type the downlevel destination domain name (**OAKTEST** for this example) and trust password (see Figure 5.37), and click OK to create the trust. After a minute or so of waiting for creation of the trust, click OK to dismiss the message that verifies the first trust.

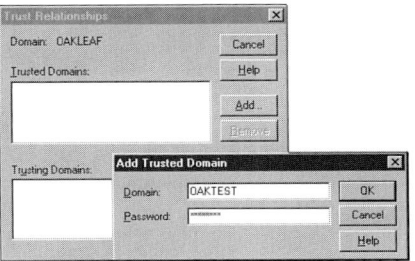

Figure 5.37
Use Windows NT's User Manager to establish the reciprocal trust of the Windows 2000 destination domain by the Windows NT source domain.

7. Repeat step 6 by clicking the lower Add button to open the Add Trusting Domain dialog. Type the domain name, trust password, and confirmation, and click OK to add the second reciprocal trust (see Figure 5.38). Click Close to close the Trust Relationships dialog.

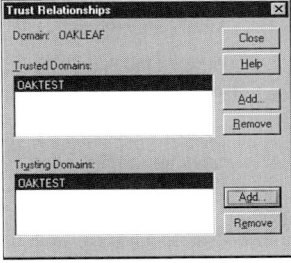

Figure 5.38
User Manager displays the reciprocal trust pair established in the Windows NT source domain.

8. In User Manager, double-click the Administrators group to open the Local Group Properties dialog, and click Add to open the Add Users and Groups dialog. Select the source domain in the List Names from list, and double-click the Domain Admins group to add it to the Add Names list. Optionally, add the Administrator account as backup (see Figure 5.39).

PART

I

CH

5

Figure 5.39
Add the Domain Admins group and Administrator account of the destination domain to the source domain's local Administrators group.

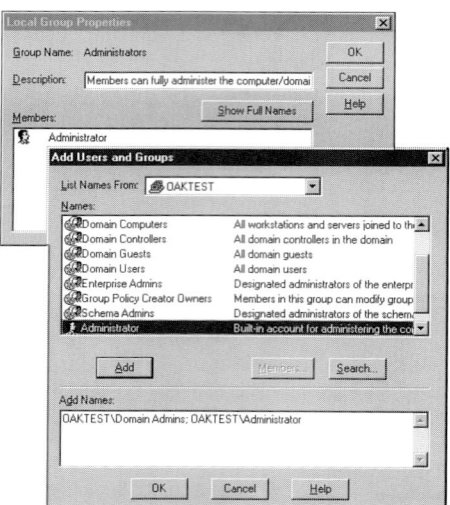

9. To turn on auditing for account management on the source PDC, in User Manager choose Policies, Auditing to open the Audit Policy dialog. Select the Audit These Events option, and mark the Success and Failure check boxes for User and Group Management events (see Figure 5.40). Click OK to close the dialog, and exit User Manager.

Figure 5.40
Set up success and failure auditing of user and group management operations in the Windows NT source domain.

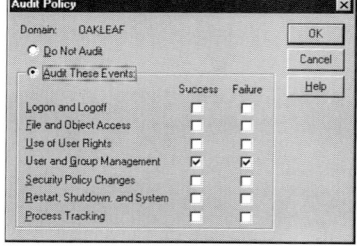

10. On the Windows 2000 DC, double-click Admt.exe in the folder in which you saved the downloaded file to start Microsoft Installer and open the Active Directory Migration Tool Setup Wizard. Click Next to bypass the Welcome dialog.

11. In the License Agreement dialog, select the I Accept the License Agreement, and click Next.

12. In the Installation Folder dialog, accept or change the default installation path, and click Next.

13. In the Start Installation dialog, click Next to begin ADMT installation. The Installing Software dialog reports installation progress. Installation time is a couple of minutes.

EMULATING DOMAIN MIGRATION WITH THE ACTIVE DIRECTORY MIGRATION TOOL | 237

14. In the Completing the Active Migration Tool Setup Wizard dialog, click Finish to dismiss the wizard.

Installing ADMT adds an Active Directory Migration Tool item to the Administrative Tools menu.

RUNNING A GROUPS AND USERS MIGRATION TEST

ADMT provides a wizard for each of its functions, the most important of which is the Group Migration Wizard. The Group Migration Wizard lets you establish an OU structure, and then migrate users and groups into the specified OU. You can add more than one group and its users to an OU, but you can't specify a subset of group members to move.

Tip from
RJ

Create your Windows 2000 domain's OU structure with Active Directory Users and Computers before you start the groups and users migration test.

The Group Account Migration Wizard, like most ADMT wizards, lets you perform a "dry run" to emulate migration without making changes to either the source or destination domain. This example uses the Windows 2000 oaktest.edu (OAKTEST) destination domain; ADMT runs on oaktest-dc1.oaktest.edu.

To give the Wizard a test drive, do the following:

1. In Active Directory Users and Computers, add a test Organizational Unit to the domain. This example uses the second-level Faculty Members, Anthropology OU.

2. Choose Programs, Administrative Tools, Active Directory Migration Tool to open ADMT's console snap-in, and right-click the Active Directory Migration Tool node to display initial options (see Figure 5.41).

Figure 5.41
The Active Directory Migration Tool's initial menu offers seven wizard choices.

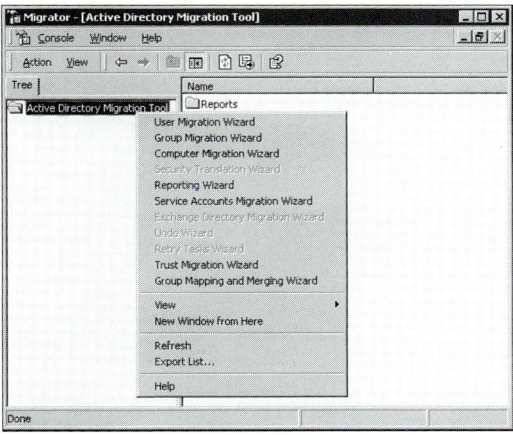

3. To verify the trust with the source domain, and migrate any additional trusts to accommodate local accounts, choose Trust Migration Wizard, and click Next to bypass the wizard's first dialog.

4. In the Domain Selection dialog, select the source (OAKLEAF) and target (OAKTEST) domains from the lists (see Figure 5.42) and click Next.

Figure 5.42
Select the source and destination (target) domains in the second dialog of the Trust Migration Wizard.

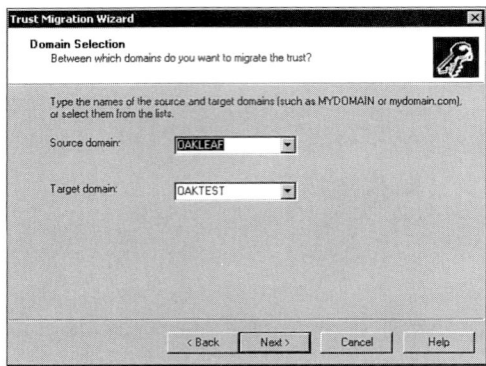

5. If you correctly established the trusts in steps 3, 4, 6, and 7 of the preceding section, the existing bidirectional trust shown in Figure 5.43 appears. If your source PDC trusts other domains, the additional trusts appear in the list. Select the additional trusts, click Copy Trust, click Next, and complete the wizard steps. This example has only a single trust, so click Cancel to exit the Trust Migration Wizard.

Figure 5.43
Verify the downlevel trust between the source and destination domains with the Trust Migration Wizard.

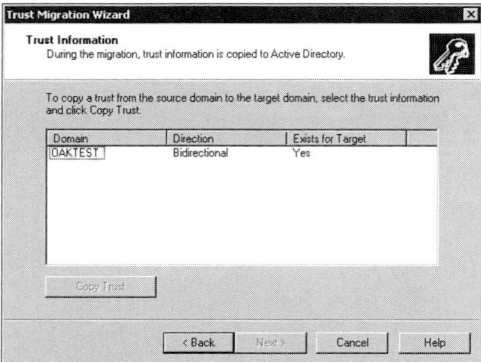

6. Right-click the Active Directory Migration Tool node, and choose Group Migration Wizard to open the Group Account Migration Wizard. Click Next to bypass the Welcome dialog.

7. In the Test or Make Changes dialog, accept the default Test the Migration Settings Now and Migrate Later option to perform the initial dry run (see Figure 5.44).

Figure 5.44
Specify a test of the user and group migration process before creating new user and group entries in AD.

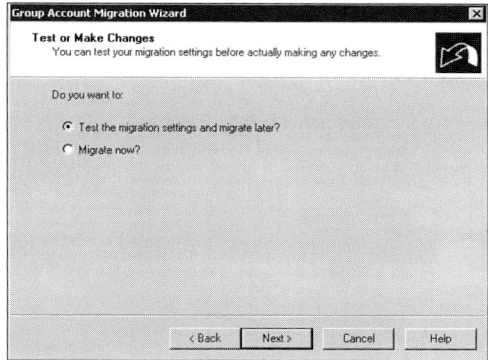

8. In the Domain Selection dialog, select the source (OAKLEAF) and target (OAKTEST) domains from the lists (refer to Figure 5.42), and click Next.
9. In the Group Selection dialog, click Add to open the Select Groups dialog, select the group and its users to migrate (Anthropology for this example), and click Add to add the group name to the list (see Figure 5.45). You can add multiple groups to a single OU by selecting and adding more groups. Click OK to close the dialog and display the group in the Group Selection dialog's Groups list (see Figure 5.46). Click Next.

Figure 5.45
Select the group(s) and their members to migrate to an OU. You can select more than one group, but only one destination OU.

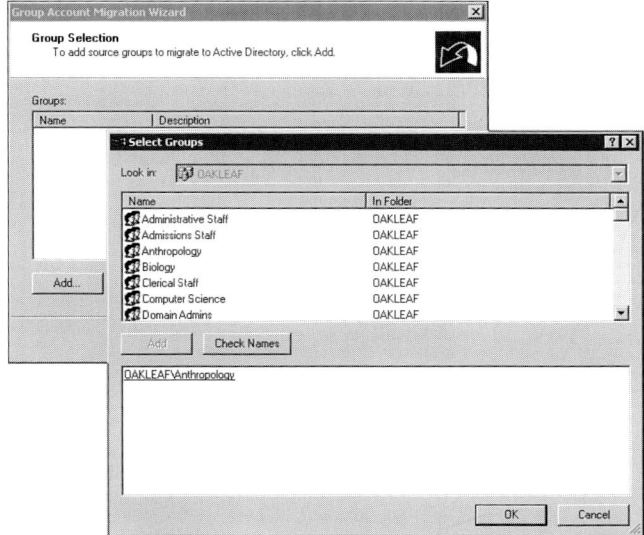

Figure 5.46
The selected source Anthropology security group is added to the wizard's Group Selection dialog.

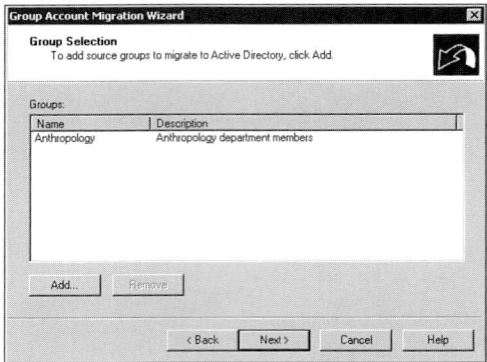

10. In the Organizational Unit Selection dialog, click Browse to open the Select a Target Container dialog, select the OU you added in step 1 (see Figure 5.47), and click OK to add the full LDAP path to the OU—called the ADsPath—to the Target OU text box (see Figure 5.48). Click Next.

Figure 5.47
ADMT requires the full LDAP path to the destination OU for the selected group and its members. Fortunately, you can browse to and select the OU, rather than typing the LDAP path.

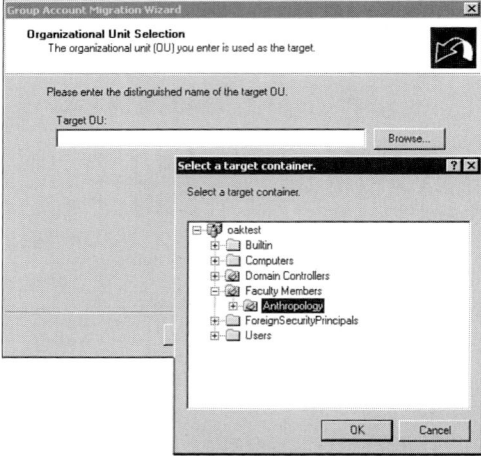

EMULATING DOMAIN MIGRATION WITH THE ACTIVE DIRECTORY MIGRATION TOOL | 241

Figure 5.48
Clicking OK in the Select a Target Container dialog (shown in Figure 5.47) adds the full LDAP `ADsPath` value added to the Target OU text box.

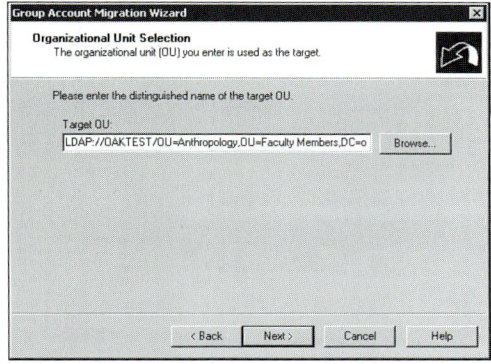

> **Note**
>
> The dialog caption in Figure 5.48 requests that you "enter the distinguished name of the target OU." The wizard actually requires an Active Directory Services Interfaces (ADSI) prefix, `LDAP://DOMAINNAME/`, for the DN of the OU, `OU=Anthropology,OU=Faculty Members,DC=oaktest,DC=edu` for this example.

11. In the Group Options dialog, mark the check boxes for the group elements you want to migrate. The most commonly used options are Update User Rights, Copy Group Members (users), and Migrate Group SIDs to Target Domain (see Figure 5.49). You don't need to be concerned with group name conflicts. Click Next.

Figure 5.49
Set standard group and user migration options in the Group Options dialog. The Copy Group Members option causes user accounts to migrate with their group membership(s) intact.

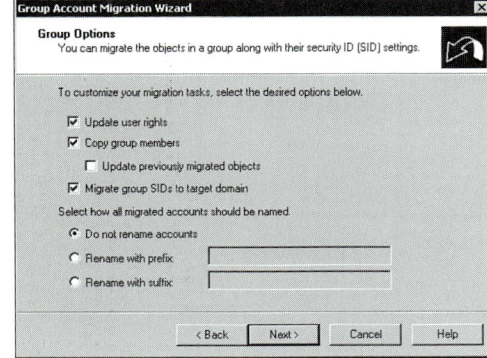

> **Note**
>
> If you don't mark Copy Group Members, the group migrates, but not its user accounts. Migrate Group SIDs generates the SID history for the group. If you mark Update Previously Migrated Objects, existing group objects are overwritten and assigned new SIDs.
>
> The Group Options dialog offers to rename accounts with a prefix or suffix to prevent conflicts with names of existing groups in the domain. This example starts with only the default AD containers and accounts, so naming conflicts aren't a consideration.

PART
I
CH
5

12. The Wizard displays three messages that offer to create the required local group, *DOMAINNAME$$$*, on the source PDC; add a TcpipClientSupport key to the Registry; and reboot the PDC to make the new Registry key effective (see Figure 5.50). Click Yes to accept each offer; if you don't let the wizard perform all three tasks, migration fails.

Figure 5.50
Acknowledge the three messages for adding a special local group and a registry key to enable TCP/IP connectivity to the source SAM, and rebooting the source PDC.

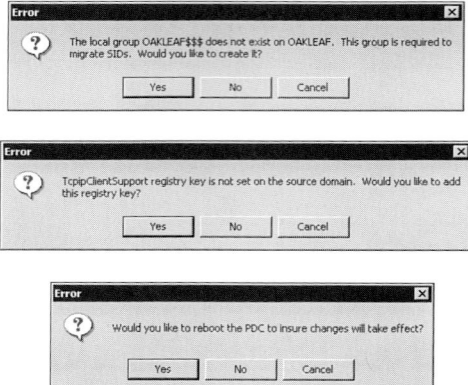

13. In the User Account dialog, type your source domain administrator logon ID and password, and accept the default domain entry (see Figure 5.51). Click Next.

Figure 5.51
Provide your administrator credentials for the source PDC.

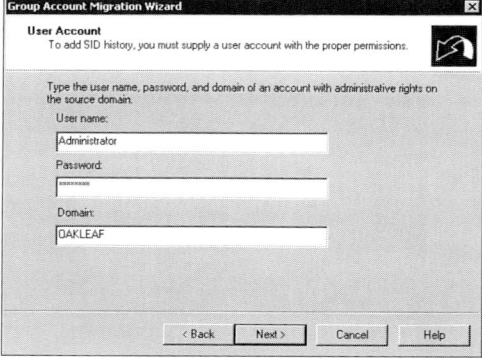

14. In the Naming Conflicts dialog for user accounts, select the Replace Conflicting Accounts option, and mark the Remove Existing User Rights and Remove Existing Members of Groups Being Replaced (see Figure 5.52). Click Next.

Figure 5.52
Specify the actions to take in the event of user account name conflicts.

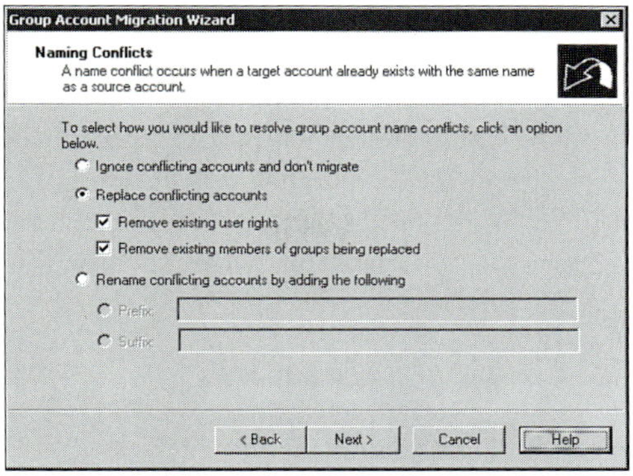

> **Note**
>
> Although the option to resolve group account naming conflicts wasn't selected in step 11, it's a good practice to re-create conflicting user accounts and their SID histories. If you decide to perform multiple migrations, re-creating the user accounts incorporates the latest SID history for the user.

15. In the Group Member Options dialog, select the Set Password to User Name option, unless you want to generate complex (secure) passwords for each user. The wizard doesn't migrate existing user account passwords. Accept the default Leave Both Accounts Active option, so users can log on to either the source or destination domain. If you've enabled roaming profiles for your Windows NT users, and you want the users to obtain profiles from the new domain, mark the Translate Roaming Profiles check box (see Figure 5.53). Click Next.

Figure 5.53
Set the new password type, enable user accounts in both domains, and specify the addition of roaming profiles to the new domain.

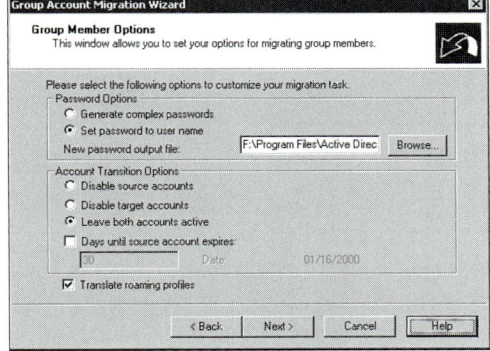

> **Caution**
>
> Make sure that the Leave Both Accounts Active option is selected before running the wizard in Migrate Now mode. If you accidentally set the Disable Source Accounts option, the users you migrate from the Windows NT domain won't be able to log on to their domain.

16. Review your selections in the Completing the Group Account Migration Wizard dialog, which confirms that changes won't be written because you chose to migrate objects later in step 7 (see Figure 5.54). The single object for migration is the group (and its members) you chose in step 8. Click Back repeatedly to make changes to your selections. When your task description is correct, click Finish to emulate the migration process. The Migration Progress dialog displays the number of objects migrated and errors, if they occur, at intervals set by the value (in seconds) in the Refresh Rate text box (see Figure 5.55).

Figure 5.54
Review group and user migration selections in the final wizard dialog before running the test migration.

Figure 5.55
The Migration Progress dialog as it appears about 10% through the process of migrating a group with about 100 user accounts.

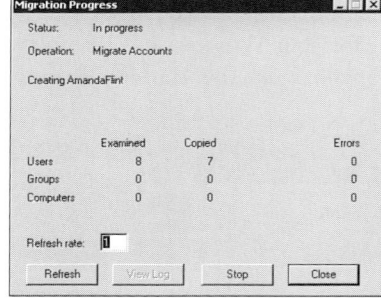

17. When the Migration Progress dialog reports Complete in the Status caption, click the View Log button to display the migration lot in Notepad. The `Account MigrationWriteChanges:No` log entry confirms that group and user accounts weren't written to the destination domain's DC (see Figure 5.56). Scroll the list to view the sequence of tasks the Wizard performs—adding the group, users and their SID histories, roaming profiles, and updating user rights. Finally, click Close in the Migration Progress dialog to exit the Group Migration Wizard.

Figure 5.56
Notepad displays the first 28 lines of the Migration.log file for the user and group migration test.

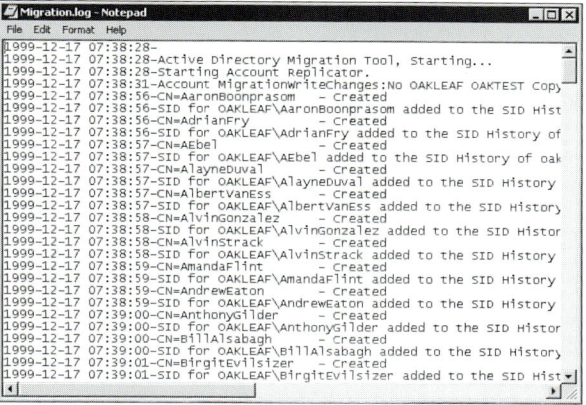

 If you receive error messages during the preceding steps or are unable to migrate accounts, see the "ADMT Refuses to Migrate Users and Groups" topic in the "Troubleshooting" section at the end of the chapter.

The preceding steps create three log files—Migration.log, Passwords.txt, and Trusts.log—in the DC's \Program Files\Active Directory Migration Tool\Logs folder. Only Migration.log and Trusts.log have entries. The Wizard adds entries to Passwords.txt only when you choose the Migrate Now option. You can verify in Active Directory Users and Computers that the wizard didn't create the new OU, group, or user accounts.

Tip from
RJ

Carefully check the Migration.log file after running migration tests and after an actual account migration operation. If you encounter log entries for migration errors, correct the problem(s), which usually occur in the source domain. If you have orphaned Windows NT user accounts (Unknown User), delete them before running a second test.

MIGRATING AN ENTIRE GROUP STRUCTURE

After you've tested migrating a single group and have set up reports for the migration operations, do the following to perform a production-scale migration:

1. Create the OU structure required to accommodate all the groups you intend to migrate.

Tip from
RJ

Create an OU for each group you intend to migrate. It's much easier to merge users into an OU than to separate a large number of users into subgroups that you move to other OUs.

2. Follow the steps in the earlier "Running a Groups and Users Migration Test" section, but select the Migrate now option in the Test or Make Changes dialog. Adding a group with 100 users takes about 8 to 10 minutes on a moderate-performance DC.

> **Tip from**
> *RJ*
>
> Be sure to change the OU name in the Organizational Unit Selection dialog each time you change the group name. The wizard persists your prior settings for all dialogs except the Group Selection and User Account dialogs.

3. Launch Active Directory Users and Computers, if necessary, to verify addition of the group and its users to the designated OU. If Active Directory Users and Computers is open during the migration process, select the domain name node, and choose Action, Refresh to display new user and group entries.

4. Repeat steps 2 and 3 for each source domain group and destination domain OU. The wizard appends log entries for each operation to the Migration.log file.

The preceding process demonstrates migrating global groups, but you also can migrate local groups, such as Administrators or Backup Operators, to the Builtin container. Often, however, it's a better policy to establish a new set of Domain Local user accounts for administration of the new Windows 2000 domain.

Preparing Migration Reports

In addition to log files, ADMT creates summary reports as Web pages. To create a report after running an actual migration, do the following:

1. Right-click the Active Directory Migration Tool node and choose Report Wizard. Click Next to bypass the Welcome dialog.

2. In the Domain Selection dialog, accept the default source and target domains, and click Next.

3. In the Folder Selection Dialog accept the default location for the report .htm files (see Figure 5.57), and click Next.

Figure 5.57
Specify the folder to hold the report pages for the migration. Report files you created prior to running the Report Wizard are located in the default \Program Files\Active Directory Migration Tool\Reports folder.

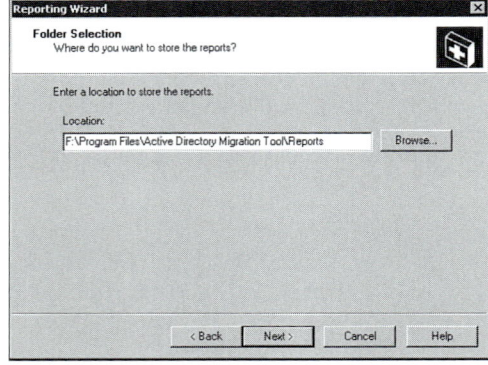

Emulating Domain Migration with the Active Directory Migration Tool   247

Tip from
RJ

> Specify individually named folders to hold the report files for each domain you migrate. If you have a large number of users in multiple domains, the reports can become quite lengthy.

4. In the Report Selection dialog, select the reports you want to create. For this example, select the Migrated User Accounts and Migrated Computer Accounts reports (see Figure 5.58). The Account References report associates computer names with user account IDs, where applicable. Click Next.

Figure 5.58
The most common initial report selection is reports for user and computer account migration.

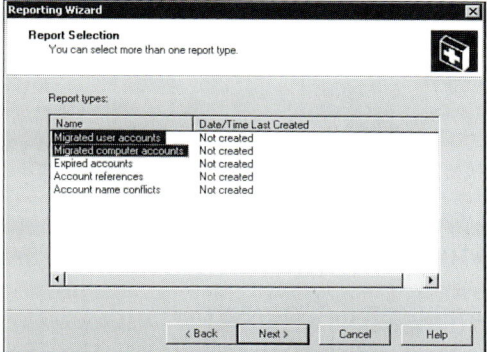

5. Review your selections in the Completing the Reporting Wizard dialog and click Finish to prepare the reports. If you haven't migrated users or computers, the reports are empty.

The wizard adds a subnode to the Reports node for each report you specified in step 4. Double-clicking the Reports subnode opens an empty report with table headers. Figure 5.59 shows the format of the Migrated User and Group Accounts report with the first few records for the accounts migrated in the preceding section.

Part I
Ch 5

Figure 5.59
The Migrated Computer Accounts report appears as shown here after migrating a few groups and their users into OUs.

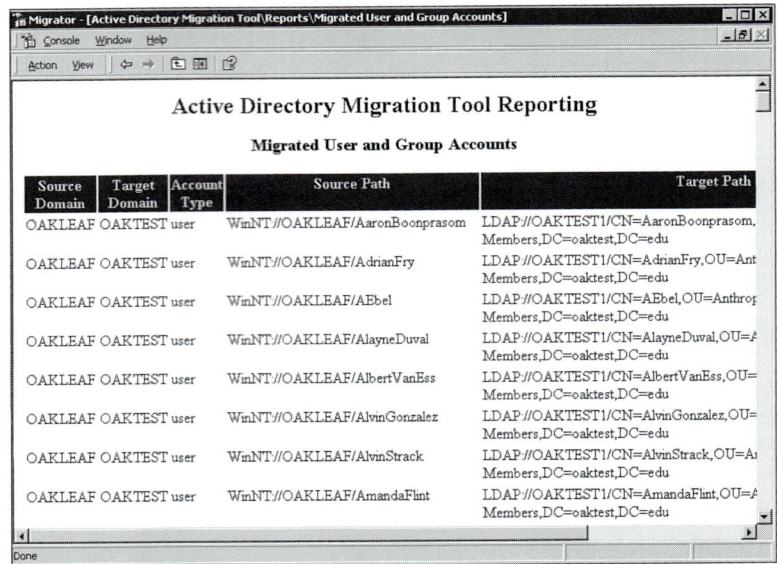

MIGRATING WINDOWS NT COMPUTER ACCOUNTS

ADMT automates migration of computer accounts to the new Windows 2000 domain, which eliminates the need for users or administrators to authorize the creation of new Windows 2000 computer accounts. You can migrate selected sets of computers into OUs or place all computer accounts in the Computers container. You can't migrate accounts for Windows NT PDCs and BDCs.

To migrate computer accounts, do the following:

1. Right-click the Active Directory Migration Tool node and choose Computer Migration Wizard. Click Next to bypass the Welcome dialog.

2. In the Test or Make Changes dialog, select Make Changes if you're ready to migrate accounts.

3. In the Domain Selection dialog, accept the default source and target domains, and click Next.

4. In the Computer Selection dialog, click Add, and select the computer accounts to migrate from the Select Computer dialog's list (see Figure 5.60).

Emulating Domain Migration with the Active Directory Migration Tool | 249

Figure 5.60
Select computer accounts without trailing dollar signs for processing by ADMT's Computer Migration Wizard.

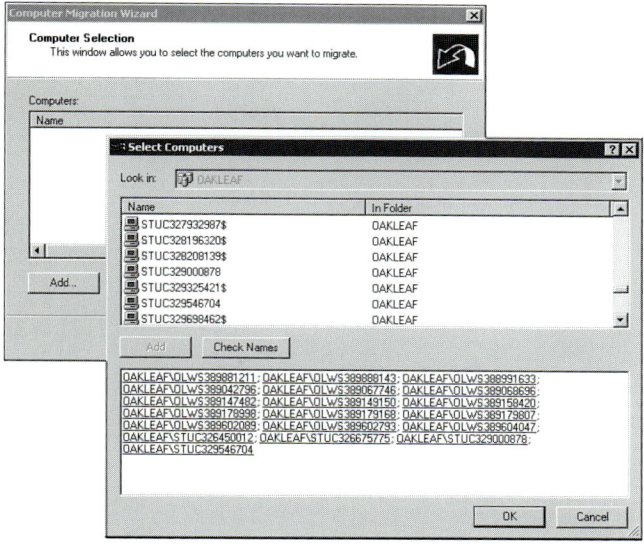

> **Note**
> Computer accounts with trailing dollar signs—such as STUC327932987$—emulate legacy accounts created by Windows 3.51 and earlier. According to the online help files, the first version of ADMT doesn't handle migrating such accounts correctly.

5. Click OK to close the Select Computer dialog and add the selected computer accounts to the Computer list (see Figure 5.61). Click Next.

Figure 5.61
The Computer Migration Wizard displays a typical set of Windows NT or 2000 computer accounts to migrate to the destination domain.

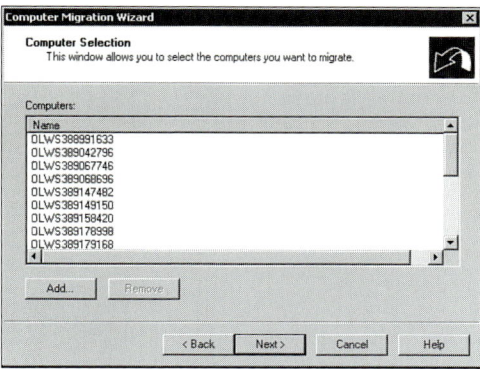

6. In the Organizational Unit Selection dialog, click Browse and, in the Select a Target Container dialog, select the container or OU to hold the computer accounts. Click OK to close the dialog. For this example, the Computers container holds the accounts (see Figure 5.62). Click Next.

Figure 5.62
Specify the default Computers container or a previously created OU to hold the migrated computer accounts.

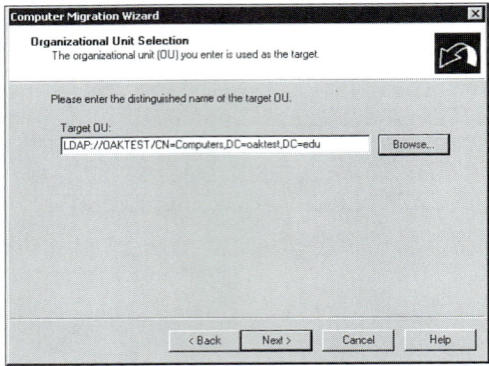

Tip from
RJ

If you plan to move computer accounts into OUs, it's a good practice to create a nested OU to hold the entries. Doing so prevents computer accounts from mixing with the user and group accounts.

---

7. If the computers you're migrating share resources, mark in the Translate Objects dialog the check boxes for the type of objects whose security descriptors you need to modify. In most cases, the safest approach is to mark all objects for translation (see Figure 5.63). Click Next.

Figure 5.63
Set the types of objects for which to add or modify security descriptors in the Translate Objects dialog. Unless you have a particular reason to do so, mark the check boxes for all objects.

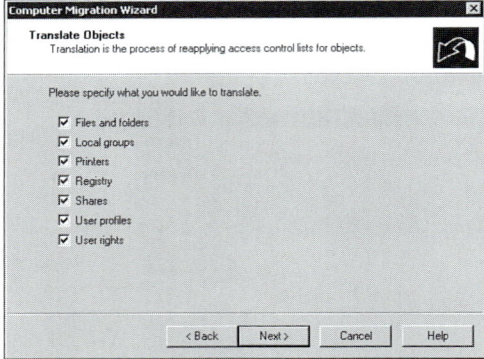

8. In the Security Translation Options dialog, mark the Add option to supplement, rather than replace or remove, the security descriptors for the objects you selected in the preceding step (see Figure 5.64). The Add option lets users and groups in both domains retain their permissions for the objects. Click Next.

Figure 5.64
Specify the addition of resource security descriptors for user and group accounts in the destination domain. Addition preserves user rights in the source domain.

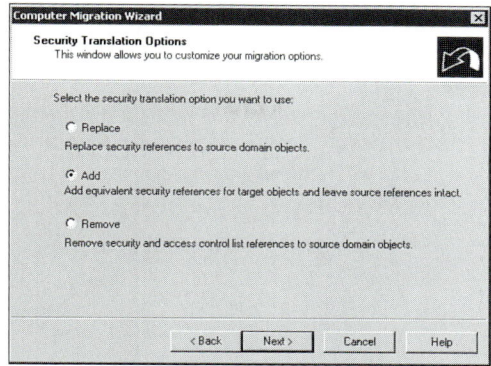

9. In the User Account dialog, type your administrator credentials in the source domain, accept the default domain entry, and click Next.

10. In the Computer Options dialog, set the elapsed time (in minutes) before dispatching the agents and restarting the specified computers with the new account information (see Figure 5.65). You also can rename computer accounts with a prefix or suffix. Click Next.

Figure 5.65
Set the period between the time you dispatch the computer account agents and the occurrence of an unattended computer reboot.

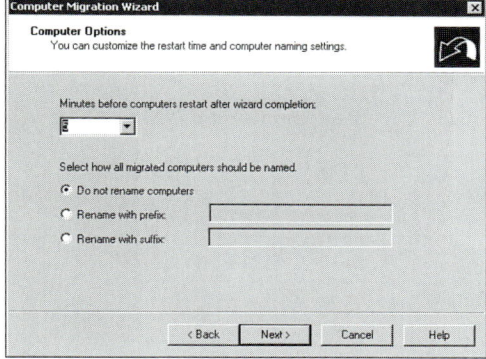

Tip from
RJ

Be sure to warn users in advance that their Windows NT workstations and, if selected, file and printer servers will perform an unattended reboot. The computers must be online and you must have Administrator privileges for each migrated computer the agent is to reboot.

11. In the Naming Conflicts dialog, accept the default Replace Conflicting Accounts option and Remove Existing User Rights. Removing existing user rights assures that the latest set of rights applies to the account (see Figure 5.66). Click Next.

Figure 5.66
Select the option to replace existing conflicting computer accounts with updated account parameters. This option is applicable only to subsequent operations on the same set of computers you move with the Computer Migration Wizard.

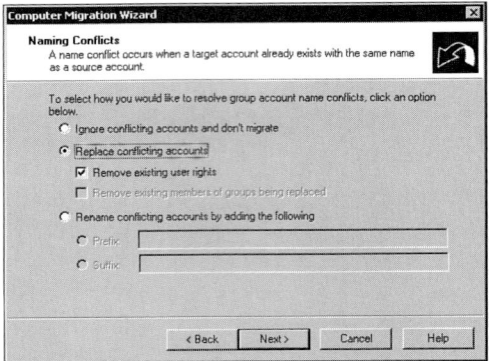

12. In the Completing the Computer Migration Wizard, review your selections and make any necessary corrections (see Figure 5.67). Click Finish to open the Migration Properties dialog and perform the initial migration steps.

Figure 5.67
The Completing the Computer Migration Wizard dialog shows a summary of the computer migration options you selected in the preceding steps.

13. Click Close to dispatch the agents to each computer you selected. After a few minutes, the Active Directory Migration Tool Agent Monitor dialog opens. If the computers aren't accessible on the network, the agent reports Install Failed in the Server List page. Click Close.

Figure 5.68
This is a list of computers for which the Computer Migration Wizard attempted to install the agent for updating account information, but failed.

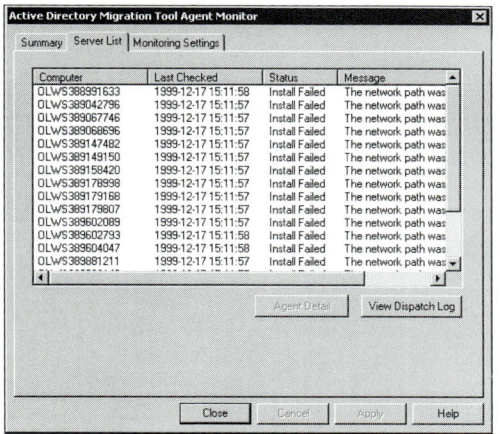

> **Tip from**
> *RJ*
>
> Use the Retry Task Wizard to rerun agents for computers that were offline during the initial computer migration step. None of the computers shown in Figure 5.68 were online when the wizard attempted to install the agent and reboot them. Ordinarily, you should make sure that all or at least most of the computers to migrate are online when you run the Computer Migration Wizard. When the missing computers are online, right-click the Active Directory Migration Tool node and select Retry Task Wizard. Click Next to display a list of uncompleted tasks. Select each computer to retry, and click Skip/Include to change the status to Include, and complete the wizard's steps.

After completion of the Computer Migration Wizard's operations, you can generate a report of those computers that you attempted to migrate. Empty entries in the Source Path column indicate computers not migrated.

UPDATING SERVICE ACCOUNTS

As an optional step, you can migrate source domain service accounts to the destination domain by running the Service Account Migration Wizard. You need only run the Service Account Migration Wizard if services in the source domain run under accounts other than Administrator or accounts already migrated. The wizard dispatches an agent to the domain controllers you specify, collects the service account list, and determines what accounts can be migrated. You must then employ the User and Group Migration Wizard to migrate the newly included accounts to the destination domain.

To prepare a list of service accounts to include in user and group migration, do the following:

1. Right-click the Active Directory Migration Tool node and choose Service Account Migration Wizard. Click Next to bypass the Welcome dialog.

2. In the Domain Selection dialog, accept the default source and target domains, and click Next.

3. In the Update Information dialog, accept the default Yes, Update the Information if you want to include service accounts when you next run the User and Group Migration Wizard. Click Next.
4. In the Service Account Selection dialog, click Add and specify the servers on which the services run—OAKLEAF0 (a BDC) and OAKLEAF1 (a PDC) for this example (see Figure 5.69). Click Next.

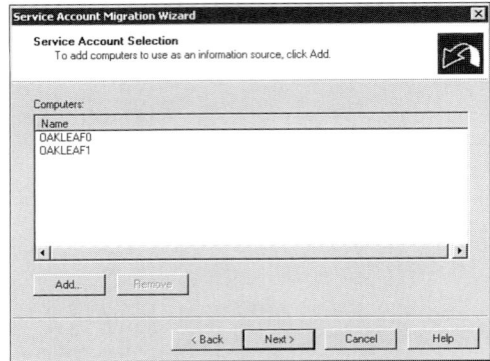

Figure 5.69
Specify the servers running the services for account migration, in this case a PDC and BDC. Only the service accounts on the PDC migrate.

5. In the User Account dialog, type your administrator credentials, and click Next.
6. After dispatching the agents, the wizard reports those accounts that it can include for migration and those that it can't presently update (see Figure 5.70). Click Next and then Finish to exit the wizard.

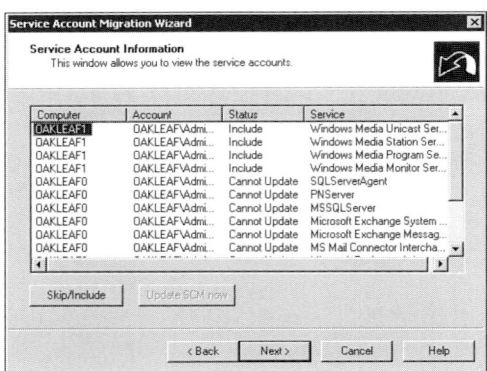

Figure 5.70
The Service Account Migration Wizard displays a list of services whose accounts are to be included in the User and Group Migration Wizard's next run and services that the Wizard can't update.

The wizard doesn't include services on PDCs or member servers that run under the Administrator or other accounts in the Administrators group. The wizard is capable of updating the service account on the PDC (OAKLEAF1), but not those on the OAKLEAF domain's PDC (OAKLEAF0).

Exploring Other ADMT Features

ADMT offers several other wizards that you might want to use in case you make an error in the migration process or encounter problems with migrated objects. Following are brief descriptions—in order of their context menu choices—of the functions of the wizards not covered in the previous sections:

- The User Account Migration Wizard lets you add individual user accounts to an OU, independently of their group membership. Use this wizard only if you don't plan to move user accounts into OUs based on group membership.

- The Security Translation Wizard lets you modify the ACLs of resources provided by computers you've migrated to Active Directory. You need to use this wizard only if you didn't correctly specify the resources to modify in step 8 of the earlier "Migrating Windows NT Computer Accounts" section.

- The Exchange Directory Migration Wizard, mentioned earlier in the chapter, modifies Exchange 5.5 mailbox security for migrated users. Use of this wizard is beyond the scope of the book.

- The Retry Tasks Wizard, mentioned in a tip in the "Migrating Windows NT Computer Accounts" section, maintains a list of objects that failed to migrate, and lets you reattempt the migration process.

- The Undo Wizard lets you reverse the last migration operation you performed. The Undo Wizard context menu choice is enabled only if the operation is reversible. Most ADMT operations, such as migrating groups and accounts, aren't reversible.

- The Group Mapping and Merging Wizard lets you move users from group(s) you specify into a new source domain group that the wizard creates (mapping) or into an existing group (merging). This wizard is intended to restructure your Windows NT domain prior to migration, which is one of the subjects of the next chapter—"Preparing NT 4.0 for Windows 2000 Server Migration."

The Active Directory Migration Tool is by far the most useful support tool that Microsoft offers to Windows 2000 Server administrators. Don't even *think* about performing an in-place upgrade or domain restructure in a Windows NT 4.0 production environment until you've become adept at using ADMT in emulated upgrade scenarios.

Troubleshooting

Hardware Faults During Upgrade

Hardware-based error messages appear during upgrade from Windows NT 4.0 to Windows 2000 Server.

The "usual suspects" that cause upgrade problems are NICs, older SCSI adapters, out-of-date BIOSes, and ancient or exotic graphics adapters. In particular, make sure your servers' NICs appear as tested in the HCL. Other components you take for granted, however, can lead to failed upgrades. For example, even fairly recent 12X CD-ROM drives that work fine under Windows NT 4.0 throw "Can't copy CDROM installer" or similar errors during upgrade. Such errors, which occurred during the writing of this chapter, are fatal.

If you encounter this error or the inability to extract Storprop.dll or other DLLs from a .cab file during an upgrade, power down the computer; don't attempt to cancel the upgrade. If you continue with the upgrade, it's a sure bet that you'll encounter problems with upgrading NIC and other specialized drivers. Replace the CD-ROM drive with an HCL-compliant device and restart the upgrade from scratch with the boot diskettes.

Replacing the CD-ROM drive with an HCL-compliant unit and continuing the original upgrade doesn't work. The Plug and Play Service fails to find a driver for the CD-ROM drive, and drivers for HCL-compliant NICs install but don't work. Attempts to install NIC drivers fail with "invalid data" messages.

ADSI25 Setup Problems

Automation error message appears when creating computer accounts under Windows 2000 or Exchange mailboxes under Windows NT 4.0.

ADSI25's Setup.exe failed to register Adssecurity.dll, which is required to associate computer accounts and mailboxes with user accounts.

The expected d:\Shared folder, subfolders, and Ad25test.txt test files are missing on the child DC.

You forgot to share the root or another folder of the child DC and map the share to a logical drive on the parent DC before clicking the Create OakLeaf Groups button of ADSI25's main form. ADSI25 doesn't throw an error if it can't create the \Shared folder and its subfolders.

Clients Are Unable to Log on to an Existing Computer Account

An "Account exists" message appears when you attempt to move a Windows 2000 client to a new domain and change its computer name to an existing account.

If you're using a test client that already has a computer account in another domain, you can't use the Network Identification Wizard or the Identification Changes dialog to change the client's computer name to another preexisting computer account and change the domain name simultaneously. You first must change the computer name, specify a temporary workgroup name, such as **WORKGROUP**, and reboot the computer. Then move the client from the temporary workgroup to the new domain in the Identification Changes dialog. You must provide a Domain Admins account name and password to join the new domain, and reboot the client a second time.

Child Domain Creation Problems

When installing the child domain, installation fails after specifying the parent and child domain names.

You didn't select the No, Just Install and Configure DNS on This Server option when installing AD for the parent domain, or the DNS Server Service failed to start. Verify that DNS is configured on the parent DC with at least a Forward Lookup Zone by running the DNS administrative tool. If the Forward Lookup Zone is missing, run the New Zone Wizard to create the zone.

If DNS is configured, launch the Computer Management administrative tool, expand the Applications and Services node, click the Services node, and check the status of the DNS Server service. If the DNS Server service is stopped, right-click its entry and choose Start. If the DNS Server startup mode is Manual or Disabled, change it to Automatic.

ADMT Refuses to Migrate Users and Groups

Error messages relating to a missing local group, Registry entry, or auditing occur during attempts to migrate user and group accounts.

The most common cause of migration failure is a missing local group, *DOMAIN-NAME*$$$—OAKLEAF$$$ for this example—on the source PDC. Ordinarily, ADMT automatically creates this group during the first test or production migration. Launch User Manager and verify that the required local group is present. If not, create the local group.

Running ADMT requires enabling TCP/IP updates to the Local Security Authority (LSA) by adding a special Registry key named `TcpipClientSupport` with a value of 1 to the source PDC's Registry. Like the local auditing account, ADMT ordinarily adds this key for you and reboots the server remotely. Use the Registry Editor (RegEdit.exe) to find this key on the source PDC. If it's missing, add the following key:

`HKEY_LOCAL_MACHINE\System\CurrentControlSet\Control\Lsa\TcpipClientSupport`

and set its Dword value to 1. Reboot the server after adding the Registry key.

Failure to enable auditing of account management events on either the source PDC or the destination DC also causes migration to fail. Verify that you completed steps 5 and 8 in the "Installing ADMT on a Windows 2000 Domain Controller" section of this chapter.

MCSE Corner: Choosing and Testing Migration Strategies

The process for upgrading from Windows NT 4.0 to Microsoft Windows 2000 is important to know for two exams: 70-215, "Installing, Configuring, and Administering Microsoft Windows 2000 Server," and 70-222, "Upgrading from Microsoft Windows NT 4.0 to Microsoft Windows 2000."

70-215   Installing, Configuring, and Administering Microsoft Windows 2000 Server

This exam tests your ability to upgrade a server from Windows NT Server 4.0 to Windows 2000 Server. The upgrade-related questions on this exam probably are light on the domain controller upgrade process and focus more on the general operating system upgrade.

You should be familiar with the section of this chapter regarding developing a migration plan, as well as a historical perspective on Windows NT upgrades. These sections help by giving you the background knowledge to prepare you for the upgrade process. You should also know the process for upgrading a single domain and upgrading domain controllers, but the use of the ADSI25 utility is not tested.

The section on troubleshooting hardware faults during upgrade is very important, because troubleshooting is always a likely topic on this exam. You should be able to recover from errors encountered during the operating system upgrade process.

70-222   Upgrading from Microsoft Windows NT 4.0 to Microsoft Windows 2000

This exam focuses more on the planning and execution of domain and multidomain upgrades than the 70-215 exam. It is important to be familiar with all the topics covered in this chapter (although the ADSI25 utility is not tested.)

You must be able to plan the upgrade of an entire enterprise Windows NT 4.0 network to Windows 2000, single or multidomain. You should be familiar with the single-domain upgrade process, including switching from mixed mode to native mode. You should also be familiar with how the upgrade process switches domain controllers from the traditional Windows NT 4.0 architecture to Active Directory, and the use of organizational units (OUs) to structure user accounts. You should also be able to optimize the migrated security groups through nesting and delegation of control.

Multidomain upgrade planning and implementation are also tested. You should be familiar with the process for upgrading domains and adding them to the forest as parent and child domains. For this exam, it is important to have a good grip on troubleshooting, both during the operating system upgrade and during child domain creation.

CHAPTER 6

PREPARING NT 4.0 FOR WINDOWS 2000 SERVER MIGRATION

In this chapter

Getting Ready for Windows 2000 Server   260

Moving from NetBEUI to TCP/IP   261

Automating Client TCP/IP Settings with DHCP   267

Enabling NetBIOS Name Resolution with WINS   272

Providing DNS Name Resolution   275

Adding Fixed DNS and WINS Addresses to Servers   282

Migrating Client PCs to DHCP, WINS, and DNS   284

Cleaning Up User and Group Accounts   287

Troubleshooting   293

MCSE Corner: Preparing NT 4.0 for Windows 2000 Server Migration   295

Getting Ready for Windows 2000 Server

Your migration schedule for Windows 2000 Server may be several Service Packs (SPs) down the road, but preparing your Windows NT network for the eventual upgrade should be one of your top administrative priorities. This chapter assumes that you're familiar with Windows NT 4.0's basic administrative tools and network management duties. If you're not upgrading an existing Windows NT network, skip to the next chapter, "Specifying Server and Data Storage Hardware."

Following are the basic guidelines to making your current Windows NT 4.0 network Windows 2000-ready:

- Install the latest Windows NT 4.0 SP—first on servers, then on client workstations running Windows NT. SP6 was current when this book was written. You can obtain the latest SP on CD-ROM or by download from http://www.microsoft.com/ntserver/.
- Move servers and clients to TCP/IP if your network currently runs only the NetBIOS Extended User Interface (NetBEUI) protocol. NetBIOS is an abbreviation for Network Basic Input/Output System; NetBIOS is NetBEUI's programming interface. Phase out NetBEUI after you've upgraded all network clients to TCP/IP.

> **Tip from**
> *RJ*
>
> You can update to TCP/IP mobile clients who connect via Remote Access Service (RAS) dialup to RAS Servers after your upgrade to Windows 2000, if you want. Windows 2000 supports NetBEUI over dialup RAS connection.

- Set up the Dynamic Host Control Protocol (DHCP) service to assign IP addresses, subnet masks, and the default gateway address to client PCs automatically. Using DHCP instead of fixed IP addresses for client PCs greatly reduces workstation setup problems and subsequent network-related help desk issues.
- Install and configure the Domain Name Service (DNS) Server service to resolve Internet-style DNS names for network hosts (computers). When you migrate to Windows 2000, DNS upgrades to Dynamic DNS (DDNS), which greatly simplifies DNS management in enterprise-scale operations.
- Use Windows Internet Naming Service (WINS) to resolve NetBIOS names to IP addresses. Windows 2000 requires DNS for server name resolution, but downlevel (pre-Windows 2000) servers and clients need WINS for NetBIOS name resolution in routed networks. WINS integrates with Microsoft DNS Server and DHCP.
- Remove unneeded and unknown user accounts from the SAM database with User Manager for Domains or the batch files described later in this chapter. Unused accounts tend to accumulate over time as a result of personnel turnover, temporary account assignments, and the like.
- Delete obsolete and disabled workstation accounts with Server Manager.
- Review membership of all current local and global groups, and remove duplicate or unneeded user accounts, especially from the Domain Admins group. Consolidate global groups that contain many duplicate users. When consolidating Windows NT global

groups, bear in mind that Windows 2000 Server lets you nest Global groups when you ultimately move to native mode.

- Restructure global groups as necessary to parallel the Organizational Unit (OU) hierarchy of your Active Directory (AD) topology. Base your Windows NT group structure and membership on the lowest level of the OU hierarchy, so you can take advantage of the User, Group Membership custom LDAP filter to move user accounts to the appropriate OUs.

→ To review the process for moving user accounts to OUs based on their group membership, **see** "Using Custom Filters to Classify Users by Group Membership," **p. 212**.

This chapter deals primarily with setting up TCP/IP, DHCP, WINS, and DNS on Windows NT 4.0 servers in preparation for an upgrade to Windows 2000 Server. Installing Windows 2000 Server on a Windows NT 4.0 Primary Domain Controller (PDC) upgrades DHCP, WINS, and DNS servers. If you need more help with Windows NT's TCP/IP configuration than this chapter offers, consider acquiring *Special Edition Using Windows NT Server 4*, Second Edition (Que, ISBN 0-7897-1388-8).

MOVING FROM NETBEUI TO TCP/IP

You can successfully run a small Windows NT network without TCP/IP, DHCP, WINS, DNS, and user policies. There are many single-location Windows NT networks in use today that continue to employ only the NetBEUI protocol. NetBEUI is fast, easy to set up, and very simple to administer. Windows for Workgroups 3.11, which is still a common Windows client operating system for many small companies, ordinarily uses NetBEUI to support basic networking features.

> **Tip from**
> *RJ*
>
> If your TCP/IP network must support Windows for Workgroups (WfW) 3.11 clients, download version 3.11b of the TCP/IP-32 upgrade for WfW from http://www.microsoft.com. At the Microsoft home page, click Support and Choose Knowledge Base to open the Knowledge Base search page. Select Windows 3.1x in the My Search Is About list, type **tcpupdate** in the My Question Is text box, and click Go to return links to TCP/IP-32 3.11b pages. Read the Update.txt page, and then go to the How to Obtain TCP/IP-32 3.11b for Windows for Workgroups page to download Tcp32b.exe, which was last updated in July 1995. Run Tcp32b.exe on each WfW client to enable TCP/IP connectivity.

The relatively low licensing cost and quick installation of Windows NT running NetBEUI, compared with Novell's NetWare and its IPX/SPX protocol, has made it a favorite of storefront "networking consultants." The primary limitation of NetBEUI is that it's not a routable protocol, which restricts its common use to workgroup environments with 25 to 50 clients at most.

> **Note**
>
> Microsoft states that NetBEUI "is usually used in small, department-size, local area networks of 1 to 200 clients." Few, if any, networks having close to 200 clients currently run NetBEUI.

Windows 2000 Server, on the other hand, relegates NetBEUI to servicing clients that dial in to remote access servers through a NetBIOS gateway. Windows 2000 Server can't use NetBEUI as the sole network protocol, because NetBEUI only understands node—not network—addresses and recognizes only NetBIOS—not DNS—names. Windows 2000 Server requires the TCP/IP protocol to support DNS and WINS to handle NetBIOS name resolution for downlevel servers and clients on routed networks. Although few administrators will be upgrading a Windows NT 3.51 or 4.0 network that runs only NetBEUI, the rules of computer book completeness, however, dictate coverage of the subject.

> **Tip from**
> *RJ*
>
> You can't upgrade Windows NT 3.1 or 3.5 servers to Windows 2000. If you encounter servers running these first two Windows NT versions, you must upgrade them to versions 3.51 or 4.0. Windows NT 3.51's TCP/IP implementation left much to be desired, so an interim upgrade from 3.51 to 4.0 saves aggravation. Apply the latest SP to all servers and thoroughly test network connectivity before adding the TCP/IP protocol, DHCP, WINS, and DNS. Immediately apply the SP again to update the added files. The examples of this chapter are based on SP5.

CHOOSING INTERNAL IP ADDRESSES

NetBEUI networks can't connect to the Internet, so you have a virtually unlimited choice of internal IP addresses to assign to servers and clients. It's a good practice, however, to use the reserved Class A IP address, 10, as the first octet of your internal network's TCP/IP address. No public Internet addresses begin with 10, so you can use the entire Class A IP address range of 10.0.0.0 through 10.254.254.254. Taking advantage of a subset of the reserved set of internal IP addresses, such as the 10.7.x.1 through 10.7.x.254 Class C addresses used in many of this book's examples, prevents potential conflicts and security problems if you later decide to provide client PCs with direct, rather than dialup, Internet connectivity. Windows 2000's Network Address Translation (NAT) capability or a firewall with NAT handles traffic between the public Internet and your internal network.

→ To learn more about Windows 2000 Server's NAT feature, **see** "Taking Advantage of Network Address Translation (NAT)," **p. 1056**.

> **Note**
>
> The Internet Engineering Taskforce (IETF) Request for Comment (RFC) 1597 defines two other private network addresses that aren't available on the public Internet. The 172.16.0.0 network reserves a block of 16 Class B addresses from 172.16.0.1 to 172.31.255.254. The 192.168.0.0 network provides 256 private Class C addresses in the range of 192.168.0.1 to 192.168.255.254. Most administrators use the 10.0.0.0 network for internal addressing.

A Class B IP address provides a total of 65,534 host (computer) addresses, which is likely to satisfy the future expansion requirements of any current NetBEUI network. You can choose any number from 1 to 255 to specify your Class B address; the examples in this chapter use 7, so 10.7.0.0 identifies the network. A Class B IP address uses a subnet mask of 255.255.0.0.

→ For a review of IP address conventions and capabilities **see** "Decoding and Assigning IP Addresses," **p. 64**.

> **Note**
>
> IP addresses whose first octet has a value of 1 through 126 are Class A addresses and have a default subnet mask of 255.0.0.0. By specifying a subnet mask of 255.255.0.0, you subnet the Class A address to Class B. If your network grows beyond 65,000 hosts, you can add more subnets.

Establish a plan for assigning individual IP addresses to servers and clients. A logical approach is to dedicate 253 addresses for servers starting with 10.7.1.2 for the Primary Domain Controller (PDC) and continuing with 10.7.1.3 and higher for Backup Domain Controllers (BDCs) and member servers. You then use DHCP to assign the first 254 clients addresses in the 10.7.2.0 network. As you add more clients or locations, you can add Class C addresses for 10.7.3.0, 10.7.4.0, and higher networks.

> **Tip from**
> *RJ*
>
> Reserve the first address of a subnet (1 in the last octet) for the default gateway (router) address, if you plan to route your network in the future. Assigning the router as the first IP address of a subnet isn't a requirement, but it's a common practice. If you specify a Class B subnet mask (255.255.0.0) for your clients, you don't need routers. When you install routers to create subnets, you change the client's subnet mask to Class C, and specify the router's address as the default gateway.

If you've decided to connect your internal Windows 2000 network directly to the Internet—a chancy proposition at best for a small organization—your Internet Service Provider (ISP) assigns you a block of IP addresses. The size of the block, usually 254 or fewer usable addresses (all or part of a Class C IP address), determines your network's subnet mask. You or your ISP then register an Internet DNS name for one of the addresses. Your Internet DNS name is unlikely to correspond to your current Windows NT domain name because someone else probably has claimed it.

> **Note**
>
> The oakmusic.com domain name used in this chapter's examples is registered with InterNIC and has a single assigned IP address of 209.249.8.35. Use of the 10.7.0.0 network address for the oakmusic.com domain is for illustrative purposes only.

ADDING THE TCP/IP PROTOCOL AND RELATED SERVICES TO A NETBEUI-ONLY SERVER

Setting up TCP/IP and related services takes less than 30 minutes, and requires two server reboots. The server is offline only during the reboot process, and adding TCP/IP and other services doesn't affect NetBEUI connectivity to BDCs, member servers, and clients. BDCs normally handle client logons, so only client access to services and shares on the PDC are affected during the installation.

To install TCP/IP and related IP-based services, do the following:

1. Launch Control Panel's Network tool and click the Protocols tab.

2. Click Add to open the Select Network Protocol dialog and select TCP/IP in the Network Protocols list (see Figure 6.1).

Figure 6.1
TCP/IP protocol is installed on a system that has only the NetBEUI protocol installed.

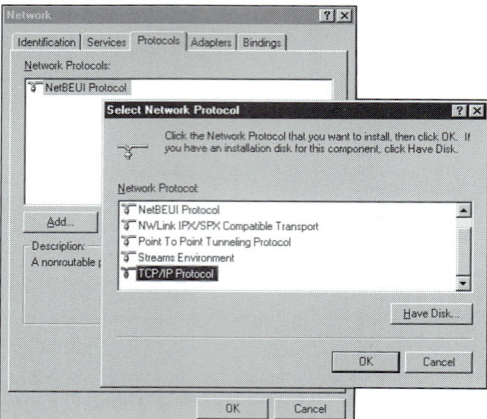

3. Click OK and click No when the TCP/IP Setup message asks if you want to use a DHCP server to assign the server's network address.

Tip from
RJ

Don't use DHCP to assign IP addresses to servers. Servers require a fixed IP address to install the DHCP Server service. Even if you don't install DHCP, using DHCP to assign server addresses is very unwise. If a server loses its lease on a DHCP-assigned IP address and receives a new address, clients and other servers that depend on reaching the server by the original IP address won't be able to connect.

4. Insert the Windows NT 4.0 distribution CD-ROM, verify the CD-ROM drive letter assignment, and click OK when requested by the Windows NT Setup input box.

   Setup installs the required files to your system partition and adds TCP/IP Protocol to the Network Protocols list.

5. Click OK in the Network dialog to start the Bindings Review process and open the Microsoft TCP/IP Properties dialog.

6. With the default Specify an IP Address option selected, type the IP address for the server in the IP Address text box. Use the right-arrow key to move from octet to octet.

7. If you use the preceding section's recommended IP addresses, accept the default `255.255.0.0` as the Subnet Mask for Class B network addresses (see Figure 6.2). If `255.0.0.0` appears as the default, change the mask value. Click Apply to store the settings.

   NetBEUI networks don't support routers, so leave the Default Gateway's IP address text box empty until you install a router.

Figure 6.2
When the new protocol is installed and you click OK on the Network properties page, assign a server address and subnet mask to the TCP/IP protocol.

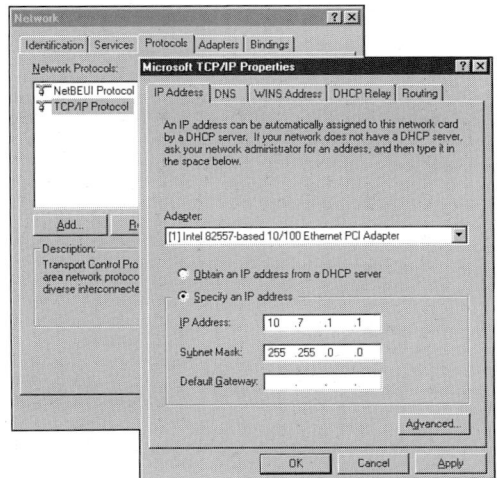

8. Click the Services tab and click Add to open the Select Network Service dialog.
9. Select Microsoft DHCP Server in the Network Service list (see Figure 6.3) and click OK.

Figure 6.3
Click Add on the Network dialog's Services page and select Microsoft DHCP Server to add the DHCP service.

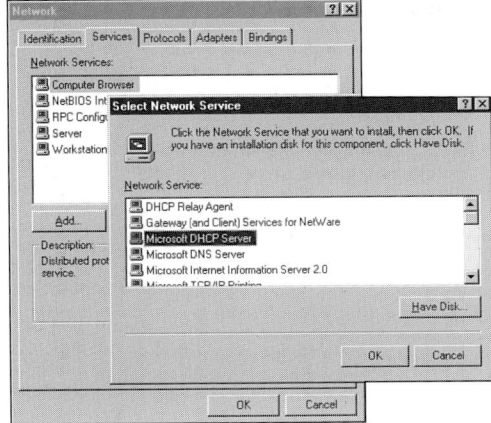

10. Click Continue in the Windows NT Setup input box to copy the required files from the CD-ROM.
11. Click OK when notified that you must assign a static IP address for the DHCP server.
12. Repeat steps 9 and 10 for the Microsoft DNS Service and Windows Internet Naming Service.
13. Click OK to close the Network tool, and click Yes to reboot your computer to start TCP/IP and the new services.

14. If you added the DHCP Relay Service, an Error message appears asking if you want to specify the IP address of the DHCP server. Click Yes to reopen the Network tool, click the DHCP Relay tab, click Add to open the DHCP Relay Agent dialog, type your server's TCP/IP address in the text box (see Figure 6.4), click Add, and then click OK and Yes to reboot the server.

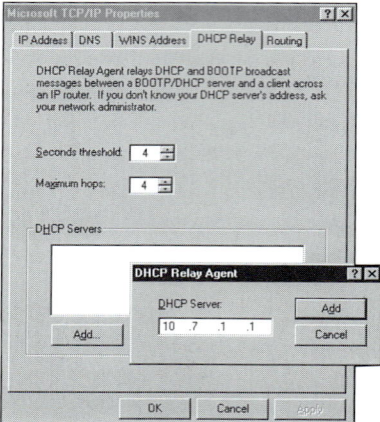

Figure 6.4
From the DCHP Relay page of the TCP/IP properties dialog, you set the addresses of DHCP servers on your network so that a multihomed server can forward DHCP requests.

15. Apply the latest Windows NT 4.0 SP to update the services you installed. You must reboot the server after installing the SP.

Check client connectivity to the PDC's resources immediately after the preceding process. Adding TCP/IP shouldn't affect NetBEUI operations, but Murphy's Law—Anything That Can Go Wrong Will Go Wrong—applies even to the simplest of networks.

Upgrading BDCs and Testing IP Connectivity

After adding TCP/IP services to the PDC, upgrade BDCs and member servers, if any, to TCP/IP following the procedure described in the preceding section. Prepare at least one Backup Domain Controller (BDC) to become a secondary WINS and DNS server, which backs up these services on the PDC. Installing the DHCP Relay Agent service on BDCs is optional.

When you've installed TCP/IP on at least two network servers, check TCP/IP connectivity between the servers with ping.exe. You use the ping utility as the first step in tracking down TCP/IP network problems. Ping's basic command-line syntax is relatively simple—type **ping**, a space, and the IP address of the target host to test at the command prompt, as in `ping 10.7.1.2`. Ping sends four sets of Internet Control Message Protocol (ICMP) echo request packets to the specified host and, if successful in finding the host, displays the time for the round-trip to the source host. Substitute the NetBIOS name of the destination host to test NetBIOS over TCP/IP (NetBT) name resolution, as in `ping oakmusic2`. You can verify the source host's IP address by supplying its name as ping's argument. Pinging the source IP address is similar to performing a loopback test, `ping 127.0.0.1`, with the added benefit of verifying the IP address you specified during the setup process.

→ For a discussion of ping and the ICMP echo request, **see** "IP Datagram Structure," **p. 73**.

Figure 6.5 illustrates running ping on the OAKMUSIC1 PDC to test its TCP/IP stack and check connectivity to the OAKMUSIC2 BDC. The first pair of entries uses IP addresses to test the PDC and BDC stacks. The second pair checks name resolution for both servers.

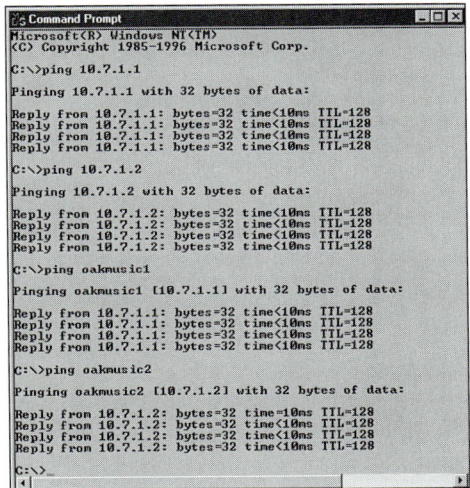

Figure 6.5
By using the ping utility as shown, you can check the TCP/IP protocol on the local machine (10.7.1.1 or oakmusic1) and check connectivity to remote machines such as 10.7.1.2, which is oakmusic2. By pinging by NetBIOS names, you can check NetBIOS-name–to–IP-address resolution.

Automating Client TCP/IP Settings with DHCP

Upgrading a Windows NT NetBEUI network to TCP/IP and installing the latest SP let you take advantage of the latest improvements and bug fixes before implementing TCP/IP on client PCs. If you're already running TCP/IP with fixed-address clients, consider moving to DHCP to assign automatically client IP addresses, subnet masks, and default gateways, if your network has routers. DHCP is especially effective when you need to move a group of clients from one subnet to another. When the moved clients boot, DHCP automatically issues each PC a lease for an IP address on the new subnet.

Note
If you're using TCP/IP and haven't installed the Microsoft DHCP Server service, follow the instructions in steps 1 through 4, 8, and 12 of the earlier "Adding the TCP/IP Protocol and Related Services to a NetBEUI-Only Server" section.

→ For a detailed explanation of Windows 2000's DCHP implementation, **see** "Understanding the Dynamic Host Configuration Protocol," **p. 586**.

Windows NT (and Windows 2000 Server) uses a special Jet 5.0 database, Dhcp.mdb in \Winnt\System32\DHCP, to store DHCP configuration data and client lease information. The …\DHCP folder also has a \Backup\Jet folder to store automatic, hourly Dhcp.mdb backups.

CREATING A DHCP SCOPE

A DHCP *scope* is one or more blocks of unassigned addresses available for client IP address reservations. You specify a scope by its beginning and ending IP addresses—10.7.2.2 through 10.7.2.254, for example. Initially, the DHCP server assigns addresses from the lowest to highest values on a first-come, first-served basis. As you add more clients, you establish additional scopes, such as 10.7.3.2 through 10.7.3.254. If some clients or servers have fixed IP addresses within the scope, you can exclude those specific addresses.

To set up the initial DHCP scope, do the following:

1. Launch DHCP Manager from the PDC's Administrative Tools menu. DHCP Manager identifies the PDC as "Local Machine."

2. Choose Scope, Create to open the Create Scope (Local) dialog.

3. Type the beginning IP address for clients in the Start Address text box, the last IP address in the scope in the End Address text box, and complete the Subnet Mask entry. The scope Name and Comment are optional scope properties (see Figure 6.6).

    If some clients have been assigned permanent IP addresses within the scope you select, specify their addresses in the Exclusion Range text boxes, and click Add to prevent DHCP from assigning these addresses.

4. Set the length of client leases in days. You can accept the default value, but 10 days is a more appropriate lease duration for most networks.

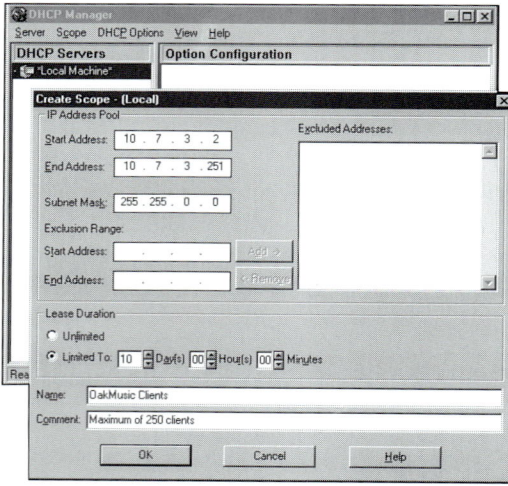

Figure 6.6
The Create Scope dialog within the DHCP Manager utility enables you to configure the initial values for a new DHCP address scope.

5. Click OK to close the Create Scope dialog. When the message box asks if you want to make the scope active, click Yes. The scope appears as a node with network address and scope name below "Local Machine."

Tip from
RJ

> Don't set the lease duration to Infinite. Specifying an infinitely long lease defeats the purpose of DHCP. If particular clients need fixed IP addresses, assign the fixed IP addresses in the clients' Network Control Panel tool.

SETTING DHCP OPTIONS AND ATTRIBUTES

DHCP can set many attribute values for scopes, only a few of which are applicable to Windows DHCP clients. The DHCP Options menu has Scope (a selected scope for a single subnet), Global (options for all subnets), and Default (all new scopes you create on the server) choices. These options control the application of all DHCP attribute values you specify.

Windows 3.11, 9x, and 2000 DHCP clients support the following options:

- 003 Router—To set the IP address of the Default Gateway for the scope's subnet.
- 006 DNS Server—To specify the IP addresses of primary and secondary DNS servers. You add the DNS Server service in the later "Providing DNS Name Resolution" section.
- 015 Domain Name—To specify the domain name for client logon, OAKMUSIC for this example.
- 044 WINS/NBNS Servers—To specify the IP addresses of primary and secondary WINS servers. NetBIOS Name Service (NDNS) is IETF's synonym for WINS. You set up WINS in the "Enabling NetBIOS Name Resolution with WINS" section that follows shortly.
- 045 WINS/NBT Node Type—To set the WINS operating mode. You must specify a value, usually `0x8` (8 in hexadecimal notation) for a type h node, when you specify a WINS Server.

Settings in a client's Network Control Panel tool override the DHCP option settings. For instance, if you specify the OAKLEAF domain name in a fixed IP address for a DNS server in the DNS page of the Microsoft TCP/IP Properties dialog, the client doesn't use the DNS address provided by DHCP.

The following steps set the five usable DHCP options:

1. Choose DHCP Options, Global to open the DHCP Options: Global dialog.
2. Select 006 DNS Server in the Unused Options list, and click Value to expand the dialog to display the Edit Array button and the disabled array list with the default value of <None>. The IP Addresses array is a list of addresses of DNS servers that are authoritative for the specified domain. In DNS context, authoritative means that servers are the primary source for name resolution within the domain.
3. Click Edit Array to open the IP Address Array Editor dialog. Type the PDC's address, `10.7.1.1`, in the New IP Address text box and click Add to add the address to the IP Addresses list (see Figure 6.7).

Figure 6.7
By configuring DHCP options, you can have DHCP automatically configure the client machines to use the specified DNS servers.

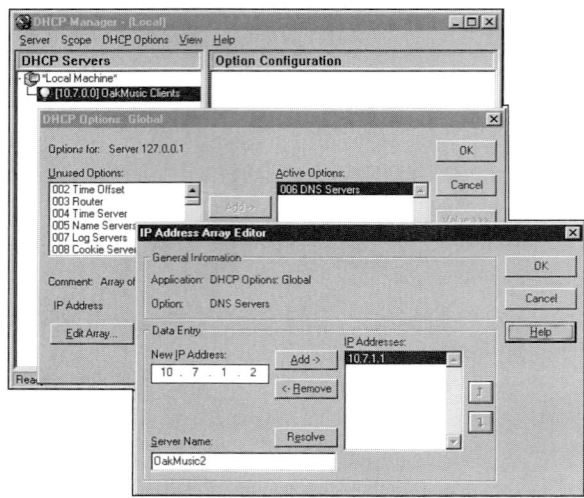

Adding the server name to test with the Resolve button doesn't work at this point, because you haven't set up the DNS Server service.

4. Type the BDC's address, **10.7.1.2**, in the New IP Address text box and click Add to add the address to the IP Addresses list.

5. Select the PDC's address in the IP Address list and click the up-arrow button to move it to the top of the list, making the PDC the primary DNS Server for clients. Click OK to return to the DHCP Options: Global dialog.

6. Select 015 Domain Name in the Unused Options list, click Add, and type the domain name, **OAKMUSIC** for this example, in the Domain Name text box to move 015 Domain Name to the Active Options list.

7. Select 044 WINS/NBNS Servers, click Add to move the attribute to the Active Options list, acknowledge the message regarding the WINS Node Type, and repeat steps 3, 4, and 5 to set the IP addresses for the primary and secondary WINS servers on the PDC and BDC, respectively.

8. Select 045 WINS/NBT Node Type and type **0x8** in the text box.

9. If the scope is subnetted with a router, select 003 Router and repeat step 3 to set a single router (Default Gateway) address.

10. Click OK to close the DHCP Options: Global dialog. The options settings you made in the preceding steps appear in the Option Configuration pane of DHCP Manager's window (see Figure 6.8).

Figure 6.8
The Global DHCP options configured for the server selected in the left pane are shown in the right pane.

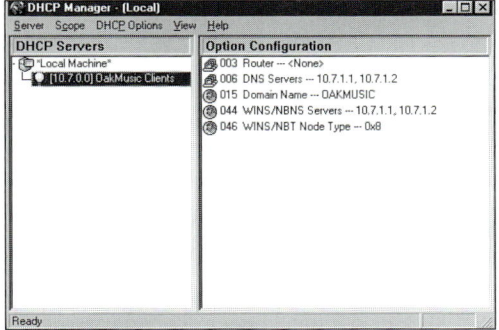

The DHCP Relay Agent, mentioned in the earlier "Adding the TCP/IP Protocol and Related Services to a NetBEUI-Only Server" section, must be running on the DHCP server to pass DHCP messages through routers.

ADDING A BACKUP DHCP SERVER

Relying on a single server to provide critical client services isn't a good network operating practice. Only one Windows NT DHCP server can assign client addresses in a particular scope, and Windows NT 4.0's DHCP server doesn't support replication of its Dhcp.mdb Jet database to other servers. Providing backup for the PDC's DHCP server requires allocating an alternative block of IP addresses to a second DHCP server that runs on the BDC.

The following steps add a backup DHCP server on OAKMUSIC2, the BDC for the example OAKMUSIC domain:

1. "Local Machine" is an ambiguous name on a BDC because it duplicates "Local Machine" on the PDC. To enable adding a backup scope, in the DHCP Manager window choose Server, Add to open the Add DHCP Server to Server list. Type the IP address of the BDC, **10.7.1.2**, in the text box, and click OK to add the 10.7.1.2 node below "Local Machine."

2. Follow the instructions in the earlier "Creating a DHCP Scope" section, but in step 3 of that procedure, specify a nonoverlapping pair of Start IP Address and End IP Address values. A Class B address provides a sufficient number of available addresses for most networks, so the backup scope uses `10.7.4.2` through `10.7.4.254`.

Note

Assigning multiple, nonoverlapping Class C (`10.7.4.n`) address blocks works if your clients use a Class B subnet mask (`255.255.0.0`), but not if your network is subnetted with Class C addresses and clients use Class C subnet masks (`255.255.255.0`). In the latter case, you would need to restrict the address ranges of the primary and secondary DHCP servers to prevent overlap. For example, use a primary DHCP server address range of `10.7.3.2` through `10.7.3.127` and a secondary address range of `10.7.3.128` through `10.7.3.254`.

3. Set option values identical to those for the BDC, following the 10 steps in the preceding "Setting DHCP Options and Attributes" section. DHCP Manager's Option Configuration pane now appears identical to that of preceding Figure 6.8.

4. Repeat step 1 of this procedure on the PDC. Adding the DHCP server to the BDC lets you administer the backup server from the PDC (see Figure 6.9).

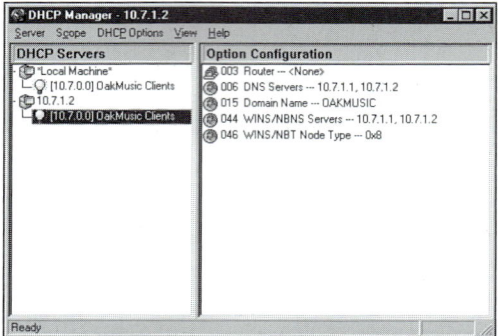

Figure 6.9
The 10.7.1.2 DHCP server shown in the left pane has been added to the local server's DHCP Manager utility so it can be administered remotely.

You also can administer the primary and backup servers from DHCP Manager installed on a PC running Windows NT Workstation with the server administrative tools installed. In this case, you add both DHCP servers to the workstation's DHCP Manager.

Enabling NetBIOS Name Resolution with WINS

The purpose of WINS is resolving computer NetBIOS names to IP addresses, such as associating OAKMUSIC1 with 10.7.1.1 in a routed network. Prior to Microsoft's addition of WINS to Windows NT, you needed a LMHOSTS file to resolve IP addresses from NetBIOS names in a routed network. LMHOSTS is a readable text file; there's a starter version named Lmhosts.sam in the \Winnt\System32\Drivers\Etc folder. LMHOSTS adds Microsoft's LAN Manager extensions to UNIX's HOSTS file. Adding DNS Server, the subject of the next section, eliminates the need for a HOSTS file.

Tip from
RJ

WINS isn't necessary in a simple, nonrouted network, because computers discover NetBIOS names and IP addresses of other hosts through broadcasts. Routers don't ordinarily pass broadcast packets, so WINS takes over beyond the local subnet. Even if you don't have a router installed, it's a good idea to set up and configure WINS. It's only a matter of time before most networks require subnetting or other router-based functionality.

Follow the instructions in steps 1 through 4, 8, and 12 of the earlier "Adding the TCP/IP Protocol and Related Services to a NetBEUI-Only Server" section to add the WINS Server service.

→ For details on Windows 2000's WINS implementation, **see** "Installing and Configuring WINS," **p. 606**.

Setting up WINS is simpler than commissioning DHCP, because PCs create their own entries in the WINS database, WINNT\System32\Wins\Wins.mdb. Wins.mdb also uses Jet 5.0 and generates automatic, hourly backups. To configure a primary WINS Server on your PDC, do the following:

1. Open WINS Manager from the Administrative Tools menu.
2. WINS doesn't automatically back up Wins.mdb until you specify a backup location. Choose Mappings, Backup Database, to open the Select Backup Directory dialog, and select in the Drive list a volume other than the system volume, if available.
3. Type the name for the new backup folder, typically **WINSBack**, in the New Directory Name dialog.
4. Click OK to create the backup folder, acknowledge the database backed up message, and close the Select Backup Directory dialog.
5. Choose Mappings, Static Mappings to open the Static Mappings (Local) dialog.
6. Click Add Mappings to open the Add Static Mappings dialog.
7. Accept the default Unique option, and type the NetBIOS name of the PDC in the Name text box and the PDC's IP address in the IP Address text box. Click Add to add the mapping.

    Alternatively, if you have an up-to-date LMHOSTS or HOSTS file, click Import Mappings, select the HOSTS file, and click OK to add mappings from the HOSTS file.

8. Repeat step 7 for the sample BDC (see Figure 6.10) and any other BDCs or member servers in the domain.

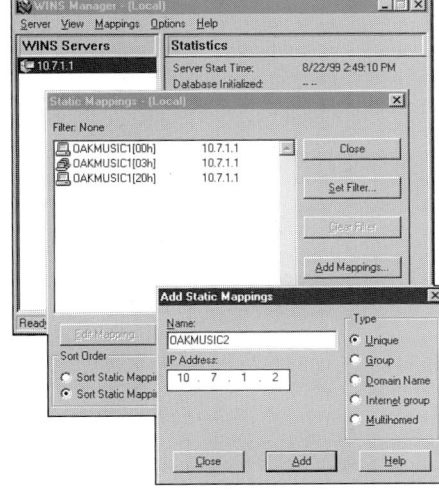

Figure 6.10
The WINS Manager utility is being used to add a static mapping for the OAKMUSIC2 server to the address 10.7.1.2 by selecting Add Mappings from the Static Mappings window.

Like the preceding example for DHCP servers, it's a good practice to configure a backup WINS Server on a BDC. Unlike DHCP, WINS supports database replication. To establish WINS replication with the BDC's WINS Server, do the following:

1. With WINS Manager open on the BDC, choose Server, Replication Partners to open the Replication Partners (Local) dialog.
2. Click Add to open the Add WINS Server dialog. Type the PDC's address, **10.7.1.1** for this example, in the WINS Server text box and click OK.
3. Repeat steps 1 and 2 on the PDC, specifying **10.7.1.2** as the sample BDC address (see Figure 6.11), and then click the Replicate button to queue the replication operation.

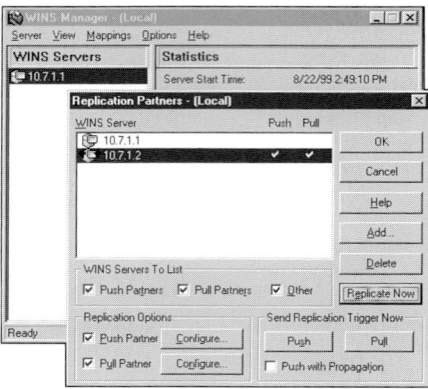

Figure 6.11
The Replication Partners dialog of the WINS Manager is used to configure push-pull replication between the two WINS servers on the network.

4. Click OK to close the Replication Partners (Local) dialog and add the BDC node to the PDC's WINS Servers list, and vice versa.

You can change timing and other parameters of the WINS Server by choosing Server, Configuration to open the WINS Server Configuration (Local) dialog, and clicking Advanced to expand the dialog (see Figure 6.12). The default configuration values are suitable for most networks.

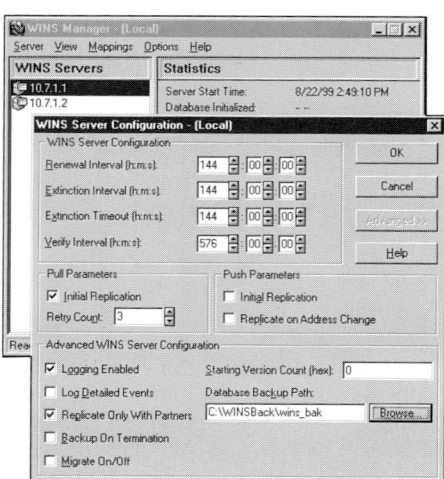

Figure 6.12
The default configuration values are shown for the PDC WINS server. Replication, WINS database entry lifetimes, and logging options can be set from this dialog.

Another useful WINS dialog opens when you choose Mappings, Show Database (see Figure 6.13). The Show Database dialog displays all mappings or only the mappings for the selected server, depending on the option you choose in the Owner frame.

Figure 6.13
The Show Database dialog displays the mappings in the WINS database. The database shown contains one dynamic WINS entry and several static mappings.

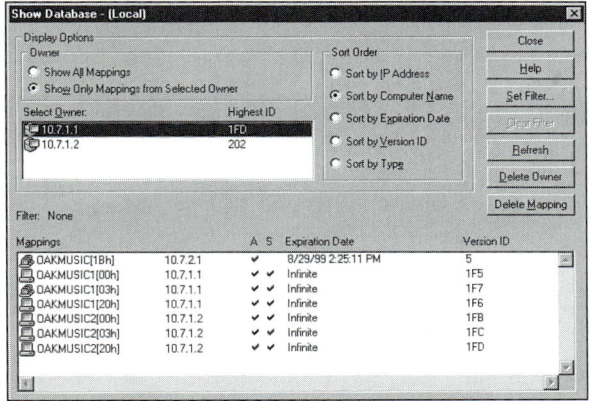

 If you run into "duplicate name" problems when setting up WINS, see the "WINS Problems" topic in the "Troubleshooting" section near the end of the chapter.

PROVIDING DNS NAME RESOLUTION

Windows NT's DNS Server service eliminates the need to manually edit the LMHOSTS file to associate domain hosts with IP addresses. You need DNS to fully support the Windows Sockets (WinSock) API used by browsers, Internet Information Server (IIS), and other Internet-compliant applications.

→ For a review of DNS basics, **see** "Resolving Names with the Domain Name System," **p. 77**.

| **Tip from** *RJ* | DNS isn't mandatory for small TCP/IP networks. It's possible to run an intranet with IIS 3+ on a DNS-less network. Instead of typing `http://www.domainname.com/`, Internet Explorer users type `[http://]servername` to open the intranet's home page. The `http://` prefix is optional and *servername* is the NetBIOS name of the machine running IIS. Setting up DNS, however, makes connecting to your intranet more closely resemble public Web navigation. Becoming familiar with DNS on Windows NT prepares you for managing Windows 2000's DNS after the upgrade. |

Windows NT's DNS Server service supports static lists of domain names. If a DNS client attempts to look up a name that isn't in the static list, DNS Server checks the WINS database for the required entry. DNS Server's interaction with WINS Server(s) minimizes manual entries to create static DNS records.

> **Tip from**
> *RJ*
>
> If the DNS Server service isn't installed, follow the instructions in steps 1 through 4, 8, and 12 of the earlier "Adding the TCP/IP Protocol and Related Services to a NetBEUI-Only Server" section to add it. Don't forget to reinstall the latest service pack after adding DNS Server from the Windows NT Server distribution CD-ROM.

CREATING A PRIMARY ZONE WITH DNS MANAGER

A primary DNS zone is required for each domain in your network. A primary DNS zone is said to be authoritative for a domain; that is, it's the primary source for translation of readable DNS names within the domain to IP addresses. DNS performs functions similar to WINS, except that the translation is from a fully qualified DNS host name, such as `oakmusic1.oakmusic.com`, rather than the NetBIOS address, OAKMUSIC1 for this example. Large DNS namespaces, such as the Internet, require division into many zones for administrative purposes. A primary master DNS name server is required for each zone; a secondary master name server(s) receives periodic updates from the primary master name server to provide redundancy.

To set up the PDC's DNS Server, do the following:

1. On the PDC, launch the DNS Manager administrative tool.

2. Choose DNS, New Server to open the Add DNS Server dialog, type the PDC's IP address in the text box, and click OK to create the name server (NS) record for the domain.

   Alternatively, you can use the `localhost` address, `127.0.0.1`, or the server's NetBIOS name in lieu of the PDC's IP address.

3. Choose DNS, New Zone to open the first of a series of dialogs to add the primary zone for the domain (`oakmusic.com` in this example). Select the Primary Zone option and click Next to open the second dialog (see Figure 6.14).

Figure 6.14
When you create a new DNS zone in the DNS Manager, you must specify whether it is a primary (shown here) or a secondary zone.

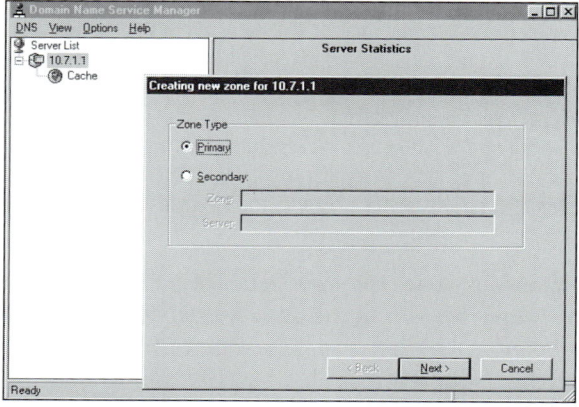

PROVIDING DNS NAME RESOLUTION

4. Type in the Zone Name text box your internal domain name, which needn't—and usually shouldn't—be your InterNIC-registered domain name for the public Internet. When you tab to the Zone File text box, the name of the DNS file, the domain name with a .dns suffix, automatically appears (see Figure 6.15).

Figure 6.15
You need to give the new zone a name and specify a zone file when creating a new DNS zone from DNS Manager.

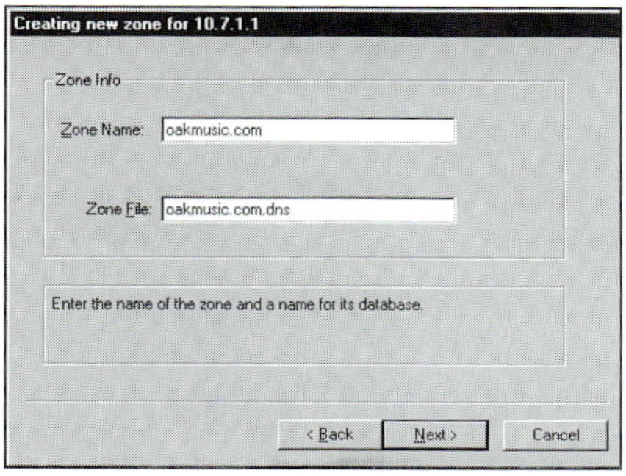

5. Click Next and then Finish to add the new primary zone.
6. Double-click the SOA (Start of Authority) record in the Zone Info list to open the DNS Server's *domainname* Properties dialog (see Figure 6.16). DNS Server properties are similar to configuration entries for WINS servers. Click OK to close the dialog.

Figure 6.16
The Properties dialog is shown for the Primary DNS server in the `oakmusic.com` domain. You can set several time values for DNS entry TTL, set expire times, and define the DNS name for the server.

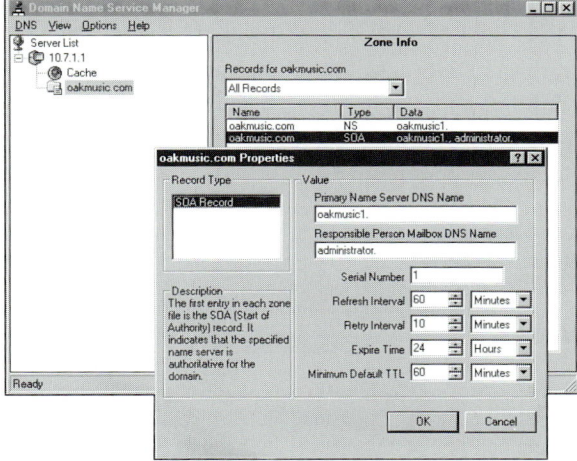

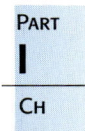

PART
I

CH
6

7. Domains also need a reverse lookup-zone, so select the server entry (10.7.1.1), and choose DNS, New Zone again.

→ For a brief explanation of reverse-lookup zones and zone files, **see** "DNS Zones," **p. 80**.

8. Select the Primary Zone option, click next, and type the reverse lookup value, **7.10.in-addr.arpa** in the Zone Name text box. Tab to the Zone File text box, and click Next and Finish to add the reverse-lookup zone.

9. To add an entry to specify the IP address of the PDC, right-click the primary domain entry and select New Record to open the New Resource Record dialog.

10. Accept the default A Record (Address record) in the Record Type list, type the NetBIOS name of the PDC in the Host Name text box, and the PDC's address in the Host IP Address text box (see Figure 6.17).

Figure 6.17
The New Resource Record dialog of the DNS Manager enables you to add an Address (A) record for the oakmusic1 server and map it to the IP address 10.7.1.1.

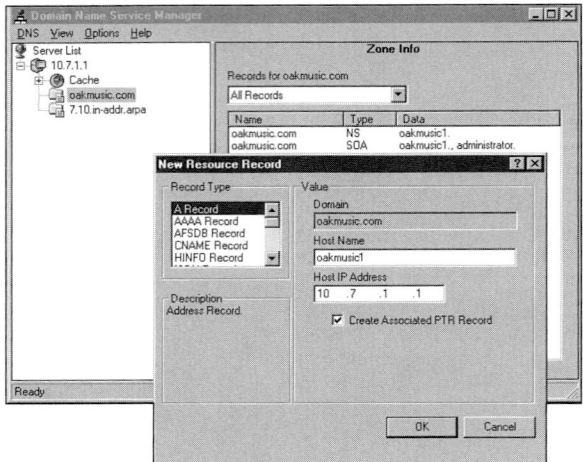

11. Repeat steps 9 and 10 for each BDC and member server in the domain.

12. Press F5 to refresh the DNS data. The PDC's and BDC's address records appear in the domain's Zone Info list and a new 1 node is added to the reverse-lookup zone.

13. Double-click the 1 node to display the pointer (PTR) record to the BDC in the reverse-lookup zone (see Figure 6.18).

Figure 6.18
The Resource Records for the oakmusic.com domain are shown in the background window, and their corresponding reverse lookup values are shown in the foreground dialog.

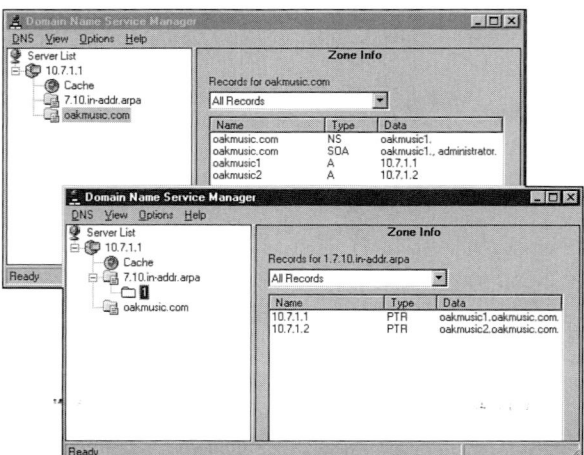

ENABLING WINS LOOKUP

The DNS Server service doesn't enable WINS lookup by default. To add WINS lookup to your DNS server(s), do the following:

1. In DNS Manager, right-click the domain zone node and choose Properties to open the Zone Properties sheet for the domain.
2. Click the WINS Lookup tab and mark the Use WINS Resolution check box to enable controls in the WINS Servers frame.
3. Type the IP address of the primary WINS Server in the text box, and click Add to add the address to the list.
4. Repeat step 3 to add the address of the secondary WINS Server to the list (see Figure 6.19).

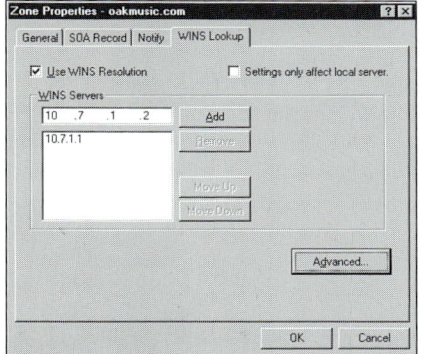

Figure 6.19
The WINS Lookup page of the Zone Properties dialog enables you to specify a WINS server to resolve names to addresses.

5. Click OK to close the Zone Properties sheet. A WINS record is added to the Zone Info pane (see Figure 6.20).

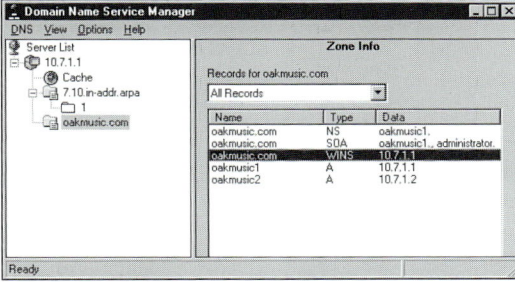

Figure 6.20
The WINS Resource Record can be seen in the right pane of the DNS Manager and can now be used for the resolution of DNS names.

WINS records don't conform to UNIX standards. You receive an error if you attempt to transfer zone records containing WINS records to a UNIX DNS server.

TESTING DNS

Use the Nslookup.exe tool to verify that your DNS Server is operational. The Nslookup (name server lookup) application emulates a client request for DNS name resolution. To run a quick diagnostic check of the PDC's DNS Server service with Nslookup, do the following:

1. Open the Command Prompt and type **nslookup**. Nslookup starts and displays the default server and its IP address. Nslookup uses a > command prompt.

2. Type `ls -d domainname` at the Nslookup > prompt to display DNS entries for the domain's zone (see Figure 6.21).

Figure 6.21
The nslookup utility is used to view the list of zone records including WINS resolved records.

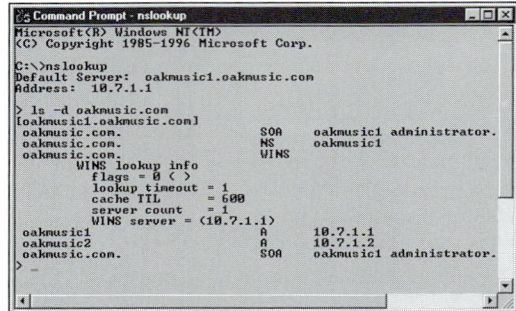

3. Type **?** to display the syntax of valid Nslookup commands (see Figure 6.22).

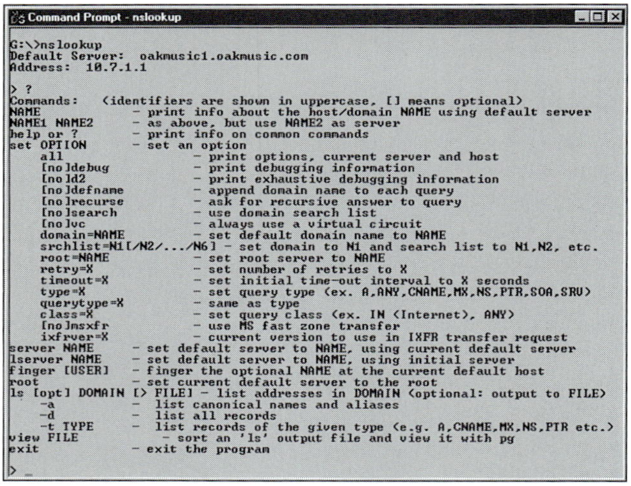

Figure 6.22
By typing **?** at the nslookup prompt (>), you can view all available commands.

⚠ *If Nslookup fails with a "can't locate server" message, see the "DNS Problems" topic in the "Troubleshooting" section near the end of this chapter.*

Adding a Secondary DNS Server

Internet domain name registries require ISPs to maintain redundant DNS servers that are authoritative for Web sites hosted by the ISP. As with DHCP and WINS, it's a good network management practice to provide a secondary (backup) DNS server. A secondary DNS server maintains a read-only copy of the resource records of the primary DNS server.

> **Note**
> Setting up a secondary DNS server isn't required for the Windows 2000 upgrade to AD. Windows 2000's DDNS automatically replicates DNS records to all servers running AD. If you intend to rely on Windows NT 4.0's DNS for an extended period prior to the upgrade, implement the secondary DNS Server service on the BDC.

To create a secondary DNS server on a BDC, follow these steps:

1. Launch DNS Manager on the BDC.
2. Choose DNS, New Server, type the server's NetBIOS name in the DNS Server text box, and click OK.
3. Repeat step 2, but substitute the primary DNS server's NetBIOS name. When you click OK, the primary DNS server's zones appear in the node list.
4. Right-click the secondary DNS server entry, choose New Zone to open the Creating New Zone for *domainname* dialog, and select the Secondary option.
5. Drag the hand from the lower frame of the dialog to the domain zone node of the primary DNS server entry. Entries from the primary zone fill the Zone and Server text boxes (see Figure 6.23). Click Next.

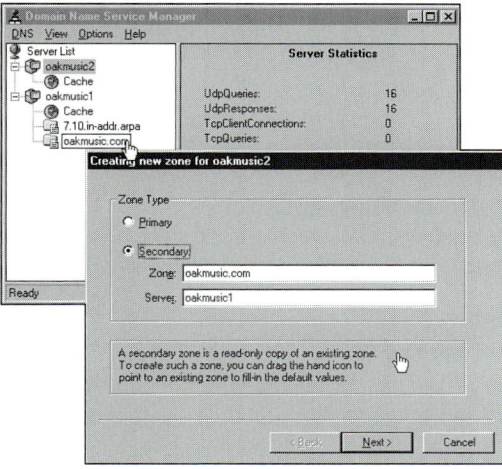

Figure 6.23
After you open the Creating New Zone dialog and specify a secondary zone, you can drag the hand icon from the primary DNS item in the DNS Manager window to the new Zone dialog. The information from the zone you select is filled in automatically.

6. Click Next to skip the Creating New Zone for *zonename* dialog, which is completed by the drag-and-drop feature.

7. Type the IP address of the primary DNS server in the IP Master text box, and click Add to add the address to the list (see Figure 6.24).

8. Click Next and Finish to complete the operation.

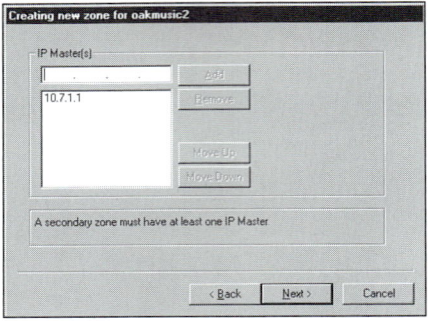

Figure 6.24
You must specify at least one IP master for a secondary zone—in this case, the primary DNS server 10.7.1.1.

ADDING FIXED DNS AND WINS ADDRESSES TO SERVERS

Once you've set up primary and secondary DNS and WINS servers, it's a good policy to designate their addresses in the TCP/IP Properties dialog of all servers. Do the following to add DNS and WINS addresses to each server:

1. Launch Control Panel's Network tool, click the Protocols tab, and double-click the TCP/IP Protocol item to display the Microsoft TCP/IP Properties page.

2. Click the DNS tab and type your domain name in the Domain text box.

3. Click the Add button to open the TCP/IP DNS Server dialog, type the IP address of the primary (PDC) DNS server in the DNS Server text box, and click OK.

4. Repeat step 3 for the secondary (BDC) DNS server, and click Apply. The DNS page appears as shown in Figure 6.25.

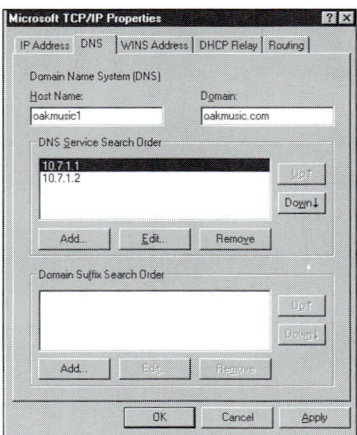

Figure 6.25
On each server, you can specify the primary and secondary DNS servers created earlier in this chapter to provide DNS name resolution.

5. Click the WINS Address tab. On WINS servers, type the IP address of the computer in the Primary WINS Server *and* Secondary WINS Server text boxes (see Figure 6.26 for the PDC example). On servers that don't run the WINS Server service, use the individual IP addresses of the primary (PDC) and secondary (BDC) WINS servers.

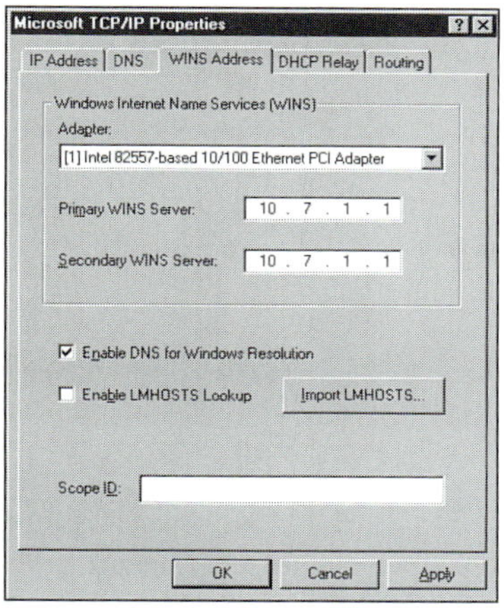

Figure 6.26 Specify both the primary and secondary WINS server addresses as the system's own IP addresses, as shown here for the server `10.7.1.1`.

Caution

Specifying the IP address of the secondary WINS server on the primary machine or the primary WINS server on the secondary machine can cause failure to replicate and renew NetBIOS entries. For more information on this "split registration" problem, search the Microsoft Knowledge Base for article Q150737, "Setting Primary and Secondary WINS Server Options."

It isn't necessary to specify a Scope ID name. You use a Scope ID to restrict NetBIOS communication to a particular group of computers with the same Scope ID.

6. Click OK to close the dialog, and click Yes when prompted to reboot the server.
7. Confirm the server's IP settings with the Ipconfig.exe diagnostic tool by typing **ipconfig /all** at the command prompt. Figure 6.27 shows Ipconfig's report for the OAKMUSIC1 PDC.

PART I

CH 6

```
Command Prompt
(C) Copyright 1985-1996 Microsoft Corp.

G:\>ipconfig /all

Windows NT IP Configuration

        Host Name . . . . . . . . . : oakmusic1.oakmusic.com
        DNS Servers . . . . . . . . : 10.7.1.1
                                      10.7.1.2
        Node Type . . . . . . . . . : Hybrid
        NetBIOS Scope ID. . . . . . :
        IP Routing Enabled. . . . . : No
        WINS Proxy Enabled. . . . . : No
        NetBIOS Resolution Uses DNS : Yes

Ethernet adapter E100B1:

        Description . . . . . . . . : Intel EtherExpress PRO/100B
        Physical Address. . . . . . : 00-A0-C9-59-CC-AA
        DHCP Enabled. . . . . . . . : No
        IP Address. . . . . . . . . : 10.7.1.1
        Subnet Mask . . . . . . . . : 255.255.0.0
        Default Gateway . . . . . . :
        Primary WINS Server . . . . : 10.7.1.1
        Secondary WINS Server . . . : 10.7.1.1

G:\>_
```

Figure 6.27 Using the ipconfig /all command from the Command Prompt, you can see that this system has primary and secondary WINS and DNS servers specified.

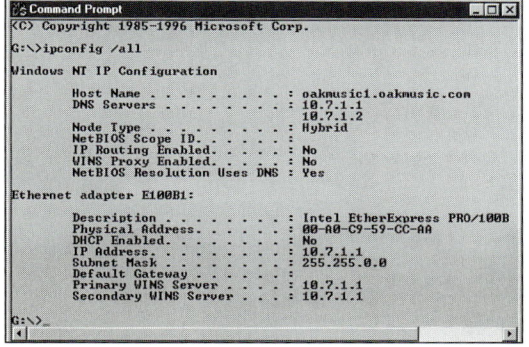

When you ping a DNS-enabled server by NetBIOS name, the server returns its full DNS name. For example, `ping oakmusic1` returns `oakleaf1.oakleaf.com`, instead of oakmusic1, as the computer name.

Migrating Client PCs to DHCP, WINS, and DNS

Changing the client network protocol from NetBEUI to TCP/IP is a three-phase project:

1. Install the TCP/IP protocol on each client.
2. Verify that the DHCP, WINS, and DNS servers are operational and that client TCP/IP protocol defaults provide TCP/IP connectivity.
3. Remove the NetBEUI protocol from all clients.

Tip from
RJ

Upgrade all WfW 3.11 and Windows 95 clients having sufficient RAM (16MB minimum) and free disk space (100MB or so) to Windows 98 SE (Second Edition) at this point, if you have the budget and time. Windows 98 includes connectivity components to connect to AD and search for objects published in AD. WfW 3.11 doesn't support AD, and you must upgrade Windows 95 with the AD client components from the Windows 2000 Server CD-ROM to AD-enable machines running Windows 95.

Installing TCP/IP

To install TCP/IP on a Windows 98 client, as an example, do the following:

1. Launch Control Panel's Network tool, and click Add on the Configuration page.
2. Select Protocol in the Select Network Component Type dialog, and click Add.
3. Select Microsoft and TCP/IP in the Select Network Protocol Manufacturers and Network Protocols lists (see Figure 6.28).

Figure 6.28
To add TCP/IP to a Windows 98 client system, click Add under the Configuration tab of the Network properties page, select Protocol and click Add, and then select Microsoft as the manufacturer and TCP/IP as the protocol.

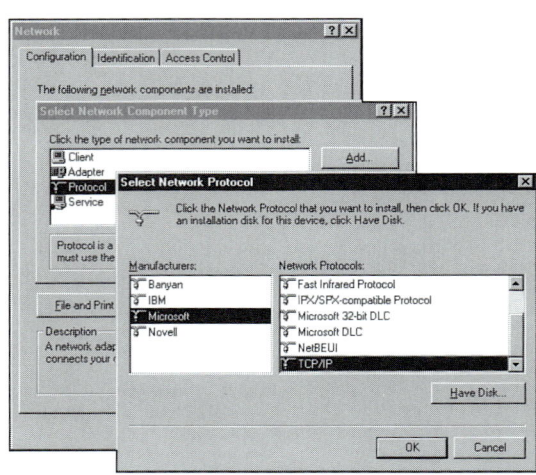

4. Click OK to install the required components from a network installation share or the Windows 98 CD-ROM.

5. Reboot the computer after completing the installation.

Rebooting the client takes a bit longer when DHCP is operational, because the DHCP client must contact and negotiate with a DHCP server to obtain its reserved IP address.

 If your clients have problems connecting to the server with TCP/IP, see the "TCP/IP Problems" topic of the "Troubleshooting" section near the end of the chapter.

Verifying DHCP, WINS, and DNS Operation

One of the advantages of DHCP is that it makes installation of TCP/IP simple enough that most users of Windows 9x and NT Workstation client PCs can handle the installation process without help desk assistance. If the client is connected to the network, runs NetBEUI, and you added the appropriate DHCP options when setting up your DHCP servers, PC users need only install the TCP/IP protocol, not configure it. The Winipcfg.exe utility included with Windows 95 OSR2 and 98 provides a graphical display of the DHCP option values provided to the client with the IP address lease.

To set up or verify proper installation of TCP/IP on Windows 9x clients and validate operation of your DHCP servers, do the following:

1. If the client runs NetBEUI, its NetBIOS name and domain name is assigned; if not, launch Control Panel's Network tool, click the Identification tab, and type in the Computer Name text box a unique NetBIOS name for the client.

    DHCP automatically provides the domain name for non-NetBEUI clients if you added the 015 Domain Name option and set its value in step 6 of the earlier "Setting DHCP Options and Attributes" section. Otherwise, you must type the domain name.

2. In the Configuration page, verify that TCP/IP is bound to the network adapter by a TCP/IP -> *Adapter Name* entry in the list. If the computer has a modem, confirm that the TCP/IP -> Dial-Up Adapter entry is present.

3. Double-click the TCP/IP -> *Adapter Name* entry to display the TCP/IP Properties dialog, and click the IP Address tab to verify selection of the default Obtain an IP Address Automatically option (see Figure 6.29).

Figure 6.29
By default, a Windows 98 TCP/IP client attempts to get an IP address assignment automatically from a DHCP server.

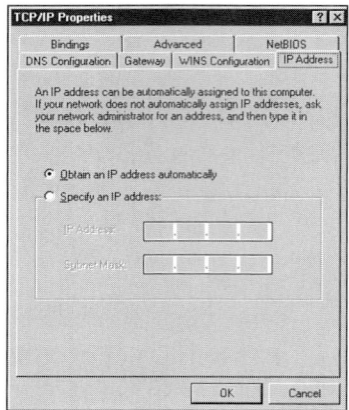

If you added the 006 DNS Server, 044 WINS/NBNS Server, and 045 WINS/NBT Node Type option values in the earlier "Setting DHCP Options and Attributes" section, you don't need to set IP addresses in the DNS Configuration and WINS Configuration pages.

4. Reboot the client if you've changed any configuration settings.
5. Choose Start, Run, type **winipcfg** in the Open text box, and click OK to run the Winipcfg.exe utility.
6. Click More Info to expand the IP Configuration dialog, and select the computer's network adapter in the Ethernet Adapter Information frame.
7. Review the Host Information to verify operation of DHCP Server service and the DHCP option values for DNS Servers (click the ... button to display the secondary address), the DHCP Server, and Primary and Secondary WINS Servers (see Figure 6.30). Then close Winipcfg.

Figure 6.30
By running winipcfg.exe on this Windows 98 client, you can see the IP address, DNS server, and WINS server settings assigned by DHCP.

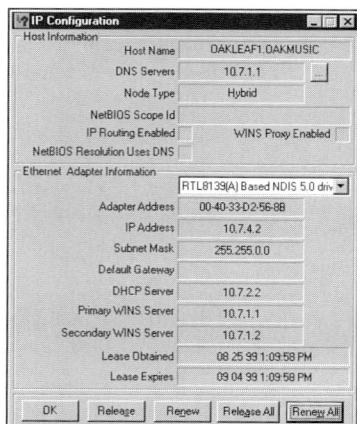

The DHCP Server address in Figure 6.30, `10.7.1.2`, is the backup DHCP server on the PDC, because the DHCP Server service on the PDC was stopped to verify operation of the backup server on the BDC. It's a good practice to verify operation of backup DHCP, WINS, and DNS servers by temporarily stopping the services or shutting down the PDC and booting a DHCP-enabled client PC.

 If your clients encounter problems obtaining IP address leases with DHCP, see the "DHCP Problems" topic of the "Troubleshooting" section near the end of the chapter.

 If your DHCP clients that use WINS can ping servers by IP address but not by NetBIOS name, see the "WINS Problems" topic in the "Troubleshooting" section near the end of the chapter.

ELIMINATING CLIENT RELIANCE ON NETBEUI

After verifying that all clients have TCP/IP installed, you can take one of two approaches to turning off NetBEUI and discovering which users have problems:

- Radical removal—You remove the NetBEUI protocol from your PDC and every BDC, and then wait for users to complain that they can't log on to the network. This approach is neither practical nor politic if you have mobile users who rely on NetBEUI as their sole dial-up protocol to your network.

- Conservative transition—You remove the NetBEUI protocol from individual client PCs on a scheduled basis. If you have mobile users running WfW 3.11 on outmoded laptops, this might be your only option because of insufficient disk space to install TCP/IP or other hardware limitations.

Unneeded protocol stacks on client PCs waste resources, slow network operations, and sometimes cause browsing problems. Visiting each client PC, removing NetBEUI, and verifying proper network logon is the most foolproof route to assuring a smooth transition to TCP/IP networking.

Tip from
RJ

> Remove the Novell IPX/SPX protocol from clients if you're not running NetWare servers. Windows 9x installs the IPX/SPX protocol by default, and experience demonstrates that many NetBEUI clients have unneeded copies of the NetWare client installed.

CLEANING UP USER AND GROUP ACCOUNTS

Over time, duplicate and obsolete user accounts accumulate in your servers' SAM databases. Similarly, groups and membership have a tendency to multiply beyond basic network requirements. Preparing for a Windows 2000 upgrade offers you an opportunity to clean up your user account database and group structure. During the cleanup process, you can create an Access database or Excel spreadsheet of user accounts and their group membership(s) to aid in assigning users to OUs after the upgrade.

LISTING AND SCAVENGING USER ACCOUNTS

A user worksheet is the quickest way to identify duplicate and obsolete accounts. The Windows NT Resource Kit's Usrstat.exe command-line tool generates a fixed-width text file with logon IDs, full usernames, and last logon dates and times. If the last logon date is more than a few months ago, the account is likely to be obsolete. You can delete or disable accounts that don't pass the last-use test. It's a safer practice, however, to disable the account until you're absolutely sure the user won't need to use the account again. Enabling an existing account is much easier than creating a new one, especially if the user has a custom logon script or special permissions for network objects.

To create a text file with Usrstat.exe that you can sort on logon IDs, usernames, and last logon dates, do the following:

1. Launch Command Prompt on the PDC and change to the \Ntreskit folder.
2. Type **usrstat** *domainname* at the command prompt to test the listing operation, where *domainname* is the name of the PDC's domain.
3. Type **usrstat** *domainname* **> usrstat.txt** to create the fixed-length text file.
4. Launch Excel and open Usrstat.txt to start the Text Import Wizard.
5. In the first Wizard dialog, accept the Fixed Width option and set Start Import at Row to 2. Click Next to define worksheet columns.

> **Note**
>
> For reasons known only to the developer who wrote the code for Usrstat.exe, the last logon date and time has the format *www mmm dd hh:nn:ss yyyy*, as in Wed Aug 25 16:05:46 1999. This format, possibly the result of a clumsy Y2K patch, unnecessarily complicates creating a worksheet that you can sort by date.

6. Follow the instructions in the Step 2 Wizard screen to add column break lines to prepare for elimination of hyphens and separate the date/time field into its components (see Figure 6.31).

Figure 6.31
The Microsoft Excel Text Import Wizard enables you to import the output from the usrstat.exe utility to a spreadsheet.

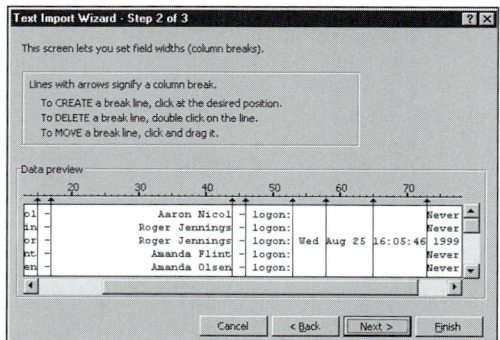

7. Select the Do Not Import Column (Skip) option for the hyphen, logon:, and day columns. Select the Date MDY format for the day-month column (see Figure 6.32). Click Finish to import the file.

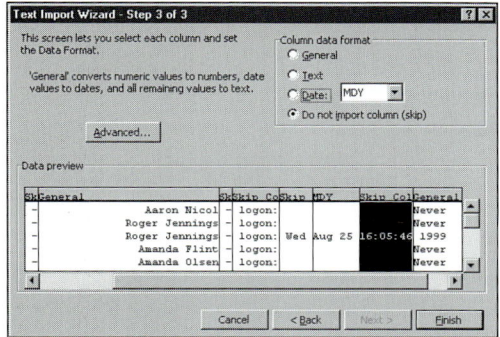

Figure 6.32
In the third screen of the Text Import Wizard, you can set the type of data contained within a column and select columns not to import into the Excel worksheet.

8. Expand the four columns in Excel's window for readability, and select all cells. Press Ctrl+C to copy the worksheet to the Clipboard.

9. Launch Word, copy the cells to a table, and choose Table, Convert, Table to Text with Tab separators.

10. With the text selected, choose Edit, Replace ^t19 with -19, and click Close to reformat the text to the mmm-dd-yyyy format suited to Excel. If you have 2000 dates, repeat the replace operation with ^t20 and -20.

11. Choose Table, Convert, Text to Table with Tab separators to regenerate the table with the proper date format (see Figure 6.33).

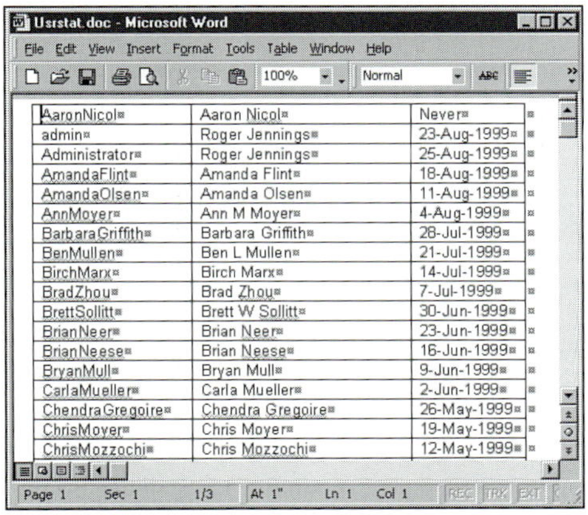

Figure 6.33
Here is the data from the usrstat.exe utility in Microsoft Word after it has been imported into an Excel worksheet and copied into a table.

The dates shown in Figure 6.33 for users, which were created with the ADSI25 Visual Basic application that's on the accompanying CD-ROM, are simulated.

→ For more information on the ADSI25 application for creating user accounts, **see** "The ADSI25 Visual Basic Application," **p. 141**.

12. Choose T<u>a</u>ble, Select, <u>T</u>able, and press Ctrl+C to copy the table to the Clipboard.

13. In Excel, choose <u>I</u>nsert, <u>W</u>orksheet, and press Ctrl+V to paste the table to the new worksheet. Adjust the column widths and row height for readability (see Figure 6.34).

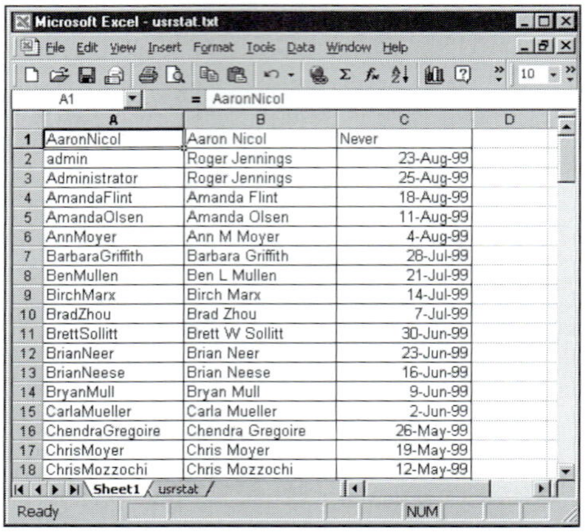

Figure 6.34
The table of Figure 6.33 has been imported back into Microsoft Excel after it has been edited in Word.

Once you've segregated the accounts to delete, you can use a batch file to perform a bulk account deletion or deactivation:

1. Copy the logon IDs to delete to a new worksheet.
2. Add a new column to the left of the logon ID column, and another column to the right of the logon ID column.
3. Type **net user** in cell A1 and copy the value to the remaining cells in column A.
4. Type **/DELETE** in cell C1 and copy the value to the remaining cells in column C (see Figure 6.35).

Figure 6.35
Column A (Logon IDs) has been copied to column B, the net user command has been copied into all rows in column A, and /DELETE has been copied into all rows in column C. The data is then copied back to Microsoft Word and changed to a text file to delete all these stagnant user accounts.

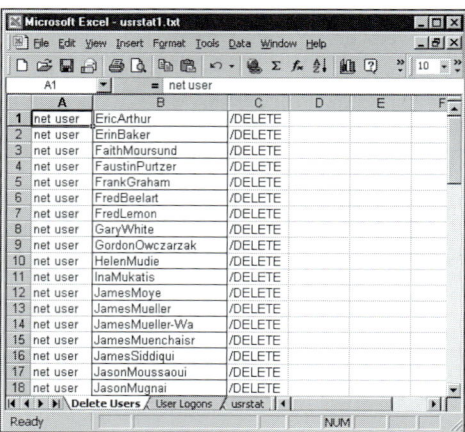

If you want to disable, rather than delete, the account, replace /DELETE with **/ACTIVE:NO**.

5. Copy and paste the worksheet cells to a table in a new Word document, and choose Ta_ble, Con_v_ert, Ta_b_le to Text.

6. Select the Other option in the Convert Table to Text dialog, type a space in the text box, and click OK to create a text file with a space separating columns A and B, and columns B and C (see Figure 6.36).

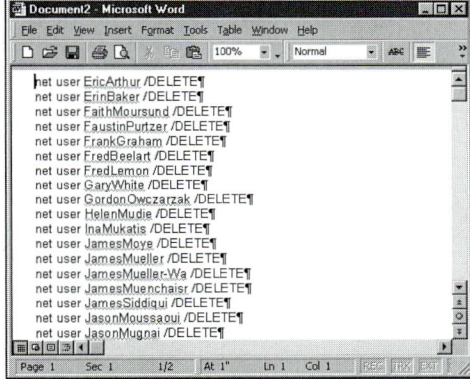

Figure 6.36
This is the final product in Microsoft Word, which can be run as a batch file to delete the user accounts listed.

7. Choose _F_ile, Save _A_s, select Text Only (.txt) in the Save as _T_ype list, navigate to the *ServerName*\Ntreskit folder, save the file as Delusers.txt or the like, and close Word.

    Word insists on a .txt extension for Text Only files.

8. In the PDC's Command Prompt, type **rename delusers.txt delusers.cmd**.

9. Run **delusers.cmd** from the prompt and observe the Command Completed Successfully message as the batch file deletes each user account.

10. Verify that the accounts are deleted or disabled with User Manager for domains.

Alternatively, you can create a comma-separated list of user accounts to delete with the Resource Kit's Adduser.exe tool. Type **Adduser /?** to display the syntax for Adduser.

CREATING GROUP MEMBERSHIP FILES

Running Net.exe with the [local]group and other optional arguments lets you create a list of groups and group membership that you can associate with users in a worksheet or add to a database table. If you create a relation table with group name and logon ID fields, you can write a query having an outer join with the users list to identify the logon IDs and usernames of accounts with multiple group memberships.

Table 6.1 lists the most useful commands for generating group-related lists and altering group membership. Use the .cmd file techniques described in the preceding section to automate changes to group membership. Unfortunately, the net group commands return three-column lists with an asterisk (*) prefix, which requires a substantial amount of manipulation to create a usable list.

TABLE 6.1   NET COMMANDS FOR LISTING GROUPS AND GROUP MEMBERSHIP, AND ADDING OR DELETING USERS FROM GROUPS

Command	Result
`net group > `*`globlist`*`.txt`	Lists all global groups in the PDC's domain
`net localgroup > `*`locllist`*`.txt`	Lists all local groups on the PDC, BDC, or member server
`net group `*`groupname`*` > `*`ggrpname`*`.txt`	Lists logon IDs for the specified global group
`net localgroup `*`groupname`*` > `*`lgrpname`*`.txt`	Lists logon IDs for the specified local group
`net group `*`groupname logonid`*` /add`	Adds the user with *logonid* to the *groupname* global group
`net localgroup `*`groupname logonid`*` /add`	Adds the user with *logonid* to the *groupname* local group
`net group `*`groupname logonid`*` /delete`	Removes the user with *logonid* from the *groupname* global group
`net localgroup `*`groupname logonid`*` /delete`	Adds the user with *logonid* to the *groupname* local group

The initial objective when creating lists of groups and group membership is to streamline group structure and minimize user accounts in local groups. Other than the Administrator and other built-in accounts, local groups should contain only global groups.

Tip from
RJ

> As you restructure and repopulate your global groups, keep in mind the Windows 2000 OU structure you plan to implement when upgrading to AD. Populating OUs from global group membership is much easier than the alternative methods described in Chapter 5, "Choosing and Testing Migration Strategies."
>
> You can use the Group Mapping and Merging Wizard of the Active Directory Migration Tool (ADMT) for Windows 2000 Server, described in Chapter 5, to alter your Windows NT group structure.

→ To review how to populate OUs based on group membership, **see** "Using Custom Filters to Classify Users by Group Membership," **p. 212**.

→ For a brief description of the Group Mapping and Merging Wizard, **see** "Exploring Other ADMT Features," **p. 255**.

Troubleshooting

TCP/IP Problems

Clients on a Class B network with IP addresses whose third octet value differs from that of the server can't connect to the server in a nonrouted network.

The client's subnet mask specifies a Class C, not a Class B, address in a nonrouted network. If, for example, you reserve the `10.7.1.0` network for hosts with fixed IP addresses, and use DHCP to assign addresses in the `10.7.2.0` network, both the server and all clients must have a Class B (`255.255.0.0`) subnet mask. Verify in the IP Address page of the server's TCP/IP Properties dialog that the subnet mask is correct. Use Winipcfg or Ipconfig to check the client's subnet mask.

Clients are unable to connect to a server in a routed network.

The most common cause of this problem is an incorrect Default Gateway entry, either in the Gateway page of the client's TCP/IP Properties sheet or, if your clients use DHCP, the 003 Router attribute of the global attributes (options). Verify with ipconfig /All or Winipcfg that the Default Gateway value corresponds to that of the client subnet's router.

If there's more than one router between the client and the server, run the Tracert.exe (TraceRoute) command-line program to identify the point of failure. At the client, specify the IP address or DNS name of the server as the argument, as in `tracert 10.7.2.2` or `tracert oakmusic1.oakmusic.com`. A "Destination host unreachable message" appears at the first instance of a router disconnect. With an active connection to the Internet, try running `tracert microsof.com` or `tracert fawcette.com` as an example of Tracert.exe's responses with packets moving through many routers.

DHCP Problems

Some DHCP clients open "The DHCP client could not renew the IP address lease" messages.

If all your DHCP clients display this or a similar message, the most likely problem is that your DHCP server is down. In that case, see the next topic for the solution. If only a single client reports the renewal problem, the client might have a problem connecting to the DHCP server. Use ping with the DHCP server's IP address from the client to verify network connectivity.

Another source of this problem is overlapping DHCP address ranges when you run two DHCP servers. In this case, it's more likely that the clients display a "Duplicate IP address detected on network" or similar message. Use DHCP Manager on each server to verify that your scopes don't have overlapping address ranges.

No DHCP clients can obtain or renew leases.

The DHCP Server service has stopped. Launch Control Panel's Services tool and scroll to Microsoft DHCP Server. If the DHCP Server service shows Stopped in the Status column, click Start to attempt to start the service. If Automatic doesn't appear in the corresponding Startup column, click Startup and select the Automatic option.

Check the Services event log with Event Viewer and check DHCP Service messages identified by DhcpServer in the Source column. The Event Detail dialog's Description text often is quite cryptic, but might help you diagnose why the service isn't starting.

If you receive a message after clicking the Start button that the DHCP Service can't be started, try running `net start dhcpserver` at the Command prompt. If this instruction doesn't succeed, turn off the power to the server for at least a minute, and then power the server back up.

WINS PROBLEMS

Clients can ping the server by IP address but not by NetBIOS name.

The most common cause of this problem is a Scope ID name mismatch between the clients and the server. Designating a WINS Scope ID lets you establish the software equivalent of a routed network by restricting communications to a group of computers with the same Scope ID value. Specifying a Scope ID in the WINS Configuration page of the TCP/IP Properties dialog isn't a common practice, especially in small networks.

If you've specified a Scope ID name for your WINS server, all client computers must specify the same Scope ID name in their WINS configuration page. Scope ID values are case-sensitive, so clients with a `Faculty` Scope ID can't use NetBIOS over TCP/IP (NetBT) to communicate with a server with a `faculty` or `FACULTY` Scope ID.

Inability to resolve NetBIOS names also can be caused by failure of the WINS Server to start. Perform a Services tool check similar to that for the DHCP Server in the preceding topic. The command-line prompt is `net start wins`.

You receive "duplicate name" errors when clients or servers attempt to reconnect to the network.

"Duplicate name" errors usually occur as a result of a static address mapping that's identical to a dynamic mapping. In WINS Manager, review the database by choosing Mappings, Show Database and select the Show All Mappings option. Delete the static mapping—indicated by an "Infinite" entry in the Expiration Date column—for any host that has a duplicate dynamic mapping—indicated by a date and time in the Expiration Date column.

DNS PROBLEMS

Clients can't locate a DNS server or other host by a fully-qualified domain name.

Running `ping hostname.domain.com` at the command prompt and receiving a "Bad IP address" error indicates that the host name isn't registered in the DNS database or that the client has an incorrect IP address for the primary DNS server. A less likely cause is that the DNS Server service isn't running on the primary DNS server, and no secondary (alternate) DNS server is specified.

From a Windows NT client, run nslookup at the command prompt to verify that the primary DNS server for the domain is operational, then type **ls *domain*.com** at Nslookup's interactive prompt to list all hosts in the domain. An address (A) record for the host you're seeking must exist in order for the client (or server) to resolve the name to the IP address. If the A record for the host is missing, use DNS Manager to add an address record for the server.

Running Nslookup.exe fails to find the default DNS server.

You probably didn't create a primary reverse-lookup zone for your domain or the reverse-lookup zone is missing PTR (pointer) record(s). Nslookup uses reverse lookup to determine the default domain name and then the IP address of the default (primary) DNS name server for the domain. The reverse-lookup zone (`7.10.in-addr.arpa` for this chapter's examples) must have a PTR record to the primary DNS name server (`oakleaf1.oakleaf.com`, `10.7.1.3`). Double-check to make sure you followed all of the steps in this chapter's "Creating a Primary Zone with DNS Manager" section. There's also the remote possibility that the DNS Server service isn't started, so use Control Panel's Services tool to verify that the DNS Service is started on the primary DNS name server.

MCSE Corner: Preparing NT 4.0 for Windows 2000 Server Migration

The topics in this chapter are tested on two exams: 70-215, "Installing, Configuring, and Administering Microsoft Windows 2000 Server," and 70-222, "Upgrading from Microsoft Windows NT 4.0 to Microsoft Windows 2000."

70-215 Installing, Configuring, and Administering Microsoft Windows 2000 Server

The blueprint for this exam lists upgrading a server from Windows NT 4.0 to Windows 2000 as one of its objectives. The topics in Chapter 6 are important to this process, but are not likely to be tested in as much detail on this exam as they are on the 70-222 exam. For the 70-215 exam, however, you should be familiar with topics in this chapter, such as switching from NetBEUI to TCP/IP and troubleshooting TCP/IP problems, because these tasks are necessary when upgrading any Windows NT 4.0 server to Windows 2000.

70-222 Upgrading from Microsoft Windows NT 4.0 to Microsoft Windows 2000

The topics in Chapter 6 relate closely to some of the items tested on this exam. TCP/IP, DHCP, DNS, and WINS become more important in Windows 2000 than they were in older versions of Windows NT because of 2000's enterprise-type distributed structure.

You must be familiar with changing a server from the NetBEUI protocol to TCP/IP, including servers using both NetBEUI and TCP/IP and servers using NetBEUI only. You should also know what to look out for when choosing IP addresses for the network. You need to be able to upgrade all the domain controllers in the network to TCP/IP and test and troubleshoot their connectivity.

You should be able to set up DHCP, WINS, and DNS, to some extent. The exam does not test your knowledge of these topics thoroughly, but they will be mentioned. Another topic covered is cleaning up user and group accounts, because it is one of the planning steps before the migration occurs. You also should be familiar with troubleshooting WINS, DHCP, and DNS.

CHAPTER 7

SPECIFYING SERVER AND DATA STORAGE HARDWARE

In this chapter

Setting Server Objectives   298

Creating a Secure, Controlled Server Environment   307

Getting the Most from Your New Server Expenditures   311

Upgrading Existing Servers for Windows 2000   313

Taking Advantage of Windows 2000 Hardware Management   315

Choosing the Optimum RAID System   325

Troubleshooting   333

MCSE Corner: An Overview of the Exams   334

Setting Server Objectives

When Microsoft launched Windows NT 3.1 Advanced Server in August 1993, no true "server-class" category of PC hardware existed. Articles in the trade press cited Windows NT 3.1's memory and fixed-disk space requirements as "monumental" and even "astronomical." Relatively few PCs of the time had the horsepower to run either the Workstation or Advanced Server version.

In the early days of Windows NT, many network administrators rolled their own servers by purchasing and assembling individual components. The objective wasn't necessarily to save money. Building custom servers allowed network administrators to mix-and-match components to optimize the server's design for their networking requirements, which usually consisted of an application server or a file- and printer-sharing server.

PC vendors soon jumped into the server fray and offered machines designed specifically to run Windows NT 3.1 Advanced Server and its successors, which often are called *purpose-built* servers. By the late 1990s, purpose-built servers from major PC suppliers had replaced almost all custom-assembled Windows NT servers. As a result of server price wars in 1998 and thereafter, along with increasing sales volume, factory-configured servers came to offer a combination of price, performance, and features that made building your own server uneconomical.

The three primary design criteria of purpose-built servers are *availability*, *performance*, and *scalability*. The sections that follow define the meaning of these terms and how your server hardware specifications determine the degree to which you meet these three objectives.

Tip from
RJ

> If you plan to upgrade an existing network to Windows 2000 Server and don't plan to purchase new hardware, skip to the "Upgrading Existing Servers for Windows 2000" section later in the chapter.

Maximizing Availability

Most administrators consider server availability to be the most important of the three server design criteria. A high-performance, super-scalable server that repeatedly drops dead and requires on-site service is a network administrator's nightmare. Availability is the ratio of operational (online) time to total time, expressed as a percentage—usually 99.5% or greater. Availability relates to reliability, but uses different units of measurement. Hardware reliability, on the other hand, commonly is expressed in hours as *mean time between failures (MTBF)* or *mean time to failure (MTTF)*. The hardware component of availability takes into account the time required to detect a server failure, travel to the server site (if necessary), make the necessary repairs, and bring the server back online. The average repair time commonly is expressed as *mean time to repair (MTTR)* in hours.

> **Tip from**
> *RJ*
>
> Take MTBF or MTTF values for computer components, especially those with moving parts, with a grain—or an entire box—of salt. Experience with the OAKLEAF network used to write this book demonstrates that MTBF for fixed-disk drives is virtually meaningless. During assembly of the original OAKLEAF0 server, a new 4.3GB SCSI drive failed within four hours of installation. The replacement drive from the same manufacturer failed after 14 days of service. These failures occurred despite an advertised MTBF of 100,000 hours (11.4 years) when purchased. The final replacement—from another manufacturer—has run for more than three years (about 30,000 hours) without a glitch. Today, fixed-disk manufacturers commonly claim an MTBF of 1,000,000 hours (114 years).

Availability also takes into account software-related downtime divided into the following two categories:

- *Scheduled downtime*—For installation of upgrades, additional services and components, or service packs. You perform these activities during periods of low network activity, usually at night or when most network users are not working.

- *Unscheduled downtime*—A result of software failures that aren't caused by hardware problems. In many cases, rebooting the server takes care of the problem, so the ability to boot remote servers from a local workstation is important. Handling more complex software problems on remote servers requires remote-control software such as PCAnywhere or software included with Microsoft SMS Server.

This chapter deals primarily with hardware, so only those elements of Windows 2000 Server that relate to server hardware requirements and configuration are discussed here.

> **Note**
>
> OAKLEAF0, the Windows NT 4.0 Primary Domain Controller (PDC) for the OAKLEAF domain used in the Active Directory (AD) examples of this book, was upgraded in 1995 for beta testing Windows NT 4.0, Exchange Server, and SQL Server. After installing the released versions of the products, OAKLEAF0 accumulated less than one hour of unscheduled downtime, excluding two prolonged power outages, in four years of continuous operation as the primary file and application server on the OAKLEAF network.

SINGLE-SERVER AVAILABILITY

The primary method of maximizing single-server hardware availability is through redundant components with automatic failover switching, where applicable. The most common redundant components are power supplies, network interface cards (NICs), Small Computer System Interface (SCSI) host controllers, and fixed-disk drives. Hot-swappable (also known as hot-plug) PCI components minimize MTTR by enabling replacement of adapters without shutting down the server.

→ For more information on SCSI components, **see** "SCSI Drives for RAID Systems," **p. 325**.
→ To learn more about automatic failover switching, **see** "Failover Clustering," **p. 300**.

The current generation of high-end servers running Windows NT 4.0 with Service Pack (SP) 4 or later appears to be able to achieve about 99.5% availability, based on mid-1999 market research reports and articles in the trade press. That rate availability is equivalent to an average (mean) server outage time of about 3.65 hours per month. (An average month is about 730 hours.) EMC's Data General Division guarantees 99.9% ("three nines") availability with Data General hardware running Windows 2000 Server (see http://www.microsoft.com/PressPass/press/2000/Feb00/EMCpr.asp). The 99.9% availability figure doesn't include network hardware failures, which commonly reduce user availability by 0.1% to 0.2%. A reasonable overall goal for a new server running Windows 2000 Server and recently purchased network switches and routers is about 99.85% availability, which corresponds to about one hour of outage per month.

Reporting mean outage times often disguises occasional lengthy outages—commonly called meltdowns—combined with frequent short-duration offline intervals. The median outage duration appears to be about the same as the outage time, or about one hour for a system with 99.85% availability. Median outage values substantially less than the mean are indicative of failure of nonredundant components, such components on the server's system board, that have a long MTTR.

Users probably can live with lack of server access for 12 one-hour periods per year, which might result from scheduled shutdowns or minor hardware glitches. A couple of seven-hour server outages during working hours, however, can provoke a user insurrection. For example, 14-hour and 22-hour outages of Sun Unix servers running eBay.com's Web auction site during mid-1999 resulted in a storm of articles in the trade press. eBay's management attributed the 22-hour June 10-11, 1999, outage to lack of a server backup system.

> **Note**
>
> Synchronous Dynamic RAM (SDRAM), the most common memory class for current servers and workstations, has achieved a very high reliability level. Few, if any, present-day PCs use parity checking to detect memory errors; a parity error results in an Error - System Halted message that immediately stops server operations in its tracks. Memory errors, although infrequent, usually result in corrupted data or a halted service. Error Checking and Correcting (ECC) memory dedicates an extra three bits per byte of RAM to detecting and correcting the most common single-bit memory errors. ECC also attempts to correct very infrequent multiple-bit errors. Almost all high-end PC servers now include ECC memory as a standard feature, and you should specify ECC memory in every server you purchase.

FAILOVER CLUSTERING

A server backup system isn't a tape drive with a backup copy of the operating system and other files stored on the fixed-disk drives. A true server backup system is a second server operating in standby mode, ready to take over almost instantly if the primary server fails. Microsoft introduced its approach to providing a standby server—called failover or availability clustering—with the Enterprise Edition (EE) of Windows 4.0. Windows 2000's failover clustering delivers two primary availability benefits:

- The ability to perform scheduled maintenance without disrupting server operation.
- Increased availability to 99.95% or better (22 minutes of server downtime per month or less) through server redundancy.

Windows 2000 Advanced Server delivers failover clustering similar to that of Windows NT 4.0 EE and supports *rolling upgrades.* You perform a rolling upgrade by shutting down one server for the upgrade, and then transferring the active cluster role to the upgraded server and upgrading the second server.

→ For more information on Windows 2000 Advanced Server's clustering capabilities, **see** "Using Clustering to Improve Service Availability," **p. 1229**.

> **Note**
>
> Several hardware vendors have extended the Microsoft Cluster Service (MSCS) to provide failover support for clusters with eight or more nodes. IBM's NetFinity servers offer Availability Extensions for Microsoft Cluster Services. An IBM white paper based on Windows NT 4.0 EE, much of which also is applicable to Windows 2000 Advanced Server, is available at `http://www.pc.ibm.com/us/netfinity/mscs.html`. Newer and larger cluster implementations substitute Fibre Channel storage-attached networks (SANs) for conventional SCSI-attached Redundant Arrays of Inexpensive Disk (RAID) subsystems.

→ For a discussion of RAID and Fibre Channel, **see** "Choosing the Optimum RAID System," **p. 325**.

Figure 7.1 illustrates the basic components of the Microsoft Cluster Service (MSCS) implemented by Windows 2000 Advanced Server. MSCS takes the shared-disk approach to clustering—an independent RAID subsystem connects via two RAID controllers to SCSI adapters in the two clustered servers, called *nodes*. Each node has its own system drive that runs the operating system and MSCS. The shared RAID drive holds a volume, called the *quorum resource*, to store MSCS configuration and administration information. The remaining volume(s) store data shared with the two nodes via Ultrawide SCSI-2 or faster connections. The private interconnect is a 10BaseT crossover connection between two dedicated network cards. A crossover connection has the transmit and received connectors reversed on one connection so a hub isn't required to make the connection. The two nodes send keep-alive signals to one another over this connection. If the active node goes down, loss of the keep-alive signal alerts the inactive node, which then assumes the active role.

Figure 7.1
The hardware components and network connections for the Microsoft Cluster Service (MSCS) include an independent RAID subsystem.

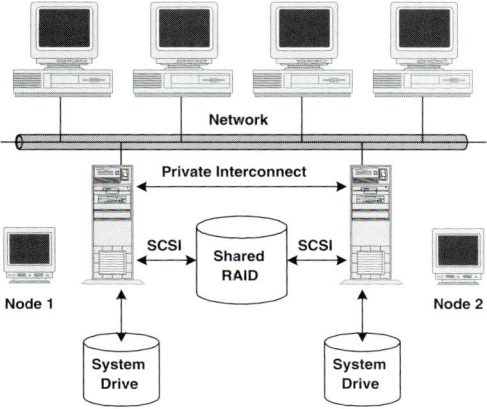

Applications usually must be modified to support clustered operation; SQL Server 7.0 and Exchange Server 5.5 were the first Microsoft applications to be upgraded to EE status with clustering support. In mid-1999, two-server failover clustering was by far the most popular means of improving server availability. The forthcoming DataCenter Server raises the failover bar to four nodes. With the substantial improvement in the stability of all Windows 2000 Server versions, four-node failover should come close to 99.99% (four nines) availability.

> **Note**
>
> Assembling your own cluster servers and RAID subsystems from individual components isn't practical for most organizations. Microsoft provides technical support only for validated cluster systems that appear on the Windows Hardware Qualification List (HQL). Before purchasing a clustering system for Windows 2000 Advanced Server, check its validation status at `http://www.microsoft.com/hcl/`. Type **cluster** in the Search For text box to generate a list of vendors and their validated cluster configurations. You can download the latest Windows 2000 HQL in text format from `ftp://ftp.microsoft.com/services/whql/win2000hcl.txt`.

IMPROVING PERFORMANCE

Prior to widespread use of the Internet, server performance played a secondary role to availability. In conventional 10Mbps 10Base2 and 10BaseT Ethernet networks of the late 1980s and early 1990s, traffic congestion—not server speed—was the bottleneck. As switches replaced hubs and 100Mbps 100BaseT became commonplace, server performance garnered more attention from information technology (IT) and network managers. Intense competition in the server hardware market during 1999 brought about rapid price erosion of high-performance boxes designed specifically to run Windows NT Server 4.0. Faster CPU speeds—800MHz and up for the Pentium Xeon—and Windows 2000 Server's improved performance result in greatly increased server throughput with hardware prices equal to or lower than those prevailing in 1999.

SINGLE-SERVER PERFORMANCE TUNING

Up to about 512MB, increasing the amount of server RAM usually is the most cost-effective method of improving server performance, regardless of the speed of the server's processor(s). If a server already employs a RAID system for high availability, the most common second step is to increase the number of processors to speed up the operating system and multiprocessing-enabled (multithreaded) applications, such as relational database management systems (RDBMSs), messaging services, and Web servers. Adding processors also requires adding RAM; 256MB per processor is the rule of thumb for the starting point. Like money, you never can have too much RAM. For uniprocessor servers, adding fixed-disk drives and implementing multiple RAID arrays usually delivers the most bang for the buck.

> **Note**
>
> Two new classes of dynamic RAM—Rambus and double-data rate (DDR) SDRAM—will gain acceptance on server system boards in 2000 and beyond. Intel is betting heavily on Rambus technology, which uses a proprietary 16-bit serial bus to deliver 1.6GBps (gigabytes per second) across today's standard 64-bit main memory buses with 400MHz chips. Advanced Micro Devices (AMD), Intel's primary U.S. competitor, says that 100MHz DDR SDRAM can deliver 1.6GBps and 133MHz chips can reach 2.1GBps.
>
> Industry pundits project that Rambus will still cost 25% more than conventional SDRAM by the end of 2000, with the price penalty for DDR SDRAM somewhat less. Regardless of which technology wins, current SDRAM bottlenecks will widen considerably in the next year or so.

Increasing the size of the Level-2 (L2) cache memory from the Pentium III Xeon's standard 512KB to 1MB or 2MB delivers a substantial performance improvement to database applications, such as Windows 2000 Domain Controllers (DCs) and member servers running SQL Server or Exchange Server. L2 cache is high-speed RAM that bridges the main (external) memory bus and the processor's built-in (Level-1 or L1) cache. Increasing the amount of L2 cache improves the *hit rate*, which is the percentage of time the processor obtains its data from the cache instead of the far-slower memory bus. Adding cache space is especially effective with multiprocessor servers because it reduces contention by multiple processors for the main memory bus. L2 cache is expensive, but vital, for enterprise-scale servers. As a rule of thumb, specify 1MB of cache per processor for 512MB of RAM, and 2MB for 1GB of RAM or more.

> **Note**
>
> In early 2000, a Dell PowerEdge 6300 server with two 550MHz Pentium III Xeon processors (512KB of L2 cache each), four 64-bit hot-plug PCI slots, 512MB of EDO ECC RAM, a quad-channel SCSI controller with a 64MB cache, six hot-plug drive bays, two 9.1GB and three 18GB Ultra-2/Low-Voltage Differential (LVD) SCSI drives, and a 100BaseT NIC had a calculated price of less than $14,500 without the operating system. A year or so earlier, almost-comparable systems from Compaq and Hewlett-Packard but with slower Pentium Pro processors, carried price tags in the range of $30,000. To check current Dell server pricing for high-end servers, go to `http://www.dell.com/us/en/bsd/products/series_enter_servers.htm`. You need Windows 2000 Server or Advanced Server to take full advantage of this server class; for instance, Windows 2000 is required to support 64-bit PCI adapters.

Achieving optimum relational database management system (RDBMS) performance with four or more CPUs requires stretching the limit of Windows NT's or 2000's 4GB memory limitation. By design, Windows NT allocates half the installed RAM to the kernel and the other half to applications. A feature called 4GB RAM Tuning (4GT) lets you allocate 3GB of RAM to applications, such as SQL Server or Exchange Server, and 1GB to the kernel. Windows 2000 Advanced Server's 4GT feature is identical in all essential respects to that of Windows NT 4.0 EE.

Microsoft's Address Windows Extensions (AWE) API supports Intel's Physical Address Extension (PAE) architecture to let 32-bit applications address up to 64GB of RAM. In Windows 2000 Advanced Server, the maximum RAM with AWE/PAE is 8GB. You can download a technical paper on AWE at http://www.microsoft.com/hwdev/ntdrivers/ awe.htm. Conventional 32-bit applications must be rewritten to support AWE, which Microsoft calls Enterprise Memory Architecture (EMA). According to Microsoft, all versions of Windows 2000 Server will accommodate AWE-enabled applications, but only Advanced Server and DataCenter Server provide 8GB and 64GB memory addressing ability, respectively. You must purchase Pentium Xeon servers specifically designed for PAE to obtain the additional maximum RAM capacity.

Performance Clusters

In December 1997, Microsoft published a press release titled "Compaq, Intel, and Microsoft Announce Completion of the Virtual Interface Architecture Specification." VIA version 1.0 purports to address the need for distributing workload over clustered servers, rather than simply providing failover for high availability. VIA 1.0 defines high-speed interconnects, called System Area Networks (SANs), between standard high-volume (SHV) servers and to Fibre Channel SANs to combine performance and failover capabilities for 16 or more nodes.

Performance clusters based on VIA 1.0 were in the development stage when this book was written. You can view a slideshow of a Microsoft SAN and VIA presentation at the 1999 Windows Hardware Engineering Conference (WinHEC) at http://www.microsoft.com/ WinHec/presents/Enterprise/Enterprise7/Enterprise7_files/frame.htm.

Delivering Scalability

The most common measure of server scalability is the maximum number of processors supported by the operating system and system board. Windows 2000 Server's symmetrical multiprocessing (SMP) features support up to four processors; Advanced Server handles four to eight CPUs; and DataCenter Server can accommodate up to 32. Unfortunately, you don't get a linear increase in performance as you add more processors to conventional SMP servers; memory management overhead and data-transfer bottlenecks cause a progressive reduction in incremental speed increases.

Pentium III Xeon servers based on the Intel Profusion chipset announced in August 1999 promise eight-way servers that deliver substantial improvement over the performance of four-way systems. In tests running the Transaction Processing Performance Council's TPC-C benchmark software, Windows 2000 Advanced Server, and SQL Server 2000, 12 Compaq 8500 ProLiant servers, each having eight Xeon 550MHz processors achieved 227,079 order transactions per minute (tpmC). Microsoft claims the test, conducted in early 2000, represents a world record for database transaction processing. For details of the test, go to http://www.microsoft.com/presspass/press/2000/Feb00/SQLSvr2000PR.asp.

What's more important, however, is the total system purchase price divided by tpmC, a value that's commonly used to compare RDBMS price-performance ratios. The $19.12/tpmC of the 12 eight-way server configuration was almost identical to the $18.93/tpmC for an eight-server configuration, which delivered 152,207 tpmC. As of March 2000, the next fastest system was a 96-processor IBM RISC System 6000 running an Oracle 8i version 8.1.6 database that delivered 135,815 tpmC at $52.70/tpmC. You can review the current list of tmpC and $/tmpC values for various combinations of hardware, operating system, and RDBMS at `http://www.tpc.org/New_Result/TPCC_Results.html`.

TCP/IP Load Balancing

In January 1999, Microsoft released the Windows NT Load Balancing Service (WLBS) as a downloadable add-on to Windows NT 4.0 Advanced Server. WLBS lets Internet Service Providers (ISPs) and large commercial Web sites distribute Internet traffic across up to 32 individual servers. Each server runs an independent copy of Internet Information Server (IIS). The multiple servers commonly act as a front end to a large failover or performance cluster running an RDBMS, such as SQL Server 7.0.

Microsoft calls Windows 2000 Advanced Server's implementation of WLBS Network Load Balancing (NLB). NLB doesn't require the specialized hardware needed for failover clustering; you can scale your system to accommodate increasing Web traffic by adding more front-end servers, up to the 32-server limit. Increasing front-end capacity, of course, requires scaling up the back-end RDBMS to handle the additional workload by adding more RAM and processors. For Web sites, you can combine NLB and failover clustering for the RDBMS to achieve a combination of server performance and availability that rivals higher-cost performance clusters.

Tip from
RJ

> NLB eliminates the need for RAID 5 arrays to provide Web content data redundancy. The optimum configuration for high-performance page serving is a RAID 1 (mirror) set for the system partition and RAID 0 striping for the paging file, logs, and Web content.

Figure 7.2 illustrates a Windows 2000-based Web server farm that combines NLB and MSCS. Four Advanced Server systems running NLB connect to a two-node failover cluster running SQL Server 7.0+ EE. Each of the four Web servers handles, on the average, 25% of the HTML and ASP traffic generated by visitors. SQL Server stores page content and handles visitor registration and, if applicable, e-commerce transactions. Optionally, the cluster also provides file-sharing services to deliver Web content, including streaming audio/video files, to the machines running NLB. Two machines running Windows 2000 Server perform Domain Controller (DC) duties, including Dynamic DNS Server (DDNS) services. Web and cluster servers are member servers of a single site and domain tree.

Figure 7.2
This diagram shows a four-node NLB Web farm and two-node MSCS cluster running Windows 2000 Server and Advanced Server.

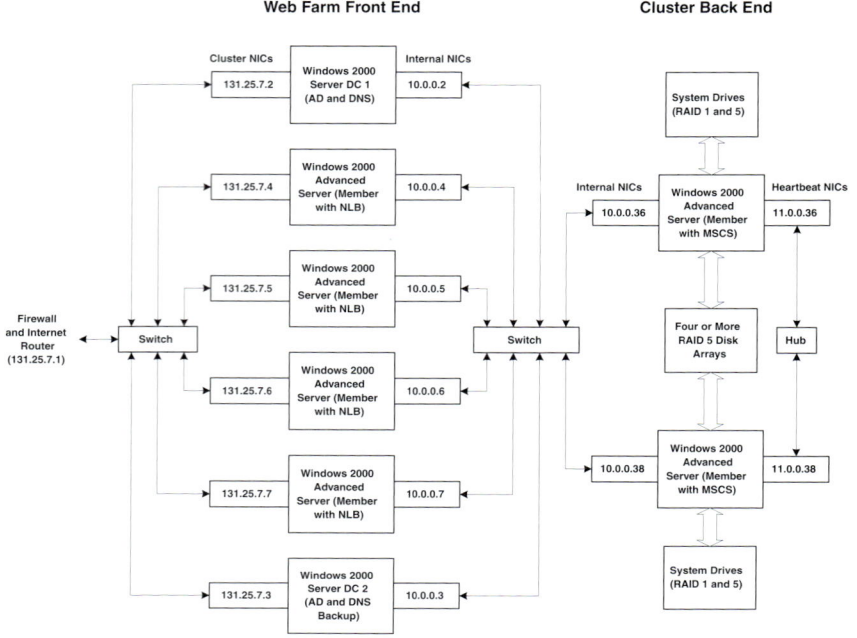

Each server is equipped with two NICs; servers with more than one NIC are called *multi-homed*. One NIC on each server (called the cluster NIC) connects to a 100Mbps Ethernet switch that, in turn, connects to the public Internet through a firewall and router. Cluster NICs must have IP addresses assigned by InterNIC; you need a slash 26 or lower Classless Internetwork Domain Routing (CIDR) network type to provide 61 IP host addresses for 32 front-end servers, the maximum that NLB supports. A slash 27 CIDR network type with 29 available host addresses accommodates up to 25 Web servers, plus the two DCs.

→ For a brief explanation of CIDR network types, **see** "IP Subnets and Routers," **p. 67**.

The other NIC on each server, called the internal NIC, isolates the back-end cluster from Internet hackers. Internal Web farm NICs run on the private 10.0.0.0 Class A network. The internal NICs of the cluster nodes transmit the *heartbeat packets* that indicate the node is alive on an arbitrary pair of IP addresses that aren't on the internal subnet. If the active node stops sending heartbeat packets, failover—which takes a minute or two—puts the previously inactive node on line.

Note

Network Engines (http://www.networkengines.com) offers an alternative approach to Windows 2000's NLB with rack-mounted WebEngine servers. WebEngines, which are one 1.75-inch rack unit in height, offer cluster-based load balancing for up to 256 servers. WebEngines run IIS on the embedded version of Windows NT, and provide automated content replication. IBM announced, in early September 1999, a license to use Network Engine's designs for its NetFinity server line. Microsoft hadn't announced an embedded version of Windows 2000 when this book was written.

Component Load Balancing

Three-tier applications, in which a business services layer—called the middle tier—separates front-end processes from RDBMSs, has become the standard architecture for Web-based transaction processing and other heavy-duty database operations. You implement business service elements as in-process Component Object Model (COM) DLLs. Visual Basic and Visual C++ are the two most common programming languages for creating COM DLLs. Windows 2000 Server's COM+ features streamline deployment and management of COM components on single or multiple servers.

→ To gain a better understanding of COM+ and component-based application design, **see** "Three-Tier Component Architecture," **p. 1141**.

The Web server system that was shown in Figure 7.2 can run middle-tier objects on individual front-end servers or on the clustered nodes. The problem with the latter approach is the resources consumed by the need to create an instance of a COM object for each user session on the Web servers. Although COM+ provides object pooling and other enhancements to Microsoft Transaction Server 2.0, running complex components can bog down the RDBMS servers.

Microsoft originally planned that Windows 2000 Advanced Server would offer Component Load Balancing (CLB). In late 1999, Microsoft announced that CLB would be removed from Advanced Server and incorporated into a new product called AppCenter Server, scheduled for release in mid-2000. CLB lets you create a group of up to eight servers devoted exclusively to running middle-tier components. The CLB servers automatically equalize the component load across members of the group. You connect the CLB servers, which run on the internal network, to the 100BaseT switch (near the center of Figure 7.2). The switch provides direct 100Mbps connections between the Web and CLB servers, and between the CLB servers and the cluster nodes.

Creating a Secure, Controlled Server Environment

You waste much—if not all—of your substantial outlay to improve server availability if you don't provide physical security, a standby power source, power conditioning, and a constant-temperature environment for your server.

Physical Security

Physical security is the key to protecting your server investment and preventing availability lapses as a result of unauthorized tampering with or deliberate damage to the server. Servers should be located in a totally enclosed area with controlled access, commonly called a *server closet*. Access control can be by a conventional key lock or Smart Card reader; if you use a Smart Card for physical access, consider adding a Smart Card reader for local server logon and for workstations used to administer the server(s).

Power Supply and Conditioning Systems

An uninterruptible power supply (UPS) to handle the entire server closet's electrical load for a predetermined time period is an absolute requirement to assure availability. Power outages have varying frequencies and durations in different geographic regions. Areas subject to frequent thunderstorms are the most prone to outages. You also must protect your server and networking hardware from lightning-induced spikes and power surges from other sources. Most server-grade UPSs provide some degree of power conditioning—at least surge supression—in addition to supplying standby power.

The original UPS designs consisted of a battery, charging circuitry, and an inverter. The load—your equipment—is never connected directly to mains power but is instead powered at all times by the inverter, driven by battery power. The battery is charged constantly as long as there's mains power (see Figure 7.3). This type of UPS is called a *true UPS* or an *online UPS*.

Figure 7.3
An online UPS isolates your servers and networking components from the utility power line by running on battery power at all times.

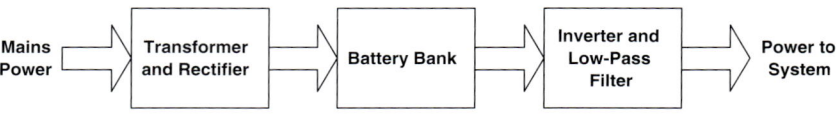

An online UPS has several advantages. First, because the load is driven directly by battery power at all times rather than switched to battery when mains power fails, there's no switch-over time. Second, because there's no switch, the switch can't fail. Third, full-time battery operation allows the equipment to be completely isolated from the AC mains power, thereby guaranteeing clean power.

Balanced against online UPS advantages are a few drawbacks. First, an online UPS is expensive, often costing 50% to 100% more than alternatives. Second, because an online UPS constantly converts mains AC voltage to DC voltage for battery charging and then back into AC to power the equipment, efficiencies are often 70% or lower, compared to near 100% for other methods. In large installations, this may noticeably increase your power bill. Third, battery maintenance becomes a more important issue with a true UPS, because the battery is in use constantly.

The high cost of online UPS technology led to the development of a less-expensive alternative that was originally called a *standby power supply* (SPS). Like an online UPS, an SPS includes a battery, charging circuitry, and an inverter to convert battery power to 120-volt AC. Unlike the online UPS, the SPS also includes a switch. In ordinary conditions, this switch routes mains power directly to the equipment being powered (see Figure 7.4, top). When the mains power fails, the switch quickly transfers the load to the battery-powered inverter, thus maintaining power to the equipment (see Figure 7.4, bottom).

Figure 7.4
A standby power supply runs your equipment on mains power (top) until a power outage occurs (bottom).

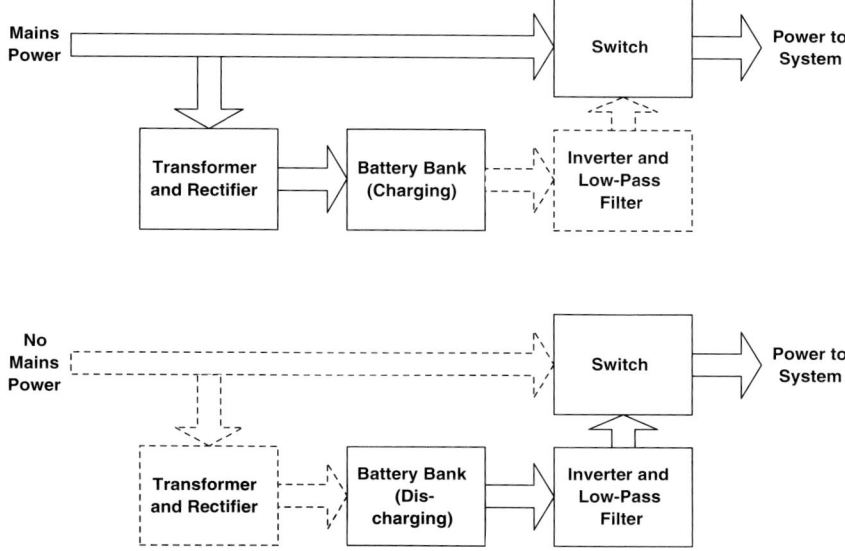

If you have an a-c ammeter, measure the current consumption of each connection to mains power and sum the readings. Alternatively, estimate the electrical load by totaling the rated power consumption in watts of all server and subsystem power supplies, the rated power consumption of monitors and networking hardware. Divide the total watts by 120 to determine the electrical current in amperes. Add at least 50% of the measured or calculated total power for future expansion. Then multiply the amperes by the number of power-outage hours to determine the required ampere-hours (Ah) of the UPS. Most electrical utilities will provide statistical data for local power outage durations on request.

Figure 7.5 shows a sample Excel worksheet for calculating the UPS load of a typical server closet or room at a primary Windows 2000 site. You obtain the rated power (Rated Watts) from the device's label, and divide by 120 (in North America) to obtain Rated Amps. Use a clamp-on digital a-c ammeter to determine the actual current consumption of each device (Measured Amps). Averaging rated and actual current consumption provides a conservative value for sizing the UPS (UPS Amps). Based on the worksheet value (51.07 A) and a 50% safety factor, the UPS must be capable of delivering 75 Amps. If you want the UPS to cover a two-hour outage, specify a 150-Ah unit.

Figure 7.5
You can use a simple Excel worksheet to determine the UPS load for a bank of servers.

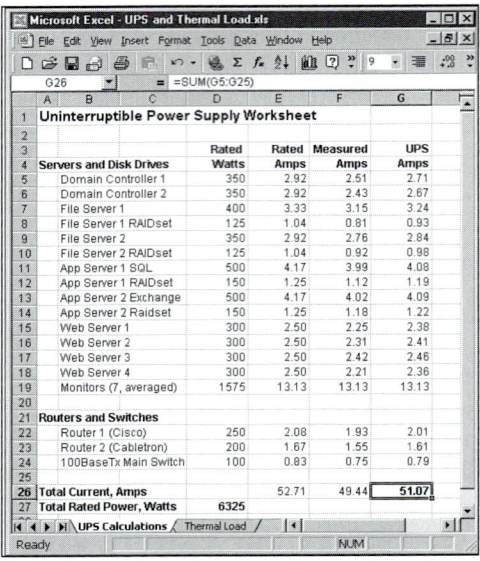

> **Tip from**
> *RJ*
>
> Don't count on standby diesel generators you install or those provided by the owners of large office buildings to take the place of a UPS or SPS, or reduce the maximum outage time you use in the capacity calculation. In many buildings, standby power is provided only to elevators, emergency lighting, and other high-priority services, such as health care facilities. Standby generators also are notorious for failing to start when an outage occurs. Another common failure point is the high-voltage, high-current switch that substitutes generator for utility power.

AMBIENT TEMPERATURE CONTROL

If the server closet has solid walls, provide air conditioning to maintain the ambient temperature at 25°C (78°F) or lower. A rule of thumb is that the incidence of component failure doubles for each 18°C (25°F) increase in ambient temperature above 25°C.

Estimate the air conditioning load by multiplying the total power consumption in Watts calculated for your UPS by 1.25 for a standby UPS or 1.5 for an online UPS. Then multiply by 3.414 to convert to British thermal units (Btu) per hour or by 0.86 for kilocalories (kcal) per hour. Add the load in Btu/hr or kcal/hr for the size of the room and the maximum expected external ambient temperature. Figure 7.6 is a sample worksheet for calculating air-conditioning requirements for the equipment shown in Figure 7.5. The calculations show that an air conditioning system with a capacity of about 30,000 Btu/hr or 7,500 kcal/hr is required. Most mechanical engineers would add a safety factor and specify an air-conditioning system with a capacity of about 50,000 Btu/hr or 12,500 kcal/hr.

Figure 7.6
Use a worksheet to help determine the thermal load for air conditioning the server closet or room.

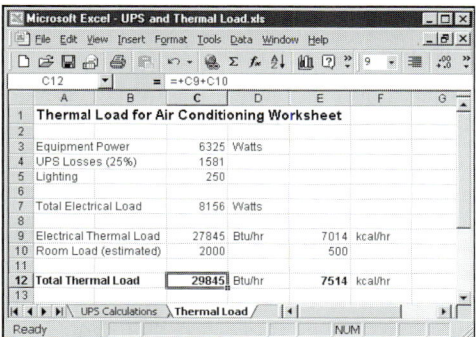

There is a growing trend toward mounting servers in standard 19-inch wide racks, rather than in floor-standing cabinets. Rack-mounted servers typically are more compact than cabinets, making them a more concentrated source of radiated and conductive heat. With a central air conditioner, orient discharge (cold air) ducts near the bottom of each rack and return plenums above the top of the rack.

If you use unit air conditioners, install a standby unit of equal capacity. Even with a central air conditioning system, provide a standby unit air conditioner to handle central system failures. In this case, you're likely to need to supplement closet air circulation with freestanding fans available at most hardware stores. Thermal inertia in a 25°C server closet of moderate size usually is sufficient to prevent the ambient temperature from rising above the server vendor's maximum, usually 35°C (95°F) to 40°C (104°F), during a 30-minute outage. To take full advantage of thermal inertia, consider installing higher-power circulating fans that run from the UPS.

Getting the Most from Your New Server Expenditures

If you have a budget to purchase new servers and associated networking hardware for your transition to Windows 2000, your goal should be to obtain the best combination of availability, performance, and scalability within budget limits.

Tip from
RJ

Before you purchase servers to run Windows 2000, read the "Hardware Design Guide Version 2.0 for Windows NT Server," co-authored by Microsoft and Intel. Version 2.0, which was written before Microsoft renamed Windows NT 5.0 to Windows 2000, is an excellent source of guidance for server purchase specifications. You can read the Design Guide online or download it from http://www.microsoft.com/hwdev/serverdg.htm. The design guide covers Basic Server, Small Office/Home Office (SOHO) Server, and Enterprise Server categories. Ensure that the server(s) you purchase conforms to Design Guide requirements by including a clause to that effect in your purchase order or bid request.

Following is a list of recommendations for getting the most bang and fewest headaches from your Windows 2000 Server purchase:

- Don't even think about purchasing a server that isn't on the Windows 2000 HCL. All legitimate manufacturers and assemblers of high-end servers are certain to have a broad range of systems on the HCL before all but the most adventuresome admins consider migrating production servers to Windows 2000 Server and its siblings.
- Beware of ISA slots in a PC purported to be a server. All high-end servers currently come with PCI-only buses that conform to the PCI 2.1 specification. The presence of even a single ISA slot on a system board indicates that system doesn't qualify for server status. The server should have a minimum of seven PCI slots.
- Walk away from any vendor who suggests using IDE fixed-disk drives in a server, regardless of the performance and MTBF specs for today's high-capacity DMA/33 and ATA/66 models. The Design Guide recommends that servers not include an ATA (IDE) host controller. IDE CD-ROM drives are acceptable, because the CD-ROM drive is used only for loading software, and SCSI CD-ROM drives occupy an otherwise-available SCSI device address. In today's server market, LVD SCSI and Fibre Channel represent server-quality drives and systems.

Tip from
RJ

Consider Network-Attached Storage (NAS) systems with SCSI-2/3 drives only for basic file-sharing applications. NAS, in which storage systems plug into a 100BaseT switch on your network, makes adding server capacity easy and quick. NAS systems are self-contained with their own operating system; the embedded version of Windows NT is a candidate for NAS devices. Bear in mind, however, that a 100BaseT connection delivers a maximum throughput of less than 10MBps to the switch, while internal Ultra2 SCSI RAID systems can sustain much higher speeds. Gigabyte Ethernet ports on 100BaseT switches are ten times faster but are *much* more expensive than conventional 100-Mbps switch ports.

- Purchase a complete server package from a single PC supplier; don't mix and match components to save a few hundred or even a few thousand dollars. Name-brand vendors guarantee interoperability of the components they supply as a package, and will install and test the Windows 2000 Server version you specify.

Tip from
RJ

Guaranteed interoperability is especially important when you opt for new technologies, such as a Fibre Channel SAN, and a new operating system at the same time. Purchasing dual servers and a SCSI subsystem with Windows 2000 Advanced Server and SQL Server EE or Exchange Server EE installed and tested by the vendor will save you many hours of grief and downtime compared with installing these products yourself.

It's a rule of thumb that you don't mix NIC suppliers on a network, but you can break the rule in the case of a packaged server purchase. The current crop of Intel 10/100BaseT NICs, for instance, mix well with their 3COM counterparts.

- Hot-swappable Ultra2 SCSI or Fibre Channel drives are one of the best availability investments. Hot-swapping lets you replace a failed member of a RAID system or subsystem without shutting down the server. RAID controller software rebuilds the RAID volume(s) from the operable data and parity drives. Hot-swappable PCI slots and adapters—especially NICs and SCSI adapters—also improve availability, although dual NICs with automatic failover drivers usually are the better choice for high-availability networking.
- Adding RAM is the fast track to increased performance. Estimate the amount of RAM you need to handle Windows 2000 Server and your server-based applications, and then add at least 50% to the estimate when you write the purchase order. Efficient operation of Windows 2000 Server takes substantially more RAM than Windows NT 4.0 Server; fortunately, even ECC SDRAM is far cheaper today than a couple of years ago. Make sure you can install up to 1GB of RAM in a single-processor server and up to 4GB with four or more processors.

Tip from
RJ

> Chapter 2 of the Design Guide requires a minimum of 128MB of ECC RAM for each processor running Windows 2000 Server and 256MB for Advanced server. Double these minimum requirements if you don't have a valid basis for estimating your initial RAM needs.

- Gain scalability by purchasing a four-way server with two processors, or an eight-way server with four processors. Buying additional processors when your server begins to run out of steam is far less expensive than replacing the entire server or its system board.
- Obtain or prepare for additional performance by specifying a server that supports Intel's Intelligent I/O (I2O) architecture. I2O consists of a Hardware Device Module (HDM), which runs on the system board's dedicated I2O Processor (IOP), and an Operating System Services Module (OSM) included in Windows 2000 Server. Special PCI adapter cards, most commonly RAID controllers and network cards, support I2O. For more information on I2O, start at `http://www.intel.com/pressroom/initiatives/i2o.htm`.

If you decide to purchase your server from a value-added reseller (VAR), rather than directly from the manufacturer, make sure the VAR can deliver the promised added value—on-site setup, outsourced server management, admin training, and the like.

Upgrading Existing Servers for Windows 2000

Most early adopters of Windows 2000 Server are faced with budgetary limitations that require the upgraded network to run on existing server hardware, if possible. If your servers are less than a couple of years old and have 128MB or more RAM, Windows 2000 Server probably will run without your upgrading the hardware, albeit more slowly than its Windows NT 4.0 predecessor. Installing Windows 2000 Server on older hardware, however, is a hit-or-miss proposition, and you don't want to miss when you're halfway through upgrading your network's PDC.

Few 1998-model servers, even those from the top-brand suppliers, are likely to appear on the Windows 2000 HCL. Vendors want to sell you new and fastest Pentium III Xeon hardware, not invest in certifying their older Pentium Pro models. The older your hardware, the less likely it—or even its major components—will appear on the HCL.

Following are recommendations to reduce the risk of a failed Windows 2000 upgrade on your existing Windows NT PDC:

- Update your system board's BIOS to the manufacturer's latest version, even it it's a year or so old. If you haven't done an upgrade to a BIOS flash-ROM, your first-time upgrade probably will be a high-anxiety event. Back up your system, and make sure to follow the system board manufacturer's instructions exactly. If the BIOS upgrade fails, recovery to your previous version sometimes is problematic.

- Obtain from the manufacturer the latest drivers for each of your server's adapter cards. The older the adapter, the less likely that the vendor will write a Windows 2000-specific driver for it. Install the latest version of the Windows NT driver for each adapter, if you can't obtain the Windows 2000 version.

Tip from
RJ

> Check the Hardware section of Relnotes.doc in the root folder of the Windows 2000 Server distribution CD-ROM for hardware known to be incompatible with Windows 2000. For example, the early Intel EtherExpress 16 ISA adapters, which shouldn't be installed in a server, cause severe problems with Windows 2000 installations. Windows 2000 doesn't support the original EtherExpress 100/PRO PCI adapter (E100A), but the replacement E100B adapter is supported, and works well on the `oakleaf2.oakleaf.edu` DC.

- Add at least 50% to your 128MB or more server's RAM inventory; consider 256MB to be the minimum RAM for a production server in anything but a home or SOHO network.

- Make sure you have sufficient space on your system volume for Windows 2000 Server. Full installation requires about 1GB of free disk space. You can specify a different volume with at least 250MB free for the AD database and \Sysvol folder. If you have a RAID set, you can gain an increase in performance by installing the AD database and \Sysvol folders on the array.

- Beware peripheral problems that arise from upgrading older servers with newer and faster components. For example, a 1997-vintage 12X IDE CD-ROM drive, which replaced an ancient 2X SCSI-1 drive on an OAKLEAF server, caused Windows 2000 Setup to fail with a "Missing Storprop.dl*" message. The 12X drive, which isn't on the Windows 2000 or Windows NT 4.0 HCL, worked fine for two years with Windows NT 4.0 Server.

> **Tip from**
> *RJ*
>
> If you encounter "Missing Storprop.dl*" or similar messages during setup, power down, replace your CD-ROM drive, and start Setup again from scratch. You can't recover by changing the CD-ROM drive and continuing Setup from the point at which the message occurred. Clicking the Cancel button when the message appears doesn't cancel the installation; it only terminates the attempt to copy Storprop.dll to the system drive, which leads to further "Missing…" errors.

- Replace older 10BaseT or 10Base2 NICs with 10/100BaseT models that appear on both the Windows NT 4.0 and 2000 HCLs before the upgrade. Server-grade NICs are much less expensive today than a year or two ago. Many early NIC drivers that work with Windows NT don't work with Windows 2000; Setup detects most, but not all, deficient drivers. There's nothing worse than upgrading a PDC to a Windows 2000 DC, and then finding it can't reconnect to your network.

Taking Advantage of Windows 2000 Hardware Management

One of Microsoft's primary objectives for Windows 2000 was to bring the Plug and Play, Universal Serial Bus (USB), laptop power management, and—to a lesser extent—the IEEE-1394 High-Performance Serial Bus features of Windows 98 to the new operating system. These new hardware-related features are of interest primarily to Windows 2000 Professional users, not server administrators. Plug and Play simplifies installing new or replacement hardware components, but Advanced Configuration and Power Interface (ACPI) power management isn't applicable to servers that—hopefully—run 24 hours per day, seven days per week. Few USB peripherals, other than mice and keyboards, are useful for servers, and the IEEE-1394 bus—called FireWire by Apple Computer and i.LINK by Sony—currently is used primarily for Digital Video (DV) data transfer and capture.

 The new or improved Windows 2000 hardware management features that server administrators commonly use are

- *Device Manager*—A component of the Computer Management Microsoft Management Console (MMC) snap-in that replaces Windows NT 4.0's Device Manager. Device Manager includes a Hardware Troubleshooter that's of limited use when attempting to diagnose server hardware problems.

- *Driver Signing*—Authenticates Windows 2000 hardware drivers with digital signatures.

Other hardware-related features, such as the Add/Remove Hardware Wizard and Found New Hardware Wizard for Plug and Play devices, are essentially identical to their Windows 98 forebears. Hardware Profiles are intended for laptop PCs, not servers. It's very uncommon to use multiple Hardware Profiles on servers, except occasionally for troubleshooting purposes.

Using Device Manager

Device Manager is your first line of defense when you suspect a hardware device failure has downed your server. As mentioned earlier in the chapter, many older and some current devices or their drivers (or both) either don't work or exhibit problems under Windows 2000. Device Manager usually can pinpoint—but not necessarily solve—these problems. You also use Device Manager to update device drivers. You can expect many third-party hardware vendors to provide a series of driver updates during the first year or two after Windows 2000's release.

To explore Device Manager's feature set, including installing a new hardware device driver, do the following:

1. Right-click My Computer and choose Manage to open the Computer Management console.

2. Choose View, Show Hidden Devices to list all device groups in Computer Management's right pane. Figure 7.7 shows Device Manager with the Network Adapters node expanded to display two network interface cards (Intel and Realtek) and hidden Direct Parallel and WAN Miniport drivers for the IP, L2TP, and PPTP protocols used by the Routing and Remote Access Service (RRAS).

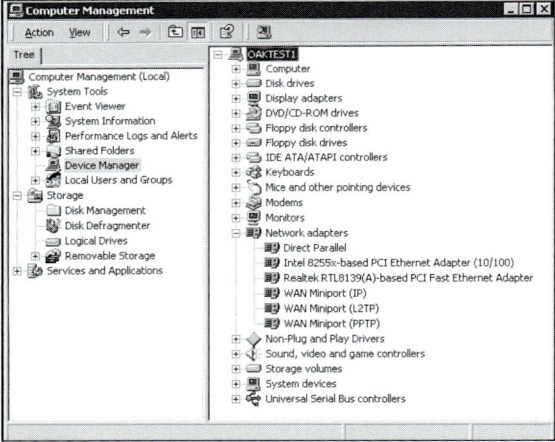

Figure 7.7
The Device Manager component of the Computer Management snap-in displays a list of network adapters and drivers, which includes hidden devices.

3. Double-click a device or driver to display the General page of its Properties dialog. Figure 7.8 shows the General page for a Realtek RTL8139(A)-based PCI 10/100BaseT adapter. The driver for adapters using this chip is included on the Windows 2000 distribution CD-ROMs.

Figure 7.8
The General page of the Properties dialog displays basic network adapter information—in this case for a 10/100BaseT network adapter using a Realtek RTL8139(A) chip.

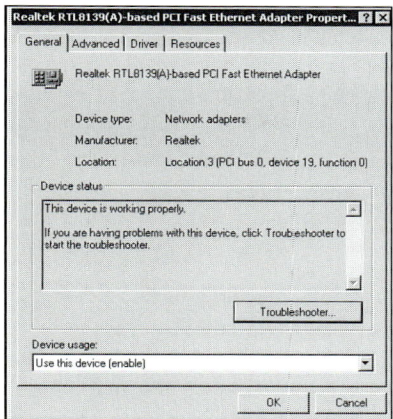

4. Click the Advanced tab to display additional settings for the device, if the device supports them. Figure 7.9 shows available settings for the Link Speed/Duplex Mode property of the Realtek adapter. Most autosensing 10/100BaseT adapters offer similar value sets for this property.

Figure 7.9
The Advanced page displays Link Speed/Duplex Mode settings for a typical 10/100BaseT autosensing network card.

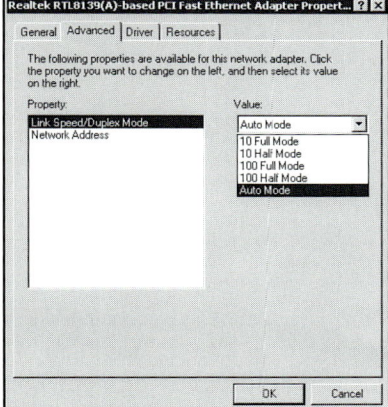

Tip from
RJ

Verify the Link Speed/Duplex Mode—sometimes called Link Speed & Duplex or the like—after you install Windows 2000 Server. You might find that the default value is 10 Full or 10 Half, instead of the autosense mode, which usually is called Automatic, Auto Mode, or Auto Detect. Unless the adapter's instruction manual states otherwise, use Auto Detect for autodetecting hubs or switches. If you specify 100 Full with some adapter and switch/hub combinations, the adapter won't communicate with the switch or hub.

> **Note**
>
> Most 10/100BaseT network cards let you specify a local Media Access Control (MAC) address for the card. By default, the local and network MAC addresses are identical. Assign a local MAC address only if your software instructs you to do so.
>
> Many adapters, such as the Intel 8255x series, have several more property settings. Don't change the default values unless you know what you're doing; it's easy to disable a network adapter by setting the wrong values. If you intend to change the default values, make a list of the defaults before proceeding.

5. Click the Driver tab to display basic information about the device driver, such as Driver Provider, (file) Date, Driver Version, and Digital Signer, if the driver is signed. Figure 7.10 shows Microsoft as the Driver Provider, because the driver is on the Windows 2000 distribution CD-ROMs.

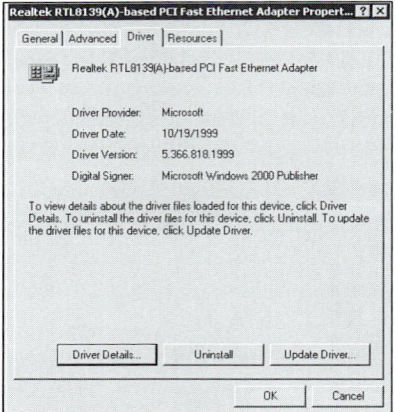

Figure 7.10
The Driver page for a network adapter shows the source, date, version, and driver signatory.

6. Click the Driver Details button of the Driver page to open the Driver File Details dialog. This dialog displays more information about the driver file(s) and the name of the person or firm that wrote and copyrighted the driver (see Figure 7.11). If you're attempting to resolve a driver problem, the device manufacturer probably will ask you to provide the information from this dialog. Click OK to close the dialog.

7. To install a replacement driver from a diskette or a network share, click the Driver page's Update Driver button to start the Update Device Driver Wizard. Click Next to bypass the Wizard's Welcome dialog.

8. In the Wizard's Install Hardware Device Drivers dialog, select the Display a List of the Known Drivers... option (see Figure 7.12), and click Next.

9. In the Select *DeviceType* dialog, click to select the item in the list, if necessary, and click Have Disk to open the Install from Disk dialog (see Figure 7.13).

TAKING ADVANTAGE OF WINDOWS 2000 HARDWARE MANAGEMENT | 319

Figure 7.11
The Driver File Details dialog displays the filename, version, and original provider of the network adapter driver.

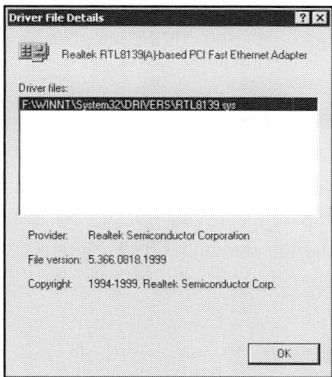

Figure 7.12
The Update Device Driver Wizard's second page allows you to select the method for installing an updated driver.

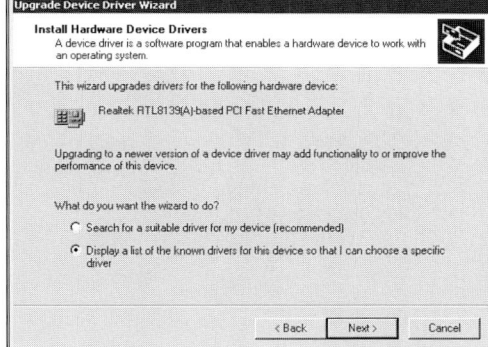

Figure 7.13
The most common method for installing drivers for an unsupported network adapter is from a diskette.

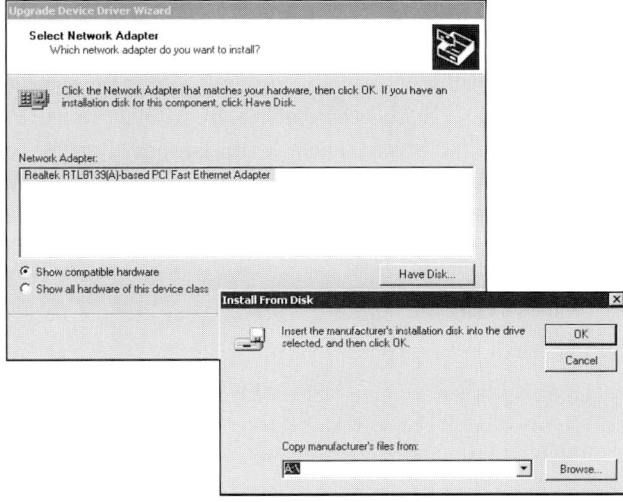

PART
I
CH
7

10. If the driver is on a diskette, click OK to run the installation process. Otherwise, navigate to the location of the driver installation package. Follow the Wizard's instructions, which vary by driver type and supplier, to complete the new driver installation.

11. Click the Resources tab of the Properties dialog to display the Input/Output Range (I/O address), Memory Range (if the driver allocates blocks of high memory), and the Interrupt Request (IRQ) number. Figure 7.14 shows the values for the Realtek network adapter. You can view but not alter the Plug and Play values for most PCI adapters; the Plug and Play manager sets these values on startup. Click OK to close the Properties dialog.

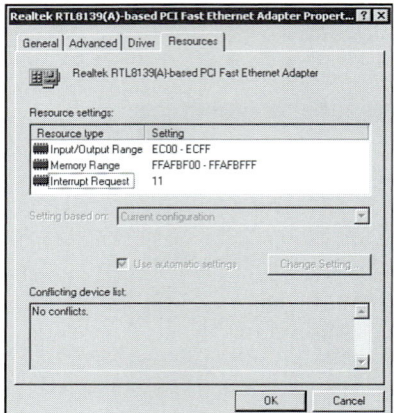

Figure 7.14
The Resources page allows you to examine the fixed I/O address range, high memory address allocation, and IRQ number for a network adapter.

DISABLING AND ENABLING DEVICES

If your server includes hardware that you don't ordinarily need to use, you can disable the device by right-clicking its node and choosing Disable from the context menu. The Intel 8155x adapter in the DC used for the preceding examples is for testing multihoming features, such as software routing, with two adapters. In ordinary operation, the network card is disabled, as illustrated by the barely visible X superimposed on the icon to the left of the highlighted description in Figure 7.15. Once disabled, you can re-enable the device by right-clicking its node and choosing Enable. You also can disable or enable a device in the General page of the device's properties dialog.

TAKING ADVANTAGE OF WINDOWS 2000 HARDWARE MANAGEMENT | 321

Figure 7.15
Device Manager shows a disabled device, in this case an Intel 8255x-based PCI Ethernet Adapter.

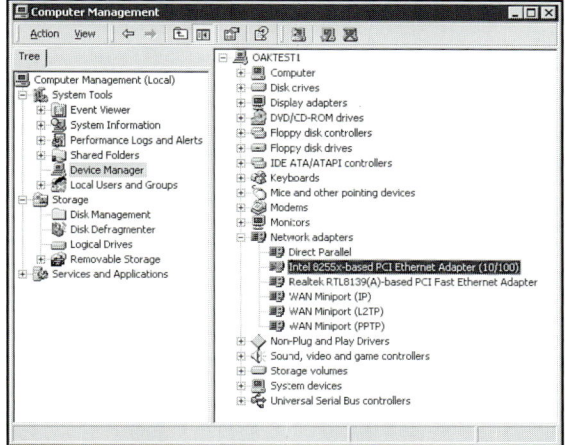

ATTEMPTING TO USE DEVICE MANAGER'S TROUBLESHOOTING FEATURE

The General page of the properties dialog for all devices has a Troubleshooter button (refer to Figure 7.8) that opens a related topic in the Troubleshooting and Addition Resources chapter of the Windows 2000 Help file. Figure 7.16 shows the troubleshooting topic for the non-Plug and Play Serial driver, which, along with the Parport (parallel port) node, indicated a problem by the appearance of a yellow exclamation point superimposed on the Serial and Parport nodes of the Non-Plug and Play drivers lists. The troubleshooting topic, "Device Manager Error Code 24," sheds little light on the reason for the problem with the two serial ports on the PC, and doesn't give you a clue as to how to go about solving the problem. The Ports node and its Communications Ports and Printer Ports subnodes are missing from Device Manager's list because of failure of their drivers to load.

Figure 7.16
The Windows 2000 Troubleshooter topic for a problem with a server's serial port sheds little light on how to correct the problem.

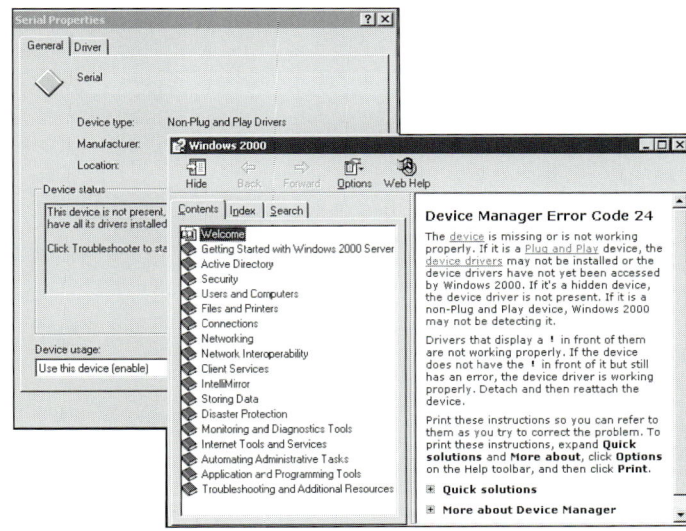

PART
I
CH
7

Viewing Devices by Connection and Resources by Type

 Device Manager offers the following four views, which you access by choosing View and selecting the one you want:

- Devices by Type—The default view. Lists hardware and software devices grouped by category as shown in preceding Figures 7.7 and 7.16.

- Devices by Connection—Lists all hardware and software devices in alphabetic order (see Figure 7.17).

Figure 7.17
Device Manager provides an alphabetical hardware list in Devices by Connection view mode.

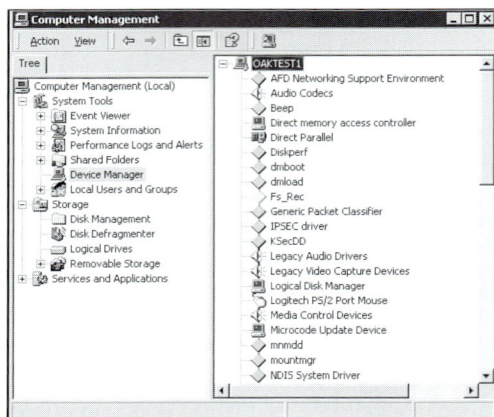

- Resources by Type—Provides a list of devices that use Direct Memory Access (DMA), Input/Output (IO) addresses, Interrupt Request (IRQ) numbers, and upper Memory addresses (see Figure 7.18). The Resources by Type display mode is useful for investigating existing or potential resource conflicts.

- Resources by Connection—Displays the same list as Resources by Type.

Figure 7.18
Resources by Type (or by Connection) displays DMA, I/O, IRQ, and memory allocations.

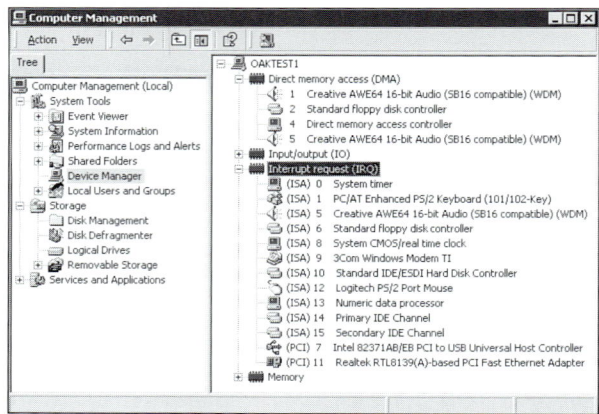

Deciding on Windows 2000 Driver Signing

Driver Signing is an element of the new Windows File Protection System, which attempts to prevent overwriting of system files with sys, .dll, .exe, .ocx, .fon, and .ttf extensions. All such files provided by Microsoft have an embedded digital signature to vouch for their authenticity and compliance with Windows 2000 device driver standards. All Windows 2000 device drivers, most of which carry a .sys extension, on the distribution CD-ROMs are digitally signed by Microsoft.

You can test whether all system files on your machine have been verified by doing the following:

1. Choose Start, Run, and type **sigverif** in the Open text box to open the File System Verification dialog.
2. Click Start to perform a scan of all system files for the Microsoft digital signature (see Figure 7.19).

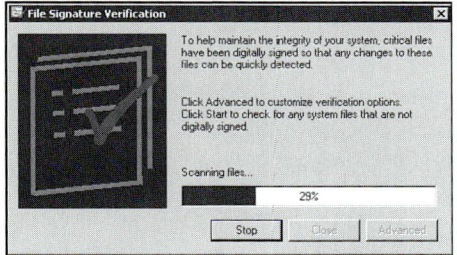

Figure 7.19
Use the File Signature Verification program (Sigverif.exe) to scan system files for the Microsoft digital signature.

3. If all files pass the verification test, you receive a SigVerif message. If not, a list of unverified files opens.
4. To check additional files for missing signatures, click the Advanced button of SigVerif's dialog to open the Search page of the Advanced File Signature Verification Settings dialog. You select the type(s) of files to scan in the Scan This File Type list, and type or browse for the path for the start of the scan in the Look in This Folder text box. Mark the Include Subfolders check box to ensure that all subfolders are tested (see Figure 7.20). You can specify scan logging options in the Logging page.

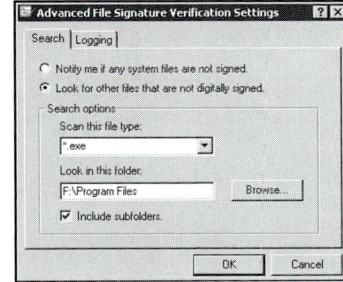

Figure 7.20
Use SigVerif to scan for digital signatures of executable files in the \Program Files folder and its subfolders.

5. Click Start to run the newly specified scan. On completion, the Signature Verification Results dialog lists the .exe files that don't pass the test (see Figure 7.21). Note that Microsoft's Internet Explorer executable (Iexplore.exe) version 4.40.1381.1 isn't digitally signed.

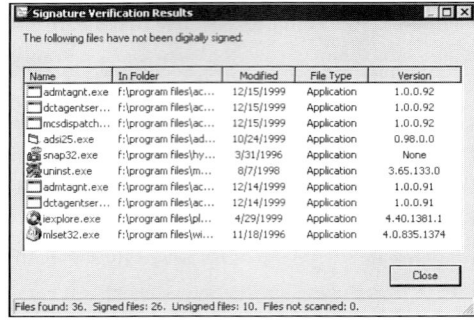

Figure 7.21
Running SigVerif generates a list of executable files in the \Program Files folder and subfolder without digital signatures.

To set the level of Driver Signing security on system files, do the following:

1. Launch Control Panel's System tool, and click the Hardware tab.
2. In the Device Manager frame of the Hardware page, click Driver Signing to open the Driver Signing Options dialog. The Ignore, Warn, or Block unsigned system files options appear in order of increasing security (see Figure 7.22).

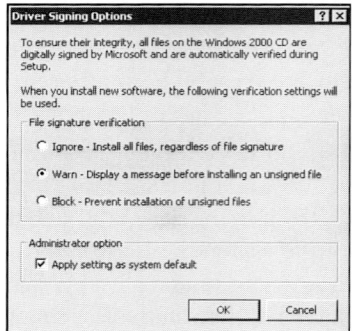

Figure 7.22
The Driver Signing Options dialog of Control Panel's System tool allows you to set the level of security on Windows 2000 system files.

3. Select the level of security you want—Warn is the default. Assuming you're logged on with Administrators privileges, mark the Apply Setting as System Default check box to apply the setting to the server.

The default Warn option is your best choice until more third-party driver suppliers climb on the Designed for Windows 2000 bandwagon.

Choosing the Optimum RAID System

Fixed-disk drives have moving parts, so drives are much more failure-prone than system boards, processors, or adapter cards. Virtually all minicomputer and PC servers use RAID to provide redundant data storage. RAID's instant access to duplicated data or ability to quickly regenerate lost data prevents unscheduled server downtime as a result of a single drive failure. Defining the RAID system that's appropriate for your server is as important as establishing your basic server specifications. The RAID system is a primary determinant of the availability and performance of your server(s).

SCSI Drives for RAID Systems

SCSI defines a general-purpose bus that allows the connection of a variety of peripherals—hard-disk drives, tape drives, CD-ROM drives, scanners, printers, and so forth—to a host adapter that occupies only a single expansion slot. You can connect up to 30 such devices to a dual-channel host adapter and install more than one host adapter in a server.

SCSI is the dominant drive technology in servers for the following two reasons:

- SCSI supports many devices, and many types of devices, on a single host adapter. Expansion slots are precious resources in a server. SCSI's capability to conserve these slots by daisy-chaining many devices from a single host adapter is in itself a strong argument for its use in servers.

- SCSI provides request queuing and elevator seeking. Other drive technologies process disk requests in the order in which they're received. SCSI instead queues and services requests in the order in which the data can be most efficiently accessed from the disk. SCSI determines the location of each requested item on the disk and then retrieves it as the read head passes that location. This method results in much greater overall disk performance and a shorter average wait for data to be retrieved and delivered to the requester.

SCSI can transfer data using one of two methods. Asynchronous SCSI, also referred to as *Slow SCSI*, uses a handshake at each data transfer to verify completion of transmission. Synchronous, or Fast, SCSI reduces this handshaking to double the throughput.

SCSI uses a variety of electrical connections, differing in the number of lines used to carry the signal. Single-ended SCSI uses unbalanced transmission, where the voltage on one wire determines the line's state. Unbalanced transmission is susceptible to errors generated by electrical noise, so the total length of cables on the bus is limited to 3 or 6 meters for the fast and slow data rates, respectively. Differential SCSI uses balanced transmission, where the difference in voltage on a pair of wires determines the line's state. Balanced transmission is much less susceptible to induced electrical noise, making practical longer cable lengths. Differential SCSI enables use of expansion cabinets to store a large number of individual drives to create disk farms.

Tip from
RJ

> Don't consider low-cost Ultra DMA/33 or ATA/66 (IDE) RAID subsystems to implement RAID 1 or RAID 5 on a server. IDE RAID subsystems implemented on special adapter cards are quite effective for implementing RAID 0 to improve workstation performance or RAID 1 for nonstop client operation, but IDE RAID isn't robust enough for production servers. Windows 2000's IntelliMirror service usually is a more cost-effective approach to achieving client data redundancy than doubling the number of workstation drives.

→ For the details on SCSI RAID controllers, **see** "Hardware RAID Controllers and Subsystems," **p. 330**.

→ To learn the basics of the IntelliMirror service, **see** "Defining IntelliMirror," **p. 828**.

SCSI Classification

Over the years, SCSI has evolved from a relatively simple system for connecting peripheral components to a very sophisticated bus for high-speed data transfer. Following is a list of the current SCSI classifications:

- SCSI-1 uses an 8-bit bus connection and 50-pin D-Ribbon (Centronix) or 25-pin DB25 connectors, and serves a maximum of seven attached devices. SCSI-1 has a maximum data transfer rate of 2.5MBps asynchronous and 5MBps synchronous. SCSI-1 is obsolete.

- SCSI-2 uses an 8-bit or 16-bit bus connection. The data-transfer rates range from 2.5MBps for 8-bit asynchronous connections to 20MBps for 16-bit synchronous connections. Fast SCSI is the term applied to SCSI-2 host adapters that support data transfers at rates of 10MBps or faster. Fast SCSI uses a 50-pin Micro-D external device connector, which is considerably smaller than the Centronix connector. SCSI-2 is obsolete, except for peripheral components with slow data rates, such as printers, scanners, and CD-ROM drives.

- Wide SCSI is a SCSI-2 option that uses a 16-bit connection to double or quadruple the data-transfer rate compared with the 8-bit connection used by SCSI-1. 16-bit Wide SCSI uses a 68-pin Micro-D connector for external devices and supports burst speeds to 20MBps. Fast, wide SCSI-2 was the standard for servers until the advent of Ultra Wide SCSI.

Note

> Wide SCSI lets you connect 15 SCSI devices to a single host adapter. Dual-host adapters, such as the Adaptec AHA-3940UW Ultra Wide adapter, consist of two host adapters on a single PCI card, so you can connect up to 30 devices to two internal and one external SCSI cables. The AHA-3940UW and similar dual-bus adapters require the server system board to support PCI bridging, which is provided by most high-end system boards produced in 1997 and thereafter.

- Ultra SCSI is a subset of the SCSI-3 specification. Ultra is Fast SCSI with a doubled clock rate, which provides twice the potential throughput. Ultra Wide host adapters, such as the Adaptec AHA-2940UW, provide data transfer rates up to 40MBps over single-ended or differential cables. The majority of servers shipped in the late 1990s came with Ultra Wide SCSI host adapters. The cable length limitations of Ultra Wide SCSI—a maximum of 1.5 meters with seven or more devices attached—makes it impractical to create very large RAID systems with many drives.

- Ultra2 SCSI uses LVD connections to increase the maximum burst data rate to 80MBps and quadruple maximum cable length to 12 meters. 80MBps reasonably can handle up to four or five of the highest-performance 10,000-rpm disk drives available in late 1999. Ultra2 SCSI is today's standard for mainstream server host adapters and internal SCSI drives. It's possible to mix SCSI-2 and Ultra2 devices, but doing so drops the data rate to SCSI-2 speeds. Popular Ultra2 host adapters, such as the Adaptec AHA-2940U2W, provide a combination of Ultra2, Ultra, and Ultra Wide internal and external connectors. The 50-pin Ultra connector supports CD-ROM drives and other slower SCSI peripherals.

> **Note**
> The Adaptec AHA-3950U2 adapter is a 64-bit PCI card that provides two Ultra2 buses on a single host adapter. The AHA-3950U2 supports a combined data transfer rate of 160MBps on the 64-bit PCI bus. The AHA-2950U2 also fits in 32-bit PCI slots, and one of the buses can be dedicated to standard, Ultra, or Ultra Wide single-ended devices.

- SCSI-3 is a major upgrade to the SCSI-2 specification that defines additional SCSI Parallel Interfaces—SPI-3 for Ultra3 and SPI-4 for Ultra4—and other high-performance serial protocols. The most important of the serial protocols for servers are those for Fibre Channel (FCP and FCP-2). Fast-80 SCSI is an extension to SCSI-3 that provides data transfer rates of up to 160MBps over a single 16-bit SCSI bus.

SCSI Bus Termination

Proper bus termination is essential for successful data transfer from SCSI devices to the SCSI host adapter card. You must terminate both the internal (ribbon cable) and external SCSI buses. If you're using only internal or only external devices, the adapter card's built-in termination circuitry must be enabled. Internal termination must be disabled if you connect a combination of internal and external devices. In most cases, you specify whether on-card termination is enabled by setting the adapter's BIOS parameters during the hardware boot process. Figure 7.23 illustrates SCSI termination for internal devices; Figure 7.24 shows termination of a combination of typical internal and external SCSI devices.

328 | CHAPTER 7 SPECIFYING SERVER AND DATA STORAGE HARDWARE

Figure 7.23
SCSI cabling of internal devices requires the last device on the cable to terminate the chain.

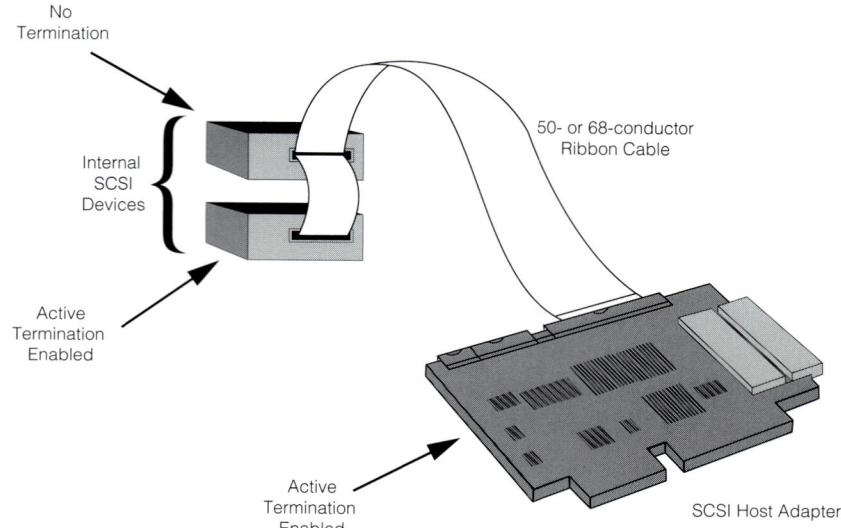

Figure 7.24
SCSI termination for a combination of internal and external devices requires a terminator on the last device of each of the two chains.

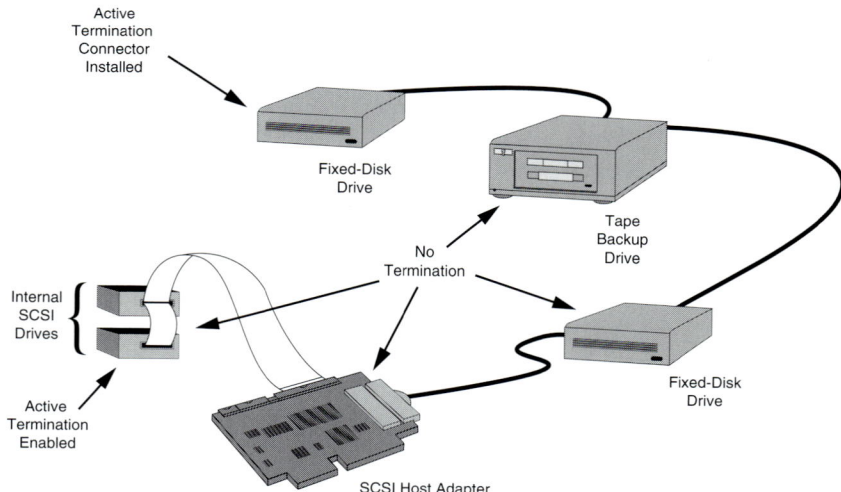

Note

Internal devices include termination circuitry, which usually is enabled or disabled with a jumper. You terminate external devices with a connector that contains the termination circuitry. Active (rather than passive) termination is necessary for Fast, Wide, Ultra, and Ultra2 SCSI devices. You must use special differential active terminators for Ultra2 buses.

Common RAID Classifications

RAID originated at the University of California at Berkeley in the late 1980s as a definition of Extended Data Availability and Protection (EDAP) techniques and classifications. Table 7.1 lists the three commonly used RAID levels and their uses for server data storage.

TABLE 7.1 THE THREE STANDARD RAID LEVELS FOR SERVER USE

RAID Level	Common Name	Primary Server Application
0	Striping	Paging, log, and other files that aren't critical to server operation, and content files of Web servers in a load-balancing configuration
1	Mirroring	Operating system and other critical files that have a very high ratio of reads to writes
5	Striping with parity	Data files that must remain on line following failure of a single drive

More detail on each of these RAID levels follows:

- RAID 0 improves performance but doesn't provide redundancy; if one drive fails, applications and services that depend on the volume fail with it. Increasing the number of drives in a RAID 0 set decreases volume reliability, because the probability of a volume failure is directly proportional to the number of drives in the volume. Drive management overhead increases as you add drives to a RAID 0 volume, so performance doesn't improve as rapidly as reliability deteriorates. RAID 0 requires a minimum of two drives.

- RAID 1 offers 100% redundancy by duplicating data on two drives of identical size. RAID 1 improves read performance at the expense of write time; writes commonly take 15% to 25% longer than to a single drive. RAID 1 is the only level on which you can install Windows 2000's system files. Like RAID 0, RAID 1 requires a minimum of two drives.

- RAID 5 is by far the most common level in use by today's servers. RAID 5 provides the data redundancy benefits of RAID 1, but with a substantial improvement in storage efficiency. The parity information needed to regenerate data lost as the result of a disk failure is only about 20% to 25% of the actual data. If a drive fails, a regeneration process based on the parity and other available data reconstructs the image on the replacement drive. RAID 5 requires a minimum of three drives.

The original Berkeley EDAP paper defined RAID levels 1 through 6, and there are many other proprietary RAID implementations, such as level 1/0 or 10 (mirrored striped sets), level 7 (a proprietary system with its own operating system), and level 53 (a combination of levels 0 and 3).

Software-Based RAID

Windows 2000 Server, like Windows NT Server, has the ability to create and manage software-based RAID volumes with the Disk Administrator snap-in for Microsoft

Management Console. Software-based RAID has the advantage of low cost; you can implement Windows 2000 RAID arrays with an Ultra Wide or Ultra2 SCSI PCI adapter, and two or three SCSI fixed-disk drives. The algorithms that implement redundancy, however, can consume a substantial percentage of your processor horsepower. Implementing Windows 2000's software RAID is one of the subjects of Chapter 9, "Installing RAID and Removable Media Systems."

Consider Windows 2000's software RAID features only in RAID 0 systems, which consume a small percentage of processor cycles, for load-balanced Web servers or for dedicated file-sharing servers that use the replication services of the Distributed File System (Dfs). To create a conventional file-sharing server at the lowest cost, you can use a combination of software RAID 1 for the system files and RAID 5 for the shared folders.

→ To learn more about Dfs replication, **see** "Using the File Replication Service with Dfs," **p. 716**.

Hardware RAID Controllers and Subsystems

All high-end servers include hardware RAID controllers, and even mid-range servers offer hardware RAID as an option. Hardware RAID controllers include one or more dedicated microprocessors and a real-time operating system (RTOS) to manage all striping and redundancy operations, including rebuilding a failed array. The majority of today's hardware RAID controllers provide four independent Ultra2 SCSI channels and up to 128MB or 256MB of cache memory shared by all channels.

Many servers incorporate an integrated RAID controller on the system board that connects to a maximum of six or eight internal drives. The internal drives plug into a printed-circuit card—called a backplane—having connectors that permit hot-swapping of a failed drive. It's a common practice to provide a *hot spare* drive that's plugged into the backplane but isn't made a member of the RAID set until a drive fails. You connect a pair of drives in a RAID 1 set for the system partition, regardless of your configuration for the data arrays. A conventional SCSI-2 controller on the system board connects to internal CD-ROM and backup tape drives. You also use the integrated SCSI-2 controller external magneto-optical disc changers (juke boxes) or backup tape changers, if you use them. Newer high-speed backup systems use the Ultra2 standard.

An optional second four-channel RAID controller on an adapter card connects additional drives housed in a separate rack cabinet with its own power supplies and cooling fans. These Ultra2 adapters typically cost about $2,000 with 128MB of cache.

One alternative to a hardware RAID controller connected to external SCSI drives is a complete RAID subsystem housed in a rack cabinet. In this case, the RAID subsystem appears to the server as a set of conventional (non-RAID) SCSI drives, and is called SCSI-to-SCSI RAID. Although SCSI-to-SCSI RAID is much more expensive than internally housed RAID sets, the added cost returns substantial availability improvement. High-availability RAID subsystems provide redundant RAID controllers, and hot-swappable power supplies and cooling fans; larger RAID subsystems include their own tape backup systems and a dedicated UPS. If you can afford the higher cost of a RAID subsystem, you gain scalability and availability by an increase in the number of drives you can add to the system and elimination of the PCI RAID adapter as a single point of failure.

> **Note**
>
> The RAID Advisory Board (RAB) has established a classification system for RAID subsystems. The primary classifications are Failure Resistant, Failure Tolerant, and Disaster Tolerant Disk Systems. Most major storage system vendors and some SCSI component vendors are RAB members. RAB's Web site at `http://www.raid-advisory.com` provides a full description of the requirements for certification to each classification and a list of certified products. The RAB Web site also links to white papers that relate classification criteria to the Berkeley EDAP levels and articles about RAID from *Computer Technology Review* magazine (`http://www.westworldproductions.com/`).

SCSI-to-SCSI RAID systems for failover clustering use controllers with a dual-attachment feature. Dual-attachment permits two server nodes to connect to the same SCSI channels. Redundant channel cabling between multiple adapters in the subsystem and server prevents cabling from becoming a single point of failure in the overall system. Purchasing a cluster-ready SCSI subsystem, even if you don't plan an early move to Windows 2000 Advanced or Datacenter Server, is a cost-effective investment in scalability.

Fibre Channel Subsystems and Adapters

Fibre Channel RAID subsystems are becoming the standard at the very high end of the server spectrum. Fibre Channel is a serial protocol that runs at a maximum of 100MBps over fibre-optic or copper cabling. The fibre-optic option provides much greater maximum distance between nodes—up to 10km for long-wave (single-mode) fiber—but costs substantially more than copper, which is limited to 30-meter node separation.

Fibre Channel offers the following three topology options:

- *Point-to-point*—Similar to the SCSI connection approach.
- *Loop*—Called Fiber Channel Arbitrated Loop (FC-AL), this option permits attached devices to communicate with and through one another.
- *Fabric*—Similar in concept to an Ethernet switch, this option permits multiple pairs of attached devices to communicate with each other at the full 100MBps bandwidth.

When this book was written, FC-AL over copper was by far the most popular Fibre Channel implementation. Fibre Channel provides a significant increase in Ultra2 SCSI's availability, performance, and scalability. FC-AL hubs with copper ports connect nodes in close proximity. A hub with a combination of copper and fibre-optic ports, illustrated by Figure 7.24, lets you separate servers having FC-AL adapters a substantial distance from the storage subsystem. In Figure 7.25, two sets of FC-AL RAID arrays connect to each other and to two servers with FC-AL adapter cards, providing each server with access to the two RAID sets. The servers, in turn, have 100BaseT connections to workstations on two physically isolated network segments. The servers and their workstations can be located up to 10 km from the RAID arrays because fibre-optic cabling connects the servers and RAID sets.

Figure 7.25
This diagram illustrates four FC-AL RAID controllers and disk sets connected by copper and two servers connected by fiber-optic ports to an FC-AL hub.

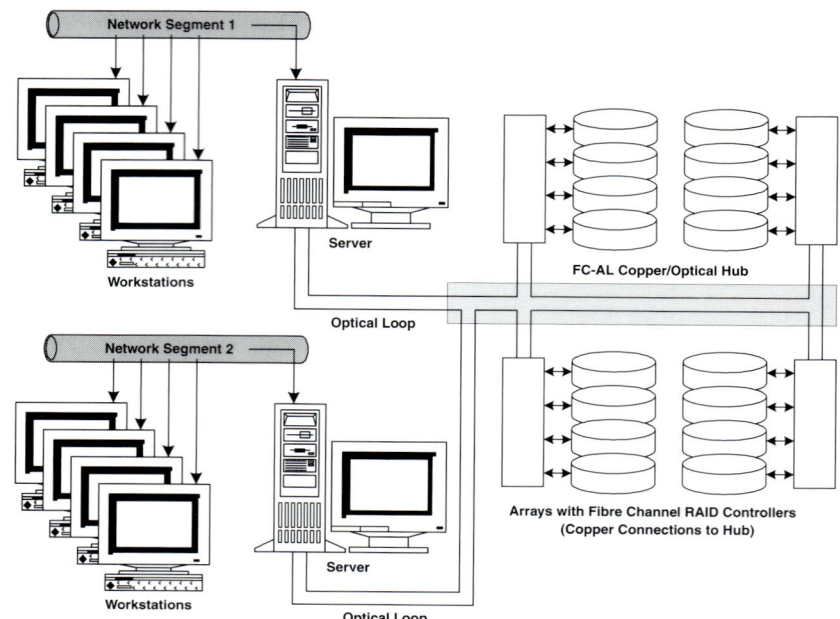

Redundant FC-AL connections increase availability by eliminating cabling as a single point of failure, and you can plug additional devices into an FC-AL hub without SCSI's requirement to reinitialize the system. FC-AL's 100MBps bandwidth is 20% greater than Ultra2 SCSI, and handles many more I/O operations per second. Finally, a single FC-AL bus can accommodate up to a combination of 126 hosts (servers) and drives. All major fixed-disk manufacturers offer FC-AL versions of their high-performance drives.

> **Note**
>
> Fibre Channel fabric systems, which implement Storage Area Networks (SANs) by interconnecting individual loops, are much more expensive than FC-AL-based RAID subsystems. A 16-port fabric expands the capacity of a storage system to about 2,000 attached devices. West World Publications' Storage Management Solutions and Storage, Inc. sites (http://www.westworldproductions.com/) are a good source of up-to-date information on SANs.

FC-AL is considerably more expensive to implement today than Ultra2 or forthcoming Ultra3 and Ultra4 SCSI systems. The cost ratio of FC-AL and Ultra2 drives is similar to that between SCSI-2 and IDE drives in the late 1990s. The added cost of FC-AL is destined to decrease rapidly in the first few years of the 21st century. If you need the ultimate in RAID availability, performance, and scalability to support large-scale, data-intensive operations, such as data warehousing, start with FC-AL.

Troubleshooting

Missing Non-Plug and Play Devices

Legacy devices, such as serial (COM) and parallel (LPT) ports, don't appear in Device Manager.

The majority of cases of missing COM and LPT ports is failure to specify in older computers' BIOS that a Plug and Play operating system is installed. A standard installation of Windows NT 4.0 doesn't support Plug and Play and the Plug and Play add-in to Windows NT 4.0 was "safe for servers." Thus, system administrators usually installed Windows NT without BIOS Plug and Play support.

Shut down Windows 2000, and change the system BIOS setting for PNP OS Installed (Award BIOS) or Plug and Play Aware O/S (American Megatrends BIOS) to Yes, and restart your server. After you log on, Found New Hardware messages appear for the serial and parallel devices, as well as diskette and other controllers in some cases. After Windows 2000 completes the "Searching for drivers" stage, you receive a System Settings Change message to reboot your computer.

Non-Plug and Play Devices Can't Obtain Required Resources

After you solved the preceding problem with missing legacy devices, some or all of the devices in Device Manager have exclamation points superimposed on their icons.

You've run out of interrupts, and must disable one or more devices to free legacy IRQs. PCI devices can share interrupts, but ISA and legacy devices can't. Figure 7.26 illustrates the result of changing the BIOS on the computer used for the Device Manager examples of this chapter to PNP OS Installed = Yes. Compare Figure 7.26 with Figure 7.7 earlier in the chapter. The LPT port and two COM ports now appear in Device Manager's list, but the COM port icons have exclamation points.

Figure 7.26
Device Manager displays added entries for COM1, COM2, and LPT1 ports. COM1 and COM2 are disabled due to resource conflicts.

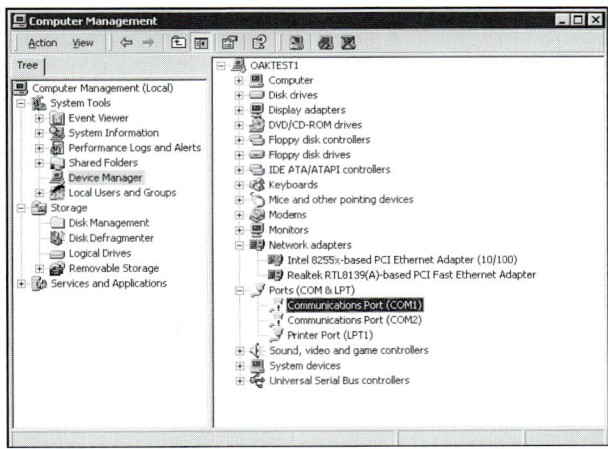

To verify that the COM ports have an IRQ problem, choose View, Resources by Type and expand the Interrupt Request (IRQ) node. Figure 7.27 shows both COM1 and COM2 attempting to use IRQ4 (the standard IRQ for COM1), because the 3COM Windows Modem TI has moved from IRQ? and now occupies IRQ3 (the standard IRQ for COM3). Note that there's no indication of disabled status in Resources by Type view. The Plug and Play manager has moved other devices to new IRQs—compare Figure 7.27 with earlier Figure 7.18.

Figure 7.27
Two legacy COM (serial) ports attempt to use IRQ4 as a result of an insufficient number of IRQs to handle installed devices.

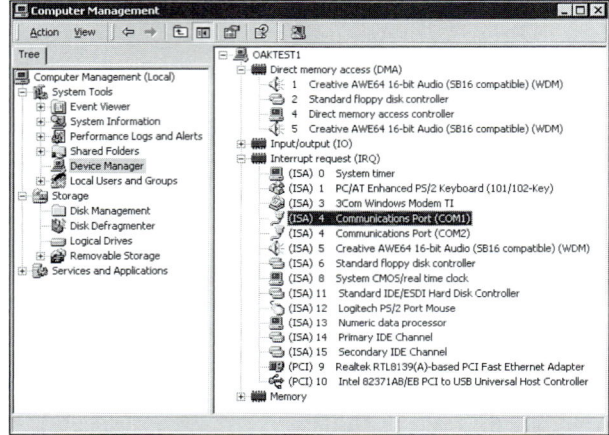

The only solution to this problem is to eliminate devices that you don't need on a server. For instance, don't install sound cards on servers, unless you intend to hide in the server closet during working hours to play PC games. If you don't need both COM ports, disable one. In the example shown in Figure 7.27, disabling COM2 and rebooting the server removed COM1's resource conflict. On reboot, the Found New Hardware displays the "Searching for drivers" message, but you don't need to reboot again in this case.

MCSE Corner: An Overview of the Exams

The following tests are scheduled to be available mid-year 2000. Some exams offer a broad overview of the functionality of Windows 2000 Server, while others are in-depth about a specific area of the Windows 2000 architecture.

70-215 Installing, Configuring, and Administering Microsoft Windows 2000 Server

Exam 70-215 is the primary exam for Windows 2000 Server. It covers most of the basics of a Windows 2000 Server system such as installation, file and printer sharing, and troubleshooting. It does not cover topics such as clustering or Active Directory.

70-216 Implementing and Administering a Microsoft Windows 2000 Network Infrastructure

Exam 70-216 covers the installation, configuration, management, monitoring, and troubleshooting of the following services:

- DNS
- DHCP
- Remote Access (RAS) and Virtual Private Networks (VPNs)
- TCP/IP and NWLink protocols (including IPsec)
- WINS
- IP Routing
- Network Address Translation (NAT)
- Certificate Services

In addition to being able to install and configure all of the these services, you must also understand how network security relates to each concept including authentication and encryption.

70-217 Implementing and Administering a Microsoft Windows 2000 Directory Services Infrastructure

Exam 70-217 covers the implementation of Active Directory services for Windows 2000 Server. You should understand the following concepts:

- Installation, configuration, and troubleshooting of Active Directory, including the use of sites, objects, and Organizational Units, and backup and restore procedures
- Optimizing Active Directory
- Active Directory Security
- Installation and administration of DNS for Active Directory
- Detailed usage of Group Policies
- Remote Installation Services (RIS)

70-219 Designing a Microsoft Windows 2000 Directory Services Infrastructure

Exam 70-219, along with 70-220 and 70-221, covers the design aspects of Windows 2000 systems, rather than the hands-on implementations. Exam 70-219, in particular, covers the analysis of business requirements and technical requirements, including size, administration, resource distribution, and data usage. You must also be able to design:

- An Active Directory forest and domain structure including trust relationships
- An Active Directory and DNS naming structure

- An Organizational Unit (OU) structure
- Active Directory replication
- Coexistence of Active Directory with other directory services
- An Active Directory implementation plan
- Placement of Operations Masters, Global Catalog Servers, Domain Controllers, and DNS servers

70-220 DESIGNING SECURITY FOR A MICROSOFT WINDOWS 2000 NETWORK

Exam 70-220 tests your ability to design a security solution for a distributed Windows 2000 network. You must be able to analyze technical and business requirements such as network layout, data usage, management topology, connectivity, the impact of implementing security policies, and security requirements. You should be proficient in the design of:

- Audit Policies
- Delegation of Authority
- Security policy location and behavior
- Data encryption strategy
- Authentication strategy
- Security groups
- Public Key Infrastructure
- Network services security
- Inter-network security
- Remote access security
- IPSec

70-221 DESIGNING A MICROSOFT WINDOWS 2000 NETWORK INFRASTRUCTURE

Exam 70-221 tests your ability to design network systems based on Windows 2000 Server given specified technical and business requirements. You should be able to recommend solutions for network topology, routing, addressing, name resolution, virtual private networks (VPNs), remote access, and telephony. You should be proficient in the design of:

- TCP/IP networking including subnetting, addressing, routing, and integration with existing WAN and LAN environments
- DHCP for both local and remote routed locations, and optimization
- Name Resolution services including DNS and WINS
- Multi-protocol implementations (IPX/SPX and SNA)
- Distributed File Systems (DFS)

- Internet access using proxy servers, firewalls, Routing and Remote Access Service (RRAS), Network Address Translation (NAT), Internet Connection Sharing (ICS), and Web and mail servers
- Remote Access solutions using RRAS and RADIUS
- VPN solutions
- Dial on Demand routing using RRAS
- Management and Implementation plans for the above solutions

70-222   Upgrading from Microsoft Windows NT 4.0 to Microsoft Windows 2000

Exam 70-222 tests your ability to perform the upgrade process from Microsoft Windows NT 4.0 systems to Microsoft Windows 2000 systems. You should be familiar with the differences in the domain models and how to move a Windows NT 4.0 domain to Windows 2000 with Active Directory. You should also be familiar with the process for moving users, groups, and shares to the new system.

70-240   Microsoft Windows 2000 Accelerated Exam for MCPs Certified on Microsoft Windows NT 4.0

Exam 70-240 is for the MCP or MCSE who has passed the Microsoft Windows NT 4.0 exams. It assumes the examinee has knowledge of Windows NT 4.0 and focuses the exam only on the parts of Windows 2000 that are different.

PART II

DEPLOYING WINDOWS 2000 SERVER

8 Deploying Windows 2000 Production Servers   341

9 Installing RAID and Removable Media Systems   413

10 Working with the Windows 2000 Registry   453

11 Setting Up Key- and Certificate-Based Security   485

12 Interoperating with NetWare Servers   519

13 Integrating UNIX and Linux Networks   545

CHAPTER 8

DEPLOYING WINDOWS 2000 PRODUCTION SERVERS

In this chapter

Planning Migration Tactics   342

Performing Domain Upgrades   343

Restructuring Domains   348

Optimizing Drive Partitioning   350

Upgrading a Windows NT 4.0 Production Server   352

Adding Other Services, Programs, and Tools to the DC   361

Promoting the PDC to Active Directory   363

Verifying the Active Directory Upgrade   367

Upgrading and Testing BDCs   376

Adding and Removing DCs in a Windows 2000 Domain   380

Installing Windows 2000 on a New Server   384

Upgrading Resource Domains   392

Throwing the Native-Mode Switch   397

Using ADMT to Restructure Windows NT Domains   398

Setting Security Policies for Domains and Domain Controllers   400

Recovering from a Disabled System   403

Seizing the FSMO Roles of a Failed DC   408

Troubleshooting   409

MCSE Corner: Deploying Windows 2000 Production Servers   410

Planning Migration Tactics

Moving your production network to Windows 2000 Server isn't a step to be taken lightly. Fortunately, Microsoft's Windows 2000 developers have made a substantial number of improvements to Windows NT 4.0's installation procedure. The number of reboots during the Windows 2000 Setup operation is reduced greatly, but the total installation time is about equal to that for Windows NT's setup plus installation of a Service Pack (SP).

As in warfare, a tactical misstep in the migration process can cause even the most elegant Windows 2000 upgrade strategy to fail. The basic tactical objectives for your migration to Windows 2000 Server, in descending priority, are as follows:

- Eliminate the possibility of a catastrophic failure, which is defined as the inability to recover from a failed server upgrade.
- Minimize disruption of user logon and access to resources—folder shares, printers, messaging services, and databases.
- Retain logon scripts, policies, and other user-oriented features so as to make the transition to Windows 2000 Server as transparent as possible to users.
- Consolidate or prepare for consolidation of upgraded resource domains into Organizational Units (OUs) and delegation of OU administrative authority to the appropriate individual(s).

Windows 2000 Server offers two approaches to migrating production domains from Windows NT 4.0—domain upgrade, which Microsoft also calls an *in-place upgrade*, and domain restructure, sometimes referred to as *domain consolidation* or *domain collapse*.

The examples in this chapter demonstrate the following production scenarios:

- Upgrading a Windows NT domain with a Primary Domain Controller (PDC) having 500 users and many groups
- Upgrading a Windows Backup Domain Controller (BDC) to a domain controller (DC) in the preceding domain
- Removing a Windows 2000 Domain Controller (DC) from a domain
- Adding a new Windows NT BDC to a Windows 2000 domain
- Creating a new Windows 2000 domain in the forest of the preceding domain as an example of domain consolidation
- Upgrading a resource domain as a child domain of the new Windows 2000 domain
- Changing the new domain to native mode
- Using the Active Directory Migration Tool (ADMT) to copy groups and users from a Windows NT to a Windows 2000 domain running in native mode

To follow the examples in this chapter fully, you need four networked servers that meet at least the minimum—and preferably the recommended—hardware requirements for Windows 2000 Server. The servers can be on the same subnet or separated into three subnets by two routers; the examples in this chapter use a single subnet.

Performing Domain Upgrades

A domain upgrade is a one-time bulk process that immediately affects all users and processes having access to the domain's resources. Upgrading a domain is easier and (usually) less costly than restructuring. Restructuring requires you to install Windows 2000 Server on new server hardware and copy Windows NT directory objects to the new domain and organizational unit (OU) structure. The bulk of this chapter is devoted to upgrading Windows NT domains.

→ To install Windows 2000 Server for domain restructuring, **see** "Installing Windows 2000 on a New Server," **p. 384**.

The upgrade process includes a recovery scenario, but there remains a definite risk that critical services—such as Windows Internet Naming Service (WINS), Dynamic Host Configuration Protocol (DHCP), or Domain Name Service (DNS)—might fail when you fall back to Windows NT 4.0.

Tip from
RJ

> Minimize the risk of a failed upgrade by verifying that the server hardware on which you intend to install Windows 2000 Server appears on the current Windows 2000 Hardware Compatibility List (HCL). If the server model doesn't appear, verify that each component is listed. Replace and test under Windows NT 4.0 Server any non-listed components before attempting to install Windows 2000 and AD.

→ For more information on use of non-HCL servers with Windows 2000, **see** "Equipment Requirements," **p. 195**.

It's particularly important that you verify operability of secondary WINS and DNS servers and the hot-spare DHCP server on at least one BDC before upgrading a PDC that serves as the primary supplier of these services. To test the BDC's WINS, DHCP, and DNS servers, you must power down or disconnect the PDC from the network, activate the hot-spare DHCP server, and check all services on one or more network PCs running each client operating system in use.

Sequencing Multiple-Domain Upgrades

Following is the recommended upgrade sequence for a Windows NT 4.0 network with two or more domains:

1. Thoroughly test non-transitive trust relationships to all other Windows 4.0 domains. Use the Domain Monitor tool (Dommon.exe) of the Windows NT 4.0 Resource Kit to verify trust validity (see Figure 8.1).

Figure 8.1
The Domain Monitor Resource Kit tool displays multimaster Windows 4.0 transitive trusts between one resource and two account domains.

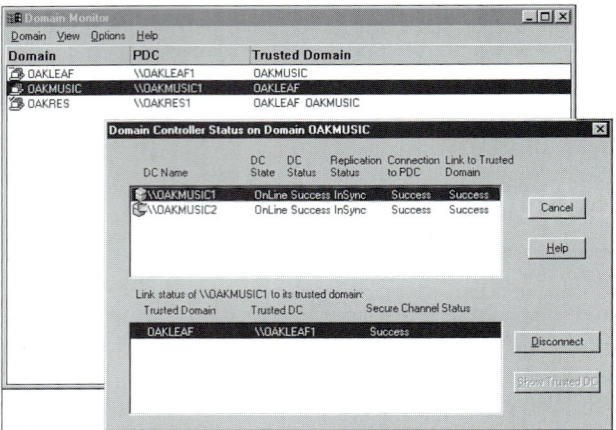

> **Tip from**
> *RJ*
>
> If you have more than one account domain, start the upgrade process with the account domain having the fewest number of users.

2. After upgrading the Primary Domain Controllers (PDCs) of all account domains, upgrade resource domains as child domains in the appropriate domain tree. Resource domains include middle-tier servers running Microsoft Transaction Server (MTS) and Microsoft Message Queue Server (MSMQ).

> **Tip from**
> *RJ*
>
> Apply the latest Windows 2000 Service Pack (SP) to each server you upgrade. SP1 was current when this book was written.

3. When the PDCs of all domains have been upgraded and are operating satisfactorily, upgrade all but one Backup Domain Controller (BDC) in each domain. You can add a Windows NT 4.0 BDC to any domain at this point if you encounter problems with client access to a domain's resources.
4. After all clients have been upgraded to Windows 2000 Professional, upgrade the remaining BDC(s), and throw the native-mode switch.
5. Restructure domains, if desired, to reduce the number of domains and enhance administrative efficiency. Restructuring domains with ADMT or third-party domain-management tools requires use of native mode's Universal Groups.

You can make minor alterations to the preceding sequence, such as upgrading all BDCs in a domain or performing a progressive upgrade of account and resource domains on a per-network basis.

> **Caution**
>
> Upgrading all BDCs to Windows 2000 DCs and changing to native mode creates a single point of failure for downlevel client logon. In native mode, the domain's PDC emulator authenticates all Windows NT and 9x user logons. If the domain's PDC emulator goes offline, downlevel clients are unable to log on to the domain. Until you've upgraded all clients to Windows 2000 Professional, maintain Windows NT 4.0 BDCs in strategic locations and retain mixed-mode operation.

UPGRADING A SINGLE DOMAIN

Upgrading an individual domain involves the following basic steps:

1. Verify that you have at least 1GB of free disk space in the PDC's Windows NT 4.0 system partition. Add 100MB to the disk space requirement for each 64MB of RAM above the 128MB minimum recommendation. Service Pack backup files require an additional 250MB of free space. You should have a system partition of 2GB or more—preferably 4GB—total space for production installations.

   If you're short on system partition disk space, you can install Windows 2000 Server's system files in a partition with about 850MB of free space, and install AD and the System Volume (Sysvol folder) on another partition with at least 300MB of free space.

→ For additional recommendations on partitioning your server's drives, **see** "Optimizing Drive Partitioning," **p. 350**.

> **Tip from**
> *RJ*
>
> PowerQuest's PartitionMagic (http://www.powerquest.com/partitionmagic/index.html) is a useful tool for altering the size and format of Windows NT partitions.

2. Carefully review the Read1st.txt and Relnotes.doc files in the root folder of the distribution CD-ROM to determine if you have any applications or hardware to which warnings apply or that require special attention during setup.

3. Become familiar with the upgrade process by performing at least one PDC upgrade on an isolated network.

→ To review step-by-step instructions for a practice upgrade, **see** "Migrating a Single-Domain Configuration," **p. 198**.

4. Mitigate the upgrade risk by ensuring that your system partition contains only Windows NT 4.0 system files. If you haven't followed this recommended practice, move shared folders—services, such as SQL Server, Exchange Server, Microsoft Transaction Server, and Internet Information Server—and important applications to another partition or physical disk(s).

5. Perform a full backup of the PDC to tape immediately before the upgrade, and verify the ability of the backup device and media to restore the files.

> **Tip from**
> *RJ*
>
> The backup drive be must be installed on a computer other than the PDC to be upgraded. If the upgrade hoses the PDC, you're not likely to be able to restore files quickly from a drive on the downed computer.

6. Add a temporary Windows NT 4.0 BDC to the domain. This computer should have sufficient horsepower to handle the PDC's load temporarily if the PDC upgrade fails. A logical choice for the backup BDC is the computer you used for practice upgrades on the isolated test network.

> **Tip from**
> *RJ*
>
> If you have sufficient disk space, create a partition on the temporary BDC to hold a mirror image of at least the PDC's boot and system partition(s). PowerQuest's DriveImage (http://www.powerquest.com/driveimage/index.html) and Symantec's Norton Ghost (http://www.symantec.com/sabu/ghost/index.html) are two of the most common third-party mirror-imaging applications.

7. Synchronize the temporary BDC and the domain's Primary Domain Controller (PDC) with Server Manager by choosing Computer, Synchronize Entire Domain. Verify in Event Viewer's System Log absence of events indicating a synchronization problem.
8. Power down the temporary BDC and disconnect it from the network.
9. Upgrade the domain's PDC, and set up AD and DNS. During the upgrade process, domain users won't be able to change passwords or perform other operations that write to the Windows NT directory.

> **Note**
>
> If all applications running on your PDC are Windows 2000-compliant, Windows 2000 Server's Setup program runs without the need for user intervention.

10. Immediately after the upgrade process completes, verify that you can change a Windows NT or 9x user's password and add a test user account. These two tests indicate that the upgraded PDC has reassumed the role of the PDC in the Windows 2000 domain.

If your Windows 2000 and AD installation succeed, the first PDC you upgrade becomes the initial root domain of the AD forest of domain trees. The upgraded PDC assumes the master Flexible Single-Master Operation (FSMO) role for all domains and the PDC emulator for the upgraded domain. As a result of the master FSMO assignment, you can't rename the Windows 2000 domain you create during the upgrade, nor can you rename the DC. The downlevel domain name, used by Windows 9x and NT clients, continues to be the domain name of the PDC you upgrade. The FSMO master also is authoritative for the Windows Time Synchronization service (Win32Time); all other Windows 2000 DCs update their system time from the FSMO master. Clients update their system time from the most accessible DC.

→ For a review of FSMO, **see** "Single-Master Operations," **p. 150**.

If you have problems with the Windows 2000 Server upgrade, see "Solving Windows 2000 Upgrade Problems" in the "Troubleshooting" section near the end of this chapter.

Tip from
RJ

> For an explanation of how Win32Time implements the requirements of the Simple Network Time Protocol (SNTP) of IETF RFC 1769, go to the Microsoft Knowledge Base (http://support.microsoft.com/search/default.asp) and read article Q224799, "Basic Operation of the Windows Time Service." The PDC emulator must have a full-time connection to the Internet to act as the primary time server for the site.

The PDC emulator performs the following three functions for downlevel computers:

- Serves in place of the PDC to replicate directory changes to Windows NT 4.0 BDCs, which retain their original domain name
- Acts as the Domain Master browser by registering the Domain<0x1B> NetBIOS master browser name
- Handles all AD write operations, such as password changes, for Windows 9x and NT Workstation users

The PDC emulator remains in effect until all downlevel clients are upgraded. Users of the upgraded network don't need to change their logon credentials, and Windows NT computer accounts upgrade intact.

Tip from
RJ

> Minimize the time between upgrading the PDC and completing tests of the upgraded domain. You must record all changes you make to AD—which also replicate to the Windows NT BDCs—after you disconnect the temporary BDC from the network. The change record is necessary in case you decide to abandon the upgrade and reconnect the temporary BDC as the domain's PDC.

The upgrade process achieves the objective of minimum user disruption and a transparent migration, but entails a finite—albeit small—probability of catastrophic upgrade failure. Upgrading usually is the fastest and most economical migration choice for simple Windows NT 4.0 networks with one or two domains and up to a few hundred clients.

Recovering from an Upgrade Disaster

In the course of more than 50 Windows NT 4.0 upgrades on the systems used to write this book, only one upgrade failed. The unrecoverable failure was caused by a CD-ROM drive that wasn't on the HCL. The failure required reformatting the system partition and starting over with a Windows NT 4.0 Server installation.

Following is the typical recovery process for a failed PDC upgrade:

1. Power down and remove the Windows 2000 Server from the network. You can't revert to a Windows NT 4.0 PDC with a Windows 2000 Server on the network.

2. Start the temporary BDC without a network connection and promote it to the PDC for the domain.
3. Reconnect the former BDC to the network as the PDC.
4. At one of the BDCs, launch Server Manager, and choose Computer, Synchronize Entire Domain. In Event Viewer's System Log, verify the absence of events indicating a synchronization problem.
5. Reconstruct changes made to the domain while the Windows 2000 Domain Controller (DC) was active. Users must revert to their original password, if changed in AD.
6. Reformat the system partition on the failed Windows 2000 computer, and reinstall Windows NT 4.0 as a BDC with the services originally provided by the PDC.
7. Optionally, return the PDC role to the downgraded BDC.

You can complete steps 1 through 3 in less than five minutes. Steps 4 through 7 take about 40 minutes, including applying the current Windows NT SP. If your original system partition included other services, such as SQL Server or Exchange Server, reinstallation and restoration of data from backup tapes can require several hours.

RESTRUCTURING DOMAINS

The domain restructure strategy lets you begin your Windows 2000 network with a clean slate, called a *pristine forest*. Your AD domain design can—and probably should—depart dramatically from your existing Windows NT domain structure. The primary justification for domain restructuring is a drastic reduction in the number of network domains. If you intend to make only minor changes to your domain structure, you can perform restructuring operations on upgraded domains, rather than starting from ground zero.

"If it works, don't fix it" is another justification for domain restructuring. The innate reluctance of IT and higher corporate management to risk disabling a functioning network is prudent, to say the least. Domain restructuring enables you to create a Windows 2000 image of your existing domain(s) to which you can migrate user and computer accounts incrementally.

Prior to Microsoft's release of ADMT in March 2000, the only method of performing an incremental migration of Windows NT security groups, and user, service, and computer accounts to a Windows 2000 domain, was a very complex set of Visual Basic scripts. The five scripts, installed as a component of the Windows 2000 Support Tools, rely on the ClonePrincipal COM DLL, Clonepr.dll, to handle the transformation of Windows NT to Windows 2000 directory objects. The cloned Windows 2000 objects receive a new security identifier (SID); sIDHistory additions to each user's access token preserve access to objects in the parallel Windows NT domain.

> **Tip from**
> *RJ*
>
> Read Clonepr.doc in the \Program Files\Support Tools folder for a more detailed explanation of how sIDHistory works. If you haven't installed the Support Tools, run 2000rkst.msi from the \Support\Tools folder of the Windows 2000 Server distribution CD-ROM.

Mission Critical Software (http://www.missioncritical.com/), now a part of NetIQ (http://www.netiq.com/), developed ADMT for Microsoft as a graphical tool for Windows NT domain consolidation and reorganization. ADMT makes domain restructuring practical by providing a Microsoft Management Console (MMC) snap-in that launches wizards to perform each operation required to duplicate Windows NT directory objects in your Windows 2000 domains. You can preview most operations without copying or moving objects; previewing creates a log file that you can inspect for migration problem entries. An undo feature rolls back most operations, although relying on an undo of accidental move (instead of copy) operations is chancy, at best.

→ For details on the use of ADMT in a test environment, **see** "Emulating Domain Migration with the Active Directory Migration Tool," **p. 231**.

Domain restructure offers the following advantages over the in-place upgrade process:

- You don't risk a failed upgrade of a PDC. The Windows 2000 domain is independent of your Windows NT domain(s). Mutual, two-way transitive trusts are the only connection between the domains.
- You can perform incremental migration of user and computer accounts from Windows NT to Windows 2000. For example, you can migrate only users running Windows 2000 Professional to the new domain.
- You can move user accounts into OUs based on Windows NT domain and group membership. In many cases, you can coalesce multiple Windows NT account domains into a single Windows 2000 domain.
- During the user account copying process, you also can copy user home folders and their contents to a new location you specify.
- Once user accounts are added to OUs, you can apply specific sets of Group Policies to OUs, and delegate management of individual OUs to particular administrators.
- If you don't like the domain or OU structure you created and populated, you can demote the DC(s) and rerun Dcpromo to create a new domain topology. Demoting and promoting the server has no effect whatsoever on the operation of your production Windows NT domain(s).

The most obvious drawbacks of domain restructure are

- New server hardware is required for each Windows 2000 domain. You need one DC—preferably two—in each domain. Additional DCs are needed for domains spanning multiple sites. If your existing PDC(s) and BDC(s) don't meet or can't be upgraded to Windows 2000 hardware standards, however, you must install new servers.

- Your Windows NT security group structure must duplicate that of your OU structure to ease the migration process. You might need to add many new Windows NT global groups and add user accounts to the groups before you run ADMT.
- ADMT doesn't copy existing user passwords to the Windows 2000 account. You can elect to assign the user's logon ID as a temporary password, which the user must change at the first logon to the Windows 2000 Server, or to generate a complex password.
- You must configure DNS—and ultimately WINS and DHCP—for the Windows 2000 domain. Users continue to obtain DHCP IP address leases and DNS and WINS address resolution from the Windows NT domain until you authorize DHCP server(s) in the Windows 2000 domain and decommission the Windows NT DHCP server. Upgrading Windows PDCs and BDCs automatically upgrades existing DNS, WINS, and DHCP configurations.
- All Windows NT computer accounts migrate to the Windows 2000 domain's default Computers container. Moving computer accounts to OUs is a manual process unless the accounts use a naming convention that permits LDAP filtering by appropriate criteria.
- If clients have home directories with roaming user profiles, you must decide whether to copy home directories and profiles to a new location when copying the user account information.

Most medium- to large-size organizations are likely to opt for domain restructure, especially if the goal is to coalesce a large number of existing Windows NT domains into one or a few Windows 2000 domains. If ADMT doesn't meet your enterprise-level domain restructuring requirements, consider using third-party migration tools, such as Mission Critical's OnePoint Domain Migration Administrator 6.1+. Version 6.1 and later migrate Windows NT user account passwords to the Windows 2000 account.

→ For more details on the use of ADMT, **see** "Using ADMT to Restructure Windows NT Domains," **p. 398**.

Optimizing Drive Partitioning

Obtaining maximum availability and performance from servers running Windows 2000 requires careful attention to partitioning your sets of fixed disks. If you're performing an upgrade to an existing Windows NT 4.0 server, your partitioning options might be limited by the server's current drive configuration. If you're adding a new server as the Windows NT 4.0 PDC to be upgraded or as the Windows 2000 DC for a domain restructure, you have the opportunity to prepare for future expansion by organizing your SCSI drives into the appropriate RAID subsystems.

Tip from
RJ

You can't change partition size or modify an existing partition structure during an upgrade. If you want to alter your existing partition structure prior to upgrading, use a third-party partition management tool.

> **Note**
>
> The "Hard Drive Configuration" topic, near the end of Microsoft's "Windows 2000: Designing and Deploying Active Directory Services for the Microsoft Internal CorpNet" white paper (http://www.microsoft.com/technet/showcase/w2kacdir.asp), describes the standard hardware configuration for DC and Global Catalog (GC) servers, regardless of the number of users in the domain.

Following are partitioning recommendations for a typical SCSI-equipped DC in a Windows 2000 network with about six servers and 200 to 300 clients:

- Use a RAID 1 mirror set of two drives of at least 4.3GB capacity for your boot and system partition(s); in most cases, the boot and system partition are the same. A hardware RAID controller lets you create the mirror set before installing Windows NT or 2000. If you use software RAID for the system partition, you create the mirror after installation. Microsoft's CorpNet uses a pair of mirrored 9GB drives.

→ To review recommendations for implementing hardware-based RAID, **see** "Choosing the Optimum RAID System," **p. 325**.

→ For details on setting up Windows 2000 software RAID, **see** "Creating a Mirror (RAID 1) Volume," **p. 439**.

- Reserve at least 2.5GB for the system partition. Don't create additional partitions in the free space until you've installed Windows NT or 2000. CorpNet creates one 4.5GB partition for the boot/system and paging files, and another 4.5GB partition for the AD log file (Ntds.log).

> **Note**
>
> A clean installation of Windows 2000 Server lets you designate physical disks as dynamic disks, which are divided into volumes, not partitions. When you upgrade the basic disk created during Windows 2000's setup process, the boot and system partition(s) become a basic volume of a dynamic disk. You can create dynamic volumes from unpartitioned (free) space, but not from partitions you create on a basic disk. You can expand dynamic volumes with unpartitioned space on additional physical drives without rebooting the server. Windows 2000 can boot from a basic volume of a dynamic disk, but not from a dynamic volume.

- If you're installing Windows 2000 and want to be able to create a dynamic partition, convert the basic disk to a dynamic disk, and then create the dynamic volume in the unpartitioned space.

→ For more information about dynamic volume management, **see** "Dynamic Disks, Basic Disks, and Volumes," **p. 416**.

- Use a RAID 5 stripe set of 9GB or greater capacity for shared folders, such as the Sysvol folder, log files, and user home directories. If you have a hardware RAID controller, consider placing the paging file on the stripe set, but compare performance with the paging file on the mirror set. CorpNet uses three 18GB drives in a stripe set to hold only the AD database (Ntds.dit) and the replicated Sysvol folder.

Note

If you plan to run Remote Installation Services (RIS) for Windows 2000 Professional on the server, you must dedicate a partition to RIS. You can create this partition on the system drive or a RAID 5 stripe set after setup completes. The RIS partition holds an image of the setup files from the CD-ROM or a copy of a prototype Windows 2000 Professional standard configuration. RIS is the subject of Chapter 21, "Using Remote Installation Services."

- If you have a hardware RAID controller, set up your RAID 5 stripe set(s) for storing Windows 2000's AD database and log files, the Sysvol folder, Exchange Server's message store, SQL Server database files, file shares, and other data requiring protection by redundancy.

Tip from
RJ

Create a separate partition to hold only the AD database and log files, and the Sysvol folder. Windows 2000 automatically disables write caching on the Sysvol folder's partition. Disabling write caching can affect the performance of other services, such as Exchange Server, and Internet Information Server. SQL Server handles its own cache operations.

- If you use software-based RAID 5 (which isn't a recommended practice for a production server), create the RAID 5 stripe set after installing Windows NT or 2000, but before you install AD. Install the paging file on the mirror set, not on the RAID 5 stripe set, because writing to a mirrored paging file consumes fewer processor resources than writing to a software RAID 5 set.

Upgrading a Windows NT 4.0 Production Server

As noted earlier in the chapter, upgrading an existing Windows NT 4.0 PDC is almost a hands-off operation, unless you have hardware or software installed that isn't compatible with Windows 2000. If your hardware complies with the Windows 2000 HCL, the only manual intervention needed is to click OK when asked if you want to upgrade, accept the license agreement, and acknowledge the presence of incompatible software, if any.

Note

Windows 2000 replaces Windows NT's Directory Replicator service (LMRepl, short for LAN Manager Replication) with the System Volume (Sysvol) or the Distributed File System (Dfs) and File Replication Service (FRS). Thus all Windows NT 4.0 servers require that you acknowledge the replacement.

The Windows NT 4.0 PDC that's upgraded in this example is OAKMUSIC1, the PDC for the OAKMUSIC domain, which appears in preceding Figure 8.1. OAKMUSIC1 is the primary WINS, DHCP, and DNS server for the Windows NT 4.0 OAKMUSIC domain. OAKMUSIC1 on network `10.7.0.0` has a two-way trust with the primary OAKLEAF domain on network `131.254.0.0`, and a one-way trust from the OAKRES resource domain. Figure 8.2 illustrates the networking components and trusts between the three domains.

OAKRES trusts the OAKLEAF and OAKMUSIC domains, creating a multi-master Windows NT domain structure. In the sample configuration OAKLEAF manages user and computer accounts for all Oakleaf University employees. OAKMUSIC is a new domain that's still under construction and serves 500 students who have enrolled in music classes. The OAKRES domain runs SQL Server, Exchange Server, IIS 4.0, and middle-tier components under MTS 2.0 to service the Web site on a PDC, BDC, and member servers, which aren't shown in Figure 8.2. OAKMUSIC and OAKRES servers communicate with the OAKLEAF network via IP routing set up on the multihomed OAKLEAF1 PDC. In a production network, conventional routers would connect the 131.254.0.0, 10.7.3.0, and 10.7.4.0 subnets. In this example, a Class B subnet mask of 255.255.0.0 lets all hosts on the 10.7.0.0 network communicate without routers.

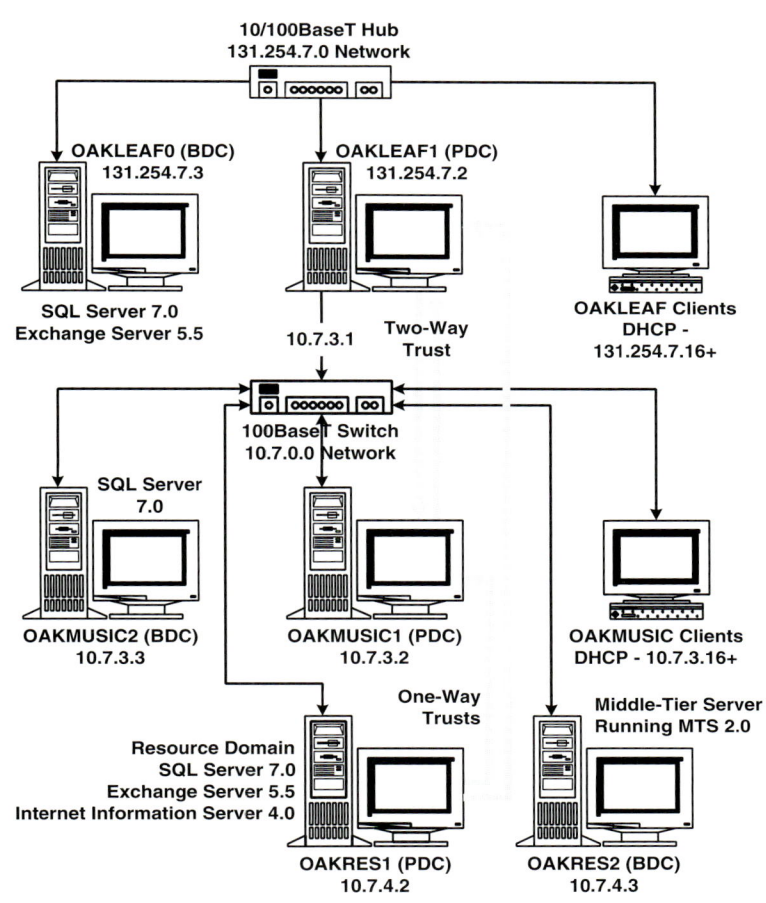

Figure 8.2
These are the network connections and trusts for the OAKLEAF, OAKMUSIC, and OAKRES domains.

> **Note**
> The upgrade sections that follow assume that you have experience with the primary administrative features of Windows NT 4.0 Server and are familiar with basic Windows network troubleshooting techniques.

STARTING THE OPERATING SYSTEM UPGRADE

To begin the first phase of the upgrade process, do the following:

1. Shut down all running applications on your server. You don't need to stop services, but be sure to temporarily disable antivirus software before starting the upgrade.

2. If you're using Windows NT's software disk mirroring (RAID 1) on your system partition, break the mirror set with Disk Manager. Re-enable mirroring after a successful upgrade.

3. If you have an uninterruptible power supply (UPS) with a management connection to the server's serial port, disconnect it. UPS management connections to serial ports might cause problems during Windows 2000's hardware detection process.

4. Insert the Windows 2000 Server distribution CD-ROM in the drive. If Autorun is enabled on your server, the splash screen and message shown in Figure 8.3 appear. If Autorun is disabled, run Setup.exe from the root folder of the CD-ROM to display the splash screen and message. Click Yes to start the upgrade.

Figure 8.3
Click Yes in the message box that appears with the opening dialog of a Windows 2000 Server upgrade.

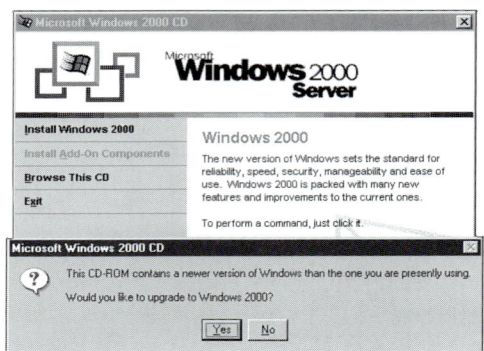

Alternatively, you can run the upgrade from a copy of the contents of the CD-ROM's \i386 folder on a network share. In this case, navigate to the installation share and run Winnt32.exe from the command prompt.

Tip from

RJ

Don't attempt to upgrade by booting from the distribution CD-ROM on a computer whose BIOS supports this feature. You can't upgrade an existing Windows NT installation by booting from the CD-ROM.

---

5. In the Windows 2000 Setup Welcome dialog accept the default Upgrade to Windows 2000 option and click Next.

   If you have insufficient disk space to perform the upgrade and install AD on the same partition, a warning message appears that advises the amount of disk space you must free to install AD. If you plan to install on another partition, you can disregard the warning.

6. In the License Agreement dialog select the I Accept the Agreement option, and click Next.
7. If your server has incompatible hardware or software, the Report System Compatibility dialog opens, similar to the example shown in Figure 8.4. Incompatible software for supported hardware, such as 3Com EtherLink XL-series network adapters and common graphics adapters, don't prevent a successful upgrade.

Figure 8.4
The Report System Compatibility dialog reports problems with 3Com software for the EtherLink XL network adapter and the Powerdesk Utilities for a Matrox graphics adapter.

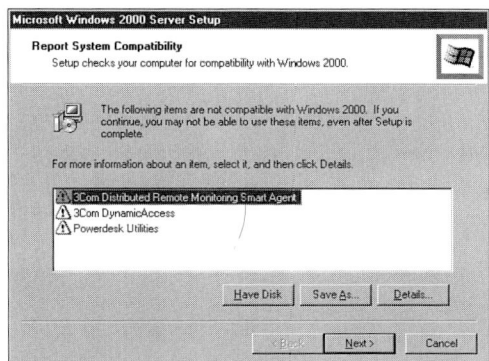

8. Click Next to continue. If a Directory of Applications dialog opens, click Next to bypass it; the Copying Installation Files dialog opens (see Figure 8.5). This is the last point in the installation process at which you can cancel the upgrade without endangering your Windows NT PDC installation.

Figure 8.5
The Copying Installation Files dialog offers your last opportunity to cancel the upgrade gracefully.

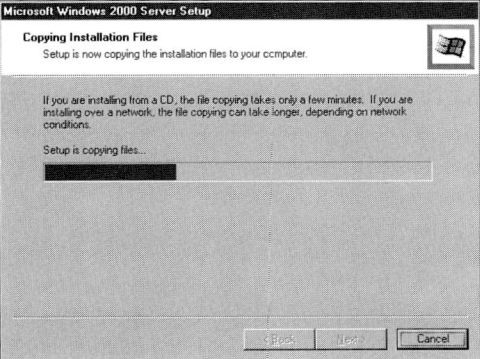

The files copied to your disk are the same as those on the four Windows 2000 Server setup disks. Windows NT shuts downs and reboots from the newly added Windows 2000 Setup entry to Boot.ini. At this point, your PDC is inaccessible from other network computers, and remains inaccessible until you complete the AD upgrade.

> **Note**
>
> You have about five seconds at the beginning of the bluescreen boot process to press F6 and install drivers for unsupported SCSI, RAID, or Fibre Channel fixed-disk adapters. If your controller isn't on the current HCL, and you have a disk or CD-ROM with Windows 2000 drivers for the controller, press F6 at the prompt and follow the onscreen and manufacturer's instructions to install the driver.
>
> If you don't install the required driver at this point, Setup detects supported devices—such as an Adaptec on-board SCSI controller—but not the unsupported controller(s). You won't be able to utilize drives connected to the undetected controller during setup.

ENDURING THE UNATTENDED SETUP CYCLE

The Windows 2000 upgrade process proceeds unattended from this point, unless Windows 2000 Setup encounters problems detecting your server hardware.

> **Note**
>
> If Windows 2000 Setup has problems detecting your network adapter(s) or can't determine current adapter settings, a Setting Up Network Components dialog opens. Older or unsupported network adapters commonly cause this dialog to open. Provide the missing information for the network adapters, then continue with the upgrade.

Plan on about an hour for the unattended part of the installation on a server with a 233MHz Pentium II processor, 16x CD-ROM drive, and multiple 4.3GB Seagate Barracuda Ultrawide SCSI drives. Your elapsed time will vary, depending primarily on the speed of your CD-ROM and fixed-disk drives. Table 8.1 lists the sequence of events that occur during the four phases of the unattended setup cycle.

TABLE 8.1 PHASE, OPERATION, AND APPROXIMATE ELAPSED TIME IN MINUTES FOR A WINDOWS NT SERVER UPGRADE ON A TYPICAL LOW-END SERVER

Phase	Operation	Time
Bluescreen	Installing files	1:00
	Checking the system disk	1:00
	Searching for prior Windows versions	1:00
	Examining the boot and system partitions	2:00
	Deleting unneeded Windows NT files	1:00
	Creating a list and copies files	6:00
	Initializing the Windows 2000 installation	1:00
	Saving the configuration	0:30
	Rebooting into Starting Up splash screen	0:30
Windows 2000 Setup	Please Wait appears on splash screen	3:00
Windows 2000 Upgrade	Installing Devices	3:00

Phase	Operation	Time
	Networking Settings	9:00
	Installing Components	8:00
	Performing Final Tasks	24:00
	Second Reboot (remove CD-ROM)	1:00
Windows 2000 Startup	Startup	1:00
	Preparing Network Connections	2:00
	Applying Your Personal Settings	1:00
	Total Time	66:00

> **Note**
>
> If your server has software RAID 1 or RAID 5 volumes, installation time increases because the setup process regenerates mirror and stripe sets. Regeneration doesn't apply to the system drive because the mirror set must be broken before installation. For more information on software RAID regeneration, see Microsoft Knowledge Base article Q231376, "Legacy FT Sets Regenerate During a Windows 2000 Upgrade."

> **Tip from**
> *RJ*
>
> If you receive a computer name conflict message during the Networking Settings phase of the upgrade, don't change the computer name. Resolve the cause of the name conflict before proceeding with the remainder of the setup process. If you can't resolve the name conflict at this point, click OK to force use of the PDC's current computer name. Changing the name of the PDC raises many problems after the upgrade, and you can't change the name of the PDC after the upgrade is completed. After the upgrade, run **Nbtstat -n** at the command prompt to determine the source of the name conflict. Nbtstat.exe is a component of the Windows Support Tools that install from the \Support\Tools folder of the distribution CD-ROM.

On average, you can expect a Windows 2000 Server upgrade to take about twice as long as a new installation of Windows NT 4.0 Server from the distribution CD-ROM.

> **Note**
>
> Windows 2000 Server Setup defaults to the Always On Power Scheme, with Turn Off Monitor set to 30 minutes and Turn Off Hard Disks set to Never. To change the default turn-off time of the monitor, launch Control Panel's Power Options tool and select a different time in the Turn Off Monitor dropdown list.

TESTING THE UPGRADE TO WINDOWS 2000

When you log on to Windows 2000 Server with your existing Administrator credentials, the Active Directory Installation Wizard's Welcome dialog opens. It's a recommended practice to verify network connectivity and investigate the cause of an "At least one service or driver failed during system startup" message, if it appears. During an upgrade, network problems are the most common causes of services failing to start. Network problems often prevent successful installation of AD.

> **Tip from**
> *RJ*
>
> Rebooting the server often cures initial service and driver startup errors. Reboot the server at least twice after the upgrade.

If you receive a "Failed during system startup" message, do the following:

1. Choose Programs, Administrative Tools, Computer Management to open the Computer Management Microsoft Management Console (MMC) snap-in.
2. Expand the Event Viewer node and double-click System Log to display System events (see Figure 8.6). Upgrading to Windows 2000 preserves your Windows NT event logs.

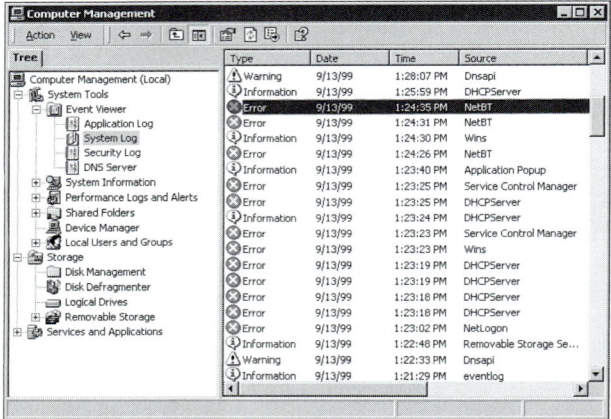

Figure 8.6
Double-clicking System Log displays a typical series of errors resulting from creating a duplicate NetBIOS name for a computer on two segments of the network.

Disregard NetLogon errors for Event ID 5721, which relate to domain controller problems. These events appear until you install AD, which enables the PDC emulator for the domain.

3. Determine the cause of error events that occurred at the approximate time of the initial boot into Windows 2000 Server. You can disregard warnings at this point.
4. Correct the problem, which often is easier said than done, and reboot the server. You can take advantage of your Windows NT troubleshooting experience to diagnose most errors that occur before installing AD.

> **Tip from**
> *RJ*
>
> Take advantage of the Windows 2000 Errors and Event Messages online help file (W2000msgs.chm) of the Resource Kit in the troubleshooting process. The Event Log, System topic lists event names in alphabetical order; Logon, Netlogon lists errors related to connections with Windows NT BDCs. Most topics have a "User Action" section that suggests a remedy for the problem.

5. Repeat steps 1 through 4 for each problem.

The Active Directory Installation Wizard opens automatically after the initial server upgrade to Windows 2000 completes. Do the following to verify network connectivity before proceeding with installation of AD:

1. Click Cancel to close the Wizard's Welcome dialog, and confirm the resulting message.
2. Wait for the first Windows 2000 Configure Your Server dialog to appear, select the I Will Configure My Server Later option, and click Next.
3. Clear the Show This Screen at Startup check box and close the Configure Your Server dialog. This prevents the dialog from reappearing on successive reboots.
4. Double-click My Network Places to open Windows 2000's replacement for the equally ineptly named Network Neighborhood window of Windows 9x and NT.
5. Choose Tools, Folder Options to open the Folder Options dialog, select the Use Windows Classic Folders option, and click OK to eliminate Web folder clutter.
6. Double-click Entire Network, then Microsoft Windows Network to display icons for your Windows NT domains and workgroups you've established, if any.
7. Double-click each domain icon to verify the presence of Windows NT servers in the domain.
8. If you experience browsing problems, type **ping** *servername* in the Command window, substituting each server on the network, including your upgraded PDC, to verify network name resolution.

At this point, your former PDC is a workstation in its original domain, and its server shares and services are inaccessible to other members of the PDC's domain and to members of other previously trusted domains. Thus it's important to continue with installation of AD as soon as you've cleared significant errors and confirmed network connectivity. You can, however, access shares on servers in another domain by providing, when requested, a logon ID and password that are valid in the other domain and have permission for the shares.

Tip from
RJ

Disable unused network adapters if you have more than one network adapter installed. Windows 2000 Setup sometimes enables all detected network adapters, regardless of whether you disabled one or more under Windows NT. Setup assigns a random IP address to the previously disabled adapter.

You can disable the Local Area Connection for the unneeded adapter by right-clicking My Network Connections and choosing Properties to open the Network and Dial-up Connections dialog. Right-click the connection on the adapter you want to disable, and choose Disable.

Verifying DNS, WINS, and DHCP Upgrades

If the PDC you're upgrading provides DNS, WINS, DHCP, or any combination of these services, verify that the service is installed and operating by doing the following:

1. Choose Programs, Administrative Tools, DNS to open the DNS snap-in. Expand the tree view to display the server's forward lookup zone(s) and reverse lookup zone(s). DNS zones upgrade to Windows 2000 primary DNS zones. You can convert the primary zone to Dynamic DNS (DDNS) after you install AD.

→ For more information on use of the DNS snap-in, **see** "Taking Advantage of Windows 2000 Server's DNS Service," **p. 82**.

2. Choose Programs, Administrative Tools, WINS to open the WINS snap-in. Expand the tree view, right-click Active Registrations, and choose Find by Name to open the eponymous dialog. Type the first letter of your domain name (**o** for this example) in the text box, and click Find Now to display the WINS database entries for matching computer names.

→ For detailed instructions on the use of the WINS snap-in, **see** "Installing and Configuring WINS," **p. 606**.

3. Right-click My Network Connections, and choose Properties to open the Network and Dial-up Connections dialog. Right-click the Local Area Connection icon for your network adapter, and choose Properties to open the *ConnectionName* Properties dialog. Select Internet Protocol (TCP/IP) in the list and click Properties to open the General Page of the TCP/IP Properties dialog. Verify that the IP Address, Subnet Mask, Default Gateway, Preferred DNS Server, and Alternate DNS Server address values are the same as those for the PDC.

Verify that the PDC's IP address appears as one of the DNS Server addresses, preferably the Preferred DNS Server address. If not, add the PDC's IP address as the Preferred DNS Server address, if that value is empty, or as the Alternate DNS Server address. Click Advanced and the DNS tab, and add the PDC's IP address to the DNS Server Addresses list if both the Preferred and Alternate values are occupied.

> **Caution**
>
> If your PDC's IP address isn't in the DNS Server Address list, installation of Windows 2000's Dynamic DNS during the AD upgrade process will fail without warning.

4. Choose Programs, Administrative Tools, DHCP to open the DHCP snap-in. Expand the tree view, and click the Address Pool, Address Leases, Reservations, Scope Options, and Server Options items to verify that the settings for each item have migrated correctly.

→ To learn how to use the DHCP snap-in, **see** "Configuring DHCP with the DHCP Snap-In," **p. 590**.

It's uncommon to encounter problems with upgrading DNS, WINS, and DHCP services that were properly configured and functioning under Windows NT 4.0. You repeat some of the preceding tests in the "Testing Primary DC Operations and Authorizing Zone Transfers" section after upgrading the server to a DC.

Adding Other Services, Programs, and Tools to the DC

Upgrading the PDC to Windows 2000 and AD adds only the networking features and services previously installed on the Windows NT PDC. Launch the Configure Your Server administrative tool, click Advanced, Optional Components, and Start to run the Windows 2000 Components Wizard. Alternatively, launch Control Panel's Add/Remove Programs tool and click the Add/Remove Windows Components button (see Figure 8.7).

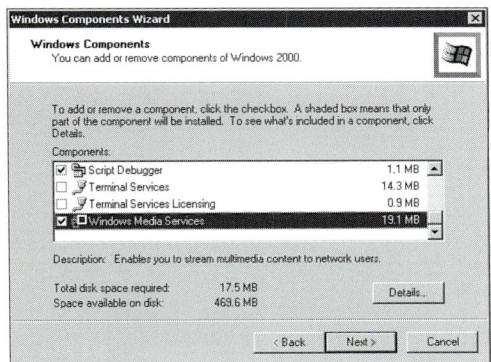

Figure 8.7
Use Windows 2000 Components Wizard to add server components, such as Windows Media Services, to the upgraded PDC.

Table 8.2 lists and describes the components you can install or remove with the wizard. A "Partial" entry in the "Default" column of Table 8.2 indicates that upgrading installs one or more of the subcomponents if present on the upgraded PDC or as the result of default setup choices.

TABLE 8.2   COMPONENTS AND SUBCOMPONENTS YOU CAN INSTALL OR REMOVE WITH THE WINDOWS 2000 COMPONENTS WIZARD

Component	Default	Subcomponents and Descriptions
Accessories and Utilities	Yes	Accessibility Wizard, Accessories (Calculator… WordPad), Communications (Chat, HyperTerminal, and Phone Dialer), Games, and Multimedia
Certificate Services	No	Certificate Server for obtaining, creating, and registering public-key certificates
Indexing Service	Yes	Full-text indexing of documents
Internet Information Server (IIS 5.0)	No	Web and FTP server and support files for Active Server Pages (ASP), database connectivity, and posting acceptance

Table 8.2 Continued

Component	Default	Subcomponents and Descriptions
Management and Monitoring Tools	No	Connection Manager Components (Connection Manager Administration Kit (CMAK), Network Monitor Tools, and Simple Network Management Protocol (SNMP)
Message Queuing Service	No	Microsoft Message Queue Server (MSMQ) 2.0 for message-based connections between components
Networking Services	Partial	You can selectively install COM Internet Services Proxy, Directory Services Migration Tool (for Netware), Domain Name System (DNS), Dynamic Host Configuration Protocol (DHCP), Internet Authentication Service, QoS (Quality of Service) Admission Control Service, Simple TCP/IP Services, Site Server ILS (Internet Locator Service) Services, and Windows Internet Name Service (WINS)
Other Network File and Print Services	Partial	File Services for Macintosh, Print Services for Macintosh, and Print Services for UNIX
Remote Installation Services	No	Enables automatic installation of Windows 2000 Professional on networked clients having network adapters that support the Remote Boot Service (usually implemented as a pluggable read-only memory chip)
Remote Storage	No	Enables storage of seldom-used files on tape drives
Script Debugger	Yes	Debugger for the VBScript or JScript code you write to automate Windows 2000 administrative operations
Terminal Services	No	Installs Windows Terminal Services on the server to enable Terminal Services clients to log on to and run applications from the server
Terminal Services Licensing	No	Enables the server to supply to clients the Terminal Services licenses you purchase from Microsoft
Windows Media Services	No	The files required to deliver streaming audio and video content on intranets and the Internet, and basic administrative tools.

Tip from
RJ

> Install the Network Monitor Tools subcomponent of Management and Monitoring Tools, and DHCP and WINS from Networking Services, if these services weren't installed on the Windows NT 4.0 PDC. Setup installs the DNS Server service by default. You can save disk space by removing all items but the Calculator, Notepad, and WordPad Accessory subcomponents in Accessories and Utilities.

After you've chosen the components to add or remove from your installation, click Next to install and set up added components, and delete unneeded subcomponents. If you elect to add components, you must insert the CD-ROM in the drive or connect to a network share holding the Windows 2000 Server setup files.

Control Panel's Add/Remove Programs tool lists Windows NT applications previously installed and those added by Windows 2000 Setup during the upgrade. Windows 2000 Support Tools, also called the Resource Kit tools, are the most important element in the list.

> **Tip from**
> *RJ*
>
> You need the Support Tools to perform operations that the Administrative Tools MMC snap-ins can't handle. For example, you can't add a new Windows NT 4.0 BDC to a Windows 2000 DC without running Netdom.exe. Upgrading doesn't add the Support Tools item to the Add/Remove Programs list, so run 2000rkst.msi in the \Support\Tools folder of the distribution CD-ROM to install them with the Support Tools Setup Wizard.

PROMOTING THE PDC TO ACTIVE DIRECTORY

After you've verified your server's network connectivity, you promote your workgroup server to a Windows 2000 DC, test replication between the new DC and the domain's Windows NT PDC(s), verify the trusts with other Windows NT 4.0 domains, and confirm client connectivity to the DC.

→ To review promoting a server to a DC in a test environment, **see** "Installing Active Directory," **p. 96**.

> **Tip from**
> *RJ*
>
> If you intend to install the AD database, log, and Sysvol folders on a conventional or RAID volume other than the system partition, verify the health of the volume with the Disk Management tool. Choose Programs, Administrative Tools, Computer Management, and double-click Storage, Disk Management to display drive volumes and partitions. Verify that each formatted partition reports Healthy status.
>
> If you haven't formatted the volume(s) for the AD database, log, and Sysvol folders, format the volume(s) now with NTFS before promoting your server.

> **Caution**
>
> You must be a member of the Enterprise Admins group to add a new domain tree to the forest. You must also add to the DNS Servers list the IP address of a DNS server in the initial root domain, usually the domain naming master DC. If you don't add this DNS server address, your server won't be able to find the domain naming master DC, and AD upgrade will fail.

> **Note**
>
> If you have set up the existing DCs for test purposes only, and want to use the upgraded PDC as the initial root domain DC for your production directory, run Dcpromo and demote all test DCs to standalone servers. You can't demote a test DC that acts as the root certificate server, so you must disconnect that test DC from the network. Reformat the system drive, and reinstall Windows 2000 before reconnecting the machine to the network.

→ For more information on the role of the domain-naming master DC, **see** "Single-Master Operations," **p. 150**.

The following procedure assumes that the PDC you're upgrading is the first DC in your enterprise network. If you already have a Windows 2000 DC anywhere on your network, verify network connectivity by pinging the DC that acts as the domain-naming master for the existing forest in which you create a new domain tree. Unless you have a very good reason to create a new forest, such as a definitive requirement for a different schema, all upgraded Windows NT domains should be in a single enterprise forest.

To promote the upgraded standalone server to the DC that creates the initial root domain, do the following:

1. Run Dcpromo.exe to start the Active Directory Installation Wizard. Click Next to bypass the Welcome dialog.
2. In the Create Tree or Child Domain dialog, accept the default Create a New Domain Tree option, and click Next.
3. In the Create or Join Forest dialog, if you have no DCs on the network, accept the Create a New Forest of Domain Trees option, and skip to step 5. If you have an existing DC, select the Place This New Domain Tree in an Existing Forest option. Click Next.
4. If you selected the Existing Forest option, the Network Credentials dialog opens. Type your Enterprise Admins logon ID, password, and the name of the initial root domain in the User Name, Password, and Domain text boxes. Click Next.

> **Note** There is a several-second delay at this point while the wizard searches for the initial root domain DC. If you receive a "Domain can not be located" error message, you didn't add the IP address of the DDNS server for the domain, or the address you added was incorrect. Click Cancel, confirm exiting the wizard, and correct the IP address error.

5. In the Install or Configure DNS dialog, accept the default Yes, Install and Configure DNS on This Computer to set up DDNS for the domain. If you intend to use an existing network DNS server, such as the PDC's upgraded DNS server, select the No, I Will Install and Configure DNS Myself option. Click Next.
6. In the New Domain Name dialog's text box, type the DNS name of the new domain, **oakmusic.edu** for this example, and click Next. (A delay of 15 to 30 seconds occurs at this point.)
7. In the Database and Log locations dialog, accept the default drive letters if you want to store the database and log in the system partition. Otherwise, change the default drive letters in the Database Location and Log Location to the appropriate volume. Click Next.
8. In the Shared System Volume dialog, accept the default system partition if it's formatted with NTFS. Otherwise, change the drive letter to the appropriate NTFS 5.0 volume. Click Next.

9. If you have Windows NT 4.0 remote access servers or other server applications in the domain that require authentication by the DC, in the Permissions dialog, accept the default Permissions Compatible with Pre-Windows 2000 Servers option. Otherwise, select the Permissions Compatible Only with Windows 2000 option. Click Next.

> **Note**
>
> You can increase the security within your domain after you promote your server to a DC by altering the Default Domain Controller's Security Options Group Policy with the Group Policy Editor.

→ For a discussion of Domain Controller security options, **see** "Setting Security Policies for Domains and Domain Controllers," **p. 400**.

10. In the Directory Services Restore Mode Administrator Password dialog, type your administrator password in both text boxes, and click Next.

11. Review the Summary dialog that displays the choices you made in the preceding steps (see Figure 8.8 for the example DC). Use the Back button to make changes to your AD configuration. Click Next to start the AD configuration process, which requires about three or four minutes.

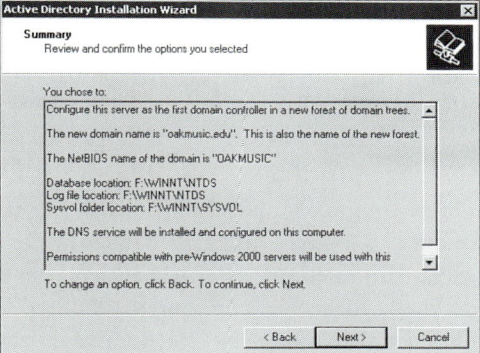

Figure 8.8
The Active Directory Installation Wizard's Summary dialog displays all parameters for the upgraded domain.

> **Note**
>
> If you receive a "DNS zone already exists" error message, click OK. This message means that you selected the "Yes, Install and Configure DNS on This Computer" option in step 5, but a primary forward lookup zone with the domain name exists.

12. When the Completing the Active Directory Installation Wizard dialog opens, click Finish and Restart Now to reboot your server as the primary DC for your first upgraded domain. You can expect the reboot process to require about five minutes.

Tip from
RJ
> Acknowledge any "failed during system startup" messages you receive during the reboot process. These messages are more common with an existing DC on the network. Booting the server again often solves the problem.

Note
> Promoting a server to active directory generates three log files—Dcpromo.log, Dcpromoui.log, and Dcpromos.log—in the server's \Winnt\Debug folder. Dcpromo.log is the most useful of the three logs for determining the source of errors. A `returned 0` entry at the end of a line indicates success; a non-zero value indicates failure. The *Windows 2000 Server Resource Kit*'s "Active Directory Diagnosis, Troubleshooting, and Recovery" chapter (http://www.microsoft.com/windows2000/library/resources/reskit/samplechapters/dsbi/dsbi_add_qouy.asp) supplies additional information on using the log files to diagnose AD promotion problems.

13. Click the Options button to display the downlevel domain name in a dropdown list. Log on to the domain with your Administrator credentials or use email style `administrator@domainname.ext` to specify the domain, in this case **administrator@oakmusic.edu**.

Note
> As with Windows NT, you can select in the Domain dropdown list any trusting domain for which you have appropriate credentials. Trusting domains might not appear in the dropdown list for up to 15 minutes after your initial logon, or after a reboot. Email-style logon is valid only for Windows 2000 domains.
>
> If you log on to the DC with administrator credentials from another Windows NT domain, you receive an error message when you attempt to use the AD administrative tools.

14. If your first DC has a fulltime Internet connection, you can synchronize the time of all Windows 2000 DCs with the U.S. Naval Observatory time. At the command prompt, type **net time /setsntp:tick.usno.navy.mil**. Alternatively, you can specify **tock.usno.navy.mil** as the time synchronization source. All other domain controllers you upgrade or add synchronize their system clocks with this domain controller.

Note
> If you don't specify a time synchronization source for the first DC of your network, multiple Win32Time errors appear in the System log.

Tip from
RJ
> To keep your Windows NT domain controllers in sync with the Windows 2000 DC, use the Winat.exe utility from the Windows NT 4.0 Resource Kit to run `net time \domain \set \yes` every day at a specified hour.

15. Apply the latest Windows 2000 Service Pack after you complete the promotion of the server to a DC.

Verifying the Active Directory Upgrade

Installing AD adds the AD management tools to the Administrative Tools menu, and copies Windows NT users, groups, computers, and trusts from the SAM database to AD's database. Object permissions, policies, and other Windows NT features ordinarily are unaffected by the upgrade. Verification of the upgrade requires testing the DC to ensure that the PDC emulator correctly performs all functions expected of a Windows NT 4.0 PDC, including providing DHCP, WINS, and DNS services to Windows 9x, NT and 2000 clients.

Testing Primary DC Operations and Authorizing Zone Transfers

Primary DC operations involve supplying PDC emulation services, managing AD security groups, user and computer accounts, and providing DHCP, WINS, and DNS services to clients. To verify that the basic PDC upgrade succeeded on the DC, do the following:

1. Choose Programs, Administrative Tools, Active Directory Users and Computers to open the Active Directory Users and Computers snap-in.

2. Expand the domain node and click the Domain Controllers node to display a list of domain controllers (DCs and PDCs) in the upgraded domain. Verify that all BDCs in the domain appear in the list, which provides initial operational confirmation of the DC's PDC emulator service.

3. Double-click the DC item to display the General page of the Properties dialog for the DC. Add a description for the DC, if you want, and verify that the Trust Computer for Delegation check box is marked (see Figure 8.9). All DCs need the capability of requesting services from other servers.

Figure 8.9
The *Computername* Properties dialog for the upgraded DC lets you add a description for the DC.

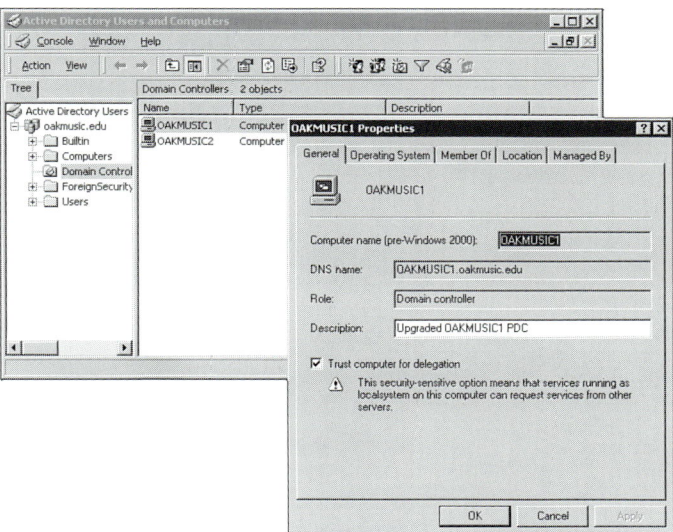

4. Repeat step 3 for each Windows NT BDC in the domain.
5. Click the Users node to display the migrated user accounts (see Figure 8.10).

Figure 8.10
Student accounts migrated from the PDC's SAM database to the Users container of the DC.

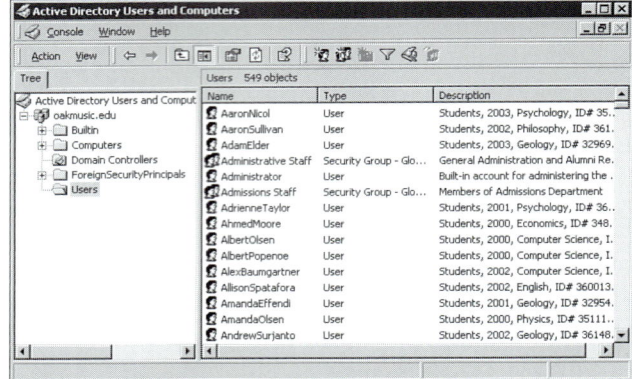

6. Click the Computers node to verify migration of Windows NT computer accounts.
7. Choose Programs, Administrative Tools, Active Directory Domains and Trusts to open the snap-in, right-click the domain node, and choose Properties to open the *domain-name* Properties dialog. Verify the lists of trusted and trusting Windows NT domains (see Figure 8.11). Click OK.

Figure 8.11
The *domainname* Properties sheet displays downlevel (Windows NT 4.0) trusted and trusting domains.

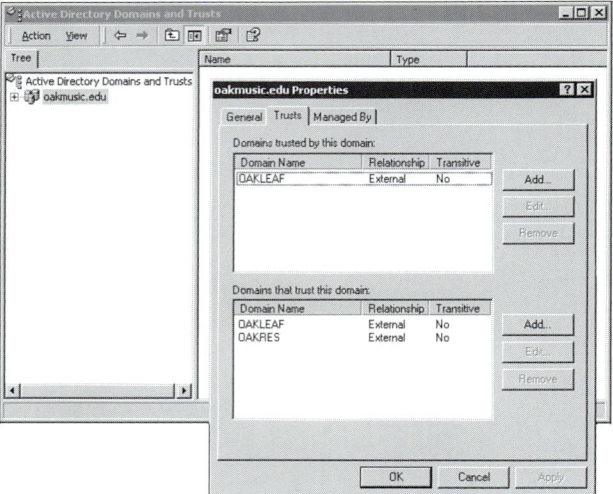

→ If one or more downlevel trusts are missing in the *domainname* Properties dialog, **see** "Checking Trusts from Windows NT Domains," **p. 373**.

8. Choose Programs, Administrative Tools, Computer Management to open the Computer Management snap-in, and navigate to the Services, DHCP node. Alternatively, you can launch the Computer Management snap-in by right-clicking My Computer and choosing Manage. Using the Computer Management snap-in lets you manage DHCP and DNS from a single point.

9. If a red dot and message in the right pane indicate that DHCP must be authorized to start, right-click the DHCP node and choose Authorize to start the DHCP service. Wait 30 seconds or so, then press F5 to refresh the snap-in.

10. If **Active** doesn't appear in the Status column for the scope, right-click the Scope node, and select Activate to enable the scope. Press F5 to verify activation.

11. Click Address Leases to check DHCP leases from your Windows NT 4.0 DHCP scope (see Figure 8.12). The DHCP snap-in (Dhcpmgmt.msc) provides the DHCP node in the Services and Applications tree of the Computer Management tool.

Figure 8.12
The Computer Management snap-in's DHCP node displays DHCP address leases migrated from the Windows NT 4.0 PDC.

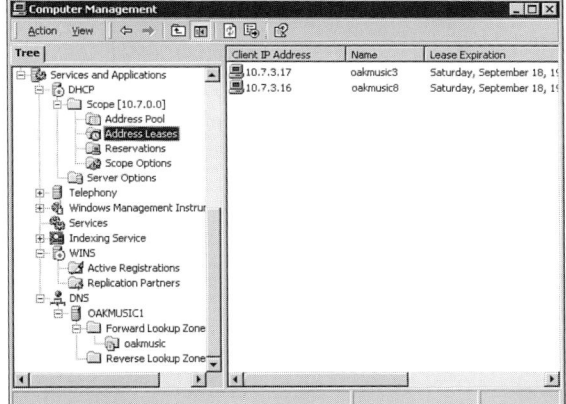

12. Navigate to the DNS, Forward Lookup Zone node for the domain, and expand the *domainname* (oakmusic.edu) node to display the Host record for the DC and any other computers imported from the Windows NT 4.0 DNS database, if you previously set up DNS.

13. Right-click the *domainname* node, and choose Properties to open the General page of the *domainname* Properties dialog. If you imported DNS records from the PDC, the forward lookup zone type is Primary. In this case, click Change to open the Change Zone Type dialog, select the Active-Directory-Integrated option, click OK, and confirm your action.

14. Select Only Secure Updates in the Allow Dynamic Updates? list (see Figure 8.13), and close the dialog.

Figure 8.13
If the forward lookup zone type is Primary, change the type to Active Directory-Integrated and specify Only Secure Updates.

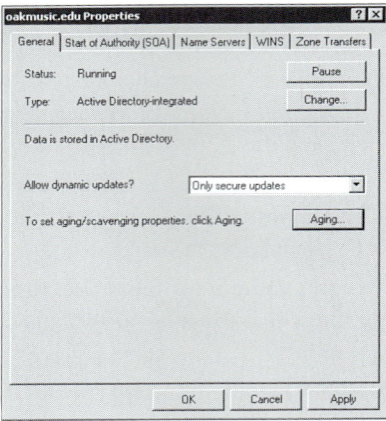

15. Verify that the four Dynamic DNS folder nodes—_msdcs, _sites, _tcp, and _udp—appear under the node (see Figure 8.14).

Figure 8.14
The forward lookup zone displays DNS records for the domain (oakmusic.edu) and DC (oakmusic1), and folders for replicating Dynamic DNS entries.

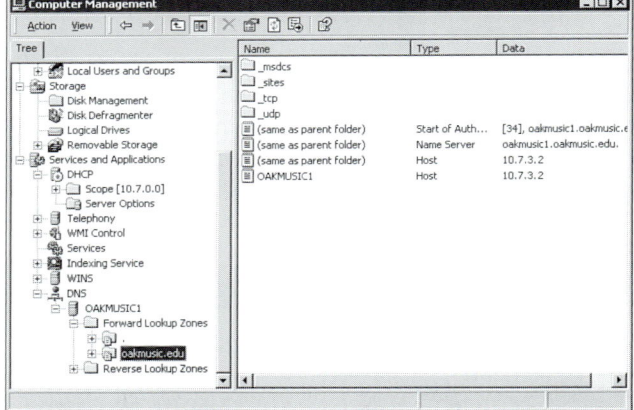

Note

It might take a minute or two to update AD with the forward lookup zone information. Press F5 periodically until the DDNS folder nodes appear.

16. Verify that DNS zone transfers to secondary forward lookup zones of other DCs are authorized. Right-click the *domainname* node, choose Properties, and click the Zone Transfers tab of the oakmusic.edu Properties dialog. Mark the Allow Zone Transfers check box, if it's cleared, and accept the To Any Server option (see Figure 8.15).

Figure 8.15
The local DC must authorize zone transfers to secondary forward lookup zones of other DCs. DDNS requires secure zone transfers.

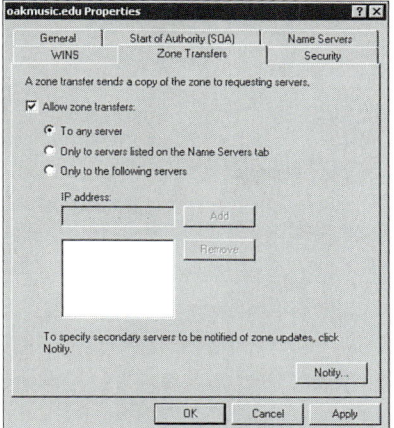

17. If no Reverse Lookup Zone entry appears for your network, right-click the node, choose Properties to start the New Zone Wizard, click Next, select the Active Directory-Integrated option, click Next, and fill in the Network Address text box with the non-zero octets of your subnet—`10.7` for this example. Click Finish to add the new reverse lookup zone.

→ For detailed information on AD's DNS forward and reverse lookup zones, **see** "Initial DDNS Configuration with Active Directory," **p. 83**.

18. Windows 2000 WINS is integrated with AD and Dynamic DNS (DDNS) services, which minimizes administrative duties. To verify the upgrade from Windows NT 4.0's WINS Server, expand the WINS node, right-click Active Registrations, choose Find by Name to open the Find by Name dialog, type your domain name in the text box, and click Find Now to display the domain's initial WINS database entries (see Figure 8.16).

Figure 8.16
Check WINS database records for the `oakmusic.edu` sample domain.

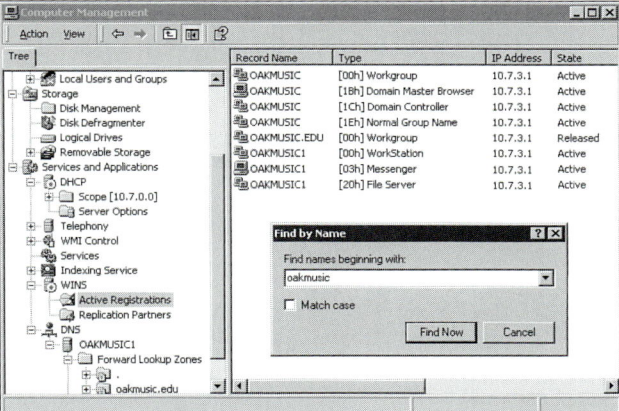

Repeat the Find by Name operation for each domain for which WINS entries existed under Windows NT.

→ If expected Windows NT WINS entries are missing from the list, **see** "Installing and Configuring WINS," p. 606.

19. Click the Replication Partners item to verify migration of Windows NT WINS replication settings for your secondary WINS server on the BDC. If the WINS server entry is missing, right-click Replication Partners, choose New Replication Partner, type the IP address of the secondary WINS server, and click OK to add the server.

20. Right-click the entry for the backup WINS Server, choose Start Push Replication, accept the Start for This Partner Only option (see Figure 8.17), click OK to close the dialog, then click OK to acknowledge the replication message. Check the Event Log to verify that WINS replication succeeded.

Figure 8.17
Check the entry for the secondary WINS server as a replication partner of the DC's WINS server.

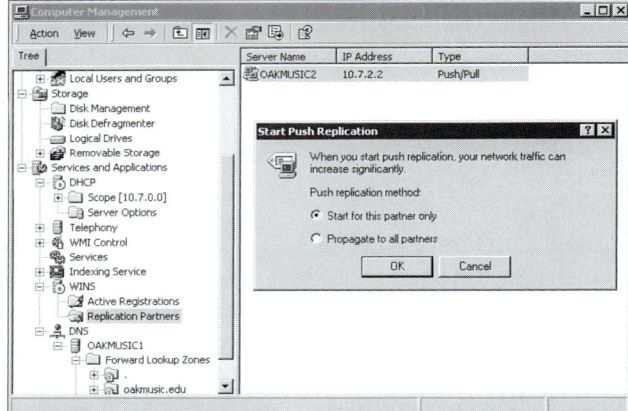

If the Replication Partners entry for your secondary WINS is missing, right-click the Replication Partners node, choose New Replication Partner, type the name or the IP address of the secondary WINS server in the text box, and click OK to close the dialog and add the partner to the list.

Tip from
RJ

If your PDC runs additional services, such as SQL Server, Exchange Server, and Routing and RAS, verify that each service is operational with the administrative tool for the service. For example, SQL Server Enterprise Manager should display the same member set in the SQL Server Group node as before the upgrade. If you're using Windows NT 4.0's Remote Access Service or the Routing and RAS add-on, test a dialup connection to the DC.

Checking Trusts from Windows NT Domains

The second phase of the DC verification procedure consists of verifying non-transitive trusts from other Windows NT domains—OAKLEAF and OAKRES for this example. If the downlevel domain trusts to the upgraded domain fail, users in the Windows NT domains won't be able to access resources in these domains.

To verify Windows NT trust relationships with the Windows 2000 DC's PDC emulator, do the following:

1. On a Windows NT 4.0 workstation with Windows NT Administrative Tools installed or a Windows NT 4.0 server in another domain trusted by your DC—the OAKLEAF1 PDC for this example—launch User Manager for Domains.

2. Choose User, Select Domain to open the Select Domain dialog. Wait a few seconds for the list box to populate and double-click the DC's domain entry, OAKMUSIC for this example. Alternatively type the domain name in the text box and click OK. After a few seconds, the Username and Groups lists populate from the DC.

3. Choose User, New User and add a temporary new user account from the Windows NT computer (see Figure 8.18).

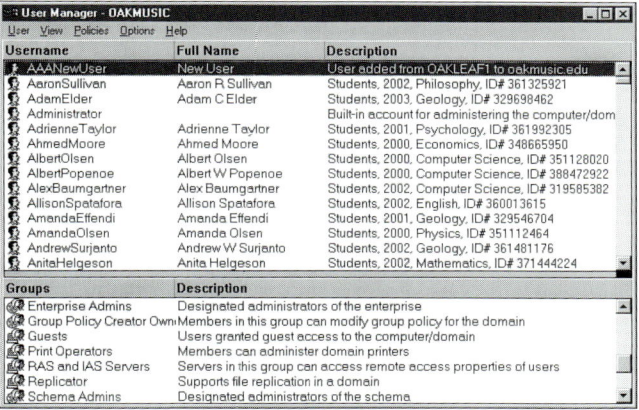

Figure 8.18
Adding a new user (AAANewUser) by a Windows NT administrator tests the trust with the upgraded domain.

4. Double-click one of the new AD local groups—such as DHCP Users—and add the new user to the group (see Figure 8.19).

Figure 8.19
Add a temporary new user to a Windows 2000 local group with User Manager for Domains.

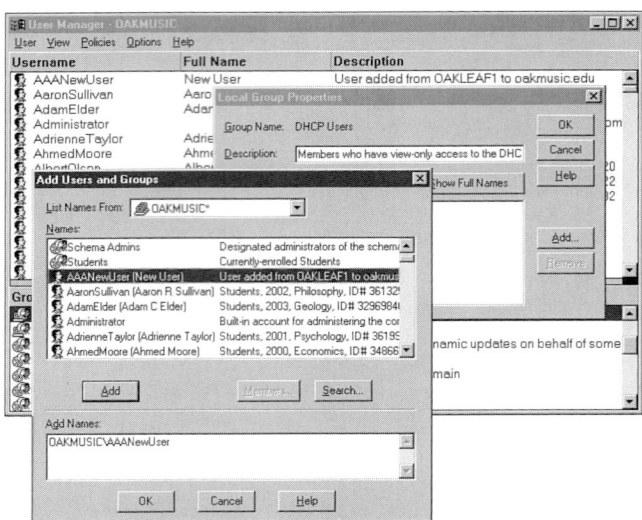

5. At the DC, verify with Active Directory Users and Computers that the new user appears in the Users container. Right-click the new user entry, choose Properties, and check propagation of the Windows NT account properties in the General Page and group membership in the Member Of page of the *NewUser* Properties dialog.

6. Log off as Administrator in the Windows NT domain, and log on with the new user's credentials in the upgraded domain. If you accepted the default security properties for the new user's account, you must change the password at logon.

   This and the following step verify the trust from the DC to the Windows NT domain.

7. Log off and log on to the Windows 2000 domain with your Windows NT Administrator account. Launch User Manager for Domains, which opens with the Username and Groups list of the DC. Delete the temporary new user account. Verify that the user account is deleted on the Windows 2000 DC by clicking Action and choosing Refresh in Active Directory Users and Computers.

8. On the Windows NT computer, launch Server Manager, choose Computer, Select Domain, and select the upgraded domain. Choose View, All if client accounts don't appear in the Computer list. Verify that the upgraded DC, identified as Windows NT 5.0 Primary, the BDC(s), and all computer accounts appear in the list.

9. Verify full connectivity to the DC by double-clicking the DC entry to open the Properties for *DCNAME* dialog, and clicking users to open the User Sessions on *DCNAME* dialog (see Figure 8.20).

Verifying the Active Directory Upgrade

Figure 8.20
Check the presence of computer accounts and full connectivity to the upgraded DC with Server Manager.

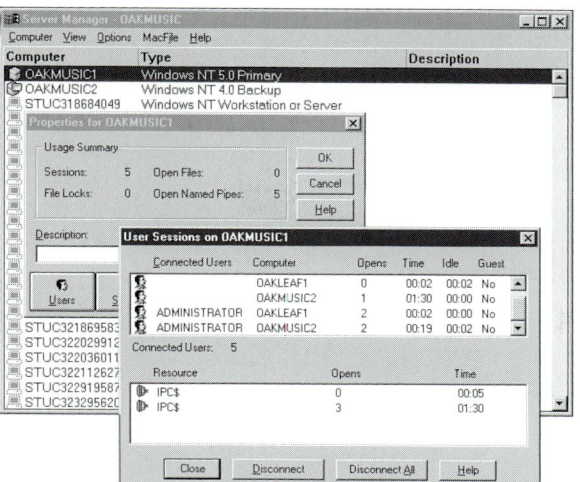

Tip from
RJ

You must use Windows NT administrative tools to administer user and computer accounts in Windows NT domains from a Windows 2000 Server DC or Windows 2000 Professional workstation. Active Directory Users and Computers won't connect to a downlevel Windows NT 4.0 domain; you receive an error message if you try.

To set up Windows NT domain administration on your Windows 2000 DC, copy Usrmgr.exe, Srvmgr.exe, and any other Windows NT administrative tools you need from the \Clients\Srvtools\Winnt\I386 folder of the Windows NT 4.0 distribution CD-ROM.

Testing Client DHCP, WINS, and DNS Services

The final testing phase of the PDC emulator for Windows 9x and NT clients is to verify operation of DHCP, client name resolution, and the ability to access server shares and other resources for which clients have permissions.

To run Winipcnf.exe or Ipconfig.exe to test DHCP, do the following:

1. Run Winipcfg.exe on a Windows 9x client, click More Info, and select the DHCP-enabled Ethernet adapter in the dropdown list.

2. Click Release to drop the current DHCP lease, and then click Renew to obtain an IP address lease from the PDC emulator (see Figure 8.21).

Figure 8.21
Obtain a new DCHP lease that returns the correct DNS Servers, Primary WINS Server, and Secondary Wins Server addresses to verify DHCP is running properly on the Windows 2000 DC.

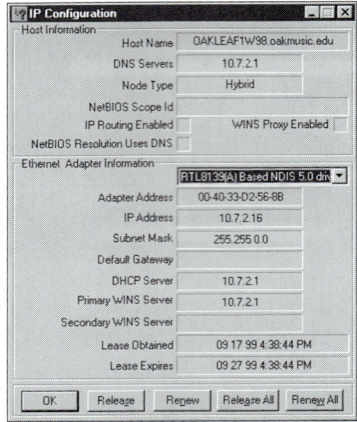

3. Reboot the client to verify access to logon scripts, server shares, and client policies, if implemented.
4. Repeat steps 1 through 3 for Windows NT clients by running Ipconfig.exe from the command prompt. Type **ipconfig /release** then **ipconfig /renew**, and finally type **ipconfig /all** to test lease renewal.

→ For an example of Ipconfig.exe's output, **see** "Adding Fixed DNS and WINS Addresses to Servers," **p. 282**.

After successful completion of client connectivity testing, you can be reasonably certain that the new Windows 2000 DC is capable of supporting the production domain and handling its PDC emulator responsibilities.

UPGRADING AND TESTING BDCS

When you've proven operability of the Windows 2000 DC by a few days of full production, it's safe to upgrade the domain's production BDC(s) to Windows 2000 and AD. You perform the BDC upgrade to Windows 2000 in the same manner as that for the first PDC. During the AD installation process, you add BDCs as DCs in the existing domain. All DCs in a domain are created equal, but the first DC you added, which assumes the FSMO role, is more equal than the other DCs.

The BDC you're upgrading is out of commission during the Windows 2000 upgrade process and installation of AD, which requires between 75 and 90 minutes, if all goes well. The DC or another BDC handles logons and the DC accepts account updates during the upgrade.

> **Tip from**
> *RJ*
>
> Reconnect the temporary Windows NT 4.0 BDC reserved for disaster recovery to the domain and synchronize it with the PDC emulator DC. Use the updated BDC as a standby system in the event of a problem with downlevel logons or failure of AD installation on the upgraded BDC. For added safety, copy logon script folders and other important shares from the BDC you're upgrading to serve as a backup.

Upgrading the BDC

The OAKMUSIC2 BDC serves as the example for this section. OAKMUSIC2 (`oakmusic2.oakmusic.edu`, `10.7.3.3`) acts as a stand-by DHCP server and a backup WINS server for the Windows NT OAKMUSIC domain. The DNS Server service isn't installed on OAKMUSIC2.

To upgrade a BDC to a DC in the new Windows 2000 domain, do the following:

1. Run a full backup of the BDC to tape, and verify the backup tape's usability. Selectively restore folders containing critical files, such as databases, to the temporary BDC, if you installed it in the domain.

2. At the command prompt, execute **net time /domain /set /yes** to synchronize the system time of your BDC with the DC. Time synchronization is necessary to ensure correct AD replication.

3. Run the Windows 2000 Server upgrade in accordance with the procedure described in the earlier "Upgrading a Windows NT 4.0 Production Server" section.

> **Note**
>
> You're likely to receive an "At least one service or driver failed during system startup" message when the upgrade completes. This message is inevitable when upgrading a BDC, because the BDC has a domain controller account and doesn't become a DC until you install AD.

4. Close the Active Directory Installation Wizard, and use My Network Places to verify network connectivity with the domain's DC and other DCs, PDCs, and BDCs. At this point, you must supply a Domain Admins username and password to display shares on other servers.

5. Right-click the Local Area Connection for the network and add the IP address of the PDC emulator DC as the Preferred DNS Server address. If the IP address of the upgraded BDC isn't present, add it as the Alternate, or click Advanced and the DNS tab, and add the BDC's IP address to the DNS Server Addresses list.

> **Caution**
>
> The DNS server addresses set in the BDC's TCP/IP Properties dialog are lost when you upgrade the BDC to Windows 2000. If you fail to provide the IP address of the PDC emulator DC for the domain, the upgrade of the former BDC to a DC fails. A missing IP address for the former BDC (now a member server) running the DNS Server service also has been found to cause AD upgrade failures.

> **Tip from**
> RJ
>
> It's a good practice to reboot the upgraded BDC after adding the DNS server addresses. In most cases, the "Failed during system startup" message doesn't reappear after rebooting.

6. You can install additional networking services at this point or after promoting the member server to a DC. If you install and configure the DNS Server service at this point, you can't create an AD-integrated forward lookup zone until you promote the server. To install DNS, DHCP, or both at this point, skip to the "Adding Backup Services" section, and then return to the next step.

7. Run Dcpromo.exe to start the Active Directory Installation Wizard, and click Next to bypass the Welcome dialog.

8. In the Additional Domain Controller or Member Server dialog, select the Make a Domain Controller option, and click Next.

9. In the Network Credentials dialog, type your Administrator account name and password for the domain you're joining, and click Next.

If you receive an error message that your upgraded BDC or new workstation server can't contact a domain controller, see "Solving Active Directory Upgrade Problems," in the "Troubleshooting" section near the end of this chapter.

10. In the Database and Log Locations dialog, specify the locations for the AD database and log.

11. In the Shared System Volume dialog, specify the location for the …\Sysvol folder.

12. In the Directory Services Restore Mode Administrative Password dialog, type and confirm your Enterprise Admins account password.

13. Confirm your preceding entries in the Summary dialog, and click Next to start the AD installation process, which requires 10 minutes or more, depending on the number of AD entries in the PDC emulator DC's database.

14. Click Finish to close the wizard and reboot your new DC when prompted.

15. Log on with your email style address, Administrator@*domainname.ext*.

16. Apply the latest Windows 2000 Service Pack.

A successful AD promotion usually indicates that critical networking services are operating satisfactorily. If you receive an "At least one service or driver failed during system startup" message, reboot both DCs, but delay booting the new DC for about five minutes. In most cases a reboot resolves service startup errors after installing AD.

> **Tip from**
> RJ
>
> Promoting your server to a DC sometimes results in persistent AD-related startup errors that you can't correct by reference to Event Viewer's description of the problem. In this case, demoting the DC to a member server with Dcpromo and promoting it again often resolves the problems.

→ For instructions on how to demote a DC, **see** "Removing a DC from a Domain with More Than One DC," **p. 383**.

Testing the Domain's Second DC

Testing the upgraded BDC follows a procedure similar to that for checking proper operation of the first DC. Perform at least the following tests:

1. Verify with Active Directory Users and Computers that all expected DCs appear in the Domain Controllers container, and that all User and Computer accounts are replicated to the appropriate container or OU.

2. Launch the WINS administrative tool and verify that records appear for both DCs. Establish the second DC as a replication partner with the first DC, then perform a push replication to all partners and verify that the new DC's records appear in the first DC's WINS pane.

    To set up the replication partnership, refer to steps 19 and 20 of the earlier "Testing Primary DC Operations and Authorizing Zone Transfers" section.

3. Verify that Windows NT, 9x, and 2000 clients have access to services and shares on the new DC.

For a more thorough test of the new DC, power down or disconnect the first DC and any other BDCs from the network, and test the ability of Windows 2000 clients to log on to the domain. Downlevel clients can't log on while the PDC emulator DC is out of service.

Tip from
RJ

> Maintain at least one Windows NT 4.0 BDC in each domain for downlevel client logons in the event of failure of the PDC emulator DC. As mentioned earlier in the chapter, the PDC emulator DC is a single point of failure for downlevel client logon. If you want additional logon insurance, add an addition BDC.

→ For instructions on adding a Windows NT 4.0 BDC, **see** "Adding a New Windows NT BDC to an Existing Domain," **p. 382**.

Adding Backup Services

If your Windows NT BDC didn't have a backup DHCP server or provide an alternative DNS server, you can add backup DHCP and DNS servers to your new DC at this point.

→ To review the process for adding network-related components to your server, **see** "Adding Other Services, Programs, and Tools to the DC," **p. 361**.

After adding DHCP and DNS services with the Add/Remove Windows Components tool, do the following:

1. Choose Programs, Administrative Tools, DHCP to launch the DHCP snap-in, which opens with an unauthorized node for your server.

2. Right-click the server node and choose New Scope to start the New Scope Wizard. Follow the wizard's instructions to create a scope with IP addresses in the same or a different range as the active DHCP server.

3. In the last wizard dialog, don't activate the scope. You authorize the server and activate the scope only in the event of failure of your first DC.
4. Choose Programs, Administrative Tools, DNS to open the DNS snap-in, and add a new secondary forward lookup zone.

→ For the details of adding a secondary DNS forward lookup zone, **see** "Establishing Secondary DNS Zones," **p. 381**.

5. Verify that the Forward Lookup Zone and Reverse Lookup Zone contain host (A) records for at least the original and new DCs.
6. Add a record for the alternative DNS server to the 006 DNS Servers option of the activated and deactivated DCHP servers.

You can test the backup DHCP server by deactivating the first DC's server, and then authorizing and activating the backup DHCP server. As a rule, only one DHCP server should be activated within a subnet; if you have sufficient spare IP addresses in the subnet, you can activate a secondary DHCP server that allocates IP addresses from a scope that doesn't overlap the scope of the primary DHCP server. To test the alternative DNS server, you must power down or disconnect the other DNS server(s) from the network.

Adding and Removing DCs in a Windows 2000 Domain

A pair of DCs within a site provides adequate availability for relatively small networks, but you might want to add another DC to share the AD load. The basic difference between adding a new DC and upgrading an existing BDC is the necessity to specify the computer name, domain name, and network configuration during Windows 2000 Setup. Installing AD is identical to that of the BDC upgrade process.

→ For the instructions on starting a Windows 2000 installation from scratch, **see** "Installing Windows 2000 on a New Server," **p. 384**.

Remote sites should have at least one DC to handle local logons and other AD operations. You also might find it necessary to add a Windows NT BDC to an AD domain. The following sections briefly describe these two processes, and how to decommission a DC in a domain with more than one DC.

Adding a Windows 2000 DC at a Remote Site

Adding a DC at a remote site connected by a WAN is a relatively simple process. If there's a BDC at an existing remote site, simply upgrade it to Windows 2000 and AD with a new site name. The upgrade process preserves all existing Windows NT network settings. Setting up a new remote site ordinarily involves installing a WAN router and one or more DCs, and then connecting new client PCs to the DCs. In the latter case, you run a new Windows 2000 Server installation for the DCs, followed by a site name change.

Tip from	If you have a large number of AD objects that you must replicate to the new DCs over a relatively slow WAN link, set up at least one DC with a direct network connection to the first (FSMO) DC. Install AD on the LAN, then disconnect the DC and transport it to the new site. When you reconnect the DC with the new site name, only changes made since the AD installation replicate to the remote DC.
RJ	

→ To review the process for changing a DC's site, **see** "Moving a Child Domain to a New Site," **p. 176**.

Creating an Additional Global Catalog Server

At least one DC at a site should act as a Global Catalog (GC) Server. Having a second GC Server is important to maximize AD availability if the first GC Server fails. You also need a second GC Server if you want to transfer to it or seize FSMO roles from the DC you created as the initial root domain server.

→ For details on transferring or seizing FSMO roles, **see** "Seizing the FSMO Roles of a Failed DC," **p. 408**.

To make the new DC a GC Server, do this:

1. Launch Active Directory Sites and Services, and expand the nodes to display the NTDS Settings leaf node for the DC you want to make a GC Server.
2. Right-click the NTDS Settings leaf to open the General page of its Properties dialog.
3. Mark the Global Catalog check box, and click OK to close the dialog and make the change effective.

Up to 15 minutes can elapse before the new DC actually assumes the GC Server role, which occurs during the next replication cycle.

Establishing Secondary DNS Zones

It's a good practice to add secondary DNS zones to DCs to back up other DNS servers in case of a failure, and to deliver better DNS lookup performance in large networks. The zone file from the primary DNS server that's authoritative for the domain replicates to other DCs in the site running DNS every 15 minutes, and to DCs in other sites on the replication schedule you specify.

To add a secondary DNS zone for a domain (`oakmusic.edu` for this example), do the following:

1. Launch the DNS administrative tool, right-click the Forward Lookup Zones node for the DC, and choose New Zone to start the New Zone Wizard. Click Next.
2. In the Zone Type dialog, select the Standard Secondary option, and click Next.
3. Type the name of the zone, `oakmusic.edu` in this case, and click Next.

4. In the Master DNS Servers page, type the IP address of the DC that's authoritative for the named zone—10.7.3.2 for this example. Click Add, Next, and Finish to add the secondary zone.

5. Verify that the secondary DNS zone is active by expanding the new node to display its four underlying nodes.

Tip from	
RJ	If you receive an error message that the primary DNS server can't be reached, verify that the Allow Zone Transfers check box is marked in the primary DNS server's property dialog's Zone Transfers page (refer to Figure 8.15).

6. If you've created a reverse lookup zone on the initial DNS server, repeat step 1—but right-click Reverse Lookup Zones—and steps 2 through 4.

7. Authorize zone transfers from other domains, if necessary, and repeat steps 1 though 6 for each domain.

You also can add optional secondary reverse lookup zones for other domains at this point.

Adding a New Windows NT BDC to an Existing Domain

If you experience client connectivity problems after upgrading all your Windows NT BDCs to Windows 2000, you might need to install a new BDC to handle the problems. For instance, if you upgrade a RAS server and remote clients no longer can connect to the domain, you can add a BDC to support Windows NT RAS or Routing and RAS (RRAS) until you resolve the problem with Windows 2000's RAS features. You must be a member of the Enterprise or Domain Admins groups to add a new DC.

Do the following to add a Windows NT BDC to your Windows 2000 mixed-mode domain:

1. At the command prompt of a DC for the domain, create a computer account for the new BDC by running the Netdom.exe support tool from the \Program Files\Resource Kit folder. Type the following entry to do so:

   netdom add *NetBIOSName* **/Domain:***DownlevelDomainName* **/DC /UserD:***Administrator* **/PasswordD:***AdminPassword*

   The following statement adds the sample OAKMUSIC3 BDC to the OAKMUSIC (oakmusic.edu) domain:

   netdom add OAKMUSIC3 /Domain:OAKMUSIC /DC /UserD:Administrator /PasswordD:Secret

2. Verify in the DC's Domain Controllers container that the new BDC's computer name you added is correct and its object class is Computer. If the BDC account isn't present, you can't add the computer as a BDC during the networking part of Windows NT setup.

3. Install Windows NT 4.0 as a BDC in the domain, using the NetBIOS name you assigned in step 1.

4. Add the networking features you need, such as Routing and RAS, and apply the latest SP.
5. Verify proper operation of the BDC with User Manager for Domains and Server Manager.

Removing a DC from a Domain with More Than One DC

It's tempting to simply disconnect from the network a second or third DC of a domain in order to devote the computer to another purpose. Don't do it—simply pulling the plug on a DC leaves its footprint in AD, and it's not easy to remove all traces of the DC from DNS, AD, and other persistent storage on the remaining DCs throughout your enterprise. Even if you delete the DC's entry in the Active Directory Users and Computers' Domain Controllers container, remnants of its prior existence remain.

To assure a clean removal of a DC, follow these steps:

1. Run Dcpromo on the DC you want to remove and click Next.
2. If you receive a message that you're about to remove the Global Catalog (GC) Server, click OK and then Cancel. Don't remove the DC that serves as the initial GC server—usually the first DC you created.
3. In the Remove Active Directory dialog, make sure to clear the This Is the Last Domain Controller in the Domain check box. If you mark this check box, and another DC exists, you receive an error message. If Dcpromo doesn't detect another DC, you run the remote chance of removing the entire domain—even if other DC(s) exist.
4. Follow the wizard's instructions from this point to remove the DC from the domain.

Wait at least 15 minutes, and then verify that the DC no longer appears in the Domain Controllers container of other DCs in the domain.

Performing Post-Upgrade Operations

After an initial production trial of the upgraded domain, the following steps let you take advantage of Windows 2000's organizational and security features:

1. Apply domain and DC security policies to increase the security of your network.
2. Create the OU structure applicable to your organization, and move user accounts into the OUs.
3. If your upgraded PDC maintains Windows NT and 2000 computer accounts, move the computer accounts into OUs.

| Tip from *RJ* | Don't combine user and computer accounts in an OU. Create separate OUs for computer accounts so you can delegate their administration and apply specific Group Policies to computer OUs. |

4. Delegate administration of the user and computer account OUs to appropriate members of the IT staff. The ability to delegate administration of OUs eliminates the need to establish or maintain Windows NT-type resource domains.

5. Reorganize your Security Group structure to prepare for application of Group Policies to Windows 2000 clients.

The preceding list covers only the basic steps involved in getting your upgraded domain up and running smoothly. The chapters of Part III, "Delivering Network Resources to Clients," describe how to expand the capabilities of your Windows 2000 domain with features such as IntelliMirror and Applications Installation Services, remote operating system installation, and other new Windows 2000 functions.

→ To learn how to designate security policies for domains and DCs, **see** "Setting Security Policies for Domains and Domain Controller," **p. 400**.

→ For more information on organizing user accounts, **see** "Moving Accounts from the Users Container to OUs," **p. 211**.

→ To review the steps for delegating control of OUs, **see** "Delegating Administrative Responsibilities for OUs," **p. 223**.

→ For more information on Windows 2000's Security Groups, **see** "Reorganizing Migrated Security Groups," **p. 220**.

INSTALLING WINDOWS 2000 ON A NEW SERVER

Running Windows 2000 Server Setup on a new computer requires more user input than upgrading an existing Windows NT PDC or BDC. You must enter at least the server's IP address and subnet mask, and the addresses for DNS and WINS servers, if these services are currently available on the network or you want the new DC to provide them.

How you install AD depends on your current network configuration. If you've previously set up AD and added a DC to the network, you can install the new server as one of the following:

- An additional DC in an existing domain.
- A new DC for a child domain of an existing domain.
- A new DC for a new domain in the same forest of domain trees that contains your existing domain.
- A new DC in the first domain of a new forest if you have no other DCs anywhere on your network. If other DCs exist, select this option only if you have a definitive need, such as a different AD schema, to create a new forest.

The sample installation described in the following sections creates a new `oakleaf.edu` domain in a new forest of domain trees, often called a *pristine forest*. Installing Windows 2000 Server from scratch as the first DC of an existing Windows NT 4.0 network is the most common method to prepare for domain restructure with ADMT.

Running Windows 2000 Server Setup

Do the following to start a new installation of Windows 2000 on a server with or without a 32-bit operating system installed:

1. If Windows NT Workstation or Windows 9x is pre-installed on the server, consider using FDISK to delete the existing partition(s), and repartition your system disk as recommended earlier in the chapter. Alternatively, delete all partitions with FDISK, which removes all content from the fixed disk, and then recreate the partitions with Windows 2000 during setup.

> **Tip from**
> *RJ*
>
> You can't upgrade a Windows 2000 Professional installation to any version of Windows 2000 Server.

2. If you don't have an operating system installed, and your server supports booting from the CD-ROM drive, insert the Windows 2000 Server CD-ROM and boot the server. You might need to change the Boot Sequence in your server's BIOS settings to CDROM/A/C or CDROM/A/SCSI to enable booting from the CD-ROM.

   Otherwise, insert the Windows 2000 Server boot disk 1 in the A drive, boot the server, and insert the remaining three Windows 2000 setup disks when prompted. During setup, you're required to accept the license agreement for Windows 2000 Server.

> **Tip from**
> *RJ*
>
> If you don't have the four disks required to start Windows 2000 Server installation, on another computer format four disks, and run Makeboot.bat (DOS and Windows 9x) or Makebt32.bat (Windows NT) from the \i386\Bootdisk folder to create the disk set.

3. When prompted, specify the system partition for the installation. If you didn't partition your system disk with FDISK prior to installation, you can create the partition structure during the bluescreen phase of Windows 2000 Setup. Format the system partition with NTFS.

> **Note**
>
> Copying files, starting Windows 2000, and setting up hardware devices requires several minutes. After Windows 2000 restarts, the Windows 2000 Setup Wizard's Welcome dialog eventually opens. Click Next or wait another 30 seconds to continue the installation, which requires another 20 minutes or so, depending on the speed of your hardware.
>
> Depending on the source of your installation CD-ROM, the wizard might open a dialog requesting you to type a 25-character product key. If the dialog appears, type the product key, and click Next.

4. In the Regional Settings dialog, accept the English (United States) locale or click the upper Customize button to change the locale and language settings. If you want to change the keyboard layout, click the lower Customize button to change to a Dvorak keyboard or a keyboard for another language. Click Next.

5. In the Personalize Your Software dialog, type your name and organization, and click Next.
6. In the Licensing Modes dialog, select the Per Server or Per Seat option. If you choose Per Server, set the number of concurrent connections for which you have client licenses in the spin box. Click Next.

Tip from
RJ
> If you haven't decided on a licensing mode for your organization, choose Per Server. You can change the licensing mode from Per Server to Per Seat, but not the reverse.

---

7. In the Computer Name and Administrative Password dialog, replace the suggested computer name with the downlevel (NetBIOS) name for your server (**OAKLEAF-DC1** for this example). The computer name must be unique on the entire network. Type and confirm your Administrator account password, and then click Next.
8. In the Windows 2000 Components dialog, select the additional components you want to install on the server. You must include at least the default Domain Name System (DNS), Dynamic Host Configuration Protocol (DHCP), and Windows Internet Naming Service (WINS) in the Networking Services category. Add at least the Network Monitor Tools from the Management and Monitoring Tools category. Click Next.
9. If you have a modem installed, in the Modem Dialing Information dialog select your country from the dropdown list, type your area or city code in the first text box, and, if required, the outside-line string—typically **9,**—in the second text box. Click Next.
10. In the Date and Time Settings dialog, verify the date and time, select your time zone, and clear the Automatically Adjust Clock for Daylight Saving Changes if you are in a region that doesn't implement daylight saving time, such as Indiana. Click Next to start installation of networking hardware and support services, which requires about three minutes.
11. In the Networking Settings dialog, select the Custom Settings option to specify a pre-established TCP/IP address for your server.

Tip from
RJ
> The alternative option, Typical Settings, establishes a private 169.254.0.0 Class B IP network with Windows 2000's Automatic Private IP Addressing (APIPA) feature. Only consider Typical Settings if you're creating a completely new, very small network for a single location (site) without routing installed. APIPA is intended only for Small Office/Home Office (SOHO) installations.

---

12. The Networking Components dialog opens with three default services—Client for Microsoft Networks, File and Print Sharing for Microsoft Networks, and Internet Protocol (TCP/IP) for the first network adapter. Select Internet Protocol (TCP/IP), and click Properties to open the Internet Protocol (TCP/IP) Properties dialog's General page.

13. Select the Use the Following IP Address option, type the server's fixed IP address and subnet mask and the default gateway (router) address if the server is connected to a router. For this example, the server's IP address is **10.7.2.2** with a Class B subnet mask of **255.255.0.0**. This first server will run DDNS for your network, so type the server's IP address as the Preferred DNS Server.

14. Click Advanced to open the Advanced TCP/IP Settings dialog, and click the WINS tab. Click Add to open the TCP/IP WINS Server, type the server's IP address, and click OK twice to close the TCP/IP dialogs.

15. Click Install to open the Install Network Component Type dialog, and double-click Protocol in the list to open the Select Network Protocol dialog. Double-click the Network Monitor Driver item in the list.

16. If you need to add additional network protocols, such as Novell IPX/SPX or AppleTalk, repeat step 14 for each protocol. You also can add Clients—Gateway (and Client) Services for NetWare—and Services—QoS Packet Scheduler and SAP Agent—. Alternatively, you can add protocols and services after you complete the initial installation for TCP/IP.

17. If you have more than one network adapter installed in a multihomed server, repeat steps 12 through 16 for each additional adapter. If you don't want to install additional adapter(s) at this time, clear the check boxes for each service on the additional adapter(s). You can disable, enable, and configure multiple adapters after you complete the setup process.

Tip from
RJ

Don't click Uninstall to disable additional NICs. Uninstall removes the service, not the NIC.

18. In the Workgroup or Computer Domain dialog, select No, This Computer Is Not on a Network or Is on a Network without a Domain. Accept the default WORKGROUP entry, and click Next to open the wizard's Installing Components dialog.

    Installing the components you chose in step 6, and the Performing Final Tasks process requires about 30 more minutes.

19. When the Completing the Windows 2000 Setup Wizard dialog opens, remove the CD-ROM, and click Finish to reboot the server into Windows 2000.

20. If you receive an "At least one service or driver failed during system startup" message, reboot the server. It's common to receive this error message during the first reboot into Windows 2000.

Caution

If you continue to receive "Failed during system startup" messages after rebooting, use Event Viewer to check the System, Applications, and DNS Server logs. You must correct any errors that cause these messages before proceeding. The first DC you create on your network is the initial root domain DC, the health of which is critical to installing AD and all subsequent AD operations, such as adding DCs.

You can ignore the DNS Server Log's warning that the DNS server machine has no DNS domain name. You add the domain name during promotion to a DC.

INSTALLING THE DC FOR THE FIRST DOMAIN

When Windows 2000 completes the reboot process, log on to the workgroup server as Administrator with the password you specified in step 7 of the preceding section. After a short delay, the Configure Your Server window opens. Close it. All the examples in this book use the Active Directory Installation Wizard (Dcpromo.exe) without the dubious assistance of Configure Your Server.

→ To review installation of AD in a test environment, **see** "Installing Active Directory," **p. 96**.

Before proceeding with AD installation, verify connectivity of the new server with all other servers on your network—or at least your subnet—by running **ping** *servername* at the command prompt. AD requires accurate system time information, so you must specify an Internet time server.

→ For instructions on connecting to U.S. Naval Observatory's time server, **see** step 14 of "Promoting the PDC to Active Directory," **p. 366**.

After confirming network connectivity and setting up the Win32Time service, do the following to set up the initial DC of a new domain:

1. Run Dcpromo to start the Active Directory Installation Wizard, and click Next to bypass the Welcome dialog.
2. In the Domain Controller Type dialog, select the Domain Controller for a New Domain option; click Next.

→ For instructions on adding a DC to an existing domain, **see** steps 5 through 16 of "Upgrading the BDC," **p. 377**.

3. In the Create a Tree or Child Domain dialog, select the Create a New Domain Tree option, and click Next.

→ For instructions on adding a child domain to an existing domain, **see** "Upgrading Resource Domains," **p. 392**.

4. In the Create or Join Forest dialog, select the Create a New Forest of Domain Trees option, and click Next.
5. In the New Domain Tree text box, type the full DNS name of the domain, `oakleaf.edu` for this example, and click Next. Expect a delay of a minute or two while the wizard tests the validity of the default downlevel domain name (the first domain component, OAKLEAF for this example). The Windows NT OAKLEAF domain exists on the sample network.
6. If a conflict exists between the wizard's default downlevel domain name and an existing domain on the network, an error message advises that the wizard proposes to add a 0 to the downlevel domain name (OAKLEAF0). Click OK to ignore the warning.
7. In the NetBIOS Domain Name dialog, type a nonconflicting downlevel domain name (**OAKLEAFU** for this example), and click Next. Another delay occurs while the wizard tests the name for conflicts.
8. In the Database and Log Locations dialog, accept or change the location for the AD database and log files. Click Next.

9. In the Shared System Volume dialog, accept or change the location for the \Sysvol folder, which must be located on a partition formatted with NTFS. Click Next.
10. You haven't configured DNS on the server, so you receive the message that you must do so. Click OK.
11. In the Configure DNS dialog, accept the default Yes, Install and Configure DNS on This Computer, and click Next.
12. In the Permissions dialog, select the option that applies to your domain configuration. If you need to support services running on Windows NT servers, which is the case for almost all Windows 2000 installations, accept the default Permissions Compatible with Pre-Windows 2000 Servers option. Click Next.
13. In the Directory Services Restore Mode dialog, type and confirm your Enterprise Admins password. (Your Administrator account becomes the only member of the Enterprise Admins group when you promote the server to the first DC on the network.) Click Next.
14. In the Summary Dialog (see Figure 8.22), review your prior selections. Click Back to make changes, if necessary, and then click Next to start the AD promotion process.

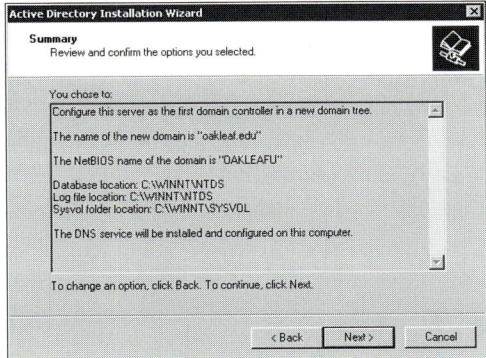

Figure 8.22
The wizard's Summary Dialog displays the profile for creating the first DC of a new domain tree in a pristine forest.

Promoting the workgroup server to AD takes several minutes; the amount of time depends primarily on the number of AD objects in existing AD domains. When the process completes, click Finish to dismiss the wizard, reboot your new DC, and log on with your email-style logon ID, **Administrator@oakleaf.edu** for this example.

Verifying Operability of the New Domain

It's almost a sure bet that an "At least one service or driver failed during system startup" message appears after your new DC reboots. Don't be alarmed; in most cases, the errors are the result of multiple unresolved service dependency errors during the initial reboot. It's a good practice, however, to launch Event Viewer, clear all of the events from each of the logs, and then reboot the DC to determine if services or drivers continue to fail.

A clean startup should show only one error in Event Viewer's System log: "The DHCP/BINL service has determined that it is not authorized to service clients on this network for the Windows domain: oakleaf.edu." This condition is normal until you decide on your DHCP strategy for the domain; Microsoft should have classified the message as a warning, not an error. If you see other, more serious-sounding error messages, attempt to solve them before entering troubleshooting mode. You must at least correct any errors that cause "Failed during system startup" messages before attempting to connect your newly promoted DC to existing Windows NT domains.

Your new DC must be able to establish trusts with existing Windows NT domains, add members of the Windows 2000 Enterprise Admins group to the local Windows NT Administrators group, and connect to Windows NT DNS servers, if DNS is implemented for the domain(s). To perform a quick check on the health of your new DC by testing its ability to interoperate with existing Windows NT domains and services, do this:

1. On a Windows NT PDC, launch User Manager, and choose Policies, Trust Relationships to open the Trust Relationships dialog. Two-way, non-transitive trusts between Windows 2000 and NT domains are required for domain restructure.

2. Click the upper Add button to open the Add Trusted Domain dialog. Type the down-level domain name (**OAKLEAFU** for this example) in the Domain text box and type a password for the trust in the Password text box. Click OK to initiate the trust. Click OK to acknowledge "The trust relationship could not be verified at this time" message.

3. Click the lower Add button to open the Add Trusting Domain dialog. Type the down-level domain name in the Domain text box, type a password for the trust in the Initial Password and Confirm Password text boxes, click OK, and click Close to close the Trust Relationships dialog.

4. At the new DC, choose Programs, Administrative Tools, Active Directory Domains and Trusts to open the snap-in of the same name. Expand the tree, right-click the domain name item (`oakleaf.edu`), and choose Properties to open the *domainname* Properties dialog.

5. Click the Trusts tab, and click the upper Add button to open the Add Trusted Domain dialog. Type the domain name of the Windows NT domain (**OAKLEAF** for this example) in the Domain text box, type the password for the trust in the Initial Password and Confirm Password text boxes, and click OK to complete the trust. Acknowledge the message that confirms the trust has been created.

6. Click the lower Add button to open the Add Trusting Domain dialog. Type the Windows NT domain name in the Domain text box, type the password for the trust in the Initial Password and Confirm Password text boxes, and click OK to attempt to complete the trust.

7. Windows NT doesn't recognize your Windows 2000 Administrator account, so an Active Directory dialog opens requesting your Windows NT administrative credentials. Type your Windows NT administrator logon ID and password, and click OK twice to complete the trust and close the dialogs. The Trusts page (see Figure 8.23) appears.

Figure 8.23
Use Active Directory Domains and Trusts to create non-transitive trusts between Windows 2000 and Windows NT domains.

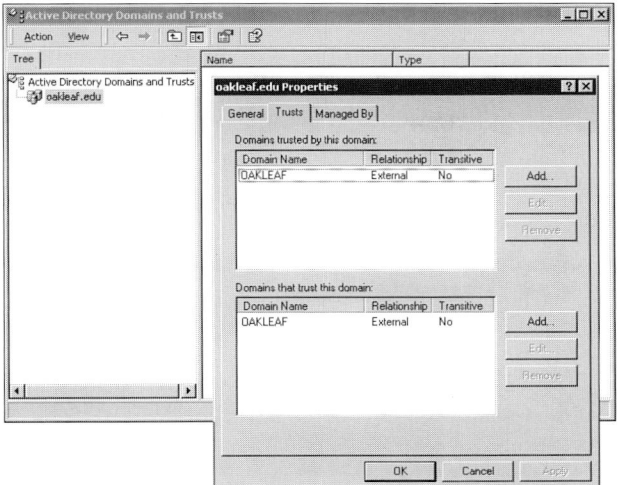

8. Click OK to close the dialog, and close the snap-in.
9. In User Manager at the Windows NT PDC, double-click the Administrators group to open the Local Group Properties dialog, and click Add to open the Add Users and Groups dialog.
10. Open the List Users From list and select the downlevel name of your new Windows 2000 domain. After a few seconds, the list fills with user and group accounts from AD.
11. Double-click the Enterprise Admins group to add it to the Add Names list (see Figure 8.24).

Figure 8.24
Use Windows NT's Add Users and Groups dialog to add Windows 2000 Security Groups and user accounts to the Windows NT domain.

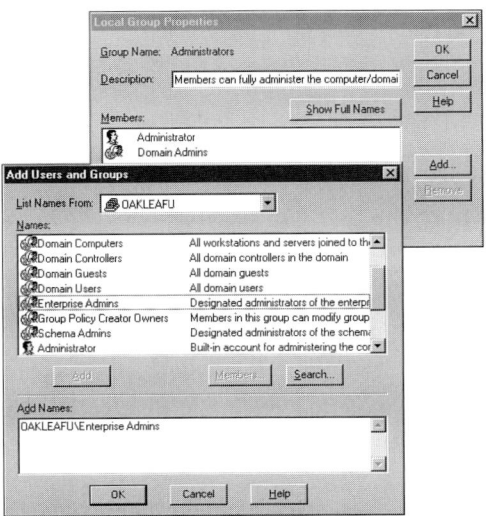

12. Click OK twice to close the dialogs and return to User manager.
13. At the Windows 2000 DC, choose Programs, Administrative Tools, DNS to open the DNS snap-in. Expand the tree to display the four folders below the domain name entry.
14. If the Windows NT domain runs the DNS Server service, right-click the Forward Lookup Zones item and choose New Zone to start the New Zone Wizard. Click Next to bypass the Welcome dialog. In the Zone Type dialog, select the Standard Secondary option, and click Next.
15. In the Zone Name dialog's text box, type the fully qualified domain name (FQDN) of the Windows NT domain, and click Next.
16. In the Master DNS Servers dialog, type the IP address of the Windows NT PDC hosting the DNS Server service, click Add, click Next, and click Finish to add the secondary zone (see Figure 8.25).

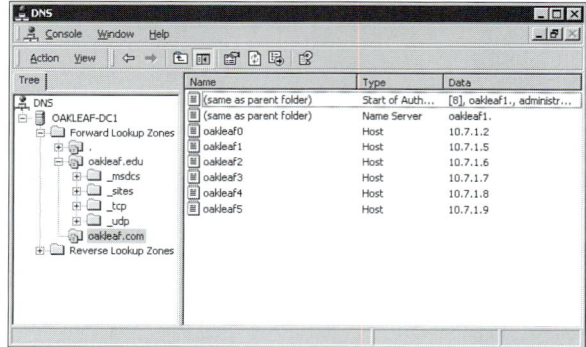

Figure 8.25
Adding a Windows 2000 DNS secondary forward lookup zone from a Windows NT DNS server confirms interoperability of the two DNS Server services.

UPGRADING RESOURCE DOMAINS

Windows NT network administrators commonly use resource domains to hold computer accounts for servers and workstations. In this case, all file, print, and application servers are members of one or more resource domains. One of the primary advantages of the use of resource domains is the ability to delegate their administration independently of that for user accounts. It's a common practice to create a resource domain in each regional facility, such as branch offices or manufacturing plants. Each Windows NT resource domain requires a PDC, plus at least one BDC to back up the PDC.

Windows NT supports the following three types of user/resource domain models:

- The *master domain model* uses a single Windows NT domain to hold all user accounts; its PDC and BDC(s) handle all user logons. In this case, each resource domain has a one-way, non-transitive trust with the master (user) domain. You place BDCs for the user account domain in each regional facility to expedite local logons. The disadvantage of this approach is that changes to every user account in the organization propagate to every regional BDC.

- The *multiple-master domain model* uses two or more domains to hold user accounts. The user account domains require two-way trusts, and each resource domain must have a single trust with each user domain. Multiple-master domains are more difficult to manage than single-master domains, but permit more user accounts than a single Windows NT domain can handle.
- The *complete-trust model* requires two-way trusts between every user and resource domain. Administration of the complete-trust model with many domains is almost impossible, so few network designers adopt this approach.

One of Microsoft's objectives in designing AD was to eliminate the need for resource domains, and the multiple-master and complete-trust domain models. AD can accommodate a very large number of user and computer accounts, which eliminates the need for multiple user account domains and the use of resource domains to hold computer accounts. As a general rule, the fewer Windows 2000 domains you create, the better.

Following are the two basic approaches to upgrading Windows NT resource domains:

- Add the resource servers as member servers of an existing Windows 2000 domain, which must run in native mode. This approach simplifies your domain structure, but requires that you clone (copy) the shared local groups of each resource domain to the Windows 2000 domain. The two copies of the groups are required to assure continuous resource access by Windows 2000 and NT servers and clients during progressive upgrading of the resource domain's servers. The group clones contain the sIDHistory of group members. You use ADMT to clone the shared local groups. You then upgrade resource domain member servers to Windows 2000, and use Dcpromo to make them member servers in the target domain. This process is quite complex, and the risks entailed by a misstep are substantial.

> **Note**
> The "Planning the Domain Restructure" chapter of the Windows 2000 Server Resource Kit (http://www.microsoft.com/WINDOWS2000/library/resources/reskit/samplechapters/dgbf/dgbf_upg_hpyr.asp) describes several alternative processes for moving resource domains to OUs.

- Upgrade the PDC of the resource domain to a Windows 2000 DC in a child domain. The upgraded PDC becomes the PDC emulator for the child domain, which runs in mixed mode. (You can create a mixed-mode child of a native-mode parent domain.) The advantages of a child domain are that AD automatically creates two-way transitive trusts, computer accounts migrate intact, and you can apply a totally different set of security policies to the resource domain. The downside of the child-domain method is the risk of failed upgrade, which can permanently disable a server running a critical application, and the need for two DCs to support the new domain.

→ To review the process of adding a child domain, **see** "Adding a Sample Child Domain," **p. 160**.

> **Tip from**
>
>
> The safest approach for either scenario is to demote all application servers—especially servers running critical email and database services—to member servers in the resource domain, even if you must add temporary PDC and BDC servers during the upgrade.

UPGRADING THE RESOURCE DOMAIN'S PDC

The procedure for upgrading a Windows NT resource domain (OAKRES for this example) to a child domain (oakres.oakleaf.edu) is quite similar to that for a conventional PDC upgrade. In this case, the OAKRES1 PDC has only local users and groups, plus 250 computer accounts. To perform a resource domain PDC upgrade, do the following:

1. Run a full tape backup of the PDC, and verify that the tape image can be restored. If you have a disk-imaging utility, generate an image of the PDC.

2. Install a temporary BDC for the resource domain, synchronize it with the PDC, and remove it from the network.

3. Upgrade the PDC of the resource domain (OAKRES1) to Windows 2000, following the procedure described in the "Upgrading a Windows NT 4.0 Production Server" section near the beginning of the chapter. Add any additional Windows 2000 networking services you want the server to run. (Promoting the PDC to DC installs and configures the DNS Service on the server.)

4. Specify in the TCP/IP Properties dialog the IP address of the parent domain's DC as the Preferred DNS Server.

5. Run Dcpromo to start the Active Directory Upgrade Wizard, and click Next.

6. In the Create Tree or Child Domain dialog, select the Create a New Child Domain in an Existing Tree option, and click Next.

7. In the Administrator Credentials dialog, type your *Enterprise Admins* logon ID, password, and the name of the parent domain—**oakleaf.edu** for this example. Click Next.

8. In the Child Domain Installation dialog, complete the Parent Domain and Child Domain entries. As you type, the Complete DNS Name of New Domain text box displays the proposed fully qualified domain name—oakres.oakleaf.edu for this example. Click Next.

9. Complete the rest of the wizard dialogs, as described in the earlier "Installing the DC for the First Domain" section.

10. Reboot the computer at least twice after installing AD; then use Event Viewer to check for AD-related errors.

11. On a DC of the parent domain, verify with the DNS snap-in that DDNS entries for the child domain appear under the parent domain's forward lookup zone node. Creating a child domain adds DDNS subnodes to a new *childdomainname* (oakres) node if the child domain doesn't run the DNS Service.

12. On the parent domain DC, launch Active Directory Users and Computers, right-click the parent domain node, choose Connect to Domain, click Browse, expand the parent domain node, and select the child domain. Click OK twice to connect to the child domain, and close the dialogs.

> **Note**
>
> You must log on to the parent domain as a member of Enterprise Admins to gain access to the child domain.

> **Tip from**
> *RJ*
>
> If you can't connect to the child domain from the parent domain, launch the DNS snap-in and add a secondary forward lookup zone that points to the child domain's DC. Similarly, if you can't connect to the parent domain from the child domain, add a secondary forward lookup zone that points to the parent DC.
>
> The need to add secondary lookup zones means that the child domain's DNS forward lookup zone isn't integrated with AD. Rebooting the child domain DC after adding a zone for the parent usually completes the integration, which is indicated by _msdcs, _sites, _tcp, and _udp nodes under the child domain's AD-integrated forward lookup zone.

13. Expand the Computers container to verify presence of the resource domain's computer accounts, if any.
14. Launch Active Directory Domains and Trusts, expand the parent domain node, right-click the child domain node, and choose Properties. Click the Trusts tab to confirm that the Child trusts with the parent domain are in place (see Figure 8.26).
15. Apply the latest Windows 2000 SP.

Figure 8.26
Active Directory Domains and Trusts displays the two-way, transitive Child trust between the parent and child domains.

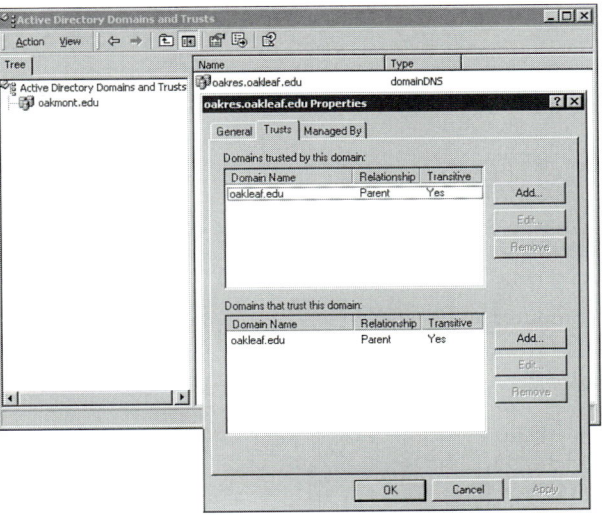

Recovering from a Failed Child Domain Promotion

If promoting the resource domain's upgraded PDC to a child domain has problems you can't correct, such as inability to gain access to the child domain from the parent, you can't recover by running Dcpromo to demote the server and starting again. DNS problems are the most common source of AD replication failures.

All local user and computer accounts disappear when you demote the server. Further, if you encounter insurmountable problems with the parent DC being unable to communicate properly with the child DC, or vice versa, you're also unlikely to be able to demote the child DC. Make sure your Preferred and Alternate DNS Server addresses are correct, and set up secondary forward lookup zones, as recommended in the preceding section, before concluding that child domain problems are insurmountable. Figure 8.27 shows the addition of a secondary lookup zone for the client on the primary domain controller.

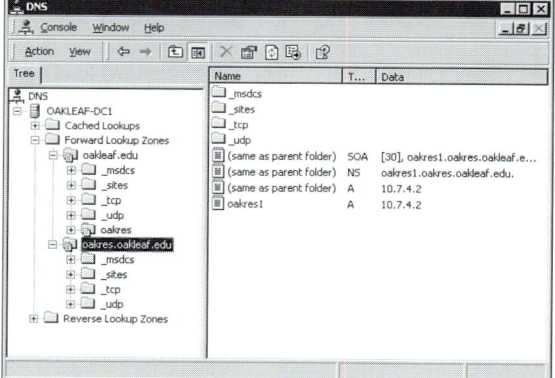

Figure 8.27
The DNS snap-in running on the sample parent domain controller (OAKLEAF-DC1) displays an AD-integrated primary zone (oakleaf.edu) and a secondary zone for the AD-integrated primary zone of the child domain (oakres.oakleaf.edu).

Tip from

> Review Dcpromo.log—and Dcpromoui.log, if necessary—to determine the source of the failure before proceeding with recovery. Copy the logs to a disk or a temporary folder on another machine for reference.
>
> You can determine whether the parent domain directory is the source of the problem by installing Windows 2000 on a test server and using Dcpromo to create a temporary child domain with a different name. Creating a temporary child domain also is helpful in diagnosing a misstep during the failed installation. Use Dcpromo to remove the child domain after you complete the test.

Following are the basic recovery steps:

1. Reformat the system partition and restore it from the disk image or tape backup. Verify that all prior Windows NT accounts and services are operational. Return the server to duty as the PDC of the resource domain, and test its operability.

2. If you were unable to demote the child DC, launch Active Directory Sites and Services on a parent domain DC, expand the tree view to display the list of servers for the child DC's site, and delete the entry for the server (OAKRES1 for this example.)

3. Repeat the upgrade of the resource domain PDC to Windows 2000, making sure to correct all errors that appear in the event logs.

4. Run Dcpromo to promote the server again. When you receive the warning message that the child domain already exists, click Yes to replace the remaining child domain information in AD.

5. Resolve all errors that occur after booting the server two or three times; then reapply the latest SP.

Throwing the Native-Mode Switch

As mentioned earlier in the chapter, changing a domain from mixed mode to native mode is a one-way process. If the new domains you added (`oakleaf.edu` and `oakres.oakleaf.edu`) don't need connectivity with Windows NT BDCs or member servers, you can change both domains to native mode. The best approach, however, is to change one domain at a time to native mode. You must change to native mode any domain to which you want to clone existing Windows NT 4.0 security principals for incremental user migration with ADMT.

Fortunately, changing a domain to native mode only affects the selected domain and doesn't alter the mode of child domains. The upgraded OAKRES PDC must remain accessible to BDCs in the domain until you've upgraded the last OAKRES BDC.

> **Tip from**
> *RJ*
>
> To ensure the ability to perform future operations requiring authentication of your Domain Admins credentials in trusting Windows NT domains, add the DC's Administrator account and Domain Admins group to the Windows NT domain's local Administrators group before changing to native mode.

To change a domain from mixed to native mode, do the following:

1. Launch the Active Directory Domains and Trust tool with the General page active.

2. Right-click the node for the domain to change and choose Properties to open the *domainname* Properties dialog.

3. Click the Change Mode button, then click Yes when the message asks for confirmation of the change to native mode. The Change Mode button disappears and the Domain Operation Mode text box indicates the change to native mode.

After you throw the native-mode switch, you can continue to view the domain's user and group accounts with Windows NT's User Manager for Domains. You can continue to add and delete native-mode users and groups in Windows NT groups. You can't, however, display in User Manager the properties of native-mode users or membership of native-mode groups. You receive an "Access is denied" error if you try either operation.

Using ADMT to Restructure Windows NT Domains

Microsoft's Active Directory Migration Tool is an effective, no-charge tool for domain restructuring and incremental migration of Windows NT user and group accounts and security groups to the new domain. If you have the budget to purchase new hardware for domain controllers, ADMT is the safest approach to moving to Windows 2000 Server. You need a minimum of two new servers—the primary DC and a backup DC—to migrate a Windows NT account domain and resource domains to a single Windows 2000 site. Additional sites require at least one DC—and preferably two.

After you've successfully migrated all users to the new domain, and set up and tested your applications on the new servers, you can retire the Windows NT servers and use them as new DCs for other domains or member servers in the Windows 2000 domain.

Before you commence the domain migration process, do the following:

1. Update the inventory of user and computer accounts, plus local and global security groups, of the Windows NT domain.
2. Create a global security group structure that corresponds to the OU structure for your Windows 2000 domain. Add each OU-based collection of users to the corresponding security group, and update the inventory. Assignment of users to OUs by ADMT is based on security group membership.
3. Create or update a diagram that describes all trusts between the domain you intend to migrate and other user and resource domains.
4. Create the OUs for user accounts. ADMT migrates all computer accounts to the Computers container, so you don't need to create OUs for computer accounts at this point.

Tip from
RJ
> Don't create in the Windows 2000 domain Domain Global Security Groups that duplicate the Windows NT global groups. If the wizard encounters a Domain Global group with the same name as a Windows NT global group being migrated, users aren't added to the Domain Global Security Group.

5. Read ADMT's online help file for interforest migration.

After you perform the migration, create all new user and computer accounts in the Windows 2000 domain. Otherwise, you must repeat the group, user, and computer account migration process to reflect the post-migration changes you make to the Windows 2000 domain.

The basic steps for domain restructure in which resource domain(s) are coalesced into a single Windows 2000 domain are as follows:

1. Download Admt.exe from `http://www.microsoft.com/windows2000/downloads/deployment/admt/default.asp`, and execute the file to install ADMT on any DC of the target (Windows 2000) domain. The target domain must run in native mode, and you must have at least Domain Admins credentials for the target domain to use ADMT.
2. Create a two-way non-transitive trust on the source (Windows NT) domain with the target domain, and verify the trust in the Active Directory Domains and Trusts snap-in.
3. Add the Domain Admins group of the target domain to the local Administrators group of the source domain.
4. Repeat steps 2 and 3 for any user or resource domains that trust the source domain.
5. If you intend to automatically migrate Windows NT workstation (and server) computers to the target domain, you must add the Domain Admins group to the local Administrators group of each computer. Migrating computer accounts individually is the more common (and conservative) practice.
6. Choose Programs, Administrative Tools, Active Directory Migration Tool to launch the ADMT snap-in.
7. Right-click the Active Directory Migration Tool node and choose Reporting Wizard. Use the wizard to specify the reports to create, usually the Migrated User Accounts and Migrated Computer Accounts reports.
8. Choose the Group Migration Wizard and add a global group and its members to the corresponding OU.

> **Caution**
> Be certain to mark the Copy Group Members check box in the Group Account Migration Wizard's Group Options dialog. If you don't mark this check box, user accounts are moved, not copied, to the new domain. If you move user accounts instead of copying them, users won't be able to log on to the Windows NT domain.

9. Repeat step 6 for each additional global group and OU you created.
10. Migrate shared local groups.
11. Run the Computer Account Migration Wizard to create copies of domain computer accounts in the source domain. Don't migrate accounts for PDCs and BDCs; you must manually migrate PDCs and BDCs after you decommission the domain.
12. If resource domains contain your computer accounts, run the Computer Account Migration Wizard to create copies in the target domain's Computers container.
13. Run the Service Account Migration Wizard to copy local service accounts to the target domain.
14. Test the new domain by progressively moving user logons from the source to the target domain.
15. After you've verified the operational status of the target domain with all user and computer accounts, upgrade resource domains in PDC–BDC–member server sequence. Run Dcpromo twice (promote and demote) on resource domain PDCs and BDCs, and manually join all resource domain servers to the target domain as member servers.

> **Caution**
>
> Don't change the name of resource domain servers when you join them to the domain as member servers. Clients, middle-tier components, and other servers continue to use the server name to specify the location of databases and message stores.

You also can use ADMT to move AD objects between domains in the same forest (intraforest migration) or from one forest of domain trees to another (interforest). The process of such migrations is basically the same as that described for migrating Windows NT domains.

→ To review the detailed steps for migrating groups and users with ADMT, **see** "Migrating Windows NT Computer Accounts," **p. 248**.

→ For details on copying computer accounts, **see** "Migrating Windows NT Computer Accounts," **p. 248**.

→ For instructions on using the Service Account Migration Wizard, **see** "Updating Service Accounts," **p. 253**.

SETTING SECURITY POLICIES FOR DOMAINS AND DOMAIN CONTROLLERS

Windows 2000 Server provides two administrative tools—Domain Security Policy and Domain Controller Security Policy—for applying standard security policies to all Windows 2000 computers within a domain and all DCs in the domain, respectively. These security policies are subsets of the Group Policies described in Chapter 15, "Establishing Group Policies, User Accounts, and Logons." The domain security policies you set apply to DCs, but you can apply more stringent policies to protect DCs by applying DC security policy. The application of security policies, like Group Policies, is local, site, domain, OU—commonly called *SDOU*. A better—but unpronounceable—acronym would be *LSDOU*. Unlike the Computers and Users containers, Active Directory Users and Computers' Domain Controllers node is an OU.

When you install the first DC of a domain, the setup process creates a Default Domain Policy and Default Domain Controller Policy. The two security policy administrative tools alter the settings of these two default policies.

The most important Group Policy security elements for domains—and thus DCs—that you set initially are Account Policies\Password Policies and Local Policies\User Rights Assignments and …\Security Options. All policies replicate to all DCs within a domain every five minutes; policies replicate every 90 minutes to member servers and Windows 2000 workstations.

You can set individual security policies manually, as shown by Figure 8.28, or take advantage of preset policy templates (.inf files in \Winnt\Security\Templates) for three basic levels of DC security.

Setting Security Policies for Domains and Domain Controllers

Figure 8.28
Use the Domain Security Policy snap-in to set the Minimum Password Length for logons in the DC's domain.

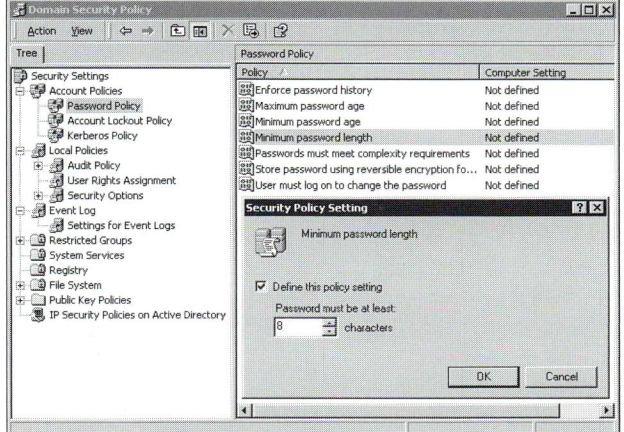

> **Tip from**
> *RJ*
>
> Test each security you apply at the DC on which you run the security tools. For example, to test the Minimum Password Length policy, add a test user account and specify a short password. When you click OK to add the new user account, you receive a message that the password violates security policy.

A prefabricated security template is a good starting point for establishing domain security. Microsoft includes templates for initial setup, workstations, and standalone (workgroup) servers, and another set for DCs. Table 8.3 lists the available security template files for DCs and the starting security levels they provide. The security settings you apply to DCs overwrite those applied by the Default Domain Security Policy object.

TABLE 8.3 DOMAIN CONTROLLER TEMPLATE FILES INCLUDED WITH WINDOWS 2000 SERVER

Template File	Security Level	Enforces
Basicdc.inf	Low	Nothing (does not apply to Domain Controllers)
Securedc.inf	Medium	42-day maximum password age 24 passwords remembered in history 2-day minimum password age 8-character minimum password length Lockout after 5 invalid attempts 30-minute account lockout reset period 30-minute account lockout duration Complex passwords required

TABLE 8.3 CONTINUED

Template File	Security Level	Enforces
		Several Security Options changes
		Audit primarily of failed account-related events
Hisecdc.inf	High	Same as above, but applicable only to all Windows 2000 domains
Setup Security.inf	None	Adds default User Rights assignments, allowing members of the Everyone group to access the server from the network

Dcpromo.exe installs the Setup Security.inf template upon promotion of a workgroup server to a DC. To achieve a moderate level of security for a DC by adding Securedc.inf policies to those of Setup Security.inf, do the following:

1. Launch the Domain Controllers Security Policy snap-in from the Administrative Tools menu.

2. Right-click the Security Settings node and choose Import Policy to open the Import Policy From dialog.

3. Double-click Securedc.inf in the file list to add medium-level security features to the DC, and close the dialog.

4. Review the changes made by Securedc.inf by inspecting each leaf node of the Account Policies and Local Policies nodes. Figure 8.29 shows changes made by Securedc.inf to Password Policies (refer to Figure 8.28).

Figure 8.29
The Domain Controller Security snap-in displays security policy changes made to Domain Controller Password policies by applying the Securedc.inf security template.

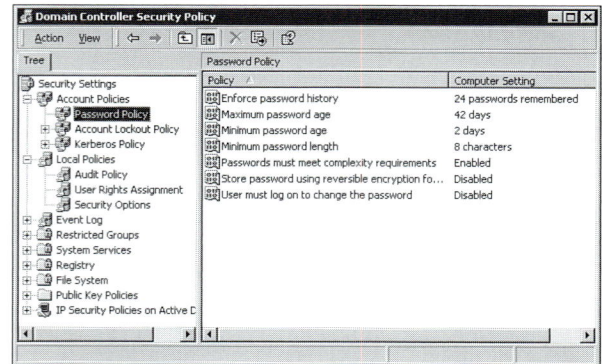

RECOVERING FROM A DISABLED SYSTEM | 403

5. Make additional changes you deem necessary to each of the six policy subnodes. Most policy names are sufficiently descriptive to let you make the decision as to whether a policy should or should not apply to your domain.

6. When you complete and test the changes, right-click the leaf nodes of interest, choose Export List, and export the settings to a tab-delimited text file for future reference (see Figure 8.30). You must create a separate .txt file for each security leaf node.

Figure 8.30
Excel 2000 displays the Security Options Group Policy settings applied by Securedc.inf.

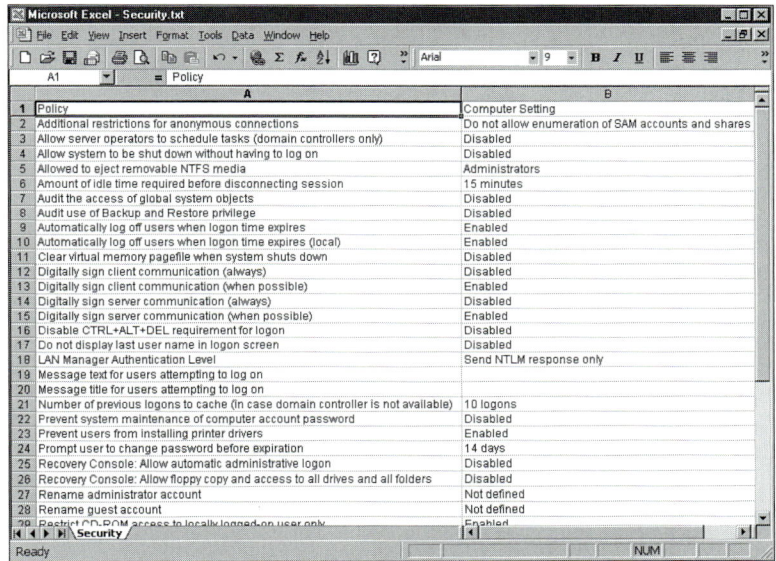

Tip from
RJ

You also can review the current Domain Controllers Group Policy by right-clicking the Domain Controllers node in Active Directory Users and Computers, selecting Properties, clicking the Group Policy tab, selecting Default Domain Controllers Policy, and clicking Edit to open the Group Policy editor. The Group Policy Editor snap-in displays the complete set of Group Policy objects (GPOs).

When you close the Domain Controllers Security Policy snap-in, you're prompted to save the changes. Changes you make to Domain Controller Group Policies require up to 5 minutes to replicate to other DCs. To apply the changes immediately across the domain, reboot the other DCs in the domain.

RECOVERING FROM A DISABLED SYSTEM

Windows 2000's system recovery approach offers more options than Windows NT. You can create an Emergency Repair Diskette (ERD) that aids in restarting a downed server or use the new System State backup feature to restore your system partition from a backup drive.

Windows 2000 also offers a Safe Mode feature similar to that of Windows 98 for recovery from the inability to boot your server normally, and a low-level Recovery Console for non-startable systems.

→ For more detailed information on Windows 2000's Backup application, **see** "Using the Windows 2000 Backup Application," **p. 965**.

PREPARING FOR RECOVERY

The ability to recover a server disabled by serious problems depends on proper preparation. Each time you make a significant alteration to your server, create a new ERD and an ASR backup. Significant alterations include hardware changes or additions and reconfiguration or resizing disk partitions. The ASR backup drive must be physically attached to your server. A transportable tape or Iomega Jaz drive is the most economical method of providing ASR restoration for multiple servers.

Unlike Windows NT, Windows 2000 Setup doesn't offer you the opportunity to create an ERD. You can, however, create an ex post facto ERD with Windows 2000's Backup tool. An ERD handles only a limited set of repairs to your server—primarily related to boot sector issues, corrupted system files, and registry damage—and won't correct any AD problems.

After you've stabilized the configuration of your server, create an ERD by following these steps:

1. Insert a blank, formatted 3.5-inch disk in the A: drive.
2. Choose Programs, Accessories, System Tools, Backup to open the Welcome page of the Backup dialog.
3. Click Emergency Repair Disk to open the Backup page and the Emergency Repair Diskette dialog.
4. Mark the Also Backup the Registry to the Repair Directory check box (see Figure 8.31). You can access this copy of the Registry when you run the Emergency Repair Process.

Figure 8.31
Using the Backup application to create an Emergency Repair Diskette.

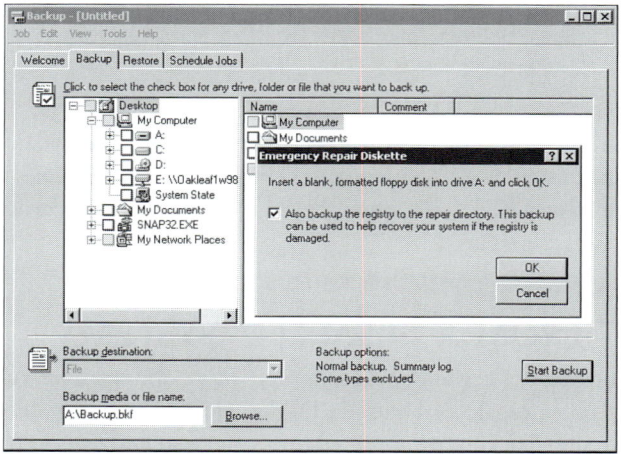

5. Click OK to create the ERD, which requires about a minute.

The ERD contains three files—Autoexec.nt, Config.nt, and Setup.log—for the Emergency Repair Process. The \Winnt\Repair folder contains these and other files. The \Winnt\Repair\RegBack folder holds current copies of each Registry hive.

BACKING UP SYSTEM STATE

The Backup utility included with Windows 2000 provides a System State backup and restore feature. System State backs up Registry data, the COM+ Class Registration database, and boot files, which include the basic system files for starting Windows 2000. System State backs up all AD-related files, including the Sysvol folder. If you have Certificate Services installed, System State adds the Certificate Services database. System State for Windows 2000 Advanced Server, AppServer, and Datacenter Server also backs up cluster service information. You restore System State to a downed server with the Backup utility.

→ For the details on backing up System State, **see** "System State and System Volume Information," **p. 953**.

RUNNING IN SAFE MODE

Safe Mode's primary function is as a troubleshooting tool for diagnosing hardware and device driver problems. There's no repair facility in Safe Mode, other than those fixes you can make by altering Registry entries, removing or replacing files, and other maintenance operations. The advantage of Safe Mode is that you can perform most Windows 2000 operations, depending on the choice you make when entering Safe Mode. You must use Safe Mode to run Windows 2000 Server without AD's lock on its database (Ntds.dit).

When you press F8 during the boot process to enter Safe Mode, the DOS-like menu offers the following choices:

- *Safe Mode* boots with only the bare minimum of files and drivers required for the keyboard, mouse, monitor (in base video mode), and fixed-disk drives.
- *Safe Mode with Networking* adds network support to Safe Mode. The Restoring Network Connections dialog appears during the startup process, regardless of the startup option you choose. The Netlogon service, however, doesn't start in Safe Mode or Safe Mode with Command Prompt. Figure 8.32 shows the Safe Mode with Networking screen with the My Network Places window open.

Figure 8.32
My Network Places are seen in the VGA-resolution display of Safe Mode with Networking.

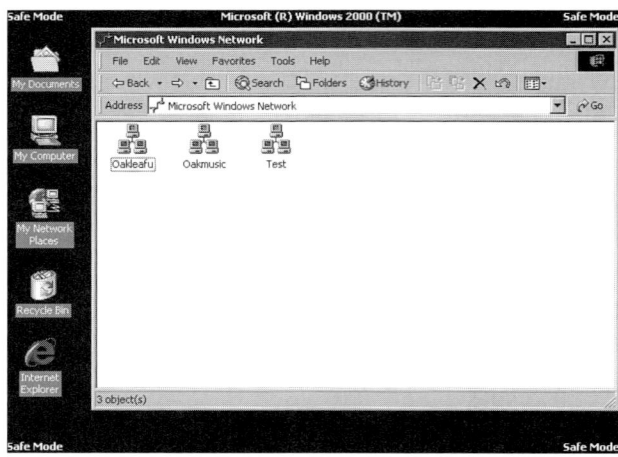

- *Safe Mode with Command Prompt* boots (without network support) into the Command window. If you close the Command window, you must restart the server to reopen it.
- *Enable Boot Logging* starts normally and creates a boot log text file (Ntbtlog.txt) in your \Winnt folder. The three preceding Safe Mode options also append records to Ntbtlog.txt. Figure 8.33 shows the first few records added to Ntbtlog.txt when starting in Safe Mode with Networking.

```
Microsoft (R) Windows 2000 (R) Version 5.0 (Build 2128)
10  1 1999 12:20:27.500
Loaded driver \WINNT\System32\ntoskrnl.exe
Loaded driver \WINNT\System32\hal.dll
Loaded driver \WINNT\System32\BOOTVID.DLL
Loaded driver pci.sys
Loaded driver isapnp.sys
Loaded driver intelide.sys
Loaded driver \WINNT\System32\DRIVERS\PCIIDEX.SYS
Loaded driver MountMgr.sys
Loaded driver ftdisk.sys
Loaded driver Diskperf.sys
Loaded driver \WINNT\System32\Drivers\WMILIB.SYS
Loaded driver dmload.sys
Loaded driver dmio.sys
Loaded driver PartMgr.sys
Loaded driver atapi.sys
Loaded driver disk.sys
Loaded driver \WINNT\System32\DRIVERS\CLASSPNP.SYS
Loaded driver Dfs.sys
Loaded driver KSecDD.sys
Loaded driver Ntfs.sys
Loaded driver NDIS.sys
Loaded driver Mup.sys
Did not load driver Audio Codecs
Did not load driver Legacy Audio Drivers
Did not load driver Media Control Devices
Did not load driver Legacy Video Capture Devices
Did not load driver Video Codecs
Did not load driver Standard PC
Did not load driver Audio Codecs
Did not load driver Legacy Audio Drivers
```

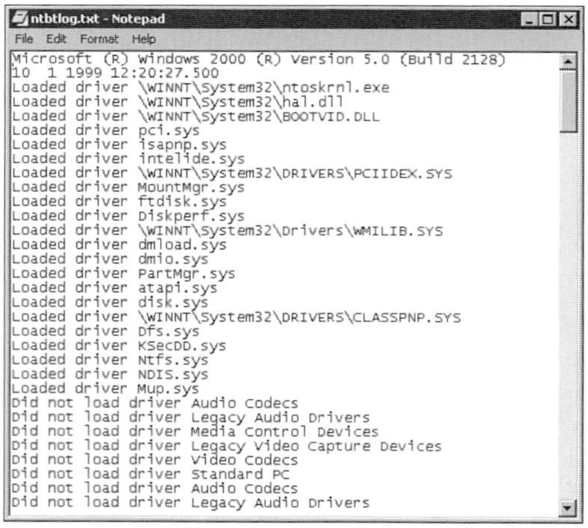

Figure 8.33
Starting in Safe Mode with Networking creates a boot log text file.

- *Enable VGA Mode* starts normally, but substitutes the basic VGA driver (640×480 resolution and 4-bit color depth) for the currently installed video driver. This mode is the equivalent of Windows NT's VGA Mode which adds the `/basevideo /sos` command-line switches.

- *Last Known Good Configuration* starts with the Registry configuration data for the last successful startup. This mode is the equivalent of Windows NT's Last Known Good Menu startup option.
- *Directory Services Restore Mode* starts with AD disabled, so you can repair a corrupted AD database (Ntds.dit) with Ntdsutil.exe in your \Winnt\System32 folder. Ntdsutil's Authoritative Restore mode performs the repair operations. Figure 8.34 shows the command syntax for Ntdsutil's basic and Authoritative Restore functions.

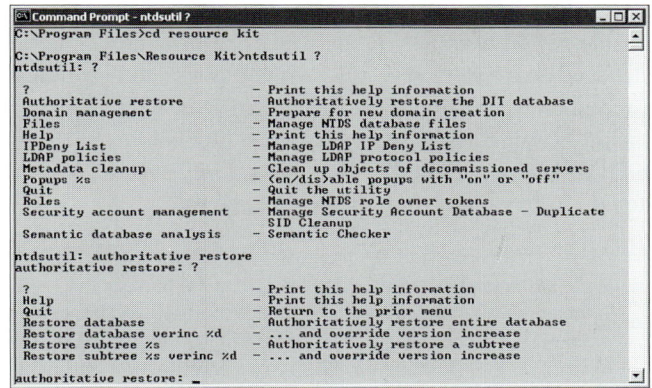

Figure 8.34
You can view the command line arguments for Ntdsutil.exe in startup and Authoritative Restore mode.

- *Debugging Mode* lets you view debug information on another computer connected to the server's serial port.

All Safe Mode choices require you to log on with your Administrator credentials.

USING THE RECOVERY CONSOLE

The Recovery Console is a new Windows 2000 feature that provides a command prompt to let you access basic command-line operations, such as COPY, DEL, DIR, and the like.

To start the Recovery Console, do the following:

1. Boot the server from the CD-ROM. If you can't boot from the CD-ROM, use the boot and setup disks. Setup loads all its files and starts Windows 2000.
2. Follow the Setup prompts until the Repair or Recover menu choice appears, and then press R.
3. Press C to start the Recovery Console.
4. At the Which Windows 2000 Installation Would You Like To Log Onto prompt, type **1**, unless you are multibooting installations.
5. Type your Administrator password at the prompt and press Enter. Windows 2000 enters Recovery Console mode with a *d*:\Winnt prompt.

6. Type **help** to obtain a list of the limited set of commands available in Recovery Console mode.

You can use the recovery console to replace files and perform low-level maintenance operations, but not much more. Type **exit** to kill the Recovery Console and reboot your computer.

Seizing the FSMO Roles of a Failed DC

If your DC that handles one or more FSMO roles drops dead, and you can't return it to service in a reasonable period of time, you must take drastic action. The time limit for missing FSMO roles depends on network activities, but you can't add new domains or perform other operations that require availability of the Schema Master, RID Master, Infrastructure Master, or Domain Naming Master roles while the DC holding the role is missing. You must seize the FSMO roles provided by the downed server with Ntdsutil.exe. AD must be running on the DC from which you want to seize the role.

> **Note**
>
> In the case of this chapter's examples, DCs in the primary `oakleaf.edu` domain, located in the administration building, are a better choice for FSMO roles than those of the `oakmusic.edu` domain, which is housed in the music building. The `oakmusic1.oakmusic.edu` DC owns the FSMO roles, because it was created by upgrading a Windows NT PDC before adding the `oakleaf.edu` domain. In this case, you would transfer FSMO roles to individual `oakleaf.edu` DCs rather than seize them.

> **Tip from**
> *RJ*
>
> You can transfer the FSMO role from an active DC holding the role to another DC on the network by substituting **transfer** for **seize** in the commands shown in this chapter's procedure for seizing FSMO roles. To maximize availability, it's a good practice to distribute the FSMO roles among DCs in the primary site. You must log on with Enterprise Admins credentials to transfer FSMO roles.

→ For a review of FSMO roles, **see** "Single-Master Operations," **p. 150**.

To seize FSMO roles, do the following:

1. Disconnect the failed server from the network. There's always a chance it might come back to life during the process.
2. At the command prompt, run Ntdsutil.exe from \Program Files\Resource Kit, and type **roles** at the ntdsutil prompt.
3. Type **?** to review the commands available at the fsmo maintenance prompt.
4. Type **select operation target**, and then **connections**.
5. At the server connections prompt, type **connect to server** *name*, where name is the NetBIOS name of the server. After a few seconds' delay, the prompt returns "Connected to name with credentials of locally logged on user."

6. Type **quit** to return to the fsmo maintenance prompt.
7. Type one or all of the following commands at the fsmo maintenance prompt:

   seize domain naming master
   seize infrastructure master
   seize pdc
   seize rid master
   seize schema master

   Click Yes to confirm your action when prompted, and check for error messages. There is no need to execute the preceding commands in a particular order, and you might want to change the operation target DC to distribute FSMO roles among other DCs in the site.

8. Type **quit** twice, and then **exit** to close the Command window.

Once you seize a FSMO role from a DC, don't reconnect the repaired DC to the network with AD running. If you can successfully demote the offline DC to a standalone server with Dcpromo, you can reconnect the repaired server to the network. If demotion is unsuccessful, delete the existing Windows 2000 Server installation, reattach the repaired server to the network, and perform a fresh Windows 2000 Server installation.

Troubleshooting

Solving Windows 2000 Upgrade Problems

Your PDC or BDC fails to reboot after copying initial files.

The Windows 2000 upgrade updates Boot.ini and installs replacement files for Ntldr. You might be able to edit Boot.ini to recover, but it's safer to reinstall Windows NT 4.0 Server as an "upgrade" to the existing installation.

To recover from an unbootable upgrade, do the following:

1. Start the installation process with the Windows NT 4.0 Server boot and setup disks.
2. When Setup detects an existing version of Windows NT, choose the Upgrade option from the menu. The Upgrade choice preserves the Registry and other files containing computer- and service-specific settings and data.
3. Disregard messages stating that your network adapters are obsolete and telling you to remove them.
4. After the Windows NT 4.0 installation completes, which takes considerably less time than a new installation—immediately reapply the latest Windows NT 4.0 Service Pack.
5. Verify trusts with replication partners, and check all services running on the PDC or BDC being upgraded.
6. Ascertain the source of the problem that prevented the reboot, which is likely to be a system board BIOS problem or an unsupported—or unreliable—CD-ROM drive.

7. If you can identify and correct the problem preventing reboot—for instance, by applying a BIOS upgrade—you can try another upgrade from within Windows 4.0 Server.

Unlike Windows NT, you can't upgrade an existing installation from the Windows 2000 Server boot and setup disks.

SOLVING ACTIVE DIRECTORY UPGRADE PROBLEMS

The server you're upgrading to AD can't connect to the DC with the domain-naming master FSMO role.

First, verify full network connectivity to the domain's FSMO DC by double-clicking My Network Places, Entire Network, Microsoft Windows Network, the icon for the domain, and finally the icon of the first DC you created. Provide your Domain Admins credentials to connect to the DC, and verify that administrative shares are visible. If you experience browsing problems, ping the DC. If you can't connect to the DC, troubleshoot the networking problem.

Next, make sure that the DNS server on the FSMO DC is operational. Check the DNS event log for error messages. Rebooting the FSMO DC usually is the fastest method of restoring the DNS service, but stopping and restarting the DNS service with the Services tool is less disruptive to network users. You must be able to log on as a member of the Enterprise Admins groups to the DC with its fully qualified DNS domain name. Connecting with the downlevel domain name doesn't verify DNS operability.

Finally, in the Internet Protocol (TCP/IP) Properties dialog, recheck that the IP address of the Preferred DNS Server points to the FSMO DC.

MCSE Corner: Deploying Windows 2000 Production Servers

There are three exams that test your knowledge of the concepts and techniques explained in Chapter 8. They are 70-215 Installing, Configuring and Administering Windows 2000 Server, 70-217 Implementing and Administering a Microsoft Windows 2000 Directory Services Infrastructure, and 70-222 Upgrading from Microsoft Windows NT 4.0 to Microsoft Windows 2000 (naturally.)

70-215   Installing, Configuring and Administering Windows 2000 Server

This exam tests your knowledge of Windows 2000 Server as a standalone server (not a domain controller) and does not touch on the topics of upgrading domain controllers, domains, and Active Directory. Some of the contents of this chapter do apply to the exam, though.

For this particular exam, you should be familiar with performing a Windows NT upgrade installation. Any references to Active Directory should not be on this exam, but there are no

MCSE CORNER: DEPLOYING WINDOWS 2000 PRODUCTION SERVERS | 411

guarantees that they won't appear. You should be comfortable upgrading an existing system, so walk through the process once or twice.

You should also be familiar with performing a complete install of Windows 2000 Server on a new server. This is another process you should walk through a few times to get the hang of it, assuming you have a spare computer. (You can multi-boot several Windows 2000 instances on the same server, if you have a large enough disk drive). You should know how to do a full install, not including Active Directory, but including services like DNS or Services for NetWare. You probably don't need to know the specifics of installing and configuring the individual services, but you should know the process for installing them.

The other vital parts of this chapter for this exam are using safe mode and using the recovery console. Due to the emphasis placed on troubleshooting ability in the newer exams, you should be comfortable in the use of both safe mode and the recovery console for restoring a disabled system and recovering data. You should also know how to troubleshoot the Windows NT 4.0 to Windows 2000 upgrade process.

70-217 IMPLEMENTING AND ADMINISTERING A MICROSOFT WINDOWS 2000 DIRECTORY SERVICES INFRASTRUCTURE

This exam covers the installation and administration of the Active Directory service on a Windows 2000 Server. It takes over where 70-215 leaves off. For this exam, you must know the process for installing Active Directory on a server and enabling it as a domain controller. You should also be familiar with Testing Active Directory servers and authorizing zone transfers.

Adding new domain controllers is also on the exam, along with creating DNS zones and creating new Global Catalog Servers. You should also know how to set group policies for domain controllers and how to back up and restore Active Directory.

70-222 UPGRADING FROM MICROSOFT WINDOWS NT 4.0 TO MICROSOFT WINDOWS 2000

This exam covers the entire process of upgrading Windows NT 4.0 machines to Windows 2000. You should be familiar with planning the upgrade process across the entire domain or group of domains. You also must know the process for bringing an existing Windows NT 4.0 PDC and any BDCs to Windows 2000 Active Directory servers functioning as domain controllers. You must be able to test the Active Directory implementations and test all inter-domain trusts that existed before the upgrade.

You should be familiar with the process of changing a Windows 2000 domain from mixed mode to native mode, and the implications of making that change. You can expect a question on the benefits and problems of changing a domain to native mode, such as compatibility issues with existing servers. You also must have excellent troubleshooting skills to find the cause of problems with Windows 2000 upgrade installations and Active Directory upgrade installations.

CHAPTER 9

INSTALLING RAID AND REMOVABLE MEDIA SYSTEMS

In this chapter

Enhancing Storage Management with Windows 2000   414

Understanding Windows 2000 Storage Concepts   416

Using the Disk Management Snap-In   418

Reviewing Fundamental Concepts of NTFS   424

Working with RAID Implementations   430

Using Removable Storage and Media Pools   442

Using Windows 2000 Disk Management Tools   448

Troubleshooting   451

MCSE Corner: Installing RAID, Backup, and Removable Media Systems   452

Enhancing Storage Management with Windows 2000

Organizations constantly struggle over costs associated with maintaining an enterprise storage solution. With the constant growth of available network services and the data associated with those services, administrators need new and innovative ways to store and maintain data. Windows 2000 provides enhanced storage services to empower administrators with a cost-effective tool to manage their data. Administrators can also organize their enterprise storage solutions while maintaining ease-of-use for their user community.

Windows 2000's enhanced storage management techniques include a new interface for disk management and some new disk and NTFS (NT File System) features. Windows 2000 also provides the ability to manage disks on both local and remote computers.

The new interface for Windows 2000 disk management is the Disk Management snap-in. This interface enables administrators to create partitions and volumes, implement software fault tolerance, and use some of the new storage features in Windows 2000. One of the key features of the Disk Management snap-in is the capability of managing disk configurations on remote systems. In most organizations, it is unrealistic to manage disks directly from the local server. Without some sort of remote control mechanism, administrators were forced to visit all servers for any disk management duties. Figure 9.1 displays the Disk Manager snap-in in Windows 2000.

Figure 9.1
The Disk Manager snap-in is used for local or Remote Storage administration. This figure displays the Disk Manager snap-in on a local server.

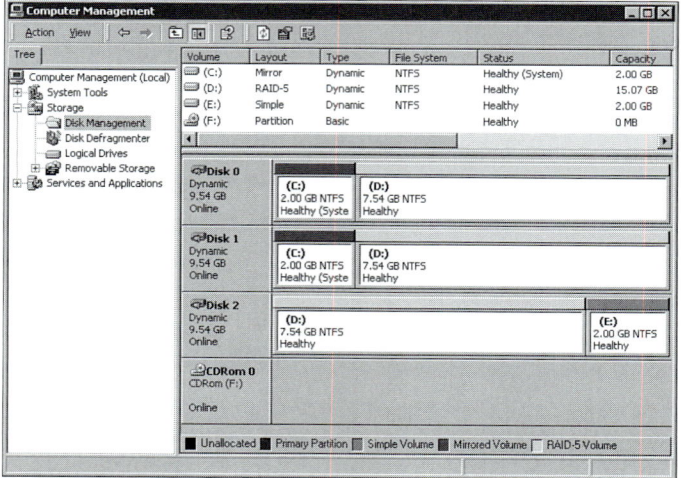

 If you encounter problems with a severed network connection when administering disks on a remote computer, see the "Problems with the Disk Management Snap-In" topic of the "Troubleshooting" section near the end of this chapter.

Windows 2000 also enhances the current storage capabilities with new features, such as:

- Dynamic Disks—Dynamic disks are a new feature to Windows 2000. Dynamic disks contain one large physical partition (also known as an *extent*) that holds all volume and configuration information within the disk. This enables the disks to be self-identifying for smooth interoperability between systems.

- Reparse Points and Filters—Reparse points and filters are used to extend the functionality of NTFS by providing the ability to implement triggers within the file system. This allows developers of third-party applications greater interoperability with storage and management mechanisms of NTFS.

- Distributed File System (Dfs)—The Distributed File System, previously an add-on to Windows NT 4.0, has been updated to provide a more scalable storage solution. Dfs provides a single logical view of distributed physical storage implementation. Dfs enables multiple physical stores to share a common namespace while providing name transparency and load balancing. This creates a high-availability enterprise storage solution for even the most complex environments.

- File Replication Service (FRS)—Windows 2000 provides an updated FRS from its predecessor. The service provides two-way replication to duplicate files, directories, and their respective attributes consistently across the network. Combining Dfs and FRS results in a highly scalable and reliable enterprise storage solution for your organization.

- Encrypting File System (EFS)—The Encrypting File System enables users to encrypt and decrypt information on the NTFS file system. This provides the file system more security in an otherwise compromised situation.

- Disk Quotas—Windows 2000 provides disk quotas inherently built into the NTFS file system. This enables administrators to monitor disk usage and define disk usage configurations for their users.

- NTFS Change Journal—Change Journals record all changes to files and folders within the NTFS file system. Applications that index or otherwise manage the file system can use Change Journals without actually reading every file and folder.

- Sparse File Support—Some applications might create very large files (Sparse Files) to allocate storage. Much of the file usually contains large amounts of unallocated data represented by consecutive 0 bits. Windows 2000 recognizes these sparse files in NTFS and uses only the storage space required by the application.

- Volume Mount Points—Windows 2000 provides volume mount points in NTFS to enhance the management of disks and namespaces. Mount points enable administrators to define a folder on one volume to point to another volume. This enables a single drive letter to point to multiple volumes.

- Remote Storage—Remote Storage is the Windows 2000 implementation of HSM (Hierarchical Storage Management). Remote storage enhances storage utilization by archiving infrequently used data to less expensive media, such as tapes.

- Removable Storage and Media Pools—Removable Storage enables administrators and developers to recognize removable devices, such as tape drives, and more precisely administer robotic tape libraries and CD jukeboxes. All Removable Storage media are part of a media pool. Media pools organize media of the same type with common management properties.

In addition to some of the new features in Windows 2000, software *RAID (Redundant Array of Independent Disks)* and NTFS have been enhanced to provide smoother interoperability with applications that use storage features.

→ To learn the benefits of Dfs, **see** "Taking Advantage of the Distributed File System," **p. 707**.
→ To gain a better understanding of FRS, **see** "Using the File Replication Service with Dfs," **p. 716**.
→ For more information on the Encrypting File System, **see** "Encrypting and Decrypting Files," **p. 489**.

Understanding Windows 2000 Storage Concepts

Microsoft has worked with many organizations to determine the majority of storage needs in today's enterprise networks. Windows 2000 introduces advanced storage techniques useful to many organizations. Additionally, Independent Software Vendors (ISVs) now have greater control within the storage subsystem of Windows 2000 to develop the next generation of storage management applications.

Dynamic Disks, Basic Disks, and Volumes

Windows 2000 enhances disk management by providing two types of disks—*Basic* and *Dynamic*.

Basic disks are disks that contain traditional primary partitions, extended partitions with logical drive letters, and fault-tolerant partitions created in Windows NT 4.0. Basic disks store data in *hard partitions*, which means the structure of the physical partitions created on the disk is the same as the logical partitions represented by the operating system. Basic disks are used for backward compatibility with MS-DOS, Windows 98, and Windows NT 4.0. All basic disks are managed by the FT Disk driver (`Ftdisk.sys`). The FT Disk driver was developed in previous versions of Windows NT for all disk operations.

Tip from
RJ

Most server implementations take advantage of the features provided with dynamic disks. If you choose to use basic disks, use only extended partitions if more than 4 storage namespaces (drive letters) are required. Most implementations of basic disks should use primary partitions. Basic disks can have a total of 4 primary partitions or 3 primary partitions and an extended partition.

Caution

If you're running a dual-boot system, use basic disks. Upgrading to dynamic disks might render the file system unreadable from operating systems other than Windows 2000.

New to Windows 2000 is the implementation of *dynamic disks*. Dynamic disks are represented by a single physical partition created on the disk. This single physical partition stores all configuration information and volumes stored on the disk. Additionally, dynamic disks provide the foundation of software RAID in Windows 2000. RAID is a technique of using multiple physical disks to provide to the system improved *fault tolerance* (the capability of gracefully recovering from a catastrophic disk failure) and performance. Dynamic disks provide many volume types, such as:

- Simple Volumes—Simple Volumes are the functional equivalent of primary partitions on basic disks. Comprised of large amounts of space defined by a drive letter or mount point, simple volumes are ideal for systems using hardware RAID. Simple volumes can be extended if additional disk space is required for the volume.

> **Tip from**
> *RJ*
>
> Simple volumes can be extended only if there's unallocated free space available on the disk and the volume selected is not a system volume.

- Spanned Volumes—Spanned volumes consist of a single volume spanned across multiple disks. This is useful if you need to create a single volume with unallocated space across multiple disks. As with simple volumes, spanned volumes can also be extended.
- Striped Volumes—Striped volumes write data across multiple disks in segments *(stripes)* to provide fast access across multiple disks. Striped volumes are the functional equivalent of RAID 0. Because data is written across multiple disks, striped volumes cannot be extended.

> **Note**
>
> Spanned volumes and striped volumes do not provide redundancy and should be used only if no other options are available or hardware RAID is in place. At least two physical disks are required for a spanned or striped volume. An alternative to using spanned volumes is volume mount points. Volume mount points are discussed later in the chapter.

- Mirrored Volumes—Mirrored volumes are the functional equivalent to RAID 1, mirroring information between two disks. Mirrored volumes provide for data redundancy by ensuring that volumes on two disks are exact copies. If a disk fails with a mirrored volume, no data is lost. Mirrored volumes require two physical disks and cannot be extended.
- RAID-5 Volumes—RAID-5 volumes require at least 3 physical disks and provide for data redundancy. RAID-5 volumes are more efficient than mirrored volumes because data is written across multiple disks in segments (stripes) providing for faster disk access. RAID-5 volumes cannot be extended.

Using dynamic disks allows the disk to be self-identifying and provides better interoperability between Windows 2000 systems. Dynamic disks are accessed from the Logical Disk Manager using the Disk Manager I/O Driver (DMIO.SYS), also new in Windows 2000.

> **Note**
>
> With the exception of system volumes, all volume management can be done online. No system reboots are required to create volumes in Windows 2000.

> **Tip from**
> *RJ*
>
> When upgrading from Windows NT 4.0, disks are initially created as basic disks. Basic disks can be upgraded to Dynamic disks. When the upgrade occurs, all partitions are upgraded to volumes. If you upgrade a Basic disk to a Dynamic disk, the physical structure of the partitions is retained. The volumes are *hard-linked*. If a dynamic disk is created without any existing partitions, the volumes are *soft-linked*.

LOGICAL DISK MANAGER

The *Logical Disk Manager (LDM)* is a new component in Windows 2000. The LDM provides access and enhances management of dynamic disks. File systems and disk management are seamlessly controlled by the LDM to provide online configuration changes in an enterprise storage system. Additionally, the LDM provides ISVs the ability to seamlessly integrate storage applications into the Windows 2000 operating system.

The LDM uses a small database on dynamic disks to read all configuration information. The database ranges from 1–8MB and contains all information about the disk configuration in the system. The LDM database is replicated to every dynamic disk in the system to allow dynamic disks to be self-identifying and self-configuring when moved between systems.

USING THE DISK MANAGEMENT SNAP-IN

The Disk Management snap-in is a new feature in Windows 2000 that enables administrators to effectively manage the disk configuration on servers. Additionally, the snap-in can be used locally or to connect to a remote server eliminating the need to physically visit each server. The Disk Management snap-in enables administrators to configure disks, volumes, and RAID implementations online. This reduces needless reboots in an enterprise storage environment.

> **Note**
>
> When you first access a new disk with the Disk Management snap-in, a Signature Wizard guides you through signing the disks. Windows 2000 (and previous versions of Windows NT) use disk signatures to identify volume and other fault-tolerant information in the registry.

IMPLEMENTING DYNAMIC DISKS

Dynamic disks enable Windows 2000 disks to be self-identifying and self-configuring. Additionally, software RAID implementations can be accomplished only with dynamic disks. To convert basic disks to dynamic disks, follow these steps:

Using the Disk Management Snap-In

1. Right-click My Computer and choose Manage to open the Computer Management console.
2. Open the Storage, Disk Management node.
3. Right-click on the disk you want to convert and select Upgrade to Dynamic Disk (see Figure 9.2).

Figure 9.2
To implement dynamic disks, you must upgrade the basic disk to a dynamic disk using the Disk Management snap-in.

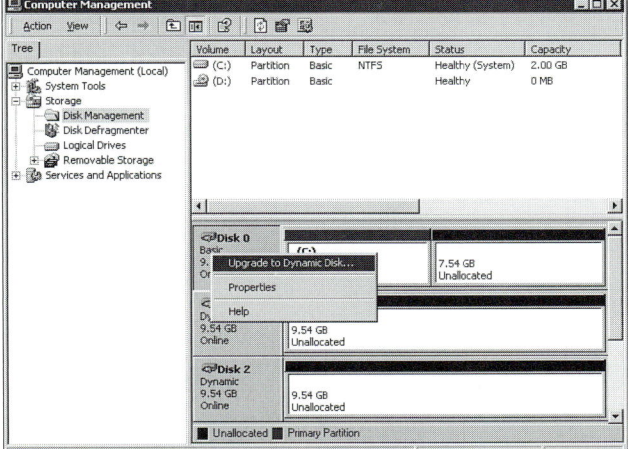

Caution

Upgrading the disk that contains the system partition is a one-way operation. When the system partition is a dynamic disk, it cannot be reverted to a basic disk. When upgrading the disk that contains the system partition, you must reboot your server for the changes to take effect.

CREATING A SIMPLE VOLUME

The implementation of Simple Volumes is new in Windows 2000, but the concept of creating a namespace on a disk remains the same. Simple Volumes are the dynamic disk equivalents of primary partitions on basic disks. Volume creation is accomplished through a wizard appropriately called the Create Volume Wizard. To create a simple volume, follow these steps:

1. From the Disk Management snap-in, right-click the disk on which you want to create a simple volume and select Create Volume to start the Create Volume Wizard. Click Next at the welcome screen to continue.
2. In the volume type dialog (see Figure 9.3), select Simple Volume and click Next.

Figure 9.3
To create a simple volume, select the Simple Volume option in the Volume Type dialog.

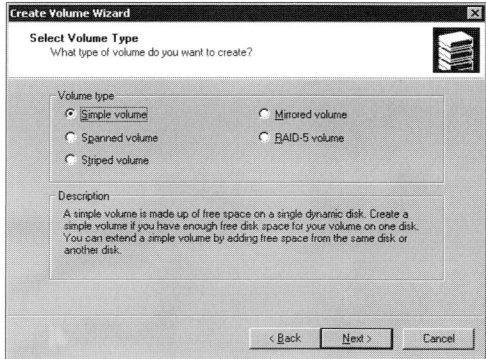

3. In the Select Disks dialog, the disk you selected should be in the Selected Dynamic Disks list (see Figure 9.4). If you want to create a simple volume on a different disk than the one selected, remove the disk from the selected list and add the appropriate disk. Enter the size of the volume in the For Selected Disk text box and click Next.

Figure 9.4
Create a new volume by selecting a disk and entering a size.

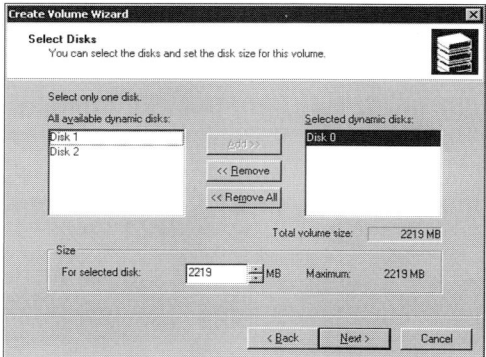

4. In the Assign Drive Letter or Path dialog, select the appropriate drive letter or mount point, or choose to assign a drive letter at a later time by not choosing a drive letter (see Figure 9.5); click Next to continue.

USING THE DISK MANAGEMENT SNAP-IN   421

Figure 9.5
To assign a drive letter, select the Assign a Drive Letter option.

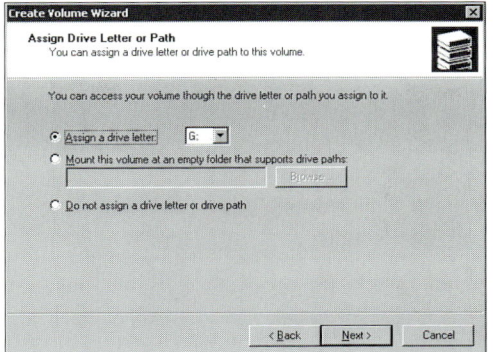

→ To learn more about creating volume mounts, **see** "Volume Mount Points," **p. xxx**. (later in this chapter)

   5. On the Format Volume dialog, you have the option of formatting the volume now or at a later point (see Figure 9.6). Select the appropriate formatting information and click Next.

Figure 9.6
To format the newly created volume, select the Format This Volume as Follows option.

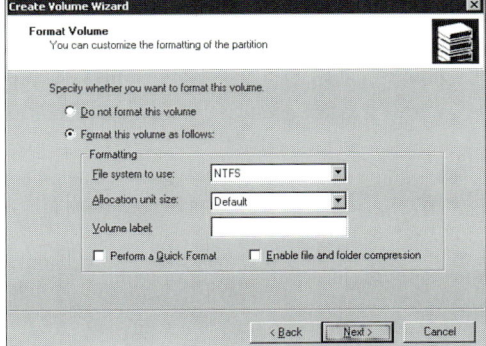

   6. Review your settings on the final completion dialog and select Finish. This creates the simple volume with the settings you selected.

 If you encounter problems viewing newly created volumes using the Windows 2000 Terminal Services Client, see the "Problems with the Disk Management Snap-In" topic of the "Troubleshooting" section near the end of this chapter.

EXTENDING THE VOLUME SIZE

If you've created a simple or spanned volume, you can extend the size of the volume automatically without taking the volume or file system offline. Extending the volume size is a new feature of Windows 2000. Follow these steps to extend the volume size:

1. From the Disk Management snap-in, right-click on the volume you want to extend and select Extend Volume to invoke the Extend Volume Wizard; click Next at the welcome dialog to continue.

2. On the Select Disks dialog, the disk containing the volume you selected should be in the Selected Dynamic Disks list (see Figure 9.7); enter the size of the extended storage in the disk size field and click Next.

Figure 9.7
To extend a volume, select a disk and size. This extends the current volume online.

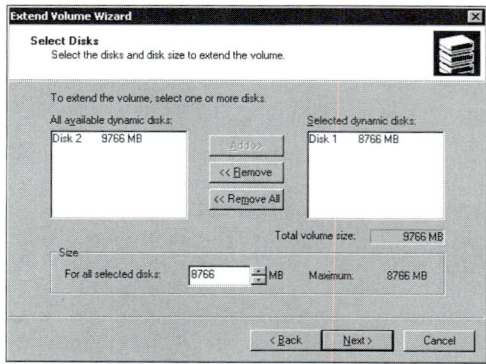

Tip from
RJ

When extending a simple volume, you can automatically convert it to a spanned volume by selecting a disk other than the disk where the simple volume exists.

3. On the completion dialog, review your changes and select Finish to extend the volume.

 If you encounter problems extending or spanning simple volumes, see the "Problems with the Disk Management Snap-In" topic of the "Troubleshooting" section near the end of this chapter.

CREATING A SPANNED VOLUME

Creating a spanned volume in Windows 2000 is as easy as creating a simple volume. Although the use for spanned volumes might not be immediately obvious, they do serve a purpose in your storage configuration. Spanned volumes are useful when creating a stacked RAID (RAID 0/1) configuration. With RAID 0/1, software RAID is used to stripe the data across multiple physical disks, and hardware RAID is used to mirror the disks. This improves I/O and provides for redundancy. To create a spanned volume, follow these steps:

1. From the Disk Management snap-in, right-click on any of the disks and select Create Volume to start the Create Volume Wizard. Click Next at the welcome screen to create the volume.

2. In the Volume Type dialog, select Spanned Volume (see Figure 9.8); click Next.

Figure 9.8
To create a spanned volume, select the Spanned Volume option in the Volume Type dialog.

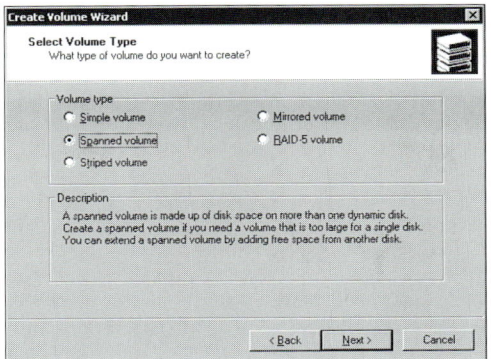

3. On the Select Disks dialog, select the disks to participate in the spanned volume and enter the size of the volume in the For Selected Disks size text box (see Figure 9.9); click Next.

Figure 9.9
When creating a spanned volume, select the disks and size for the volume.

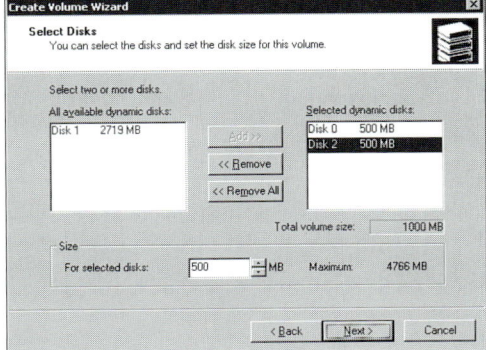

4. The remaining steps are the same for Spanned volumes as those for simple volume creation (steps 4 through 6 in that procedure), in which you assign a drive letter, format the volume, and review your changes.

DELETING A VOLUME

Administrators are sometimes required to delete volumes to better organize storage utilization or to reconfigure storage support. To delete a volume, follow these steps:

1. From the Disk Management snap-in, right-click on the volume you want to delete and select Delete Volume.
2. A warning dialog opens (see Figure 9.10); click yes to confirm your changes and delete the volume.

Figure 9.10
To delete a volume, right-click on the volume you want to delete and select Delete Volume from the Disk Management snap-in.

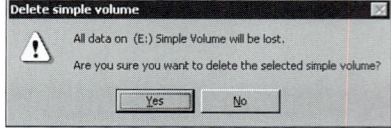

> **Caution**
>
> Deleting volumes results in permanent data loss unless you've previously backed up your data. Delete volumes only after you've performed appropriate measures to save the data.

> **Note**
>
> System volumes cannot be deleted. A system volume is a volume marked with a special attribute that identifies it as a volume containing operating system files or folders.

Reviewing Fundamental Concepts of NTFS

Windows 2000 provides an updated version of NTFS, a core component of the Windows 2000 operating system. Much of the extended storage functionality in Windows 2000 requires NTFS.

> **Note**
>
> This chapter focuses on the features of NTFS 5 in Windows 2000. When compared with its predecessor, the term NTFS refers to NTFS 5. NTFS 4 refers to the NTFS implementation in Windows NT 4.0.

NTFS 5 Clusters

Windows 2000 uses 64-bit addresses for clusters of physical storage sectors that range from 512 bytes to 4KB, depending on the size of the volume and its sector size. (The standard sector size for drives manufactured in the U.S. is 512 bytes.) The maximum volume size for NTFS is 2^{64} bytes or roughly 16EB (exabytes, 2^{60} bytes). Large volume and file sizes are especially important for storing full-screen, full-motion video for editing and broadcast applications. Although NTFS 5 theoretically supports 16EB, the current limitation is 2TB because of hardware limitations. Table 9.1 outlines the default cluster sizes based on the size of the volume.

Table 9.1 NTFS Cluster Sizes Based on Volume/Partition Size

Volume/Partition Size	Cluster Size	Sectors per Cluster
512MB or less	512 Bytes	1
513MB–1GB (1024MB)	1KB	2

REVIEWING FUNDAMENTAL CONCEPTS OF NTFS | 425

Volume/Partition Size	Cluster Size	Sectors per Cluster
1025MB–2GB (2048MB)	2KB	4
2049MB–4GB (4096MB)	4KB	8
4097MB–8GB (8192MB)	8KB	16
8193MB–16GB (16,384MB)	16KB	32
16,385MB–32GB (32,768MB)	32KB	64
More than 32GB	64KB	128

Tip from
RJ

You might choose to change the default cluster size to a larger cluster if you anticipate extending a volume beyond the recommended cluster size for the current volume size (the change option is available through the format command). NTFS compression is not available on clusters greater than 4KB. If you want to implement compression on a drive larger than 4GB, you might want to adjust the cluster size. To obtain optimal performance with compression, it's better to create many 4GB volumes (with default cluster size of 4KB) and create volume mount points from a parent volume.

MASTER FILE TABLE

NTFS uses an object-oriented database in the boot sector called the *master file table (MFT)*. The MFT contains records of all files and directories located on the volume. A mirrored version of the MFT is also stored on the drive. Thus, if the original version of the MFT becomes corrupted due to a hardware failure (typically, a bad disk sector), the copy automatically is used on boot, and the operating system creates a new original from the copy. NTFS uses a transaction log to maintain file consistency in the event of a hardware problem (such as a power failure) or system failure during the write process. NTFS uses the transaction log to return the disk to a consistent state during the next disk access. Figure 9.11 shows a simplified representation of the MFT file and directory record structure for an NTFS volume.

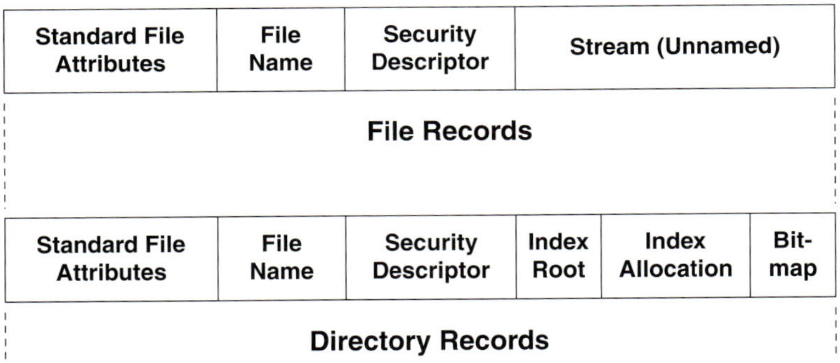

Figure 9.11
The simplified structure of the file and directory records of the master file table for an NTFS volume.

Standard File Attributes	File Name	Security Descriptor	Stream (Unnamed)		
File Records					
Standard File Attributes	File Name	Security Descriptor	Index Root	Index Allocation	Bit-map
Directory Records					

NTFS Security

Files and folders in Windows 2000 are treated as objects. Security is provided in NTFS through the use of security descriptors. *Security descriptors*, shown in Figure 9.12, are special attributes of objects that contain a *Discretionary Access Control List (DACL)* and a *System Access Control List (SACL)*. Commonly referred to as *ACL*, the DACL contains a list of SIDs and access permissions. Each entry in an ACL is called an *Access Control Entry (ACE)*. ACEs with the No Access attribute are always located at the top of the DACL. During file access, the Security Reference Monitor compares the file's ACEs to the user's security context (Access Token) to determine permissions. The Security Reference Monitor then passes the user's security privileges the appropriate process in the operating system. The SACL is used to record auditing information when the object is configured to audit events.

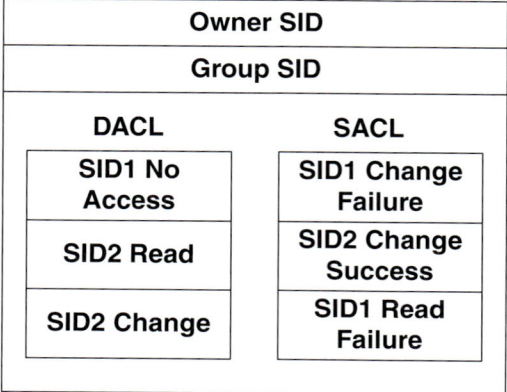

Figure 9.12
This diagram illustrates a simplified structure of a security descriptor.

Sparse File Support

Sparse files are large files with consecutive sections of 0 bits. For example, applications might create large data files to allocate storage. If the application doesn't need all the storage, the allocated storage is a combination of 0 and 1 bits and the unallocated storage consists of large sections of consecutive 0 bits. NTFS provides support for sparse files by saving only meaningful data on the file system and automatically inserting the large sections of 0 bits when the file is requested.

NTFS Change Journals

NTFS Change Journals record all changes made to files and folders in the file system. The Change Journal can be used by applications to determine which files have changed in the file system. When a file is created, modified, or deleted, NTFS adds a record to the NTFS Change Journal. This enables software developers to enhance file system operations—such as indexing, virus checking, and backup—without accessing every file and folder.

> **Note**
> Although the APIs and documentation for using the NTFS Change Journal are available, Microsoft recommends that the NTFS Change Journal be used only by independent software vendors (ISVs) developing software that requires close integration with the NTFS file system.

Reparse Points and File System Filters

Reparse points have been implemented in NTFS to provide the Windows 2000 operating system and applications with notifications when files are accessed. Reparse points are special tags that are applied to an NTFS file or folder. When a file with a reparse point is accessed, the I/O subsystem invokes a trigger that executes a *file system filter*. A file system filter is an installable filter that software developers can use to extend the functionality of NTFS.

Software vendors can implement filters to capture the file before the user accesses it. This enables developers to seamlessly interact with the NTFS file system and improves performance of Windows 2000 server. Because the reparse point is activated only when the file is accessed, software developers can concentrate their development toward the file system filter instead of monitoring the file system for user activity.

> **Note**
> Development of file system filters and reparse point integration is primarily for independent software vendors (ISVs). To maintain the integrity of the file system and avoid software conflicts, Microsoft assigned reparse tags to ISVs. For more information about developing file system filters and reparse points, obtain the Microsoft Windows Installable File System Kit from `http://www.microsoft.com/hwdev/ntifskit`.

Volume Mount Points

NTFS mount points provide the functionality of multiple volumes to be accessed from a single namespace. Administrators can define volume mount points to increase disk capacity without redirecting users to a different drive or share. To create a volume mount point, follow these steps:

1. From the Disk Management snap-in, right-click on the volume you want to mount and select Change Drive Letter and Path.
2. In the Change Drive Letter and Paths dialog, shown in Figure 9.13, select Add.

Figure 9.13
To change a drive letter to a mount point, use the Change Drive Letter and Paths dialog in the Disk Management snap-in.

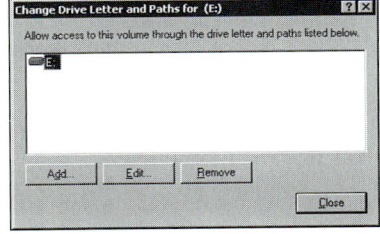

3. In the Add New Drive Letter or Path dialog, the Mount in This NTFS Folder option is selected by default (see Figure 9.14); click Browse to select the folder.

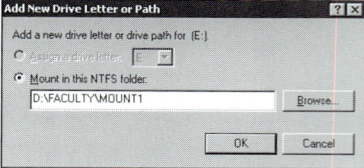

Figure 9.14
To specify the location of a mount point, use the Add New Drive Letter or Path dialog in the Disk Management snap-in.

Note

To mount a volume, the folder must be empty and exist on an NTFS volume. You can also mount volumes when you're formatting the volume. Although the volume that contains the mount point must be NTFS, the mounted volume can be FAT or FAT32 in addition to NTFS.

4. Click OK to mount the volume.

NTFS Data Streams

NTFS permits subdividing the data in a file into individual *streams* of data. The most common application of multistream files is for storing Macintosh files on Windows 2000 servers. Macintosh files have two streams (called *forks*): the data fork and the application fork. The application fork contains information on the program that created or can edit the file. (In Windows 2000, the Registry associates applications with file extensions, serving a purpose similar to that of the Macintosh's application fork.)

Unicode Support

NTFS supports Unicode filenames. Unicode uses 16 bits to specify a particular character or symbol, rather than the 7 or 8 bits of ASCII and ANSI characters. 16 bits accommodate 64KB characters and symbols, so Unicode doesn't depend on changing code pages for national language support (NLS).

Implementing NTFS Compression

NTFS provides an option for inherent data compression on the file system. This option automatically compresses selected files and folders without user intervention. Although compression operations are transparent to the user, the use of compression can reduce file access performance on your servers. Administrators should implement compression only if no other storage options are available.

To compress files and folders in Windows 2000, two options are available—compression through the Windows Explorer user interface or compression through using the Compact.exe command. Although the Windows Explorer user interface is a great tool for compressing files and folders, the COMPACT command enables an administrator to view compression ratios of the compressed files and folders. To implement NTFS compression through the use of Windows Explorer, follow these steps:

1. Open Windows Explorer and right-click the folder to compress; select Properties to open the *FolderName* Properties dialog.
2. In the General page, click Advanced to open the Advanced Attributes dialog.
3. Mark the Compress Contents To Save Disk Space check box to enable compression of the specified folder and its current or future subfolders (see Figure 9.15).

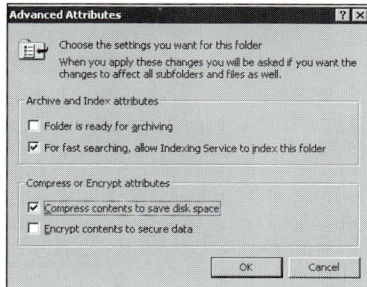

Figure 9.15
To compress a file or folder, select the compression attribute in the Advanced Attributes dialog.

4. Click OK to close the Advanced Attributes dialog and click OK again to close the *FolderName* Properties dialog; if the folder contains subfolders and files, the Confirm Attribute Changes dialog opens (see Figure 9.16).

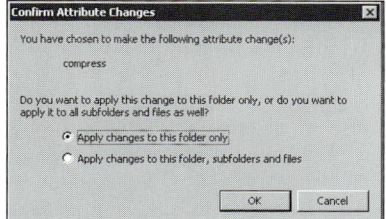

Figure 9.16
When compressing a folder with subfolders, the Confirm Attribute Changes dialog appears.

Tip from
RJ

Although a check box exists for both compression and encryption, they are mutually exclusive. Compressed files and folders cannot be encrypted, and encrypted files and folders cannot be compressed.

5. Select the Apply Changes to This Folder, Subfolders and Files option and click OK.

NTFS compression can also be performed from the command prompt. The COMPACT command enables you to compress and decompress files and folders while also providing compression ratio information. To implement NTFS compression through the use of the COMPACT command, follow these steps:

1. Open the command prompt and open the directory that contains the file or folder you want to compress.

2. To compress a folder, type **compact /C** *foldername*.
3. To display a list of compressed and uncompressed files and folders and their compression ratios, simply type **compact** without any additional parameters.
4. To uncompress a folder, type **compact /u** *foldername*.

> **Tip from**
> *RJ*
>
> To alternately compress or uncompress folders and subfolders, use the **/s** switch of the **compact** command.

Although NTFS compression is a cost-effective tool for reducing utilized storage space, it should be used sparingly because of performance degradation of the file system. On servers, compression usually is reserved for infrequently accessed files or very large files. Compressing and decompressing frequently accessed files reduces server performance by a significant margin.

ADDITIONAL NTFS FEATURES

NTFS also provides additional features, such as file and folder security, Encrypting File System (EFS), and disk quotas. File and folder security provides administrators with the ability to secure files and folders on the file system for a given user or group of users. EFS provides added security by allowing users to encrypt and decrypt their files with industry accepted encryption techniques. Disk quotas enable administrators to define and enforce user- and group-based quotas for storage utilization. These features are covered in other chapters of this book.

→ To learn more about shared folder and file security, **see** "File Sharing Security," **p. 678**.
→ For an introduction to the Encrypting Files System, **see** "Encrypting and Decrypting Files," **p. 489**.
→ To get acquainted with disk quotas, **see** "Disk Quotas," **p. 844**.

> **Note**
>
> One recurrent theme in this book is "Use NTFS, not FAT, for servers." In the early days of Windows NT, some network administrators were reluctant to abandon FAT in favor of NTFS because they wanted to be able to boot a server with a DOS disk and gain access to files in case of a problem booting Windows NT. The emergency repair disk you create when you install Windows 2000 and the Windows 2000 Setup program's Repair facility is much more effective than booting from DOS to recover from a system failure.

WORKING WITH RAID IMPLEMENTATIONS

RAID uses multiple fixed-disk drives, high-speed disk controllers, and special software drivers to increase the safety of your data and to improve the performance of your fixed-disk subsystem. RAID is a form of fault tolerance. RAID protects your data by spreading it over multiple disk drives and then calculating and storing parity information. This redundancy enables any one disk drive to fail without causing the array itself to lose any data.

RAID also increases disk subsystem performance by distributing read tasks over several disk drives, allowing the same data to be retrieved from different locations, depending on which location happens to be closest to the read head(s) at the instant the data is requested.

RAID can be implemented in hardware or as add-on software. Modern network operating systems, such as Windows 2000 Server, provide native support for multiple RAID levels (discussed in the section that follows).

Windows 2000 RAID administration is performed through the Disk Management snap-in. Windows 2000 provides two options for RAID redundancy—RAID 5 and RAID 1. The Disk Management snap-in is also used to recover from disk failure in a RAID implementation.

Understanding RAID Levels

There are different levels of RAID, each of which is optimized for various types of data handling and storage requirements. RAID levels define how data is divided and stored on the disk drives comprising the array and how and where parity information is calculated and stored. Six levels are recognized in RAID, numbered 0 through 5. RAID levels aren't indicative of the degree of data safety or increased performance (the higher number isn't necessarily better); they simply define how the array is implemented.

Depending on the application, the disk subsystem may be called on to do frequent small reads and writes; or the disk drive might need to do less frequent, but larger, reads and writes. An application server running a client/server database, for example, tends toward frequent small reads and writes, whereas a server providing access to stored images tends toward less frequent, but larger, reads and writes. RAID levels vary in their optimization for small reads, large reads, small writes, and large writes. Although most servers have a mixed disk access pattern, choosing the RAID level optimized for the predominant environment maximizes the performance of your disk subsystem.

> **Note**
> Although RAID levels are implemented across disks, Windows 2000 provides RAID for volumes. Implementing RAID on a volume basis enables the physical disks to participate in many RAID levels. This chapter focuses on RAID levels as they apply to disks, but the same concepts apply to volumes.

RAID levels 1 and 5 are very common in PC LAN environments. All hardware and software RAID implementations provide at least these two levels. RAID level 3 is used occasionally in specialized applications, and it is supported by most hardware and some software RAID implementations. RAID levels 2 and 4 are seldom, if ever, used in PC LAN environments, although some hardware RAID implementations offer these levels.

> **Note**
> This chapter focuses only on RAID levels 0, 1, and 5, because you can implement them with software in Windows 2000 Server. For more information on RAID and RAID levels, visit the RAID Advisory Board at http://www.raid-advisory.com.

RAID 0

RAID 0 is a high-performance, zero-redundancy array option. RAID 0 isn't properly RAID at all. It stripes blocks of data across multiple disk drives to increase the throughput of the disk subsystem, as shown in Figure 9.17, but it offers no redundancy. If one disk drive fails in a RAID 0 array, the data on all disk drives on the array is inaccessible. RAID 0 is used primarily for applications needing the highest possible reading and writing data rate.

Figure 9.17
This diagram illustrates an example of RAID 0 (sector striping) with two disk drives.

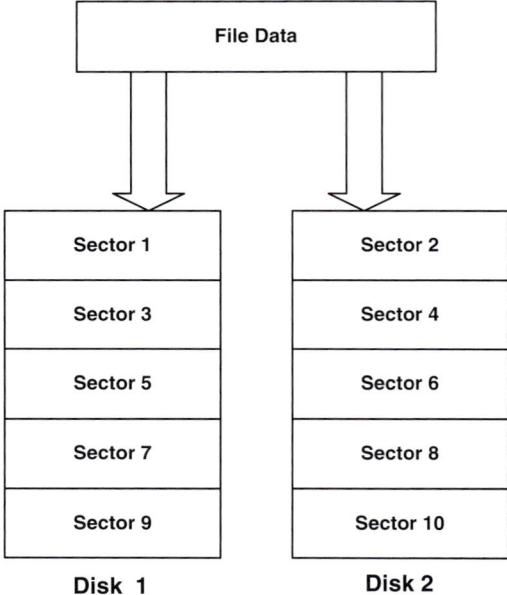

RAID 0 uses striping to store data. *Striping* means that data blocks are alternately written to the different physical disk drives that make up the logical volume represented by the array. The same striping mechanism used in RAID 0 is used to increase performance in other RAID levels, such as RAID 5. RAID 0 is inexpensive to implement for two reasons:

- No disk space is used to store parity information, eliminating the need to buy either larger disk drives or more of them for a given amount of storage.
- The algorithms used by RAID 0 are simple ones that don't add much overhead or require a dedicated processor.

RAID 0 offers high performance on reads and writes of short and long data elements. If your application requires large amounts of fast disk storage and you've made other provisions for backing up this data to your satisfaction, RAID 0 is worth considering.

RAID 0 and striping addresses this problem of unequal workload distribution among physical disk drives by distributing the workload evenly and eliminating any single disk drive as a bottleneck. What RAID 0 doesn't do is protect your data. There's no redundancy, and the loss of any single disk drive in a RAID 0 array renders the contents of the remaining drives useless. Windows 2000 provides RAID 0 functionality through the use of striped volumes.

RAID 1

RAID 1 protects data by making two physical copies of every disk operation. All data stored in a RAID 1 configuration is stored on two physical disks providing 100% redundancy in a catastrophic drive failure. The main function of RAID 1 is mirroring. *Mirroring* means that anything written to one drive is also written to the second drive simultaneously, providing 100% duplication of your drives. RAID 1, shown in Figure 9.18, offers the greatest level of redundancy, but at the highest cost for disk drives.

Figure 9.18
In this diagram, you see an example of RAID 1 (mirroring) with two disk drives.

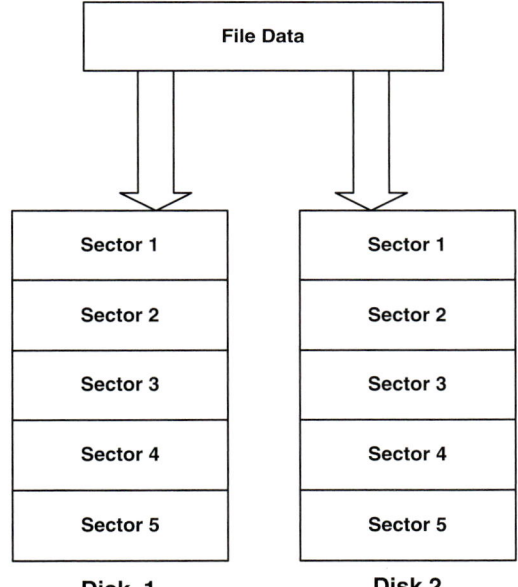

Before you implement mirroring, consider the following:

- Data is safely duplicated on two physical devices, making catastrophic data loss much less likely.
- Read performance is greatly increased, because reads can occur by the drive whose heads happen to be closest to the requested data.
- Mirroring yields 50% total storage utilization of your drives. To provide a certain storage capacity, twice as many drives are required.
- The process of writing to both drives and maintaining coherency of their contents introduces overhead, which reduces performance during write operations.

> **Note**
>
> *Duplexing* is similar to mirroring, but it adds a second host adapter to control the second drive or set of drives. The only disadvantage of duplexing, relative to mirroring, is the cost of the second host adapter. Duplexing eliminates the host adapter as a single point of failure.

RAID 1 is the most common level used in mainframes, where cost has always been a low priority relative to data safety. The rapidly dropping cost of disk storage has made RAID 1 a popular choice in PC LAN servers as well. Conventional wisdom says that RAID 1 is the most expensive RAID implementation, due to the requirement for buying twice as many disk drives. In reality, RAID 1 can be either the most or least expensive way to implement RAID, depending on your environment.

> **Tip from**
> *RJ*
>
> If you have a choice between using either Windows 2000 Server native software RAID 1 support or that provided by your SCSI host bus adapter, choose the hardware solution. Implementing RAID in hardware offers better performance and doesn't put any additional load on the server.

STACKED RAID—RAID 0/1

One characteristic of all RAID implementations is that the array is seen as a single logical disk drive by the host operating system. This means that it's possible to *stack* arrays, with the host using one RAID level to control an array of arrays, in which individual disk drives are replaced with second-level arrays operating at the same or a different RAID level. Using stacked arrays allows you to gain the individual benefits of more than one RAID level while offsetting the drawbacks of each. In essence, stacking makes the high-performance RAID element visible to the host while concealing the low-performance RAID element used to provide data redundancy.

One common stacked RAID implementation is referred to as *RAID 0/1*, which is also marketed as a proprietary implementation called *RAID 10* (see Figure 9.19). This method combines the performance of RAID 0 striping with the redundancy of RAID 1 mirroring. RAID 0/1 simply replaces each individual disk drive used in a RAID 0 array with a RAID 1 array. The host computer sees the array as a simple RAID 0, so performance is enhanced to RAID 0 levels. Each drive component of the RAID 0 array is actually a RAID 1 mirrored set; thus, data safety is at the same level you would expect from a full mirror set.

Figure 9.19
A diagram of RAID 0/1 (sector striping to mirrored target arrays) with four drives demonstrates that this RAID implementation offers the benefits of both striping and redundancy.

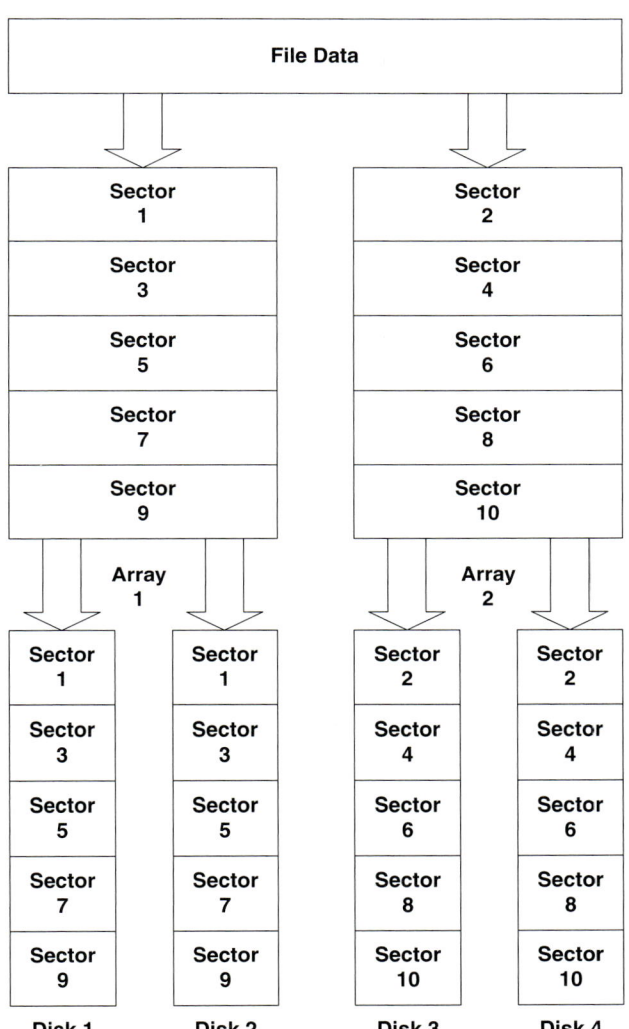

RAID 5

RAID 5, shown in Figure 9.20, is the most common RAID level used in PC LAN environments. RAID 5 stripes both user and parity data across all the drives in the array, consuming the equivalent of one drive for parity information. Windows 2000 implements RAID 5 through the use of RAID-5 volumes.

Figure 9.20
This diagram of RAID 5 (sector striping with distributed parity) with five drives demonstrates RAID 5's striping of both user and parity data across all drives in the array.

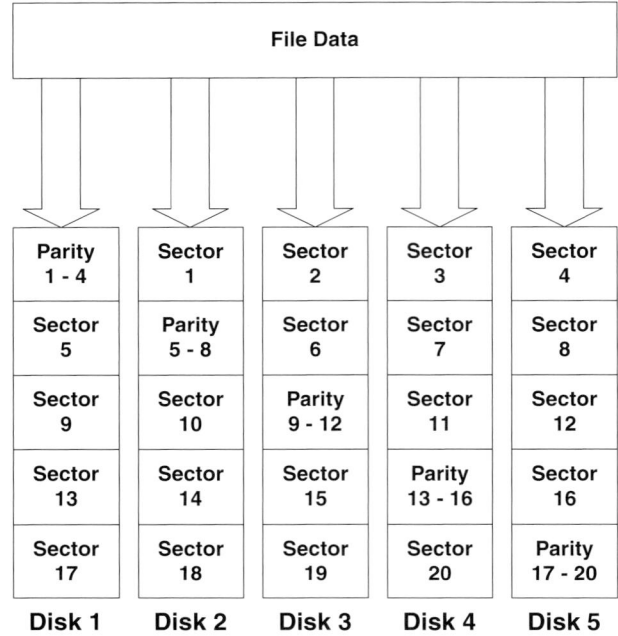

With RAID 5, all drives are of the same size, and one drive is unavailable to the operating system for storage. RAID 5 is optimized for transaction processing activity, in which users frequently read and write relatively small amounts of data. It's the best RAID level for nearly any PC LAN environment, and is particularly well suited for database servers.

RAID 5 offers random read performance that matches or improves upon that of RAID 0. RAID 5 also matches or exceeds RAID 0 performance on sequential reads because RAID 5 stripes the data across one more physical drive than does RAID 0.

RAID 5 writes are more problematic. A RAID 0 single-block write involves only one access to one physical disk to complete the write. With RAID 5, the situation is considerably more complex. In the simplest case, RAID 5 requires two reads and two writes. Completing a single write, therefore, requires a minimum of four disk operations, compared with the single operation required by RAID 0.

RAID 5 uses a two-phase commit process to ensure data integrity, further increasing write overhead. It first does a parallel read of every data block belonging to the affected stripe set, calculating a new parity block based on this read and the contents of the new data block to be written. The changed data and newly calculated parity information are written to a log area, along with pointers to the correct locations. After the log information is written successfully, the changed data and parity information are written in parallel to the stripe set. When the RAID controller verifies that the entire transaction completed successfully, it deletes the log information.

RAID Recovery

So far, this chapter has discussed redundancy, but it hasn't explained in detail what happens when a drive fails. In the case of RAID 0, the answer is obvious. The failed drive was an exact duplicate of the remaining good drive, all your data is still available, and all your redundancy is gone until you replace the failed drive. With RAID 5, the issue becomes much more complex.

RAID 5 uses parity to provide data redundancy. Reads of data formerly stored on the failed drive must be reconstructed using the contents of the other data drives and the parity drive. This results in a greatly increased number of read accesses and correspondingly lowered performance. Because every drive in a RAID 5 array contains data and parity information, the failure of any drive results in the loss of both data and parity. An attempt to read data formerly residing on the failed drive requires that every remaining drive in the array be read and parity used to recalculate the missing data.

When the failed drive is replaced, its contents must be reconstructed and stored on the replacement drive. This process, usually referred to as *automatic rebuild*, normally occurs in the background while the array continues to fulfill user requests. Because the automatic rebuild process requires heavy disk access to all the other drives in an already crippled array, performance of the array can degrade unacceptably. The best way to limit this degradation is to use a reasonably small stripe width, limiting the number of physical drives in the array to five or six at most.

Creating a RAID-5 Stripe Set

To create RAID-5 volumes, you must have a minimum of three physical disks installed on the system, and all disks used in the stripe set must be dynamic disks. Follow these steps to create a RAID-5 volume:

1. From the Disk Management snap-in, right-click on any of the disks and select Create Volume to start the Create Volume Wizard; click Next at the welcome screen to continue.
2. In the volume type dialog, select RAID-5 (see Figure 9.21); click Next.

Figure 9.21
To create a RAID-5 volume, select the RAID-5 volume option in the volume type dialog.

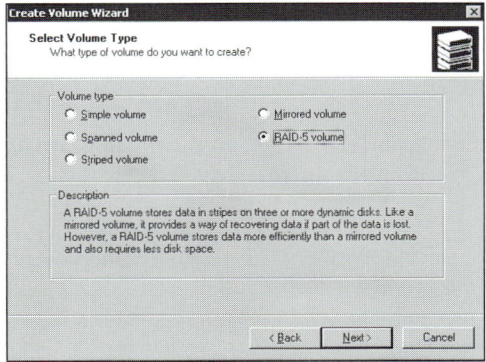

3. In the Select Disks dialog, select at least three disks to participate in the stripe set and enter the size of the volume in the disk size field (see Figure 9.22); click Next.

Figure 9.22
When creating a new RAID-5 volume, select the disks and size for the volume.

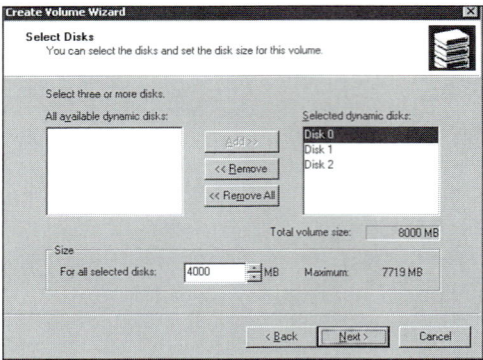

4. Follow the remaining wizard instructions to assign a drive letter, format the volume, and review your changes.

Recovering from Disk Failure with RAID 5

RAID 5 is a powerful solution that provides redundancy in the event of disk failure. If a single disk fails in a RAID 5 configuration, the data stored on the RAID 5 array is still available. If two disks fail, the data is lost. Many hardware RAID solutions alleviate this problem by providing hot-spares that are automatically configured when a disk fails. To recover from a software RAID 5 implementation, follow these steps:

1. Add a new physical disk and reboot your system. When Windows 2000 is loaded, open the Disk Management snap-in.
2. You'll be prompted to sign the new disk with the Write Signature and Upgrade Disk Wizard. Follow through the wizard to sign the disk.
3. Right-click on the failed redundancy of the failed dynamic disk, shown as Missing in the Disk Management snap-in (see Figure 9.23); select Repair Volume to open the Repair Volume dialog.
4. In the Repair Volume dialog, select the disk you want to use to regenerate the RAID-5 volume; click OK.
5. In the Disk Management snap-in, right-click on the missing dynamic disk and select Remove Disk; click OK to complete the process.

 If you encounter problems with the Disk Management snap-in when deleting a fault-tolerant volume during the regeneration process, see the "Problems with the Disk Management Snap-In" topic of the "Troubleshooting" section near the end of this chapter.

 If you encounter problems deleting a disk after recovering from a RAID 5 failure, see the "Problems with RAID Implementations" topic of the "Troubleshooting" section near the end of this chapter.

Figure 9.23
Failed disks appear as Missing in the Disk Management snap-in.

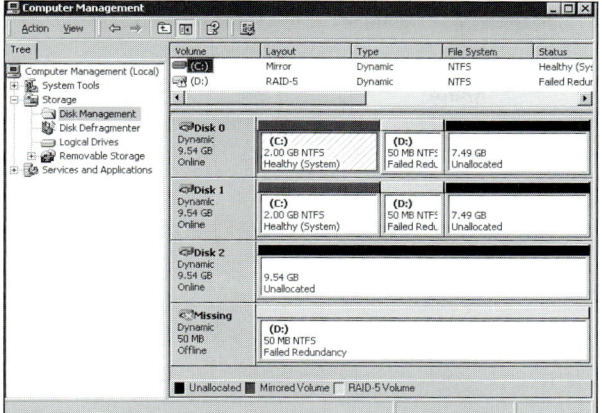

Creating a Mirror (RAID 1) Volume

As described earlier in this chapter, mirror volumes provide two disks with exact copies of each other. This implementation is called RAID 1. Windows 2000 enables administrators to mirror an existing simple volume or create new mirrored volumes. To create a new mirrored volume, follow these steps:

1. From the Disk Management snap-in, right-click on any of the disks and select Create Volume to start the Create Volume Wizard. Click Next at the welcome screen to continue.
2. In the Select Volume Type dialog, select Mirrored Volume; click Next.
3. In the Select Disks dialog, select the two disks to use in the mirror set and enter the size of the volume in the For All Selected Disks size field; click Next.
4. Follow the remaining Wizard instructions to assign a drive letter, format the volume, and review your changes; this completes the creation of the Mirrored volume.

You might also want to create a mirror of an existing volume, such as the system volume. Follow these steps to create a mirrored volume from an existing simple volume:

1. From the Disk Management snap-in, right-click on the volume you want to mirror and select Add Mirror to open the Add Mirror dialog.
2. In the Add Mirror dialog, shown in Figure 9.24, select the disk to participate in the mirror and select Add Mirror to create the mirror set.

Figure 9.24
To add a mirrored disk, select a disk in the Add Mirror dialog.

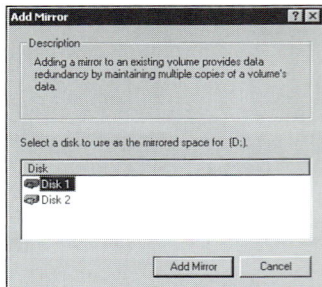

Breaking the Mirror

Administrators might decide to break a mirror to regain disk space used by a mirrored disk. Breaking a mirror is an uncomplicated process. To break a mirror, follow these steps:

1. From the Disk Management snap-in, right-click on the mirrored volume you want to break and select Break Mirror.

2. A warning dialog informs you that the data will no longer be fault tolerant (see Figure 9.25); click Yes to confirm your choice.

Figure 9.25
A Warning dialog appears when breaking mirror sets.

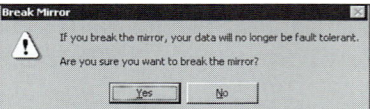

> **Note**
> When you break a mirror with Windows 2000, the mirrored volume is automatically converted to two simple volumes. The volume without a drive letter is assigned the next available drive letter on the server.

 If you encounter problems when trying to delete a previously mirrored volume, see the "Problems with RAID Implementations" topic of the "Troubleshooting" section at the end of this chapter.

Recovering from System Disk Failure with RAID 1

Recovering from disk failure with mirrored sets is mostly straightforward when a disk other than the system disk fails. However, if the system disk fails, the recovery process is a bit more complicated. To recover from a system disk failure with a mirrored volume, you must replace the failed disk, boot the system with a Windows 2000 boot disk, and re-create the mirror.

> **Tip from**
> *RJ*
>
> It's a good idea to have a Windows 2000 server boot disk on hand, but if you don't have one, you can create one from another computer running Windows 2000 server.

To create a Windows 2000 boot disk, follow these steps:

1. Format a standard floppy disk with the Windows 2000 format command or applet.

> **Caution**
>
> You must format the disk with Windows 2000. Disks formatted with a different operating system don't have the correct information in the boot sector of the floppy for Windows 2000.

2. Copy NTLDR, NTDETECT.COM, and BOOT.INI from the root of the system volume to the floppy disk.

> **Note**
>
> If you're using a SCSI card without a BIOS, you must also copy the NTBOOTDD.SYS mini-driver to the floppy. This allows NTLDR to communicate with SCSI drives without a SCSI BIOS.

3. Edit the BOOT.INI file to point to the disk containing your mirrored system volume. The BOOT.INI file is used to determine where your Windows 2000 instance is installed. In the event of a system disk failure, you might need to point the BOOT.INI to the mirrored system disk.

> **Note**
>
> For more information about the BOOT.INI and editing ARC paths, see "Fixing a boot failure" in the Windows 2000 Server online help.

After you have a floppy boot disk configured to boot to the mirrored copy of the system disk, restart your computer and boot from the floppy disk. After Windows 2000 is loaded, you can remove the floppy disk. The instance of Windows 2000 was loaded from the mirrored version; now you must delete the mirror, delete the missing disk, and rebuild the mirror on the new disk to correctly repair your system. To do so, follow these steps:

1. Add a new physical disk and reboot your system using the boot floppy. When Windows 2000 is loaded, open the Disk Management snap-in.
2. You're prompted to sign the new disk with the Write Signature and Upgrade Disk Wizard. Follow through the wizard to sign the disk.
3. From the Disk Management snap-in, right-click on the failed redundancy of the failed dynamic disk and select Remove Mirror.
4. Right-click on the missing dynamic disk in the Computer Management snap-in (see Figure 9.26); select Remove Disk.

Figure 9.26
A missing dynamic disk appears in the Disk Management snap-in when the system disk fails.

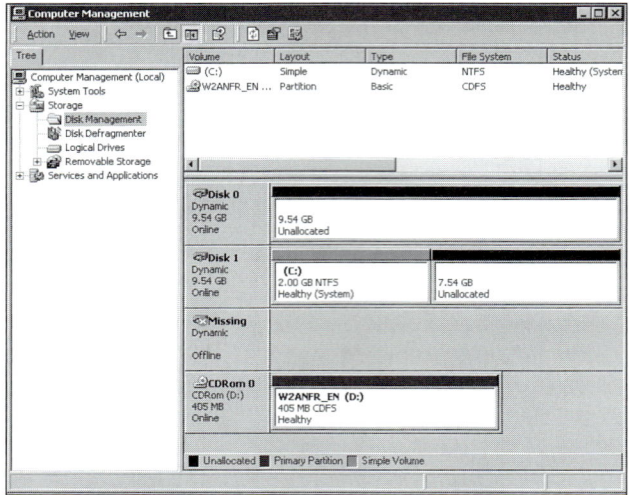

5. Re-create the mirror set with the new disk and reboot the system to load Windows 2000 to the new disk.

Using Removable Storage and Media Pools

Removable storage and media pools are new features to Windows 2000. Through the Removable Storage Management (RSM) snap-in, administrators can now fully configure CD jukeboxes, robotic tape libraries, and single-instance media from within Windows 2000 server. Additionally, Removable Storage is responsible for management of all removable media used by Windows 2000 backup and Remote Storage Services (RSS). Administrators and developers can also take advantage of Removable Storage and media pools by integrating storage applications into an existing storage infrastructure. Media pools enable administrators to classify Removable Storage devices with common administrative functions.

→ For more information on the Windows 2000 Backup Program, **see** "Using the Windows 2000 Backup Application," **p. 965**.

Removable Storage Management Snap-In

All administration for Removable Storage is done through the Removable Storage Management (RSM) snap-in (see Figure 9.27). The RSM snap-in provides administration of the following Removable Storage features:

- Media Pools—Media pools are logical groups of media that contain similar management attributes. Media pools can contain media or other media pools. Three basic types of media pools exist: Free, Import, and Unrecognized. Additionally, application-specific media pools exist based on the application.

- Physical Locations—The Physical Locations folder specifies the physical media devices installed on your system. The Physical Locations folder also enables you to inject (insert) or eject media, delete physical media from the system, assign security privileges to media, and view device information.

- Work Queue—The Removable Storage work queue displays a log of the functions performed and pending by the removable media system. The work queue log displays operations, time to complete operations, and the state of an operation. Administrators can use the work queue to move pending jobs up in the queue, determine bottlenecks in their storage system, or troubleshoot problems.

- Operator Requests—Operator requests are requests made by the Removable Storage service as drive maintenance, including failure and servicing, notification of media that is not online, requests for media, and other administrative tasks required by applications.

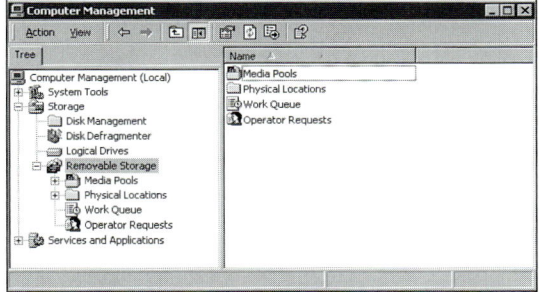

Figure 9.27
The Removable Storage snap-in in Computer Management is used for all administration of Removable Storage.

Media Pools

All removable media in a Windows 2000 server belong to a media pool. As stated earlier, each media pool can hold other media pools or media of the same type (such as tapes or discs). This enables you to create hierarchies of media pools to be used by different applications. RSM contains two types of media pools—system pools and application pools. Media used by applications are stored in application pools, and media not used by applications or unrecognized media are stored in system pools. There are three classifications of system pools:

- Free Pools—Free pools contain media that are not used by application pools on your system. All media in free pools are available for use.

- Unrecognized Pools—Media that are not recognized by the system are stored in the unrecognized pools. Additionally, new media, such as tapes, are stored in the unrecognized pool until moved to the free pool.

- Import Pools—Import media pools contain media that are recognized by Remote Storage, but not yet allocated on the current system. Media from other Remote Storage systems are initially placed in the import pools. All media in the import pools can be moved to the free pools or application-specific pools.

When using new media, the media is placed in the import pool of its type. To move the media to a free pool, you must prepare the media. Follow these steps to prepare the media:

1. In the tree pane of the Removable Storage snap-in, select the Import media pool that contains the media you want to prepare.
2. Right-click on the media and select Prepare (see Figure 9.28).

Figure 9.28
To prepare the media in the Import Pool, right-click on the media.

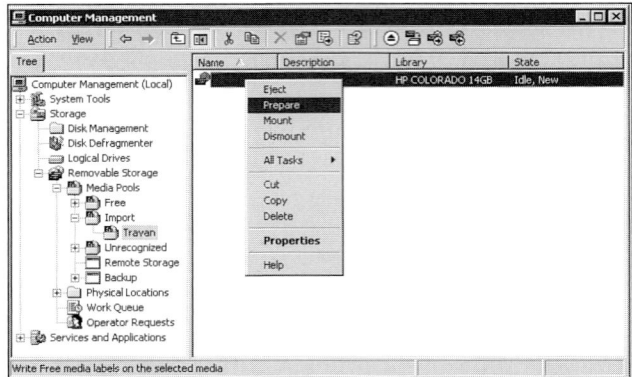

3. A warning message notifies you that all data on the media will be destroyed and moved to the Free pool (see Figure 9.29). Click Yes to prepare the media. A second dialog asks you to confirm your confirmation; click Yes to continue.

Figure 9.29
A confirmation message opens when you are preparing media; after you click Yes here, another dialog opens asking for another confirmation.

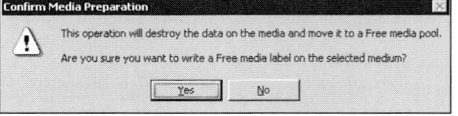

Application pools are media pools created by storage management applications on your server, such as backup and Remote Storage. Application pools contain media currently used by applications in your system. Media allocated to an application pool cannot be shared between application pools.

To create an application pool for Remote Storage, follow these steps:

1. From the Removable Storage snap-in, traverse to the Remote Storage media pool.
2. Right-click on the Remote Storage media pool and select Create Media Pool (see Figure 9.30); the Create New Media Pool properties dialog opens.

Figure 9.30
To create a media pool for Remote Storage, right-click on the Remote Storage media pool and choose Create Media Pool.

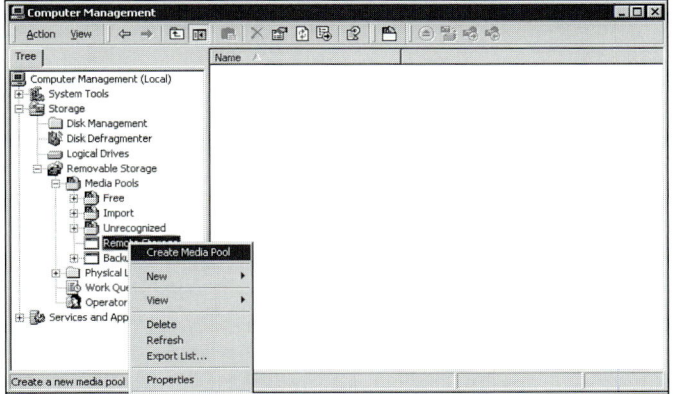

3. In the General page, enter a name and description for the media pool.
4. In the Media Information section of the General page, select Contains Media Of Type and choose the media type from the drop-down to enable the Allocation/Deallocation policy section of the page.
5. Select the Allocation/Deallocation policies on the General Page (for example, you might want to allocate media from the Free Media Pool).
6. Click OK to save your media pool.

Tip from
RJ

Media allocated to an application pool cannot be shared between application pools. If you plan to use multiple storage applications on your server, you should plan on using a robotic tape library or move applications to application-specific servers. For example, if you're using Windows 2000 backup with a single tape backup drive, you cannot use Remote Storage with the same media used by the backup process.

Physical Locations

The Physical Locations folder enables administrators to configure the physical media devices installed on the server. With the Physical Locations folder, administrators can

- Specify the media type of library—Storage devices that support multiple types of media can be configured for different media depending on the function of the device.
- Configure port timeouts of the device—The port timeout determines how long Removable Storage will wait when injecting/ejecting media.
- Specify the door timeout—When using a robotic tape library, the door timeout determines how long Removable Storage will wait when a door is opened on the tape cabinet before displaying a warning.
- Specify Media Inventory configuration—Removable storage will inventory libraries when media is mounted. The inventory configuration determines which method

Removable Storage uses to inventory the libraries. Three inventory methods are available—none, fast, and full. Depending on your system configuration, you may change this configuration.

- Enable the library—If a library fails, Removable Storage disables the library. Libraries that are disabled are not available for use.
- Specify Door Access—When using storage devices such as robotic tape libraries, you must specify that the door will be opened to Removable Storage. This allows Windows 2000 to properly handle any media requests.
- View and Prepare Offline Media—When media is offline, administrators can view and prepare offline media for use.

The configuration of physical devices is accomplished through the device properties dialog. To change the port timeout of a Removable Storage device, follow these steps:

1. From the Removable Storage snap-in, open the Physical Locations folder.
2. Right-click on the device and select Properties.
3. On the Components page, specify the port timeout in the Ports section (see Figure 9.31).

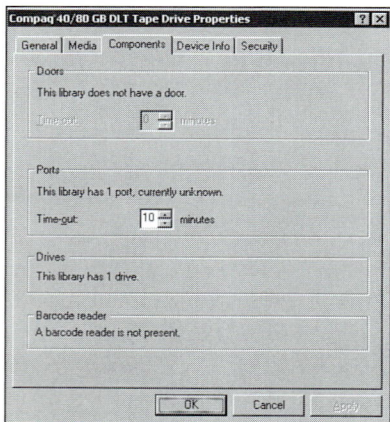

Figure 9.31
You configure the port timeout of a Removable Storage device in the Components page of the device's Properties dialog.

4. Click OK to save your changes.

Work Queue

The Work Queue displays information about Removable Storage requests (see Figure 9.32). When Removable Storage performs an operation, the operation is placed in the Work Queue.

Figure 9.32
The Work Queue in the Removable Storage snap-in displays information about Removable Storage requests.

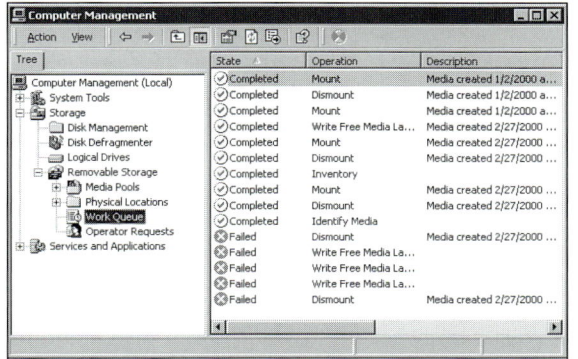

The Work Queue will display the current state of the request, the time to complete, and any actions that must be taken by the operator. Removable storage contains five states for work requests:

- Waiting—The request is waiting for a device or process currently in use by another request.
- In-Process—The request is currently being processed by Remote Storage.
- Queued—The request has been issued, but Removable Storage has not yet examined the request.
- Completed—The request has been successfully completed.
- Failed—The request has failed.

Operator Requests

Operator requests are requests submitted by the Removable Storage system that require operator intervention. A request could consist of a media mount request that is offline or a library that has failed. By default, operator requests are displayed as pop-up messages through the messenger service and tray icons on the server. Administrators may also configure operator requests so that the messenger service and tray icons are not used during a request. Additionally, administrators can specify whether requests are deleted and the threshold to delete a request. To prevent Removable Storage from sending operator requests with the messenger service, follow these steps:

1. From the Removable Storage snap-in, right-click on Removable Storage and select Properties.
2. On the General page, uncheck the option Send Operator Requests to Messenger Service; click OK to save your changes.

When an operator request is submitted, the operator might choose to complete or refuse the request depending on the request. To complete requests follow these steps:

1. From the Removable Storage snap-in, open the Operator Requests folder.
2. In the details pane, right-click on the request and select Complete.

Administrators may choose to configure completed requests to be deleted and configure the deletion threshold of failed requests. When troubleshooting Removable Storage, you might choose to temporarily save completed requests. Follow these steps to configure the completed requests to be saved:

1. From the Removable Storage snap-in, right-click on the Operator Requests folder and select Properties.
2. On the General page, uncheck the Automatically delete completed requests check box; click OK.

Using Windows 2000 Disk Management Tools

Windows 2000 provides new and improved tools for disk management, such as Disk Defragmenter, Chkdsk, and Disk Cleanup. The Disk Defragmenter enables administrators to achieve better performance on their NTFS file system by freeing up unused space and rearranging files and programs to run faster. Disk Cleanup deletes unnecessary temporary files that might be taking up space on your volume. Chkdsk examines the disk and file system for errors and fixes errors that exist on your drives by marking bad sectors.

Tip from
RJ

> An additional disk management tool in the Windows 2000 resource kit is Disk Probe. Disk Probe is a low-level disk management tool included in the Windows 2000 resource kit to modify the actual bytes of the file system. Disk probe can be useful to help administrators troubleshoot problems on the disk. Disk Probe should be used with extreme caution because it bypasses the disk management interface and reads the disk on a byte level.

Disk Defragmenter

Disk Defragmenter is a new feature in Windows 2000 that enables administrators to defrag their NTFS volumes to achieve better performance and more efficient use of storage. Disk fragmentation occurs when the operating system writes data to the file system. Often files are stored in large areas of contiguous sectors. When files are modified, contiguous sectors are not always available, so the operating system must spread the file across multiple sections of contiguous sectors. Disk defragmenter examines the storage utilization of the file system and rearranges files to use contiguous disk space. During the disk defrag process, the defragmenter analyzes the disk for fragmentation and defrags the disk when specified.

> **Caution**
> When using Disk Defragmenter on large NTFS volumes with a high amount of user activity, it's best to defrag during a time when utilization is low. Disk Defragmenter can considerably degrade performance if run during peak hours.

Follow these steps to open Disk Defragmenter:

1. Open the Disk Defragmenter from the Start menu by selecting Programs, Accessories, System Tools.
2. In the Disk Defragmenter, select the drive you want to defrag and select Analyze.
3. If the disk is heavily fragmented, as shown in Figure 9.33, Disk Defragmenter prompts you to defrag.

Figure 9.33
A fragmented disk in Disk Defragmenter displays which sections of your disk are fragmented.

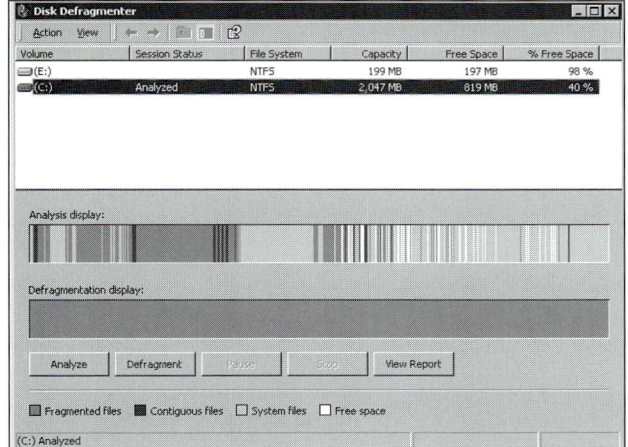

4. When prompted to defrag the disk, select Defragment (see Figure 9.34).

Figure 9.34
The defrag dialog in Disk Defragmenter enables you to defragment your disk.

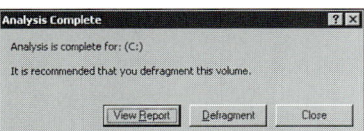

When the Disk Defragmenter completes, a dialog informs you that the process is complete. The dialog enables you to view a report of the defrag process.

> **Note**
> Depending on the size of the volume and the defragmentation of the files on the volume, Disk Defragmenter might take a considerably long time to complete the defrag process.

Chkdsk

Chkdsk is used to examine your physical disks for errors and correct the errors by marking bad sectors so they're not used by the operating system. When Chkdsk is examining the disk to fix errors, the volume is dismounted and users are unable to access the files stored on the volume.

To examine and fix errors on your disk, follow these steps:

1. From the command prompt, type **chkdsk *DriveLetter:* /F**.
2. When prompted to dismount the volume, enter **Y**.

> **Caution**
>
> Chkdsk locks the volume during the repair operation. If running Chkdsk on large NTFS volumes, the volume might be unavailable to users for several days. Chkdsk should be used only if known errors exist on the disk. To determine whether errors exist on the disk, run Chkdsk in read-only mode by not specifying the **/F** switch.

Disk Cleanup

Disk Cleanup is a new feature in Windows 2000. Many applications create temporary files used for the functionality of the application, but abandon the files when the application has completed. Disk Cleanup improves disk utilization by deleting unnecessary files, such as Windows 2000 temporary files, Internet cache files, unused program files, files in the Recycle Bin, and other files unneeded by the operating system.

To use Disk Cleanup, follow these steps:

1. Open the Disk Cleanup from the Start menu by selecting Programs, Accessories, System Tools to open the Select Drive dialog.
2. In the Select Drive dialog, select the drive you want to clean and click OK. Disk Cleanup then analyzes your file system to determine files that can be deleted.
3. After Disk Cleanup analyzes your drive, the Disk Cleanup property dialog opens (see Figure 9.35). This dialog informs you of free space you'll regain and the specific actions needed to regain free space.

Figure 9.35
The Disk Cleanup property dialog for drive C shows folders that Disk Cleanup will free up.

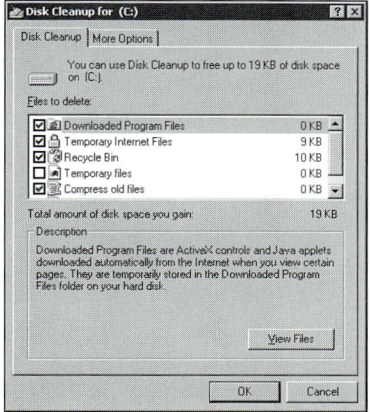

4. After you select the options to clean up, select OK. You are prompted to confirm the file deletion process; click yes to continue. When the Disk Cleanup process completes, it automatically exits.

> **Caution**
>
> Disk Cleanup is a useful tool to clean up disk space on your volume, but it should be used with caution on servers. Many server applications require the presence of temporary files to properly function.

TROUBLESHOOTING

PROBLEMS WITH THE DISK MANAGEMENT SNAP-IN

Newly created volumes do not appear under the remote administration feature of the Terminal Service Client.

When creating volumes through the Terminal Service Client, volumes do not appear in My Computer. To resolve this problem, exit the Terminal Service Client and reestablish the session.

Simple volumes cannot be extended or spanned.

Simple volumes converted from partitions on basic disks cannot be extended or spanned after the disk is converted to a dynamic disk. This occurs because the volume is hard-linked. To extend a hard-linked volume, you must first delete the volume, revert to a basic disk, upgrade to a dynamic disk, and re-create the volume. Be sure to back up your data if you're deleting the volume.

When using the Disk Management snap-in on remote computers, the console will not reconnect if the connection is temporarily severed.

When administering disks on a remote computer, the Disk Management snap-in must be restarted if a connection to the remote computer is temporarily severed. A message stating `Failed to connect to Logical Disk Manager` appears if this occurs.

The Disk Management snap-in hangs or crashes when deleting a fault-tolerant volume during the regeneration process.

If you try to delete a fault-tolerant volume during the regeneration process, the disk management snap-in might not respond—or even crash. To work around this problem, restart the Disk Management snap-in.

PROBLEMS WITH RAID IMPLEMENTATIONS

Cannot remove a volume previously a mirror of the system volume.

When breaking a mirror of the system volume, the shadowed volume (not the system volume) is still marked as a system volume and cannot be deleted. To resolve this problem, delete the volume in RAW mode through the Windows 2000 recovery console.

After recovering from RAID 5 failure, two instances of the same disk appear in the Disk Management snap-in. The unused instance cannot be deleted.

To resolve this problem, back up your data, remove the RAID-5 volume, revert the disk to a basic disk, upgrade the disk to a dynamic disk, and re-create the volume.

MCSE Corner: Installing RAID, Backup, and Removable Media Systems

Managing disk drives and RAID sets is covered in exam 70-215 Installing, Configuring and Administering Windows 2000 Server. Knowledge of several concepts from this chapter is tested on the exam.

You should be familiar with basic disk drive management and using the disk management portion of the Computer Management application. You should know how basic and dynamic disks work, and how to convert and configure dynamic disks. You should also understand simple, spanned, striped, mirrored, and RAID-5 volumes and how to add disks to and configure volumes. It helps if you know the different types of RAID (especially 0, 1, and 5).

As with most of the other chapters, troubleshooting is especially important to know here. You should be able to create an Emergency Repair Disk and know how it works. Another important thing to know is how to use the Boot.ini file and how the disk and partition naming convention works. You should be especially familiar with the ARC naming convention—multi(0)disk(0)rdisk(0)partition(1)\WINNT—and how it works. Don't be surprised to see a question with ARC naming thrown into the exam.

Another thing to be familiar with is adding and troubleshooting tape devices and removable media. You should be able to install a tape or other Removable Storage device and its drivers using the Removable Storage portion of the Computer Management snap-in. Make sure you know how to troubleshoot a failed Removable Storage device installation or a nonfunctioning device as well.

CHAPTER 10

WORKING WITH THE WINDOWS 2000 REGISTRY

In this chapter

What's New in Windows 2000 Server's Registry   454

Tracking Configuration Settings in the Registry   454

Viewing the Registry's Organization   459

Understanding Important Root Keys, Keys, and Subkeys   466

Using the Windows 2000 System Information Tool   474

Backing Up the Registry   476

Inspecting Another Computer's Registry   478

Maintaining Server Registry Security   479

Troubleshooting   481

MCSE Corner: Exam Types   482

What's New in Windows 2000 Server's Registry

Windows 2000 Server makes only minor alterations to the structure of the Windows NT Server 4.0 Registry but adds many new keys to support new hardware-related features. The initial size of the System Registry file is about twice that of its predecessors. Much of the added System file overhead is the result of adding keys for Plug and Play (PnP) features added in Windows 2000.

Following are the primary changes that Windows 2000 makes to Windows NT 4.0's Registry:

- Domain-level account, group, and alias information moves from the SAM Registry hive to Active Directory. In Windows 2000 Server, only information for local accounts, groups, and aliases remains in SAM.

- Location of `NTUser.dat files`, which store user-specific information, depends on the Windows 2000 installation. If you install on a clean machine, Windows 2000 stores `NTUser.dat` and `NTUser.dat.log` files in `d:\Documents and Settings\UserName` folders. Upgrading Windows NT Server 4.0 to Windows 2000 Server retains user-related Registry files in their original `d:\Winnt\Profiles\UserName` folders.

- Group Policies, a new feature of Windows 2000, specify computer and user configurations by altering Registry settings during the boot process (Netlogon) and user logon, respectively. Active Directory (AD) links to Group Policy Objects (GPOs), which Windows 2000 enforces at the local computer, site, domain, and organizational unit level. Administrative Templates set the attribute values of Registry-based GPOs.

- Performance improvements take the form of transparent enhancements to Windows 2000 manipulation of the Registry's contents. To compensate for the increased size of the System file, which affects the time Windows 2000 takes to boot, internal links to keys use a shorthand method to identify *key control blocks*, the basic storage element of the Registry. The Windows 2000 Configuration Manager, which reads from and writes to the Registry, caches in a memory-based table frequently used key control blocks.

Tracking Configuration Settings in the Registry

The Registry keeps track of all configuration information for each computer, including installed applications, hardware, device drivers, and network protocols. The Registry is a set of databases organized in a hierarchy. Windows 2000 uses the Registry during the boot process to determine which device drivers to load and in what sequence to load them. Registry entries also store desktop settings for one or more local users. Most of the administrative tools you use to configure Windows 2000 Server and keep it running smoothly alter Registry entries. The following sections briefly describe how Windows 2000 Server reads and updates the Registry.

Types of Registry Information

The Registry is the one place that stores virtually everything that Windows 2000 needs to know about your server hardware, software, and the users who locally log on to the machine. The Registry stores the following types of information:

- Information about your hardware and the device drivers required by the hardware.
- A list of services, such as SQL Server and Exchange Server, to start immediately after the boot process.
- Network information, including details about each network interface card and protocol in use.
- Object linking and embedding (OLE), Automation, ActiveX, and COM+ component information, such as the filename and location of local Automation servers and ActiveX components.
- File association information that relates the file type extensions with the application(s) that open or edit them.
- The time zone and local language for the server.
- For each local user, program folders and other Start menu settings.
- For each local user, desktop settings, such as colors and wallpaper.
- For each local user, all preferences in all user applications, unless the applications are older 16-bit applications that use .INI files. Preferences include the "recent files" list on the File menu.
- All local user profiles.
- Local user and group security information.

Registry-Based Configuration Management

Windows 2000's Registry keeps everything in one place, eliminating the need for the individual initialization files required by 16-bit Windows. The *Configuration Manager* is a kernel-based subsystem that handles the interaction between Windows 2000, 32-bit services, and applications, and the Registry. You can view all Registry settings by using one tool—the Windows 2000 Server Registry Editor. Windows 2000 Server provides two versions of the Registry Editor: `Regedit.exe`, a single-document interface (SDI) Explorer-type tool derived from Windows 9x's RegEdit application (see Figure 10.1), and `Regedt32.exe`, a multiple-document interface (MDI) version that originated in Windows NT 3.1 (see Figure 10.2).

`Regedit.exe` offers the advantage of a more flexible Find feature; `Regedt32.exe` offers advanced administrative features, such as the capability of setting security and audit properties of individual keys. The choice of versions is up to you. If you want to search quickly for specific Registry elements (keys) or values, use `Regedit.exe`; most Windows 2000 administrators opt for `Regedt32.exe`. This chapter uses `Regedt32.exe`, except as noted.

456 | Chapter 10 Working with the Windows 2000 Registry

Figure 10.1
The `regedit.exe` application shows its use of the Single Document Interface (SDI) style window. The tree of keys is in the left pane, while the values in the selected key are shown in the right pane.

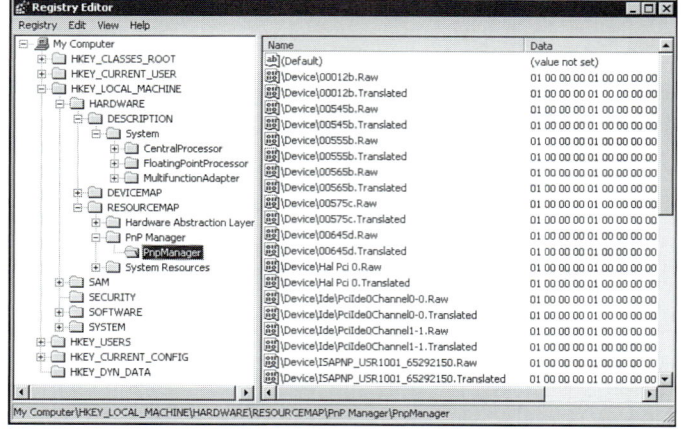

Figure 10.2
The `regedt32.exe` application shows the default cascade arrangement of its Multiple Document Interface (MDI) style windows.

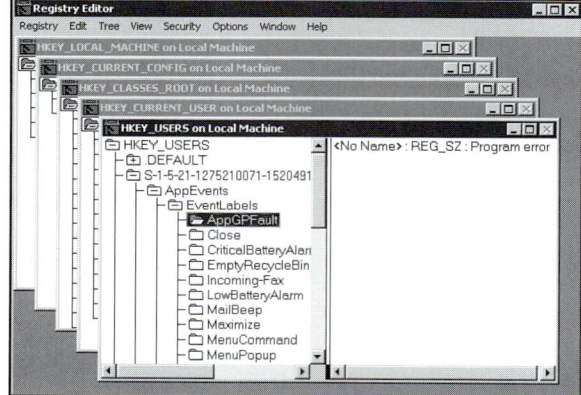

Tip from
RJ

Create a desktop shortcut for one or both of the Registry Editor versions on your server to speed access. Neither version of the Registry Editor appears as a choice in the default Start menu hierarchy. Microsoft deliberately "hides" the Registry Editor to discourage users from manually altering Registry data. `Regedit.exe` is located in the `\Winnt` folder; `Regedt32.exe` is located in `\Winnt\System32`.

Registry Organization

The Registry is arranged in a logical and straightforward way that clearly distinguishes among the following three classes of settings:

- *Systemwide, for all applications and all local users*—for example, your computer's microprocessor type

- *Systemwide, for one local user*—for example, your Windows Desktop color scheme and shortcuts

- *Per application for each local user*—for example, the last few query files you opened in SQL Server Query Manager

Although you continue to use various tools to change Registry values in Windows 2000 Server, don't underestimate the value of using just one tool to view any of the settings. Navigating such a large collection of settings and configuration information can be a bit intimidating, but understanding the structure and content of the Registry is *very important* when administering Windows 2000 Server.

The Danger of Changing Registry Values

Changing many entry values in the Registry with RegEdit or RegEdt32 can cause your server to be unstartable. Manually altering other values can lead to serious problems with applications and services that are very hard—sometimes almost impossible—to troubleshoot and correct. Microsoft and third-party software or hardware vendors often recommend or require that you change the value of, add, or delete a Registry value. For example, there are many Registry settings dedicated to performance tuning that require manual Registry value changes.

Rather than change Registry entry values directly, use Windows 2000 features or tools to change these values when possible. Following are the elements of Windows 2000 that operate directly on the Registry:

- *Device Manager*—Most hardware settings are handled by the hardware recognition process when you boot the server. For example, PCI adapter cards configure themselves automatically during startup. Windows 2000 Server supports Plug and Play ISA cards, including legacy ISA adapters that use jumpers or semipermanent software configuration methods. When you install hardware drivers, the Registry stores all driver configuration information. Changing settings for a hardware component in Device Manager alters the Registry settings for the device.

→ For a review of Device Manager basics, **see** "Using Device Manager," **p. 316**.

- *Setup*—New applications and services set many system configuration settings when you run the appropriate setup program. For this reason, it's important not to relocate applications by simply moving their files. Registry entries aren't updated when you move an application's executable and support files, so you must remove and reinstall most applications and services to change their location.

- The Start, Programs, Administrative Tools menu (see Figure 10.3) contains menu items that lead to applications or wizards for server configuration and maintenance. Using these wizards and other dedicated tools to interact with the Registry is far safer and more intuitive than adding or changing entries with the Registry Editor.

Figure 10.3
Most of the applications in the Administrative Tools group manipulate values in the registry to save configuration settings.

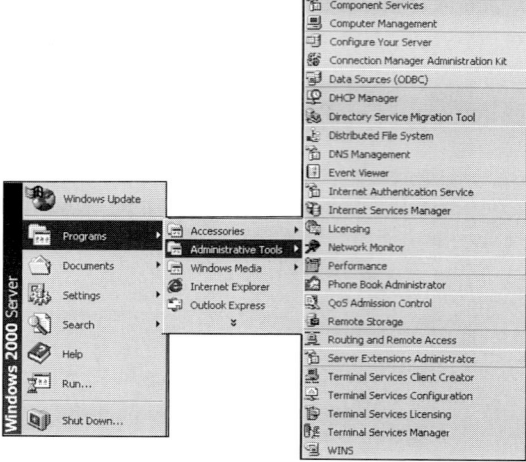

- Control Panel tools (see Figure 10.4) interact primarily with the hardware and software configuration elements of the Registry—for example, the Keyboard tool changes the computer's keyboard settings in the Registry. Manually changing configuration values can render a device—or an entire device category—inoperable.

Figure 10.4
Most of these Control Panel applets also make changes to values in the registry for storing configuration settings.

- Many applications change the Registry. For example, the list of recent files is generated automatically as you open files in a document-oriented application.
- Most OLE and Automation servers and ActiveX components register themselves when they're installed or run for the first time.

Tip from
RJ

> Avoid making inadvertent changes to Registry values when using `Regedt32.exe` to view the Registry by choosing Options, Read-Only Mode. Remove the read-only attribute only when you must alter a Registry value, and then reapply it immediately. Unfortunately, `Regedit.exe` doesn't offer a read-only option.

How the Windows 2000 and Windows 9x Registries Vary

In many important ways, the Windows 2000 Registry is similar to the Windows 9x Registry. Certainly, the concepts are the same. The same tools and applications read from and write to the Registry, and the `Regedit.exe` Registry Editor of Windows 9x and Windows 2000 Server is quite similar. The names for specific collections of information stored within the Registry, however, aren't identical. Nonetheless, experience with the Windows 9x—and Windows NT 4.0—Registry is readily transferable to Windows 2000 Server's Registry.

Note

> Both Windows 2000 Server and Windows 9x use Registry files, but the internal (binary) structure of the files varies greatly between the two operating systems. The difference in file structure is the primary reason that Microsoft didn't provide an automatic upgrade utility from Windows 95 to Windows NT 4.0. Upgrading creates or preserves the Registry information for installed applications.
>
> The new capability of upgrading automatically from Windows 95 or 98 to Windows 2000 is more important for the Professional than the Server version. Few users are likely to upgrade to Windows 2000 Server a Windows 9x client having a large number of productivity applications installed.

Viewing the Registry's Organization

Understanding the Registry requires you to learn another new vocabulary. The Registry is a hierarchy of *root keys* and *subkeys*. Subkeys have *value entries*, and groups of subkeys and their value entries are gathered into a *hive*, which corresponds to a specific Registry file; each hive contributes to a Registry Editor root key. The Registry is a hierarchical (not a relational) database; in the more familiar relational database terminology, root keys correspond to tables, and subkeys correspond to records (rows) in the tables. *Cells*, which hold the key name and related data, relate to fields (columns) of database records, but an individual cell can hold multiple data types (entities), which is not permitted in the relational model for fields.

Table 10.1 summarizes the most important Registry terms by providing Windows 2000 Registry examples and descriptions of the examples. The rows of Table 10.1 are arranged in descending hierarchical order.

TABLE 10.1   COMMON REGISTRY TERMS WITH EXAMPLES FROM THE WINDOWS 2000 REGISTRY

Term	Example	Description
Hive	`Ntuser.dat`	File containing the current user's profile information—desktop configuration, Start menu contents, Control Panel settings, local and network printer definitions, and software settings.
Root Key	`HKEY_CURRENT_USER`	Contains all user-specific settings for the current logged-on user imported from the user's `Ntuser.dat` hive.
Key	`Software`	Holds subkeys of `HKEY_CURRENT-USER` for standard classes of software.
Subkey	`Microsoft`	Holds subkeys of the `Software` key for Microsoft software installed by the current user.
Cell	`Notepad`	Element of the `Software\Microsoft` subkey that contains a list of value entries for Notepad.
Value Entry	`fWrap`	Entry that specifies whether Notepad's word-wrap feature is enabled.
Value	`0x00000000 (0)`	Value for `fWrap` that specifies word wrap is disabled. A value of `0x00000001 (1)` enables word wrap.

REGISTRY EDITOR ROOT KEYS

The Registry Editor displays the contents of the Registry in a hierarchy quite similar to a folder tree. At the top of the hierarchy are the following six root keys:

- `HKEY_LOCAL_MACHINE` contains systemwide hardware information and configuration details stored in the SAM, Security, Software, and System configuration files.

- `HKEY_CLASSES_ROOT` contains OLE and ActiveX information and file associations.

- `HKEY_CURRENT_CONFIG` links to `HKEY_LOCAL_MACHINE\SYSTEM\CurrentControlSet\Hardware Profiles\Current`, which stores configuration information for the computer's hardware, as well as Font and Internet Settings data.

- `HKEY_DYN_DATA` is a placeholder for temporary (dynamic) data that Performance Monitor uses to generate graphical displays of counter values. `HKEY_DYN_DATA` doesn't appear in Windows 2000's `Regedit.exe` or `Regedt32.exe`.

- `HKEY_CURRENT_USER` contains all the settings specific to the current user, which are stored in the `Ntuser.dat` file located in the `\Documents and Settings\`*UserName* or `\Winnt\Profiles\`*UserName* folder.

- `HKEY_USERS` contains all settings for all users, stored in `Ntuser.dat` files, including the current user and a default user, which is stored in the `\Documents and Settings\Default User` or `\Winnt\Profiles\Default User` folder.

Figure 10.5 shows `Regedt32.exe` displaying each of the five visible root keys and its topmost keys and subkeys in a tiled window. Individual sections later in this chapter discuss each root key.

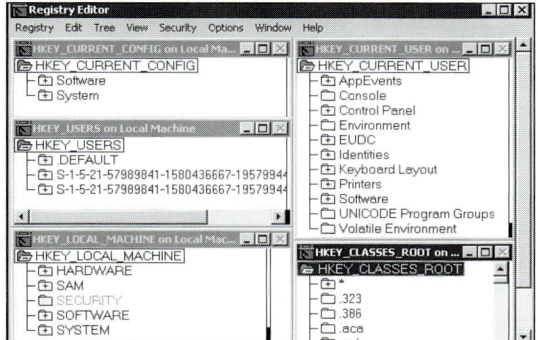

Figure 10.5
The `regedt32.exe` application is open to display the five primary root keys and their top-level subkeys.

REGISTRY FILES AND HIVES

Configuration files that hold Registry hives are stored in the `\Winnt\System32\Config` folder. Figure 10.6 highlights the four System files that store the contents of the `HKEY_LOCAL_MACHINE` and `HKEY_CURRENT_CONFIG` hives. Configuration files use the following extensions:

- Files without an extension hold the current version of the configuration information.

- `.alt` files hold a backup copy of the `HKEY_LOCAL_MACHINE\System` key, which is critical to starting Windows 2000. Only the System file (discussed in the next section) has an `.alt` version.

- `.alt` files contain the transaction log that holds all changes made to the configuration file until the change is made permanent.

- `.dat` files contain user information. Only the `Ntuser.dat` files have the `.dat` extension. `Ntuser.dat` replaces the `Usernamexxx` and `Adminxxx` files of Windows NT 3.51 and earlier. `Ntuser.dat.log` is the log file for `Ntuser.dat`.

- `.sav` files are created by the text mode part of Windows 2000 Server Setup and come into play if the graphics mode part of Setup fails.

Figure 10.6
The \Winnt\System32\Config\ folder contains the registry hive files, as well as log files that contain logs of the changes made to the registry.

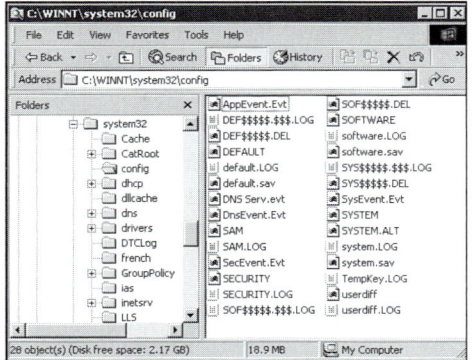

> **Note**
>
> Userdiff and Userdiff.log aren't associated with a Registry hive or key. Windows 2000 Server employs Userdiff files when updating user profiles created with Windows NT 3.51 and earlier.
>
> The .evt files in \Winnt\System32\Config hold records for the Event Viewer entries generated during Windows 2000's startup process. Windows 2000 creates .DEL and other files with dollar signs in their names as temporary files to be used during the setup process.

As mentioned earlier, pairing hive and .log files helps ensure that the Registry can't be corrupted. For example, if the power fails as your change to a value entry is written, the value might be changed, but the date stamp might still contain the old date and time, or the size of the entry might not be correct. The hive and log approach guarantees that the Registry retains consistent information.

A low-level service called Configuration Manager handles all changes to Registry hive files. When it's time to write changes to a hive file, Configuration Manager inserts a few extra steps:

1. Configuration Manager writes to the .log file the new data and its destination location in the appropriate Registry file.
2. Configuration Manager writes a special mark at the beginning of the Registry file to indicate that the file is in the process of being altered.
3. The changes are written to the Registry file and, on completion of the alteration, Configuration Manager removes the mark.

If a power failure or other serious problem occurs during the process, Configuration Manager notices when opening the file that the "being changed" mark exists, re-creates the changes from the .log file, and then removes the mark. This process maintains the consistency of the Registry file.

> **Note**
>
> The relationship between the Registry and log files is similar to that between SQL Server's device and log files. Log files record all transactions (operations that modify database values) since the last backup. In the event of a failure that requires restoration of the backup copy, the backup copy is loaded and the transaction log is run against the database to add the post-backup entries. In SQL Server, log files are stored on a physical device (disk drive) separated from the device containing the database(s). Windows 2000 hive and log files are stored on the same disk.

Table 10.2 lists the direct association of Registry Editor HKEY_LOCAL_MACHINE and HKEY_USERS member keys with Registry hive files, when hive files exist for the keys. Configuration Manager works with hive files; Registry Editor uses root keys to organize the hives into a structure that's more convenient for administrators. Configuration Manager creates and stores *nonpersisted* (also called *volatile*) keys and subkeys in RAM or virtual memory.

TABLE 10.2 REGISTRY EDITOR KEYS AND CORRESPONDING HIVE FILES, WHERE APPLICABLE

Registry Editor Keys	Hive File Path and Name
HKEY_LOCAL_MACHINE\SYSTEM	\Winnt\System32\Config\System
HKEY_LOCAL_MACHINE\SAM	\Winnt\System32\Config\SAM
HKEY_LOCAL_MACHINE\SECURITY	\Winnt\System32\Config\Security
HKEY_LOCAL_MACHINE\SOFTWARE	\Winnt\System32\Config\Software
HKEY_LOCAL_MACHINE\HARDWARE	Nonpersisted hive (key) created during the boot process
HKEY_LOCAL_MACHINE\SYSTEM\Clone	Nonpersisted subkey replica of the HKEY_LOCAL_MACHINE\SYSTEM key (not visible in RegEdit)
HKEY_USERS\.DEFAULT	\Winnt\System32\Config\Default
HKEY_USERS\User	...\NTUser.Dat file for the logged-on (local) user, identified by a security ID code

This book uses the term *root key* for the six Registry Editor categories—including HKEY_LOCAL_MACHINE and HKEY_USERS—and *key* for the hive names—SYSTEM, SAM, SECURITY, HARDWARE, and DEFAULT—which Registry Editor displays as uppercase. This book calls *subkeys* HKEY_USERS\User and HKEY_LOCAL_MACHINE\SYSTEM\Clone, as well as all entries under the uppercase keys. The hierarchy of subkeys often is many levels deep.

By convention, root key, key, and subkey names are gathered into fully qualified names that are separated with backslashes in a manner similar to folder pathnames. An example is a subkey called HKEY_LOCAL_MACHINE\HARDWARE\DESCRIPTION\System\MultifunctionAdapter\3\DiskController\0\FloppyDiskPeripheral\0.

> **Note**
> Key names can contain spaces, just as spaces are permissible in Windows 9x, Windows NT 4.0, and Windows 2000's long filenames (LFNs). Registry Editor root keys use underscores in place of spaces.

VALUE ENTRIES

To continue the analogy of a file structure, a key can contain value entries and subkeys, just as a folder can contain files and subfolders. *Value entries* in keys resemble files in folders. A value entry contains the information to examine or change, just as a file contains the data you display or edit. A key can (and often does) support more than one value entry.

A value entry has three components:

- The name of the value entry
- The type of information it contains (numerical or character data, for instance)
- The value of the information (`c:\program.exe` or `0`, for example)

The following sections describe each of these components.

VALUE ENTRY NAMES

Microsoft chose reasonably comprehensible names for most value entries; you probably can guess what `CurrentUser`, `InstallDate`, `LogFilePath`, and `DiskCacheSize` contain without any need for documentation. Much of the information is added to the Registry when you install programs on the system, and application vendors might not choose sensible or easy-to-understand names.

When there's only one value entry in a key, it's possible—but not necessarily wise—that the programmer who added the key left the name unassigned. When omitting a single value name, RegEdit shows (`Default`) in place of the missing value entry name. This practice is quite common in the file association entries of the `HKEY_CLASSES_ROOT` key. If the value name is omitted, use the name of the key to imply the type information of the value entry.

DATA TYPES

The data type must be one of the following six data types:

- `REG_BINARY` is raw binary data, which is displayed by the Registry Editor in hexadecimal format.
- `REG_DWORD` is 4 bytes of binary data. The Registry Editor can display these values as binary, decimal, or hexadecimal numbers.
- `REG_SZ` is a string of characters terminated by a `NULL` character; `SZ` is an abbreviation for "string, zero-terminated."
- `REG_MULTI_SZ` contains multiple strings of characters separated by `NULL` characters and terminated by 2 `NULL` characters.

- `REG_EXPAND_SZ` is a string of characters that contains a symbol to be expanded when the value is used. The symbol begins and ends with a `%` character.

- `REG_FULL_RESOURCE_DESCRIPTOR` is a special data type reserved for the `Configuration Data` value hardware resources. The `HKEY_LOCAL_MACHINE\HARDWARE\DESCRIPTION\System\MultifunctionAdapter\0` and other hardware subkeys use this data type for `Configuration Data`. Double-clicking a `Configuration Data` value opens a Resources dialog to display DMA, Interrupt, Memory, Port, and Device Specific Data (see Figure 10.7).

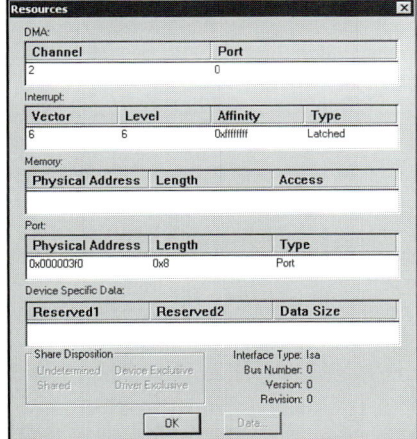

Figure 10.7
The Resources dialog shows configuration data values in several different data types.

The `REG_EXPAND_SZ` symbols correspond to environment variables—for example, `%PATH%` expands to the value of the `PATH` environment variable. Most environment variables also are stored in the Registry but aren't all under the same key. Some environment variables are in the `HKEY_LOCAL_MACHINE\SYSTEM\CurrentControlSet\Control\Session Manager\Environment` key, and others appear under `HKEY_CURRENT_USER\Environment`.

Value entries depend on the specified data type. Binary numbers are difficult for nonprogrammers to read in the Registry Editor, but specific tools, such as Windows 2000 system diagnostics feature—discussed in the "Using the Windows 2000 System Information Tool" section later in this chapter—can display these value entries in a more meaningful format. Entering new or changing binary values correctly is even more challenging.

Making changes to the Active Directory schema with the Schema Management snap-in is an example of a situation where you must add a new Registry value. To enable schema modifications, you must add a new `Schema Updates Allowed` key to `HKEY_LOCAL_MACHINE\System\Current Control Set\Services\NTDS\Parameters` and set its `REG_DWORD` (binary) value to 1.

→ For more information on the Active Directory Schema snap-in, **see** "Using the Active Directory Schema Manager," **p. 124**.

Understanding Important Root Keys, Keys, and Subkeys

It's not possible to list all subkeys in your Registry, because subkeys are added every time you install hardware or software. Publication limits on page count preclude such a listing. It's also not useful to provide a list of all Registry keys; when you know roughly where to look, it's quicker to use the Registry Editor to search for the exact key or value entry. Thus, this section doesn't attempt to describe all Registry keys, but it suggests appropriate locations to search for particular classes of Registry entries.

The HKEY_LOCAL_MACHINE Root Key

HKEY_LOCAL_MACHINE contains systemwide hardware information and configuration details. This root key has five important keys, four of which appear in the standard hive list you've already seen (refer to Figure 10.6). In addition to SAM, SECURITY, SOFTWARE, and SYSTEM—the standard hive keys of HKEY_LOCAL_MACHINE)—there's also a Hardware subkey.

SAM and SECURITY

SAM was an acronym for Security Account Manager in early versions of Windows NT. This key contained the database of user and group information, as well as security information for the domain. In Windows NT 4.0, Microsoft referred to SAM as the *directory services database*, in preparation for Windows 2000's Active Directory. In a Windows 2000–only network, SAM contains only local user accounts; Active Directory stores domain user and group information. If you install Windows 2000 Server as a standalone server, however, SAM contains all user and group information for the workgroup server, because standalone servers don't implement Active Directory. SAM has one subkey, also named SAM.

The SECURITY key contains policy information for the local machine as well as a link to the local SAM database. SAM is a *protected subsystem* of the Registry, so the HKEY_LOCAL_MACHINE\SAM\SAM subkey and HKEY_LOCAL_MACHINE\SECURITY key are disabled in RegEdt32 and display (Default) and (Value Not Set) in RegEdit. You use the Administrative Tools, Computer Management (Local), System Tools, Local Users and Groups tool to add or modify subkeys of the SAM subkey and SECURITY key.

> **Note**
>
> Windows NT 4.0-and-earlier clients in mixed-mode domains that include Windows NT Server 4.0 backup domain controllers (BDCs) make internal SAM routine (SAMR) calls to the Registry's SAM database and encapsulate Remote Procedure Calls (RPCs) for authentication and other SAM operations. Mixed-mode domains retain the SAM database, which limits to about 40,000 the sum of the numbers of users, groups, and computers—called security-principal objects—in a domain. Moving to a native-mode domain by migrating all BDCs to Windows 2000 Server overcomes the 40,000 security-principal object limit.

Software

The SOFTWARE key stores systemwide configuration information for each application installed on the computer. For example, if you install Windows Media Player, Setup adds a subkey called HKEY_LOCAL_MACHINE\Software\Microsoft\MediaPlayer with Control, Player, PlayerUpgrade, and Setup subkeys. The ...\MediaPlayer subkey has four value entries that specify the folders that store the application and media files. These subkeys don't contain any user-specific settings; user-specific entries appear under HKEY_CURRENT_USER\Software (discussed later). For example, user-specific MediaPlayer settings appear in the HKEY_CURRENT_USER\Software\Microsoft\MediaPlayer\Player\Settings and ...\ MediaPlayer\Setup\ CreatedLinks subkeys.

Tip from
RJ

> The Registry must be updated if you move software from one location to another—for example, between disk volumes on the same machine. Thus, it's usually quicker and easier, and always safer, to uninstall the software and then reinstall the software in the new location. Depending on the application, many different keys might need to be modified to point to the new location. Let the uninstall and reinstall software do the work, and heed the general rule: *Don't change the Registry manually unless you have no alternative.*

System and the Last Known Good Menu

The SYSTEM key contains information generated during startup that can't be fully determined by Windows 2000 Server until startup completes. All but three of System's subkeys are called *control sets*. The Select and Setup subkeys aren't control sets; Windows 2000 uses these subkeys to choose which control set to use on startup. MountedDevices, a subkey that's new with Windows 2000, specifies the drives and assigned drive letters for each local fixed-disk partition.

A control set contains information needed to start the system. SYSTEM maintains 2–4 control set subkeys, with names such as ControlSet001 and ControlSet002. There's also a CurrentControlSet, which links to one of the other control sets. This linkage enables you to switch back to a control set that works if you (or an application you run, or a system crash) make changes to the Registry that prevent the computer from starting.

Fortunately, during startup you have a chance to press F8 or the spacebar to use the Last Known Good menu, a specific control set. The subkey that implements the Last Known Good feature, called Select, has four value entries:

- Current holds the number of the control set that was used this time at startup.
- Default contains the number of the control set—a value of 0x2 means use ControlSet002—to be used at the next startup unless the user chooses Last Known Good.

- `Failed` holds the number of the control set that was used during a failed startup. When you choose Last Known Good, the `Failed` control set no longer is current. By storing the number of a bad control set as the `Failed` value, Windows 2000 enables you to know where to look for the bad setting that caused startup to fail.

- `LastKnownGood` contains the number of the control set that represents the values that succeeded most recently.

The `Clone` subkey of the `SYSTEM` key, which usually isn't visible, builds the `LastKnownGood` value. During startup, the current control set is copied into `Clone`. If startup succeeds, it copies `Clone` into `LastKnownGood`.

> **Tip from**
> *RJ*
>
> If your Registry is corrupted, press F8 and choose Last Known Good Configuration during startup to start Windows 2000 Server so that you can (or might be able to) correct the problem that caused the corruption. Your Registry might become corrupted for various reasons, but bad sectors on your fixed disk or—far more frequently—user errors usually are the culprits. If you edit your Registry by hand and make a serious mistake, you may leave your server unbootable. Using `LastKnownGood` saves you from a complete reinstall.

Although boot problems differ greatly, here's a typical scenario for using the Last Known Good control set with Windows 2000's new Advanced Options menu:

1. A power failure or hardware error requires a reboot, or you perform a routine reboot after changing Registry entries with the Registry Editor or some other tool. System startup won't boot Windows 2000 Server.
2. Power down and, on powerup, watch for the `For troubleshooting and advanced startup options for Windows 2000, press F8` prompt.
3. Press F8 to display the Windows 2000 Advanced Options menu.
4. Select the Last Known Good Configuration option.
5. Press Enter to boot with the Last Known Good control set.

> **Tip from**
> *RJ*
>
> You can eliminate some hardware and driver issues as the source of the boot problem by trying one of the Safe Boot options. Start with the Safe Boot option; if the system boots successfully, try Safe Boot with Networking or Safe Boot with Command Prompt. If the problem appears related to drivers, select the Enable Boot Logging option to create `Ntbtlog.txt` in your `\Winnt` folder. `Ntbtlog.txt` lists each installed driver as loaded or not loaded. You must have a dual boot configuration to read `Ntbtlog.txt` with Notepad under an alternate operating system if your computer won't boot in Safe Mode.

If you've created multiple hardware profiles, which are described in the "HKEY_CURRENT_CONFIG and Hardware Profiles" section that follows shortly, you can select an alternate hardware profile or the Last Known Good Configuration. To use the traditional Windows NT boot selection method, which Windows 2000 continues to support, do the following:

1. Press the spacebar during the Windows 2000 boot process to open the Hardware Profile/Configuration Recovery Menu.
2. Press L to select the Last Known Good control set.

    Alternatively, select a hardware profile you saved previously, if you suspect corruption of the Registry subkeys for the current hardware profile.

3. Press F3 to reboot with the Last Known Good control set or new hardware configuration.

When you've booted the server successfully, you can examine both the current control set and the failed one to see what differs between the two versions. The comparison enables you to determine what changes you need to make to your current configuration (if any) that will achieve the effect you originally wanted without preventing a successful boot.

> **Caution**
>
> If you make changes to any of the control sets discussed in this section (other than `CurrentControlSet`) within the Registry Editor, you can nullify the insurance that these keys provide you. Use Server Manager or Control Panel's Devices, Network, Server, or Services tool to make the required changes. Use the Registry Editor to *look* at entries, not *change* them.

Each control set contains four subkeys—`Control`, `Enum`, `Hardware Profiles`, and `Services`. If you have problems booting your server after making a hardware change or addition, the hardware vendor's technical service representative may request values or ask you to alter values of one or more of these subkeys. The exact subkeys in each key vary, but some of the more important subkeys in the `Control` subkey are

- `BootVerificationProgram` tells the system how to define "succeeded," if you don't want to use the default definition.

    Make sure that you know what you're doing before you alter this key value.

- `ComputerName` contains the `ComputerName` and `ActiveComputerName` subkeys. Change the values of these subkeys only with Control Panel's Network tool.
- `GroupOrderList` points to a list of the order in which to start services groups.
- `HiveList` contains the location of the hive files, usually `\Winnt\System32\Config`.

    Do not *change any values in this subkey, even if requested to do so by a vendor representative.*

- `Keyboard Layout` and its subkeys define the keyboard language layout. You change it with Control Panel's Regional Settings tool.
- `Lsa` is used by the local security authority. *Do not change.*
- `NetworkProvider` defines the order of network providers. You change this value with Control Panel's Network tool.
- `Nls` defines national language support. Change it with Control Panel's Regional Settings tool.

- `Print`—with its subkeys `Environments`, `Monitors`, `Printers`, and `Providers`—defines the printers and printing environment for the system. You change it with the Start menu's Printers folder.
- `PriorityControl` defines the priority separation. Change it with Control Panel's System tool.
- `ProductOptions` shows the `ProductType` (for example, `ServerNT`) and `ProductSuite` (`TerminalServer`).
- `SessionManager` contains global and environment variables. Its `Environment` and `MemoryManagement` subkeys can be changed with Control Panel's System tool.
- `ServiceGroupOrder` lists the order in which groups of services should be started.
- `Setup` contains hardware settings for the initial boot process.
- `TimeZoneInformation` contains time-zone settings. You change it with Control Panel's Date/Time tool.
- `Virtual device drivers` contains information about virtual device drivers (VxDs), which Windows 2000 replaces with Windows Driver Model (WDM) drivers.
- `Windows` contains paths and other data needed by the system to boot.
- `WOW` contains Windows on Windows subsystem options for running 16-bit applications.

The `Services` subkey of each control set has 100 or so subkeys, so these subkeys aren't listed here. The `Services` subkeys describe device drivers, file system drivers, service drivers, and other hardware drivers. Use Windows 2000 System Information to view the information in these subkeys. Use Computer Management or Control Panel tools to change the information in these subkeys.

HARDWARE

All the information in the `HKEY_LOCAL_MACHINE\HARDWARE` key is written into the Registry during startup, disappears when you shut down the machine, and then is recalculated and rewritten during the next startup. That makes it meaningless to change `HARDWARE` values in an attempt to solve a system problem, and that's also why the `HARDWARE` key isn't stored in a hive file. To view `HARDWARE` key values in a more readable format, use the Windows 2000 System Information utility, described later in the section "Using the Windows 2000 System Information Tool."

The `HARDWARE` key contains the following standard subkeys:

- `DESCRIPTION` describes the hardware recognized automatically by the system.
- `DEVICEMAP` points to the location in the Registry where the driver for each device is located. Typically, this is in the `Services` subkey of one of the control sets.
- `RESOURCEMAP` points to the location in the Registry where the driver for each resource is located. Typically, this is in the `Services` subkey of one of the control sets.

HKEY_CURRENT_CONFIG AND HARDWARE PROFILES

 Windows 2000 implements *hardware profiles*, which make it simple for users to switch a number of settings related to hardware at once. For example, a laptop user might have *docked* and *mobile* profiles, with the mobile profile using a lower-density screen, different color scheme, and so on. This use of hardware profiles has been supplanted by Windows 2000's new Plug and Play feature set, which provides automatic docking management, and is unlikely to be of interest on a server. Servers ordinarily maintain the same hardware configuration for long periods.

Saving the existing hardware configuration, however, is important when you decide to alter your server's hardware complement, such as changing network interface cards (NICs) or changing from IDE to SCSI drives. If your new hardware configuration fails, you can revert to your old hardware to keep your server in operation while investigating the cause of the problem.

Do the following to create a copy of your existing hardware profile before reconfiguring your server:

1. Double-click Control Panel's System tool to open the System Properties dialog.
2. Click the Hardware tab, and then click Hardware Profiles to open the Hardware Profiles dialog.
3. With the default Profile 1 (Current) selected, click Copy to open the Copy Profile dialog.
4. In the To text box, type a descriptive profile name, such as `Original Profile`, and click OK to return to the Hardware Profiles dialog with the new profile added (see Figure 10.8).

Figure 10.8
The Hardware Profiles dialog shows a copy of the current profile, Profile 1, saved as Original Profile, which can be loaded on boot from the Hardware Profiles boot menu.

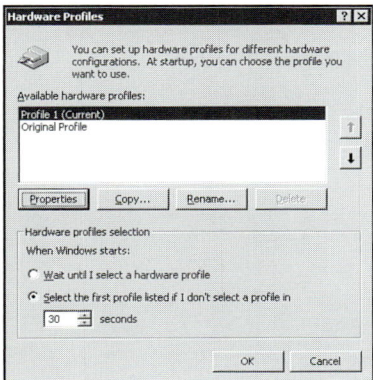

Tip from
RJ

You can alter the sequence of hardware profile selection during the boot process by selecting a profile and clicking the up- or down-arrow key.

5. If you want to choose from multiple hardware profiles during the boot process without having to press the spacebar, select each profile, click Properties, and mark the Include this profile as an option when Windows starts check box (see Figure 10.9).

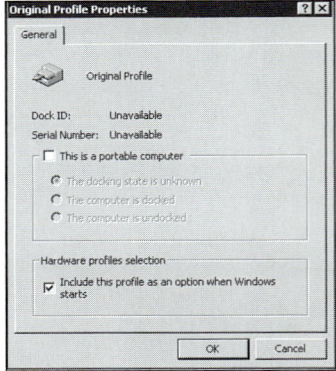

Figure 10.9
Selecting the Include This Profile as an Option when Windows starts check box on the properties dialog of the selected hardware profile causes the profile to appear in the Hardware Profiles boot menu.

HKEY_CLASSES_ROOT AND FILE ASSOCIATIONS

The HKEY_CLASSES_ROOT key, linked to the HKEY_LOCAL_MACHINE\SOFTWARE\Classes subkey, contains file association and OLE and ActiveX server information. The file association keys all have a name that starts with the period (.) separator and represent a file extension, such as .bmp (bitmap) or .txt (text). Each key has one value entry, typically with no name, that contains the name of a key for the primary application that launches files with that extension. To change file association keys, use the File Types page (see Figure 10.10) of Explorer's Folder Options property dialog by choosing Tools, Options.

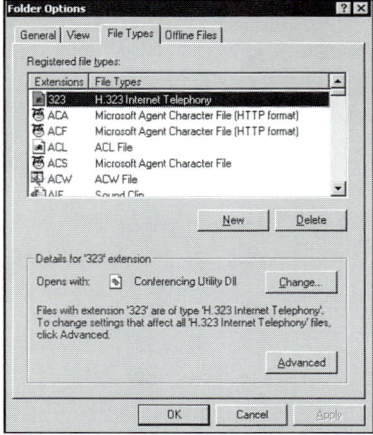

Figure 10.10
The File Types page of the Folder Options dialog for any folder allows you to associate a file type with an application.

The OLE- and ActiveX-related keys have names that don't start with a period. The subkeys vary from application to application, but all have a `CLSID` subkey for the OLE or ActiveX Class ID. A Class ID is a 32-byte identifier, called a *globally unique ID* (GUID, pronounced "goo-id"), that's guaranteed to be different each time a developer generates a value. To obtain property values for the component, you must search for the `CLSID` value; thus, `RegEdit.exe` is a better choice than `RegEdt32.exe` for verifying settings for OLE and ActiveX components.

> **Tip from**
> *RJ*
>
> Use the Windows 2000 System Information Tool to obtain the filename and location of OLE servers for document types identified by name, rather than the cumbersome `CLSID` value.

> **Caution**
>
> Don't edit `CLSID` values unless specifically directed to do so by your application vendor or Microsoft. You could leave the application unusable.

HKEY_CURRENT_USER AND User Profiles

The `HKEY_CURRENT_USER` key stores all the current profile information for the user who's logged on to the server at the moment. A *user profile* is a collection of keys that contains all the information about one user. The current user profile information overrides prior user profile settings in `HKEY_LOCAL_MACHINE`. Primary subkeys of `HKEY_CURRENT_USER`—none of which you should change with the Registry Editor—are as follows:

- `Console` defines the base options, window size, and so on, for character-based applications, such as Telnet.
- `Control Panel` retains all user-specific information set by Control Panel tools (such as colors, wallpaper, and double-click rate).
- `Environment` stores environment variables set with Control Panel's System tool.
- `KeyboardLayout` specifies the user's keyboard layout that you set with Control Panel's Keyboard tool.
- `Printers` specifies local and network printers, set by Control Panel's Printers tool, available to this user.
- `Software` contains all settings (options, preferences, customizations, recently opened files, window sizes, and more) for all the software to which this user has access. The structure of this subkey is the same as the `HKEY_LOCAL_MACHINE\Software` key, but the names of the keys under the product name and of the value entries differ. These entries are changed by the applications that use them.

When a user logs on, Configuration Manager copies his or her profile from `HKEY_USERS` into `HKEY_CURRENT_USER`. If the correct profile for a user isn't found, Configuration Manager uses the default profile, which the next section covers.

hkey_users for Local Logons

The HKEY_USERS key contains all active local user profiles, each under a key with the same name as the user's Security ID string. HKEY_USERS also contains a .DEFAULT subkey with all the default settings for a new local user. The subkeys under each user and under .DEFAULT are the same as those listed in the preceding section for HKEY_CURRENT_USER.

Using the Windows 2000 System Information Tool

In many of the preceding sections, you read warnings against modifying Registry values. Sometimes, however, you need to know the value of a Registry setting, particularly a hardware setting. One way to look at all your hardware-related Registry settings at once is to use the Windows 2000 System Information (SysInfo) tool, one of the System Tools, which replaces Windows NT 4.0's Windows NT Diagnostics tool (Winmsd.exe) and Windows 98's Microsoft System Information (Msinfo32.exe). Typing either Winmsd.exe or Msinfo32.exe in the Run dialog opens Microsoft Management Console with the System Information snap-in (msinfo32.msc) active. Choosing Administrative Tools, Computer Management, and expanding the System Tools node provides an alternative method to opening SysInfo.

SysInfo helps you diagnose the behavior of your system by examining a multitude of Registry values at once in an easy-to-read format. SysInfo gathers various settings into the following five categories, which replace the nine tabbed pages of Winmsd.exe:

- System Summary delivers operating system, processor, BIOS, and memory information (see Figure 10.11).
- Hardware Resources displays information on interrupt (IRQ), direct memory addressing (DMA), input/output addresses (I/O), and memory reserved by device drivers, such as SCSI miniports, graphics adapters, and sound cards (see Figure 10.12).
- Components includes information on multimedia software and hardware, such as ports, drives, and printers.
- Software Environment displays a list of drivers, environmental variables, servers, OLE server registrations, and other driver- and task-related elements.
- Applications lists productivity software, such as the components of Microsoft Office 2000, installed on the server. It's not a common practice to install productivity applications on a server, unless you're writing a book such as this.

USING THE WINDOWS 2000 SYSTEM INFORMATION TOOL | 475

Figure 10.11
With the System Summary object selected in the left pane of the System Information tool, the System Summary information is displayed in the right pane.

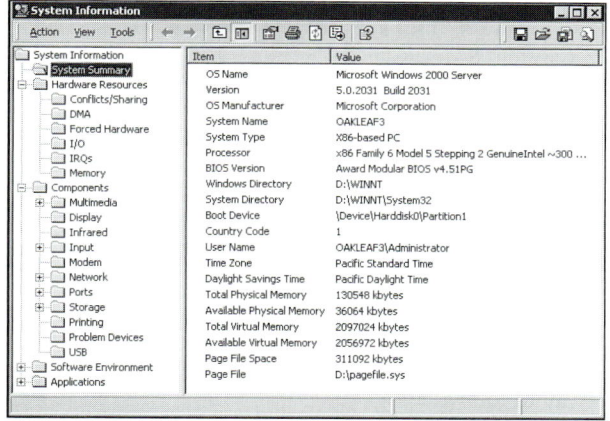

Figure 10.12
Select the Hardware Resources node in the left pane of the System Information tool's IRQ page to view the system IRQ usage in the right pane.

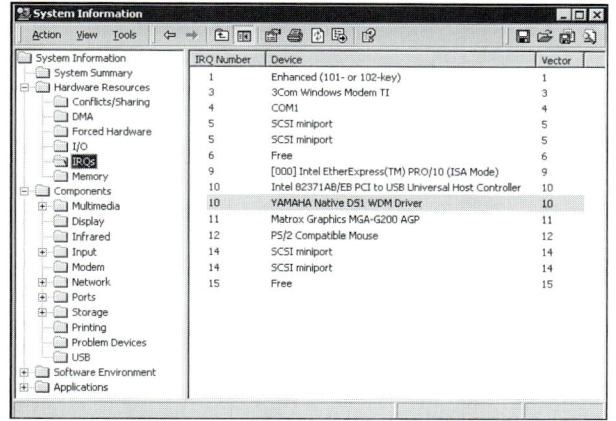

If you aren't sure which Control Panel tool or Registry key to use to check a Registry value, use SysInfo. SysInfo is quick, and you can't accidentally change a value. If you want to keep a record of the settings described in the preceding list, use the printed reports from SysInfo rather than compiling a written list from values displayed by the Registry Editor.

Tip from
RJ

A Microsoft or other software vendor's technical service representative may request that you save and upload the SysInfo data, either as a binary .nfo file or a readable .txt file. Right-click System Information, and choose Save As System Information File or Save As Text file to save a copy of your current server configuration.

PART
II
CH
10

Backing Up the Registry

Backing up the Registry often is very important, especially before you change anything to try to fix a problem. Some, but not all, of the Registry information is saved on the emergency repair disk. The following are five ways to back up the Registry:

- Use the Windows 2000 Backup application to create a System State backup on tape, on a share on another computer, or on high-capacity removable storage, such as an Iomega Jaz drive or CD-RW. System State data ranges from about 300MB to more than 500MB, depending on the software and services running on your server. Use Backup's Restore feature to restore the System State files.

- If you back up the system partition to tape by using the Backup application, the Registry is backed up to tape together with all other files, unless you specifically exclude Registry hive files. To restore from this backup, use Windows 2000 Backup's Restore feature.

→ For additional details on backing up and restoring the Registry, **see** "Using the Windows 2000 Backup Application," **p. 965**.

> **Tip from**
> *RJ*
>
> Use the Windows 2000 Backup and Recovery Tools to create a new Emergency Repair Disk (ERD) after making server hardware changes and backing up the Registry.

- From within the `Regedt32.exe` Registry Editor, choose Registry, Save Key and save the key to alternate media, such as tape or a drive elsewhere on the network. Most configurations files won't fit on a 1.44MB disk; an Iomega Zip or Jaz drive is well suited to local backup of Registry files. To restore from this backup, choose Registry Restore Key from the Registry Editor's Registry menu. You must individually select each hive window and save its associated configuration file.

  In `Regedit.exe`, choose Registry, Export Registry File to open the Export Registry File dialog. Select the All option in the Export Range frame to export the contents of the entire Registry to a single text file with a `.reg` extension (see Figure 10.13). Using `Regecit.exe` to export Registry files is simpler than using `Regedt32.exe`. Saving the OAKLEAF3 Registry resulted in an 18MB text file; Figure 10.14 shows the first few lines of the file in Notepad. To restore the Registry from the backup copy, choose Registry, Import Registry File.

Figure 10.13
The `regedit.exe` application can be used to save the registry to a man-readable text file, which can be edited and merged back into the registry later if needed.

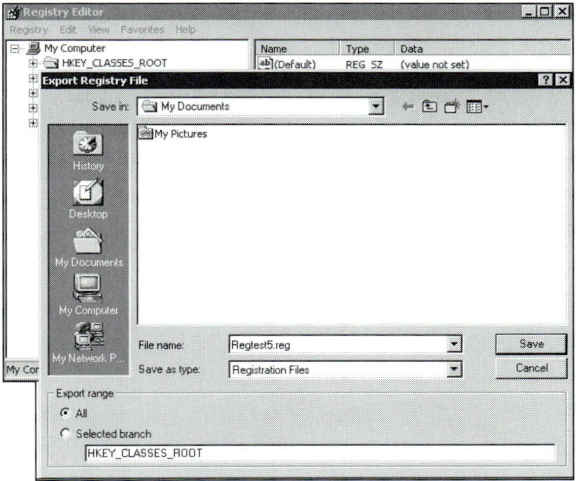

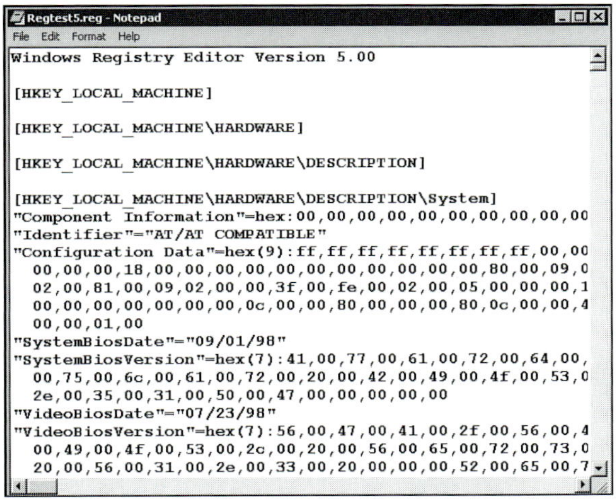

Figure 10.14
Windows Notepad shows the text contained in a registry file saved with the `regedit.exe` utility. Key names are contained in brackets and values within the keys must each be on a new line.

> **Note**
> You can save Registry files in version 5.0 (Registry Files, the default) or 4.0 (Win9x/NT4 Registration Files) format. Unless you have a specific reason for using the 4.0 format, always accept the default version 5.0 file type.

- Use the `Reg.exe` command-line tool in `\Program Files\Support Tools` to save and restore individual hive subkeys. Type **reg save /?** and **reg restore /?** to display the `Reg.exe` command-line syntax.
- Copy the files in the `\Winnt\System32\Config` folder to alternative media. Also copy the user information hives from each `\Winnt\Profiles\`*Username* folder. To restore the Registry, use the other operating system to copy the backups into their original location.

Inspecting Another Computer's Registry

The primary purpose of Windows 2000's remote Registry feature is to inspect and alter values of machines in server closets or installed in cages at an Internet service provider (ISP) co-location facility. By default, you must be a member of the Domain Admins group of the local and remote domains or a member of the Enterprise Admins group to gain access to another computer's Registry.

To edit a remote Registry from a Windows 2000 machine, start Regedt32.exe and use the Registry menu's Select Computer command (see Figure 10.15) to open windows with the HKEY_LOCAL_MACHINE and HKEY_USERS keys of the remote computer (see Figure 10.16). Alternatively, start Regedit.exe and choose Connect Network Registry from the Registry menu. Then inspect or change the keys and value entries of the remote computer; you must have Administrator privileges to view or alter Registry keys and values from a remote Windows 2000 computer. The changes you make take effect immediately, so use extra care—especially if the remote computer is in use while you're changing the Registry. You might want to save this task for a time when the remote machine isn't in use, or arrange such a time with your users.

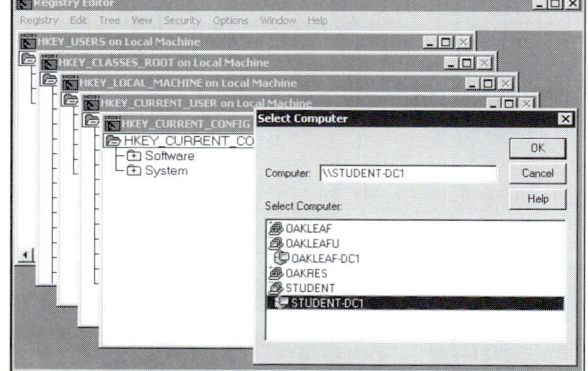

Figure 10.15
The Select Computer dialog is used to open the registry of another computer on the network, STUDENT-DC1 in the STUDENT domain in this case.

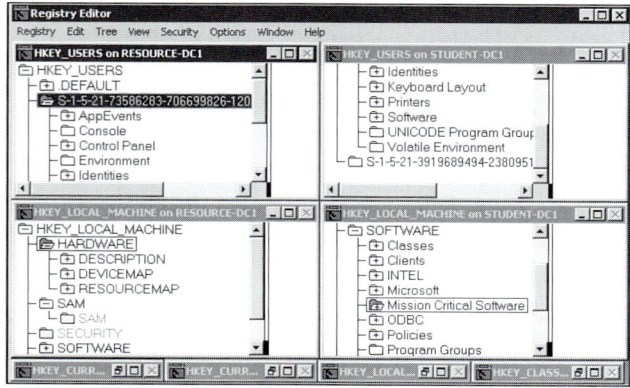

Figure 10.16
The regedit32.exe application shows the HKEY_USERS and HKEY_LOCAL_ MACHINE hives of two remote DCs, RESOURCE-DC1 and STUDENT-DC1.

> **Caution**
> As mentioned earlier, take great care, especially when changing settings on a server. A single keystroke could inconvenience a large number of users by making the server unavailable.

Maintaining Server Registry Security

You can restrict users' ability to change a server's Registry values in a number of ways. Such restrictions should be part of an overall security plan that allows users to access only those administrative features they need. It's especially important to restrict to Domain Admins local and remote changes to each server's Registry hives.

> **Note**
> If you allow users other than members of the Domain Admins to log on locally to the server, you can compromise Registry security. Although Authenticated Users—typically members of the Domain Users group—can't view Registry permissions, such users can change permissions when logged on to the server. Thus, it's important not to modify server User Rights to allow anyone other than Domain Admins to log on locally. Further, servers should be located in a secure area with access restricted to only those persons necessary for its operation and maintenance.

To control access to individual keys, you can add or remove names from the Access Control List (ACL) for each key. If you care enough about a particular key's value to restrict access, you should audit at least failed access attempts.

> **Caution**
> Excessive access restrictions can make applications unusable or the system unbootable. Always make sure that the Administrator and System accounts have Read and Full Control access to all keys. Back up the Registry before implementing any security restrictions.

Only `Regedt32.exe` provides access to the security properties of keys. Follow these steps to set up auditing and security for one or more key values:

1. Select a hive key and choose Permissions from the Security menu to open the Permissions for *KEYNAME* dialog with default permissions assigned to the groups listed (see Figure 10.17). Mark the Allow or Deny check boxes to alter basic permissions for the selected group; Deny is a more aggressive alternative to leaving a check box empty. To add another group, OU, or user, click Add; to remove a group, OU, or user, click Remove. When the permissions for the selected key are correct, click OK.

Figure 10.17
Set basic access permission with the Permissions for KEYNAME dialog.

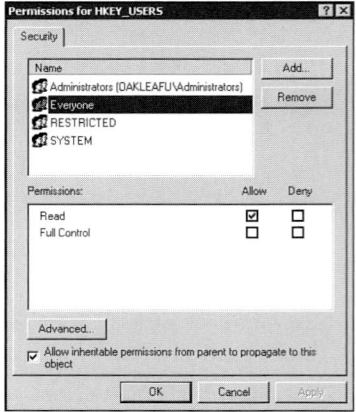

The two available basic permissions are as follows:

- *Full Control*—Users in the group can view, change, take ownership, and alter permissions. Administrators and the System group should have Full Control on every key.
- *Read*—Users in the group can only read the key.

2. Click Advanced to open the Access Control for *KEYNAME* dialog and click the Auditing tab.
3. Click Add to open the Select User, Computer or Group dialog, and double-click the group for auditing to open the Auditing Entry for *KEYNAME* dialog.
4. Select the types of accesses you want to be logged for the group, OU, or user (see Figure 10.18).
5. Click OK to close the dialog and apply the security logging attributes.

Figure 10.18
Set auditing selections in the Auditing Entry for *KEYNAME* dialog.

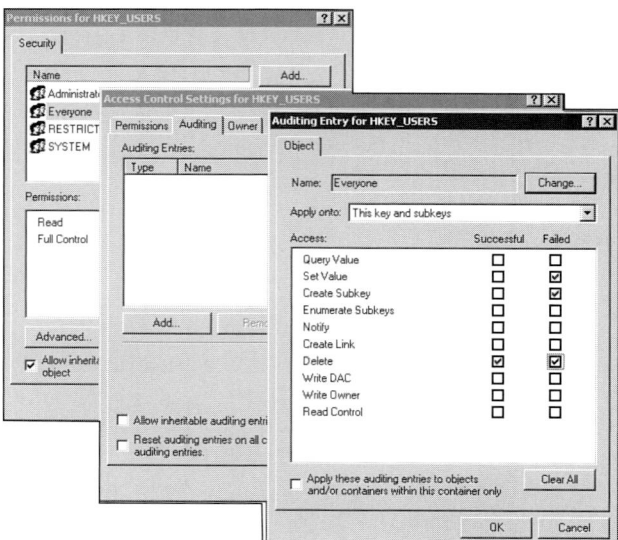

You probably wouldn't want to log successful accesses, because there might be a large number of accesses. For example, many keys are updated every time you run a server application, and each update may generate several log entries. Logging failed accesses enables you to discover applications that are no longer working or administrators who are trying to change keys for which they don't have Set Value permission.

The types of access audits are as follows:

- *Query Value*—An attempt to learn the value of the key.
- *Set Value*—An attempt to change the value of the key.
- *Create Subkey*—An attempt to make a subkey within the key.
- *Enumerate Subkeys*—An attempt to list the subkeys of this key.
- *Notify*—Notification events from the key.
- *Create Link*—An attempt to create a link within a key.
- *Delete*—An attempt to delete the key.
- *Write DAC*—An attempt to change the permissions (Discretionary Access Control) on a key.
- *Write Owner*—An attempt to change ownership of a key.
- *Read Control*—An attempt to learn the permissions on a key.

To view the audit logs with Computer Management, expand the System Tools and Event Viewer nodes, and then double-click Security Log to display the entries.

Tip from
RJ

> You also can apply Registry security with the Domain Controller Security or Domain Security snap-in by right-clicking the Registry node, choosing Add Key, and selecting a root key. The default security properties assign Full Control privileges to Everyone, which defeats all Registry security. If you downgrade the Everyone group to the Read privilege only, you must add Full Control privileges manually to all other groups that need them. If you fail to add all required Full Control privileges, software installation and other server operations are likely to fail. Thus, using Group Policy settings for Registry security isn't a recommended practice for inexperienced administrators.

TROUBLESHOOTING

WRONG REGISTRY EDITOR

An `Error Connecting Network Registry` message appears when attempting to connect to a remote computer's Registry.

You're using `Regedit.exe` instead of `Regedt32.exe` to perform remote Registry edits. `Regedit.exe` requires enabling the Remote Registry Service. Use `Regedt32.exe` for all administrative operations on the Registry; use `Regedit.exe` only for subkey name and value searches.

MCSE Corner: Exam Types

There are two types of exams in the Microsoft Certified Professional curriculum: the static exam and computer adaptive tests (CATs.) A regular static exam contains a predetermined number of questions from which the final score is calculated. Regular exams usually take 90–120 minutes, and have approximately 50–100 questions. The specific types of questions are listed in Chapters 13 and 27.

A computer adaptive test is a recent innovation in the Microsoft Certified Professional program. CATs are becoming more prevalent in the MCP testing environment.

CATs, which are usually referred to just as adaptive tests, do not have a predefined number of questions. A CAT uses an algorithm to determine the ability of the person taking the exam and tailors the exam to his abilities. Here is how a CAT works:

1. The exam system has a bank of questions, each with a difficulty rating. The first question asked is one of moderate difficulty.
2. If the examinee answers the question correctly, the next question is a more difficult question. If the answer is incorrect, the next question is easier.
3. The process continues. If the examinee continues with wrong answers, the exam continues to get easier. If the right answers are given, the test gets harder.
4. The exam ends on one of two conditions. Either the predetermined maximum number of questions is reached, or the exam system has enough information to accurately gauge the examinee's ability.

The catch to the CAT is that the exam does not give "points" to each answer, but uses an algorithm to determine the overall ability of the examinee, on a scale of 0–1000. The ability level starts in the middle, 500 for a Microsoft Exam. Correct answers to more difficult questions raise the ability score, while answering easier questions lowers the score. Remember that answering an easy question may lower the ability level, but the next question will be more difficult, and answering correctly will raise the level.

An exam ends when it has enough data to accurately estimate the examinee's ability. This is determined using a standard error of measurement calculation. As a test progresses, the standard error of measurement moves from a high number (closer to 1.0) to a low number (closer to zero). A standard error of measurement of .3 equates to a test reliability of around 90%. This is accurate enough so that the exam will have approximately the same results if it is taken multiple times. The standard error of measurement value at which an exam ends is predefined when the test is released.

The exams also calculate two other functions: the Item Characteristic Curve and the Test Information function. The Item Characteristic Curve shows the probability of a correct answer across the ability range (from 1–1000). At the end of the exam, this curve will show the probability (0–1.0, across the y-axis) of an examinee of any ability level (0–1000, across the x axis) of getting a correct answer in the given test. It shows the difficulty of the CAT that was just presented. An easy test (with many easy answers) will have a high curve, with lower ability levels having a higher probability of getting a correct answer. A difficult test will have the opposite trend.

The Test Information function shows how much information is given to an examinee for each question. The information value is shown on the y axis, and the ability level is shown on the x axis. A simpler explanation of this graph is that it explains how useful the given exam would be for a specified ability level. An easier exam would have a lower information value for a higher ability level. A more difficult exam would have a higher overall graph.

The final result of an adaptive test is to determine the examinee's level of ability to a fairly high level of accuracy in as few questions as possible. It is not uncommon for a CAT to have as few as 10 questions, or as many as 30. The questions on a CAT are usually more difficult and longer than questions on a regular exam.

CHAPTER 11

SETTING UP KEY- AND CERTIFICATE-BASED SECURITY

In this chapter

Enhancing File and Network Security   486

Understanding Public Key Encryption   486

Encrypting and Decrypting Files   489

Configuring Servers for Encryption   495

Providing Encrypted File Recovery   501

Establishing and Managing Certificate Authority Servers   506

Working with User Certificates   512

Troubleshooting   515

MCSE Corner: Setting Up Key- and Certificate-Based Security   516

Enhancing File and Network Security

Maintaining internal network security is one of the most important duties of a network administrator. Sophisticated network intrusion technology is readily available on the Internet, so administrators need to constantly examine their internal security implementations while maintaining interoperability with the many application services provided on the network. An additional concern for administrators is the link between security and ease-of-use. As security increases, ease-of-use traditionally decreases. Windows 2000's built-in Public Key Infrastructure (PKI), Encrypting File System (EFS), Internet Protocol Security (IPSec), and Certificate Services features greatly simplify setting up and administering internal file and network security.

Note This chapter is limited to securing the content of files stored on your internal network, and preventing compromise of network security within the organization's premises and on private telecommunication links. Chapter 26, "Setting Up a Virtual Private Network," covers secure communication over the Internet.

Understanding Public Key Encryption

In most organizations, the network administrators hold the key to all sensitive information available in the company. With the IT job market constantly growing, a relatively new employee could have access to a myriad of private information. Furthermore, there's not much to stop a savvy administrator from viewing or even changing personal information in corporate databases. The encryption services provided in Windows 2000 alleviate this problem. With proper implementation, data encryption keeps this private data from the hands of administrators while allowing them to retain control of their network infrastructure.

Cryptography and Key-Based Encryption

More commonly called encryption, cryptography is the science of keeping data private. When you *encrypt* data, you conceal it. Encryption is the method of taking readable data, commonly referred to as *plaintext* in the cryptography world, and obscuring it in one way or another. The hidden data is called *ciphertext*. Decryption is the opposite method, converting ciphertext back to plaintext.

Modern cryptography algorithms use keys to conceal or reveal data. Two types of key algorithms exist—symmetric and asymmetric. *Symmetric key* algorithms use a single key, often called a *shared secret*, to encrypt and decrypt data. Encryption and decryption are very fast using a single, symmetric key, but security can be compromised because the key needs to be passed in a secure manner to prevent unauthorized access. Anyone who obtains the key can immediately decrypt the data.

Asymmetric key algorithms use two keys to encrypt or decrypt data. This is also known as *public and private key cryptography* or *key pair cryptography*. With public and private keys, the public key is known to everyone, while the private key—which is related to the public key—

is known to just the owner of the key pair. Data encrypted with the sender's private key and both public keys can be decrypted by the recipient using a different decryption key that's related to the public keys. Some implementations of cryptography use the asymmetric key algorithm to encrypt shared-secret keys used in symmetric key algorithms. The sender generates a random number that represents half of the shared-secret key and encrypts the half with his or her public key. The recipient generates the random number for the other half of the shared-secret key, encrypts it with her or his private key, and the two parties exchange the halves to generate a temporary full shared-secret key for successive encryption and decryption operations. This provides a secure mechanism for transporting the symmetric key between two parties.

Many factors determine the strength of your encryption, which determines how secure your data is. The two most common factors are the encryption algorithm used and the key bit length. Some of the more common encryption algorithms are DES (Data Encryption Standard), MD5 (Message Digest 5) and SHA (Secure Hash Algorithm). Generally, the more secure an encryption algorithm, the slower it performs. The key bit length determines the strength of the algorithm. Common key lengths are 40-bit, 56-bit, and 128-bit.

> **Note**
> Exporting commercial encryption products is regulated by the Bureau of Export Administration in the U.S. Department of Commerce. If your organization extends outside of the United States and Canada, you should keep abreast of the current federal export regulations for encryption. For more information, visit `http://www.bxa.doc.gov/encryption`. To implement higher encryption levels in Windows 2000, you can download the Windows 2000 High Encryption Pack (128-bit) from `http://www.microsoft.com/downloads/default.asp`.

Windows 2000 supports many different cryptography algorithms and key sizes. This is facilitated by Microsoft's *CryptoAPI* (Cryptography Application Programming Interface). CryptoAPI is a set of libraries in the Windows 2000 operating system that lets developers embed cryptography into their applications while adhering to the standards of Windows 2000. The implementation of EFS, IPSec, and Certificate Services is based on the CryptoAPI.

Certificate Authorities and PKI

While key pair encryption is a very secure way of passing data, it's not foolproof. When exchanging information using key pairs, the sender must know the recipient's public key. The key must be obtained through some secure mechanism or else the sender isn't assured that the public key actually came from the recipient. There's nothing to stop potential hackers from exchanging their public keys for the recipient's.

Certificate Authorities guarantee authenticity of keys through the use of digital certificates. A (digital) certificate is an encrypted attachment to your encrypted file. The certificate contains the public key of the sender and other identifying information.

A Certificate Authority (CA) is a trusted computer system that can perform many functions within an organization. The main function of a CA is to issue certificates and certificate revocation lists (CRLs). Users and systems trust the CA to provide accurate and secure information. To facilitate this, the CA provides its public key to any requester within the organization. When a user needs to send an encrypted message, the user sends a certificate request to the CA. When the request is approved, the CA replies with a certificate encrypted with the CA's private key. This certificate contains the public key of the sender and other identifying information. When the sender encrypts a file, the certificate is also attached to the file. When the recipient receives the file, the certificate is decrypted using the CA's public key. This reveals the sender's public key, which in turn is used to decrypt the file. The recipient can then use the sender's public key to reply with encrypted information.

> **Note**
>
> Public Certificate Authorities are also available to users outside your organization. Windows 2000 provides the ability to define public CAs through Certificate Services. You can also use a third-party certificate authority such as VeriSign or Thawte.

Due to the explicit trust of Certificate Authorities by users and systems in your organization, the CA must be protected from compromises in security. Protection could be accomplished by securing the systems in a special area of the computer room or implementing CA hierarchies. A CA hierarchy is designed to add levels of abstraction to your most trusted CA. CA hierarchies consist of *root* and *subordinate* CAs. A root CA is the most trusted CA in your organization. A subordinate CA is a node or leaf in the hierarchy. A node CA is called an *Intermediate CA* while a leaf CA is called an *Issuing CA*. An Intermediate CA trusts the CA directly above it in the hierarchy and issues certificates to other Intermediates or Issuing CAs. An Issuing CA trusts the CA above it and issues certificates to users and systems in your organization.

> **Tip from**
> *RJ*
>
> When defining CA hierarchies in your organization, it's best to create at least three levels of certificate authorities—root, intermediate, and issuing. This provides a greater amount of flexibility and protects your root from malicious users.

Public Key Infrastructure (PKI) is the implementation of Certificate Authorities, CA hierarchies, encryption technologies, and other secure mechanisms of providing security and authenticity within an organization through the use of digital certificates.

→ To learn more about implementing CA hierarchies, **see** "Choosing a Certificate Authority Type," **p. 506**.

Windows 2000 Encrypting File System (EFS)

Encrypting File System (EFS) is a new feature in Windows 2000 that provides users with a transparent mechanism for encrypting and decrypting files and folders on their workstations or servers. Because these operations are transparent to the user, no extra training is required. If a workstation or server is compromised, the files on the system remain unseen. EFS uses a symmetric file encryption key (FEK) to quickly encrypt or decrypt the file. The FEK is then encrypted with the user's public key. When implementing EFS in your organization, a certificate authority is not required. EFS functions with inherent keys installed on your Windows 2000 server or workstation. EFS uses the DESX encryption algorithm developed by RSA Laboratories. This encryption algorithm is an extension of the U.S. Data Encryption Standard (DES).

IP Security (IPSec) in Windows 2000

New to Windows 2000, IP Security (IPSec) provides secure communication between servers and workstations. IPSec encrypts and decrypts packets below the transport layer of the IP stack. This allows your distributed applications to take full advantage of secure communications without additional updates. Additionally, all encrypted communication is transparent to the user; this benefit of IPSec reduces training costs while maintaining ease-of-use. Windows 2000 IPSec is designed and compatible with the Internet Engineering Task Force (IETF) specifications of IP Security. In order to use IPSec, both the client and the server must be Windows 2000 operating systems.

> **Note**
> For a detailed list of the IPSec drafts developed by IETF, visit http://www.ietf.org/ids.by.wg/ipsec.html.

Windows 2000 Certificate Services

Windows 2000 Certificate Services let you create and administer private or public certificate authorities in your organization. Windows 2000 provides functionality to create CA hierarchies in your organization through root and subordinates, while also providing additional functionality to create *Enterprise* or *Standalone* CAs.

An Enterprise CA is fully integrated with Active Directory. If you want to use certificates within your organization and you're using Active Directory, you should choose Enterprise CA. A Standalone CA does not require Active Directory. This is useful when you place a certificate authority on the Internet to allow external users to request certificates.

Once installed, Windows 2000 Certificate Services can be administered directly through an MMC snap-in or from the command line. The MMC snap-in installed with Certificate Services is called "Certification Authority." It allows you to create policies for your certificate server, revoke certificates, and approve pending certificate requests. It also allows you to view all revoked requests, issued certificates, pending requests, and failed requests, and (if installed as an Enterprise CA) view policy certificate settings for your Windows 2000 environment.

Encrypting and Decrypting Files

Windows 2000 provides the Encrypting File System (EFS) to easily allow users to encrypt and decrypt information. EFS is useful to conceal information not only in the event that the corporate network security is compromised, but also in the event that a user's laptop is stolen. When a user's laptop is stolen, the thieves don't necessarily intend to sell the hardware. Some thieves may be looking for sensitive corporate secrets and strategies. If, by chance, the thief is able to compromise the NTFS security system, the encrypted files remain encrypted and are unreadable.

Because most of the encryption happens behind the scenes, EFS is ideal for users. While EFS prevents the average administrator from reading the content of files, administrative tasks are not hindered through its use. Additionally, file recovery is built into the architecture of EFS. A small set of administrators can be defined as *recovery agents*. A recovery agent can decrypt files in the event that the user leaves the company or loses his private key.

Understanding the Encrypting File System

EFS provides encryption of files or folders on the hard drive. When a file or folder is encrypted, the operating system randomly generates a file encryption key (FEK) that is used to encrypt and decrypt the file or folder.

During the encryption process, the FEK is encrypted with the user's public key. The encrypted FEK is stored in a special attribute of the encrypted file called the *Data Decryption Field* (DDF). Another operation during the encryption process is the creation of the *Data Recovery Field* (DRF), an additional attribute of the encrypted file. The data recovery field encrypts the FEK with the recovery agent's public key. Both the DRF and DDF are tightly bound to the encrypted file, making them difficult to extract. Figure 11.1 shows the EFS encryption process.

Figure 11.1
EFS encryption involves three keys—user and recovery public keys and a random file encryption key.

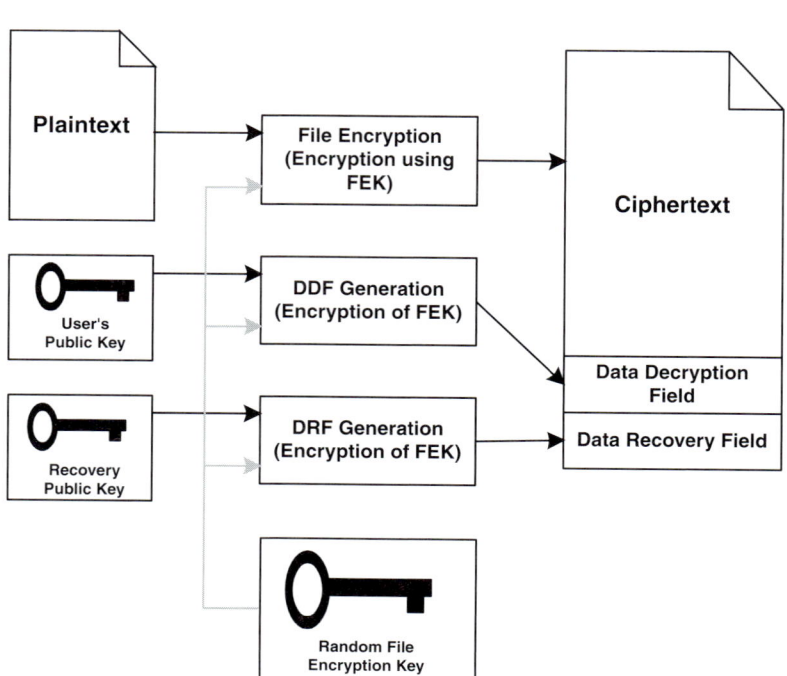

During the decryption process of EFS, the DDF is extracted from the file. The user's private key is used to decrypt the DDF and extract the FEK. The FEK is then used to decrypt the file. Figure 11.2 shows the EFS decryption process.

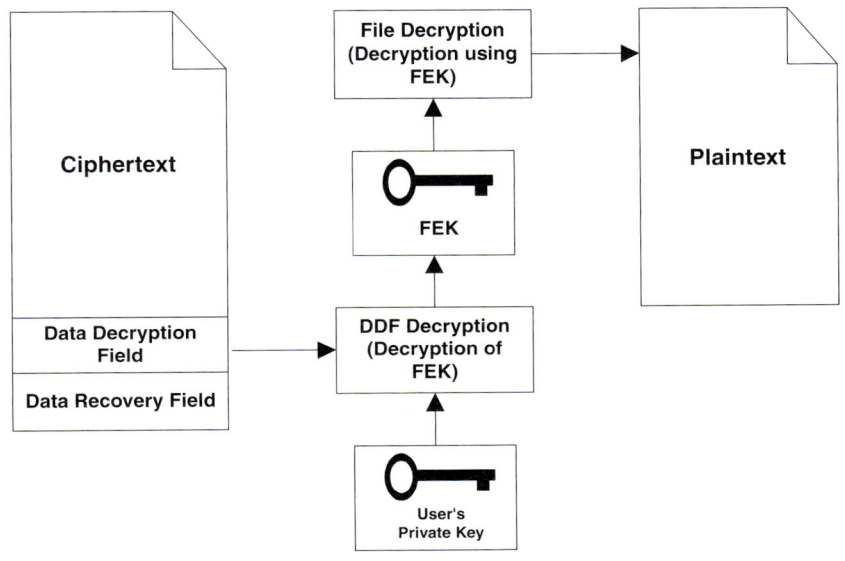

Figure 11.2
The decryption process requires the user's private key and the file encryption key.

Tip from
RJ

Encryption and decryption of the FEK are based on your public/private keys. If you encrypt a file with your local computer account, you might not be able to decrypt it with your domain account. To solve this problem, log on with your local user account to decrypt the file.

ENCRYPTING FILE SYSTEM ARCHITECTURE

Encrypting File System Architecture consists of many different components, most of which exist in kernel mode of the operating system. The following components are part of the Encrypting File System:

- *EFS Driver*—The EFS driver sits on the NTFS file system and issues requests for file encryption keys, DDFs, and DRFs from the EFS service. This information is passed to the EFS file system run-time library (EFS FSRTL).

- *EFS FSRTL*—The EFS FSRTL performs multiple operations on the file: It manipulates the file transparently to the user, and it opens, saves, reads, writes, encrypts and decrypts information to the file or folder. It also writes the special EFS attributes to the file, such as the DDF and DRF.

- *EFS Service*—The EFS service is a component of the Windows 2000 security subsystem and serves purposes in both kernel mode and user mode of the Windows 2000 operating system. In kernel mode, it uses the Local Security Authority (LSA) to communicate with the EFS driver. In user mode, it communicates with the CryptoAPI libraries.

Encrypting Folders and Files in Windows Explorer

The Windows 2000 EFS service is relatively easy to set up. You must be using an NTFS file system to encrypt files and folders. As with permissions, auditing, and compression, encryption is solely a feature of NTFS.

When implementing EFS, always encrypt folders instead of files. This ensures that all files within the directory inherit the encryption attribute of the directory. You also should encrypt all temporary directories used by the application to ensure that no remnants of unencrypted files are left on the file system.

Tip from	
RJ	Encryption polices can be set so that EFS doesn't automatically encrypt files moved to encrypted folders. This is done from a Group Policy within the computer configuration.

Tip from	
RJ	If mandatory profiles are implemented in your organization, you might not have access to EFS functionality. This occurs because your public/private key pair is stored within your profile, and mandatory profiles cannot be edited.

To use Windows Explorer to encrypt files within a folder, do the following:

1. Open Windows Explorer and navigate to the folder to be encrypted.
2. Right-click the folder and select Properties to open the *FolderName* Properties dialog.
3. In the General page, click Advanced to open the Advanced Attributes dialog.
4. Mark the Encrypt Contents to Secure Data check box to enable encryption of the specified folder and its current or future subfolders (see Figure 11.3).

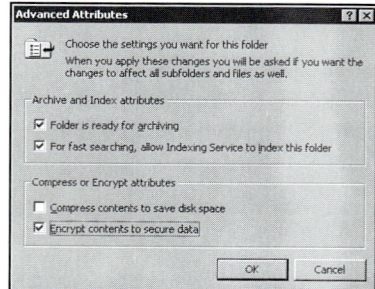

Figure 11.3
To encrypt the contents of a folder, select the encryption option on the Advanced Attributes dialog.

Tip from	
RJ	While a check box exists for both encryption and compression, they are mutually exclusive. Encrypted files and folders cannot be compressed, and compressed files and folders cannot be encrypted.

ENCRYPTING AND DECRYPTING FILES   493

5. Click OK to close the Advanced Attributes dialog.

6. Click OK to close the *FolderName* Properties dialog. If the folder contains subfolders and files, the Confirm Attribute Changes dialog opens (see Figure 11.4).

Figure 11.4
Once a folder is marked for encryption, you must confirm the change and determine if you want subfolders to be encrypted.

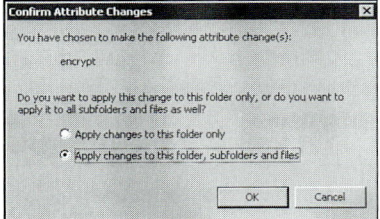

7. Select the Apply Changes to This Folder, Subfolders and Files option and click OK.

 If you encounter problems encrypting files, see the "Problems with Encrypting File System" topic of the "Troubleshooting" section near the end of this chapter.

When a file or folder is encrypted, the Encrypted attribute is added to the detail pane of Windows Explorer if Web View is selected for the folder (see Figure 11.5).

Figure 11.5
The Encrypted attribute can be viewed from Windows Explorer in Web View.

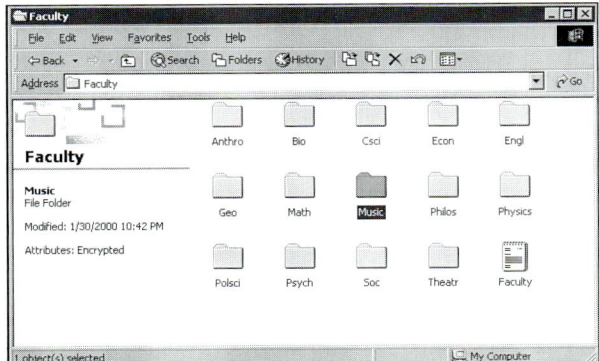

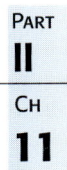

As with permission and compression attributes, you should always encrypt folders. All files created in encrypted folders automatically inherit the encryption attribute of the folder. If you want to encrypt an individual file, follow the same steps used to encrypt folders (see the preceding steps), but select a file, rather than a folder. In step 6, the Encryption Warning dialog offers you the choice of encrypting the file you selected or the file and the parent folder (see Figure 11.6).

Figure 11.6
The Encryption Warning dialog allows you to encrypt the file or the file and the parent folder.

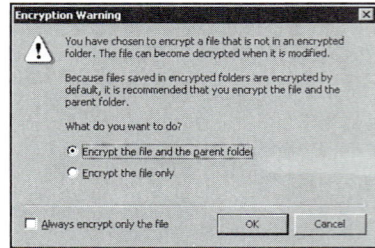

Tip from
RJ

To decrypt files and folders, simply go to the Advanced Attributes dialog and clear the Encrypt Contents To Secure Data check box.

 If you encounter problems decrypting files, see the "Problems with Encrypting File System" topic of the "Troubleshooting" section near the end of this chapter.

ENCRYPTING FOLDERS AND FILES WITH THE CIPHER COMMAND

You can also encrypt and decrypt folders and the files they contain from the command prompt by using the cipher command. You might choose to use the cipher command when encrypting or decrypting multiple folders on your file system. The cipher command can be used in a batch file for bulk encryptions or decryptions.

To perform encryption operations with the cipher command, do the following:

1. Open the command prompt and type **cipher /e** *foldername* to encrypt the folder (see Figure 11.7).

Figure 11.7
The cipher command can be used to encrypt folders from the command prompt.

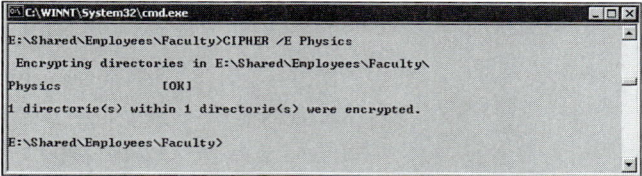

2. To display a list of encrypted and unencrypted files and folders, simply type **cipher** without any additional parameters (see Figure 11.8).

Figure 11.8
Use the cipher command to view a list of encrypted and unencrypted files and folders. Encrypted files are preceded by the letter E in the list, and unencrypted files are preceded by the letter U.

3. To decrypt a folder, type **cipher /d** *foldername*.

Tip from
RJ

To encrypt or decrypt folders and subfolders, use the **/s** switch of the cipher command in addition to the **/e** or **/d** switches. For example, **cipher /e /s** *foldername* encrypts the folder and subfolders.

CONFIGURING SERVERS FOR ENCRYPTION

The secure and straightforward process of implementing EFS on a local computer becomes more complicated when you introduce a distributed environment. Most organizations implement file services to centralize administration and provide a flexible environment to their users. When working in a distributed environment, a more complex security infrastructure is required. Organizations not only need to consider the confidentiality of the data stored on the server, but also the data flowing across the transmission systems.

EFS uses a public/private key pair to encrypt and decrypt data. If the key pair is located on the local computer and the file is located on the remote server, security of either the key pair or the remote file would be compromised during a distributed encryption/decryption process. To provide secure encryption, Windows 2000 permits the server to encrypt and decrypt on behalf of the user. While this provides a secure mechanism for encrypting and decrypting files on a remote computer, the applications used to read and write the data are still left unsecured. To address this problem, Windows 2000 provides encrypted data transmission through IPSec.

DISTRIBUTED EFS—UNDERSTANDING THE TRUSTED FOR DELEGATION OPTION

Implementing EFS for distributed operations requires some additional configuration. During the encryption process, EFS uses the public key of the user to encrypt the FEK and store it in the DDF. This process doesn't compromise security because the user's public key is generally available. However, during the decryption process, EFS extracts the DDF and decrypts the FEK with the user's private key. This presents a security concern since the EFS process on the server must obtain the user's private key. To enable EFS on the server to decrypt with the user's private key, the server must be configured to impersonate the user. This requires the server to be Trusted for Delegation.

Trusted for Delegation allows the server to impersonate the user by requesting the user's master key from the Kerberos KDC (Key Distribution Center). By default, this option is set on all Domain Controllers (DCs) in the organization to enable trust relationships between domains.

→ For a brief description of the Kerberos KDC, **see** "Kerberos Authentication," **p. 38**.

Tip from
RJ

Be sure to enable Trusted for Delegation on all computers participating in EFS. By default, DCs are trusted for delegation, but member servers and workstations aren't. If this option is not configured, the EFS service isn't available for users to encrypt and decrypt files. Additionally, the shared folders must be on an NTFS partition to use EFS.

To enable Trusted for Delegation, follow these steps:

1. Open Active Directory Users and Computers on a DC or a Windows 2000 workstation with the AD administrative tools installed, and navigate to the Computers container.
2. Right-click the computer to configure and select Properties to open the *ComputerName* Properties dialog.
3. In the General page, mark the Trust Computer For Delegation check box to enable delegation (see Figure 11.9).

Figure 11.9
Enabling a computer to be trusted for delegation is done through the Trust Computer For Delegation check box on the General page of the computer's Properties dialog.

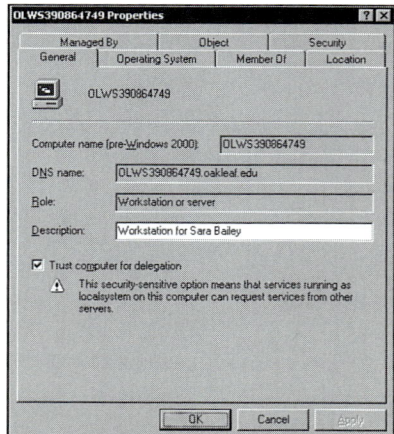

4. A message box opens warning that this option is a security-sensitive operation; click OK to close the dialog.
5. Click OK to close the *ComputerName* Properties dialog. Restart the computer you just configured to immediately download the new security policy.

Before you start encrypting files and folders, you must set the folder attribute to Encrypt Contents To Secure Data and assign only the *CREATOR OWNER* and *Administrators* Full Control on the folders. This ensures that the encrypted files can't be renamed or deleted by a malicious user.

→ For instructions on how to set security on shared folders, **see** "High-Level Folder and File Permissions," **p. 680**.

PROVIDING ENCRYPTED DATA TRANSMISSION WITH IPSEC

Network devices, such as firewalls, have prevented external users from accessing sensitive business information on servers, but firewalls can only control so much. Reading or "sniffing" the data flowing across the wires is one way to breach security. Much of the data traveling across the network wires is in clear text. This means any user with a good network "sniffer" can easily interpret much of the data traveling across the network. While many administrators concentrate on preventing external users from violating their network integrity, fewer are watching the internal users, with whom many security problems originate.

EFS secures sensitive data on the server, but it doesn't secure the network transmission systems. Security on the network wires must be configured to prevent malicious users from viewing information from applications across the network.

For example, a user might edit a Word 2000 document on a secured share with EFS enabled. While the document is encrypted on the server, network traffic is not. When the user saves the document, the contents are transmitted in clear text and then encrypted on the server. This allows a malicious user to read any packet sent between the two computers even if the document is stored on an encrypted share.

Tip from *RJ*	To view a document transmitted across the network, install Network Monitor, included in Windows 2000. Start a network capture and open a word document on the remote server. Look for the frame with the "NBT" protocol and the "SS: Session Message ...." description. The capture includes all text in your file.

→ For an example of using Network Monitor to view text transmitted on the network, **see** "Running the Add-Users Test," **p. 1001**.

As mentioned previously, Windows 2000 provides IPSec to configure encryption on your transmission systems. IPSec allows you to encrypt all data transmitted between a client and a server. If you decide to implement trusted servers for your EFS configuration, you should consider requiring secure communication with these servers. Windows 2000 conforms to the IP Security drafts defined by the Internet Engineering Task Force (IETF).

The architecture of IPSec includes the following components:

- *Oakley/ISAKMP*—Oakley is a key determination protocol defining how keys are used during the secure communication. The Internet Security Association and Key Management Protocol (ISAKMP) is used to create a security association (SA) between two computers. The SA is a specification of the required information used to pass encrypted data. The SA must be established before encrypted communication can occur. Once the SA is defined between two computers, the IPSec driver passes secure packets between the two computers by use of the Authentication Header or Encapsulating Security Protocol methods.

- *IP Authentication Header*—The IP Authentication Header (AH) is used to transmit authentic and unmodified data between two computers.
- *IP Encapsulating Security Protocol*—The IP Encapsulating Security Protocol (ESP) is used to transmit authentic, unmodified, and confidential data between two computers. The ESP provides authentication by using the DES encryption algorithm to encrypt the packets.

CONFIGURING IPSEC

To install IPSec, you must have TCP/IP installed. During the configuration of IPSec, you're presented with three options for the IP Security policy:

- *Client (Respond Only)*—This option allows your computer to participate in unsecured communication with all other computers unless the remote computer requests secure communication.
- *Server (Request Security)*—This option always requests secure communication for your computer. If the remote computer does not support IPSec, unsecured communication occurs.
- *Secure Server (Requires Security)*—This option requires secure communication for your computer. If the remote computer does not support IPSec, no communication occurs. Unsecured communication isn't accepted.

When configuring IPSec for use with EFS, you should ensure the server is set to Secure Server. This requires any clients to use IPSec when saving encrypted information to your EFS file server.

> **Note**
> By default, Windows 2000 computers are set not to use IPSec. If you choose the Secure Server policy for your EFS file server, you must choose the Client (Respond Only) policy for all of your clients. If you do not set the option on the clients, communication doesn't occur.

Follow these steps to configure secure communication using IPSec:

1. Open Network and Dial-up Connections.
2. Right-click the connection you want to configure and select Properties to open the *ConnectionName* Properties dialog.
3. In the General page, highlight Internet Protocol (TCP/IP) and select Properties to open the Internet Protocol (TCP/IP) Properties dialog.
4. In the General page, select Advanced to open the Advanced TCP/IP Settings dialog.
5. In the Options page (see Figure 11.10), highlight IP Security and click the Properties button to open the IP Security dialog (shown in Figure 11.11).

Figure 11.10
IP Security (IPSec) is configured from the Advanced TCP/IP Settings dialog.

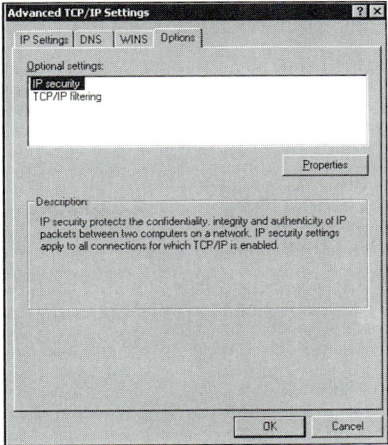

6. From the Use This IP Security Policy drop-down list, select the policy you want to implement.

Figure 11.11
The IP Security dialog is used to select the IP Security policy implemented on the computer.

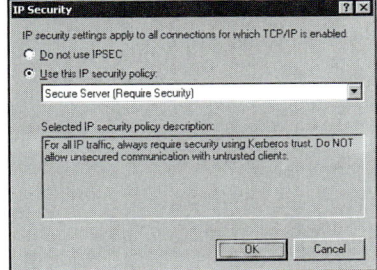

7. Click OK to close all dialogs and return to Network and Dial-up Connections.

UNDERSTANDING IP SECURITY POLICIES

Implementing IP security policies can be tedious if you need to physically configure each server and workstation in your organization. For most organizations, physically visiting every workstation is unrealistic. Windows 2000 allows IP security policies to be configured as part of a Group Policy.

Depending on your AD configuration, you may choose to create a separate OU for EFS file servers. This allows you to create IP security policies specific to your EFS servers. Other options include setting your EFS file servers on their own subnet, creating separate domain-level policies for EFS file servers, or applying the policy based on DNS entries. Using the Group Policy editor, you can configure different IP security policies based on IP address, DNS name, subnet, and many other metrics.

→ For more information on the Group Policy Editor, **see** "Using the Group Policy Snap-In to Edit Group Policy Objects," **p. 622**.

Note
This chapter covers the basic steps for implementing IP security policies with the Group Policy Editor. As with all security implementations in your network, IP security policies should be properly planned for ease of administration and flexibility. For more information on IP security policies, please refer to the IP Security section of the Windows 2000 documentation.

IMPLEMENTING IP SECURITY POLICIES

The following steps demonstrate how to define a Domain Group Policy for IP security on your workstations (in this example, servers have been configured manually to require a secure connection):

1. Open Active Directory Users and Computers.
2. Right-click your domain name and select Properties to open the *DomainName* Properties dialog.
3. On the Group Policy page, highlight the Default Domain Policy and select Edit to open the Group Policy Editor.
4. Open the Computer Configuration, Windows Settings, Security Settings, IP Security Policies node (see Figure 11.12).

Figure 11.12
The Group Policy Editor is used to define IP Security Policies. In this example, the Default Domain policy is selected.

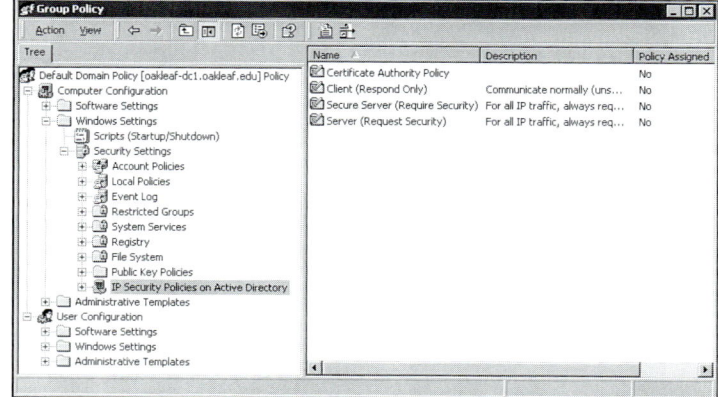

5. In the detail pane, right-click Client (Respond Only) and then select All Tasks, Assign. This configures all computers in the domain to use secure communications when requested by the remote computer (see Figure 11.13).

PROVIDING ENCRYPTED FILE RECOVERY | 501

Figure 11.13
To assign the IP Security policy, right-click the policy and select All Tasks, Assign.

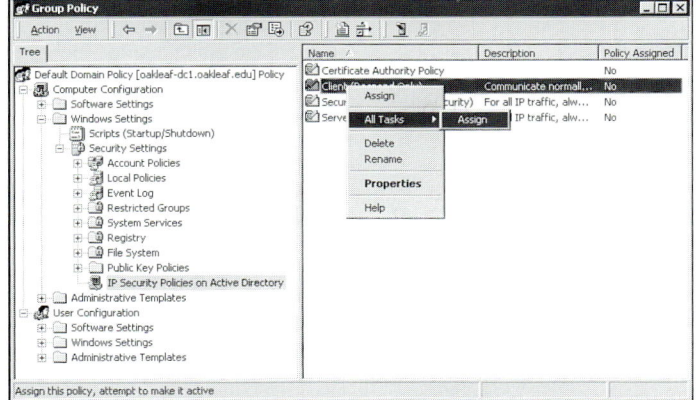

6. Close the Group Policy Editor and select OK on the *DomainName* Properties dialog.

> **Caution**
> IP security policies can become very complex and possibly cripple the network communication in your organization. Before implementing complex IP security configurations, it's best to create a "sandbox" to test the different implementation techniques before deploying your enterprise solution.

 If your clients encounter problems communicating with servers, see the "IP Security Communication Problems" topic of the "Troubleshooting" section near the end of this chapter.

PROVIDING ENCRYPTED FILE RECOVERY

An essential feature of the EFS design is the ability to seamlessly recover files that have been encrypted by users. When a user's certificate is revoked, a mechanism for recovering previously encrypted files is required. Recovery functionality is built into the EFS architecture to provide organizations with a method for decrypting files that have been encrypted by users.

During the encryption process, EFS provides the *Data Recovery Field* (DRF) to recover encrypted files. The DRF is a special attribute in the encrypted file that allows the *Data Recovery Agent* (DRA) to decrypt the file. A Data Recovery Agent is usually a trusted administrator in your organization. EFS uses the DRA's public key to encrypt the FEK during the encryption process. If file recovery is needed, the private key of the DRA is used to decrypt the FEK. With the FEK, the DRA can decrypt the file (see Figure 11.14).

During the recovery process, only the FEK is available to the recovery agent. No information about the user or user's private key is available to the DRA. Organizations may have more than one DRA. A corresponding DRF is created for each DRA during the encryption process. During the decryption process, the DRA's corresponding DRF is extracted from the encrypted file. This allows multiple DRAs to decrypt the file without compromising the security of their individual private keys.

PART
II
CH
11

Figure 11.14
The recovery process of EFS uses the Data Recovery Agent's private key to decrypt the FEK stored in the DRF. The FEK is then used to decrypt the file.

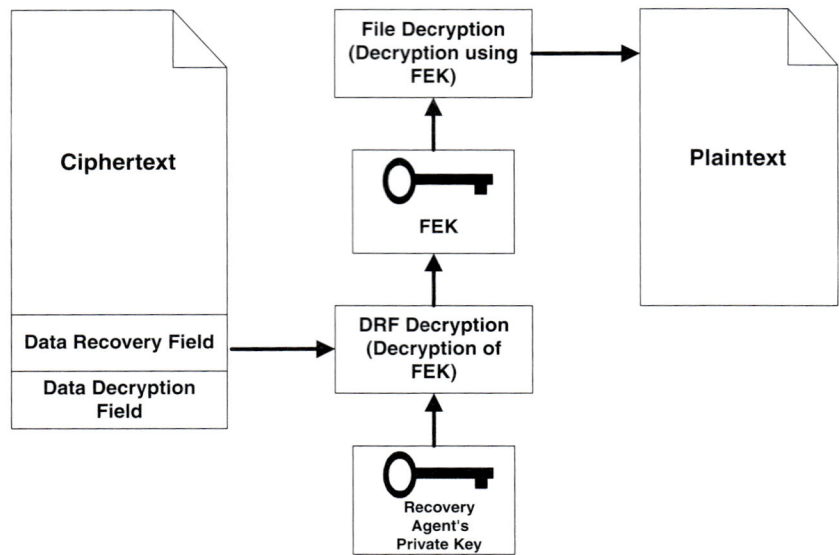

IMPLEMENTING DATA RECOVERY AGENTS

Data Recovery Agents are defined using the Encrypted Data Recovery Policy (EDRP) in the Group Policy Editor. Since data recovery is an integral part of the EFS architecture, recovery agents are required for EFS to function properly. If a recovery agent is not defined, EFS isn't functional.

→ For more information on the Group Policy Editor, **see** "Using the Group Policy Snap-In to Edit Group Policy Objects," **p. 622**.

When Windows 2000 is initially installed, an inherent recovery key is assigned to the administrator account. To prevent possible security breaches, you should remove the administrator account from the EDRP and add elected recovery agents in your organization. Before adding a recovery agent to your domain, the elected agent must request an EFS Recovery Agent certificate from your certificate authority and must be a member of the Domain Admins Global group.

→ For more information on Certificate Authorities, **see** "Establishing and Managing Certificate Authority Servers," **p. 506**.

→ For more information on requesting EFS Recovery Agent certificates, **see** "Working with User Certificates," **p. 512**.

The following steps demonstrate how to add recovery agents to your EDRP.

1. Open Active Directory Users and Computers.

2. Right-click your domain name and select Properties to open the *DomainName* Properties dialog.

3. On the Group Policy page, highlight the Default Domain Policy and select Edit to open the Group Policy Editor.

Providing Encrypted File Recovery 503

4. Open the Computer Configuration, Windows Settings, Security Settings, Public Key Policies, Encrypted Data Recovery Agents node (see Figure 11.15).

Figure 11.15
Encrypted Data Recovery Agents are configured in the Group Policy Editor.

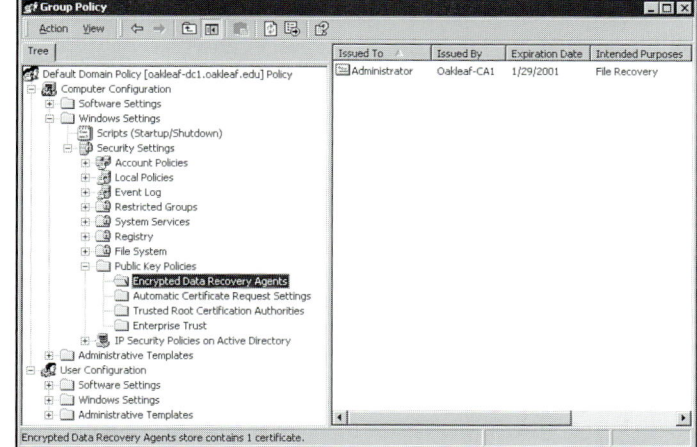

5. Right-click Encrypted Data Recovery Agents and select Add to initialize the Add Recovery Agent Wizard. Select Next to continue.
6. In the Select Recovery Agents dialog, select Browse Directory to find the elected recovery agent (see Figure 11.16).

Figure 11.16
Use the wizard to select recovery agents for the policy.

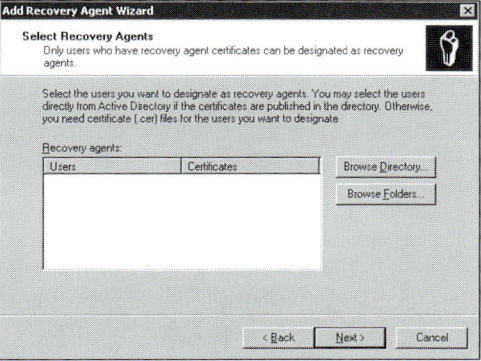

7. In the Find Users, Contacts, Groups dialog, enter the name of the elected recovery agent in the Name field and select Find Now.

⚠ *If you encounter problems selecting a recovery agent, see the "Problems with Encrypting File System" topic of the "Troubleshooting" section at the end of this chapter.*

8. Select the account you want to add as a recovery agent and click OK. In the Select Recovery Agents dialog, select Next to continue.

PART
II

CH
11

9. Verify the correct user account is in the recovery agent list and select Finish.
10. Close the Group Policy Editor and close on the *DomainName* Properties dialog.

Removing recovery agents from the EDRP can be useful to prevent users from using EFS in your organization. If you remove the EDRP, users don't have a valid recovery agent for EFS. This causes the encryption operations to fail.

To disable EFS in your domain, follow these steps:

1. Open Active Directory Users and Computers.
2. Right-click your domain name and select Properties to open the *DomainName* Properties dialog.
3. On the Group Policy page, highlight the Default Domain Policy and select Edit to open the Group Policy Editor.
4. Open the Computer Configuration, Windows Settings, Security Settings, Public Key Policies, Encrypted Data Recovery Agents node.
5. Right-click Encrypted Data Recovery Agents and select Delete Policy. When a message confirming the deletion appears, select Yes.
6. Right-click Encrypted Data Recovery Agents and select Initialize Empty Policy.
7. Close the Group Policy Editor and select OK to close the *DomainName* Properties dialog.

> **Note**
> Deleting the policy is quite different from initializing an empty policy. When you delete a policy, EFS is available to the local users of workstations in your domain. When you initialize an empty policy, EFS is disabled for both domain accounts and local accounts.

> **Caution**
> Removing Data Recovery Agents might prevent your files from being recovered. Be sure to examine your EFS implementation before removing DRAs to prevent this problem.

> **Tip from RJ**
> Your organization may choose to disable EFS for local accounts of the user workstations. This prevents users from logging in locally and creating encrypted files that are unrecoverable by the DRA. To implement this configuration, simply remove the EDRP from the local workstations.

Securing the DRA Private Key

The DRA's private keys are possibly the most important keys in your organization. These keys can be used to decrypt all sensitive information in your organization, so securing them is imperative. It's likely you may need to store the DRA's private key on external storage media such as a tape or disk. To accomplish this, you must export the certificate and private key information.

Providing Encrypted File Recovery

To export the DRA certificate, follow these steps:

1. Open the Certificates snap-in and open the Certificates - Current User, Personal, Certificates node.

→ For more information on the Certificates snap-in, **see** "Working with User Certificates," **p. 512**.

2. In the detail pane, right-click the DRA certificate you want to export. Select All Tasks, Export to initialize the Certificate Export Wizard; select Next to continue.

3. In the Export Private Key dialog, select the Yes, Export The Private Key option (see Figure 11.17); click Next.

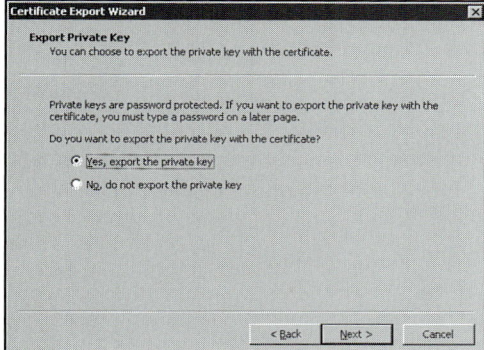

Figure 11.17
When exporting certificates, you can export the private key from the Export Private Key dialog in the Certificate Export Wizard.

4. In the Export File Format dialog, verify that the Enable Strong Protection check box is marked (see Figure 11.18); select Next.

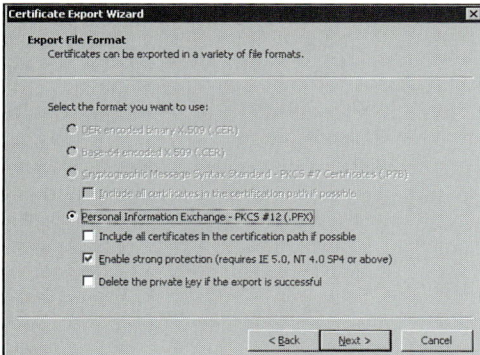

Figure 11.18
Mark the Enable Strong Protection check box in the Export File Format dialog of the Certificate Export Wizard.

5. In the Password dialog, enter a password in the Password and Confirm Password fields. Click Next to continue.

6. In the File to Export dialog, enter the path and filename you want to associate with the certificate you are exporting (the file must end with the extension .PFX).

7. Verify the correct certificate information is in the export list and select Finish. A message appears indicating that the export was successful.

Establishing and Managing Certificate Authority Servers

Windows 2000 allows organizations to design a public key infrastructure (PKI) through the use of Certificate Services. Certificate Services allow administrators to create a multitier Certificate Authority (CA) hierarchy to maintain a high level of control and flexibility with the different cryptography services implemented throughout their enterprise. This section concentrates on the installation and administration basics of Certificate Services.

During the installation of Certificate Services, you'll need some essential information. Certificate Services may be part of your initial Windows 2000 deployment or additional functionality to an existing implementation. Before you install Certificate Services, you should plan your CA implementation. Many of the installation options depend on how you plan to use certificate authorities in your organization. During the installation of Certificate Services, the following configuration options are available:

- *Certificate Authority Type*—Windows 2000 provides four options for certificate authorities: Enterprise Root CA, Enterprise Subordinate CA, Standalone Root CA, and Standalone Subordinate CA.
- *Advanced Options*—Advanced installation options allow you to choose your Cryptographic Service Provider, hash algorithm, and key length. Additionally, you can use an existing certificate for your CA.
- *CA Identifying Information*—Identifying information is used to provide information to the users of the certificate authority.
- *Specifying CA Database Location*—When installing a CA, you can specify where the CA database resides.

Caution

Before you begin the installation of Certificate Services, choose a computer name and domain membership that is not likely to change. Once Certificate Services are installed, you cannot change the computer name or domain membership.

Choosing a Certificate Authority Type

Windows 2000 Certificate Services provide you with the flexibility of choosing either a root or subordinate CA type, based on the function of the CA and the structure of your organization. As explained earlier, a root CA is the most trusted CA in your organization. Depending on the size and structure of your organization, you may choose to create multiple roots. A subordinate CA is a child of the root CA. Implementing a subordinate CA allows you to create a CA hierarchy in your organization, which you may choose to do based, again, on the size of your organization. If your CA hierarchy consists of multiple subordinate CAs, you should consider implementing a three-level hierarchy for maximum flexibility and security.

> **Note**
>
> To install subordinate certificate authorities, you must have at least one root certificate authority.

After determining whether to install a root or subordinate, you must decide between an Enterprise CA or a Standalone CA. An Enterprise CA is fully integrated with Active Directory. Any user that logs on to your domain trusts an Enterprise CA by default. Additionally, when a user in the domain requests a certificate from an Enterprise CA, the default action is to issue the certificate. If you're installing a CA to be used solely by your organization, you should choose an Enterprise CA.

A Standalone CA is not integrated with Active Directory. Standalone CAs are best suited for public implementation on the Internet. If a user in your organization requests a certificate from a Standalone CA, the request is set to pending until it can be reviewed by the administrator. Additionally, users in your domain do not automatically trust Standalone CAs; this trust must be configured manually.

Choosing Advanced Options

The Advanced Options in Certificate Services are provided to let you better control the configuration of your CA. Within the Advanced Options, you can change your cryptographic service provider (CSP), hash algorithm, and key length. All of these options are used when the CA generates keys for requesters. The default CSP for certificate authorities is Microsoft Base Cryptographic Provider and the default hash algorithm is SHA-1 (Secure Hash Algorithm). For most implementations, you should keep the default CSP and hash algorithm. If your security requirements conflict with the defaults, you may choose to change this information.

> **Tip from**
> *RJ*
>
> The default key length is 512 bits for the Microsoft Base Cryptographic Provider. If installing a root CA, you should increase this length to at least 2048 bits. If installing a subordinate CA, you should increase the key length to a minimum of 1024 bits. The longer the key length, the more secure your CA. CAs are the most trusted systems in your organization and should be secured as much as possible.

> **Note**
>
> If you're using Smart Cards in your organization, you might want to choose a different CSP, one that is compatible with your Smart Cards. Please refer to the manufacturer for more information.

Entering CA Identifying Information and Choosing a Data Storage Location

Identifying information must be entered to install your CA. This information is mostly used to determine where their certificates are issued from. Only two fields are required in this form—CA name and validity period.

During the installation, you are provided with the ability to change the location of the CA database and log files. By default, the CA database is stored under Winnt\System32\Certlog. While most large organizations back up servers nightly, most backup schemes do not include system or program files. Consider changing where the CA database is stored to assure regular backups through the Windows 2000 backup program. If a system failure occurs and you need to reinstall Windows 2000, you could potentially lose your CA database.

Installing Certificate Services

The installation of Certificate Services is an easy process when all required information is gathered beforehand.

To install certificate services, follow these steps:

1. Open Control Panel and select the Add/Remove Programs tool.
2. In the Add/Remove Programs dialog, select Add/Remove Windows Components. This initializes the Windows Components Wizard.
3. Mark the Certificate Services check box; a warning dialog appears informing you that computer name and domain membership cannot be changed after Certificate Services is installed. Click Yes to install Certificate Services and then click Next.
4. In the Certificate Authority Type dialog, choose the CA type you want to install and mark the Advanced options check box (see Figure 11.19); click Next.

Figure 11.19
The Certificate Authority Type dialog allows you to select a CA type.

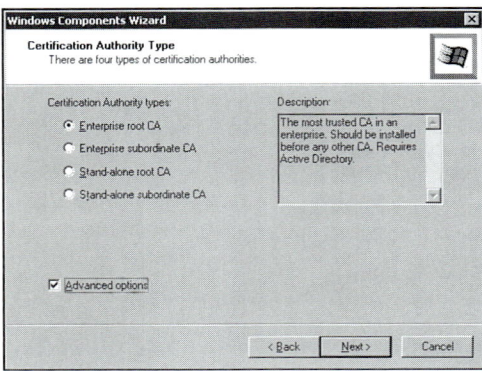

5. On the Public and Private Key Pair dialog, select the desired key length from the drop-down list (see Figure 11.20); click Next.

Note

The CSP and Hash Algorithm allow you to further configure your CA based on specific requirements you have identified in your organization. For most configurations, the default values for CSP and Hash Algorithm are adequate. If you're using an existing key for your CA, the Use Existing Key option is available to enhance the flexibility of Certificate Services.

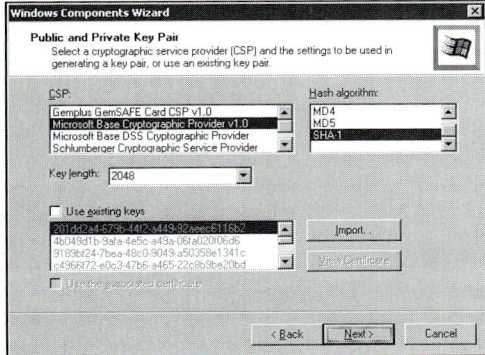

Figure 11.20
Select a key length through the (Advanced Options) Public and Private Key Pair dialog.

6. Enter your CA identifying information in the CA Identifying Information dialog (see Figure 11.21) and click Next.

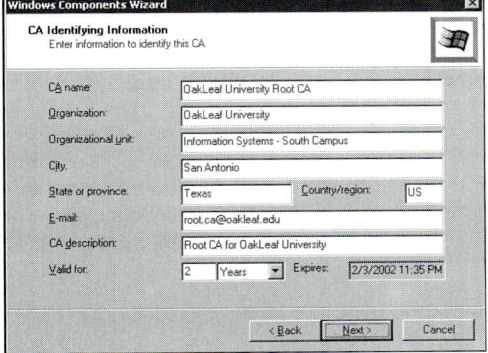

Figure 11.21
Identifying information for every certificate issued by your CA is entered in the CA Identifying Information dialog.

7. On the Data Storage location dialog, verify the correct installation paths of the CA database and log. You may choose to change the location of the data storage. Select Next to continue.

8. Immediately after you select Next, you're prompted with a warning message about stopping Internet Information Services. Click OK to continue. Once the installation is complete, Internet Information Services is restarted.

9. The installation process copies all required files to your system. Once the installation process concludes, select Finish to complete your installation. At the Add/Remove Programs dialog, select Close.

Tip from
RJ

If you installed an Enterprise CA, it's automatically added to the Trusted Root Certification Authorities of your domain Group Policy.

USING THE CERTIFICATION AUTHORITY MMC SNAP-IN

After the installation of Certificate Services is completed, a new MMC snap-in, Certification Authority, is available from the Administrative Tools menu. This snap-in allows you to configure and administer your CA. The following operations are available from the Certification Authority snap-in:

- *View Certificate Information*—The Certificate Authority snap-in allows you to view information about the certificates in your CA database such as revoked certificates, issued certificates, pending requests, and failed requests.

- *Approve Certificate Requests*—If you installed your CA as a Standalone CA or changed a policy so that certificate requests are not automatically approved, you may need to approve certificate requests.

- *Revoke Certificates*—When security is compromised, you may want to revoke a previously issued certificate. The Certification Authority snap-in enables you to revoke issued certificates and create certificate revocation lists (CRLs). A CRL is a list of certificates that have been revoked for some reason or another due to compromised security situations. When a system or user uses a certificate, it first checks the CRL to see if the certificate has been revoked.

Note

CAs can revoke certificates in a number of different ways. For example, a CA may revoke individual certificate or a node of a subordinate CA. If a CA revokes a node of a subordinate CA, all certificates issued by the subordinate are revoked.

- *CA Policy Settings*—If your CA was installed as an Enterprise CA, you can view and modify the list of certificates issued by your CA. You may choose to implement your CA hierarchy to issue different types of certificates based on the CA. For example, a CA could be configured to only issue Code Signing certificates.

- *Define Exit and Policy Modules*—Policy modules are used to define how certificate requests should be processed, such as automatically approving, denying, or pending certificate requests. Policy modules also indicate where users can find certificate revocation lists and where they can obtain the certificate information for the CA. Exit modules are used to add additional processing of certificates once the request is approved, such as publishing the certificate to the file system or Active Directory.

- *Backup and Restore the CA*—Windows 2000 CAs have their own backup and restore processes. These processes can be used to back up or restore the CA from a local directory or shared directory on the network. While this functionality is provided with the Certification Authority snap-in, you should only use it if you want to back up the CA to a particular location on the file system. For normal backup operations, the Windows 2000 backup program is adequate.

ESTABLISHING AND MANAGING CERTIFICATE AUTHORITY SERVERS | 511

> **Note**
> This chapter focuses on viewing the certificate information and revoking certificates of an Enterprise CA. For more information on Certificate Services, refer to "Certificate Services" in the Windows 2000 documentation.

The task of implementing an Enterprise CA for your organization is simplified by integration with Active Directory. Once installed, all certificate requests are automatically approved and most cryptography functions in your organization should be functional. Nearly all administration of the CA revolves around viewing certificate information for your users and revoking certificates.

VIEWING CERTIFICATE INFORMATION USING THE MMC SNAP-IN

Viewing certificates can be useful in evaluating different attributes of the certificate such as root CA, expiration date, and public key. To view certificate information using the MMC snap-in, follow these steps:

1. Open the Certification Authority MMC snap-in from the Administrative Tools folder.
2. Expand the *ServerName* certificate authority to view CA certificate information (see Figure 11.22).

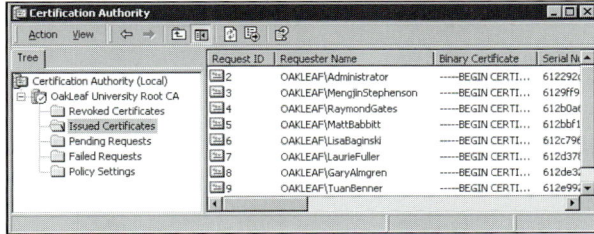

Figure 11.22
The Certification Authority Snap-In is used to administer certificates issued by your CA.

3. Select the certificates you want to view—Revoked Certificates, Issued Certificates, Pending Requests, or Failed Requests.
4. On the details pane, right-click a certificate and select Open to open the Certificate dialog (see Figure 11.23).

Figure 11.23
The Certificate dialog allows you to view information about certificates issued by your CA.

Revoking Certificates Using the MMC Snap-In

Part of the administration of your CA is revoking certificates. Certificates occasionally need to be revoked if security is compromised within your organization. When you revoke a certificate, it is no longer available for use and is published to the CRL.

To revoke certificates, follow these steps:

1. Open the Certification Authority MMC snap-in and navigate to the Issued Certificates Folder.
2. Right-click the certificate you want to revoke and select All Tasks, Revoke Certificate to open the Certificate Revocation dialog (see Figure 11.24).

Figure 11.24
Reasons for revoking certificates can be selected in the Certificate Revocation dialog.

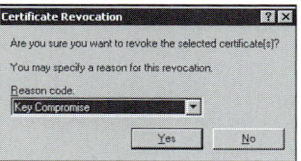

3. Select a reason code for revoking the certificate from the Reason Code drop-down list and then select Yes.

Working with User Certificates

Digital Certificates are used to verify the authenticity of encryption keys. While Windows 2000 provides built-in (digital) certificates for Encrypting File System, Encrypted File Recovery, and IP Security, certificates can also be requested from a Certificate Authority. Windows 2000 provides an interface for users to manage their existing certificates and request new certificates.

The Certificates MMC Snap-In is a new feature in Windows 2000 that allows users to manage their personal certificates and trusted Certificate Authorities. With the Certificates snap-in, users can request certificates for a variety of uses such as Encrypting File System, Secure Email, Code Signing, and File Recovery. The Certificates snap-in also provides users with the ability to import certificates for Trusted Root Certificate Authorities, Intermediate Certificate Authorities, and Active Directory User Object Certificates.

Configuring the Certificates Snap-In

To access and configure the Certificates snap-in, follow these steps:

1. From the Start menu, select Run to initialize the Run dialog.
2. At the Run dialog, enter **mmc.exe** in the Open field and click OK to open the Microsoft Management Console with a blank console root.
3. From the Console menu, select Add/Remove Snap-in. This initializes the Add/Remove Snap-in dialog.
4. In the Add/Remove Snap-in dialog, select Add to display a list of available snap-in modules in the Add Standalone Snap-in dialog.
5. In the Add Standalone Snap-in dialog, select Certificates from the snap-in list and click Add to initialize the Certificates snap-in configuration dialog.
6. Select the My User Account option and click Finish. This will add the Certificates snap-in to the Standalone snap-in page.
7. Close the Add Standalone Snap-in dialog by selecting Close, and click OK on the Add/Remove Snap-in dialog.

The Certificates snap-in allows users to access their personal certificates from an MMC interface. Certificates are stored on the local computer of the user's workstation or in Active Directory. To obtain a certificate, the user must have access to a certificate authority. Using the Certificates snap-in, users can request and install certificates.

Tip from
RJ

Certificates installed on the local computer are stored in the Certificate Store. The Certificate Store is located in Applications and Settings*UserName*\\Microsoft\\Application Data\\Certificates\\My.

Requesting a Certificate

During the request process, the user specifies the type of certificate requested. The certificate type, also known as the Certificate Template, defines the usage of a certificate. The user also can specify special attributes of the certificate such as Friendly Name and Description. These attributes are included in the request and as part of the issued certificate. After a request is approved, the certificate is sent back to the user.

To request a certificate for Encrypting File System, follow these steps:

1. Open the Certificates snap-in, and then open the Certificates - Current User, Personal, Certificates node, shown in Figure 11.25.

Figure 11.25
The Certificates snap-in allows you to administer certificates installed with your account.

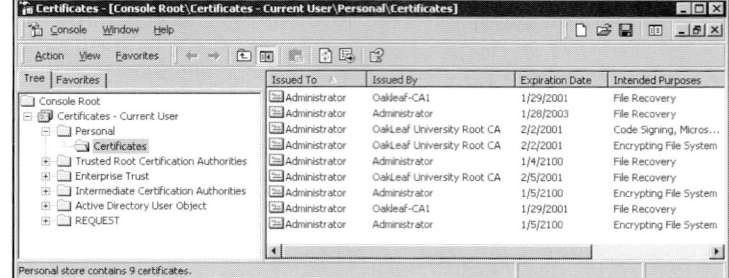

2. Right-click the Certificates node and select All Tasks, Request New Certificate to initialize the Certificate Request Wizard; click Next to begin the request.
3. At the Certificate Template dialog, select the type of certificate you want to request from the list of available templates (see Figure 11.26); select Next.

Figure 11.26
The Certificate Template dialog in the Certificate Request Wizard allows you to select the type of certificate you want to request.

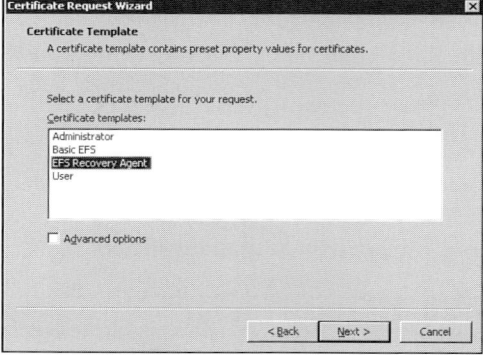

4. In the Certificate Friendly Name and Description dialog, enter a friendly name for the new certificate and a description; select Next to continue.
5. Verify that all the correct information is in the request list and select Finish to initialize the request with the Certificate Authority. If the request succeeds, a message indicating a successful request appears (see Figure 11.27).

Figure 11.27
The wizard displays a successful certificate request message.

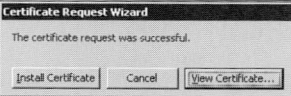

Troubleshooting | 515

6. Select Install Certificate to install the certificate into your Certificate store.

 If you encounter problems requesting certificates, see the "Certificate Authority Issues" topic of the next section.

Users can request many different types of certificates. The valid certificate templates are determined by the certificate templates offered by a certification authority.

Tip from *RJ*	When requested certificates are approved, a 10-minute window is added to the Valid to and Valid from fields of the certificate to consider a time difference of the real-time clock between different computers.

Troubleshooting

Problems with Encrypting File System

You can't encrypt files using EFS.

If problems occur when trying to encrypt files using EFS, verify the file system is NTFS. EFS is only available on the NTFS file system. If the problem persists, verify the EDRP is configured with a valid recovery agent. An empty EDRP prevents users from encrypting files.

You can't access previously encrypted files with EFS.

Users may experience problems accessing files previously encrypted with EFS. If the user was logged on locally during the encryption process, the encrypted file was encrypted with his key pair from his local account. When a user logs on with his domain account, a different key pair is used. To resolve this problem, the user should log on locally and decrypt the file, then log on to the domain and encrypt the file with his domain key pair.

When Adding a Data Recovery Agent, the elected recovery user does not appear in the search results.

If the elected recovery agent does not have a certificate for file recovery or the certificate is not valid (expired or not yet active, for instance), the user doesn't appear when you browse the directory. To resolve this problem, ensure that the elected recovery agent has a valid certificate for file recovery.

IP Security Communication Problems

Clients can't communicate with servers using IPSec.

Clients that are not configured with the IP Security setting Client (Respond Only) cannot communicate with servers that are configured for Secure Server communication. If a server is configured with the IP Security option Secure Server, IP Security is required.

Certificate Authority Issues

Failures occur using Certificate Services.

Fully-qualified domain names (FQDN) with more than 64 characters could prevent Enterprise Certificate Authorities from functioning. To resolve this problem, ensure that the FQDN is less than 64 characters.

You can't find a Certification Authority that can process your request.

If users cannot find a Certification Authority that can process requests, either the Certificate Services are not installed and configured or your certificate authority is not in the Trusted Domain Certificate Authorities list. To resolve this problem, verify that Certificate Services have been installed and an Enterprise Root CA exists.

You can't request EFS Recovery Certificates.

EFS Recovery Certificates are only available to users with membership in the Domain Admins global group. Ensure the recovery agent is in the Domain Admins group and request the EFS Recovery Certificate.

MCSE Corner: Setting Up Key- and Certificate-Based Security

The use of symmetric and asymmetric keys and third-party certificates has become an important part of many security models. Key and certificate security is tested on three exams: 70-215 Installing, Configuring, and Administering Microsoft Windows 2000 Server; 70-216 Implementing and Administering a Microsoft Windows 2000 Network Infrastructure; and 70-220 Designing Security for a Microsoft Windows 2000 Network.

70-215 Installing, Configuring, and Administering Microsoft Windows 2000 Server

The required knowledge for this exam from Chapter 11 is the use of the Encrypting File System (EFS) for encrypting data on the hard disk of a system. First of all, you should know what the EFS is and how it works. You should also be familiar with the different methods of encrypting data using EFS, such as use of Windows Explorer and the Cipher command.

70-216 Implementing and Administering a Microsoft Windows 2000 Network Infrastructure

The first topic covered on the blueprint for exam 70-216 is IPSec. You need to be able to enable IPSec and configure it for both transport mode and tunneling mode. You should also be familiar with IPSec policies and rules and managing and monitoring IPSec. Lastly, you should be familiar with troubleshooting IPSec connections.

The use of Certificate Services also is tested on this exam. You need to be able to install and configure the Certificate Authority, and create, issue, and revoke certificates. You must also be able to troubleshoot Certificate Services.

Finally, familiarity with EFS is important for this exam. The only explicit topic related to EFS on this exam, however, is the use of EFS recovery keys.

70-220   Designing Security for a Microsoft Windows 2000 Network

Exam 70-220 tests your ability to design an overall security strategy for a network. You must be familiar with EFS for this exam, and have the ability to design a strategy for the use of EFS as a security method.

Designing authentication methods is also tested on this exam. You need to be familiar with the different types of authentication and encryption, including symmetric and asymmetric keys and certificates. By assessing a network and its requirements, you should be able to recommend the best authentication strategy.

You should be familiar with public key infrastructure and Certificate Services. You need to be able to design a Certificate Authority structure and Certificate Server roles. You should also be able to manage certificates and be familiar with integrating third-party certificate authorities.

Finally, you should be familiar enough with IPSec to design an IPSec strategy for a network. You should be able to design an IPSec encryption scheme, management strategy, and negotiation and security policies. You should also be able to design IP filters and security levels.

CHAPTER 12

INTEROPERATING WITH NETWARE SERVERS

In this chapter

Introducing NetWare   520

Comparison of Protocols   521

Comparing NetWare and Windows 2000   522

Integrating Windows 2000 Server into a Predominantly NetWare Environment   524

Integrating NetWare Server into a Predominantly Windows Environment   529

Directory Synchronization   534

Troubleshooting   542

MCSE Corner: Interoperating with NetWare Servers   544

Introducing NetWare

If you manage a network environment that contains only one network operating system, you're one of the lucky few. You have only one set of tools, protocols, and server problems, and you're the envy of network administrators everywhere. If that one network operating system (NOS) happens to be Windows NT or Windows 2000, this chapter is not for you.

Most of you, however, administer heterogeneous environments with two or three different network operating systems. NetWare, UNIX, Linux, and OS/2 are only some of the other NOSs that may abound in your network. UNIX is covered in Chapter 13, "Integrating UNIX and Linux Networks," and OS/2 is slowly disappearing; so this chapter strives to help you understand how to integrate *NetWare* and Windows 2000. This chapter gives you a brief history of NetWare, compares NetWare and Windows 2000, and shows you the tools you need to manage a mixed environment.

When the computing world swung over to the client/server model, Novell was a pioneering leader. NetWare, its flagship product, ushered in the dawn of the Local Area Network (LAN) revolution. Companies quickly saw the benefit of a network operating system that would allow their new personal computers to communicate and share data. Built on the technology of ShareNet, Advanced NetWare, and SFT NetWare, NetWare became the de facto standard for corporate LANs. The fact that some companies still have NetWare 3.11 and 3.12 servers running in their environments testifies to the enormous popularity of the 3.x line in the early 1990s.

> **Note**
> NetWare 3.11 and 3.12 won't be around for long. Administrators will be forced to upgrade to NetWare 3.2 or higher to avoid Y2K problems with NetWare 3.1x.

In 1994, Novell again became a pioneer in the computer industry with the introduction of Novell Directory Services (NDS). The 4.x version line brought the first extensible directory for network administration. NDS allowed administrators to easily move users, add new servers, and manage large, complex networks—all of which were the bane of the administrator's existence with NetWare 3.x.

Novell continued its popularity by releasing NetWare 5.0 in the autumn of 1998. NetWare's latest incarnation offered IP-only environments, a built-in Java Virtual Machine, and, of course, an improved Novell Directory Services. NetWare was—and continues to be—the vehicle for Novell's success.

Table 12.1 compares the various NetWare versions and the features introduced in each.

Table 12.1 NetWare Versions and Features

NetWare Version	Protocols Used	Features Introduced to NetWare Line
2.x	IPX/SPX	16-bit NOS Introduced the Transaction Tracking System (TTS), which logged server operations and re-created events in the event of server failure Fault tolerance with disk mirroring and duplexing
3.x	IPX/SPX, TCP/IP	32-bit NOS NetWare Loadable Modules (NLMs) to allow software add-ons Support for TCP/IP; however, server and client communication remained entrenched in IPX Support for DOS and OS/2 Enhanced server management tools
4.x	IPX/SPX, TCP/IP	Novell Directory Services Scalable server able to handle from 5 to 1,000 workstations per server Support for TCP/IP; however, server and client communication remained entrenched in IPX/SPX communication Macintosh support Graphical administration utilities Disk compression Enhanced network security Built-in support for CD-ROM drives Foreign language support
5.x	IPX/SPX, TCP/IP	Support for TCP/IP-only environment Built-in Java Virtual Machine to allow running Java-based programs LDAP-compliant NDS Oracle 8 Database Engine Netscape's FastTrack Web Server ZENWorks Desktop Management Suite

Comparison of Protocols

Until the late 1990s, the integration of different network operating systems meant the administration of different network protocols. Thankfully, today most NOSs have migrated to TCP/IP as a standard. Although this should eliminate the need for other protocols, most NetWare versions are still grounded in using IPX/SPX for critical NOS communication. Unless you've upgraded to NetWare 5 or above, you must still plan your NetWare integration with the IPX/SPX protocol suite in mind. Table 12.2 is a brief comparison between the two protocol suites.

Table 12.2 TCP/IP and IPX/SPX Comparison

	TCP/IP	IPX/SPX
Origin	Created by the Department of Defense to allow government systems to easily communicate.	Developed by Novell; based on Xerox's Xerox Network Systems (XNS) and Sequenced Packet Protocol (SPP) protocols.
Most popular use	All systems connected to the Internet use TCP/IP to communicate; most NOSs also use TCP/IP for LAN communication.	Until NetWare 5, served as native protocol for NetWare NOS communication; previous versions of NetWare even routed TCP/IP over IPX/SPX.
Primary function	TCP is responsible for establishing communication between systems; IP is responsible for transferring data.	SPX is responsible for establishing communication between systems; IPX is responsible for transferring data.
Open System Interconnection (OSI) Model classification	TCP falls into the Transport layer, and IP lies in the Network layer.	Neither IPX nor SPX fit neatly into the OSI layers; however, both fall into the Transport and Network layers.

Comparing NetWare and Windows 2000

Despite the rhetoric from Novell and Microsoft, both NetWare and Windows 2000 have a place in the NOS marketplace. NetWare used to rule the file and print services domain, and Windows NT dominated the application server market. For the most part, that statement still holds true. However, both Novell and Microsoft are in a race to gain market share. NetWare 5.x was built with features to allow it to serve as an application server, and Windows 2000's Encrypting File System and Active Directory make it more palatable as a file and print server. To avoid the propaganda, it's important to see the pros and cons of each operating system to understand how each can work for you (as shown in Table 12.3).

Table 12.3 NetWare and Windows 2000 Comparison

Features	NetWare	Windows 2000
Centralized directory services	Novell Directory Services is a mature DS that has proven its worth in the marketplace and corporate environments.	Although relatively new, Active Directory promises to deliver a single-sign-on technology across Microsoft applications (for example, SQL Server, Exchange, Windows authentication, and so forth).

Features	NetWare	Windows 2000
Application serving	Still relatively immature in serving applications, NetWare 5.x can run Java applications on its Java Virtual Machine. Netscape FastTrack Server and Oracle 8 have been included with NOS.	Windows NT built its NOS empire on serving applications. Microsoft Windows NT and BackOffice Suite have propelled Microsoft's success in the NOS market. Windows 2000 continues the application-serving tradition with new features.
File and Print services	Originally, NetWare could run few programs and could not act as a workstation. This simplicity and focus allowed the server to be placed in a corner without attention from administrators. Later versions have complicated this vision, but have not distracted NetWare from its core competency of file and print services.	Lacking the centralized administration, Windows NT lagged behind NetWare 4.x in file and print services. Windows 2000 remedies those problems with Active Directory and seeks to offer the benefits of NetWare 4.x to a homogeneous Windows environment.
Third-party application development	Until now, NetWare was rarely the platform of choice for software developers. With NetWare 5.x and its JVM, Novell should see more takers in developing software for the NetWare platform.	With its marketplace domination, Windows has always been a magnet for third-party application developers. Even in Beta, Windows 2000 has garnered the attention and software development efforts of most major software companies.
Desktop administration	The inclusion of ZENWorks allows administrators to track asset information, remotely control workstations, and remotely deliver software.	Although it's not free, Systems Management Server also allows asset tracking, remote control, software distribution, network monitoring, and software metering. The inclusion of Terminal Services in Windows 2000 also allows remote administration of workstations.

Integrating Windows 2000 Server into a Predominantly NetWare Environment

There are many challenges involved in bringing a new network operating system into your environment. You have to ensure that all the appropriate users can connect to this new server and have the proper network client software. This section is designed to help those of you that would like to integrate a Windows 2000 server in an environment that has NetWare servers and users who authenticate only through NetWare.

> **Note**
> This chapter employs examples to demonstrate the real-world applications of Windows 2000 and NetWare integration and shows you the how and when of using Microsoft's integration utilities.

When integrating Windows 2000 into an existing NetWare environment, there are several items to plan and consider. As an example, you are a network administrator of one of Oakleaf University's Business computing labs (Lab 024). The lab contains 100 workstations running Windows 9x, the IPX protocol, and Novell's NetWare client for Windows 9x. You have one NetWare 4.11 server (OAKLEAF_NWFPS1) to perform authentication and provide NDS services to all the lab's workstations. The NetWare server, however, is at full capacity and unable to store additional data.

In an effort to cut costs and keep the number of servers low, the IS department has decided to share disk space on a Windows 2000 server running in Lab 015. Users from Lab 024 will still authenticate to OAKLEAF_NWFPS1; however, they will also be able to share files and printers from the Windows 2000 server (OAKLEAF-DC1) in Lab 015. You have been directed to ensure that all Lab 024's workstations can log on to OAKLEAF-DC1 and share files on this new Windows 2000 server.

Installing IPX

For those NetWare environments using only IPX for client-to-server communication, Windows 2000 server can integrate seamlessly by communicating via IPX. This seamless integration allows clients to connect to shares and printers and even use Windows 2000 as an application server (provided that the application running on the Windows 2000 server can also communicate via IPX). As with Windows NT, you must install the NWLink protocol in order to modify your Windows 2000 server to communicate via IPX. NWLink is Microsoft's own implementation of the IPX/SPX protocol.

For your computing lab, IPX provides the necessary glue to allow communication from the Windows 9x workstations to the NetWare 4.11 server. For the purposes of this example, the addition of NWLink on the Windows 2000 server enables clients to communicate seamlessly to both Lab 024's NetWare 4.11 server and Lab 015's Windows 2000 server.

INTEGRATING WINDOWS 2000 SERVER INTO A PREDOMINANTLY NETWARE ENVIRONMENT | 525

Tip from	If you're running NetWare 5 in an IP-only environment and Novell's NetWare Client for
RJ	Windows 2000, you don't need IPX. The client lets you authenticate to both NDS and AD. If,
	however, you use Microsoft's NetWare client for Windows 2000, you must install IPX.
	Microsoft's implementation of the NetWare client still requires IPX to communicate.

To install IPX on the Windows 2000 server, follow these steps:

1. Right-click the My Network Places icon and choose Properties to open the Network and Dial-up Connections window.
2. Right-click Local Area Connection and click Properties to open the Local Area Connection Properties dialog, shown in Figure 12.1.

Figure 12.1
The General page of the Local Area Connection Properties dialog displays installed networking components and allows you to add new components.

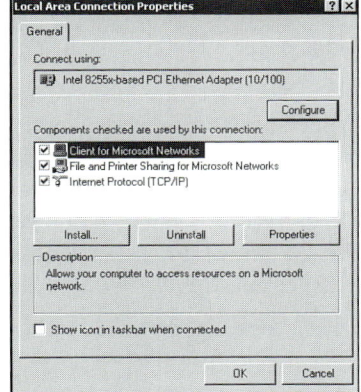

3. Click Install to open the Select Network Component Type dialog.
4. Select Protocol, as shown in Figure 12.2, and then click Add to open the Select Network Protocol dialog.

Figure 12.2
Select a category of Network Components available for installation.

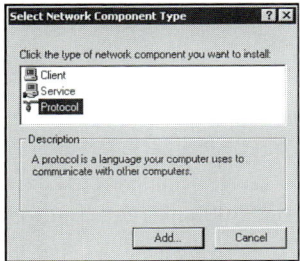

5. Select NWLink IPX/SPX/NetBIOS Compatible Transport Protocol, as shown in Figure 12.3, and then click OK; the installation of the IPX protocol on your server begins. There is no need to reboot the server after the installation completes.

PART
II
CH
12

Figure 12.3
By choosing Protocol from the Select Network Component Type dialog, you can choose a protocol from the list of protocols included with Windows 2000, or click Have Disk to install a third-party protocol.

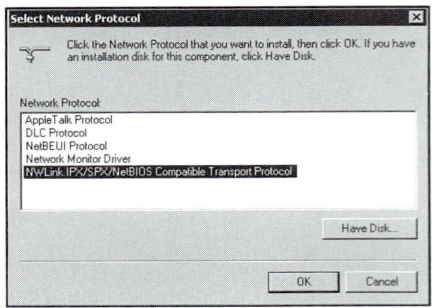

 If you have trouble using IPX to connect to NetWare server from Windows 2000, see "IPX Connection Problems" in the "Troubleshooting" section near the end of this chapter.

SHARING WINDOWS 2000 FILES AND PRINTERS

If your lab's workstations have only Novell's NetWare Client for Windows 9x installed, you have to install the Microsoft Client for Microsoft Networks to allow the workstations to access the Windows 2000 server. Without this client, the workstations will not be able to authenticate into the Windows domain and cannot access any Windows resources. Now that your clients can talk to the server via IPX and ask for authentication via the Microsoft client, the third step is to add user accounts to the Windows 2000 server. To keep life simple, make the user account names the same in both NDS and AD.

→ For more information on creating user accounts for Windows 2000, **see** "Adding Groups and Users," **p. 118**.

Tip from *RJ*	There are a couple of ways you can avoid having to maintain two sets of computer accounts. The first is to use Microsoft's Directory Synchronization tool. This utility allows you to automatically synchronize user accounts between NDS and Active Directory. (Read more about this tool later in this chapter.)
	The second way is to use Novell's NDS for NT product. This allows you to maintain computer accounts for Windows 2000 within the NDS tree. The benefit is that you have only one account per user to maintain, but the drawback is that NDS for NT is a rather pricey product.

As mentioned earlier, you can share files on a Windows 2000 server regardless of whether clients authenticate solely to NetWare. The good news is that clients can log in to NDS and still be able to access files on a Windows 2000 server. The bad news is that you have to have an additional Active Directory or local Windows 2000 user account to allow client access to files stored on the Windows 2000 server. So the fourth and final step is to allow the NetWare users to access resources on the Windows 2000 server.

Using the previous example, follow these steps to share a folder with the NetWare clients:

1. Create a share. In Figure 12.4, the Templates folder is shared to allow students and faculty access to common Oakleaf University Microsoft Word templates.

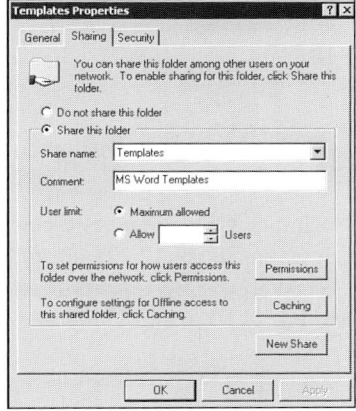

Figure 12.4
From the Sharing page of the Properties page for the Templates directory, you can share the folder with NetWare users.

2. Click the Permissions button in the Sharing page of the Templates Properties dialog to open the Permissions for Templates dialog, as shown in Figure 12.5. Assuming that you've created accounts to mimic the NDS accounts, you can assign rights to the share based on group membership. When you have finished assigning permissions, click OK.

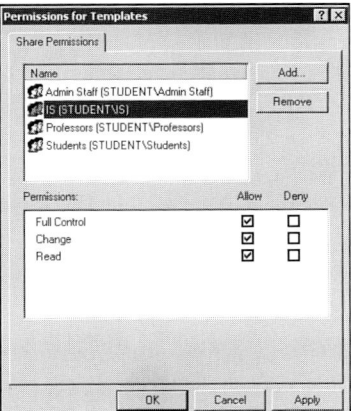

Figure 12.5
Assign the appropriate permissions to the Templates share.

3. From the NetWare client, you can test client connectivity by mapping a drive to the new share on OAKLEAF-DC1 through Windows Explorer (see Figure 12.6).

Figure 12.6
Clients see no difference between NetWare and Windows 2000 drives.

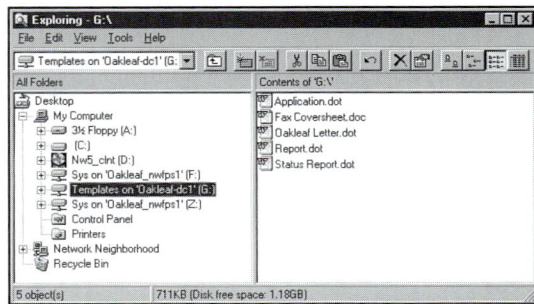

You can use the same procedure to share printers. Give the users access and share the printer with the proper permissions. As you can see in Figure 12.7, a printer connected to the Windows 2000 server is visible from the NetWare-connected workstation. For Windows 9x clients, you must install the printer drivers. For NT 4.0 and Windows 2000 workstations, the drivers install automatically with the printer.

Figure 12.7
A printer shared on a Windows 2000 server is visible from the workstation authenticated only to NetWare.

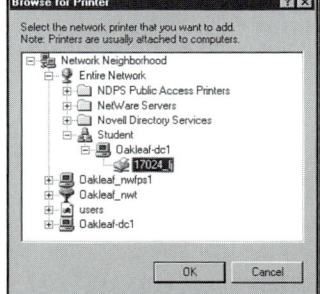

FILE AND PRINT SERVICES FOR NETWARE

Some NetWare environments have Microsoft's Client for NetWare Networks and Service for NetWare Directory Services instead of Novell's client. Unlike the example outlined earlier, these workstations aren't able to directly share files and printers.

> **Tip from**
> *RJ*
>
> Older versions of Windows 95 did not ship with the Service for NetWare Directory Services. For these workstations, you must download Msnds.exe from Microsoft's Web site at http://support.microsoft.com/download/support/mslfiles/MSNDS.EXE.

In these cases, Microsoft offers File and Print Services for NetWare (FPNW) to integrate the Windows 2000 server into the NetWare environment. FPNW offers the following features:

- Adds File and Print Services for NetWare to the Windows 2000 server (there is no need to install additional software on client workstations)
- Allows the Windows 2000 Server to appear as a NetWare server to clients
- Shares files and printers from the Windows 2000 server to Windows clients
- Allows clients to log in to NetWare only and still attain access to Windows 2000 resources

Integrating NetWare Server into a Predominantly Windows Environment

If your environment runs Windows 2000 Server with Windows 9x clients, your situation is the reverse of the one previously described. Your environment includes only Windows 2000 servers, and all workstations authenticate through Active Directory. However, for whatever reason, you want to integrate a new NetWare server into the computing environment. This section outlines the concepts and utilities you need to integrate a NetWare server into your Windows 2000 environment.

As stated previously, the situation is now reversed. You are the administrator of Lab 015. You currently administer a Windows 2000 server—OAKLEAF-DC1—and a number of Windows 9x clients. However, the IS department, in its fiscal conservatism, has decided to turn OAKLEAF-DC1 into a dedicated domain controller for most of the building. Instead of sharing files and printers, the server will provide domain authentication to two of the four labs within the Business School housed in Building 17.

You now must attach your Lab's Windows 9x clients to the NetWare server in Lab 024 to share files and printers. To accomplish this task, you could load a NetWare client on every workstation and give yourself several hours' or days' worth of work. Or with Microsoft's Gateway Services for NetWare, you can have a Windows 2000 server share NetWare resources to the Windows clients within a few minutes. No additional software is necessary on the client machines; the software is simply installed once on the Windows 2000 server.

Installing Gateway Services for NetWare (GSNW)

Gateway Services for NetWare is incredibly beneficial to administrators because it allows Windows clients to access NetWare directories. The Windows 2000 server connects to the NetWare server and reshares the directory via the standard Windows Share. The clients do not require additional clients or NWLink.

To install Gateway Services for NetWare, follow these steps:

1. Right-click the My Network Places icon, and choose Properties to open the Network and Dial-up Connections window.
2. Right-click Local Area Connection, and select Properties to open the Local Area Connection Properties dialog.

3. Click Install to open the Select Network Component Type dialog.
4. Select Client, and then click Add to open the Select Network Client dialog, as shown in Figure 12.8.

Figure 12.8
The Select Network Client dialog is displayed when you choose Clients from the Select Network Component Type dialog. The Gateway (and Client) Services for NetWare client is visible in this dialog.

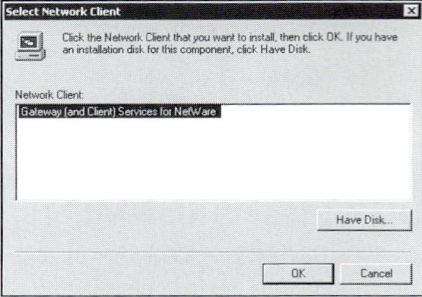

5. Choose Gateway (and Client) Services for NetWare and then click OK. This begins the installation of GSNW on your server.

> **Note**
> You might have noticed that the installation dialog lists Gateway (and Client) Services for NetWare. With Windows 2000 Server, Client Services for NetWare accompanies GSNW to allow the server itself to connect to the NetWare server. On workstations running Windows 2000 Professional, Client Services for NetWare is the only service installed.

6. After the installation is complete, the Select Netware Logon dialog prompts you for the server or NDS tree information (see Figure 12.9). Fill out the Preferred Server section for NetWare servers using Bindery services (NetWare 3.x servers). Enter the tree and context information if using NDS (NetWare 4.x servers and above). Click OK to complete the configuration. You may be required to reboot your server.

Figure 12.9
The Select NetWare Logon dialog enables the administrator to enter the proper NetWare authentication information.

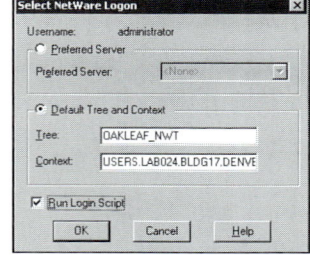

Using Gateway Services for NetWare

After the installation of Gateway Services, you must configure GSNW to connect to the NetWare server and enable Windows Shares of the NetWare directories or volumes.

INTEGRATING NETWARE SERVER INTO A PREDOMINANTLY WINDOWS ENVIRONMENT | 531

Before you set up the Windows 2000 Share, you must first create a user with the proper rights to log in to the NetWare server and a user group to control GSNW access to NetWare resources. To do this, follow these steps:

1. Log in as an NDS administrator and launch NetWare Administrator from a PC running the Novell client.

2. Right-click the context that you specified during step 7 of the GSNW installation, select Create, and click User; the New Object dialog opens (see Figure 12.10).

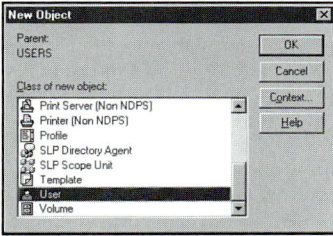

Figure 12.10
The New Object dialog enables administrators to create new objects within a NetWare NDS context.

3. Fill in the appropriate information for this user (see Figure 12.11). You probably won't want to use the standard template or create a home directory because this user simply will be acting as the Windows 2000's gateway account. All users will use this account to log in to the NetWare server, so all options and security settings that you choose apply globally to clients using GSNW.

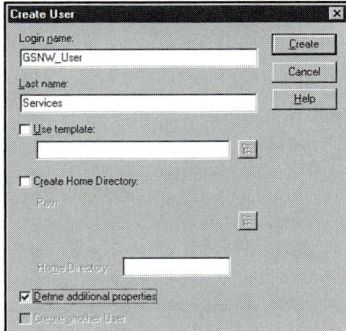

Figure 12.11
Selecting User from the New Object dialog brings up the Create User dialog from which you can create a new user within the NetWare NDS context.

> **Note**
> The gateway account for GSNW is a simple NetWare user account. The Windows 2000 server running GSNW logs into the NetWare server and accesses NetWare resources using this username and password. It allows a great number of Windows users to access NetWare resources without additional clients.

PART
II
CH
12

4. To create an NTGATEWAY group that controls appropriate access to the NetWare server, right-click again on the context where you'd like to create the group. (It does not have to reside in the same context as the gateway user account.) Select Create and click Group. Type **NTGATEWAY** as the group name and click Create.

5. After you've created the group, add the gateway user account to the group. Right-click the new NTGATEWAY group and select Properties. Click the Members tab and then click Add. Highlight the gateway users account (see Figure 12.12). Click OK to finish the configuration of the gateway user account and group.

Figure 12.12
The Group properties page for NTGATEWAY shows the gateway user account that has just been added.

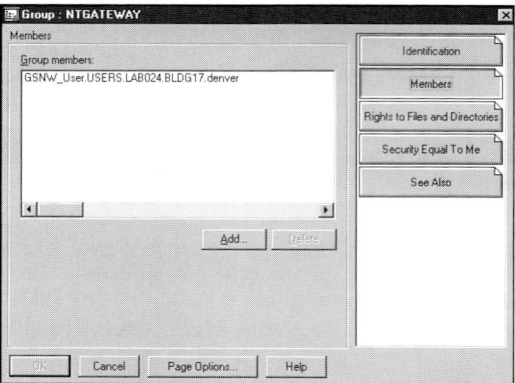

You use this NTGATEWAY group to control all permissions and security options. On the Windows 2000 server, administrators can use Share security to limit which Windows users have access to the GSNW gateway. With the NTGATEWAY group, the administrator can set trustee rights to the files and directories that users can access. You can further restrict security settings by setting permissions on the gateway user account.

Now that you've done the preparatory work on the NetWare server, you can configure GSNW on the Windows 2000 server—for example, to change the authentication properties, NDS context, server names, and other NetWare properties. To reconfigure GSNW, follow these steps:

1. Launch Control Panel from Windows 2000, and double-click the GSNW icon to open the Gateway Service for NetWare properties dialog, shown in Figure 12.13.

2. The GSNW dialog is similar to one you saw during installation. Figure 12.13 shows the variety of choices to allow you to change the GSNW authentication options. The Preferred Server section is for NetWare servers using Bindery or Bindery emulation. Check Default Tree and Context section for NDS servers. Print Options allows you to modify properties for print jobs submitted to a printer attached to the NetWare server. Login Script Options allows you to run the NetWare login script when logging on to the Windows 2000 server. You do not have to modify any of these options to start GSNW; this dialog simply allows you to modify these options if needed.

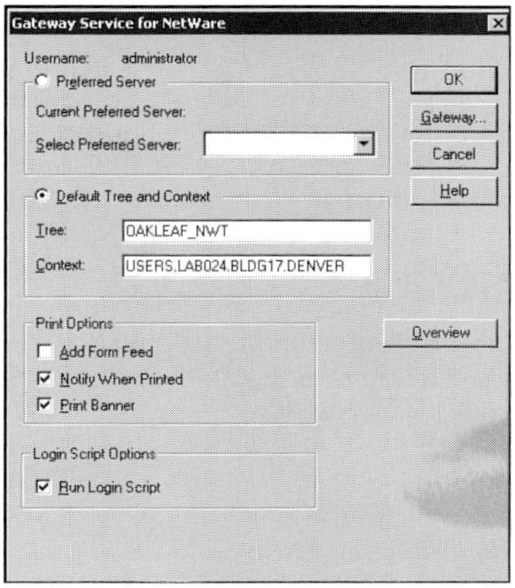

INTEGRATING NETWARE SERVER INTO A PREDOMINANTLY WINDOWS ENVIRONMENT | 533

Figure 12.13
The Gateway Service for NetWare control panel applet shows the configuration details for the service.

3. Click Gateway to configure the gateway user account and Windows Shares. Check Enable Gateway, and then enter the NDS gateway user account you created previously (see Figure 12.14). Type the password for the gateway user account in the Password text box and then retype in the Confirm Password text box to confirm.

Figure 12.14
From the Configure Gateway dialog, you provide the user account and password required to log in to the NetWare server.

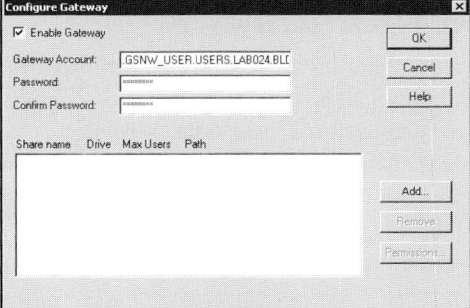

4. Click Add to open the New Share dialog (see Figure 12.15). This allows you to add Windows Shares that point to the NetWare server. Enter the appropriate path and share name for the data stored on the NetWare server. The drive mapping applies only to users that log on to the Windows 2000 server. Click OK.

Figure 12.15
From the New Share dialog, you can create a Windows 2000 share that points to a resource on the NetWare server.

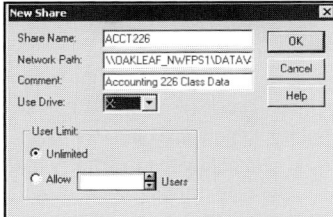

PART
II
CH
12

5. Click OK until you are out of the dialogs. The Share is now complete. Windows clients are now able to access data stored on the NetWare server without additional software!

As you can see from Figure 12.16, Windows clients can easily map drives via Windows Explorer to the Windows 2000 server and, in turn, share data on the NetWare server.

Figure 12.16
The newly mapped share originating from the NetWare server is visible in the Network Neighborhood in Windows Explorer.

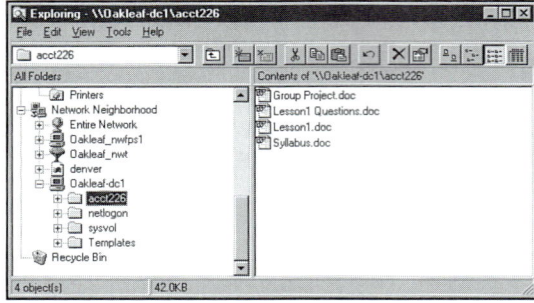

 If you can't get GSNW to connect to the destination NetWare server, see "Gateway Services for NetWare Problems," in the "Troubleshooting" section near the end of this chapter.

Directory Synchronization

So far, this chapter has covered integrating a NetWare server into a Windows 2000 environment and integrating a Windows 2000 server into a NetWare environment. Each section outlined the tools necessary to perform these tasks; however, there is one tool that does not fit cleanly into either section: Microsoft Directory Synchronization Services (MSDSS). This utility is another important tool in the arsenal of NetWare and Windows 2000 integration utilities. It can be used for integration of NetWare and Windows 2000 in a mixed environment or to help migrate from NetWare to Windows 2000. This is Microsoft's all-purpose NetWare integration tool.

Note

MSDSS is a component of the Microsoft Services for NetWare 5.0 add-on for Windows 2000 Server, which also includes the new Microsoft File Migration Utility (MSFMU) for NetWare. Microsoft announced on January 10, 2000, the addition of MSFMU, which is based on technology Microsoft licensed from FastLane Technologies Inc. MSFMU replaces Windows NT Server 4.0's Migration Tool for NetWare and the Directory Services Migration Tool that Microsoft included with early beta versions of Windows 2000 Server. Microsoft's Services for NetWare 5.0 press release promises availability "shortly after the launch of Windows 2000."

MSFMU, like the Migration Tool, is designed to simplify the tasks involved in a one-way migration from NetWare to Windows 2000 Server. MSFMU handles the migration of files from NetWare servers and maintains the original directory structure. MSFMU uses MSDSS to apply Windows 2000 security access settings as it migrates the NetWare files.

Directory Synchronization

> MSFMU is based on FastLane's DM/Consolidator for interserver data movement projects. FastLane also offers DM/Manager 5.0, which has a feature set similar to that of the Active Directory Migration Tool (ADMT) described in Chapters 5, "Choosing and Testing Migration Strategies," and 8, "Deploying Windows 2000 Production Servers." You can learn more about FastLane's utilities for Windows 2000 migration and management at http://www.fastlane.com/.

→ To review the use of ADMT to migrate domains from Windows NT to 2000, **see** "Emulating Domain Migration with the Active Directory Migration Tool," **p. 231**.

The main idea behind directory synchronization is that there is both a publisher and subscriber—as there is with Microsoft SQL Server 7+ and other products that offer replication features. The publisher pushes out data and the subscriber pulls in the publisher's data. The publisher can be considered the master data store and subscribers are the client data stores. This arrangement allows an administrator to automatically propagate changes from one directory to the other and ensure that all data remains accurate.

In the case of Microsoft Directory Synchronization Services, Active Directory is the publisher, and the NetWare Bindery or NDS is the subscriber. If the NetWare Bindery is the subscriber, MSDSS performs only one-way synchronization: Bindery to Active Directory. The tool cannot publish AD objects back to the Bindery. With NDS, however, you have the option of two-way synchronization. Active Directory pushes changes to NDS, and NDS can then push any changes back to AD.

There are several things to keep in mind when using Directory Synchronization Services:

- The tool can be used only to synchronize users, groups, and organizational unit changes between NDS and AD. Other objects are excluded from the synchronization process (for example, printers, print queues, templates, and so forth).
- Directory Synchronization can support only one-to-one relationships. You can't translate one NDS object into two AD objects.
- *Forward synchronization* refers to the process of propagating AD objects to NDS. *Reverse synchronization* pulls data from NDS (or NetWare Bindery) into Active Directory. As mentioned previously, only reverse synchronization is supported for NetWare 3.x servers.
- NetWare 4.x (and above) servers require a schema extension to allow the tool to assign a unique identifier to all objects that must be synchronized.

Installing Microsoft Directory Synchronization Services

You must install Directory Synchronization Services on a Windows 2000 Domain Controller. The DC must also have NWLink and Novell's Client for Windows 2000 installed. If your server meets these two requirements, use the following steps to install Directory Synchronization:

1. You must extend the AD schema to allow the inclusion of additional attributes in Active Directory. Before you do so, however, you must first ensure that you are a member of the Schema Admins group. Members of the Enterprise Admins group also are Schema Admins, so use your Enterprise Admins account.

2. Launch the command prompt and type **msiexec /a {drive}:{path}\dirsync.msi SCHEMAUPDATE=1**. This creates the necessary schema extensions.

3. From the Directory Synchronization CD, launch the setup program.

4. You are prompted with the usual Welcome, License Agreement, and Identification dialogs. Enter the appropriate information and click Next on each screen.

5. The Setup Type dialog prompts you for the type of installation you'd like to perform. For most administrators, the Typical setup should suffice. Check Typical and then click Next.

6. Click Next again to begin the installation.

7. After the installation has completed, click Next. You are then prompted to reboot. The Directory Synchronization takes effect when the server is restarted.

> **Tip from**
> *RJ*
>
> If you ever need to change the installation options that you chose for Directory Synchronization, simply rerun setup.

 If you have trouble installing Directory Synchronization, see "Directory Synchronization Problems," in the "Troubleshooting" section near the end of this chapter.

CREATING A SYNCHRONIZATION SESSION

The Directory Synchronization client is the utility you use to define synchronization sessions and perform the information exchange. You can install the client on any computer running Windows 2000; it doesn't have to run on a Domain Controller or member server.

To begin the synchronization, follow these steps:

1. Launch Directory Synchronization from the Administrative Tools Start Menu group.

2. Right-click Directory Synchronization, select All Tasks, and click New Session.

3. Click Next on the Welcome dialog; the New Session Wizard prompts you to select a directory to act as the master directory (see Figure 12.17).

4. With this dialog, you have the option of modifying only the subscriber. The publisher is always AD. For subscribers, you can choose Novell Bindery or Novell Directory Services. With NDS, you have the option of allowing two-way synchronization; Bindery allows only reverse synchronization. Click Next.

5. Choose the AD container to synchronize and the DC that will perform the synchronization, as shown in Figure 12.18. Click Next.

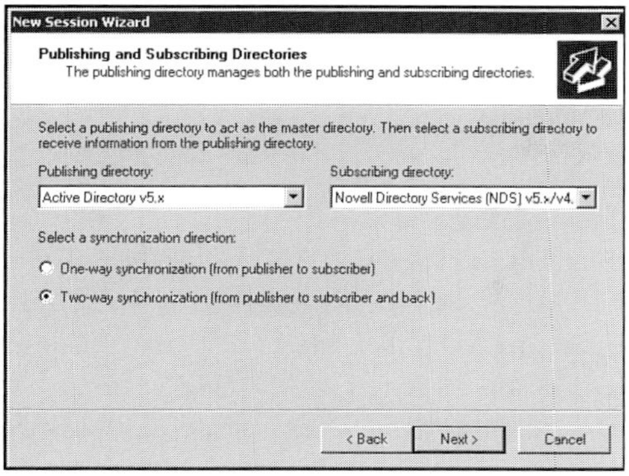

Directory Synchronization | 537

Figure 12.17
By using the New Session Wizard, you can configure the Publishing and Subscribing directories and direction for directory synchronization.

Figure 12.18
From the Container and Domain Controller dialog of the New Session Wizard, you can specify the AD container and Domain Controller for synchronization.

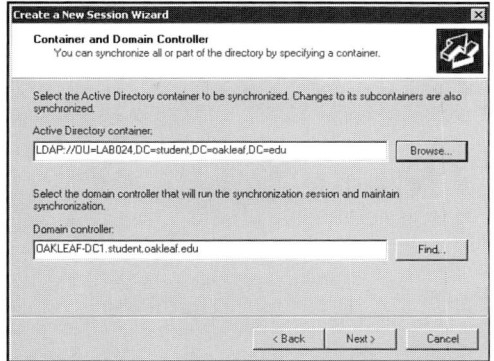

6. In the Subscribing Container screen, select the NDS context that you'd like to synchronize (see Figure 12.19). Also fill in the information for the administrative login. You must specify an account using the fully qualified NDS syntax (that is, Jdoe.Users.OU.O).

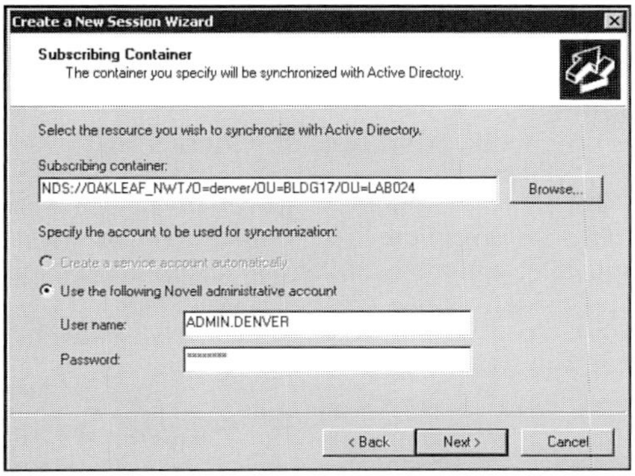

Figure 12.19
In the Subscribing Container dialog, you can set the NDS source context and administrative login for directory synchronization.

Part
II
Ch
12

> **Caution**
>
> You must use an account that has access to modify the schema of the source NDS context. Directory Synchronization modifies the schema so that NDS objects can be assigned unique identifiers used in the synchronization process.

7. The Initial Synchronization dialog, shown in Figure 12.20, allows you to perform an initial Reverse synchronization (NetWare to AD) before beginning the normal synchronization routine. For Bindery servers, the Reverse synch is the only method that allows you to import Novell objects to AD. Click the User Passwords button to set the policy for passwords when the users are migrated to AD. (For example, you can have all the passwords created to mimic the username after migration.) Click Next.

Figure 12.20
In the Initialization Synchronization dialog, select a one-time reverse synchronization to copy any data in the subscribing directory into the publishing directory, which is helpful for one-way synchronizations.

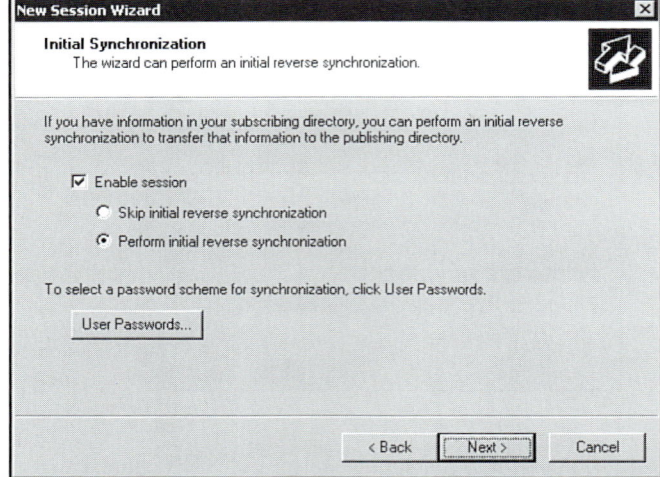

8. The Object Mapping Scheme is for those administrators that need to synch objects based on attributes other than username. For example, if you have one or two users that have different user accounts between AD and NDS, you can specify that specific mapping using the Custom Object Mapping. For most, the default name mapping should suffice. Click Next.
9. Choose a name for this synchronization session. Click Next.
10. The Synch tool then begins the initial reverse synchronization, as you specified in step 7. After the synchronization is complete, you should view the logs and determine whether any objects did not synch properly, as shown in Figure 12.21. Click OK.
11. After the initial synchronization is complete, you have finished the setup of the session. Click Finish.

Figure 12.21
Click Finish to dismiss the New Session Wizard.

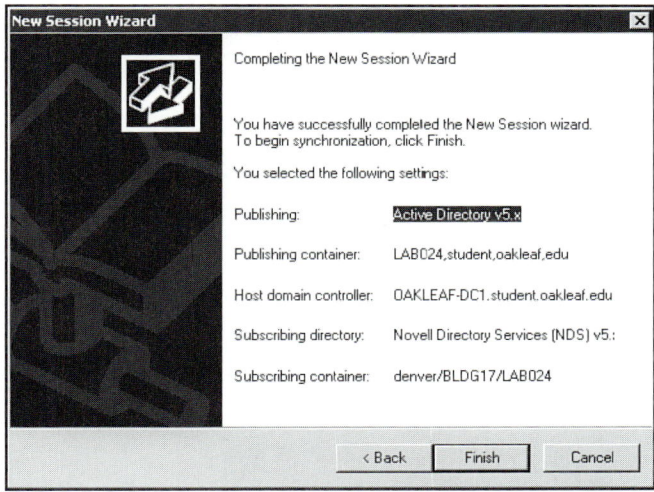

Performing the Synchronization

Now that you've created the session, it's time to use it. You can use this session to continually update both directory services. Directory Synchronization Services affords you two options to perform the actual synchronization: You can manually perform the synchronization, or you can schedule the synch to happen automatically.

For example, you can see in Figures 12.22 and 12.23 that Student01 exists in both AD and NDS. For this example, Student01 is manually removed from the NDS tree. You can then manually run Directory Synchronization Services to propagate changes to the Active Directory container.

Figure 12.22
This Active Directory Users and Computers snap-in view shows the Lab024 container prior to the removal of Student01.

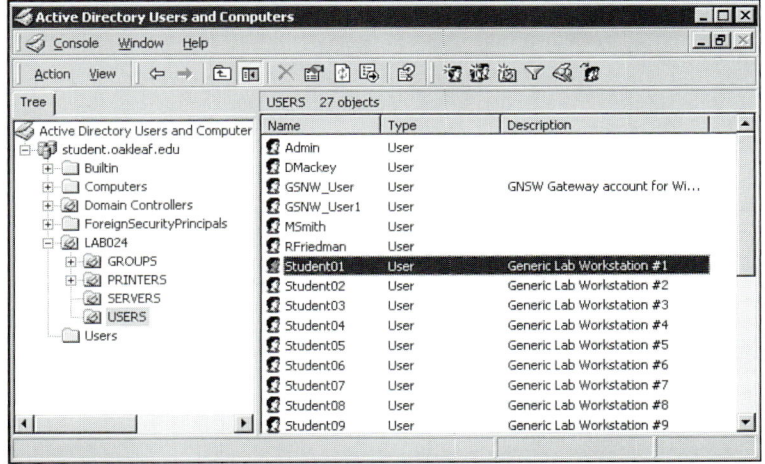

Figure 12.23
This NetWare Administrator view shows the Lab024 context before the removal of Student01.

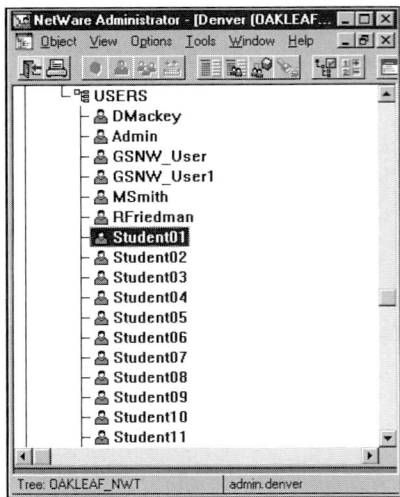

To perform a manual synch from NDS to AD (Reverse Synch):

1. Right-click the newly created session and choose Synchronize Publisher Changes. This begins the synchronization process. After the process is complete, click View Logs to view any errors or warnings.
2. After the synch is completed, notice that the user is now missing from AD (see Figure 12.24).

Figure 12.24
This view of the Active Directory Users and Computers snap-in shows the Lab024 container after Student01 was removed from NDS and the changes propagated through directory synchronization.

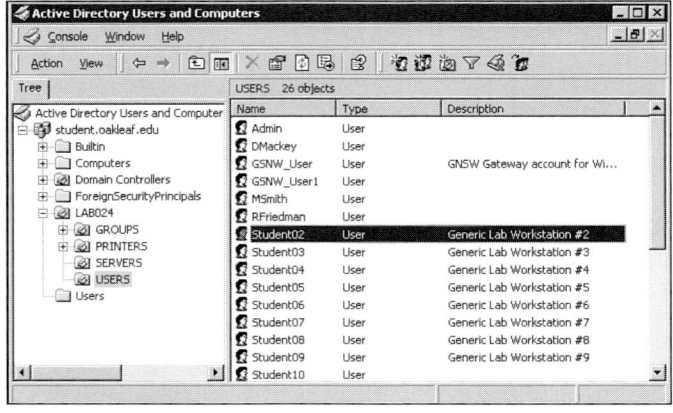

The following example outlines forward synchronization. To outline the process, Student02 and Student03 have been removed from Active Directory. To perform a manual synch from AD to NDS (Forward Synch):

1. Right-click the newly created session and choose Synchronize Subscriber Changes. This begins the synchronization process. After the process is complete, click View Logs to view any errors or warnings.
2. After the synch is completed, notice that the users are now missing from NDS (see Figure 12.25).

Figure 12.25
NetWare Administrator shows that the removal of Student02 and Student03 from AD has propagated to NDS.

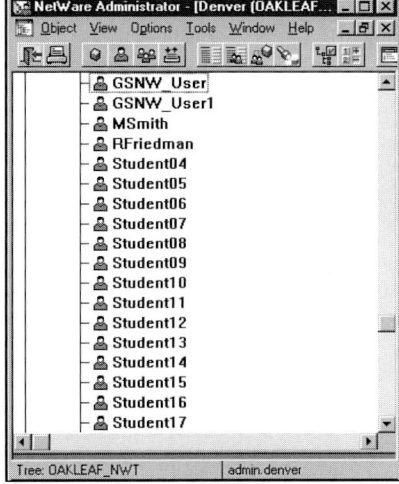

You can also schedule synchronization to take place automatically. To do so:

1. Right-click the session and click Properties.
2. Click the Settings tab (see Figure 12.26). To schedule forward synchronization, click Schedule under Active Directory v5.x to Novell Directory Services (NDS) v5.x/v4.x. To schedule reverse synchronization, click Schedule under Novell Directory Services (NDS) v5.x/v4.x to Active Directory v5.x.

Figure 12.26
The Settings page of the Properties page for the Lab024 container allows the configuration of synchronization session properties, such as schedules and filters.

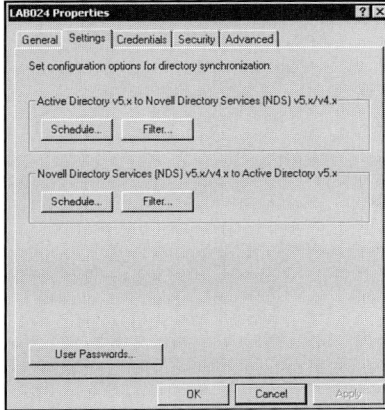

3. Select each time period by clicking an area and expanding the outlining area over the time boxes. Select the time block that you'd like to modify and click Synchronize or Don't Synchronize. For example, in Figure 12.27, the administrator setup synchronization takes place every day from 2 a.m. to 7 a.m. Click OK.

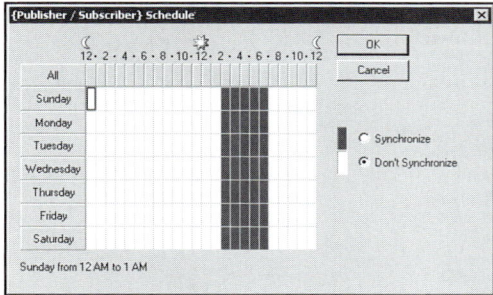

Figure 12.27
The Schedule dialog allows you to set an automated schedule for directory synchronization.

This completes the steps to schedule the synchronization process.

Note

If you selected scheduled synchronization, the Directory Synchronization utility checks for updates every 15 minutes.

Tip from
RJ

You can customize which objects are synchronized on an automated schedule. From the Synchronization Session Properties page, click the Settings tab. Click the Filter button and choose the objects you'd like to synchronize.

 If you can't get the two-way synchronization to perform correctly, see "Directory Synchronization Problems" in the following section of this chapter.

TROUBLESHOOTING

IPX CONNECTION PROBLEMS

You can't connect to NetWare Servers from Windows 2000 via IPX.

You might have to set the external or internal NetWare network number to ensure that other NetWare servers running IPX can identify the Windows 2000 server. To do so:

1. Launch Control Panel.
2. Double-click Network and Dial-Up Connections.
3. Right-click Local Area Connection and click Properties.
4. Select NWLink IPX/SPX/NetBIOS Compatible Transport Protocol and click Properties.

5. The internal network number is normally used only if GSNW is installed on the server. Modify this unique number to identify the Windows 2000 server to other NetWare servers. Otherwise, skip this step.

6. Check Manual Frame Type and click Add. Choose the IPX frame type and type the external network number. NetWare 3.x servers normally use the 802.3 frame type; 802.2 is used by NetWare 4.x and above. The external network number is a common number that NetWare servers use to communicate with other NetWare servers. Click OK.

7. Click OK to finish the modification.

GATEWAY SERVICES FOR NETWARE PROBLEMS

GSNW will not connect to the destination NetWare server.

When installing GSNW, you receive an error stating that the specified user does not exist.

To solve this problem, ensure that you entered the correct user, context, and NDS tree information in the GSNW Properties screen. If all information is correct, ensure that the user exists in the NDS tree and is a member of the NTGATEWAY group. The NTGATEWAY group must then also have access to the destination NetWare directory.

DIRECTORY SYNCHRONIZATION PROBLEMS

You can't install Directory Synchronization.

Because the Directory Synchronization installation modified Active Directory's Schema, you must log in with a user that is a member of the Schema Admins group.

You've set up Directory Synchronization to perform a two-way synchronization between AD and NDS; however, forward synch (AD to NDS) is the only option working.

The Directory Synchronization installation tries to modify the NDS tree's schema. If you've logged into the NDS tree without the proper administrative rights to modify the schema, the installation completes successfully; however, the two-way synch doesn't complete successfully.

You must extend the NDS schema manually. To do so:

1. Launch a Command Prompt.
2. From the \WINNT\SYSTEM32\DIRECTORY SYNCHRONIZATION\CLIENT directory, type **NDSEXT** using the following syntax:

    NDSEXT {EXTEND|CHECK} *Treename Username.Context {Password|*}*

    Use the **EXTEND** argument to Extend the Schema of the specified tree.

    Use the **CHECK** argument to check whether the specified tree has been extended already.

MCSE Corner: Interoperating with NetWare Servers

For exam 70-215, "Installing, Configuring and Administering a Microsoft Windows 2000 Server," you are required to know how to install and configure network services for interoperability.

The first thing to know for this exam is the difference in function between File and Print Services for NetWare and Gateway Services for NetWare and where each of them should be used. You should also be familiar with installing and configuring both of these services and installing the IPX protocol. In addition, you must know the process for troubleshooting IPX connections and Gateway Services for NetWare.

The final concept to be familiar with for this exam is upgrading a NetWare server to Windows 2000. This is not a concept explicitly specified on the exam blueprint, but it is important to know to increase your understanding of the subject. This leads us to the next two exams for which NetWare interoperation is important: 70-217, "Implementing and Administering a Microsoft Windows 2000 Directory Services Infrastructure," and 70-219, "Designing a Microsoft Windows 2000 Directory Services Infrastructure."

For the 70-217 exam, you should know the process of installing and using the Directory Service Migration tool, and installing and using directory synchronization. You should also be familiar with troubleshooting directory synchronization. For 70-219, you must have an understanding of how Active Directory and NetWare can coexist, mainly by using the Directory Synchronization tool.

Finally, 70-216, "Implementing and Administering a Microsoft Windows 2000 Network Infrastructure," requires that you know how to install the NWlink (IPX) protocol, and 70-221, "Designing a Microsoft Windows 2000 Network Infrastructure," requires you to be able to design a multiprotocol strategy, including using IPX with TCP/IP.

CHAPTER 13

INTEGRATING UNIX AND LINUX NETWORKS

In this chapter

Introducing UNIX Integration Methods   546

Using Telnet   546

Taking Advantage of X Window   556

Integrating Windows and UNIX Printers   558

Using the File Transfer Protocol   561

Running Microsoft Services for UNIX   563

Troubleshooting   580

MCSE Corner: Question Types, Part 1   581

Introducing UNIX Integration Methods

There are many different methods of integrating UNIX computers and networks into Windows 2000 networks. This chapter begins with the simplest methods, such as telnet, and ends with the more complex methods, including Microsoft Services for UNIX (SFU) 2.0.

The examples in this chapter use Windows 2000 Server as a Domain Controller (DC) and a RedHat 6.1 Linux server. The examples apply, with minor changes in a few cases, to any UNIX flavor or commercial Linux release. Your UNIX or Linux server should support a telnet client and server, a File Transfer Protocol (FTP) server, X Window client programs, Network File System (NFS) servers and clients, and Network Information Service (NIS).

Windows 2000, as shipped, offers basic UNIX integration in the form of command-line utilities—telnet and FTP. More sophisticated integration mechanisms that display graphical output of UNIX programs on a Windows 2000 machine or provide file sharing similar to Windows 2000 shares require third-party commercial or freeware programs. This chapter uses Hummingbird Ltd.'s Exceed for X Window integration and SFU 2.0 from Microsoft for NFS and Active Directory/NIS integration.

Using Telnet

The base level of command-line connectivity for UNIX systems is telnet. When no other mechanism for connectivity is available or working, telnet usually allows an administrator access to a remote machine. Although telnet is among the least-sophisticated methods for executing commands on a remote host, telnet almost always works. When you've logged on to the remote machine via telnet, you usually are able to execute other commands that provide a friendlier, more familiar user interface for remote host administration.

Telnet was one of the first networking methods on the UNIX scene. It came about from the need for users to be able to administer or access a remote host without having physical access to the host. Telnet, put simply, is a networking program and protocol that permits commands typed on a client machine to be executed on a remote computer; the text output of the command is then sent from the remote computer back to the client and displayed on the client computer. Technically, telnet combines a set of programs and a protocol.

The Telnet Client Program

Telnet is a program whose display appears to the user as if he or she is sitting in front of the remote computer's character-mode console. Telnet prompts you to type a command, you type a command and press Enter, and the remote computer sends you the output from the command followed by another prompt. Communication occurs at a character level, so users can run telnet on even "dumb" ASCII terminals.

THE TELNET SERVER PROGRAM

A telnet client accepts input from the user sitting at the keyboard and sends those keystrokes to a telnet server program running on the remote host. This server waits at a known TCP port on the remote computer (usually 23), accepts the input from the telnet client, passes it to the remote computer's operating system, and returns whatever output the operating system generates from the command to the client computer. UNIX telnet server processes are typically called *telnetd*, which stands for Telnet Daemon.

> **Note**
> Daemons in UNIX are quite similar to services in Windows 2000; the name is loosely based on the concept of a demon, which is behind the scenes and invisible.

THE TELNET PROTOCOL

Although the telnet protocol is not technically part of the TCP/IP protocol suite, telnet uses TCP/IP and has been around for so long that the protocol is considered part of the TCP/IP family. The telnet protocol is simply a set of conventions allowing two computers to pass requests and responses between a client and server machine. The protocol also supports basic command interchange between the two. The telnet protocol can be almost painful over very slow communication lines because the protocol is fairly simple; if a single character needs to go between client and server, an entire Ethernet frame, IP header, and TCP header is required in addition to the byte for the single character—a highly inefficient prospect.

WINDOWS 2000 TELNET CLIENT SUPPORT

Windows 2000 has two integrated telnet client programs: a command prompt–like telnet client harking back to the early UNIX days, and a new telnet client integrated with Windows 2000's HyperTerminal program.

USING THE COMMAND-LINE TELNET CLIENT

To start a telnet session on your Windows 2000 computer and list telnet's available commands, do the following:

1. Choose Start, Run, type **telnet** in the Open text box, and click OK to open the Command Prompt - telnet window.
2. Type ? at the Microsoft Telnet > command prompt to display the commands you can use (see Figure 13.1).

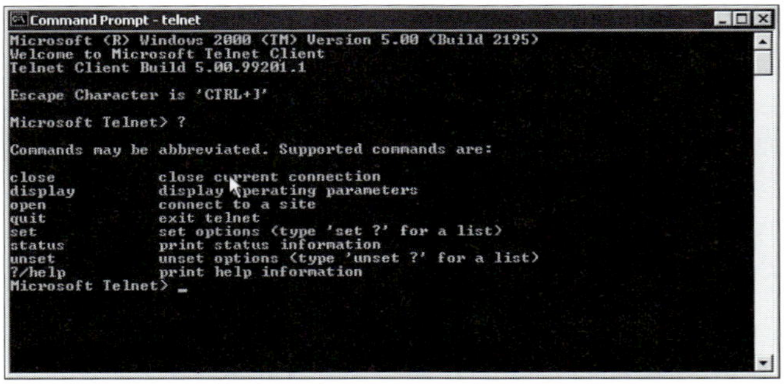

Figure 13.1
Typing **?** at the Windows 2000 telnet command line lists the supported commands.

When you have the telnet client program running, follow these steps to make a connection to a Linux, UNIX, or Windows 2000 host:

1. Type **open** at the telnet client program prompt and press Enter.
2. Type the IP address or the name of the Linux or UNIX host at the prompt (see Figure 13.2), and press Enter. If the remote host is accessible and its telnet server is running, the host sends a login: prompt.

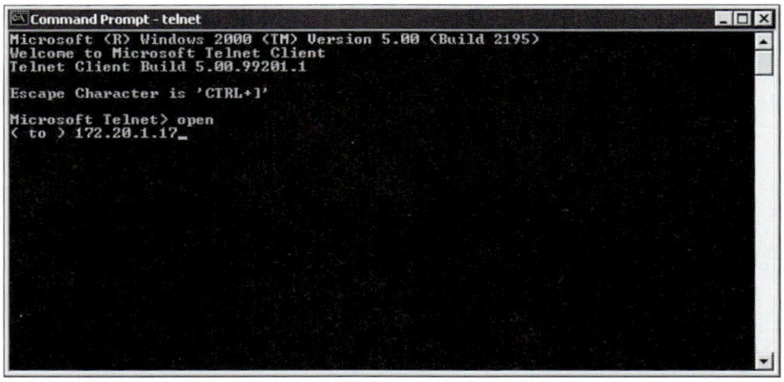

Figure 13.2
Type the IP address of the remote host at the (to) prompt of the open command to establish the initial connection to the machine.

3. Type your username for the remote host at the login: prompt and press Enter. Linux prompts you with a password: prompt; type your password and press Enter.

> **Note**
> The Linux server prompts you for your username and password on the Linux server; this distinction regarding username and password is important. The open standard version of telnet doesn't have a method of synchronizing user credentials on client and server computers.

4. A prompt appears telling you that you have logged in to a Linux server. Typing **pwd** places you in the home directory for username (see Figure 13.3). The pwd command in UNIX is short for Print Working Directory, and shows you where you are in the directory tree.

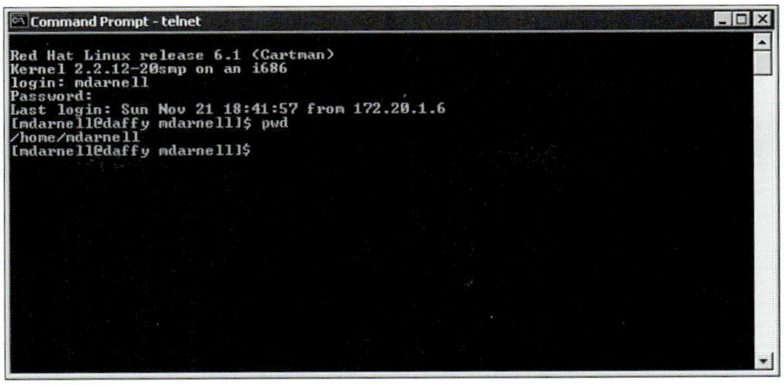

Figure 13.3
Typing **pwd** after connecting to the telnet server places you in the home directory for the username you specify—in this case, /home/mdarnell.

⚠ *If you encounter problems with connecting to a telnet server, see the "Telnet Problems" topic of the "Troubleshooting" section near the end of the chapter.*

The administration capabilities accessible at this point are almost unlimited, if you have administrative privileges on the remote computer. Telnet can be run from a client anywhere in the world to a server anywhere else in the world if the two computers are connected by a TCP/IP connection. The command-line version of the telnet client has ANSI terminal support, which means that UNIX programs, such as vi (visual, an early but very fast UNIX text editor), can be run from this telnet client.

TELNET MODES

Telnet effectively has two modes: connected and unconnected. Your telnet session is in unconnected mode when you have not connected to a telnet server; otherwise, you are in connected mode. Unless you provide an IP address or hostname on the telnet command line, telnet starts in unconnected mode. Telnet moves into connected mode when you actually establish a connection to another machine by entering the open command. For example, Figure 13.3 shows telnet in a connected mode, indicated by the Linux host having requested your *username* and password. When you are in connected mode, you return to unconnected mode in one of the following ways:

- You terminate your session on the remote host by typing an **exit** or **logout** command at the telnet prompt.
- The host disconnects you or the network connection breaks.

If you're in connected mode and want to enter a command to the telnet client instead of the server, hold the Ctrl key and press]. This combination maintains the connection to the remote computer but allows you to type commands to the telnet client program. After you've finished typing commands to the telnet client, you type **connect** to resume your connection to the remote computer.

The telnet client program accepts the commands shown in Table 13.1.

Table 13.1 Telnet Commands

Command	Description
Ctrl+]	Temporarily escapes from that host's command line and lets you type commands to your telnet client. (This command can be executed only when you're connected to another host.)
Close	Closes the connection to the currently connected host.
Display	Displays current options on your telnet client program, such as authentication types, terminal emulation preferences, and so on.
Open	Opens a connection to another host.
Quit	Exits the telnet client program.
Set	Allows you to set telnet client program options.
Status	Tells you whether you're connected or not. This command is useful if you can't remember whether you used Ctrl-] to escape a current connection.
Unset	Allows you to reverse options modified by the set command.
?/help	Displays a summary of client commands.

HyperTerminal's Telnet Client

In Windows 2000, Microsoft has packaged more sophisticated telnet capabilities integrated with HyperTerminal than were available in Windows NT.

> **Note**
> If you don't have HyperTerminal installed, use the Add/Remove Windows Components feature of Control Panels' Add/Remove Programs tool to install it. HyperTerminal is a member of the Accessories, Communications program group.

To access the telnet feature of HyperTerminal, follow these steps:

1. Choose Start, Programs, Accessories, Communications, HyperTerminal to launch the program and open the Connection Description dialog.

> **Note**
> If you haven't previously entered the telephone area code for the computer running HyperTerminal, a dialog opens that prompts you for the area code.

2. Type a descriptive name for the telnet session in the Name text box, and select one of the icons (see Figure 13.4). Click OK to close the dialog and open the Connect To dialog, which defaults to settings for a dial-up modem connection, if a modem is installed on the computer.

USING TELNET 551

Figure 13.4
Specify a name and choose an icon for the telnet session in HyperTerminal's New Connection dialog.

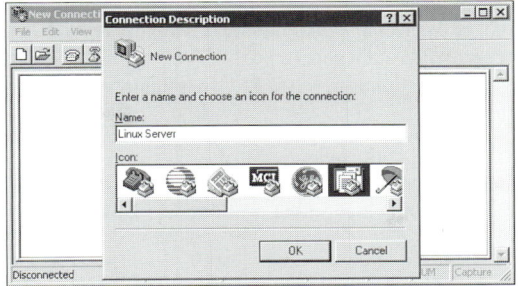

3. In the Connect To dialog, select TCP/IP (Winsock) in the Connect Using list to display Host Address and Port Number text boxes.

> **Note**
> If you don't have a modem installed in your computer, the TCP/IP (Winsock) option is the default connection method.

4. Type the host address (or hostname if you have a properly configured DNS server on your network) in the Host Address text box. Type **23** in the Port Number text box; 23 is the standard TCP port for telnet (see Figure 13.5).

Figure 13.5
Type the IP address or name of the remote host and specify **23** as the telnet port to establish a telnet connection.

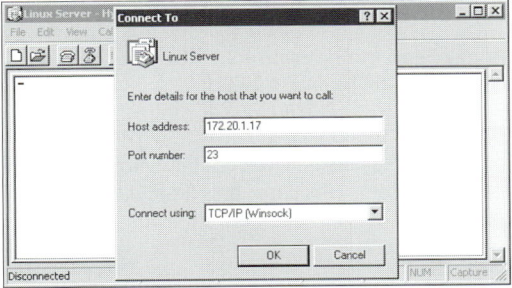

5. Click OK. If you entered the remote host's address correctly, and the host supports telnet, HyperTerminal's window appears, as shown in Figure 13.6.

Figure 13.6
HyperTerminal's window for a telnet session with a Red Hat Linux telnet server.

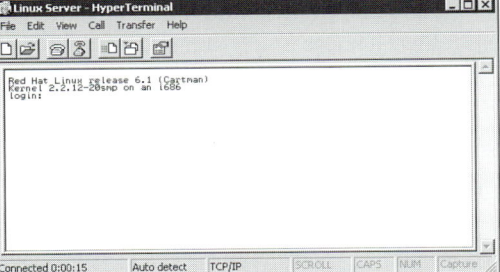

PART
II
CH
13

> **Note**
>
> If you attempt to connect to a Windows 2000 telnet server with default settings, you receive a "Server allows NTLM authentication only. Server has closed connection" message. You must change the telnet server's NTLM Registry settings with the Telnet Server Administration tool.

→ To change the Windows 2000 telnet server authentication method, **see** "Configuring the Telnet Server on Windows 2000 Server," **p. 554**.

6. Type your *username* followed by your password for the remote host, as you did to log on with the command-line version of telnet.

You're now logged on to the remote host and can perform any administrative or other operation authorized for your user account. When you complete the session, choose File, Save, and save your session as a HyperTerminal (.ht) file for future use.

> **Tip from**
> *RJ*
>
> A major benefit of HyperTerminal's telnet implementation is that you can send and receive text and binary files from your Windows 2000 machine to and from the UNIX host.

Telnet Advantages

Telnet sessions are useful for the following additional reasons:

- You can capture text files of session operations with many telnet programs, including HyperTerminal.

> **Tip from**
> *RJ*
>
> Don't rely on valid text capture until you test this function with a long, detailed session. The text capture feature of some telnet programs drops data because of buffer overflow on the receiving system.

- Telnet is supported by many operating systems and by many types of networking hardware, such as routers.
- Telnet is an excellent debugging tool for many UNIX-based services.

As a debugging example, assume you want to find out whether the Simple Mail Transfer Protocol (SMTP) server on a Linux machine is running. A quick way to verify the health of your SMTP server is to use telnet. Choose Start, Run and, in the Open text box, type **telnet**, a space, the host's IP address, a space, and **25**, as in **telnet 172.20.1.17 25**. The trailing 25 specifies the TCP port; SMTP usually runs on port 25. Click OK. If telnet is able to connect, the SMTP service is running.

You can type additional SMTP commands to further test the health of your SMTP server. Figure 13.7 shows an example of connecting to the SMTP server on a Linux box from a

Windows 2000 machine, and then typing a **HELO** SMTP command at the prompt. Note that the **HELO** command doesn't appear in the window, because SMTP servers don't echo commands; they only send the output of the commands.

Figure 13.7
The Windows 2000 telnet client is connected to an SMTP server (Sendmail), as indicated by the first line in the Command Prompt window. The second line is the server's response to a HELO command.

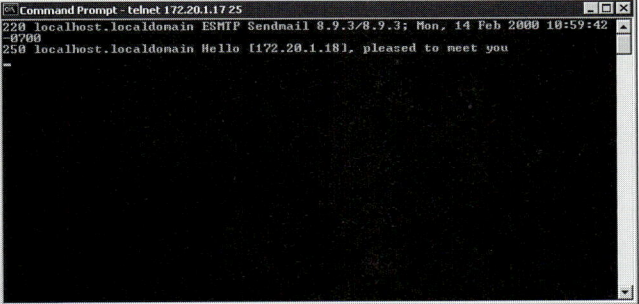

TELNET DISADVANTAGES

Despite telnet's advantages, the following are two of the primary disadvantages of using telnet:

- Telnet has a rudimentary user interface and a cryptic command set.
- Telnet sends clear-text passwords across the network; clear text can easily be intercepted and read by network "sniffers," such as Windows 2000 Server's Network Monitor. This is a serious flaw in telnet, but necessary to maintain its cross-platform capabilities.

→ For more information on how to use Network Monitor as a network sniffer, **see** "Monitoring Network Activity with NetMon," **p. 911**.

Note
Windows 2000's support for NTLM authentication in both the Windows 2000 telnet client and server doesn't qualify as cross-platform. Similarly, Linux's telnetd offers an encryption option, but the encryption prevents interoperation with most other operating systems.

CONFIGURING WINDOWS 2000 FOR TELNET SERVER OPERATION

Remote administration of Windows 2000 servers is the rule, not the exception. Using a client running Windows 2000 Professional with the Administrative tools added from Adminpak.msi or using a Terminal Services client are two common methods of remote server administration. If an RPC service failure occurs or an Active Directory DC is unable to authenticate your client machine, tools such as the command-line rcmd service or shutdown utility are inoperable. The client is unable to connect to the server to execute the command. A simple interface is required that allows you to execute a command on the remote Windows 2000 server as if you were sitting at the server console.

All versions of Windows 2000 Server ship with a telnet server that runs as a service and supports only command-line operations. The Administrative tools include a Telnet Server

Administration tool, which has a two-user license. The two-user license should be more than sufficient for ordinary administrative duties. If you need more than two simultaneous connections, you must purchase SFU, which is described later in the chapter.

CONFIGURING THE TELNET SERVER ON WINDOWS 2000 SERVER

To configure the telnet server on Windows 2000, follow these steps:

1. Choose Start, Programs, Administrative Tools, Telnet Server Administration to open the Command Prompt window shown in Figure 13.8.

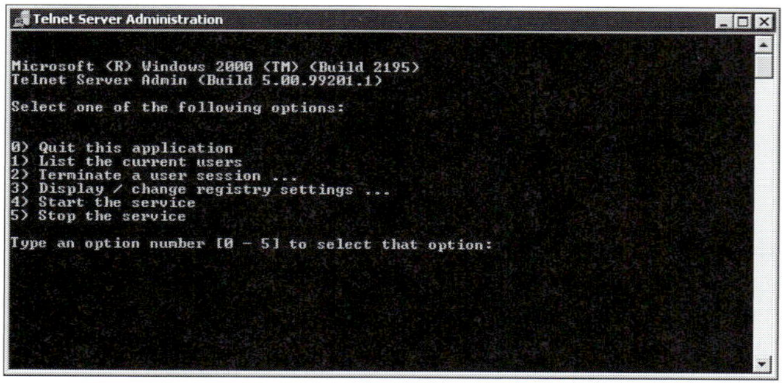

Figure 13.8
You administer the telnet server included with Windows 2000 Server with the Telnet Server Administration program.

2. Type **3** and press Enter to display the configuration options for the telnet server, which are stored in the server's Registry. Figure 13.9 shows the configuration options menu.

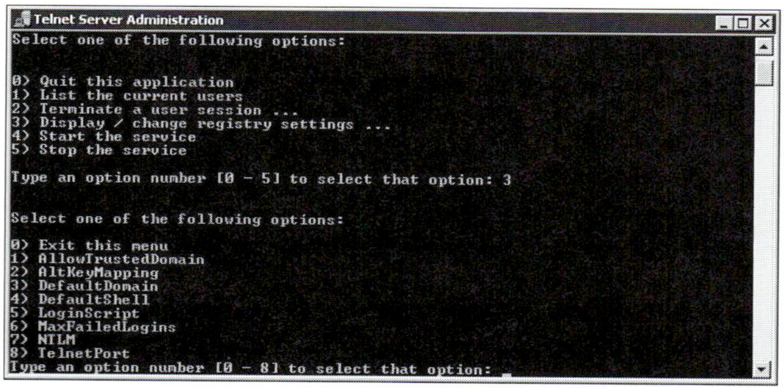

Figure 13.9
The configuration options supported by the Windows 2000 built-in telnet server are shown here.

3. Set the options on the telnet server for the configuration you want by typing a number between 1 and 8, and press Enter. The following list describes the available configuration options and their allowed values.

- `AllowTrustedDomain`—Set this parameter to 1 if you want to allow users from all trusted domains to log in to your server via telnet. Set it to 0 if you want to allow only users from the server's domain to log in via telnet.
- `AltKeyMapping` is used to change how the Alt key is treated for Alt commands. The default value, 1, maps Ctrl+A as the Alt key; 0 doesn't map Ctrl+A.
- `DefaultDomain` is used to determine which domain to validate the *username* and password of connecting users. To use the domain of the server, set this parameter to a period (.). Otherwise, type the domain name.
- `DefaultShell` is the fully qualified path of the command processor used to interpret commands sent to this machine by the telnet client program. The default command processor configured in Windows 2000 is Cmd.exe, the standard command prompt processor.
- `LoginScript` is the fully qualified path of a login script that will be executed by the DefaultShell when a user logs in to the telnet server.
- `MaxFailedLogins` sets the maximum number of wrong *username*s or passwords the remote user can enter during a single login attempt before the telnet server disconnects them. The default is 3.
- `NTLM` sets the type of authentication used during a login attempt. The default value is 2, which supports only Windows' NTLM authentication. Set `NTLM` to 0 to support only standard clear-text user/password authentication, which is what most UNIX machines use. Most administrators in mixed Windows/UNIX environments choose 1 to support mixed NTLM and clear-text authentication.
- `TelnetPort` is the TCP port on which the telnet server listens for client requests. The default is 23, which is the standard for telnet servers. Set `TelnetPort` to a different value only if you have another telnet server running on port 23 of your server already, or you don't want to use the standard port number for security reasons.

> **Note**
> You must type **y** and press Enter to confirm you want to change an option value, and then type **y** and press Enter again after you make the change to confirm the new value.

4. After you have the telnet server options configured correctly for your network, type **0** and press Enter to return to the main menu.
5. Start the telnet server by selecting main menu choice 4. Alternatively, you can use the Services snap-in in Administrative Tools to set the telnet service to start automatically.

> **Tip from**
> *RJ*
> If the telnet service is running, you must stop (5) and start (4) the service for the option changes you made to take effect.

6. Type **0**, and press Enter to close the Telnet Server Administration window.

When the telnet server is correctly configured and started on your Windows 2000 server, you can telnet to the server and use command-line utilities to administer the server. Figure 13.10 shows a telnet client on a Windows 2000 client sending a shutdown command to the telnet server on a Windows 2000 server.

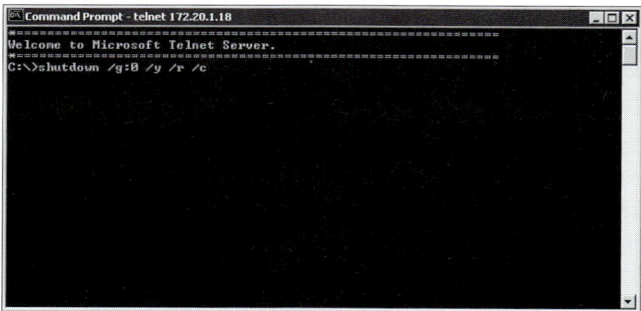

Figure 13.10
You can telnet from a Windows 2000 client machine or a UNIX host to your Windows 2000 server and execute administrative command-line utilities, such as shutdown.

Taking Advantage of X Window

Although telnet is useful for showing character-mode output from a remote system, X Window is a sophisticated, cross-platform means of executing programs on one machine and displaying graphical output on another. In this sense, X Window is a "better telnet" for administering UNIX hosts from a Windows 2000 workstation or server. If you're familiar with Microsoft Terminal Server, you'll find the architectures of X Window and Terminal Server are remarkably similar. Both systems allow programs to run on a centralized server and display on client machines, and allow clients to simultaneously run programs on multiple servers.

Tip from
RJ

Here are a few terms that will help you if you are new to X Window.

X Window Client   This is the executing portion of an X Window program. Many platforms support X Window clients, but UNIX is the most common client platform.

X Window Display   This is a device capable of displaying output from an X Window client and passing keyboard and mouse input back to the client. Common displays include X Window servers running on a UNIX or Windows 2000 computer.

X Window Server   A synonym for X Window Display.

Note

The X Window client and server labels actually appear to be misplaced. A technically accurate sentence is as follows: "The X Window xclock client program running on the Linux (or any other UNIX) server displays its output on the X Window server running on the Windows 2000 client machine." This appears counter-intuitive. A simple explanation is that the X Window display provides display services to the X Window client program. Thus, the display device is a server, and the code executing on the UNIX or Linux server machine is really a client.

X Window History

X Window development started at MIT in the first half of the 1980s. Digital Equipment Corporation (DEC, now owned by Compaq) also contributed major development effort to the X Window project. The goal was a cross-platform technology to allow programs running on different types of machines to be displayed on a single display device. The team succeeded in its efforts, and X Window was adopted by the major UNIX players of the time—such as HP, Sun, IBM, AT&T, and DEC—as the primary windowing system for their UNIX workstations.

In spite of the UNIX market fragmentation and Windows' dominance, the fact remains that UNIX-based servers are popular and becoming increasingly so. Therefore, it is important for a Windows 2000 administrator to have a good way to administer or at least access UNIX servers from the familiar Windows 2000 console.

X Window Servers for Windows 2000

Although there are several X Window servers available for Windows 2000, the product that has the longest history is Exceed from Hummingbird, Ltd. Hummingbird's Web site (http://www.hummingbird.com) describes the company's products that focus on application-layer network integration between UNIX and Windows NT, and recently Windows 2000. Hummingbird version 6.2 and above runs under Windows 2000.

Exceed is a high-performance X Window server for Microsoft Windows that supports industry-standard X Window Version 11 Release 6.4. It uses the Windows 2000 video adapter driver to render X Window graphics, so the product supports a wide array of video cards. Exceed supports multiple keyboard and mice, but—most importantly—it can emulate a three-button mouse with a standard two-button Windows mouse. This capability is significant, because the X Window standard mouse has three buttons.

Exceed 2.6 also supports two styles of windowing: single-window and multiple-window. Single-window style should be familiar to Windows Terminal Server users—all X windows programs display inside a single large window. Single-window is a much more integrated environment, because an X Window program displays in a window managed by Windows 2000, so the UNIX program appears to be a Windows 2000 program. Figure 13.11 shows an example of xterm (a terminal program much like telnet), xclock, and xtrojka (a game) running simultaneously on a Linux server and displaying in Windows 2000.

Figure 13.11
Hummingbird's Exceed allows you to run programs on one or more UNIX servers and interact with them from your Windows 2000 computer. Here, you see the windows of a terminal emulator, clock, and game running on a Linux server.

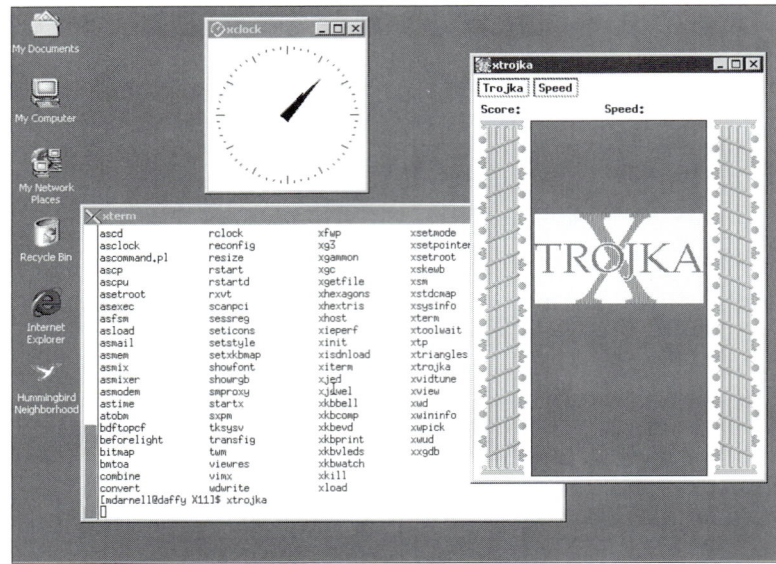

Installing and configuring Exceed or other third-party X Window software is beyond the scope of this chapter. You can order a CD-ROM with a trial copy of Exceed 2.6 from http://www2.hcl.com/html/forms/nc/exceed/request.html.

INTEGRATING WINDOWS AND UNIX PRINTERS

UNIX print spooling uses a TCP/IP-based print spooler called lpr/lpd. *lpr* is the name for the client program and protocol to print a job to a remote printer. *lpd* is the name of the remote print service or daemon.

Windows 2000 Server's Print Services for UNIX component provides lpr print services to remote UNIX clients so UNIX clients can print to Windows 2000-hosted printers, and allows you to add LPR ports so Windows 2000 machines (servers and workstations) can connect to UNIX-hosted printers. Print Services for UNIX, which also is included with Windows 2000 Professional, delivers very flexible printer configurations; a Windows 2000 print server can share one of its attached printers with UNIX clients. Alternatively, a Windows 2000 server can access a UNIX-hosted printer as a local printer and share that printer with other Windows clients.

PROVIDING PRINT SERVICES TO UNIX CLIENTS

Follow these steps to make printers connected to Windows 2000 print servers accessible to UNIX clients:

1. Launch Control Panel's Add/Remove Programs tool and click the Add/Remove Windows Components button to start the Windows Components Wizard.

2. Select Other Network File and Print Services in the Components list and click Details to open the dialog of the same name.

3. Mark the Print Services for UNIX check box in the Subcomponents… list (see Figure 13.12), and click OK to close the Other Network File and Print Services dialog.

Figure 13.12
Installing Print Services for UNIX allows you to share your Windows 2000–hosted printers with UNIX clients.

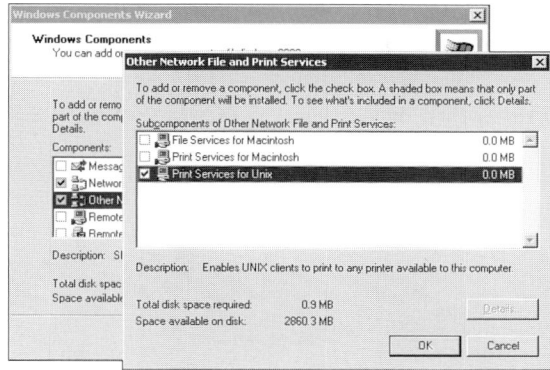

4. Click Next in the Windows Components dialog. The Wizard prompts you to insert the Windows 2000 Server distribution CD-ROM or specify a network share location for installation.

5. Click OK, specify the location of the setup files, if necessary, and complete installation of Print Services for UNIX.

6. If you've already shared the printer under Windows 2000, you're done. Otherwise, choose Start, Settings, Printers and locate the printer you want to share with UNIX (and Windows) clients.

7. Right-click the icon for the printer to share, and choose Properties to open the *PrinterName* Properties dialog.

8. Click the Sharing tab, select the Shared As option, and type a descriptive share name for the printer in the Shares As text box.

9. Click OK to close the Properties dialog.

Your printer is now shared with UNIX clients via the lpr protocol.

The Windows 2000 service responsible for this functionality is named TCP Print Server. This service presents an lpr protocol interface (which most UNIX machines need to print) to the TCP network and allows UNIX servers to access any of the printers shared by Windows 2000. The Windows 2000 printer share name is the name UNIX clients use to access the printer.

Accessing Printers on UNIX Servers for Windows 2000 Clients

To configure a Windows 2000 workstation or server to access printers that use or emulate UNIX print services:

1. Launch Control Panel's Printers tool, and double-click the Add Printer icon to start the Add Printer Wizard. Click Next to bypass the Welcome dialog.
2. In the Local or Network Printer dialog, select Local Printer, clear the Automatically Detect and Install My Plug and Play Printer check box, and click Next.
3. In the Select the Printer Port dialog, select the Create a New Port option, and select LPR Port from the Type list (see Figure 13.13).

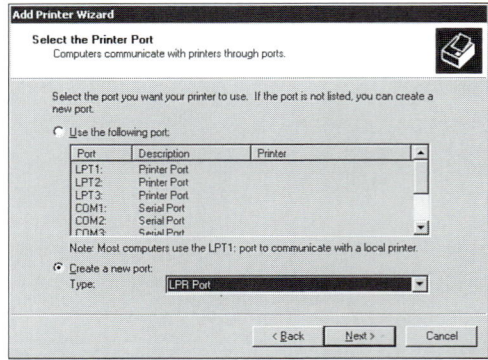

Figure 13.13
Create a new local printer port with the LPR Port type.

4. Click Next to open the Add LPR Compatible Printer dialog.
5. Type the IP address of the UNIX print server or emulator and the printer or queue name for the LPR printer in the two text boxes (see Figure 13.14), and click OK.

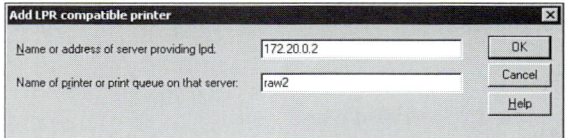

Figure 13.14
Enter the name or IP address of your print server and the name of the queue. For this example, the server's IP address is 172.20.0.2 and the printer queue name is raw2.

 If you have problems setting up the LPR Port for your printer, see the "UNIX Printing Problems" topic of the "Troubleshooting" section near the end of the chapter.

The process from this point forward is the same as for any typical printer addition. Select the printer type, insert your Windows 2000 CD-ROM if prompted, and complete the process as usual for adding a local printer. If you run the procedure of this section under

Windows 2000 Server, you can share the UNIX printer with network clients by following steps 6 through 9 of the preceding section.

The lpr protocol, unfortunately, doesn't provide security mechanisms for printers, so Windows 2000 Professional users with Administrator privileges can install Print Services for UNIX and connect to the printer. Print Services for UNIX doesn't appear in the Domain Security Policy snap-in's Services list, because the services are implemented as printer drivers. You can, however, restrict Windows 2000 Professional users from adding new printers with Group Policies. If you share the UNIX printer from a Windows 2000 server, which is the most common approach, you can apply Windows 2000's printer share security.

→ For more information on implementing Group Policies, **see** "Using the Group Policy Snap-In to Edit Group Policy Objects," **p. 622**.

Using the File Transfer Protocol

File Transfer Protocol (FTP) is a UNIX-based method for sending and receiving text and binary files. FTP originated about the same time as telnet, and remains the most popular method of downloading files from and uploading files to IP hosts running any of today's common server operating systems. The primary advantages of FTP are its standards-based operation and ubiquity; FTP is widely used for file transfer over the Internet. All versions of Windows 2000 include a command-line FTP client; Internet Explorer and other popular browsers act as graphic FTP clients.

Tip from
RJ

Obtain one of the many freeware or shareware graphical FTP clients if you intend to use FTP regularly, especially to upload files to an FTP server. Graphical FTP clients automate the FTP process and eliminate the need to type a series of somewhat arcane commands in the FTP client's command-line window. One of the most popular graphical FTP clients is FTPx Corp.'s FTP Explorer. FTPx offers a no-charge license for noncommercial, home use; commercial use requires payment of a moderate license fee. To download a copy of FTP Explorer, go to `http://www.ftpx.com/`.

Internet Information Server (IIS) 5.0, included with Windows 2000 Server, provides a high-performance FTP Server service that's very easy to administer. Setting up IIS 5.0's FTP service is one of the subjects of Chapter 27, "Administering Internet Information Server 5.0."

→ To learn more about IIS 5.0's FTP Server service, **see** "Setting Up the Default FTP Site," **p. 1125**.

The FTP Command-Line Client

Windows 2000's command-line FTP client is useful for exchanging files between Windows 2000 and any other machine that acts as an FTP server. To launch the FTP client, explore its command set, and make a test connection to the Microsoft FTP server, do the following:

1. Choose Start, Run; type **ftp** in the Open text box, and press Enter to launch the Command Window with Ftp.exe running.

2. Type **?**, and press Enter to display a list of commands available at the ftp> prompt.
3. With an active connection to the Internet, type **open ftp.microsoft.com**, and press Enter at the ftp> prompt to connect to the Microsoft FTP site. The site returns a User...: prompt.
4. Type **anonymous**, and press Enter at the User...: prompt. Some, but not all, FTP sites accept logons from all users. The site returns a Password: prompt.
5. Type your *email address*, and press Enter at the Password: prompt, which logs you on to the site, returns a message, and displays the ftp> prompt.
6. Type **dir**, and press Enter to display entries in the root directory of the site (see Figure 13.15). Entries with a dr- prefix are directories, and -r- signifies a file in the directory.

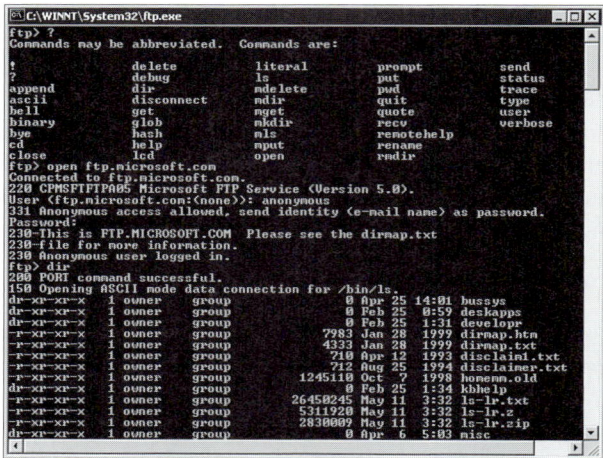

Figure 13.15
The command-line FTP client displays a list of available FTP commands, a test connection to the Microsoft FTP site, and a partial list of subdirectories and files in the site's root directory.

7. Type **get dirmap.htm**, and press Enter to download an HTML file with links to the Microsoft site's first- and second-level directories. The default location for downloaded files is in the root (\) folder of the current drive.
8. Type **close** and press Enter, and type **quit** and press Enter to close the connection and the Command Prompt window.

Using the command-line FTP client effectively requires users to learn many additional commands. To obtain a terse description of the purpose of each command, type **help** *commandname*, and press Enter at the ftp> prompt. For more detailed information on ftp command syntax, search for "ftp commands" in Windows 2000's online help.

FTP Support in Internet Explorer 5.0+

Internet Explorer (IE) has included FTP download capability for individual files since version 1.0. IE 5.0+ allows you to retrieve a full directory tree, which includes all files and subdirectories, from a remote server. This feature is very convenient for retrieval of a large directory tree on an FTP server, but can involve long download times.

To retrieve a directory tree or a single file from an FTP server, in this case from the Microsoft FTP site, do the following:

1. Launch IE 5.0+ and type an FTP server URL, such as `ftp://ftp.microsoft.com`, in the Address text box.
2. Navigate to a folder whose contents you want to download.
3. Right-click the folder icon, and select Copy to Folder. If the folder permits anonymous access, the Browse for Folder dialog opens (see Figure 13.16).

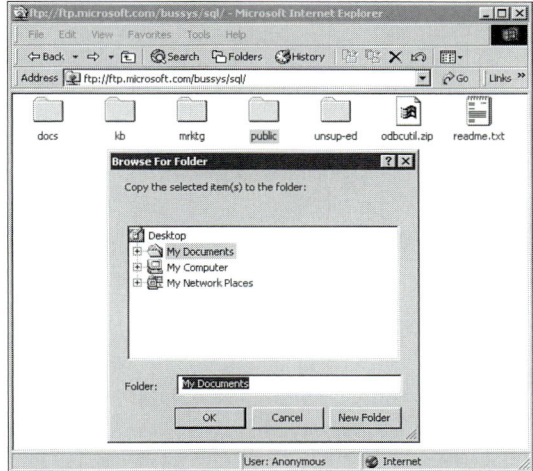

Figure 13.16
The Browse for Folder dialog allows you to specify a location in which to save a directory tree from an FTP server.

4. Navigate to the folder on your computer where you would like the downloaded directory to be created, select the folder icon, and click OK to open a message box that displays the download progress.
5. Click Cancel to terminate the download at any time.

The process for downloading individual files is similar; in preceding step 3, right-click a file icon instead of a folder icon.

Running Microsoft Services for UNIX

Microsoft Services for UNIX (SFU) 2.0, released in May, 2000, is a complete UNIX integration toolset. This Windows 2000 (and NT) add-on product includes the Network File System (NFS, a UNIX file sharing protocol) and UNIX–to–Active Directory integration and synchronization. Pricing and availability information is available at `http://www.microsoft.com/windows2000/sfu/`.

SFU 2.0 Contents

SFU 2.0's components logically divide into an integration group and a utility group. Following are the components of the integration group:

- Client for NFS allows a Windows 2000 computer to access NFS shares from UNIX computers in the same manner as accessing a Windows 2000 network share. UNIX servers must run NFS for client access.

- Gateway for NFS allows computers running Windows 2000 Server to connect to an NFS network share (called an *NFS export*) on a UNIX computer running NFS, and republish it as a Windows 2000 share for Windows 2000 clients that don't have the NFS Client installed. You can't run Client for NFS and Gateway for NFS on the same machine.

- Server for NFS allows Windows 2000 to publish shared folders to the network as NFS shares (exports) accessible to UNIX clients.

- Server for PCNFS allows Windows 2000 to serve as a *username*/password authentication service for PCs running PCNFS. PCNFS has lost much of its former popularity, so install Server for PCNFS only if you need it.

- Server for NIS allows Windows 2000 to act as a Network Information Services (NIS) server to a UNIX network. This feature provides UNIX and Windows 2000 directory integration by using the AD to manage NIS domains. Server for NIS must be installed on a Windows 2000 Server configured as a DC.

- NIS to Active Directory Migration Wizard is a tool for moving an existing NIS structure to Server for NIS. You can do a single move of an entire NIS environment or perform an incremental migration.

- Password Synchronization allows users to maintain common passwords between UNIX and Windows. Precompiled single-sign-on daemons are included for HP-UX 10.3+, Sun Solaris 2.6+, IBM AIX 4.3+, Digital True64 UNIX, and RedHat 5.2 and 6.0 versions of Linux. Password Synchronization must be installed on an AD domain controller (DC) or Windows NT primary or backup domain controller (PDC or BDC).

- Server for NFS Authentication Mapping provides Windows 2000–hosted services to authenticate NFS users.

When installing SFU 2.0, it's a common practice to install all but the Client for NFS and Server for PCNFS components on a single DC or a combination of a DC and one or more member servers.

The following utilities and tools aren't necessary for Windows 2000/UNIX integration, so installation is optional:

- *Telnet Client* is similar to the client discussed earlier in this chapter.

- *Telnet Server* is similar to the server shipped with Windows 2000 Server. It allows you to connect more than two users to your telnet server. This is a licensing rather than a functional difference, so we will not install this.

- UNIX Utilities are a subset of commands from the Mortice Kern Systems (MKS) toolset that are familiar to all UNIX administrators and users. A Windows-compatible, case-insensitive version of the Korn shell (sh.exe) supports DOS-style drive letters.
- ActiveState Perl is a practical extraction and reporting language (Perl) interpreter. Perl is a scripting language popular in the UNIX world; it excels at processing text files.

SFU 2.0 Installation

To install selected SFU 2.0 components from the distribution CD-ROM, do the following:

1. Run Setup from the SFU 2.0 distribution CD-ROM, and click Next to bypass the Welcome dialog.
2. In the Customer Information dialog, type your name, organization, and CD key code and click Next.
3. In the License dialog, select the Accept option and click Next.
4. In the Ready to Install dialog, select Customize to enable selection of the options to install. Click Next.
5. In the Select Features dialog, select Not Available in the drop-down list for those features in the Available Features list you don't want to install on the destination machine (see Figure 13.17).

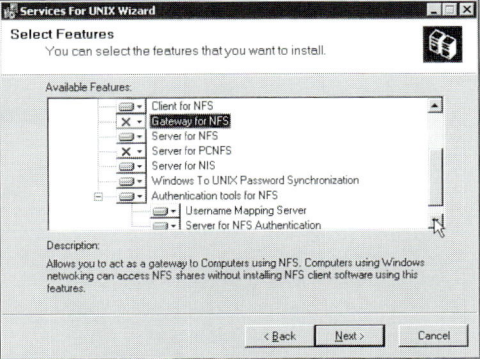

Figure 13.17
By default, all SFU 2.0 components install to the local computer's disk. Select the feature(s) you don't want to install, such as Gateway for NFS and Server for PCNFS, and choose Not Available.

6. In the Installation location dialog, type the drive and folder in which you want SFU installed, and click Next.

> **Caution**
> Don't include spaces in the path to the folder to hold the SFU files. If you include a space, such as in *d*:\Program Files\SFU, SFU 2.0 doesn't function correctly.

7. In the final installation dialog, click Install Now. After a minute or two, a message box opens with a "Services for UNIX were successfully installed" message.

Configuring the Mapping Server

The first item that must be completed before NFS client access to the Windows 2000 NFS server can be enabled is the mapping server configuration.

UNIX uses numerical IDs to identify users, one ID for a user and one ID for a group. Windows 2000, however, uses a much more complex set of objects to identify users and groups. For Windows 2000 to allow a UNIX user to access its shared files, Windows 2000 must understand how to map the numerical user and group IDs from UNIX into Windows 2000 Active Directory objects.

If the text versions of the UNIX user and group names match those of your Windows 2000 domain, you can use simple user maps in the mapping server.

To create a simple user map, do the following:

1. Obtain your passwd and group files from the UNIX machine. This process varies depending on the variant of UNIX in use. You might need to rely on one of your UNIX administrators to get these files for you. Copy the passwd and group files into a folder, such as \SFU\maps on your Windows 2000 Server.

2. Choose Start, Programs, Windows Services for UNIX, Services for UNIX Administration to open the SFU Management snap-in (see Figure 13.18).

Figure 13.18
Use the SFU Management snap-in to administer installed Services for UNIX components.

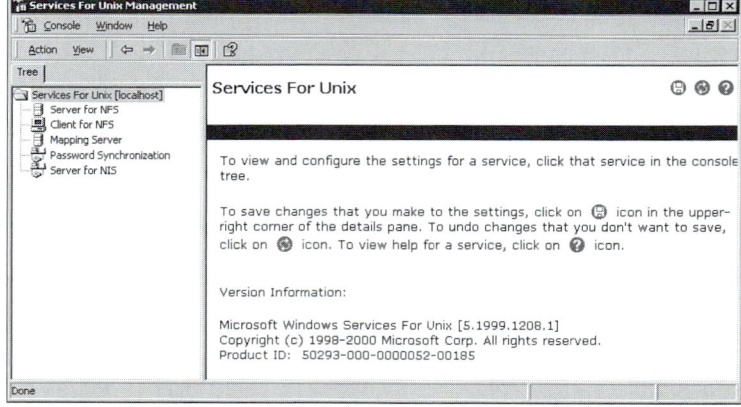

3. Click the Mapping Server node in the tree view pane to open the Mapping Server on localhost page in the right pane. Choose Simple User Maps from the menu at the top of the page.

4. With the Password and Group Files option selected, browse for the passwd file you copied from your UNIX server in step 1.

5. Repeat step 4 for the group file you obtained from your UNIX server in step 1. Figure 13.19 illustrates typical Mapping Server entries.

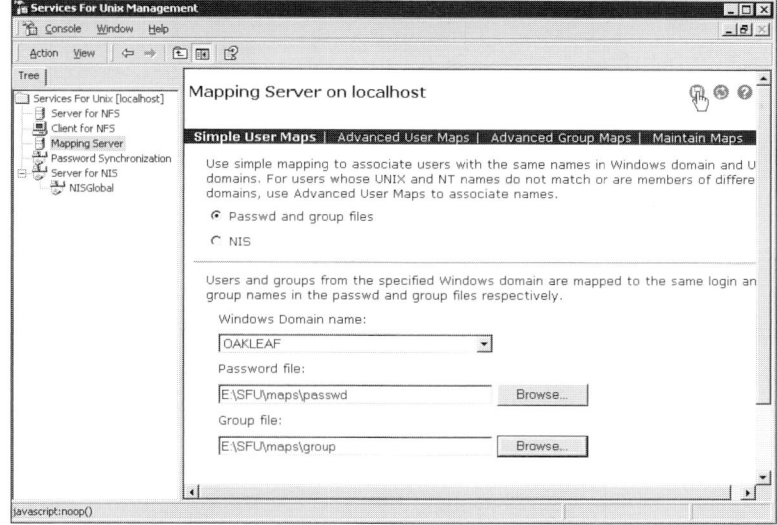

Figure 13.19
The Simple User Maps portion of the SFU snap-in allows you to map UNIX accounts to Windows 2000 accounts so long as the names textually match.

6. Click the red disk icon in the upper-right corner of the page to save your settings and enable the mapping server.

If the text names of your Windows 2000 and UNIX accounts don't match, you should use the Advanced Mapping capabilities under the Mapping Server node. In the following example, the UNIX account name, markd, should map to the Administrator account in the Windows 2000 OAKLEAF domain.

To create an advanced map, do the following:

1. Launch the SFU Management snap-in, if it's not open, and click the Mapping Server node.
2. Choose Advanced user Maps from the menu in the right pane to open the page shown in Figure 13.20.

Figure 13.20
Use the Advanced User Maps page to allow UNIX usernames to obtain permissions of Windows 2000 accounts with different names.

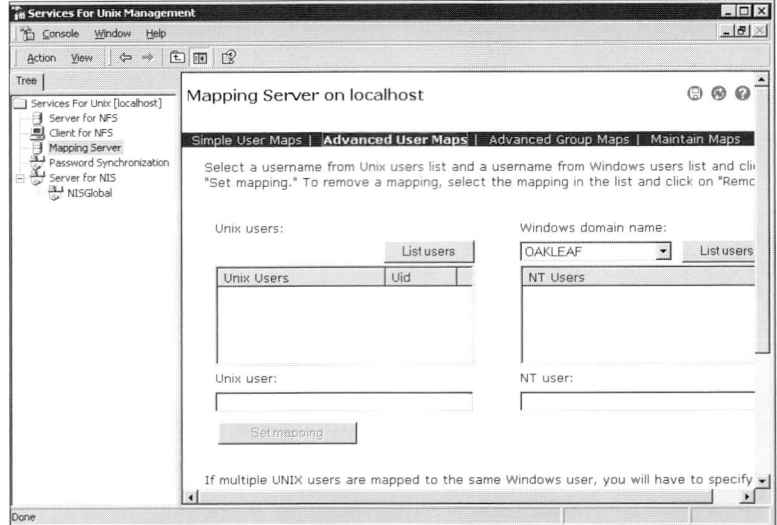

3. Click the List Users button in the UNIX Users column to load the user information from the passwd file.
4. Click the List Users button in the NT Users column to obtain the list of users in your Windows 2000 domain.
5. Select the UNIX username and the corresponding Windows username in the two lists. As you make the selections, the selections appear in the text boxes below the list boxes (see Figure 13.21). Click the Set Mapping button to create the UNIX to Windows mapping.
6. Repeat step 5 for each additional UNIX to Windows username mapping.

Figure 13.21
After mapping between the markd UNIX account name and the Windows 2000 Administrator account, the markd account on a UNIX client accessing an NFS share from a Windows 2000 server has the file access permissions of the Administrator account.

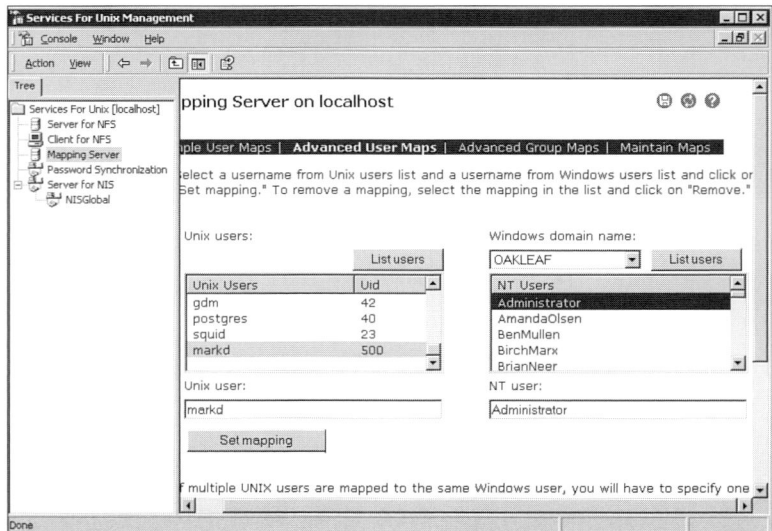

Configuring the Windows 2000 NFS Server

Before you can configure the NFS server, make sure that your mapping server is configured correctly. Perform the appropriate steps in the preceding section if you haven't configured your mapping server.

Follow these steps to configure the NFS server:

1. Launch the Services for UNIX Administrative snap-in, if necessary.
2. Click Server for NFS in the tree view pane, and choose User Mapping in the Server for NFS localhost page.
3. Type the name of your Windows 2000 server in the Mapping Server text box (see Figure 13.22).

Figure 13.22
Specify in the Server for NFS on localhost page the name of the server on which you established the UNIX-to-Windows 2000 account mapping.

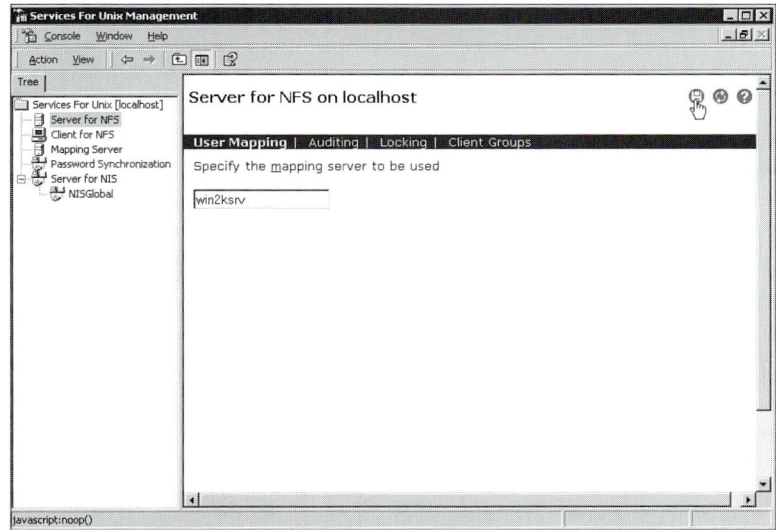

4. Click the red disk icon in the upper-right corner of the page to save the settings.

Following are three other configuration pages you access by menu choices to customize the behavior of your Windows 2000 NFS server:

- *Auditing* options (see Figure 13.23) are useful if you want to determine what NFS activities have occurred, or check the source of problems with file sharing between a UNIX client and your server.

Figure 13.23
The Auditing page configures logging of events triggered by your NFS server.

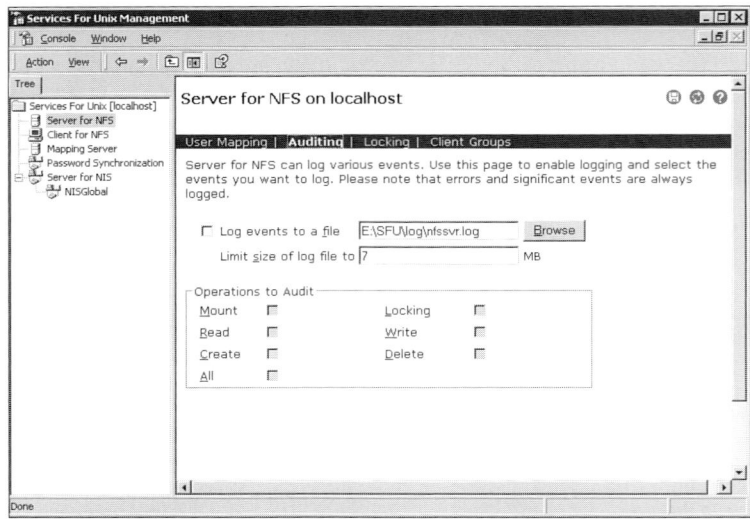

- *Locking* options (see Figure 13.24) are useful in determining which UNIX clients have locks on your server files. You can force these locks to be removed using this dialog.

Figure 13.24
This page allows you to administer UNIX locks on your Windows 2000 server's files.

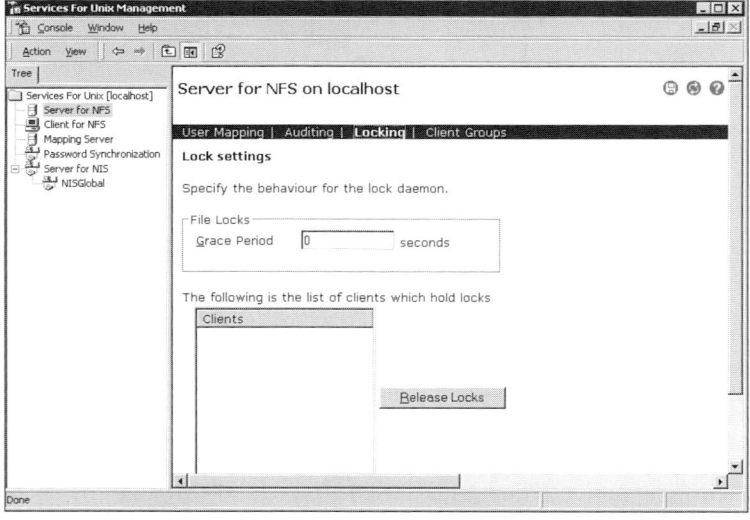

- *Client Groups* options (see Figure 13.25) allow you to create groups of machine names. When assigning permissions of who can access NFS shares later, you can assign permissions to these group names.

If you've made changes in any of the preceding three option pages, click the red disk icon to save the changes.

RUNNING MICROSOFT SERVICES FOR UNIX | 571

Figure 13.25
This page allows you to create groups of UNIX NFS client computers so that you can administer permissions on NFS shares using groups rather than individual computer names.

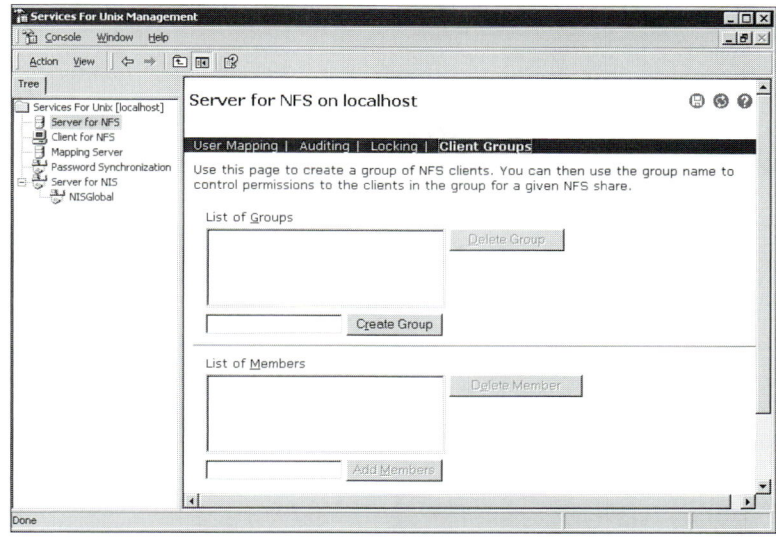

SHARING A WINDOWS 2000 FOLDER WITH NFS CLIENTS

To share a folder with NFS clients, your mapping server and NFS server must be configured as described in the two preceding sections. Follow these steps:

1. Launch Windows Explorer or navigate from My Computer to the folder you want to share.

2. Right-click the folder to share, select Properties to open the *FolderName* Properties dialog, and click the NFS Sharing tab.

3. Select the Share This Folder option and type a share name for the folder in the text box (see Figure 13.26).

Figure 13.26
Configuring the NFS server adds an NFS Sharing page to the properties dialog of all Windows 2000 folders. To share a folder with NFS clients, select the Share This Folder option and specify a share name.

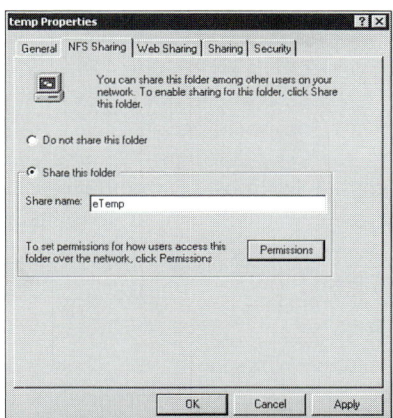

PART
II
CH
13

4. Click the Permissions button to open the NFS Share Permissions dialog shown in Figure 13.27.

Figure 13.27
By default, all NFS clients have read-write permissions for Windows 2000 shares. Click Add to assign NFS share permissions by a computer name or group basis.

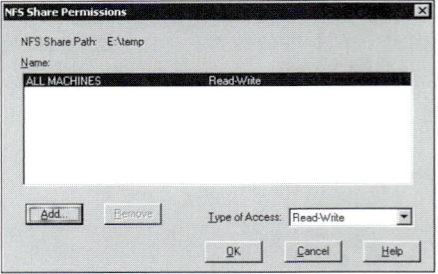

5. Click the Add button to allow only certain computers to access this share. Otherwise, click Cancel to dismiss the dialog and assign all NFS clients read-write permissions for the share.
6. Click OK to close the FolderName Properties dialog and apply your settings.

Figure 13.28 illustrates with Exceed's xterm program the UNIX mkdir and mount commands required to connect an NFS client to the Windows 2000 NFS share.

Figure 13.28
Use the UNIX mkdir and mount commands on the NFS client to mount a Windows 2000 share.

Configuring the Windows 2000 NFS Client

The Windows 2000 Client for NFS component most commonly is installed on workstations, not servers. You must configure the mapping server, as described in the earlier "Configuring the Mapping Server" section, and the Windows 2000 NFS Client before you can use it to connect to a UNIX NFS server. Follow these steps to configure the NFS Client:

1. Launch the Services for UNIX Management snap-in, if necessary, and click Client for NFS in the tree view pane to open the default Client for localhost page.
2. Type in the text box the name of the server configured as the mapping server, and click on the red disk icon to save the configuration (see Figure 13.29).

Running Microsoft Services for UNIX | 573

Figure 13.29
You must specify the name of the mapping server that converts Windows 2000 usernames to UNIX user IDs.

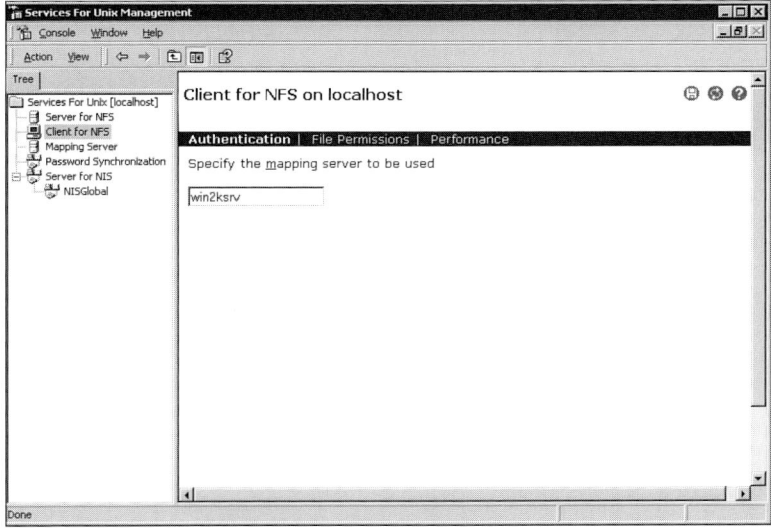

3. Choose File Permissions to display the page that enables you to set the permissions for newly created directories or files on any NFS share the client creates. Figure 13.30 shows the default permissions for new NFS directories and files.

Figure 13.30
The NFS client user who creates a file or directory has default read (R), write (W), and execute (X) permissions. Members of the user's group and all others have default read and execute permissions.

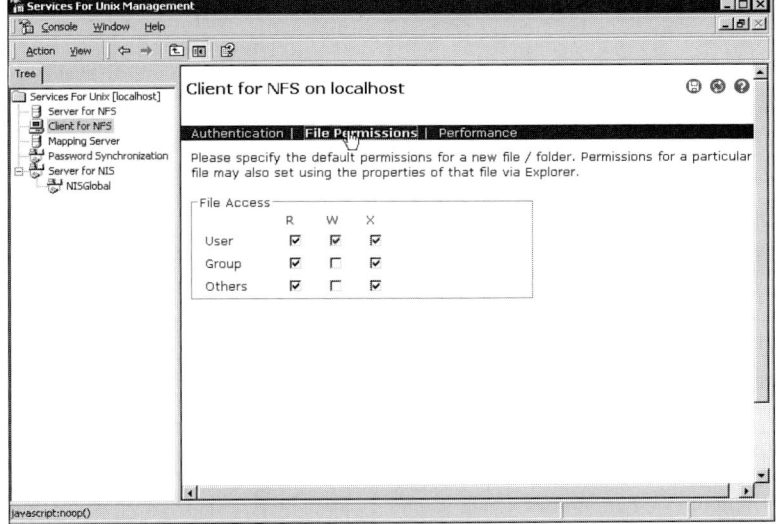

4. Choose Performance tab to open the page—shown with default settings—in Figure 13.31. Table 13.2 explains how to set each Performance parameter.

PART
II
CH
13

Figure 13.31
You can specify values for six performance parameters for the NFS Client.

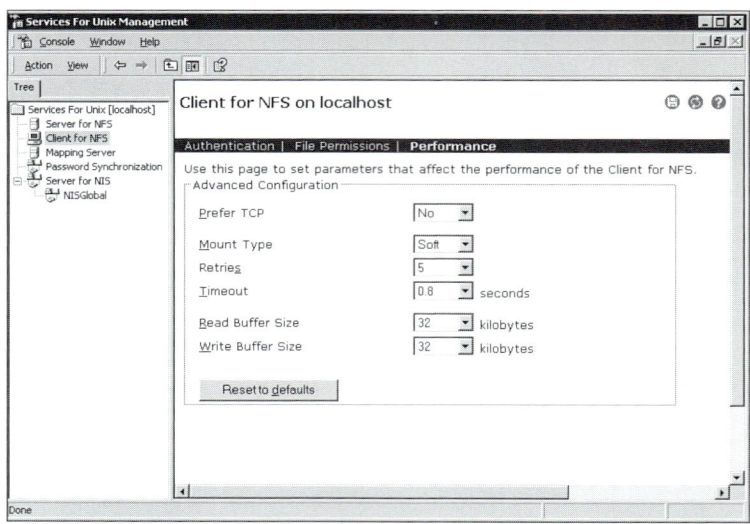

Table 13.2	NFS Performance Parameters
Parameter	**Description**
Prefer TCP	NFS can run over UDP or TCP (UDP is the default). Setting this parameter to Prefer TCP causes the NFS client to attempt to run NFS over TCP. TCP is more reliable in certain cases, but is slower than UDP-based NFS.
Mount type	Soft mount is the default. Soft mounts time out after a configurable number of retries (see the Retries parameter). Hard mounts guarantee that a write or read data request from the Windows 2000 machine to the UNIX server doesn't return control to the requesting application until the UNIX machine responds. If the UNIX server is inaccessible from the network, the Windows 2000 application hangs until the UNIX server is once again reachable.
Retries	The Retries parameter applies only to soft mounts. If a UNIX machine becomes unreachable and a read or write request to the UNIX server is outstanding, the NFS client retries the operation for the number of Retries, waiting Timeout seconds between each retry.
Timeout	The number of seconds between retries on a soft mount.
Read Buffer Size	Size of the Windows 2000 buffer that holds data being read from the UNIX server. The larger the buffer, the more data that can be cached locally without incurring another network round-trip to the server.
Write Buffer Size	Size of the Windows 2000 buffer that can hold data being written to the UNIX server. The larger the buffer, the more data that can be cached locally without incurring another network round-trip to the UNIX server.

In most cases, you can accept the default File Permissions and Performance values for the NFS client. If you make changes on either of these two pages, click the red disk icon to save the configuration.

Connecting to a UNIX NFS Server

Client for NFS adds a new folder, NFS Network, to the My Network Places folder and an NFS Attributes page to the properties dialog for NFS shares. To connect with the Windows 2000 NFS client to a UNIX NFS server using Windows Explorer, follow these steps:

1. Launch Windows Explorer, and expand the My Network Places, Entire Network, NFS Network, and Favorite LAN nodes (see Figure 13.32).

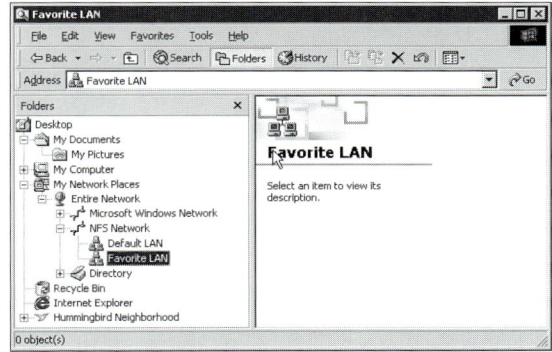

Figure 13.32
My Network Places has been expanded to show the NFS Network folder added by the Client for NFS.

2. Right-click the Favorite LAN pane, and choose Add/Remove Hosts to open the dialog of the same name.
3. Click Add Host, and type a hostname, IP address, or both in the Add Host dialog (see Figure 13.33). Click OK twice to add the host to the Favorite LAN node.

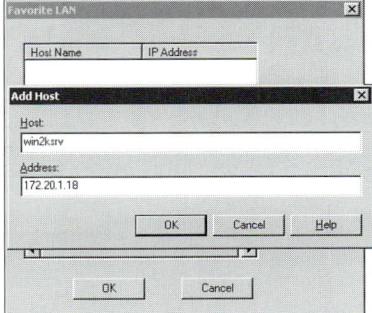

Figure 13.33
The Add Host dialog allows you to add UNIX machines running an NFS server to your NFS Network node.

Tip from
RJ

If you're serving an NFS share from the NFS server configuration created earlier in the chapter, you can connect to the Windows 2000 NFS share to test an NFS client. This configuration is shown in Figure 13.33 and is used in the steps that follow. Alternatively, you can connect directly to an NFS share on a UNIX host.

4. Press F5 to refresh Windows Explorer, which displays the added host under the Favorite LAN node. Expanding the host's node displays the available NFS shares.

5. Right-click a file or folder in the NFS share, choose Properties to display the *FileOrDirectory* Properties dialog, and click the NFS Attributes tab (see Figure 13.34).

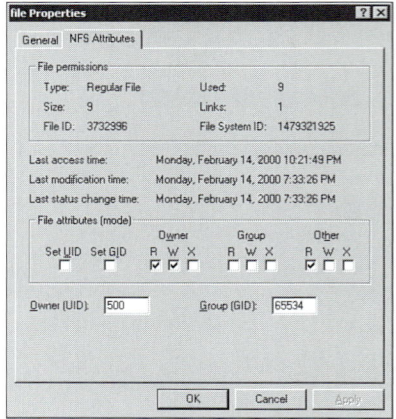

Figure 13.34
The NFS Attributes page for a shared file uses UNIX—not Windows 2000—permissions for the file's owner (creator), the owner's group, and all other users.

The NFS Attributes page of the *ShareName* Properties dialog is specific to NFS shares and shows the UNIX file or folder permissions, as well as the numerical IDs for the user (UID) and the user's group (GID). Figure 13.34 illustrates several changes made to the default permissions that are described in the preceding section.

Any new files created on the UNIX server are owned by their creator's user account, and you can access only files or directories for which your UNIX user account has permissions. Table 13.4 describes the primary differences between NFS and Windows 2000 shares and text files.

TABLE 13.4   DIFFERENCES BETWEEN NFS AND WINDOWS 2000 SHARES

Feature	Difference
Security	The security model in NFS is far less sophisticated than that of Windows 2000 (or NT). Some UNIX variants use a DACL (Discretionary Access Control List) model similar to that supported by NTFS, but DACLs don't appear to have reached the NFS.
Text files	UNIX text files use only a line-feed character (hex `0x0a`) to denote the beginning of a new line. Windows text files use a carriage-return followed by a line-feed (hex `0x0d` followed by hex `0x0a`).
Property pages	The NFS Attributes properties page shown in Figure 13.34 differs greatly from the standard Windows 2000 *FileOrFolder* Properties dialog's Security page. Windows NT 4.0 attempted to integrate NFS security into the NTFS model. SFU 2.0 running under Windows 2000 adopts the UNIX security model.

Integrating UNIX and Windows Directories

Sun Microsystems developed the Network Information System (NIS) for UNIX, which uses a protocol originally called Yellow Pages (yp). NIS uses a collection of maps—stored in a special database format called DBM—to create simple, flat (nonhierarchical) directories. UNIX NIS directories can be integrated with the Active Directory, which provides network administrators with a single, unified source of user and group information for both UNIX and Windows 2000 Servers.

> **Tip from**
> *RJ*
>
> For a more extensive discussion of NIS migration and management, download the "Server for NIS Overview" white paper from http://www.microsoft.com/WINDOWS2000/sfu/nis.asp.

Directory integration requires UNIX administrators to accept Windows 2000 Server as the master NIS server in the NIS domain. Few UNIX administrators are likely to acquiesce to such a drastic step, especially with a relatively new operating system. If you're the network administrator for UNIX and Windows 2000, you have the option of migrating the NIS directories to the AD.

To integrate UNIX NIS information into the Active Directory, follow these steps:

1. Obtain text (not DBM-format) copies of all the NIS maps you want to integrate into the Active Directory.
2. Place the NIS map files into a directory of your choosing on the Windows 2000 server.
3. Choose Start, Programs, Windows Services for UNIX, NIS Server Migration to start the NIS Data Migration Wizard on the domain controller that you want to act as the master NIS server. Other DCs for the domain become subordinate NIS servers.
4. Click Next to bypass the Welcome screen and display the Domain Selection dialog.
5. In the Domain Selection dialog, type the NIS domain name to migrate into the Active Directory in the UNIX NIS Domain Name text box, and click Next.
6. In the Administrator Authentication dialog, type your Windows 2000 administrator username and password in the two text boxes, and click Next.
7. In the NIS Map Selection dialog, select each map to migrate in the Standard UNIX NIS Maps list, and click Add to move the map to the Maps to Migrate list (see Figure 13.35). The maps you must migrate depend on the NIS configuration; group, passwd, protocols, and services are the most common minimum set. Click Next.

Figure 13.35
Select the maps you want to migrate from NIS into the Active Directory in the Wizard's NIS Map Selection dialog.

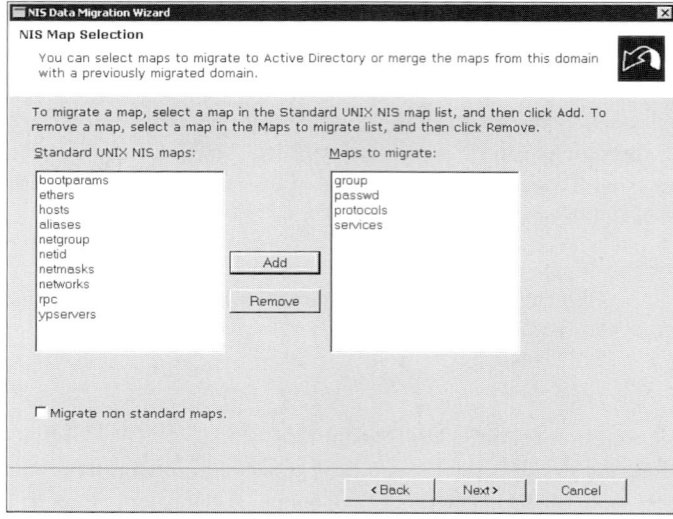

8. In the UNIX NIS Directory Name dialog, type the full path to the folder, which you created in step 2, that contains the NIS map text files. Click Next.

9. In the Target Domain for Migration dialog, accept the default NIS Domain Name option and NISGlobal (or another selection from the list), if you want to preserve your original NIS domain name. Otherwise, select Migrate to a New Domain and type the AD domain name to use in the adjacent text box, as shown in Figure 13.36. Click Next.

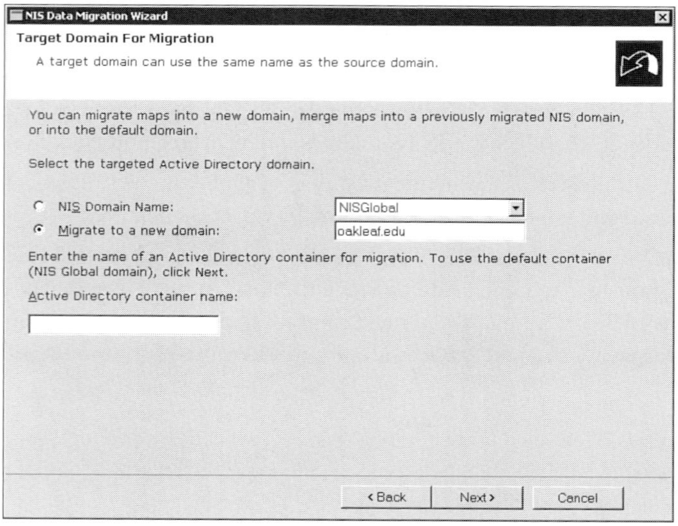

Figure 13.36
For the example shown in this figure, the NIS and AD domain names are NISGlobal and `oakleaf.edu`, respectively, and migration creates AD objects based on the NIS maps for the `oakleaf.edu` NIS domain.

10. In the Managing Conflicts During Migration dialog, select the method you want to use to handle conflicts during NIS map integration. If you select Overwrite, map entries for objects with the same name as those already in the AD replace those in the AD. This option has the potential to overwrite Windows 2000 account information with UNIX account data. Alternatively, select Preserve, which doesn't overwrite existing Active Directory information with incoming map entries. The Do Not Migrate option—the most conservative choice—creates a log file that you can use to determine conflicts before performing an actual migration (see Figure 13.37). Click Next.

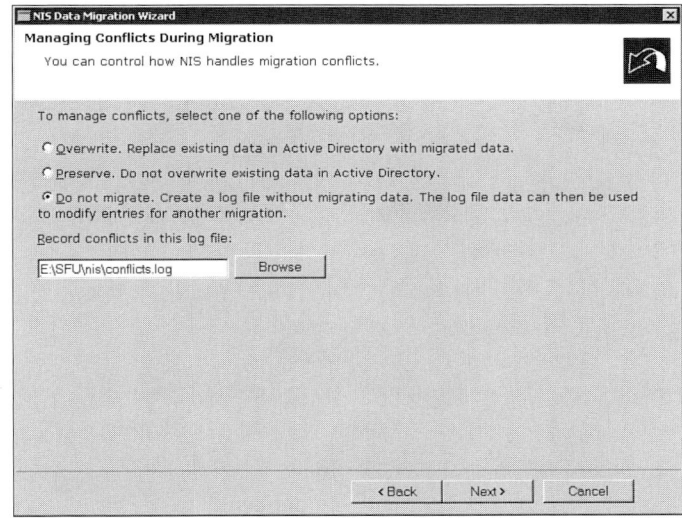

Figure 13.37
The Managing Conflicts During Migration option allows you to select how you want migration conflicts to be handled.

11. The Migration Logging dialog allows you to either log only or log and actually execute the migration process (see Figure 13.38). It's a good practice to run a test migration, examine the log files, resolve any errors or conflicts, and then restart the Wizard to perform an actual migration. Click Next.

Figure 13.38
Specify in the Migration Logging dialog whether you want to run a test migration (Log only) or perform the NIS migration (Migrate and Log) at this point.

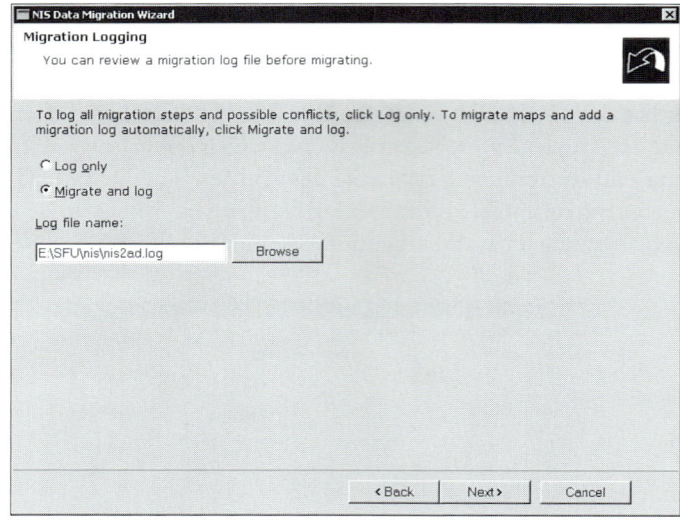

12. In the Completing the NIS Data Migration Wizard, click Finish to execute the migration process you configured in the preceding steps.

When the Migration Wizard completes its operation, review the log file created during the migration process. Fix any failed map entries and retry the migration or manually integrate failed entries into the Active Directory.

A DC running the Active Directory for the domain with the migrated NIS maps now must assume the role of the master NIS server. You or a UNIX administrator must reconfigure UNIX NIS servers as slave NIS servers that point to a Windows 2000 DC for the NIS domain to receive NIS map updates from the Windows 2000 Server.

Troubleshooting

Telnet Problems

You receive a "Could not open a connection to host:" message when attempting to connect to a telnet server.

The most common source of this message is that the telnet server daemon or service isn't running on the remote host. If the remote host runs UNIX, make sure the telnet daemon is started. If you're testing telnet between two Windows 2000 hosts, the default startup type for the Windows 2000 telnet service is Manual. Start the server service on the remote host from the Services list of the Computer Management snap-in. Unless you intend to use telnet to manage a server routinely, don't change the startup type to Automatic. Running the telnet service is an invitation to hackers to attempt to gain unauthorized access to your server.

UNIX Printing Problems

No LPR Port option appears in the list adjacent to the Create a New Port Type option in the Add Printer Wizard's Select the Printer Port dialog.

The LPR Port item doesn't appear if you haven't installed Print Services for UNIX. In this case, the Type list includes only Local Port and Standard TCP/IP Port items. Cancel the Wizard, complete steps 1 through 5 of the "Providing Print Services to UNIX Clients" section to install Print Services for UNIX, and then restart the Add Printer Wizard.

MCSE Corner: Question Types, Part 1

There are several types of questions asked on MCP exams. It's important to be familiar with each type of question before you take your first exam so you don't have to spend your limited exam time learning how the questions work. Here's a list of the question types:

- Multiple choice
- Choose all that apply
- Select and place
- Case study
- Scenario
- Simulation

The first three are covered in this chapter, and the case-study, scenario, and simulation types are covered in Chapter 27; they are similar to each other, but complex enough to be discussed in a separate MCSE corner.

Multiple Choice

The multiple-choice question is the most basic type of question. You are presented with a question and several answers and are expected to choose the correct one. Here is a sample:

Disk mirroring is which level of RAID?

a. RAID-0
b. RAID-1
c. RAID-5
d. RAID-10

Choose All That Apply

The choose-all-that-apply questions are similar to multiple-choice questions, except you can choose more than one answer. Sometimes the question states "Choose three" or "Choose two," but most of the time it does not specify how many answers are correct.

Select and Place

This is a fairly new question type in the MCP exams. This is a graphical-type question that tests the examinee's ability to "synthesize the information required to complete a task and assemble the correct solution."

Select-and-place questions first present you with a scenario. After you've reviewed the scenario, you click the Select and Place button to bring up a palette of potential answers and answer areas marked Place Here. You drag your selections from the potential answers and into the answer locations.

With select-and-place questions, you can't go back and change individual answers. To go back and review the question, all answers are cleared and you must place all answers again. There are no partial points given for select-and-place questions if multiple answers are required. All answers must be correct to receive points for that question.

Delivering Network Resources to Clients

14	Providing Clients with DHCP and WINS xx
15	Establishing Group Policies, User Accounts, and Logons xx
16	Managing Server Shares and the Distributed File System xx
17	Installing Network Printers xx
18	Connecting Windows 2000, NT, and 9x Clients xx
19	Serving Macintosh, Windows 3.11, and DOS Clients xx
20	Supplying IntelliMirror and Application Installation Services xx
21	Using Remote Installation Services xx
22	Monitoring and Tuning Your Network xx
23	Optimizing, Backing Up, and Restoring Your Servers xx

CHAPTER 14

PROVIDING CLIENTS WITH DHCP AND WINS

In this chapter

Assigning IP Addresses and Resolving NetBIOS Names   586

Understanding the Dynamic Host Configuration Protocol   586

Installing the DHCP Service   589

Configuring DHCP with the DHCP Snap-In   590

Using the DHCP Relay Agent   601

Understanding the Windows Internet Naming Service   604

Installing and Configuring WINS   606

Troubleshooting   613

MCSE Corner: Providing Clients with DHCP and WINS   615

Assigning IP Addresses and Resolving NetBIOS Names

The logical addressing system provided by the Internet Protocol (IP) poses some interesting challenges for the Windows 2000 network administrator. The first is assigning unique IP addresses to all nodes on your network—servers, clients, printers, routers, and other networking devices. Depending on your IP network class (Class B with 65,534 hostids as opposed to Class C with only 254), you might be responsible for an extremely large pool of IP addresses, so assigning and keeping track of the addresses in the pool can become problematic.

→ For more information on TCP/IP and IP addressing, **see** "Decoding and Assigning IP Addresses," **p. 64**.

Another problem area related to TCP/IP on Microsoft networks is the strategy used by Windows 3.x, 9x, and NT hosts to resolve NetBIOS names to IP addresses. The broadcast traffic generated by downlevel computers on the network as they attempt to match a NetBIOS computer name to an IP address can result in the loss of substantial network bandwidth.

Two Windows 2000 services—Dynamic Host Configuration Protocol (DHCP) and Windows Internet Naming Service (WINS)—provide network administrators with solutions for address pool management and NetBIOS traffic problems, respectively. DHCP dynamically assigns IP addresses to nodes on the network, making the management of the IP pool much more efficient and straightforward. The use of a WINS server to resolve NetBIOS names to IP addresses greatly reduces NetBIOS broadcasts on a network segment. Windows 2000 Server's DHCP and WINS services are the primary subjects of this chapter; Chapter 18, "Connecting Windows 2000, NT, and 9x Clients," covers the client side of DHCP and WINS.

> **Note**
>
> Working with enterprise Windows 2000 TCP/IP networks in an enterprise really requires a thorough understanding of routing and how IP subnetting works. For a good general discussion of LAN, WAN and routing issues on networks and an overview of TCP/IP and IP subnetting, check out the book *Practical Cisco Routers*, published by Que.

Understanding the Dynamic Host Configuration Protocol

DHCP provides the ability to automate and administer the assignment of IP addresses to hosts on the Windows 2000 network. The DHCP server supplies all TCP/IP-related information needed by a client—such as the leased IP address, subnet mask, default gateway, Domain Name Service (DNS) server address, and, if required, WINS server address.

DHCP is an extension of the UNIX BOOTP protocol, which was an early method for assigning IP addresses to computers—including diskless workstations—on a network using the TCP/IP protocol. BOOTP, however, didn't provide the dynamic assignment of IP addresses, which is the primary feature of DHCP.

> **Note** The BOOTP protocol, which is still used to assign IP addresses to diskless workstations, requires you to create a BOOTP table that consists of Media Access Control (MAC) addresses (the 48-bit address burned onto the ROM of each network adapter on your network) cross-referenced to specific IP addresses. The BOOTP table is kept on a BOOTP server. When a BOOTP client boots up, it requests an IP address from the BOOTP server. The server, recognizing the client's MAC address, supplies a permanent IP address to the client.

The advantage of using DHCP to dynamically assign IP addresses to network hosts is that the problems associated with the manual assignment of IP addresses go away. These problems range from the potential for errors when typing IP parameters for a large number of client machines to inadvertently assigning the same IP address to more than one computer. DHCP also simplifies reconfiguring computers with new IP parameters when you move them from one subnet to another.

DHCP Client and Server Communication

DHCP supplies IP addresses from a fixed pool of addresses (called a scope) to subscribing hosts on a first-come, first-served basis. Addresses from the available pool can be reserved, however, for particular computers on the network such as servers or the routers that typically serve as default gateways.

> **Tip from** *RJ*
> Always assign fixed IP addresses to every server on your network(s). The DHCP Server service requires that the machine on which it's installed have a fixed IP address. Although the Windows 2000 Server setup program offers a DHCP option, never use DHCP to assign IP addresses to Domain Controllers (DCs) or member servers. Reserve DHCP for assigning IP addresses to clients.

The process that takes place when a client requests an IP address from a DHCP server is as follows:

1. When a DHCP client (a computer needing an IP address) initializes, it broadcasts a request for an IP lease by means of a DHCPDISCOVER message addressed to 255.255.255.255, which is received by all nodes on the client's subnet. The message contains the client's NetBIOS name and its MAC hardware address. The term *lease* indicates that the client possesses the address for a limited period of time, and eventually returns the address to the server for issuing again.

2. A DCHP server (or servers, if more than one is available) on the subnet responds with a DHCPOFFER message that includes an offered IP address, an accompanying subnet mask, the length of the lease, and the IP address of the DHCP server.

3. The DHCP client accepts the first appropriate offer that it receives for a DHCP server. It does this by sending another broadcast message (DHCPREQUEST) to accept a particular offer. At this point all other DCHP servers that have offered IP addresses retract their offers.

4. The DHCP server that supplied the accepted offer broadcasts an acknowledgement message (DHCPACK) to the client, which contains a valid IP address and other TCP/IP configuration information. A 32-bit client stores this information in its Registry; 16-bit clients store the information in a configuration file.

Figure 14.1 shows the process of a DHCP client obtaining an IP address lease from a DHCP server. DHCP client requests come in the form of User Datagram Protocol (UDP) datagrams. Using UDP makes sense because it's a connectionless protocol and the client doesn't have an assigned IP address at the time of the broadcast.

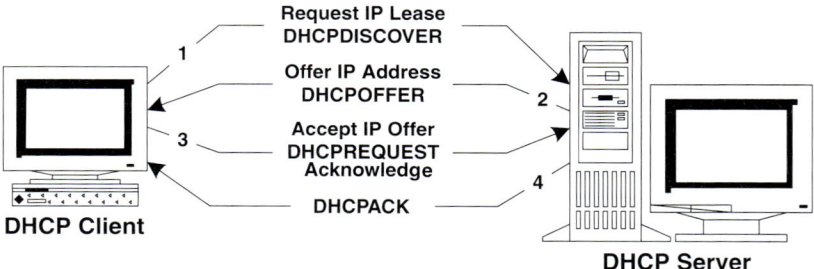

Figure 14.1
The four broadcast messages shown are required for a client workstation to receive a dynamically allocated IP address from a DCHP server.

→ For more information on UDP, **see** "Taking Chances with UDP Delivery," **p. 89**.

Note
You must DHCP-enable network clients that are to receive their IP addresses from a DHCP server. This requires that the TCP/IP software used by the computer include a DHCP client. Windows NT 4 clients (Workstation and Server), Windows 9x, and Windows 2000 Professional clients are DHCP-ready. Windows 3.11 clients require the Microsoft 32-bit TCP/IP stack be installed to be DHCP clients. MS-DOS clients running Network Client version 3.0 require installing the real-mode TCP/IP driver. Both TCP/IP client stacks are included on the Windows NT Server 4.0 CD-ROM.

NEW FEATURES OF WINDOWS 2000 DHCP

Windows 2000 Server offers the following DHCP features that aren't included in Windows NT Server 4.0's DCHP implementation:

- Better integration of DHCP with DNS—In Windows 2000, DHCP servers can register with the Dynamic DNS service (DDNS) integrated with Active Directory (AD). DHCP provides information to DNS that maps client IP addresses to their fully qualified domain names.

- Improved monitoring capabilities of DHCP servers—For example, you can view the number of available versus assigned addresses. You also can monitor the number of requests for addresses, acknowledgements, and declines.
- Automatic client configuration—A Windows 2000 DHCP client is designed to automatically configure itself when it can't find a DHCP server. This means that new workstations brought online and configured to dynamically obtain TCP/IP information are able to communicate on the IP network even if you haven't brought a DHCP server online. In cases where a lease was obtained from a DHCP server that is currently down, the client attempts to determine if the lease is still usable by pinging its default gateway.

> **Note**
> Windows NT DHCP clients and Windows 98/95 clients do not self-configure. If these clients can't find a DHCP server on the network, they attempt to find a server every five minutes until they can lease an IP address.

- Rogue DHCP server detection—DHCP servers on a network must be authorized by AD. An unauthorized Windows 2000 DHCP server coming online in the domain contacts the initial root domain controller to see if it is on the authorized DHCP list. If not, the unauthorized DHCP server doesn't respond to client requests.

Like most other Windows 2000 services, you manage DHCP with a Microsoft Management Console (MMC) snap-in that's added to your Administrative Tools menu when you install the DHCP service.

→ For more information on configuring the DHCP server service, **see** "Configuring DHCP with the DHCP Snap-In," **p. 590**.

Installing the DHCP Service

If you perform an in-place upgrade of a Windows NT 4.0 Primary Domain Controller (PDC) that has DHCP installed and operating, the setup process automatically updates DHCP to the Windows 2000 version. All your DCHP configuration parameters remain intact when setup upgrades the Windows NT DHCP (Dhcp.mdb) database to the new Jet 5.0 version used by Windows 2000. If you're working with an upgraded server, skip to the "Configuring DHCP with the DHCP Snap-In" section of this chapter to verify your DHPC configuration parameters.

You can install DHCP on any Domain Controller (DC) or member server of the domain. Typically, you configure a DHCP server on each subnet of your network. DHCP operates using broadcast messages that usually aren't forwarded from subnet to subnet by the routers connecting the network segments. However, you can configure the DHCP Relay service to accommodate routers.

→ For information on installing and setting up the DHCP Relay service, **see** "Using the DHCP Relay Agent," **p. 601**.

If you didn't specify adding the DHCP service during the Windows 2000 setup process, you can install DHCP using Control Panel's Add/Remove Software Control Panel and the Windows Components Wizard. After the necessary DHCP server files have been copied to your server's disk, restart your system before specifying the IP address scope and setting the other parameters related to the DHCP server.

Tip from
RJ

You can also start the Windows Component wizard from the Windows 2000 Configure Your Server dialog, which provides a quick way to get more information about server components, such as DHCP. Click Start, Programs, Administrative Tools, Configure Your Server to open the dialog. Click the Networking link on the left side of the dialog, and then select DHCP from the list. You have the option of an overview of DHCP (the Learn more about DHCP link) or starting the Windows Component Wizard.

CONFIGURING DHCP WITH THE DHCP SNAP-IN

Launching the DHCP snap-in from the Administrative Tools menu opens the window shown in Figure 14.2, if your server is the initial root DC and the in-place upgrade process hasn't set up DHCP. AD automatically adds the entry for the DC, oakleaf-dc1 (`10.7.2.2`) for the examples of this chapter. The default status of the DHCP server is unauthorized and stopped, which is indicated by a down-pointing red arrow in the DC's node.

Figure 14.2
The DHCP snap-in is shown opened for the first time on a newly installed DHCP server.

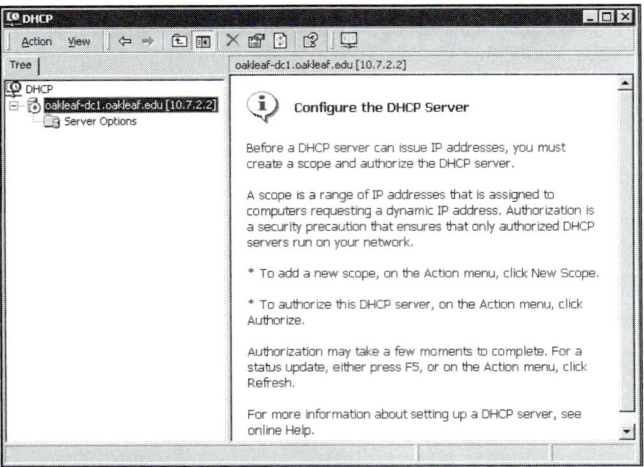

Note

If you're setting up DHCP on a server in a child domain, you see a DHCP entry for the parent domain's DHCP server and an entry for the child domain's server. The DHCP server in the child domain automatically adds a subnode with a backup copy of the parent domain's scope.

An in-place upgrade to a Windows NT PDC with DHCP installed and operating adds subnodes for the existing scope(s).

Setting up DHCP for a domain or subnet involves the following basic activities:

1. Define the range of IP addresses to assign to clients and create a new scope.
2. Set DHCP options for the new scope.
3. Set DNS options for clients having IP address leases.
4. Activate the DHCP scope.
5. Authorize the DHCP server.

The sections that follow describe how to perform each operation with DHCP installed on a newly-created DC. If you're working with a DC that's been upgraded from a Windows NT PDC, you can skip the scope definition process. However, you should verify the DHCP and DNS options after the upgrade, and add values for the new options offered by Windows 2000.

CREATING A DHCP SCOPE WITH THE NEW SCOPE WIZARD

To set up your first DHCP scope for the domain and subnet on your DC, do the following:

1. Right-click the server node and choose New Scope to start the New Scope Wizard. Click Next to bypass the Welcome dialog.
2. In the Scope Name dialog, type a short name for the new scope and add an optional description. Click Next.
3. In the IP Address Range dialog, type the starting and ending IP address for the scope, and the subnet mask in the text boxes. Alternatively, you can specify the subnet mask by its length in bytes, such as 16 for a Class B network. Figure 14.3 shows settings for a Class C network (10.7.2.0) with the first 15 valid addresses (10.7.2.1 through 10.7.2.15) reserved for routers and servers, which leaves 239 addresses available for clients. Click Next.

Figure 14.3
The IP Address Range dialog has the information necessary to create a scope spanning from 10.7.2.16 to 10.7.2.254. All addresses in the scope are valid for assignment to workstations.

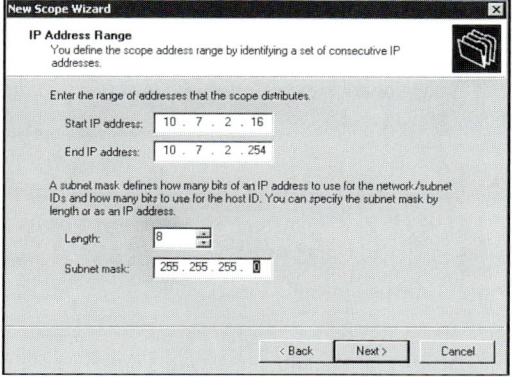

Tip from
RJ

When assigning the starting IP address reserve the network address (x.x.x.0), default gateway (usually x.x.x.1), and current and future servers (x.x.x.2 through x.x.x.15). Reserving a group of addresses when you specify a scope eliminates the need to alter your scope later when you add new hosts with fixed IP addresses.

4. The Add Exclusions dialog lets you specify one or more ranges of IP addresses within the scope to exclude from client assignment. The first 16 addresses are excluded already, so click Next.

5. In the Lease Duration dialog, set the length of the lease in days (see Figure 14.4). Click Next.

Figure 14.4
Set the lease duration for addresses assigned from this scope in the Lease Duration dialog.

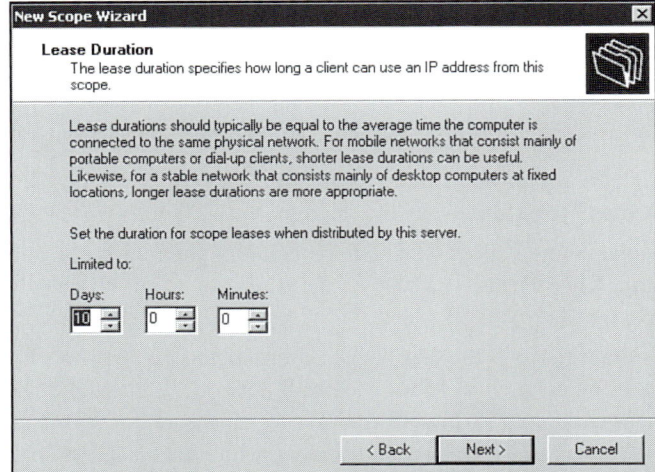

Tip from
RJ

Set the lease duration to two or three days, if you have a large number of mobile or dial-up users and a shortage of IP addresses. When you set the least duration to a much shorter value, such as eight hours, network users who log off at night must obtain a new lease every morning. Many users attempting to obtain a new lease at 8:00 a.m. can cause a large network traffic burst.

6. The Configure DHCP Options dialog offers the choice of configuring options in the Wizard now or later. Select the No, I Will Configure These Options Later option, because using the Scope Options dialog is easier. Click Next and Finish to dismiss the Wizard.

7. Expand the Scope Node to display its subnodes (see Figure 14.5). Click the Address Pool node to show the address range you set in step 3.

Figure 14.5
The newly created scope appears in the DHCP snap-in, but is not yet authorized.

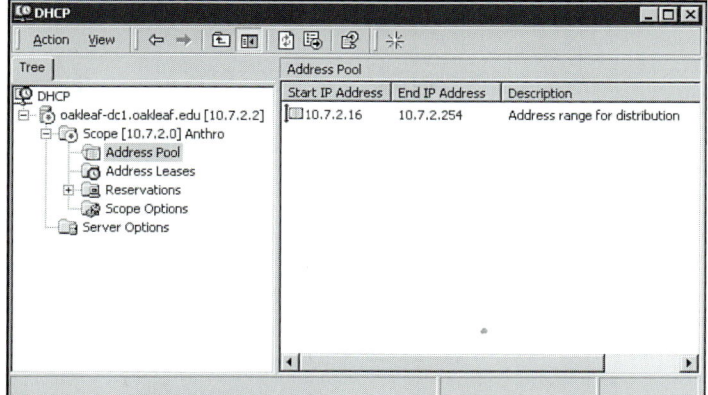

Specifying DHCP Options

Setting a DHCP scope supplies clients with IP address leases, but nothing more. To take full advantage of DHCP, you must specify a set of options that supply important addresses, such as the addresses of the domain's DNS and WINS server(s), the default gateway address for a routed subnet, and the fully-qualified domain name (FQDN) for downlevel clients.

→ For a description of the common DHCP options available in Windows NT Server 4.0's DHCP implementation, which also apply to Windows 2000, **see** "Setting DHCP Options and Attributes," **p. 269**.

You can specify options that apply to all scopes you create on a DHCP server (global options) or individually to each scope (local options). Applying global option values minimizes the effort required to add new scopes, but it's likely that only a few options—typically DNS and WINS server addresses, and domain names—are amenable to global definition. Other option values, such as the default gateway address for a subnet scope, require local options. Thus, it's more common to set all option values at the scope level.

To set the most common options for a new Windows 2000 DHCP scope, do the following:

1. In the DHCP snap-in for the scope you created in the preceding section, right-click the Scope Options node, and select Configure Options to open the General page of the Scope Options dialog.

2. If your scope applies to a routed subnet, mark the 003 Router item's check box, type the router's IP address in the text box, and click Add to add the default gateway value for the scope (see Figure 14.6). Click Apply to add the value.

Figure 14.6
Setting the 003 Router Address parameter defines the default gateway which is assigned to a workstation when it receives an address from this scope.

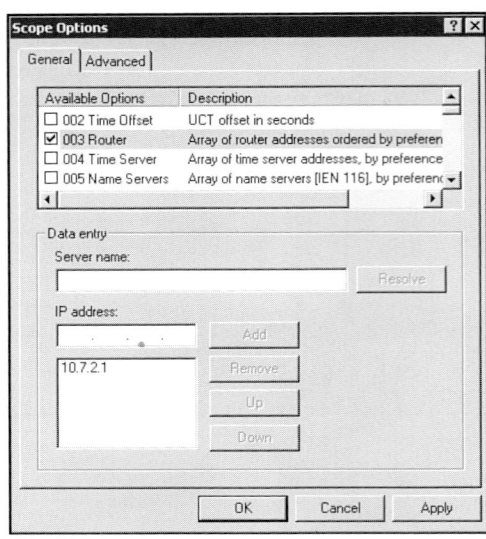

3. Scroll to 006 DNS Servers and mark the check box. Type the name of the primary DNS server for the domain, and click Resolve to verify the server name to its IP address. Click Add to add the DNS server to the list. Repeat the process for a secondary DNS server, if present (see Figure 14.7). Click Apply.

Figure 14.7
The primary and secondary DNS servers are assigned to workstations receiving addresses from this scope.

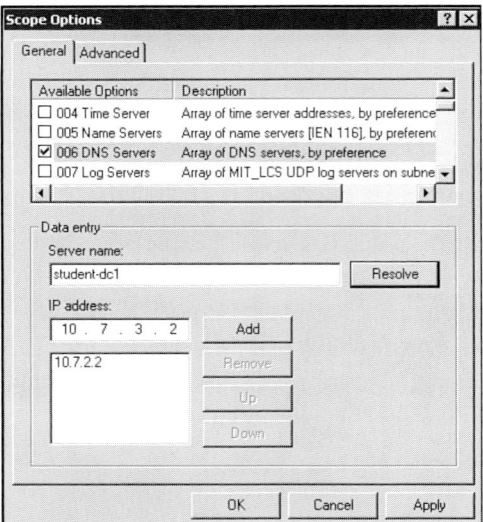

4. Scroll to 015 DNS Domain, mark the check box, and type the client's FQDN, `oakleaf.edu` for this example, in the String Value text box (see Figure 14.8). Click Apply.

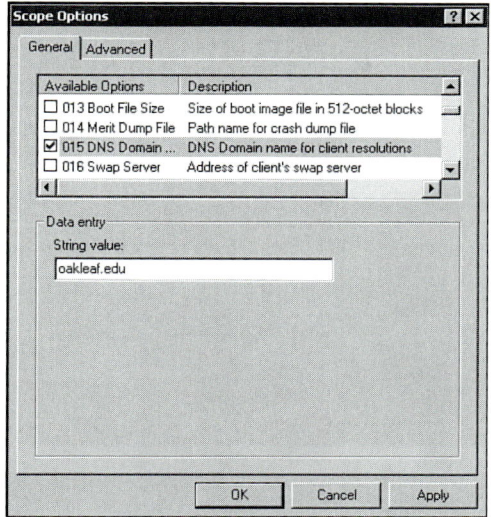

Figure 14.8

The 015 DNS Domain Name value sets the assigned domain name suffix to clients receiving addresses from this scope.

5. Mark the 044 WINS/NBNS Servers check box, type the IP address of the primary WINS server for the domain, `10.7.2.2` for this example, and click Resolve. Click Add, and Apply. If you have more than one WINS server, repeat this step.

> **Note**
>
> You can't type the server name and click Resolve to add the IP address for a WINS server unless the WINS server is set up and accessible. You set up a WINS server for Windows 3.x, 9x, and NT clients later in the chapter.
>
> Only downlevel clients require WINS server addresses; Windows 2000 clients use DNS, not WINS, for name resolution.

6. When you specify a WINS server, you *must* set the node type; failure to set the node type causes the WINS client to fail. Mark the 046 WINS/NBT Node Type check box and type `0x8` for H-node (see Figure 14.9). H-node (Hybrid) is the node type preferred by most network administrators, because it supports all common Windows DHCP clients. Click OK to save this setting and close the Scope Options dialog.

7. Click the Scope Options node, if necessary, to display a list of the option values you set in the preceding steps (see Figure 14.10).

Figure 14.9
The 046 WINS/NBT Node Type value is necessary when specifying a WINS server for clients receiving addresses from a scope or the WINS client will fail. The value of 0x8 for H-Node (Hybrid) is specified here.

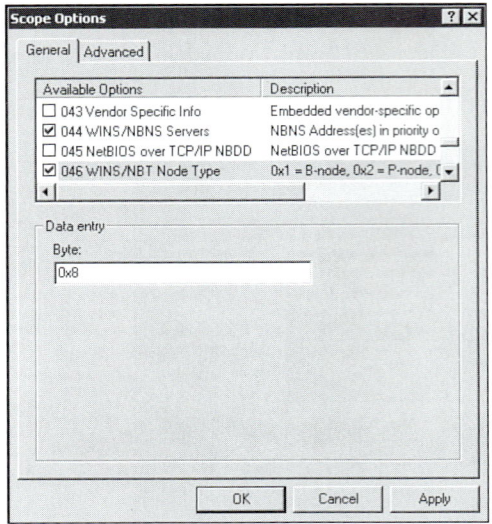

Figure 14.10
The defined scope options are shown in the right pane of the DHCP snap-in when the Scope Options node is selected in the left pane.

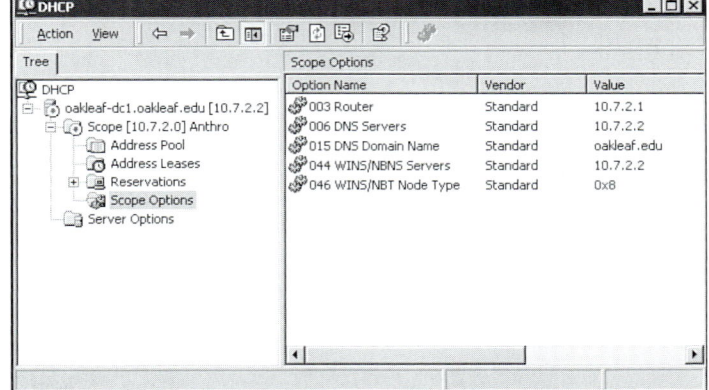

> **Note**
> The Advanced page of the Scope Options dialog lets you set special-purpose DHCP options for BOOTP, dial-up, and Windows 2000 clients. You seldom need to set these special-purpose values.

8. Right-click the Scope node, choose Properties to open Properties dialog for the Scope, and click the DNS tab. The DNS page lets you set options to automatically register DHCP clients in Windows 2000's AD-enabled DDNS. Figure 14.11 shows the DDNS values you set to cause all clients to register their resource records in DDNS, regardless of the operating system in use.

Figure 14.11
Setting the properties as shown on the DNS page of the Scope Properties dialog allows downlevel (Windows 9x and NT) clients to dynamically update their DNS records.

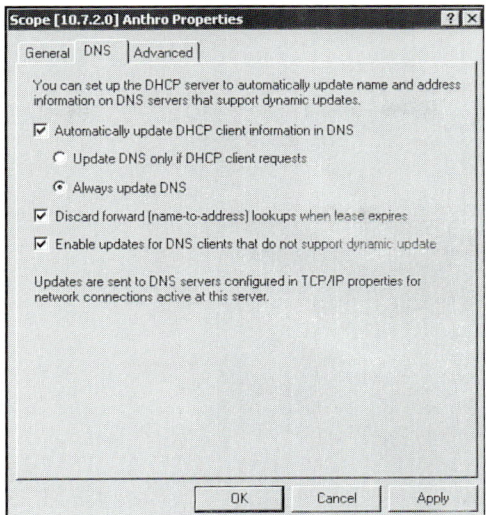

Windows 2000 clients automatically register DNS Host (A) and Pointer (PTR) records for their IP address when you accept the default options of the Scope Properties' DNS page. If you want all clients to register their resource records in DNS, select the Always Update DNS option and mark the Enable Updates for DNS Clients That Do Not Support Dynamic Updates check boxes as shown in Figure 14.11.

ACTIVATING AND TESTING THE NEW DHCP SCOPE

After you set the scope range and options, you must start the DHCP server and activate the scope before you can test your work with a typical client. To test the DHCP server, do the following:

1. Right-click the server node and choose Authorize to start the authorization process. Wait a few seconds to start the DHCP service, and then press F5 to refresh the display. An up-pointing green arrow indicates the service is running and the server is authorized.

2. Right-click the scope node and choose Activate to activate the scope you created in the preceding two sections. A folder icon replaces the down-pointing red arrow.

3. Use Control Panel's Network tool to configure a Windows 9x or NT test client to use DHCP. The DHCP server you're testing must be the only DHCP server on the network during the test.

→ For instructions on setting up a downlevel client to test DHCP, **see** "Verifying DHCP, WINS, and DNS Operation," **p. 285**.

4. Reboot the test client, and verify with Winipcfg.exe (Windows 9x) or Ipconfig.exe (Windows NT) that the client received an IP address within the scope you set and obtained the correct IP addresses for the DNS server, default gateway, DHCP server,

and primary WINS server. Figure 14.12 shows Windows 98 Second Edition's Winipcfg.exe dialog displaying the DHCP option values set in the preceding sections.

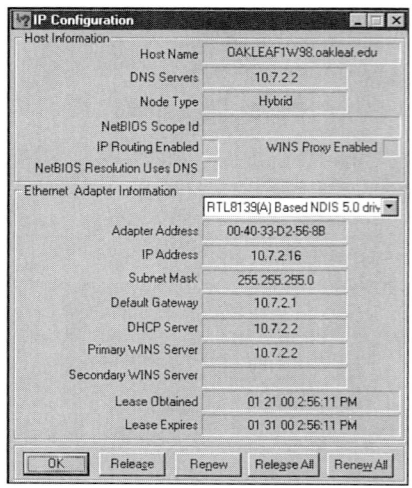

Figure 14.12
The Winipcfg.exe application is shown running on a Windows 98 client which has received an address from the Windows 2000 DHCP server configured in the preceding steps. The address is within the defined scope, and the default gateway, DNS and WINS servers, and WINS node type are as specified in the scope options.

5. Verify that the client has registered its IP address with the AD-integrated DNS server you specified in the preceding section. Launch the DNS snap-in from the Administrative Tools menu, expand the domain nodes, and check for a Host entry with the client's NetBIOS name and IP address. Figure 14.13 shows the Host record for the test DHCP client.

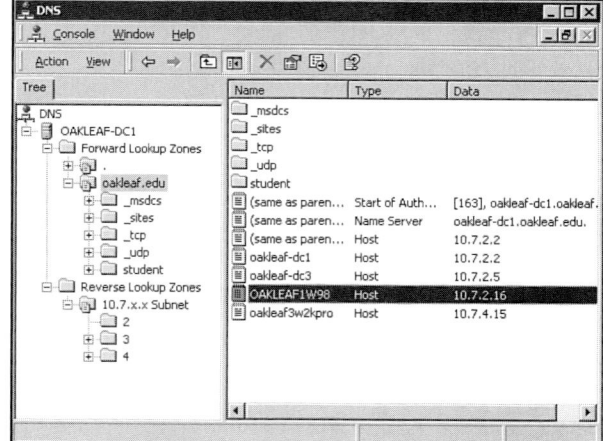

Figure 14.13
The DNS snap-in is shown with the Windows 98 client shown in Figure 14.12 selected in the right pane. When the Windows 98 client was given a DHCP address by the server, its information was recorded in DNS.

6. If you created a reverse-lookup zone for your domain, click or expand the appropriate subnet node to display the host records for the DHCP subnet. The DHCP client adds

a pointer that relates the leased IP address to the fully-qualified DNS name of the client (see Figure 14.14).

Figure 14.14
The DNS snap-in shows a reverse lookup pointer record for the Windows 98 client from Figure 14.12.

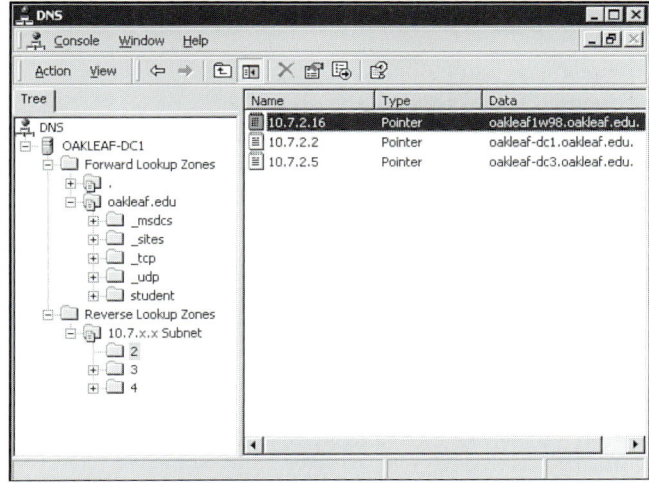

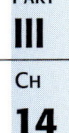 *If your DHCP clients don't receive a valid IP address within their scope and subnet, see the "DHCP Problems" topic in the "Troubleshooting" section at the end of the chapter.*

If you run Network Monitor (NetMon) on the DHCP server during the test client's initial start-up, you can capture the DHCP request and acknowledgment packets that establish the client's lease. Figure 14.15 shows the NetMon trace for the DHCPREQUEST and DHCPACK operations, with the DHCPACK (ACK) packet details in the lower frame. The test client connects to the network with an ADDTROD2568B 10/100BaseT network card.

Figure 14.15
The packet shown here captured in Network Monitor is an example of a DHCP Acknowledgement (ACK) packet sent to the client when an address is requested. The request message (REQUEST) is seen above the ACK packet in the upper pane of the window.

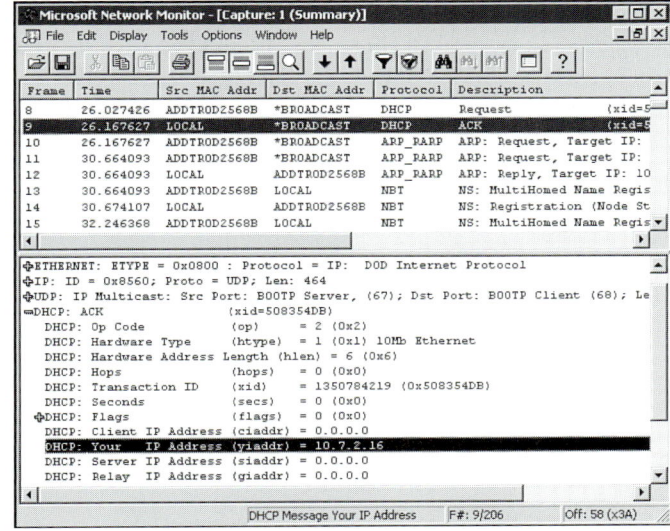

Viewing DHCP Statistics and Properties

Once your DHCP is running and you've set up one or more DHCP clients on a test or production subnet, you can track DHCP statistics at the scope or server level. To view DHCP statistics, do either or both of the following:

- To view the relatively limited number of statistics for a scope, right-click the scope node, and choose Display Statistics to open the Scope (*Subnet IP*) Statistics dialog (see Figure 14.16). This dialog is useful for monitoring In Use and Available addresses in the scope. If the Available value falls below 5 or 10, it's time to create a new scope to service newly-added clients.

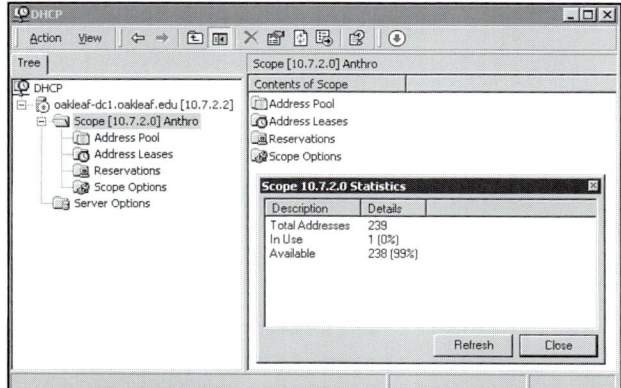

Figure 14.16
Statistics are shown for the selected DHCP scope showing the total number of addresses as well as those in use and those available.

- To view the overall statistics for the server, right-click the server node and choose Display Statistics to open the Server (*IP Address*) Statistics dialog (see Figure 14.17). Uptime is the number of hours since the last server reboot (Start Time), not the number of hours the DCHP server has run. If you receive a large number of Nacks (not-acknowledged messages) or Declines, you might have a scope that's run out of addresses to lease or a problem with the DHCP server.

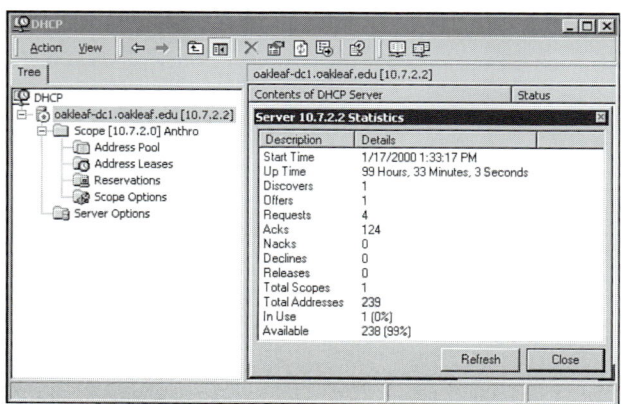

Figure 14.17
The statistics window for an entire DHCP server shows the total numbers for all scopes defined on that server as well as general server statistics, such as requests and acknowledgements.

You can alter the properties of individual scopes, as well as server properties, by right-clicking the appropriate node and choosing an action from the context menu. Following are the most common actions for managing a DHCP server with many clients:

- Add exclusion ranges. Right-click the Scope, Address Pool node and choose New Exclusion Range to open the Add Exclusion dialog. Type the beginning and ending IP addresses you want to exclude from assignment to clients.

- Add client IP address reservations. Right-click the Scope, Reservations node and choose New Reservation to open the New Reservation dialog. You can reserve particular IP addresses in the scope for clients that need fixed IP addresses. You must know in advance the client's MAC address to add the reservation.

- Assign multicast scopes. Right-click the server node, and choose New Multicast Scope to start the New Multicast Scope Wizard. Windows 2000 adds the Multicast Address Client Allocation Protocol (MADCAP) for automatically providing clients and servers with multicast addresses.

→ For more information on Windows 2000 multicasting, **see** "Establishing a Multicast Broadcast Station," **p. CD36**, on the CD-ROM.

- Create superscopes. Right-click the server node and choose New Superscope to start the New Superscope Wizard. Superscopes let you expand the IP address range available to clients by collecting individual scopes within a superscope.

- Authorize or unauthorize a local or remote DHCP server. Right-click the DHCP node and choose Manage Authorized Servers to open the dialog of the same name. All authorized DHCP servers on your network appear in the dialog's list; you can unauthorize a server or authorize another DHCP server.

Online help for the DHCP snap-in supplies descriptions of the lesser-used actions not included in the preceding list.

Using the DHCP Relay Agent

DHCP relies on broadcasts, so a DHCP server on a routed subnet ordinarily can't serve clients on other subnets. If you set up a DHCP server for each subnet or your router passes BOOTP forwarding, you don't need to be concerned with other subnets. All new routers support BOOTP forwarding, also called RFC 1542-compliance, and most older routers can be upgraded to provide BOOTP forwarding.

If you're running a multihomed Windows 2000 server—a server with two or more network adapters—as a software router, or your router doesn't support BOOTP forwarding, you have another option. Use the DHCP Relay Agent feature of the Routing and Remote Access Service (RRAS) to supply client IP address leases on another subnet. In the preceding examples, the DHCP server is oakleaf-dc1 (`10.7.2.2`) on the `10.7.2.0` subnet. In this example, you want the oakleaf-dc1 DHCP server also to supply IP leases to clients on the `10.7.3.0` subnet, which doesn't have a DHCP server.

> **Caution**
>
> You can't run the DHCP Relay Agent on a server that runs the DHCP Server service. If you attempt to do so, you disable the DHCP server. You also can't run the DHCP Relay Agent on a server that uses RRAS's Network Address Translation (NAT) with automatically assigned addresses.

To install and set up the DHCP Relay agent and establish the DHCP scope for the other subnet, follow these steps:

1. Launch the Routing and Remote Access snap-in from the Administrative Tools menu on a server in the second subnet—student-dc1 (`10.7.3.2`) for this example.
2. If Routing and RAS isn't configured on the server, right-click the server name node and choose Configure and Enable Routing and Remote Access Service to start the Routing and Remote Access Setup Wizard. Click Next to bypass the Welcome dialog.
3. In the Common Configurations dialog, select the Network Router option, and click Next.
4. In the Network Protocols dialog, accept the default TCP/IP entry and Yes, All of the Available Protocols Are on This List option, and click Next.
5. In the Demand-Dial Connections dialog, accept the No (demand-dial connections) option, click Next, and then Finish to dismiss the Wizard and start the RRAS service.
6. Expand the server node and its subnodes to display the IP Routing, General node, which shows the router interfaces on the server. Right-click the IP Routing, General node, and choose New Routing Protocol to open the dialog of the same name. Select the DHCP Relay Agent in the Routing Protocols list (see Figure 14.18), and click OK to add the protocol to RRAS.

Figure 14.18
The Routing and Remote Access snap-in is shown adding the DHCP Relay Agent as a new RRAS routing protocol to route DHCP requests across multiple subnets.

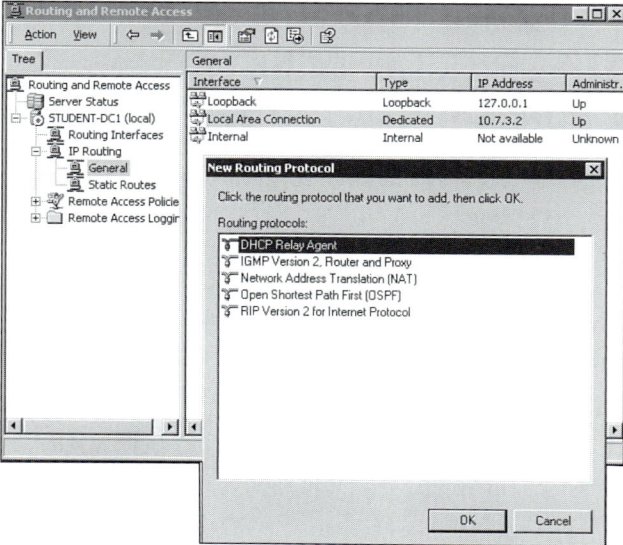

7. Right-click the added DHCP Relay Agent node, and choose New Interface to open the New Interface for DHCP Relay Agent dialog (see Figure 14.19). Select the Local Area Connection—the network adapter assigned the 10.3.2.2 address and a gateway address of 10.3.2.1 for this example—and click OK to add the router interface for the 10.3.2.0 network. Click OK to add the interface and open the DHCP Relay Agent Properties dialog.

Figure 14.19
The New Interface window is shown for the DHCP Relay Agent, selected in the left pane. It is used to specify the interface on which the agent should run.

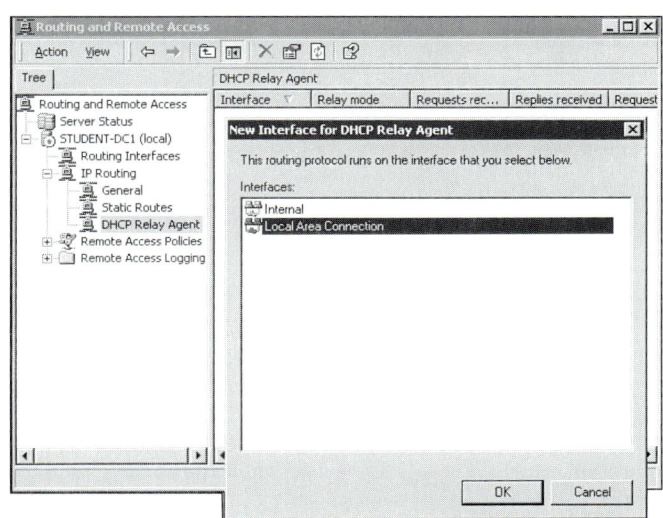

8. Accept the default Relay DHCP Packets selection, the 4 Hop-Count Threshold, and the 4-second Boot Threshold values. These values are appropriate for most networks. Click OK to return to the RRAS snap-in, which now displays an item for the Local Area Connection interface in the DHCP Relay Agent list.

> **Note**
> The Relay Mode item states that the interface is enabled, but DHCP forwarding doesn't occur until you specify the DHCP server's address in the next step.

9. Right-click the DHCP Relay Agent node, and click Properties to open its properties dialog. Type the IP address of the DHCP server on the other subnet (10.7.2.2 for this example) in the text box, and click Add (see Figure 14.20). Click OK to close the dialog and enable software BOOTP forwarding.
10. Launch the DHCP snap-in and add a new scope with an address range in the second subnet—such as 10.7.3.16 to 10.7.3.254—following the instructions in the earlier "Creating a DHCP Scope with the New Scope Wizard" and its following sections.
11. Test operation of the DHCP Relay Agent with a test client in the second subnet, as described in the earlier "Activating and Testing the New DHCP Scope" section.

Figure 14.20
Specify the local area network interface of the DHCP Relay Agent server.

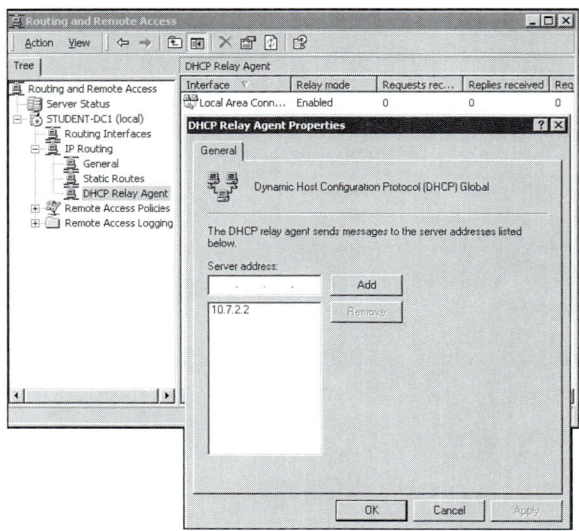

Fortunately, the DHCP Relay Agent and BOOTP recognize that clients on the second subnet need IP addresses within the subnet range. When the router sends the request message to the DHCP server (10.7.2.2), it includes a field that identifies the requestor as being in a different subnet (10.7.3.0). The DHCP server then leases the client an IP address from the appropriate (newly-added) scope.

Understanding the Windows Internet Naming Service

The Windows Internet Naming Service (WINS) is a networking component of Windows 2000 server that resolves NetBIOS names to IP addresses. NetBIOS name resolution is required only for downlevel clients; Windows 2000 clients use DNS for name resolution. You can dispense with WINS only after you upgrade all clients and servers on your network to Windows 2000. Many current 32-bit Windows applications depend on NetBIOS networking, thus most organizations must run WINS for many more years.

Sytek developed the Network Basic Input/Output System (NetBIOS) for IBM in 1983 to serve as the foundation of a networking infrastructure (PC-NET) for IBM's early PC product line. Microsoft adopted NetBIOS and the NetBIOS Extended User Interface (NetBEUI) in the mid-1980s for its original PC networking product, MS-NET, and the later LAN Manager. Windows 3.x, 9x, and NT use NetBIOS, NetBEUI, and NetBIOS over TCP/IP (NBT) as Microsoft Networking components.

NetBIOS provides a method of identifying resources—primarily clients, servers, and printers—on a network. Each device running on the network is assigned a unique name with a maximum length of 15 characters that defines the particular computer or printer to the network. You assign a NetBIOS name when you install any current Windows operating system on a computer. Windows 2000 prefers DNS names for network hosts, so Microsoft refers to NetBIOS names as downlevel. Despite the emphasis on DNS names, Windows 2000 makes extensive use of NetBIOS names. Windows 3.x, 9x, and NT hosts running NBT require translation of NetBIOS names to IP addresses, a process called NetBIOS name resolution. Before the advent of WINS, Microsoft networks handled NetBIOS name resolution by one or more of the following methods:

- *NetBIOS broadcasts* require the requesting host to broadcast its IP address and the NetBIOS name of the destination host. The destination host returns its IP address to establish a network session. In a large network, broadcast traffic can consume a substantial part of the network bandwidth. Most routers don't pass broadcasts, so this approach to name resolution usually is restricted to a single subnet.

- *NetBIOS name caching* stores the most recently used sets of NetBIOS names and their IP addresses at the host. Before sending a broadcast, the host checks the cache for the NetBIOS name. If found, the host establishes the connection with the cached IP address; if not, a host without an LMHOSTS file broadcasts its request. You use the Nbtstat.exe command-line utility with the -c argument (type **nbtstat -c**) to read the contents of the name cache. Typing **nbtstat -r** lists the names of all accessible hosts.

- *LMHOSTS files* are static text files that contain a list of NetBIOS names and corresponding IP addresses. If a host can't find the NetBIOS name in its cache, it consults the LMHOSTS file. The advantage of LMHOSTS is that it can store IP addresses on other networks; the drawback is that each host must store a local copy of a manually created LMHOSTS file. Keeping every client's LMHOST file up to date is a major administrative undertaking.

In each of these methods, the Address Resolution Protocol (ARP) translates the IP address to the host's MAC address. ARP uses broadcasts and caching to associate IP and MAC addresses.

→ For a review of ARP, **see** "Matching IP and NIC Addresses with ARP," **p. 76**.

Microsoft designed WINS to eliminate NetBIOS broadcast traffic and the need for administrators to distribute updated LMHOSTS files to clients. When you attach hosts to a network with a WINS server, the host registers its NetBIOS name and IP address with the WINS server. When a client on the network wants to communicate with another host, usually a server, the client communicates with the WINS server to handle NetBIOS name resolution.

Windows 2000 offers many improvements to the Windows NT 4.0 WINS implementation. The most important new features and enhancements are

- An Improved management tool—Like DHCP, the WINS manager now is an MMC snap-in for the Microsoft Management Console. The WINS snap-in lets you dynamically delete duplicate records in the WINS database, if present, and remove statistics for computers no longer on the network or moved to another subnet.

- Persistent replication connections between WINS servers—Larger networks using multiple WINS servers require synchronization of the WINS database between servers. Prior to Service Pack 4, Windows NT required that each WINS synchronization between replication partners open a new connection. The Windows 2000 WINS implementation lets you establish a persistent connection between replication partners.

- Better fault tolerance—Like Windows 98, Windows 2000 WINS clients (servers and workstations) can be configured to specify up to 12 WINS server IP addresses. Windows 95 and NT limit the choice to two WINS servers.

- Manual tombstoning of WINS records—This feature lets you mark an entry in the WINS database for deletion by all WINS servers on the network. Deletion occurs immediately on the local WINS server. When the WINS servers on the network synchronize their database, the "tombstoned" record is removed from all copies of the WINS database.

Installing and Configuring WINS

If you upgrade a Windows NT 4.0 PDC, BDC, or member server running WINS, the setup process automatically updates the Jet 4.0 WINS database (Wins.mdb) to the Jet 5.0 version. In a new server installation, it's the most common practice to specify adding WINS during the setup's Networking Components phase. If you didn't add WINS during Windows 2000 setup, you can add the service from the Configure Your Server dialog or Control Panel's Add/Remove Programs tool.

Tip from
RJ

> If you're running WINS in a large network with many Windows 9x and NT clients, don't run WINS on a DC if you have a member server–preferably a file server–in the domain that can handle WINS traffic. When a large number of downlevel clients log on at 8:00 a.m., the DC must handle WINS requests from computers and logon requests from users simultaneously. If WINS doesn't respond to a client request within a few seconds because the DC is busy authenticating user accounts, the WINS client reverts to NetBIOS broadcasts, which adds to the early-morning burst of traffic.

Unlike DHCP, Windows 2000 Server starts WINS automatically. The earlier DHCP sections of this chapter assume that WINS is running, but you can install the WINS server after setting up DHCP. You don't need to authorize or activate the WINS server, and there's not much to manage in the WINS snap-in.

Managing Local and Remote WINS Servers

Windows 2000's WINS snap-in bears little resemblance to Windows NT 4.0's WINS Manager application. The WINS snap-in presents a much more logical approach to displaying WINS status database records in a Window with a layout that's consistent with other service management snap-ins.

After installing WINS, if necessary, you can check the initial status of the WINS server by doing the following:

1. Launch the WINS snap-in from the Administrative Tools menu. Click the Server Status node to display an entry in the Server Status list that indicates the server is responding.
2. Expand the server node, right-click Active Registrations, and choose Find by Owner to open the Find by Owner dialog.
3. Accept the default This Owner option, select the entry for the local server in the list, and click Find Now to display all WINS entries in the local server's database in the Active Registrations pane (see Figure 14.21).

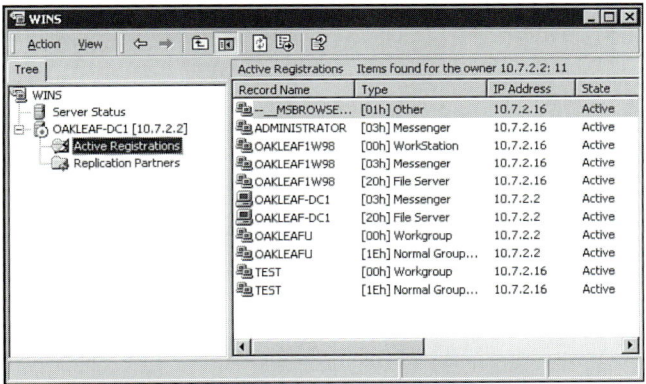

Figure 14.21
The WINS snap-in shows WINS records for a server in the sample `oakleaf.edu` domain, which has one DC and one workstation as members.

Note

By default, WINS displays only entries for clients and servers in the WINS server's domain. Figure 14.21 shows entries for the sample oakleaf.edu (OAKLEAFU) domain with one DC (OAKLEAF-DC1), and one Windows 98 workstation (OAKLEAF1W98), which also is a member of the Test peer workgroup. If your domain includes many clients, the Find by Owner list can become quite lengthy and, ultimately, unmanageable.

4. To shorten the list by displaying only records that begin with a specific set of characters, right-click the Active Registrations node, and choose Find by Name to open the dialog of the same name. Type the first few characters in the Find Names Beginning With text box, and click Find Now to restrict the number of records displayed.
5. To add entries from another WINS server to the WINS snap-in, right-click the WINS node, and choose Add Server to open the Add Server dialog. Type the NetBIOS or IP address of the server in the text box, and click OK to add the server entries. Figure 14.22 shows the WINS snap-in with entries for servers in the Windows 2000 `oakleaf.edu` and `student.oakleaf.edu` (STUDENT) domains, and the Windows NT OAKLEAF domain. You can manage Windows NT WINS servers from the WINS snap-in, despite the difference in Jet database versions.

Figure 14.22
Multiple WINS servers can be administered from the oakleaf-dc1 DC of the `oakleaf.edu` domain.

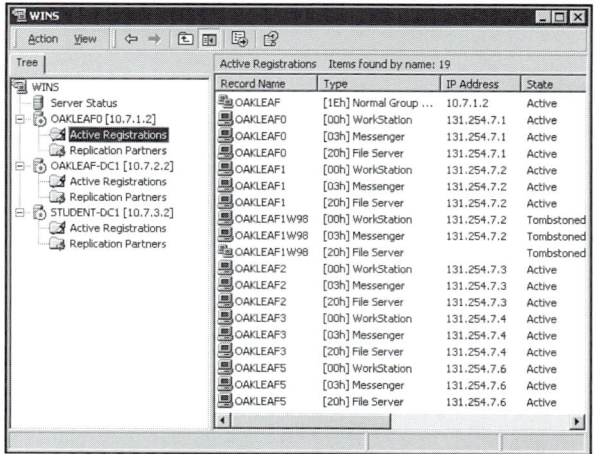

Note

The OAKLEAF0 BDC for the OAKLEAF domain is multihomed to the `10.7.1.0` and `131.254.7.0` networks. The record for the OAKLEAF1W98 test workstation is tombstoned, because its IP address changed from 131.254.7.2 to 10.7.2.16 by DHCP in the earlier "Activating and Testing the New DHCP Scope" section. A Find By Name criterion of "OAK" restricts the number of record entries for the OAKLEAF domain.

6. To remove tombstoned records from the database, right-click the server node, choose Scavenge Database, and click OK to acknowledge the "Queued on server" message.

Tip from
RJ

Scavenge your WINS databases for moderate-size networks (100 to 250 clients) monthly. Larger networks with thousands of clients deserve weekly housecleaning. Scavenging the database on OAKLEAF0 removes the tombstoned OAKLEAF1W98 records.

7. Back up your WINS database(s) periodically, especially after you make a large number of changes to or additions of records. To back up the database on the local server, right-click the server node, choose Backup Database, and specify the drive and folder to hold the backup in the Browse for Folder dialog.

Tip from
RJ

Back up the database to a drive other than the system drive on your server, or to a network share on another server or your administrative workstation. You must map the backup destination share to a local drive letter, because the Browse for Folder dialog doesn't have a Network option.

8. To alter default WINS server properties, right-click a server node, and choose Properties to open the General page of the *ServerName* Properties dialog. Accept the default 10-minute statistics refresh interval, specify the folder for WINS database backup, and mark the Backup Database During Server Shutdown check box (see Figure 14.23).

INSTALLING AND CONFIGURING WINS | 609

Figure 14.23
The General page of the properties dialog for a WINS server allows you to specify a location to which to back up the WINS database, and allows you to force a WINS database backup upon server shutdown.

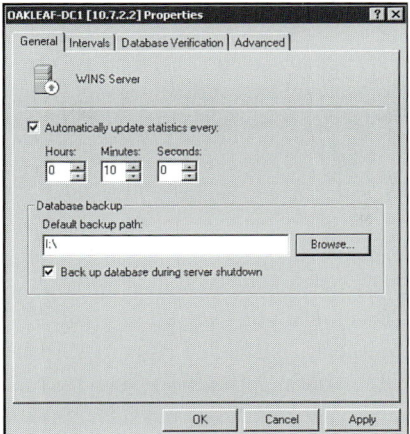

Note

The server properties dialog's Intervals page lets you change the default values for updating the WINS database. The default values are satisfactory for small networks (250 hosts or fewer); if you have more hosts, you might need to tune the update intervals.

The Database Verification page lets you enable—and specify the interval between—scans of the server's database for consistency; the default interval is every 24 hours.

The Advanced page lets you enable detailed WINS event logging for troubleshooting, set burst handling options, change the path to the local WINS database, and remove the restriction on computer names to those compatible with Microsoft LAN Manager.

9. To view initial server statistics, right-click the server node, and choose Display Server Statistics to open the WINS Server '*ServerName*' Statistics dialog (see Figure 14.24).

Figure 14.24
The WINS server statistics are shown for a newly created WINS server.

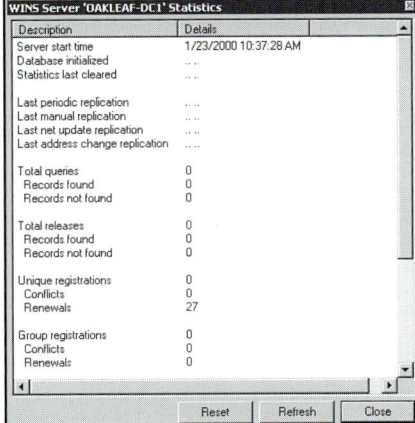

PART
III

CH
14

Tip from
RJ

Check statistics daily for each WINS server you set up until you're certain that WINS is operating correctly. Keep a watch on Records Not Found and Conflicts; these statistics should be 0 or a very low number. Server statistics are your first line of defense against WINS server problems—especially replication failures. WINS replication statistics appear at the bottom of the statistics text box.

DESIGNATING REPLICATION PARTNERS

Unlike DHCP servers, only one of which can have an activated scope with an IP address range that overlaps the range of other servers, you can add as many WINS servers as you want to a domain. Better yet, you can specify individual pairs of Windows 2000 and NT WINS servers in the same or other domains as replication partners. Like AD's replicated directory, WINS replication maintains synchronization between all databases. WINS replication lets you designate replication partners as push (send changes), pull (accept changes), or push/pull (send and accept changes). Push/pull, the default replication type, is satisfactory for most WINS configurations in networks of moderate size (up to 1,000 or so clients).

Tip from
RJ

It's a good practice to designate a single server—preferably a member server, not a DC—as a single replication partner for all other WINS servers. Establishing a central WINS server creates a hub-and-spoke replication configuration that prevents loops in the replication topology. A loop occurs if, for example, you replicate between WINS servers on oakleaf-dc1 and student-dc1, student-dc1 and OAKLEAF0, and OAKLEAF0 and oakleaf-dc1. Loops cause re-replication, which can corrupt your WINS database.

To set up WINS replication, using the three WINS servers shown in Figure 14.22 for the example, do the following:

1. Right-click the Replication Partners icon for the server you designate as the central server (oakleaf-dc1 for this example), and choose New Replication Partner to open the dialog of the same name. Type the IP address of the WINS server to become a partner in the WINS Server text box (see Figure 14.25). Click OK to add the entry to the Replication Partners list.

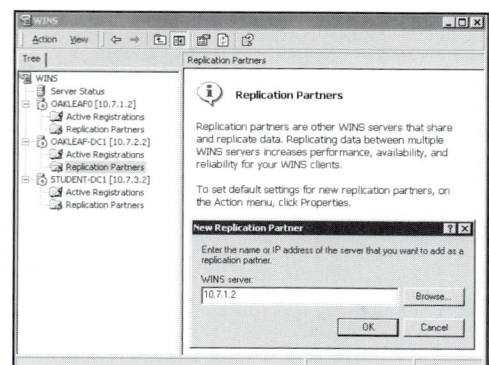

Figure 14.25
The New Replication Partner dialog allows you to add a replication partner for the WINS server. Here, 10.7.1.2 is being added as a partner for 10.7.2.2.

INSTALLING AND CONFIGURING WINS | 611

2. Repeat step 1 for each of the other replication partners of the central server. For this example, the replication partners are OAKLEAF0 (10.7.1.2, Windows NT 4.0) and student-dc1 (10.7.3.2, Windows 2000).

3. If you added the other WINS servers to the DHCP snap-in step 5 of the preceding section, right-click the partner's server node, and add the central server (oakleaf-dc1, 10.7.2.2, for this example) as a replication partner. Repeat this step for each replication partner you specified in steps 1 and 2.

Tip from
RJ

If you didn't add nodes for the other WINS server in your network, do it now. It's much easier to set up and verify replication from a single snap-in than to go to each remote server and specify a replication partner. You also can manage multiple WINS servers from a workstation running Windows 2000 Professional with the server administrative tools installed.

Note

Setting up WINS replication partners is similar to establishing Windows NT interdomain non-transitive trusts. You must establish a reciprocal partnership on the replication pairs. If you don't specify a partnership on both participating WINS servers, replication fails.

4. Right-click the Replication Partners node for the central WINS server, and choose Properties to open the Replication Partners Properties dialog. Accept the default Replicate Only with Partners option, and click the Push Replication tab. Mark the At Service Startup and When Address Changes check boxes, and set the Number of Changes in Version ID Before Replication value to a number greater than 0—5 is a good starting point (see Figure 14.26). Accept the default Use Persistent Connections for Push Replication Partners option.

Figure 14.26
The Push Replication page of the Replication Partner properties dialog for the selected partner enables you to configure the replication parameters. Here, replication occurs on startup, on address change, and after five changes to the WINS database.

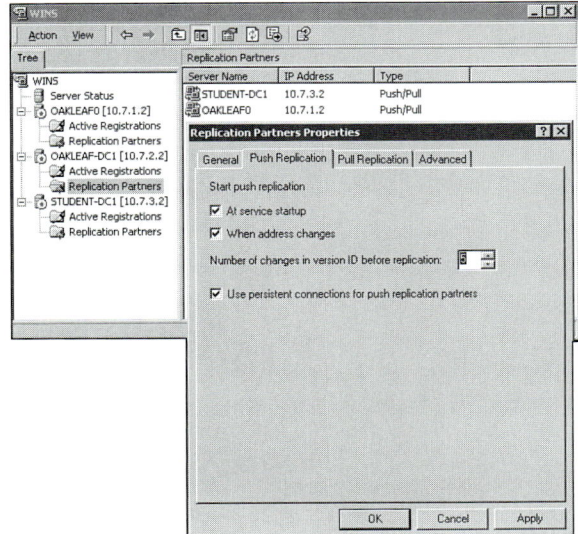

PART
III
CH
14

> **Note**
>
> The Pull Replication page of the properties dialog sets the interval for time-based pull replication from partners. The default for the pull replication interval is 30 minutes. In a large network, a setting of an hour or two is more suitable.
>
> The Advanced page lets you block replication from specific servers, and configure automatic discovery of replication partners. It's a better practice to manually configure replication partners; manual configuration lets you determine your own replication topology.

5. Repeat step 4 for each of the central WINS server's replication partners.
6. Right-click the central WINS server's node, choose Replicate Now, and acknowledge the messages by clicking Yes and OK. Replication isn't instantaneous, so you might need to wait a few minutes for replication to occur.
7. Verify that the central WINS server's database has received records from its replication partners. Right-click the server node, choose Refresh, right-click Active Registrations, choose Find by Name, and type a criterion that returns records from a replication partner. Figure 14.27 shows records received by oakleaf-dc1 from OAKLEAF0 and, at the bottom of the list, the original records for the `oakleaf.edu` domain created when setting up oakleaf-dc1 as a WINS server.

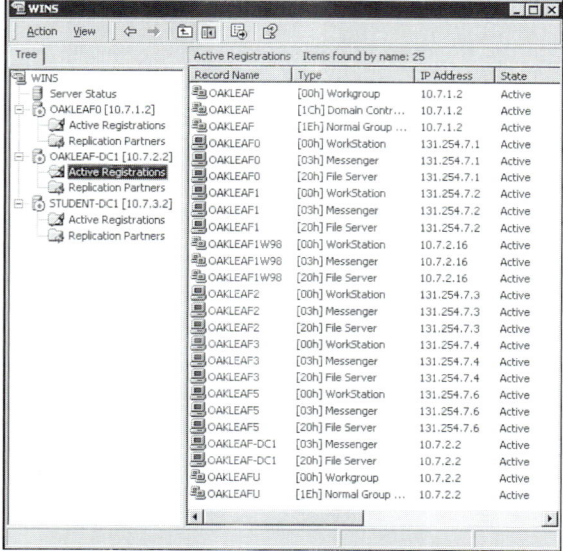

Figure 14.27
WINS database records were pulled by the central WINS server (oakleaf-dc1) from a Windows NT WINS server (OAKLEAF0).

8. Repeat steps 6 and 7 for each of the other WINS servers.
9. Right-click the server node, and choose Display Server Statistics. The WINS Server '*ServerName*' Statistics dialog shows the date and time of the last periodic and manual replication near the top, and the number of successful and failed replications at the bottom (see Figure 14.28).

Figure 14.28
The server statistics dialog shows the date and times of replications at the top, and the number of replications and failures for each partner at the bottom.

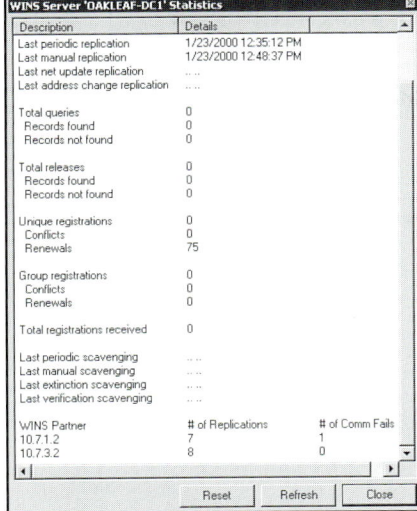

Tip from
RJ

The WINS Partner, # of Replications, and # of Comm(unication) Fail(ure)s data at the bottom of the server statistics text box is your best source for determining the health of WINS replication. If more than 20% of replication attempts fail, you probably have a connectivity problem with the replication partner on a LAN. You can expect a higher percentage of replication failures over unreliable WAN connections.

10. Use your DHCP test client to verify connectivity with one or more hosts in each of the external subnets by pinging each host with the NetBIOS name. Testing by pinging hosts within the client's subnet doesn't test WINS, because name resolution can succeed by conventional NetBIOS broadcasts.

 If you encounter problems with client connectivity outside the local subnet, see the "WINS Problems" topic in the following "Troubleshooting" section.

Troubleshooting

DHCP Problems

All DHCP clients on the subnet fail to obtain a DHCP address.

The most common cause of this problem is forgetting to activate the scope for the subnet or failing to authorize the DHCP server that manages the scope. Another possibility is that you set an incorrect value for the 003 Router option (default gateway) for the subnet, or there is a problem with the subnet mask.

A more remote possibility is that you have two DHCP servers authorized with active scopes with IP address ranges that overlap one another. In this case, decide which scope is the most appropriate for your subnet and deactivate the other scope with the IP address range overlap. If you need the deactivated scope, change its IP address range to exclude the overlapping addresses and reactivate it.

If the server is on a different subnet than the clients requesting IP addresses, make sure BOOTP forwarding is enabled on the subnet's router. If you can't get the router to forward BOOTP broadcasts, set up a DHCP Relay Agent on the clients' subnet.

A few clients on a large subnet don't receive IP addresses.

The most probable cause is that the maximum number of IP leases in the scope has been assigned to clients, and additional clients can't obtain a lease. In this case, revoke leases for clients no longer on the subnet to free their addresses. If you still don't have enough addresses to service all clients, review the start and end of your scope's IP range to see if you can gain a few addresses. Similarly, review excluded addresses to determine if you can free a few of those addresses for use by clients.

Overlapping IP address ranges in two scopes on one server—which shouldn't be possible but sometimes is—or on another activated DHCP server also can cause clients within the overlap region to fail to obtain leases.

WINS Problems

Clients can't resolve NetBIOS names of all computers outside their own subnet.

The client isn't able to connect to a WINS server that stores information for computers on other subnets. This issue can arise from several sources, such as a required WINS server being offline, long-term replication failures, an incorrect gateway address, or WINS database corruption. There's also the chance that DHCP has delivered the clients an incorrect WINS server address.

Like most other problems that might involve network connectivity, run Winipcnf.exe or Ipconfig /All on the client to determine the WINS server that the client is attempting to reach. Ping with the server's IP address to verify network connectivity, and then ping with the WINS server's NetBIOS name to check name resolution. The IP address tests connectivity, and using the server name checks name resolution of the remote server. If both pings succeed, it's likely that the WINS server's database is corrupt, so use the WINS snap-in to verify the server's database integrity.

A client can't resolve NetBIOS names of some computers outside their own subnet.

A common cause of this problem is impatience. If the client is attempting to reach a newly added host on a subnet whose WINS server replicates with the client's designated WINS server, a record for the new host won't appear until the replication process completes. This can take up to an hour or more, depending on replication interval settings on both WINS servers.

> **Note**
>
> WINS causes major headaches that reach migraine proportions for network administrators in large, distributed networks with extensive WAN links. WINS replication isn't nearly as robust as AD replication. Like Windows NT trusts, WINS replication often fails for no apparent reason, and the WINS error messages in the System event log don't explain why the failure occurred. In many cases, simply rebooting the WINS server(s) restores a broken replication link. Alternatively, you might need to use the WINS snap-in to dissolve and recreate the replication partnership.
>
> One of the primary incentives for upgrading *every* computer in your organization to Windows 2000 is to eliminate NetBIOS and NBT, replacing NetBIOS name resolution with DNS name resolution. In the long run, you might save the entire upgrade cost by eliminating the troubleshooting time and aggravation caused by WINS. As economist John Maynard Keynes stated in the mid-1930s, "In the long run, we are all dead."

MCSE Corner: Providing Clients with DHCP and WINS

DHCP becomes especially important when a network is large enough to use multiple subnets and multihomed servers. For this reason, DHCP is a concept that is thoroughly tested in many of the Windows 2000 Server–related exams. WINS is an element of Windows NT that has been superseded by the addition of Dynamic DNS to Windows 2000 Server, but still is necessary to service downlevel clients. Many Windows NT 4.0 networks already have functioning WINS servers, and most administrators are familiar with setting up and troubleshooting WINS. Make sure you are familiar with WINS, and especially DHCP, for any Windows 2000 Server exam; both are an integral part of a successful network implementation. A thorough understanding of WINS and DHCP also helps you administer actual networks.

70-216 Implementing and Administering a Microsoft Windows 2000 Network Infrastructure

Most questions pertaining to what you learned in this chapter about WINS and DHCP are found in the 70-216 exam. You are required to know everything about installing, configuring, and troubleshooting the two services. You will probably be asked questions about installing the DHCP server service and creating and managing DHCP scopes. It is likely that you will have to perform one or more of these operations in a simulated environment for the exam and answer theoretical questions. You should also be familiar with monitoring the DHCP server.

The exam requires you to understand how to install, configure, and troubleshoot the WINS server service. You should know how to install the service and configure both basic WINS installation and WINS replication.

An important skill to have for this exam is the ability to troubleshoot both WINS and DHCP. The Microsoft exams are adding more and more troubleshooting questions to better prepare potential MCPs for the real world. You will probably be presented with at least one question in which you are given a set of symptoms of a nonfunctioning DHCP or WINS server and will be expected to determine the cause of the problem.

70-221   Designing a Microsoft Windows 2000 Network Infrastructure

The 70-222 exam assesses your ability to analyze the requirements of a complex network environment and make suitable architectural recommendations. You must be familiar with all aspects of DHCP. You must be able to integrate DHCP and the DHCP Relay Agent into a Windows 2000 network with routers joining remote locations, and therefore separate IP subnets. You should also be able to determine the optimum design for a DHCP implementation, given a specified environment.

You are required to know how to design a WINS implementation in a distributed network, including WINS security. You should also be able to optimize a WINS implementation and plan the implementation of WINS on a network.

CHAPTER 15

ESTABLISHING GROUP POLICIES, USER ACCOUNTS, AND LOGONS

In this chapter

Understanding Windows 2000's Group Policies   618

Using the Group Policy Snap-In to Edit Group Policy Objects   622

Creating New Group Policy Objects   632

Designing and Populating Security Group Structures   643

Filtering GPOs with Security Groups   650

Working with User Accounts   654

Specifying User Profiles for Downlevel Clients   658

Implementing Downlevel System Policies   663

Setting Up User Home Folders   670

Troubleshooting   672

MCSE Corner: Establishing Group Policies, User Accounts, and Logons   673

Understanding Windows 2000's Group Policies

Microsoft promotes Group Policies as one of the most important new Change and Configuration Management and Total Cost of Ownership (TCO) features of Windows 2000. The purpose of Group Policies is to apply specific sets of options—most commonly restrictions—to collections of users and computers within an Active Directory (AD) container. These restrictions typically are based on the user's or computer's membership in an AD domain and organizational unit (OU). These Group Policy restrictions establish centrally managed Windows 2000 Professional desktops. For example, you can restrict the ability of some users to install applications on client PCs, but assign such permission to others. Preventing users from installing unauthorized software on company-owned client PCs is one of the most effective—but controversial—methods of reducing TCO. On the other hand, preventing a telecommuter who works on his or her own PC from installing the latest PC game software isn't an acceptable policy.

Another means of reducing TCO is to automate installation of Windows 2000 Professional on client PCs with the Remote Installation Service (RIS). You can use RIS to distribute Windows applications to client PCs and to provide automatic updates to the applications with IntelliMirror. Group Policies and IntelliMirror also let you install special-purpose software, such as statistical or computer-aided design applications, on the computers of only those users who need them. Prior to Windows 2000, you needed Microsoft Systems Management Server (SMS) to automate these tasks.

→ To learn more about automating software installation with Group Policies and RIS, **see** "Setting Group Policy for RIS Installation," **p. 879**.

→ For additional details on IntelliMirror and Group Policies, **see** "Using the Application Installation Service," **p. 846**.

> **Note**
> Group Policies apply only to computers running Windows 2000, and this chapter covers only Group Policies that apply to Windows 2000 clients. Chapter 8, "Deploying Windows 2000 Production Servers," describes how to apply Group Policies to AD domain controllers (DCs).

Client Computer and User Settings

Group Policies fall into two classes: computer settings and user settings. Computer settings, which go into effect during Windows 2000's initialization, let you specify the following parameters:

- Computer startup and shutdown scripts, which, if implemented, let you run Visual Basic Scripting Edition (VBScript) or JavaScript/ECMAScript (JScript) scripts from the Windows Scripting Host (WSH).

- Security settings, which affect account policies, local (client) Security Policies, system services, Registry keys, the file system (disk quotas), and other security-related objects.
- Assigned (mandatory) applications, which install on the computer during the initialization process and become available to all users. You also can update assigned applications automatically.
- Desktop appearance, including desktop shortcuts and start menu choices that apply to all computer users.

The client's HKEY_LOCAL_MACHINE Registry key holds computer settings that apply to all users.

User settings, which are applied when a user logs on from any Windows 2000 computer, determine the following settings:

- User logon and logoff scripts, if implemented
- Special folder redirection settings for Application Data, Desktop, My Documents and My Pictures, and Start Menu folders
- Published applications, which let the user choose whether to install the application
- Internet Explorer maintenance for the browser, Internet connection, URLs (Favorites and Links, Important URLs and Channels), and access to programs (HTML Editor, E-Mail, Newsgroups, Internet Call, Calendar, and Contact List)
- Remote Installation Service options for the Client Installation Wizard
- Public Key Security Policies for clients

The client's HKEY_CURRENT_USER Registry key stores most computer settings for the currently logged on user, and user policies override most user-related computer policies, unless you specify otherwise. DCs send computer and user policy settings changes to clients at a specified interval; the default Group Policy refresh interval is 90 minutes.

Folder redirection, offline folders, application installation and maintenance, and other computer settings that apply to a specific user and his or her local computer, rather than to classes of users and computers, are IntelliMirror functions.

> **Note**
>
> Downlevel clients running Windows NT, 95, and 98 continue to use Windows NT System Policies that you create with the System Policy Editor (Poledit.exe). System Policies are limited to client desktop lockdown. Windows 2000 Server Setup installs Poledit.exe in your \Winnt folder, but doesn't add a System Policy Editor choice to the Administrative Tools Menu.
>
> Windows 2000 Server supports System Policies for downlevel clients and, if you do an in-place upgrade from a Windows NT 4.0 PDC to Windows 2000, the prior System Policies remain intact.

Group Policy Hierarchy and Inheritance

Windows 2000 applies Group Policies to Windows 2000 clients in the following sequence:

1. Local computer
2. Site
3. Domain
4. Organizational unit
5. Subordinate OU(s)

The application sequence determines Group Policy priority, and you can apply Group Policies at any level in the preceding list. AD objects inherit settings from the top of the list down. For instance, if you apply a Group Policy at the Site level, all members of the site's domain(s) receive the site settings, unless you assign different Group Policies at a lower level. This characteristic is called *policy inheritance*. You can block inheritance, but doing so isn't a recommended practice.

Tip from
RJ

Child domains don't inherit domain-level Group Policies from the parent domain. If you want one or more child domain to share a common Group Policy, you must create a link from the child domain to the parent's Group Policy object.

Group Policies applied at the Domain level override Local Computer- and Site-based settings; settings applied at the lowest level of an OU hierarchy override all other settings. Some settings, such as those for password security, are accessible only at the Domain level, so they can't be overridden by OU-level settings. As with inheritance blocking, you can specify that lower-level objects cannot override settings, but doing so isn't recommended.

Note

Blocking inheritance, specifying no override, or (even worse) both isn't recommended because doing so can make troubleshooting Group Policy problems very difficult. Troubleshooting problems under these circumstances arise primarily as a result of the difficulty in determining what policies apply to a specific container or object. In almost all cases, accepting the default Group Policy inheritance and override attributes is the best practice.

Security Group Filtering

Security Groups are collections of users to whom you grant permissions to access specific domain resources, such as file shares and printers. The basic characteristics of Windows 2000 security groups are almost identical to those of Windows NT. An Access Control Entry (ACE, pronounced "ace") represents each security group in the Access Control List (ACL, pronounced "akkel") for a resource. When a user requests use of a resource, the system checks for the presence of an ACE for the user account. If the user ACE isn't in the ACL, the system checks the user's group membership(s) for a group's ACE in the ACL. When it is found, the user has access to the resource with the permissions granted to the group.

→ For a brief introduction to Windows 2000's Security Groups, **see** "Security Groups," **p. 29**.

Substituting group for individual user permissions to access a resource greatly reduces administrative workload. Windows NT offers two group classes—local and global. Windows 2000 has three types of AD-based Security Groups—Domain Local, Global, and Universal. Windows 2000 lets you place Security Groups within OUs and, if your domain runs in native mode, provides very useful group nesting options.

You can exempt members of a particular Security Group from specific Group Policies. For example, if you define a relatively stringent Group Policy for the domain, you can prevent members of the built-in Domain Admins groups from receiving the domain-level policy. This process is called *group filtering*, and is an important feature to consider when you create and apply Group Policy Objects (GPOs). Using group filtering is much more efficient than creating additional OUs and GPOs to accommodate specific users' requirements.

→ To learn more about Security Groups and filtering, **see** "Filtering GPOs with Security Groups," **p. 650**.

AD Structures for Group Policy Optimization

When you design your AD domain topology, you can take one of two basic approaches—geographic or functional. The *geographic* method organizes domain trees by region, such as `oakleaf-us.edu`, `oakleaf-ca.edu`, and `oakleaf-uk.edu`, each of which might constitute a single site. *Functional* organization classifies domain structure along organizational lines, such as this book's examples of the `oakleaf.edu` domain for OakLeaf University employees and the `student.oakleaf.edu` child domain for students. Of course, you can add child domains, such as `student.oakleaf-ca.edu`, to segregate students from employees in each region. Adding a child domain lets you specify different logon and password policies for the parent and child domains.

If you elect the geographic approach, which reduces intersite replication traffic, you or the regional administrator(s) must create and manage GPOs for each domain and, optionally, site. Geographic organization implies decentralized administration, which might be necessary to satisfy jurisdictional politics, which are especially common in universities and colleges.

The alternative, functional organization, permits the use of subordinate OUs to classify employees and students by region—a highly centralized administrative model. In this case, a typical OU hierarchy might be `/Faculty Members/Anthropology/`*Region*. This structure permits applying a GPO at the Faculty Members level that applies to all faculty members in all departments at all locations. You install DCs as Global Catalog (GC) servers for each domain at each location. If you correctly design your replication topology—routing changes from the U.S. (Texas) to Canada (Toronto) to the U.K. (Mumbles)—you minimize the effect of the added intersite replication traffic. You alter GPOs infrequently, and only changes to GPOs replicate, so centralized GPO management doesn't add much replication overhead.

→ For a description of how to measure intersite replication overhead, **see** "Setting Up a Test to Estimate Replication Traffic," **p. 990**.

You must also consider Security Group membership when optimizing domain topology for Group Policy application. The first issue you face is limiting the membership of Security Groups to Microsoft's recommended "few thousand users." From a practical standpoint, security groups should be limited to about 2,000 or 3,000 users. In the OakLeaf U context, this means that a Students Security Group having all students in all regions as members is impractical for an institution of substantial size. One option is to establish Global Security Groups with a smaller membership based on graduation year or major subject. If your domain runs in native mode, you can nest the smaller Global groups within a Global or Enterprise group.

> **Note**
>
> You might have heard that Windows 2000 limits group size to 5,000 accounts or fewer. This isn't the case; you can use the ADSI25 for Active Directory application to create groups with 20,000+ users. Such large groups, however, can reduce performance substantially. Therefore, you should stick with the 2000–3000 limit recommended by Microsoft.

Another new feature of Windows 2000 is that you can assign selected computer accounts to Security Groups, in addition to placing them in OUs. If you establish GPOs for computer settings, you can exempt computers in a particular Security Group from the GPO. Bear in mind, however, that GPOs apply only to PCs running Windows 2000; it's unlikely that all hosts in your domain will run Windows 2000 until sometime in the (perhaps distant) future.

Using the Group Policy Snap-In to Edit Group Policy Objects

The Administrative Tools menu has Domain Controller Security Policy and Domain Security Policy choices, but not a Group Policies choice. The reason for this omission is that you open the Group Policy snap-in within the context of the container to which you want to apply the GPO. The standard practice is to open the Group Policy snap-in from a qualified container in Active Directory Users and Computers. The domain, Domain Controllers, and OUs you've added are the only containers to which you can assign (link) GPOs; the properties sheet of these containers has a Group Policy tab. Builtin, Computers, Foreign Security Principals, and Users containers don't have this tab, which indicates that they don't permit assigning GPOs.

> **Note**
>
> One of the major issues associated with in-place upgrades of Windows NT domains is that all user accounts fall into the Users container during the upgrade process. You can't apply–and wouldn't want to apply–a single GPO to every member of the domain. Fortunately, you can use Windows NT group membership to filter accounts into OUs you create, and then apply GPOs to the OUs as needed.

→ To review how to move Windows NT user accounts from the Users containers to OUs, **see** "Using Custom Filters to Classify Users by Group Membership," **p. 212**.

USING THE GROUP POLICY SNAP-IN TO EDIT GROUP POLICY OBJECTS | 623

 The "Establishing Security Policies for a Child Domain" section of Chapter 4, "Optimizing Your Active Directory Topology," gave you a preview of the process for assigning a GPO to a sample child domain. The sections that follow describe GPO creation and linking in a Windows 2000 production environment with two domains having a total of about 7,500 user and computer accounts. The examples take advantage of the OUs and Security Groups created by the ADSI25 for Active Directory application that's on the accompanying CD-ROM, but the examples are applicable to any domain topology of moderate complexity.

PART
III
CH
15

Note

An alternative to working with the example of the ADSI25 domain structure is to use the Active Directory Migration Tool (ADMT) to copy user, group, and computer objects from your current Windows NT domain(s) into an empty Windows 2000 domain.

→ To review use of ADMT for copying Windows NT objects, **see** "Emulating Domain Migration with the Active Directory Migration Tool," **p. 231**.

NAVIGATING THE DEFAULT DOMAIN POLICY

A useful approach to getting acquainted with AD's Group Policy management features is to navigate the Group Policy console's default configuration after you promote a server to a DC with `Dcpromo.exe`. Default GPOs have a collection of standard option groups for computer and user objects, but don't apply settings to the majority of the options.

To open the Group Policy snap-in (`Gpedit.msc`) for a domain and view and alter the default GPO options for domain-level security settings, do the following:

1. Launch Active Directory Users and Computers, right-click the domain node (`oakleaf.edu` for this example), and choose Properties to open the *DomainName* Properties dialog.

2. Click the Group Policy tab, and select Default Domain Policy in the Group Policy Object Links list (see Figure 15.1). Click Edit to open the Group Policy snap-in.

Figure 15.1
The Group Policy page of the Domain Properties dialog enables you to add, delete, and edit Group Policy Objects. The Default Domain Policy is selected here.

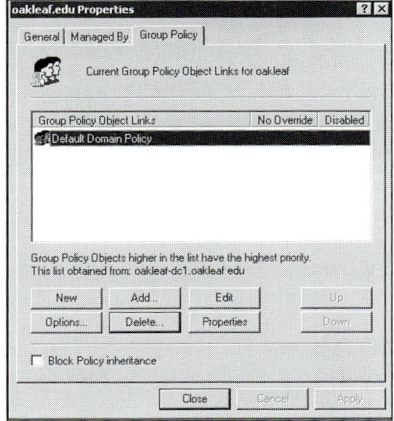

3. Expand the second- and third-level nodes in the tree view pane of the Group Policy snap-in to display the fourth-level nodes. At this level, you can compare Computer and Users setting options (see Figure 15.2).

Figure 15.2
Specific policies are defined in the Group Policy Console. The Computer Configuration and User Configuration containers are expanded in the left pane, showing some of the available types of configuration options.

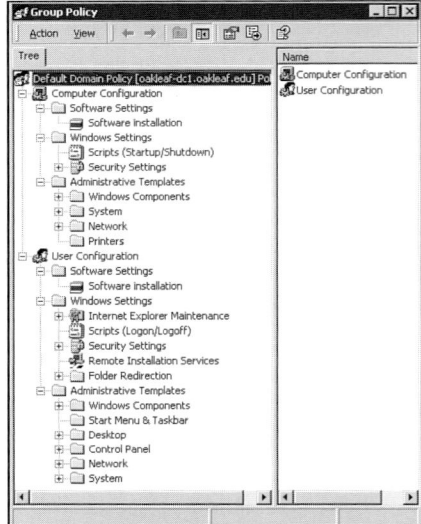

4. Expand the Computer Configuration Windows Settings, Security Settings, Account Policies node; click Password Policy to display the default history, age, length, complexity, and encryption policies for passwords in the Policy list.

5. A Minimum Password Length of 0 Characters lets users log on to the domain with an empty password. To change the minimum password length, double-click the entry in the Policy list to open the Template Security Policy Setting dialog.

6. Use the spin button or type the minimum number of characters in the spin box (see Figure 15.3) and click OK to close the dialog and change the policy.

Figure 15.3
The Template Security Policy Setting dialog enables you to configure the specific settings within a Group Policy Object. In this example, the minimum password length is selected in the background window and is being set to 8 characters.

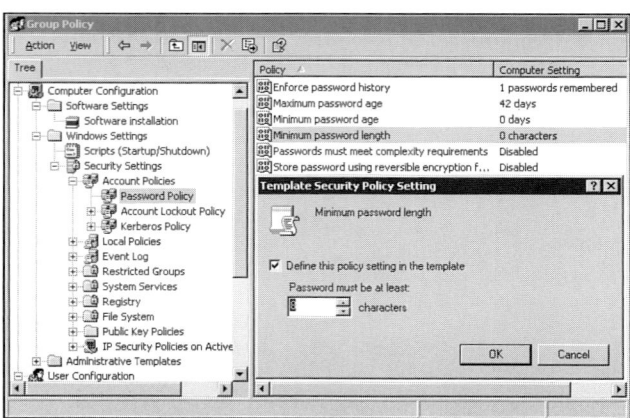

If you encounter problems after changing password policies, see the "Password Policy Problems" topic of the "Troubleshooting" section at the end of the chapter.

Tip from
RJ

It's a good practice to retain default policy settings; you may need to revert to the defaults in the event you run into a Group Policy problem. Thus, you should repeat steps 5 and 6 and revert to the Minimum Password Length value to 0. You create a new domain Group Policy later in the chapter.

ENFORCING COMPUTER SECURITY POLICIES

You must be a member of the Group Policy Creator Owners default Global group to create or modify GPOs in the domain, and to link GPOs to objects. By default, only the local Administrator account of a domain's DC is a member of this group. To permit other members of the Enterprise Admins and Domain Admins groups to modify GPOs, add these groups as members of the Group Policy Creator Owners group. Nesting these two Global groups requires that your domain operate in mixed mode.

Computer Security Settings are the most important of the Group Policies you apply at the domain level. Following are brief descriptions of the Computer Security Settings options:

- Account Policies set password, account lockout, and Kerberos options. Always configure Account Policies to establish basic domain logon security. Unless you have a reason to do otherwise, accept the default values for Kerberos Policy.

Note

Changing password options has an immediate effect only on the addition of new users to the domain. As user passwords established prior to the policy change expire, new passwords must meet the age, length, and complexity requirements of the new or modified Group Policy object.

Tip from
RJ

If you intend to use ADMT to migrate Windows NT groups and user accounts to a new Windows 2000 domain, don't apply password restrictions to Account Policies until after you successfully migrate the users. By default, ADMT sets the user's new password to his or her logon ID. If you specify complex passwords, ADMT creates random passwords meeting complexity requirements, but you must supply each user a written copy of his or her logon password from the appropriate entry in a passwords log file that ADMT generates.

- Local Policies establish auditing, group and user rights, and security settings for the local computer—a DC for this example. All but one setting—Security Settings, Automatically Log Off Users When Logon Time Expires, which is set to Disabled—are Not Defined by default. Not Defined means that the Group Policy option isn't applied to the currently selected AD object.

> **Note**
>
> Migrating accounts with the Active Directory Migration Tool (ADMT) or cloning AD objects with Clone Principal scripts requires that you enable auditing of account management operations. Windows 2000 audit policies are similar to those you set in Windows NT's User Manager for Domains.

→ For an example of setting domain account auditing policy, **see** "Installing ADMT on a Windows 2000 Domain Controller," **p. 233**.

- Event Log has a subnode, Settings for Event Logs, in which you can set many logging options for the local machine.
- Restricted Groups is a feature that lets you limit the membership of built-in and other groups having administrative permissions to a particular set of users.
- System Services opens a list in which you specify the startup mode—Automatic, Manual, or Disabled—of all server services. In addition, you can restrict the ability of local computer groups or users to alter service startup mode.
- Registry lets you apply security settings to specific Registry hives and keys.
- File System enforces selected drive, folder, and file permissions by restricting the ability to modify permissions to specific groups or users.
- Public Key Policies handle encrypted file data recovery, certificate options, and other public-key infrastructure settings.
- IP Security Policies on Active Directory enforce security rules for TCP/IP communication with AD for clients, servers, and secure servers.

Several Security Settings nodes, such as Restricted Groups and File System, don't have default entries in their policy lists. To add options to nodes without list entries, right-click the node and choose Add *Object* to open a dialog in which you specify the object to add to the list. For example, to set and enforce a particular set of permissions on an existing folder or file, do the following:

1. Right-click the File System node, and choose Add File to open the Add a File or Folder dialog.
2. Select the folder or file in the list (see Figure 15.4), and click OK to open the Database Security for Drive\Folder[\File] dialog.

Figure 15.4
Using the Add File or Folder dialog, you can select a file or folder (the folder "Shared" in this case) whose permissions you want to restrict with a GPO.

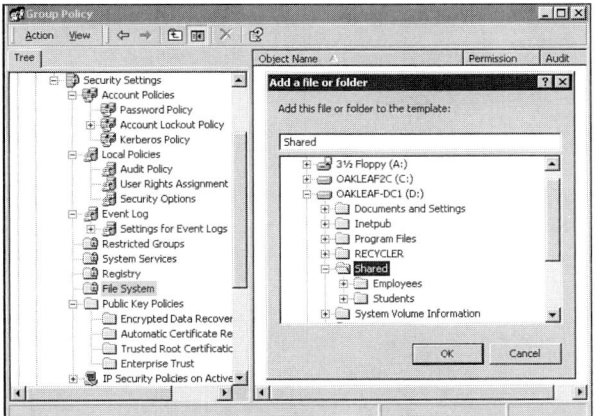

3. By default, Everyone has Full Control permissions for file system objects, unless you've previously set permissions. You can limit the Everyone group's permissions by clearing Allow or marking Deny check boxes.
4. To add groups or users to the permissions list, click the Database Security dialog's Add button to open the Select Users, Computers, or Groups dialog; select the group(s) to add, and click OK to close the dialog.
5. Select the added group in the Database Security dialog's Name list, and mark the Allow check boxes for the permissions to enforce. For instance, you usually grant members of the local Administrators group Full Control permissions for folders and their files (see Figure 15.5).

Figure 15.5
Use the Database Security dialog to enforce the Local Administrators group's Full Control permissions for the Shared folder.

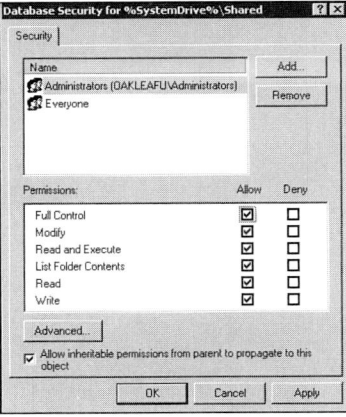

6. Click OK to close the Database Security dialog and display the Template Security Policy Setting dialog. The default options (see Figure 15.6) allow permission inheritance. In this case, changes to permissions for the folder's parent (the D: drive) propagate to the Shared folder.

Figure 15.6
The Template Security Policy Setting dialog displays the default settings to allow permission inheritance from parent file system objects.

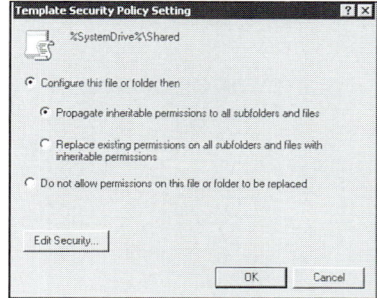

7. If you want to enforce permanently the specific security settings you applied in steps 3 through 6, select the Do Not Allow Permissions on This File or Folder to Be Replaced Option.

8. Click OK to apply the options.

You add settings for other objects, such as Registry hives and keys, and Restricted groups by methods similar to those for setting File System options.

Understanding Administrative Templates

Administrative Templates are a bit confusing because they appear out of context with other Computer Configuration and User Configuration options groups. Figure 15.7 illustrates the Administrative Template nodes and subnodes for domain-level Computer Configuration. Windows Components has options for setting NetMeeting, Internet Explorer, Task Scheduler, and Windows Installer options on clients. Logic dictates that options of this type be included under the Software Settings node.

Figure 15.7
The Group Policy snap-in displays the elements of the Administrative Templates for domain-level Computer Configuration with containers in the left pane and individual settings in the right pane.

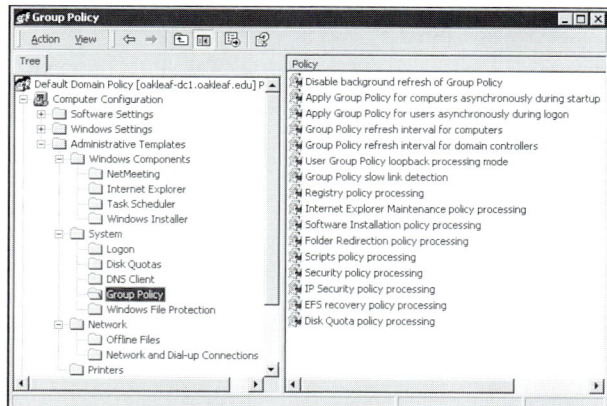

Administrative Templates are similar to Windows NT System Policies. As with Windows NT and Windows 9x Group Policy files, Windows 2000 stores Administrative Templates in .adm files; it stores changes to Computer Configuration templates in `HKEY_LOCAL_MACHINE\Software\Policies` keys and User Configuration changes in `HKEY_CURRENT_USER\Software\Policies` keys. Active Directory stores the changes you make to settings other than Administrative Templates options. The schizophrenic nature of Group Policies—some stored in AD and some in the Registry—gives rise to the unintuitive organization of Group Policy editor nodes.

> **Note**
>
> Using ...Policies keys lets Windows 2000 circumvent *tattooing* the Windows NT and 9x Registry. Tattooing results from applying a System Policy and then removing the policy without deliberately reversing the prior option. For instance, if you enable the Allow Shutdown from Authentication Dialog Box policy and then create a new System Policy file that doesn't configure the option, the option remains in the client's Registry. You must specifically negate the option by clearing the check box for the appropriate entry in the new policy.

Windows 2000 stores Administrative Template files in the `\Winnt\Inf` folder and copies of the template files in the shared `\Winnt\Sysvol\Domain\Policies` and `\Winnt\Sysvol\Sysvol\`*DomainName*`\Policies` folders. Windows 2000's File Replication Service copies the contents of the `Winnt\Sysvol` folders between DCs. Thus, changes you make on one DC propagate to the other DCs every five minutes, but you can change the interval in the Group Policy node (see the Group Policy Refresh Interval for Domain Controllers item in the list of Figure 15.7).

Following is a list of Windows 2000's commonly used standard template files:

- `System.adm` is the standard template for Windows 2000 client PCs.
- `Inetres.adm` sets Internet Explorer options for Windows 2000 clients.
- `Conf.adm` sets NetMeeting and related conferencing options for Windows 2000 clients.
- `Winnt.adm` is the template used by the System Policy Editor to set System Policies for Windows NT clients.
- `Windows.adm` is the Windows 9x version of `Winnt.adm`.
- `Common.adm` is a template that contains the options that are common to Windows NT and Windows 9x.

The Group Policy snap-in loads only `System.adm`, `Inetres.adm`, and `Conf.adm`. `Poledit.exe` loads `Winnt.adm`, `Windows.adm`, and `Common.adm`.

Each Administrative Template option has a properties dialog whose appearance varies with the type of setting. Figure 15.8 shows the Policy page of the Group Policy Refresh Interval for Computers Properties dialog. This page lets you change the refresh interval for clients—not DCs—and specify a randomizing interval to minimize the chance that all clients will request a GPO refresh at the same time. To alter the default refresh and randomizing intervals—the defaults are 90 minutes and 30 minutes, respectively—select the Enabled option and change the values in the spin boxes.

Figure 15.8
This policy page of the Properties dialog for the "Group Policy refresh interval for computers" policy allows you to enable or disable the policy. You also can configure the interval at which group policies are refreshed on domain computers and the maximum random time added to the interval to prevent network traffic floods.

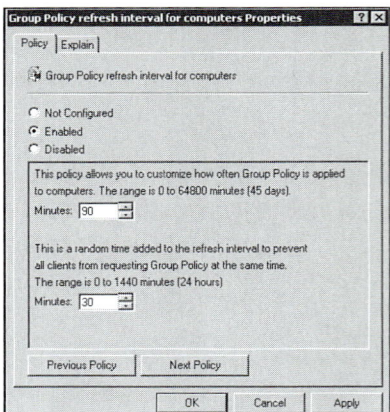

A helpful feature of Administrative Template options that's missing in other nodes is the Explain page, which provides a description of the effect of altering the default values for an option. Figure 15.9 shows the lengthy instructions for setting refresh intervals.

Figure 15.9
The Explain page of the Group Policy Refresh Intervals for Computers Properties dialog explains the purpose of the policy and the function of the individual settings.

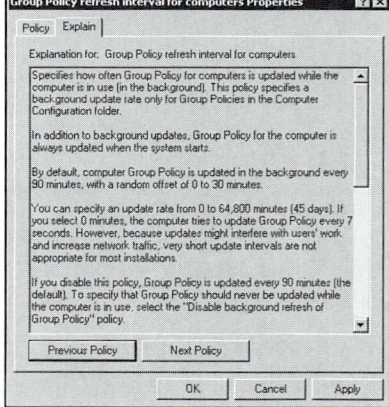

Tip from
RJ

If you want computer policies to prevail over user policies on a specific group of clients in an OU, open the Group Policy snap-in from the OU in Active Directory Users and Computers. Enable the User Group Policy Loopback Processing Mode option of the Computer Configuration, Administrative Templates, System, Group Policy node. Select Merge from the Mode list if you want Computer Configuration settings to override User Configuration settings. Select Replace if you want to apply only Computer Configuration settings, regardless of who logs on to the computer.

Exploring User Configuration

The nodes under User Configuration have properties dialogs that enable you to specify settings that apply when a user logs on to a client. The most interesting of these options to network administrators are those that let you lock down elements of computer configuration. For example, the Windows Settings, Folder Redirection, Desktop node offers the option of redirecting the user's Desktop folder to a server share. If you select the Advanced—Specify Locations for Various Users and Groups setting, you can redirect the Desktop folder for all members of selected group to a share you specify (see Figure 15.10). The share contains a central copy of the Desktop folder with shortcuts you create. You also can specify redirection of the Application Data, My Documents, and the Start menu to a centralized location.

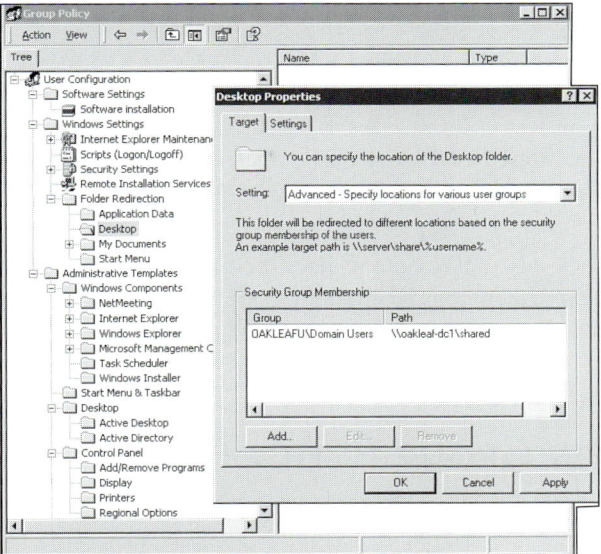

Figure 15.10
The Desktop Properties dialog under the Folder Redirection container allows you to configure a shared desktop stored on a common server share for groups of users (the oakleaf\Domain Users group in this case).

Nodes under Administrative Templates provide the ability to further restrict user modification of the client environment, including setting Active Desktop, Active Directory, and access to Control Panel tools. The most useful option of this group is Disable Active Desktop. Figure 15.11 shows the options available to restrict the user's access to Control Panel's Add/Remove Programs tool and its features.

Figure 15.11
With the Control Panel, Add/Remove programs container selected in the left pane, there is a group of options for disabling or limiting the features of the Add/Remove Programs Control Panel tool shown in the right pane.

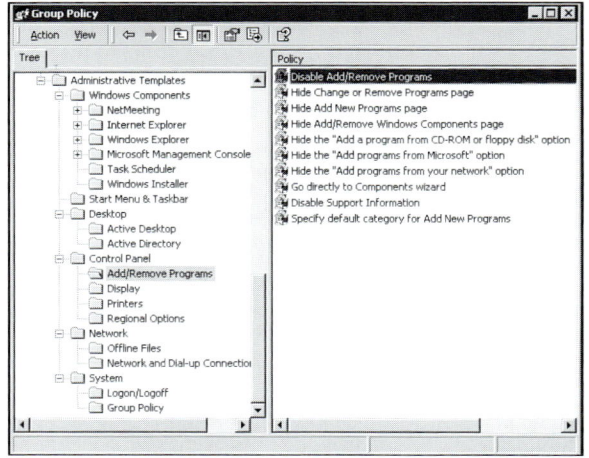

> **Note**
> You access the ultimate lock-down setting—Run Only Allowed Windows Applications—from the User Configuration, Administrative Templates, System node.

Most of the User Configuration options have self-explanatory descriptions, and the user Administrative Template options have extensive Explain text. The methods for altering default option values are similar to those described earlier for Computer Configuration options.

CREATING NEW GROUP POLICY OBJECTS

As noted earlier in the chapter, it's a good practice to retain the unmodified Default Domain Policy GPO for reuse in case you have a problem with inappropriate or conflicting option settings. Keeping the Default Domain or any other default GPO requires that you create a new GPO.

To create a new GPO for the domain, do the following:

1. Close the Group Policy snap-in, if it's open, to display the *DomainName* Properties dialog (oakleaf.edu Properties for this example). Otherwise, right-click the DomainName node in Active Directory Users and Computers and choose Properties.

2. Click the Group Policy tab—if necessary—to display the Group Policy page, select the Default Domain Policy entry in the Group Policy Object Links list, and click Options to open the Default Domain Policy Options dialog.

3. Mark the Disabled check box (see Figure 15.12), click OK to disable the policy, and click Yes to acknowledge the resulting Confirm Disable warning message.

CREATING NEW GROUP POLICY OBJECTS | 633

PART
III
CH
15

Figure 15.12
Clicking the Options button on the Group Policy tab of the Oakleaf.edu Properties page brings up this dialog, where the "Default Domain Policy" GPO is being disabled.

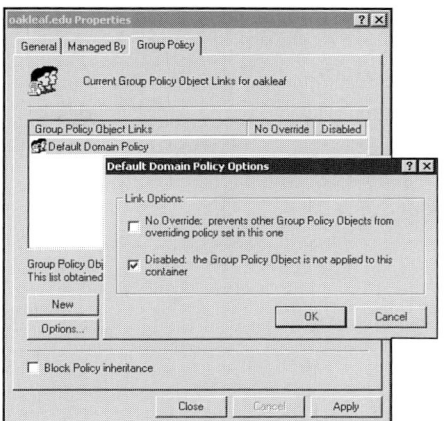

4. Click the New button to add a New Group Policy Object to the list. Rename the GPO as appropriate to its purpose, and click the Up button to move the new GPO to the top of the list (see Figure 15.13). If you have multiple, enabled GPOs, they apply in bottom-to-top order.

Figure 15.13
The new domain GPOs are added to and moved to the top of the Group Policy Object Links list.

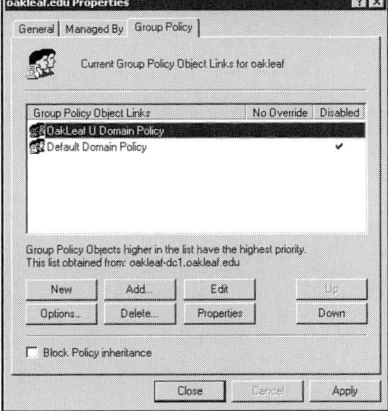

5. With the new GPO highlighted in the GPO Links list, click Properties to open the General page of the *GPOName* Properties dialog (see Figure 15.14). If you intend to apply only User Configuration policies, mark the Disable Computer Configuration settings check box, and vice versa. If you mark both check boxes no policies apply, so option buttons would be the more appropriate control type for this choice.

Figure 15.14
The General page of the OakLeaf U Domain Policy Properties dialog displays summary information for the new GPO and lets you disable unused elements of the GPO.

6. Click the Links tab, and then click the Search button to verify that AD recognizes the new GPO as applicable to the domain in which you created it. If you add links to this GPO from other sites, domains, or OUs, their names appear in the list; this list is very handy for troubleshooting GPOs having multiple links. Stop the search after the domain name appears (see Figure 15.15).

Figure 15.15
By using the Links tab of the Oakleaf U Domain Policy Properties dialog, you can select a domain and perform a search that locates all sites, domains, and OUs that use the "Oakleaf U Domain Policy" GPO.

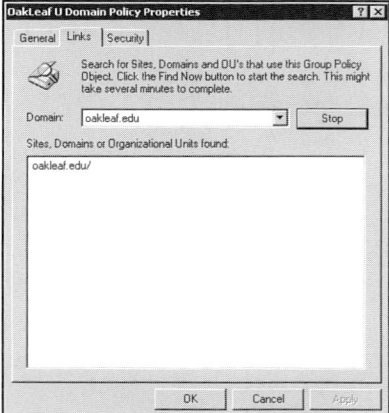

7. Click the Security tab to verify permissions for the new GPO. All groups have Allow Read permissions. Members of the Domain Admins and Enterprise Admins, by default, are exempted from application of User Configuration elements of GPOs (see Figure 15.16). Authenticated Users is the only group with the Apply Group Policy's Apply box marked by default. Close the *GPOName* Properties dialog.

CREATING NEW GROUP POLICY OBJECTS   635

Figure 15.16
The Security page of the Oakleaf U Domain Policy Properties dialog allows you to view and change the permissions assigned to the GPO. The permissions for the Domain Admins group are selected here.

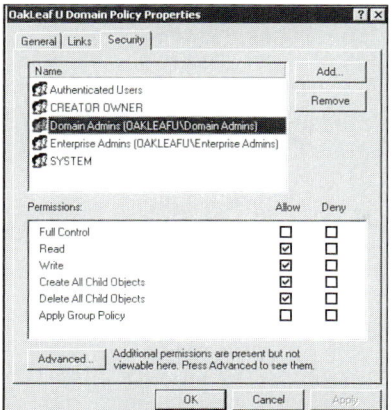

PART
III
CH
15

Tip from
RJ

After changing the default values of the domain-level GPO or any other GPO that applies to Authenticated Users, make sure to assign Deny Apply Group Policy rights for all Admins groups. All members of Admins groups become Authenticated Users when they log on, and the security settings for Authenticated Users override no setting for Apply Group Policy.

→ For instructions on how to prevent Admins accounts from receiving GPOs, **see** "Exempting Administrators from GPO Application," **p. 650**.

IMPORTING WORKSTATION SECURITY SETTINGS POLICIES

Windows 2000 Server comes with a collection of Security Settings templates stored in the \Winnt\Security\Templates folder. These templates, which carry an .inf extension, have names that attempt to describe their purpose. Unfortunately, Microsoft didn't add a Title attribute to the .inf files to describe their purpose explicitly.

Following is a list of the commonly used Security Settings templates that apply to client PCs:

- Basicwk.inf sets security properties to the default values for a Windows 2000 workstation or server (refer to Figure 15.3).

- Compatws.inf sets security properties similar to Basicwk.inf, but disables audit operations, and sets the LAN Manager Authentication Level policy to Send LM and NTLM responses for authentication by downlevel server.

- Securews.inf applies high-level security with 24 passwords remembered, 42-day maximum password age, 2-day minimum password age, 8-character minimum password length, and complex (strong) passwords. Strong passwords require combinations of upper- and lowercase letters, numerals, and symbols. This template also enforces auditing operations.

- Hisecws.inf applies the highest level of security to workstations, but differs only slightly from the settings of Securews.inf in Local Security and a few other policies.

> **Note**
>
> You ordinarily use the workstation versions of the Security Settings templates for domain- or OU-level GPOs. You apply one of the templates for DCs—Basicdc.inf, DC Security.inf, hisecdc.inf, or securedc.inf—to the GPO you create for the Domain Controllers OU. Domain Controllers is an OU, so its security settings override the domain-level settings for clients running Windows 2000 Professional.

To apply one of the Security Settings templates to the new domain GPO, do the following:

1. Click Edit in the *DomainName* Properties dialog to open the Group Properties snap-in for the new GPO.
2. Expand the Computer Configuration, Windows Settings node to display the Security Settings node, right-click the node, and choose Import Policy to open the Import Policy From dialog (see Figure 15.17).

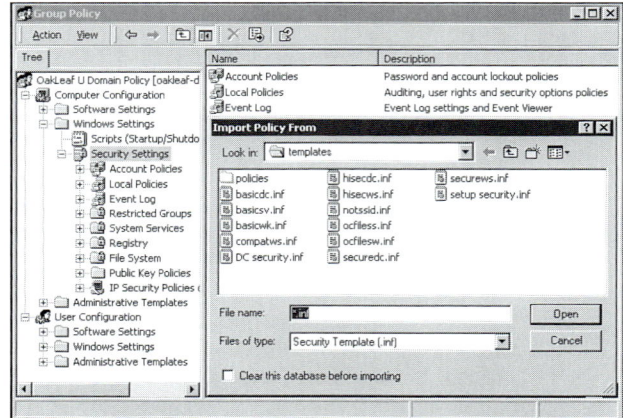

Figure 15.17
The Import Policy From dialog allows you to import policy template files. In this instance, the policy files are the template files included with Windows 2000 Server.

3. Double-click the template to import—Securews.inf or Hisecws.inf are the best choices—to apply the template and close the Import Policy From dialog.
4. Review the settings added by the template to the subnodes of Security Settings, and make changes to suit the level of domain security you want. Figure 15.18 shows the values applied by Securews.inf or Hisecws.inf to the Password Policy options.

CREATING NEW GROUP POLICY OBJECTS | 637

PART
III

CH
15

Figure 15.18
The Password Policy values shown in the right pane of the Group Policy snap-in were applied by the `Securews.inf` Security Settings template.

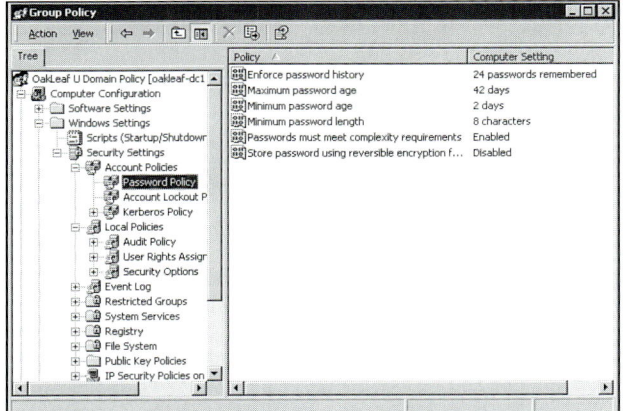

> **Tip from**
> *RJ*
>
> If you want to replace Security Settings applied by one template with those from another, mark the Clear This Database Before Importing check box (refer to Figure 15.17). Marking this check box resets all Security Settings to Not Defined before applying the policies in the new `.inf` file.

After you've established your basic domain security GPO settings, log on from a Windows 2000 Professional client joined to the domain. Verify at least that Password and Account Lockout policies are enforced correctly. Test Password policies by attempting to change your password in a way that conflicts with your password policy settings. To change your password, press Ctrl+Alt+Delete to open the Windows Security dialog, click Change Password to open the Change Password dialog, and type your old password, new password, and new password confirmation in the text boxes. Test Account Lockout Policy by typing various combinations of bad user logon IDs and passwords until the computer locks you out.

Finally, set any additional Computer Configuration or User Configuration policies that you want to apply to all clients, as described in the earlier "Enforcing Computer Security Policies," "Understanding Administrative Templates," and "Exploring User Configuration" sections of this chapter. Bear in mind that the more policies you establish, the greater the network traffic when users boot up and log on, as well as during periodic Group Policy refresh cycles.

> **Tip from**
> *RJ*
>
> Be conservative when applying restrictive policies to a new or newly upgraded Windows 2000 domain. Testing the effects of many policy settings applied at one time is a daunting process. The best approach is to roll out incremental changes to a few users in a single OU, test them, and then apply the policies to other OUs or the entire domain.

Linking Group Policies Across Domains

One of the advantages of storing GPOs in AD is that you can create and test a GPO for one domain, and then apply the same GPO to other domains in the same domain tree or forest. One of the primary reasons for creating multiple domains is the ability to apply a different set of Security Policies to individual domains, so cross-domain GPO linking isn't a common practice. Child domains based on organizational function—for example, `faculty.oakleaf.edu`, `staff.oakleaf.edu`, and `student.oakleaf.edu`—might use the same domain Security Settings. However, it's unlikely that most other policies for faculty and staff members would apply to student accounts.

> **Note**
>
> You must be logged on with an Administrator account that's a member of the Enterprise Admins group to link a GPO to or edit the GPO of another domain. If you log on to the GPO source domain with a Domain Admins account, you obtain read-only access to AD Users and Computers in the destination domain.

→ For more information on linking privileges, **see** "Delegating Administrative Control of GPO Linkage," **p. 653**.

To test linking an existing domain-level GPO (for `oakleaf.edu`) to another domain (`student.oakleaf.edu` for this example), do the following:

1. Launch Active Directory Users and Computers (if necessary) in the source domain, right-click the topmost node, and choose Connect to Domain to open the Connect to Domain dialog.
2. Mark the Save This Domain Setting for the Current Console check box, and click Browse to open the Browse for Domain dialog.
3. Select the domain to which you want to link the GPO—the destination domain—in the list (see Figure 15.19), and click OK twice to close the two dialogs.

Figure 15.19
Using the Connect to Domain dialog, you can select a child domain to link to a domain-level GPO in the parent domain.

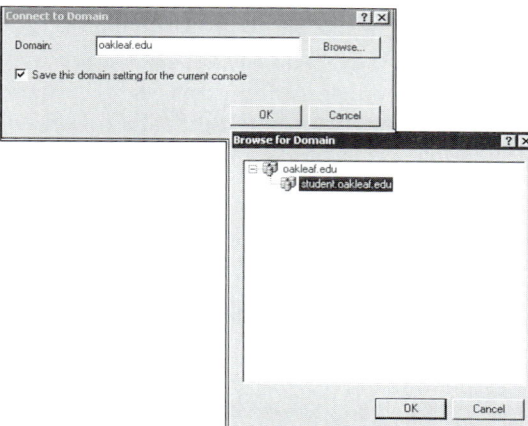

4. Right-click the domain node in Active Directory Users and Computers, choose Properties to open the *DomainName* Properties dialog, and click the Group Policy tab.
5. Select Default Domain Policy, click Options to open the Default Domain Options dialog, mark the Disabled check box, click OK, and click Yes to dismiss the warning.
6. Click Add in the Group Policy page to open the Add a Group Policy Object Link dialog with the Domains/OUs page active; select in the Look In list the domain in which you created the GPO to link. In the Domains, OUs, and Linked Group Policy Objects list, select the GPO item (see Figure 15.20).

Figure 15.20
From the Group Policy page of the Properties dialog of the child domain selected in Figure 15.19, you can select the GPO to link from the parent domain after clicking the Add button.

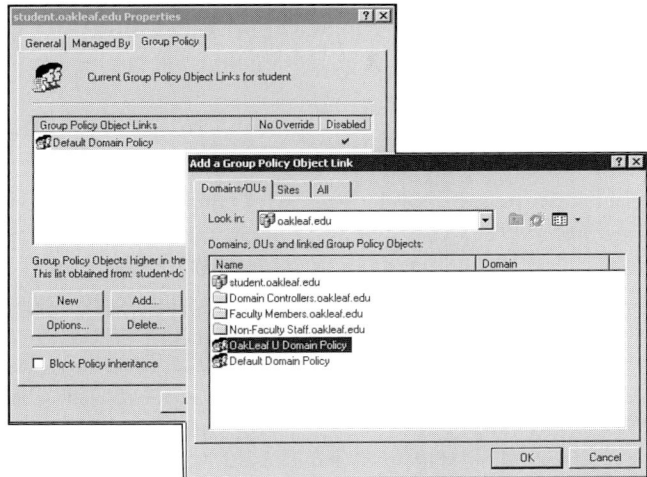

7. Click OK to close the dialog and return to the Group Policy page. Select the new linked GPO entry in the Group Policy Object Links list and click Up to move the entry to the top of the list (see Figure 15.21).

Figure 15.21
The Group Policy page of the child domain Properties dialog shows the newly linked GPO from the parent domain at the top of the list. The domain it was linked from is shown in parentheses.

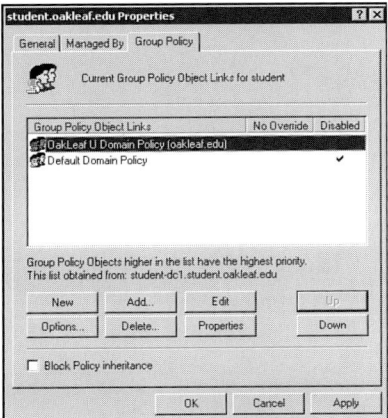

8. Reboot the DC for the domain with the link (student-dc1.student.oakleaf.edu for this example) or wait five minutes or so for the GPO to replicate.

 9. Launch AD Users and Computers on the DC with the GPO link, open the *DomainName* Properties dialog, and click the Group Policy tab to verify that the newly linked GPO is present and active.

If you log on to the newly linked domain controller with a Domain Admins account in the destination domain, the Edit button of the Group Policies page of the *DomainName* Properties dialog is disabled. By opening the Security page of the *GPOName* Properties dialog, you can view, but not alter, security settings for the linked GPO. You must log on as a member of the Enterprise Admins group to edit or change security settings of GPOs linked from other domains. This group membership requirement is similar to that for creating links to out-of-domain GPOs.

Establishing Group Policies for OUs

One of the better features of Group Policies gives you the ability to apply them to particular sets of user and computer accounts defined by inclusion in OUs. For example, you might want to severely restrict the ability of clerks and typists to modify their desktops, add applications to their workstations, or run any program they choose. If you're responsible for computers located in a publicly accessible area, such as a library or Internet café, you need to lock down the workstation totally with Computer Configuration policies. To complete the client PC lockdown, you also must prevent the processing User Configuration policies by enabling the User Group Policy Loopback Processing Mode option described in the tip at the end of the earlier "Understanding Administrative Templates" section.

Tip from

RJ

> If you want to set Computer Configuration properties for a particular set of PCs, put the computer accounts in a dedicated OU. Doing so lets you add OU-level Group Policies that override domain-level Computer Configuration policies. Combining user and computer accounts within an OU isn't a good practice; only similar objects with a common set of attributes belong in an OU. AD treats `Computer` objects as a subclass of the `User` object, but users and computers aren't similar objects.

On the other hand, it's common to give executives, managers, and software developers wide latitude in configuring their computers. Executives and—to a lesser extent—managers have the authority to demand computer configuration flexibility. Software developers usually require total control of their workstations to perform their duties. If your domain Group Policy has User Configuration restrictions, consider creating subordinate OUs to contain user accounts that require exemption from domain User Configuration policies.

To restrict severely the options available to members of a given OU (in this example, the Non-Faculty Staff, Clerical Staff OU of the oakleaf.edu domain), close the Group Policy snap-in and *ContainerName* Properties dialog (if they're open), and then follow these steps:

1. Right-click the OU to which you want to apply the new GPO, and choose Properties to open the *OUName* Properties dialog.
2. Add the new GPO by following steps 1 through 5 of the procedure in the preceding "Creating New Group Policy Objects" section.
3. Click the Edit button of the Group Policy page of the *OUName* Properties dialog to open the Group Policies snap-in, and fully expand the User Configuration nodes.
4. To make sure that clerical staff users receive and install current versions of the productivity applications they need (Microsoft Word, Excel, Access, and Outlook for this example), right-click the Software Installation node to display its properties dialog.
5. Specify the UNC location of the Microsoft Installer files for clerical workers in the Default Package Location text box. To force installation of new or updated packages, select the Assign option in the New Packages frame.
6. Accept the Basic option in the Installation User Interface Options frame to minimize user interaction with the installation process (see Figure 15.22). Click OK to close the dialog and add the policies.

→ For more information on creating packages and installing applications automatically, **see** "Setting Up a Typical Software Installation," **p. 848**.

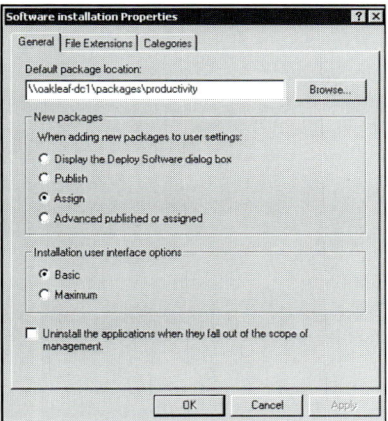

Figure 15.22
Using the Software Installation Properties dialog, you can configure settings that force users to accept installation of new and updated application installation packages.

7. To enable users to run only the applications they require for their day-to-day work, navigate to the User Configuration, Administrative Templates, System node, and double-click the Run Only Allowed Windows Applications policy to open its properties dialog.
8. Select the Enabled option and click the Show button to open the Show Contents dialog.
9. Click the Add button to open the Add Item dialog and, in the text box, type the name of the executable file to make it operable. Click OK to add each file to the list (see Figure 15.23). Click OK twice to close the two dialogs and return to the Group Policy console.

Figure 15.23
From the Run Only Allowed Windows Applications Policy Properties dialog, you can specify a list of applications that will run on workstations. Any programs not listed won't run.

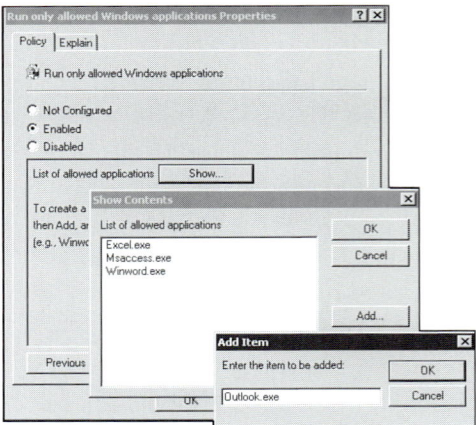

Tip from
RJ

Only very authoritarian regimes lock down users' desktops to the point where they run only Microsoft Office components, but doing so isn't unheard of. If you don't want users to have access to games included with Windows 2000—Freecell, Minesweeper, Pinball, and Solitaire—don't install them. If they're already installed, you can prevent users from running them by enabling the Don't run specified Windows applications and adding the names of the executables for restricted programs.

10. Before leaving the System node, enable the Disable the Command Prompt and Disable Registry Editing Tools policies. It's a good idea to enable these two policies for all but power users.

Other policies for locking down workstations are those in the Start Menu/Taskbar category. Figure 15.24 shows some of the policy settings that you might want to apply to employees who need to perform only a limited range of tasks. You should apply restrictions to the Control Panel tools to prevent use of Add/Remove Programs and unauthorized changes to display and regional settings. You also can customize the appearance and behavior of Internet Explorer (IE) for specific users.

Figure 15.24
When the Start Menu and Taskbar container is selected in the left pane of the Group Policy snap-in, a number of policies are displayed in the right pane that allow you to restrict changes to the Start Menu and Taskbar.

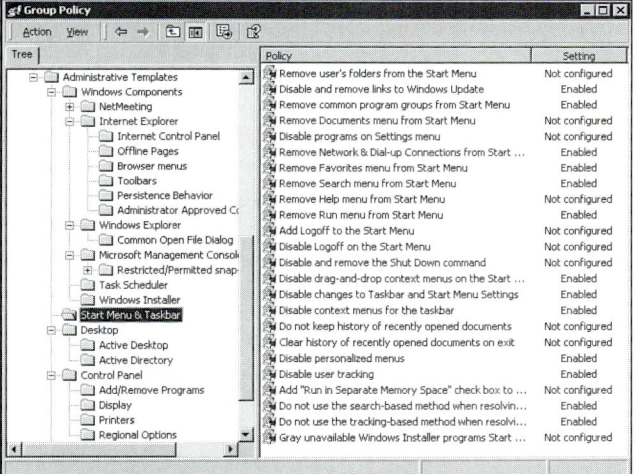

Designing and Populating Security Group Structures

When you perform an in-place upgrade to a Windows NT 4.0 PDC, or use ADMT or Clone Principal scripts to add users and groups, your Windows 2000 Security Groups upgrade or import intact as Domain Local or Global groups. If you're starting with an entirely new Windows 2000 network, it's a good practice to design and implement a security group structure before you add a substantial number of user accounts. In a new Windows 2000 network, you can design your security groups with your OU structure and Group Policies in mind; Windows NT administrators upgrading existing domains don't share this benefit.

Earlier chapters of the book cover Security Groups, primarily in the context of domain upgrade, migration, and installation strategies. This chapter concentrates on methods of designing security group structures that take maximum advantage of Windows 2000's AD features.

→ For the basics of Windows 2000's Security Group structure, **see** "Security Groups," **p. 29**.

If you create OUs based on organizational function, you have the opportunity to create Security Groups that classify users by their level in the organizational hierarchy. Using OakLeaf U as an example, you might assign faculty members to Deans, Department Heads, Professors, and Teaching Assistants groups. If your domain runs in native mode, you can nest Global groups—a feature not available in Windows NT. If you've placed all faculty members in a single Security Group and the user accounts have attribute(s) on which you can create LDAP filters, you can assign users to new Security Groups in bulk. If you don't like the groups structure you create, it's easy to reorganize the groups—but only if you have an LDAP attribute on which to filter for the new group structure.

> **Note**
>
> Security Group design precedes the subject of adding user accounts in this chapter, because it's important to determine which User object attributes to populate when adding accounts. It's a relatively easy task for an experienced Visual Basic for Applications programmer to write an Excel application that uses the Active Directory Service Interfaces (ADSI) to generate new user accounts from a company directory worksheet. It's unfortunate that Microsoft didn't include such an application with the Support Tools.

→ For an example that assigns OakLeaf U students to OUs and Security Groups based on school year, **see** "Reorganizing Migrated Security Groups," **p. 220**.

→ To learn more about using LDAP filters, **see** "Applying LDAP Filters," **p. 138**.

If you have multiple domain trees or forests, you can nest Global groups within Universal groups. However, you should limit the number of members and changes to membership of Universal groups to minimize replication traffic. One of the objectives of creating hierarchies of Global groups is to minimize Domain Local group membership and keep Global groups within the recommended "few thousand" limits.

Creating a New Global Group Structure

The following example for establishing a Global group hierarchy uses the OakLeaf University Faculty OUs you create with the ADSI25 application that's on the accompanying CD-ROM. The process is applicable, however, to almost any OU hierarchy in a production domain. The only limitation in a production environment is that the domain must run in native mode, which doesn't support Windows NT Backup Domain Controllers (BDCs). It's a good practice, however, to perform a test run of creating or modifying group structures before you attempt the process on a production domain.

→ If you haven't installed ADSI25, created the OU structure, and added employee users at this point, **see** "Installation on a Windows 2000 DC or Workstation," **p. 1259**.

> **Note**
>
> You can run ADSI25 in a test domain that you add to a new domain tree or forest of domain trees on a new DC in a production Windows 2000 environment. Adding a large number of users contributes a substantial amount of replication traffic, so it's best to add users during periods of relatively low network traffic.

The Faculty Members OU of the sample oakleaf.edu domain has a Faculty Members Domain Local group whose membership includes the entire faculty. Each department-based OU—such as Anthropology or Computer Science—has a Global group whose membership encompasses the entire department. A group structure of this type might be useful for assigning permissions for department-level shares and printers, but it doesn't permit filtering domain-level GPOs by organizational rank. Figure 15.25 illustrates a grid or mesh of functional and rank-based Security Groups for OUs contained in the Faculty Members OU. You can elect to use either or both types of security grouping.

Figure 15.25
Functional and rank-based Global Security Groups are applied to the OUs contained in the sample Faculty Members OU.

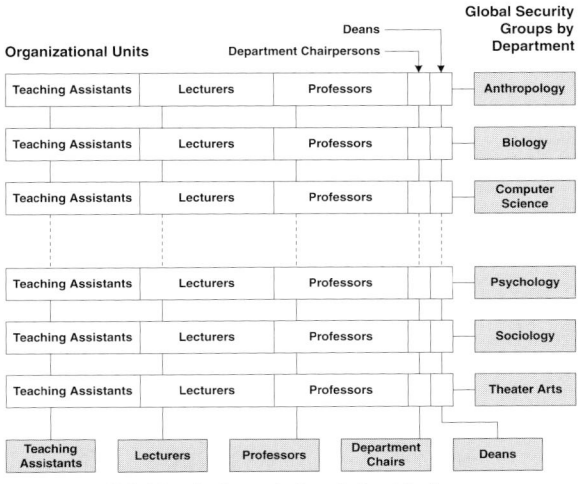

Filters shorten the task of adding a large number of users to groups, but you need a rank-based attribute by which to select or sort the users. Faculty member user accounts have a Display Name attribute with a "Prof." prefix for professors, and a Title attribute for filtering other academic ranks. The time you take to add Title attribute values—Vice President, Director, Manager, and the like—when you add user accounts pays big dividends when you need to create or re-create rank-based group structures.

The "Reorganizing Migrated Security Groups" section of Chapter 5, "Choosing and Testing Migration Strategies," used filters to select student user accounts to OUs and groups. This section uses an alternate method for selecting users by attribute value to add to groups. Active Directory Users and Computers lets you add attribute value columns to the list and sort the columns in ascending or descending order by the selected column values. Because this method eliminates the need to apply, remove, and reapply filter criteria for group membership, it's usually faster than using filters.

To create a new set of attribute-based nested groups from sorted columns of attribute values, do the following:

1. If your test domain is running in mixed mode, change it to native mode. To do so, launch Active Directory Domains and Trusts, right-click the domain node, and choose Properties. Click the Change Mode button on the General Page and exit Active Directory Domains and Trusts. Changing a test domain to native mode doesn't affect any other domains in the tree or forest.

2. Right-click the appropriate OU node for the new groups (Faculty Members for this example) and choose New, Group to open the New Object—Group dialog.

3. Type a name for the group containing the nested groups (Faculty), accept the default Global scope and Security group type options, and click OK to close the dialog.

4. Repeat step 2 for each nested group (in this example, Deans, Department Chairs, Professors, Lecturers, and Teaching Assistants).

5. Click View and select Columns to open the Modify Columns dialog. Double-click in the Hidden Columns list each attribute column you want to add to the Displayed Columns list—Job Title and Display Name for this example.

6. In the Displayed Columns list, select the attribute columns you added and click the Move Up or Move Down button to place the columns in the order you want (see Figure 15.26). Click OK to close the dialog.

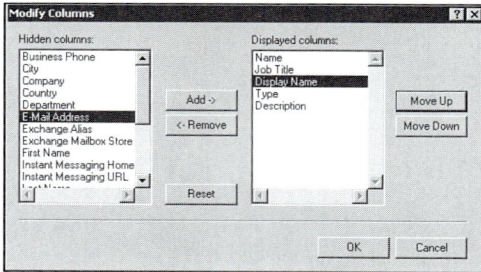

Figure 15.26
By using the Modify Columns dialog, you can add columns containing attribute values by which to sort the user account list.

Tip from
RJ

Adding Last Name and First Name columns, if you populate the lastName and firstName user attributes, is the best method of alphabetizing users by name. Click the First Name header and then the Last Name header to sort by the combination of last and first names.

7. Click the header of the column you want to sort (Display Name for this example), select the first qualifying item, and press Shift+click the last qualifying member to multiselect the accounts.

8. Right-click your selection and choose Add Users to a Group to open the Select Group dialog. Select the group (in this example, Professors) to which to add the users (see Figure 15.27).

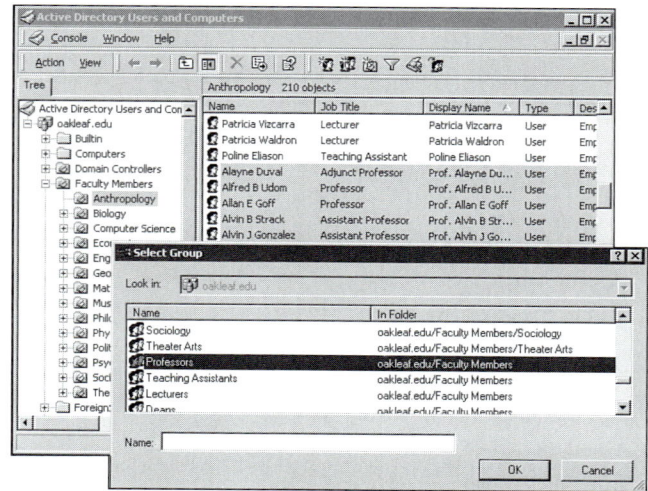

Figure 15.27
The users selected in the background window have been sorted by job title and are added to a Global Security Group selected in the foreground window.

DESIGNING AND POPULATING SECURITY GROUP STRUCTURES 647

PART
III
CH
15

9. Click OK to add the selected users to the group and click OK to dismiss the message that acknowledges the addition.

10. Double-click the entry for the group to which you just added the users, and click the Members tab of the *GroupName* Properties sheet to verify addition of selected users to the group (see Figure 15.28).

Figure 15.28
Verify the addition of the users from multiple OUs.

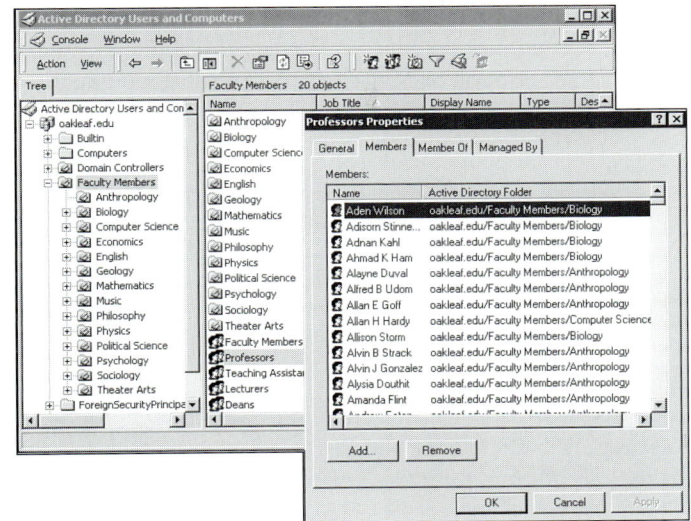

11. Repeat steps 7 through 10 for each group that contains user accounts that meet the group's criterion.

12. Repeat steps 7 through 11 for adding other OUs.

Tip from
RJ

Avoid duplication of user accounts in lower-level groups of a ranked Security Group structure. Restricted permissions of the lower-level group might override the higher-level permissions. In the preceding example, department chairpersons also are professors; adding them to the Department Chairs group duplicates their membership in the Professors group. Deselect the Department Chairperson in the sorted list when adding members to the Professors account, or delete the chairperson from the Members list of the Professors group.

Steps 5 through 12 are nested loops of group addition operations. In a production domain, it's obvious that you must complete all iterations of the outer and inner loops—a total of 70 group assignments for the Faculty Members OU example. Sorting user accounts by attribute value is a tedious task if you have many groups and OUs, but it's much less daunting than applying LDAP filters to accounts.

Adding Computer Accounts to New Security Groups

As noted earlier in the chapter, `Computer` objects are a subclass of the `User` object, so you can add computer accounts to Security Groups you create. By default, all Windows 2000 and NT computer accounts in the domain—except DCs—are members of the Domain Computers Global group. Unfortunately, you can't add computer accounts to Global groups you create by the method described in the preceding section. The Adds the Specified Object to a Group You Specify toolbar button is disabled, and there's no Add Members to a Group context menu choice for `Computer` objects. Further, the Hidden Columns list doesn't include attributes—such as Description or Managed By—on which you might sort computer accounts (refer to Figure 15.26).

> **Note**
>
> The lack of Active Directory Users and Computers' ability to add selected groups of computers to a new Group Policy doesn't affect your ability to filter computer accounts and move them to a new OU. The problem is that computer accounts have very few attributes suitable for filter criteria. Description is the best attribute on which to search, but you must design the description text to accommodate the filter's limited Condition selections—Starts With, Is Exactly, or Ends With—suited to this use.

The upshot of Active Directory Computers and Users' disdain for adding computer accounts to groups is that you must add individual computer accounts manually to Security Groups. Doing so is not fun, primarily because the list from which you must select computer accounts includes virtually every AD object in your domain.

To add computers to a new group, do the following:

1. If you identify computers by a number, such as an asset tag, or other code that's not easy to classify, prepare a written list of the NetBIOS computer names to add to the new group.
2. Create a Security Group for the computer accounts (Faculty Workstations for this example) in the appropriate OU.
3. Double-click the group entry in the OU to open its properties dialog, and click the Members tab.
4. Click the Add button of the Members page to open the Select Users, Contacts, Computers, or Groups dialog.

> **Note**
>
> If you have a large number of objects in your domain, it might take a minute or two to fill the list. It's very difficult to scroll to the computer account you want to add, because the accounts appear in no discernable sort sequence in the brain-dead Add Users, Contacts, Computers, or Groups dialog. It's bad enough to have no control over what types of objects the list displays, let alone having the class of objects you're looking for appear in random order.

5. Replace the default highlighted text in the bottom pane of the dialog with a list of the NetBIOS names of the computers to add. Separate the names with semicolons.

6. Click Check Names to check your typing. If you type an invalid NetBIOS name, an Invalid Name dialog opens to let you correct the error, if you can, or omit the entry (see Figure 15.29). Click OK to close the dialog.

Figure 15.29
The Invalid Name dialog reports a typographical error in a computer's NetBIOS name during the addition of new computers to a group.

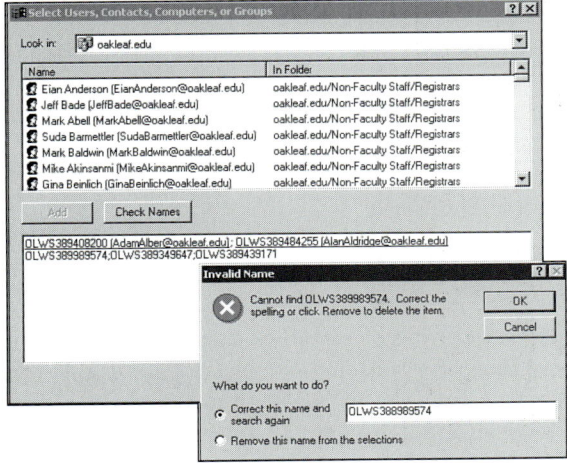

Note

The ADSI25 application used to add the computer accounts shown in Figure 15.29 associates each computer account with a domain user account. The user principal name (UPN) of the associated user account follows the NetBIOS name. The only operation where UPNs for computer accounts appear is when you add the accounts to groups. For unknown reasons, the UPN doesn't appear on any page of the *ComputerAccount* Properties sheet. It would be quite helpful to network administrators if the General page displayed the UPN for the user account.

7. Click OK to close the Add Users, Contacts, Computers, or Groups dialog. The computer accounts you added appear in the Members list.

Tip from
RJ

If you need to exempt only a few computer accounts from a GPO, don't bother adding the accounts to a special Security Group. You can add individual computer (and user) accounts to the GPO's Security page list and exempt the accounts from GPO application.

Reorganizing Existing Groups

Group membership detritus often results from reworking Domain Local and Global group structure after in-place upgrades of Windows NT PDCs. ADSI25's Domain Local and Global group approach, for instance, is a very inefficient method of handling group membership, because Faculty Members group membership duplicates the entire user list of the department-level groups. In addition, the Faculty Members Domain Local group also has nested OU-based Global groups that have the same icon as users. Using identical user and group icons makes identifying potential user and group overlaps difficult. If you didn't take the earlier advice to clean up your group structures before upgrading a PDC, some after-the-fact housekeeping is required.

→ For recommendations on pre-upgrade sanitation, **see** "Cleaning Up User and Group Accounts," **p. 287**.

The general approach to reorganizing and cleaning up Domain Local and Global group membership depends on the extent to which you've granted group permissions to network resources. The following are the two most common group cleanup methods:

- If you haven't granted the Domain Local group permissions to many network resources, create a new Global group and then nest the existing department-level groups within the new group. Delete the original Domain Local group, and change the name of the new Global group to that of the deleted group. Reassign resource permissions to the new parent or outer Global group.

- If you want to preserve existing Domain Local group permissions to many network resources, promote this parent group to a Universal group and demote it to a Global group. You can't promote a Domain Local group directly to a Global group, and you can't promote a Domain Local group to a Universal Group if the Domain Local group contains other Domain Local Groups. Nest the subordinate groups in the new Global group, if they're not already present, and then delete any individual user accounts from the parent group.

Caution

Never remove a group or users from a group until you've verified that users have joined another group and the group's permissions for important network resources are intact. Those users who are missing appropriate group membership immediately lose their network resources permissions.

Filtering GPOs with Security Groups

One of the primary purposes of the preceding sections that cover creating or altering Security Groups is to prepare for GPO group filtering. You can apply Group Policy filtering to Security Groups containing users or computers, or both.

Exempting Administrators from GPO Application

The first step after applying any GPO that might have *even a chance* of affecting Enterprise Admins or Domain Admins group members, is to deny application of the GPO to these groups. As mentioned earlier, the Apply check box for Admins groups' Apply Group Policy permission is clear. However, clearing the check box isn't sufficient to ensure that restrictive GPOs *never* apply to administrators.

Administrative User Accounts

To prevent the possibility of GPO restrictions to administrative user accounts, do the following:

1. Open in Active Directory Users and Computers the Group Policy page of the domain's properties sheet, and select the active GPO for the domain.
2. Click Properties, and then click the Security tab of the *PolicyName* Properties dialog.
3. Select Domain Admins in the Name list, and mark the Deny check box for the Apply Group Policy item of the Permissions list (see Figure 15.30).

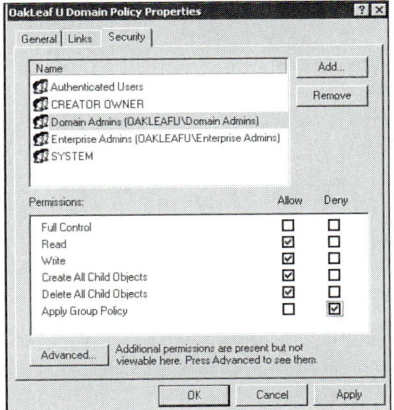

Figure 15.30
From the Security page of the selected domain's Properties dialog, you can select the Apply Group Policy Deny check box for the selected group (Domain Admins in this case.) This causes the group to be excluded from the Group Policy.

4. Repeat step 3 for the Enterprise Admins group.
5. Click OK and acknowledge the warning message that Deny permissions supercede Allow permissions, which is what you want to happen.
6. Repeat steps 1 through 5 for any other GPO that might apply to administrators, such as a GPO for an OU that contains administrators or has a subordinate OU with administrative accounts.

Administrative Computer Accounts

If you've applied restrictive Computer Configuration policies to domain computers, you also must exempt administrator's workstation accounts from the GPOs. Doing so raises the issue of assuring the physical security of administrators' computers, because unauthorized users might be able to log on to those computers. Using Smart Cards for access to administrative workstations provides adequate security for most organizations.

To exempt specific administrative workstations from the Computer Configuration policies of domain-level and other GPOs, do the following:

1. Open in Active Directory Users and Computers the Group Policy page of the domain's properties sheet, and select the active GPO for the domain.

2. Click Properties, and then click the Security tab of the *PolicyName* Properties dialog.
3. Click Add to open the Select Users, Computers, or Groups dialog, scroll to and select the computer to exempt, or type its NetBIOS name in the text box.
4. Repeat step 3 for other accounts to exempt, if any; click Check Names, and then click OK to close the dialog and add the computer account(s) to the Name list.
5. Select each computer account you added, and mark the Deny check box for the Apply Group Policy item of the Permissions list (see Figure 15.31).

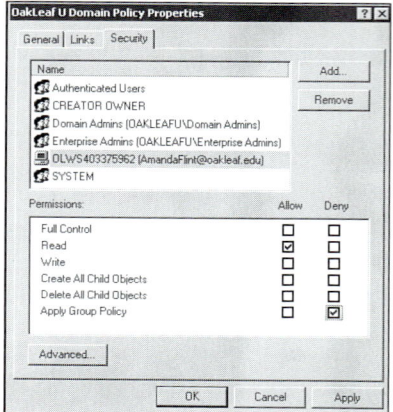

Figure 15.31
By selecting the same deny box as in Figure 15.30, but for a computer account, the computer can be excluded from the GPO's computer account policies.

6. Click OK and acknowledge the warning message.
7. Repeat steps 1 through 6 for each GPO that might apply to administrative computers.

Exempting Other Groups from GPO Application

You filter other GPOs you've created by Security Group by the method outlined in the earlier "Administrative Computer Accounts" section. If you've created increasingly restrictive GPOs as the rank in the organization hierarchy decreases, you must filter lower-level GPOs if you organize your users into a functional OU structure.

For example, OakLeaf U's Faculty Members are organized into subordinate OUs by academic department. However, groups by rank—Deans, Department Chairs, Professors, Lecturers, and Teaching Assistants—have members from all departments. Thus, you must go through the exercise of exempting each higher-level group from application of the lower-level GPOs.

Creating a mesh of group and OU structures, adding many Group Policy Objects, and then exempting several groups from the groups' application is a very chancy proposition at best. Don't over-engineer your Security Group structure, and be cautious when applying Group Policies, especially restrictive ones. Troubleshooting such a structure is an onerous task. Establish a test OU, and add some user and computer accounts within the OU. Then create and modify the GPO within the test OU and test it thoroughly from a workstation with one of the test user and computer accounts. After you complete the test, you can link the GPO to the appropriate OU, exempt higher-level groups, and hope you don't hear too many complaints from your users.

DELEGATING ADMINISTRATIVE CONTROL OF GPO LINKAGE

Just as you delegate OU administration, you can delegate administrative control of GPO links to others. Delegating links to GPOs doesn't require you to relinquish control of the policies enforced by the GPO; only members of the Group Policy Creator Owners group have such permissions. You might delegate control of GPO links that apply to a particular department's OU to a group vice president, but not to a department manager. Delegating GPO linkage authority permits removing GPO links to the OU, which then inherits its Group Policy from the next higher OU or, if there are no OUs above it, the domain. Letting a member of the OU remove or alter its GPO links isn't a good administrative policy.

→ To review delegation of administration of an OU, **see** "Using the Delegation of Control Wizard," **p. 223**.

You use the Delegation of Control Wizard at the OU level to assign rights to create or modify GPO links. To delegate such authority, do the following:

1. Right-click the OU node and choose Delegate Control to open the Delegation of Control Wizard first dialog. Click Next to open the Users or Groups dialog.

2. Click Add to open the Users, Computers, and Groups dialog. (Why computer accounts are included in the list is a mystery.) Select or type the logon ID of the delegate user account, and click OK to close the dialog and add the account (see Figure 15.32). Click Next to open the Tasks to Delegate dialog.

Figure 15.32
You can select users and groups in the Delegation of Control Wizard to assign rights to perform selected administrative tasks.

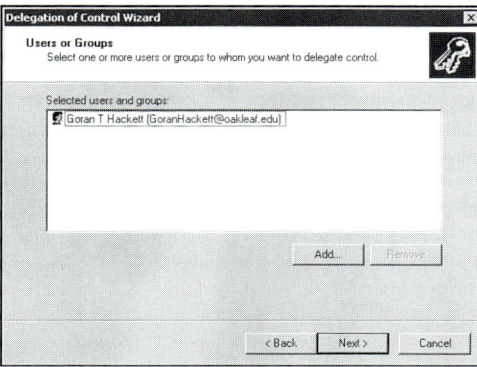

3. Mark the Manage Group Policy Links check box and, if you filter GPOs by group, the Modify the Membership of a Group check box (see Figure 15.33).

Figure 15.33
This screen in the Delegation of Control wizard enables the specified user to add, delete, or change group policy links and Security Group membership.

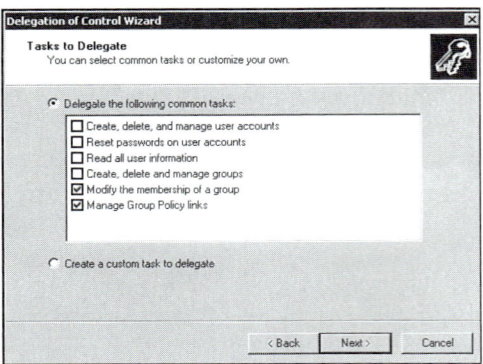

4. Click Next to review your choices, and then click Finish to dismiss the Wizard.

WORKING WITH USER ACCOUNTS

When you upgrade existing Windows NT PDCs, current user accounts and their attributes (such as logon scripts, user profiles, and home directories) remain intact. If your in-place upgrade doesn't encounter serious problems, existing Windows NT and 9x users in the domain probably won't notice the change to the server's OS. When you implement Group Policies, the initial logon by Windows 2000 Professional users is delayed while the client downloads the entire Group Policy from the server. After the initial logon, only policy changes replicate to Windows 2000 PCs. Subsequent policy changes occur through background refresh operations.

Tip from
RJ

Encourage mobile Windows 2000 users to log on initially to the LAN to receive their Group Policy and assigned and published applications. Remote users won't be happy if they must download 100MB or more of software over a 56kbps modem connection before being able to use their new laptop PC.

An initial local logon is especially important if you implement IntelliMirror's roaming user profiles, one of the subjects of Chapter 20, "Supplying IntelliMirror and Application Installation Services." Windows 2000 uses a locally cached copy of the roaming user profile when a slow link is detected.

ADDING NEW USER ACCOUNTS

Adding new Windows 2000 user accounts is a piece of cake, at least compared with designing Group Policies and Security Group structures. The New Object—User dialogs require only that you specify a name, logon ID, and password to start a new user account. After adding the account, you can change the name and logon ID, but you can't change the password.

→ For the basics of adding user accounts to AD, **see** "Adding Groups and Users," **p. 118**.

To add a new user account, do the following:

1. In Active Directory Users and Computers, right-click the OU in which to create the new user account, and choose New, User to open the first page of the New Object—User dialog.
2. Type entries in the First Name, Initials (if applicable), and Last Name text boxes. The Full Name text box fills automatically with the Display Name attribute as you type the other name entries.
3. Type a unique logon ID in the User Logon Name text box. The User Logon Name (Pre-Windows 2000) text box fills simultaneously. Click Next to open the second dialog.

> **Note**
> You must add a name to at least one of the text boxes of step 2 and provide a logon ID in step 3 to enable the Next button. The user's logon ID must be unique within the domain.

4. Type and confirm an initial password for the user. The password must meet the length and complexity policies you specified for the domain and OU of the user's account.
5. Mark the User Must Change Password at Next Logon check box, and click Next to review your entries.
6. Click Finish to close the dialog and add the new account with its mandatory attributes.

 If you receive an Active Directory error message stating that Windows can't set the password for the new user, see the "Password Policy Problems" topic of the "Troubleshooting" section at the end of the chapter.

ADDING OPTIONAL ATTRIBUTE VALUES

Windows 2000 user accounts have an extraordinary number of optional attributes compared with Windows NT and 9x accounts. You add the optional attribute values in the *UserName* Properties pages after upgrading or creating the user account. Many of the new Windows 2000 account attributes—Display Name, E-mail Address, Job Title, Address, City, Region, Telephone Number(s) and the like—are similar or identical to those of a Microsoft Exchange mailbox. Because AD stores the optional attributes, they apply to all user accounts, not just Windows 2000 users. The preceding sections of this chapter demonstrate the value of some of these attributes to sort or filter users. Following is a list of the four dialog pages for entering additional demographic and organizational data and for specifying group membership:

- The General page's First Name, Initials, Last Name, and Display Name text boxes are filled when you create the user account. The remainder of the text boxes are empty. Figure 15.34 illustrates optional attribute values added by the ADSI25 application. Telephone Number (work) and Web Page are multivalued attributes; click Other to open the *AttributeName* (Others) dialog to add additional phone numbers or URLs.

Figure 15.34
The General page of the *UserName* Properties dialog with all optional attributes populated.

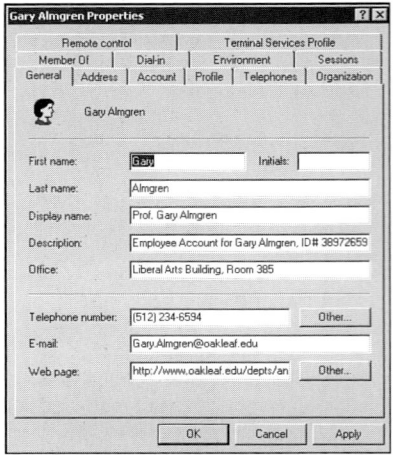

- The Address page for residence information has Street (multiline), P.O. Box, City, State/Province, and Zip/Postal Code text boxes. A Country/Region list lets you select from a fixed list of countries.

- The Account page's controls are populated by the initial user account settings (see Figure 15.35). You can alter the User Logon Name, Account Options, and Account Expires attributes. To restrict the user to specific days and hours of network use, click Logon Hours to open the Logon Hours for UserName dialog, drag over the hours of each day that the user isn't allowed to log on, and select the Logon Denied option.

Figure 15.35
The Account page of the selected user's Properties dialog shows only the attributes populated when the account is first created.

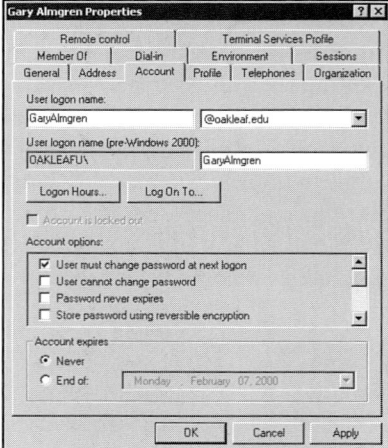

To create a mandatory profile for a group of Windows NT clients in a Windows 2000 domain, do the following:

1. Create a share on the server to store profiles, typically \Profiles. If you want to use separate profiles for Windows 2000, NT, and 9x clients, create a separate subfolder or different share for each OS. Create a subfolder named for each profile you copy. This example uses \Profiles\WinNT\TAs as the folder for the Teaching Assistants group.

2. On a Windows NT client in the Windows 2000 domain (or in a Windows NT domain with a two-way trust to the Windows 2000 domain), create a new user account named for the OU or group to which the profile applies; this example uses TAProfileNT for Teaching Assistants running Windows NT Workstation.

3. Log on with the new account, configure the desktop for the mandatory profile, and log off.

4. Log on as a member of the local Administrators group and launch Control Panel's System tool.

5. Click the User Profiles tab, select the profile you created in steps 2 and 3, and click Copy To to open the Copy To dialog.

6. Click Browse to open the Browse for Folder dialog, navigate to the profile share you created in step 1, and click OK to close the Copy To dialog.

7. Click Change in the Permitted to Use frame to open the Choose User dialog, select the domain in the List Names From list, if necessary, and select the Security Group to which the profile applies (Teaching Assistants for this example).

8. Click Add and then click OK to close the dialog. The User Profiles page and Copy To dialog appear as illustrated in Figure 15.39.

Figure 15.39
By clicking the Copy To button on the User Profiles page of the System Properties dialog, a user profile can be copied from the local machine to a central profile server.

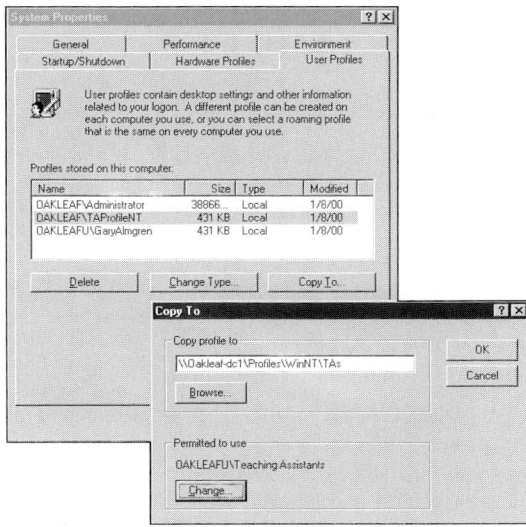

Note

Assigning the profile to a Windows 2000 security group is only a formality; you can skip step 7 if you want. Windows NT clients logging on to a Windows 2000 domain can't query AD for user group membership during the Netlogon process.

9. Click OK twice to copy the profile to the server and close the two dialogs.
10. On the server, oakleaf-dc1.oakleaf.edu for this example, rename the folder containing the profile to add the .man extension (\Profiles\WinNT\TAs.man). Assign the Everyone group read-only permissions and the Domain Admins group full-control permissions to the Profiles share.

Tip from
RJ

Verify that the profile you copied to the server folder with the .man extension includes the new folders required for Windows 2000 profiles, such as Application Data.

11. In Active Directory Users and Computers, open the properties dialog for the account of a member of the group to which the profile applies and click the Profile tab.
12. Type the full path to the shared profile in the Profile page's Profile Path text box, **\\oakleaf-dc1\Profiles\WinNT\TAs.man** for this example (see Figure 15.40). Click OK to add the mandatory profile to the user account.

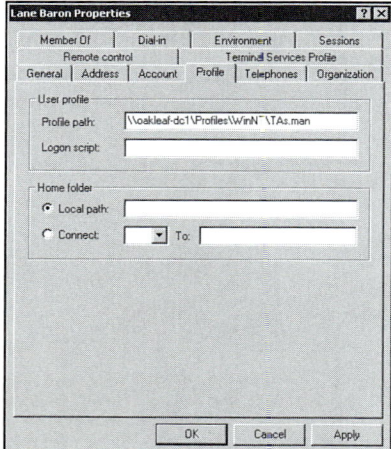

Figure 15.40
On the Profile page of the selected user's Properties dialog, you can specify the location of a mandatory user profile to be used.

13. Log on to the Windows NT client with the account to which you assigned the mandatory user profile in the preceding step. The client downloads the mandatory profile during the Netlogon process.

 If you receive a User Environment error message stating that "The operating system is unable to log you on because your roaming mandatory profile is not available," see the "Mandatory Profile Problems" topic of the "Troubleshooting" section at the end of the chapter.

IMPLEMENTING DOWNLEVEL SYSTEM POLICIES | 663

14. Verify that the client is using the mandatory profile by launching Control Panel's System tool and clicking the Profiles tab. The entry for the profile in the Profiles Stored on This Computer list displays Mandatory in the Type column (see Figure 15.41).

PART
III
CH
15

Figure 15.41
Look in the Type Column the System Properties dialog's User Profiles page to verify that a user profile is in fact mandatory.

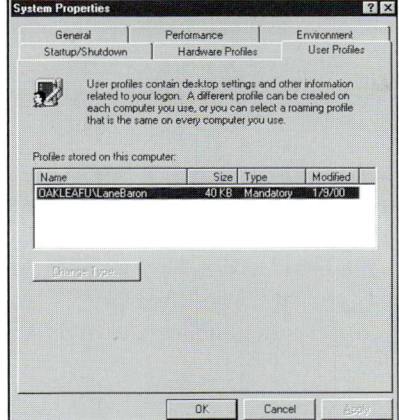

Tip from	
RJ	Remember to delete or change the Profile Path for each user whose computer you upgrade to Windows 2000 from Windows NT or 9x. If you specify a mandatory user profile, the user receives the same mandatory profile when you upgrade his or her computer to Windows 2000 Professional. Windows 2000 Group Policies replace user profiles, so deleting the profile path works for Windows 2000–only users. However, if you have users that log on to both Windows 2000 and NT machines, you might want to retain their Windows NT profiles.

Unfortunately, Windows 2000 offers no easy way to automate assignment of a mandatory profile to a group of users. You must manually add the Profile Path entry for each user. The alternative is to write a script that uses the Active Directory Service Interfaces (ADSI) 2.5 to add the entry to user accounts in a specified group or groups.

Note	
	ADMT offers the option of automatically copying Windows NT roaming user profiles to the DC when you migrate groups and users to a new Windows 2000 domain.

 If your users can't log on after you assign them a mandatory profile, see the "Mandatory Profile Problems" topic of the "Troubleshooting" section at the end of the chapter.

IMPLEMENTING DOWNLEVEL SYSTEM POLICIES

You can apply system policies to Windows NT or 9x clients in a Windows 2000 domain to restrict users' access to a limited selection of Windows 2000 features. System policies, an element of Microsoft's Zero Administration Windows (ZAW) initiative of the late 1990s, form the foundation of Windows 2000's Group Policies. As with Group Policies, you can apply system policies to specific computers and users, but system policies offer far fewer setting options.

When a Windows NT user logs on, Netlogon checks for an Ntconfig.pol policy file in the \\ServerName\Netlogon share. If found, the logon process copies Registry entries in the Ntconfig.pol system policy file to the Windows NT client's local Registry. Windows 9x clients follow a similar approach, but look for a Config.pol file. Windows NT system policies don't apply to Windows 2000 clients.

You create and edit Ntconfig.pol files with Windows NT 4.0's System Policy Editor, Poledit.exe, which Windows 2000 Server installs in the \Winnt folder during the Administrative Tools setup process. You create or edit a Config.pol compatible with Windows 9x clients by running Poledit.exe under Windows 98 or 95, and then copying the Config.pol file to the Netlogon share of the DC. The Windows NT and 9x versions of Poledit.exe are identical, but Poledit creates system policy files in different formats, depending on the OS under which it runs.

Note

To install Windows 98's version of `Poledit.exe` with the appropriate administrative templates for Windows 9x, insert the Windows 98 (original or Second Edition) distribution CD-ROM. Launch Control Panel's Add/Remove Programs tool, click the Windows Setup tab, click Have Disk, click Browse, and run `Poledit.inf` from the `d:\Tools\Reskit\Netadmin\Poledit` folder. Select Group Policies and System Policy Editor in the Have Disk dialog, and click OK to complete the installation.

Windows NT 4.0 PDCs and BDCs store Ntconfig.pol and Config.pol files in the \Winnt\System32\Repl\Import\Scripts folder, which the system shares as \\ServerName\Netlogon. Windows 2000 Server's Netlogon share is the \Winnt\Sysvol\Sysvol\Domain.ext\Scripts folder. When you do an in-place upgrade on a Windows NT 4.0 PDC, running Dcpromo.exe moves the system policy files to the new location, which causes the policy files to replicate to every DC in the domain. If you create a new Windows 2000 domain and want to use existing Windows NT 4.0 system policy files, you must manually copy the policy file(s) from the Windows NT to the Windows 2000 Netlogon share. Just remember not to try editing your existing Config.pol files with Poledit running under Windows 2000.

Tip from
RJ

Decide early whether you want to use mandatory user profiles or system policies for Windows NT clients. If you specify a Profile Path to a mandatory user profile, the Windows NT client won't load the `Ntconfig.pol` file to change the local Registry settings. If you start with system policies and then specify a Profile Path for a user account, you can't reverse the `Ntconfig.pol` Registry settings from the server. You must log on the client with local Administrator privileges and alter the Registry settings manually.

IMPLEMENTING DOWNLEVEL SYSTEM POLICIES | 665

PART
III
CH
15

Caution

The release version of Windows 2000 Server doesn't support assignment of system policies to Windows NT clients by Windows 2000 Security Groups. When Windows NT clients log on to a Windows 2000 DC, the clients can't determine their Windows 2000 group membership from AD during the Netlogon process. This means you must add an entry to Ntconfig.pol for each Windows NT user account, just as you must add an entry to Config.pol for each Windows 9x account. If you have a large number of Windows NT users who require application of system policy, and you previously used Windows NT groups to assign the policy, be prepared to spend many hours adding individual user entries to Ntconfig.pol with Poledit.

APPLYING SYSTEM POLICIES TO USER ACCOUNTS

If you haven't been dissuaded from assigning system policies to your Windows NT and 9x users, do the following to run Poledit on the Windows 2000 DC that serves as the PDC emulator and apply policies to existing user accounts:

1. Use the Run command to open Poledit.exe's window; there's no menu shortcut for Poledit.
2. If you have an existing Ntconfig.pol file on your DC, choose File, Open Policy and load the file. Otherwise, choose File, New Policy to start the policy creation process.

Tip from
RJ

Policy files contain Default Computer and Default User policies. Don't use either unless you want a particular set of policies to apply to *all* Windows NT computers, including Windows NT BDCs, and users in the domain.

3. To create an Ntconfig.pol entry for a user account, choose Edit, New User to open the New User dialog, and click Browse to open the Add Users dialog.
4. Accept the default domain in the List Names From list, select a user, and click Add to add the user's account to the Add Names list. You can add multiple users by multiselecting or double-clicking names (see Figure 15.42).

Figure 15.42
The System Policy Editor is being used to add three users for system policy application.

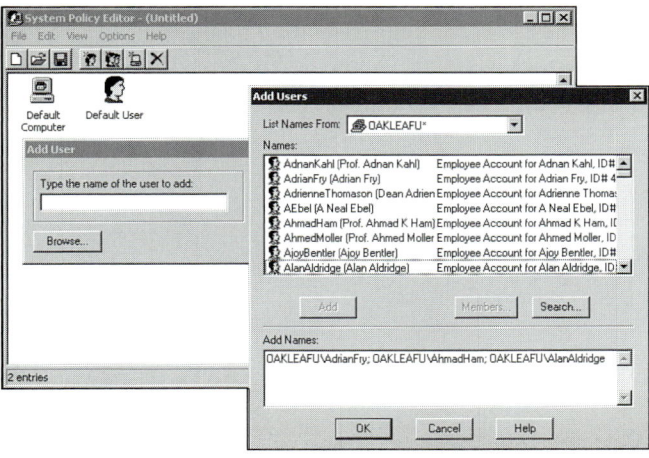

5. Click OK twice to close the dialog and add icons for the user(s) to Poledit's window.
6. Double-click a new user icon to open the *UserName* Properties dialog with the seven standard top-level policy nodes (see Figure 15.43).

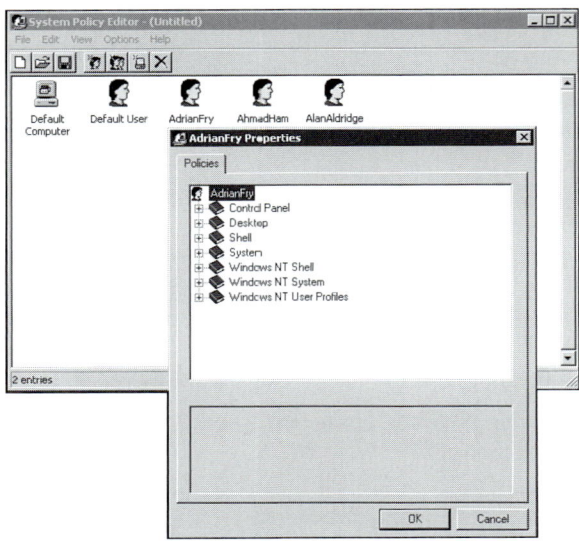

Figure 15.43
The initial configuration of the Properties dialog is shown for the first of the three new user accounts added to the System Policy Editor's window.

Like Group Policies, system policies use administrative template (.adm) files to specify node names and their settings. The format of system policy .adm files differs from that used by the Group Policy snap-in. Common.adm contributes the first four nodes—Control Panel, Desktop, Shell, and System—which are the same for Windows NT and 9x policies. The last three nodes—Windows NT Shell, Windows NT System, and Windows NT User Profiles—come for Winnt.adm and are used only by Ntconfig.pol files. When you expand the nodes, it's evident that the Shell node's Restrictions subnode offers the widest array of user-based restrictions; Figure 15.44 shows the 11 options. The System, Restrictions subnode lets you disable the user's Registry editing tools—the most commonly used option—and apply the notorious Run Only Allowed Windows Applications option.

→ To review how to limit users to running specific applications, **see** "Establishing Group Policies for OUs," **p. 640**.

Figure 15.44
The Properties dialog shows the 11 optional restrictions you can apply from the Shell, Restrictions subnode.

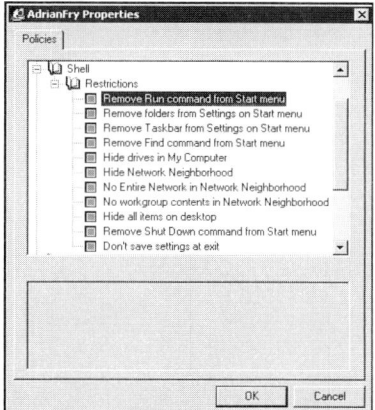

Fortunately, Poledit has copy and paste capabilities, so you can create a standard set of user restrictions, copy them to the Clipboard, and paste them to other user entries. To apply system policy options to multiple user accounts, do the following:

1. In the *UserName* Properties dialog, expand the node that contains the restrictions you want, and click to mark the items' check boxes. Clicking the check box multiple times causes the restriction status to change from applied (checked), removed (cleared), and not specified (gray square). Figure 15.45 illustrates application of three user restrictions—Hide Network Neighborhood, Remove Shutdown Command from Start Menu, and Disable Registry Editing Tools. The remainder of the restrictions visible in Figure 15.45 are not specified. Click OK to close the dialog and add the restrictions.

Figure 15.45
The Properties dialog shows typical system policy restrictions to be applied to a Windows NT user's account.

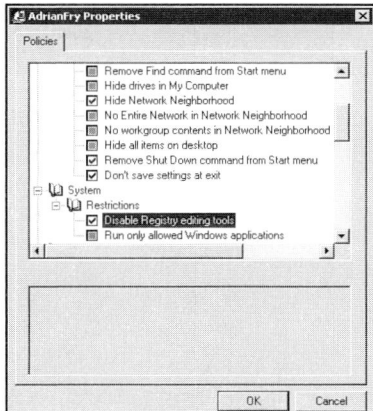

2. Select the user icon to which you just applied the restrictions and choose Edit, Copy. Select another user icon and click Edit, Paste to apply the same set of restrictions.

3. After you paste the restrictions to all users, choose File, Save As to open the Save As dialog; navigate to the \Winnt\Sysvol\Sysvol*domain.ext*\Scripts folder and save the file as Ntconfig.pol.

Note

If you create policies on a remote workstation, save Ntconfig.pol to the DC's Netlogon share. By default, you must log on to the domain as a member of the local Administrators group to write to the Netlogon share. Change the Netlogon share permissions to suit your administrative needs.

4. On a Windows NT workstation in the domain, log on with one of the user accounts and verify that the policies you specified are applied.

To create Windows 9x system policies, run Poledit on a Windows 98 PC under your Administrators group account. In step 3, save the policy file as Config.pol to the Windows 2000 DC's Netlogon share.

Tip from

If you're creating a new set of system policies, create a test user account, specify the policies you want to apply to actual user accounts, and then evaluate the effects of applying the policy before applying it to a large number of users. You might find that some of the restrictions cause unanticipated problems for users.

Working with Computer System Policies

You apply computer-specific system policies by methods similar to those described for user accounts. Unfortunately, you can't multiselect computer accounts, and the computer must be online—or in the browser list—in order to add its account to the policy file.

Note

The reason you can't add multiple Windows NT computer accounts is that the Browse for Computer dialog's subnodes that hold computer accounts, such as AD's Computers container, don't expand to display the accounts. The only accessible computer nodes appear in the My Network Places tree. Windows 9x computers don't use computer accounts, so it's logical to require adding those computers from My Network Places. It's illogical not to provide access to multiple computer accounts through the Directory node.

To add policies for computer accounts, do the following:

1. With Ntconfig.pol open in Poledit, choose Edit, Add Computer to open the Add Computer dialog, and Click browse to open the Browse for Computer dialog. Expand the nodes to display the browser's list of computers in the domain, and select the computer you want to add (see Figure 15.46).

Implementing Downlevel System Policies 669

Figure 15.46
Poledit's Browse for Computer dialog lets you select an online computer in the Windows 2000 domain for which to apply system policies.

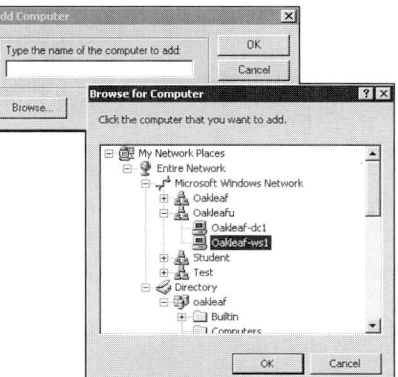

2. Click OK twice to close the two dialogs and add an icon for the computer account to Poledit's window.

3. Double-click the computer icon to open the *ComputerName* Properties dialog and expand the nodes.

4. Select the restrictions to apply, and save Ntconfig.pol (or Config.pol) as you did when adding user accounts in the preceding section. Figure 15.47 shows the first-level nodes for Windows NT computers accounts, with the Windows NT Remote Access node expanded.

Figure 15.47
The Properties dialog for the selected computer shows the first-level nodes for computer-based system policies with options for the Windows NT Remote Access policy.

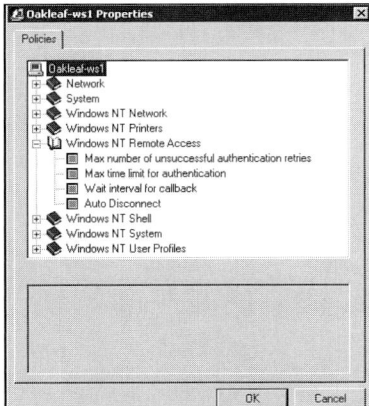

5. Test application of the computer system policy at one of the workstations to which you applied the policy.

> **Note** This book is devoted almost entirely to Windows 2000 Server, so detailed descriptions of individual system policy options for user and computer accounts is beyond the book's scope. For more information on Windows NT and Windows 9x system policies, search the Microsoft Knowledge Base. To navigate to the Knowledge Base Search page, choose Support, Knowledge Base in the Microsoft Web site's top menu of the home page. Select Windows NT 4.0 Server in the My Search Is About list, accept the default I Want To Search By option, type **system policies** in the My Question Is About text box, and click Go.

SETTING UP USER HOME FOLDERS

Setting up home folders for users of downlevel clients is a trivial process compared with establishing user profiles or applying system policies. If you set up individual roaming profiles for Windows NT or 9x users, it's a common Windows NT practice to place the roaming profile files and folders in the user's home folder. Home folders—like user profiles—can grow quite large, so you should devote at least one volume with disk quotas to home folders.

COMMON VERSUS INDIVIDUAL HOME FOLDER SHARES

Sharing each home folder individually can lead to a very large number of shares on a server and, as a consequence, a substantial increase in browser network traffic. Thus, it's a common practice to create a hidden common share—such as *ServerName*\USERS$—to hold a large number of individual home folders, which ordinarily have a name identical to the user's logon ID. Adding the $ suffix to the share name hides the share from the browser. You map the *ServerName*\USERS$*LogonID* share to a client drive letter, commonly U. The user sees only *LogonID* as the default folder for storing his or her files. Figure 15.48 illustrates assigning the \\oakleaf-dc1\USERS$\LaneBaron share to the U: drive of an OakLeaf U teaching assistant's Windows NT workstation.

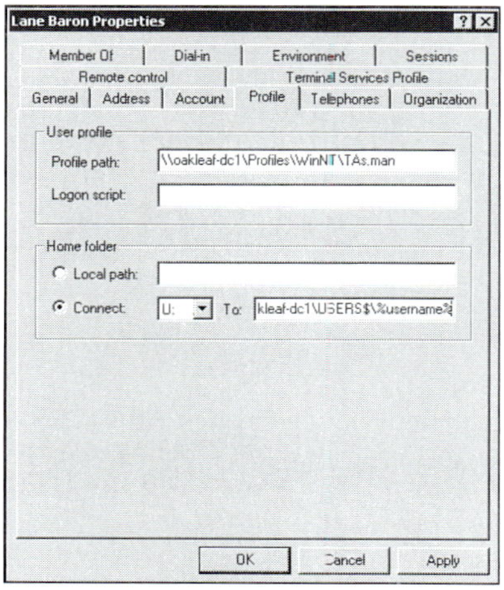

Figure 15.48
From the Profiles page of the selected user's Properties dialog you can create a home folder which is automatically mapped upon login. This folder is on the domain controller under the USERS$ share.

> **Note**
> The full entry in the Home Folder frame's To text box is \\oakleaf-dc1\USERS$\%username%. The %username% element is an environmental variable that points to the properties dialog's user name. In the example shown in Figure 15.48, when you click Apply or OK, LaneBaron replaces %username%. Logon scripts make extensive use of environmental variables.

The problem with this single-sharepoint approach is that all subfolders of the share are visible to every user in My Computer or Explorer, although the share isn't visible in Network Neighborhood. The advantage of this method is that you automatically generate a home folder when you specify the Connect *d*: To *FolderPath* in the Profile page of the user's account properties dialog. The automatic home page method also applies security to the folder. Only members of the Administrators group and the user have permissions for the subfolder; other users can't read from or write to it. Missing in Windows 2000 is a View permission for folders.

The alternative is to create individual shares for home folders. Most network administrators place a limit of 250 to 500 shares on a server, but tests show that 1,000 or 2,000 shares are practical for high-performance file servers configured as Windows 2000 member servers. Specifying a 100MB quota for each user isn't unrealistic when you consider that today's workstations come with at least 9GB of fixed disk space, and 32MB is the most common flash memory capacity of digital cameras. A quick calculation shows that 250 home directories of 100MB each potentially consume 25GB, and 2,000 require 200GB of server drive space. Your file server probably can handle 1,000 shares, so creating individual shares is practical.

The problem with individual-user sharepoints is that you must manually create each LogonID home folder as a subfolder of a nonshared folder and share it as LogonID$. The Home Folder feature of the Profile page expects to create home folders under the share you specify in the To text box. If the share is missing, you receive an error message when attempting to Connect U: To \\*ServerName**LogonID*$.

After you create the individual share, you must set share and folder permissions manually by removing the Everyone group and giving the user account and the Administrators group Full Control permissions. You also must revoke inherited permissions for the folder, delete the Everyone group, and give the user and Administrators Full Control. You can write a script to accomplish these tasks, but revoking and assigning share and folder permissions with ADSI 2.5 scripting isn't easy.

Logon Scripts for Mapping Home Folders

Windows 9x won't map a share based on entries you make in the Connect list and To text box. You must write a logon script for Windows 9x clients and specify the path to and name of the script in the Logon Script text box. A typical logon script to synchronize the client's clock with the server and set the home folder is

```
net time \\ServerName /set /yes
net use u: /home
```

The /home argument designates the assigned logical drive as the user's home folder and causes the client to query the server for the location of the user's home folder for the mapping.

Write your logon script—in this case, a simple DOS batch file—in Notepad and save it as *Filename*.bat in the \Winnt\Sysvol\Sysvol*domain.ext*\Scripts folder to make it accessible via the Netlogon share, which is the default location for common logon scripts as well as for the common mandatory user profile discussed earlier in the chapter.

To set up and map home folders for Windows 9x (and Windows for Workgroups) clients, do the following:

1. Create the user's home folder using one of the two methods described in the preceding section. You don't need to remove the Connect *d:* To *HomeFolder* entry.

2. Type **Filename.bat** in the Logon Script text box of the Profiles page, and click Apply or OK to save the change to the account.

3. On a Windows 9x machine, log on as the user for whom you created the new home folder and verify that the logon script executes properly. A brief Windows NT Logon Script message appears during execution of the logon script. Type **net use** at the command prompt to verify the mapped logical drive, or check for a U: drive letter in Explorer.

> **Tip from**
> *RJ*
>
> Create another logon script with the `net time` line only, and specify its name in the Logon Script text box for your Windows NT clients. Windows 2000 clients automatically synchronize their clocks with the DC's clock, but Windows NT clients don't.

Troubleshooting

Password Policy Problems

When you attempt to add a new user account, you receive an Active Directory error message saying that Windows can't set the password for the new user.

The password you typed and confirmed doesn't meet the length or complexity requirements you assigned in the Account Policies node of the Computer Configuration section. If you change the policy to reduce the restrictions for domain or OU passwords, you might have to wait up to five minutes or more for the change to take effect.

Tests with the initial release version of Windows 2000 Server indicate that reversing password complexity options in Account Policies sometimes fails. In this case, you probably are faced with creating initial user passwords that meet the original requirements.

Mandatory Profile Problems

Your users receive this User Environment error message: "The operating system is unable to log you on because your roaming mandatory profile is not available."

The most common cause of this message is an error in specifying the path to the mandatory roaming profile folders. Verify that the Profile Path value in the Profile page for the user account matches exactly the \\ServerName\ProfileShare location of the profile folders.

Another cause of this message is forgetting to share the ProfileShare folder or failure to grant Read permission for the share to the Everyone group.

MCSE Corner: Establishing Group Policies, User Accounts, and Logons

The topics covered in Chapter 15 are important for two specific reasons: for background to understand other topics such as file sharing, and for working with users and groups. Because one of the most common administrative tasks in the real world is working with users and groups, it is tested on the base Windows 2000 Server exam 70-215, "Installing, Configuring, and Administering Microsoft Windows 2000 Server."

You need to be familiar with adding users to the domain. You should know how account options work and how to configure profiles. Configuring and managing user profiles is listed explicitly on the exam blueprint for managing storage use, so you should be familiar with configuring home directories and profile locations.

You also need to be familiar with the three different types of groups and how they are used. It is quite common to find questions about how group memberships affect permissions and what groups can be contained where; also common are questions about group nesting.

Finally, you should know about the use of local groups and user accounts on member servers and how they can be used in a security role. The exam is likely to have quite a few questions on user accounts and security groups, so it is an important topic to know thoroughly.

For this exam, you need to know troubleshooting of groups and user accounts. You will most likely be required to determine the cause of a user being unable to access a resource caused by group membership problems.

CHAPTER 16

MANAGING SERVER SHARES AND THE DISTRIBUTED FILE SYSTEM

In this chapter

Understanding the Principles of File Sharing   676

Creating New Shared Folders   683

Mapping Shares to Drives with Windows 2000 Logon Scripts   694

Sharing Folders on Your Intranet   697

Publishing Shares in Active Directory   701

Indexing File Contents   703

Taking Advantage of the Distributed File System   707

Using the File Replication Service with Dfs   716

Troubleshooting   719

MCSE Corner: Managing Server Shares and the Distributed File System   720

Understanding the Principles of File Sharing

A fundamental purpose of a network server is to provide a repository for files for access by networked client PCs. Novell's Netware continues to be Microsoft's major competitor in the network operating system (NOS) business. Windows NT made its mark primarily in the application server market. *Application servers* run services—such as Internet Information Server, SQL Server, and Exchange Server—to which other clients and servers connect. This chapter is devoted to Windows 2000 Server's file server and other file-related functions—Indexing Service, Distributed File System (Dfs), and the File Replication Service (FRS).

Default Shares and Their Properties

When you install Windows 2000 Server, Setup creates a basic group of common or standard shares, most of which are visible only on the server. To view the common shares, on the server right-click My Computer, choose Manage to open the Computer Management snap-in, and expand the Shared Folders and Shares nodes. Figure 16.1 shows the standard set of common shares that appear immediately after installing a Windows 2000 member server that has two disk volumes and a network printer. You seldom, if ever, need to be concerned with common shares, and you can't alter their properties. You should, however, be aware of their existence or disappearance; loss of a common share is very uncommon, but it can occur as a result of a system failure.

Figure 16.1
Installing a new member server creates a set of common shares that you can view from the Shared Folders, Shares node of the Computer Management snap-in.

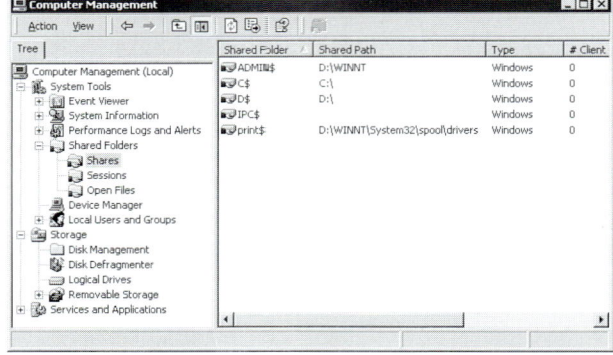

> **Note**
> If you upgrade a Windows NT Primary Domain Controller (PDC), Backup Domain Controller (BDC), or member server to Windows 2000, all shares on the upgraded server are preserved. Depending on the type of server you upgrade, you might see many more shares.

Following are brief descriptions of each common share shown in Figure 16.1:

Understanding the Principles of File Sharing

- ADMIN$ is an administrative share for the \Winnt folder of the server, called the *system root*. Only members of the local Administrators and Server Operators groups have access to administrative shares. The dollar sign ($) suffix creates a *hidden share*; hidden shares don't appear when users browse the Entire Network from My Network Places or Network Neighborhood. ADMIN$ primarily is used for remote administration of the server.

> **Note**
>
> If you double-click an administrative share to display its properties dialog, you receive a message stating: `This has been shared for Administrative Purposes. The share permissions and file security cannot be set.` The ShareName Properties dialog that opens when you acknowledge the message displays only a single, General page. The only property value you can change is the Comment text.

- C$ and D$ are administrative shares for the root of the two fixed-disk volumes. Additional volumes appear as E$, F$, and so on. Removable media drives—such as CD-ROM, DVD, and tape drives—don't receive an administrative share.
- IPC$ is the interprocess communication (IPC) share that lets remote servers and applications communicate by the *Named Pipes* protocol. Named Pipes has been the default network protocol for many Microsoft server applications, such as SQL Server, but the Windows Sockets (WinSock) protocol now is more common in TCP/IP networks.

→ For a brief description of TCP/IP ports and the WinSock protocol, **see** "TCP Ports and Processes," **p. 87**.

- print$ is a share that points to the \Winnt\System32\spool\drivers folder that contains subfolders for print drivers for the installed printer(s). The print$ share appears only if a printer is attached to the server or the server acts as a spooler for a network printer. Clients automatically download from this share a print driver for their operating system, if the required driver isn't available locally on the client.

→ For more information on the network printing process, **see** "Understanding the Printing Process with a Shared Printer," **p. 725**.

When you upgrade a member server to a Domain Controller (DC), `Dcpromo.exe` adds the following shares:

- NETLOGON is a visible share that clients automatically inspect when logging on to the Windows 2000 network. NETLOGON points to a ...\Scripts folder that contains logon scripts, profiles, policy, and other files that apply to all downlevel (Windows NT and Windows 9x) clients. The location of the ...\Scripts folder depends on whether you performed a clean install or upgraded a Windows NT server.

→ To review use of the NETLOGON share, **see** "Implementing Downlevel System Policies," **p. 663**.

- SYSVOL is a visible share that points to the \Winnt\SYSVOL\Sysvol*DomainName.ext* folder that contains Policies and Scripts subfolders to store Group Policy files and logon scripts, respectively. The contents of the SYSVOL share automatically replicate between DCs.

> **Caution**
>
> Don't alter properties of the NETLOGON and SYSVOL shares. Administrators have access to the Share Permissions and Security pages of the properties dialog for these shares, but there is no reason to change property values. Doing so might make client logon impossible.

If you upgrade a Windows NT 4.0 server that has the file replication feature installed, a hidden REPL$ administrative share also appears in Computer Management. Windows 2000 uses FRS for replication and doesn't support Windows NT 4.0's export/import replication methodology.

File Sharing Security

Supplying the contents of server-stored files to remote clients is a relatively simple process. The complex part is providing a security mechanism to precisely control which files users can see, execute, read, modify, copy, or delete. Windows 2000's new Kerberos authentication mechanism, certificate services, and other enhanced security features apply equally to serving files and applications. The new Encrypting File System (EFS), which requires user certificates, applies only to file sharing.

> **Note**
>
> This chapter discusses file, folder, and share security in the context of Windows 2000's NTFS version 5.0 only. There is no justification for using the FAT or FAT32 file systems on a production server. FAT and FAT32 provide very limited and easily penetrated security.

→ For a brief discussion of how NTFS handles file and folder security, **see** "NTFS Security," **p. 426**.

NTFS file sharing security has the following three components:

- Share security, which determines access by groups or individual users to shares. When you create a new share manually, the Everyone group has full control over the share by default. Folder security overrides share security.

- Folder security, which applies to the folder itself and the files and other folders it contains. When you create a new folder to share, the Everyone group has full control by default, unless you alter the security properties of a parent folder, if present, or the fixed-disk volume. Windows 2000 treats a volume as a top-level folder for security purposes.

- File security, which applies to individual files within a folder and overrides folder permissions.

> **Caution**
>
> After performing a new installation of Windows 2000 Server, none of your server volumes have any security. The Everyone and Administrators groups have full permissions on every volume, and every new folder and share you create inherits this unlimited—and potentially dangerous—access to files.
>
> When you upgrade a server from Windows NT, the existing Windows NT security settings and permissions are applied to volumes, shares, folders, and files.

Before placing a new Windows 2000 server into production, do the following to secure your server volume(s) against unauthorized access:

1. In My Computer or Explorer, right-click the icon of the server volume to be secured, and choose Properties to open the *ComputerName (DriveLetter)* Properties dialog.
2. Click the Security tab and select the Everyone group in the Name list (see Figure 16.2).

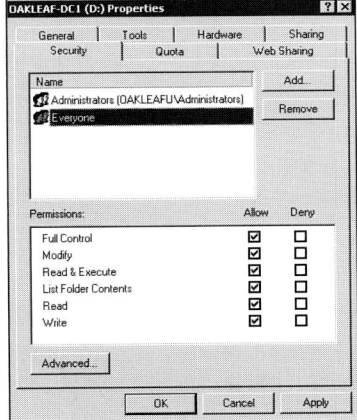

Figure 16.2
To prevent unauthorized access to and modification of your server files, select and remove the Everyone group from each volume.

3. Click Remove to remove the Everyone group from the list.
4. Optionally, click Add to open the Users, Computers and Groups dialog and double-click the Server Operators and Backup Operators to add their entries to the list. Click OK to close the dialog and add the groups to the Name list.
5. Select the Server Operators group and mark the Modify, Read & Execute, List Folder Contents, and Read check boxes. Marking the Modify check box marks the Write check box (see Figure 16.3). The following section provides a description of each of the permissions shown.

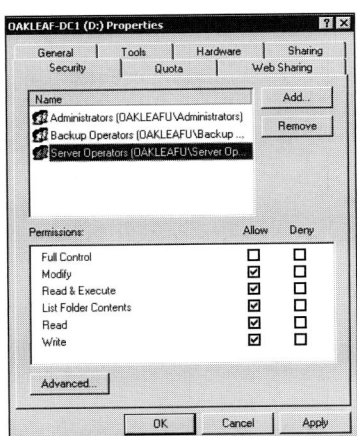

Figure 16.3
If you've assigned administrative personnel who aren't members of the Administrators group to the Server Operators, Backup Operators, or both groups, grant members of these groups limited permissions for the volume.

6. Repeat step 5 for the Backup Operators group, but click the Modify check box to clear it.
7. Click OK to close the properties dialog and effect the permission changes. Repeat steps 1 through 3 or 6 for each volume on the server.

Your volumes are now secure—except from mistakes by administrators—and the folders and files you create won't have default access by the Everyone group.

High-Level Folder and File Permissions

Following is a list, in order of increasing authority, of the high-level permissions that apply to folders and files:

- List Folder Contents lets members of the specified group read a list of the files in the folder, but doesn't allow them to open (read) the files. List Folder Contents applies only to folders.
- Read permission enables members to open files in read-only mode.
- Read & Execute adds to Read permission the ability to run an executable (.exe) file and gain access to other files, such as .dll files, required by the executable.
- Write permission enables members to create new folders, subfolders, or files, as well as open existing files in read/write mode.
- Modify is the equivalent of Read & Execute and Write permissions, plus the authority to delete files.
- Full Control combines Modify permissions with the right to take *ownership* of files and folders.

Ownership of file and folder objects is a very important security feature. The owner (officially called the CREATOR_OWNER) of the object, has Full Control permissions for the object, regardless of subsequent changes to group or user permissions. By default, the Administrators group is the owner of all files and folders created on the server. Users who create their own folders and files are the owners of the objects they create. If you have Full Control permission of the parent container, such as the drive on which the folder is created, you can change the ownership of a folder to the Administrators group or a member of the Administrators group.

To take ownership of a folder created by an owner whose account no longer exists in Active Directory (AD), called an *orphaned folder*, do the following:

1. Right-click the folder icon and choose Properties to open the *FolderName* Properties dialog.
2. Click the Security tab, and acknowledge the message that advises that you can't change the security properties of the folder, but you can change its ownership.

Understanding the Principles of File Sharing | 681

3. Click the Advanced button to open the Access Control Settings for *FolderName* dialog. The Current Owner of This Item text box contains Unable to Display Current Owner, because the owner's account no longer is present in AD.

4. Select the Administrators group, mark the Replace Owner on Subcontainers and Objects dialog (see Figure 16.4), and click OK.

Figure 16.4
Members of the Administrators group can take ownership of an orphaned folder in the Access Control Settings for *FolderName* dialog.

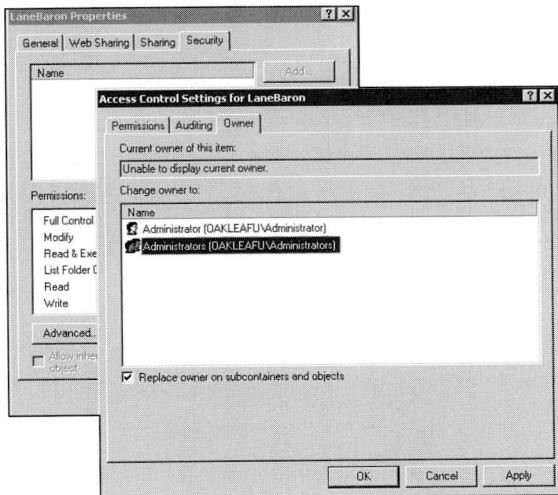

Part
III
Ch
16

5. Click Yes when asked whether you want to replace permissions on the folder with Full Control for the selected group, and then click OK to close the *FolderName* Properties dialog.

6. Reopen the *FolderName* Properties dialog, which displays the permissions inherited from the parent container, the D: volume for this example (see Figure 16.5).

Figure 16.5
Taking Administrators group ownership of an orphaned folder adds the other groups and their permissions to the folder.

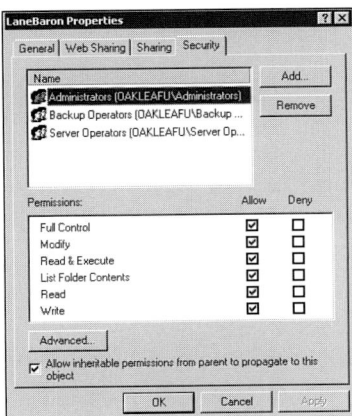

Low-Level Folder and File Permissions

High-level folder and file permissions aren't actual permissions; they link to sets of low-level permissions. Low-level permissions are more *granular* (meaning more precise) than the high-level versions. You seldom, if ever, need to alter low-level permissions; the high-level permissions are adequate for ordinary file sharing operations.

To view low-level permissions for a folder or file, do the following:

1. Open the properties dialog for the folder or file, and click Advanced to open the Access Control Settings for *FileOrFolderName* dialog.

2. In the Permissions page, select a group or user and click the View/Edit button to open the Permission Entry for *GroupOrUser* properties dialog, which contains a list of 13 low-level permissions (see Figure 16.6). The Traverse Folder/Execute File permission appears only for folder objects.

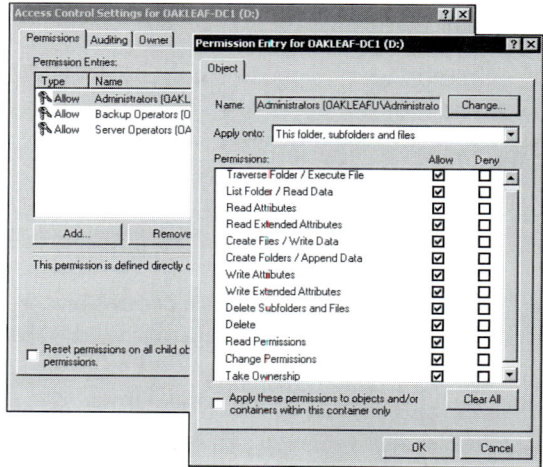

Figure 16.6
You can view and alter low-level permissions for a folder or file in the Permission Entry for *GroupOrUser* properties dialog.

3. Click OK three times to close all dialogs.

Following is a brief description of the relationship of low-level and high-level permissions:

- Read Attributes (Read-Only, Hidden, System, and Archive for a file), Read Extended Attributes (for example, the properties of a Word .doc file), and Read Permissions (all NTFS permissions of a file or folder) allow members to read property values of files and folders.

- Write Attributes, Write Extended Attributes, and Change Permissions are the write-only versions of the preceding read-only permissions.

- List Folder/Read Data and Traverse Folder/Execute File combine to form the Read & Execute high-level permission.

- Create Folders/Append Data and Create Files/Write Data combine as the Write high-level permission.
- Delete and Delete Subfolders and Files, together with the four preceding permissions, form the Modify high-level permission.
- Take Ownership, together with all preceding permissions, comprise the Full Control high-level permission.

CREATING NEW SHARED FOLDERS

Setting permissions on individual shares and their folders is a relatively simple process. Gaining a full understanding of the interaction of inherited share and folder permissions, however, requires experimenting with multiple nested shares. Nesting related shares and their folders in a multitier hierarchy simplifies administrative tasks. Nesting also provides users with a shared file structure that emulates the local folder topology of their client PC.

If you've run the ADSI25 for Active Directory application, you already have a hierarchy of shared folders for the faculty members and students of OakLeaf University, the sample organization used in the book. ADSI25 needs only a single shared folder to hold the Faculty, Staff, and Students subfolders it generates. ADSI25 then adds multiple department subfolders to the Employees and Staff subfolders and major subject subfolders to the Students subfolder. Each folder contains a `FolderName.txt` file that you can use to verify file permissions. Using ADSI25 to generate a share and folder hierarchy is much faster and easier than creating these objects manually.

Note

Creating shared folders and subfolders before removing Everyone permissions from their volume results in unsecured server shares, because file and folder permissions are inherited from the volume permissions. You can clear the Allow Inheritable Permissions from Parent to Propagate to This Object check box of the Security page for the volume, but creating a new set of shares with appropriate default permission is the better practice. Creating a new set of shares with ADSI25 doesn't affect your existing AD objects.

USING THE ADSI25 APPLICATION TO GENERATE A FOLDER HIERARCHY

To create a set of sample shares with ADSI25, follow these steps:

1. Delete any ADSI25 or other test shares you created prior to removing the Everyone group from the volume permissions.
2. If you haven't removed the Everyone group from the volume security list, use the process described in the earlier "File Sharing Security" section.

Tip from
RJ

Remove the default Everyone group as the first step after placing a share on a folder. Granting Allow permissions to the Everyone group results in no security at all on the share. If you want every user on the network, regardless of domain membership, to have access to the share, replace Everyone with the Authenticated Users group.

3. Create a new folder in the root of the server volume you use for file sharing. You can create the share on the DC running ADSI25 or, preferably, a Windows 2000 member file server. For this example, the name of the folder is **OakLeaf**.

4. Right-click the folder and choose Sharing to open the OakLeaf Properties dialog, click the Sharing tab, select the Share This Folder option, and type **OakLeaf$** in the Share Name dialog to create a hidden share (see Figure 16.7). Adding a share description is optional.

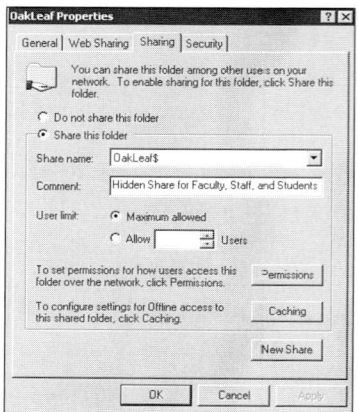

Figure 16.7
Use the OakLeaf Properties dialog to create a hidden share on the root folder of the three-tier folder hierarchy.

5. Click Permissions to open the Permissions for OakLeaf dialog, select the default Everyone group, and click Remove. Click Add to open the Users, Computers and Groups dialog; double-click the Administrators group to add it to the list and click OK to close the dialog.

6. With Administrators selected in the Permissions for OakLeaf$ dialog, mark the Full Control permission (see Figure 16.8).

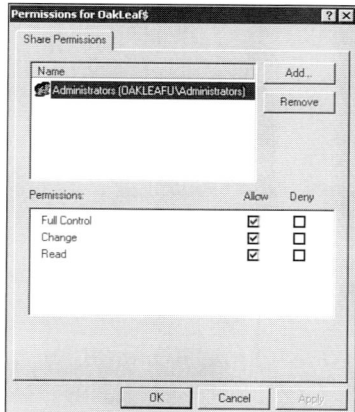

Figure 16.8
Give the Administrators group Full Control permissions on the root folder share.

7. Click the Security tab to confirm that the Administrators group and, if you added them to the volume permissions, the Server Operators and Backup Operators groups have corresponding inherited folder permissions.

8. Run the ADSI25 application to open the ADSI25: Create Groups, Users and Computers dialog. Type in the domain text boxes your DC's domain name for Employees and Students, **oakleaf.edu** for this example, and type the UNC path to the share you added in steps 4 through 7 in both share text boxes (see Figure 16.9).

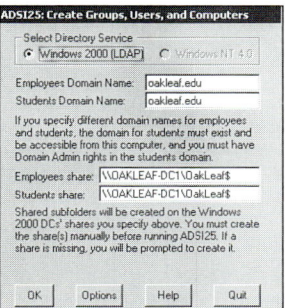

Figure 16.9
Prepare to add ADSI25 subfolders by specifying the domain name of your DC and the root share name.

→ For instructions on installing and running the ADSI25 for Active Directory application, **see** "ADSI25.msi for Windows 2000," **p. 1262**.

9. Click OK to check the share, close the dialog, and open ADSI25's main window.

10. Click the Add OUs and Groups button to create the new shares. If you have fewer than 500 Employee and Student users, type **250** or more in the two user text boxes, and click Add Employee Users and Add Student Users to create a few hundred user accounts (see Figure 16.10.)

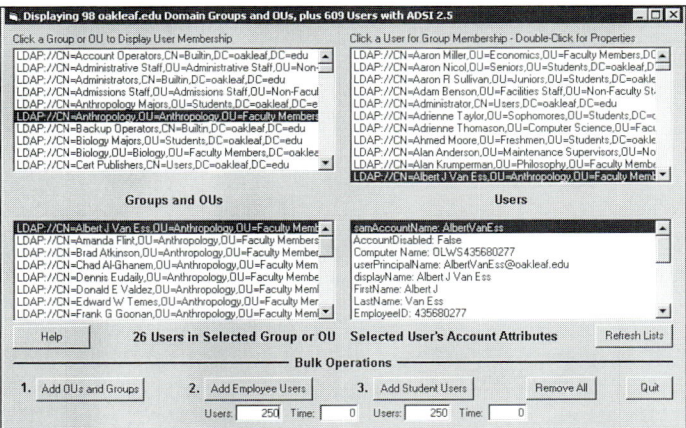

Figure 16.10
In ADSI25's main window, click Add OUs and Groups to regenerate the folder hierarchy, and then add a few hundred user accounts with ADSI25.

11. Open Explorer and expand the Faculty, Staff, and Students subfolders to display the folders added by ADSI25 (see Figure 16.11).

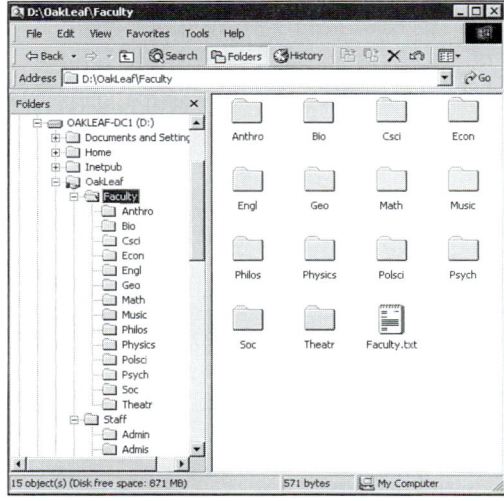

Figure 16.11
The ADSI25 application adds 14 academic department subfolders to the Faculty and Students subfolders, and 10 subfolders to the Staff subfolder.

Note

If you add subfolders manually, create the OakLeaf folder and the second-tier Faculty, Staff, and Students subfolders; then, add only their first two third-tier subfolders—Anthro and Bio, Admin and Admis, and AnthroMajors and BioMajors, respectively. You also must create the Security Groups described in the following section and add at least one user to each group for testing.

Assigning Hierarchical Share and Folder Permissions

Permission inheritance is a powerful feature that enables you to control access to multiple shares within a hierarchical structure. One of the advantages of folder hierarchies is that you can add a very restrictive set of folder permissions at the root level and then exempt individual Security Groups from specific restrictions at lower levels in the hierarchy. This approach assures that you don't compromise folder and file security by inadvertent creation of shares with Read permissions for the default Everyone group.

For the following example of permissions in a folder hierarchy, OakLeaf U's administrative staff members have decided on the following policies:

- For maximum security, Deny Full Control folder permissions for three primary Global groups—Faculty, Staff, and Students—are applied to the first-tier OakLeaf$ hidden share. Second- and third-tier folders inherit the Deny Full Control permissions from the first tier. Allow permissions for Administrators, Server Operators, and Backup Operators to inherit from the volume permissions.

- To the extent possible, shared folders should be hidden from users who don't have access to them. Hidden shares require adding a logon script to map the appropriate share(s) to local (client) drive letters. Alternatively, users or help-desk personnel can map the appropriate shared folder to a drive letter.

> **Note**
> You can add a `net use d: \\servername\sharename[\foldername]` line to a logon script specified in the Group Policy for members of the organizational unit (OU) that corresponds to the Security Group. This method works for Windows 2000, but not down-level clients. Downlevel clients require individual logon scripts that reflect their group membership.

→ For instructions on how to use Group Policy to automatically map shares to Windows 2000 clients, **see** "Mapping Shares to Drives with Windows 2000 Logon Scripts," **p. 694**.

→ To review how to create logon scripts, **see** "Logon Scripts for Mapping Home Folders," **p. 671**.

- Faculty members are allowed to read all third-tier subfolders of the Faculty and Students folder. The second-tier Faculty folder has a hidden share (Faculty$) with Read share and folder permissions for the Faculty Members group. These Read permissions override the inherited Deny Full Control permissions. Students and Non-Faculty Staff members are prohibited from accessing the Faculty$ share.

- All faculty members are allowed to read all Faculty and Students third-tier subfolders. Thus, the Faculty Members group requires Read share, and List Folder Contents and Read folder permissions for the Faculty and Students subfolders.

- Non-faculty staff members have Read access to a hidden Staff$ share, but are restricted to reading only the third-tier subfolder that matches their job classification, such as Admissions Staff. Only members of the Executive Officers group can add to or modify the contents of these subfolders.

- Students have Read access to the hidden Students$ share, and, like staff members, are restricted to reading only their particular third-tier major subject share. Members of the corresponding academic department can add contents to major subject shares, but only the department chairperson can modify (delete) items.

A problem arises with inherited folder permissions when you have overlapping or nested Security Groups. ADSI25 creates sets of Domain Local Security Groups with overlapping membership. For example, the Students group's membership consists of every member of the Anthropology Majors through Theater Arts Majors groups. Read permissions for the Students group on the Students$ share give members Read permissions on all major subject shares, despite the inherited Deny Full Control permissions on the third-tier folders. Windows 2000's application of least-restrictive permissions doesn't allow you to restrict that ability to read third-tier subfolders based on membership in another group. Thus, inherited permissions aren't appropriate for the third-tier Staff department and Students major subject subfolders. Figure 16.12 shows the share and folder permissions for the three tiers.

688 Chapter 16 Managing Server Shares and the Distributed File System

Figure 16.12
The three-tier OakLeaf U folder hierarchy has hidden shares on the first two tiers. Inheritance applies to the third-tier subfolders of the Faculty$ share, but not to the Staff$ or Students$ shares.

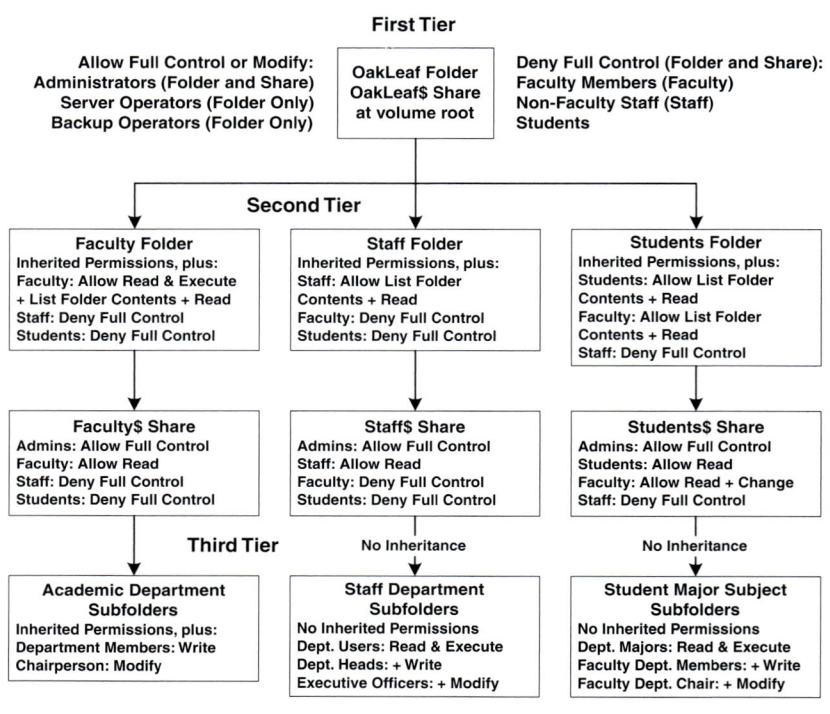

> **Note**
> Deleting the group with overlapping membership doesn't solve the least-restrictive permissions problem. For instance, deleting the Students group, re-creating it as a Global group, and then adding all the major subject groups as members of the group isn't a solution.
>
> An alternative approach is to not share the Staff and Student folders, and instead create individual shares for their third-tier subfolders. Such a design permits you to control access to shares by membership in other groups, but involves considerably more effort to implement.

Creating Second-Tier Faculty$, Staff$, and Students$ Shares with Read Permission

Granting or denying Read permission is the primary method of controlling user access to a share. To create the second-tier shares and set permissions for the three second-tier shared folders, do the following:

1. In Explorer, right-click the Faculty folder and choose Sharing to open the Sharing page of the Faculty Properties dialog.

2. Mark the Share This Folder option, add the **$** suffix to Faculty in the Share Name text box, and, if you want, add a description of the share.

3. Click Permissions to open the Permissions for Faculty$ dialog. Select the default Everyone group and click Remove.

4. Click Add to open the Users, Computers and Groups dialog, and type **Administrators; Faculty Members;Non-Faculty Staff;Students** in the text box. Click Check Names to verify your typing, and then click OK to close the dialog and add the four Security Groups to the Names list.

5. In the Permissions for Faculty$ dialog, select Administrators and mark the Full Control Allow check box. Administrators have full control of all shares in the three tiers.

6. Select Faculty (Members) and verify that the group's Read Allow check box is marked. Read Allow is the default share permission.

7. Select Non-Faculty Staff and mark the Full Control Deny check box (see Figure 16.13). Do the same for Students. Denying Full control prevents the Non-Faculty Staff and Students groups from gaining access to the Faculty$ share. Close the Permissions for Faculty$ dialog.

Figure 16.13
Marking the Full Control Deny check box for a Security Group prevents access to the share by group members.

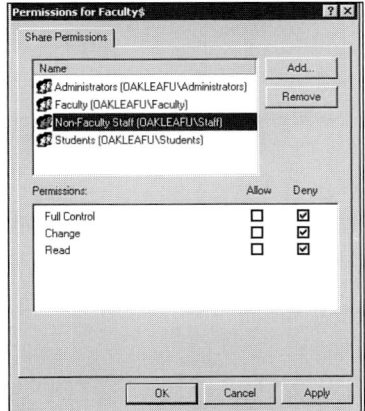

8. In the Faculty$ Properties dialog, click the Security tab. Inherited permissions, indicated by shaded boxes, appear for Administrators, Backup Operators, and Server Operators.

9. Click Add to open the Users, Computers and Groups dialog and type **Faculty Members;Non-Faculty Staff;Students** in the text box. Click Check Names, and then click OK to close the dialog and add the three groups to the Names list.

10. Select Faculty and mark the Read & Execute Allow check box, which also marks the List Folder Contents and Read Allow check boxes (see Figure 16.14). Allow permissions override inherited Deny permissions.

Figure 16.14
Setting explicit folder permissions at the second or lower folder tier overrides permissions inherited from the first tier.

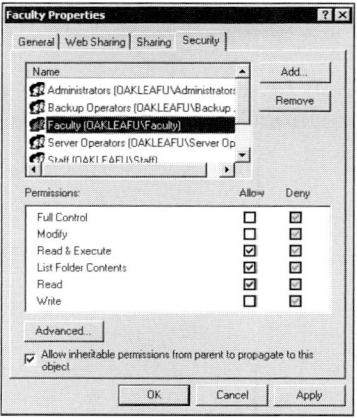

11. Select Staff to verify the inherited Deny permissions. Do the same for Students and then click OK to close the dialog and apply the security settings to the folder.

12. Repeat steps 1 through 11 for the Staff$ share and Staff folder, but make the following changes: In step 7, mark the Full Control Deny check box for the Faculty and Students groups. In step 10, mark the List Folder Contents and Read Allow check boxes for the Staff group (refer to Figure 16.12).

13. Repeat steps 1 through 12 for the Students$ share and Students folder, but make the following changes: In step 7, mark the Full Control Deny check box for the Staff groups and mark the Read and Change Allow check boxes for the Faculty group. In step 10, mark the List Folder Contents and Read Allow check boxes for the Faculty and Students groups (again, refer to Figure 16.12).

To verify the shares, log on as a member of the Administrators group at any network client, launch Explorer, and verify in My Network Places or Network Neighborhood that none of the shares you added is visible. Then click Map Drive and map the shares to local drive letters with *servername**sharename*$ as the path. Expand each mapped share to display the contained folders. Figure 16.15 illustrates in Windows 98 Explorer the three mapped shares with the Faculty$ share expanded. Verify that you have full control of each share by modifying a *Foldername*.txt file and then moving one of the text files between two folders. Do the same for one of the subfolders of the share.

Creating New Shared Folders

Figure 16.15
After mapping the three second-tier shares to local drive letters on a client, test your Administrator permissions for the shares and their sub-folders.

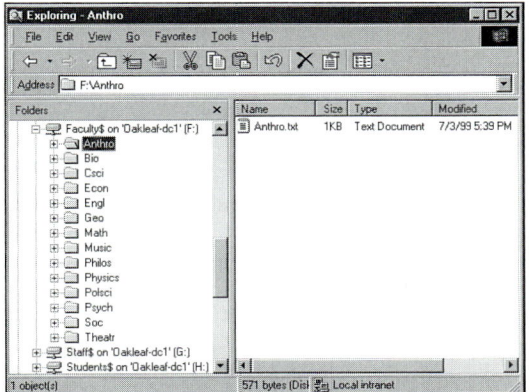

One of the basic tenets of network administration is to fully test each change you make to the properties of an object—in this case, shared folders. To test second-tier folder and file permissions for a typical user, log on to a client as a user who's a member of one of the groups to test access restrictions. For example, use the **GaryAlmgren** account; Prof. Almgren is the chairperson of the Anthropology department. The default password for all users added by ADSI25 is **password**. With this account, you can open department files, such as Anthro.txt, but you can't make changes to existing files or add new files or subfolders to department folders. You receive a somewhat misleading You don't have permission to open this file message if you attempt to save changes you make to a file. You receive an Access is denied message when you attempt to add a new file or subfolder to the Faculty or Anthropology folder. You see the same message if you map or attempt to open the Staff$ share, but you can map and open the Students$ share.

Creating Third-Tier Faculty$ Shares with Write and Modify Permissions

Permissions to write and, especially, modify files in a shared folder should be granted sparingly. Modify permissions permit users to delete files, so a disgruntled user with modify permissions on a folder could delete its entire contents. In the following example, faculty members are permitted read access to all subfolders of the Faculty$ share by inheritance of Allow Read & Execute permissions from the Faculty folder. Members of each academic department need permission to write (add files and folders), and the department chairperson needs modify permission to be able to delete outdated or objectionable files and folders. Adding these permissions for one or two academic departments enables you to verify the behavior of Write and Modify permissions.

Tip from
RJ

The next two sections require specific user accounts to test for correct share and folder permissions. If you haven't added at least 250 employee and 250 student accounts with ADSI25, do it now.

To add Write permission (Anthropology department faculty members for this example) and Modify permission (here, for the departmental chairperson, Prof. Gary Almgren), do the following:

1. On the server, right-click the Anthropology subfolder of the Faculty folder, choose Properties to open the Anthropology Properties dialog, and click the Security tab. All permissions in the list are inherited from the OakLeaf and Faculty folders.

2. Click Add to open the Users, Computers and Groups dialog; type **Anthropology;GaryAlmgren** in the text box; and click Match Names to open the Select Matching Names dialog. Select Anthropology in the list, and click OK to close the dialog and add the group and user to the Names list.

3. Select Anthropology, and mark the Write Allow check box to add Write permission to the default Read & Execute, List Folder Contents, and Read permissions.

4. Select Gary Almgren and mark the Modify Allow check box, which adds Modify and Write permissions to the defaults (see Figure 16.16). Click OK to save the security changes and close the dialog.

Figure 16.16
The department chairperson of each academic department has Modify permissions for the department subfolder.

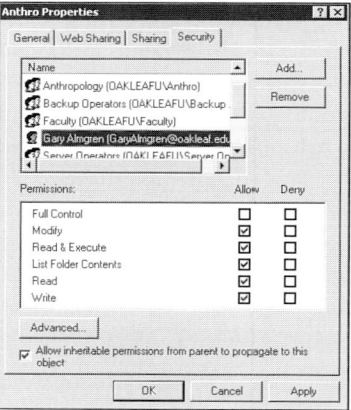

5. Log on to a network client with the department chairperson user ID and password **GaryAlmgren** and **password**, if you aren't already logged on with that account.

6. Map the Faculty$ share to a drive letter and test your ability to add a new subfolder to Anthropology, add a file, and modify an existing file under the department chairperson's account.

7. Log off the client, and then log on with another Anthropology department account—such as **AmandaFlint**, an assistant professor—and map the Faculty$ share to a drive letter.

8. As Amanda Flint, you can edit existing files, such as Anthro.txt, but you can't delete them. Similarly, you can add a new folder to Anthropology, but you can't delete it.

> **Tip from**
> *RJ*
>
> Thoroughly test the share and folder permissions you grant groups and users with logon credentials for test users within each Security Group before releasing shared folders to production. You might find that you've created conflicting Allow and Deny permissions at different levels in the hierarchy. Conflicting permissions can inadvertently permit or prevent appropriate access.

In a production environment, you need to repeat the preceding steps for each subfolder. If you want to verify that Geology department members can't edit or delete objects in the Anthropology folder, repeat steps 1 through 6, substituting **Geology** for Anthropology and **JacobMarvin** for GaryAlmgren.

CREATING THIRD-TIER STUDENTS$ SHARES WITH MULTIPLE GROUP PERMISSIONS

It's a common practice to grant members of one group Read permissions on a set of shares, give other groups Read or Read and Write permission on a particular share in the set, and enable individuals to modify a share. A permission structure of this type is the most complex you're likely to encounter as a network administrator.

To illustrate this process, we return to the OakLeaf example. Students in that example, unlike faculty members, don't have permissions to read third-level shares in departments other than their major academic subject. (A similar restriction on Staff subfolders applies to members of the Non-Faculty Staff group.) At this point, students are able to read all Students subfolders by virtue of permissions inherited from the Students folder. In addition, faculty members must be able to read all Students subfolders. Department members must have Write permission, and the department chair requires Modify permissions on corresponding major subject subfolders.

To restrict students from reading all subfolders and add appropriate permissions for faculty members, using AnthroMajors for the example, do the following:

1. Expand the Students folder, right-click the AnthroMajors subfolder, choose Properties, and click the Security tab.

2. Clear the Allow Inheritable Permissions from Parent to Propagate to This Object check box to eliminate all inherited permissions. In the Security message box, click Remove to confirm the action, and remove all groups from the Names list.

3. Click Add to open the Users, Computers and Groups dialog. Type **Administrators;Anthropology Majors;Faculty Members;Anthropology; GaryAlmgren** in the text box, click Match Names, select Anthropology in the Select Matching Names dialog, and click OK to add the five groups to the list. Adding Backup Operators and Server Operators is optional.

4. Select Administrators and mark Full Control Allow, select Anthropology and mark Write Allow, and finally select Gary Almgren and mark Modify Allow. Default Read & Execute, List Folder Contents, and Read Allow permissions are adequate for StuAnthro and Faculty (refer to Figure 16.12). Click OK to close the AnthroMajors Properties dialog and effect the security changes.

5. From the client PC at which you're logged in as **GaryAlmgren**, map the Students$ share to a drive letter and verify that you have modify permissions on the AnthroMajors share. Do the same when you log on as **AmandaFlint**, but verify only Read and Write permissions.

6. Finally, log on with an Anthropology Major student account, such as **DavidCrosby**, map the Students$ share to a drive letter, and confirm that you have only Read & Execute permissions.

> **Note**
>
> Subfolders of the Staff$ share and Staff folder require a permissions procedure similar to that for the Students$ share and Students folder. The primary difference is that all members of the Executive Officers group have Modify permissions on all subfolders.

Mapping Shares to Drives with Windows 2000 Logon Scripts

Creating Security Groups with membership identical to a corresponding OU enables you to use Group Policy to automatically map shares to logical drive letters on Windows 2000 clients. OakLeaf U's Faculty Members, Non-Faculty Staff, and Students OUs have a one-to-one correspondence with users in the Faculty (Members), (Non-Faculty) Staff, and Students groups. You use Notepad to write a `net use d: \\servername\sharename$` logon script for each group, which you save as a `GroupName.cmd` file in the ...\Scripts\Logon subfolder of the Group Policy that's buried deep in the \Sysvol\... folder hierarchy.

To create and test logon scripts (in this example, `Faculty.cmd`, `Staff.cmd`, and `Students.cmd`) to map user shares, do the following:

1. In Active Directory Users and Computers, right-click the OU node for the logon script (Faculty Members for the initial example), choose Properties, and click the Group Policy tab.

2. If you haven't added a Group Policy for the OU, click New to add a New Group Policy Object (GPO) item, and rename it to better describe its purpose, such as **Default OUName Policy**.

3. With the GPO selected, click Edit to open the Group Policy Editor and expand the User Configuration, Windows Settings, User Settings node; click Scripts (logon/logoff) to display Logon and Logoff entries in the Name list.

4. Double-click the Logon item to open the Logon Properties dialog with an empty list of logon scripts.

5. Click Show Files to open an empty Explorer window for the buried subfolder that contains logon scripts for the OU's GPO (see Figure 16.17).

Figure 16.17
Use the Group Policy Editor to add a logon script that maps a share to a common drive letter for all members of an OU.

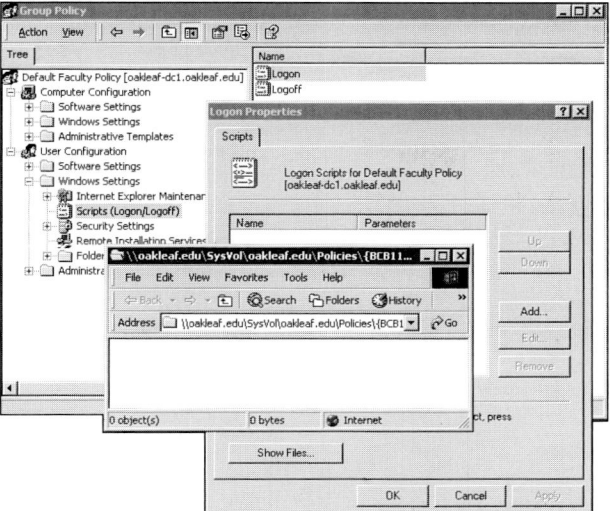

6. In the Explorer window, choose File, New, Text Document to add a New Text Document.txt file to the folder, and double-click its icon to open the file in Notepad.

7. Type **net use d: \\servername\sharename$** where **d:** is the drive letter to map the share on the client. For this example, type **net use m: \\servername\Faculty$**. Faculty members need a drive mapped to the Students$ share, so add a **net use n: \\servername\Students$** line (see Figure 16.18). Save the file as *GroupName*.cmd (**Faculty.cmd**) and close Notepad.

Figure 16.18
Use the Group Policy Editor to add a logon script that maps a share to a common drive letter for all members of an OU.

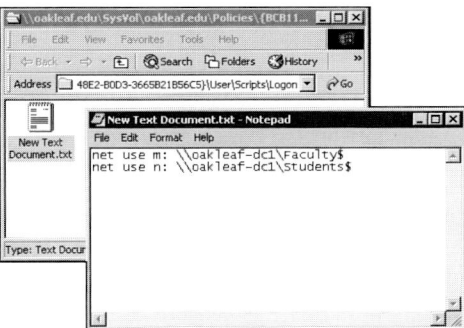

8. Delete the New Text Document.txt file and close the Explorer window.

9. In the Logon Properties dialog, click Add to open the Add a Script dialog, click Browse, and double-click *GroupName*.cmd in the Browse dialog to add the file to the Scripts list of the Logon Properties dialog (see Figure 16.19).

Figure 16.19
The logon script(s) specified in the Logon Properties dialog run when a member of the OU logs on to a client.

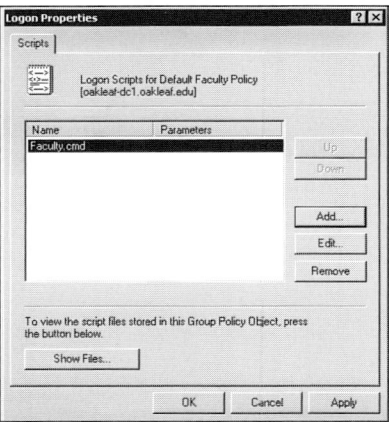

10. Click OK to close the Logon Properties dialog and save your changes, close the Group Policy Editor, and finally click Close to close the *OUName* Properties dialog.
11. At a test client PC running Windows 2000 Professional, log off, and then log on as a member of the OU to which you added the logon script. Open My Computer or Explorer to verify operation of the logon script (see Figure 16.20).

Figure 16.20
The logon script added to the GPO of the Faculty Members OU maps the Faculty$ share to Windows 2000 client's M: drive and the Students$ share to the N: drive.

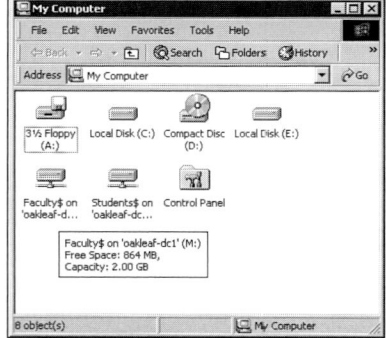

12. Repeat steps 1 through 11 for the Staff and Students OUs, creating **Staff.cmd** and **Students.cmd** logon files with single-line **net use m: *servername*\Staff$** and **net use n: \\*servername*\Students$** statements, respectively.

The ability to easily add logon scripts that apply to all members of specific OUs is another incentive to migrate your client PCs to Windows 2000 Professional. Mapping shares with logon scripts enables you to set a Group Policy option to hide the My Network Places

(NetHood) dialog, which prevents users from browsing the network. If users can browse the network, they will—even when there's no reason for them to do so.

 If clients encounter problems with mapped share or folder permissions, see the "File Sharing Problems" topic of the "Troubleshooting" section near the end of this chapter.

Sharing Folders on Your Intranet

Web sharing allows you to make shared folders available to users of your intranet. You must have Internet Information Server (IIS) 5.0 running on a networked server to take advantage of Web sharing. Setup installs IIS 5.0 by default, so at least one of your DCs or domain member servers probably has IIS 5.0 installed.

Web sharing of conventional folder hierarchies containing text files or Word documents isn't likely to interest your users. Folders without HTML or Active Server Pages (ASP) default files appear as a simple list of files and subfolders. All folders and files are read-only. On the other hand, Web sharing is a quick and easy method of making folder contents available to remote users who have an Internet connection to your Web site but don't have a dialup connection to your network.

→ For instructions on setting up and managing IIS 5.0, **see** "Upgrading to or Installing IIS 5.0," **p. 1106**.

> **Note**
> The following example assumes that you have completed the procedures in the earlier "Using the ADSI25 Application to Generate a Folder Hierarchy" section, including the Third-Tier Faculty$ Shares section.

To make a folder—Faculty for this example—accessible from your Default Web Site and test the share with Internet Explorer (IE) 5.0 on a client PC, do the following:

1. In My Computer or Explorer, right-click the shared folder you want to add to the Web site, choose Properties, and click the Web Sharing tab of the *FolderName* Properties dialog.
2. Accept the Default Web Site option in the Share In list and Select the Share This Folder option to open the Edit Alias dialog.

> **Note**
> The Share In list has two standard entries: Default Web Site and Administration Web Site. If you've added another Web Site for testing or other purposes, you can select it for the location of the Web sharing alias.

3. In the Edit Alias dialog, accept or edit the default name in the Alias text box. (Don't add spaces or other punctuation to the alias name.) Accept the default Read in Access Permissions and mark the Directory Browsing check box.
4. For added security, mark the Application Permissions None option to prevent execution of scripts (see Figure 16.21). Click OK twice to close both dialogs.

Figure 16.21
You set the IIS equivalents of conventional sharing permissions in the Edit Alias dialog of the *FolderName* Properties dialog's Web Sharing page.

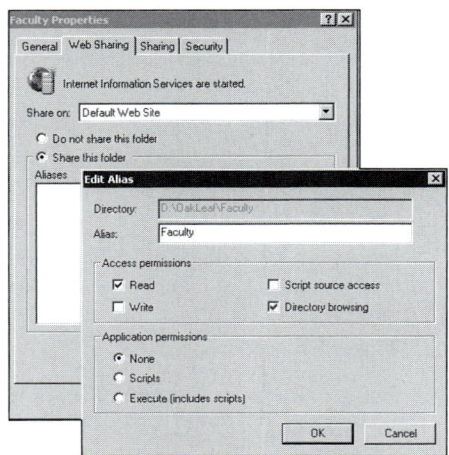

> **Note**
> Web sharing respects the security settings you apply to the folder and its subfolders. Write permission allows users to upload content, including scripts, to the folder. If you enable Write permission for Web sharing, make sure to set folder security to allow only members of authorized groups to upload content to the share.

5. Choose Programs, Administrative Tools, Internet Services Manager to open the Internet Information Services snap-in, and expand the Default Web Site node. The Faculty alias, which points to the shared folder, appears below the Printers nodes in both lists (see Figure 16.22).

Figure 16.22
When you specify Web sharing for a folder, its alias appears as a node of the Default Web Site.

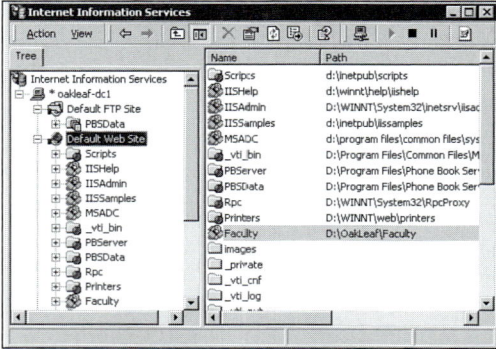

6. Right-click your new alias to display the Virtual Directory page of its Properties dialog to verify the security and application settings you specified in step 3 (see Figure 16.23).

Sharing Folders on Your Intranet

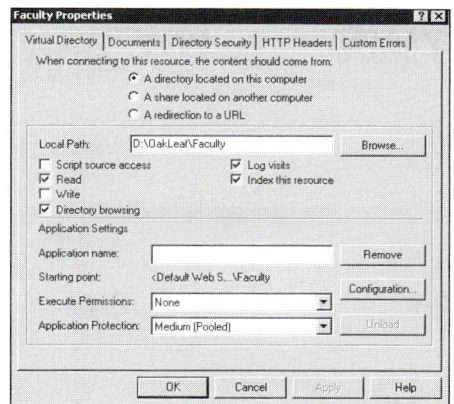

Figure 16.23
The Virtual Directory page of the *AliasName* Properties dialog allows you to alter the alias settings you specified in the Web Sharing page's Edit Alias dialog.

7. Click the Directory Security tab, and click the Edit button of the Anonymous Access and Authentication Control frame to open the Authentication Methods dialog.

8. To increase security of the share, clear the Anonymous Access check box and mark the Integrated Windows Authentication check box (see Figure 16.24). These settings require authentication of the user account when someone attempts to open the share. Click OK twice to close the two dialogs.

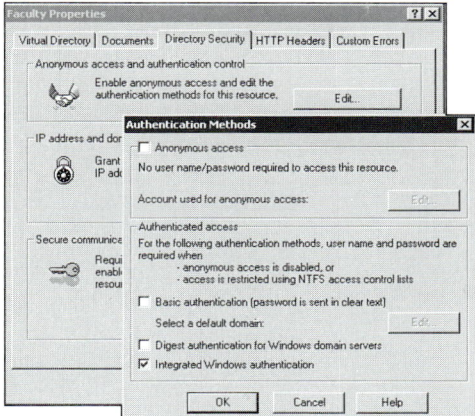

Figure 16.24
Require Integrated Windows Authentication for the virtual directory if you want to prevent anonymous users from gaining access to the share.

Note
If you've applied folder security to the share, it's not necessary to specify Integrated Windows Authentication. Only members of groups with Read and View Folder Contents Allow permissions can browse folders and display their contents. In an Internet or intranet environment, it's a good practice to apply all available security features.

9. At a test client PC, log on as a member of the Faculty Security Group (**GaryAlmgren**, **password**) and launch IE.

10. In the Address text box, type the intranet address of the alias, `http://servername/faculty/` for this example, to open the *servername* - /faculty/ folder (see Figure 16.25). Members of the Faculty group can browse the subfolders and read their contents.

Figure 16.25
Subfolders and files of the share appear in IE 5.0 in a list format with creation date and time, <dir> or file size in bytes, and the name of the folder or file.

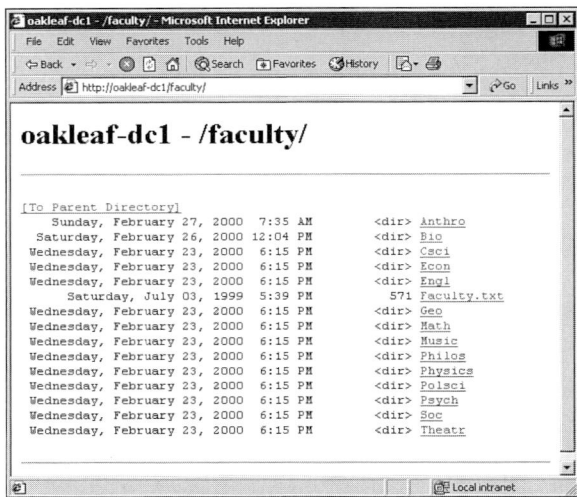

11. Click a .txt file to display its contents (see Figure 16.26). Authorized Web users can open in IIS any file type for which they have a reader—such as Word Pad for .doc and .rtf files—or the appropriate application—Excel for .xls files, for example.

Figure 16.26
Shared files open in IE with the associated reader for the file type. By default, text files display in 12-point Courier New, not the standard Times New Roman font of HTML files.

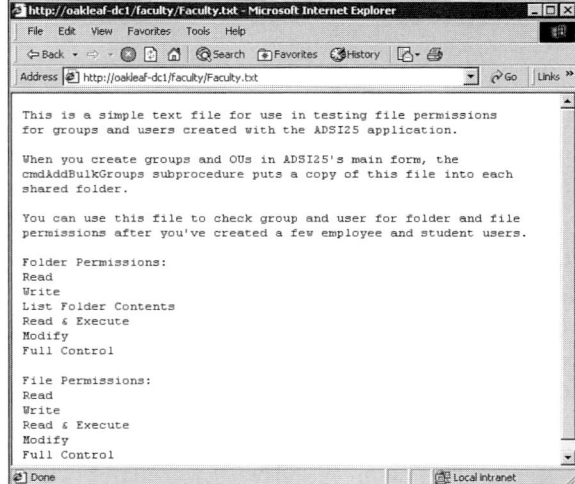

12. Log off the client and log on as a member of the Students group (**DavidCrosby**, **password**). When you attempt to connect to `http://servername/faculty/`, the Enter Network Password dialog opens (see Figure 16.27). This dialog appears because members of the Students group have Deny Full Control permissions for the Faculty folder.

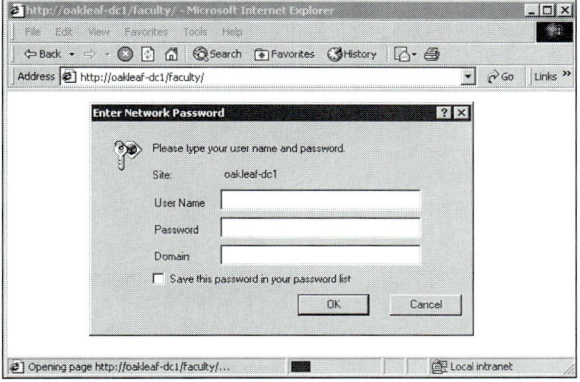

Figure 16.27
If a user who doesn't have permissions for the shared folder attempts to gain access to the folder's Web share, the Enter Network Password dialog requests a valid user name, password, and domain name.

Tip from
RJ

If you place a `Default.htm` (or `Iisstart.htm`) file in a Web-shared folder, the HTML file replaces the contents list. You can retain the list format by giving `Default.htm` a different name or clearing the Enable Default Document check box in the Documents page of the *WebShareName* Properties dialog.

Publishing Shares in Active Directory

You can add entries for shares in most AD containers, a process that Microsoft calls "publishing shared folders." The most common container for publishing a shared folder is the OU to which it pertains. When you run the ADSI25 application for the first time, the program code automatically publishes entries for the Faculty, Staff, and Students shares and their subfolders in the corresponding OUs. The only property values of a published shared folder at the time you create it are the display name you assign it and the UNC path to the share.

Publishing shared folders is useful only to server administrators who have access to the server administrative tools. As an administrator, you can search in Active Directory Users and Computers for shared folders at the Entire Directory or any lower level in the OU hierarchy. Unlike published printers, ordinary users can't search for published shares—there's no "Shared Folders" or similar option in Windows 2000 Search window.

Following are your share publishing options:

- Search for Published Folders in AD by clicking the toolbar's Find Objects in Active Directory button to open the Find dialog, selecting Shared Folders in the Find list, and clicking Find Now to display all published shared folders. Double-clicking an entry in the list opens an Explorer window that displays the folder's contents (see Figure 16.28). You can search by name, including leading and trailing DOS wildcards (* or ?). If you've added a keyword to the published share properties, you also can search for the keyword.

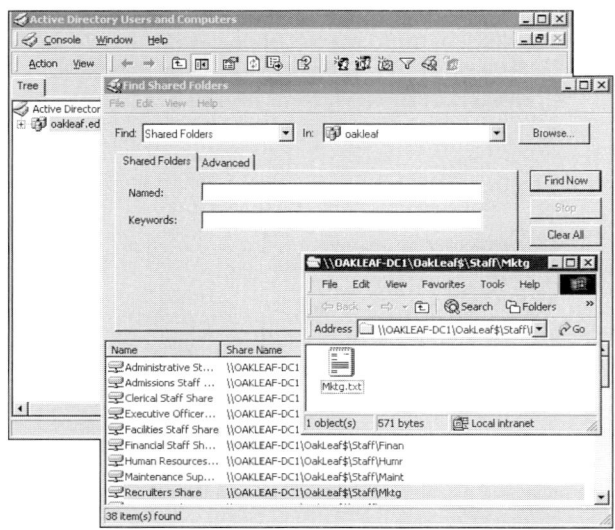

Figure 16.28
The Find Shared Folders dialog displays a list of all shared folders you've published in AD, starting at any point in the domain hierarchy.

- Publish a new shared folder by right-clicking the appropriate OU node and choosing New, Shared Folder to open the New Object—Shared folder dialog. Type a descriptive name for the share and the UNC path to the share in the Name and Network path text boxes, respectively (see Figure 16.29); click OK to add the object to AD.

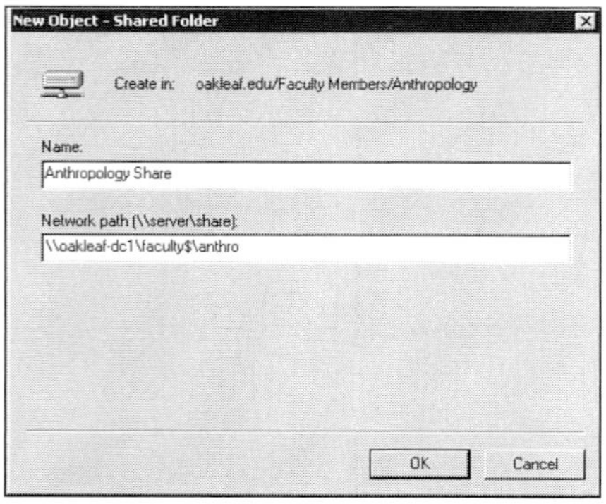

Figure 16.29
The New Object–Shared Folder dialog allows you to specify only the display name and UNC path to the share.

- Add or edit properties of a published shared folder by opening the *PublishedShareName* Properties dialog. Setting more than the name and path to the share requires editing. You can add a description of the share and, by clicking the Keywords button, add a list of words on which you can search (see Figure 16.30). As with most other AD objects, you can specify a user as the manager of the share.

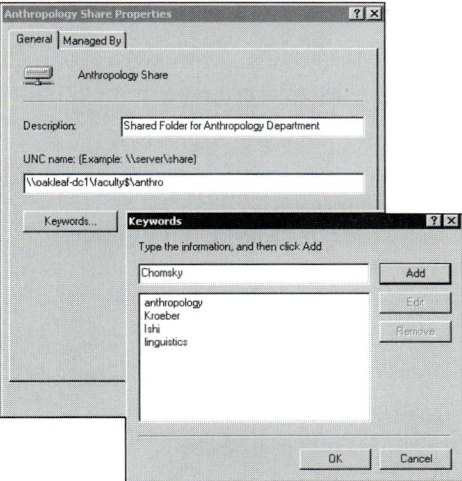

Figure 16.30
You add or edit a few additional published share properties in the General page of its properties dialog, which also enables you to add keywords for searching.

> **Note**
> Inability of ordinary users running Windows 2000 Professional to take advantage of published shared folders indicates that this feature probably is a work in progress.

INDEXING FILE CONTENTS

Windows 9x and NT's Find feature, and Windows 2000's Search dialog enable basic searches for folders and files with names that match a simple character-string criterion, such as Stu*.txt. You also can search for text strings contained in files. Basic searches, especially for specific text in many large files, can become a very slow process when searching network shares.

Windows 2000's Indexing Service can automatically generate full-text indexes on specific types of files; the indexes are stored in special folders called Catalogs. The release version of Windows contains indexing filters for text, HTML, and Office 95 or later file types (.doc, .xls, and .ppt, but not Access/Jet .mdb files). Full-text indexes speed users' searches for character strings contained in a file, and permit use of more complex (Boolean) search criteria not offered by the basic search feature.

The Indexing Service is a disk- and processor-intensive service, so it runs in the background at a low priority. After you start the service, it's easy to forget that the service is running until something goes wrong with your server. Following is a list of more important Indexing Service caveats:

- If you have many large documents to index on a production file or Web server, don't start the initial indexing operation during normal business hours. Creating a large initial set of indexes, especially of Web sites, can bring your server to its knees.
- Microsoft recommends that you don't run antivirus software simultaneously with Indexing Service. Indexing Service hangs when attempting to index a file locked by antivirus software.
- Don't store the catalog(s) for a Web site in the \Inetpub\Wwwroot folder or a folder for any other virtual Web root. You can locate the catalog in \Inetpub, which is its default location.
- Encrypted files aren't indexed. If you encrypt files after indexing clear-text versions, the index no longer contains references to the encrypted files.
- Folders specified in the index by their UNC share names display filenames to all users, regardless of their permission(s) for the folder or files. This is the equivalent of giving the Everyone group List Folder Contents permission.
- On an NTFS volume, the catalog consumes about 15% of the total size of the files indexed.

Configuring Index Service Prior to Startup

The Indexing Service doesn't autostart by default, because administrators should determine what to index before running the service for the first time. Before you enable the Indexing Service, you should indicate the specific drives or, preferably, folders to index.

To set up the Indexing Service before running it, do the following:

1. Right-click My Computer and choose Manage to open the Computer Management snap-in. Expand the Services and Applications and the Indexing Service nodes to display the default System and Web catalogs.

Note When you install Windows 2000 Server, the location of the System catalog is on the volume with the greatest amount of free space and the Web catalog is in IIS's default \InetPub folder (see Figure 16.31).

Indexing File Contents 705

Figure 16.31
Setup automatically places the System index on the volume with the largest amount of free space. The standard location of the Web index is IIS 5.0's default \Inetpub folder.

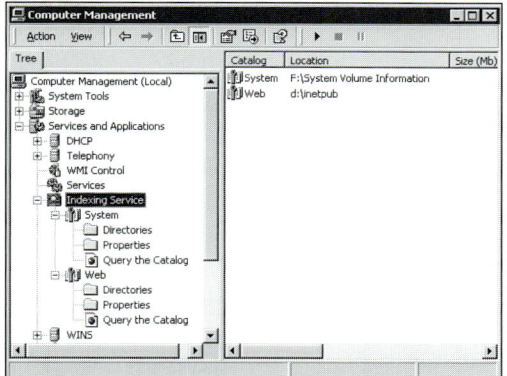

2. To specify the System directories to be processed by Index server, click the Directory node under the System node to display the default folders to index and those excluded from the index.

> **Note**
> By default, all drives (and their folders, with a few exceptions) are indexed by System. Most administrators remove all objects from the System Directories list and start over.
>
> Web indexes all \Inetpub subfolders, plus several \Program Files subfolders. You might not see the folders in the Web, Directories list until you run Index Server for the first time.

3. Select each default drive or folder you don't want to index, press Delete to remove it from the list, and confirm your action.
4. To add a specific folder hierarchy to index, right-click the Directories node and choose New, Directory to open the Add Directory dialog. Type or browse the path to the folder to index and, if shared, add the UNC path to the folder (see Figure 16.32). Click OK to add the folder to the Directories list.

Figure 16.32
Remove all default folders from the System, Directories list, and then add the specific folders or subfolders that contain the files you want to index.

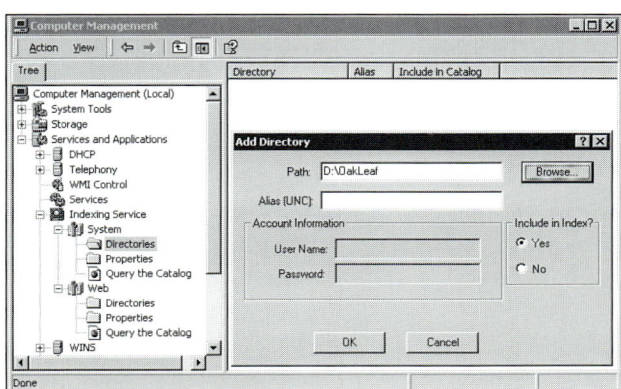

STARTING AND TESTING THE INDEXING SERVICE

To start and quickly test the success of the indexing process, do the following:

1. Right-click the Indexing Service node and choose Start. Click Yes in the Enable Indexing? message box if you want the Indexing Service to autostart on booting. After a few seconds to minutes—depending on the number and size of files being indexed—of heavy CPU activity, a set of properties for the installed document filters appears in the Properties lists of the System and Web nodes (see Figure 16.33).

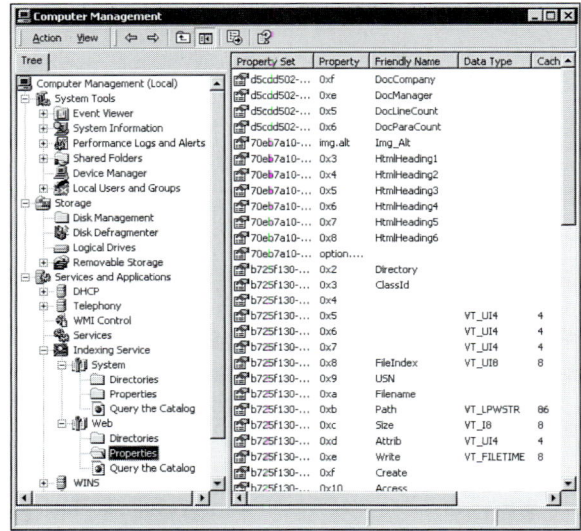

Figure 16.33
When the initial indexing operation completes, a set of properties and values appears in the Web, Properties list. You might not see the full set of properties until you reboot the server.

2. To verify that the Indexing Service is operating properly, click the Web, Query Catalog node to open the Indexing Service Query Form in the snap-in's right pane.
3. Mark the Advanced Query option and type a query, such as **active NEAR interface**, that you expect to return a result set from the sample HTML files installed with IIS 5.0.
4. Click Search to display a list of files that meet the query criterion (see Figure 16.34).

Figure 16.34
Active Directory Service Interfaces (ADSI) appears in several of IIS 5.0's sample HTML files, so you receive several records for an `active NEAR interface` search criterion.

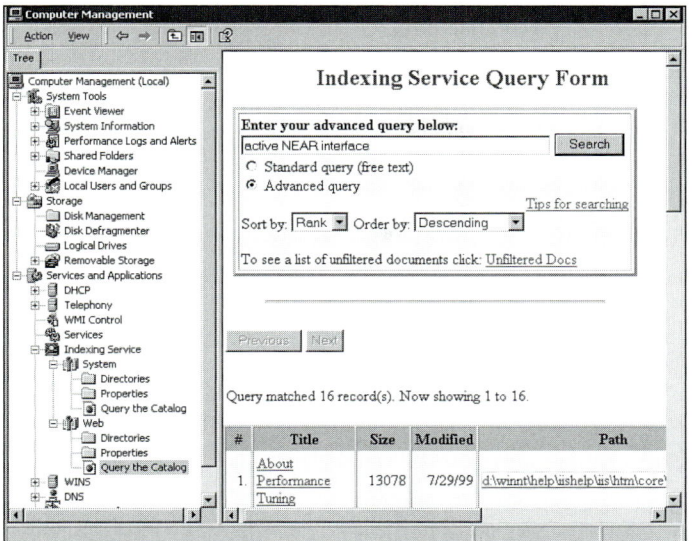

Tip from
RJ

If a small VBScript dialog with a `No Results` message opens when you run the query shown in Figure 16.34, reboot the server. Rebooting the server after the initial indexing operation assures that the Indexing Service completes the indexing process. The potential need to reboot the server is another reason to start the Indexing Service during off-hours.

The Indexing Service Query Form's Standard (Free Text) option enables you to search for a word or phrase. The Advanced option enables you to use Boolean operators, such as AND, OR, NEAR, and the like. The Sort By list enables you to select Rank (relevancy), Title (only), Path, Size, or Modified (date) order for the result set. You also can select Ascending or Descending order for any Sort By selection.

If you've used the advanced searching features of Web search sites, such as `Altavista.com`, you're probably familiar with Boolean search syntax. If not, click the Tips for Searching link to open a page that discusses query methods, and then click the Query Syntax button to open the "Making Queries" topic of the online help for Indexing Service.

 If you have problems with the Indexing Service's query feature, see the "Indexing Service Problems" topic of the "Troubleshooting" section near the end of this chapter.

Taking Advantage of the Distributed File System

Network administrators in growing firms face a continuing need to add more file server disk drives or connect additional file servers to the network. Windows 2000's Dynamic Disks and Volume Mount Points ease the problems of expanding storage capacity by adding physical drives. When your file sharing operations need additional servers to deliver better performance under heavy network load, however, it's often necessary to move sets of popular shares to the new server(s). Users are dismayed when shares mapped to local logical drive letters display Network path not found messages.

→ To review the features of Dynamic Disks, **see** "Dynamic Disks, Basic Disks, and Volumes," **p. 416**.
→ For more information on the benefits of Volume Mount Points, **see** "Volume Mount Points," **p. 427**.

You can solve the Network path not found messages for Windows 2000 Professional users by altering the net use commands of logon scripts in GPOs. You also can alter logon scripts in individual or mandatory user profiles for downlevel clients. Making these modifications without causing users temporary problems requires exquisite timing. In the real world, it's seldom practical to completely restructure all existing server shares to provide users with a cogent hierarchical view of a complex network. Lack of structured shares also causes users to run out of logical drive letters for mapping. In many cases, Dfs can solve most or all of the problems you encounter as you increase file sharing capacity and incrementally reorganize share and folder hierarchies.

Windows NT 4.0 introduced Dfs as an optional add-on; Dfs now is an integral element of Windows 2000 Server's NTFS file services. Dfs gives you, in Microsoft's words, "a logical view of physical storage," letting shares on multiple Windows 2000 servers "appear as one giant hard drive." Most network administrators probably won't use the single giant drive option but will use Dfs to set up a limited number of hierarchical shares that deliver specific categories of information to particular groups of users.

Understanding Dfs Terminology

Before you attempt to set up Dfs on a server, you should become familiar with the following Dfs-related terms:

- *Dfs root volumes* are shares on a DC or member servers that represents the top of the Dfs hierarchy on the server. A server can have only one Dfs root volume.
- *Dfs leaf folders* are folders linked to a Dfs root volume. A Dfs root volume can contain only leaf folders or junctions.
- *Inter-Dfs junctions* connect Dfs leaf folders and Dfs root volumes on other servers. (Windows NT 4.0's Dfs called this type of junction a *junction point*.)
- *Mid-level junctions* are the Windows 2000 replacement for Inter-Dfs junctions. You must have AD enabled to use mid-level junctions.
- *Post-junction junctions* point to the leaf folders of Dfs root volumes connected by inter-Dfs or mid-level junctions.
- *Alternate volumes* are pairs of leaf folders having identical contents. If one of the alternate volumes is inaccessible, the client connects to the other alternate volume by a process called fail-over. Alternate volumes are best suited to read-only or write-seldom content, because replication of alternate volume content is manual and, therefore, unreliable.
- *Fault-tolerant volumes* use Windows 2000 Server's File Replication Service (FRS) to replicate a volume's contents between two servers. FRS replaces Windows NT 4.0's LMRepl export/import replication scheme, and FRS doesn't provide direct backward compatibility with LMRepl running on downlevel servers in mixed mode. Like mid-level junctions, fault-tolerant volumes rely on Windows 2000's multimaster replication

capability. Fault-tolerant volumes replace alternate volumes; FRS automatically synchronizes the contents of the volumes based on time-stamped entries in the NTFS 5. FRS synchronization has considerable latency, so it's best suited to write-seldom files. FRS also provides load balancing between fault-tolerant volumes.

- *Downlevel volumes* are linked shares on machines running Windows 2000 Professional, NT Workstation, or 9x. These operating systems can't host Dfs root volumes.

- *Partition knowledge tables (PKTs)* are sorted lookup tables that map logical Dfs names to physical Dfs referrals. Dfs clients cache PKT records to speed access to previously visited folders; if a record is missing from the client's cache, it retrieves the required information from the PKT. The client cache expires in 60 minutes, unless you change the default expiration time. Windows 2000's AD stores the PKT for *fault-tolerant Dfs*; in a non-AD environment, the Registry stores the PKT records for *standalone Dfs*.

- *Dfs referrals* map junctions to the physical location of folders. The referral is the UNC path to the folder.

Figure 16.35 illustrates a Dfs hierarchy for the Faculty, Staff, and Students folders and shares used in the examples of earlier sections of this chapter. OakShare is the primary Dfs root volume, which points to an empty OakShare folder. Mid-level junctions connect the OakShare root to the Students share on the oakleaf-ps1 server and to the Employees Dfs root on the oakleaf-fs1 server. Post-junction junctions connect the Employees Dfs root to the Faculty and Staff leaf volumes (shares) on oakleaf-fs1. Fault-tolerant (F-T) volumes are replicas of the original Faculty, Staff, and Students folders.

Figure 16.35
This diagram depicts a Dfs hierarchy with the Dfs root volume on a DC (oakleaf-dc1) with links to another Dfs root on member file server (oakleaf-fs1) and a shared folder on a member print server (oakleaf-ps1).

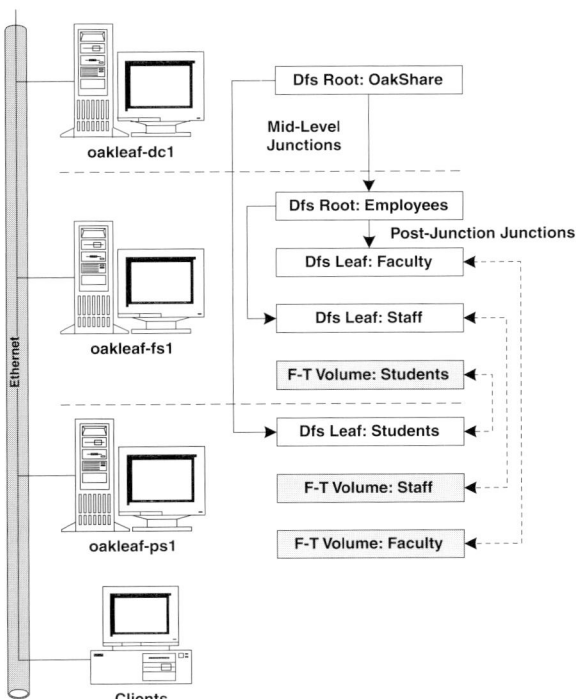

> **Note**
> Folder replicas provide fault tolerance, but you must have at least two DCs for the domain to prevent a single point of Dfs failure. If you have only one DC for the domain and that DC fails, clients can't connect to Dfs shares after their cache times out.

Creating Dfs Roots

The first step in setting up and configuring Dfs is to create a primary Dfs root volume on a designated server. You can place the Dfs root volume on a DC, because the leaf folders or Dfs roots connected by mid-level junctions can be located on other servers that deliver shared files to clients. In this case, the DC provides referrals only when the client PKT caches require updating, so the Dfs load on the DC is minimal.

> **Note**
> You must be a member of the local Administrators group of the server(s) on which you install a Dfs root. You can administer Dfs from any Windows 2000 server or a client running Windows 2000 Professional that has the Administrative Tools installed.
>
> Figure 16.35 and the example of this section use the folder structure created by ADSI25, but you can substitute existing shares for the Faculty, Staff, and Students shares.

→ For instructions on installing ADSI25 and creating the sample shared folders, **see** "Using the ADSI25 Application to Generate a Folder Hierarchy," **p. 683**.

To create a new Dfs root, such as the OakShare root shown in Figure 16.35, do the following:

1. Choose Programs, Administrative Tools, Distributed File System, to open the Dfs snap-in (Dfsgui.msc).

2. Right-click the Distributed File System node, and choose New Dfs Root to open the New Dfs Root Wizard. Click Next to bypass the Welcome dialog.

3. In the Select the Dfs Root Type dialog, accept the default Create a Domain Dfs Root option. A domain Dfs root enables you to use fault-tolerant Dfs to replicate Dfs shares. Click Next.

4. In the Select the Domain for the Dfs Root dialog, accept the default or change the domain name, oakleaf.edu for this example. If you change the value in the Domain Name text box, you must choose one of the domains in the Trusting Domains list. Click Next.

5. In the Specify the Host Server for the Dfs Root dialog, accept the default fully qualified domain name (FQDN) if you're running the Wizard on the host server. The host server for this example is oakleaf-dc1.oakleaf.edu. Otherwise, click Browse to open the Computers dialog, and double-click the host server's entry in the list to add it to the Server Name text box. Click Next.

TAKING ADVANTAGE OF THE DISTRIBUTED FILE SYSTEM | 711

6. In the Specify the Dfs Root Share dialog, select the Create a New Share option, and type the local path (**d:\OakShare** for this example) in the Path to Share text box and its name (**OakShare**) in the Share Name text box (see Figure 16.36). Click Next, and click Yes when asked whether you want to create the new folder.

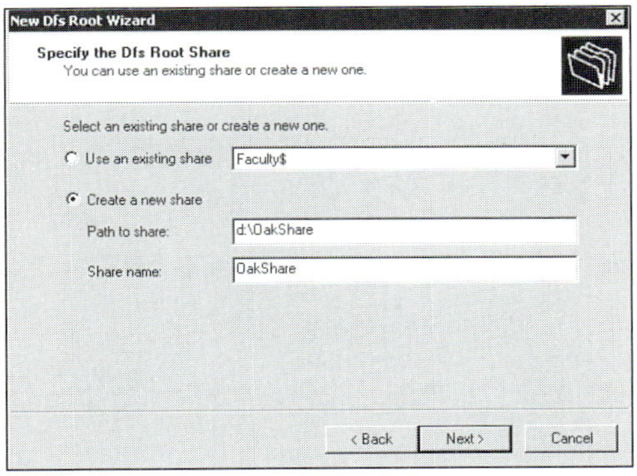

Figure 16.36
Create a new, empty share with the New Dfs Root Wizard to serve as the Dfs root share.

PART
III
CH
16

Tip from
RJ

Dfs root shares, like roots of other volumes, shouldn't contain files. You can specify an existing share for the Dfs root share, but it's a better policy to create a new share with a short name that reflects the scope of the Dfs root share.

7. In the Name the Dfs Root dialog, accept the default Dfs Root Name from the name of the shared folder and add an optional description of the share in the Comment text box (see Figure 16.37). Click Next.

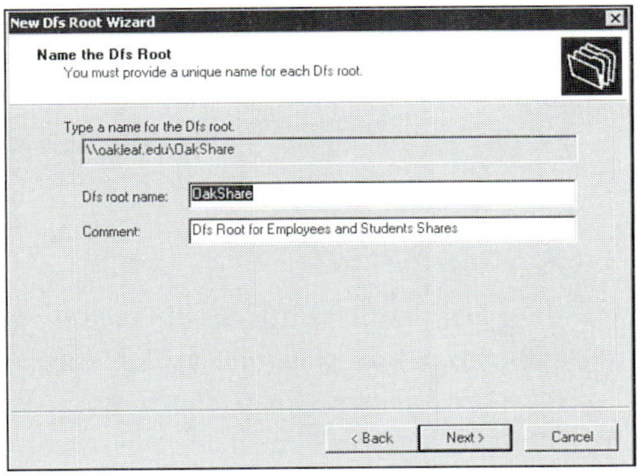

Figure 16.37
Specify the Dfs root name and its description. Unlike conventional shares, domain Dfs shares use the domain name (oakleaf.edu), not the server name (oakleaf-dc1), as the share location.

8. In the Completing the New Dfs Root Wizard, review your choices and click Finish to create the new Dfs root and dismiss the Wizard. Your new Dfs root appears as a node below the Distributed File System entry in the list.

9. Right-click the Dfs root node and choose Check Status to verify the root node is functional. A check mark in a circle at the lower-left of the icon indicates a healthy Dfs root.

10. Right-click the Dfs root node, choose Properties, and click the Security tab of the RootName Properties dialog. New Dfs roots don't inherit volume-level permissions; instead, the root has a default set of permissions for the primary domain groups and a new *SERVERNAME$* user account (see Figure 16.38). Review the default permissions for each group and then click OK to close the dialog.

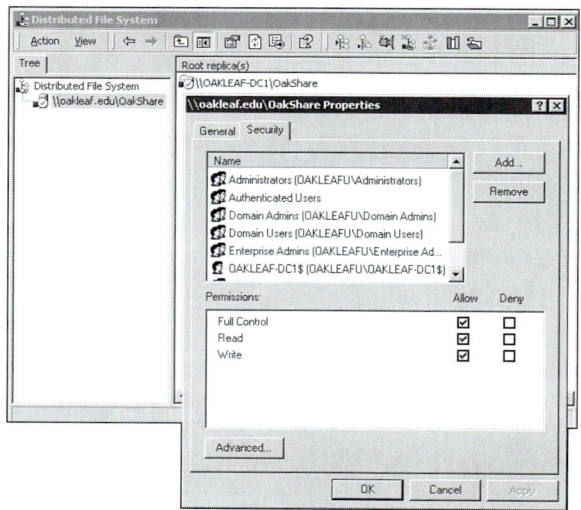

Figure 16.38
When you create a new Dfs root, the Wizard automatically adds groups and sets default permissions for each group.

If you have two servers in the domain, repeat the preceding process on the second server (oakleaf-fs1 for this example) and create an Employees Dfs root and folder. Copy the Faculty and Staff folders from the location in which you created them with ADSI25 to the second server. The location to which you copy the folders isn't important.

If you have three servers available in your domain, copy the Students folder to the third server (oakleaf-ps1).

Populating Dfs Roots by Linking Shares

You build Dfs hierarchies by adding leaf shares or mid-level junctions to the root. This example uses three servers to demonstrate how to connect a Dfs root and a shared folder to a Dfs root on a DC, but two servers are adequate for test purposes. After you create them, you can add Dfs roots on other domain servers to the primary server's Distributed File System snap-in.

To populate the Dfs root volume by creating mid-level junctions to other servers, do the following:

1. On the primary Dfs server (oakleaf-dc1), right-click the Dfs root node and choose New Dfs Link to open the Create a New Dfs Link dialog.

2. Type the name of the Dfs root node on the second server (**Employees**) in the Link Name text box. Click Browse to open the Browse for Folder dialog, navigate to the shared Employees folder (\\oakleaf-fs1\Employees), and click OK to add the UNC path to the Send the User to This Shared Folder text box.

Tip from
RJ

The Dfs online documentation states that the proper UNC syntax to specify a root node is \\domain.ext\RootName (in this example, \\oakleaf.edu\Employees). This UNC syntax works with Windows 2000 clients, which use Dfs version 4, but not with downlevel Windows clients that use Dfs version 3. You receive an error message from Windows NT and 9x clients if you use the domain syntax with Dfs version 3.

3. Type an optional comment and accept or change the client cache expiration time in seconds (see Figure 16.39). Click OK to close the dialog.

Figure 16.39
When you create a new Dfs link, you can set the amount of time that clients can cache the referral.

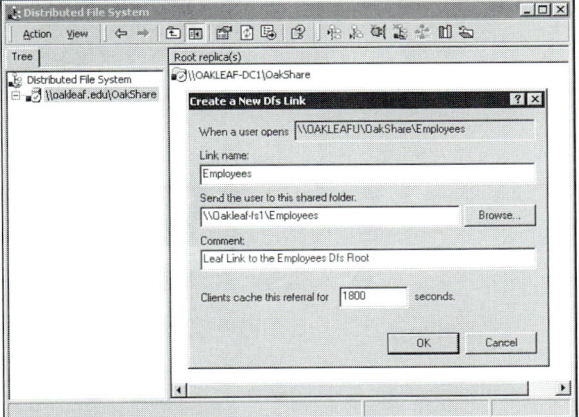

4. On the second server, right-click a folder to share (the copied Faculty folder) and choose Sharing to open the *FolderName* Properties dialog. Select the Share This Folder option, accept the default share name (Faculty), and click OK to close the dialog.

5. Repeat step 4 for each additional folder to share—Staff for this example.

6. Right-click the second server's (Employees) Dfs root node and choose New Dfs Link. Type the name of the link (**Faculty**) in the Link Name text box.

7. Click Browse to open the Browse for Folder dialog, navigate to the folder you shared in step 4, and click OK to add the link location. Add an optional description in the Comment text box and click OK to close the dialog.

8. Repeat steps 6 and 7 for each additional link to add—**Staff** for this example.

9. Return to the primary server (oakleaf-dc1), right-click the Distributed File System Node, and choose Display an Existing Dfs Root to open the eponymous dialog. Expand the nodes and select the Dfs root of the second server (see Figure 16.40). Click OK to add the second Dfs root.

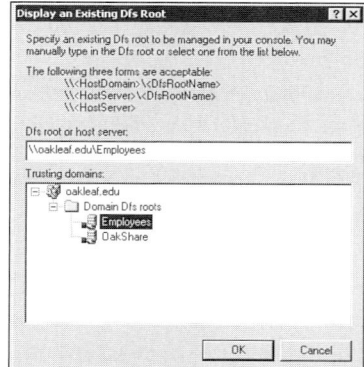

Figure 16.40
The Display an Existing Dfs Root dialog enables you to add nodes to the Distributed File System snap-in for other Dfs roots in your domain.

10. Expand the second server's root node to display its leaf nodes. Right-click one of the leaf nodes and choose Open to display the contents of the share (see Figure 16.41).

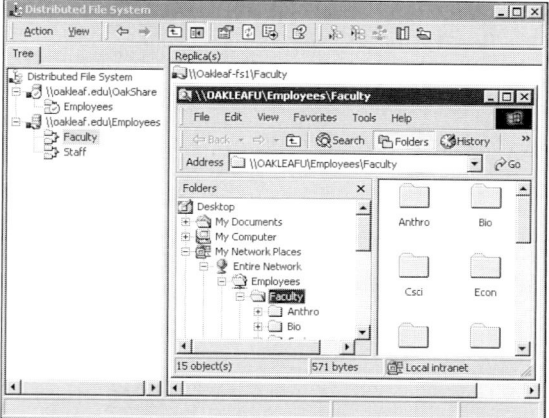

Figure 16.41
In an Explorer window, the path to a root node uses the downlevel domain name (OAKLEAFU instead of oakleaf.edu).

11. Right-click the primary Dfs root volume (oakleaf-dc1), and choose New Dfs Link to open the dialog. If you have a third server (oakleaf-ps1) with the shared Students folder, create a Students link to the share (\\oakleaf-ps1\Students). If not, share the local Students folder and create a link to it.

Despite Windows 2000 Server's current limitation of a single level of leaf folders within a Dfs root folder, you can create a deeply nested share hierarchy if you have enough file

TAKING ADVANTAGE OF THE DISTRIBUTED FILE SYSTEM | 715

servers to host the required number of subordinate Dfs root folders. Microsoft has committed to the ability to nest leaf folders and to support multiple Dfs roots on a server in a future upgrade to Windows 2000.

> **Note**
>
> You publish a Dfs root volume in AD by the process for publishing any other share. Specify the domain-based UNC path to the share (`\\domain.ext\RootName`) when publishing Dfs root volumes in AD.

→ To review how to publish a shared folder in AD, **see** "Publishing Shares in Active Directory," **p. 701**.

PART
III
CH
16

TESTING DFS SHARES WITH WINDOWS 2000 AND DOWNLEVEL CLIENTS

Windows 2000, Windows NT 4.0 with Service Pack 3+, and Windows 98+ include native support for Dfs. Windows 95 clients must have the DFS Services for Microsoft Windows Client or its equivalent installed. `Dsclient.exe` for Windows 9x includes the Dfs Services, so it's a good practice to remove DFS Services from Windows 98 and install `Dsclient.exe` if you want to support both AD and Dfs.

→ For instructions on installing `Dsclient.exe`, **see** "Installing and Testing the Directory Services Client for Windows 9x," **p. 786**.

Following are the two UNC address syntaxes for connecting Windows clients to a Dfs root volume:

- Windows 2000 clients and Windows NT and 9x clients that are configured to use DNS—either through assignment by the Domain Host Control Protocol (DHCP) or manual configuration—use the `\\domain.ext\RootName` UNC syntax to map a local drive to the Dfs root. The mapping appears in Explorer as `RootName` on `'servername.domain.ext' (D:)`. Figure 16.42 illustrates the appearance in Windows 98 SE Explorer of the example of the Dfs root share created in the preceding two sections.

Figure 16.42
Windows clients with DNS configured use the `\\domain.ext\RootName` UNC syntax to map local drive letters to Dfs root volumes.

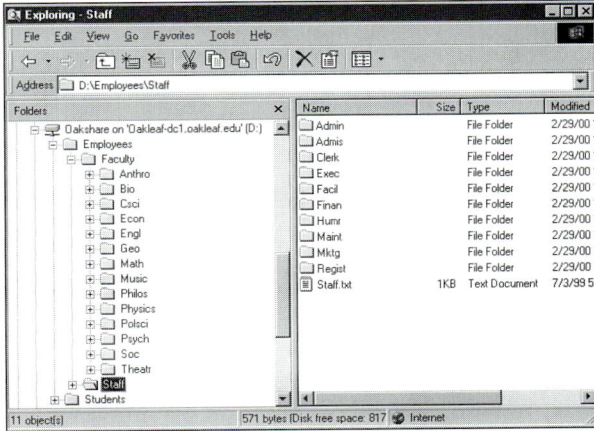

- Windows NT and 9x clients that don't have DNS configured use the downlevel \\DomainName\RootName syntax to map a local drive. In this case, the mapping appears in explorer as RootName on 'ServerName' (D:).

Tip from RJ	If your Windows NT client that uses the \\domain.ext\RootName UNC syntax displays the Students, Employees, Faculty, and Staff shared folders, but not their files and subfolders, change to the \\DomainName\RootName syntax.

 If you encounter problems mapping client drive letters to Dfs shares, see the "Dfs Configuration Problems" topic of the "Troubleshooting" section near the end of this chapter.

Using the File Replication Service with Dfs

One of the advantages of using Dfs for file shares is the ability to replicate shared folders to achieve fault tolerance. A fault-tolerant share consists of a mirror image of the shared folder on two servers. A Jet database (Ntfrs.jdb) in the \Winnt\System32\Ntfrs\Jet folder holds records to store the date and time that each replicated file was last modified and a calculated checksum value of the file's contents. If the checksum value of the mirrored files differ, a change has occurred, and FRS replaces the older file with the newer version. If you add a new file to one of the replicated shares, FRS automatically copies it to the replication partner share.

Fault-tolerant Dfs allows you to remove a file server for maintenance and replacement without affecting the availability of shares to your users. Fault tolerance is especially important for shares containing mandatory user profiles, because Windows 2000 and NT users can't log on if their computers can't connect to a profile share. The price you pay is a doubling of disk storage space for the mirrored shares.

Creating a Fault-Tolerant Share Replica Set

To establish a fault-tolerant replica set, do the following:

1. On an alternate server, create a shared folder with the same name as the original shared folder (Students on oakleaf-fs1 for this example).
2. Share the alternate folder with a share name identical to the folder name.
3. Copy all the files and subfolders of the original share to the alternate share to create an identical share structure.
4. In the Distributed Files System snap-in, right-click the entry for the original Dfs share (Students), and choose New Replica to open the Add a New Replica dialog.
5. Click Browse to open the Browse for Folder dialog, navigate to and select the alternate share you added in step 2, and click OK to add the share to the Send the User to This Shared Folder text box.
6. Mark the Automatic Replication option (see Figure 16.43), and click OK to close the Add a New Replica dialog and open the Replication Policy dialog.

Figure 16.43
You specify the replication partner share and select automatic replication in the Add New Replica dialog.

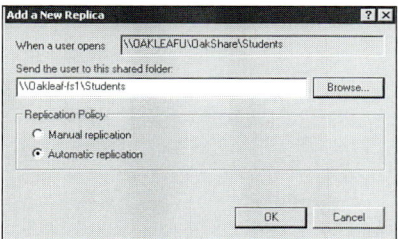

7. In the Replication Policy dialog, select each replication partner in the list and click Enable to enable replication.
8. Select the original share and click Set Master to make the original share of the primary replication partner (see Figure 16.44). Click OK to close the dialog and begin the replication process.

Figure 16.44
You must enable replication of the contents of the two shared folders and specify the primary partner in the Replication Policy dialog.

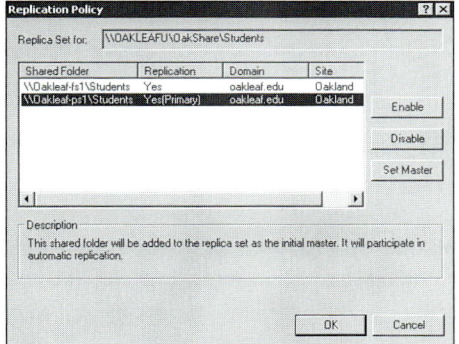

Note

Downlevel Dfs clients always attempt to connect to the primary (master) replication partner's share; if the primary partner is offline, the client connects to the alternate share. Windows 2000 clients in the same site connect at random to the primary or alternate share. If only one of the shares is on a server in the client's site, a Windows 2000 client first attempts a connection to the in-site share.

FRS moves the original shared files into a folder named NTFrs_PreExisting___ See_EventLog and adds a hidden DO_NOT_REMOVE_Ntfs_PreInstall_Directory to the share (see Figure 16.45). When users first connect to the preexisting shares on the alternate server, FRS compares their time stamp and checksum with the original version. If the files are identical, FRS moves the files and their folders to their proper location under the share. If not, FRS copies the updated version(s) from the primary partner to the share.

Figure 16.45
The NTFrs_
PreExisting___
See_EventLog folder
holds the folders and
files you copy to the
alternate share. If the
date/time and check-
sum match the origi-
nal file data, FRS
moves the folders and
files to their original
location under the
share.

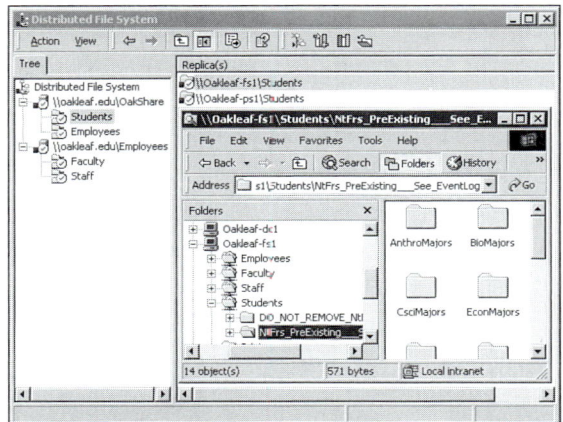

Tip from
RJ

After a week or so of production use, you can delete the remaining files in NTFrs_PreExisting... folders to conserve disk space. FRS automatically replicates any files missing from the alternate shared folder. For more information on files in NTFrs_PreExisting..., open Event Viewer's File Replication Service log on the alternate replication partner, and double-click the Warning to display the Event ID 13520 properties dialog.

You can test FRS replication by adding a file to either replication partner's shared folder and verifying that it replicates to the other share. You must delete the temporary file from both shares to prevent future replication.

Tip from
RJ

After you've tested Dfs and FRS on a production share, set the sharing, folder, and file permissions for the share. Be sure to verify with test user accounts that the appropriate security settings exist before releasing the Dfs share to users.

→ To review share and folder permission, **see** "File Sharing Security," **p. 678**.

VIEWING FRS ENTRIES IN ACTIVE DIRECTORY

You can check the information that FRS stores for replication partners under the System node of Active Directory Users and Computers. To view FRS entries in AD, do the following:

1. Launch Active Directory Users and Computers. If the System node doesn't appear in the tree-view pane, choose View, Advanced Features.

2. Expand the System, File Replication Service, Dfs Volumes, *RootName* nodes to display entries for replication partners. Figure 16.46 illustrates the two replication partners for the example of the Students share.

Figure 16.46
Active Directory stores entries for replication partners under the File Replication Service, Dfs Volumes, *RootName* node.

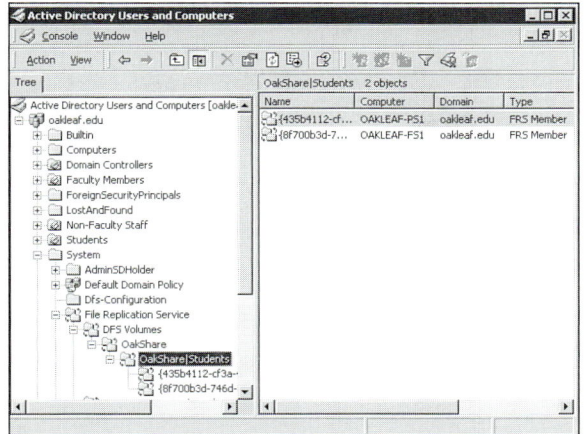

3. Click the Dfs-Configuration node to view single-line entries for all fault-tolerant Dfs root volumes in the domain.

TROUBLESHOOTING

FILE SHARING PROBLEMS

Folders have explicit or inherited Write or Modify permissions, but users in the appropriate Security Groups can't edit or delete files.

You forgot to add Change Allow permission on the share. You must permit changes at the share level to enable editing or deleting lower-level folders or files.

Users who are members of authorized groups can't read or modify shared files.

If you've set restrictive permissions at the drive root folder level or any other level in the share hierarchy above the share, you forgot to override folder or file inherited permissions with explicit Read, List Folder Contents, or Write permissions, or all three.

INDEXING SERVICE PROBLEMS

The Search for Files and Folders feature states that the Indexing Service is running, but you receive a No results *message with a query that you know should return links to files.*

Reboot the server after the initial indexing operation, and try the query again. If the query still doesn't succeed, you probably haven't added the appropriate folders to the list of folders to index.

DFS CONFIGURATION PROBLEMS

Downlevel clients can connect to conventional Dfs shares, but receive an error message when attempting to connect through mid-level junctions to other Dfs root volumes.

You used the `\\domain.ext\ShareName` UNC syntax instead of the `\\ServerName\ShareName` UNC path to the Dfs root folder on another server. This syntax works for Windows 2000 clients, but not Windows NT or 9x. Delete and re-create the Dfs link with the correct syntax.

Windows 95 clients throw errors when attempting to map the Dfs root volume or open a share from the Dfs root.

The client is missing the DFS Services for Microsoft Network Client or `Dsclient.exe` isn't installed. Install `Dsclient.exe` on the client.

Windows NT clients display empty folders when users open a drive mapped to a Dfs root volume.

Use the `\\DomainName\ShareName` syntax—for example, `\\OAKLEAFU\OakShare`—to map the shares.

MCSE Corner: Managing Server Shares and the Distributed File System

The topics covered in Chapter 16 are tested on the base Windows 2000 Server Exam, 70-215 Installing, Configuring and Administering Microsoft Windows 2000 Server. File sharing is one of the most likely reasons to implement a network, along with printer sharing, and it is an important feature to be familiar with. The Windows 2000 Distributed File System (Dfs) now is a built-in component of Windows 2000, instead of a separate add-on. Dfs is closely integrated with file sharing and permissions topics. With the explosion of the size and number of files being stored on most networks, Dfs undoubtedly will become a widely used service.

The exam covers file and folder security in detail. You can expect several questions on file permissions and file sharing. You should be familiar with sharing folders, including setting share permissions. You should also know how to set permissions on files and folders for access control. You may also be asked about hidden shares (share names ending with $) and the default hidden administrative shares created when you install Windows 2000 (c$ for C:, d$ for D:, and so on, for each partition on each drive).

It's important to know how permissions are inherited and how they affect files and folders. Permission inheritance defines how a permission affects each file and subfolder when you apply permissions to a folder. Permission inheritance can be controlled, and it is important to know how it works so that you never change permissions on an important file by accident. There can be disastrous results caused by changing permissions on an object and having those permissions inherited by its child objects.

You also should be able to determine what permissions a user has to a file by looking at the permissions granted to the user and the permissions granted to each group that the user is in. You should be able to answer a question such as "Jane is explicitly allowed read and write access to a file. She is a member of the Marketing group, which is explicitly denied write access to that file. What access does Jane have to the file?"

Also tested on the exam is the configuration of a standalone or domain-based Distributed File System (Dfs.) You should be able to perform the initial setup of a Dfs as well as the configuration of an in-place Dfs.

As noted in the other MCSE corners, troubleshooting plays a large role in the newer Microsoft Certified Professional exams, including the Windows 2000 series. You should be able to diagnose and repair problems with file sharing, permissions, and Dfs. You may be presented with situations on the exam where a user cannot access a file, and from the given details, you should be able to determine if the problem is with sharing or permissions, and what the specific problem is. You'll find that troubleshooting plays a large role both in the exam environment and when you're working with a real-life network.

Dfs also is covered in 70-221, Designing a Windows 2000 Network Infrastructure. For this exam, you should have the ability to design a Dfs structure and a strategy for the implementation of Dfs. You should be able to determine the optimum place for the Dfs root and determine a strategy for the replication of Dfs information.

CHAPTER 17

INSTALLING NETWORK PRINTERS

In this chapter

What's New in Windows 2000 Network Printing   724

Understanding the Printing Process with a Shared Printer   725

Installing the Three Types of Shared Printers   726

Configuring a Shared Printer After Installation   734

Configuring Print Server Properties   739

Connecting Clients to Shared Printers   742

Taking Advantage of Internet Printing   748

Establishing Group Policies for Printing   752

Troubleshooting   754

MCSE Corner: Installing Network Printers   756

What's New in Windows 2000 Network Printing

If you have experience installing network printers under Windows NT 4.0, you'll appreciate Windows 2000's new and improved printing features and tools for sharing printers. The basic steps for installing and sharing printers under Windows 2000 Server are the same as for those of Windows NT 4.0 Server. Windows 2000 streamlines the printer setup process and provides much more granular control over printer security and user permissions. The ability to publish shared printers in Active Directory (AD) simplifies finding and connecting to shared printers from Windows 2000 and updated downlevel clients.

Changes to Printer Setup

Here's what's new for network printing setup in Windows 2000:

- A new Add Standard TCP/IP Port Wizard simplifies installation of network-attached TCP/IP printers.
- Added Plug and Play features detect server-attached printers having Universal Serial Bus (USB) or IEEE 1394 Serial Block Protocol (SBP) interfaces. Windows 2000 recognizes and has drivers for more than 3,000 printer models.
- The enhanced Print Server and PrinterName Property dialogs make it easier for administrators to set up and manage printers.
- Remote Port Administration lets you set up and administer networked printers from any Windows 2000 machine.

Administration Improvements

Windows 2000 Server offers the following improvements to Windows NT 4.0 printer administration:

- Printer pooling allows a single print server to host multiple printers of the same type and general capabilities (preferably the same model), and share them as a single printer. Print jobs are assigned to the first available (non-busy) printer in the pool.
- Standard Port Monitor is a new client that communicates to network-attached printers running TCP/IP. The Standard Port Monitor replaces Windows NT 4.0's LPRMON, and improves performance by about 50%.
- The Print Queue object added to System Monitor (SysMon) records the total number of pages printed, errors, bytes printed per second, and other performance-related values for print servers.
- Delegation of printer management responsibility with AD makes life easier for network administrators. Print servers can be placed in their own organizational unit (OU), and administrators can assign members of the Print Operators Builtin group to manage a group of print servers without granting them Administrators privileges.

User Benefits

Windows 2000 offers the following important improvements for users of networked printers:

- Internet Printing allows Windows 2000 Professional users to specify a URL to print over the Internet or an intranet to any Windows 2000 print server. All the features that are available in Windows NT 4.0's print monitor can be accessed via a Web browser. Web Point and print provides administrators single-click Web installation of a shared printer. Users automatically install printer drivers from the Web site.
- Active Directory publishing makes all shared printers in a domain available as directory objects. Publishing a printer to AD allows users to search for the resources by location, type of printer, and other attributes.
- User Print Preferences enables Windows 2000 Professional users to modify their own print preferences. This feature of Windows 98 isn't available to Windows NT 4.0 Workstation users.
- The tabbed Print Dialog has been enhanced to support Active Directory features, such as printer searching. Windows 2000 also lets users add network printers directly from the Print Dialog.

Understanding the Printing Process with a Shared Printer

A print job takes a labyrinthine journey between the workstation sending the job and the document's ultimate arrival on paper. Understanding the route a document follows from its file to the printer's rendering engine helps you troubleshoot printing problems.

When a print job is sent from a Windows 2000 workstation, the following processes occur:

1. The workstation downloads the print driver from the print server, if the driver hasn't been downloaded in the current session or if the driver has been updated since the last time it was downloaded.
2. The file is modified by the Graphics Device Interface (GDI) in conjunction with the printer driver and converted to Enhanced Metafile Format (EMF); EMF makes the file smaller and easier to transmit over the network.

> **Note**
> The GDI is a part of the Windows 2000 operating system that generates the graphical representation of an object for the monitor or printer. The GDI provides a layer of abstraction between the printer and the program requesting the printing by generating an intermediary file in EMF, RAW, or TEXT format. Windows 2000 and NT clients can use all three versions; Windows 9x clients support only RAW and TEXT formats. The printer driver handles the device-specific elements of the encoding from EMF, RAW, or TEXT formats required for printing.

3. After being partially encoded, the print data, now in the form of an EMF file, is examined by the Print Provider. The Print Provider resides on the workstation and is responsible for creating, scheduling, starting, or stopping print jobs, as well as managing print queues, ports, printer drivers, print monitor, forms, and print processors.

> **Note**
>
> Microsoft provides four print providers with Windows 2000: the Local Print Provider to handle local printing, Windows Network Print Provider to handle jobs sent over the network, Novell Netware Print Provider to handle jobs sent to Novell Netware print servers, and the HTTP Print Provider to take care of print jobs sent across the Internet or intranet.

4. The Print Provider determines whether the print job is local or must be sent across the network. If the job is local, the Print Provider delivers it directly to the printer. If not, the job is transferred over the network to the print server, and the following steps apply.
5. The EMF file is sent to the print spooler on the print server. The spooler's functions include converting the network data to a file, selecting the appropriate physical printer from a printer pool (if there is one), and translating data from EMF to a format that can be read by the particular printer model.
6. The spooler sends the file to a component of the print server called a *router*. The router examines the file and forwards it to the proper print processor.
7. The print processor de-spools and converts the file from EMF or TEXT (ASCII) into RAW.
8. Depending on its data type, the job goes to the appropriate print monitor. The print monitor connects to the proper printer port and controls the flow of data to that port. Windows has four standard types of print monitors:
    - Local Port Monitor for jobs sent to the local ports, including printing to file.
    - Hewlett Packard (HP) Port Monitor for printers using the HP JetDirect language.
    - Macintosh Print Monitor for Apple printers on AppleTalk networks.
    - Standard TCP/IP Port Monitor for TCP/IP printers connected to the network.
9. The printer finally prints the file.

Installing the Three Types of Shared Printers

Following are the three most common types of shared printers on a Windows 2000 network:

- *Network-attached printers* contain a network card and plug directly into a network hub or switch. These can be placed in any location where you would normally place a workstation. Network printers normally have a fixed IP address that's reserved by Dynamic Host Control Protocol (DHCP). The advantage of using network-attached printers is that they can be located a long distance from the print server, which usually is placed in a locked server closet.

- *Server-connected printers* are the easiest to install, but are becoming less commonly used. These printers connect directly to the server by a printer (parallel or LPT), serial (COM), or USB cable. They're most useful in very small environments where the print server is in close proximity to the printer(s), usually within five meters or less.

- *Workstation-owned (shared) printers* are printers managed by a workstation and connected to the workstation with a printer, serial, or USB cable. Users often share a printer with other members of their workgroup. Workstation-owned printers are accessible to other users in the same or different domains, but you can't publish these printers in AD.

> **Note** To add a local printer to a print server, you must log on as a member of the Administrators group. Printer and Server Operators can add only networked printers.

Installing with Plug and Play

Windows 2000 includes a Driver.cab file, which contains device drivers for most common printers manufactured before the Windows 2000 release date. This means, for the most part, that users don't need additional media (in the form of disks or Internet downloaded drivers) to install printer drivers. The operating system searches the Driver.cab file for the appropriate driver, rather than asking the user to supply the file.

Driver installation is handled by the Plug and Play manager, which runs as a service. Because it runs as a service, Plug and Play recognizes and sets up the printer without an administrator having to log on—a real benefit for administrators. The Add Printer Wizard handles non–Plug and Play printers. The Wizard-based installation process requires information from the installer, such as printer manufacturer, printer model, and printer port. If Windows 2000 doesn't have a printer driver for the particular make and model, you must have a disk or CD-ROM with the vendor's driver.

Installing a Network-Attached Printer

Most network printers can be configured with several different protocols. Among the most common protocols are TCP/IP; DLC, the original network protocol for HP printers; IPX for Novell networks; and AppleTalk for Macintoshes. Windows NT 2000 can accommodate all these protocols, but doesn't install DLC, IPX, or AppleTalk by default. To install DLC or IPX:

1. Open the Network and Dial-up Connections window, right-click the icon for the print-server's network adapter, and choose Properties.

2. Click Install to open the Select Network Type dialog, select Protocol, and click Add to open the Select Network Protocol dialog.

3. Select DLC Protocol or NWLink IPX/SPX/NetBIOS Compatible Transport Protocol (IPX), and click OK to add the protocol. If you select IPX, configure the protocol with the Network Number by selecting the IPX item and clicking the Properties button.

→ For the details of configuring IPX under Windows 2000, **see** "Integrating NetWare Server into a Predominantly Windows Environment," **p. 529**.

4. Close the dialogs and the Network and Dial-up Connections window.

→ For more information on AppleTalk and printing to Apple printers, **see** "Adding Print Services for Macintosh," **p. 799**.

Most network-capable printers can be configured for static IP addresses or IP addresses assigned by DHCP. If you've configured DHCP to support network clients, DHCP is the better choice. To avoid printer connectivity problems that result from changes to dynamically assigned IP addresses, reserve a DHCP address within the appropriate scope for each printer. To reserve a DHCP address, you must know the Media Access Control (MAC) address of the printer's network adapter, which usually is on a label on the back of the printer.

→ For additional background on DHCP, **see** "Configuring DHCP with the DHCP Snap-In," **p. 590**.

To reserve an address within a DHCP scope for the printer's subnet, do the following:

1. Launch the DHCP manager snap-in from the Administrative Tools menu, and expand the node for the scope of the printer's subnet.

2. Right-click Reservations, and choose New Reservation to open the New Reservations dialog.

3. Type the name of the printer in the Reservation Name text box, the IP address to reserve in the IP Address text box, and the printer MAC address in the MAC Address text box.

4. Accept the Both option in the Supported Types frame, click OK to add the reservation, and close the DHCP snap-in.

5. Plug the printer's network cable into the hub or switch, and turn on the printer power.

Refer to the printer manufacturer's documentation for information on configuring a network printer with a fixed IP address.

CONFIGURING A NETWORK-ATTACHED PRINTER

To configure the network-attached printer, log on a member of the local Administrators group and follow these steps:

1. Choose Start, Settings, Printers to open the Printers window.

2. Double-click the Add Printer icon to start the Add Printer Wizard. Click Next to bypass the Welcome dialog.

3. Select Local Printer (see Figure 17.1), leave the Automatically Detect my Plug and Play Printer check box cleared, and click Next.

INSTALLING THE THREE TYPES OF SHARED PRINTERS | 729

Figure 17.1
A network-attached printer is physically remote from the print server, but the server treats it as a local printer.

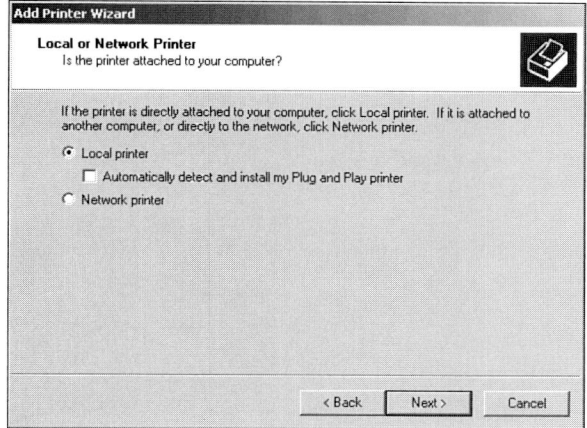

4. In the Select the Printer Port dialog, select the Create a New Port option. In the Type list, select the Standard TCP/IP Port item (see Figure 17.2). Click Next to start the Add Standard Port Wizard, and click Next to bypass its welcome dialog.

Figure 17.2
Select Create a New Port and use the drop-down list to add a Standard TCP/IP printer port.

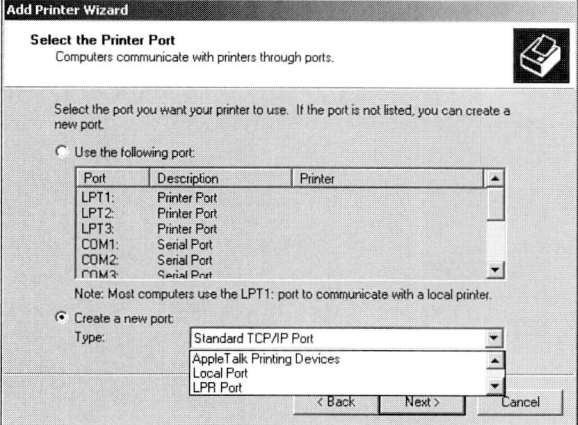

5. In the Add Port dialog, type the reserved or fixed IP address of the network printer in the Printer Name or IP Address text box (see Figure 17.3). Type the printer name in the Port Name text box, and click Next.

PART
III
CH
17

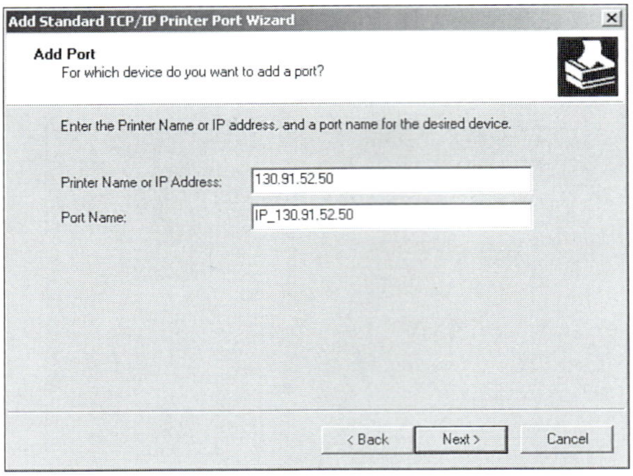

Figure 17.3
Add the IP address and a name for the new printer port.

6. In the Completing the Add Standard TCP/IP Printer Port Wizard dialog, review the printer properties you set (see Figure 17.4) and click Finish. The Add Standard TCP/IP Printer Port wizard closes, and you return to the Add Printer Wizard.

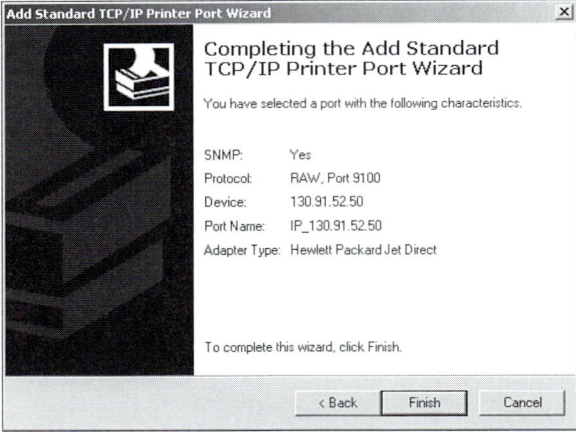

Figure 17.4
The Port Wizard's last dialog summarizes your TCP/IP printer port setup.

Note

If the Port Wizard doesn't detect a printer with the IP address you provide, an Additional Port Information dialog opens with suggested reasons for failure to find the printer, such as the power is off or it's not connected to the network.

7. In the Add Printer Wizard dialog, select the printer manufacturer and model (see Figure 17.5). If Manufacturers and Printers lists don't have entries for the printer, click Have Disk, insert the printer driver disk or CD-ROM, and follow the instructions in the dialogs to load the proper driver.

Figure 17.5
Select the printer manufacturer and model in the Wizard's lists.

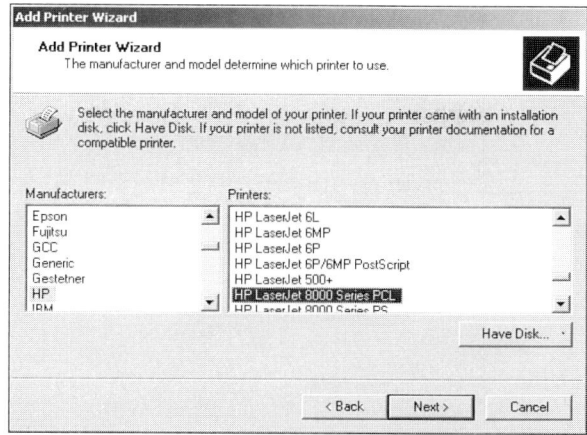

8. After installing the driver, the Wizard requests a name for the printer that appears in the Printers window. Add a descriptive name with optional location information, such as a building and room number. The option to make this the default printer applies to the print server, not clients. Click Next.
9. In the Printer Sharing dialog, select the Share As option and type a name for the printer share (see Figure 17.6).

Figure 17.6
When you share the printer, give the printer share a name that users can recognize.

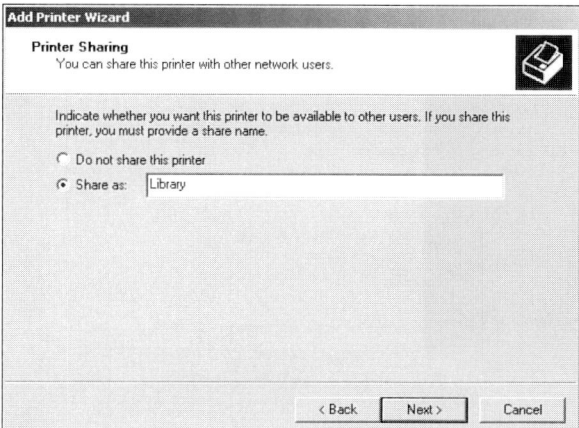

10. In the Location and Comment dialog, complete the two text boxes (see Figure 17.7). Click Next.

Figure 17.7
Provide brief descriptions of the printer's location and capabilities in the Location and Comment text boxes.

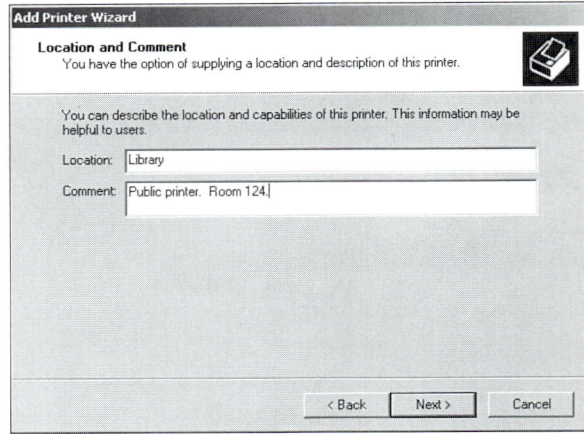

11. The next Wizard dialog offers the option to print a test page, which is highly recommended. Click Next.
12. The Completing the Add Printer Wizard dialog summarizes the installation process (see Figure 17.8). Verify that the settings information is correct, and click Finish to dismiss the Wizard.

Figure 17.8
Review the network-attached printer properties in the last Wizard dialog.

Configuring a Server-Connected or Workstation-Owned Printer

Installing printers physically connected to computers running Windows 2000 Professional and Server are quite similar. In both cases, log on as a member of the Administrators group. The primary user-related difference between printers shared by the two Windows 2000 versions is that a workstation-owned and shared printer isn't automatically added to AD.

Installing the Three Types of Shared Printers 733

Following are the differences between installing a server-connected and workstation-owned printer and the process for installing a network-attached printer:

- Plug and Play is likely to detect and automatically install server-connected printers without intervention by you.
- You connect these printers using an existing port, most commonly LPT1, rather than creating a new port.

After you've connected the printer to the USB, parallel or serial connector and turned on the power, follow these steps:

1. Choose Start, Settings, Printers to open the Printers window. Windows automatically installs most Plug and Play printers and adds a printer icon with the manufacturer name and model to the Printers window.
2. If the new printer installs automatically, proceed to the next section to configure the new printer. Otherwise, proceed to the next step.
3. Double-click the Add Printer icon to start the Add Printer Wizard. Click Next to bypass the Welcome dialog.
4. Select the Local Printer printer option, and mark the Automatically Detect And Install My Plug And Play Printer checkbox (see Figure 17.9). Click Next. If Windows 2000 successfully detects and installs the printer, go to the next section to configure it.

Figure 17.9
Server-attached printers are local and can be detected by Plug and Play.

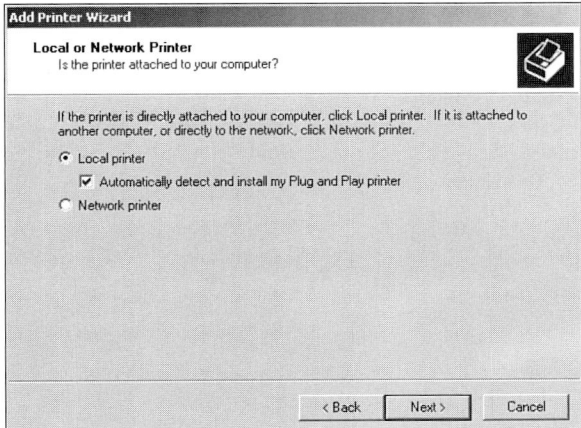

5. If the printer doesn't install automatically at this point, the New Printer Detection dialog opens, as shown in Figure 17.10. Click Next.

Figure 17.10
If Windows can't locate a driver for the printer in the Driver.cab file, you must install it manually.

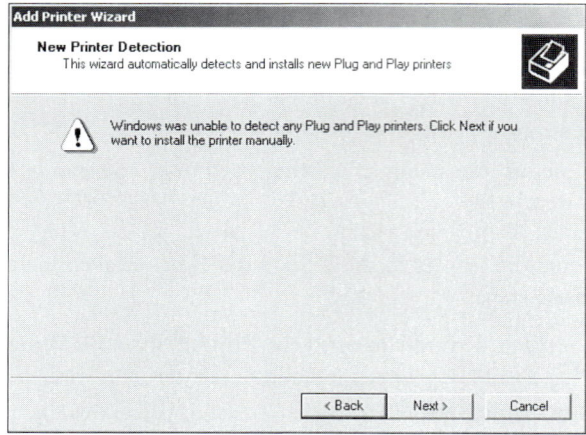

6. Select the Use The Following Port option, and select a port from the list (see Figure 17.11). Click Next.

Figure 17.11
Installing a printer manually requires you to select the port to which the printer is connected.

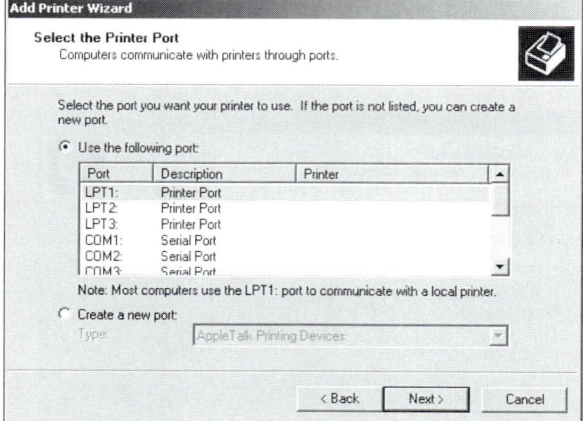

From this point, printer installation is identical to the installation of a network-attached printer. Follow steps 7 through 12 in the preceding section, "Configuring a Network-Attached Printer," to complete the installation of the server-attached printer.

CONFIGURING A SHARED PRINTER AFTER INSTALLATION

Automatic or manual printer installation applies a default set of basic properties to the printer. The default printer properties usually are satisfactory for basic laser and ink-jet printers, but you might need to change the properties for high-production or color printers, or plotters. The multipage *PrinterName* Properties dialog lets you specify property values common to all types of printers and those that are specific to a particular category of printer, its manufacturer, and its model. You also can make changes to the property values you set in the Add Printer Wizard dialogs during printer installation.

Tip from
RJ

The most important page of the PrinterName Properties dialog is Sharing, where you add printer drivers for operating systems other than Windows 2000 and Windows NT 4.0. If you didn't share the printer in the Printer Sharing dialog of the Add Printer Wizard, do so on this page.

Follow these steps to review and alter the properties of an individual printer. A server-attached laser printer is used for this example.

1. Right-click the printer icon in the Printers window, and choose Properties to open the General page of the *PrinterName* Properties dialog (see Figure 17.12).

Figure 17.12
The General page of the *PrinterName* Properties dialog lets you alter the settings made during installation, specify detailed default printing preferences, and print a test page.

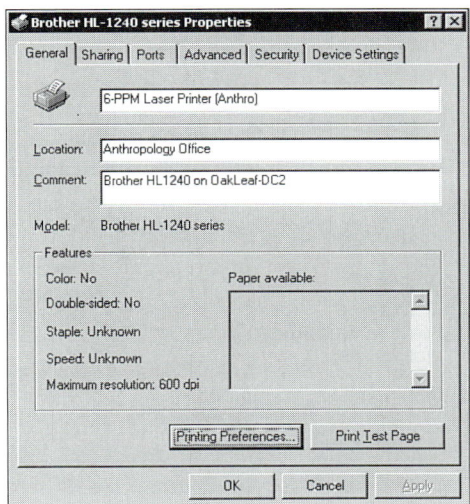

2. Change the description, name, and location of the printer, if you want, in the three text boxes. Clicking Printing Preferences opens a tabbed dialog for setting common default printer properties, such as page orientation. Clicking Advanced opens another dialog with printer-specific properties that you set by clicking an underlined value (see Figure 17.13).

Figure 17.13
The contents of the Printing Preferences and Advanced Options dialogs depend on the printer's type, manufacturer, and model.

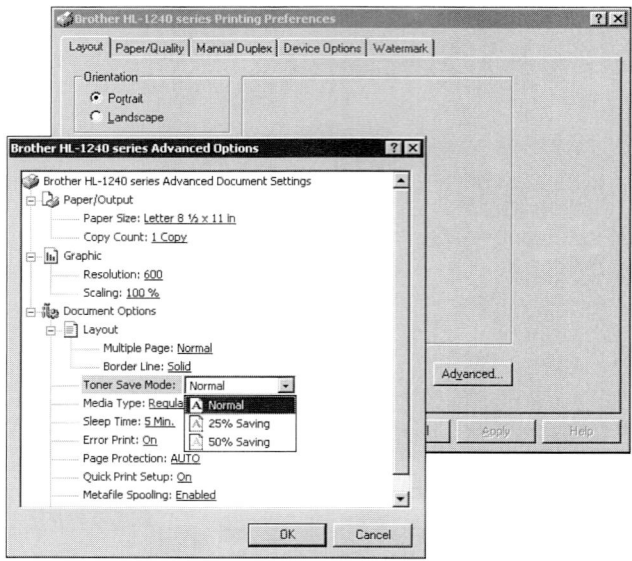

3. Click the Sharing tab to enable sharing or change the share name. The List in the (Active) Directory check box is marked by default. If you need to support operating systems other than Windows 2000 and NT 4.0, click Additional Drivers to open the dialog of the same name. Mark the check boxes in the list for the additional drivers you need to service various clients (see Figure 17.14). Be prepared to obtain the drivers from the Windows 2000 Server installation share or distribution CD-ROM, or a disk or CD-ROM provided by the printer manufacturer.

Figure 17.14
Click the Additional Drivers button to open the dialog that lets you add printer drivers for operating systems other than Windows 2000 and NT 4.0. The Additional Drivers dialog obscures the button in this figure.

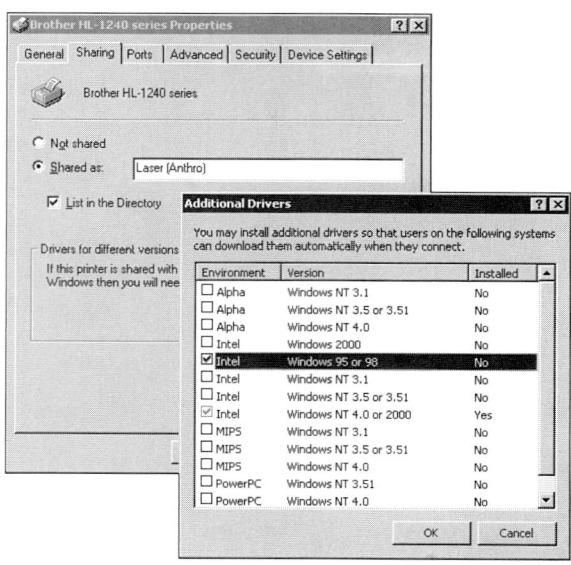

CONFIGURING A SHARED PRINTER AFTER INSTALLATION | 737

Tip from

Alternatively, you can add printer drivers for other operating systems in the Server Properties dialog, which is the subject of the next section.

4. Click the Ports tab to add and configure additional types of ports, such as Standard TCP/IP port(s) for additional network-attached printers. The printer you've set up has the Port check box marked. To enable multiple printers managed by the server to be pooled, mark the Enable Printer Pooling check box. Enabling printer pooling lets you mark an additional Port check box for each pooled printer (see Figure 17.15). Pooled printers appear to users as a single shared printer.

Note

By default, the Ports list has entries for legacy LPT1 through LPT3, COM1 through COM4, and FILE. A legacy port is any port type other than USB and IEEE-1394. The default ports are software, not hardware, ports. Conventional PCs come with a single LPT1 and COM1 and COM2 ports installed. Ports you add with the Add Printer Wizard also appear in the list.

PART
III
CH
17

Figure 17.15
The Ports page lets you add more ports, such as those for network-attached TCP/IP printers. You can add and enable multiple ports for printer pooling if you mark the Enable Printer Pooling check box. This figure illustrates pooling three identical parallel-port printers.

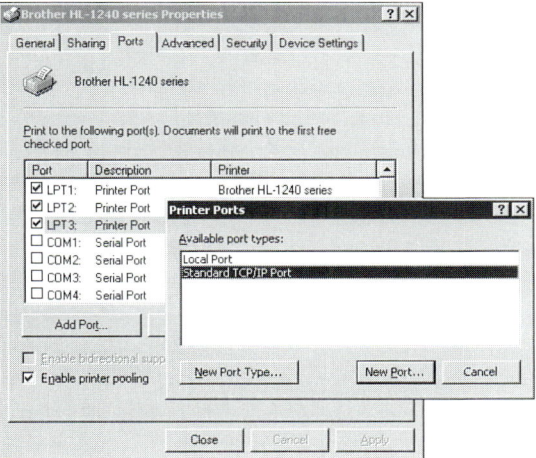

Tip from

Make sure the additional printers are connected and powered on before adding and configuring additional ports. Your life as a printer administrator will be much easier if you pool identical make and model printers that appear to users as a single shared printer.

5. Click the Advanced tab to alter printer availability hours, default print job priority, spooler settings, and other printer options (see Figure 17.16). Clicking Print Processor opens a dialog that lets you change the default processor from RAW to NT EMF 1.003, and other processors. You also can add separator pages here.

738 Chapter 17 Installing Network Printers

Figure 17.16
Alter spooling properties, if necessary, on the Advanced page. The default values shown are satisfactory for most printers and common types of print jobs.

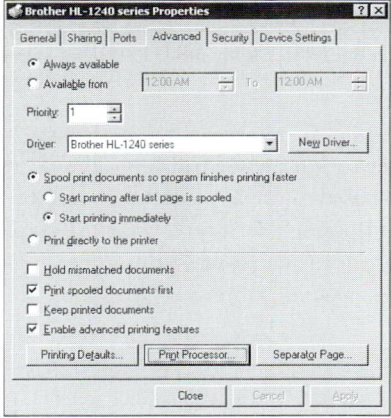

Tip from
RJ

Don't change the default print processor unless you understand the ramifications of doing so. For instance, if you specify NT EMF 1.003, Windows 9x clients can't print to the printer.

6. Click the Security page to control which group members can print and manage the printer. By default, Administrators, Print Operators, and Server Operators have Allow Print, Manage Printers, and Manage Documents permissions. The CREATOR OWNER group, which contains the account of the person who added the printer, has only Allow Manage Documents permission. All other groups, including Everyone, have default Allow Print permission.

7. If you want to restrict printing to members of a particular Security Group, click Add to open the Select Users, Computers or Groups dialog, double-click the group to add to the list, and click OK to close the dialog. The added Security Group is given Print permission by default (see Figure 17.17). Select the Everyone group, and clear the Print check box in the Allow column to prevent Everyone (else) from using the printer.

Figure 17.17
Use the Security page to add one or more group(s) whose members can use the printer, and then remove Allow Print permissions from the Everyone group.

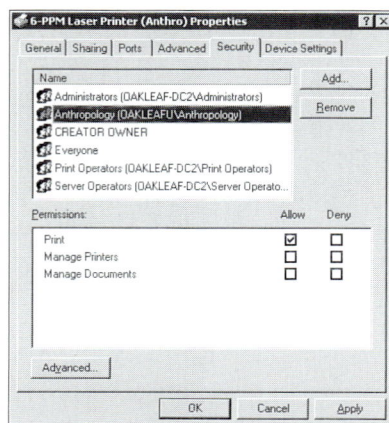

Configuring Print Server Properties 739

> **Tip from**
> *RJ*
>
> If you want to make absolutely sure members of the Everyone group can't print to the printer, check the Deny Print check box. Deny overrides an Allow permission that's inherited from another group.

8. Click the Device Settings page to display a list of device-specific options. The format of the list is similar to that shown previously (refer to Figure 17.13).

> **Note**
>
>
>
> You can assign printers to handle specific paper sizes or preprinted forms in one or more paper trays. Using Windows 2000 forms is one of the subjects of the next section.

9. After making the appropriate changes to property values, click OK to close the dialog and save your change. You can save changes incrementally by clicking the Apply button on each page.

> **Tip from**
> *RJ*
>
> If you alter printer security to restrict use by group membership, log on to a domain workstation as a member of the group(s) with the Allow Print privilege and print a test page. Then log on as a member of a group without this privilege, and verify that you can't print with the secured printer.

 If you have problems setting up and sharing a printer, see the "Printing Problems" topic of the "Troubleshooting" section near the end of the chapter.

Configuring Print Server Properties

In addition to configuring individual printers, you can configure print server properties, which apply to all printers managed by the server, in the Server Properties dialog. To view and adjust printer server properties:

1. In the Printers window, choose File, Server Properties to open the Forms page of the Server Properties dialog. Scroll the Forms in the *ServerName* list to view the large number of international and *de facto* standard paper and envelope sizes.

> **Note**
>
> Forms are a new printer feature of Windows 2000 that let you specify paper sizes and printer margins that apply to all printers managed by the server or only specific printers designed to handle a particular form in one or more paper trays. North American 8 1/2- by 11-inch paper is called Letter in the list; 8 1/2- by 14-inch paper is called Legal. The list also offers forms for common envelope sizes. Virtually every common paper and envelope size in the world appears in the list, including engineering drawing sizes for plotters.

Part III
Ch
17

2. To generate and name a new form, mark the Create a New Form check box, which enables the Paper Size and Printer Area Margins text boxes, and type a name in the Form Description For text box, which enables the Save Form button. Type the dimensions for the form (see Figure 17.18), and click Save Form to add the new form to the list.

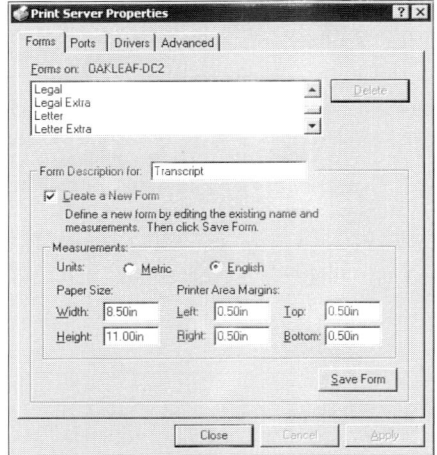

Figure 17.18
You can add new forms by marking the Create a New Form check box, typing a name for the new form, changing dimensions, and clicking Save Form.

3. To assign a form to a paper tray of a printer, open the *PrinterName* Properties dialog, and click the Advanced tab. Under the Form To Tray Assignment node, open the tray that holds the paper for the form—usually Paper Cassette or a similar term (see Figure 17.19). If the list displays the form names you saw in step 1, your printer driver is compatible with Windows 2000 forms. If not, determine whether the vendor has a printer driver that's been updated for Windows 2000. Click OK to close the dialog and return to the Server Properties dialog.

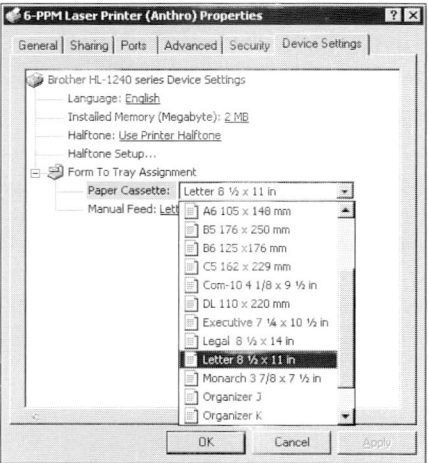

Figure 17.19
If your printer's drivers have been updated to Windows 2000 standards, you see those forms having sizes within the printer's capability in the list. The Brother HL-1240 used for many of the examples in this chapter has early 1999 Windows 2000 drivers and doesn't display the Windows 2000 forms list.

Configuring Print Server Properties   741

4. Click the Ports page to view and reconfigure printer ports of the print server. Like the Ports page of the *PrinterName* dialog (refer to Figure 17.15), the Server Properties dialog displays a list of the ports configured on the server and lets you add, delete, and configure the selected port.

5. Click the Drivers tab to display the list of drivers for the printer(s) installed on the server. Clicking Add starts the Add Printer Driver Wizard, which lets you add printer drivers to the server independently of the Add Printer Wizard. You also can delete and update drivers from this page.

6. Double-click a driver item in the list to open the Driver Properties dialog, which lists files required for the print driver (see Figure 17.20). Double-click a file item in the list to display the *FileName* Properties dialog, which lets you inspect the date, version, and security properties of the file.

Figure 17.20
The Driver Properties dialog lists the files that comprise the selected printer driver. Double-clicking a file item lets you check the date, version, and other properties of the driver file.

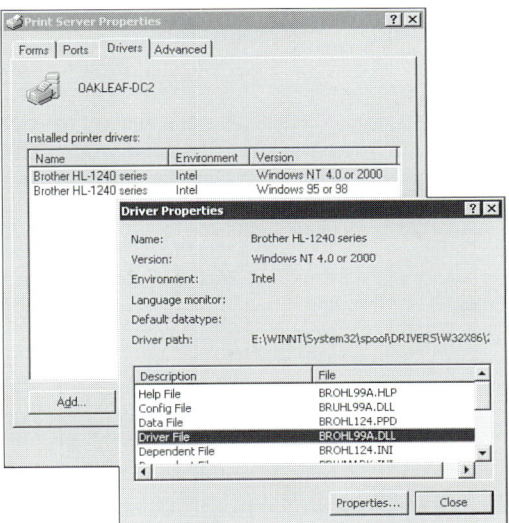

Part III
Ch 17

Tip from
RJ

If you encounter a printer driver problem and request technical service from the vendor, you're likely to be requested to provide the driver files' dates and versions. The Drivers page of the Server Properties dialog is the only convenient source of this information.

7. Click the Advanced tab to change the location of the print spool folder and change event logging and notification properties. The default values shown in Figure 17.21 are satisfactory for low- to medium-duty print servers.

Figure 17.21
The Advanced page of the Print Server Properties dialog lets you change the location of the printer spooling files and specify event logging and notification options.

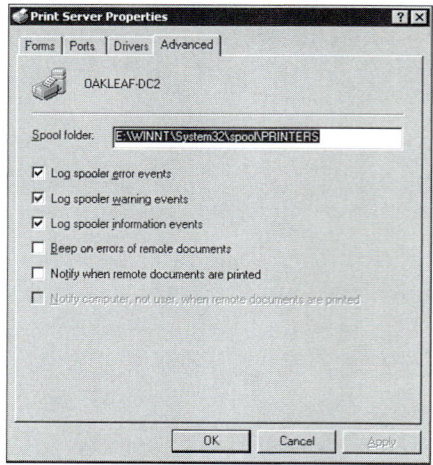

Tip from	
RJ	If your print server manages a large number of printers or has plotters for computer-aided design (CAD) programs, you can improve printing performance by moving the spool folder to a physical drive other than that which holds the system volume. Consider using a pair of RAID 0 (striped) drives to improve input/output performance.

→ For the details of implementing RAID 0 in software, **see** "Working with RAID Implementations," **p. 430**.

Connecting Clients to Shared Printers

When you have printers shared on the network, connecting clients to the printers is a simple process, especially if the printer is published in AD and all clients run Windows 2000 Professional. You can take advantage of AD printer publishing with Windows 9x and NT clients, if you install the Directory Service Client on these computers.

 If you have problems connecting clients to shared printers, see the "Network Problems" topic of the "Troubleshooting" section near the end of the chapter.

Installing the Directory Service Client on Downlevel Computers

The Directory Service Client (DS Client) for Windows 9x, Dsclient.exe, is located in the \Clients\Win9x folder of the Windows 2000 Server distribution CD-ROM or the network installation share. Installing the AD client also installs the Distributed File System Redirector services provided by Windows 2000 Server.

> **Note**
>
> Microsoft has committed to providing the DS Client for Windows NT 4.0 in Service Pack (SP) 7, which wasn't released when this book was written. You can expect the process for installing this client software to be identical or very similar to that for Windows 9x.

To install the Directory Services Client for Windows 9x:

1. Navigate to \Clients\Win9x on the Windows 2000 Server distribution CD-ROM of the installation share.
2. Double-click Dsclient.exe to start the Directory Service Client Setup Wizard. Click Next to bypass the Welcome dialog.
3. In the Ready to Install dialog, click Next to copy the required files to the client.
4. In the Installation Completed dialog, click Finish to dismiss the Wizard.
5. Click Yes to acknowledge the message that asks you to reboot the client.

The examples in the following section assume that you've installed the DS Client on clients running downlevel operating systems.

Publishing Printers Shared by Downlevel Servers or Workstations

You can publish in AD printers shared by Windows NT servers or workstations and Windows 9x clients. For Windows NT, your Windows 2000 account must have Administrators credentials on the Windows NT machine, which requires nontransitive trusts between the Windows NT domain and your Windows 2000 domain.

→ For instructions on creating trusts between Windows NT and 2000 domains, and adding your Windows 2000 administrative account to the Windows NT domain, **see** steps 3 and 4 of "Installing ADMT on a Windows 2000 Domain Controller," **p. 233**.

Follow these steps to publish the printer in AD:

1. On a Windows 2000 DC or a workstation with the Administrative Tools installed, log on with Domain Admins credentials and launch Active Directory Users and Computers.
2. Right-click the *DomainName* or an OU node, and choose New, Organizational Unit to open the New Object - Organizational Unit dialog.
3. Type the name of the OU, **NT Printers** for this example, in the Name text box, and click OK to add the OU.
4. Right-click the new printers OU, and choose Add, Printer to open the New Object - Printer dialog.
5. Type the full UNC path to the printer, **\\OAKLEAF0\BrotherLaser** for this example, in the Network Path of the Pre-Windows 2000 Print Share text box. Click OK to add the entry to the OU.

Note

Downlevel Printer objects in AD are identified by the server name, a hyphen, and the share name for the printer. The name of the sample printer added in step 5 is OAKLEAF0-BrotherLaser.

You can't add a printer shared by Windows 2000 to an OU. You receive an error message if you try.

6. Double-click the added Printer object to open the General page of the *PrinterShareName* Properties dialog, which shows values only for the Model and Maximum Resolution attributes.

7. Type Location and Description values, mark the appropriate feature check boxes (Color, Staple, and Double-Sided), and add the Printing Speed value (see Figure 17.22). Click OK to close the dialog.

Figure 17.22
Add values for the Location, Description, features, and Printing Speed in the properties dialog for the newly added shared printer.

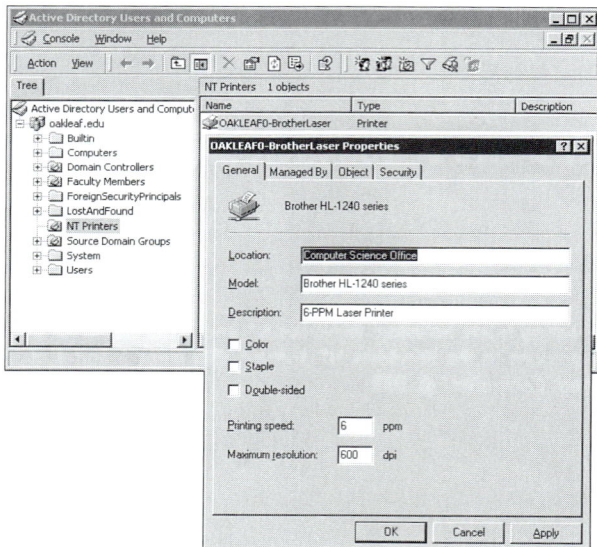

8. Click the Managed By tab if you want to identify the person responsible for managing the printer, and click Security to verify or change permissions for the printer by Windows 2000 Security Groups.

Note

Permissions for downlevel printer shares are similar to those for Windows 2000 shared printers, but Authenticated Users (rather than Everyone) have print access.

Printers shared by downlevel computers appear together with those shared by Windows 2000 machines in the Find Printers list described in the following section. When you install a printer shared by Windows NT 4.0, Windows NT and 9x clients automatically download the appropriate drivers for the printer.

Finding and Installing Shared Printers Published in Active Directory

With the Windows 2000 Search or Windows 9x Find feature, users can search for published shared printers based on any following criterion or combinations of criteria:

- Name (text box)
- Location (text box)
- Model (text box)
- Duplexing capability (Can Print Double-Sided check box)
- Color (Can Print Color check box)
- Stapling capability (Can Staple check box)
- Resolution (Resolution At Least list)
- Paper size (Has Paper Size list)
- Output speed (Speed At Least spin-button box)

Entries users make in text boxes can include DOS * and ? wildcards, and aren't case-sensitive. For example, you can search for any printer with "Office" in the location by typing ***Office*** in the Location text box.

You also can use the AD filter feature to search by a large number of additional printer attribute values, such as Server Name or Share Name.

→ For instruction on how to use AD's filter feature, **see** "Applying LDAP Filters," **p. 138**.

To find and install on a client a shared printer that's published in AD, do the following:

1. Choose Start, Search (for Windows 2000 or Start, Find for Windows 9x or NT), For Printers to open the Find Printers dialog with Entire Directory selected in the In list and the Printers tab active.
2. To obtain a list of all published printers in all AD domains, click Find Now. If your network has only a few shared printers, users don't need to search for one.
3. If you want to restrict the search to a particular domain, open the In list and select the domain name. The domain extension (such as .com or .edu) doesn't appear in the list. Click Find Now.
4. To limit the list to printers with names, locations, or models that meet your criteria, type a search string in one of the three text boxes. Figure 17.23 illustrates a search for all printers whose location includes the word "office."

Figure 17.23
Type a criterion fragment and use the DOS * wildcard to search for printers by location. The Brother HL-1240 Series entry is the printer shared by a Windows NT 4.0 server in the OAKLEAF domain.

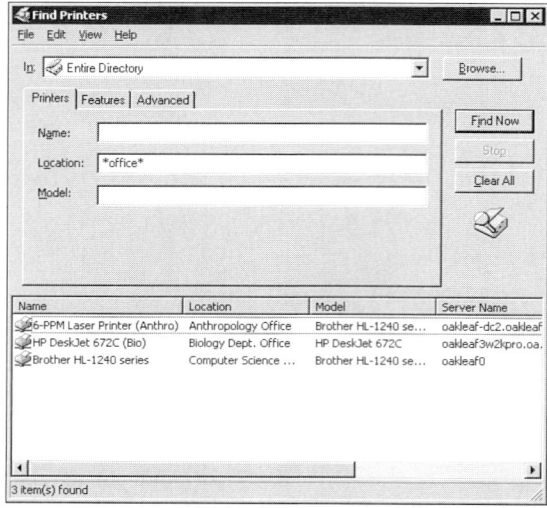

5. To further refine the search by printer attributes—such as color capability, resolution, and the like—click the Feature tab. Specify the features required by the user in the check boxes and lists and click Find Now. Figure 17.24 illustrates a search for color printers having at least 300 dots per inch (dpi) resolution and a speed of 4 pages per minute (ppm) or more.

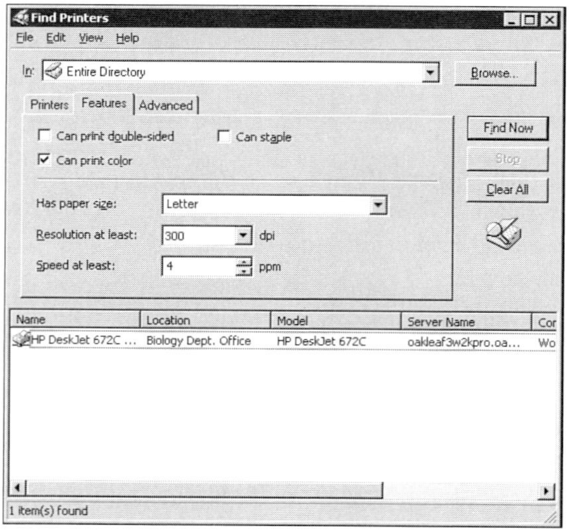

Figure 17.24
Select the printer characteristics needed by the user in the Features page. The Features criteria are added to those specified in the Printers page.

Tip from
RJ

Don't encourage users to find printers by specifying LDAP attribute values in the Advanced page of the Find Printers dialog. LDAP filters use an arcane method to specify filter criteria, and few of the available attributes are populated with values. A further limitation of LDAP filters is that the current version doesn't support *criterion* syntax. You're limited to Begins With (*criterion*) or Ends With (criterion*) conditions.

6. To install a printer from the list, and add it to the Printers window, double-click its list entry. The client downloads the required printer drivers and adds an icon for the printer to the Printers window.

Note

Under Windows 2000, the printer installs automatically and silently. If the client runs Windows 9x, the Add Printer Wizard appears with a dialog that asks whether you print from MS-DOS–based programs. Select Yes or No, and click Next. Accept or change the default printer name, which is the Model not the Name in the printers list, and click Next. In the final Wizard dialog, select Yes or No for a test page, and click Finish to complete the installation by installing the server-stored Windows 9x driver files on the client. If you specified a test page, click Yes to acknowledge the test page message.

INSTALLING UNPUBLISHED PRINTERS

If you don't publish shared printers in AD or the client doesn't have the DS Client extensions installed, the user must run the Add Printer Wizard to add the shared printer to the Printers window. The user also must know the server name and printer name to specify the UNC path (*ServerName**PrinterName*). The following example is for a Windows NT 4.0 client (because of initial lack of the DS Client), but the process for Windows 9x is similar.

To install an unpublished printer, do this:

1. Choose Start, Settings, Printer to open the Printers window.
2. Double-click the Add Printer icon to start the Add Printer Wizard.
3. Select the Network Printer Server option, and click Next to open the second dialog.
4. Expand the node for the domain and server in the Shared Printers list to display the shared printer to add. Click the item to add the shared printer's path to the Printer text box (see Figure 17.25). Alternatively, type the UNC path to the printer in the text box. Click Next to open the third dialog.

Figure 17.25
Navigate to and select the shared printer to add or type the UNC path to the printer in the text box to connect the shared printer to the client.

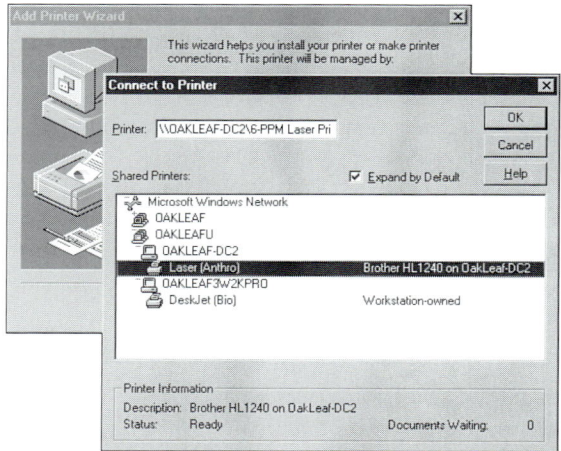

Tip from
RJ

If you've just booted the client onto the network, you won't see the list of domains and servers to which the client has access. The browser takes a few minutes to collect printer information from the network.

5. Select Yes if you want to make the printer the default printer for the client, and click Next to install the printer and its drivers, and add an icon for the printer to the Printers window.

6. Click Finish in the final dialog that confirms the printer is installed.

 If you have problems connecting downlevel clients to Windows 2000 shared printers, see the "Driver Problems with Downlevel Clients" topic of the "Troubleshooting" section near the end of the chapter.

Taking Advantage of Internet Printing

 Windows 2000 allows documents to be printed across the Internet by typing a printer's URL in a browser Address text box. This means not only that users can print across an intranet by using a URL, but users on completely different networks or on the road can send jobs to remote printers. The user must know the URL and have been granted permissions to the printer through group membership. For Internet Printing to work, Internet Information Server (IIS) 5.0 must be installed on the print server or, if the printer is connected to a Windows 2000 Professional workstation, Microsoft Peer Web Services (PWS) must be installed. Windows 2000 Server installs IIS 5.0 by default, and PWS is an installation option for Windows 2000 Professional.

→ For a brief introduction to IIS 5.0, **see** "Internet Information Server 5.0," **p. 44**.
→ For detailed information about installing IIS 5.0, **see** "Upgrading to or Installing IIS 5.0," **p. 1106**.

Following are the primary benefits of Internet printing:

- Printing to a URL—Users can print across the Internet or an intranet to a shared printer, if they know the URL for the printer and are using Internet Explorer 4.0+.
- Web Browser Integration—You can use any Web browser to view printers or manage print jobs. Administrators can manage print queues, and users can check the status of the printer, as well as view, pause, resume, or delete their own jobs.
- Multiple Security Methods—Security in Internet printing is handled by IIS or PWS. Supported authentication methods include Secure Sockets Layer (SSL) 3, Kerberos, Digest, and Microsoft challenge/response. Kerberos is the default authentication protocol for Windows 2000 clients.

→ To learn more about the Kerberos protocol, **see** "Kerberos Authentication," **p. 38**.

- Internet Point-and-Print—Using a Web browser, users can add any printer served by a Windows 2000 Server with a single click.

How Internet Printing Works

When a Windows 2000 client sends a document to a printer URL, the content follows this route:

1. The client sends the content to the local print spooler.
2. The HTTP Print Provider (part of the local print spooler) prepares the content for transmission across the Internet or intranet in Internet Printing Protocol (IPP) format.
3. The client sends the IPP data to IIS 5.0 running on the print server (or PWS if the printer is connected on a Windows 2000 workstation), where it is converted to RAW data and sent to the HTTP Print Server.
4. The print server sends the data to the server's print spooler for printing.

Installing Internet Printing

Before you can install Internet printing to a network, IIS must be running on the print server to service the IPP connection, and users must have permission to use the printer.

With these conditions met, follow these steps to install Internet printing on the client:

1. Open the Printers window, double-click the Add Printer icon to start the add Printer Wizard, and click Next.
2. In the Local or Network Printer dialog, select the Network Printer option, and click Next.
3. In the Locate Your Printer dialog, select the Connect to a Printer on the Internet or Your Intranet option, and type the URL for the printer in **http://servername/printers/printersharename/.printer** format for your intranet or **http://www.domainname.ext/printers/printersharename/.printer**. (You can substitute an IP address for **www.domainname.ext** if you don't have a public domain name). The period

preceding **printer** is required. This example connects to **http://oakleaf-dc2/ printers/laser (anthro)/.printer** (see Figure 17.26). Click Next, and wait while the Wizard makes the connection to the printer share.

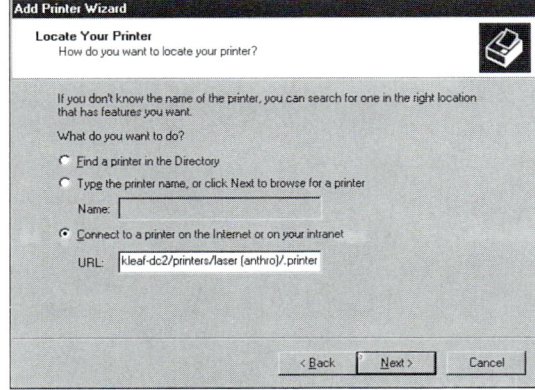

Figure 17.26
Select the Internet/intranet option and type the URL for the printer in Internet Printing format to connect to the shared printer by IPP.

4. In the Default Printer dialog, select Yes if you want to make the IPP-connected printer the default printer. Click Next and Finish to add the printer icon to the Printers window.

The caption for the new icon is the printer name followed by "on http://*servername*" for an intranet and "on http://www.*domainname.ext*" or "on http://*xxx.xxx.xxx.xxx*" for an Internet connection. You might need to reconfigure your Web server authentication methods to allow clients to connect via the public Internet.

→ For instructions on setting Web server authentication methods, **see** "Setting Master IIS Properties," **p. 1110**.

Managing a Printer over the Internet or an Intranet

A useful function of Internet printing is the ability of administrators or print operators to manage printers remotely with a Web browser. Users must have permission to manage the printer to take advantage of this feature.

Tip from
RJ

Shared printers must be published in AD to permit Internet-based management. The Active Server Pages (ASP) that handle printer management use the Active Directory Services Interfaces (ADSI) to connect to the printer.

→ To review the capabilities of ADSI, **see** "Programming Directory-Enabled Applications with ADSI," **p. 139**.

TAKING ADVANTAGE OF INTERNET PRINTING | 751

To manage a printer over the Internet or an intranet with IE 4.0+, follow these steps:

1. Launch IE and type **http://www.*domainname.ext*/printers/** as the management URL. You can substitute the IP address of your Web server for **www.*domainname.ext***, if you don't have an assigned domain name. If you're managing the printer on an intranet, type **[http://]*servername*/printers/**.

2. If you use your intranet to manage the printer, the All Printers on *servername* page opens. If you connect via the Internet, the Enter Network Password dialog opens. Type your administrative logon ID, password, and domain name, and click OK to display the All Printers on *domainname* or *IPAddress* page (see Figure 17.27).

Tip from
RJ

Don't mark the Save This Password in Your Password List check box. If you type the wrong password, you won't be able to easily correct the error in the saved password.

PART
III
CH
17

Figure 17.27
The All Printers on *IPAddress* Active Server page for an Internet connection lets you select the shared printer to manage. The two shares shown here point to the same laser printer.

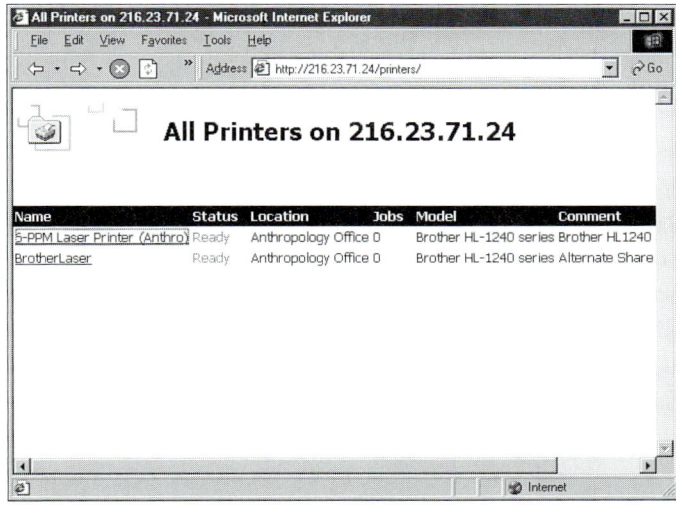

If you receive an error message when attempting to manage printing via the Internet, see the "Internet-Based Printer Management Problems" topic of the "Troubleshooting" section near the end of this chapter.

3. Click the name of the printer to manage to open the Document List page. This page displays the printer queue status and lists all pending print jobs in the server's print spooler queue. You can pause or resume printing, or cancel printing of all pending documents. Alternatively, select a pending document, and pause, resume, or cancel printing it.

4. Click the Properties link to open a page that shows the AD attribute values for the shared printer (see Figure 17.28).

Figure 17.28
The Properties page for a shared printer displays queue status and the AD attribute values for the printer.

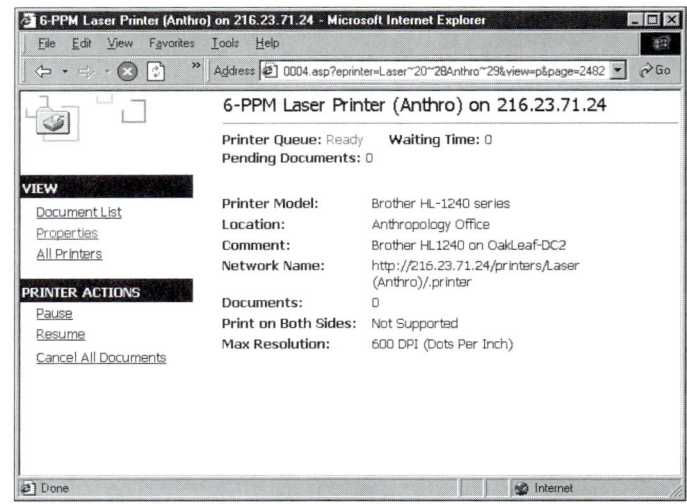

ESTABLISHING GROUP POLICIES FOR PRINTING

You can use Windows 2000 Group Policies to control many of Windows 2000's new printer features, providing that the shared printers are published in AD. You normally configure Group Policy for shared printers at the domain level to cause the policies to apply to all print servers in the domain. By default, Group Policies relevant to printers aren't configured when you install AD on your DC(s).

→ For an overview of Group Policies, **see** "Understanding Windows 2000's Group Policies," **p. 618**.

> **Note**
>
> Group Policies apply only to printers shared by computers running Windows 2000 Server and Professional. A few of the policies, such as Web-based Printing, apply to downlevel shared printers published in AD.

To view and optionally specify Group Policies for shared printers at the domain level:

1. Launch Active Directory Users and Computers from the Administrative Tools menu.
2. Right-click the *DomainName* node, choose properties to open the *DomainName* Properties dialog, and click the Group Policy tab.
3. With the Default Domain Policy item selected in the Group Policy Object (GPO) Links list, click Edit to open the Group Policy Editor with the selected GPO active.
4. Expand the Computer Configuration, Administrative Templates nodes, and click the Printers node to display the list of 13 policies applicable to domain-shared printers in the Policy list (see Figure 17.29).

Establishing Group Policies for Printing   753

Figure 17.29
No Group Policies for shared network printers are configured by default. Not configuring a Group Policy causes the underlying objects (shared printers in this case) to exhibit default behavior.

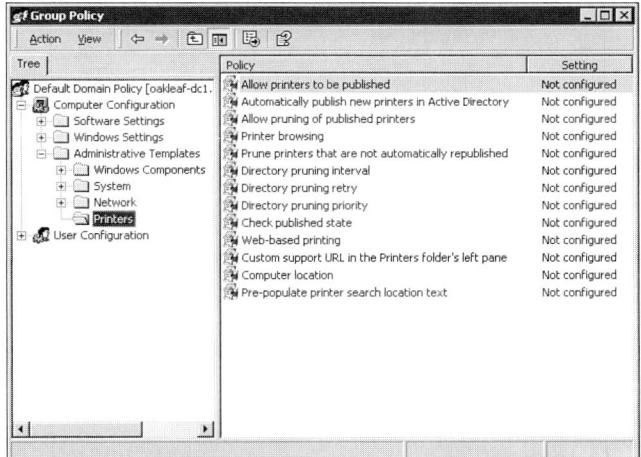

5. The names of printer policies are reasonably self-explanatory, but you can obtain a lengthy explanation of the effects of configuring a policy (either Enabled or Disabled), by double-clicking a policy entry to open its *PolicyName* Properties dialog and clicking the Explain tab (see Figure 17.30).

Figure 17.30
The Explain page delivers a verbose description of the consequences of enabling, disabling, and not configuring a policy.

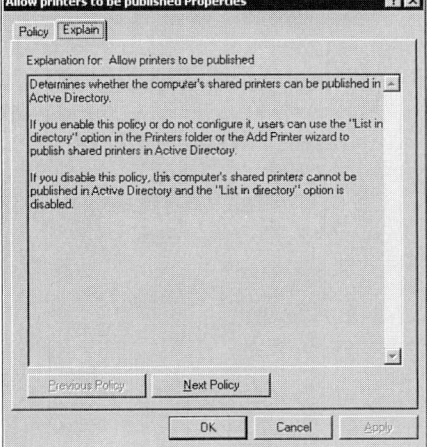

6. The most important two policies to enable are Allow Printers To Be Published and Automatically Publish New Printers in Active Directory. Setting these two policies assures that shared printers get published. To enable or disable a policy, click the Policy tab, select the Enabled or Disabled option, and click Apply or OK.

7. When you've configured all policies you want to apply to the domain's shared printers, click OK to close the PolicyName Properties dialog, the Group Policy snap-in, and finally the Active Directory Users and Computers snap-in.

During initial configuration of shared printers, most administrators omit configuration of printer Group Policies. Possible exceptions are to disable Web-based Printing and Printer Browsing, if these features are deemed undesirable. Disabling printer browsing prevents users from discovering printers that the administrator wants hidden, such as color laser printers. Unless you're administering a very large number of printers within the domain, you can leave printer pruning and the other more obscure policies unconfigured.

TROUBLESHOOTING

PRINTING PROBLEMS

The printer prints documents, but prints gibberish or prints some characters incorrectly.

The wrong printer driver is installed or is corrupt. Delete the printer from the Printers window, and reinstall it. When asked whether you want to use the current driver, select the option to install a new copy of the driver.

The printer stops printing jobs, and print jobs build up on the queue.

Take one or more of the following actions to solve disabled printer problems:

- Check to make sure that the printer has not been paused by the printer monitor. Double-click the printer icon to display the monitor's window, and open the Printer menu. If the Pause choice is checked, choose Pause to remove the check mark. (Print, Pause toggles between paused and not paused.)

- Stop and start the Print Spooler service on the print server. Right-click My Computer, choose Manage, expand Computer Management's Servers and Applications node, click Services, and double-click Print Spooler in the list to open the Print Spooler Properties dialog. Click Stop and, after the service stops, click Start.

- Turn the printer power off and then on to clear any errors buffered by the printer.

- Check the printer cable to the server or its network connection. Ping the IP address of a network-attached printer.

- If the printer uses DHCP for address assignment, make sure your DHCP server hasn't leased the printer's original IP address to another client. Use the Administrative Tool's DHCP snap-in to verify the printer's address.

- If the printer is attached to a workstation that receives its IP address via DHCP, run the preceding tests for the workstation.

DRIVER PROBLEMS WITH DOWNLEVEL CLIENTS

Users can't install a printer on their network client or are prompted for unavailable drivers during installation.

Open the *PrinterName* Properties dialog, click the Sharing Tab, and click Additional Drivers to verify that the drivers required for the client's operating system are installed.

If the proper driver appears to be installed, clear the driver's check box and click OK to remove the driver. Then reopen the *PrinterName* Properties dialog and add the driver again.

ACTIVE DIRECTORY

Users can't find a printer in AD with the Find, Printers or Search, For Printers menu choices.

Verify that the printer has been published in AD. Open the PrinterName Properties dialog, click the Sharing tab, and verify that the List in the Directory check box is marked. If not, mark the check box and click OK. You might need to wait five minutes for the change to replicate to the DC with which the client communicates.

NETWORK PROBLEMS

A shared printer is visible on some workstations, but not others.

First, verify in My Network Places that other network resources, such as network shares, are available. Next, verify that the client can see the print server in My Network places. If you reboot the client, wait at least five minutes for the shared printer to appear in the Add Printer Wizard's networked printers dialog.

A shared printer is visible, but the client can't connect to it.

Verify that the client's user is logged on to the network and has Print permission for the printer. The next most probable cause of this problem is a client DNS error. Run Winipcfg.exe or Ipconfig.exe, and verify that the client has the proper fixed or DHCP-assigned primary DNS server address (and secondary DNS server address, if your network runs more than one DNS server).

INTERNET-BASED PRINTER MANAGEMENT PROBLEMS

You receive the "An error occurred processing your request" message, with an error code of 80070034, "Get ADSI Printers," when you attempt to connect to the Web site to manage printers.

This problem is the subject of Microsoft Knowledge Base article Q252416, "Internet Printing May Not Work on a Network Address Translation Server." If you use Network Address Translation (NAT) to enable clients to connect to the Internet and NAT is running on the server sharing the printer, you can't manage printers over the Internet without enabling File and Print Sharing for Microsoft Networks on the external network adapter.

→ For more details on NAT, **see** "Taking Advantage of Network Address Translation (NAT)," **p. 1056**.

Enabling File and Print Sharing on an external network adapter creates a serious security risk. If you want to use the Internet to manage shared printers, move the printers to a server that's not running NAT.

MCSE Corner: Installing Network Printers

Being able to print from any node on the network is a major user requirement in almost every network. The ability to install, configure, and troubleshoot printers is tested in the exam 70-215, "Installing, Configuring, and Administering Microsoft Windows 2000 Server," which is the base exam for Windows 2000 Server concepts. You certainly will be asked at least one question about printers, and there will likely be several. You are expected to know how to install network printers and their drivers and enable them for shared access. You also are required to know how to control access to the shared printers, including the meaning of each permission setting and how it affects the users. You might need to perform these operations in a simulation-type question.

One of the most important elements to know is the troubleshooting process for a network printer. You must be able to determine whether the problem is with the printer, the print server, or the network. You probably will be presented with a scenario including a list of symptoms, and you must determine the cause of the printer problem. Being able to monitor and manage printers and print jobs is also important to know for the test exam, as well as important to the troubleshooting process.

CHAPTER 18

CONNECTING WINDOWS 2000, NT, AND 9X CLIENTS

In this chapter

Assessing the Networking Requirements of 32-Bit Windows Clients   758

Preparing for Windows 2000 Client Upgrades   759

Creating Windows 2000 Client Computer Accounts   762

Delegating Authority for Computer Account Creation   764

Setting Up Windows 2000 Client Networking   765

Connecting Windows NT 4.0 Clients   775

Accommodating Windows 9x Clients   780

Installing and Testing the Directory Services Client for Windows 9x   786

Troubleshooting   788

MCSE Corner: Connecting Windows 2000, NT, and 9x Clients   789

Assessing the Networking Requirements of 32-Bit Windows Clients

It's not surprising that the optimum Windows 2000 network consists of servers and clients running only Windows 2000. You only gain the advanced features of Windows 2000—such as IntelliMirror functions and full Active Directory (AD) integration—when you install Windows 2000 Professional on your client PCs. If you're responsible for setting up and administrating a network for a startup organization with no existing servers and workstations, you have the luxury of specifying that Windows 2000 be installed on all your computers. If your budget's approved, your homogeneous Windows 2000 network will be the envy of most of your system administrator colleagues. Even in this case, you're faced with issues surrounding Windows 2000 Professional upgrades to Windows 95, 98, and NT clients. You must also handle "clean installs" of Windows 2000 Professional on newly purchased or refurbished PCs.

Unfortunately, most administrators must support heterogeneous networks that encompass clients running Windows 9x, Windows NT 4.0 Workstation, and—sooner or later—Windows 2000 Professional. Estimates from IT market research organizations vary, but the consensus is that Windows 2000 Professional won't become the dominant business desktop and laptop operating system until late 2001 or thereafter.

This chapter begins with a description of hardware requirements for new or upgraded Windows 2000 clients, and how to minimize network-related problems when installing Windows 2000 Professional. The remainder of the chapter covers client-side networking issues you're likely to encounter when moving from a Windows NT Server 4.0 network, or upgrading from Windows 9x or NT peer-to-peer networking.

Note

The examples of this chapter assume that you have at least one Windows 2000 Domain Controller (DC) with the Domain Name Service (DNS), Dynamic Host Control Protocol (DHCP), and Windows Internet Naming Service (WINS) running on your network. DHCP is the preferred method of assigning IP addresses to client PCs. Windows 2000 clients don't require WINS, but Windows 9x and NT clients need WINS to resolve NetBIOS names to IP addresses of computers on other subnets.

→ For a review of DNS installation during Active Directory setup, **see** "Taking Advantage of Windows 2000 Server's DNS Service," **p. 82**.

→ To install DHCP on your DC, **see** "Installing the DHCP Service," **p. 589**.

→ For instructions on setting up WINS, **see** "Installing and Configuring WINS," **p. 606**.

PREPARING FOR WINDOWS 2000 CLIENT UPGRADES

Microsoft designed Windows 2000 Professional to provide a direct upgrade path for downlevel (Windows 9x and NT 3.51/4.0) clients. Unfortunately, not all machines that run Windows 9x or NT Workstation can be upgraded painlessly to Windows 2000. You must determine which of your client PCs can successfully run Windows 2000 Professional before developing a full-scale client migration plan.

> **Tip from**
> *RJ*
>
> Download Microsoft's Windows 2000 Readiness Analyzer (Chkupgrd.exe) from `http://www.microsoft.com/windows2000/upgrade/compat/RAread.asp`. **The Readiness Analyzer is a tool that runs on Windows 9x and NT 3.51 or 4.0 and prepares a report that lists potential incompatibility problems. The analysis is similar to that conducted by Windows 2000's setup programs. Unfortunately, the Readiness Analyzer won't run with antivirus software installed or on dual-boot Windows 9x/NT systems. If you can't run the Readiness Analyzer, go to the Product Compatibility Search page (**`http://www.microsoft.com/windows2000/upgrade/compat/search/`**) to check whether your clients' hardware meets Windows 2000's requirements.**

Following are some of the most common hardware-related issues you're likely to encounter when upgrading existing clients to Windows 2000:

- Insufficient RAM—128MB of RAM is required for optimum client performance. Microsoft's original minimum RAM requirement for Windows 2000 Professional was 32MB; the recommendation as of the February 17, 2000, release date was 64MB. Power users won't be satisfied with the responsiveness of a PC with 64MB.

- Inadequate fixed disk capacity—Microsoft requires a 2GB or larger fixed disk with a minimum of 650MB free space to install Windows 2000 Professional. Many older laptops and some of your inventory of desktop PCs probably have 1GB or smaller drives.

- Adapter cards or their laptop equivalents that don't have Windows 2000-compliant drivers—Older ISA adapters (now called *legacy cards*) and many special-purpose PCI adapters such as high-end, multichannel audio subsystems and high-resolution video capture devices aren't supported. Legacy network adapters are particularly likely to cause upgrade problems. You also might encounter problems with on-board or Personal Computer Memory Card International Association (PCMCIA or PC Card) audio and video input/output devices.

- Advanced Configuration and Power Interface (ACPI) problems with laptop PCs—ACPI provides standby and hibernate modes to conserve battery power. Older laptops don't support ACPI, and even recent models might require a BIOS upgrade to enable Windows 2000's power management features.

- Application incompatibility—Only about 30 commercial applications had gained the Microsoft seal of approval (Certified for Windows 2000) on Windows 2000's release date. Most shrink-wrapped applications that run under Windows NT 4.0 probably will run under Windows 2000, but you must be especially careful to test custom programs written expressly for your organization.

Tip from
RJ

Don't confuse the term Windows 2000-Ready, which is an Independent Software Vendor (ISV) self-test and self-certification program, with applications that carry the Certified for Windows 2000 logo. Applications must pass a rigorous set of tests, the results of which are verified by an independent testing lab (VeriTest). For more information on the Certified for Windows 2000 program, go to http://www.microsoft.com/PressPass/press/1999/Jul99/certificationPR.htm.

- BIOS incompatibilities of older PCs—Microsoft's minimum CPU requirement is a 133MHz Pentium, which Intel introduced in early 1995. You're likely to need to upgrade the BIOS of ancient (1997 or earlier) Pentium PC system boards to install Windows 2000 Professional.

Tip from
RJ

If you must upgrade a PC's BIOS to install Windows 2000 Professional, you're better off not making the upgrade attempt. Performing a flash upgrade to the BIOS stored in nonvolatile RAM (NVRAM) is a risky process if you don't have prior experience with BIOS upgrades.

After you've completed an inventory of client PCs that meet or can be upgraded to accommodate Windows 2000 Professional hardware requirements, you can develop a short-term upgrade plan for these clients. One element of the short-term plan should be to standardize network access of those PCs that aren't amenable to upgrades and must continue to run downlevel Windows versions. The final step is to develop a long-term budget and schedule for replacing all downlevel PCs with Windows 2000-compliant systems.

Upgrades Versus Clean Installations

Migrating clients to Windows 2000 Professional offers the opportunity to implement policy-based management to standardize users' PC environments. Group Policies, IntelliMirror, folder redirection, and other Windows 2000-only features offer the promise of lower Total Cost of Ownership (TCO). You can't take full advantage of policy-based management with PCs on which users have already loaded their own set of favorite applications, such as PC games, audio (MP3) jukeboxes, and image editors for digital snapshots. Performing a clean installation of Windows 2000 and a standard set of applications on a freshly partitioned and formatted drive leads to increased user productivity and reduced helpdesk trouble tickets.

Tip from
RJ

Use the Remote Installation Service (RIS) to perform a network installation of Window 2000 Professional on new or refurbished client PCs. RIS lets you design a standard corporate desktop configuration and specify a standard set of applications for installation on all or specific groups of client PCs. RIS requires that clients use Dynamic Host Configuration Protocol (DHCP) for IP address assignment, so you must have DHCP running on your Windows 2000 Server network.

PREPARING FOR WINDOWS 2000 CLIENT UPGRADES | 761

> **Note**
> RIS repartitions and formats the client PC's entire fixed disk, so you can't use RIS to perform Windows 2000 upgrades.

→ For a description of how to create and deploy a customized version of Windows 2000 Professional, **see** "Using RIPrep to Create a Corporate-Standard Installation Image," **p. 882**.

Obviously, users accustomed to configuring their own PCs and storing their documents and other files wherever they want—rather than in the recommended My Documents folder—might resist client standardization. Thus, the decision to perform a clean Windows 2000 installation versus an upgrade involves organizational politics. To justify clean installations to your users, emphasize the dramatic changes to the feature set of Windows 2000. If your political clout isn't sufficient to overcome user resistance to starting with a clean Windows 2000 slate, sell users on immediately moving their documents and other working files to subfolders of Documents and Settings, My Documents. Standardizing on storing files in My Documents lets users take immediate advantage of Windows 2000's IntelliMirror features.

→ For an introduction to IntelliMirror and its feature set, **see** "Defining IntelliMirror," **p. 828**.

> **Note**
> Several client upgrade tests were conducted on a vintage 200MHz Pentium MMX and 1998-99 Pentium II PCs during the writing of this book. Clients running Windows 95 Original Equipment Manufacturer Service Release 2 (OSR2), Windows 98 Second Edition (SE), and Windows NT 4.0 Workstation with Service Pack (SP) 4 or 5 upgraded satisfactorily. The test clients had Office 2000 Professional Edition, Visual Studio 6.0, Front Page 98, several special-purpose commercial applications, and a few custom-written Visual Basic 6.0 applications installed. The Setup program detected noncompliant graphics adapter utilities, but the graphics cards performed satisfactorily with the Windows 2000 drivers installed by Setup.

PART
III

CH
18

NETWORK INTERFACE CARD ISSUES

Most of the examples of this chapter make the assumption that client PCs have network interface cards (NICs) installed prior to installing Windows 2000 Professional. Windows 2000 provides drivers for current 10/100BaseT dual-speed PCI and PCMCIA/PC Card models from major NIC suppliers, such as 3Com and Intel. These two types of NICs are Plug and Play-compliant; Windows 2000 Setup recognizes them and automatically installs the required networking driver during the hardware-detection phase.

> **Tip from**
> *RJ*
> The "Upgrading from Windows NT 4.0" section of the Readme.doc file in the root folder of the Windows 2000 distribution CD-ROM lists six NICs that Windows 2000 Setup might report as not supported during an upgrade from Windows NT 4.0. Only the following four of the six adapters are likely to be installed in client PCs:
> - 3Com EtherLink 905x 10/100 adapters
> - Compaq Ethernet or Fast Ethernet PCI adapters

continues

continued

- Hewlett-Packard EN1207-D-TX 10/100 adapters
- Intel EtherExpress PRO/10 adapters

The Readme.doc file says that after Setup completes, these adapters work properly. Upgrade tests with two of these adapters (3Com and Intel) confirm the file's statement. You might encounter problems, however, if you perform a clean Windows 2000 installation with the Intel EtherExpress PRO/10 adapter installed.

You'll probably encounter problems with older 10BaseT and 10Base2 (coax or Thin Ethernet) ISA NICs. Some of these adapters meet early versions of the Plug and Play (PnP) specification, but Microsoft considers all ISA adapters to be legacy devices; Windows 2000 provides minimal support for legacy devices. You're *guaranteed* to have problems with early 10Base2 or 10BaseT NICs that use jumpers or nonvolatile RAM (NVRAM) to set interrupt request (IRQ) and input/output (I/O) address range. NVRAM NICs, such as early Intel EtherExpress adapters, use setup diskettes to specify IRQ and I/O values. Fixed IRQ and I/O addresses often interfere with other devices on the computer's system board, such as serial (COM) and parallel (LPT) ports.

Some legacy ISA NICs *might* work with Windows 2000, but you're far better off replacing them with dual-speed 10/100BaseT PCI NICs from a well-known manufacturer. You can purchase name-brand NICs that appear on the Windows 2000 HCL for $60 or less. Install the NIC in the PC before running Windows 2000.

Tip from
RJ

Don't choose a NIC based on cost alone. Many bargain-priced NICs aren't on the Windows 2000 HCL, and you're likely to encounter problems installing them. The better policy is to purchase name-brand NICs for all the clients in your network and use a single model for all desktops and one model for all laptops. You might currently have clients with a variety of NICs installed, but you should standardize NICs as you upgrade or replace the PCs.

If you want to take advantage of Windows 2000 Server's Remote Installation Service (RIS) to automatically install Windows 2000 Professional, select one of the NICs that Microsoft has approved for RIS.

→ For the list of RIS-compatible NICs that was current as of Windows 2000's release date, **see** "Client Requirements for RIS," **p. 862**.

Creating Windows 2000 Client Computer Accounts

Before you start installing new or upgrading Windows 2000 client PCs, you need a strategy for handling user and computer accounts. The strategy you use is dictated by your existing Windows client PCs, unless you're building a completely new network. Following are the primary factors to consider in setting your client networking strategy:

Creating Windows 2000 Client Computer Accounts

- If you've upgraded a Windows NT 4.0 Primary Domain Controller (PDC) or used the Active Directory Migration Tool (ADMT) to migrate the domain to Windows 2000, existing computer accounts for PCs running Windows NT 4.0 Workstation remain valid. Users can log on to the new or upgraded domain with their existing credentials. PCs running Windows NT Workstation 4.0 use their existing computer accounts.
- If you've established a new network or want to add users to an existing network, you must create a new user account for each user who is to become a member of the domain. PCs running Windows 2000 Professional or Windows NT Workstation 4.0 require a computer account; Windows 9x clients don't use computer accounts.

→ To review the process for adding new user accounts to a domain, **see** "Adding Groups and Users," **p. 118**.

- You can pre-create and enable a computer account for each Windows 2000 Professional or Windows NT Workstation 4.0 PC you add to the network. Alternatively, you can have a help-desk person or the user who installs the operating system create the computer account. In either case, someone must type the computer name in Setup's Computer Name and Administrator Password dialog.

> **Note**
>
> If you use RIS to install the operating system, you can choose from several naming options to automatically create new Windows 2000 Professional computer accounts during the RIS process.

→ For a description of RIS computer naming methods, **see** "Configuring RIS Server Properties," **p. 868**.

Pre-creating a new computer account is similar to adding a new user account; AD treats computers as a subclass of the user object. To add a computer account to the domain, do the following:

1. In Active Directory Users and Computers, right-click the container for the computer account, and choose New, Computer to open the New Object - Computer dialog.

> **Tip from**
> *RJ*
>
> Create multiple containers to hold computer accounts, preferably in a Computers container under the organizational unit (OU) to which the computer belongs. If you place all computer accounts in the default Computers container, Active Directory Users and Computers' performance deteriorates, and you might find it cumbersome to locate a specific computer account.

2. Type the name of the client in the Computer Name text box; the Computer Name (Pre-Windows 2000) text box fills with the characters you type.
3. If you want the client's user or members of a specific Security Group to be able to add the account, click Change to open the Users and Computers dialog, select the user or group from the names list, and click OK to close the dialog.

> **Note** The default group permitted to add computer accounts is Domain Admins. The next section describes how to delegate permission to add computer accounts to Domain Users or another Security Group. If you delegate the permission, you don't need to change the default Domain Admins setting in step 3.

4. To enable Windows NT 4.0 clients to use the computer account, mark the Allow Pre-Windows 2000 Computers to Use This Account check box. Click Next.
5. Click Next to bypass the Managed dialog, and click Finish to close the dialog and add the new computer account.

Delegating Authority for Computer Account Creation

By default, only members of the Enterprise and Domain Admins groups have the permissions required to join new Windows 2000 computers to a domain, even if a computer account exists for the user's workstation. You can delegate this authority to other administrator(s), or permit the user to join his or her workstation to the domain. To let users join their computers to the domain, do the following:

1. Launch Active Directory Users and Computers on the server, right-click the *DomainName* node, and choose Delegate Control to start the Delegation of Control Wizard. Click Next to bypass the Welcome dialog.

> **Note** If you want to delegate control for a specific OU and have a Security Group that contains only members of the OU, right-click the *OUName* node instead of the *DomainName* node. Substitute the name of the Security Group for Domain Users in step 3.

2. In the Users or Groups dialog, click Add to open the Add Users, Computers or Groups dialog.
3. Type **Domain Users** in the text box, click Check Names to verify your entry, and then click OK to close the dialog and add *DOMAINNAME*\Domain Users to the Selected Users and Groups list (see Figure 18.1). Click Next.
4. In the Tasks to Delegate dialog, mark the Join a Computer to the Domain text box (see Figure 18.2). Click Next, and then Finish to dismiss the Wizard.

Setting Up Windows 2000 Client Networking   765

Figure 18.1
The Users or Groups dialog lets you specify the Security Group whose members you want to be able to join computers to the domain.

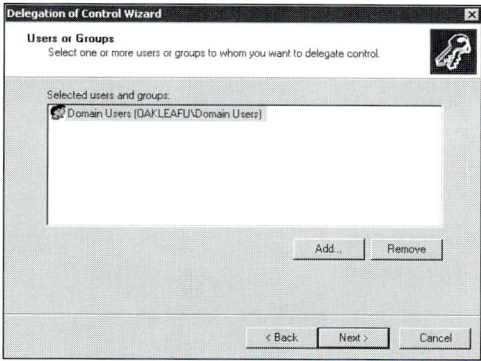

Figure 18.2
Delegate the Join a Computer to the Domain task to the previously specified Security Group.

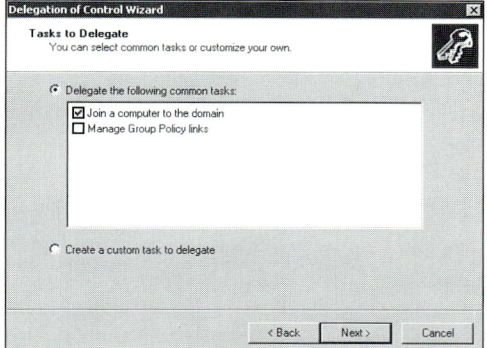

Setting Up Windows 2000 Client Networking

Windows 2000 Professional's Setup program defaults to DHCP for good reason. DHCP eliminates the administrative burden of manually setting client IP, default gateway (if applicable), and DNS server addresses. If Windows 2000 Setup correctly detects the client's NIC and you elect during setup to use DHCP, network installation proceeds without the need for further intervention.

Unless you have a compelling reason to assign fixed IP addresses to clients, plan to take full advantage of the Windows 2000 DHCP service. If your network currently has fixed client IP addresses, consider moving to DHCP before or during the server upgrade process. You can set up and test DHCP on your Windows NT 4.0 servers and begin client migration to DHCP before you upgrade to Windows 2000 Server. The upgrade process preserves all existing DHCP settings.

 If you encounter problems with Windows 2000 client networking, see the "Networking Problems with Windows 2000 Clients" topic of the "Troubleshooting" section near the end of the chapter.

PART
III

CH
18

Performing a Standard Installation of Windows 2000 Professional

It's a good practice to perform a test of the installation process before assigning the client setup responsibility to help-desk personnel or your users. Following is an accelerated set of instructions for installing Windows 2000 Professional on clients without an existing operating system:

1. Start the installation process from the distribution CD-ROM, partition the fixed disk, and format the system partition with NTFS.
2. Complete the Regional Settings, and Personalize Your Software dialogs.
3. In the Computer Name and Administrator Password dialog, type the computer name you've assigned to the client, regardless of whether you've pre-assigned computer names.
4. Complete the Date and Time Settings dialog.
5. In the Network Settings dialog, accept the default Typical Settings option to use DHCP for IP, DNS, and WINS address assignment.
6. In the Workgroup or Computer Domain dialog, select the Make This Computer a Member of the Following Domain option, and type the DNS name of the domain in the text box. Click next to open the Join Computer to Domain Name dialog.
7. If you delegated the Join a Computer to the Domain to members of the Domain Users group or the Security Group for an OU, type a user's pre-assigned logon ID and password in the text boxes, and click OK to create or bind to the computer account. Otherwise, this step requires entry of a logonID and password for a member of the Enterprise or Domain Admins groups.

Tip from
RJ

Type the fully qualified DNS name of the domain in the Domain text box, **OAKLEAF.EDU** for this example. Note that the text box forces your entry to uppercase, but Windows 2000 domain names aren't case-sensitive. If you type the downlevel domain name (OAKLEAFU), the attempt to join the domain fails.

Expect a several-second delay while the Wizard checks the logon ID and password; it then continues with installation of networking components. From this point forward, no manual intervention is required until the Completing the Windows 2000 Setup Wizard dialog opens. Click Finish to dismiss the Wizard and reboot into Windows 2000. Log on with the user ID and password for the account you specified in preceding step 7. If you've specified Group Policies, IntelliMirror services, or both for clients, the initial logon might require a couple of minutes to complete.

Tip from
RJ

Run **ipconfig /all** from the Command Prompt to verify that the DHCP settings for DNS and WINS server addresses, default gateway (if specified), and domain name(s) are correct. If client DHCP settings aren't correct, launch the DHCP snap-in on the server, and change incorrect option values for the subnet's DHCP scope. Then run **ipconfig /renew** and **ipconfig /all** on the client to make and verify the changes.

Setting Up Windows 2000 Client Networking

Exploring Network Adapter Device Properties

Once you've installed Windows 2000 Professional on a client, it's a good practice to gain familiarity with Device Manager's network adapter property dialog. Some network adapters require that you alter their default properties to obtain improved network performance, so a quick check of the default settings for the NIC is important. This and the following sections of this chapter assume that you're logged on to the Windows 2000 or NT client as Administrator or as a member of the local Administrators group.

To review the properties of an installed NIC, a Linksys Ether16 LAN Card (10BaseT/10Base2) for this example, do the following:

1. Right-click My Computer and choose Manage to open the Computer Management snap-in.
2. Click Device Manager in the tree pane to display the list of device classes in the right pane.
3. Expand the Network Adapters node to show the entry for the installed NIC (see Figure 18.3).

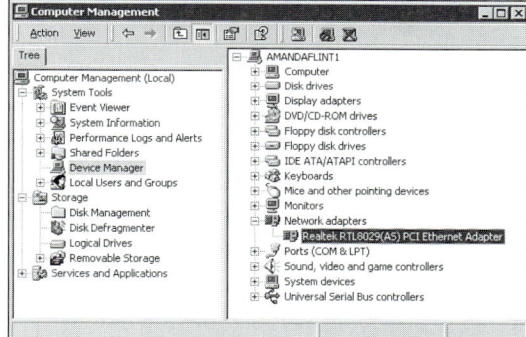

Figure 18.3
Installed NICs appear under the Computer Management snap-in's Device Manager, Network Adapters node.

PART
III

CH
18

> **Note**
> The Linksys Ether16 LAN Card and PCI NICs from many other manufacturers use a Realtek RTL8029-series chip for which Microsoft provides a driver. Most NICs using RealTek chips appear as a Realtek RTL8029(AS) PCI Ethernet Adapter, not the manufacturer's name. The Linksys Ether16 LAN card is listed in the HQL, but the entry for this device states that an upgraded driver might be needed. Upgraded drivers aren't required for NICs using the RTL8029-series chips.

4. Double-click the NIC entry to open the General page of its properties dialog, which displays basic information obtained from the driver and the status of the NIC. The device usage list lets you disable or re-enable the NIC (see Figure 18.4).

Figure 18.4
The General page of the *AdapterName* Properties dialog shows type, manufacturer, PCI bus location, and status information for the NIC.

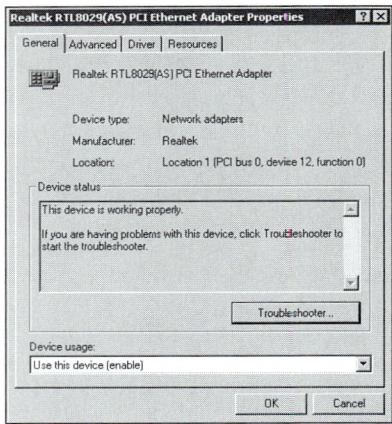

> **Note**
>
> Clicking the Troubleshooter button opens the "Hardware Troubleshooter" topic of the Windows 2000 online help file. Once there, selecting the My Network Adapter option, and clicking Next opens the "Does Windows 2000 Support Your Device?" topic.

5. Click the Advanced tab to display a list of NIC property values you can set. The list's items vary by the type of NIC and its driver; RTL8039 single-speed NICs usually have only a single (misnamed) Line Speed property. In this case, the Line Speed property Value setting specifies the type of network connection—AUI, BNC for 10Base2, or TP (twisted pair) for 10BaseT (see Figure 18.5). Most low-end NICs don't include a multi-pin AUI connector.

Figure 18.5
Set the type of connection for RTL8039 dual-media (10BaseT/10Base2) adapters in the Advanced page of the adapter's properties dialog.

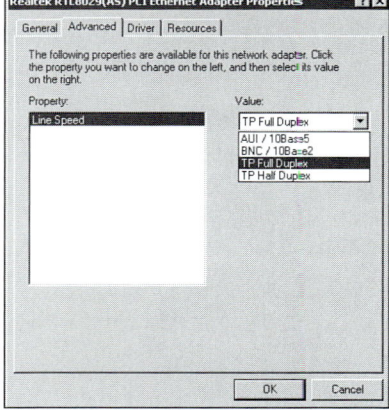

SETTING UP WINDOWS 2000 CLIENT NETWORKING | 769

Tip from

Be sure to verify that the media property setting is correct for your network. Most NICs automatically detect the active connector (BNC for 10Base2 or RJ-41 for 10/100BaseT), but you might have to change the setting manually.

When installing 10BaseT or 10/100BaseT NICs, verify that the NIC is set for full-duplex operation, which permits simultaneous transmission and reception of network packets. The default for most NICs is half-duplex, which reduces network performance because of the lack of simultaneous receive/transmit capability.

6. Click the Driver tab to display basic information about the Windows 2000 driver provided by Microsoft for the NIC. Clicking the Driver Details button opens the Driver File Details dialog that shows the original source of the driver file, in this case REAL-TEK Semiconductor Corp., and the vendor's version number (see Figure 18.6).

Figure 18.6
The Driver page of the *AdapterName* Properties and the Driver File Details dialog display NIC driver installation and file data.

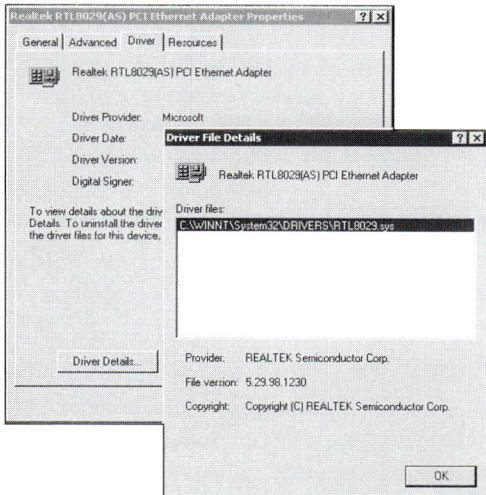

Note

Windows 2000 supports *driver signing* to verify that device drivers have been validated for use with Windows 2000. To specify the level of device driver security, right-click My Computer, choose Properties to open the System Properties dialog, click the Hardware tab, and then click Driver Signing to open the Driver Signing Options dialog. The three options are Ignore (disregard signing), Warn (notify if unsigned), and Block (prevent unsigned driver installation).

7. Click the Resources tab to display the I/O address range and IRQ assigned by the PnP service to the adapter (see Figure 18.7). You might need to know these values if you encounter conflicts with other adapters in the client. The Change Settings button isn't enabled for PCI NICs, so you can't alter the PnP settings for them. Close the dialog and the Computer Management snap-in.

PART
III
CH
18

Figure 18.7
The Resources page of the *AdapterName* Properties dialog displays the Input/Output (I/O address) range and Interrupt Request (IRQ) assigned by the PnP service to the NIC.

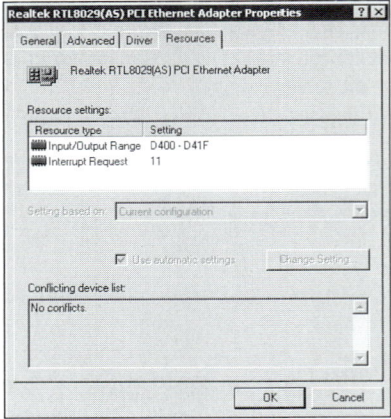

Tip from
RJ

Always run a full test of network connectivity after changing NIC property values. Changing NIC property values no longer requires a reboot, but it's a good practice to reboot the client to verify operability of logon and other network operations.

SETTING LOCAL AREA CONNECTION PROPERTIES

Installing a NIC in a client—either before or after setting up Windows 2000 Professional—automatically adds a Local Area Connection icon to the Network and Dialup Connections window. To verify or change the properties of the connection, including changing the client to a fixed IP address, do the following:

1. Right-click My Network Places and choose Properties to open the Network and Dial-Up Connections window. If the client's NIC is enabled and connected to the network, the Local Area Connection icon is present and enabled.

Tip from
RJ

If you've installed and then uninstalled a network adapter, the icon might be labeled Local Area Connection 2. In this case, rename the connection to Local Area Connection or Local Area Connection 1 to prevent users from inferring that a connection is missing.

2. Right-click Local Area Connection to open the Local Area Connection [1] Properties dialog. The default components, shown in Figure 18.8, are Client for Microsoft Networks, File and Printer Sharing for Microsoft Networks, and Internet Protocol (TCP/IP).

SETTING UP WINDOWS 2000 CLIENT NETWORKING | 771

Figure 18.8
The Local Area Connection *n* Properties dialog displays the network adapter name and networking components installed by default on the client.

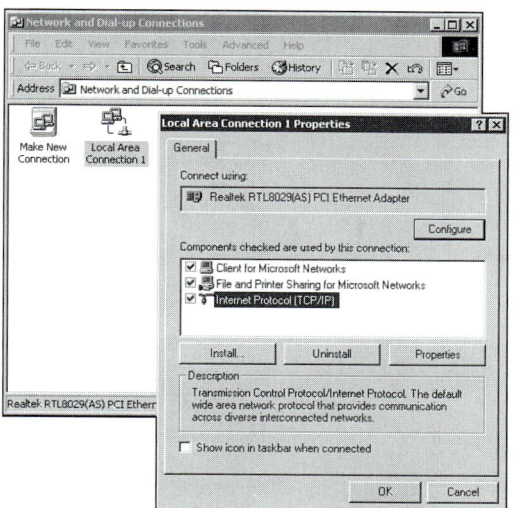

3. To add a component, click the Install button to open the Select Network Component Type dialog. Double-click Client, Service, or Protocol to open a dialog that displays currently uninstalled standard components for that component class; an example of such a dialog is the Select Network Protocol dialog shown in Figure 18.9. Unless you want to install a component, click Cancel twice to close the two dialogs and return to the Local Area Connection [1] Properties dialog.

Figure 18.9
The Select Network Protocol dialog shows protocols available for installation on the client from the Windows 2000 Professional distribution CD-ROM.

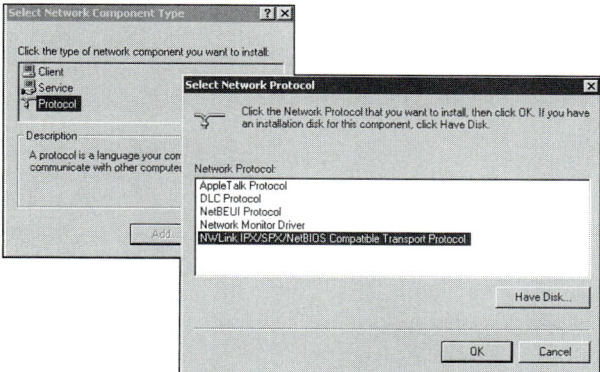

PART
III
CH
18

> **Note**
>
> The only standard Client option you can add is the Client Service for NetWare. The standard Service options include the QoS Packet Scheduler (for clients that require Quality of Service features) and the SAP Agent (Service Advertising Protocol for NetWare). If you add the Client Service for NetWare, you must also add the NWLink IPX/SPX/NetBIOS Compatible Transport Protocol. Click the Have Disk button of the selection dialog to install a nonstandard network component from a diskette or network share.

4. Double-click the Internet Protocol (TCP/IP) component entry to open its properties dialog with default entries for DHCP address assignment (see Figure 18.10). If you accept the Obtain IP Address Automatically and Obtain DNS Server Address Automatically options, click OK to close the dialog, and skip to the "Changing Network Adapters" section. Otherwise, continue to the next section.

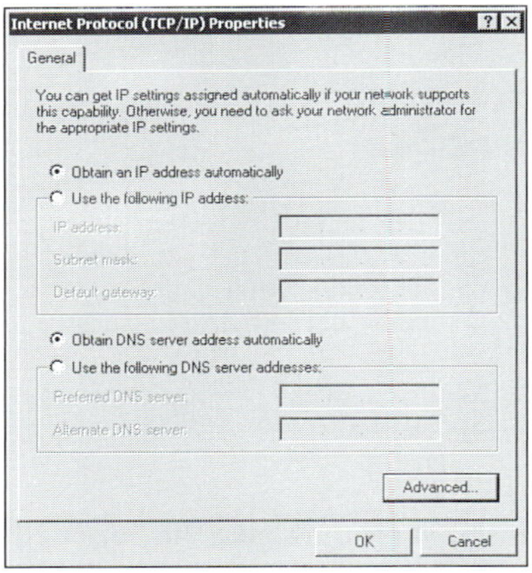

Figure 18.10
Accepting the default Obtain IP Address Automatically and Obtain DNS Server Address Automatically options sets the client up to use DHCP for all address assignments.

SPECIFYING FIXED IP ADDRESSES FOR CLIENTS

If you *must* specify fixed IP addresses for your clients, do the following in the Internet Protocol (TCP/IP) Properties dialog:

1. Mark the Use the Following IP Address option, which automatically selects the Use the Following DNS Server Address option.

2. Type the IP address, subnet mask, and default gateway address for the client's subnet. Clients need a default gateway address only if their subnet is connected to a router or you've installed Network Address Translation on the server.

→ For more information on using NAT to provide Internet access to clients, **see** "Taking Advantage of Network Address Translation (NAT)," **p. 1056**.

3. Type the address of the primary DNS server, usually the first DC for the client's domain (the PDC emulator), in the Preferred DNS Server text box. If you have a backup DNS server, type its address in the Alternate DNS Server text box (see Figure 18.11).

4. Click the Advanced button to open the Advanced TCP/IP Settings dialog and click the DNS tab.

5. If you want the client to be able to resolve unqualified DNS computer names in multiple domains, select the Append These DNS Suffixes (in Order) option, and click Add to open the TCP/IP Domain Suffix dialog. Type the name of the client's primary domain (`oakleaf.edu` for this example) in the Domain Suffix text box, and click OK to add the domain to the list.

Figure 18.11
When you specify a fixed IP address for a client, you must also add at least one DNS server address. The default gateway address is required only if your network is subnetted by a router or you've implemented NAT on the server.

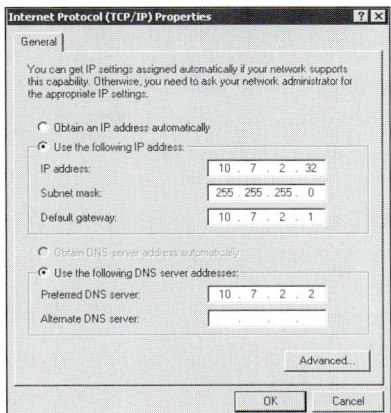

> **Note**
> An unqualified DNS computer name is the computer name only, such as oakleaf-dc1. The fully qualified domain name (FQDN) for oakleaf-dc1 is `oakleaf-dc1.oakleaf.edu`. The `oakleaf.edu` component is the DNS suffix.

6. Click Add again, type the name of the next domain to add (`student.oakleaf.edu`), and click OK to add the suffix. Repeat this step for each DNS suffix for the client to test to resolve an unqualified computer name.

7. If you specified multiple domains in the preceding two steps, type the client's domain name in the DNS Suffix for This Connection text box. Mark the Register This Connection's Addresses in DNS and the Use This Connection's DNS Suffix in DNS Registration check boxes (see Figure 18.12). Marking both check boxes assures that the client is registered with its correct DNS suffix (`oakleaf.edu` for this example).

Figure 18.12
Add the DNS suffixes for domains that the client should test to resolve an unqualified (computer name only) DNS IP address lookup request.

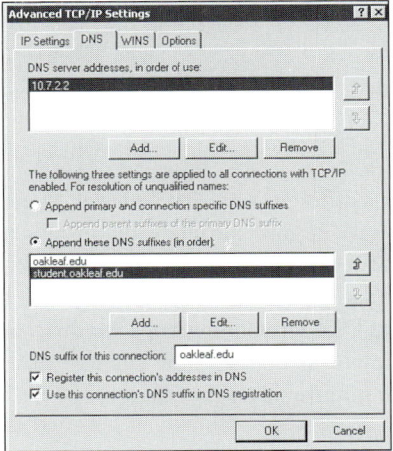

774 CHAPTER 18 CONNECTING WINDOWS 2000, NT, AND 9X CLIENTS

8. If clients must resolve NetBIOS names of downlevel computers to IP addresses and you've set up WINS on a server, click the WINS tab, click Add, type the IP address of the primary WINS server in the text box, and click OK to add the WINS server address to the list. If you have more than one WINS server, add additional address(es).

9. In the unlikely event that your Windows 2000 clients use an LMHOSTS file for IP address resolution, leave the Enable LMHOSTS Lookup check box marked. Otherwise, clear the check box. Accept the default Enable NetBIOS Over TCP/IP option to handle network communication with downlevel clients (see Figure 18.13). Click OK twice to close the two properties dialogs.

10. Reboot the computer to test the new network settings.

Figure 18.13
Set up WINS for clients that must resolve IP addresses of networked computers running Windows 9x and NT.

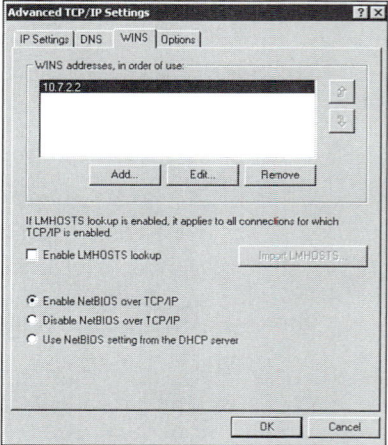

> **Note**
> In most cases, you don't need to modify values in the IP Settings and Options pages of the Advanced TCP/IP Settings dialog. The Options page lets you establish IP security (IPSec) for network connections, and filter IP packets destined for the client.

CHANGING NETWORK ADAPTERS

If you exchange an existing NIC for a different supported model, Windows 2000 detects the hardware change during the startup process and automatically installs the drivers for the new adapter. In most cases, you don't see a message box or other notice that a new adapter is in use. The only indication of an adapter change at the client is that the Local Area Connection icon in the Network and Dial-Up Connections windows has been replaced with Local Area Connection 2. As recommended earlier in the chapter, rename the icon to Local Area Connection 1 to prevent user confusion after the change.

Tip from
RJ

Conserve IP addresses in your DHCP scope by running **ipconfig /release** in the Command Window before powering down the client to exchange NICs. When you install a new NIC, DHCP clients receive a new IP address, because the Media Access Control (MAC) address of the adapter has changed. If you don't release the replaced NIC's address, the client consumes two IP address leases until the first lease expires.

Connecting Windows NT 4.0 Clients

When you upgrade the PDC of the client domain to Windows 2000 and AD or take advantage of ADMT to migrate existing user and computer accounts to a new Windows 2000 domain, clients running Windows NT Workstation 4.0 with Service Pack (SP) 4 or higher connect via TCP/IP without the need to change their network configuration.

You only need to alter client network settings in the following three cases:

- If you're installing a new Windows NT 4.0 client, you must add an account for the user and a computer account for the workstation. You specify the client NIC and other network configuration parameters during the networking phase of the setup process.

- If your Windows NT network runs only the NetBEUI protocol, you must install and configure TCP/IP on the client. It's uncommon to run only NetBEUI except in small, peer-to-peer workstation networks.

- If your existing Windows NT TCP/IP clients have fixed IP addresses and you haven't implemented DNS on the Windows NT server(s), you should specify the DNS server address for the clients' Windows 2000 subnet.

In all three of these situations, specify DHCP for IP address assignment unless you have a compelling reason to use fixed client IP addresses. If you choose DHCP during setup or change the TCP/IP properties from fixed to DHCP-assigned addresses, you don't need to specify the DNS server address; DHCP does this for you.

Caution

When using the Windows 2000 DHCP service to assign Windows NT and 9x client IP addresses, make sure that the IP subnet mask of the DC acting as the PDC emulator for your domain matches the subnet mask assigned to your clients by DHCP. When you create a Class C DHCP scope, DHCP manager assigns the scope a fixed 255.255.255.0 (/24) subnet mask. If your DC has an IP subnet mask other than 255.255.255.0, downlevel clients can't connect to the DC to validate their domain name. The same problem occurs if you specify a fixed IP address and have a subnet mask mismatch with the DC.

Setting Up a New Windows NT 4.0 Client

Starting installation of Windows NT 4.0 Workstation from the distribution CD-ROM or a network share containing the setup files is similar to the process for installing Windows 2000 Professional. Following are accelerated instructions for completing the network-related elements of Windows NT 4.0 Workstation setup and connecting the client to a Windows 2000 domain:

1. In the Computer Name dialog, type the name you've assigned to the new computer account, whether or not the account exists in Active Directory. If the computer account exists, it must be enabled.

2. In the first Network Adapter dialog, click Start Search to detect the network adapter. If search finds your adapter, go to step 4.

3. If Setup doesn't automatically detect the network adapter, which is likely, click Select From List to open the Select Network Adapter dialog. Insert the driver diskette for your NIC, click Have Disk to open the Insert Disk dialog, and click OK to accept the A:\ drive.

> **Tip from**
> *RJ*
>
> Don't bother looking up your network adapter in the Select Network Adapter dialog's list, which dates from about 1996. Setup scans the items in the list for a match with the installed adapter. Unless your clients are equipped with obsolete or obsolescent NICs, be ready to insert the manufacturer's latest driver diskette during the network setup process.

4. In the Select OEM Option dialog's list, select the driver that applies to the client's NIC, and click OK to add the driver to the Network Adapter's list. Click Next.

5. In the Network Protocols list, accept the default TCP/IP protocol, and click Next.

6. In the Network Services list, accept the four default services. If you want to add additional services, click Select from List to open the Select Network Service dialog, select the service to add, and click OK. After you've added all the services your client needs, click Next twice to install the NIC drivers.

7. When the DHCP Setup message appears, click Yes to use DHCP for address assignment. If you click No, you must provide TCP/IP property settings at this point.

8. When the dialog with the Show Bindings For list opens, click Next twice to continue with starting the network.

9. In the dialog with the Make This Computer a Member Of frame, select the Domain option, type the downlevel domain name in the Domain Text box and mark the Create a Computer Account in the Domain check box. Click Next.

10. In the Create a Computer Account in the *DomainName* Domain dialog, type a logon ID and password of an account that has permission to add Computer accounts, then click OK. Delegating the task to Domain Users or another Security Group also works with Windows NT clients.

Connecting Windows NT 4.0 Clients | 777

> **Note**
> You must mark the Create a Computer Account in the *DomainName* Domain dialog regardless of the existence of a pre-created computer account. If the computer account exists, the client uses it; otherwise, a new computer account is created at this point.

11. Click Next and then Finish to continue with Windows NT Workstation 4.0 installation.
12. Log on with the Domain User account to test client connection to the domain with the user's credentials. You can select the client's domain, local computer, and other trusted domains from the Log On To list.
13. Run **ipconfig /all** from the Command Prompt to verify the client's IP address and related properties.
14. Install any other required services or drivers, then apply the latest Windows NT 4.0 service pack to the client.

When you complete the installation process, the client has full access to the network. Network Neighborhood's windows display all visible shares of servers in its domain.

> **Note**
> You must install the Directory Service client included with SP7 to enable Windows NT clients to obtain limited AD services.

 If your Windows NT clients have problems connecting to the network, see the "Networking Problems with Windows NT 4.0 Clients" topic of the "Troubleshooting" section near the end of the chapter.

ALTERING THE NETWORKING PROPERTIES OF WINDOWS NT CLIENTS

Windows NT enables you to view and alter TCP/IP and NIC properties with Control Panel's Network tool. This differs from Windows 2000, which uses different properties dialogs for TCP/IP (Network and Dial-Up Connections, Local Area Connection) and NIC (Device Manager, Network Adapters) for this purpose. If you have problems connecting to the network, you might need to change TCP/IP or NIC property values.

To inspect and, optionally, alter the client's TCP/IP and NIC property values, do the following:

1. Launch Control Panel's Network tool, which opens with the Identification page active. To change the computer name, click the Change button to open the Identification Changes dialog (see Figure 18.14).

Figure 18.14
Change the name of the workstation or revert to a workgroup in the Network tool's Identification Changes dialog.

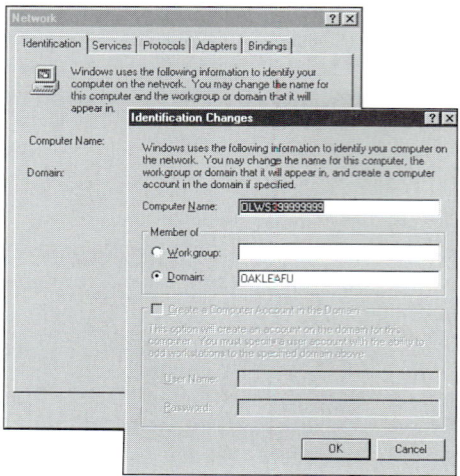

> **Note**
> If you change the computer name, you receive a warning that a network administrator must change the name of the computer account, or the user won't be able to log on to the domain. The warning is only partly correct, assuming that an account exists for the new computer name.

2. Type a new name in the Computer Name text box, and click OK; a warning message states that an administrator must change the name of the account, or the user won't be able to log on to the domain. Acknowledge the warning, click OK when the message box confirms the name change, click OK to close the Network tool, and reboot the computer.

3. If you receive a message during logon that the computer account or its password is invalid, select Active Directory Users and Computers, right-click the computer account, choose Reset Account, click Yes to confirm your action, and then click OK on the client to dismiss the acknowledgment message. Retry the logon with the new computer name, which now works as expected.

4. To change domains, demote the client to a workgroup, reboot, return to the Identification Changes dialog, change the computer and domain names, add the logon ID and password of a user account with the appropriate permissions, and reboot again.

5. To alter TCP/IP properties, click the Protocols tab, and double-click the TCP/IP item in the Network Protocols list to open the Microsoft TCP/IP Properties dialog. If the client has a fixed IP address and you've wisely decided to use DHCP, mark the Obtain an IP Address from a DHCP Server option (see Figure 18.15). Acknowledge the message that advises DHCP settings override the current TCP/IP property values, click OK twice to close the two dialogs, and reboot the server.

CONNECTING WINDOWS NT 4.0 CLIENTS | 779

Figure 18.15
Select the Obtain an IP Address from a DHCP Server option to disable an existing fixed IP address and related DNS and WINS settings.

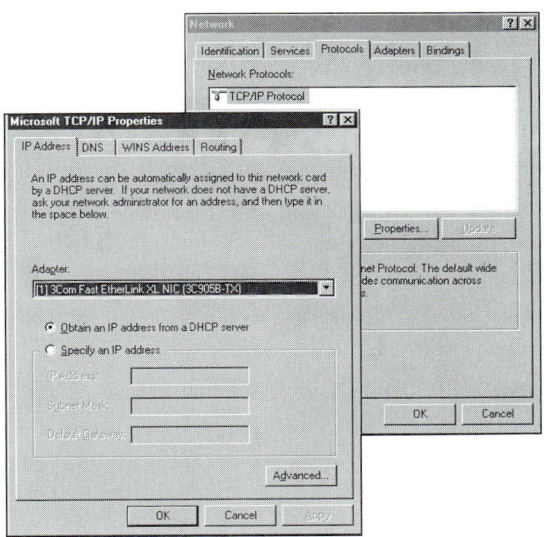

Tip from
RJ

If you insist on specifying or retaining a fixed IP address for the client, make sure to specify the correct IP addresses for the DNS and WINS server(s). Add the domain suffix of the client (oakleaf.edu for the examples of this chapter) in the DNS page.

PART
III

CH
18

6. To check the client's NIC settings, click the Adapters tab, and then double-click the applicable entry in the Network Adapters dialog to open the properties dialog for the NIC. High-end NICs such as the 3Com 3C905 series offer built-in diagnostic programs. Set your NIC for full-duplex operation, even if Auto Select is an option (see Figure 18.16). Reboot the client and test network connectivity if you make any changes to NIC property values.

Figure 18.16
Force full-duplex operation of your 10/100BaseT NIC in the Properties page of the *AdapterName* Diagnostics dialog.

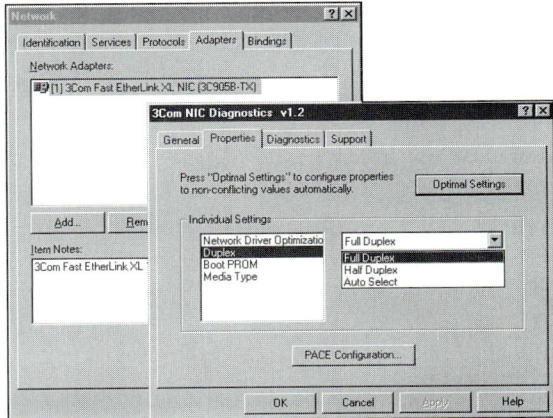

You can add or remove network services in the Services page of the Network properties dialog, and prioritize or modify bindings between devices and protocols in the Bindings page.

Accommodating Windows 9x Clients

Setting up Windows 9x clients is simpler than the process for Windows 2000 and NT, because Windows 9x doesn't offer the added security of a computer account for each client. Like Windows NT, you set network adapter and TCP/IP settings in Control Panel's Network tool. Unlike Windows NT clients, Windows 9x clients don't belong to a specific Windows 2000 domain. You specify authentication of the user's password in a Windows 2000 domain that contains the user's account to obtain access. Authentication by a DC of the domain gives the user access to domain resources.

If your Windows 9x clients previously were connected to a Windows NT network, you need not make any changes to the client PCs' network or NIC settings when you upgrade the network to Windows 2000. If your Windows 9x clients currently have fixed IP addresses, seriously consider adopting DHCP for address assignment.

> **Note** The sections that follow use Windows 98 Second Edition (SE) for the example Windows 9x client. Setting network and NIC property values in Windows 95 and the two 98 versions is very similar.

Setting Up a New Windows 98 Client for Networking

When Windows 98 Setup detects an installed PnP-compliant network card, or you add a network card after an initial installation without a NIC, Windows automatically adds TCP/IP networking with DHCP for client IP address assignment. The computer and workgroup name entries you make during the setup process are for network identification only.

Windows 9x provides Ipconfig.exe and a graphical version of ipconfig named Winipcfg.exe. To verify the client's DHCP settings, do the following:

1. Choose Start, Run, type **winipcfg** in the Open text box, and click OK to open the IP Configuration dialog with the PPP Adapter settings visible.
2. Select your NIC in the drop-down list.
3. Click More Info to expand the dialog and display all DHCP-assigned IP address settings (see Figure 18.17).
4. Verify the DHCP-assigned values, and then close the dialog.

Accommodating Windows 9x Clients | 781

Figure 18.17
Use the graphical Winipcfg.exe application (IP Configuration) to display client IP address settings provided by DHCP.

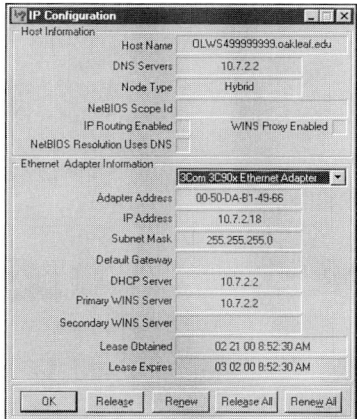

The client doesn't have access to resources in a Windows 2000 domain until you alter the user's logon properties of the Client for Microsoft Networks component. To authenticate the user in the domain, do the following:

1. Launch Control Panel's Network tool.
2. Double-click the Client for Microsoft Networks item in the components list to open the Client for Microsoft Networks dialog.
3. Mark the Log On to Windows NT Domain check box, and type the domain name in the Windows NT Domain text box.
4. Select the Logon and Restore Network Connections option (see Figure 18.18), and click OK twice to close the two dialogs.

Figure 18.18
Specify the Log On to Windows NT Domain option and type the Windows 2000 domain name to authenticate the Windows 9x user.

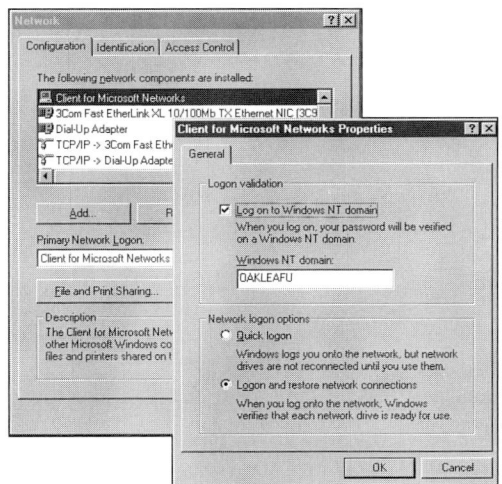

PART
III
CH
18

5. Click Yes to reboot the computer. Like Windows NT, Windows 9x requires a reboot after any change to networking properties.
6. When Windows 9x restarts, the Enter Network Password dialog opens with the domain name you entered in step 3 in the Domain text box. Type the user's password, and click OK to log on to the domain.
7. To enable the client to map network shares to logical drives, open My Computer, and choose View, Folder Options to open the Folder Options properties dialog.
8. Click the View tab, and mark the Show Map Network Drive Button in Toolbar check box. You can change other My Computer view options for the client at this point (see Figure 18.19). Click OK to close the Folder Options dialog.

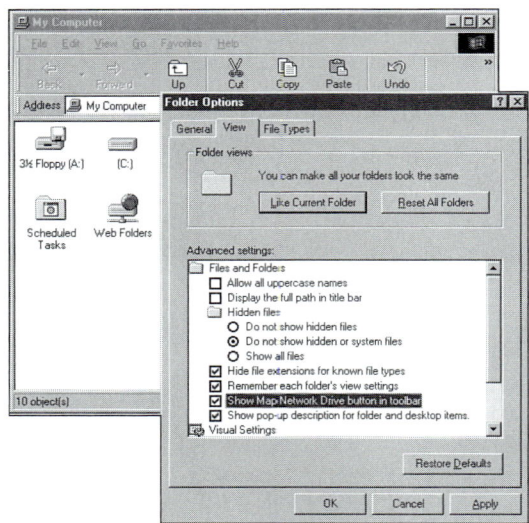

Figure 18.19
Mark the Show Map Network Drive Button in Toolbar option to allow users to map network shares to local logical drive letters.

9. Check accessibility of folder shares by clicking the Map Network Drive button to open the Map Network Drive dialog. Accept the default next available drive letter, type the UNC path to a share, and click OK to add an icon for the mapped drive to My Computer and open a new window showing the share's contents. Close all windows.
10. Wait a few minutes for the master browser to recognize the new client, then open My Network Places, which displays icons for computers in the client's workgroup (Test, for this example).

Note
If computer icons aren't visible when you open My Network Places, or you receive a "Network is not available" message when you click Entire Network, wait a few more minutes for network browsing to activate. After the initial connection to the browse master DC, the client caches the network topology locally.

11. Double-click Entire Network to open a window with icons for the domain and the workgroup. Double-click the domain to view the domain's servers, and then double-click one of the server icons to display its visible shares (see Figure 18.20). Close all windows.

Figure 18.20
Network Neighborhood displays the network topology hierarchy in a series of windows. You can specify single-window display with a custom setting in the General page of the Folder Options dialog.

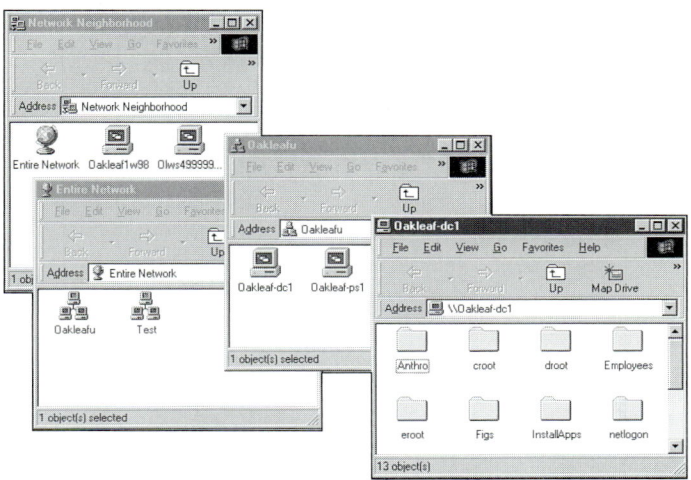

ADDING A NETWORK PRINTER

To connect to a remote printer on the Windows 2000 network, do the following:

1. Choose Start, Settings, Printers to open the Printers window.
2. Double-click the Add Printer icon to open the Add Printer Wizard, and click Next to bypass the first dialog.
3. In the second dialog, select the Network Printer option, and click Next.
4. In the third dialog, click the Browse button to open the Browse for Printer dialog.
5. Expand the Entire Network node. If you have a network-attached printer, select it. Otherwise, expand the domain and server nodes to display a printer attached to a server (see Figure 18.21). Select the printer, and then click OK to return to the Wizard dialog.
6. Click Next and accept or change the name of the printer.
7. Click Next for an option to print a test page, and then click Finish to dismiss the Wizard and add the printer to the Printers window.

Figure 18.21
Use the Browse for Printer dialog to locate network-attached or server-attached printers. In this figure, the BrotherLaser printer is attached to the Oakleaf-ps1 print server.

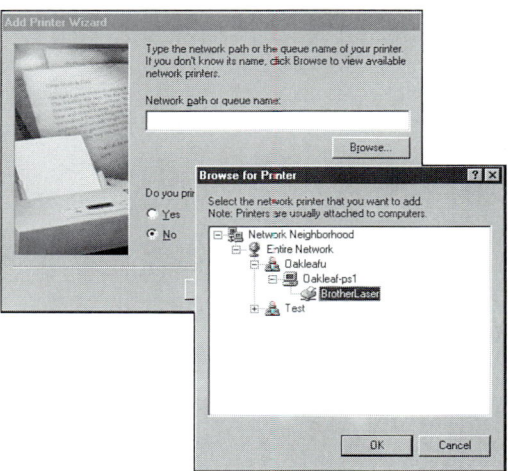

The first printer you add becomes the default printer for the client.

 If you run into problems connecting Windows 9x clients to the Windows 2000 network, see the "Networking Problems with Windows 9x Clients" topic of the "Troubleshooting" section at the end of the chapter.

SETTING NETWORK AND NIC PROPERTIES

If you use DHCP to assign client IP addresses, and your Windows 9x clients have recent-vintage PCI NICs, you seldom need to alter network settings—other than domain logon—or change NIC property values. As with other client operating systems, though, it's a good practice to become familiar with the dialogs for setting networking property values.

To review or alter networking settings of Windows 9x clients, do the following:

1. Launch Control Panel's Network tool, and double-click the TCP/IP -> *Network Adapter Name* item in the Configuration page's list to open the IP Address page of the TCP/IP properties dialog (see Figure 18.22).

2. To assign a fixed IP address to the client, select the Specify an IP Address option, and type the IP address and subnet mask values in the two preformatted text boxes.

3. If you specify a fixed IP address, click the DNS Configuration tab, mark the Enable DNS option, and type the computer name in the Host text box and the DNS domain name in the Domain text box. Enter the IP address of the DNS server in the DNS Server Search Order text box, and click Add to add the server to the list.

4. Click the WINS Configuration tab, select the Enable WINS Resolution option, type the IP address of the WINS server in the text box, and click Add to add the server to the list. If you have a routed network, go to step 5; otherwise, skip to step 6.

5. Click the Gateway tab, type the router's address in the New Gateway text box, and click Add to add the default gateway address.

Accommodating Windows 9x Clients — 785

Figure 18.22
The seven pages of the TCP/IP Properties dialog let you reconfigure the client's network settings.

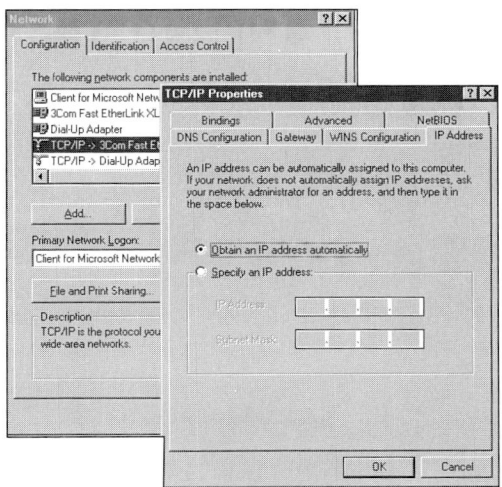

6. Close the TCP/IP Properties dialog, and double-click the Network Adapter Name entry in the component list to open the NIC's properties dialog, which varies with the NIC's manufacturer and model.
7. Click the Advanced page to check the NIC's speed and duplex settings, which often are specified as values of the Media Type property. Select 100Mbps Full-Duplex or its equivalent for other 10/100BaseT NICs (see Figure 20.23).

Figure 18.23
Specify 100Mps Full-Duplex mode for dual-speed 10/100 BaseT NICs to assure optimum network performance.

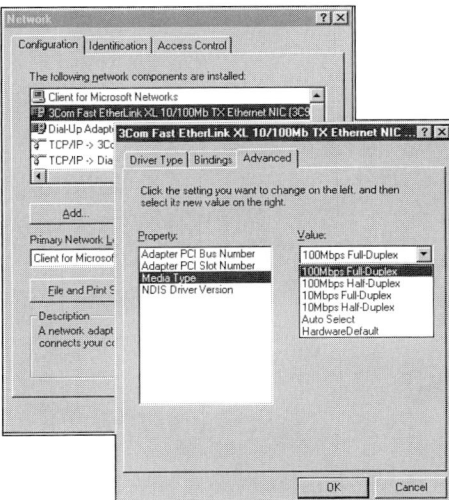

8. Click OK to accept the NIC property changes, click OK to close the Network tool, and click Yes to reboot the computer to effect your changes.

Installing and Testing the Directory Services Client for Windows 9x

The Directory Services Client (Dsclient.exe) in the \Clients\Win9x folder of the Windows 2000 Server distribution CD-ROM provides the ability to find people (users) and printers published in AD.

> **Note**
> Installing Dsclient.exe on a Windows 9x client also installs the files—Secur32.dll, Msnp32.dll, Vredir.vxd, and Vnetsup.vxd—required to support NTLM 2 authentication and session security. NTLM 2 is more secure than the conventional NTLM security used by Windows 9x to log on to Windows NT and 2000 domains. Installing the files doesn't enable NTLM 2 security on the client. You must change a Registry setting to enable NTLM 2. For more information on enabling NTLM 2, go to http://www.microsoft.com, choose Support, Knowledge Base, and search for article Q239869, "How to Enable NTLM 2 Authentication for Windows 95/98 Clients."

To install and test Dsclient.exe, do the following:

1. Navigate to the \Clients\Win9x folder of the Windows 2000 Server distribution CD-ROM in the client's CD-ROM drive or to a network share containing the server files.
2. Double-click Dsclient.exe to start the Directory Service Client Wizard. Click next to bypass the Welcome dialog.
3. In the Ready to Install dialog, click Next to open the Installation dialog and complete the Dsclient setup.
4. In the Installation Completed dialog, click Finish to dismiss the Wizard, and click Yes to reboot the client.
5. Log on to the domain, and choose Start, Find, People to open the Find People dialog, and select Active Directory from the Look In list.
6. Type a search criterion, such as a first name, in the Name text box, and click Find Now to list matching user Name entries in AD (see Figure 18.24).
7. Double-click a list entry to display the Summary page of the *UserName* Properties dialog (see Figure 18.25).

Figure 18.24
Use the Find People dialog to list AD user accounts matching a name or email search criterion.

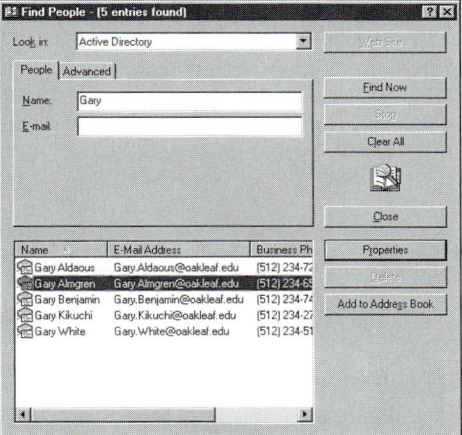

Figure 18.25
Double-clicking an item in the Find People list opens a read-only property dialog that displays some—but by no means all—properties of the AD user account.

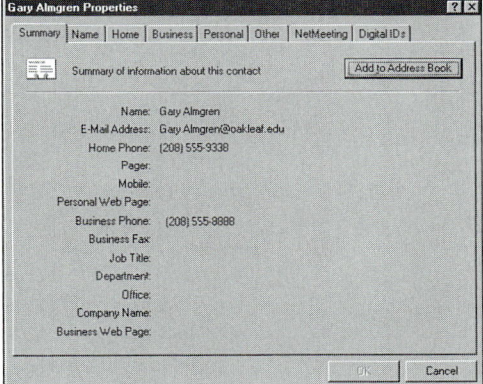

> **Note**
>
> Many property values that exist in AD don't appear in the Summary or other pages of the *UserName* Properties dialog. For instance, Gary Almgren's Job Title property value is Department Chairperson, his Department is Anthropology, his Office is Liberal Arts Building, Rm. 385, and his personal Web site is http://www.oakleaf.edu/depts/anthro/GaryAlmgren.htm. None of these property values that are present in Active Directory Users and Computers' Gary Almgren Property dialog appear in the properties pages added by Dsclient.exe.

8. If you want to add a contact record for the user to your personal address book, click Add to Address Book to open an editable version of the *UserName* Properties dialog. Make the changes you want to the contact data, then click OK to add the entry to your address book. Click Close to close the Find People dialog.

9. To find printers published in AD, choose Start, Find, Printers to open the Find Printers dialog. The default (and only) choice of the In list is Entire Directory.

10. Type a search criterion based on the name of the printer in the Name dialog and click Find Now to provide a list of printers that match the criterion. Double-click a network printer to add it to the Printers collection of the client.

The Advanced page of the Find People and Find Printers dialogs lets you perform limited Lightweight Directory Access Protocol (LDAP) searches for user accounts and published printers.

→ For instructions on the use of the advanced search features, **see** "Searching for AD Objects with LDAP," **p. 135**.

> **Note**
>
> Windows 9x clients with Dsclient.exe installed can take advantage of the additional security offered by Microsoft NTLM 2 authentication by Windows 2000 and Windows NT 4 SP4+ domain controllers. For instructions on changing Registry settings to enable NTLM 2 authentication, go to www.microsoft.com and search the Knowledge Base for article Q239869 ("How to Enable NTLM 2 Authentication for Windows 95/98 Clients").

TROUBLESHOOTING

NETWORKING PROBLEMS WITH WINDOWS 2000 CLIENTS

When upgrading a Windows NT 4.0 or Windows 9x client to Windows 2000 Professional, the network adapter isn't recognized or doesn't work after manual installation.

Most NICs with operational Windows NT 4.0 drivers upgrade satisfactorily to Windows 2000, regardless of whether they're on the HCL. Windows 2000 supports most miniport drivers that comply with the 32-bit Network Device Interface Specification (NDIS). Try to obtain a Windows 2000-compliant NIC driver from the card's manufacturer. If a Windows 2000 driver isn't available, download the latest Windows NT driver, and attempt to install the NIC.

If you can't install the NIC with the latest Windows NT 4.0 driver, you probably need to replace the NIC with a more current device.

The NIC appears to install satisfactorily, but the client can't connect to a domain controller.

Open the Command Prompt and run a loopback test (**ping 127.0.0.1**) on the adapter. If the loopback test fails, the driver isn't operational or the NIC is defective. Obtain a new driver for the NIC, or replace it with a NIC on the Windows 2000 HCL.

If the loopback test succeeds, try pinging a DC, first by IP address, then by computer name, and finally by the server's FQDN. If the IP address test fails, the client probably has an incorrect IP address or subnet mask value. Run **ipconfig /all** to verify the client's IP address settings. If the computer name and FQDN tests fail, the client has a DNS problem. Verify that DNS is running on the server, and that the client's IP address for the DNS server is correct.

For a more detailed test of the NIC and your TCP/IP settings, install the Windows 2000 Support Tools on the client and run **netdiag** in the Command Window. You install the Support Tools by running \Support\Tools\2000rkst.msi from the Windows 2000 Professional distribution CD-ROM. For more information on netdiag's command syntax and output, type **netdiag /?** or read the online help for Netdiag.exe.

NETWORKING PROBLEMS WITH WINDOWS NT 4.0 CLIENTS

The client can ping the server by IP address, computer name, and FQDN, but can't connect to a DC in the site.

The most common source of this problem is an error in the IP property values provided by DHCP. Try running **ipconfig /release**, and then **ipconfig /renew** to obtain a new IP address lease with the latest DHCP scope options.

This problem also might be caused by the subnet mask mismatch described in the Caution element of the "Connecting Windows NT 4.0 Clients" section of this chapter. Verify that the DC's subnet mask is the same as the subnet mask reported when you run **ipconfig /all** on the DC and the client.

NETWORKING PROBLEMS WITH WINDOWS 9X CLIENTS

A "Network is not available" message appears when attempting to browse the Windows 2000 network.

The most likely cause of this problem is impatience when performing the initial network connectivity test with the client. Verify network connectivity by mapping a server share to a client driver. If this test succeeds, wait a few more minutes, and then try network browsing again. If the test fails, the network logon probably failed. Try logging off and then logging on to the domain again.

Another possibility is that you didn't specify Log On To a Windows NT Domain option and add the domain name in the properties dialog for the Windows Network Client.

MCSE CORNER: CONNECTING WINDOWS 2000, NT, AND 9X CLIENTS

The exams that cover the topics in this chapter are 70-215 Installing, Configuring, and Administering Windows 2000 Server, which is the base Windows 2000 Server exam, and 70-210 Installing, Configuring, and Administering Windows 2000 Professional, which is the base exam for Windows 2000 Professional. The exam 70-210 is not mentioned in any of the other MCSE corners as this is the only chapter that covers topics on it. Some topics in this chapter are also covered on the Microsoft exams 70-064 Implementing and Supporting Microsoft Windows 95, 70-073 Implementing and Supporting Microsoft Windows NT Workstation 4.0, and 70-098 Implementing and Supporting Microsoft Windows 98. Items covered in this chapter are also included in the 70-217 Implementing and Administering a Microsoft Windows 2000 Directory Structure.

70-064 Implementing and Supporting Microsoft Windows 95, 70-073 Implementing and Supporting Microsoft Windows NT Workstation 4.0, 70-098 Implementing and Supporting Microsoft Windows 98, and 70-210 Installing, Configuring, and Administering Microsoft Windows 2000 Professional

These exams cover the Windows Desktop operating systems, but the topics in Chapter 18 relate heavily to these exams. The important part of the chapter to be familiar with for these exams is the section on configuring clients for network connections to the network, and connecting clients to the Domain Controllers. You should be able to set up the client system with the correct network protocols for the environment and connect to the domain controller and access domain resources. You should also be familiar with the theory and application of the TCP/IP, IPX/SPX, and NetBEUI protocols.

70-215 Installing, Configuring, and Administering Microsoft Windows 2000 Server

For the Windows 2000 Server exam, the important concept in Chapter 18 is the knowledge gained about the TCP/IP, IPX/SPX, and NetBEUI protocols. In addition, the sections on configuring Windows 2000 Professional clients and connecting Windows 2000 clients to the domain also apply to Windows 2000 servers which are configured in a standalone form.

70-217 Implementing and Administering a Microsoft Windows 2000 Directory Services Infrastructure

This exam tests your knowledge of working with computer accounts in the Active Directory. You should be familiar with the general theory and process of adding computers to the domain as well as the use of the Active Directory Users and Computers tool for working with computer accounts.

Troubleshooting

As for all of the new Microsoft exams, the troubleshooting section of this chapter is important, especially so for the Windows 2000 Server and all of the Professional exams. You need to be able to troubleshoot a client connection including the physical link, the network adapter, and the network protocols.

CHAPTER 19

SERVING MACINTOSH, WINDOWS 3.11, AND DOS CLIENTS

In this chapter

Integrating Other Clients with Windows 2000   792

Understanding the Macintosh Networking System   792

Integrating a Macintosh Client into the Network   795

Adding Print Services for Macintosh   799

Installing, Configuring, and Using File Services for Macintosh   803

Upgrading Windows for Workgroups 3.11 Clients to TCP/IP   815

Adding TCP/IP to the Network Client v3.0 for MS-DOS and Windows   820

Troubleshooting   823

MCSE Corner: Serving DOS, Windows 3.11, and Macintosh Clients   825

Integrating Other Clients with Windows 2000

Windows 9x and NT clients predominate on today's Windows NT and 2000 networks. In the long term, Windows 2000 Professional and its successors will replace most Windows 9x and NT clients. Many organizations, however, must continue to support clients running other operating systems—primarily Apple Computer's MacOS and Windows for Workgroups 3.11. Apple's Macintosh computers traditionally have dominated the content-creation market—desktop publishing, graphic design, high-end audio processing, and digital video production. 32-bit Windows operating systems continue to expand their share in the creative arts market segment, but it's improbable that Windows-based PCs will totally displace the Macintosh. Mac users are a determined breed, and most vehemently resist adoption of Windows. If you're a network administrator for a sound studio, magazine or book publishing firm, or video postproduction organization, count on supporting Macintoshes forever. Thus, this chapter concentrates on integrating computers running the MacOS into Windows 2000 networks.

A declining—but still significant—number of Windows for Workgroups (WfW) 3.11 clients remain attached to Windows networks. Many of these machines run legacy 16-bit Windows applications with pre-Pentium processors—Intel 80486s and even 80386s. Auctions on eBay.com and Amazon.com demonstrate a continuing demand for MS-DOS 6.22 and WfW 3.11. The distribution version of WfW 3.11 supports only NetBEUI and NetWare IPX/SPX protocols. To avoid the need to run NetBEUI on your Windows 2000 network, you must upgrade WfW 3.11 to support the current MS-DOS version of TCP/IP. Sections at the end of this chapter cover adding TCP/IP connectivity for WfW 3.11 and MS-DOS.

> **Note** The Windows 2000 Server distribution CD-ROM doesn't include the required upgrade files for WfW 3.11. You must have a copy of the Windows NT Server 4.0 CD-ROM to create the files required to add TCP/IP connectivity to WfW 3.11 clients.

Understanding the Macintosh Networking System

Networking Macintosh clients in a Windows 2000 system requires familiarity with *AppleTalk*. AppleTalk is a family of protocols for the Macintosh that offers functionality similar to that of Microsoft's Windows 9x networking.

AppleTalk runs on the following three types of physical media:

- *LocalTalk*, which is both a protocol and a physical medium, runs on a daisy-chain or bus connection. Physically, LocalTalk is a serial connection running at a speed of 230Kbps. A single LocalTalk network can support a maximum number of 255 nodes, but the practical limit is about 50 clients. To support LocalTalk, you must install a LocalTalk network adapter in your server. LocalTalk is obsolete, so it isn't covered in this book.

- *TokenTalk* runs on a Token Ring network. As is the case with a LocalTalk network, if any connecting cable in a TokenTalk network breaks, the entire network goes down. Like LocalTalk, TokenTalk is an obsolete protocol.
- *EtherTalk* is an Apple link layer access protocol running on 10BaseT or 100BaseT Ethernet. Ethernet is by far the most popular connection method for all networks, so this chapter covers only TCP/IP over EtherTalk.

Understanding the AppleTalk Protocol Layers

As stated earlier, AppleTalk is a family of protocols. You can think of this family as a stack of protocols, with each stack offering a different type of protocol service. Figure 19.1 illustrates the three AppleTalk Protocol Layers.

Figure 19.1
The AppleTalk family of protocols is represented here as a layered stack; each layer delivers a different type of protocol capability.

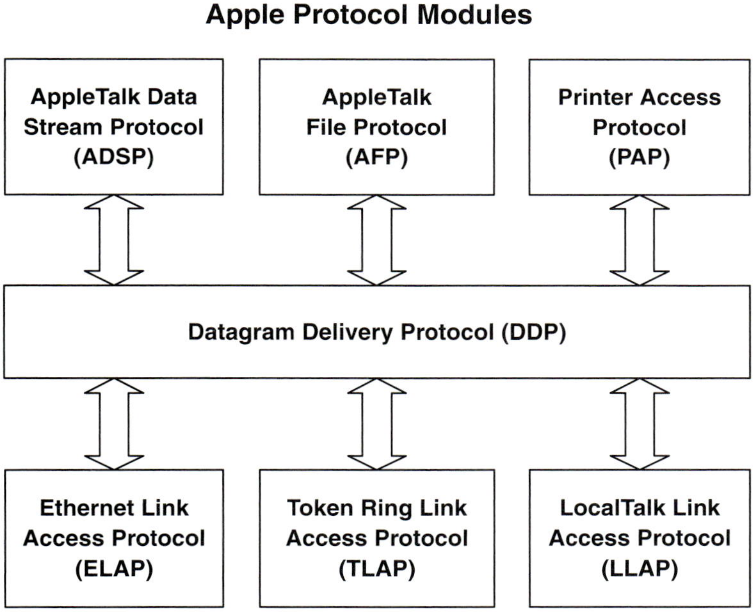

Apple Protocol Modules

```
┌─────────────────┐  ┌─────────────────┐  ┌─────────────────┐
│  AppleTalk Data │  │    AppleTalk    │  │  Printer Access │
│  Stream Protocol│  │  File Protocol  │  │     Protocol    │
│      (ADSP)     │  │      (AFP)      │  │      (PAP)      │
└─────────────────┘  └─────────────────┘  └─────────────────┘
         ⇅                    ⇅                    ⇅
┌───────────────────────────────────────────────────────────┐
│            Datagram Delivery Protocol (DDP)               │
└───────────────────────────────────────────────────────────┘
         ⇅                    ⇅                    ⇅
┌─────────────────┐  ┌─────────────────┐  ┌─────────────────┐
│  Ethernet Link  │  │ Token Ring Link │  │  LocalTalk Link │
│ Access Protocol │  │ Access Protocol │  │ Access Protocol │
│      (ELAP)     │  │      (TLAP)     │  │      (LLAP)     │
└─────────────────┘  └─────────────────┘  └─────────────────┘
```

At the bottom of the AppleTalk network protocol stack are the Link Access Protocols (LAP): the Token Ring Link Access Protocol (TLAP), Ethernet Link Access Protocol (ELAP), and LocalTalk Link Access Protocol (LLAP) modules. These three protocol modules allow computers to communicate with each other over more than one physical media type. For example, two AppleTalk computers communicating with each other over Ethernet use ELAP.

Above the LAP layer is the Datagram Delivery Protocol (DDP) protocol layer. This layer provides nonguaranteed delivery of datagrams between computers, which means the receiving computer might or might not receive the packet. For example, if a router between two computers fails while the datagram is in transit, the datagram might not arrive at the receiving computer.

The nonguaranteed delivery of data might, at first glance, appear to render the DDP protocol unusable, but there are many areas in modern networking where nonguaranteed protocols are useful. Streaming audio and video servers commonly use nonguaranteed datagram protocols, such as the User Datagram Protocol (UDP), because momentary audio or video dropouts are less bothersome than lengthy pauses to retransmit missing datagrams. Datagram protocols offer better performance and lower overhead than guaranteed-delivery protocols. DDP corresponds to the IP component of TCP/IP.

→ To review characteristics of the UDP protocol, **see** "Taking Chances with UDP Delivery," **p. 89**.

Above the DDP layer are Apple protocol modules. The most important of these modules is the AppleTalk Data Stream Protocol (ADSP). Technically, ADSP is a symmetric, connection-oriented protocol supporting order of delivery, flow control, and duplicate elimination. A computer using this protocol is assured that the data it sends to another computer arrives just as it was sent, even if the data is divided into small packets for transmission across the network.

ADSP is a higher-overhead, lower-performance protocol than DDP, but the performance tradeoff is worthwhile for applications that require reliable data transmission between two computers. ADSP corresponds to the TCP element of TCP/IP.

Apple Computer includes several other protocol modules in its AppleTalk protocol suite, but only two are relevant to Windows 2000 integration: the Printer Access Protocol (PAP) and the AppleTalk File Protocol (AFP). These two protocol modules implement for Macintoshes the functionality provided by the SMB (Server Message Block) protocol, which is the native Windows 2000 protocol for file and printer sharing.

The AppleTalk Numbering and Zone Systems

A network in AppleTalk is equivalent to a TCP/IP subnet. As in TCP/IP, multiple networks or subnets can share a single physical cable. Unlike TCP/IP subnets, AppleTalk networks are numbered using a 16-bit integer having a value between 1 and 65,279.

Each computer in an AppleTalk network is assigned a node number. As is the case with hosts that use TCP/IP, this node number must be unique within a network. AppleTalk node numbers are represented by an eight-bit byte, which means that the theoretical maximum number of nodes per network is 256.

Tip from
RJ
> Node numbers 0 and 255 are reserved for unknown and broadcast addresses, respectively, which leaves 254 node numbers per physical network cable.

Nodes in the AppleTalk network are uniquely identified by a 24-bit number that results from the addition of the 16-bit network and eight-bit node numbers. AppleTalk is comparable to a fixed Class C IP network with the potential for 65,279 networks, instead of IP's approximately 16 million Class C networks.

AppleTalk nodes boot onto the network and self-assign node numbers (making sure no node number conflicts exist), and routers provide network numbers to these clients. No networking configuration is required on a computer in an AppleTalk network, although you may opt to set a default zone name. *Zones* are human-readable names for groupings of computers and peripherals; these names help users find specific resources on the network.

AppleTalk Routing

Understanding AppleTalk routing is critical for the Windows 2000 administrator. Once you understand AppleTalk routing, you easily can keep your Windows 2000 and Macintosh networks playing together nicely. Without this understanding, it's almost impossible to integrate AppleTalk and Windows networks.

A *non-routed* AppleTalk network is one where all nodes on the network effectively share a common cable. This shared cable can be interconnected via switches or hubs, but the cable can't pass through a router or between two network cards in a multihomed computer. A router or multihomed computer with multiple network cards typically places your network into the category of a routed network.

A *routed* AppleTalk network includes one or more devices configured as an AppleTalk router. The AppleTalk router enables you to partition your network into multiple physical networks. Partitioning enhances your network's security and performance, and minimizes node count on a single shared cable.

An AppleTalk router, like an IP router, is responsible for examining the network number in packets and passing those packets destined for other networks to the appropriate location.

AppleTalk routers come in two varieties: seed and non-seed. A *seed* router advertises zones for a physical network as well as the network numbers supported on the physical cables attached to the seed router. A *non-seed* router asks seed routers for information regarding the network configuration and uses that information to route packets and assign network numbers to computers booting onto the network.

Tip from
RJ

> Windows 2000 administrators may find it easiest to think of a seed router as a Windows NT Primary Domain Controller (PDC) and a non-seed router as a Backup Domain Controller (BDC). The PDC or seed router replicates network topology information to the BDC or non-seed router.

Integrating a Macintosh Client into the Network

Your first task as a Windows 2000 administrator enabling Macintosh support is to install the AppleTalk protocol. Windows 2000 Server's Services for Macintosh (SFM) includes full AppleTalk server support for the AppleTalk protocol and Macintosh print and file services. During SFM installation, you must determine what type, if any, of routing support Windows 2000 should provide. A Windows 2000 Server can play the role of an end-node (no routing support), a non-seed router, or a seed router. To configure AppleTalk routing, you first must have installed Windows 2000 Routing and Remote Access Services (RRAS).

→ For the instructions on setting up RRAS on your server, **see** "Installing Windows 2000 RRAS," **p. 1027**.

INSTALLING THE APPLETALK PROTOCOL

To install the AppleTalk protocol component of SFM, follow these steps:

1. Right-click My Network Connections and choose Properties to open the Network and Dial-up Connections window.

2. Right-click the network connection icon for the network adapter connected to your Macintosh clients, and choose Properties to open the *ConnectionName* Properties dialog.

3. On the General page, click Install to open the Select Network Component Type dialog, and select Protocol (see Figure 19.2).

4. In the Select Network Protocol dialog, select AppleTalk Protocol. Click OK to close both dialogs and return to the *ConnectionName* Properties dialog.

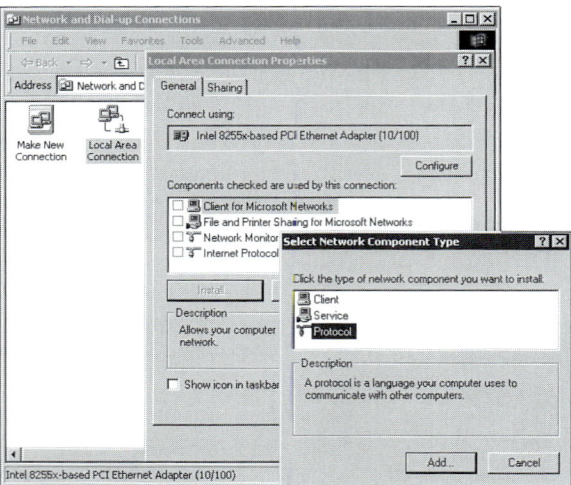

Figure 19.2
The Select Network Component Type dialog enables you to add additional protocols to a selected network adapter.

5. The Components Checked Are Used by This Connection list shows AppleTalk as an installed protocol. Click Close to close the properties dialog, and close the Network and Dial-up Connections window.

CONFIGURING APPLETALK ROUTING

If your network requires AppleTalk routing support, you add it after you've installed AppleTalk on your server. Use Table 19.1 to determine the type of AppleTalk router to set up, if any.

INTEGRATING A MACINTOSH CLIENT INTO THE NETWORK | 797

TABLE 19.1   WINDOWS 2000 APPLETALK NODE TYPES AND ALTERNATIVE CONDITIONS FOR THEIR SELECTION

Windows 2000 Node Type	Conditions for Selection
End-Node	You have a single, shared-cable network, require only file or print services, and there are fewer than 254 nodes.
	The AppleTalk network already has one or more routers.
Non-seed Router	You have a multi-cable network, want Windows 2000 to act as a router to convey packets from one network to another, and want other AppleTalk routers to perform seed duties.
	Windows 2000 Server has multiple network interface cards connecting AppleTalk networks, and these networks must communicate.
Seed Router	You have a single- or multi-cable network, no other seed routers on the network, and more than 254 nodes on the network.
	The AppleTalk network needs to be divided into zones, and another router is not already providing zone and network number information.

If your Windows 2000 Server serves as an end-node, skip the remainder of this section; you don't need router support.

To configure AppleTalk routing, follow these steps:

1. Choose Programs, Administrative Tools, Routing and Remote Access to open the Routing and Remote Access snap-in.
2. In the tree view pane, expand the *ServerName* node, and click the AppleTalk Routing node to display the routing status (see Figure 19.3).

Figure 19.3
If the status of the AppleTalk network adapter shown in the detail pane is Network Not Seeded, there is no AppleTalk seed router on the network.

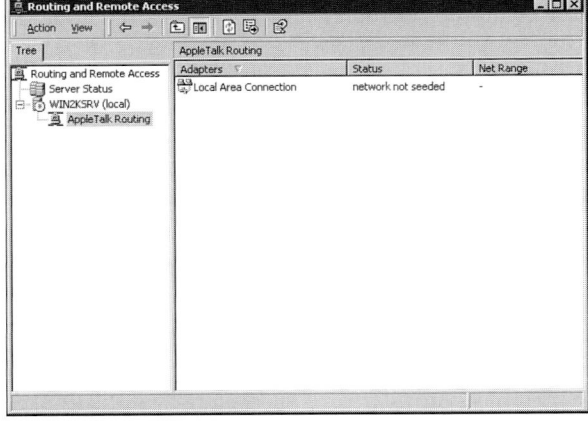

PART
III
CH
19

3. Right-click the AppleTalk Routing node, and choose Enable AppleTalk Routing to change the adapter's status to Routing (Default). The default status is a non-seed router.

4. In the Adapters list of the pane, right-click the AppleTalk adapter's icon, and choose Properties to open the empty *ConnectionName* Properties dialog, which lets you add AppleTalk configuration options (see Figure 19.4).

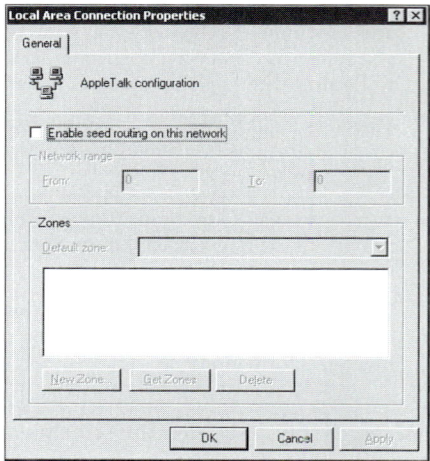

Figure 19.4
The *ConnectionName* Properties dialog in the Routing and Remote Access snap-in contains the options for enabling and configuring your AppleTalk seed router.

5. To enable the server as a seed router, mark the Enable Seed Routing on This Network check box, which enables the Network Range From and To text boxes and the controls in the Zone frame.

6. Type network numbers for the networks to which this adapter is connected in the From and To text boxes. For this example, the numbers are from 100 to 105, which provides six networks of up to 254 hosts each. This configuration allows a theoretical limit of 1,518 AppleTalk devices on the connection to this network adapter.

Tip from

Be sure not to duplicate network numbers assigned by other seed routers (if any seed routers exist on your AppleTalk network) and don't allocate more network numbers than you need. The example of 100 to 105 numbers is arbitrary; for a small routed network, a few network numbers accommodate a very large number of AppleTalk clients.

7. Click the New Zone button to open the Add New Zone dialog. Type the AppleTalk zone name for the network in the text box, and click OK. This example uses Oakleaf as the AppleTalk zone name.

8. Open the Default Zone and select the new zone name as the default zone.

9. Click Apply to complete the configuration process. Figure 19.5 shows the completed AppleTalk routing configuration for the network.

Figure 19.5
AppleTalk seed routing is enabled, the network number range is specified, and the default zone name is set.

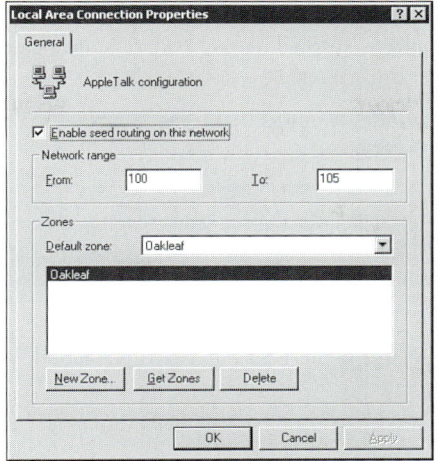

10. Click OK to close the *ConnectionName* Properties dialog and return to the Routing and Remote Access configuration utility.

At this point, your AppleTalk network is seeded by your Windows 2000 Server, and you can establish Macintosh file, print, and remote access services.

 If you have problems with Mac client connectivity to or authentication by Windows 2000 DCs, see the "AppleTalk Networking Issues" topic of the "Troubleshooting" section near the end of the chapter.

ADDING PRINT SERVICES FOR MACINTOSH

Windows 2000 includes the following two types of printer support:

- *Windows 2000 printer client support* allows Windows 2000 to act as an AppleTalk printer client. Windows 2000 Server can share printers connected to AppleTalk clients with Windows clients. The printers appear to Windows clients as conventional network printers.

- *AppleTalk printer server support* allows Windows 2000 to expose printers, whether on the AppleTalk or Windows network, to Macintosh clients as AppleTalk printers.

CONNECTING WINDOWS 2000 SERVER TO APPLETALK PRINTERS

Windows 2000 Server has rudimentary AppleTalk client capabilities. For instance, you can't attach to AppleTalk servers using AFP without add-on third-party software, which means Windows 2000 machines cannot read files from or write files to a Macintosh server. All versions of Windows 2000 can, however, connect to AppleTalk printers as a client.

Once connected to an AppleTalk printer, a Windows 2000 Server can share the AppleTalk printer to other Windows clients that don't have AppleTalk printer support installed. For example, a typical network design might use one Windows 2000 Server machine with the

AppleTalk protocol installed. Windows 95, 98, NT, and 2000 clients can print to the AppleTalk printer(s) without requiring AppleTalk to be installed on each of the client workstations.

→ For an overview of setting up printers under Windows 2000, **see** "Configuring a Server-Connected or Workstation-Owned Shared Printer," **p. 732**.

Caution

Disable print spooling on Macintosh clients when sharing network-attached AppleTalk printers with Windows 2000 Server. Mac clients create a local printer spool, which interferes with print jobs queued by the Windows 2000 Server's print spooler.

To connect a Windows 2000 Server as a client of a network-attached AppleTalk printer, follow these steps:

1. Choose Settings, Printers to open the Printers window.
2. Double-click the Add Printer icon to launch the Add Printer Wizard. Click Next to bypass the Welcome screen.
3. In the Local or Network Printer dialog, select the Local Printer option, clear the Automatically Detect and Install my Plug and Play Printer check box, and click Next.
4. In the Select the Printer Port dialog, select the Create a New Port option, and select AppleTalk Printing Devices in the Type list (see Figure 19.6). Click Next to open the Available AppleTalk Printing Devices dialog.

Figure 19.6
Create a new port for a local printer and specify AppleTalk Printing Devices to connect to a printer on the AppleTalk network.

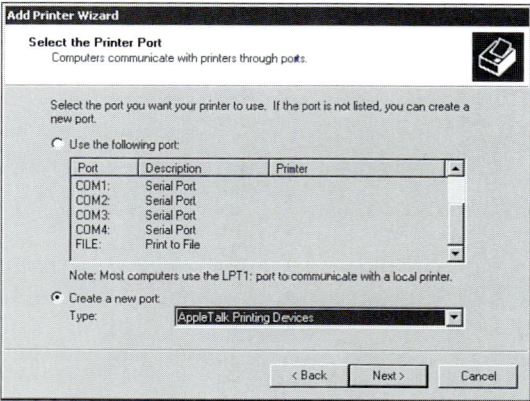

5. In the AppleTalk Printing Devices list, double-click the zone where the AppleTalk printer is located, or expand the list to find other available Apple printing devices. Select the desired device, and click OK.
6. A message box, shown in Figure 19.7, asks if you want to capture the AppleTalk printer. If you click Yes to capture the device, the Windows 2000 Server owns the printer and no AppleTalk clients can connect to it directly. AppleTalk clients must connect through Windows 2000's Print Services for Macintosh, the subject of the next section.

Adding Print Services for Macintosh   801

If you click No, and don't capture the device, Macintosh users and other computers with native AppleTalk support can bypass the Windows 2000 Server's print queue and print directly to the AppleTalk printer.

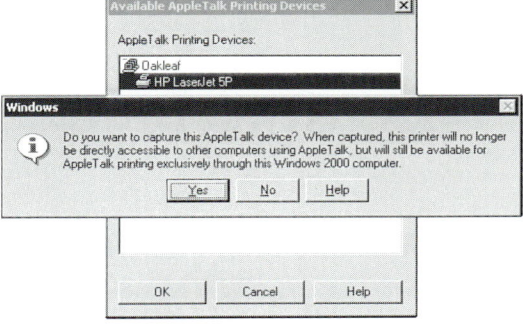

Figure 19.7
Capturing the printer ensures that all printing operations use the Windows 2000 Server's print queue, but might compromise special printer features accessible only to Macintosh printer clients.

Tip from
RJ

> Capture the AppleTalk printer to prevent the casualties of LaserPrep wars—printer performance problems that result from client sending different preparation instructions to the printer, which radically reduces printer throughput. Capturing the printing device also allows the Windows 2000 administrator to monitor all printer jobs in the Windows 2000's *PrinterName* or *ServerName* windows.

7. In the Add Printer Wizard dialog, select your printer type from the list of supported printers and click Next.
8. In the Name Your Printer dialog, type the Windows 2000 name for the printer, select whether to make the printer the default for the server, and click Next.
9. In the Printer Sharing dialog, select Yes to share the printer with Windows clients, and type a share name in the text box. Click Next.
10. In the Location and Comment dialog, type an optional location and comment in the two text boxes. This information is stored in Active Directory and lets users view additional information about this printer. Click Next.
11. In the Print Test Page dialog, select Yes if you want to print a test page on completion. Click Next and Finish to dismiss the Add Printer Wizard and add an icon for the printer to the Printers window.

If you shared your AppleTalk printer in step 9, Windows network clients are able to print to the AppleTalk printer through the Windows 2000 Server by connecting to the Windows 2000 printer share name you supplied.

Part III
Ch 19

Caution

If you have Printer Services for Macintosh installed, you share this printer, and you didn't capture the printer in step 6, the AppleTalk network displays both the Windows 2000 AppleTalk printer share name and the name of the AppleTalk printer on the AppleTalk network. In this case, it's important to choose printer share names carefully in order not to confuse users.

Tip from
RJ

Append or prefix Win2K or W2K to the share name for AppleTalk printers shared by Windows 2000.

Connecting Macintoshes to Windows 2000 Printers

Print Services for Macintosh is focused specifically at providing Macintosh computers on an AppleTalk network with access to printers managed by Windows 2000 Servers.

To install and configure Print Services for Macintosh, follow these steps:

1. Launch Control Panel's Add/Remove Programs tool, and click the Add/Remove Windows Components button to start the Windows Components Wizard.

2. Select the Other Network File and Print Services item in the Components list (see Figure 19.8), and click Details to open the Other Network File and Print Services dialog.

Figure 19.8
You install File and Printer Services for Macintosh through the Windows Components Wizard's Other Network File and Print Services option.

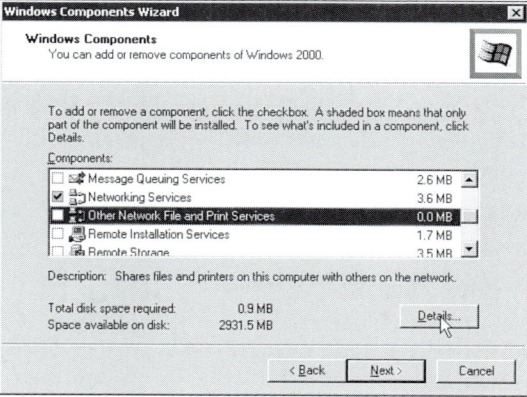

3. Mark the Print Services for Macintosh check box. You also can add File Services for Macintosh at this point. Click OK to close the dialog.

4. Click Next to complete installation of Print Services for Macintosh, and File Services for Macintosh if you selected the latter in the preceding step.

5. Click Finish to dismiss the wizard, click Close to exit the Add/Remove Programs tool, and close Control Panel.

Sharing a Printer

Sharing Windows 2000 printers with Macintosh clients requires installing Print Services for Macintosh. All printers shared on the Windows 2000 network appear to Macintosh clients as shared printers on AppleTalk.

> **Note** You can't share a printer to an AppleTalk network without sharing it to Windows network clients as well. This limitation also applies to Windows NT Server.

Connecting a Macintosh Client to a Windows 2000 Macintosh Printer

After you've set up the Windows 2000 Server to expose printer(s) to the AppleTalk network, the following steps connect Mac clients to the printer:

1. Open Chooser on the Macintosh.
2. Select the zone in which the Windows 2000 Server resides.
3. Select the printer, an Apple LaserWriter for this example, from the Chooser's resource type.

> **Note** Windows 2000 shares the printer to the AppleTalk network as AppleTalk *PrinterName*, in this case AppleTalk LaserWriter. Accessing an Apple printer from Windows 2000 might adversely affect Macintosh clients that need to take advantage of Macintosh-only printer capabilities. If the Macintosh clients must print directly to the printer to access advanced capabilities, don't capture the AppleTalk printer.

4. The name of the shared Windows 2000 printer appears in Chooser's right pane.
5. Select the Windows 2000 shared printer and exit Chooser.

⚠ *If you encounter problems with client connectivity to AppleTalk printers, see the "Macintosh Printer Problems" topic in the "Troubleshooting" section near the end of the chapter.*

Installing, Configuring, and Using File Services for Macintosh

File Services for Macintosh enables a Windows 2000 Server to act as a file server for Macintosh clients. File Services for Macintosh uses AFP, the protocol Macintoshes use to share files. Following are the prerequisites for installing File Services for Macintosh:

- Installation of the AppleTalk protocol and configuration of routing, if your network needs AppleTalk routing.

→ To review the AppleTalk installation and configuration process, **see** "Installing the AppleTalk Protocol," **p. 796**.

- At least one partition or volume formatted with NTFS 5.0 to store files shared with Macintosh clients. You can't share files on FAT partitions with Macs.

Installing File Services for Macintosh

If you didn't install File Services for Macintosh when you set up Print Services for Macintosh, do the following:

1. Launch Control Panel's Add/Remove Programs tool, and click Add/Remove Windows Components to start the Windows Components Wizard.

2. In the Windows Components dialog, select Other Network File and Print Services, and click Details.

3. In the Other Network File and Print Services dialog, mark the File Services for Macintosh check box (see Figure 19.9), and click OK.

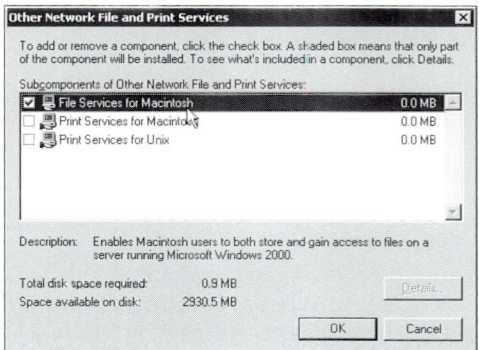

Figure 19.9
Enable File Services for Macintosh in the Windows Components Wizard's Other Network File and Print Services dialog.

4. Click Next to install File Services for Macintosh, click Finish to dismiss the wizard, click Close to exit the Add/Remove Programs tool, and close Control Panel.

Setting System-Wide File Server Parameters

Installing File Services for Macintosh sets default values for five important parameters (property values) that apply to all Macintosh clients that connect to any share on the Windows 2000 Server. The following list describes these property settings and how they affect Macintosh clients:

- Server Name for AppleTalk Workstations—This parameter sets the AppleTalk server name Macintosh clients select in Chooser to connect to the Windows 2000 Server running File Services for Macintosh. The default value is the downlevel (NetBIOS) name of the server.

Tip from

If you intend to move shared folders from a Macintosh server to the Windows 2000 Server, accept the default name. After you verify Macintosh client access to the new files, decommission the Mac server, and change the AppleTalk server name to that of the decommissioned server. Doing this eliminates the need for Mac users to change their server connections.

Installing, Configuring, and Using File Services for Macintosh

- Logon Message—This optional message appears when a Macintosh client connects to the Windows 2000 Server and authenticates correctly. You can use this message to present information such as scheduled server downtime or upgrade information. The default value is no message.

- Allow Workstations to Save Password—A Macintosh client can be configured to save username and password information for each of the shared volumes the client uses. Saving passwords compromises security, because the passwords for Windows 2000 user accounts are stored on clients' fixed disks. You must balance the convenience of simple server logon with the security risk of client-stored passwords. The default value is Don't Allow Saved Passwords.

- Enable Authentication—This option allows you to determine the type of authentication your Windows 2000 Server requires of Macintosh clients. The MacOS supports clear text or encrypted passwords natively. The default value is Apple Clear Text or Microsoft authentication. Clear text lets persons running Network Monitor or other network sniffers to intercept authentication packets and read passwords. Use either AppleTalk's encrypted authentication or Microsoft's authentication encryption for Macintosh.

> **Tip from RJ**
> Select the Microsoft authentication option if your Macintosh users need to be able to log in to different Windows 2000 domains. The Microsoft authentication option allows Macintosh users to log on with domain-qualified account names in the downlevel *DOMAINNAME\UserName* format. Another reason for using Microsoft encryption is storage of Macintosh-encrypted passwords in Active Directory as clear text, which compromises security. Enabling Microsoft encryption on clients is the subject of the next section.

> **Note**
> Versions of AppleTalk used by older MacOS clients don't support the Macintosh or Microsoft-encrypted login options.

- Sessions—This option allows you to limit the number of simultaneous users connected to the file server. This option setting applies only to Macintosh clients and not to Windows clients. The default value is an unlimited number of connections.

To specify the system-wide file server property values, follow these steps:

1. Right-click My Computer, and choose Manage to open the Computer Management snap-in.
2. Right-click the Shared Folders node under System Tools, and choose Configure File Server for Macintosh to open the General page of the File Server for Macintosh Properties dialog with default system-wide property values.

> **Note**
> The property values you set are global to a server. You can't set different property values for individual shared volumes.

806 | Chapter 19 Serving Macintosh, Windows 3.11, and DOS Clients

3. Specify the property values to apply to shared files for Macintosh clients in the General page (see Figure 19.10). The most important setting is Enable Authentication, which defaults to Apple Clear Text or Microsoft (encrypted). Click Apply to set the values.

Figure 19.10
You set values for the five system-wide file-sharing properties in the General page of the File Server for Macintosh Properties dialog. Opening the Enable Authentication list displays the five options for Macintosh user authentication.

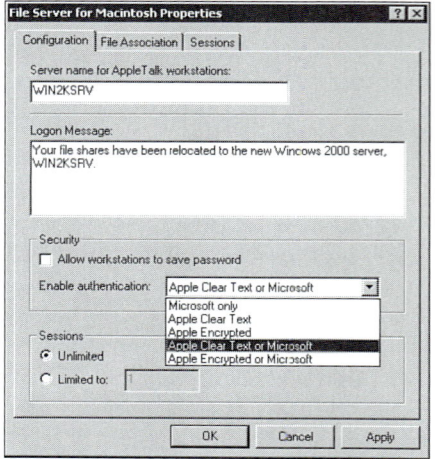

4. Click the File Association tab to display a default set of Macintosh application extensions. You can add or edit extensions, and associate MS-DOS file extensions with Macintosh applications that also have Windows versions.

→ For more information on Macintosh file associations, **see** "Setting File and Creator Types on Shared Files," **p. 812**.

5. Click the Sessions tab to display the number of sessions, open file forks, and file locks applied by Macintosh clients. You also can send a message to all Mac clients by typing the text of the message in the text box and clicking Send.

→ For the details of Macintosh session values, **see** "Monitoring Macintosh Sessions," **p. 814**.

6. Click OK to close the File Server for Macintosh Properties dialog, and close the Computer Management snap-in.

Enabling Microsoft Authentication on Macintosh Clients

When you install File Services for Macintosh on your Windows 2000 Server, setup creates a Macintosh volume in the root directory of your server's C: drive, which is shared as Microsoft UAM Volume. This volume holds a Macintosh executable, which installs a Microsoft-supported authentication extension onto the Macintosh client. The default permissions on this volume allow guest access so you don't need to make changes for your Macintosh clients to be able to connect to this volume.

> **Note**
> If your Macintosh clients have been using the executable from a Microsoft UAM Volume on a server upgraded from Windows NT 4.0 Server, the clients must reinstall the UAM executable.

You must install this authentication extension on your Macintosh clients if you elect to use Microsoft authentication. If you use Apple Clear Text or encrypted authentication, you can skip this section. In order to install Microsoft UAM on your Macintosh, execute the following steps on each Macintosh client:

1. Select Chooser from the Apple Menu.
2. Select AppleShare servers in the left panel. If more than one zone exists on your AppleTalk network, you might need to select the default zone in the lower-left panel. The Windows 2000 Server appears in the default AppleTalk zone.
3. Select the server name in the right panel and click OK.
4. Select the Microsoft UAM Volume. If requested to enter a username and password, type the username and password for a Windows 2000 account on your server.

> **Note**
> Macintosh users are required to enter a valid Windows 2000 username and password if the Guest account on the server has been disabled. The Guest account is disabled by default.

5. Run the Microsoft UAM Installer. This installer checks the current version of AppleShare on your Macintosh client and installs Microsoft UAM only if your MacOS version supports Apple-encrypted authentication.
6. Reboot the client.

ENABLING MACINTOSH USER ACCOUNTS TO INTERACT WITH WINDOWS 2000 ACCOUNTS

A Macintosh client must provide a username and password to connect to an AppleShare server, unless using the Guest account. This username and password can be different for each server, but once a volume is accessed on a server, the username and password are used for all other connections to that AppleShare server. The only way to enter a new username and password for a particular server is to disconnect from all shares on that server.

> **Note**
> The Macintosh username and password connection scheme is almost identical to that used in Windows NT 4.0 networking; once a connection to a share on an NT server is established by a client NT workstation, the credentials used when establishing the session are used for all future connections to that server.

The username and password typed in the authentication dialog on the Macintosh must map to a valid Windows 2000 account. This mapping enables Windows 2000 to determine whether the Macintosh user has access to requested volumes, folders, and files.

SHARING VOLUMES WITH MACINTOSH CLIENTS

Volume is a Macintosh equivalent of Windows' *share*. Volume identifies a network resource that can contain files, folders, or both. Part of the administrator's responsibility when integrating Macintosh clients to the Windows 2000 Server network is to enable sharing of volumes with Macintosh clients.

→ To review basic file sharing operations and Windows 2000 file/folder permissions, **see** "Understanding the Principles of File Sharing," **p. 676**.

The following procedure shares one of the folders (*d:\ShareName\Faculty\Csci*) that's created by running the ADSI25 for Active Directory application on the Windows 2000 Server. The folder contains a single test file, Csci.txt. The procedure adds from a Macintosh client a text file, Grades. Members of the Computer Science Faculty Security Group have read-write access, but members of the Computer Science Major Students Group have only read access to this file. The account used by the Macintosh client to connect to the volume and create the file is CraigGeiger, a member of the Computer Science faculty, with the default ADSI25 password (password).

Tip from
RJ

If you haven't installed ADSI25 on a Windows 2000 Domain Controller (DC), you can create the folder manually and substitute other Security Groups for those described in the procedure. Installing ADSI25 takes only a few minutes. If you've installed ADSI25, but haven't run the Add OUs and Groups operation (or you ran Remove All), add the OUs and Security Groups. Then add a minimum of 25 employee users and 75 student users to create a few user accounts in the Computer Science Faculty and Computer Science Majors groups.

→ For instructions on installing ADSI25, **see** "Installation on a Windows 2000 DC or Workstation," **p. 1259**.

Note

Microsoft provides a command-line utility, Macfile.exe, that you can use to administer File Services for Macintosh. For more information on Macfile.exe, search the index for **macfile**.

To create a sample shared volume for Macintosh users only, follow these steps:

1. Open the Computer Management snap-in, expand the Shared Folders node, right-click the Shares node, and choose New File Share to open the Create Shared Folder dialog.

2. In the Folder To Share text box, type the well-formed path to the folder on the server. Alternatively, click Browse to navigate to the folder. The shared folder must be on an NTFS volume.

3. In the Accessible from the Following Clients frame, mark both Microsoft Windows and Apple Macintosh check boxes if you want to share the folder with all users. For this example, the share is accessible only by Macintosh clients. Changing client access enables the appropriate text boxes.

Installing, Configuring, and Using File Services for Macintosh

> **Caution**
>
> Executing step 3 correctly is extremely important, because Windows 2000 doesn't allow you to later modify the share to add Windows clients to a Mac-only share or vice versa. To alter client types, you must delete the existing share and re-create it, or create a second share only for the new client type(s) you want to support.

4. Type a share name in the Macintosh Share Name text box. For this example, the folder path is **e:\share\faculty\csci**, and the share name is Csci (see Figure 19.11). Click Next.

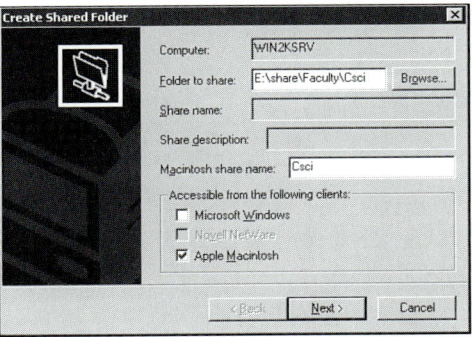

Figure 19.11
The Create Shared Folder dialog lets you specify the type of clients that can access the share. After you make the client type selection, fill in the enabled share-related text boxes.

5. Only the Customize Share and Folder Permissions option is enabled in the second dialog. Click the Custom button to open the Customize Permissions dialog.

> **Note**
>
> You can't set conventional Windows 2000 share permissions for Macintosh clients; only NTFS folder permissions apply to the Mac volume. The General page of the Share Permissions page states, "There are no share permissions for shares accessible from Apple Macintosh clients." After you create the volume, you can set Macintosh-specific properties for the volume, as described in the next section, "Setting Volume Properties."

6. Click the Security tab to display the default set of NTFS permissions, which are inherited from the parent folder or drive.

7. Customize the security on the share by granting the Computer Science group Full Control, the Computer Science Majors group Read & Execute, and Administrators Full Control permissions. Allowing Read & Execute permission also allows List Folder Contents and Read permissions.

8. After adding the permissions for specific groups, clear the Allow Inheritable Permissions from Parent to Propagate to This Object check box to prevent inherited permissions from applying to the volume. Click Remove when the Security message box opens. Figure 19.12 shows the permissions set for the sample volume.

9. Click OK twice to close the two dialogs, and click Finish to complete sharing this folder as a Macintosh volume. Click No when asked if you want to create another shared folder.

Figure 19.12
The Permissions page of the Access Control Settings for Csci dialog shows the permissions granted to the Administrators, Computer Science, and Computer Science Majors Security Groups.

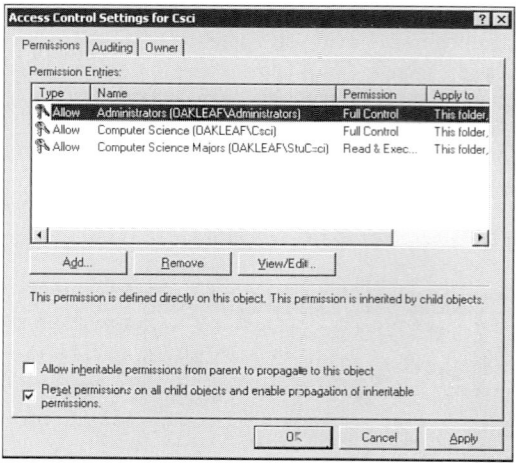

After completing these steps, a volume named Csci appears on the AppleTalk network.

To test Macintosh client access to and permissions for the folder, do the following:

1. Log on to the server from a Macintosh client. For this example, type **CraigGeiger** (a Computer Science faculty member) as the username and **password** as the password.

2. Create a text file in the volume (called Grades for this example), using the Macintosh SimpleText text editor to demonstrate Craig A. Geiger's Write permission.

3. On the server, open My Computer, navigate to the newly added text file, right-click the file's icon, and choose Properties.

4. Click the Security tab of the *FileName* Properties dialog, and click Advanced to open the Access Control Settings for the *FileName* dialog (see Figure 19.13). By default, the permissions on the file are inherited from the folder permissions.

Figure 19.13
Permissions for a file created by a Macintosh client in a shared volume inherit the permissions of the volume.

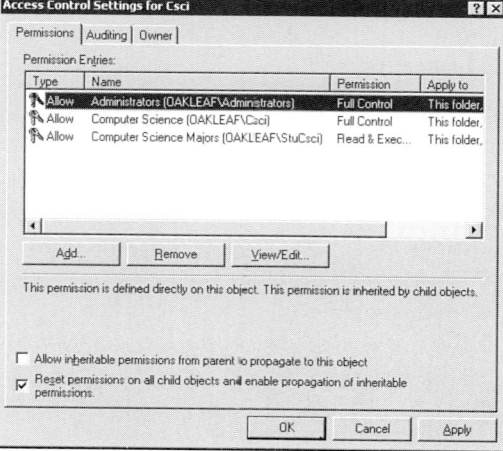

The Computer Science Majors group only has Read & Execute and Read permissions for the text file; Csci faculty and administrative groups have Full Control permission for the file. These permissions were inherited from the containing volume, Csci. If you log on to the Macintosh client as a Computer Science student (for example, MichelleHollowell), you can read the file but not modify it. Clicking the Owner tab shows the owner as CraigGeiger, which demonstrates mapping of the Macintosh user account to the Windows 2000 account.

Setting Volume Properties

You can configure additional property settings on Macintosh volumes, but these settings are not accessible during the initial volume creation. You configure these settings in the volume's Properties dialog. To access the Properties dialog, right-click the volume item in the Shared Folders, Shares node of the Computer Management snap-in, and choose Properties. Figure 19.14 shows the Csci Properties dialog with default volume property values. The Share Name and Path values are read-only.

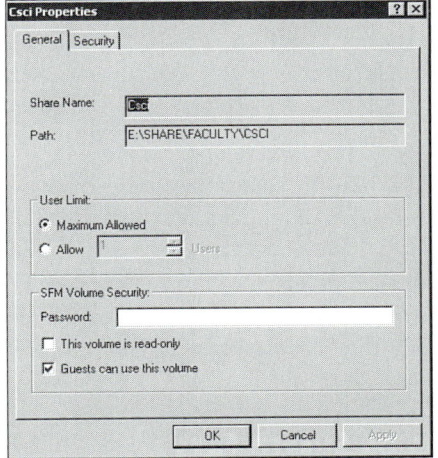

Figure 19.14
The *VolumeName* Properties dialog for a Macintosh volume shows the per-volume properties, which are not accessible during the volume creation process.

Use the following information to set the volume property values:

- *User Limit* limits the number of connections to the share. This limit is independent of the server-wide session-limit value discussed earlier, but the server-wide value prevails if it is set lower than the share limit. To allow an unlimited number of users to connect to the share, select Maximum Allowed, which inherits the server-wide value. To limit the number of concurrent connections, select Allow and type the maximum number of users in the text box.

- *Password* sets a volume password. This feature is useful if you want to allow users to access the share without requiring a user account on the server, but want basic protection for the volume. To set a volume password, type a password into the password field.

- *This Volume Is Read-Only* is a shortcut to specifying that files and folder contents can be read but not modified by Macintosh users. This option can be used to prevent write access on normally writable files, but cannot be used to allow write access on files with read-only permission.

- *Guests Can Use This Volume* allows Macintosh clients to access the volume without entering a username and password. The Windows 2000 Server Guest account must be enabled for this option to function correctly. The Macintosh client must also select Guest Access in the authentication dialog.

When you have selected the volume access properties of your choice, click OK to apply them, and close the Computer Management snap-in.

WORKING WITH THE MACINTOSH FILE STRUCTURE

Macintosh file structures are more complex than those of files in most other operating systems. Unix files, for example, are flat streams of bytes, as are MS-DOS (FAT) files. Each Macintosh file has two regions, called *forks*. The *resource fork* of a Macintosh file holds bitmaps, sounds, executable code, and whatever other resources the program creating the file stores there. The *data fork* of a Macintosh file is where data, such as Microsoft Word documents, end up.

Windows 2000 supports the dual-fork Macintosh file format quite well. Situations occur, however, where Windows 95, 98, or 2000 client machines have problems reading data from files created by Macintosh clients and shared by Windows 2000. The problems are the result of the multi-fork Macintosh file structure—the data the Windows client user seeks might reside in the resource rather than the data fork of the file, and Windows programs open the data fork of files by default. If this situation occurs, you can use a utility like ResEdit on the Macintosh to extract the information from the resource fork and save it to the data fork of another file.

SETTING FILE AND CREATOR TYPES ON SHARED FILES

One of the Macintosh's ease-of-use features is encapsulation of a file's origin into the file itself. The resource fork contains both a File code and Creator code. Each value consists of a four-byte sequence, similar to the four-character code (FOURCC) of Windows .avi files. Windows substitutes file extensions for File codes and Registry entries associated with the File code for the Creator code value. In Windows, for example, double-clicking an .xls file item launches Microsoft Excel.

Windows 2000 Server enables Windows and Macintosh users on an integrated network to exchange data easily by using the Registry database that associates Windows file extensions with Macintosh File and Creator types. Figure 19.15 shows the File Association page of the File Server for Macintosh Properties dialog displaying 12 associations between the XCEL Creator code and various File type codes.

Figure 19.15
The File Association page of the File Server for Macintosh Properties dialog lists a default set of Creator and File (Type) codes for Macintosh applications. You can associate standard MS-DOS file extensions with default entries or new Macintosh association entries you add.

Selecting an entry, such as XLS, in the Files with MS-DOS Extension list and clicking Associate selects the corresponding Macintosh File (Type) code in the With Macintosh Document Creator and Type list.

The Registry stores the file association entries for the With Macintosh Document Creator and Type list in the \HKEY_LOCAL_MACHINE\SYSTEM\CurrentControlSet\Services\MacFile \Parameters\Type_Creators key. The number in the Name column is a unique (primary) key for the file association records. Figure 19.16 shows the association between the XLS3 File type, MS Excel 3.0 Spreadsheet, with the XCEL Creator.

Figure 19.16
Value entries in the ...\MacFile\ Parameters\Type_ Creators key provide the associations between Type and Creator codes. Each association has a unique key value (Name).

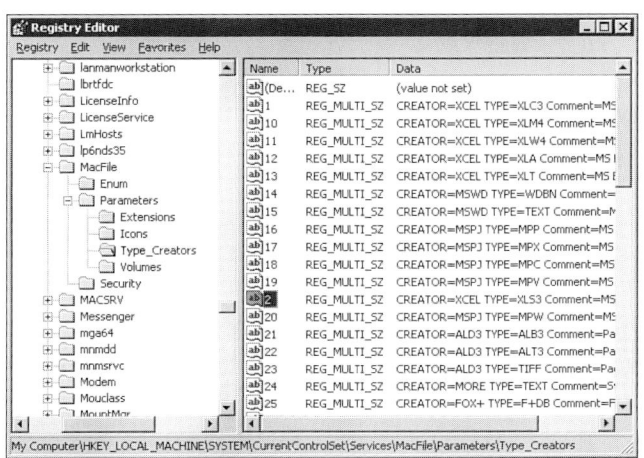

Value entries in the ...\MacFile\Parameters\Extensions key relate MS-DOS file extensions with the File type entry. In this case, the data (ID=) value is the foreign key that matches the Name key of the file association entry. Values in the Type_Creators and Extensions keys have a one-to-one relationship; each extension has only a single corresponding File type, and vice-versa.

You can use the File Association page controls to associate new creators and types with extensions of newly installed programs on your server. The description of this process is beyond the scope of this book; refer to Windows 2000 online help for more information on adding and editing file associations.

Monitoring Macintosh Sessions

Windows NT Server 4.0 offers only rudimentary session monitoring capabilities for Macintosh clients. Windows 2000 adds to those features and exposes session data in a more cohesive manner.

Figure 19.17 shows the session information available in Computer Management. To open this dialog, launch the Computer Management snap-in; expand System Tools, Shared Folders; and click the Sessions node. Items for Windows 9x, NT, 2000, and Macintosh clients appear in the session monitor in the right pane.

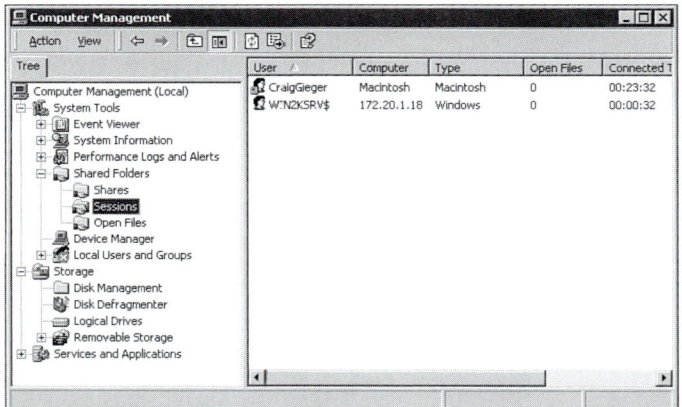

Figure 19.17
The session monitor in Windows 2000 is dramatically improved over that in Windows NT 4.0, especially for Macintosh clients.

You also can monitor file usage in the Computer Management snap-in. Select Open Files under the Shared Folders node to display a list of files opened by all connected users (see Figure 19.18).

Figure 19.18
The Open Files monitor feature of the Computer Management snap-in shows CraigGieger having opened the Grades file. Two entries appear for this file because both the resource and data forks of the file are open.

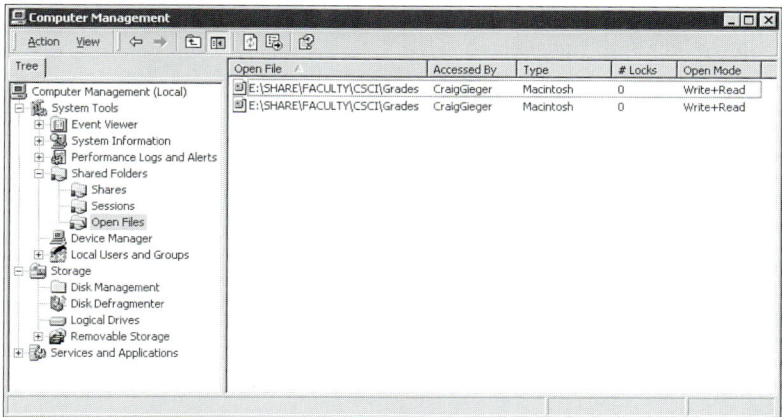

Using Remote Access to Support Macintosh Dial-in Clients

Windows 2000's Routing and Remote Access (RRAS) feature now supports dial-in Macintosh clients. The PPP protocol, a low-level serial protocol that allows multiple simultaneous high-level protocols to share a serial line, handles AppleTalk via modem connections in Windows 2000.

To enable this capability, you must install one or more modems in your Windows 2000 Server, and run RRAS. Enable AppleTalk over PPP for Macintosh dial-in clients by running Routing and Remote Access from the Administrative Tools menu, selecting Configure and Enable Routing and Remote Access to start the Routing and Remote Access Setup Wizard, and specifying Remote Access Server in the wizard's Common Configurations dialog.

Upgrading Windows for Workgroups 3.11 Clients to TCP/IP

As mentioned at the beginning of this chapter, the retail version of WfW 3.11 includes support for NetBEUI and NetWare 3.x networks, but doesn't include the 32-bit protocol stack required for TCP/IP networking. If you upgrade a Windows NT 4.0 PDC that runs NetBEUI, Setup automatically adds the NetBEUI protocol to the Windows 2000 Server. If you perform a clean install (not an upgrade), you can continue to support networked WfW 3.11 clients by adding the NetBEUI protocol to a Windows 2000 DC in each subnet.

Running NetBEUI in an otherwise all-TCP/IP network, however, adds a substantial amount of network broadcast traffic and consumes valuable server resources. NetBEUI isn't routable, and your ability to reconfigure your network is very limited. Thus, you should plan to upgrade your WfW 3.11 clients to TCP/IP and DHCP during your transition to

Windows 2000 Server. Using TCP/IP and DHCP results in a consistent network configuration for all Windows clients.

> **Tip from**
> *RJ*
>
> Don't use Windows NT 4.0's 3.11 version of TCP/IP-32 to upgrade WfW 3.11 clients with disks created by the Network Client Administrator (refer to Figure 19.24). The current version (3.11b) corrects several bugs in the original Microsoft TCP/IP-32 stack.

Microsoft TCP/IP-32 includes most of the Windows 9x TCP/IP command-line tools—arp, ftp, ipconfig, nbtstat, netstat, ping, route, telnet, and tracert. TCP/IP-32 defaults to DHCP for IP address assignment.

OBTAINING THE TCP/IP-32 SETUP FILES

Follow these steps to obtain the required installation files for the current version (3.11b) of Microsoft TCP/IP-32:

1. At the home page of the Microsoft Web site (http://www.microsoft.com), click Support, Knowledge Base to open the Knowledge Base Search page.
2. Select Specific Article ID Number in the I Want To Search By section; type **Q111682** in the My Question Is text box; and click Go to open the Search Results page.
3. Click the Q111682 entry in the list to open the "WFWG 3.11: How to Obtain Microsoft DLC and Microsoft TCP/IP" topic page.
4. Click the Tcp32b.exe link to download the self-extracting archive file to a temporary folder.
5. In Explorer, double-click Tcp32b.exe to extract the files to a server share accessible to networked WfW 3.11 clients. Alternatively, extract the files to an installation diskette.
6. Review the Readme.txt and Mtcpip32.hlp file.

INSTALLING TCP/IP-32

To install TCP/IP-32 on WfW 3.11 clients, follow these steps:

1. Open Program Manager's Network window, and double-click Network Setup to open the Network Setup dialog.
2. Click the Drivers button to open the Network Drivers dialog.
3. Select the network adapter for TCP/IP, if more than one adapter is installed, and click Drivers to open the Network Drivers dialog.
4. Click Add Protocol to open the Add Network Protocol dialog, and select Unlisted or Updated Protocol (see Figure 19.19).

Figure 19.19
Select Unlisted or Updated Protocol in WfW 3.11's Add Network Protocol dialog to prepare for installation of TCP/IP-32.

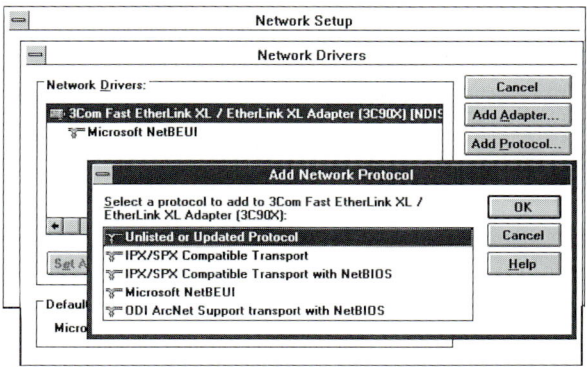

5. Click OK to open the Install Driver dialog. Accept A:\ or navigate to the network share with the TCP/IP-32 files, and click OK.

6. With Microsoft TCP/IP-32 3.11b selected in the Unlisted or Updated Protocol dialog, click OK to copy the required files. The Network Setup dialog displays file copy progress, and returns to the Network Drivers dialog when copying completes.

7. In the Network Drivers dialog, select Microsoft TCP/IP-32 3.11b, and click the Set as Default Protocol button.

8. Click the Setup button to open the Microsoft TCP/IP Configuration Dialog. Mark the Enable Automatic DHCP Configuration check box (see Figure 19.20), and click Yes to close the Microsoft TCP/IP message confirming use of DHCP.

Figure 19.20
Mark the Enable Automatic DHCP Configuration check box to use DHCP for IP address assignment. Specifying IP addresses for Default Gateway and WINS servers override DHCP option values, if set in Window 2000's DHCP snap-in.

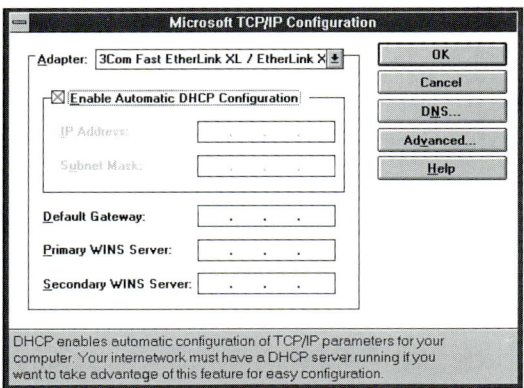

→ To review setting up the Windows 2000 DHCP service, **see** "Configuring DHCP with the DHCP Snap-In," **p. 590**.

9. If you want to override DHCP settings for the subnet's default gateway (router), WINS servers, or both, type the IP addresses in the text boxes.

818 | CHAPTER 19 SERVING MACINTOSH, WINDOWS 3.11, AND DOS CLIENTS

10. To override DHCP DNS settings, click DNS to open the Microsoft TCP/IP Connectivity Configuration dialog. The previously assigned NetBIOS computer name appears in the Host Name text box. Add the domain name, specify the IP addresses of DNS server(s), and add domain name suffixes (see Figure 19.21). Click OK to close the dialog.

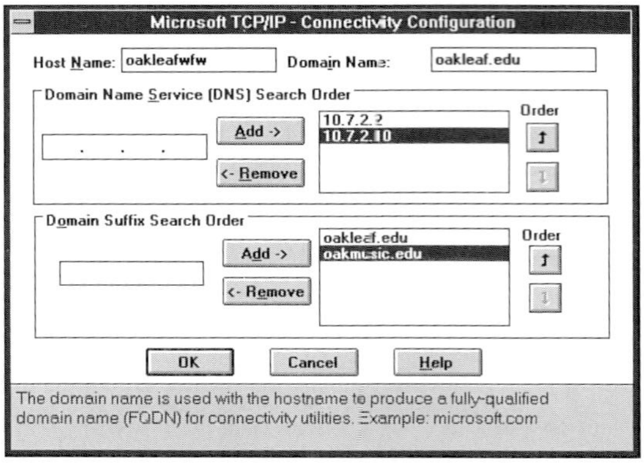

Figure 19.21
DNS settings you add in the Microsoft TCP/IP Connectivity Configuration dialog override DHCP option values.

11. Click Advanced to open the Advanced Microsoft TCP/IP Configuration dialog. Mark the Enable DNS for Windows Name Resolution check box. You can specify up to five default gateway addresses in this dialog (see Figure 19.22). Click OK to close the dialog.

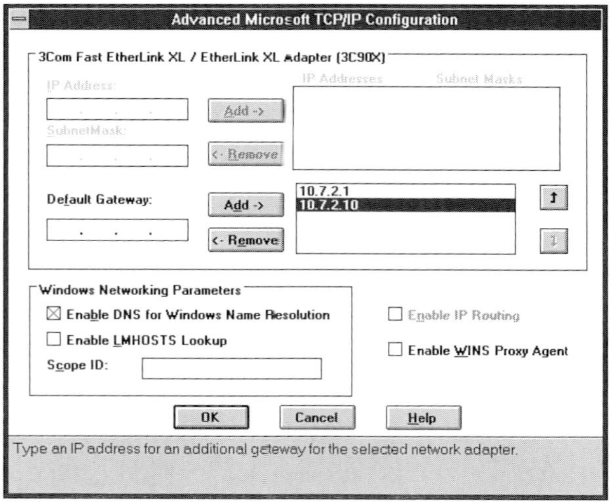

Figure 19.22
Marking the Enable DNS for Windows Name Resolution lets WfW 3.11 clients take advantage of Windows 2000 Dynamic DNS capability.

12. Click OK to return to the Network Drivers dialog. You can remove the Microsoft NetBEUI protocol at this point, if you want. Click Close, and click OK to close the Network Setup dialog.

13. Click OK to acknowledge the message that the SYSTEM.INI and PROTOCOL.INI files have been changed, and click Restart Computer in the second message box. Log on to the network during startup.
14. If you need to change user logon credentials or the default domain name, launch Control Panel's Network tool to open the Microsoft Network dialog. Change the Default Logon Name value, if necessary.
15. Click Startup to open the Startup Settings dialog, which displays settings for former NetBEUI sessions. Change the Domain Name value to the downlevel name of your Windows 2000 domain, if necessary (see Figure 19.23). Close all dialogs, and reboot the client.

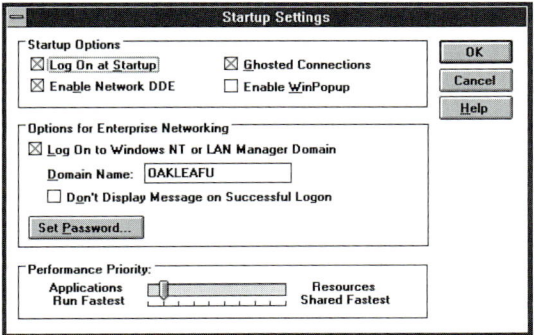

Figure 19.23
Change the default domain name in the Startup Settings dialog. You can change the user's default logon ID before or after changing the domain name.

Tip from
RJ

Remove the NetBEUI protocol from the client at this point to verify TCP/IP connectivity. If the NetBEUI protocol is running on your network, logging on to a DC running NetBEUI doesn't verify that TCP/IP-32 is working correctly.

Testing WfW 3.11 TCP/IP Clients

If your Windows 2000 DHCP server properly leases addresses to Windows 9x, NT, and 2000 clients, you probably won't encounter problems with WfW 3.11 clients failing to obtain a lease. To verify properties of the IP address lease obtained when the client first logs on to the network with TCP/IP, type **ipconfig /all** at the DOS prompt. Following are the IP address and option values for the test client, as set up in the preceding section:

```
Windows IP Configuration

    Host Name . . . . . . . . . : oakleafwfw.oakleaf.edu
    DNS Servers . . . . . . . . : 10.7.2.2
                                  10.7.2.10
    Node Type . . . . . . . . . : Hybrid
    NetBIOS Scope ID. . . . . . :
    IP Routing Enabled. . . . . : No
    WINS Proxy Enabled. . . . . : No
    NetBIOS Resolution uses DNS : Yes
```

```
Ethernet adapter 3Com 3C90x Ethernet:

    Physical Address. . . . . . : 00-50-DA-B1-49-66
    DHCP Enabled. . . . . . . . : Yes
    IP Address. . . . . . . . . : 10.7.2.17
    Subnet Mask . . . . . . . . : 255.255.0.0
    Default Gateway . . . . . . : 10.7.2.10
                                  10.7.2.7
    DHCP Server . . . . . . . . : 10.7.2.2
    Primary WINS Server . . . . : 10.7.2.2
    Secondary WINS Server . . . :
    Lease Obtained. . . . . . . : Mon 12th. Jun 2000  10:13:11 am
    Lease Expires . . . . . . . : Thu 22nd. Jun 2000  10:13:11 am
```

As noted earlier, option values you set in the TCP/IP configuration dialogs override the DHCP values.

To test DNS name resolution, at the DOS prompt type **ping** followed by the fully qualified domain name (FQDN) of the DCs on your network, as well as that of the client. For this example, typing **ping oakleafwfw.oakleaf.edu** and receiving replies verifies DNS registration of the new host.

Adding TCP/IP to the Network Client v3.0 for MS-DOS and Windows

Despite the fact that Microsoft no longer supports MS-DOS, there are a surprising number of networked DOS machines running legacy point-of-sale and other character-based applications under MS-DOS 5.0 and 6.22. Many of these applications—written in dBASE, FoxBase, and Clipper—connect to networked shared-file databases.

Microsoft provides the Network Client v3.0 for MS-DOS 5.0+ and Windows 3.1, which offers optional support for TCP-IP with DOS 5.0+, Windows 3.1, and WfW 3.11. The Network Client's TCP/IP components include DHCP services and basic DOS TCP/IP tools, such as ping and an early version of ipconfig. The sections that follow assume that DOS clients have the Network Client v3.0 installed and run NetBEUI, NWLink for NetWare, or both protocols. Your objective is to replace NetBEUI and (optionally) NWLink with TCP/IP to establish an all-TCP/IP Windows 2000 network.

During initial installation, the Network Client is configured with a computer name, one or more logon IDs (usernames), and the names of the client's domain and workgroup. When you upgrade a Windows PDC to Windows 2000, DOS clients continue to use their logon IDs and passwords for the TCP/IP connection. You must create a new user account for each client if you perform a clean install of Windows 2000 and don't use ADMT to migrate Windows NT groups and user accounts.

CREATING CLIENT INSTALLATION DISKS

If you don't have the second Network Client v3.0 disk handy, which is likely, you need the Windows NT Server 4.0 distribution CD-ROM and two high-density disks to create the two DOS setup disks for installing the Network Client v3.0 for MS-DOS and Windows. Only the second disk is required to add the TCP/IP protocol. If you have the second disk, skip to the next section.

Follow these steps to create the installation disks:

1. If you haven't previously copied the client installation files to a shared \Clients folder for server-based installation, insert the Windows NT Server 4.0 CD-ROM into your CD-ROM drive.
2. From the Windows NT Server 4.0 Start menu, choose Programs, Administrative Tools, Network Client Administrator to open the Network Client Administrator dialog.
3. Select Make Installation Disk Set and click OK to open the Share Network Client Installation Files dialog.
4. In the Path text box of the Share Network Client Installation Files dialog, type the path to the \clients folder. If you use the CD-ROM, type or browse to the *d:*\clients folder, where *d:* is the drive letter for your CD-ROM drive. Select the Use Existing Path option and click OK to open the Make Installation Disk Set dialog.
5. The Network Client or Service list box of the Make Installation Disk Set dialog lets you choose the client drivers to copy. Select Network Client v3.0 for MS-DOS and Windows (see Figure 19.24). Make sure that the disk destination drive is correct, and click OK to create the two disks. If the disks aren't formatted, mark the Format Disks check box.

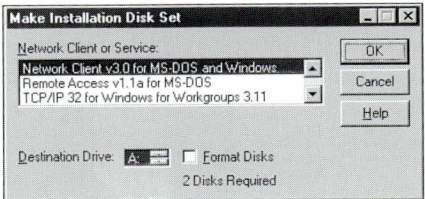

Figure 19.24
Select the Network Client v3.0 for MS-DOS and Windows in the Network Client or Service list of the Make Installation Disk Set dialog.

Tip from
RJ

If you anticipate the need to create additional sets of network install disks, copy the files from the *d:*\clients folder to a \clients folder on your server. Creating a \clients folder is one of the options of the Share Network Client Installation Files dialog.

ADDING TCP/IP TO THE CLIENT FOR DOS

Now that you've created the installation disks, the next step is to install TCP/IP on your Windows 3.1x or DOS client. The following procedure assumes that the client currently uses the NetBEUI or NetWare protocol and the network adapter drivers are installed and operating.

To add TCP/IP as a new protocol, do the following:

1. If you're running Windows, exit to the DOS prompt. You must run the Network Client's Setup program from DOS.
2. Change to the network directory, usually C:\NET, type **setup**, and press Enter.
3. The screen displays a list of the default values for Names, Setup Options, and Network Configuration. Use the arrow keys to select Change Network Configuration, and press Enter. The screen displays under the name of the client's network adapter the current protocol(s) in use.
4. Select Add Protocol and press Enter. Scroll to Microsoft TCP/IP, and press Enter.

Tip from
RJ

Don't delete the only existing protocol before adding TCP/IP. Doing so deletes the entry for the network adapter. Remove the existing NetBEUI, NWLink IPX, or both protocols, if you want, after you add TCP/IP.

5. Select Network Configuration is Correct, select Setup Options, and press Enter to review the Microsoft Client setup options.

Note

If you need to change the logon ID or domain name, highlight the Names option and press Enter. Change the User Name to the new logon ID and the Domain Name to the Windows 2000 downlevel domain name. Change the workgroup name to the domain name, unless you want to permit peer-to-peer networking. After altering the names, use the tab and arrow keys to accept changes.

6. Select The Listed Options Are Correct and press Enter. You are prompted to install the Network Client disk, which is the second disk in this case. When you press Enter, Setup adds the files to support TCP/IP, modifies AUTOEXEC.BAT, CONFIG.SYS, PROTOCOL.INI, and other files.
7. Reboot the computer to start the TCP/IP service, which is implemented by several DOS terminate-and-stay-resident (TSR) programs.

DOS's startup screen for TCP/IP includes the following lines added to those that appear when running NetBEUI or NWLink:

```
Microsoft DOS TCP/IP Protocol Driver 1.0a
Copyright (c) Microsoft Corporation, 1991. All Rights Reserved.
Copyright (c) Hewlett-Packard Corporation, 1985-1991. All Rights Reserved.
Copyright (c) 3Com Corporation, 1985-1991. All Rights Reserved.
Microsoft DOS TCP/IP NEMM Driver 1.0
The command completed successfully.

MS-DOS LAN Manager v2.1 Netbind
Initializing TCP/IP via DHCP....
Microsoft DOS TCP/IP 1.0a
```

If you receive a "Not enough memory" message during network startup, see the "Insufficient Memory to Run DOS TCP/IP" topic of the "Troubleshooting" section near the end of the chapter.

You can verify TCP/IP connectivity by typing **ping** with the numeric IP address the Windows 2000 DCs on the subnet. Running **ipconfig c:\net**, the approximate equivalent of Windows 2000 and WfW 3.11's ipconfig /all, returns the following typical data:

```
IP Address          : 10.7.2.18
Subnet mask         : 255.255.0.0
DefaultGateway0     : 10.7.2.10
DefaultGateway1     : 10.7.2.7
DefaultGateway2     :
DefaultGateway3     :
DefaultGateway4     :
Primary WINS Server : 10.7.2.2
Backup  WINS Server :
Primary DNS Server  : 10.7.2.2
Backup DNS Server   :
Domainname          : oakleaf
Lease issued        : Sun Jun 11 17:24:45 2000
Lease expiry        : Wed Jun 21 17:24:45 2000
Lease length        : 864000 sec. (10 days)
Server ID           : 10.7.2.2
```

Windows 2000's DHCP snap-in displays the entry for the TCP/IP client in the Address Leases node. MS-DOS TCP/IP clients don't display a Name value in the list.

Finally, verify the ability to connect to Windows 2000 and other shared folders by typing **net share * ***servername******sharename* for shares required by the client and for which the logged-on user has appropriate permission.

TROUBLESHOOTING

APPLETALK NETWORKING ISSUES

The Windows 2000 Server can't access AppleTalk resources.

AppleTalk network numbering and named zones are the most common cause of Macintosh connectivity problems. If there's an existing AppleTalk router on the subnet, make sure your Windows 2000 DC AppleTalk adapter settings correspond to those of the router. The network number and zone name must exactly match those established by the AppleTalk router.

Macintosh clients can't authenticate with the Windows 2000 DC.

Installing the Microsoft UAM Volume and running the contained executable on Macintosh clients involves a bit of extra work, but pays long-term dividends. Using Microsoft UAM authentication solves almost all Macintosh authentication issues.

If Macintosh clients can't log on to a DC that's been upgraded from a Windows NT PDC running SFM, users must install a new version of UAM authentication.

Macintosh Printer Problems

Print jobs merge pages from mutiple documents or fail to print on AppleTalk network-attached printers.

The most likely cause of this problem is Mac clients spooling print jobs on the local computer that conflict with jobs spooled by Windows 2000 Server. You must disable local spooling of print jobs on Mac clients to prevent "printer chaos."

To disable spooling on the Macintosh client, run Chooser, select the appropriate printer, and disable background printing.

AppleTalk print jobs arrive at the Windows 2000 spooler, but don't print.

Verify that you've set up the Printer Server for Macintosh service with a valid Startup user account. This user account must have full permissions for the printer.

Insufficient Memory to Run DOS TCP/IP

A DOS "Not enough memory" message occurs after the `Initializing TCP/IP via DHCP....` *message.*

You need to free up DOS low memory by loading some of the executables in high memory. MS-DOS 6.22's MemMaker program automates the process, but you must be careful to load high only SETVER.EXE and NET.EXE. Loading the TCP/IP TSR programs in high memory causes errors. Following are the contents of the DOS 6.22 CONFIG.SYS and AUTOEXEC.BAT files used for testing the DOS TCP/IP protocol with Windows 2000 Server:

```
DEVICE=C:\DOS\HIMEM.SYS
DEVICE=C:\DOS\EMM386.EXE NOEMS
BUFFERS=15,0
FILES=30
DOS=UMB
LASTDRIVE=Z
FCBS=4,0
DEVICEHIGH /L:1,12048 =C:\DOS\SETVER.EXE
DOS=HIGH
device=C:\NET\ifshlp.sys

LH /L:0;1,40352 /S C:\NET\net initialize
LH /L:0;1,45456 /S C:\DOS\SMARTDRV.EXE /X
@ECHO OFF
PROMPT $p$g
PATH C:\NET;C:\DOS
SET TEMP=C:\DOS
C:\NET\netbind.com
C:\NET\umb.com
C:\NET\tcptsr.exe
C:\NET\tinyrfc.exe
C:\NET\nmtsr.exe
C:\NET\emsbfr.exe
LH /L:0;1,976 /S C:\NET\net start
```

With the preceding CONFIG.SYS and AUTOEXEC.BAT files, MEM.EXE reports the following on a computer with 64MB RAM:

```
Memory Type         Total   =   Used   +   Free
----------------    -------     -------    -------
Conventional          640K        182K       458K
Upper                 155K        153K         2K
Reserved              384K        384K         0K
Extended (XMS)     64,357K      2,418K    61,939K
----------------    -------     -------    -------
Total memory       65,536K      3,136K    62,400K

Total under 1 MB      795K        334K       461K

Largest executable program size       458K  (469,264 bytes)
Largest free upper memory block         2K    (2,336 bytes)
MS-DOS is resident in the high memory area.
```

MCSE Corner: Serving DOS, Windows 3.11, and Macintosh Clients

For exam 70-215, "Installing, Configuring, and Administering a Microsoft Windows 2000 Server," you are required to know how to install and configure network services for interoperability. This includes Apple Macintosh clients, although the likelihood of questions on this topic being on the exam is slim.

For this exam, you should be familiar with the AppleTalk protocol and its function, including naming and addressing with numbering and zones. You should be able to install the AppleTalk protocol and configure it with an address. Understanding AppleTalk routing is also helpful. You should also be able to install and configure print services for Macintosh so that Mac clients can print to printers on Windows 2000 servers and Windows clients can print to Mac printers.

You should be able to install File Services for Macintosh to allow Microsoft Authentication on Mac clients and access from Mac clients to files on Windows 2000 servers. Also important is accessing Mac files from Windows clients with File Services for Macintosh.

Finally, you should know how to create client installation disks for MS-DOS and Windows 3.11 clients to allow them access to the Windows 2000 Server resources.

CHAPTER 20

SUPPLYING INTELLIMIRROR AND APPLICATION INSTALLATION SERVICES

In this chapter

Defining IntelliMirror   828

Managing User Settings   829

Providing User Data Management   835

Using the Application Installation Service   846

Setting Up a Typical Software Installation   848

Redirecting Folders   852

Troubleshooting   854

MCSE Corner: Supplying IntelliMirror and Application Installation Services   855

Defining IntelliMirror

For several years, Microsoft has attempted to design a set of features and tools to define and stabilize the user environment of networked PC clients, which Microsoft calls Change and Configuration Management (CCM). Some of the more important elements of CCM are synchronizing client data files with copies stored on servers, maintaining a consistent Start menu and desktop when users change computers, keeping each user's Internet favorites, and the like. These CCM tools are all designed for one purpose—productivity. The more consistent a user's environment remains, the more productive he or she becomes. This concept of maintaining a consistent user environment, which originated in Zero Administration Windows (ZAW) and the Zero Administration Kit (ZAK) for Windows NT 4.0, gains a new Windows 2000 name: IntelliMirror.

> **Note** The full set of IntelliMirror features are available only to Windows 2000 clients, so taking advantage of new CCM functions within an organization requires upgrading all clients to Windows 2000 Professional. Setting PC upgrade priorities is certain to be a major economic and political issue in medium- to large-size firms.

IntelliMirror isn't a singular service that you start and stop with Control Panel's Services tool. IntelliMirror is a framework for several other Windows 2000 services. Windows 2000 provides a full suite of technologies that work together to keep the user environment consistent and stable despite network outages or workstation changes. In order to accomplish its objectives, IntelliMirror integrates the following four functions:

- User settings management
- User data management
- Software installation and maintenance using the Application Installation Service, which uses the Windows Installer
- Remote Installation Service

This chapter covers the first three topics; Remote Installation Service is the subject of the next chapter.

All the IntelliMirror components rely on Windows 2000's Active Directory (AD) and Group Policies in effect on your Windows 2000 network. You need a clear understanding of AD and group policies before delving into IntelliMirror services.

> **Note** Chapter 3, "Introducing the Active Directory and LDAP" and Chapter 4, "Optimizing Your Active Directory Topology," cover AD basics. It's recommended that you read those chapters first if you're new to the Active Directory. Group Policies from the server perspective is one of the subjects of Chapter 15, "Establishing Group Policies, User Accounts, and Logons."

Following are the six basic components of IntelliMirror:

- Group Policies—Group Policies administer the user's environment and are at the core of the IntelliMirror Services. This chapter covers Group Policies from the Windows 2000 client perspective.
- Offline Files—Offline Files let users continue to work with network files, such as Word documents or Excel worksheets, when not connected to the network.
- Synchronization Manager—The Synchronization Manager service ensures that the Offline Files are synchronized with the most recent versions of files and that the changes made by the user are replicated to the network copy when the user reconnects to the network.
- Disk Quotas—Disk Quotas allow administrators to keep track of and control their users' disk usage.
- Roaming User Profiles—Roaming User Profiles provide a familiar desktop environment to the user when the user moves between computers.
- Windows Installer—Windows Installer delivers all necessary applications to the user, regardless of which Windows 2000 computer he uses. Users also can install optional, published applications.

Managing User Settings

IntelliMirror user settings management ensures that your users always receive their correct user and computer settings along with any files necessary to make them functional. IntelliMirror is not concerned with whether the settings are mandatory settings made by the administrator or personal preferences of the user, only that the settings always are available to the user.

User settings management is accomplished with the following elements:

- Group Policies—These ensure the settings on your users' computers are correct.
- Roaming User Profiles—These ensure that your users have their user environment settings no matter what computer they use.
- Offline Files—These ensure that your users have the files they need to utilize those settings, no matter what computer they use.

Group Policies

Group Policies are used by IntelliMirror to ensure that your users' computer settings are correct no matter what computer at your site they log in to. If the computer settings are not correct, then no amount of data or application mirroring will gain your users the access to files that they need. This means that all of your basic computer settings should be inherently specified as well as your basic user settings.

As noted in Chapter 15, user and computer Group Policies are applied in the following order:

1. Windows NT 4.0-style system policies (NTConfig.pol) for compatibility with Windows NT 4.0 clients. You can disable applications of Windows NT system policies by selecting Disable System Policy in the Group Policy Editor's Administrative Templates, System, Group Policy node.

→ For more information on system policies for Windows NT and 9x users, **see** "Implementing Downlevel System Policies," **p. 663**.

2. Local Group Policies.
3. Site Group Policies.
4. Domain Group Policies.
5. Organizational unit (OU) Group Policies.

The further down this list that your policy resides, the higher its priority. Domain Group Policies take precedence over settings in the site Group Policies which take precedence over settings in the local Group Policies. Group Policies are cumulative—that is, policies set at lower priority levels apply to higher levels, unless you specifically override lower-level policy settings. This means that you must be careful where you place each of your policy settings in the hierarchy.

→ For more information on the hierarchy of Group Policy application, **see** "Group Policy Hierarchy and Inheritance," **p. 620**.

Settings for each Group Policy Object (GPO) reside in a pair of Registry.pol files, one for user settings and one for computer settings. The client downloads the contents of each applicable computer Registry.pol file and combines their Registry settings into a local Registry.pol file stored in the \Winnt\System32\GroupPolicy\Machine folder. The local Registry.pol file adds its entries to the Registry's HKEY_LOCAL_MACHINE root key. When a user logs on, the client combines the Registry entries from the user-related Registry.pol files into the \Documents and Folders*Username*\Ntuser.dat file that contributes its entries to HKEY_CURRENT_USER. Figure 20.1 illustrates the sequence of applying GPO settings for computers and users. Windows NT system policies are applied only if they exist on an upgraded Primary Domain Controller (PDC) and you haven't set Disable System Policy with the Group Policy Editor.

→ For a review of Registry subkeys, **see** "Understanding Important Root Keys, Keys, and Subkeys," **p. 466**.

Managing User Settings | 831

Figure 20.1
Windows 2000 applies computer GPOs when the user boots the client, and applies user GPOs when the user logs on to the domain. Group Policy settings propagate to Registry entries in the HKEY_LOCAL_MACHINE and HKEY_CURRENT_USER root keys.

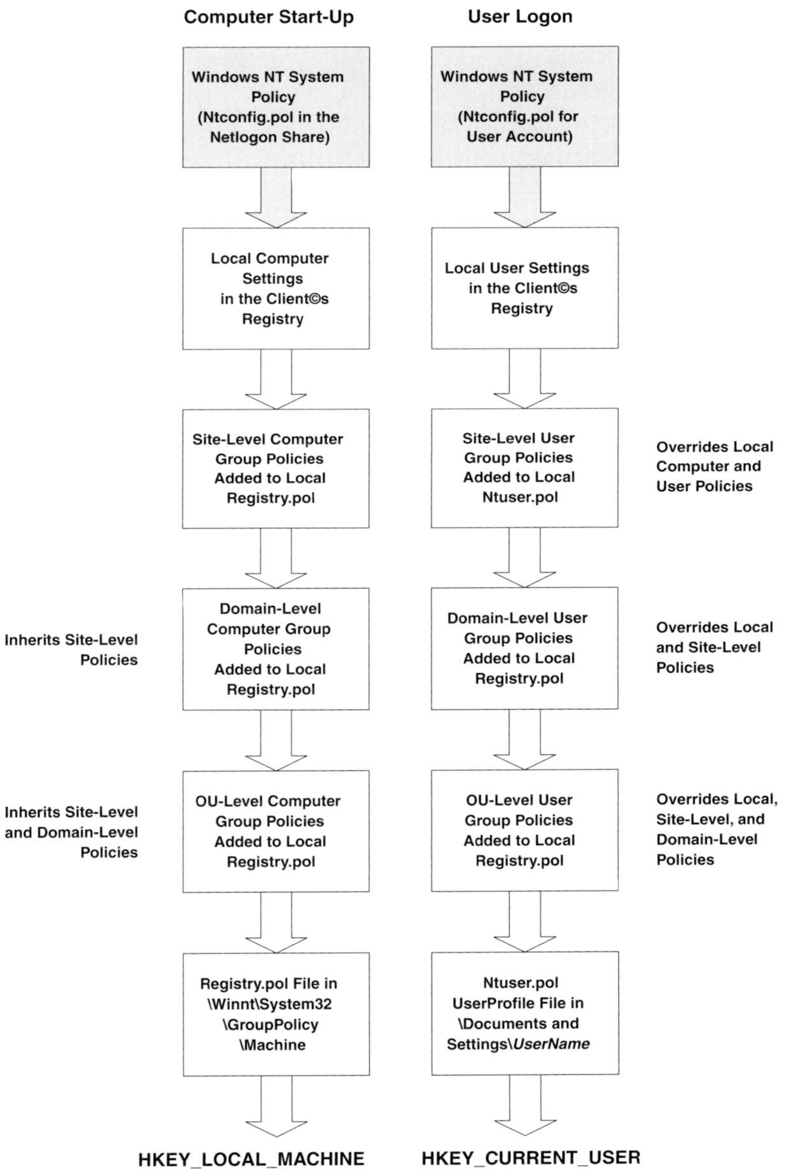

Chapter 15 contains specific information on how to set up Group Policies. This chapter contains guidelines to make your Group Policies most effective with IntelliMirror. The objective of IntelliMirror is to provide a consistent environment to your users, regardless of the workstations they use, their application needs, or how they connect to the network. Maintaining consistent Group Policies makes IntelliMirror services much easier to implement and maintain.

SITE GROUP POLICY

If you have only a single site, a default policy for every user and computer in your site should be created at the site Group Policies level. If you have multiple sites, it's a better practice to create your initial Group Policies at the domain level. The site-level policy should be the absolute minimum set of enforced items you want to be sent to every user with the exception of administrators. To create this policy, think about what *every* user in your site must have access to, be restricted from, and have specified in his or her computer/user settings. This set of policies is for your users, not administrators; keep in mind that in this policy you are establishing a set of *no exceptions* policies. Once you've created a set of policies that work for every user in your site—with the exception of administrators—you have a good site Group Policy and are ready to set up domain Group Policies if you have multiple domains in the site.

> **Tip from** *RJ*
>
> Group Policy filtering allows you to prevent application of restrictive Group Policies to administrators.

→ To review how to exempt members of the Domain Admins and other administrative groups from Group Policies, **see** "Filtering GPOs with Security Groups," **p. 650**.

> **Caution**
>
> Avoid using No Override or Inheritance Blocking in your policies. The use of No Override in your site policy causes you not to be able to override settings for your systems administrators or developers who need the freedom to escape those policies. Use of Inheritance Blocking causes administrative confusion, because it overrides the standard hierarchical structure. Try to set up your policies in such a manner that the natural inheritance provides an acceptable environment at the user level without the use of No Override or Inheritance Blocking.

DOMAIN GROUP POLICY

In most organizations, domains are divided functionally. These functional divisions often are defined by workgroups, such as Development, Sales, and Finance. In other organizations these functional divisions are by the type of services provided by the domain, such as Mail, Internet, and Database. If your domains are of the workgroup type, then domain Group Policies serve you well. If they are organized by service type, don't use domain Group Policies; rely on site-level and organizational unit policies.

After establishing the policies for your site, you need to determine the minimum set of enforced settings for every user in your domain. Again, when developing a domain-level policy, consider users, not administrators. Administrators' policies are set at the organizational unit level or by Group Policy filtering.

Don't duplicate domain settings from the site Group Policy at the domain level. If a setting already exists from the site Group Policy for an item, make sure that policy is set to Not Configured in the domain-level Group Policy. Setting the policy to Not Configured passes through the settings from the site Group Policy. If this causes an undesirable result for your users, then the site Group Policy isn't correctly configured and should be adjusted accordingly.

ORGANIZATIONAL UNIT GROUP POLICIES

The OU Group Policies are the settings that most directly affect your users. In an organization where there are many users who perform the same job functions and don't need to change their desktop settings or install new software, the OU Group Policy is where you can restrict users' desktops to only display the elements they need and to standardize their environment to have a common look and feel.

The first OU Group Policy to create is for the OU that contains members of the Domain Admins group. In this policy you want to remove any restrictions to changing computer or desktop settings that you applied in previous policies. This is the only time that you will want to specifically set every policy item so that the other policies are not passed down.

For other OUs, set applicable items while avoiding duplicating settings from the site- or domain-level Group Policies. With well-configured site and domain Group Policies, it shouldn't be necessary to override higher-level policies.

ROAMING USER PROFILES

Roaming User Profiles allow your users to log in to any computer in your domain and keep their desktop settings, start menu configuration, Internet Explorer favorites, and many other user-specific settings. This saves a lot of time for the users because it makes their computing environment consistent regardless of what computers they log in to.

To establish Roaming User Profiles you must provide disk space on a server for the profile information to be stored. This area usually is called a User Area and is shared as Users. Once you have an area set aside on your server for the user profiles, you can make users' profiles roam by putting the path to the users' profile directories into the Profile Path of their User accounts. You can establish a common mandatory profile for users in a particular OU or provide each user with an individual user profile in his or her home directory.

→ For instructions on how to set up typical user profiles, **see** "Establishing Mandatory User Profiles," **p. 660** and "Common Versus Individual Home Folder Shares," **p. 670**.

→ To enable users of mandatory profiles to store the contents of their My Documents folder on a server, **see** "Redirecting Folders," **p. 852**.

HOW ROAMING USER PROFILES WORK

Once the profile path is entered in a user's account, the next time the user logs on to the network, Windows 2000 automatically searches the designated profile folder on the server for the Ntuser.dat file in the location specified by profile path. This file contains the entire HKEY_CURRENT_USER Registry root key for the user. If the file isn't found, the client defaults to the local computer's Ntuser.dat file, which contains entries from applicable user GPOs, to obtain its settings. If this file isn't found, Windows 2000 creates a new profile from the default user profile in the \Documents and Settings\Default User folder of the local computer. If Ntuser.dat is found on the server, its contents merge with the content of the HKEY_CURRENT_USER Registry root key. Figure 20.2 illustrates the logon process for roaming profiles.

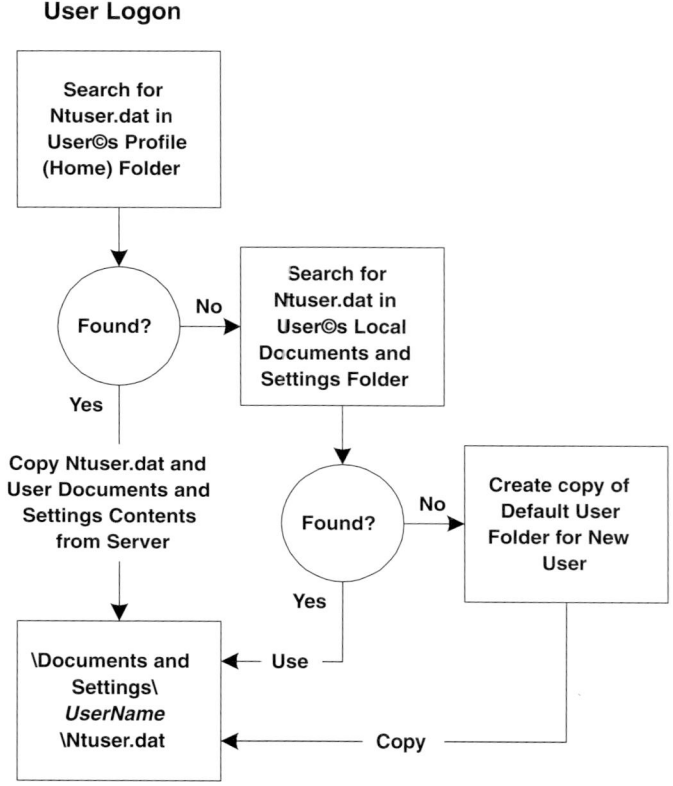

Figure 20.2
If a user has an existing roaming profile, its contents are copied to the client PC. Otherwise, the PC uses the local user profile, if it exists. If the user has no roaming profile and no local profile, Windows 2000 creates a copy of the Default User profile for the user.

At this point, a local profile folder exists on the client, whether Windows just created it or found the profile on the server. During the user's session, all changes to the profile are maintained in this local folder. When a user with an individual profile logs off the network, the entire profile—including the Ntuser.dat file and all other contents of your profile directory (Temporary Internet Files, My Documents, SendTo, and the like)—are copied to the user's profile (home) folder. If the user is assigned a mandatory profile, Windows copies all but Ntuser.dat and My Documents to the user's home folder. Figure 20.3 illustrates the logoff process.

Figure 20.3
When the user with a roaming profile logs off, Windows 2000 copies the contents of the user's local profile folder to the user's profile folder on the server. Ntuser.dat and the My Documents folder aren't copied if the user is subject to a mandatory profile.

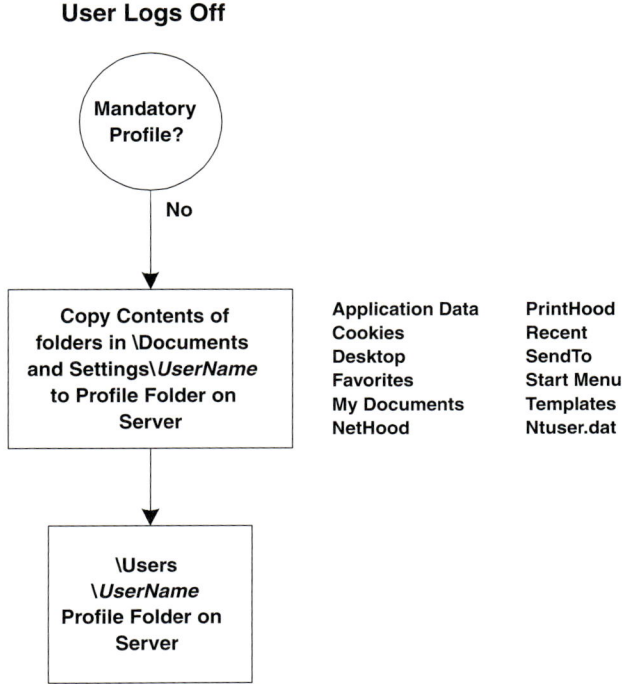

Tip from
RJ

Set quota limits in the range of 20MB to 40MB for individual user profiles. Copying the server-stored profile to the local profile can cause long logon and logoff times as the size of profiles expands.

→ For more about establishing disk quotas, **see** "Disk Quotas," **p. 844**.

Providing User Data Management

IntelliMirror defines user data management as providing your users with access to their data regardless of network connectivity. Offline Files, managed by the Synchronization Manager, store copies of server-based files locally to make the files available to users when disconnected from the network. Disk Quotas maintain records of the amount of server file storage users consume and limit the amount if necessary. Roaming User Profiles also provide access to some data files while offline. These IntelliMirror features, described in the sections that follow, ensure that your users have access to their personal data files at all times.

Offline Files

Offline Files make your users' files available to them even when the network is not. In the context of user settings management this means that any files necessary for user settings (.ini files, logon scripts, and so forth) are available regardless of network connectivity. The versions of the files differ as a result of any changes made after a user last synchronized his files with the server. Synchronization is covered later in the chapter.

Setting Up Offline Files on Your Server

To set up Offline Files for a single user or all members of a Security Group, you must first share a folder specifically for this purpose. You can use a folder that you already have shared or create a new one and share it. Offline Files shared by all members of a workgroup or project-based Security Group are useful for collaborative projects.

To enable a folder to support Offline Files, do the following:

1. In My Computer or Explorer, create a new folder, if necessary.
2. Right-click the folder, choose Properties, and click the Sharing tab. For a new folder, select the Share This Folder option, and complete the Share Name and Description text boxes.
3. Click Permissions to open the Select Users, Computers or Groups dialog. Select or type the individual user or the Security Group(s) who have access to the share, and click OK. Then set appropriate permissions for the user or Security Group(s).
4. Click Caching to open the Caching Settings dialog, and select the type of caching for clients to use (see Figure 20.4). The default caching type, Manual Caching for Documents, is the best choice for most users.

Note You can clear the Allow Caching check box later to disable client caching of files in the share.

5. Click OK twice to return to My Computer or Explorer.

Following is a description of each of the three caching methods:

- Manual Caching for Documents—This method caches only those files that the user specifically selects to use offline. This method uses the fewest resources on client computers but might result in some important files not being available offline.

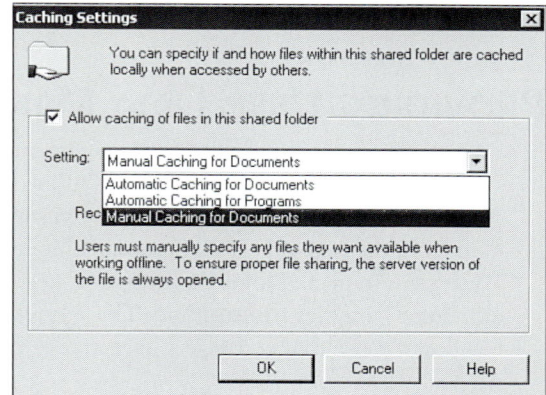

Figure 20.4
Choose one of the three Offline Files caching methods for the shared folder.

- Automatic Caching for Documents—This method automatically caches any file that the user opens in the folder, but doesn't cache unopened files. This is an alternative that ensures availability of necessary documents while not caching every file in the shared folder.
- Automatic Caching for Programs—This method is designed for folders that contain read-only information, such as application installations, help files, and the like. This option caches the entire contents of the directory to each user's hard drive, so use this option sparingly.

SETTING UP OFFLINE FILES ON WINDOWS 2000 PROFESSIONAL CLIENTS

By default, the client side of Offline Files is enabled for Windows 2000 Professional and, as expected, disabled on Windows 2000 Server. To specify how the Windows 2000 Professional clients handle Offline Files, do the following:

1. Launch My Computer or Explorer, and choose Tools, Folder Options to open the Options dialog.
2. Click the Offline Files tab to display the default settings for the user's handling of cached file shares (see Figure 20.5).

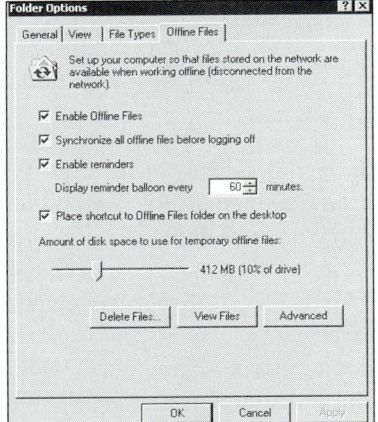

Figure 20.5
The Offline Files page of the Folder Options dialog displays default user settings for cached file shares.

The controls of the Offline Files page provide users the following options:

- Synchronize All Offline Files Before Logging Off—Ensures that any files that have changed during the user's online session are copied to the local hard drive before disconnecting from the network. Users with read/write access to files should mark this check box.

- Enable Reminders—Places an icon in the user's taskbar when he or she is disconnected from the network. A balloon reminding the user that he or she is offline appears at preset intervals. Set the reminder time period by using the spinner buttons. Users with permanent network connections should mark this check box; mobile users of laptop PCs should clear the check box.
- Place Shortcut to Offline Files Folder on the Desktop—Places on the desktop a shortcut to the Offline Files Folder. The Offline Files folder offers a list of all Offline Files and their current synchronization status.

Note

The default cache size for Offline Files is 10% of your available drive space. You can change this setting in the Offline Files page of the Folder Options dialog. Most users will need about 100 MB of space for offline files but space requirements may vary depending on the size and quantity of documents that users need when offline.

Tip from
RJ

The default storage area that Windows 2000 Professional uses to store Offline Files is the root of C:\ drive. You can change the location of offline files to another folder or drive with the Offline Files Cache Mover (cachemov.exe) application of the Windows 2000 Professional Resource Kit.

The Advanced settings are covered in the next section.

SPECIFYING OFFLINE FOLDER BEHAVIOR

Clicking the Advanced button of the Offline Files dialog opens the Offline Files - Advanced Settings dialog that allows you to select how your client will respond to a server going offline. You can select Notify Me and Begin Working Offline to be notified that one or more of the servers sharing cached files is offline, and begin working offline. If you prefer to never go offline, even if the server is offline, choose Never Allow My Computer to Go Offline, meaning the network files are never available when you lose network connectivity. The settings that you choose here are default settings for how your client will react to servers going offline. You can add specific computers to be exceptions to this default behavior.

Exceptions are useful for servers whose files should not be used while offline. Different users may need different servers available offline so each client must be set up individually with exceptions. For example, users in accounting might need the accounting files available when they are offline but never need the sales files server when offline. To configure exceptions on a client workstation, do the following:

1. Click the Advanced button to open the Offline Files - Advanced Settings dialog.
2. Click the Add button in the Exception List frame to open the Offline Files - Add Custom Action dialog.

3. Type the computer name of the server for the current exception. A Browse button makes it easier to find the computer that you want to add to the list.
4. Select the action to occur when the specified server goes offline (see Figure 20.6).
5. Repeat steps 2, 3, and 4 for each server for which the client needs an exception.
6. Click OK three times to close all open dialogs, save your changes, and return to Explorer or My Computer.

Figure 20.6
You specify Offline Files client exceptions for specific servers in the Offline Files - Add Custom Action dialog.

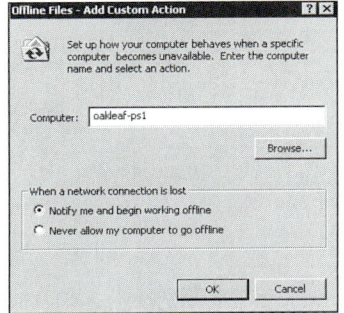

MAPPING OFFLINE FILES TO LOGICAL DRIVES ON CLIENTS

Mapping a server file share with caching enabled to a logical drive on a Windows 2000 Professional client is similar to that for ordinary shares. To map a cached folder share (Anthro for this example) to a client logical drive and view the result of the mapping in the client's Offline Files folder, do the following:

1. In My Computer or Explorer, choose Tools, Map Network Drive to open the Map Network Drive dialog, browse to the server share (\\oakleaf-dc1\anthro), and click OK to add the logical drive (F:\) and close the dialog.

> **Note**
> When the user maps a cached file, the Synchronization Manager window opens automatically to perform an initial file synchronization. The time required for synchronization depends on the size of the file, but usually is very brief.

2. Double-click the mapped drive icon to display the shared cached file(s). The icons for cached shares and files have a shortcut box with a double arrow at the lower left (see Figure 20.7).

Figure 20.7
Windows 2000 identifies shared folders and files with caching enabled by a double arrow symbol at the lower left of their icons.

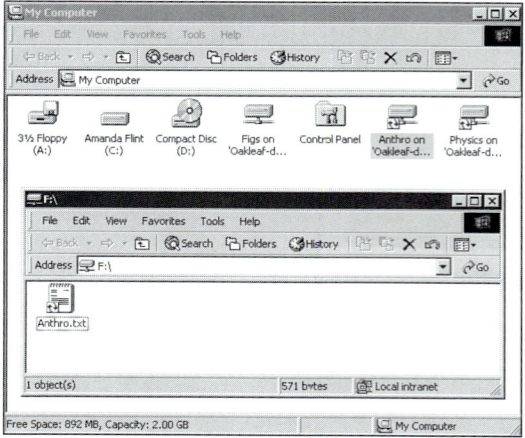

3. Repeat step 2 for each cached folder to which the client requires access.
4. Double-click the Offline Files desktop shortcut you added in the preceding section to open the Offline Files window. Each Offline file you added in steps 3 and 4 appears as an item in the file list.
5. Double-click one of the items in the Offline Files list to open the file for editing (see Figure 20.8).

Figure 20.8
The Offline Files window displays a list of the shared cached files and allows the user to open a file by double-clicking it.

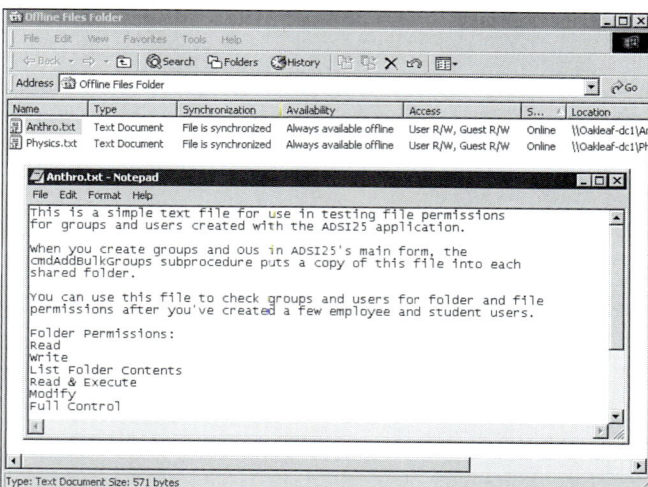

Managing Offline Files Synchronization Conflicts

There are several conflicts that can arise when more than one user uses the same file offline:

- When the user synchronizes files that he or she had opened or updated while offline, the files are compared to the files on the network. If the file on the network was not changed while the user was offline, then the updated file is simply copied from the user's computer to the server. Conflicts arise if another user modified the file while the first user was offline. If the file on the network was modified, then the last user is prompted to make a choice; he or she may keep his or her version, keep the version on the server, or keep both. This is an area in which your users must be educated in order to prevent lost work. In most cases, it's probably wise to save both but most users will have a tendency to save their own.

- Another type of conflict that can arise is when someone deletes a user's cached file from the server. In this case, the user may save his or her version of the file to the server in place of the file that was deleted. This feature also can cause some confusion to users, but doesn't cause data loss when the user chooses to save the file.

- If a user deletes an offline file on his or her computer while offline, but someone else modifies the network copy of the file, the file remains on the network, but is removed from the computer from which it was deleted.

- If a user is offline and another user creates a new file in a shared network folder that you have made available offline, the file follows the caching rules to determine whether or not the new file is copied to offline computers during synchronization on reconnection. Manual Caching for Documents only copies (caches) new documents to a computer if the user specifically requests caching of the document. Automatic Caching for Documents copies to file to the user's computer only if he or she opens the document.

Synchronization Manager

Synchronization Manager is the engine that performs comparisons of users' Offline Files with their networked counterparts. Synchronization Manager updates the user's computer with the most recent copies of the files while connected and then places the modified files onto the server when the user goes offline.

Synchronization Manager controls when the user's Offline Files are synchronized with the server copy. You can set synchronization to happen every time the user logs on or off the client computer (or both), while the user's computer is idle, or at scheduled times. You can set various combinations of these options for offline files from different shares and under different network connectivity conditions.

To modify which items are synchronized, how often they are synchronized, and by which method, do the following:

1. On a Windows 2000 Professional client, choose Start, Accessories, Synchronize to open the Items to Synchronize dialog.
2. Select or clear the check boxes of the cached folders to synchronize (see Figure 20.9).

Figure 20.9
Users specify the cached folders to synchronize in the Items to Synchronize dialog.

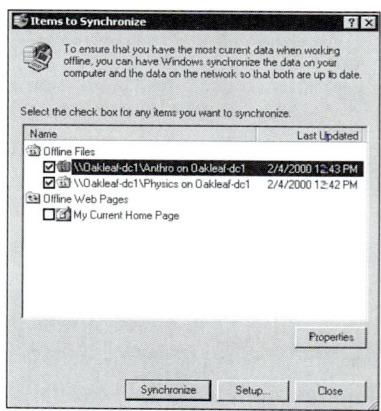

3. If the user's computer is connected to the network, click Synchronize to perform an immediate synchronization.

4. Select one of the folders under the Offline Files node, and click Setup to open the Synchronization Settings dialog's default Logon/Logoff page. Mark or clear the When I Log On To My Computer or When I Log Off My Computer check box, or both to suit the user's requirements (see Figure 20.10).

Figure 20.10
Specify the folders to synchronize on user logon and logoff in the Logon/Logoff page of the Synchronization Settings dialog.

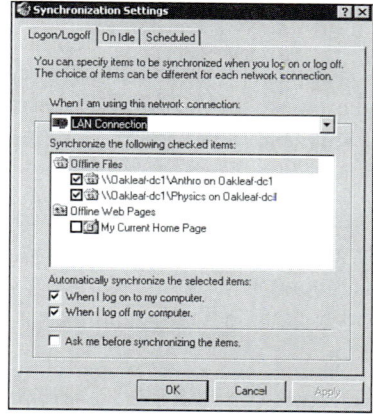

Note

If the user has established dialup connections in My Network Places, you can select different options for dialup and the LAN Connection. Select the type of connection in the When I Am Using This Network Connection list, and specify the options for each connection.

5. If the user needs more frequent synchronization than that offered by the Logon/Logoff page, click the On Idle tab, mark the Synchronize the Selected Items While My Computer Is Idle check box, click the Advanced button, select the folder in the list, and set the synchronization frequency in the Idle Settings dialog (see Figure 20.11).

Providing User Data Management 843

Figure 20.11
To synchronize files more frequently than user logon/logoff, use the Idle Settings dialog to synchronize files during inactivity of the client PC.

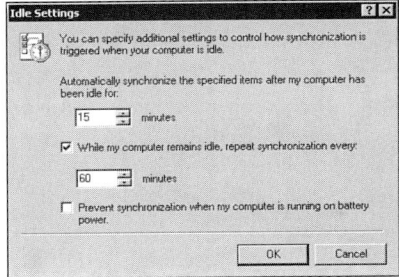

6. If the user needs access to very large files that change infrequently, click the Scheduled tab, mark the folder(s) to schedule synchronization, and click Add to start the Scheduled Synchronization Wizard. Click Next to bypass the first dialog.

7. In the Wizard's second dialog, mark the folder for scheduled synchronization (see Figure 20.12). Mark the If My Computer Is Not Connected When This Scheduled Synchronization Begins, Automatically Connect for Me check box for users with dialup connections. Click Next.

Figure 20.12
Use the Scheduled Synchronization Wizard to cause synchronization of large files to occur at a time when network activity is low or dialup connections incur minimum cost.

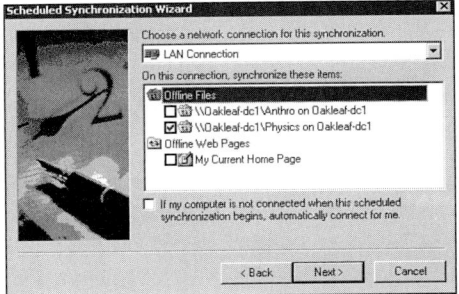

8. In the Wizard's third dialog, set the time at which synchronization is to occur, the frequency of synchronization, and the date on which scheduled synchronization is to start (see Figure 20.13). Click Next.

Figure 20.13
Set the user's synchronization properties.

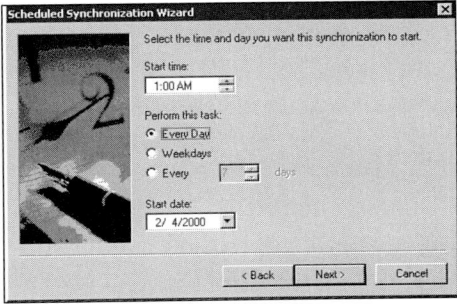

PART
III
CH
20

9. In the fourth dialog, type a meaningful name for the schedule in the text box, and click Finish to dismiss the Wizard and add the schedule to the list of the Scheduled page.

10. Click OK to close the Items to Synchronize dialog and save the user's changes.

> **Tip from**
> *RJ*
>
> You can apply multiple synchronization options to cached folder(s). The Logon/Logoff, Idle, and Schedule settings are additive, not exclusionary.

 If you encounter problems synchronizing Offline Files, see the "Offline Files and Synchronization Manager Problems" topic of the "Troubleshooting" section near the end of the chapter.

DISK QUOTAS

Disk Quotas allow you to monitor and control the amount of disk space that your users consume on your servers. Disk quotas are useful to administrators in a variety of scenarios—billing clients for usage, monitoring departmental usage, or limiting home page sizes on Web servers. With IntelliMirror, quotas are most useful for limiting the size of user profiles. Several improvements in Windows 2000 make Disk Quota management more useful than many third-party quota management applications for Windows NT. Only partitions formatted with NTFS 5.0 support Disk Quotas.

Quotas are set on a per-volume basis, which means that you can set a quota on an entire drive such as your D:\ drive but not on a specific folder on that drive. You must keep this in mind when setting your quotas, because often the users have access to multiple shared folders on any given server volume.

TURNING ON QUOTA MANAGEMENT

To set or view quotas you must be logged in as a member of the Administrators group of the server. To manage quotas, open My Computer, right-click the icon of any NTFS 5.0 volume, select Properties, and then click the Quota tab. Mark the Enable Quota Management check box to enable the other controls on the page (see Figure 20.14).

Figure 20.14
The Quota page on a server volume's properties dialog holds all controls for Quota Management.

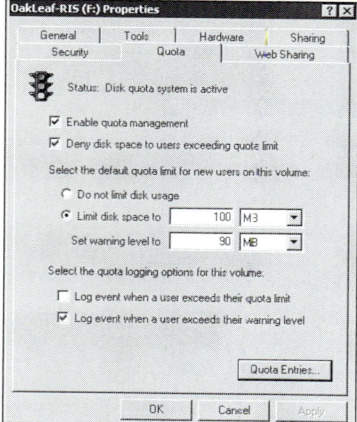

If you don't want to set limitations on your users but need to track usage for billing, statistical, or general curiosity purposes, select the Do Not Limit Disk Usage option.

Set your quota in the Limit Disk Space To text box and units dropdown list. Set the level at which you notify users of an impending freeze on disk space usage in the Set Warning Level To text box and units list.

Tip from RJ	Remove Full Control from your users and give them all other rights to their profile/home folders. The only difference between Full Control and setting all other rights is the ability of users to change permissions on the folders and files. If you allow users Full Control, they can remove your Administrator access to their folders. In this case, you must take ownership of the folder and all files that it contains to regain control of the folder. If you take ownership of the folder, Quota Management doesn't subtract the size of these files from the user's quota. Instead, the size is deducted from the Administrator's quota, because Quota Manager determines disk space usage based on the owner of the files. By default, however, the Administrator account is exempted from quotas on any drive.

The last two options are for logging quota events to the Windows 2000 event log. If you want to log an event when users reach the warning level, select Log Event When User Exceeds Their Warning Level. Similarly, to log an event when users reach the quota limit, select Log Event When User Exceeds Their Quota Limit.

If your user profile folders reside on a separate volume from other data, set quotas for the volume with user profiles. Setting a 10MB or 25MB quota keeps profiles from growing too large and causing excessively long logons and logoffs.

Note	You can set your global setting to Do Not Limit Disk Usage so that by default your users are not limited on a volume and then turn on limits for individual users in the Quota Entries dialog. You can also set your global setting to Limit Disk Space To and turn off limits for individual users in the Quota Entries dialog. Viewing and setting individual quotas is the subject of the next section.

Tip from RJ	It can take a long time to scan a volume when you set up quotas, so you may want to turn on quota management for all your volumes before enforcing any limits. If you need quota limits at a later date, you can turn on the limits without a re-scan of the entire volume.

VIEWING AND SETTING INDIVIDUAL QUOTAS

To view the information collected by quota management, click the Quota Entries button located at the bottom of the Quota page of the properties dialog for the partition (refer to Figure 20.14). When you open the Quota Entries window, it takes a few seconds to load a few user account names, and much longer to load a few hundred or thousand names. Once the usernames are loaded you can manage individual quotas from this window (see Figure 20.15).

Figure 20.15
Use the Quota Entries window to add and adjust quotas for individual users.

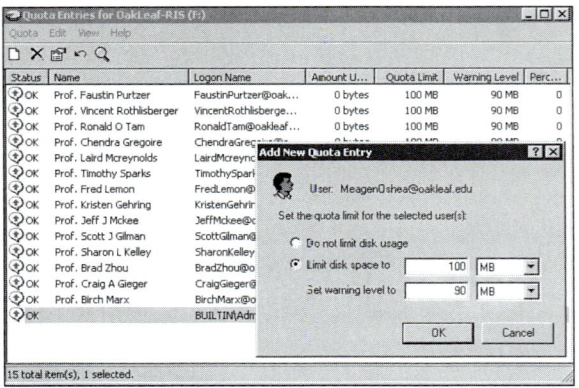

In the Quota Entries window, you can change individual user quota properties, such as increasing, decreasing, or disabling quota limits. You also can delete individuals from the quota list but only if the user account you want to delete isn't the owner of any files on the volume.

From the Quotas menu you can add new individual entries, import quota settings from other volumes, or export your settings to other volumes. For example, choose Quotas, New Quota Entry to open the Select Users dialog. Select the user(s) for whom to establish a quota with uniform settings. When you click OK to close the dialog, the Add New Quota Entry dialog appears to let you set limits for the user(s) you add.

> **Tip from**
> *RJ*
>
> Be careful not to surprise your users with quotas just because they're available in Windows 2000 Server. Implement quotas carefully so that you don't disrupt your users' workflow. Implementing 20MB limits on your users in order to ensure your servers don't run out of disk space isn't a good idea if your company president is currently using 35MB. Warn users in advance that the limitations are coming and, if feasible, set the standard quota at or above the current maximum that any of your users are using.

 If you have difficulties with user quota management, see the "Disk Quota Problems" topic of the "Troubleshooting" section near the end of the chapter.

Using the Application Installation Service

Conventional 32-bit Windows applications use the Setup.exe file, a collection of installation helper files, plus the executable and other files required by the particular application being installed. For example, the Windows NT version of the ADSI25 for Active Directory application in the \Seuw2ks\ADSI25 folder of the accompanying CD-ROM requires Setup.exe, Setup.lst, Ads_nt.exe, and Adsi25.cab to complete the installation on Windows NT 4.0 SP4+. Adsi25.cab is a compressed cabinet (archive) file that contains the executable and source code, and many other files required to run the application. Complex applications, such as Microsoft Office 2000, require copying several hundred individual files during installation.

The Application Installation Service allows you to make prepackaged software installations available to your users as a single Microsoft Installer (.msi) file. Prepackaged means that you set some or all of the installation options in order to standardize installations in your environment. The ADSI25.msi file for installation of ADSI25 under Windows 2000 is a typical example of a Microsoft Installer file. Windows 2000 Server's Administrative tools (Adminpak.msi) in your \Winnt\System32 folder is another example of a Microsoft Installer file.

Group Policies and the Windows Installer service let you specify packages to be automatically installed when the user logs on (required or mandatory applications) or made available for users to choose to install (published applications). One of the most innovative features of this service is that packages can be set to associate themselves with certain file extensions (such as .doc for Microsoft Word) and only install if the user attempts to open a document having that extension. Another advantage of using the Windows Installer service is that you can automatically repair, upgrade, or remove previously installed applications.

The Application Installation Service is tied directly to AD. All settings for packages to be distributed are made in Group Policy page of the properties dialog for the domain or OU to receive the application and in the Group Policy Editor.

→ For an overview of Group Policy settings and use of the Group Policy Editor, **see** "Client Computer and User Settings," **p. 618**.

REQUIREMENTS OF APPLICATION INSTALLATION SERVICE

Windows Installer delivers all of its features only for .msi files, so you need a Microsoft Installer version of the application. Providing an .msi file for use by Windows Installer is one of the requirements of Microsoft's "Certified for Windows" program. When Microsoft released Windows 2000, there were only a few certified applications that met the requirements of the Desktop Specification 1.0a or Server Specification 1.2. You can download copies of these two specifications from `http://msdn.microsoft.com/certification/appspec.asp`. VeriTest is the independent testing organization Microsoft has selected to award the "Certified for Windows 2000 Logo." You can learn more about VeriTest's certification process at `http://www.veritest.com/mslogos/windows2000/`.

The lack of certified status doesn't prevent developers from providing .msi versions of their applications. Microsoft offers a no-charge add-on to Visual Studio 6.0 called the Visual Studio Installer 1.0 for creating Windows Installer versions of Visual Basic, Visual C++, Visual J++, and Visual Interdev applications. The installer is included on the Windows 2000 Developer Readiness Kit CD-ROM, which you can order from `http://msdn.microsoft.com/vstudio/downloads/vsi/ordering.asp`. You also can use Veritas's WinINSTALL Limited Edition (LE) application that's included in the \ValueAdd\3rdParty\Mgmt\ Winstle folder of the Windows 2000 Server distribution CD-ROM to create .msi files from existing applications. Creating .msi files is beyond the scope of this book.

Some Windows Installer packages include .mst transform files to customize installations without having to rebuild the .msi file. The .mst file is the equivalent of the answer file(s) used for conventional unattended installations of operating systems and applications. You also can assign or publish application patches—bug-fixes or minor upgrades—with .msp files.

You can shortcut the .msi process by using a ZAP file. A ZAP file is a simple text file with a .zap extension, which is similar in structure to a Windows initialization (.ini) file. The .zap file specifies the network path to the Setup.exe program for an application. If you only need to install the application's executable file, and don't need online help or other support files for the application, you can specify the application's .exe file and, optionally, a file extension association. For example, if you have a site license for Niko Mac Computing's WinZip and want to publish the setup program for the beta version of WinZip 8.0, use Notepad to create a Winzip8b.zap file with the following text:

```
[application]
FriendlyName = "WinZip 8.0 Beta"
SetupCommand = \\ServerName\ShareName\AppName\Wzbeta32.exe
DisplayVersion = 8.0
```

Like .msi files, you specify the .zap when publishing the application. You can't assign ZAPped applications to users, nor automatically upgrade, repair, or remove the application.

Setting Up a Typical Software Installation

To set up a test installation using the Application Installation Service to publish or assign Adminpak.msi to every member of the Domain Admins group for your domain, regardless of the computer he or she uses, do the following:

1. Create a server share to hold the .msi and other files for applications that you want to assign or publish.

2. Copy the .msi, .mst, .msp, .zap, or other Windows Installer file(s) to the shared folder or a subfolder named for the application. For this example, Adminpak.msi is copied to the \Shared\Apps folder of the oakleaf-dc1 domain controller, shared as InstallApps.

3. Launch Active Directory Users and Computers, right-click the domain node (oakleaf.edu), and choose Properties. Click the Group Policy tab, and then click New to add a new domain-level Group Policy. Rename New Group Policy Object to a more descriptive name, such as **Administrator Assigned Apps**.

4. With the new Group Policy selected, click Edit to open the Group Policy Editor with the new GPO loaded. Expand the User Configuration, Software Settings node (see Figure 20.16).

5. Right-click Software Installation, and choose New, Package to open the Open dialog. Type the UNC network path and filename of the .msi file (**oakleaf-dc1****InstallApps**\ **Adminpak.msi**) in the File Name text box, and click Open to close the dialog and open the Deploy Software dialog.

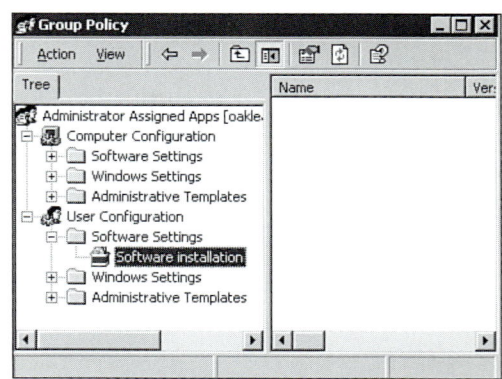

Figure 20.16
The Software Installation node of the Group Policy Editor for the new GPO is where you specify the network location and name of the package to assign or publish.

SETTING UP A TYPICAL SOFTWARE INSTALLATION | 849

> **Caution**
> You must use the UNC path and filename to specify the location of the .msi file for the application to assign or publish. If you specify a local drive, folder, and filename, then installation fails.

6. In the Deploy Software dialog, select the Assign option to make installation mandatory (see Figure 20.17) or Publish for optional applications that you want to appear in Control Panel's Add/Remove Software tool. Click OK to close the dialog. After many seconds, an entry for the package appears in the right pane of the Group Policy Editor.

7. Double-click the newly added package item to open the *ApplicationName* Properties dialog. The General page lets you rename the package. Click the Deployment tab to explore other package properties (see Figure 20.18).

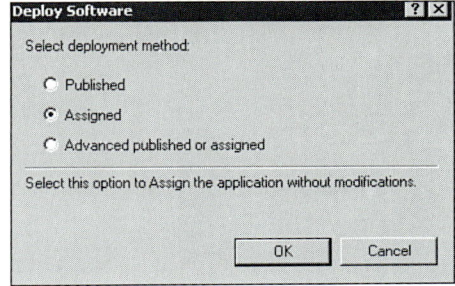

Figure 20.17
Select the installation method (Assigned or Published) in the Deploy Software dialog. Advanced Published or Assigned enables you to specify additional package properties.

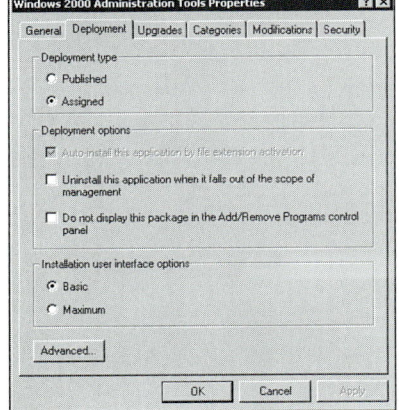

Figure 20.18
After adding a package to assign or publish, you specify deployment and other properties in the package's properties dialog.

VIEWING AND CHANGING PACKAGE PROPERTIES

The Deployment page enables you to change whether the package is published or assigned, and select other deployment options for the package. The options of the deployment page are

- Deployment Type—Select Published or Assigned. Published means that the package will be made available but is not mandatory for the user to install. Assigned means that the package installation is mandatory.

- Auto-install This Application by File Extension Activation—Marking this check box causes file extension(s) for the packaged software to be associated with the package, and start menu shortcuts that the software creates are placed in the Start menu. The remainder of the package (including the application files) isn't installed on the client until the user either selects the application from the start menu or opens a file associated with the application. This check box is disabled for assigned applications.

- Uninstall This Application When It Falls Out of the Scope of Management—When application installation services are used in conjunction with the other IntelliMirror services for application management, marking this check box removes the application automatically when it is no longer managed by the Application Installation Service.

- Do Not Display This Package in the Add/Remove Programs Control Panel—Marking this check box prevents the application from appearing in Add/Remove Programs. This selection is useful to prevent users from uninstalling the application.

- Installation User Interface Options—Select Basic or Maximum. Selecting the Basic option minimizes the dialogs presented to the user during installation; maximum display all installation dialogs.

Clicking Advanced on the Deployment page opens the Advanced Deployment Options dialog (see Figure 20.19), which offers the following choices:

- Ignore Language When Deploying This Package—Marking this check box deploys packages in the language of the computer on which the application resides, rather than other languages specified for the clients.

- Remove Previous Installs of This Product for Users if Not Installed by Group Policy-Based Software Installation—Marking this check box removes prior installations not specified by a Group Policy. This ensures that all installations are standardized by removing the software that a user installed.

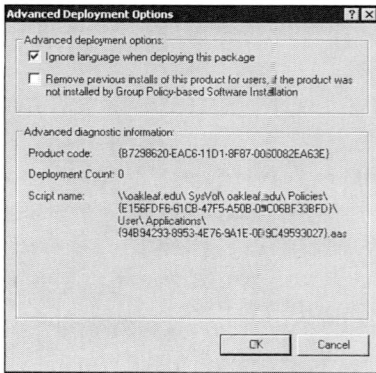

Figure 20.19
The Advanced Deployment Options dialog offers two additional installation options.

You seldom need to alter settings in the other four pages of the *ApplicationName* Properties dialog, unless you're installing a complex or special-purpose application. Following are brief descriptions of the remaining four pages of the dialog:

Setting Up a Typical Software Installation

- The Upgrades page allows you to designate prior versions of the software that the current package upgrades or replaces, or packages that upgrade the application.
- The Categories page classifies published applications in Control Panel's Add/Remove Programs tool. The Categories page isn't active for assigned applications.
- The Modifications page contains a list of transform files applicable to the package, if required.
- The Security page lets you set security on the application object. These security settings don't apply to the GPO, folder, file, or share.

Completing and Testing the Software Installation

To complete and test installation of an assigned application, do the following:

1. Close the *ApplicationName* Properties dialog and the Group Policy Editor to return to the Group Policy page of the *DomainName* Properties dialog.
2. Select the Group Policy for the application installation, click Properties to open the *GroupPolicyName* Properties dialog, and click the Security tab.
3. Select each group having the members to whom you want to distribute the application, and mark the Apply Group Policy check box in the Permissions list. By default, Group Policies don't apply to Domain Admins and Enterprise Admins. The sample Adminpak.msi installation is intended for administrators, so you must mark the Apply Group Policy check box for these two groups (see Figure 20.20).
4. Select each group whose members should not receive the application, and clear the Apply Group Policy check box. For this example, clear the Apply Group Policy check box of Authenticated Users.
5. Click OK twice to close the two Group Policies dialogs and return to Active Directory Users and Computers.
6. Log on to a domain workstation with Domain Admins or Enterprise Admins credentials. During the login process, an "Applying Software Installation Settings" message appears.
7. If you chose to assign the application, verify that the Programs menu includes a choice (Administrative Tools) for the newly added application.

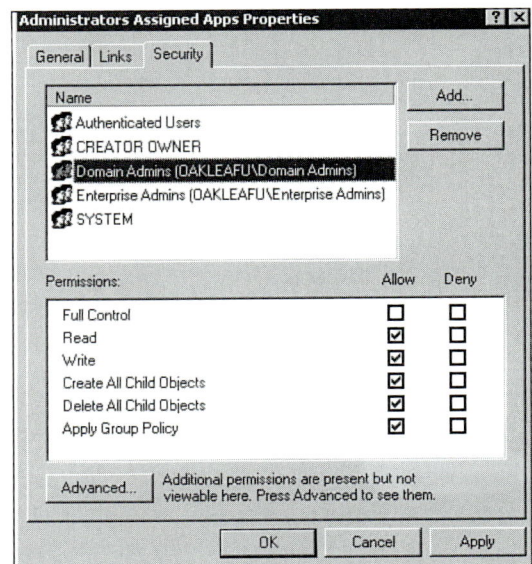

Figure 20.20
Determine the groups to receive the assigned or published application by marking or clearing the Apply Group Policy check box for each group.

For published applications, verify that the application appears in Control Panel's Add/Remove Programs list.

 If you encounter difficulties with installing applications, see the "Application Installation Service Problems" topic of the "Troubleshooting" section near the end of the chapter.

REDIRECTING FOLDERS

Technically, Folder Redirection isn't an IntelliMirror feature, because Roaming User Profiles perform a similar function to Offline Folders. If you assign a mandatory profile to users, however, users don't automatically save the contents of their My Documents and other Documents and Settings folders to their home folders. Administrators commonly use folder redirection to maintain users' important documents only on a server, which assures regular backup of each user's files.

Once you move the user's Documents and Settings files to the server, the user is dependent on a functioning network connection and server to perform almost any useful work on his or her workstation. The alternative is to copy the users' Documents and Settings folders to the server, but this results in users having different versions of documents and settings in two locations. If you want users to have synchronized file copies on their local computer and the server, use IntelliMirror's Offline Files feature, not Folder Redirection.

→ For a brief discussion of Folder Redirection in the overall Group Policy context, **see** "Exploring User Configuration," **p. 631**.

Folder Redirection applies to the following subfolders of the Documents and Settings (local profile) folder:

- Application Data
- Desktop
- My Documents and, optionally, its My Pictures subfolder
- Start Menu

In most cases, redirecting only the My Documents folder is the best practice, and you should redirect only My Documents when employing mandatory user profiles. If you redirect the Application Data, Desktop, or Start Menu folders, loss of a server connection might prevent the user from gaining access to local applications. It's not common to redirect the My Pictures folder because of the very large size of the bitmap files stored by users of digital cameras.

Caution

Exclude all laptop computers from Folder Redirection. If you move Documents and Settings subfolders to a server share, laptop users won't have access to the contents when disconnected from the network. Provide Offline Files for laptop users.

To redirect any of the Documents and Settings subfolders to users' home folders, do the following:

1. Launch Active Directory Users and Computers, and right-click the domain or OU node that contains the user accounts whose folders you want to redirect. If you use site-level Group Policies, launch Active Directory Sites and Services, and right-click the site.

2. Choose Properties to open the *ContainerName* Properties dialog, the `oakleaf.edu` domain for this example, and click the Group Policy tab.

3. Select an existing Group Policy or click New to add a new policy, and click Edit to open the Group Policy Editor. Expand the User Configuration, Windows Settings, Folder Redirection nodes to display the list of folders you can redirect.

4. Right-click the folder to redirect (My Documents for this example), and choose properties to open the *FolderName* Properties dialog.

5. To apply Folder Redirection only to members of particular Security Groups or specify a different server for particular groups, select Advanced - Specify Locations for Various User Groups in the Setting list.

6. Click Add to open the Specify Group and Location dialog, click Browse to open the Groups dialog, and double-click the Security Group to which Folder Redirection applies.

7. In the Target File Location text box, type the UNC path to the server share to store the folder, followed by `\%username%` (see Figure 20.21), and click OK.

8. Repeat steps 6 and 7 for each Security Group needing folder redirection, and then click the Settings tab.

9. In the Settings page, select the options to apply to folder redirection for the groups you specified in steps 6 through 8. Figure 21.22 shows the most commonly selected options.

10. Click OK to close the *FolderName* Properties dialog to save your new settings. Select another folder to redirect or click OK to close the Group Policies dialog.

Figure 20.21
Specify the UNC path to the user's home folder to store redirected folders for individual Security Groups.

Log on at a workstation as a user in one of the security groups you selected, and verify that the user My Documents folder appears in the *\\ServerName\ShareName\UserName* folder.

Figure 20.22
Set the Folder Redirection options to apply to the selected group.

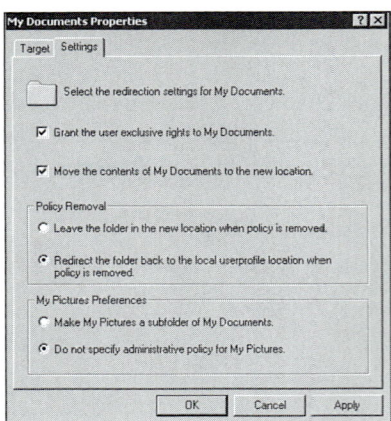

TROUBLESHOOTING

OFFLINE FILES AND SYNCHRONIZATION MANAGER PROBLEMS

User files don't synchronize with those on the server.

Check the settings of the Synchronization Manager on the user's workstation to ensure that it is enabled and correctly configured to synchronize the files. Also ensure that the user has access to the files on the server.

DISK QUOTA PROBLEMS

User files don't deduct from disk quotas.

Check the ownership of the files in question. The most likely problem is that the Administrator owns the files. Give the user access to the Take Ownership privilege for the files, and then have the user assume the Creator Owner role.

APPLICATION INSTALLATION SERVICE PROBLEMS

After removing a remote installation package, the application becomes unusable by any users, even those who had previously installed it.

Most likely when removing the application package from remote installation you selected Uninstall from Clients. This is the default option for removing applications. Select Prevent Future Installations rather than Uninstall from Clients if you want your users to be able to continue to use the application. Otherwise, the only solution is to have the users manually reinstall the application from server share or re-create the package.

The remote installation package doesn't install.

Check the properties of the package, and ensure that you specified the file location by its full UNC path. Verify that the share containing the .msi file is accessible to the user. Also check to make sure that the user has sufficient rights on the workstation to install the application. You can test accessibility and user rights by navigating to the share containing the .msi file and performing a manual installation on the client.

MCSE Corner: Supplying IntelliMirror and Application Installation Services

IntelliMirror and the services it provides are covered on several exams, including 70-215, "Installing, Configuring, and Administering Microsoft Windows 2000 Server," 70-217, "Implementing and Administering a Microsoft Windows 2000 Directory Services Infrastructure," and 70-219, "Designing a Microsoft Windows 2000 Directory Services Infrastructure." For each of these exams it is important to understand exactly what IntelliMirror is and all the services that it entails. The exams test the features of IntelliMirror separately, but understanding how all the services work together will help you understand the individual services. You should be familiar with working with offline files and folders, although it is not explicitly listed in these exam blueprints.

70-215 Installing, Configuring, and Administering Microsoft Windows 2000 Server

User profiles and disk quotas are the two topics related to IntelliMirror and covered in this chapter that are tested on this exam. You should have an understanding of the use of user profiles in a non-directory–enabled environment (that is, standalone servers and workstations), because this exam covers only servers configured as member servers and not domain controllers. You also need to be able to configure disk quotas using quota management and to monitor disk quotas.

70-217 Implementing and Administering a Microsoft Windows 2000 Directory Services Infrastructure

You need to have a complete understanding of working with group policies for this exam. You need to be able to create group policy objects for various containers, such as organizational units, and to configure behaviors, such as inheritance, for these group policy objects. You should be able to apply the newly created group policy objects by configuring user settings and environments, and you should be familiar with configuring roaming user profiles. You should also be very familiar with the Remote Installation Service and how to use group policy for Application Installation. The exam requires you to be able to deploy and maintain software with group policies and use Remote Installation Services to deploy Windows 2000. You should also be familiar with using group policies to apply security policy to users and computers and managing network configuration.

70-219   Designing a Microsoft Windows 2000 Directory Services Infrastructure

This exam requires a higher level of understanding of group policies than exam 70-217. You need to be able to plan the management of group policies for both users and computers. You should be familiar with organizational units and delegation. You will most likely be given an exam question (or several) in which you must analyze a fictitious environment and plan group policies to meet certain functionality goals, yet minimize the amount of management necessary.

CHAPTER 21

USING REMOTE INSTALLATION SERVICES

In this chapter

Simplifying Standardized Installations with Remote Installation Services   858

Preparing for Installation: RIS Components Checklist   860

Installing and Configuring RIS   865

Creating and Testing a Remote Installation Boot Disk   872

Setting Group Policy for RIS Installation   879

Using RIPrep to Create a Corporate-Standard Installation Image   882

Troubleshooting   886

MCSE Corner: Using Remote Installation Services   888

Simplifying Standardized Installations with Remote Installation Services

Many of the important new features offered by Windows 2000 Server are available only to clients running Windows 2000 Professional. It's not unrealistic for system administrators to prepare for installation of Windows 2000 Professional on 33% to 50% of an organization's client PCs during the first year of a wholesale upgrade to Windows 2000.

Client PCs usually come with a specified operating system installed by the assembler, but most large organizations prefer to install a standardized version of the OS to establish a uniform desktop configuration and provide a standard set of applications. Disk imaging software, typified by Symantec's Norton Ghost, is a common means of accomplishing these standardized installations. You create an image of the standard OS and application files from the fixed disk of a standard client. Desktop support personnel then install the image from a copy on a CD-ROM or a server share. In either case, a PC support person usually must visit the client location to run the PC from an MS-DOS boot disk that includes a CD-ROM driver or network client software.

> **Note**
>
> Prior to the disk-imaging approach, a common method for installing a standard OS and set of applications was to use a hardware disk duplicator to create an image on a fixed disk that technicians then installed in the desktop or laptop PC. This distribution method has become uncommon due to the cost of the duplicator and the labor cost involved in removing, duplicating, and reinstalling drives.

One of the primary problems with the disk-image approach is differences in desktop and laptop client hardware configuration—you need individual disk images for each PC group that has significant hardware differences and driver requirements—typically a mixed bag of display adapters, network cards, and modems. Even with the benefits of Plug and Play technology, the support technician must remain on the scene to verify the successful install (New Hardware Found messages on the first boot after completing the OS installation). Installing the OS and standard applications usually requires about an hour—if no serious hardware-related problems occur—plus travel time and expense.

Windows 2000 Remote Installation Services (RIS) offers a very significant improvement over the disk-image approach for installing Windows 2000 Professional. Assuming your PC users have functioning workstations with a network connection—and a network adapter supported by RIS—or are capable of unpacking and connecting a newly delivered PC to the network, they can install the OS without PC helpdesk assistance. Once Windows 2000 Professional is running, IntelliMirror's Application Installation Service downloads a specified set of required applications. Alternatively, you can use RIS to install a set of applications.

Simplifying Standardized Installations with Remote Installation Services 859

Tip from
RJ

You can use RIS to install other operating systems, applications, or both if you download the 3Com Menu Editor from `http://www.3com.com/technology/key_net/dynamic/ris_overview.html`. The 3Com Menu Editor lets you add new choices to the Automatic Setup or the Maintenance and Troubleshooting menus of the Client Installation Wizard that starts the RIS process.

→ For examples of Client Wizard Installation menus, **see** "Performing a Test of Automatic OS Installation," **p. 872**.

If your client PCs comply with the Microsoft/Intel/Compaq Office PC98 or later System Design Guide—or the Network PC Design Guide—you need only instruct the user to press F12 for a network installation when booting a new client. PC98+ requires that clients have a network adapter that supports Intel's Wired for Management (WfM) initiative and its Preboot eXecution Environment (PXE). The network adapter stores the PXE code in ROM.

Note

You can read the full PC98 System Design Guide at `http://www.microsoft.com/hwdev/xpapers/pc98/00wel98.htm`. The Network PC Design guide is at `http://www.microsoft.com/hwdev/xpapers/netpc/netintro.htm` and includes "Attachment B: Preboot Execution Environment," which defines the PXE requirements. Links to the PC99 and proposed PC 2001 System Design Guides are at `http://www.pcdesguide.org/`.

If your client PCs have supported network adapters but don't have the required PXE boot ROM for diskless startup, RIS includes a command-line program that creates a 3.5-inch boot disk. You can use the disk to establish a connection to a Windows 2000 server running the Dynamic Host Control Protocol (DHCP) service, and then to the RIS server that delivers over the network the OS and other files you specify. Almost all PC users probably are capable of inserting the boot disk, following the onscreen instructions, and installing their own OS. Whether booting from PXE on the network adapter or from the disk, installation is an almost totally automatic process. Even if you have PXE boot ROMs on some PCs, the boot disk method provides a consistent installation method across all conforming PCs; providing users with boot disks usually doesn't present a significant problem.

Tip from
RJ

Don't even *think* about using RIS to install Windows 2000 Professional on PCs attached to the network by a low-speed Remote Access Service (RAS) connection. Although it's conceivable that such an approach *might* succeed, the connection time required to download the 300MB of OS files, plus any other files you decide to include in the setup image, can require several days. Even with a 128kpbs ISDN connection, downloading 300MB of OS files requires about 50 hours.

Part III
Ch 21

Preparing for Installation: RIS Components Checklist

Before you begin the installation, you need to ensure that all RIS server and client components are available and meet the minimum requirements for RIS installation. You also can help prepare for a smooth installation by understanding how the RIS components interact in the Windows 2000 environment.

The server side of RIS consists of the following three components:

- *Boot Information Negotiation Layer (BINL)* is the boot service that negotiates with the client and AD to enable network logon with an IP address provided by DHCP. BINL also makes the client connection with a RIS server and ensures that appropriate Remote Installation Group Policy is applied to the client's RIS installation based on the user's site, domain, and OU membership, or all three. BINL runs as a service (BINLSVC) on Windows 2000 Server.
- *Trivial File Transfer Protocol Daemon (TFTPD)* services client requests for downloading OS and application files from the RIS server's share. Microsoft's TFTPD is based on UNIX's standard Trivial File Transfer protocol (TFTP).
- *Single Instance Store (SIS)* is a service that resides on the partition hosting the RIS files. SIS checks all the files in multiple RIS folders for duplicates. If SIS finds a duplicate file, it creates a link to the original copy and deletes the duplicate. SIS saves a substantial amount of disk space when you store multiple OS installation packages.

Client components consist of the following elements:

- *Network adapter* to connect the client to the Windows 2000 network. Clients need not be on the same subnet as the RIS server, but must have at least a 10Mbps—preferably 100Mbps—connection to the server. Network adapter requirements are one of the subjects of the next section.
- *PXE boot ROM* or a 3.5-inch disk drive to load the PXE software into the client's RAM from a boot disk.
- *BIOS that supports Boot Load Order.* All PCs with system boards manufactured after about mid-1997 support Boot Load Order.

Following is a simplified description of how the client and server components interact in a Windows 2000 RIS environment:

1. On startup, the client sends a broadcast to all Windows 2000 servers in its subnet requesting a response from any DHCP server that's reachable, is running BINLSVC, and offers the name of the boot image file specified by the client.

2. The DHCP server responds by providing an IP address from its address pool, attaching the name of the boot image file, and the IP address of the RIS server holding the boot image file.

3. The client acknowledges receipt of its IP address and sends a request to the BINL service on the RIS server to deliver the boot image file, which the client stores in RAM or a temporary RAM drive. The boot image file includes optional RIS configuration information.

4. Pressing F12 causes the PC to boot from the stored boot image and opens the first of a set of character-mode screens for selecting the type of installation, if specified, and a screen to enter a preassigned username, password, and domain name. The user account must be present and enabled in AD for installation to proceed. Microsoft refers to the initial boot screens as the Client Installation Wizard (CIW).

5. After authenticating the user, the client receives its computer name. RIS lets you choose from several methods for automatically generating computer names. Alternatively, you can pre-create computer accounts for clients based on the client PC's Universally Unique ID (UUID), which is similar to Windows' Globally Unique ID (GUID).

6. The client repartitions and formats the fixed disk, and downloads the startup (bluescreen) components of Windows 2000 Professional. These components are identical to those on the four boot disks that you can create from the Makeboot.bat command file on the Windows 2000 Professional distribution CD-ROM. If a boot disk is used, the client's attendant must remove the disk before rebooting the computer.

7. The client runs the initial setup program, reboots, and copies the full set of Windows 2000 Professional installation files from the RIS server to the C:\Winnt folder. No user intervention is required during the blue-screen part of setup. Depending on the type of installation and the source of the RIS setup files, interaction with a user at the client workstation might be required during the final Windows-based setup process.

8. The computer reboots into Windows 2000 Professional.

Figure 21.1 illustrates the boot process. This figure is based partly on information provided by Microsoft's "Remote Installation System Installation" white paper (RemoteOS.doc) and the "Managed Boot Agent (MBA) User's Guide" (3Com_MBA_UGa.doc) from Lanworks Technologies (a subsidiary of 3Com).

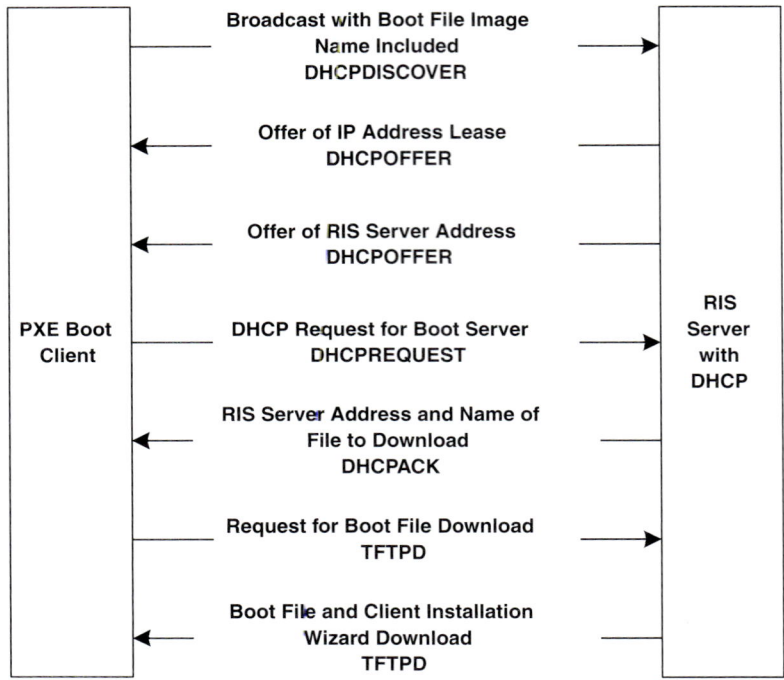

Figure 21.1
The PXE boot client and a RIS server use the DHCP service to download the initial boot file to start the RIS installation.

Client Requirements for RIS

RIS clients must, of course, comply with the resource and hardware requirements for Windows 2000 Professional. The basic client system requirements and recommendations are as follows:

- 133MHz or faster Pentium-compatible CPU. 300MHz+ Pentium II CPUs are recommended.
- 64MB of RAM, minimum. 128MB of RAM provides a more responsive system.
- 2GB fixed disk having a minimum of 650MB of free space.
- BIOS, network, and other adapters, and peripheral components that comply with the Hardware Compatibility List (HCL). You can check computer, hardware devices, and software compatibility at http://www.microsoft.com/windows2000/upgrade/compat/search/default.asp.
- For preassigned computer accounts, a BIOS that contains the UUID for the computer. Computers that meet the Network PC specification have a UUID that you can read from the BIOS setup screen. The UUID usually is included on an identification sticker or tag on the back of the PC. It's a common practice to provide a barcode for scanning the UUID into a handheld reader.

Preparing for Installation: RIS Components Checklist

> **Note**
>
> Although several of the computers used to write this book have system boards manufactured in early 1999, none of those or earlier system boards were equipped with a Network PC-compliant BIOS.

> **Caution**
>
> RIS wipes out all existing data on the client's first physical drive. If the client PC dual-boots another OS on a second physical drive, installing RIS kills the ability to boot to the OS on the second (usually D:\) drive. Tests on dual-boot machines indicate that the Boot.ini file remains and displays the OS selection screen on reboot. You receive a "Windows 2000 could not start because of computer disk hardware configuration problem" error if you attempt to boot the second operating system—Windows 2000 Server or Professional in this example.
>
> RIS automatically repartitions the client's primary fixed disk to a single C:\ active partition, regardless of the size of the drive, and formats the partition with NTFS 5.0.

In addition to the preceding requirements, your PC clients must have network adapters supported by RIS. Unfortunately, relatively few network interface cards (NICs) were on the supported list when this book was written.

Following is a list of the supported NICs on the Windows 2000 release date:

3Com 3C900B-Combo	3Com 3C900B-FL	3Com 3C900B-TPC
3Com 3C900B-TPO	3Com 3C900-Combo	3Com 3C900-TPO
3Com 3C905B-Combo	3Com 3C905B-FX	3Com 3C905B-TX
3Com 3C905C-TX	3Com 3C905-T4	3Com 3C905-TX
AMD PCnet Adapters	Compaq NetFlex 100	Compaq NetFlex 110
Compaq NetFlex 3	DEC DE450	DEC DE500
HP JetDirect 10/100 TX	Intel Pro 10+	Intel Pro 100+
Intel Pro 100B	SMC 8432	SMC 9332
SMC 9432		

> **Tip from RJ**
>
> Run Rbfg.exe from the \Winnt\System32\Reminst folder and click Adapter List to obtain a current list of supported adapters. Windows 2000 service packs probably will add more adapter models to the list.

The RIS examples of this chapter use the 3Com 3C950B-TX 10/100BaseT autosensing NIC, which carries a street price of about $50 from Internet retailers. The standard version of this NIC doesn't include a boot ROM. The 3C950B-TX is one of the most popular PCI NICs among Windows NT network administrators—because of its reliability and 3Com's excellent technical support—and is a common choice of PC assemblers serving the commercial market. The ubiquitous $20 to $30 10/100BaseT PCI NICs installed in some name-brand home PCs and by local assemblers have boot ROM sockets, but aren't RIS-compliant.

Tip from
RJ

Don't spend your money on boot ROMs for 3C950B-TX or other NICs that have empty ROM sockets. The 3Com Managed PC Boot Agent (MBA) ROM, part number 3C90X-MBA for the 3C950B series NICs, requires reprogramming the ROM to enable PXE. This chip has a street price of about $12 from Internet vendors. The instruction sheet for the MBA chip is a 103-page Microsoft Word document, and you can't program the ROM from a DOS window or the Windows NT command prompt.

If you absolutely need PXE network boot capability, try a 3C950B-TX-M or 3C950C-TX-M; both models have embedded PXE code in the network chip. Test these NICs before you make a quantity purchase, because they don't appear in Microsoft's supported list.

SERVER REQUIREMENTS TO SUPPORT RIS

Computers that meet the requirements for Windows 2000 Server installation obviously are necessary to provide RIS to clients, but there are additional requirements for RIS installation. Thus, the Windows 2000 Server setup program doesn't install RIS by default.

Following are additional server requirements to support RIS:

- A disk partition other than the system partition—the boot partition or partition that contains the \Winnt folder—that's formatted with NTFS 5.0. Microsoft recommends a minimum partition size of 2GB, which can hold several installation images.

Note

You can install RIS on a primary partition or an extended partition. For a test RIS installation, you need a minimum of about 500MB for the RIS partition. The standard Windows 2000 Professional image consumes about 300MB. The RIS setup program attempts to find a suitable partition and usually succeeds. You can choose any available disk partition that meets the RIS requirements.

- Membership in a domain with Active Directory–integrated DNS (Dynamic DNS or DDNS) configured and operating.

→ For the basics about setting up Active Directory's DDNS, **see** "Initial DDNS Configuration with Active Directory," **p. 83**.

- DHCP fully configured to support DHCP clients with an authorized server and an activated scope.

→ To review the process of setting up and enabling DHCP for clients, **see** "Configuring DHCP with the DHCP Snap-In," **p. 590**.

Note

The server NIC need not be PXE-compliant or appear in Rbfg.exe's Adapter List. Any network adapter on the Windows 2000 HCL or that you've tested with Windows 2000 Server and found to work correctly is satisfactory for supporting the RIS server components.

You can install RIS on a Domain Controller or a member server of the domain in which you intend to install the clients. Delivering copies of Windows 2000 Professional to clients is a very disk- and network-intensive process, so it's highly preferable to install RIS on a member server. If you have a very tight schedule for installing a large number of RIS clients, you can install RIS on multiple servers.

> **Tip from**
> *RJ*
>
> If you install RIS on a member server, also install the DHCP service. The member DHCP server must have an active scope, and the server must be authorized to service DHCP clients in the domain. If you don't set up DHCP on the RIS member server, clients are likely to receive a "No reply from a server" message during the initial DHCP stage of the initial boot process. Although Microsoft states that DHCP can be located on another server, all attempts to service RIS clients without DHCP installed on the RIS member server failed.
>
> Make sure the IP address range of the member server's scope doesn't overlap the IP address range of other DHCP servers on the network. You only need to specify values for 006 DNS Servers (10.7.2.2 for this chapter's examples) and 015 DNS Domain Name (`oakleaf.edu`) as Scope Options for the member's DHCP server. If your RIS server is on a subnet different from the clients, add a value for the default gateway (003 Router) option.

INSTALLING AND CONFIGURING RIS

Providing basic RIS for clients is a three-step process—installing the RIS components from a Windows 2000 CD-ROM or from a network share, configuring RIS files on your server(s), and setting RIS server property values in Active Directory Users and Computers. You must be a member of the server's local Administrators group to install and configure RIS.

INSTALLING RIS

Windows 2000 Server Setup doesn't install RIS by default, and it's very uncommon to include RIS when making an initial server installation. You install RIS on a member server or DC with the Windows Components Wizard; you can't use the Configure Your Server administrative tool to add this server component. You must have the Windows 2000 Server distribution CD-ROM available or have access to a network share holding the Windows 2000 Server installation files.

To install RIS, do the following:

1. Launch Control Panel's Add/Remove Programs tool, and click Add/Remove Windows Components to start the Windows Components Wizard. Click Next to bypass the Welcome dialog.
2. In the Windows Components dialog, scroll to and mark the Remote Installation Services check box.
3. Click Next to open the Configuring Components dialog and finish the installation, which requires about a minute and consumes 1.7MB of disk space.
4. Click Finish to dismiss the Wizard. You must reboot the server to complete the installation.

Installation of the RIS components takes only a few minutes, including reboot time.

Configuring an RIS Share for Testing

Installing RIS doesn't add a choice to the Administrative Tools menu, so you must start the Remote Installation Services Setup Wizard from the Run dialog. Alternatively, you can configure RIS from the Add/Remove Windows Components feature of Control Panel's Add/Remove Programs tool. Configuration involves specifying the full path to the RIS folder, the name of the folder containing the first set of image files, and the name and description of the image. You must have the Windows 2000 Professional distribution CD-ROM or access to a network share with the CD-ROM files to configure RIS, and you must run the setup program on the RIS server.

→ If you use the retail CD-ROM to create the image and want to eliminate the startup dialog that requests a product key, **see** "Editing the SIF File," **p. 877**.

To configure an initial RIS share with the wizard for testing or limited production use, do the following:

1. Choose Start, Run, type **risetup** in the Open text box, and click OK to start the Remote Installation Services Setup Wizard. Click Next to bypass the Welcome dialog.

2. In the Remote Installation Folder Location dialog, specify the path to the drive and folder to contain all RIS files. The wizard determines the default location by analyzing the partitions of the local drive (see Figure 21.2). If the drive letter corresponds to the correct partition, accept the default; otherwise, edit the path. Click Next.

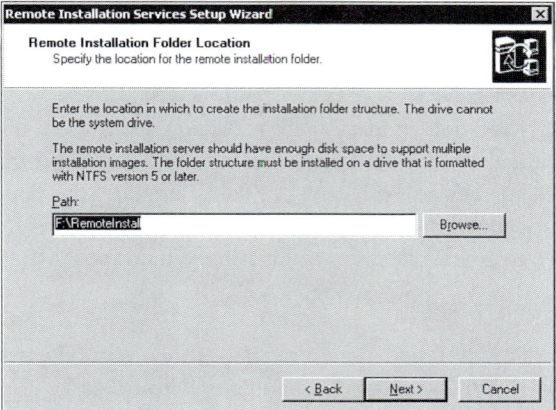

Figure 21.2
You specify the drive and path for RIS installation images in the Remote Installation Folder Location dialog.

3. In the Initial Settings dialog, mark the Respond to Client Connections Requesting Service check box only in a test scenario (see Figure 21.3). Click Next.

Figure 21.3
To create your testing environment, enable RIS to support clients prior to installing the Windows 2000 Professional setup files. In a production environment, you enable the RIS server after you've installed the file images and set additional RIS server properties.

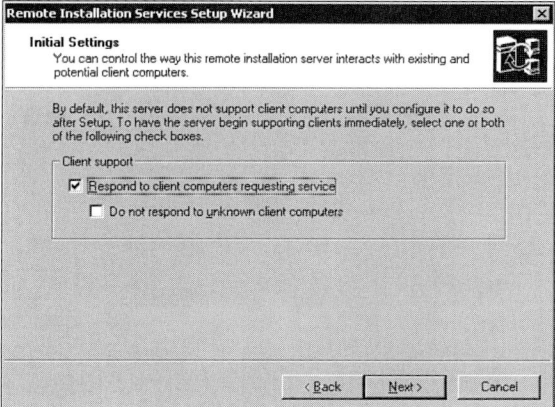

4. In the Installation File Source Location dialog, accept the default CD-ROM location or type the path to the share with the Windows 2000 Professional setup files. Click Next.
5. In the Windows Installation Folder Name dialog, accept the default folder name, win2000.pro for the image files. Click Next.
6. In the Friendly Description and Help Text dialog, accept the default text values or change them to describe the installation more specifically (see Figure 21.4). Click Next.

Figure 21.4
Add description and help text. These two text strings appear only if you enable users to view an initial installation choices screen.

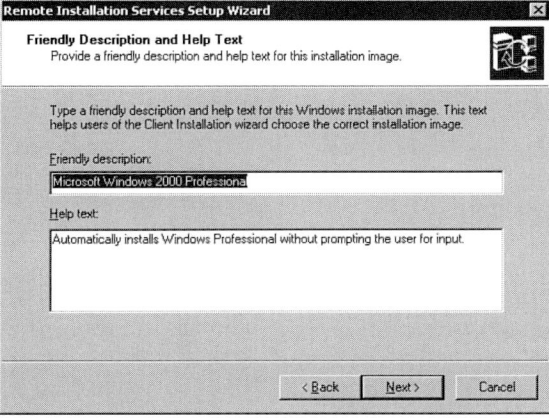

7. In the Review Settings dialog, verify the entries in the preceding steps. Click Finish to let the wizard begin installing the required files and configuring RIS. A progress dialog displays completed and current steps in the process (see Figure 21.5).

Figure 21.5
The Remote Installation Services Setup Wizard displays a progress dialog that follows along with the installation process.

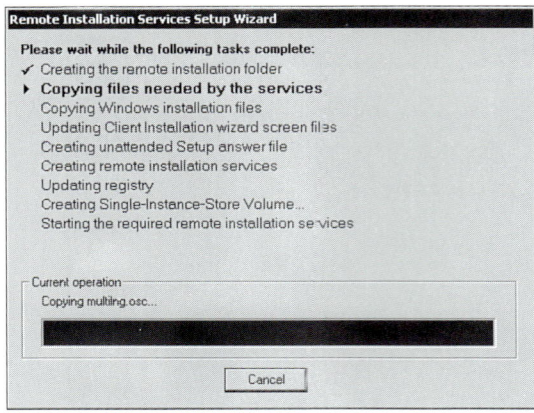

Initial RIS configuration requires about 15 to 20 minutes to complete, depending on the speed of your CD-ROM or network connection and your drive.

→ If you use the retail CD-ROM to create the image, **see** "Editing the SIF File," **p. 877**.

> **Note**
> The initial automatic installation described in the preceding steps is a plain-vanilla version of Windows 2000 with default display adapter settings (640×480 resolution and 15-bit color depth). All initial language, hardware, time-zone, and other settings are the default values for a conventional CD-ROM installation of Windows 2000 Professional.

CONFIGURING RIS SERVER PROPERTIES

The default property settings for a RIS server are adequate for initial testing, but you should establish computer account naming conventions and other RIS server properties in a production environment. Installing RIS adds a Remote Installation page to the server's properties dialog; the page lets you configure the following RIS server properties:

- The naming convention for new client computer accounts
- The location of new client computer accounts in the AD hierarchy
- OS images stored on the server, including addition or deletion of images, and changing some properties of current images
- Addition of third-party tools, if you have any, to be installed with the OS image
- Enabling the server to respond to client requests for OS installation

You can set the server properties for any RIS server on your network from any DC. If you install RIS on a member server, you must set its properties from a DC—setting RIS server properties requires access to Active Directory Users and Computers.

To complete configuration of the RIS server, do the following:

Installing and Configuring RIS

1. Launch Active Directory Users and Computers, navigate to the node for your RIS server, double-click the node to open its *ServerName* Properties dialog, and click the Remote Installation tab.

2. Click Verify Server to open the Check Server Wizard. Click Next to bypass the Welcome dialog, run a diagnostic test, and display the result in the Remote Installation Services Verification Complete dialog. Click Finish to dismiss the wizard, and Done after the BINLSVC service restarts.

> **Note**
> The Check Server Wizard performs only a limited test of RIS components by stopping and starting the BINLSVC and checking the presence of required folders and files. You can't run the Check Server Wizard on a remote RIS server; the Verify Server button is enabled only on the server that's running RIS.

3. Click Advanced Settings to open the default New Clients page of the *ServerName*-Remote-Installation-Services Properties dialog.

> **Note**
> By default, client computer accounts are named by the user's logon ID combined with a sequentially numbered suffix to prevent duplicate computer account names. The default location of computer accounts is the AD Computers container. Alternatively, you can add new computer accounts to the location of the user account, but mixing users and computers in a single OU isn't a recommended practice.

4. To designate a specific location for the new computer accounts, select The Following Directory Service Location option, click Browse to open the Browse for a Directory Service Folder, navigate to the desired container, and click OK to insert the AD path to the container in the text box to the left of the Browse button (see Figure 21.6).

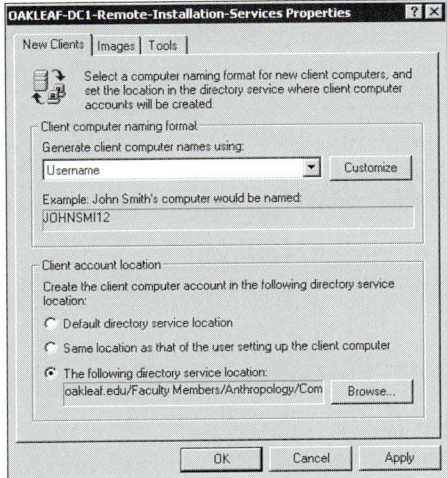

Figure 21.6
Designate a specific location for the new computer accounts.

5. Open the Generate Client Computer Names Using list to select from several alternative methods of creating new client computer names based on user first and last names or the Media Access Control (MAC) address of the client's network adapter.

> **Tip from**
> *RJ*
>
> Don't specify first-name and last-name combinations if your user accounts don't have attribute values for First Name and Last Name. The safest standard naming conventions are Username or NP plus MAC (the letters NP followed by 12 characters of the MAC address).

6. If you want to specify your own computer account naming convention, click Customize to open the Computer Account Generation dialog. Combine %-prefixed variables in the Format text box to generate the computer names (see Figure 21.7). Click OK to close the dialog and set the custom naming convention.

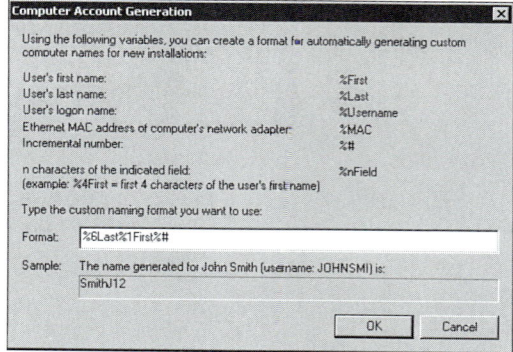

Figure 21.7
You can create custom computer account naming conventions. Here, the **%6Last%1First%#** format combines the first six characters of the user's last name, the first initial, and an appended sequential number.

7. Click the Images tab to display a list of OS images stored on the RIS server. In the Image page, you can add or delete references to image files, or you can open the Image Properties dialog to change the description and help text for a selected image (see Figure 21.8). Close the dialog to return to the *ServerName* Properties dialog.

> **Tip from**
> *RJ*
>
> Deleting a reference to an image doesn't delete the image folder and the files it contains. You must manually delete image folders that you no longer need. Manually deleting an image folder is a lengthy process because of the number of files it contains.

INSTALLING AND CONFIGURING RIS | 871

Figure 21.8
You can edit a selected image's description and help text in the Image Properties dialog.

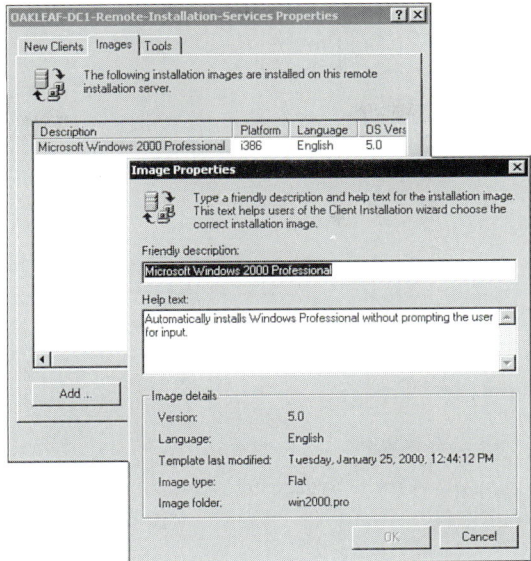

8. If you didn't enable the RIS server during the initial setup process, mark the Respond to Client Computers Requesting Service check box now (see Figure 21. 9), and close the dialog.

> **Caution**
>
> Don't mark the Do Not Respond to Unknown Client Computers check box unless you've pre-created individual computer accounts identified by the computer's UUID. If you mark this check box, computers that don't have UUID values in their BIOS can't connect to the RIS server.

Figure 21.9
If you haven't already done so, mark the Respond to Client Computers Requesting Service check box now.

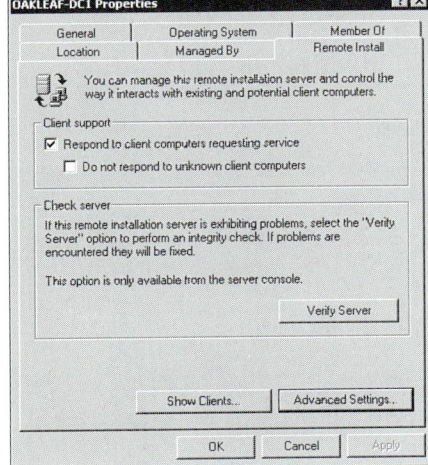

PART
III
CH
21

At this point, RIS server configuration is complete. When this book was written, there were no third-party tools available to add in the Tools page of the *ServerName*-Remote-Installation-Services Properties dialog.

Creating and Testing a Remote Installation Boot Disk

Once you've installed your RIS server(s), you must create boot disks for distribution to users who don't have PXE-compliant boot ROMs installed in their computers' NIC socket. In many organizations, most users must receive boot disks and a simple set of instructions to automatically install the OS. After you create the boot disk, it's a good practice to test automatic installation on a sacrificial client PC.

To create a boot disk, do the following:

1. Choose Start, Run, type **d:\Winnt\System32\Reminst\Rbfg.exe** in the Open text box, and click OK to open the Windows 2000 Remote Boot Disk Generator dialog.

2. Insert a 3.5-inch formatted disk in the specified drive, and click Create Disk to copy the single 90KB Risdisk file to the disk.

3. Click Yes if you want to make additional boot disks, or click No and then click Close to exit Rbfg.exe.

> **Caution**
>
> As mentioned earlier in the chapter, completing the OS installation process repartitions and reformats your test client's first fixed-disk drive.

Performing a Test of Automatic OS Installation

Insert the disk in the test client and reboot the PC. If your DNS and DHCP servers are operating properly, and the client can connect to the new RIS server, the following message—with a different node ID—appears on the client's display:

```
Node: 0050DAB14966
DHCP...
TFTP..........
Press F12 for network service boot
```

 If all four lines of the preceding message don't appear, see the "Client Boot Problems" topic of the "Troubleshooting" section near the end of the chapter.

You have less than five seconds to press F12 after the last line of the message appears; if you wait longer, you get the following message:

```
Exiting Remote Installation Boot Floppy[sr]

Please remove the floppy disk and reboot the workstation
```

In this case, you must reboot and decrease your F12 response time.

CREATING AND TESTING A REMOTE INSTALLATION BOOT DISK | 873

You can view the IP address that DHCP assigns to the computer at this point by launching the DHCP administrative tool, expanding the Scope node, and clicking Address Leases. The test client lease appears without a name. The Unique ID value is the Node Name that appears during the initial boot process (see Figure 21.10). At this point, the client hasn't been assigned a DNS name.

Figure 21.10
The test client lease is listed in Address Leases, although it has yet to be assigned a DNS name.

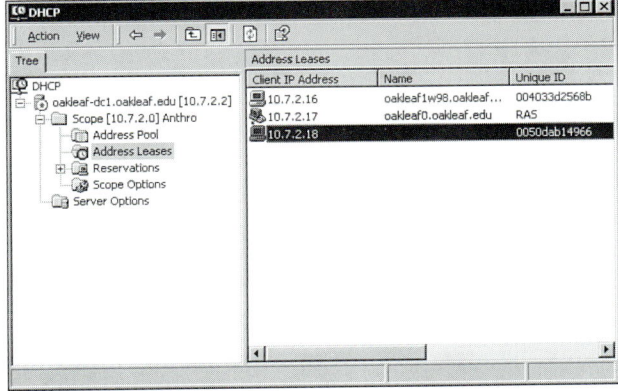

> **Note**
>
> If you take more than about 10 minutes to complete the steps that follow, the connection to the server times out and you must reboot the computer. The timeout provides a limited degree of security if the user walks away from the computer after starting the installation process.

After pressing F12 to download and start the character-based Client Installation Wizard (CIW) for an automatic install, do the following:

1. In the CIW's Welcome screen (see Figure 21.11), press Enter to advance to the next screen.

Figure 21.11
The Client Installation Wizard displays an initial Welcome screen for an automatic installation on a test client.

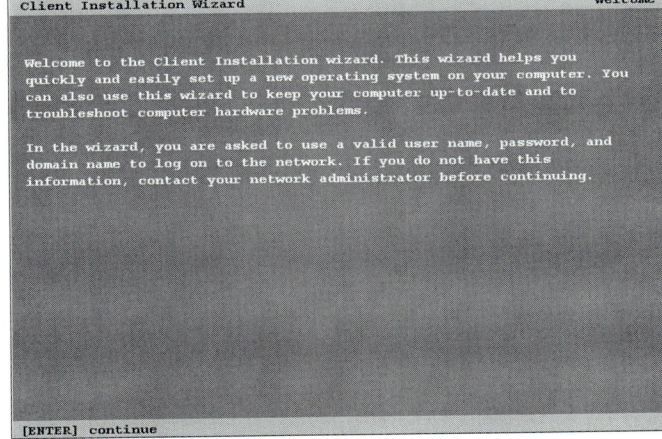

PART
III
CH
21

2. In the Logon screen, type the logon ID for a valid user account, the password, and the user's downlevel domain name (see Figure 21.12). Press Enter to authenticate the user and advance to the last CIW screen. If authentication fails, press Enter to try again.

Figure 21.12
Provide logon credentials for an existing user account in the client's domain.

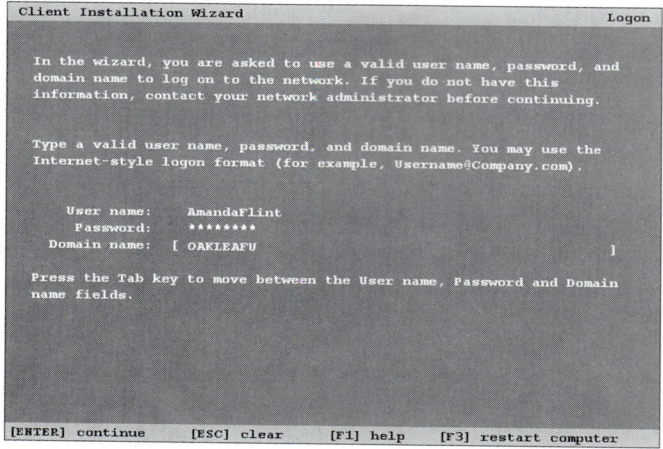

Tip from

RJ

Don't believe the "You may use the Internet-style logon format..." advice in the Logon screen. Attempts to use AmandaFlint@oakleaf.edu, a valid logon ID for the examples of the chapter, failed, as did using the DNS domain name (oakleaf.edu). Using the downlevel logon ID (AmandaFlint) and domain name (OAKLEAFU) works fine.

3. In the Caution screen (see Figure 21.13), press Enter to continue with installation, or press F3 to exit the install process and reboot. Pressing Esc doesn't work in this screen.

Figure 21.13
The wizard displays a Caution screen before wiping out the client's fixed disk.

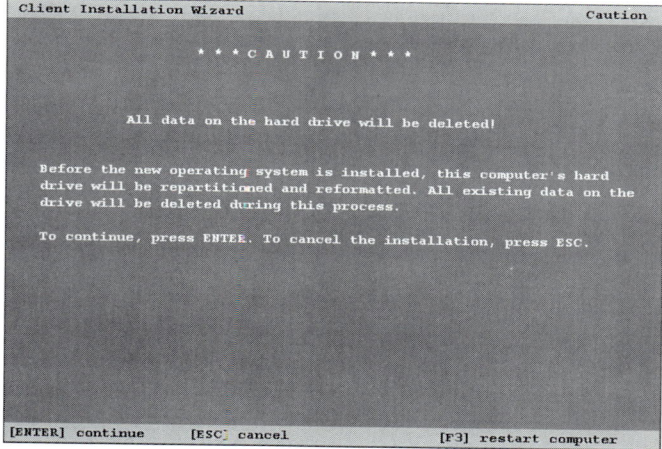

4. In the Installation Information screen, review the computer account name, GUID for the account, and the downlevel name of the RIS server handling the client's request (see Figure 21.14). Press Enter to start installation; to bail out, restart the test client.

Figure 21.14
Confirm computer account property values in the final Installation Information screen.

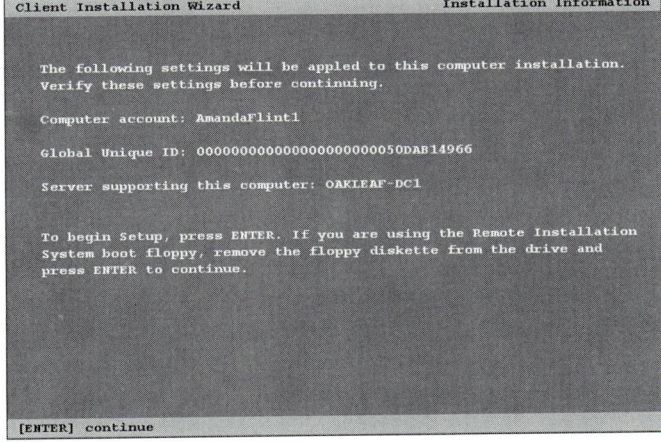

> **Note**
> Windows 2000 service packs issued after the initial release might solve the logon ID, domain name, and failure of Esc problems mentioned in the preceding process.

The TFTPD begins downloading the initial setup files. The user at the client PC has the usual few seconds to press F6 and install a special disk driver. Setup then formats the C:\ partition, using the Fast Format option if the fixed disk is already formatted, then proceeds with automated installation of Windows 2000 Professional. The setup process takes approximately 45 minutes, depending on network and disk performance.

> **Tip from**
> *RJ*
> When the client reboots, the default logon is the local Administrator account, which has an empty password. Advise users in the instruction sheet that accompanies the RIS boot disk to replace Administrator with their user ID and to log on to the domain by clicking Options and selecting the domain name in the Log On to Windows dialog's Log On To list.

> **Caution**
> The default empty password that RIS installation creates for the local Administrator account is a security risk. Instruct users to open the Computer Management console, expand the System Tools, Local Users and Groups nodes, right-click the Administrator account, and choose Change Password to establish a local Administrator password for the client.

→ For instructions on how to add a slightly more secure default password or to prevent users from gaining access to the local Administrator account, **see** "Editing the SIF File," **p. 877**.

Adding the Domain User Account to a Local Group

Depending on the responsibilities and capabilities of the user whose PC you're installing, you might want to grant the user more privileges than granted to the Domain Users group. You can manage the computer accounts you create with RIS from a server or a workstation having the Administrative Tools installed. In either case, you must be a member of the Domain Admins or Enterprise Admins group to manage computer accounts.

To add the user account to another local group on the workstation, do the following:

1. In Active Directory Users and Computers, right-click the entry for the computer account you added with RIS, and choose Manage to open the Computer Management console for the remote computer.

2. Expand the Local Users and Groups node, click Groups, right-click the group—such as Power Users—to which to add the user, and choose Add to Group to open the *GroupName* Properties dialog.

3. Click Add to open the Add Users or Groups dialog, select the domain from the Look In list, and select or type the username in the list. Click Add to add the user to the local group, and then Click OK twice to return to Active Directory Users and Computers.

> **Note**
> Unfortunately, the standard RIS setup file contains no documented provision for automatically adding each new user to a local group that has added privileges.

Reviewing the New Client Computer Account Properties

During the installation process, you can verify in the server's DHCP tool that the client received the correct DNS computer name (AmandaFlint1.oakleaf.edu, for this example). The client also is registered in DDNS. If you examined the IP lease at the beginning of this section, press F5 to refresh the DHCP console and view the computer name.

You also can check the new computer account properties by opening the *ComputerName* Properties dialog for the account in Active Directory Users and Computers. Figure 21.15 shows the Remote Install page with the GUID that identifies the computer in AD. You can assign the account to a specific RIS server in the domain by typing the server name in the Remote Installation Server text box or browsing for the server. Clicking the Server Settings button opens the *ServerName*-Remote-Installation-Services Properties dialog.

Figure 21.15
Designate a specific RIS server in the Remote Install page of the new computer account's Properties sheet.

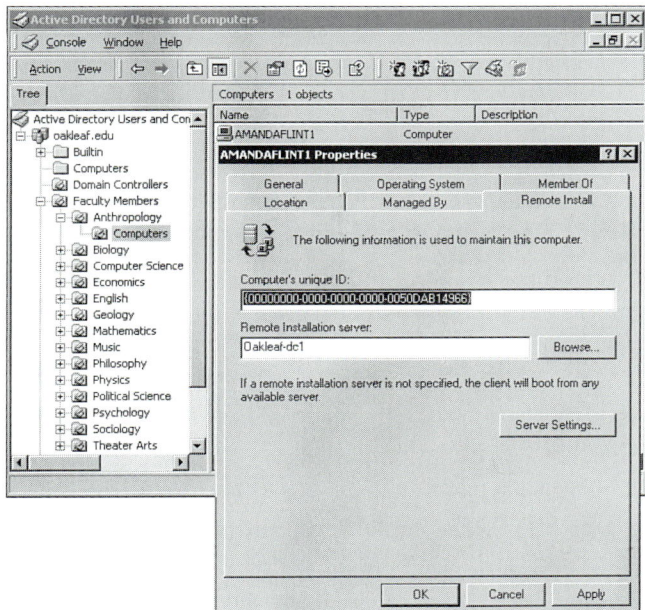

EDITING THE SIF FILE

If you use the retail version of the Windows 2000 Professional CD-ROM, setup requests that the user enter the 25-character product key to continue the setup process. The dialog opens about 25 minutes after starting the setup process. This dialog doesn't appear if you create the image from a copy of the product acquired with Microsoft's Select or OEM licenses.

You can edit the setup information file (.sif) for the RIS OS installation to add a line that eliminates the need to enter the product key during installation by adding the product key string from the sticker on back of the retail CD-ROM's jewelcase. The product key consists of five alphanumeric fields of five characters each, with the fields separated by hyphens.

Tip from
RJ

Don't believe the "Creating an installation image" topic in the Windows 2000 Server online help file. This topic advises you to use the ProductID value, which has a format similar to 82503-000-0000025-00123. You must use the 25-character product key value, *not* the ProductID value that appears in the General Page of the System Properties dialog. You can expect many changes in Windows 2000's online help files from Windows Update.

While you're editing the .sif file, you can also change the client's default display resolution to 800×600 or 1024×768 pixels. Even if you don't need the product key entry, you might want to change the initial display resolution. You also can add a default password for the Administrator account. Specifying a complex (upper/lowercase letters, numerals, and punctuation symbols) password provides increased security.

> **Caution**
>
> A standard password isn't adequate to protect clients against unauthorized access to the Administrator account, because all Administrator-level users know the password. If more than a few folks know an important password, it's only a matter of time before everyone learns it.

To remove the product key requirement from a standard OS installation and, optionally, change other default installation values, do the following:

1. Open in Notepad the Ristndrd.sif file in your *d*:\RemoteInstall\Setup\Images\ *win2000.pro*\i386\Templates folder (where *d* is the RIS drive letter). Change *win2000.pro* to the image folder name you chose, if you didn't accept the default location.

2. Scroll to the [UserData] data section and add the following line below the [TimeZone] = %TIMEZONE% entry:

   ProductID = "RBDC8-VTRC7-D7971-J97JZ-PRVMH"

   Substitute your PID for the invalid key of the preceding example.

3. To change the default display resolution, alter the pixel values of the [Display] section's XResolution and YResolution values to 800 and 600 or 1024 and 768, respectively.

4. To add a default Administrator password, replace the asterisk (*) of the [GUIUnattended] section's AdminPassword = "*" line with the password you want.

5. Save the edited version of the file, and rerun the client installation to test the modified Ristndrd.sif file.

> **Tip from**
> *RJ*
>
> You can change the default 60Hz display refresh rate to the more common 72Hz in the [Display] section's VRefresh line. You also can increase the color depth from the default 8-bit (256 colors) to 15, 16, or 24 bits by altering the BitsPerPel entry. If you change these default values, make sure all the PCs on which you intend to perform a RIS OS installation support the altered settings.

Figure 21.16 shows typical changes described in the preceding steps. The display resolution doesn't change from 640×480 until you reboot the computer at the end of the setup process.

Figure 21.16
Eliminate the product key entry requirement, and change the default password and display resolution by editing the Ristndrd.sif file.

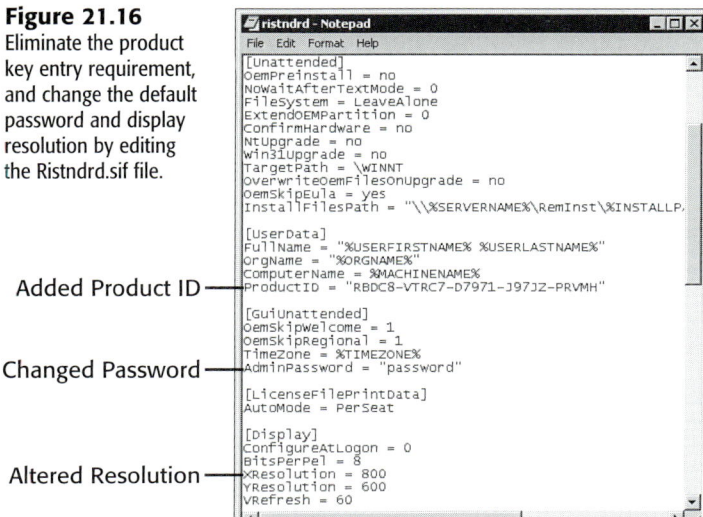

Added Product ID

Changed Password

Altered Resolution

 If client PCs ignore changes you make to the Ristndrd.sif, see the "Standard RIS OS Installation Problems" topic of the "Troubleshooting" section near the end of the chapter.

Setting Group Policy for RIS Installation

The default Group Policy for domains restricts all domain users (including members of Domain Admins) to automated installation of Windows 2000 Professional. You can change the group policy setting to permit selecting between automated and custom installations, restarting a failed installation, or using troubleshooting or other third-party tools that you installed with the OS image files.

You can enable one or more of these options with Group Policy at any AD level—site, domain, or OU. For instance, you can create a special OU for helpdesk personnel and enable members of the HelpDesk OU to choose from custom options. Another alternative is to enable custom installation options at the domain level, and then deny the options for members of particular OUs.

→ To review Group Policy editing methods, **see** "Using the Group Policy Snap-In to Edit Group Policy Objects," **p. 622**.

To enable custom installation options at the domain level by editing the Default Domain Policy, do the following:

1. Launch Active Directory Users and Computers, right-click the domain node, and choose Properties to open the *DomainName* Properties dialog.

2. Click the Group Policy tab, select the Group Policy to edit in the Group Policy Object Links list, and click Edit to open the Group Policy snap-in.

3. Expand the User Configuration, Windows Settings nodes, click the Remote Installation Service node, and then double-click the Choice Options icon to open the Choice Options Properties dialog (see Figure 21.17).

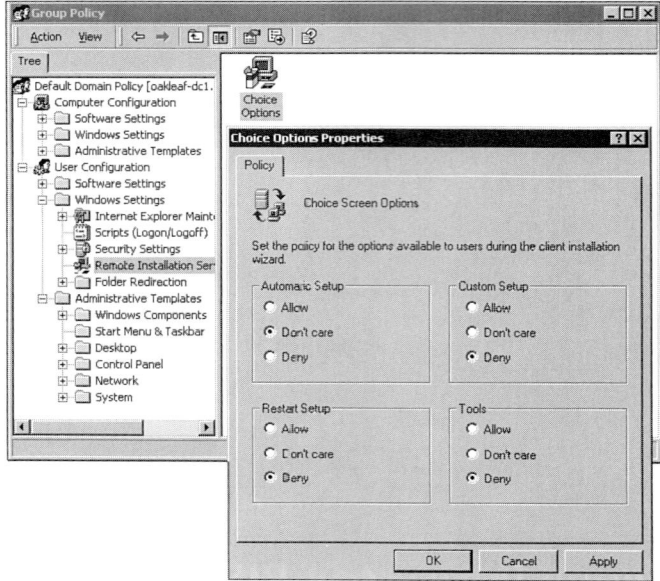

Figure 21.17
You can set the Automatic Setup, Custom Setup, Restart Setup, and Tools options that will be available to users during the client installation wizard.

4. Mark the Allow option for custom installation options you want to provide—typically Automatic Setup, Custom Setup, and Restart Setup.

5. Click OK to close the dialog and save the new settings, close the Group Policy snap-in, and click OK to close the *DomainName* Properties dialog.

You can test the effect of changing the Group Policy by rebooting the test client with the boot disk. After entering the logon ID, password, and domain name in the CIW Login dialog, and pressing Enter, a Main Menu screen appears (see Figure 21.18) in place of the Caution screen.

SETTING GROUP POLICY FOR RIS INSTALLATION | 881

Figure 21.18
Your changes to the Group Policy are reflected in the Client Installation Wizard Main Menu.

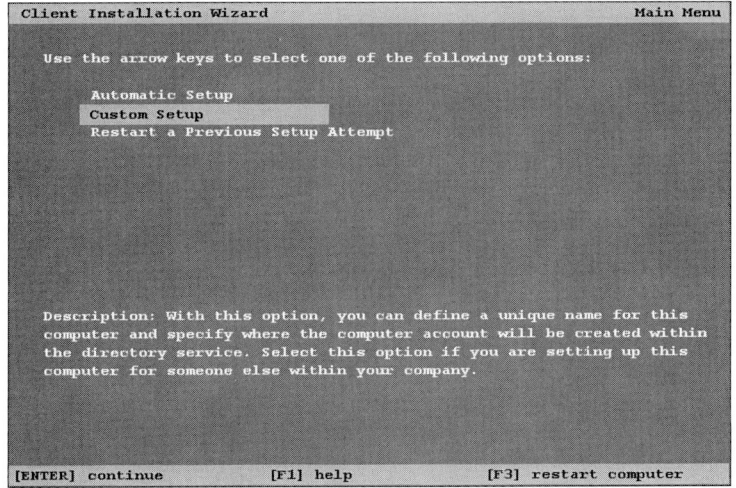

Selecting Custom Setup and pressing Enter opens another added CIW screen—Custom Setup. You type a custom name in the Computer name field and the full path to the OU in which to create the computer account (see Figure 21.19). Click Enter to continue with the remaining CIW screens and begin installation.

Figure 21.19
Specify a custom computer name and place the computer account in an OU.

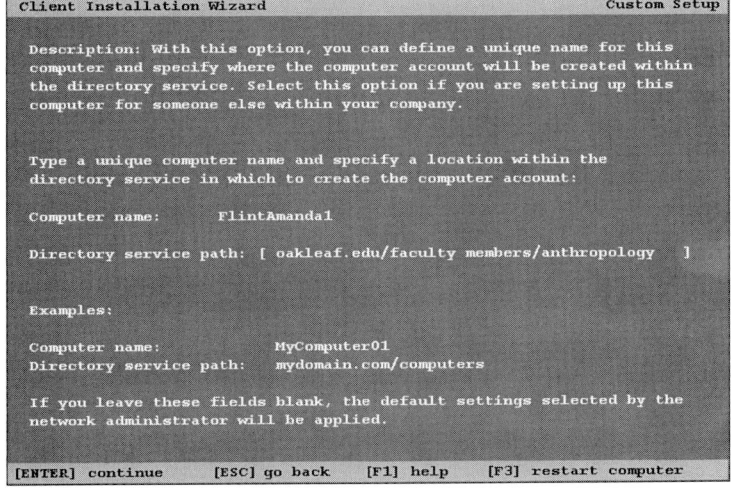

PART
III
CH
21

Note

When you boot the same client computer again from the boot disk, the DNS computer name disappears from the computer's IP address lease displayed in the DCHP administrative tool. Each time you run RIS custom setup for a computer, you create a new computer account for the computer with the same GUID. A warning screen appears that advises you to manually remove prior accounts for the client computer. This warning doesn't appear if you repeatedly run automatic setup on the same client PC.

Using RIPrep to Create a Corporate-Standard Installation Image

The Remote Installation Preparation Wizard (Riprep.exe) lets you create a RIS installation image that conforms to your organization's standard desktop. You also can add a standard set of productivity and other Windows 2000-compliant applications to the image, rather than relying on IntelliMirror to install required applications when booting the client for the first time.

Instead of a flat image file of the Windows 2000 Professional CD-ROM, RIPrep creates a set of SYSPREP (system preparation) files that the wizard copies from a RIS client running Windows 2000 Professional. The wizard strips all personal information from the Registry and elsewhere on the RIS client before copying the files to the RIS server. One of the advantages of substituting RIPrep for the standard RIS OS installation is speed—setup runs much faster with a RIPrep image than with a standard RIS OS setup image.

Unlike the standard automatic or custom RIS OS installation, you must create individual RIPrep images for each type of Hardware Abstraction Layer (HAL) in use by your PC clients. The two most common client HALs are ACPI (for laptop PCs that support the new Advanced Configuration and Power Interface specification) and the standard (non-ACPI) HAL for desktop PCs.

Caution

You must use an ACPI-compliant laptop PC to create RIPrep ACPI images. If you don't use RIS to install the OS image, the RIPrep process fails.

Tip from
RJ

Creating successful RIPrep images that work for all users isn't a job for the faint of heart. You'll probably need to spend many hours testing RIPrep images and tweaking them to suit collective user requirements. Consider using RIPrep to deliver a baseline set of applications for all your users, then take advantage of IntelliMirror's Application Installation Services to add those applications required by users in specific OUs.

→ To review IntelliMirror's application installation process, **see** "Setting Up a Typical Software Installation," **p. 848**.

USING RIPREP TO CREATE A CORPORATE-STANDARD INSTALLATION IMAGE | 883

Following are the basic steps for creating and deploying RIPrep images:

1. Use RIS to install Windows 2000 Professional on the test client that you use to create the RIPrep image. You must use an ACPI-compliant laptop PC to create RIPrep ACPI images. If you don't use RIS to install the OS image, the RIPrep process fails.

> **Tip from**
> *RJ*
>
> Make sure that the edited Ristndrd.sif file in the ...\Templates folder has the modifications you want for the installation. RIPrep copies the current Ristndrd.sif file to its ...\Templates folder when you create the image.

→ For the details on customizing the Ristndrd.sif file, **see** "Editing the SIF File," **p. 877**.

2. Configure Windows 2000 Professional with the desktop layout, Start menu contents, Internet Explorer options, and other elements that comprise your corporate-standard desktop.
3. Install and configure Windows 2000-compliant versions of productivity and other applications that each user is to receive. Microsoft recommends that you use IntelliMirror to install applications on the RIPrep client.

> **Tip from**
> *RJ*
>
> Don't encrypt any files on the RIPrep client. If the client installation process encounters copies of encrypted files, automatic or custom setup fails.

4. Run a full backup of the client to tape or other backup media. If the RIPrep Wizard fails to create the image on the RIS server, you lose your client image in the process.
5. Run the RIS server's RIPrep Wizard from the client to copy the RIPrep image files to a specified subfolder of the RIS server's Images folder. The client test account you use for creating the RIPrep image must have at least Domain Admins privileges.
6. Use the PXE boot disk to test the RIPrep image on the original RIPrep client or another test client. Check that all of the applications are present and operable.
7. After further testing and, if necessary, modification of the SYSPREP image, roll out to your users the boot disks for the installation.

Setting up the applications and generating the SYSPREP files on the RIS server usually takes only a few hours. You should budget a substantial amount of time—perhaps a week or more—for testing the resulting installation. It's a good practice to let a small group of users with varying levels of computer skills test the installation before a major-scale deployment.

USING THE REMOTE INSTALLATION PREPARATION WIZARD

After you've completed the first three steps of the basic RIPrep installation process described in the preceding section, do the following to create the SYSPREP files for your automated or custom setup process:

PART
III
CH
21

1. On the client PC, launch My Network Places and navigate to the *ServerName*\Reminst\Admin\i386\ folder of the RIS server on which to install the SYSPREP image. Double-click the Riprep.exe icon to run the Remote Installation Preparation Wizard. Click Next to bypass the Welcome dialog.

2. In the Server Name dialog, accept the default RIS server name from which you ran Riprep.exe, or change the name to that of another RIS server. Click Next.

3. In the Folder Name dialog, type a descriptive name for the folder to hold the RIPrep image, and click Next.

4. In the Friendly Description and Help Text dialog, type the installation menu choice and description text (see Figure 21.20) that users see when they run the CIW and reach the OS Choice menu. Click Next.

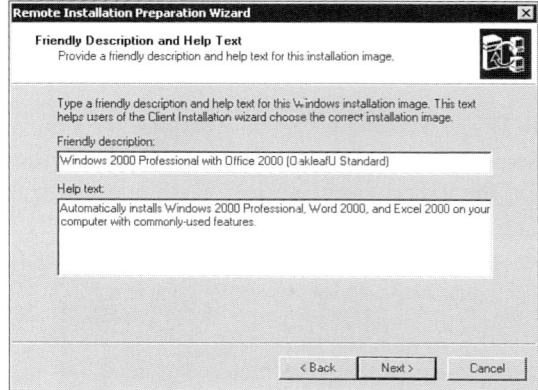

Figure 21.20
Add the menu choice and the description text to appear in the client's OS Choices menu during the installation process.

5. If any programs are running at this point, the Programs or Services are Running dialog appears. The wizard can't copy any files that are locked, so close the application in the list. If a service appears in the Process Name list, open Computer Management's Services node, and stop the process. Click Next.

6. In the Review Settings dialog, check your prior entries, click Next, and then click Finish to start the PIRep process. The wizard displays a progress dialog during the six PIRep operations.

7. At the end of the process—which usually takes 30 minutes or more, depending on the applications you install—an Error Log window might open. If you see lines *other* than the following, you probably need to verify that you installed all application software correctly, and rerun the PIRep process.
```
*01/31/2000 11:31:32
*
*Client shutdown started
```

8. Close the Error Log window, if it appears, to reboot the client. If the error log doesn't appear, the client shuts down, awaiting a reboot.

Using RIPrep to Create a Corporate-Standard Installation Image | 885

When the client reboots, it enters a Mini-Setup installation that requires you to complete Windows 2000 Setup dialogs that contain all personal and computer-related data for the client. You can't connect to the domain during the initial client setup process. When the computer reboots after Mini-Setup, you must complete required Network Identification Wizard entries to rejoin the domain.

> **Tip from**
> *RJ*
>
> If you're conducting a RIPrep test and don't need to save the test client configuration, you can dispense with the Mini-Setup operation. Use the PXE boot disk to test the RIPrep image immediately.

To verify or alter the properties of your new SYSPREP image, open in Active Directory Users and Computers the properties dialog for the RIS server, click the Remote Install tab, and click Advanced Settings to open the *ServerName*-Remote-Installation-Properties dialog. Click the Images tab, select the new SYSPREP image in the Description list, and click Properties to open the Image Properties dialog (see Figure 21.21).

Figure 21.21
The Image Properties dialog displays most of the property values for your newly created SYSPREP installation image.

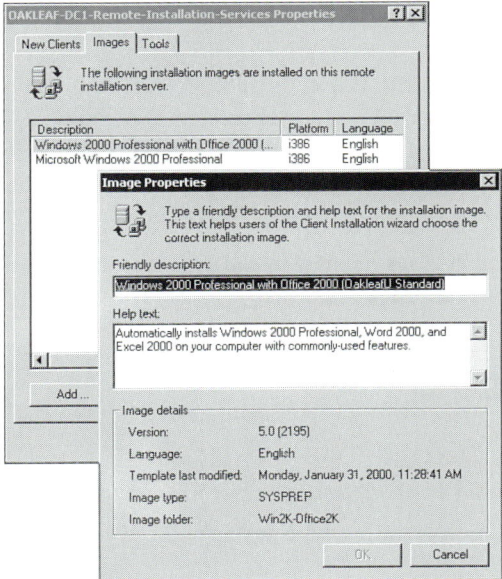

Testing the SYSPREP Image

The PXE boot process for a SYSPREP installation image is identical to that for a conventional flat OS installation image. The only significant difference in the Client Installation Wizard screens is the addition of an OS Chooser screen that appears after the Logon screen and, if you let users choose a custom installation, after the Main Menu. Figure 21.22 shows the CIW's OS Chooser screen with the standard OS installation and SYSPREP installation choices.

Part
III
Ch
21

→ To review CIW's standard set of screens, **see** "Performing a Test of Automatic OS Installation," **p. 872**.

Figure 21.22
The Client Installation Wizard's OS Chooser screen lets users choose between a standard OS installation and a SYSPREP installation.

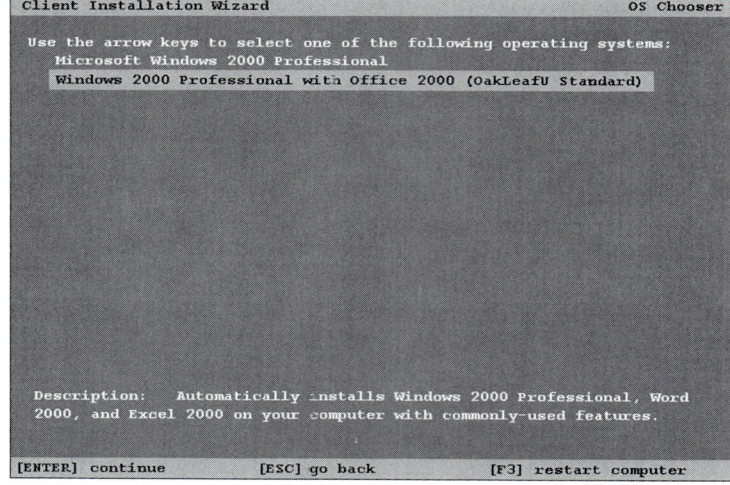

During the blue-screen period of the Windows 2000 Professional Setup operation, RIPrep repartitions and formats the client's drive, and then copies Windows 2000 and the added application files to the client PC. Instead of setup files, RIPrep copies duplicates of the client's original \Winnt, \Program Files, and other folders to the client. Only the Registry and files with personal information differ in the RIPrep copy.

When the user of the client PC logs on after installation, the desktop, menu choices, and other options—except display settings—appear.

TROUBLESHOOTING

CLIENT BOOT PROBLEMS

You receive an error immediately upon attempting to boot from the PXE disk.
Following is the most common error message at this point in the installation process:

```
Error: Could not find a supported network card. The boot floppy currently
supports a limited set of PCI based network cards for use with the Windows
2000 Remote Installation Service. Ensure this system contains one of the
supported network cards and try the operation again. For assistance, contact
your system administrator.
```

The error is self-explanatory, but you're the system administrator. If you have a network adapter that's on the RIS-approved list, create another boot disk and try again. If you still receive the error message, the adapter probably is defective. Replace the network adapter with another card that's on the approved list.

You receive an error during the initial DHCP stage of the boot process.

Your boot screen appears as follows:

```
Node: 0050DAB14966
DHCP...   No reply from a server
Press a key to reboot system
```

The client can't connect to an authorized RIS server. This is the most common error message when you've set up RIS on a member server, but haven't installed, set up, activated, or authorized DHCP. Make sure that DHCP is running on the RIS server, a scope for the client's subnet is activated, and the DHCP server is authorized for DHCP/BINL services.

You receive an "Access denied" error message when attempting to use a different user account to rerun the RIS OS installation.

Use the original user account that you used for the previous OS installation. Alternatively, delete the existing computer account from AD. If you continue to receive "Access denied" messages, delete the computer's IP lease in the DHCP administrative tool.

STANDARD RIS OS INSTALLATION PROBLEMS

Changes made to the Ristndrd.sif file for product ID, Administrator password, or display resolution aren't applied when using RIS to install the OS on the client.

You probably changed the Ristndrd.sif file in the *d*:\RemoteInstall\Setup\Images\ *win2000.pro*\i386 folder. This file is overwritten by the template file each time you run the RIS installation. Make the changes you want to the *d*:\RemoteInstall\Setup\Images\ *win2000.pro*\i386\Templates\Ristndrd.sif file. During the installation process, use Notepad to verify that the Ristndrd.sif file in the two folders is the same.

RIPREP IMAGE CREATION PROBLEMS

The Remote Installation Preparation Wizard starts to create the image, then fails when attempting to copy image files to RIS server.

The account you're using to create the RIPrep image doesn't have at least Domain Admins privileges. Unfortunately, the wizard usually attempts to continue the installation process, wipes out the client's registry, and then Mini-Setup fails with files-not-found errors. Your client no longer is operable. You must rerun the standard RIS OS install, and then reinstall client files from your backup tape.

MCSE Corner: Using Remote Installation Services

There are two exams that cover the Windows 2000 Remote Installation Service: 70-217, "Implementing and Administering a Windows 2000 Directory Services Infrastructure," and 70-220, "Designing Security for a Microsoft Windows 2000 Network." 70-217 covers RIS in the most detail.

70-217 Implementing and Administering a Windows 2000 Directory Services Infrastructure

Remote Installation Services (RIS) is an important part of Windows 2000, because it greatly reduces administrative overhead. You must be familiar with several details related to deploying Windows 2000 using RIS.

You must be able to create a RIS boot disk. Be able to use RIS to install an operating system image on a system and familiarize yourself with configuring RIS options. Also tested on the exam is the management of multiple RIS images for performing remote installations. As is the norm on the Windows 2000 exams, troubleshooting knowledge is essential. Know how to troubleshoot problems with system booting from the created boot disks and problems with RIS image installation.

The other topic tested on this exam is RIS security. You should be able to authorize a RIS server and grant computer account creation rights.

70-220 Designing Security for a Microsoft Windows 2000 Network

This exam requires you to design security for Windows 2000 RIS. You should be familiar with the security structure of RIS, including the use of user and computer accounts, and group policy as it applies to RIS.

CHAPTER 22

MONITORING AND TUNING YOUR NETWORK

In this chapter

Staying Ahead of Network Problems   890

Using Performance Monitor's Network Counters   890

Simulating Network Traffic Load for Performance Testing   896

Recording Network Traffic Data with Counter Logs   902

Setting Alerts on Out-of-Bounds Counter Values   907

Monitoring Network Activity with NetMon   911

Understanding the Browsing Process   914

Troubleshooting   916

MCSE Corner: Monitoring and Tuning Your Network   917

Staying Ahead of Network Problems

Today's 100BASE-T network adapters, hubs, and switches combine with high-performance routers to achieve LAN communication speeds that were unheard of just a few years ago. Digital video production and animation firms deliver gigabit Ethernet (1000BASE-T) to editors' and artists' desktop workstations. C. Northcote Parkinson's First Law, "Work expands to fill the time available," however, has a corollary that applies to LANs: Traffic expands to fill the bandwidth available.

> **Note**
> There also is a "Parkinson's Law of Data"—Data expands to fill the space available for storage. You can ameliorate storage space problems by taking advantage of Windows 2000's Quotas and Remote Storage features. It isn't as easy to discourage (or prevent) your users from monopolizing your network's bandwidth by listening to Internet radio or, worse yet, watching streaming music videos during working hours.

No matter how well you design your LAN and how much you spend on upgrading network hardware, users inevitably complain that your finely crafted Windows 2000 network has problems. When users encounter bottlenecks with WAN connections, especially to the Internet, you're likely to encounter a maelstrom of complaints in your email inbox. Obviously, you can improve WAN connectivity by increasing the available bandwidth, but moving from a T-1 to a T-3 connection to your ISP is an option only for network administrators working for large organizations or wealthy small firms. The first step in handling network performance issues is monitoring network activity to obtain baseline traffic data. When you develop a picture of daily traffic peaks and valleys, you have a starting point for tuning and modifying your network for top performance.

> **Tip from**
>
> Upgrading all 10BASE-T clients with 100BASE-T network adapters should be your first priority, especially if your subnets use autosensing 10/100BASE-T hubs. Depending on the hub's age and feature set, mixing 10BASE-T and 100BASE-T connections can seriously affect total network throughput. Replacing hubs with switches also can deliver a substantial improvement in subnet performance. Switches use Media Access Control (MAC) IDs to create a direct 100MBps connection between a pair of endpoints (server and client), which takes maximum advantage of server capabilities and greatly reduces packet collisions.

Using Performance Monitor's Network Counters

Performance Monitor (PerfMon) is Windows 2000 Server's basic tool for determining network traffic load on local or remote servers. Network servers usually are located in server closets or data centers, so you usually run PerfMon under Windows 2000 Professional on a workstation that has the Administrative Tools installed. Running PerfMon on a workstation instead of the server has the benefit of reducing the resource load on the server, but adds to the network traffic baseline. PerfMon measures only the network traffic generated by packets sent from or received by the network adapter(s) installed on a particular server. You can, however, add network counters from each of your servers to provide a reasonable estimate of total network traffic.

Tip from *RJ*	Install the Windows 2000 Server Administrative Tools on a workstation by running `AdminPak.msi` from the `\Winnt\System32` folder of any Windows 2000 server on your network.

→ To automatically install the Administrative Tools when a member of the Domain Admins group logs on to a workstation running Windows 2000 Professional, **see** "Setting up a Typical Software Installation," **p. 848**.

PerfMon provides the following monitoring features:

- System Monitor (SysMon, also called System Performance Monitor) delivers a graphic, time-based display of the instantaneous values of counters that monitor one or more properties of performance objects. Typical hardware performance objects are CPUs and physical disks; you also can monitor services, such as Internet Information Server (IIS) and SQL Server. Counters provide the graphed values of performance objects, which usually are captured individual measurements averaged over a short time period. SysMon provides printable line graph and histogram views of real-time performance data. This chapter concentrates on PerfMon's network-related counters, but it also includes examples of other counters that impact network performance.

- Counter Logs record counter data at intervals you set. You can view saved counter logs in SysMon or open them in a spreadsheet program for numeric analysis. You use counter logs to generate baseline network performance data. PerfMon includes a sample System Overview log that records Memory Pages/sec, Average Disk Queue Length, and Average Process Time counters.

- Trace Logs record specific sets of local computer counter data continuously. Windows 2000 Server doesn't include a reader for trace logs; you must use the Windows 2000 Server's Resource Kit's `Tracedmp.exe` and `Reducer.exe` to generate readable versions of trace logs. The capability of creating trace logs is a new Windows 2000 feature.

- Alerts trigger when a counter value exceeds or falls below a predetermined threshold setting. Alerts can send a message to a client, start a counter log, or launch an application when the counter value crosses the threshold you set.

Counter Logs, Trace Logs, and Alerts are components of PerfMon's Performance Logs and Alerts feature. Trace logs require complex additional processing to deliver useful data and are beyond the scope of this book.

INSTALLING THE NETWORK MONITOR DRIVER

A Network Monitor Driver is required on each server whose network counters you want to monitor with PerfMon. Before you run PerfMon to analyze network traffic, the Network Monitor Driver must be running on each server in the network segment you want to monitor.

You can verify whether the Network Monitor Driver is installed on a server—and install it, if necessary—by following these steps:

1. On each server in the subnet, right-click My Network Places, and choose Properties to open the Dial-Up and Network Connections window.
2. Right-click the Local Area Connection icon, and click Properties to open the Local Area Connection Properties dialog.
3. If Network Monitor Driver doesn't appear in the Components Checked Are Used by This Connection list, click Install to open the Install Network Component dialog.
4. Select Protocol and click Add to open the Select Network Protocol dialog.
5. Select Network Monitor Driver in the Network Protocol List, click OK to install it, and close all dialogs. By default, installation enables the driver.

> **Tip from**
> *RJ*
>
> If you have users who regularly share files within a workgroup, consider adding the Network Monitor Driver to workstations having heavily used shares.

STARTING PERFMON AND ADDING BASIC NETWORK COUNTERS TO SYSMON

PerfMon is a Microsoft Management Console (MMC) snap-in (`Perfmon.msc`) that performs the same basic functions as Windows NT 4.0's executable version (`Perfmon.exe`) and adds Trace Logs as a new component. If you're familiar with Windows NT 4.0's PerfMon, you won't have any difficulty adapting to SysMon.

> **Note**
>
> Windows 2000 doesn't include Windows NT 4.0's Network Segment performance object and its associated counters.

Do the following to launch PerfMon and add Network performance object counters to SysMon:

1. Choose Programs, Administrative Tools, Performance to launch MMC with the PerfMon snap-in in its default configuration with a SysMon graph in the right pane.
2. Click the + button of the toolbar—or right-click the right pane and choose Add Counters—to open the Add Counters dialog.
3. If you're monitoring a remote server, pick the Select Counters from Computer option and type the computer name in the combo list. Otherwise, select the Use Local Computer Counters option.

USING PERFORMANCE MONITOR'S NETWORK COUNTERS | 893

PART
III
CH
22

> **Note**
>
> For this and the following examples in the chapter, PerfMon runs on oakleaf-ws5, a workstation running Windows 2000 Professional, and connects to Network Monitor Drivers and other counters on oakleaf-ps1 and oakleaf-ms3 servers.

4. Select Network Interface in the Performance Object list and the network adapter that's connected to the subnet whose traffic you want to monitor.

5. Select the counter to monitor in the Select Counters from List—Bytes Total/sec for this example (see Figure 22.1). You can obtain a brief description of the counter's function in a text box below the Add Counters dialog by clicking Explain. Click Add to add the counter to the SysMon graph and the list below the graph.

Figure 22.1
Select the remote server's name, performance object, network adapter, and the counter that you want to graph in the Add Counters dialog.

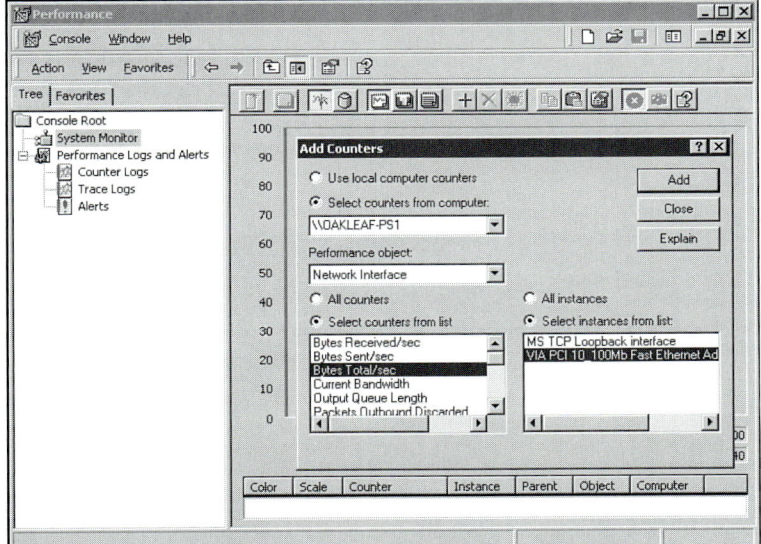

> **Note**
>
>
>
> Windows 2000's Add Counters dialog identifies multiple network interfaces by name; Windows NT's Add counters dialog displays a zero-based index number if you have multiple network interfaces.

6. Repeat steps 2 through 5 for each server to monitor.

7. Click Close to return to PerfMon and start displaying data from each of the two servers.

ALTERING THE SCALE AND APPEARANCE OF THE GRAPH

Servers generate a modest amount of background traffic (usually less than 10kBps) as a result of the monitoring process and other periodic communication activities, including broadcasts. Occasional spikes occur when replicating changes to Active Directory (AD) data between domain controllers (DCs). The default scale for the Bytes Total/sec counter is 0.0001, which divides the actual counter value by 10,000. The Y-axis of the graph has a maximum value of 100 units, so full-scale (100) corresponds to 100×10,000 or 1MBps. Thus, the graph displays idle-server background traffic as a continuous line at 0 and you must change the scale to see the background traffic display.

To make the background traffic visible on an idle server and alter the appearance of the graph, do the following:

1. Right-click anywhere in the right pane, choose Properties to open the System Monitor Properties dialog, and click the Data tab.

2. Select a counter in the Counters list and select a larger multiplier in the Scale list. Changing the scale from the default 0.0001 to 0.001 changes the graph's full-scale value from 1MBps to 100kBps.

3. Optionally, choose a new color for the counter's line and histogram bar from the Color list, and change the thickness or pattern of the line by making a selection in the Width or Style lists. If you change the Width value, you can't change the line's pattern (see Figure 22.2).

Figure 22.2
Change the color, scale, thickness, and pattern of the line for the selected counter in the Data page of the System Monitor Properties dialog.

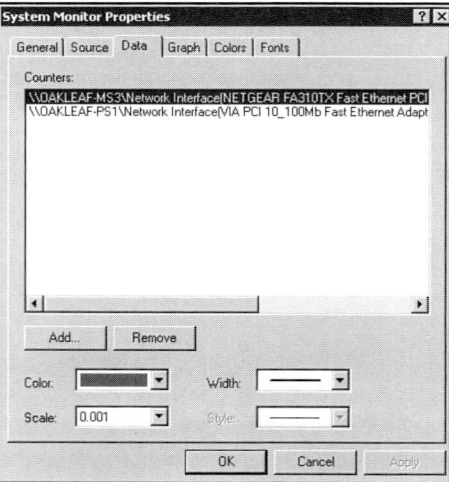

4. Click the Graph tab to add a description of the graph in the Title text box, and mark the Vertical Grid and Horizontal Grid check boxes if you want the display to emulate graph paper (see Figure 22.3). You also can add an optional title to the vertical axis and change the graph's full-scale value.

Using Performance Monitor's Network Counters | 895

Figure 22.3
Add graph and vertical axis titles and gridlines, and change the numbering for the full-scale value of the graph in the Graph page.

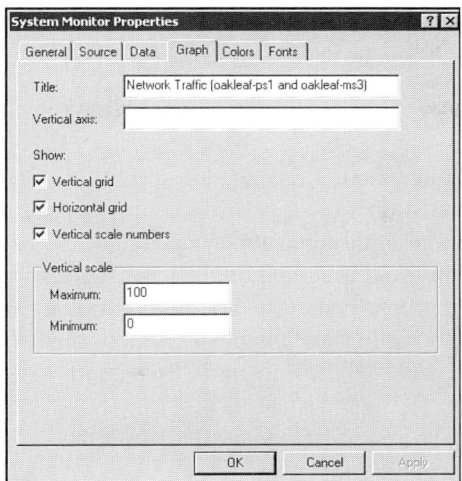

PART
III
CH
22

5. Repeat steps 2 and 3 for each additional counter in the list and then click OK to close the dialog. The SysMon display for two servers appears similar to that shown in Figure 22.4.

Figure 22.4
SysMon displays background network traffic on two idle servers after expanding the scale of the Y-axis, altering line thickness, and adding horizontal and vertical gridlines.

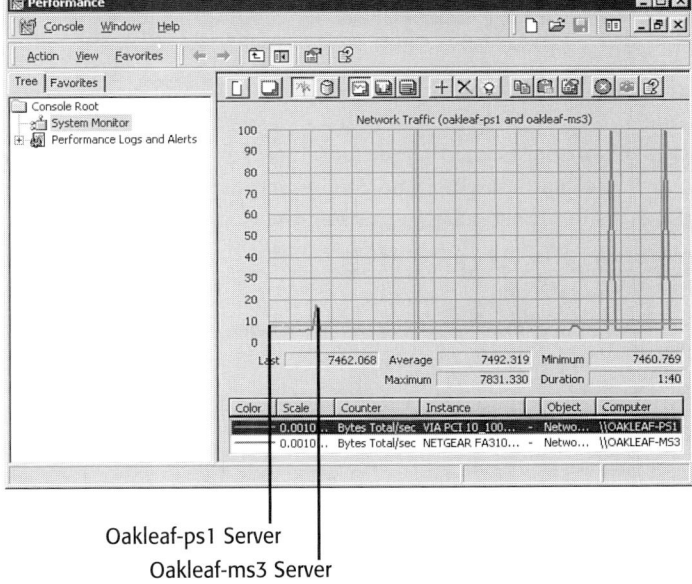

Oakleaf-ps1 Server
Oakleaf-ms3 Server

6. Select a counter in the list below the graph to display the Last, Average, Minimum, and Maximum values since closing the System Monitor Properties dialog. Numerical values in the labels below the graph aren't scaled by the multiplier you selected in step 2.

Tip from	Remove unneeded counters by selecting the counter in the list below the graph and pressing Delete. There's no context menu choice to delete a counter. You also can remove counters in the Data page of the System Monitor Properties dialog.

SysMon's default measurement interval is 1 second, which results in the horizontal axis having a full-scale Duration value of 1:40 (100 seconds). You can change the measurement interval to decrease background monitoring traffic by opening the General Page of the System Monitor Properties dialog and changing the Update Automatically Every text box value to a higher number, such as 5 seconds. The background traffic displayed by the graph and the value text boxes decreases approximately by the ratio of the default to the new interval, and the Duration value increases by the same ratio (to 8:20 for a 5-second interval).

SAVING AND REUSING A CUSTOM PERFMON CONFIGURATION

After you've created a custom PerfMon configuration for measuring your network traffic, save the MMC console for future reuse by following these steps:

1. Choose Console, Save As to open the Save As dialog. The default location for MMC console (.msc) files is \Winnt\System32.

2. Type a name for your console, such as **NetTraffic**, in the File Name text box, click OK to save the custom console, and then close PerfMon.

3. Choose Start, Run and type the console name with the **.msc** extension (**NetTraffic.msc**) in the Open text box.

4. Click OK to launch the custom console.

If SysMon can connect to each server for which you added Network Interface counters, the console opens and starts displaying data automatically. One or more failed server connection(s) causes a substantial delay in opening the console and freezes the graphic display.

Tip from	To run SysMon with a missing server connection, remove the counters for the downed server, save the console with a different name, and then close and reopen it. Simply removing the inoperative counters doesn't result in a working SysMon console.

SIMULATING NETWORK TRAFFIC LOAD FOR PERFORMANCE TESTING

If you're testing a new network configuration or must verify the scalability of an existing network, you need the ability to simulate network load. Simulated loads also enable you to analyze relationships between fixed-disk performance and network throughput for Windows 2000 file servers. There are several commercial and freeware network load simulation programs available for Windows NT 4.0 Server. Ziff-Davis Benchmark Operations' NetBench

6.0 (http://www.zdnet.com/zdbop/netbench/netbench.html) is one of the most widely used freeware programs for analyzing file server performance with multiple client PCs. Tests conducted while writing this book demonstrate that NetBench also works with Windows 2000 servers. If you have 20 or more client PCs available for testing, NetBench 6.0 generates a reasonably constant network load. With only a few clients, however, the simulated network traffic varies substantially during execution of the standard test suite. A constant, predictable network traffic load simplifies initial analysis of network performance.

One of the easiest methods of generating predictable network traffic for network performance testing is to continuously copy a large (100MB or more) file from servers to clients. The large file size minimizes the effect of client caching on the traffic load. Two 300MHz Pentium II servers with high-performance SCSI fixed drives and two or three clients with fast (DMA/33 or ATA/66) IDE drives easily can saturate a standard 10/100BASE-T hub. You need more or faster servers and clients to bring a switched subnet to its knees.

Tip from
RJ

The best source of 100MB+ files is an audio CD having tracks with a duration of nine minutes or more. Use a shareware ripper, such as Jackie Franck's Audiograbber (http://www.dezines.com/audio/), to create a .wav file from the Redbook audio content of the track. Audiograbber 1.62+ runs under Windows 2000 Professional or Server. Copy the .wav file(s) to a shared folder of the test server(s).

Note

The network performance testing examples that follow use the NetTraffic (NetTraf.exe) Visual Basic application that's in the \Seuw2ks\NetTraf folder of the accompanying CD-ROM. Run NetTraffic.msi to install the NetTraffic application on Windows 2000 clients. You must copy the large .wav file to a client-accessible share on each server you use to generate network traffic.

ADDING BASELINE NETWORK TRAFFIC WITH THE NETTRAFFIC APPLICATION

To use the NetTraffic application to create a steady-state network load with one or more servers and clients, do the following:

1. Create a share on each server and copy the large test file to the shared folder (Traffic\BP5.wav for this example).

2. For clients running Windows 2000 Professional, double-click the accompanying CD-ROM's \NetTraf\NetTraffic.msi icon to install the application with Windows Installer.

3. Choose Shortcut to NetTraf.exe from the Windows 2000 Start menu or NetTraffic from the Windows 9x/NT Programs menu to open the application's single form.

4. Type in the Source File text box the UNC path to the test server's file (\\oakleaf-ps1\Traffic\BP5.wav).

5. Type in the Destination File text box the path to a local folder and filename for the client file copy (d:\Test\Traffic.wav).

6. Click Start Traffic to begin repetitive copying of the source file to the client.

Note
When you connect to the server file, the File Size (MB) text box displays the length of the file in MB. When the first copy completes, data for a single copy appears in the Copies, Seconds, and kBytes/sec text boxes. The kBps Average text box maintains a running average of the copy operation's data rate. Figure 22.5 shows NetTraffic running on a workstation running Windows NT 4.0.

Figure 22.5
The NetTraffic client displays the test file length, seconds/copy, and average data rate for each copy operation, plus the average data rate for multiple copy operations in kBps.

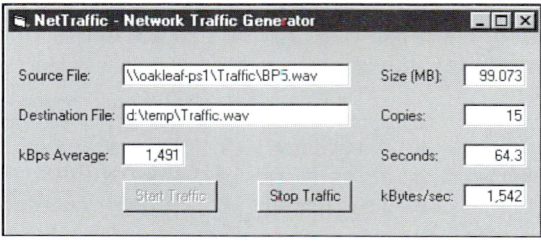

7. Repeat step 1 for each server and steps 2 through 6 for each network client.

Click Stop Traffic to halt the copy operation at the completion of the current copy. You encounter a delay before NetTraffic acknowledges clicking the Stop Traffic button, because the button doesn't regain the focus until the current copy operation completes. Similarly, if you hide NetTraffic's form behind another window, the form might not repaint until the end of a copy operation.

Note
You can run multiple instances of the NetTraffic application on clients to increase the network load, up to the maximum effective speed of your subnet. Use the same source file, but assign client files a different Destination Filename for each instance of NetTraffic. If you connect servers and clients with a hub, the maximum effective network speed is considerably less than the rated speed (100MBps for this example).

 If you encounter error messages when running one or more instances of NetTraffic on the client, see the "Problems with the NetTraffic Application" topic of the "Troubleshooting" section near the end of this chapter.

MEASURING SIMULATED NETWORK TRAFFIC WITH SYSMON

The custom PerfMon console described in the earlier "Starting PerfMon and Adding Basic Network Counters to SysMon" section enables you to measure heavier traffic loads with only minor modification. You can create the load with the NetTraffic application or by manually copying very large files from servers to clients. The following example uses four instances of NetTraffic on two clients to saturate a hub-based 100MBps network.

To measure heavy traffic loads with SysMon, do the following:

1. If you didn't save a custom console, launch PerfMon on a Windows 2000 client and add the Network Interface, Bytes Total/sec counter for each test server's network adapter.
2. In the Data page of the System Monitor Properties dialog, change the scale for each Bytes Total/sec counter to 0.00001 to make the full-scale graph value 10MBps.
3. In the General page, change the update interval to 2 seconds to set the horizontal scale to 3:20 (200 seconds) total, making each division 10 seconds.
4. Optionally add a Physical Disk, % Disk Time counter for each server. Disk time data is useful for determining whether drive performance limits a server's network traffic. Close the properties dialog.
5. Start a single NetTraffic instance on a client connected to the server with the best network performance and note the Average value of the Bytes Total/sec counter (2.430MBps for this example.)
6. After network traffic stabilizes, add another client connection to the server to observe the increase in network traffic. Figure 22.6 illustrates SysMon's display for two clients (oakleaf-dc1, the Windows 2000 machine running PerfMon, and OAKLEAF1, which runs Windows NT in this example) connected to the oakleaf-ms3 server. The second client started copying at the horizontal midpoint of the graph.

Figure 22.6
Adding a second test client connection to the same server almost doubles the average network traffic. The server's disk drive temporarily limits the data rate at about 2:20 from the start of measurement.

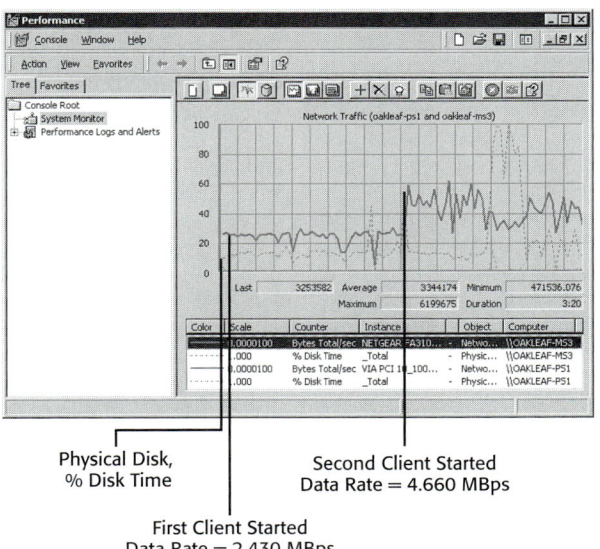

Physical Disk, % Disk Time

First Client Started
Data Rate = 2.430 MBps

Second Client Started
Data Rate = 4.660 MBps

> **Note**
>
> With a hub that has a network collision indicator visible from your working area, you see periodic collisions that result from servers sending counter and file data to the client running PerfMon and NetTraffic. When you connect the second client to its server, the frequency of collisions increases significantly.

7. After the traffic values reach a reasonably steady-state condition, click the Clear Display button of the toolbar (the second button from the left in the SysMon pane) to reset the counter data.

8. After about a minute, record the Average value of the Bytes Total/sec counter (4.660MBps for this example).

9. Launch another instance of NetTraffic on one of the clients and connect it to the same or another test server.

10. Wait for traffic to stabilize and then add another instance of NetTraffic.

Tip from
RJ

To save the SysMon data for later review, right-click the graph pane and choose Save As to save a snapshot of your data in HTML format (as an `.htm` file). Double-click the saved file's icon to open the SysMon data in Internet Explorer. The SysMon graph is an ActiveX control (`Sysmon.ocx`). The HTML file you save contains the graph data points in tab-separated text format in `<PARAM NAME>"Counter.00001.Data ... >"` fields that return property values to the `Sysmon.ocx` control.

Your maximum effective network throughput in MBps occurs when the total of the Average Bytes Total/sec counters remains constant after adding another test client. Figure 22.7 illustrates measurements made with two servers and four clients on the subnet. Traffic added by the second server decreases the bandwidth available to the first server. The average network throughput is 2.694MBps for the oakleaf-ms3 server and 2.036MBps for oakleaf-ps1—a total of 4.730MBps. The 4.730MBps value is only 1.5% more than the 4.660MBps achieved with a single server and two clients, so it's safe to assume that the effective network throughput is about 4.75MBps.

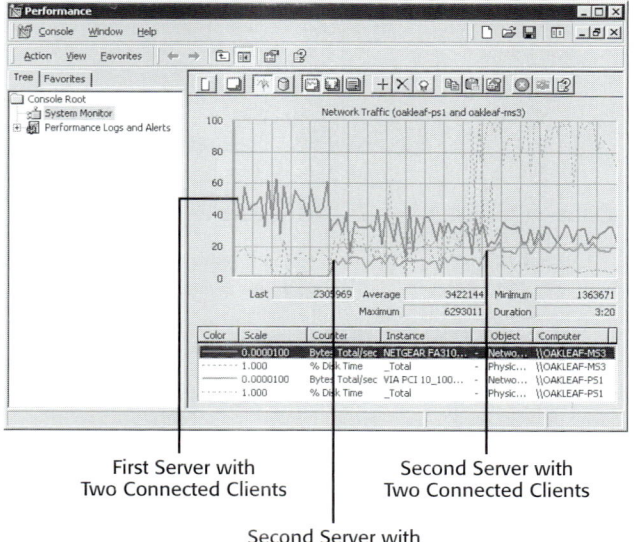

Figure 22.7
In a hub-based network operating close to its maximum effective capacity, adding traffic from a second server decreases the bandwidth available to the first server.

Tip from
RJ

Verify that fixed-disk performance isn't a performance bottleneck when measuring network throughput. Figure 22.7 shows that the disk data rates aren't a controlling factor in the results. The oakleaf-ms3 drive's % Disk Time averages about 15%. The oakleaf-ps1 drive % Disk Time averages about 85% in the figure, but drops to about 65% under steady-state conditions.

→ If your average % Disk Time values exceed 90%, **see** "Tuning Fixed-Disk Drives and RAID Arrays," **p. 926**.

 If SysMon doesn't behave the way you expect, see the "Problems with System Monitor" topic of the "Troubleshooting" section near the end of the chapter.

Using Effective Network Performance Data

The preceding steps create a standard SysMon measurement scenario and a baseline value for your current effective network throughput. Armed with the baseline data, you can make changes to server hardware and accurately measure the incremental performance gain or loss. In the majority of cases, increasing effective network throughput requires upgrading your server hardware.

Following are a few server hardware upgrade recommendations, in the approximate order of potential performance improvement:

- Replace the network hub with a switch, as mentioned earlier in the chapter. A switch greatly reduces the effect on performance when adding additional servers to a subnet, because each server has its own private connection to a client. You achieve only a modest increase in performance on connections between a single server and many clients, because the server must share its single 100MBps connection.

- Replace low-end network adapter cards with server-grade versions. Network adapters designed specifically for servers are more costly than those commonly used for clients, but offer improved manageability and performance. If your server hardware includes support for Intel's Intelligent I/O (I2O) architecture, consider upgrading to an I2O network adapter, which has an onboard processor. For more information on I2O, start at http://www.intel.com/pressroom/initiatives/i2o.htm.

- Add a processor, if you have a multiprocessor server with an empty socket. Adding extra CPU power is especially important for application servers running SQL Server, Exchange Server, or Internet Information Server. These applications consume a substantial amount of processor time, which competes with the resources required for network communication.

- Add RAM, especially if you add a processor. Paging file operations consume resources that otherwise could be devoted to handling network traffic.

→ For a detailed discussion of RAM, **see** "Optimizing Memory Management," **p. 940**.

Another real-world use for baseline-loading your network is to test its scalability. For example, if you use NetBench to analyze file server performance with multiple clients, you can add unrelated traffic to the network with an instance of NetTraffic running on a client connected to a server that's not running NetBench. The added traffic simulates the network load of, for instance, application servers.

Recording Network Traffic Data with Counter Logs

Counter logs enable you to collect network performance data over long periods of time and then analyze the data by importing the log file to SysMon or a spreadsheet application, such as Microsoft Excel. Long-term data is useful for analyzing network usage patterns and checking for periodic network bottlenecks, such as at the beginning of the workday when a large number of users log on to the network simultaneously.

You can save counter logs in either of the following basic formats:

- Comma-separated values (.csv) or tab-separated values (.tsv) text files for importing into the SysMon graphs, spreadsheets, or databases—PerfMon automatically saves the text file when the test stops. Each time you start a test, you create a new text file.
- Binary files (.blg) or binary circular files (also .blg) that you can import only into SysMon for viewing—Both file types support stopping and restarting the log operation. Binary files accumulate data continuously; binary circular files contain only the latest values for the set of counters you specify.

Configuring Counter Logs

The process of configuring counter logs is similar to that for the SysMon network traffic displays described earlier in the chapter. You specify the name of the counter log, which automatically generates the name of the counter log file, add counters, and specify how you want to start and stop the logging process.

To create a counter log that records values of interest for monitoring network traffic, do the following:

1. If you saved a PerfMon custom console, open it from the Run dialog; otherwise, launch PerfMon. Expand the Performance Logs and Alerts node, right-click Counter Logs, and choose New Log Settings to open the dialog of the same name.

2. Type a description in the Name text box and click OK to open the General page of the *LogName* Properties dialog. The default log filename, created from LogName with a serial number and .blg extension appended, appears in the Current Log Filename text box. The default location for log files is `d:\PerfLogs`.

3. Click Add to open the Select Counters dialog, select the Select Counters from Computer option, and select or type the name of the local or remote server to log in the combo list.

RECORDING NETWORK TRAFFIC DATA WITH COUNTER LOGS | 903

PART
III
CH
22

4. Select Network Interface from the Performance Object list, select Bytes Total/sec in the Select Counters from List box, select the server's network adapter in the Select Instances from List box (see Figure 22.8), and click Add to add the counter to the Counters list.

Figure 22.8
You use the Select Counters dialog to specify the data to include in the counter log.

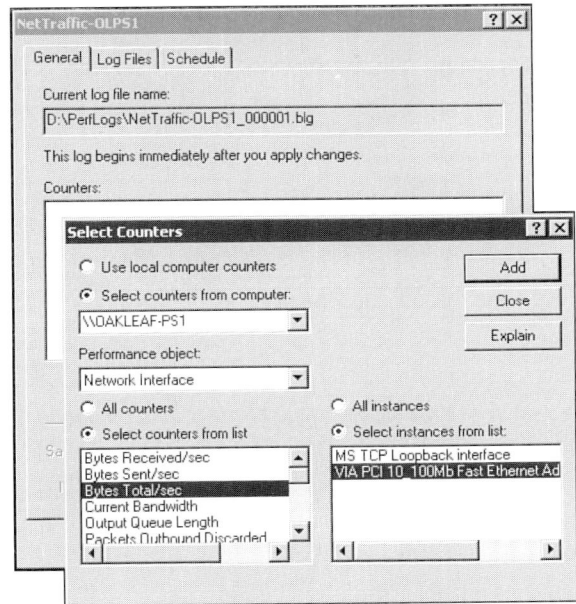

5. Repeat step 4 for each additional counter value to log (Physical Disk, % Disk Time and Server, Bytes Total/sec). Add additional servers and their counters, if needed, and then click Close to dismiss the Select Counters dialog.

6. Type the sample period you want in the Interval text box and select the time scale from the Units list. The default is a sample every 15 seconds, which is appropriate for an initial test of logging operations.

7. Click the Log Files tab to specify filename and type options. Accept or change the log file folder in the Location text box, and select the numbering convention for successive files in the End File Names With list.

8. Select the type of file to create (.csv, .tsv, or one of the two .blg formats) in the Log File Type list, and add an optional description of the counter log in the Comment text box. You also can limit the log file size, if you want, but for the initial test, the default values are satisfactory (see Figure 22.9).

Figure 22.9
Accept or alter the default values for log file location, name, format (type), and size in the Log Files page of the *LogName* Properties dialog.

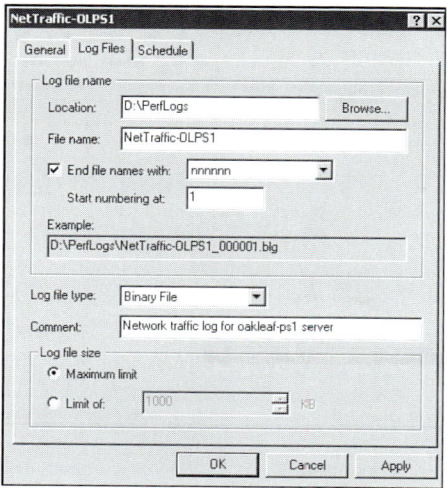

Tip from
RJ

If you want to view the log file data in a SysMon graph and import the log file into an Excel worksheet or Access database, select either the `.csv` or `.tsv` format.

9. Click the Schedule tab. If \PerfLogs or the folder you specified to store log files doesn't exist, a message box asks whether you'd like to create it.

10. Select the Start Log Manually option for the initial logging test (see Figure 22.10). Alternatively, you can set a starting and ending time for automated logging. Click OK to save the counter log configuration and add the new log item to the Counter Logs' list pane.

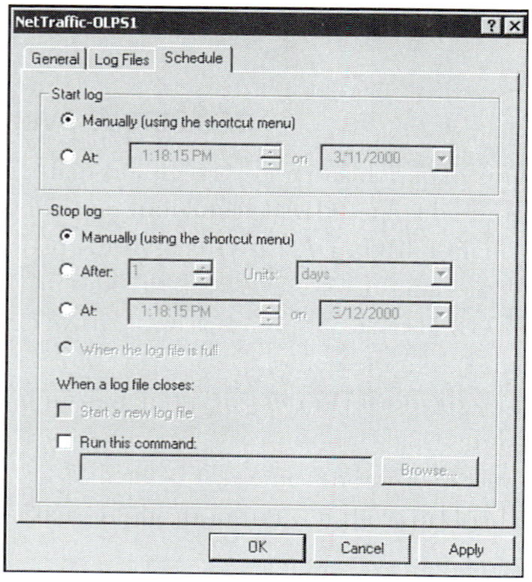

Figure 22.10
Select the Schedule page's Start Log Manually option for initial testing of counter logs.

Recording Network Traffic Data with Counter Logs | 905

If you attempt to start your first counter log file at this point, you receive an error when attempting to connect to counters on a remote server. If you didn't select Start Log Manually in step 10, you will receive an error message that advises that you don't have privileges to gather performance data from the remote server.

Enabling the Performance Logs and Alerts Service to Connect to Remote Servers

Performance logs and alerts use the Performance Logs and Alerts service to capture data from the local computer or remote server. By default, this service runs under the LocalSystem account. The LocalSystem account doesn't have logon rights to remote PCs, so you must change the account under which the service starts. The account under which you start the service must have at least logon rights to the remote server.

Tip from
RJ

The Performance Logs and Alerts service defaults to Manual startup. The service doesn't start until you start a performance log or alert.

To change the logon account for the Performance Logs and Alerts service, do the following:

1. Right-click My Computer and click Manage to open the Computer Management snap-in.
2. Expand the Services and Application and Services nodes to display the list of services in the snap-in's right pane, and double-click the Performance Logs and Alerts item to open its properties dialog.
3. Click the Log On tab and type the name of an administrative account, such as **DOMAIN\Administrator**, having logon privileges for the remote computer (see Figure 22.11). Alternatively, click Browse and double-click the account to use in the Users, Computers, and Groups dialog.

Figure 22.11
You must change the logon account for the Performance Logs and Alerts service to an account with at least logon rights to each remote server you want to monitor.

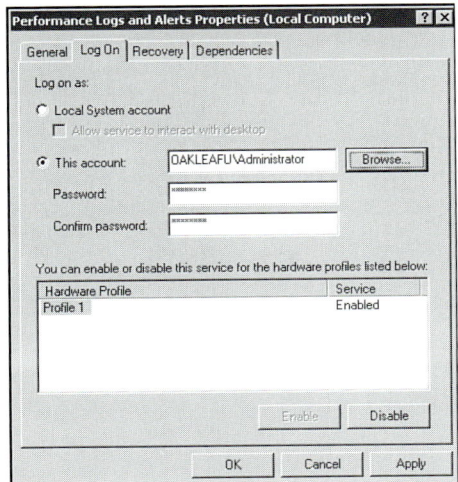

4. Click Apply to change the logon account. A message indicates that the account has been granted the Log On As a Service privilege on the local computer.

5. Click the General tab and click Start to test the new logon account. The service starts and then automatically shuts down, which is the correct behavior for the service.

6. Close the properties dialog and Computer Management snap-in.

Logging and Viewing Counter Data

To give your counter log a test run and view the saved data in SysMon's graph or an Excel worksheet, run this drill:

1. If you want to generate more than background traffic, launch an instance of NetTraffic on a client and connect to the server you're logging. Alternatively, manually copy a very large file from the server to a client.

2. Right-click the entry for your counter log and choose Start to start the logging operation. After a second or two, the Performance Logs and Alerts service starts, and the entry's icon changes color from red (stopped) to green (started).

3. After a few minutes, right-click the entry for your counter log, and choose Stop to save the .blg or .csv/.tsv file you specified when you configured the counter log.

4. To open the log file in SysMon, click the SysMon toolbar's View Log File Data button (fourth from the left with the cylinder icon) to open the Select Log File dialog.

5. Navigate to the location of your log files (usually d:\PerfLogs) and double-click the file to open. The file data replaces the current contents of SysMon's graph (see Figure 22.12). The time base of the graph adjusts to display all data points in the log.

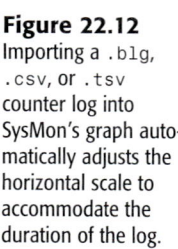

Figure 22.12
Importing a .blg, .csv, or .tsv counter log into SysMon's graph automatically adjusts the horizontal scale to accommodate the duration of the log.

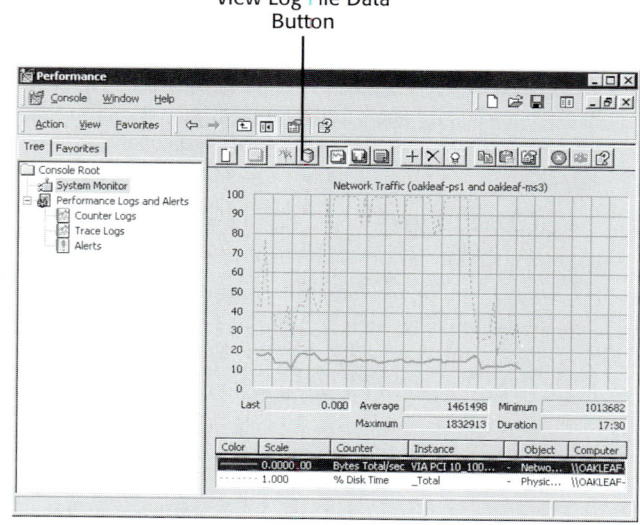

Note

SysMon calculates the Average, Minimum, and Maximum values shown in Figure 22.12. The log file stores only instantaneous counter values.

6. To view numerical data in Microsoft Excel or another spreadsheet application, open the `.csv` or `.tsv` file. If you use Excel, the Text Import Wizard opens to enable you to specify import parameters. When you accept the Wizard's defaults, the imported file opens, as illustrated by Figure 22.13.

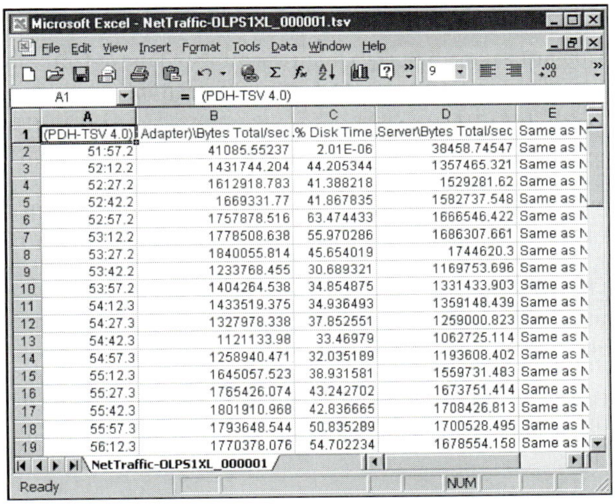

	A	B	C	D	E
1	(PDH-TSV 4.0)	Adapter)\Bytes Total/sec	% Disk Time	Server\Bytes Total/sec	Same as N
2	51:57.2	41085.55237	2.01E-06	38458.74547	Same as N
3	52:12.2	1431744.204	44.205344	1357465.321	Same as N
4	52:27.2	1612918.783	41.388218	1529281.62	Same as N
5	52:42.2	1669331.77	41.867835	1582737.548	Same as N
6	52:57.2	1757878.516	63.474433	1666546.422	Same as N
7	53:12.2	1778508.638	55.970286	1686307.661	Same as N
8	53:27.2	1840055.814	45.654019	1744620.3	Same as N
9	53:42.2	1233768.455	30.689321	1169753.696	Same as N
10	53:57.2	1404264.538	34.854875	1331433.903	Same as N
11	54:12.3	1433519.375	34.936493	1359148.439	Same as N
12	54:27.3	1327978.338	37.852551	1259000.823	Same as N
13	54:42.3	1121133.98	33.46979	1062725.114	Same as N
14	54:57.3	1258940.471	32.035189	1193608.402	Same as N
15	55:12.3	1645057.523	38.931581	1559731.483	Same as N
16	55:27.3	1765426.074	43.242702	1673751.414	Same as N
17	55:42.3	1801910.968	42.836665	1708426.813	Same as N
18	55:57.3	1793648.544	50.835289	1700528.495	Same as N
19	56:12.3	1770378.076	54.702234	1678554.158	Same as N

Figure 22.13
Microsoft Excel 2000 displays five columns for a `.tsv` log file having three counter values. The first column (A) is the time of the measurement (in minutes and seconds), and the last column (E) is comment text.

Tip from *RJ*

Don't sort the data in an Excel worksheet on column A. The minutes value in column A rolls over from 59:59.9 to 00:00.0, so sorting on time scrambles the time sequence of your data.

The advantage of importing numerical data into Excel is that you can use Excel's statistical functions and other data manipulation methods to display custom tabular data or generate graphs and charts, including three-dimensional views of data from multiple log files.

If your counter log won't start or you have logging troubles, see the "Problems with Counter Logs" topic of the "Troubleshooting" section near the end of this chapter.

Setting Alerts on Out-of-Bounds Counter Values

PerfMon's Alerts feature enables you to log an event, send a message, start a performance log, launch an application, or do all four when the value of a counter exceeds or falls below a preset limit. The process of adding an alert log is quite similar to that for creating a counter log. You name the alert, add counters and threshold values, specify what you want to happen when the counter value goes above or below the limit, and pick the method you want to start and stop the alert. Alerts are very useful for troubleshooting intermittent network problems that otherwise would require you to analyze very large counter file logs to find the problem.

> **Tip from**
> *RJ*
>
> As is the case for performance logs, you must change the logon account for the Performance Logs and Alerts service to enable alerts on remote computers.

→ For instructions on changing the server logon account, **see** "Enabling the Performance Logs and Alerts Service to Connect to Remote Servers," **p. 905**.

To set an alert on a local or remote computer, do the following:

1. If you saved a PerfMon custom console, open it from the Run dialog; otherwise, launch PerfMon. Expand the Performance Logs and Alerts node, right-click Alerts, and choose New Alert Settings to open the New Alert Settings dialog.

2. Type a short alert description in the Name text box and click OK to open the General page of the *AlertName* Properties dialog. Add an optional longer alert description in the Comment text box.

3. Click Add to open the Select Counters dialog, select the Select Counters from This Computer option, and select or type the name of the local or remote server to log in the combo list.

4. For this example, select Physical Disk from the Performance Object list, % Disk Time in the Select Counters from List box, and Total in the Select Instances from List box. % Disk Time values near 100 indicate that disk performance is limiting network traffic. Click Add to add the counter to the Counters list, and then click Close to dismiss the Select Counters dialog.

5. Choose Over or Under from the Alert When the Value Is list, and type the threshold value in the Limit text box (see Figure 22.14). You can specify 100 for the % Disk Time threshold, because the counter value can exceed 100 with heavy disk loads.

6. Optionally, repeat steps 3 through 5 to add additional counters and alert thresholds for one or more servers.

7. Accept or change the default 5-second sampling rate in the Interval text box and Units list. In a production environment, it's common to specify a sampling interval of 1 to 5 minutes to minimize consumption of server resources by the alert process.

SETTING ALERTS ON OUT-OF-BOUNDS COUNTER VALUES | 909

PART
III

CH
22

Figure 22.14
Add an alert description and counter(s), set the threshold for each counter, and specify the sampling interval for all counters in the General page of the *AlertName* Properties dialog.

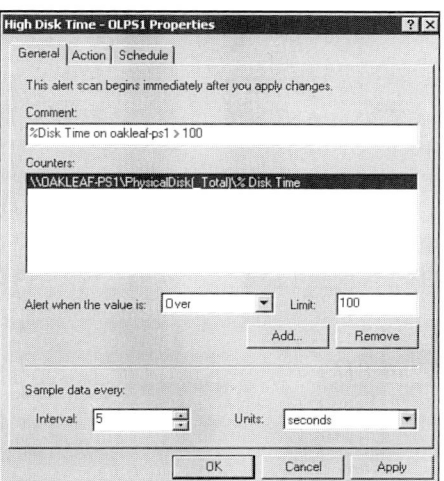

8. Click the Action tab to specify what happens when an alert triggers. Accept the default Log an Entry in the Application Event Log action. If you also want to use the Messenger service to send a message to a particular Windows 2000 or NT client, mark the Send a Network Message To check box and type the name of the client in the text box. To start a previously defined counter log when the alert triggers, mark the Start Performance Data Log check box and select the Counter Log in the list (see Figure 22.15). You also can launch a custom application and supply it with optional command-line arguments.

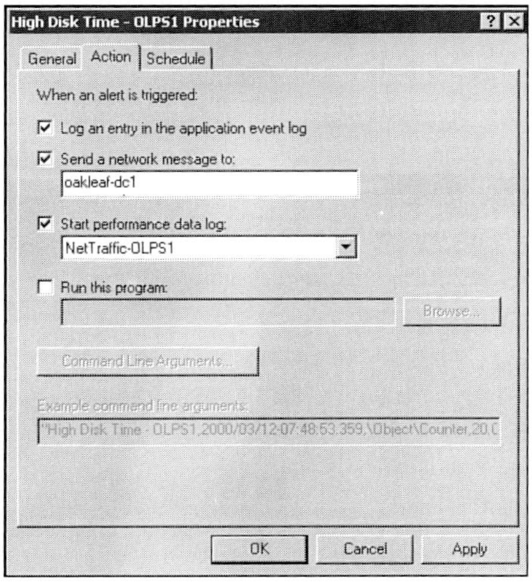

Figure 22.15
Specify the operations you want to occur when an alert fires in the Action page.

Tip from
RJ

Consider increasing the sampling interval if you mark the Send a Network Message To check box. The client receives a message each time the alert fires, so you might encounter hundreds of message boxes on an unattended machine. Also, verify that the Messenger service is running on the client you specify in the associated text box.

9. Click the Schedule tab and select the Start Scan Manually and Stop Scan Manually options for alert testing (see Figure 22.16). Alternatively, you can set starting and ending times or test duration and mark the Start a New Scan check box to run the alert during specified hours of the day.

Figure 22.16
Select the manual start and stop options for alert testing in the Schedule page. In production, you can schedule the start time and duration of alert operations.

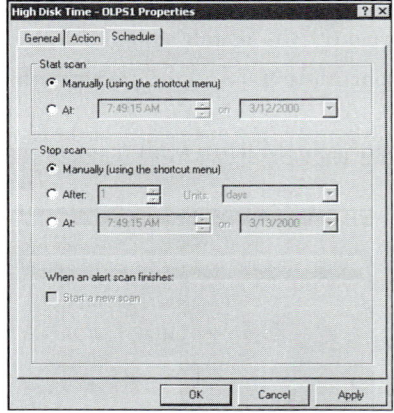

10. Click OK to save your settings and return to the Performance snap-in. Chose File, Save to save the configuration if you've created a custom console.

To start the new alert, select the Alerts node, right-click the new alert item in the list pane, and choose Start. The Performance Logs and Alerts service starts and the alert's icon changes from red to green. After a few minutes, open Event Viewer and check the application log for SysmonLog entries with event ID 2031, which indicates an alert has triggered; event ID 2023 indicates the alert has started a counter log. If you marked the Action page's Send a Network Message To check box, messages similar to that shown in Figure 22.17 appear on the specified client.

Figure 22.17
If you select the Send a Network Message To feature, the Messenger service opens a message box on the specified client each time an alert triggers.

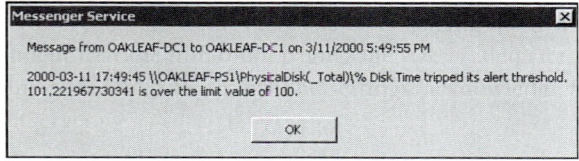

Monitoring Network Activity with NetMon

Network Monitor (NetMon) is intended primarily for network troubleshooting, not performance monitoring. You should, however, become familiar with NetMon's basic features, because you might need to use NetMon to determine sources of excessive network traffic. For instance, you can quickly find computers that are sending an extraordinary number of broadcasts. Excessive broadcast traffic degrades subnet throughput.

The version of NetMon included in Windows 2000 Server's Administrative Tools enables you to capture and analyze network Ethernet frames that travel to and from the local computer's network adapter. NetMon provides summary network data during the frame capture process. When you stop the capture, NetMon delivers a very detailed analysis of captured frames. You can filter the frames to display only packet types of immediate interest.

> **Note**
> The version of NetMon included with Microsoft Systems Management Server (SMS) enables you to connect to and capture data from any computer on the network. Each instance of NetMon measures only a single computer's traffic, so you must run multiple instances of NetMon if you want to simultaneously capture data from more than one server.

Setting Up NetMon

To start NetMon, connect to the appropriate network adapter, and capture summary network data, do the following:

1. Choose Programs, Administrative Tools, Network Monitor to launch the `Netmon.exe` application. Unlike most other Windows 2000 tools, NetMon isn't an MMC snap-in.

2. If you're opening NetMon for the first time, click OK to acknowledge the Select Default Network message and open the Select a Network dialog. Expand the Local Computer node to display a list of the network adapter(s) on the computer. If you have more than one adapter, select the device with the appropriate Blob Tag Value (see Figure 22.18). Click OK to close the dialog.

Figure 22.18
Select a network adapter to monitor when opening NetMon for the first time.

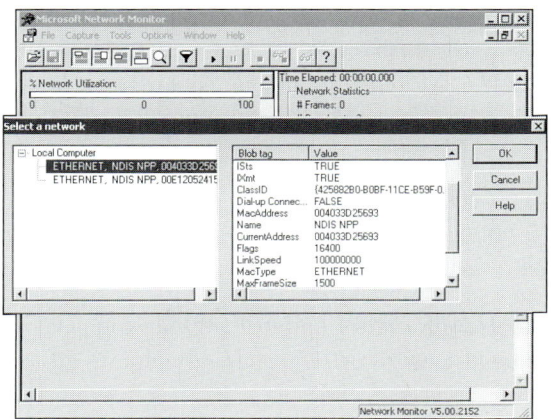

Tip from
RJ

To change network adapters after your first selection, choose Capture, Networks to open the Select a Network dialog.

3. Click the Start Capture toolbar button to begin the capture process. The Graph pane (top left) displays instantaneous traffic data. After a few minutes, entries for most or all of the computers on the network appear in NetMon's Session Statistics (middle left) and Station Statistics (bottom) panes. The Total Statistics pane (top right) displays accumulated values.

4. To make it easier to identify computers on the network, right-click one of the Media Address Control (MAC) entries in the Station Statistics pane and choose Edit Address *MACAddress* to open the Address Information dialog. Replace the MAC address in the Name text box with the computer name, mark the Permanent Name check box, and add an optional descriptive comment (see Figure 22.19). Optionally, change the LOCAL name to the name of the computer running NetMon.

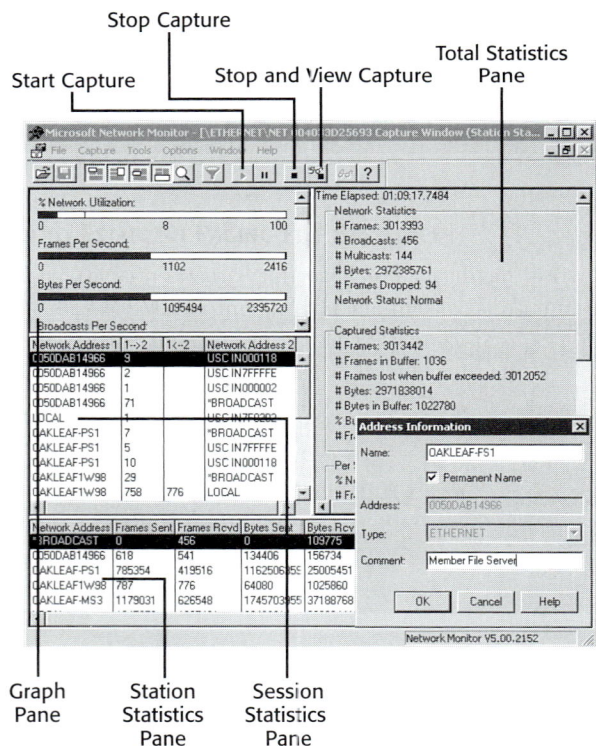

Figure 22.19
Use the Address Information dialog to translate computers' MAC addresses to computer names. The OAKLEAF-PS1, OAKLEAF-MS3, and OAKLEAF1W98 computer names are translated.

DISPLAYING AND ANALYZING CAPTURED FRAME DATA

To display and analyze the data in NetMon's temporary capture file, do the following:

MONITORING NETWORK ACTIVITY WITH NETMON | 913

1. Click the Stop and View Capture button to open the capture function's Summary pane, which lists the captured Ethernet frames. Scroll the display and double-click one of the frame entries in the list to add the Detail (middle) and Hex (bottom) panes to the display.

Note

You can apply a filter to display only a single type of Ethernet frame, such as SMB, in the display.

→ For instructions on how to use NetMon capture filters, **see** "Applying a Frame Type Filter," **p. 1008**.

2. Double-click one of the + icons in the Detail pane to expand the frame display. Figure 22.20 illustrates a Server Message Block (SMB) frame that delivers file data from the oakleaf-ps1 server to the client running NetMon.

Figure 22.20
NetMon's Capture display enables you to examine the contents of either net frame. In this example, 1,397 bytes of waveform audio (.wav) data in a file copy operation follow the highlighted values in the hex pane.

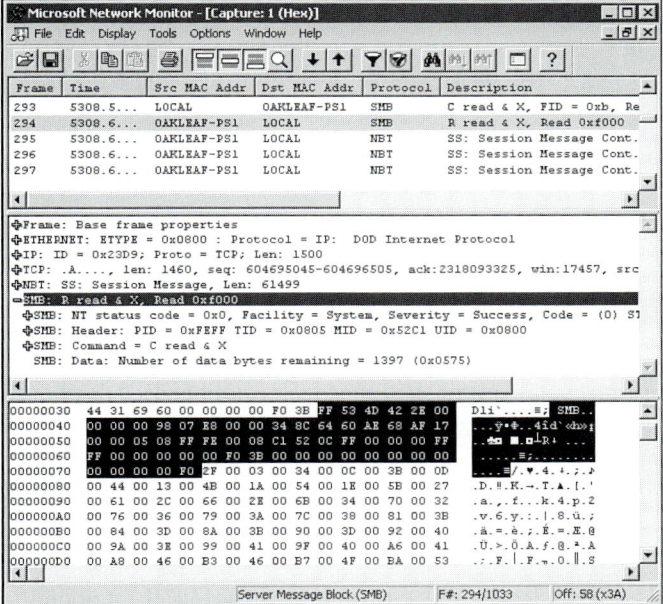

3. Close the Capture window to return to NetMon's primary window.
4. To find the computer sending the most broadcast traffic, right-click in the Station Statistic's pane's Broadcasts Sent column, and click Sort column to display the entries in descending order of frames sent (see Figure 22.21).

PART
III
CH
22

Figure 22.21
Sorting the Broadcasts Sent column displays the computer sending the most broadcast frames during capture at the top of the list. None of the computers in this example have originated an abnormal number of broadcasts.

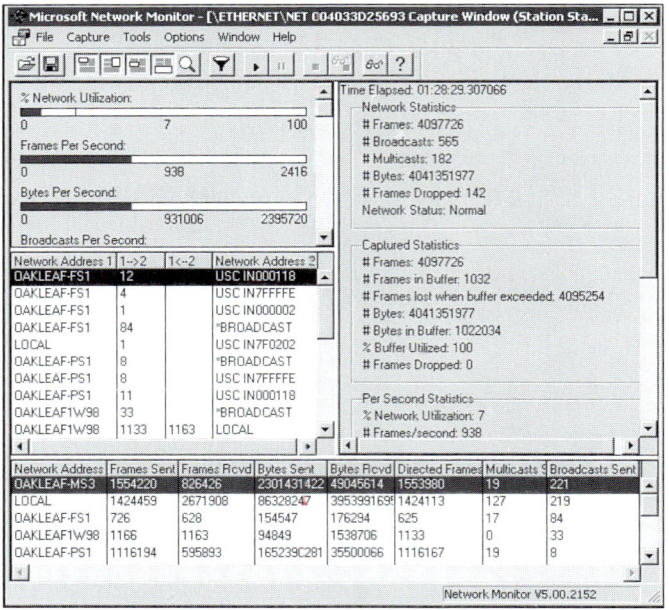

All computers on the subnet receive broadcast frames, so NetMon's inability to connect to remote computers doesn't present a problem in this case. If you suddenly encounter an unexplained loss of effective network throughput, use NetMon to check for broadcasts. You also can use NetMon to find computers that are playing streaming media files from the Internet. Run NetMon on the server that's connected to your Internet Service Provider (ISP) and check for a large number of HTTP frames addressed to TCP port 4046 or UDP frames on ports 4824 and 4639, which indicate Windows Media video traffic. Windows Media audio sends HTTP frames to TCP port 1660. Source and destination addresses of the captured frames enable you to track the originating servers and the clients receiving the streaming media content.

Tip from
RJ

One source of excessive broadcast traffic is configuration of network routers to pass broadcasts. This isn't a common occurrence, because it defeats one of the primary incentives for subnetting networks—isolating broadcast traffic.

UNDERSTANDING THE BROWSING PROCESS

In a fully upgraded Windows 2000 network, network browsing isn't an issue—all servers and clients obtain their lists of shared resources from those you publish in AD. Windows 2000's Browser service is provided for backward compatibility. If you have computers running Windows 9x and NT on the network, the Browser service must continue to run, even if you install the Directory Services Client on the downlevel computers. You also must run the Windows Internet Naming Service (WINS) if your Windows 2000 domain has a subnetted network.

When a downlevel client or server starts, it broadcasts a request that computers identified as master browsers report their computer name. By default, the DC holding the Primary Domain Controller (PDC) emulator role is the domain master browser, which holds the browse list for the entire domain. In a subnetted network, each subnet has its own master browser, which obtains its list by replication from the domain master browser.

If a master browser is unavailable, backup browsers—which obtain their list from the master browser—accommodate the request. Assignment of domain master, master, and backup browser status is automatic. The default list replication rate is 4 minutes, so it can take a substantial period of time for new service announcements to replicate from domain master to master to backup browsers. Advise network users to be patient when browsing for a newly added resource; it might take up to 20 or 30 minutes for the newly shared resource to appear in Network Neighborhood or the Printers window.

> **Note**
>
> When a server joins the network for the first time or after a long absence, it forces a browser election. The server acting as a Windows 2000 PDC emulator has the priority to obtain domain (master) browser status. If the PDC emulator is down, Windows 2000 DCs are next in line for master browser status, followed by member servers. Windows NT servers and workstations, as well as Windows 9x computers sharing files or printers, can become master browsers under exceptional circumstances.

The browse list contains entries for each domain server and its shared resources—primarily folder and printer shares. When the master browser responds to the requesting computer, it delivers its browse list, which the requesting computer caches locally. Downlevel computers display the cached browse list in Network Neighborhood (NetHood) and the Printers list (PrintHood).

The command-line `Browstat.exe` application enables you to check the status of all browser computers on your network. If network browsing isn't working properly for downlevel clients, run `Browstat.exe` to verify that the expected Windows 2000 server(s) have the master and backup browser roles for your domain.

To list the browsers on your network segment, type **browstat status** at the Command Prompt to display a report similar to that shown in Figure 22.22 for the computer's domain. If the domain's PDC emulator isn't the master browser or expected computers are missing from the list, schedule a reboot of the domain master browser in an attempt to force a new election. If no backup browsers are present in a domain with multiple Windows 2000 servers, you also might need to reboot the other servers.

Figure 22.22
The browstat status command displays a list of computers serving as browsers in the domain. The network isn't routed, so the PDC emulator, OAKLEAF-DC1, serves as the master browser. OAKLEAF-PS1 and OAKLEAF-FS1 are backup browsers. One member server, OAKLEAF-MS3, doesn't participate in the browser service.

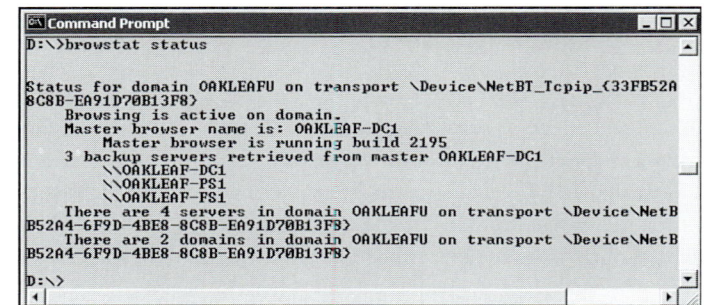

Troubleshooting

Problems with the NetTraffic Application (NetTraf.exe)

NetTraffic throws a `File Not Found` *error immediately after you click the Start Traffic button.*

The server name, share name, or filename you typed in the Source File text box isn't valid, or the network connection to the server has failed. Verify the UNC path to the server share containing the file to copy.

NetTraffic opens a `Path Not Found` *error after you click the Start Traffic button.*

The local drive letter or folder name you typed in the Designation File isn't valid. Use Explorer or My Computer to verify the drive and folder name.

NetTraffic throws a `Permission Denied` *error a few seconds after you click Start Traffic in a second instance of the program.*

You must specify different destination file names for each open instance of NetTraffic. Change the Destination File value for the second instance to `d:\FolderName\Traffic2.wav` or the like. The Source File value, but not the Destination File value, can be the same for multiple instances.

Problems with System Monitor

SysMon's graphical display freezes when you open a custom console with counters running on remote server(s).

The client on which you're running PerfMon can't connect to one of the remote servers you specified in the Add Counters dialog. Failure to connect to one remote server disables performance measurements from all other remote servers.

Problems with Counter Logs

You receive an error message when attempting to start a counter log for a remote server.

The most likely cause of the error is failure to change the logon account for the Performance Logs and Alerts service, as described in this chapter's "Enabling the Performance Logs and Alerts Service to Connect to Remote Servers" section. Launch the Event Viewer snap-in and check the Application log for warnings from the SysmonLog source. Event IDs 2046 and 2029 indicate that the Performance Logs and Alerts service's logon account doesn't have logon privileges for the remote server.

You will receive the same error message if the remote server you're attempting to log isn't running. In this case, when you acknowledge the message, the icon for the counter log in PerfMon's list turns green. A SysmonLog Information event (ID 2023) appears in the Application log indicating that logging has started or restarted. When you attempt to open the log file in SysMon, you receive an error message stating that the file contains less than two records.

MCSE Corner: Monitoring and Tuning Your Network

Troubleshooting has become an important focus of the Windows 2000 exams—more important than it has been in the past (on older exams). The System Monitor is an essential part of many Windows 2000 troubleshooting operations, and questions about the System Monitor are asked on exam 70-215, "Installing, Configuring, and Administering Microsoft Windows 2000 Server." Some of these topics also apply to exam 70-216, "Implementing and Administering a Microsoft Windows Network Infrastructure."

The most important skill that you learned in this chapter was the use of the System Monitor tool for monitoring both local and remote servers. This chapter explained how to use the System Monitor and how to add counters and monitor performance. It also explained how to use the System Monitor graph and customize its output. It explained a concept important to almost all troubleshooting: establishing baselines. Several exams cover the use of System Monitor.

70-215 Installing, Configuring, and Administering Microsoft Windows 2000 Server

The first essential thing to know for the exam is the basic use of the System Monitor, including the different ways to collect information (for example, views and alerts.) You should know how to add counters and how to use the important counters. A basic understanding is required about how to interpret the data returned by the System Monitor and how to use that data to optimize your system. You should also know how to configure all the different methods of displaying data—such as graphs, logs, and alerts—and be able to troubleshoot the System Monitor and logs.

70-216 IMPLEMENTING AND ADMINISTERING A MICROSOFT WINDOWS 2000 NETWORK INFRASTRUCTURE

Knowing how to use the Network Monitor tools and drivers is important for this exam. You need to know how to configure these tools and use them to monitor network traffic. You should be able to use the monitor data to identify and repair network traffic bottlenecks. Being able to simulate load and establish baselines will also help. You should be able to use the NetMon tool to capture and analyze network packets and perform traffic analysis.

CHAPTER 23

OPTIMIZING, BACKING UP, AND RESTORING YOUR SERVERS

In this chapter

Adapting to the Optimization and Backup Routine   920

Server Optimization—Sizing and Tuning   920

Tuning Fixed-Disk Drives and RAID Arrays   926

Optimizing Memory Management   940

Understanding the Backup Process   948

Developing a Backup Strategy   956

Organizing Backup Tape Rotation Methods   959

Using the Windows 2000 Backup Application   965

Restoring from Windows 2000 Backups   971

Automating Backup Operations with the Task Scheduler   976

Troubleshooting   978

MCSE Corner: Optimizing, Backing Up, and Restoring Your Servers   979

Adapting to the Optimization and Backup Routine

After you've gotten your Windows 2000 servers up and running with Active Directory (AD), connected your client PCs, and tuned your network, it's tempting to sit back, relax, and contemplate your successful upgrade or new installation of Windows 2000. Unfortunately, relaxation isn't included in a system administrator's job description. You now must embark on the next two phases of the system lifecycle—server optimization and system backup.

Server optimization and backup/restore operations are included in a single chapter because both are routine—but very important—elements of a system administrator's duties. Server optimization is a continuous process of tuning your hardware and software to accommodate increasing system load that occurs as a result of growth in the number of networked users, their individual demand on your servers, and the addition of new server-hosted applications and services.

Server backup is a daily activity that's amenable to almost total automation, but the routine nature of backup operations can lead to a false sense of security. Backup operations require periodic evaluation of your ability to fully restore the servers from backup tapes in the minimum amount of time. Restoring production servers is the only nonroutine event covered in this chapter. If performing full restoration of servers becomes a routine operation, you are in deep trouble.

Note: Automatic System Recovery (ASR), one of the topics covered in Chapter 8, "Deploying Windows 2000 Production Servers," is an alternative to using the Windows 2000 Backup application to back up and restore only your system partition. You normally use ASR to store the system partition backup copy on a partition of another disk drive; ASR doesn't back up data in any other server volumes. This chapter covers conventional tape backup and restore operations with the new Windows 2000 Backup program.

Server Optimization—Sizing and Tuning

Optimizing the performance of Windows 2000 Server—like its Windows NT predecessors—is more an art than a science. Server optimization involves two basic operations—sizing and tuning. *Sizing* primarily encompasses adding RAM, increasing the number of processors, and adding or augmenting fixed-disk drives and arrays. *Tuning* is the process of adjusting operating system and application parameters to gain the maximum performance from your existing hardware. In many cases, resizing your servers also requires retuning them.

Server optimization involves the following three elements:

- *Hardware* elements include the system BIOS, CPU(s), RAM, fixed-disk subsystems, and network and other adapters. Chapter 7, "Specifying Server and Data Storage Hardware," delivers sizing recommendations for acquiring or upgrading Windows 2000 servers. Chapter 22, "Monitoring and Tuning Your Network," offers topology recommendations and hardware advice for removing bottlenecks from your WAN and LAN. This chapter covers only those hardware-related problems you can tune by altering BIOS or operating system parameters, and sizing paging files.
- *System processes* encompass tuning Windows 2000 memory management, disk I/O operations, file defragmentation, and service priorities. This chapter concentrates primarily on optimizing operating system services.
- *Server applications* include optimizing Web servers (Internet Information Server 5.0), relational database management systems (SQL Server 7+), messaging systems (Exchange 2000 Server and Microsoft Message Queue Server), and COM+ applications and components. Tuning Internet Information Server (IIS) 5.0, SQL Server 7+, and Exchange 2000 Server is beyond the scope of this book. Chapter 28, "Managing Transaction and Messaging Services," provides brief coverage of tuning techniques for Microsoft Message Queuing 2.0 and COM+ applications running on application servers.

Clearly, the preceding three elements interact to determine overall performance of a particular server. As mentioned in Chapter 7, having adequate RAM are the primary key to server performance. Next in line usually are the speed and number of processors installed. Finally, fixed-disk configuration and speed play a significant role in server performance. This is especially true for application servers that run disk-intensive services such as databases, message stores, and Active Server Pages. Even if you have the latest and greatest hardware, optimizing system processes usually delivers a perceptible performance boost.

Server Tuning Tools

Microsoft includes basic server tuning tools with Windows 2000 Server and its higher-end siblings (Advanced Server, AppCenter Server, and Datacenter Server). The Support Tools add-in and the Windows 2000 Server Resource Kit sold by Microsoft Press provide additional tuning tools. Microsoft doesn't categorize all the tools listed in the following sections as performance or tuning tools, but each of these applications or snap-ins can be useful for optimizing your server and the applications it runs.

Tools Installed by Setup

Windows 2000 Server Setup installs the following applications and a snap-in to aid the server tuning process:

- Task Manager (Taskman.exe)—Displays lists of running applications and processes, graphic display of CPU and memory usage and usage history, and text-based details of running processes and memory status (see Figure 23.1). Windows 2000's Task Manager is essentially identical to the version included with Windows NT 4.0.

Figure 23.1
The Performance page of the Task Manager shows CPU Usage and Memory Usage details. This system is a domain controller performing Active Directory replication tasks.

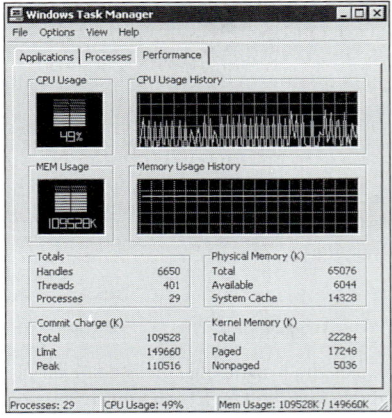

- Network Monitor (Netmon.exe)—Provides a graphic display of network utilization and traffic, and tabular network traffic summaries between computers. NetMon also captures and displays data on individual frames crossing the network.

→ For details on the use of NetMon to display and capture network traffic data, **see** "Monitoring Network Activity with NetMon," **p. 911**, and "Setting Up Network Monitor," **p. 997**.

- System Performance Monitor (Perfmon.msc)—A Microsoft Management Console (MMC) snap-in that provides a graphic display of performance data for a local or remote computer. (Running Windows 2000's Perfmon.exe launches MMC with Perfmon.msc installed.) PerfMon reads counter data from the registry and charts the dynamic behavior of CPUs, physical and virtual memory, processes, and process threads. Chapter 22 introduces you to the use of PerfMon in a network-tuning context. This chapter concentrates on using the PerfMon counters to tune your servers.

- Disk Defragmenter (Dfrg.msc)—Improves load-from-disk time for applications and components by reorganizing files so that their clusters are in sequential physical order on the drive (see Figure 23.2). Unfortunately, Dfrg.msc doesn't defragment the Windows 2000 paging file.

Server Optimization—Sizing and Tuning

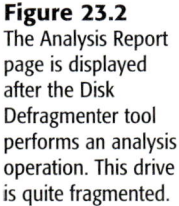
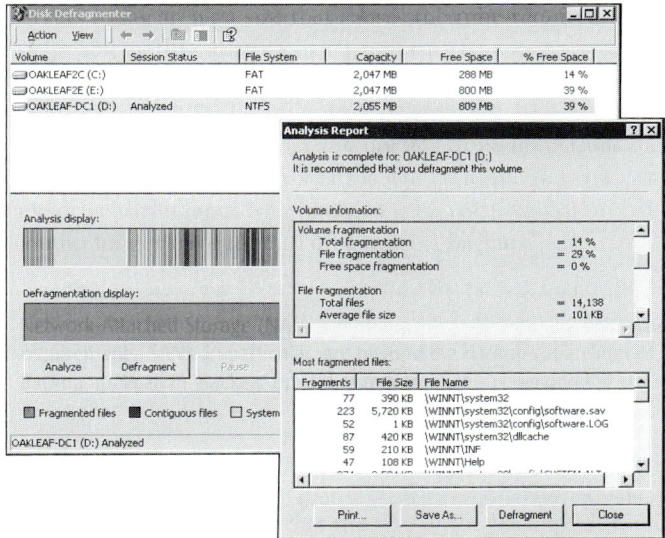

Figure 23.2
The Analysis Report page is displayed after the Disk Defragmenter tool performs an analysis operation. This drive is quite fragmented.

Support Tools' Tuning Applications

Windows 2000 Support Tools are a collection of applications that in prior versions would have been provided in the Windows Resource Kit. Microsoft determined early in the development cycle that administrators would need a basic set of tools and documentation to design, install, and manage Windows 2000 Server systems.

Installing the Support Tools from the distribution CD-ROM adds the following performance-related applications to your \Program Files\Support Tools folder:

- Process Viewer (Pviewer.exe)—An advanced version of TaskMan's Process's page. Choose Programs, Support Tools, Tools, Process Viewer to launch the application. PViewer provides extensive, detailed information on the process you select (see Figure 23.3). PViewer's memory page lets you select a process component and display its memory usage. You use PViewer primarily to troubleshoot applications and components that exhibit performance problems.

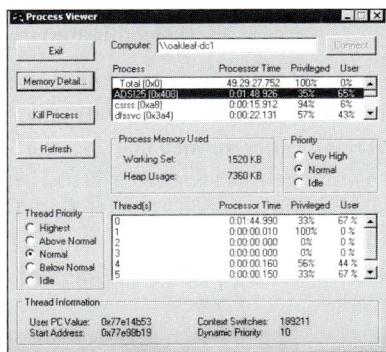

Figure 23.3
The Process Viewer tool is open and displaying the processor time for each thread of the selected Visual Basic application and the application's total processor time.

- Memory Profiling Tool (Memsnap.exe)—A command-line tool that writes entries detailing memory resource consumption to a log file. Like many other Support and Resource Kit Tools, MemSnap is useful for determining the source of memory leaks. A memory leak is the result of an application, component, or service that consumes increasing amounts of memory as it runs—usually as a result of failing to release memory allocations.

- Pool Monitor (Poolmon.exe)—Another command-line tool that you use primarily for detecting memory leaks. PoolMon writes memory allocation (Allocs) and releases (Frees), along with other memory-related data for a tagged process. You use the Enable Pool Tagging option of the Global Flags Editor (Gflags.exe) to enable PoolMon's process tagging.

- Process Resource Monitor (Pmon.exe)—A command-line tool that writes a list of CPU and memory usage values to the Command window or, by redirection, to a file you specify. PMon is another useful tool for finding memory leaks.

- Task List Viewer (Tlist.exe)—A command-line utility that writes a list of currently running processes to the Command window or to a file.

> **Note**
> The emphasis of Support Tools on detecting memory leaks is the result of the prevalence of leakage in custom-written and even commercial components and applications. In many cases, deterioration in a server's performance over time is the result of memory consumption by a leaky component or application written in C or C++. Rebooting releases the over-allocated memory, but rebooting servers periodically isn't a long-term solution to a leakage problem.

Performance Tools in the Windows 2000 Resource Kit

The Windows 2000 Server Resource Kit, a multivolume set of books and CD-ROMs, is an essential resource for system administrators. The majority of the tools in the Windows 2000 Resource Kit are duplicates of—or minor upgrades to—those in the Windows NT 4.0 Server Resource Kit and its supplements.

The Resource Kit adds the following performance-related tools in your \Program Files\Resource Kit folder:

- Performance Monitor 4 (Perfmon.exe)—The Windows NT 4.0 version of PerfMon. When you launch Performance Monitor from \Program Files\Resource Kit, you have the option of using Windows 2000's standard PerfMon version or the Resource Kit's version 4.0.

- Windows 2000 Performance Counters Reference (Counters.chm)—An HTML Help file that provides lists of all standard counters defined by Windows 2000 Server (see Figure 23.4). The Bottleneck-Detection Counters topic offers links to lists of the most-used counters for the specified object. The entry for each counter includes its name, a description of its purpose, and the type of counter—such as PERF_COUNTER_RAW_COUNT or PERF_RAW_FRACTION. The Performance Counters Reference is one of the most valuable tuning-related features of the Resource Kit.

Server Optimization—Sizing and Tuning | 925

Figure 23.4
The Resource Kit Counters.chm help file is open in the Help Viewer showing the counter table for the Memory Object in the right pane.

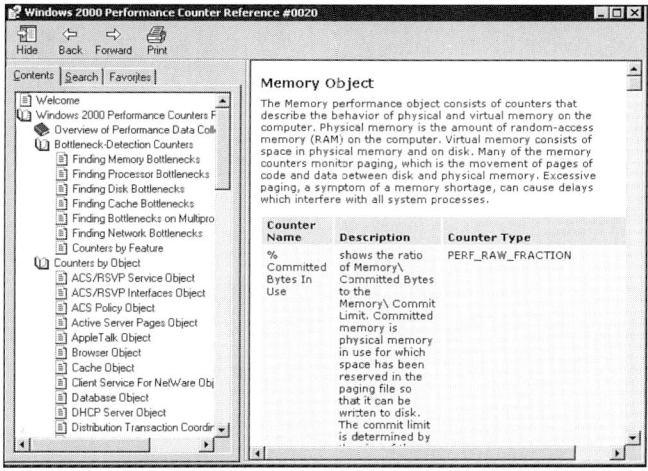

PART
III
CH
23

- **Extensible Counter List (Exctrlst.exe)**—Opens a window that displays a list of the Performance Registry entries for counters provided by Microsoft and third-party software vendors. If you believe a counter is missing from PerfMon's list, use Exctrlst.exe to check for the required dynamic link library (DLL). Figure 23.5 shows a missing DLL for Terminal Service (TermSvc) object counters; the counters are missing because Terminal Services aren't installed on the OAKLEAF-DC1 server.

Figure 23.5
The Extensible Counter List dialog shows a .DLL file, which is required to support the Terminal Services counters but is missing or not installed.

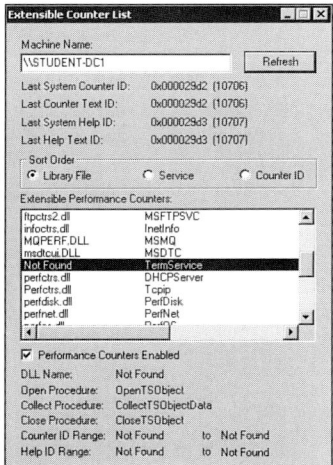

- **Performance Meter (Perfmtr.exe)**—A command-line tool that delivers tabular performance statistics at a rate of about two readings per second. You can obtain real-time data on CPU, virtual memory (VM), file cache, pool, and I/O usage; Cache Manager read/write operations; and Virtual Device Manager and server statistics. Pressing a key specified in the report header lets you change the report type on-the-fly.

- Process Explode (Pview.exe)—A more comprehensive version of PViewer that displays memory details for each running process and lets you display and alter the security context under which each process runs.

- Install Remove Service (Srvinstw.exe)—A handy tool that quickly removes unneeded or unwanted services from your server. Removing services your server doesn't need is one of the first steps in system optimization.

- LeakyApp (Leakyapp.exe)—A simple graphical tool that emulates an application with such a severe memory leak that it consumes all available memory in its own process. Use LeakyApp to test the effect of low memory on other running applications. LeakyApp releases its memory lock on command or when you close it.

You probably won't need to use all or even most of the tools in the preceding lists—many of them are very specialized and oriented to developers, not administrators. You should, however, be aware of the tools' availability in case you're requested by a software vendor to run detailed tests aimed at solving elusive performance problems.

Tuning Fixed-Disk Drives and RAID Arrays

Assuming you followed Chapter 7's recommendations for the minimum amount of RAM in your single- or multi-processor server, you probably can get best results from your initial optimization efforts by tuning your drives or RAID arrays. The following sections describe, in order of most probable performance improvements, recommendations for tuning your fixed-disk storage subsystem.

Tip from
RJ

Don't use file compression or encryption if you want to maximize disk read-write performance. Compression or encryption consumes large amounts of processor cycles, and slows disk write operations substantially. Encryption eliminates the repeated groups of characters on which compression depends, so the normal 20% to 40% disk space saving for compressed files doesn't apply to encrypted files. Encrypt only those files that contain truly confidential or sensitive information.

Altering the Default Cluster Size

All common fixed-disk drives now use 512KB sectors, but NTFS isn't concerned with sector size. Windows NT uses the term *allocation unit* interchangeably with cluster. The operating system's file system groups one or more sectors into clusters. Increasing the cluster size makes read and write operations more efficient at the cost of increased wasted (slack) space, especially in files whose size is appreciably less than the cluster size. Files with slack space are said to be *internally fragmented*.

Table 23.1 lists the default number of sectors per cluster, and cluster size for NTFS-formatted volumes of varying sizes. Default cluster sizes up to 4GB have remained the same since Microsoft introduced Windows NT 3.1. Microsoft added default cluster sizes for larger drives as their use became more common.

TUNING FIXED-DISK DRIVES AND RAID ARRAYS | 927

TABLE 23.1 DRIVE CLUSTER SECTORS AND SECTOR SIZE AS A FUNCTION OF TOTAL VOLUME SIZE

Volume Size	Sectors per Cluster	Cluster Size
<= 512MB	1	512KB
> 512MB <= 1GB	2	1KB
> 1GB <= 2GB	4	2KB
> 2GB <= 4GB	8	4KB
> 4GB <= 8GB	16	8KB
> 8GB <= 16GB	32	16KB
> 16GB <= 32GB	64	32KB
> 32GB	128	64KB

PART
III
CH
23

4GB is the minimum common size of fixed disks in today's servers and workstations, and 10,000-RPM 32GB Ultra2 or Ultra160+ SCSI with less than 6ms seek time are now available from Seagate (Cheetah 36), Quantum (Atlas 10K), and IBM (Ultrastar 36). IBM released a 72GB drive (Ultrastar 72) in late 1999. As drive size increased and cost/GB fell, slack space lost its significance in determining cluster size. You now base the cluster size for your drives or arrays solely on performance.

Tip from
RJ

Microsoft says the default cluster sizes shown in Table 23.1 are optimum, and you should approach changing cluster sizes with caution. The reality is that standard cluster sizes are the same for Windows 2000 Professional and Server—products that support entirely different application types. File servers, for instance, usually benefit by formatting drives that store shares, regardless of their capacity, with 64KB clusters. Similarly, volumes that hold large database files also should be formatted with 64KB clusters, which hold 16 4KB data pages.

CHANGING CLUSTER SIZE WITH FORMAT.EXE

The Windows 2000 Disk Manager's Format feature lets you choose the cluster size during the formatting process. Your Disk Manager options are the default cluster size listed in Table 23.1 and smaller. In some cases, however, you might want to make the cluster size larger than the default. Larger clusters are especially beneficial for storing streaming audio and video files. You're likely to find that increasing cluster size improves the performance of most file and application servers.

Note

You can't use NTFS compression on volumes with a cluster size larger than 4KB. As noted earlier, you should avoid file compression if you need optimum read-write performance from individual drives or arrays.

To increase the cluster size, you must reformat the disk with Windows 2000's Format.exe command-line tool. To reformat volume *d:* with a larger cluster size, such as 8KB, type

format *d:* /FS:NTFS /A:8192

Other valid cluster size arguments are /A:16K, /A:32K, and /A:64K. If Format.exe determines that the cluster size is inappropriate for the volume, it refuses to proceed with formatting.

Tip from RJ	Run Windows NT's or Windows 2000's Chkdsk.exe on the NTFS-formatted volume on which you plan to install or reinstall Windows 2000 Server. In some cases, you might find that the cluster size on 1+GB disks is 512KB, not the expected 2KB or larger value. When you install Windows 2000 Server, Setup accepts the existing cluster size. It's usually difficult to pinpoint the cause of cluster misallocation; running Chkdsk.exe from a diskette prior to installing Windows 2000 and reformatting with the default cluster size, if necessary, can prevent the need for later reinstallation of Windows 2000.

DETERMINING OPTIMUM CLUSTER SIZE WITH PERFMON

Before you change the cluster size, which requires reformatting your disk(s) and reinstalling your files from backup tapes, use PerfMon with the PhysicalDisk object counters to determine the average size of disk transfers on your server. Start with the PhysicalDisk object's Avg. Disk Bytes/Read and Avg. Disk Bytes/Write counters, then run a baseline test with your current cluster size.

Tip from RJ	The safest and usually fastest method for determining optimum cluster size is to partition a disk of a test server into two 2GB or larger volumes. Using relatively small volumes on a large physical drive minimizes the effect of drive geometry on your results. Format the first volume with the default cluster size of your production server, install Windows 2000, add test application(s), and perform the following baseline tests. Then format the second volume with the optimum—presumably larger—cluster size, do the installation chores, and repeat the tests. Plan on devoting a minimum of three hours to the tests.

To measure the average size of server read and write operations under normal or simulated operation, do the following:

1. Choose Administrative Tools, Performance to open PerfMon.
2. Click the toolbar's plus (+) button to open the Add Counters dialog.
3. Accept the default Select Counters from This Computer option, which displays the NetBIOS name of the local computer in the associated list. Alternatively, select the Use Local Computer Counters option.
4. Select PhysicalDisk from the Performance Object list, accept the default Select Counters from List option. In the counters list, click Avg. Disk Bytes/Read, and then press Ctrl and click Avg. Disk Bytes/Write. Click the Explain button to add a window that displays a brief description of the last counter you select.

5. If you have more than one physical drive or RAID set, accept the default Select Instances from List option, select the volume(s) you want to monitor in the list (see Figure 23.6). For a single physical drive, you can select the All Instances option.

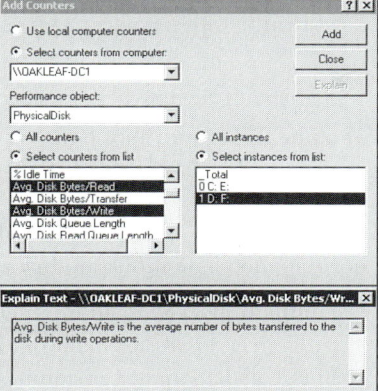

Figure 23.6
The Add Counters dialog shows the Avg. Disk Bytes/Read and Avg. Disk Bytes/Write counters selected for the second physical disk on the system (disk 1), which contains the D: and F: volumes.

> **Note**
> In Figure 23.6, system files are on drive 0's C: volume, and drive 1 stores applications and shared files on the D: and F: volumes, respectively.

6. Click Add and then Close to add the counters, close the Add Counters dialog, and begin collecting data (see Figure 23.7).
7. If your server is running in production, collect data over a sufficient period to return a representative average value of the two counters. Otherwise, use test clients to emulate production conditions and note the average value at the end of the test period (see Figure 23.7).

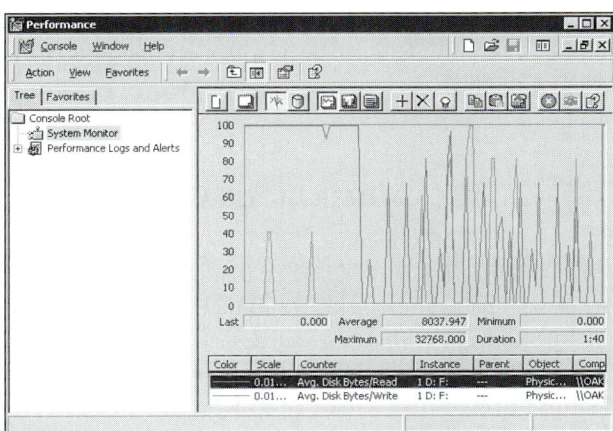

Figure 23.7
This System Monitor graph view shows the Maximum and average values of bytes per read operation during addition of 100 OakLeaf University employee users with the ADSI25 application.

Note

The Last, Average, Minimum, and Maximum values under the graph are those for the counter you select in the list at the bottom of the window. Make sure to review the averages for both read and write operations during the test.

→ For more information on the ADSI25 Visual Basic application that's on the accompanying CD-ROM, **see** "ADSI25 Application Description," **p. 1255**.

Tip from
RJ

Run a stress-testing application, such as Bluecurve's Dynameasure/File on networked clients to emulate a production file-serving environment. You can download a time-limited test version of Dynameasure/File from http://www.bluecurve.com/download/trialProducts/trialproducts.htm. A stress-testing application provides much more accurate performance comparisons, because you can duplicate exactly test conditions with different cluster sizes.

8. To obtain approximate baseline data on data transfer rate with a particular application, add the Disk Bytes/sec counter to the graph and run a disk-intensive application (see Figure 23.8). Record the maximum value during the period that the application is active.

Figure 23.8
The System Monitor now contains a Disk Bytes/sec counter.

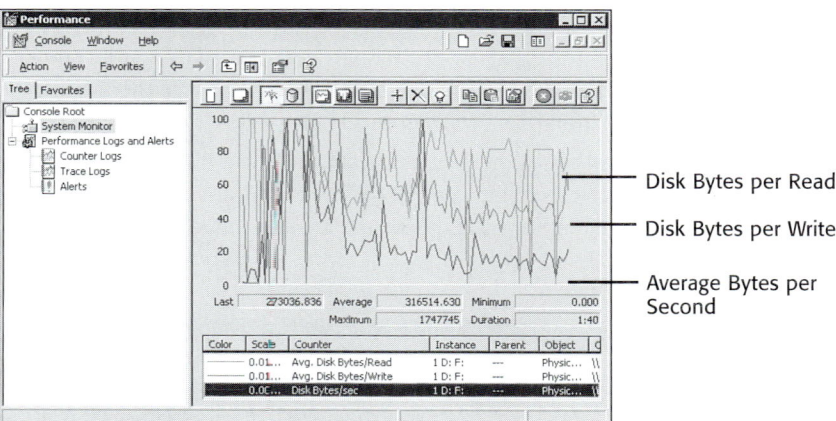

→ For more information on installing and running the ADSI25 application, **see** "Installation on a Windows 2000 DC or Workstation," **p. 1259**.

9. Click the Report button of the toolbar to display counter data in tabular form.
10. Right-click the report and choose Properties to open the System Monitor Properties dialog. You can specify only one type of value for the entire report or histogram view, so select Average, and click OK. Figure 23.9 is an example of a simple report for the average values of the three counters that were shown in Figure 23.8. The values update at the rate specified in the Properties dialog.

Tuning Fixed-Disk Drives and RAID Arrays

Figure 23.9
The System Monitor report view shows the average values of the defined counters—in this case Avg. Disk Bytes/Read, Avg. Disk Bytes/Write, and Disk Bytes/sec.

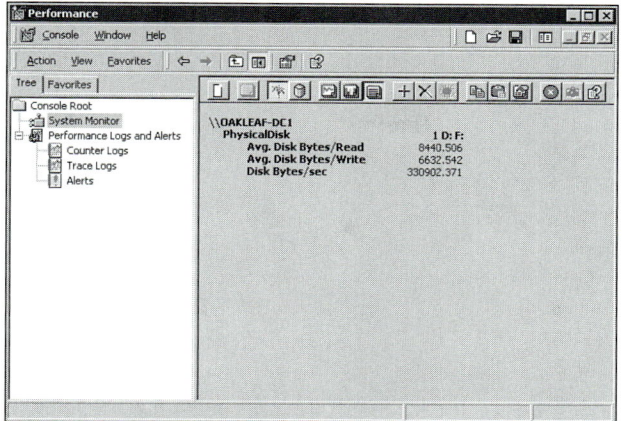

> **Note**
> You can save the report in HTML (.htm) or tab-separated-value (.tsv) format by right-clicking the report and choosing Save As.

11. Save the counter setup for reuse by choosing Console, Save As and saving the console file with a descriptive name, such as DiskBytes.msc. By default, PerfMon saves .msc files in your \Winnt\System32 folder.

After you've determined the average size of disk data transfers, you might want to alter the cluster size to increase performance. Follow these steps:

1. Once you've determined the average size of disk data transfers, perform a full backup of your production server's application or file-sharing drives.
2. Next, reformat those drives with a cluster size greater than the larger of the two Avg. Disk Bytes values, but no smaller than the default cluster size shown earlier in Table 23.1.
3. Restore your server files and compare the results by viewing Disk Bytes/sec and comparing the perceived or measured response speed of applications. Increasing the cluster size from the default 4KB to 16KB reduced the ADSI25 Visual Basic application's time to add 100 employee accounts to AD by about 25%, a significant improvement.

> **Tip from**
> *RJ*
> Format physical drives or arrays as a single volume, if feasible. Partitioning individual drives or RAID sets into multiple volumes requires large head movements when alternating reads or writes between volumes. Formatting individual drives or RAID sets as a single volume also makes PerfMon measurements for physical drives more meaningful.

Organizing Drives and RAID Sets by Read- and Write-Mostly Operation

If you've invested in a large RAID 5 disk subsystem with a hardware RAID controller, it's tempting to run all your applications and share all files from multiple volumes on the RAID 5 set. RAID 5, however, isn't as efficient for write operations as a RAID 1 mirror set, because writing to a RAID 5 set adds reading and writing parity data to the data writing task.

> **Note**
> Windows 2000's software RAID 0 arrays (stripe sets) increase performance for disk-intensive applications like capturing high-quality digital video content. RAID 0 involves very little CPU overhead, but applications like video capture are better reserved to workstations. Software RAID 1 arrays (mirror sets) have moderate overhead, but hardware RAID controllers are a better choice. Avoid software RAID 5 arrays (stripe sets with parity); the parity operations required to read and write RAID 5 consume an excessive percentage of CPU cycles.

Following are general recommendations for the types of data to store on RAID 5 subsystems:

- Read-only or read-mostly files, such as application executables, static Web pages, graphics, and read-only shares and their replicas.
- Decision-support databases, including most types of Online Analytical Processing (OLAP) databases. Read operations on decision-support databases commonly outnumber writes by two or three orders of magnitude.
- Exchange Server public folders and other relatively static information stores.
- Active Directory's database file (Ntds.dit). After you stabilize your AD topology, the read-write ratio of AD operations is similar to that of decision-support databases. Store Ntds.dit in its own volume, because AD turns off disk write caching on this volume.
- COM+ components of n-tier applications, including transactional components.

→ For disk write caching details, **see** "Setting Drive Properties," **p. 937**.

Store the following types of data on RAID 1 sets:

- Windows 2000's paging file. Your server should have a sufficient amount of RAM to eliminate paging under most circumstances. If you can't afford enough RAM to eliminate paging, put the paging file on a different physical RAID 1 set than for the operating system.
- Operating system log and capture files—especially large ones generated by PerfMon and Network Monitor (NetMon). These log files aren't critical, so they're candidates for storage on a non-RAID drive or RAID 0 stripe set.
- Online transaction processing (OLTP) database and log files. OLTP combines read and write operations, so you need to analyze file operations to determine the ratio of writes to reads to make the RAID 1 versus RAID 5 decision. Always store OLTP log files on a different physical RAID 1 set than the set you use to store the data files.

- Internet Information Server, Exchange Server, Message Queue Server, and Active Directory log files.
- Collaborative documents to which multiple users make frequent changes.

Use PerfMon's % Disk Read Time, % Disk Write Time, and % Disk Time (total time) counters to determine whether the physical disk runs in read-mostly or write-mostly mode. Even a read-mostly disk with a 2:1 ratio of read to write times is a good candidate to move from RAID 5 to RAID 1. It's difficult to obtain accurate read-write ratios with PerfMon on physical drives with multiple volumes in production environments, because the % Disk Read Time and % Disk Write Time values apply to the disk as a whole. Figure 23.10 shows typical values for the three disk counters during addition of users with ADSI25.

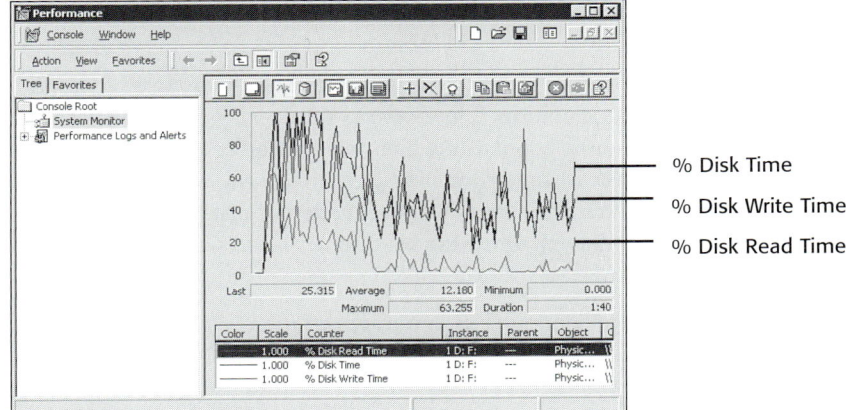

Figure 23.10
This System Monitor graph view displays the % Disk Read Time, % Disk Time, and % Disk Write Time. This graph is created during a batch addition of users to the Active Directory, which is a write-intensive operation.

Tip from
RJ

Defragment your drives with Disk Defragmenter or a third-party Windows 2000-compliant disk defragmentation utility before running % Disk Times tests. Disk Defragmenter is the subject of the next section. Installation of Windows 2000 on a newly formatted disk usually displays some fragmentation, and you're certain to have fragmentation if you remove and add applications or Windows components with Control Panel's Add/Remove programs tool.

Note

Adding users and other directory objects to AD as a bulk operation with ADSI or the Active Directory Migration Tool (ADMT) involves much more disk writing than reading. Bulk addition of AD objects isn't a common procedure, so don't base your storage location decision on data that includes bulk addition operations.

You should run multiple tests spanning several hours to obtain accurate measurement of read-write ratios on individual physical drives. Save the PerfMon Counter Log for each test run with the % Disk Times counters formatted as a comma- or tab-separated text file, which you can import into Microsoft Excel for statistical analysis.

→ To review creating Counter Logs, **see** "Configuring Counter Logs," **p. 902**.

DEFRAGMENTING FILES

When Microsoft introduced Windows NT 3.1, the company claimed that NTFS didn't suffer from file fragmentation, and thus there was no need for the popular defragmentation utilities offered by third-party vendors for DOS and Windows 3.x.

Helen Custer's *Inside the Windows NT File System* (Microsoft Press, 1964) mentions only internal file fragmentation, inferring by omission that external fragmentation doesn't occur with NTFS.

Users of Windows NT 3.1 and its successors quickly discovered that NTFS did, indeed, suffer from file fragmentation. Thus, several third-party defragmentation utilities appeared on the market, the most popular of which was Executive Software's Diskeeper for Windows NT Server. There is some controversy regarding the mathematical relationship between the percentage of file fragmentation and reduction of disk I/O performance, but there is no doubt that periodic defragmentation of server—and workstation—drives is an absolute necessity.

Microsoft finally abandoned its "no fragmentation" claim and included the Disk Defragmenter utility with all versions of Windows 2000. Disk Defragmenter is a licensed subset of the full Diskeeper utility familiar to most Windows NT 4.0 administrators. Disk Defragmenter appears in two incarnations, depending on how you start it. Choosing Programs, Accessories, System Tools, Disk Defragmenter opens Dfrg.msc in a single-pane MMC console. Right-clicking My Computer, choosing Manage, and clicking Disk Defragmenter in Computer Management's tree view pane opens the Disk Defragmenter window in the right pane.

Tip from	Don't defragment a production server volume during working hours. Defragmentation consumes a substantial amount of CPU horsepower and % Disk Time that won't be available to your server applications.
RJ	

To defragment a volume, do the following:

1. Launch Disk Defragmenter, select the volume to defragment in the Volume list, and then click Analyze.

2. After a few minutes—the number of which depends on disk size and space used—you receive a message recommending that you defragment or not defragment the volume (depending on the amount of fragmentation). Click OK to dismiss the message and view the color-coded defragmentation Analysis Display (see Figure 23.11).

Figure 23.11
The Analysis Display of the Disk Defragmenter utility shows the results from a highly fragmented disk.

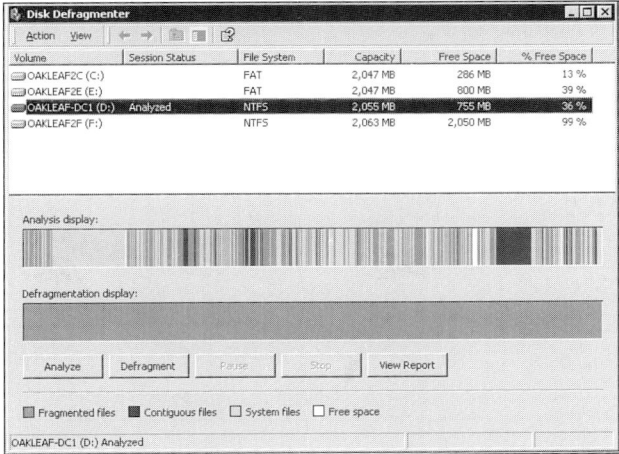

3. Click View Report to open the Analysis Report dialog. If File Fragmentation is more than about 25%, defragmentation returns significant performance dividends. Figure 23.12 shows the Analysis Report for the volume analyzed in Figure 23.11.

Figure 23.12
The Analysis Report from the same volume as in Figure 23.11 gives you detailed information about which parts of the file system are most fragmented and which files are most fragmented.

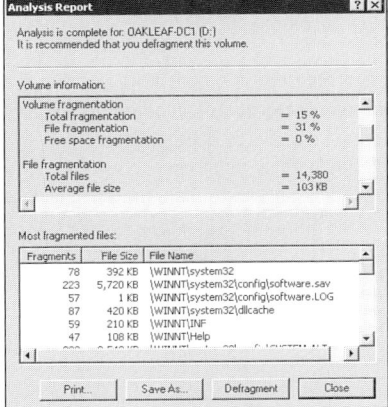

4. If you're interested in checking resources consumed by the defragmentation process, launch PerfMon and add % Processor Time, % Disk Time, and, optionally, Avg. Disk Queue Length counters.

5. Click Defragment to reanalyze the volume and start the defragmentation process. Figure 23.13 shows PerfMon's display during defragmentation of an UltraDMA/33 IDE system volume. Defragmenting a SCSI drive of similar performance and size requires about half the processor and disk times of the IDE drive.

Figure 23.13
This System Monitor graph view monitors the % Processor Time, % Disk Time, and Avg. Disk Queue Length counters for an IDE hard disk being defragmented.

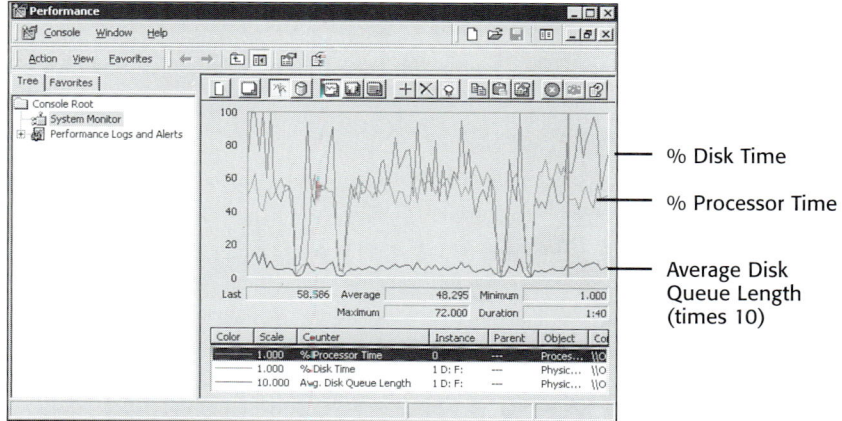

6. When defragmentation completes, click Report to check the result.

For this example, file fragmentation for the IDE drive with system files decreased from 31% to 18%. Repeating the process reduced file fragmentation to 9%, and a third pass reduced the value to 8%. It's evident from these results that Disk Defragmenter compromises defragmentation efficiency for a shorter operational cycle, and that more than two defragmentation passes accomplish very little.

> **Note**
> Defragmentation is less efficient for volumes containing system files than for volumes that store file shares. Ordinarily, you need only defragment the system volume occasionally—usually after removing and then adding applications. Disk Defragmenter doesn't defragment the paging file or the NTFS Master File Table (MFT) that's located in about the middle of the system volume, because these two files are locked for exclusive use by Windows 2000 at all times.

SPREADING THE DRIVE WORKLOAD

If you have more than one RAID set, consider analyzing your drive workload with the goal of balancing the load on individual RAID sets. The most important PerfMon counter for analyzing drive load is Physical Disk's Avg. Disk Queue Length, which specifies the number of disk read or write operations waiting for execution. Compare the Avg. Disk Queue Length—together with % Disk Time—of each RAID set, then move applications or shares to the set with the lowest Avg. Disk Queue Length value. Moving applications, of course, usually requires uninstall and reinstall operations to set new Registry key values. Moving conventional shares requires re-creating the shares and setting their permissions; the Distributed File System (Dfs) simplifies the process of moving shares to another volume. Dfs also enables share replication to even the workload on drive sets.

→ For more information on Dfs, **see** "Taking Advantage of the Distributed File System," **p. 707**.

Setting Drive Properties

Windows 2000 adds the following three options on two physical disk hardware property pages. The last two options appear only for SCSI drives:

- Marking the Enable Write Caching check box of the hardware properties dialog's Disk Properties page lets you take advantage of the disk controller's or drive's hardware write-back cache, if present. Write caching accepts sector data to memory, the controller or drive reports to the operating system that the data was written to the disk, and then the drive performs the physical write-to-disk operation.

   Write-back caching can speed write operations significantly, but at the risk of data loss in the event of a power failure or system malfunction before the cached data is written to the disk. You can overcome power failure data losses by installing an uninterruptible power supply with a controlled shutdown feature. Write-back caching is independent of the Windows 2000 disk caching performed by Cache Manager, the subject of the next section.

> **Note**
> As mentioned earlier in the chapter, promoting the computer to an AD Domain Controller automatically disables write-back caching. If you demote the computer to a member server, re-enable write-back caching if you want to use this feature.

- Marking the Disable Tagged Queuing check box of the SCSI Properties page turns off sorting of I/O commands in a sequence that minimizes head travel. Marking this check box reduces drive performance, but might be useful as a temporary setting for troubleshooting drive problems.

- Marking the Disable Synchronous Transfers check box of the SCSI Properties page causes the SCSI drive to operate in asynchronous mode. Asynchronous data transfers require that the drive acknowledge successful completion of the prior data transfer before allowing Windows 2000 to perform another data transfer. Synchronous mode is considerably faster than the alternative, so mark this check box only when troubleshooting.

To open the properties dialog for a drive, do the following:

1. Right-click My Computer, choose Manage, and click Disk Management.
2. Right-click any volume in the upper pane's list or an icon in the lower pane, and choose Properties to open the properties dialog for any volume.
3. Click the Hardware tab, select the volume's physical drive in the All Disk Drives list, and click Properties to open the properties dialog for the drive. Figure 23.14 shows the SCSI page of the hardware properties sheet for a Seagate Barracuda UltraWide SCSI drive.

Figure 23.14
The Properties dialog includes the SCSI Properties page for a Seagate 15150W Barracuda Ultra Wide SCSI disk drive.

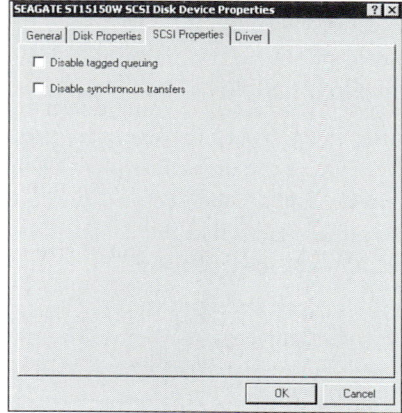

ANALYZING DISK CACHING

Windows 2000's Cache Manager automatically creates a virtual memory file cache that dramatically increases the efficiency of local and network file I/O operations. Cache Manager uses *virtual block caching* to store disk sector data in the sequence in which it's used, rather than by physical sector location on the drive. This type of caching eliminates the need to calculate sector offsets for nonsequential (fragmented) sectors and the resulting increase in drive head movement. *Logical block caching* is an alternative—and less efficient—technique used by Windows 9x and older UNIX versions. Logical block caching caches data in sector order, so file fragmentation plays a major role in cache performance.

> **Note**
> Microsoft SQL Server and most other client/server relational database management systems (RDBMSs) create their own cache when the service starts. RDBMSs use very specialized cache allocation and optimization processes. Applications that allocate their own block of RAM for caching don't rely on Cache Manager or Memory Manager for their management. The following discussion is valid only for applications and services that rely on Windows 2000 for disk cache management.

The default address space of the VM cache is 512MB for computers with 64MB or more RAM, and up to 960MB with 128MB or more, if you don't have Terminal Services installed. When an application or a user requests file reads or writes, Cache Manager loads the VM cache from the drive by a disk I/O request. Cache Manager then makes guesses about the data the application wants next and loads these sectors into the VM cache—a process called *read-ahead caching*. If the guess is correct, the application or user receives data from the cache, instead of from a disk I/O request—called a *cache hit*. Otherwise, a *cache miss* occurs and Memory Manager calls the disk driver and obtains the required data from the drive.

Cache Manager also implements *lazy writes*—a process by which file updates are stored in the cache, then written asynchronously to the disk as a background activity. The NTFS transaction log assures that a power failure immediately before or during a cache flush operation doesn't corrupt files. Hardware-based write-back caching doesn't offer the protection afforded by the transaction log.

The large address space allocated the VM cache is somewhat misleading. The real (not virtual) cache resides in a block of RAM called the *cache working set* reserved by Windows 2000's Memory Manager. Memory Manager establishes the initial size of the cache working set during the boot process, and adjusts its size based on the amount of installed RAM less the RAM Windows 2000 allocates to the kernel, device drivers, application code, and other processes running. Task Manager's Performance page displays the current size of the cache working set as System Cache in the Physical Memory frame (refer to Figure 23.1). An idle server with 128KB of RAM typically allocates about 50MB to the System Cache. Cache hits require the data to be stored in the working set, not in the much larger VM address space.

Cache Manager and Memory Manager cooperate to allocate the cache working set dynamically, so you can't tweak your server's cache size to improve performance.

There's only one Registry key that affects the cache working set—HKEY_LOCAL_MACHINE\ SYSTEM\CurrentControlSet\Control\Session Manager\MemoryManagement\LargeSystemCache.

Windows 2000 sets this key value to 0 or 1, depending on the amount of RAM and whether you've installed Terminal Services. Changing the key value from 0 to 1 on a server with 128MB of RAM increases the initial cache working set by about 30%—from about 50MB to 64MB.

PerfMon offers several Cache object counters for analyzing cache operations:

- Copy Read Hits %, which indicates the percentage of read operations from the cache, is the most important of these. Average values of 80% or higher indicate good cache utilization.
- Copy Reads/sec and Lazy Write Flushes/sec indicate the rate of cache reads and writes, respectively.
- Read Aheads/sec is the rate at which the read-ahead cache must deliver.

Figure 23.15 illustrates PerfMon's display of these four counters during the addition of 100 employee users with the ADSI25 application—a very disk-intensive operation. The Average Copy Read Hits value (90%) shows excellent cache usage. Read Aheads/sec is close to 0, because almost all reads come directly from the cache. File-server operations are likely to have substantial Read Aheads/sec values.

Figure 23.15
The System Monitor snap-in includes four Disk Caching counters during a batch addition of User and Computer accounts to the Active Directory.

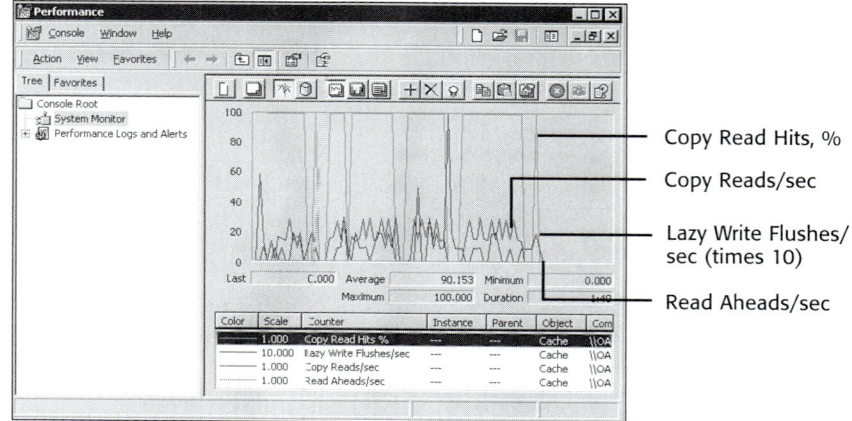

Tip from
RJ

Read the "Monitoring the Cache" topic of the Windows 2000 Resource Kit Online Books Help file (W2krkbook.chm) for a detailed description of the Cache object's counters and additional recommendations for their use in analyzing cache performance.

There's little you can do to improve caching efficiency, short of adding more RAM to your server. Use RegEdit to check the value of the HKEY_LOCAL_MACHINE\SYSTEM\CurrentControlSet\Control\Session Manager\MemoryManagement\LargeSystemCache key. If it's 0 and Terminal Services aren't running on your server, change the value to 1 to see if performance improves. If changing the key value doesn't increase Copy Read Hits to 80% or better for the majority of your applications and services, plan on adding RAM in 128KB or larger increments until you achieve reasonable Copy Read Hits values.

Optimizing Memory Management

Optimizing memory management is similar to optimizing personal cash management—like money, you never can have too much RAM. The wild fluctuations in Static DRAM (SDRAM) pricing during mid- to late-1999 made RAM purchases chancy at best. DRAM pricing probably will settle down by mid-2000, in time for your new Windows 2000 server purchases. There are few, if any, memory management problems you can't cure by specifying a minimum of 512MB of DRAM for your new server. Go for 1GB or more for multiprocessor servers running a large Web site or a large-scale database application.

Tip from
RJ

If you have sufficient memory, you can optimize server performance by adding more processors. Most firms purchase multiprocessor servers with at least two, and usually the full complement of CPUs supported by the system board. If you have empty processor slots and at least 256MB—preferably 512MB—of RAM for each processor slot, occupied or not, consider adding CPUs. As a rule, adding memory is more cost effective than adding processors, at least up to 512MB.

Sizing Paging Files

If you don't have an unlimited RAM budget or your older server has insufficient free memory slots to accommodate your RAM requirement, you must live with VM paging operations. Paging is anathema for system administrators; the necessity to swap blocks of memory between RAM and the paging file is a primary cause of server slowdown. Disk paging operations require a minimum of the drive's seek time—usually an average of about 10 milliseconds—plus data transfer time—roughly 10ms/sector. Data transfer time for 512 bytes to or from RAM, on the other hand, is a few microseconds.

The Resource Kit documentation states that Windows 2000 automatically creates Pagefile.sys having a size equal to the amount of the server's RAM plus 12MB. Installation of Windows 2000 Server on machines with 64MB and 128MB of memory resulted in default paging files of 96MB and 192MB, respectively. This indicates that Windows 2000 uses a formula of 1.5 times RAM for the default size. Recommended sizes were 94MB and 190MB; there's no explanation in the Resource Kit or other Windows 2000 documentation for the 2MB difference between default and recommended sizes.

Running Out of Virtual Memory

If you have a paging file of insufficient size, the result usually is total server failure. You can emulate running out of paging file space with the Leakyapp.exe application, mentioned earlier in the "Performance Tools in the Windows 2000 Resource Kit" section, by following these steps:

1. Start PerfMon and add the two PagingFile counters, % Usage and % Peak Usage.
2. Run Leaklyapp from the \Program Files\Resource Kit folder, and click the Start Leaking button. It takes several minutes to consume a moderate-size (100MB) paging file.
3. When the "Windows - Out of Virtual Memory" error message appears (see Figure 23.16), attempt to run another application. Most applications fail to start.

Figure 23.16
The Leakyapp.exe program consumes all available virtual memory to simulate what would happen if a real application with a memory leak consumed all virtual memory.

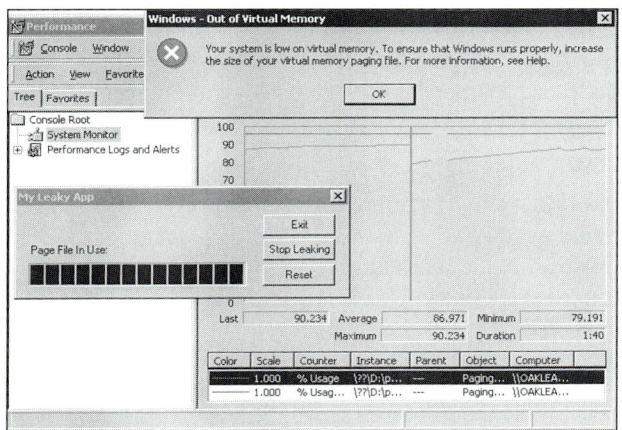

Running out of paging file space is catastrophic, especially for Domain Controllers (DCs). If a site has only one DC, users must log on to a DC in another site. If your network has only one DC—which isn't a recommended practice—users can't log on at all. Under ordinary circumstances, servers shouldn't run out of virtual memory, but services or applications with memory leaks do occur. You're quite likely to encounter memory leakage with some first releases of services and applications specifically designed for Windows 2000. It often takes a service pack or other fix, such as a version upgrade, to eliminate the memory leaks.

Changing Paging File Size and Location

You set the paging file's size and, optionally, change its location, in the Virtual Memory dialog. To view and change virtual memory settings, do the following:

1. Right-click My Computer and choose Properties to open the System Properties dialog.
2. Click the Advanced tab, and click Performance Options to open the dialog of the same name.
3. Click Change to open the Virtual Memory dialog (see Figure 23.17).

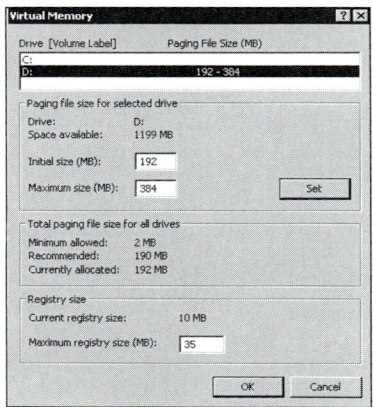

Figure 23.17
The Virtual Memory dialog shows the default Virtual Memory settings for a system with 128MB of RAM. The default size is 1.5 times the amount of RAM present.

The Paging File for Selected Drive frame displays Initial Size and Maximum Size values; for Windows 2000 Server, the default Maximum Size is twice the default Initial Size, if you have sufficient free disk space on the system volume.

4. Type new Initial (minimum) and Maximum Size values in KB in the text boxes.

   Setting equal Initial and Maximum Size values prevents the paging file from fragmenting when Windows 2000 decides to expand the paging file from the Initial Size. If you're confident that the minimum paging file size is adequate, type the same value for the maximum size, click OK to save the settings, acknowledge the reboot message, and reboot your server.

5. To divide the paging file between two volumes on separate drives, set equal Initial and Maximum Size values for the volume on the system drive. Acknowledge the warning message that appears if you set the Initial Size to less than installed RAM plus 12MB.

There's no performance benefit to dividing the paging file into two volumes on the same physical drive.

Alternatively, to move the entire paging file to a different volume, type **0** for both minimum and maximum values, and acknowledge the warning message.

6. To create or add a new paging file on another NTFS volume, select the volume in the Drive list, then specify the Initial and Maximum Size values.
7. If the new paging file volume contains files, defragment the volume at this point. If you reboot the server before defragmenting the volume, it's very likely that the new paging file will be fragmented.
8. Click OK to accept the changes, acknowledge the reboot message, and reboot the server.

For initial server testing, accept Windows 2000's default paging file size of 150% of installed RAM. Before you change the paging file size or location, read the "Improving Paging File Performance" section later in this chapter.

> **Note**
>
> Windows 2000 requires a paging file of at least 2MB in the system folder in order to accommodate system shutdown entries in the Event Log, send administrative alerts, and automatically restart Windows 2000 after a system Stop error occurs. To maintain server recoverability, set the Initial and Minimum Size values to 2MB on the system volume, then add the second paging file to a volume on another drive.
>
> If you want Windows 2000 to capture an image of the paging file during shutdown, the size of Pagefile.sys in the system folder must be equal to or greater than the amount of installed RAM plus 12MB. Saving a paging file image is valuable only for debugging applications or services that cause Stop messages.

Checking Virtual Memory Settings with Taskman and Winmsd

Task Manager's Commit Charge frame provides three dynamic values—Total, Limit, and Peak—that you can monitor to determine whether your current paging file size is adequate for your server's process activity (refer to Figure 23.1). Following are descriptions of the three values:

- Commit Peak is the maximum amount of memory (RAM plus paging file) in KB that your server has consumed since the last reboot.
- Commit Limit is the total memory available to running services and applications without enlarging the paging file.
- Commit Total is the server's current memory consumption. When Commit Total exceeds Physical Memory, paging occurs.

When Commit Total approaches the Commit Limit value, Memory Manager attempts to increase the paging file size, up the Maximum Size limit you've specified.

You can check static virtual memory settings by running Winmsd to open the System Information console, and clicking System Summary. The Winmsd.msc snap-in's data, however, is a bit misleading—Total Virtual Memory and Page File Space are based on the paging file's Maximum Size value, not the current—usually minimum—size. Figure 23.18 illustrates System Information displaying data for a server with 128MB of RAM and a paging file with 192MB Initial and 384MB Maximum Sizes. Subtracting Available Physical Memory from Available Virtual Memory results in 215,460KB. Dividing by 1,024KB/MB indicates a 210MB paging file, which is close to the actual 192MB.

Figure 23.18
The System Information snap-in shows the Virtual Memory settings for a system at the bottom of the right pane when System Summary is selected in the left pane.

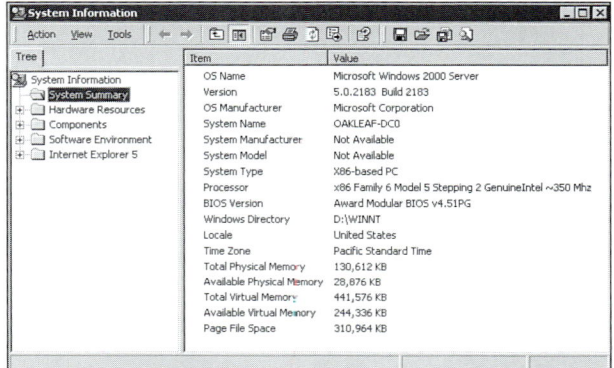

USING PERFMON TO ESTABLISH PAGING FILE BASELINES

It's tempting to take the conservative approach and specify an Initial Size value that's double or triple your installed RAM. Setting a total page file size substantially larger than required, however, wastes disk space and can cause a decrease in system performance. Once you have your server(s) running in production or in production simulation mode, use PerfMon to determine the optimum paging file size.

The most interesting Process object counters for establishing a paging file baseline value are Page Faults/sec, Page File Bytes, and Page File Bytes Peak for all processes (_Total). The Memory object's Commit Limit and Committed Bytes also are important (see Figure 23.19).

Figure 23.19
Use the System Monitor snap-in with the necessary counters to determine the optimum size for the paging file.

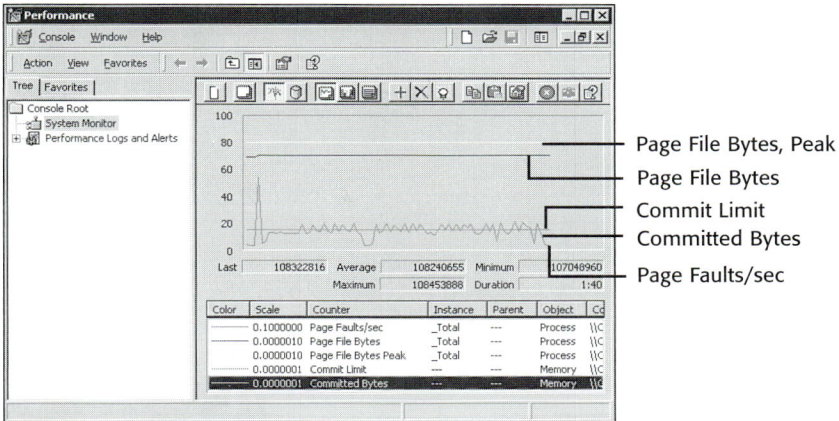

Page File Bytes Peak is the most important value for paging file sizing. Run your server under a production load for several hours before accepting the peak value. Add a safety factor in the range of 50% of the peak as the Initial Size for your new paging file. For example, the Page File Bytes Peak value shown in Figure 23.19 for a 64MB server is about 80MB, so a total of 120MB—rather than the default 96MB—is a good starting point for both Initial Size and Maximum Size values.

> **Note**
> Throughout this book, 128MB of RAM is the recommended minimum for Windows 2000 servers. A 64MB bank of memory was removed from the test server in order to demonstrate paging file operations under low-memory conditions.

Commit Limit and Commit Peak values are the same as those that TaskMan's Performance page displays. Page Faults/sec indicates the paging rate; if this value consistently exceeds 60 or so, you should take whatever action is required to add RAM to the server. Page File Bytes is useful for determining memory leakage; if this value shows a continuing increase over long periods of server operation, you probably have a leaking application or service.

SETTING A LOW-VIRTUAL-MEMORY ALERT

One of the most important PerfMon alerts is that for low virtual memory. If the PagingFile object's % Peak Usage counter exceeds 80%, your server's in trouble. The server begins to throw Windows - Out of Virtual Memory messages after consuming about 90% of the available paging file space (refer to Figure 23.16), and you can expect total server failure to occur shortly.

To receive an email warning of impending server doom, do the following:

1. Expand PerfMon's Performance Logs and Alerts node, right-click Alerts, and choose New Alert Settings to open the eponymous dialog with the General page active.

2. Type a name for the alert, such as **OAKLEAF-DC1 Low VM** in the text box, and click OK to open the alert's properties dialog.

3. Type a full description of the alert in the Comment text box.

4. Click Add to open the Select Counters dialog and add the Paging File object's % Usage Peak Counter, then close the dialog.

5. Select Over from the Alert When the Value Is list, and type **80** (or a more conservative 70 or 75) in the Limit text box.

6. Type the time between checks in the Interval spin box, and select a time units value from the Units list (see Figure 23.20); 30 minutes is satisfactory for a 70% or 75% Usage Peak setting; use 15 minutes or less for an 80% setting.

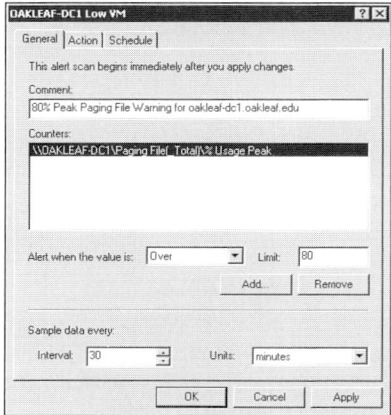

Figure 23.20
The General page of the properties dialog for an alert is designed to signal when the system uses more than 80% of its virtual memory and is set to scan every 30 minutes.

7. Click the Action tab, and mark the Log an Entry in the Application Event Log check box.

8. To use the Messenger service to send a message to your administrative workstation, mark the Send a Network Message to check box, and type the NetBIOS name of the computer in the text box.

9. To have the alert start a predefined performance log, mark the Start Performance Data Log check box, and select the previously saved log definition from the list.

10. If you have a third-party pager or email executable application, mark the Run This Program check box, and type the path and name of the executable in the text box. Click Command Line Arguments, mark the check boxes for the information to include as the argument, with an optional custom text message (see Figure 23.21). Click OK to close the dialog.

OPTIMIZING MEMORY MANAGEMENT   947

Figure 23.21
The Action page of the properties dialog (shown here in the background) for the alert enables you to specify what actions should be taken when the event defined in the alert occurs. The foreground dialog shows the Command Line Arguments that are passed to the program defined in the Run this program: box.

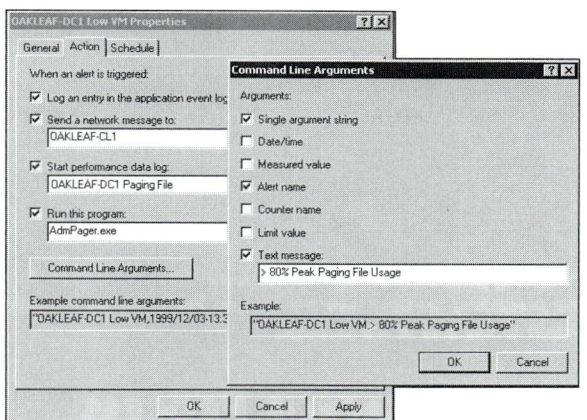

PART
III
CH
23

11. To change the schedule for the alert—or start the alert scan manually—click the Schedule tab, and set your preferences.
12. Click OK to close the alert's properties dialog.

When the alert triggers, you receive on the designated computer messages similar to that shown in Figure 23.22 at the selected interval until you fix the problem and reboot the server, you manually stop the alert, or the server dies. The Messaging service must be enabled on both the server and client PCs; Windows 2000 enables the Messaging service by default. Use Computer Management's Services feature to set the Messenger service's startup type, or start or stop the service.

Figure 23.22
This alert is displayed by the messenger service when the alert defined in Figures 23.20 and 23.21 is tripped.

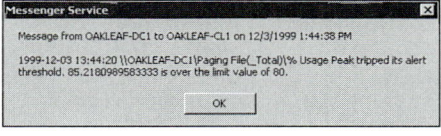

IMPROVING PAGING FILE PERFORMANCE

If circumstances dictate that you run your server with a substantial amount of paging file activity, you can gain a performance edge by dedicating a physical drive or two to the paging file. Paging files can make good use of older 1GB or 2GB SCSI-2 UltraWide drives that you've replaced with larger, higher-performance units. You might find that installing an UltraDMA/33 or UltraATA/66 IDE drive for the paging file delivers a significant boost.

If you have room—and spare cooling capacity—in your server, add a pair of drives and set them up in a hardware or software RAID 0 (striped-set) configuration. You should be aware, however, that using a RAID 0 array doubles the probability that a paging file disk failure will disable your server. A safer alternative is to install the drives as separate paging file volumes to balance the paging file load and provide a degree of fault tolerance. It's a reasonably simple task to set up PerfMon to compare paging performance of a RAID set versus two individual drives.

Dedicating a RAID 0 array or drive(s) to the paging file delivers two major benefits—the paging file doesn't compete with file sharing or application disk I/O, and you can expand the paging file as necessary without encountering fragmentation.

 If you run into disk thrashing problems at high server loads after having performed the disk-related optimizing steps in the preceding sections, see the "Server Performance Problems" topic of the "Troubleshooting" section at the end of the chapter.

Understanding the Backup Process

 Windows 2000's new Backup application is a subset of Seagate Software's BackupExec, which was one of several popular third-party applications for backing up Windows 9x and NT systems. VERITAS Software acquired BackupExec when the company purchased Seagate Software's Network and Storage Management Group in mid-1999. Many workgroup-level backup tape drives, such as Aiwa's BOLT drive, come with an original equipment manufacturer (OEM) version of BackupExec. Computer Associates' ARCserve backup applications also are popular with Windows NT administrators.

The success of third-party backup applications for Windows NT offers proof beyond reasonable doubt that Microsoft's Ntbackup.exe for Windows NT was inadequate for enterprise-scale—or even most workgroup—environments. Windows 2000's Backup application is a major improvement to Ntbackup, but most system admins are likely to opt for a third-party backup application. Commercial backup programs offer a variety of features necessary for enterprise-level backup of local and remote servers. Nonetheless, Windows 2000 Backup is a good starting point for protecting the valuable data and applications stored on your servers.

Before you determine a backup strategy and establish routine backup operations, you need to understand the backup process and its terminology.

The Archive Bit

Every file, regardless of the file system you use, has an *archive bit*, sometimes called an archive flag, which plays a crucial role in backup operations. The file system automatically sets the archive bit to 1—on, meaning not yet backed up—when you or an application create or modify a file. During ordinary backups, the backup application clears the archive bit to 0 (off). Bits or flags of this type that alternate between 1 and 0 are called *toggles*.

You can test the archive bit of any NTFS file by right-clicking the file in Explorer, choosing Properties, and clicking Advanced on the General page of the File Properties sheet to display the Advanced Attributes dialog (see Figure 23.23). If a mark appears in the File Is Ready for Archiving check box, the archive bit is set to 1. You can manually set or clear the archive bit of a file in the Advanced Attributes dialog to determine whether the file is to be backed up during the next backup operation.

Understanding the Backup Process 949

Figure 23.23
The Advanced Attributes page for the file ADSI25.exe shows that the archive attribute is set.

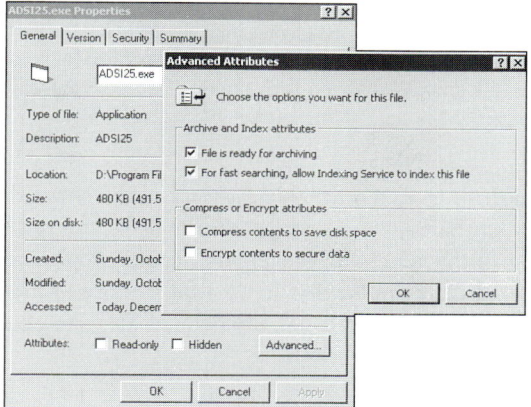

PART
III

CH
23

> **Note**
>
> The examples in this chapter use the NTFS 5.0 file system, which offers user access to Read-Only, Hidden, Archive, Index, Compress, and Encrypt attributes. The FAT32 file system doesn't have Index and Encrypt attributes, and FAT16 also is missing Compress. Several attribute bits for internal use by NTFS aren't accessible for user inspection or modification.

Normal Backups

A *normal backup* copies all selected files, regardless of the state of their archive bits, to the tape drive or other backup media, and then turns off the archive bit on all files that have been copied (see Figure 23.24). Most third-party backup software refers to this process as a *full backup*.

Figure 23.24
Notice that in a Normal (or Full) backup, all files are copied to the backup media and their archive bits are turned off.

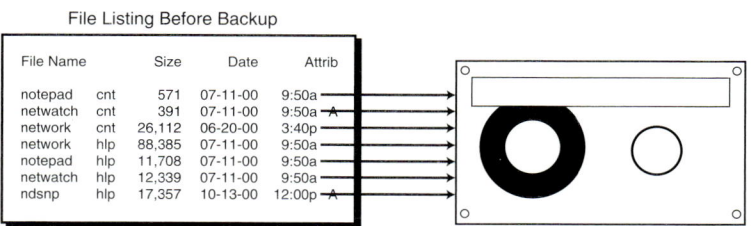

> **Note**
>
> A normal backup doesn't necessarily copy all files from a particular volume or disk drive, but it may simply copy a file or set of files from a specified folder or folders on the selected volume or disk drive. What determines a normal backup is that all *selected* files are copied without regard to the state of their archive bit.

Re-creating a failed hard drive from a normal backup set of the entire drive is straightforward. If the system drive has failed, you must replace the drive and reinstall Windows 2000 Server before proceeding. If the system drive is operable, after replacing the data drive, use the Windows 2000 Server Backup application to do a full restore of the tape to the new drive. Partial restores, such as those of accidentally deleted files, are equally straightforward.

Copy Backups

A *copy backup* is identical to a normal backup, except that copy backups skip the final step of resetting all of the archive bits on backed-up files to off (see Figure 23.25). Most third-party backup software refers to this process as a *full copy backup*. The resulting backup tape is identical to what would have been created by a normal backup, but the archive bit status of the files on the disk remains unchanged. The main purpose of a copy backup is to allow you to create an archive or off-site backup set without affecting your main backup set's rotation process.

Figure 23.25
A Copy backup is like a Full backup because files are copied to the backup media; it differs from a Full backup because the state of the archive bit is left unchanged.

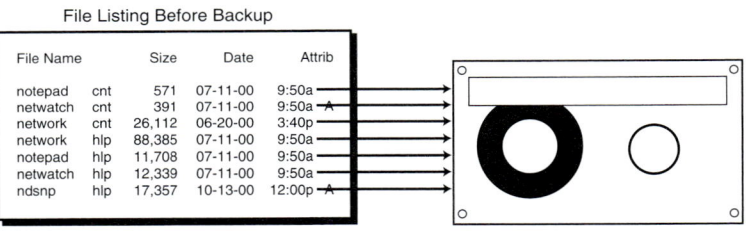

The contents of a copy backup set are indistinguishable from those of a normal backup set, so restore procedures are identical for these two types of backups.

INCREMENTAL BACKUPS

An *incremental backup* copies to the backup media all selected files that have their archive bit turned on, and then turns the archive bit off for the files that have been copied (see Figure 23.26). The tape from the first incremental backup done after a normal backup contains only those files altered since the last normal backup. Subsequent incremental backup tapes contain only those files that changed since the last incremental backup. After completing each incremental backup, all files have their archive bits turned off, as though a normal backup had been done.

Figure 23.26
An Incremental backup turns on an archive bit and copies all changed files to the backup media, then turns off the archive bit.

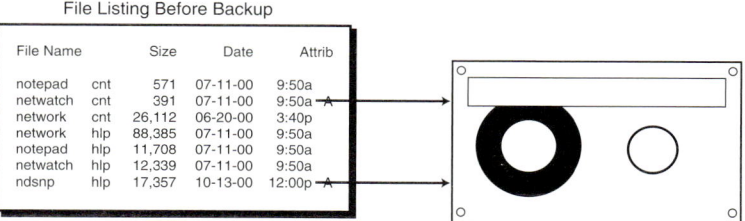

Re-creating a failed hard drive from incremental backup sets is a bit more involved than using a normal backup set, because each incremental backup tape contains only some of the changed files, and different incremental backup tapes may contain different versions of the same file. To re-create a failed disk drive, you first restore the most recent normal backup set to the replacement disk. Then you restore all incremental backup sets created after the normal backup set, beginning with the earliest, and proceeding sequentially to the latest incremental backup set.

Restoring an accidentally deleted file is a more complex process. To ensure that you get the latest version of the file, you must start by examining the most recent incremental backup set and work backward until you locate the most recent occurrence of the file on an incremental backup set. If the file in question hasn't changed since the last normal backup, you may have to work all the way back to the last normal backup set before you locate the file. Fortunately, most backup software makes this process somewhat easier by allowing you to search backup logs to locate the file so that you can load the proper tape directly.

Tip from
RJ

The incremental backup is best suited to environments where a relatively large number of different files change each day. Because the incremental backup sets the archive bit to off after each of these files is backed up, each file is backed up only on the day that it's changed. This may reduce the number of tapes needed for each daily tape set, and also cuts down on the time required for daily partial backups.

DIFFERENTIAL BACKUPS

A *differential backup* copies to the backup media all selected files that have their archive bits turned on, but then leaves the archive bits unchanged on the files that have been copied (see Figure 23.27). This means that each differential backup set contains all files changed since the last normal backup. It also means that each differential backup set is larger than the preceding set, because later sets contain all the files previously backed up, plus all files changed since that last backup.

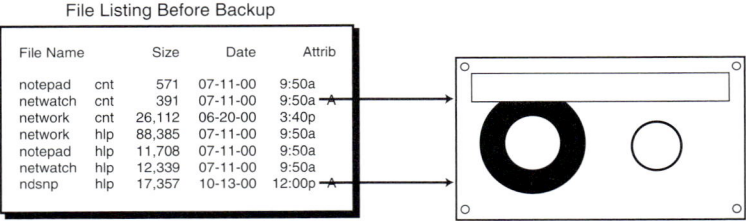

Figure 23.27
A Differential backup is like an Incremental backup because it copies only changed files to the backup media. Unlike an Incremental backup, the archive bit is not changed.

Re-creating a failed hard drive using a differential backup set is relatively straightforward. As with an incremental backup set, you begin by restoring the last normal backup set. Because each differential backup set contains all files changed since the last normal backup, however, you need to restore only the most recent differential backup set. Restoring an accidentally deleted file is similarly straightforward. If the file is listed on your most recent differential backup log, restore from the latest differential backup set. Otherwise, restore from the last normal backup.

DAILY COPY BACKUPS

A *daily copy backup* copies all selected files that have been modified that day, but leaves the archive bits unchanged on the files that are copied (see Figure 23.28). The daily copy backup uses file date and time stamps to determine their eligibility for backup, rather than examining the status of the archive bit.

Figure 23.28
A Daily Copy backup uses the file-modified date to back up only files modified on the current date. This type of backup ignores the state of the archive bit and leaves it unchanged after completion.

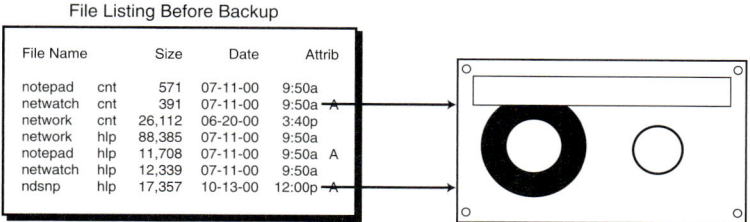

Unlike the incremental backup, which copies all files changed since the last normal backup or incremental backup was done, the daily copy backup must be run at least once each day if it's to be successfully used to archive files changed since the last normal backup. If you fail to run the daily copy backup on one particular day, none of the files changed on that day is written to tape until the next normal, copy, incremental, or differential backup is done. Because it ignores the state of the archive bit, the daily copy backup also fails to back up changed files if the file date stamp wasn't altered at the time the file was changed.

SYSTEM STATE AND SYSTEM VOLUME INFORMATION

Windows 2000 Backup adds the following two new elements to backup operations:

- *System State* backs up Registry data, the COM+ Class Registration database, and boot files, which include the basic system files for starting Windows 2000. For DCs with AD installed, System State backs up AD files, including the Sysvol folder. Backup suspends AD replication services during the backup interval. If you have Certificate Services installed, System State adds the Certificate Services database. System State for Windows 2000 Advanced Server, AppServer, and Datacenter Server also backs up cluster service information.

- *System Volume Information* backs up the protected Catalog.wci folder created by Windows 2000's Indexing Service. Catalog.wci holds files that store index information and properties for the set of directories indexed automatically by the Indexing Service. Indexes include document properties and a full-text index for HTML, email, newsgroup article, word processing, and other text files. The size of the full-text index ranges from about 15% to 30% of the size of the source file.

You can back up System State with Windows 2000 Backup only on the local computer—that is, the computer to which the backup tape drive is connected physically. You can overcome this serious limitation by backing up System State to a backup file on a share of the computer with the backup tape drive, and then backing up the shared folder. You must then restore the remote computer's System State from the restored file, not directly from the backup tape.

Tip from
RJ

Install the backup tape drive, if possible, on the initial root domain DC. Doing so lets you quickly restore this DC in the event of a hardware failure. This is especially important if you have only one DC in a domain, which is not a recommended practice. When restoring the operating system state to other DCs in a domain, AD automatically replicates changes made while the DC was offline.

Choosing Among the Backup Types

A normal backup has the considerable advantages of thoroughness and simplicity. Each normal backup set contains all the selected files on your hard drive. No juggling of tapes is required to locate a particular file. If a problem occurs, simply retrieve the last normal backup tape and do a full or partial restore, as appropriate. The primary problem with normal backups is that they consume large numbers of backup tapes and take a long time to complete.

Note

Doing a proper backup with Windows 2000 Backup requires that the contents of the server disk be static—that is, that files not be in use and subject to change by users while the backup process proceeds. Many third-party backup applications have advanced features that let you back up open, dynamic files. If you don't have open-file backup capability, the best time to do backups is during evening hours and on weekends. Assuming that the server can be taken down for backup at 10 P.M. and must be back in service by 6 A.M., the backup must be completed within eight hours.

Today's digital linear tape (DLT) drives used for production backup operations can transfer data at a sustained rate ranging from about 36GB/hour to more than 180GB/hour. If your server disk "farm" is several hundred GB, if you have multiple servers to back up to a single tape drive, or if your company's hours of operation are longer, you don't have time to complete a normal backup each night. Backing up a Web server that must run 24 hours everyday, of course, requires backup software that can handle open, dynamic files.

Although most servers today aren't a size that causes the time required to do a backup to be an insurmountable problem, this situation is changing as larger server disk storage subsystems become the norm. Only a few years ago, 4GB was considered a large amount of disk storage for a PC server. Today, 30GB arrays are common and 100GB and larger servers are available. The increasing use of multimedia and document imaging, plus the decreasing cost of disk storage, means that most server disk farms will continue to grow over the next few years. Because tape drive throughput isn't likely to keep pace, you're probably going to find, ultimately, that you no longer have time to do a normal backup overnight.

> **Note**
>
> Network-Attached Storage (NAS) and Storage Area Networks (SANs) have special backup requirements. SANs, in particular, are beyond the backup capabilities of the Windows 2000 Backup application. Backing up NAS boxes and SANs is beyond the scope of this book.

The second reason that it may not be feasible to use only normal backup sets is tape capacity. Unless your IS department or computer room is staffed 24 hours a day, 7 days a week (24×7), overnight backups require either that the size of the backup set not exceed the capacity of a single tape, or that expensive "jukebox" tape changers are used to do unattended backups.

It's for these reasons that the concepts of incremental and differential partial backups were developed. Using either incremental or differential backups with less-frequent normal backups allows only changed files to be backed up routinely, whereas the unchanged bulk of the disk contents are backed up only weekly, or monthly, typically over the course of a weekend. Because only a subset of the full disk is copied to tape each night, the time and tape capacity factors become lesser issues.

The choice between using incremental backup or differential backup for your partial backups depends on how many files are changed, how frequently the files are changed, the size of the files, and how frequently you expect to need to do restores. If most of your files are large and change infrequently, choosing incremental backup minimizes the total amount of data that must be written to tape. That is because this data is written only once each time the file changes when using incremental backup (instead of each time a backup is done with differential backup). Conversely, if you have many small files that change frequently, the storage economy of incremental backup is likely to be outweighed by the ease of file retrieval with differential backup.

If the daily copy backup has any valid application, it's to run quick, supplementary "snapshot" backups during the course of the working day. If your main backup rotation does a normal backup each day, you can use either incremental or differential backup to make snapshot backups, because the state of the archive bit doesn't matter to the normal backup run each night. If instead your main backup rotation uses either incremental or differential backup on some nights, any partial backup you do during the day must not alter the archive bits of any files. Incremental backups reset the archive bit and are, therefore, unusable for snapshot backups in this environment. Differential backups don't reset the archive bit; however, using differential backups defeats the purpose of a quick snapshot backup, because the process backs up not just the day's work, but all preceding work as well. If your main backup rotation uses partial backups and you need to do snapshot backups during the course of the day, the daily copy backup may be a useful tool, provided that you keep its limitations in mind. Otherwise, don't consider using daily copy backup.

If you're fortunate enough to have a tape drive large enough to do a normal backup on a single tape, and you have the time each night to complete a normal backup, then do so. Using only normal backups makes it much easier to manage the backup process and much less likely that you might accidentally overwrite the wrong tape or otherwise compromise the integrity of your backup sets. If—as is more common—you must depend on less frequent normal backups and daily partial backups, decide whether using incremental backup or differential backup better suits your data; then use the method that best matches your needs. For typical Windows NT servers, a program using normal backups, with differential backups, is the best choice.

Developing a Backup Strategy

Developing a coherent backup strategy that reliably safeguards your data requires more than simply deciding to do a normal backup each weekend and a partial backup every night. You must also consider several other factors, discussed in the following sections, that bear on data integrity and managing the backup process.

Organizing Disk Storage

The first issue to consider when developing a backup strategy is how you arrange the data on your server's fixed-disk drives. If you have only a single disk volume on your server, there's nothing to decide. If, however, you have multiple volumes, you can decide what type of data resides on each volume. Figure 23.29 shows one possible arrangement of data on volumes intended to make backup easier. Making the correct data organization decisions eases the entire backup process; making the wrong decisions can complicate backup operations needlessly.

A satisfactory organization places user home directories and other areas with files that frequently change on one or more volumes but segregates system files and other files that change infrequently in a separate volume of their own. Depending on the number of volumes you've created and the types of data you must store, you can extend this file segregation process. For example, if you have a large database that's updated infrequently, you might decide to place it on a dedicated volume, thereby minimizing the need for regular backup of that volume. Similarly, if you have large imaging files that change frequently, you may allocate a volume to them and then use incremental backup for only that volume, using differential backup for other volumes where its use is more appropriate. Always manage your volumes with backup issues in the back of your mind.

Figure 23.29
The data on these disk volumes is organized so that different types of data are stored on different volumes. This makes backup and restore operations easier.

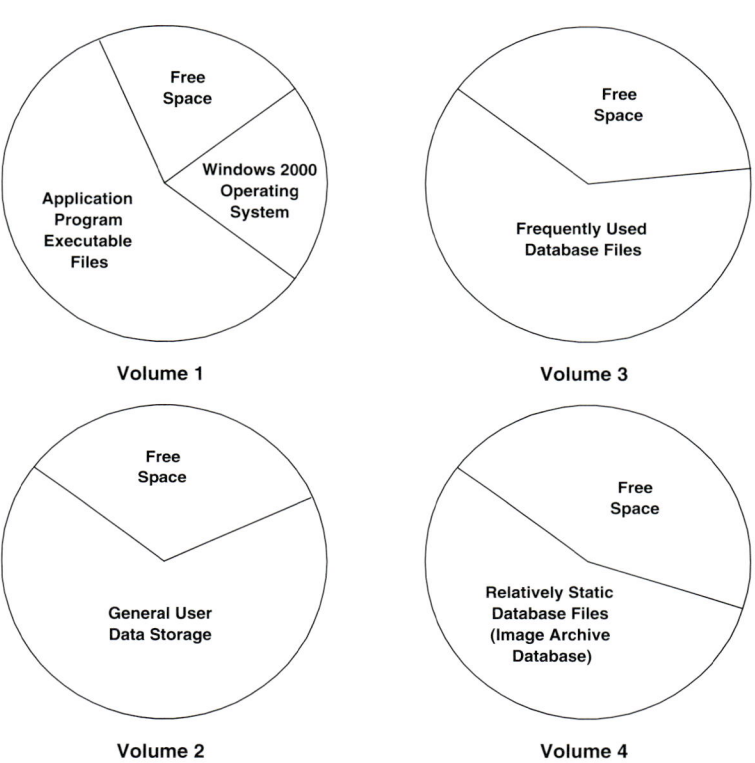

> **Note**
>
> Client/server relational database management systems (RDBMSs), such as Microsoft SQL Server 7+, present special difficulties in backing up data because their files remain open whenever the RDBMS is running. Most RDBMSs therefore provide a backup system independent of the Backup application supplied with Windows 2000 Server.
>
> RDBMS backup procedures use a periodic *database dump*, which is equivalent to a normal backup. Incremental backups save the content of a transaction log, which lists all modifications to the database since the last dump. On completion of a database dump, the transaction log file is deleted. RDBMS transaction logs vary from the transitory transaction logs created by Windows 2000's Log File Service for NTFS volumes.

ENSURING BACKUP INTEGRITY

The second issue to consider when developing a backup strategy is how you verify the integrity of your backups. Many system administrators have found, to their sorrow, that the backup tape they relied on to restore a failed drive is unreadable. You don't want to find this out when it's too late to recover your data. The way to avoid this problem is to perform a compare operation to verify that the contents of the backup tape correspond to the contents of the disk drive.

Inexpensive tape drives use a single head to perform both read and write operations. Doing a compare with these tape drives requires a second complete pass of the tape through the drive, doubling backup time. More expensive tape drives have separate read and write heads, accommodating a process called *read-after-write*. With these drives, the write head records the backup data to tape, which is then read immediately by the second read head and compared with the data stream coming from the fixed-disk drive. Read-after-write tape drives definitely are preferred, because such drives can perform both a backup and compare during a single tape pass, assuming that read-after-write is supported by the backup software.

If you find yourself forced to use a tape drive that requires a second pass to compare files, take the extra time to do the compare. Otherwise, you may find yourself with a failed disk drive and no backup from which to restore your data. Many administrators with low-cost tape drives compromise between running a compare after every backup and never running a compare operation. A common procedure is to run a compare after each normal backup but run partial backups without doing the compare. Another, somewhat riskier, method is to do the compare on partial backups, where a compare runs more quickly, and not run the compare on the larger, multitape normal backups. Whichever method you choose, make sure that you do a compare at least occasionally, to verify that your tape drive is really writing readable data to your tapes.

Tip from
RJ

> Periodically reading backup tapes created by one tape drive on another tape drive that accommodates the same format is a necessity to ensure that you don't have tape interchange problems. If you have an undiscovered interchange problem and your source tape drive fails or is destroyed in a calamity, you can't restore your backup by using another tape drive. Interchange problems usually occur as a result of mechanical changes in the tape path or head alignment that don't affect compare operations on the same drive. Interchange problems are more likely to occur with high-density tape formats, such as 4mm DAT and 8mm.

DEALING WITH OPEN FILES AND WINDOWS 2000 BACKUP

The third major issue to consider when developing a backup strategy is how to handle the backup of open files. Open files on the network pose a difficult problem for network administrators who want to make sure that all files are successfully backed up. Most commercial backup programs let you specify how to handle open files on the network, but Windows 2000 Backup doesn't.

Backing up an open file also isn't practical for Windows 2000 Backup because the file may be written to and closed while being written to the tape drive. This results in a corrupted file stored to tape. Consider the result of backing up an open database file that has related index files open. The main database file is successfully written to tape in its current state, and the backup software continues to read other files from the disk. A user saves data, modifying both the main database file and one or more index files. (Separate data and index files are used by desktop database systems such as dBASE, FoxPro, and Paradox.) Because the main database file has already been written but the index files haven't, the resulting backup tape contains an older version of the main database file and newer versions of the index files. If you then restore this database and its associated index files, the index files don't match the database files, and applications can't access the database files.

The only way to handle the open-file backup problem—other than purchasing software that handles open files—is to use a RAID subsystem to provide built-in redundancy for your disk storage. Other than the additional cost, RAID has two drawbacks:

- When a drive does fail, your data is completely vulnerable until that drive has been replaced and the parity information rebuilt. This problem can be solved—albeit at significant expense—by building an array of arrays to give you two levels of redundancy.
- Of the four main reasons for backing up—protecting against drive failure, allowing recovery of accidentally deleted files, providing a historical archive copy, and letting you store a copy of your data off site—RAID addresses only the first.

Matching Backup Media Capacity to Disk Size

Before purchasing a tape drive or other means of backup, carefully consider the size of the largest backup you're likely to need. Ideally, the capacity of the tape drive you select should exceed by a comfortable margin the size of the largest backup data set you make during the life of the tape drive. The goal is to ensure that any backup set, regardless of its size, can be written to a single tape. Avoiding backup sets that span multiple tapes makes backup administration and tape rotation considerably easier and minimizes the chance for using the wrong tape by mistake.

When selecting a tape drive, keep in mind that the disk storage on your server is likely to grow larger as time passes. Remember also that the nominal capacities stated for tape drives assume 2:1 compression of the data being backed up. A tape drive rated at 14GB capacity may have only a 7GB native capacity, depending on file compression to gain the remaining 7GB. If you back up a typical mix of files on a server used primarily for office automation tasks, you may find that the drive achieves the estimated 2:1 compression ratio. If you're backing up a disk drive dedicated to fixed images or video files, which usually are stored in a compressed format, you may find that you achieve compression ratios of 1.1:1 or less. Encrypted files seldom compress at all.

Organizing Backup Tape Rotation Methods

Tapes should be rotated in an organized manner to satisfy the following goals:

- The tape containing the most recent backup of that data is quickly available so that the server can be restored to use with minimum delay.
- Older copies of the current data can be archived for the period necessary to ensure that damage or deletion of important data, which isn't noticed immediately, can be retrieved from the most recent archived backup where the data still exists in a usable form.
- A backup copy of critical data can be stored off site to guard against catastrophic damage to the server and on-site backup copies.

- The integrity and usability of the backup sets is preserved if one or more tapes break or are lost.
- Wear on tapes is equalized, avoiding continuous use of some tapes and infrequent use of others.

Various tape-rotation schemes have been developed. Some are quite simple in concept, at the expense of inadequately meeting one or more of the preceding goals. Others are quite complex and meet all the goals for a good rotation scheme, but are difficult to administer on a day-to-day basis.

Some tape-rotation methods use normal backups exclusively; others use less frequent normal backups with daily incremental or differential backups; still others can be used either way. You may be forced to use a rotation that includes partial backups if your tape drive can't store a normal backup set to a single tape, or if time constraints don't allow daily normal backups. If neither condition applies, you're better served by a rotation that uses normal backups exclusively.

The following sections describe five different types of rotation methods. Each method assumes that a normal backup can be done to a single tape and that your organization operates on a five-day-per-week schedule. The methods may be modified if one or both of these conditions can't be met.

Weekly Normal Backup with Daily Differential Backup (Four-Tape Method)

The four-tape rotation method, shown in Figure 23.30, very commonly is used for small servers. The backup tape set comprises at least four tapes, labeled *Weekly A*, *Weekly B*, *Daily A*, and *Daily B*. The rotation begins with a normal backup to Weekly A on Friday of Week 1, followed by a daily differential backup to Daily A on Monday through Thursday of Week 2. On Friday of Week 2, a normal backup is done to Weekly B, followed by daily differential backups to Daily B on Monday through Thursday of Week 3. On Friday of Week 3, a normal backup is done to Weekly A, and the cycle begins again.

Figure 23.30
This weekly Normal backup with a daily Differential backup uses four tapes, which enable you to keep a week-old archive of data at all times.

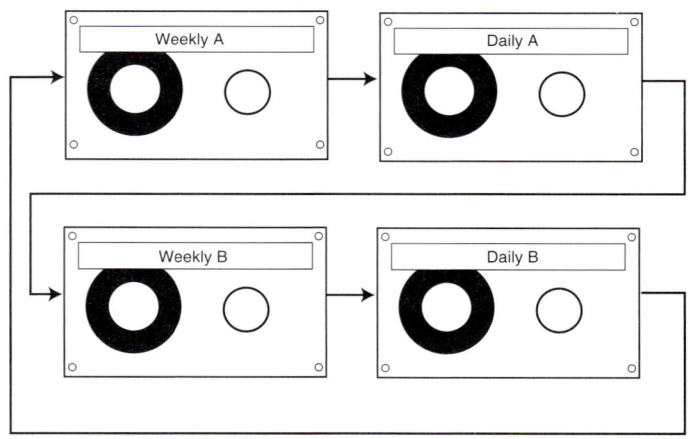

Although the four-tape method is simple to administer and uses a minimum number of tapes, it suffers the following drawbacks:

- Retrieval of historical copies of your data is limited to a two-week span.
- You're faced with the choice of either storing the normal backup off site, where it's not quickly accessible, or having the normal backup readily available for use, but at risk.
- All daily backups are written to a single tape over the course of a week, so you must return to the last weekly tape if the daily tape in use fails.
- Daily tapes are used four times more often than are weekly tapes, making the daily tapes much more likely to fail.

You can make the following minor modifications to this rotation scheme to address the preceding problems without substantial complication of the backup administration process:

- A copy backup can be processed monthly to a tape that's then stored off site, addressing the first two problems of the preceding list. Depending on your need for historical data, this set can comprise 12 tapes labeled January through December, cycled on a yearly basis, or three tapes labeled Month 1 through Month 3, cycled on a quarterly basis.
- By adding two tapes to the set, you can provide two daily differential backup tapes in each set and alternate using them. Using this method, label tapes *Weekly A*, *Weekly B*, *Daily A—Odd*, *Daily A—Even*, *Daily B—Odd*, and *Daily B—Even*. You make weekly normal backups as before but alternate using daily tapes—use the Odd tape if the day of the month is odd, and the Even tape if the day of the month is even. This way, when you run a differential backup, the tape you're writing to is never the one containing the most recent backup set. This eliminates the third problem described earlier. Because it alternates daily backups between two tapes, it also reduces uneven tape wear.
- You can extend the preceding method to use eight tapes labeled *Monday A* through *Thursday A* and *Monday B* through *Thursday B* for daily differential backups. At the small cost of six additional tapes, you eliminate the third and fourth problems of the preceding list. If a daily tape fails, you lose only that day's backup, rather than have to return to the last prior full weekly backup. Each tape is used once every two weeks, equalizing wear, although the daily tapes from later in the week and (in particular) the weekly tapes will still be used somewhat more heavily due to the larger size of the backup sets written to them.

Weekly Normal Backup with Daily Incremental Backup (10-Tape Method)

This version of the 10-tape rotation method, shown in Figure 23.31, uses 10 tapes, labeled *Weekly A*, *Weekly B*, *Monday A* through *Thursday A*, and *Monday B* through *Thursday B*. The rotation begins with a normal backup to Weekly A on Friday of week 1, followed by a daily incremental backup to the appropriately labeled daily A tape on Monday through Thursday of week 2. On Friday of week 2, a normal backup is done to Weekly B, followed by daily incremental backups to the appropriately labeled daily B tape on Monday through Thursday of week 3. On Friday of week 3, a normal backup is done to Weekly A, and the cycle begins again.

Figure 23.31
This tape rotation scheme shows daily Incremental backups with a weekly Normal backup using 10 tapes, which also provides a week-old data archive.

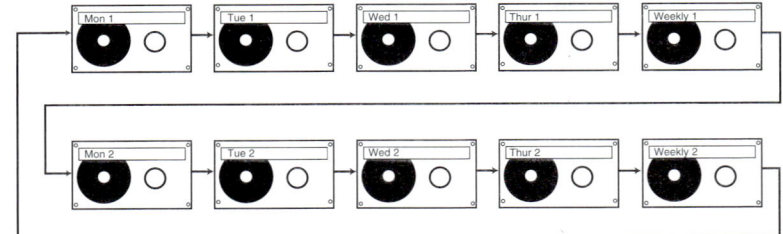

This version of the 10-tape method shares the first two drawbacks of the four-tape method, allowing only two weeks of historical data and making no provision for off-site storage. These problems can be addressed by making a copy backup each month, which is stored off site and rotated on a quarterly or annual basis. The third problem, loss of a daily tape, is more difficult to address. Because a daily incremental backup tape contains only a subset of the files changed during that week, loss of one daily incremental backup tape may require you to return to the last normal backup to retrieve a copy of a particular file. Also, if you need to restore a failed hard drive, loss of one incremental backup tape, which happens to contain critical or interdependent files, may force you to roll your restore back to the last preceding normal backup. The only way to protect against this problem is to run the incremental backup twice each day to different daily tapes, defeating the purpose of using a partial backup rotation scheme.

Although this version of the 10-tape method is commonly used, it offers the worst of all worlds. It puts your data at risk, uses no fewer tapes than other methods, and saves very little time compared to using differential backups. Don't consider using this version of the 10-tape method.

DAILY FULL BACKUPS WITH TWO SET ROTATION (AN ALTERNATE 10-TAPE METHOD)

This alternate 10-tape method, shown in Figure 23.32, is the simplest tape-rotation system in common use that uses normal backups exclusively. It uses 10 tapes, labeled *Monday A* through *Friday A* and *Monday B* through *Friday B*. A normal backup is done each day to the appropriate tape, and the full set is cycled every two weeks. The major drawback to this method is that it limits historical data to a two-week span. Again, the historical problem can be addressed simply by doing a biweekly or monthly normal backup to a separate tape and archiving the tape. The archive tapes can be rotated on a quarterly or annual basis.

Figure 23.32
This example of daily Full backups features two-set rotation using 10 tapes. This method also allows a week-old archive of data.

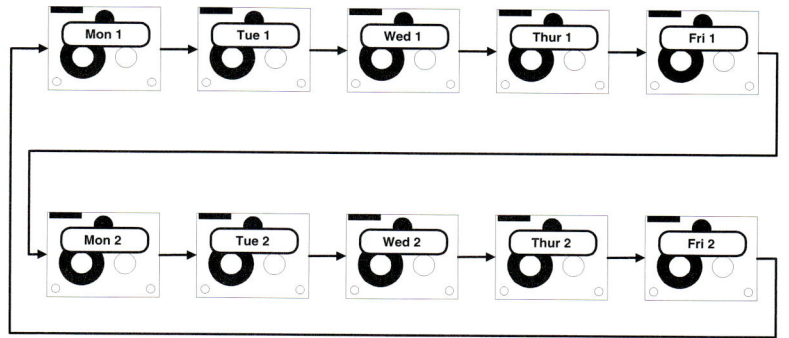

Grandfather-Father-Son Rotation (21-Tape Method)

The grandfather-father-son (or GFS) method, shown in Figure 23.33, is probably the most commonly used tape-rotation method. It's relatively easy to manage, fairly efficient in terms of the number of tapes required, and is supported by almost every backup software package on the market. A GFS rotation can use normal backups exclusively, or can use a combination of normal backups and partial backups.

Figure 23.33
A grandfather-father-son–type backup tape rotation uses 21 tapes and keeps monthly, weekly, and daily archives. Using this method, it is possible to recover data for up to a year if the monthly tapes are reused.

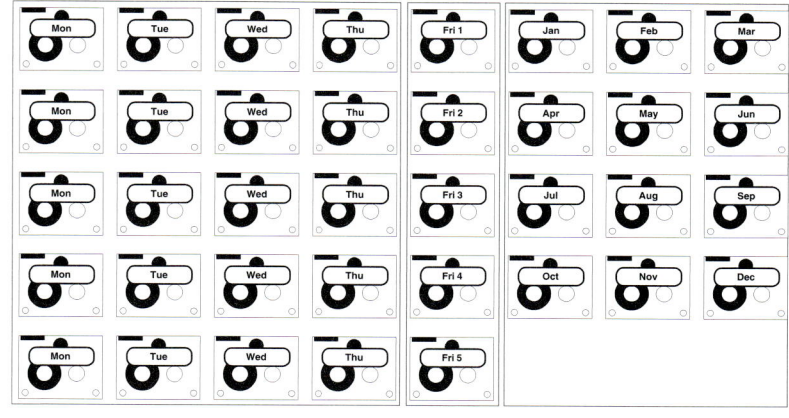

GFS is nearly always an acceptable, if not optimum, choice for a small- or medium-size Windows 2000 server. The two primary drawbacks to GFS are that it uses some tapes more heavily than others and that, in its unmodified form, it makes no provision for balancing off-site storage needs with quick retrieval requirements.

A typical GFS rotation scheme requires 21 tapes to be used over the course of a year, although this number can be altered depending on your particular archiving needs. Four daily tapes are labeled Monday through Thursday. Five weekly tapes are labeled Friday 1 through Friday 5 (the fifth Friday tape accommodates months with five Fridays). Twelve monthly tapes are labeled January through December.

The daily tapes are used on the day corresponding to the tape label, and are overwritten every week. Each Friday, the correspondingly numbered Friday tape is used, meaning that Friday tapes are overwritten only once each month. On the last day of each month, a normal backup is done to the corresponding Monthly tape, which is therefore overwritten only once per year.

> **Tip from**
> *RJ*
>
> Depending on your needs, you can alter the time span between archival backups. Firms for which archiving is less critical can substitute quarterly tapes for monthly ones. Firms for which archiving is very important may choose to substitute biweekly or even weekly archive tapes for the monthly tapes described here.

TOWER OF HANOI ROTATION (TOH)

The Tower of Hanoi (TOH) rotation method, shown in Figure 23.34, is named for a game that uses three posts and several rings of various diameters. The object of the game is to relocate the rings by using a minimum number of moves so that the rings are placed in sequence on a post, with the largest ring on the bottom and the smallest on the top. The TOH backup model introduces new tapes to the backup set periodically, using the newly introduced tape every other rotation. TOH doubles the time before the previous tape comes back into the rotation, consequently doubling the time before earlier tapes are introduced back into the rotation.

Figure 23.34
The Tower of Hanoi tape rotation is the most complex—but also the most advantageous—of the tape rotation methods.

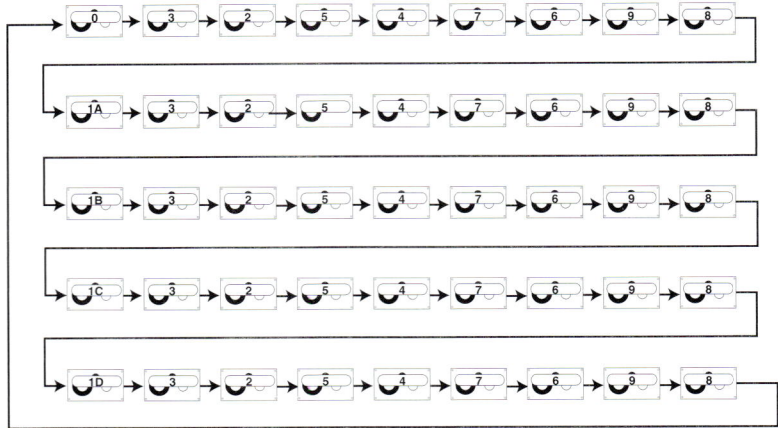

The TOH rotation has many advantages, but at the cost of considerable complexity in terms of managing the tape rotation. Wear on individual tapes is distributed relatively evenly over time using this method, but the real advantage of TOH versus GFS and other methods is that TOH saves many versions of each file, allowing you to selectively retrieve different versions of the file.

> **Note**
>
> The TOH rotation originated for mainframe and minicomputer backup, and has since migrated to the PC LAN environment. For a long time, Palindrome's PC Backup software was the only product supporting this rotation, although TOH rotation is now becoming more common. Backup software from Symantec and other third parties offer automated TOH implementation.
>
> If the backup software you select supports a Tower of Hanoi rotation, consider using it for its many advantages, particularly if yours is a medium or large LAN. If your software doesn't provide TOH, don't even consider an attempt to implement TOH rotation manually. You will almost certainly use the wrong tape at one time or another, destroying the integrity of the rotation.

Using the Windows 2000 Backup Application

Windows 2000 supports a very large number of tape backup drives, ranging from the early quarter-inch cartridge (QIC) to modern DLT, 4mm, and 8mm drives. The Windows 2000 Hardware Compatibility List—Hcl.txt in the \Support folder of the distribution CD-ROM—lists about 125 supported tape drives. The Backup application automatically detects the type of tape drive installed. The sections that follow use an old-but-reliable QIC SCSI-2 tape drive for the examples.

> **Note**
>
> If you don't have a backup tape drive available, you can create a local \Backup folder or a remote share and generate a backup file, if you have sufficient free disk space. Alternatively, you can cancel the backup operation before your backup destination volume fills, then delete the backup folder.

Running an Initial Full Backup

You must be a member of the local Administrators or Backup Operators group to back up files; Domain and Enterprise Admins have full administrative privileges on domain and all servers, respectively.

To perform your first backup operation as a test, do the following:

1. Insert a new or used backup tape in the drive.
2. Choose Programs, Accessories, System Tools, Backup to open the Backup window with the Welcome page active. Most administrators prefer to bypass the Backup Wizard for routine backups, so click the Backup tab.
3. Mark the check boxes of the folders on the local server you want to back up (see Figure 23.35). Be sure to include System State in the backup and, if you've installed the Indexing Service, System Volume Information.

Figure 23.35
The Backup page of the Windows 2000 backup utility enables you to select the files and folders to back up, specify the target tape device, and define a name for the media.

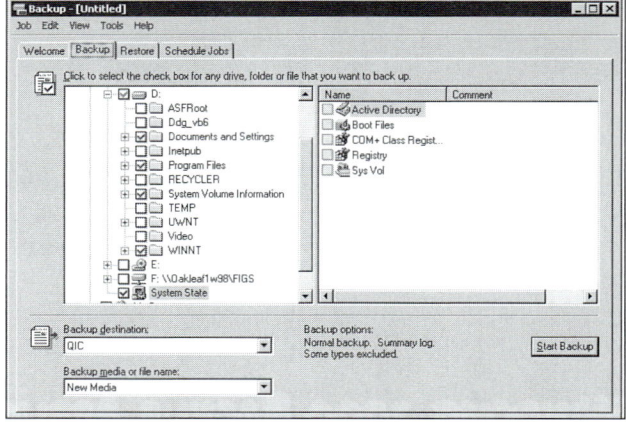

> **Note**
> Windows 2000 Server is installed on drive D: for this example. Windows Media Services (\ASFRoot) and Internet Information Server 5.0 (\Inetpub) are installed but not in use on this server. The other folders not selected in Figure 23.35 contain archived material previously backed up.

4. If File appears in the Backup Destination list, select your tape drive. For the first backup, accept the New Media default in the Backup Media or File Name list.
5. Choose Tools, Options to open the Options dialog with the Backup Type page active, and click the General tab. Figure 23.36 shows the default backup options, which are satisfactory for the initial test.

Figure 23.36
This example of the General page of the Options dialog for a backup job shows the default options checked.

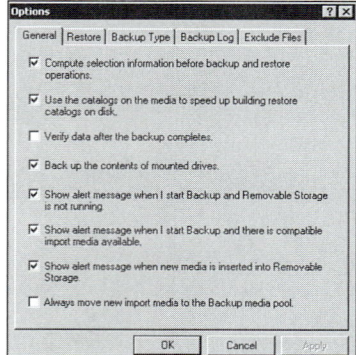

6. Click the Backup Type tab to select a Normal (full), Copy, Differential, Incremental, or Daily backup type (see Figure 23.37). Select Normal for the initial backup.

→ If you want to learn more about backup types, **see** "Understanding the Backup Process," **p. 948**.

Figure 23.37
Specify one of the five backup types to perform in the Backup Type page of the Options dialog for a backup job.

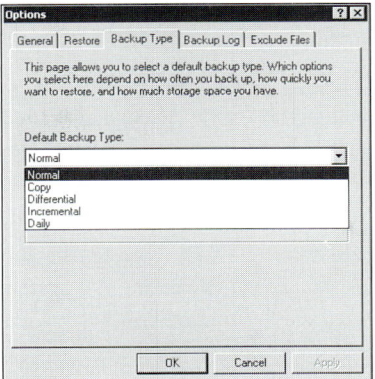

7. Click the Backup Log tab to select the type of log file to create. Always create and print at least a Summary log file for each backup (see Figure 23.38). Store the printed log file with the backup tape(s).

Figure 23.38
The Backup Log page of the Options dialog for a backup job, enables you to specify what type of logging should be output for the job.

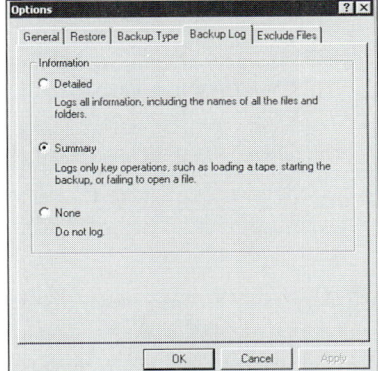

8. Click the Exclude Files tab to review the standard set of files that Backup excludes from ordinary backup operations. The most important of the excluded files is Pagefile.sys, which Backup can't restore because it's always open, and which isn't needed to restore the server. To exclude additional classes of registered file types, click Add New to open the Add Excluded Files, select the file types from the list, and click OK twice to return to the Backup window.

> **Note**
> Backup stores the names of excluded files and Registry keys in the HKEY_LOCAL_MACHINE\SYSTEM\CurrentControlSet\Control\BackupRestore\FilesNotToBackup and HKEY_LOCAL_MACHINE\SYSTEM\CurrentControlSet\Control\BackupRestore\KeysNotToRestore keys of the Registry.

9. Choose Job, Save Selections to open the Save Selections dialog and save your backup specification with a descriptive filename and the default .bks extension. You can't save your backup specification after backup completes.

10. Click Start Backup to open the Backup Job Information dialog, and click Advanced to open the Advanced Backup Options dialog. Amend the Backup Description to include the type of backup you're performing, Normal for this example.

11. Accept the first three default options, but clear the Automatically Backup System Protected Files check box to exclude about 200MB from the backup operation, if the check boxes are enabled (see Figure 23.39). In the event of a system drive failure, you must reinstall Windows 2000 Server, which includes the System Protected Files, on a new drive before you can restore from the tape.

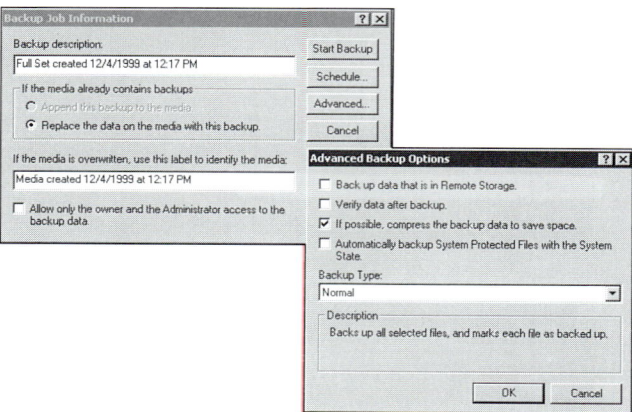

Figure 23.39
From the Advanced Backup Options dialog, you can exclude protected Windows system files from the backup by deselecting the Automatically Backup System Protected Files with the System State check box.

Tip from
RJ

Once you've installed a Windows 2000 Service Pack (SP), consider backing up the System Protected Files. The SP is likely to alter most, if not all, of these files, and backing them up eliminates the need to reapply the SP after a restore operation.

12. Click OK to close the Advanced Backup Options dialog, and click Start Backup. If your media is new, you are prompted to prepare the media; otherwise, you are prompted to select previously used media. In either case, the Waiting for Tape message appears for a few seconds while Backup writes the tape header.

After the backup operation starts, the Backup Progress dialog opens and displays elapsed and estimated remaining backup time, and the number of files and bytes processed and the estimated totals (see Figure 23.40).

USING THE WINDOWS 2000 BACKUP APPLICATION   969

Figure 23.40
In this example of the Backup Progress dialog during a backup, 1/3 of the total number of files and 1/5 of the total number of bytes have been backed up.

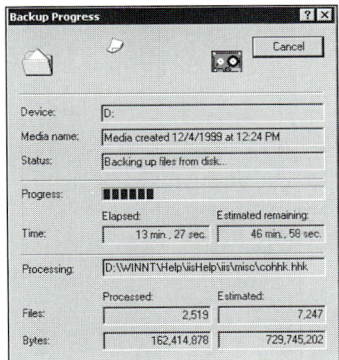

PART
III
CH
23

13. If you need more than one tape to complete the backup, the Required Media Missing message appears. Do *not* click Cancel (or any other button) at this point.

Note The Required Media Missing message doesn't appear if you're using a tape changer and haven't run out of tapes.

14. Insert another tape in the drive. If the tape is used, the Required Media Missing message closes, and you receive a Backup message, which gives you the option to select the new media you just inserted. Click OK and then click OK again to acknowledge the Replace Data message.

Note If the succeeding backup tapes are new, you are prompted to prepare the media just as you did in step 12.

When backup completes, the Backup Progress dialog changes to that shown in Figure 23.41. Click Report to launch Notepad and open the log type you specified in step 7 (see Figure 23.42).

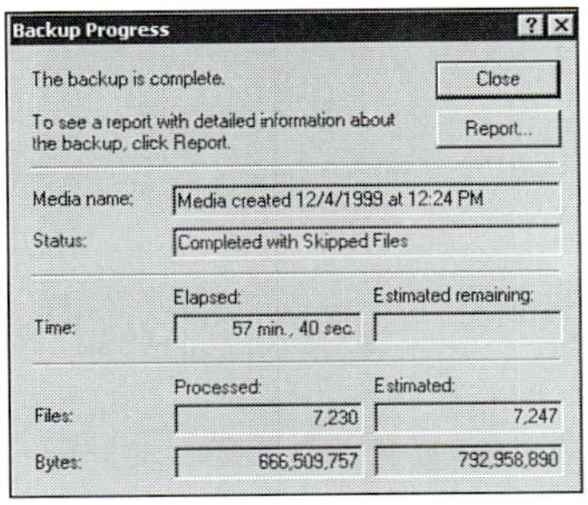

Figure 23.41
When the backup job is complete, the Backup Progress dialog shows a summary report of the backup job. More details are available by clicking the Report button.

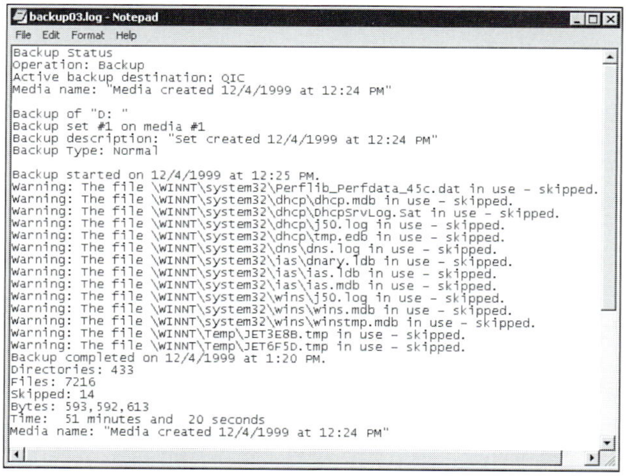

Figure 23.42
The log file for a Normal backup is shown in Windows Notepad. Notice that files in use (open files) were skipped.

The most important of the 14 skipped files shown in Figure 23.42 are Dhcp.mdb and Wins.mdb. If your server runs DHCP and WINS, it's a good policy to use DHCP Manager and WINS Manager to make backup copies of the DHCP and WINS databases immediately before running a system backup.

BACKING UP REMOTE SERVERS

You can include remote server shares in your backup regimen by expanding the My Network Places node to display shares on other DCs and member servers on the network. If you're a member of the Domain Admins group, you can use the administrative share—D$ for this example—and select folders to be backed up (see Figure 23.43). You also can back up shares on Windows 2000, NT, and 9x domain or workgroup clients, assuming you have permissions for the shares.

Figure 23.43
The Backup page of the Windows Backup tool is ready to back up subdirectories of the D$ administrative share on a remote domain controller.

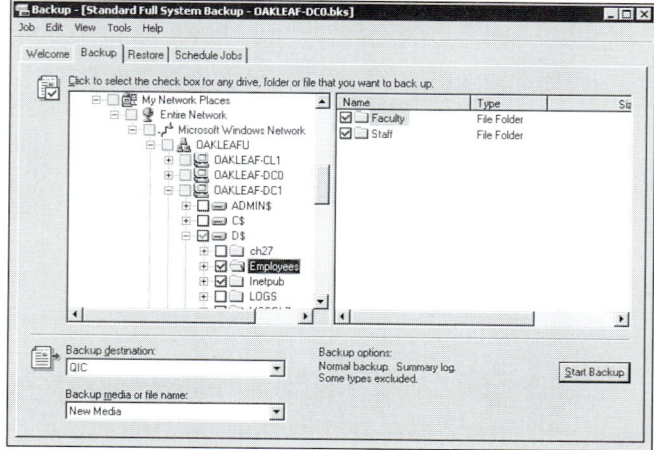

Restoring from Windows 2000 Backups

Your need to restore files from backup tapes most commonly arises from one of the following problems:

- A nonrecoverable mechanical drive failure occurs. Failures of this type are uncommon for arrays other than RAID 0, but are a regular occurrence with individual drives, despite manufacturers' mean time between failure (MTBF) representations.
- Drives become corrupted as a result of a disk controller failure or software glitch.
- A pernicious virus infects your network and deletes or overwrites files.
- Someone deletes a server file or folder and later finds he, she, or someone else needs it. This is the most common cause of restore operations.

The first three problems require reinstalling Windows 2000 Server and a full restore from tape, after you replace defective hardware in the case of a drive or controller failure. To solve the fourth problem, you locate the tape with the latest copy of the file or folder and restore the data to its previous location.

Restoring Member Servers

Restoring the System State and data on file or application (member) servers that don't have AD installed usually is a piece of cake. The basic process requires these steps:

1. Insert the first tape of the last full backup into the drive.
2. Launch the Backup application, and wait briefly while Backup reads the tape header.
3. Click the device node (D: for the preceding test backup) and System State, and be prepared to insert additional tapes for the backup to create a catalog (called a *set list*) of the folders and files from the backup. Creating the catalog takes several minutes if you've backed up a large number of folders and files.
4. If you're restoring on the server that has the backup drive connected, accept the Original Location default in the Restore Files To list. Otherwise, select Alternate Location to display the Alternate Location text box and Browse button to specify the destination drive or share(s) for restoration.
5. Select the device or individual folders or files to restore in the treeview list (see Figure 23.44).

Figure 23.44
Select the files to restore from the backup device and the target for the restore in the Restore page of the Windows Backup tool. You can restore files to their original locations or redirect them.

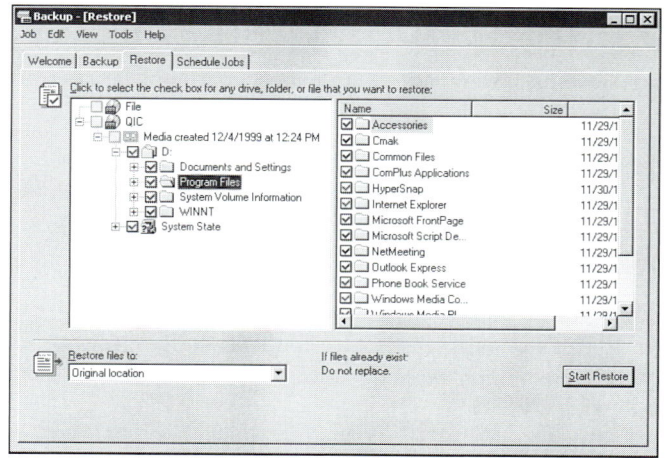

> **Note**
>
> If you select System State on a computer running AD, you receive a message stating that you must reboot, press F8, and select Directory Services Restore mode. Restoring System State on a DC is the subject of the following section.

6. Click Tools, Options to open the Options dialog with the Restore page active. For a full restore, you can accept the default option for overwriting existing files—Do Not Replace the File on My Computer for testing (see Figure 23.45).

   Choose one of the other two options—Replace the File on Disk Only if the File on Disk Is Older or Always Replace Files on My Computer—when restoring a production server. System State automatically replaces existing files, regardless of the restore option you select.

Figure 23.45
The Restore page of the Options dialog for a restore job enables you to set the default action when a file to be restored already exists on the target drive.

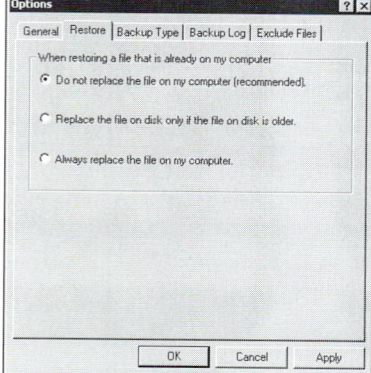

RESTORING FROM WINDOWS 2000 BACKUPS | 973

Tip from
RJ

Choose Always Replace Files on My Computer on a test server installation if you want to perform a more exhaustive test of your backup tape drive.

7. Click Start Restore, and acknowledge the Warning message if you're restoring System State, to display the Start Restore message box and click OK to open the Advanced Restore Options dialog. Accept the default options (see Figure 23.46). If you're restoring a replica file set, the When Restoring Replicated Data Sets, Mark the Restored Data as the Primary Data for All Replicas check box is enabled, but not marked.

Figure 23.46
This Advanced Restore Options dialog has the default options checked for a restore job, which does not contain replica file sets.

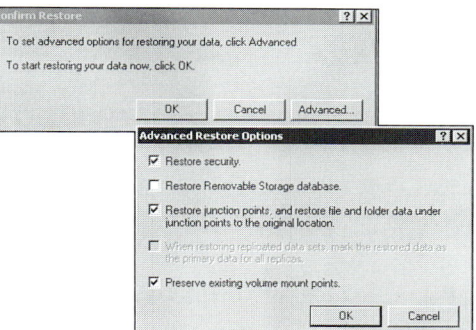

PART
III
CH
23

8. Click OK twice to start the restore process. If you left the last tape in the drive, you are prompted to replace the tape. Replace the tape and click OK to start the tape loading process, and open the Restore Progress dialog (see Figure 23.47).

Figure 23.47
Use the Restore Progress dialog for a restore of the Full backup created in the "Running an Initial Full Backup" section, earlier in this chapter.

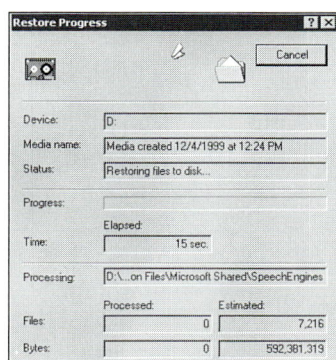

Note

The number of files and bytes processed is 0 at the point shown in Figure 23.47, because you instructed Backup not to restore existing files in step 6 and this example is a test restore operation.

9. If the backup set spans more than one tape, insert the additional tape(s) as directed by Backup's messages. At the end of the restore operation, the Restore Progress dialog changes to the format shown in Figure 23.48.

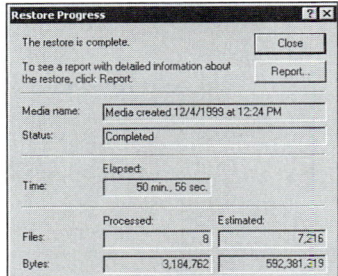

Figure 23.48
When a restore job is complete, the Restore Progress dialog shows a summary of the restore operation. For a more detailed summary, click the Report button.

Note Figure 23.48 shows 8 restored files and 3.1MB, despite instructions in step 6 not to overwrite existing files. The restored files probably are backup/restore catalog files.

10. Click Report to display the restore log in Notepad. Figure 23.49 shows the Catalog Status and Restore Status reports for the preceding test restore operation. Backup doesn't offer a detailed restore report option. Click Close to return to the Backup window. If you restored System State, you receive a message that you must reboot the server.

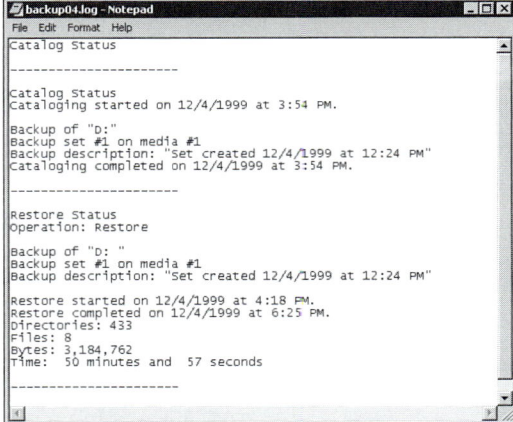

Figure 23.49
The log file is shown in Windows Notepad for the restore operation completed in Figure 23.48.

11. Repeat steps 1 through 10 for the appropriate daily or incremental backup tape(s) required to bring the disk files to the status as of the date and time of the last backup.

> **Caution**
>
> Be sure to change the Restore option in step 6 to Replace the File on Disk Only if the File on Disk Is Older or Always Replace Files on My Computer when restoring from daily or incremental backup sets. If you don't make this change, daily or incremental data for modified files, excluding System State, doesn't write to the disk.

Restoring Files and System State on Domain Controllers

Active Directory locks the Ntds.dit database for exclusive use, and restricts access to files in the \Sysvol folder during and after the conventional boot process. Restoring System State is an all-or-nothing process—you can't just restore the Registry or COM+ Class Registration database. To restore System State on a DC, you must boot the server into Directory Services Restore Mode, and then run the restore operation with Windows 2000 Backup.

> **Caution**
>
> Don't attempt to restore system files and System State as a two-step process. The default Registry settings established when you install Windows 2000 and AD might be inconsistent with the system files you restore. When restoring a DC, restore all system files—preferably all files from the backup set—and the System State as a group. This recommendation applies to both full and incremental restorations.

To restore a DC, do the following:

1. Install Windows 2000 Server, run Dcpromo.exe, and specify the original DC role. If the DC you're restoring isn't the only DC for the domain in the site, replication from another DC occurs during the AD promotion process.
2. Reboot the server normally when the Active Directory Installation Wizard completes the installation.
3. Verify with Active Directory Users and Computers that AD is working correctly.
4. Reboot the server again, but this time press F8 to display the Windows 2000 Advanced Options Menu, select Directory Services Restore Mode, and press Enter. The system boots into Safe Mode.
5. Install the first tape of the backup set, run Backup, click the Restore tab, and mark the device and System state check boxes.
6. Choose Tools, Options, and select the Replace the File on Disk Only if the File on Disk Is Older or Always Replace Files on My Computer option. As noted in the preceding section, System State replaces the existing files, regardless of the restore option you select.
7. Click Start Restore and acknowledge the Warning message regarding restore overwriting the current System State.
8. Click OK to start the restore operation. Refer to steps 8 through 11 of the preceding section for the remainder of the restore process.

9. Reboot the server normally. If you have another DC in the site, replication of updates to AD subsequent to the date and time of the backup occur during the Establishing Network Connections period.

10. Verify with Active Directory Users and Computers, Sites and Services, and Domains and Trusts that the restore process succeeded.

If the DC you're restoring previously handled Flexible Single Master Operations (FSMO) roles, and you seized these roles on another DC, you might encounter an FSMO conflict when you reboot the server after the restore operation. Use the Ntdsutil.exe system tool to resolve FMSO problems.

→ To review FSMO operations with Ntdsutil.exe, **see** "Seizing the FSMO Roles of a Failed DC," **p. 408**.

Depending on the state of AD at and after the time you backed up System State, you might need to perform an Authoritative Restore with Ntdsutil.exe to assure that all AD objects from your restored version replicate properly to other DCs.

AUTOMATING BACKUP OPERATIONS WITH THE TASK SCHEDULER

Once you've verified that your tape drive and the Windows 2000 Backup program are adequate for your backup requirements, you can automate the backup regimen with Backup's Scheduling feature. Automated backup, however, implies that you have a tape changer to automate media operations. A corollary of this hypothesis is that firms investing in $5,000+ tape changes usually purchase third-party backup applications to support them. Automated backup with manual media changes is a dangerous game, because you might forget or be unable to change the media in the drive.

Windows 2000 Backup uses the Task Scheduler to run backup operations at intervals and times you choose. Windows 2000 installs the Task Scheduler service by default and sets its Startup Type attribute to Automatic.

To schedule automatic backup operations, do the following:

1. Launch the Backup application, if necessary.
2. If the media is used, click the Restore tab, select the name of the tape in the list, and choose Tools, Media, Erase. Erasing the media assures that the scheduled backup operation won't attempt to append data or fail because of a media name mismatch.
3. Click the Backup tab, and select the folders and files to back up automatically, including System State, if applicable.
4. Choose Tools, Options, and set the backup options for the job. System State runs as a Copy backup, regardless of the backup type you select for the entire tape backup job.
5. Click Start Backup to open the Backup Job Information dialog, make any changes you want to the job and media description, and click Schedule.

6. Click Yes in the message box to save the job description as a .bks file. Type a descriptive filename in the Save Selection dialog, and click Save.

7. In the Set System Account information, accept or change the default *DomainName*\Administrator entry in the Run As text box. The account must have Administrators or Backup Operators privileges. Type and confirm the account password, and click OK to open the Scheduled Job Options dialog.

8. Type a job description in the Job Name text box and click Properties to open the Schedule Job dialog. Select Daily in the Schedule Task list, specify the Start Time, and accept the default Every 1 Day(s) value (see Figure 23.50). Click OK twice to add the task to the Task Manager's list.

Figure 23.50
The Schedule Job dialog shows that a Full backup is being scheduled every day at 11:30 P.M.

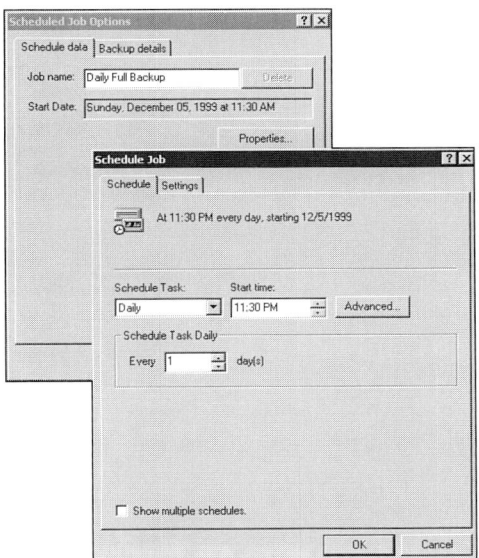

9. Test your backup task by running Control Panel's Scheduled Tasks tool to open the Scheduled Tasks explorer window (see Figure 23.51). Right-click the job entry in the list, and choose Run to start the backup task immediately.

Figure 23.51
The results of the Schedule Job operation from Figure 23.50 can be seen in the Scheduled Tasks window. The job will run daily at 11:30 P.M.

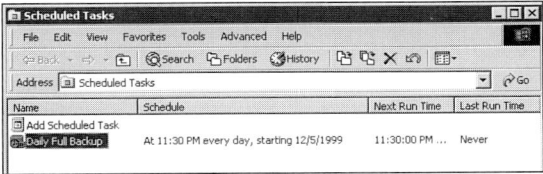

If you encounter a 2D error code or System Files are backed up—despite your having excluded them from the backup list—when using scheduled backups, see the "Backup and Restore Problems" topic of the "Troubleshooting" section that follows.

> **Note**
> You can alter the schedule and other task properties by right-clicking the task entry and choosing properties to open the tabbed properties dialog for the task.

The backup task automatically launches the Backup program with the parameters specified by the designated backup specification file. When the backup operation is complete, Backup's window closes.

TROUBLESHOOTING

SERVER PERFORMANCE PROBLEMS

Disk thrashing—constant disk reads and writes—occurs when server load increases.

Thrashing occurs when active processes run out of RAM and compete with each other for access to the paging file. This causes hard page faults to occur at a very high frequency. Application servers running middle-tier COM+ components encounter this problem when client applications attempt to create more instances of components than can be accommodated by installed RAM. Using object pooling and limiting the number of object instances in the pool can reduce thrashing at the expense of forcing clients to wait for an available components instance from the pool.

If you can't install more RAM, attempt to move the most memory-intensive applications or components to another server or implement simple load balancing by installing copies of components on another server with a relatively low memory load. Redirect half of the client DCOM requests to the second server.

→ For more information on COM+ and application servers, **see** "Brokering Objects and Processing Transactions," **p. 1147**.

BACKUP AND RESTORE PROBLEMS

Scheduled backups fail with an error code of 2D (0x2D).

The media in the drive hasn't been initialized by Windows 2000. You must initialize new media or used media that was written by a program other than Windows 2000 Backup. Run the backup manually the first time, initialize the media, and then let Task Scheduler take over.

Another cause of a 2D error code is a mismatch between the name of the media and the name expected by the backup specification. To assure reliable scheduled backups, erase the media before using it in a scheduled backup environment.

Scheduled backups include 200MB of system files even if excluded in the Advanced Backup Options dialog.

The released version of Backup doesn't save the Advanced Backup Options in the backup specification (.bks) file. Thus, automated System State always includes the protected system files. This problem might be rectified in a Service Pack.

MCSE Corner: Optimizing, Backing Up, and Restoring Your Servers

Several of the concepts covered in this chapter are contained in the blueprint for exam 70-215 Installing, Configuring and Administering Windows 2000 Server. Be prepared for this exam with a thorough knowledge of disk administration in Windows 2000 Server, especially using Windows Backup.

One of the abilities tested on the exam is that of optimizing disk performance. You should be comfortable determining the best changes to make to disk volumes, either on a single disk or RAID array. Know how changing cluster sizes affects disk performance, as well as how to determine the optimum cluster sizes, by both estimating from the size of the volume and using the system monitor.

You should also be familiar with optimizing disk volumes by defragmenting and load balancing. Know how to organize disk volumes by read-mostly and write-mostly operations as well as how disk caching settings affect disk performance. Knowing the drive properties page is also important.

For this exam, you should know how to optimize the system paging file. It is important to know how the optimum size and location of a paging file is determined, and how to set these parameters. You should also be familiar with establishing page file baselines using the system monitor, and improving the performance of the paging file.

The third operation to know, and possibly the most important, is using the Windows Backup tool. You can expect to be asked at least one question on the exam about Windows Backup. Know the theory behind the tool first, including the best methods to organize disk storage and to ensure good backups, including the backup of open files. There probably won't be a question directly related to that on the exam, but it's important to know for the more difficult topics. It is vital that you are familiar with the different types of backups and tape rotations. It is common to get a question on the differences between differential and incremental backups, and less commonly, the differences between full and copy backups. You might also need to know what a daily backup is. A sample question would be "If you have been performing full backups every Monday night, and differential backups every night, which tapes do you need to perform a restore of a file deleted on Thursday?" This would be a multiple-choice type question, and the answer, of course, would be Monday's and Wednesday's.

To pass the exam, you must also know how to use the Windows Backup utility, in addition to the concepts already mentioned. Be able to run different types of backups on local and remote servers, as well as restore from those backups. You should be comfortable restoring files to a server, as well as restoring a disk or an entire server from a complete data loss. The ability to schedule Windows Backup jobs with the task scheduler service is also important.

As with the other sections on the exam, troubleshooting of disks and backups is important. You should be able to troubleshoot disk and paging-file performance issues and determine their cause and remedy, as well as troubleshoot failed backups and restores. With backup and restore issues, it is important to know if problems are caused by permissions issues, open files, or any other problem.

PART IV

WIDE-AREA NETWORKING, INTRANETS, AND THE INTERNET

24 Communicating with Remote Sites and Domains   983

25 Managing Remote Access and Routing Services   1023

26 Setting Up a Virtual Private Network   1075

27 Administering Internet Information Server 5.0   1105

CHAPTER 24

COMMUNICATING WITH REMOTE SITES AND DOMAINS

In this chapter

Analyzing Intersite Replication Requirements and Administration   984

Choosing an Intersite Communication Method   987

Setting Up a Test to Estimate Replication Traffic   990

Performing the AD Replication Traffic Tests   1000

Analyzing NetMon Replication Capture Files   1005

Using the Active Directory Replication Monitor Support Tool   1011

Troubleshooting   1020

MCSE Corner: Communicating with Remote Sites and Domains   1022

Analyzing Intersite Replication Requirements and Administration

Active Directory (AD) multimaster replication between domain controllers (DCs) within a local area network (LAN) ordinarily consumes a relatively small percentage of the network's 100BASE-T—or even 10BASE-T—bandwidth. AD-originated traffic spikes occur when you bring additional DCs on line for the same or new domains, and when adding AD objects in bulk to a domain with more than one DC. When the initial traffic surge subsides, only changes to AD replicate. The routine LAN traffic that occurs as a result of typical AD administrative operations contributes only a fraction of the traffic associated with file and printer sharing, Internet and intranet access, messaging, and other elements of everyday network usage.

Microsoft defines an AD site as "a collection of well-connected machines—based on Internet Protocol (IP) subnets." Sites represent AD replication boundaries, so a better definition of a site might be "a collection of well-connected Windows 2000 DCs." For example, a small business might have two DCs and one or two member (resource) servers, 50 clients connected to the LAN, and 15 telecommuters and mobile users using dial-up modem connections to the LAN. Unless the telecommuters have cable modem or DSL connections and the mobile users have high-speed wireless connections to the LAN, these folks aren't "well-connected" by any stretch of the imagination.

In some cases, even well-connected DCs might be placed in separate sites. For example, the fictional OakLeaf University's on-campus and nearby DCs are well-connected through gigabyte Ethernet and optical fiber network backbones. OakLeaf U. designates a separate site for each building, however, in order to control replication traffic on the backbone. Dedicated fiber-optic cabling between buildings is limited to relatively short distances—usually 1km or less. This chapter deals primarily with multiple Windows 2000 LANs that are separated by a substantial distance—10km or greater—and thus are connected by a relatively low-speed dedicated or switched telecommunications link.

> **Note**
>
> If you're running Microsoft Exchange Server at multiple sites and are satisfied with your current intersite replication performance, you probably won't need to make major alterations to your existing telecommunication infrastructure. AD's routine intersite replication traffic is likely to be only a fraction of that for replicating Exchange public folders and transporting messages.

Site Requirements

Every site requires at least the following hardware components and Windows 2000 services:

- *Domain controller* configured as a Global Catalog (GC) server—A GC server provides local logon capabilities for users with accounts in any domain of any forest. DCs that act as gateways for replication between sites are called *bridgehead servers*. Each site should have at least two DCs to assure local logon capability in the event that one DC fails. The dual-DC requirement is similar to the PDC-BDC (primary domain controller-backup domain controller) combination of remote Windows NT domains. If the site hosts multiple domains, plan on at least one DC—and preferably two DCs—for each domain.

- *Domain Name Service (DNS)*, preferably with AD-integrated DNS—DNS is required to resolve local and remote host names to IP addresses. For maximum efficiency, host records are required for at least every DNS server on the network that's authoritative for a zone. For redundancy, you should run DNS on at least two DCs in a site.

- *Windows Internet Naming Service (WINS)* to handle NetBIOS name resolution for Windows NT, 9x, and other downlevel clients, if present: Ordinarily, you run WINS on at least two DCs.

- *Dynamic Host Control Protocol (DHCP)*, if clients require DHCP services—Only one DC running DHCP server is required per site subnet, because lease expiration intervals usually are much longer than the time-to-repair of a server or the time needed to set up DHCP on another server. However, it's a good practice to provide a second, unauthorized DHCP server that you can authorize if the primary DHCP server goes down.

- *Router and telecommunication adapter* for the site's subnet—You specify the site's subnet address in Active Directory Sites and Services. The intersite telecommunication service you choose determines the type of adapter, which often is built into the router. Several firms offer a hub, router, and telecommunication adapter combined in a single package that's designed specifically to support small branch offices.

Providing fault-tolerant Distributed File System (Dfs) services to remote sites is optional. Fault-tolerant Dfs uses intersite replication to support the Content Replication Service, which synchronizes the content of Dfs alternate volumes.

Site Administration

Sites are geographic—but not administrative—entities. Many Windows NT administrators set up remote sites as individual domains with a PDC and BDC to localize administration. Another reason for including a PDC at a remote Windows NT site is to permit changes—such as adding, altering, or deleting user accounts and privileges—to the Security Account Manager (SAM) database when the intersite communication link fails. BDCs have read-only SAM databases; all security principal changes must occur on the PDC and then replicate to the BDC.

With AD, domain administration is totally independent of site topology. Every DC is writable, so you can alter AD objects without regard to the existence of a live communication line between servers in different sites. A user with Domain Admins membership can administer a domain at a Windows 2000 server or workstation in any site that hosts a domain, and Enterprise Admins can administer any domain in any forest from any site. Administering a remote domain from a site without a DC for the remote domain requires a live (synchronous) connection to the DC in the remote site. If you centralize management of domains at remote sites, placing a DC for each remote site domain at the management site enables you to make large-scale domain changes quickly on the local DC. These changes replicate to the remote DC at the frequency you determine for the intersite link.

A single domain can span multiple sites. If you assign organizational units (OUs) on a geographic basis, you can delegate administrative responsibility for the site's OU to a member of the Domain Users or another Security Group you create. Changes made to the OU at the remote site replicate to other DCs in the domain, plus all DCs that act as GC servers.

Synchronous Intersite Operations

Intersite replication uses a messaging approach; at each replication interval—the default is 180 minutes—a DC, on which changes to a domain have been made since the last successful replication, attempts to contact its replication partner DC(s). If the intersite circuit is live, replication takes place; if the link is dead, the DC reattempts to contact its partner(s) until the circuit is restored and replication succeeds. Replication occurs in multiple bursts, which prevents the operation from consuming the entire bandwidth of the circuit.

> **Note** Windows 2000 offers two intersite replication protocols—Internet Protocol (IP) and Simple Mail Transport Protocol (SMTP). IP is the default transport; you use SMTP only for replication between systems that don't support remote procedure calls over an IP transport. Microsoft Exchange 2000 uses SMTP for message transport, but it's unlikely that you'll encounter a need to use SMTP for AD replication.

In contrast, synchronous operations require a direct and immediate connection between DCs in different sites and use the Remote Procedure Call (RPC) protocol. Synchronous intersite communication between DCs runs at the maximum data rate (also called *wire speed*) of the telecommunication link between the sites, assuming lack of competing network traffic. If the circuit between the sites is down, you can't perform tasks that require synchronous operations.

Following are the most common intersite operations that require a synchronous connection:

- Adding a local member server or workstation to a domain without a local DC—You must log on to the remote DC with Domain Admins privileges to add computer and, optionally, new user accounts. Without a local DC, computer and user authentication traffic travels over an intersite circuit to a DC acting as a GC server.

- Setting up a local DNS server on a member server as a primary or secondary server for a zone, or as an AD-integrated DNS server—DNS servers other than AD-integrated continue to communicate synchronously; AD-integrated DNS replicates between sites.

- Reading attribute values of objects that reside on remote DCs and whose values aren't replicated between GCs.

- Promoting or demoting a local DC, whether as the first DC for a domain or as an additional DC in a domain that spans sites—Promoting a remote DC for a domain containing many objects is the most bandwidth-intensive of these three operations.

Tip from
RJ

Defer a substantial part of the replication traffic by clicking the Replicate Later button when displayed in an Active Directory Installation Wizard dialog. Deferring replication enables you to complete the AD installation process for a large or complex domain in a much shorter time. Replication continues when you reboot the server after the Wizard completes its task.

Tip from
RJ

Create additional DCs for remote sites at the site with the first DC for the domain, if the domain contains a large number of objects—for example, 10,000 or more—or you have a very complex domain structure. Using a LAN connection for the initial AD replication process is very fast and enables you to troubleshoot AD, DNS, site configuration, and other problems near the original DC. If you're implementing a fault-tolerant alternate Dfs volume, creating the volume locally saves a substantial amount of initial replication traffic. After you set up and test the DC for the remote site, you ship it to its new location and connect it. Replication updates all changes made at the central DC during the disconnected period.

→ To determine for yourself which operations are synchronous and which replicate, **see** "Performing the AD Replication Traffic Tests," **p. 1000**.

Choosing an Intersite Communication Method

Dealing with remote sites—such as domestic branch offices or overseas manufacturing facilities—requires careful analysis of bandwidth requirements. Unlike LANs, where bandwidth is cheap, wide area network (WAN) connections to remote sites are costly. Traditionally, the higher the bandwidth and the greater the distance, the more the connection costs. Use of the public Internet to provide WAN connectivity eliminates—or at least mitigates—the effect of distance on connection cost but introduces its own security issues. Some WAN communication services assess usage charges based on the total megabytes of traffic per month. Most on-demand connections, such as Integrated Services Digital Network (ISDN), extract time and distance charges from users.

The Regional Bell Operating Companies (telcos) and independent Network Service Providers (NSPs) offer a variety of local and long-distance telecommunication services that are suited to interconnecting AD sites. Following are brief descriptions of the three most popular telecommunication services that offer sufficient bandwidth for intersite replication for small- to moderate-size firms:

- *T-1* is a conditioned, permanent, point-to-point private circuit that you lease by the month from a telco or local exchange carrier (LEC). T-1 lines have a bandwidth of 1.544Mbps and connect to IP routers at both termination points. T-1 dedicated circuits have relatively high one-time installation charges, commonly between $500 and $1,000, and a monthly charge based on the distance between sites. Competition between telcos and NSPs in the T1 business has resulted in declining monthly charges, but typical bills range from a few hundred to several thousand dollars per month, depending on distance.

- *Frame relay* is a switched packet service that connects access links. An access link usually is a relatively short T-1 connection between your router and a telco or LEC frame relay switch. The advantage of frame relay over T-1 is that you can order multiple permanent virtual circuits (PVCs) to connect several WANs in a star configuration. Frame relay connections have a port speed that's equal to or less than that of the access link, and a committed information rate (CIR) that's guaranteed but less than the port speed. For example, you can split a T-1 access link into four 256Kbps ports with a CIR of 200Kbps or so each to serve four remote sites. Another advantage of frame relay is that you pay only for the bandwidth you need and the time you use the bandwidth. Flat-rate frame relay tariffs substitute a fixed monthly fee for variable time and distance charges.

- *Digital Subscriber Line (DSL)* is a relatively new technology that uses conventional telco voice lines to provide connections at data rates up to T-1 speeds, but at substantially lower cost. Telcos are expanding the availability of ADSL (Asymmetric DSL) services throughout North America to compete against cable modems for consumer Internet access. ADSL delivers substantially higher download than upload speed, typically 384/128Kbps or 1.5Mbps/384Kbps. NSPs and some telcos also provide commercial SDSL (symmetric DSL), which offers the same upstream and downstream data rates—from 144Kbps to 1.5Mbps. DSL modems and routers ordinarily connect through the telco's central office to an ISP or NSP, so distance-based charges don't apply. NSPs provide virtual private networks (VPNs) with DSL endpoints; encryption provides data security on the public Internet. Windows 2000-based VPNs are the subject of Chapter 26, "Setting Up a Virtual Private Network."

Tip from
RJ

DSL is poised to become the branch-office and telecommuter connectivity method of choice in 2000 and beyond. DSL delivers the best cost-performance ratio of all "last mile" technologies—the copper connection between remote facilities and the local telco's central office. New "intelligent" DSL access multiplexers (DSLAMs) currently becoming available to telcos and NSPs enable businesses to combine Internet access, data transfer via VPNs, and voice services. High-end DSLAMs connected at the central office to ATM backbones deliver Quality of Service (QoS) features to prioritize traffic and offer frame relay over DSL.

Note

Asynchronous Transfer Mode (ATM), cable modems, Integrated Services Digital Network (ISDN), and 56Kbps dedicated lines are alternatives to the three services in the preceding list. The primary application for ATM is creating network backbones, such as those used by NSPs. Most network administrators consider cable modem connections unreliable because of the notoriously poor service response of large cable multiple service operators. ISDN, with a basic data rate of 112Kbps or 128Kpbs, carries per-minute and distance charges that make ISDN uneconomical for most point-to-point connections. The low data rate of ISDN and 56Kbps lines make them unsuited for connecting sites having substantial replication and traditional WAN traffic.

CHOOSING AN INTERSITE COMMUNICATION METHOD 989

Figure 24.1 illustrates interconnection by a frame-relay PVC of two sites that host a parent and a child domain—`oakleaf.edu` (Oakland site) and `student.oakleaf.edu` (Berkeley site). Frame relay PVCs connect other domains and sites—`research.oakleaf.edu` at the Lihue (Kauai, HI) site and `oakmusic.com` at the Sausalito (CA) site—to the Oakland site. DSL interconnections are similar to those for frame relay. DSL routers connect to your ISP or an NSP, and VPN packets travel over the Internet, instead of the frame relay switched network.

Figure 24.1
This example of a network with two sites contains separate domains connected by a frame relay link.

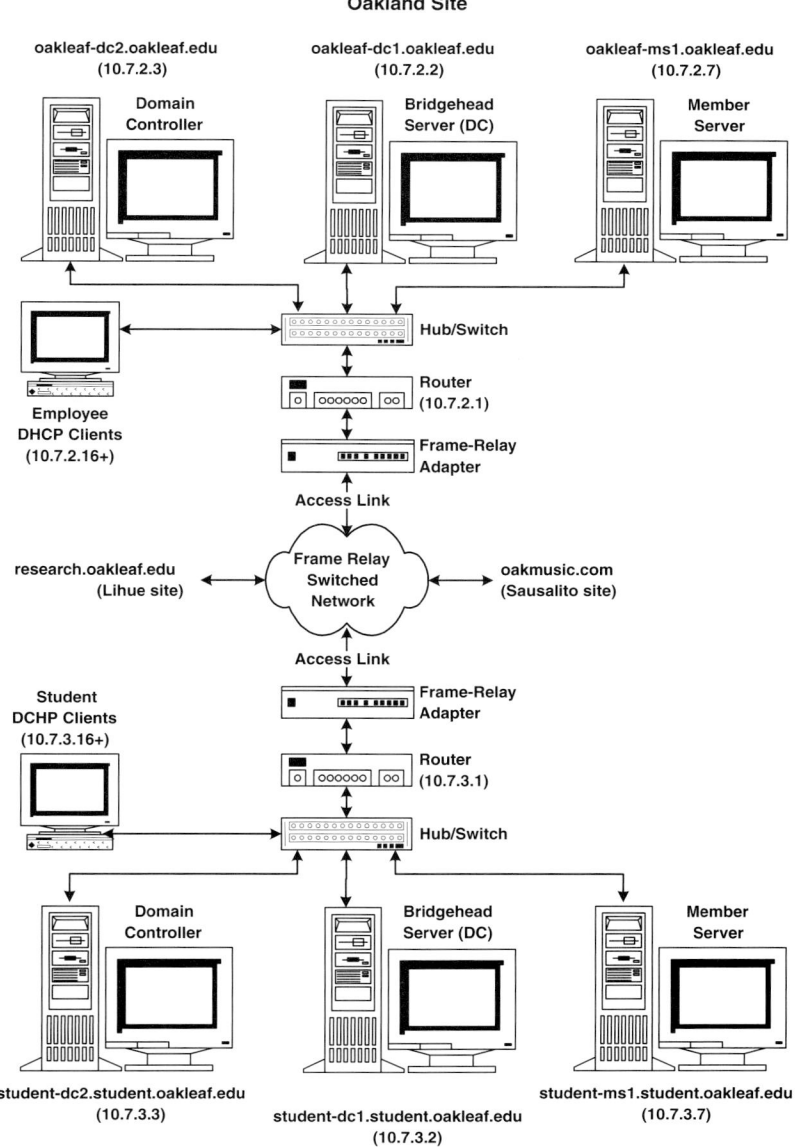

PART
IV
CH
24

Setting Up a Test to Estimate Replication Traffic

Microsoft designed the intersite AD replication process to minimize traffic and, accordingly, bandwidth requirements. Intersite replication of AD updates is compressed, which trades added processor cycles for reduced bandwidth requirement and the added security of not sending network information in the clear. Intrasite replication between DCs isn't compressed, which increases speed and minimizes processor usage.

> **Tip from**
> *RJ*
>
> Don't rely on data compression for network security when using the Internet to replicate between sites. Compression substitutes tokens for repeated groups of bytes and other relatively simple techniques to compress data. Data compression algorithms are relatively easy for hackers to reverse-engineer. If you use a public network for intersite communication, take advantage of VPN's encryption capabilities, despite the increased bandwidth requirement.

Only a subset of the attribute values of objects in other domains replicates between GCs. The replicated attribute values are those needed for logon to other domains in the enterprise and for locating objects. The bandwidth saved by replicating only a subset of attribute values is a function of how many of the object attribute values you populate.

Microsoft provides little in the way of hard data on the amount of replication traffic generated by the common synchronous operations described earlier and replication of AD changes. Microsoft's reluctance to provide traffic estimates is understandable when you consider the number of independent variables that determine the amount and frequency of replication traffic.

The only reliable method of estimating replication traffic between your sites is to emulate a typical replication scenario and measure the number of bytes sent over the circuit for a specific set of typical intersite operations. You measure the intersite traffic with Windows 2000's Network Monitor. It's desirable, but not required, to set up a router for each site and simulate the circuit between the routers. In an isolated test network, the routers and the circuit between them affect only the replication data rate, not the amount of traffic.

> **Note**
>
> A few broadcast frames, which don't propagate between routers, usually are sent during the replication period. The amount of broadcast traffic isn't sufficient to cause significant errors in the replication traffic estimates. If you have other DCs or Windows NT servers connected to your test network, disconnect them to prevent spurious network activity.

Designing an Intersite Replication Test Network

Your replication test network configuration should emulate your production network topology, if you have a sufficient server and network hardware to accomplish the objective. You need two DCs at the primary site to measure intrasite replication traffic. A single DC at each remote site is sufficient for monitoring intrasite traffic. Comparing the volume of intrasite and intersite traffic requires an application that automates typical AD operations, such as adding a large number of users. If you have a Windows NT domain with many user accounts, you can use the Active Directory Migration Tool (ADMT) to add Windows NT user accounts to your test domain. Windows NT user accounts have very few attribute values compared to Windows 2000 accounts. Using ADMT to add user accounts in bulk underestimates traffic, if you take full advantage of AD's User object attributes.

→ To review use of ADMT to generate user accounts in an AD OU, **see** "Emulating Domain Migration with the Active Directory Migration Tool," **p. 231**.

Figure 24.2 illustrates the configuration of the domain controllers for the examples of this chapter. The central Oakland site hosts the oakleaf-dc1 DC in the parent `oakleaf.edu` domain. The Berkeley site, housed in student Dormitory 1, hosts the flexible single-master operations (FSMO) DC—student-dc1 of the `student.oakleaf.edu` child domain. The Dormitory-2 site hosts the second DC, student-dc2. All three DCs are GC servers. The sites connect in the star configuration that's required to support Dfs replication. The example configuration is typical of site topology for a small- to medium-size company with two branch sales offices or manufacturing facilities.

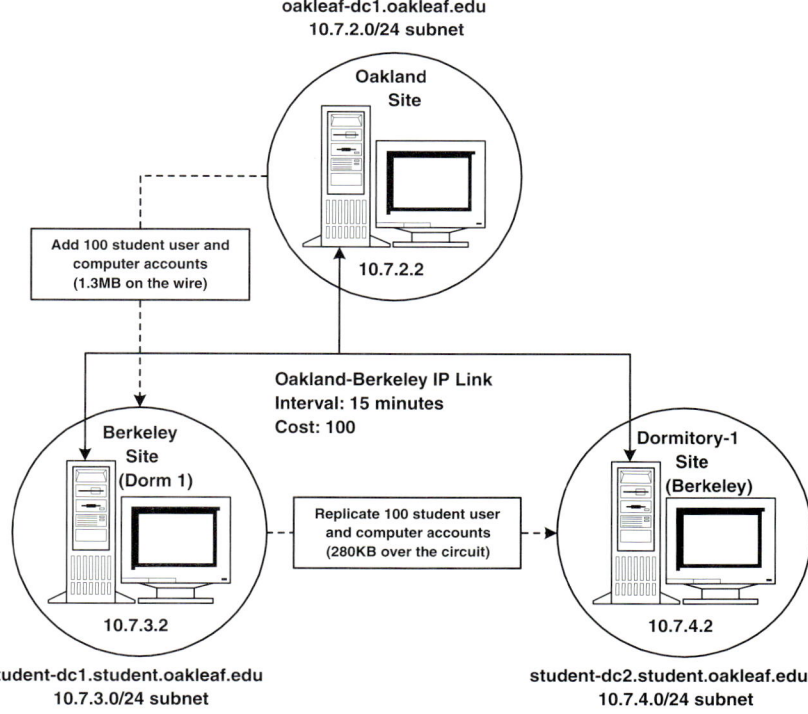

Figure 24.2
Three sites contain two domains with the replication path and replication configuration details for an example of a procedure adding 100 users.

The ADSI25 application, used in many of the other chapters of this book, runs on oakleaf-dc1 and synchronously adds new employee accounts to oakleaf-dc1, and student user and computer accounts to student-dc1. The replication process adds the accounts to student-dc2 at a frequency you specify—15 minutes for this example. The configuration of

Figure 24.2 enables you to independently compare traffic generated for GC operations, such as adding employee users to `oakleaf.edu`, synchronous account additions, and intersite account replication.

→ For instructions on installing the ADSI25 for Active Directory application, **see** "Installation on a Windows 2000 DC or Workstation," **p. 1259.**

> **Note**
> You can test simple replication scenarios with two DCs in the same domain, but that configuration doesn't let you determine GC-only traffic resulting from adding users to other domains.

The sections that follow describe a test scenario, but the testing process closely follows the steps you take to implement intersite and evaluate replication in a production environment. The test configuration is equally applicable to measuring replication traffic generated by Microsoft Exchange Server 5.5 or 2000. Exchange Server replication, however, is beyond the scope of this book.

> **Caution**
> It's possible to run ADSI25 on a production network, because ADSI25 creates it own set of user and computer accounts, OUs, and Security Groups. ADSI25 has a Removal All button that deletes only the objects it adds to AD. If you have Security Groups or OUs with the same names as those used by ADSI25, the Remove All operation deletes them. Running ADSI25 or any other third-party application that makes a large number of changes to AD on a production network entails a substantial risk of corrupting the directory, requiring reconstruction of your domain(s). It's strongly recommended that you run ADSI25 only within test domains. You can, however, use your existing LAN and WAN infrastructure for the tests.

Configuring Active Directory Sites and Services

After setting up the sample `oakleaf.edu` and `student.oakleaf.edu` or equivalent parent/child domains, if necessary, make sure AD-integrated DNS is running correctly on each DC. If you haven't installed `ADSI25.exe` on the `oakleaf-dc1.oakleaf.edu` DC, run `ADSI25.msi` from the `\Seuw2ks\Adsi25` folder of the accompanying CD-ROM. Then use `Dcpromo.exe` to add a second DC to `student.oakleaf.edu`. The DCs for testing don't need big-time RAM or processors, because replication speed isn't an issue—it's the total number of bytes that count in this scenario. Even plain Pentium 200s with 64MB of RAM can run replication tests, if you don't mind waiting 15 seconds or so for administrative snap-ins to open.

→ To review how to implement child domains, **see** "Adding a Sample Child Domain," **p. 160**.

You must add the new test sites, select the site connection type (IP is the default), specify the subnet for each site, and set the replication interval—15 minutes for the test setup. Subnets are specified to emulate a routed network. If you don't have routers installed, make sure each DC's TCP/IP subnet mask is set to 255.255.0.0, the default value for the nonrouted network used in the earlier chapters of this book. The class B address causes the DCs to disregard the subnet address for purposes other than replication.

Do the following to set up the three sites, optionally substituting your own site, domain, and DC names:

1. Launch Active Directory Sites and Services.
2. If you haven't renamed the Default-First-Site-Name site, select its node, press F2, and rename the site Oakland.
3. Right-click the Sites node, and select New Site to open the New Object—Site dialog. Type the name of the first new site—Berkeley—in the text box, and select the IP link name—Oakland-Berkeley if you renamed DEFAULTIPLINK previously (see Figure 24.3). Click OK to create the site.

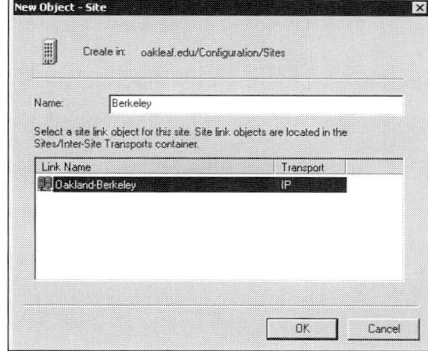

Figure 24.3
The New Object–Site window shows a new site being created called Berkeley with the Oakland-Berkeley site link selected.

4. Under the Servers node of the Oakland site, right-click the server for the Berkeley site, STUDENT-DC1, and choose Move to open the Move Server dialog. Select the Berkeley site and click OK to move the student-dc1 DC to the Berkeley site.
5. Right-click the NTDS Settings node under STUDENT-DC1 and choose Properties to open the NTDS Settings Properties dialog. Mark the Global Catalog check box and click OK to close the dialog. Leave the Description text box and Query Policy list empty for the test.
6. Repeat steps 3 through 5 for the Dormitory-2 site, moving STUDENT-DC2 to the Dormitory-2 site.
7. Right-click the Subnets node and choose New Subnet to open the New Object - Subnet dialog. Type the network address for the Berkeley subnet—10.7.3.0 for this example—and the subnet mask, 255.255.255.0 (see Figure 24.4). Click OK to close the dialog and set the Subnet attribute value, 10.7.3.0/24 for the Berkeley site.

Figure 24.4
The New Object - Subnet window enables you to specify the subnets contained in the selected site. In this example, the Berkeley site contains the 10.7.3.0 subnet with a mask of 255.255.255.0.

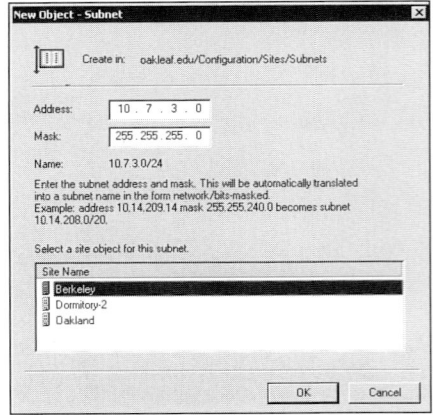

8. Repeat step 5 for the Dormitory-2 site (10.7.4.0) and, if you haven't done so previously for the Oakland site (10.7.2.0).

9. Click the IP node under the Inter-Site Transports node, right-click the Oakland-Berkeley site link in the right pane, and choose Properties to open the link's Properties dialog.

10. Multiselect the site items in the Sites Not in This Link list and click Add to add the sites to the Sites in This Site Link list. Add a description for the link, if you want. Set the Replicate every value to 15 minutes for the test (see Figure 24.5) and click OK to close the dialog.

Figure 24.5
The properties page for the Oakland-Berkeley site link enables you to add the sites that are contained in the site link and set the link cost and replication interval.

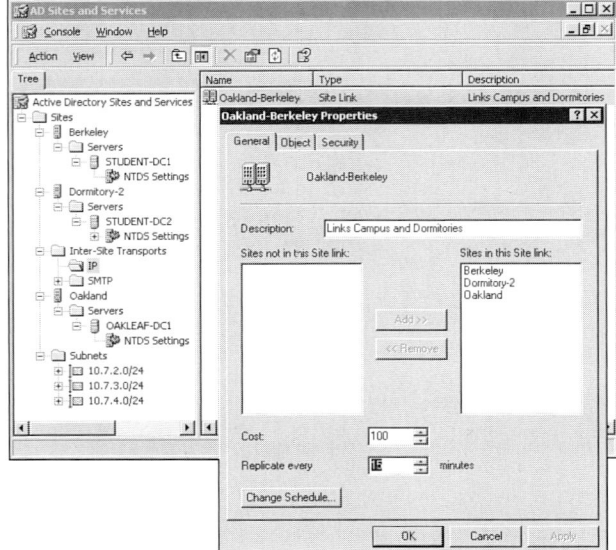

11. Verify the connections between the sites by clicking NTDS Settings node for each site, right-clicking the <automatically generated> connection item in the right pane, and choosing Properties to open the Properties dialog for the connection. Add a description to the connection to aid in identifying the connection. Figure 24.6 shows typical values for the replication connection from the Dormitory-2 site to the Dormitory-1 (Berkeley) site.

Figure 24.6
The Active Directory Connection properties page shows the automatically generated connection between Dormitory-1 and Dormitory-2.

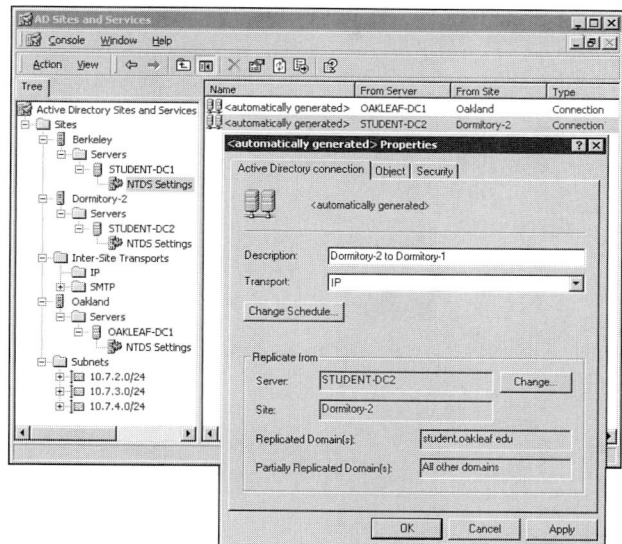

12. Right-click the NTDS node of the Berkeley site and choose Properties to open the NTDS Settings Properties dialog. Mark the Global Catalog check box to make student-dc1 the GC server for the site. Do the same for student-dc2 in the Dormitory-1 site. By default, oakleaf-dc1 (the initial root DC) is a GC server.

Replication is bidirectional, so each site ordinarily has two connections. The Berkeley site has two automatically generated connections—one from the Oakland site (`oakleaf-dc1.oakleaf.edu`) and one from the Dormitory-2 site (`student-dc2.student.oakleaf.edu`). Similarly, the Oakland site has automatically generated connections from the Berkeley and Dormi-tory-2 sites. The Dormitory-2 site needs only to replicate to and from the Berkeley site to keep its GC up-to-date, including GC updates from the parent `oakleaf.edu` domain sent to `student-dc1.student.oakleaf.edu`. Thus, Dormitory-2 receives by default only a single IP connection from Berkeley.

Automatically adding connections is a duty of AD's Knowledge Consistency Checker (KCC), which is responsible for assuring that replication can occur within and between all sites, regardless of common errors in configuring replication topology. If the KCC doesn't create a needed connection during the preceding process, you must add a connection manually. You also must add or remove one or more connections if you want to change the replication topology from a typical star configuration.

> **Note**
>
> A full star configuration requires two-way connections between each site. A full star usually results in inefficient use of bandwidth, but offers high reliability. The KCC attempts to optimize the star by taking into account connection cost when eliminating redundant connections. If a connection fails, the KCC attempts to substitute a higher-cost connection. Star configurations work best with frame relay links.
>
> A ring configuration replicates sequentially from one site to the next. Each site in the ring has a two-way connection with two adjacent sites. The DC that initiated the AD changes ignores its own changes when it receives them from the adjacent site. Ring configurations are better suited to point-to-point T-1 lines.

To add a connection manually, do the following:

1. In Active Directory Sites and Services, right-click the NTDS node of the site to which you want to replicate, and choose New Active Directory Connection to open the Find Domain Controllers dialog.

2. Select the name of the DC from which you want to replicate in the list (see Figure 24.7), and click OK to open the New Object—Connection dialog.

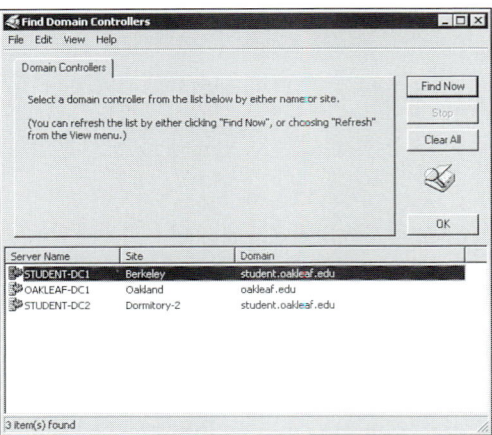

Figure 24.7
From this dialog, you select the source Domain Controller for a manually added Active Directory connection.

3. Accept the default DC name as the name of the connection, or change it and click OK to close the dialog and add the connection.

4. Right-click the new connection item in the right pane and choose Properties to open the connection's Properties dialog. IP is the default protocol for automatically generated connections, and RPC is the default for new connections.

5. If IP isn't the specified value in the Transport list, change RPC or SMTP to IP for intersite replication (see Figure 24.8). Add a description for the connection, if you want, and then click OK to close the dialog.

Figure 24.8
From the properties page for an Active Directory connection, you can specify the transport protocol and the description for the connection.

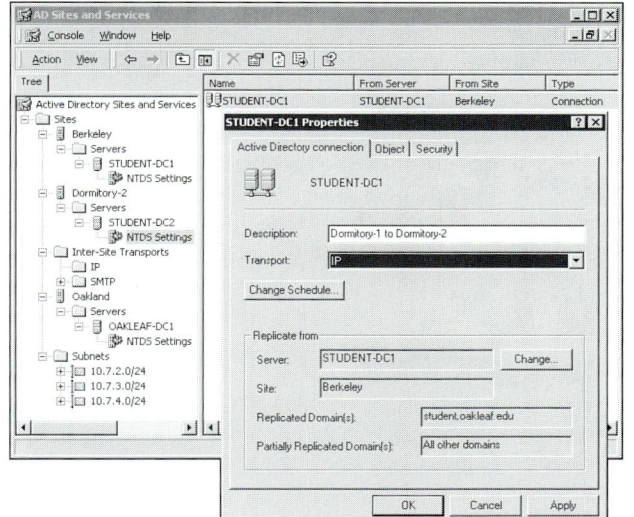

> **Note** RPC is a synchronous connection type that replicates immediately upon receiving AD change notifications. An RPC connection ignores the intersite replication schedule you set.

To remove a connection, right-click the connection item in the right pane and choose Delete. If you delete a connection required to maintain replication consistency between all DCs, the KCC automatically creates a new connection.

 If you encounter replication-related error messages in the Directory Services when establishing your initial replication topology, see the "Replication Topology Problems" topic of the "Troubleshooting" section near the end of the chapter.

Setting Up Network Monitor

As noted in Chapter 22, "Monitoring and Tuning Your Network," the Network Monitor (NetMon) administrative tool included with Windows 2000 Server is almost identical to the Windows NT 4.0 version. The standard version of NetMon included with Windows 2000 monitors network traffic only on the local PC. To determine the number of bytes needed to add 100 new student users to a DC in one site by network transfer (where student-dc1 is the site and uncompressed RPC is the network) and to a DC in another site (student-dc2) by IP replication (compressed) transport, you set up NetMon on both DCs. Using the DC on which you add the users (oakleaf-dc1) instead of the RPC-connected child domain site (student-dc1) provides a more accurate indication of network traffic and lets you measure GC-only replication traffic.

→ For NetMon basics, **see** "Monitoring Network Activity with NetMon," **p. 911**.

To set up NetMon on the parent domain's DC (oakleaf-dc1), do the following:

1. Launch Network Monitor from the Administrative Tools menu. If you haven't configured NetMon previously or your DC is multihomed, the Select a network dialog opens.

2. Select the network card to monitor. Figure 24.9 shows the Select a network dialog for a multihomed server with a 100BASE-Tx adapter selected and a second 10BASE-T/10BASE-2 adapter. Click OK to close the dialog and click the Start Capture button (with the small arrow, as shown in Figure 24.10) to begin a test capture. After a minute or two, frames between Network Address 1 and Network Address 2 appear in the left-middle pane. The machine on which NetMon runs is called LOCAL.

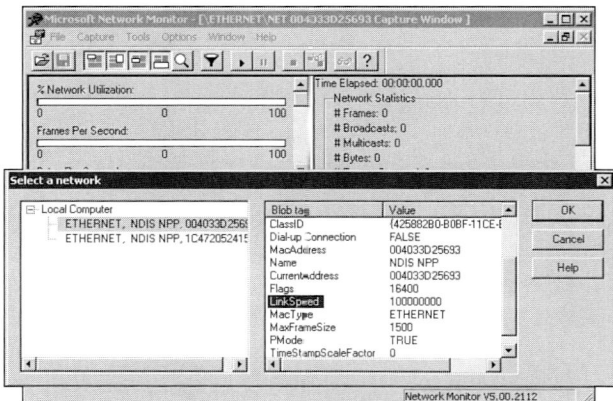

Figure 24.9
When Network Monitor is first opened on a server with multiple network interfaces, the foreground dialog opens; from here you select the network adapter to monitor.

3. By default, NetMon uses the Media Access Control (MAC) address or the adapter's vendor ID to identify network addresses other than local. In the lower pane, right-click the Network Address column of the row with the MAC address of student-dc1 and choose Edit Address '*MAC address*' to open the Address Information dialog.

4. Type the name of the DC, **STUDENT-DC1** for this example, in the Name text box, mark the Permanent Name check box, and type an optional comment (see Figure 24.10). Click OK to change the name to that of the DC.

5. Repeat steps 3 and 4 for the LOCAL adapter, changing its name to OAKLEAF-DC1.

6. Click the Stop Capture button (with the small square), and choose Capture, Addresses to open the Addresses dialog. Verify that entries for the two DCs appear at the bottom of the list.

7. To add optional IP addresses for the two DCs, click the Add button to open the Address Information dialog. Type the name of the DC in the Name dialog, select IP in the Type list, type the IP address in the Address text box, and add an optional description in the Comment box (see Figure 24.11). Click OK to add the address.

Setting Up a Test to Estimate Replication Traffic   999

Figure 24.10
In Network Monitor, you can rename a remote adapter with a descriptive name, STUDENT-DC1 in this case. By default, interface names are their respective MAC addresses.

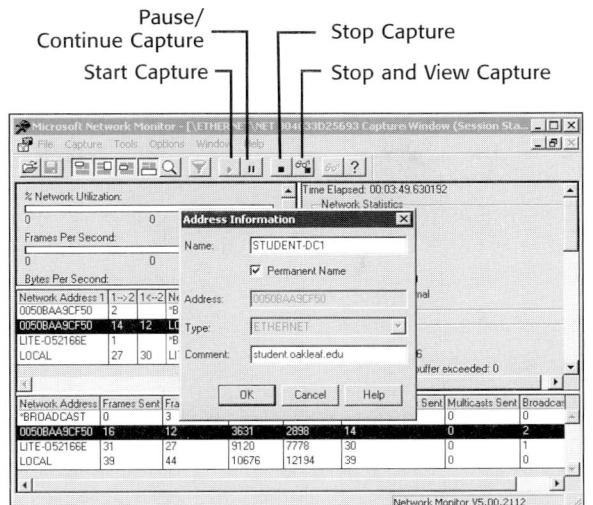

Figure 24.11
For ease of use, you can optionally add IP addresses of adapters in Network Monitor's address database.

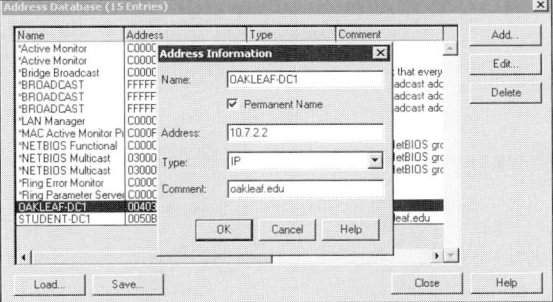

8. In the Address Database dialog, click Save to open the Save Addresses As dialog, select `Default.adr` in the `\Winnt\System32\Netmon` folder as the filename, and click OK to overwrite the existing default address file. Your Address Database dialog appears, as shown in Figure 24.12.

Figure 24.12
In this view of the Network Monitor address database, you can see the MAC and IP addresses of the two newly renamed systems.

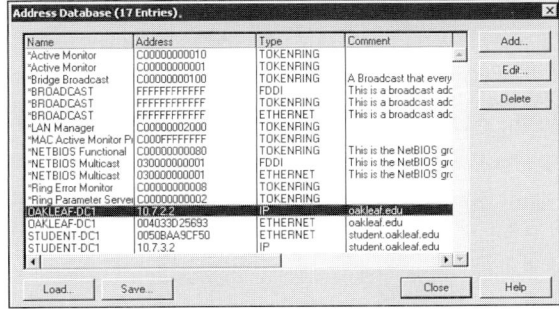

PART
IV
CH
24

9. Choose Capture, Save Configuration to save the network adapter settings you made in step 2.

10. Close and reopen NetMon without saving the capture, and verify that your configuration and address list are correct. Capture frames for a few minutes to verify the connection between the two DCs.

After you configure NetMon on the replication source DC (oakleaf-dc1), repeat the preceding process for the destination DC (student-dc2). On the destination DC, you rename the addresses for the LOCAL and the source (student-dc1) network adapters.

> **Tip from**
> *RJ*
>
> Set up NetMon on each production DC. NetMon is the primary troubleshooting tool for diagnosing replication problems. If you request replication technical assistance from Microsoft or an independent software vendor, you probably will be requested to supply NetMon capture files for analysis. NetMon captures are a subject of the sections that follow.

Performing the AD Replication Traffic Tests

Determining the amount of traffic generated by AD replication involves these two elements:

- Measuring the number of bytes replicated to add a typical user and computer account within a domain
- Measuring the number of bytes replicated to add an entry in the GC for a user in another domain

These measurements deliver worst-case data, because adding a user and computer account involves much more traffic than other routine operations. User accounts created by running the ADSI25 application have values for all common LDAP attributes. Some multivalued attributes, such as `directReports`, can contain very large arrays of references to other user accounts. Modifying or deleting user and computer accounts creates very little replication traffic. Tests show that moving a user from one OU to another generates about half the traffic associated with creating a new user account.

Setting Up ADSI25 for the Test

You can use any application or script that's capable of creating a large number of user and, optionally, computer accounts to generate the replication test traffic. The ADSI for Active Directory application, however, is designed specifically for conducting these types of tests.

If you haven't installed the ADSI25 for Active Directory application on the parent DC (oakleaf-dc1), do the following:

1. Run `ADSI25.msi` from the `\Seuw2ks\Adsi25` folder of the accompanying CD-ROM on the parent DC.

2. Add the required shares—`\\Oakleaf-dc1\Employees` and `\\Student-dc1\Students` for this example—to the parent and child DCs.

3. Run ADSI25 for Active Directory from the Programs menu. Figure 24.13 illustrates the settings in ADSI25's startup window for the examples of this and the following sections.

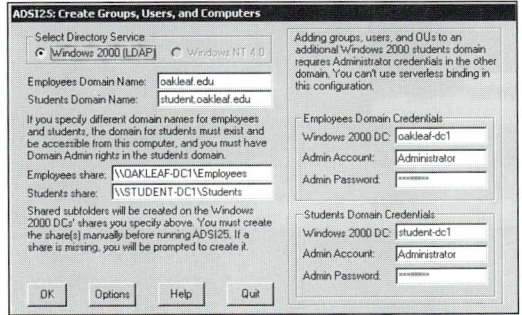

Figure 24.13
The domain and domain controller name settings are shown for the ADSI25 application running on the OAKLEAF-DC1 domain controller in the oakleaf.edu parent domain.

4. If you don't want to add computer accounts, click Options to open the ADSI25 Options dialog, and clear the three check boxes in the Computer Accounts frame. Click OK to return to the setup dialog.

5. Click OK in the setup dialog to open ADSI25's main window.

6. Click Add OUs and Groups to create the shared subfolders, add the sample text files (Adsitest.txt) to the subfolders, and generate the standard set of OUs and Security Groups in the parent and child domains.

7. Click Add Employee Users to test the addition of five employee user and computer accounts to the oakleaf.edu domain.

8. Click Add Student Users to test the addition of 25 students to the student.oakleaf.edu child domain. The student accounts replicate to student-dc2.student.oakleaf.edu within the 15-minute replication interval you set previously.

9. Verify in Active Directory Users and Computers running on student-dc2 that the student accounts have replicated.

RUNNING THE ADD-USERS TEST

Capturing the traffic data to compare synchronous and replicated operations requires running NetMon simultaneously on both the parent DC and the replication target DC. You can add any number of new student accounts—up to about 25,000—with ADSI25. To run a typical test that adds 100 student accounts, do this:

1. Type **100** in the Users text box under the Add Student Users button.

2. Launch NetMon on the parent DC and the replication target DC, and click Start Capture on both NetMon instances.

3. Immediately click Add Student Users to start the addition process. After a few seconds, synchronous traffic frames that create student accounts begin traveling between oakleaf-dc1 and student-dc1 (see Figure 24.14).

Figure 24.14
Network Monitor running on the parent Domain Controller shows the traffic between the Domain Controllers as directory replication occurs.

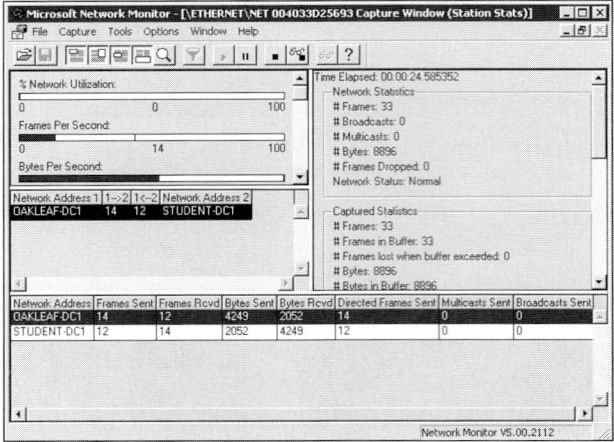

4. Observe the NetMon window on the replication target. After a few minutes, a substantial number of replication frames begin to arrive from the source DC.

5. After the replication interval expires, click Stop Capture on both NetMon instances; choose File, Save and save your capture for later analysis to an appropriately named .cap file in the DC's \Winnt\System32\Netmon\Captures folder.

At completion of the account addition operation on the replication source—student-dc1—NetMon's window appears as illustrated by Figure 24.15. Adding 100 student user and computer accounts generates about 1.3MB (3,808 frames) of synchronous LAN traffic from the Oakland to the Berkeley site, and about 930KB (3,207 frames) of return traffic from Berkeley to Oakland.

Figure 24.15
This view of Network Monitor shows the network traffic statistics between the two Domain Controllers after replication has occurred.

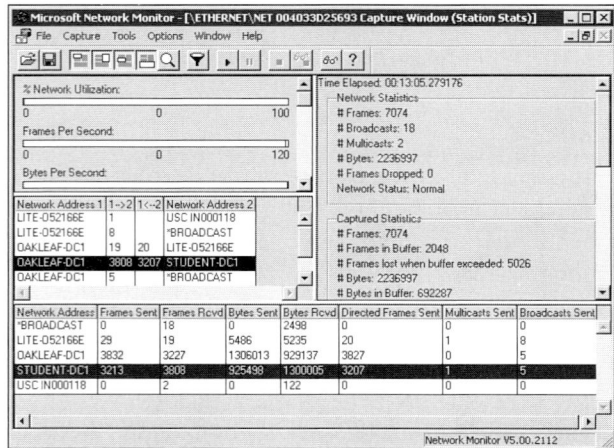

When replication between the source and target DCs completes, you can compare the amount of synchronous and replication traffic for user account addition. Figure 24.16 shows NetMon's window on the replication destination DC. Compression reduces replication traffic to the destination from 1.3MB to about 875KB, a compression ratio of about 1.5:1 or 67%. The primary decrease in traffic occurs in the return channel—930MB to about 71KB—more than a 10:1 reduction. Observe in Figure 24.16 that although the number of return frames is about half the sent frames, the return frame payload is much less than that for the synchronous operation.

Figure 24.16
These Network Monitor statistics between two Domain Controllers in the same domain were generated by the replication that occurred after a user addition process on one of the controllers.

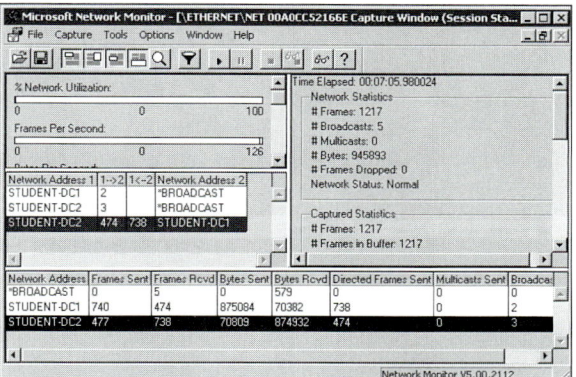

Most replication transports run in full-duplex mode, which permits traffic to flow simultaneously in both directions, so return traffic isn't a major factor in determining network bandwidth requirements for replication. Replication to a remote site of 100 new user accounts over a 56Kbps circuit, which provides a net transport rate of about 5Kbps, requires about 180 seconds, which is only 1/5 of the 15-minute test replication interval. The replication interval between production sites ordinarily is 1 hour or greater, so adding 1,000 or more new user accounts replicates well within the replication period, assuming no other traffic on the telecommunications link.

TESTING GLOBAL CATALOG TRAFFIC

One of the primary purposes of GC servers is to authenticate users having accounts in other domains. When you add or delete user accounts in domains for which no DC exists at the site, updates to each GC server in the enterprise contribute replication traffic. As noted earlier in the chapter, GC entries for out-of-domain objects possess only those attribute values necessary for user logon and finding common AD objects in other domains and forests. Thus, out-of-domain GC traffic between sites isn't a major consideration unless you perform a large-scale domain restructure.

To analyze out-of-domain GC traffic in the sample student.oakleaf.edu domain by adding Employee user accounts to the oakleaf.edu domain, do the following:

1. Close both instances of NetMon, saving your capture file if you didn't do so previously.
2. Type **100** in the Users text box under the Add Employee Users button.
3. Launch NetMon on the parent and child DCs and start capturing.
4. Click Add Employee Users to add user and computer accounts to the `oakleaf.edu` domain.
5. After the employee accounts are added to `oakleaf.edu` and the replication interval expires, stop capture on both DCs and save the capture files.

Figures 24.17 and 24.18 compare the synchronous (from OAKLEAF-DC1 to STUDENT-DC1) and replicated (from OAKLEAF-DC1 to OAKLEAF-DC2) traffic. STUDENT-DC2 receives replication traffic from both OAKLEAF-DC1 and STUDENT-DC1 via two connections. Despite the multiple connections, it's clear from the two captures that the amount of replication traffic for out-of-domain GC operations is much less than that for in-domain replication.

Figure 24.17
These statistics are the result of Global Catalog traffic between a parent and child domain after adding 100 users to a Domain Controller in the parent domain.

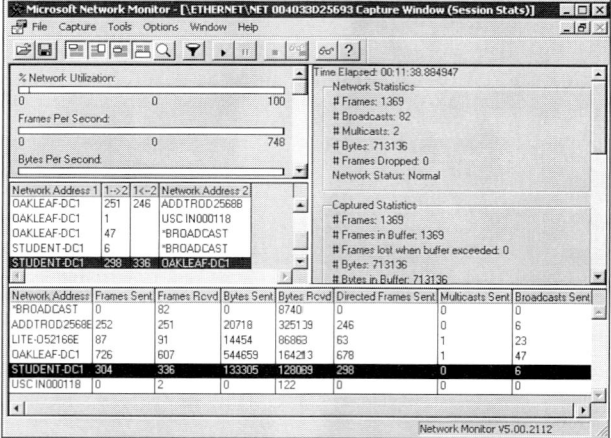

Figure 24.18
This view of Network Monitor shows the traffic between OAKLEAF-DC1, STUDENT-DC1, and STUDENT-DC2 after adding 100 users to the Global Catalog.

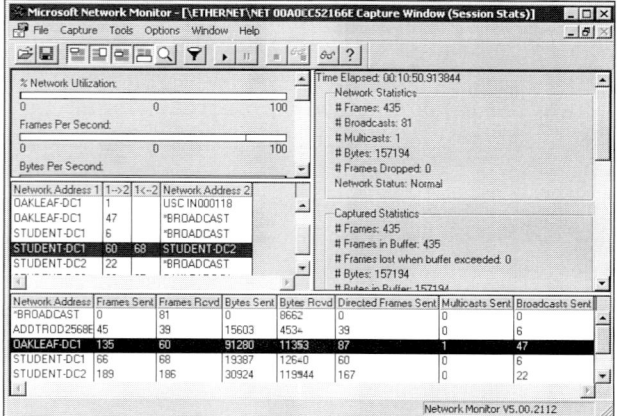

Testing Domain Restructuring Traffic

You can estimate the amount of replication traffic resulting from a major change in your domain structure by deleting all objects that the ADSI25 application adds to the parent and child domain and then re-creating the objects. Adding a few hundred (or thousand) employee and student accounts generates much more network and intersite traffic than is generated by deleting those accounts.

To run a domain reconstruction test, do this:

1. Close and reopen both instances of NetMon, saving your capture file if you didn't do so previously, and start capturing traffic.
2. Click ADSI25's Remove All button to delete all OUs and the objects they contain, and remove all computer accounts.
3. Record the number of bytes replicated. Deleting OUs performs a bulk deletion of the Security Groups and user accounts they contain.

    Deleting computer accounts requires a command for each computer, because you can't—and shouldn't be able to—delete the built-in Computers container. The amount of synchronous and replication traffic to delete 2,500 ADSI25 objects is less than half that for adding 100 student accounts.
4. Click Add OUs and Groups to re-create the standard set of OUs and Security Groups for the parent and child domains. This operation generates less than 100KB of synchronous and about 70KB of replication traffic.
5. Type **1000** in the text box below the Add Student Users button, and then click the button to add the student user and computer accounts.

LAN traffic from oakleaf-dc1 to student-dc1 is approximately 12.8MB for the preceding sequence of operations. Replication traffic from student-dc1 to student-dc2 is about 2.6MB, about 20% of the number of bytes sent over the LAN. You can conclude from these results that replication efficiency, including the effect of compression, increases dramatically with bulk addition of a large number of AD objects.

 If error messages appear in the Directory Services after you've successfully configured and tested replication between your sites, see the "Replication Connectivity Problems" topic of the "Troubleshooting" section near the end of the chapter.

Analyzing NetMon Replication Capture Files

Up to this point, the replication test has disregarded the content of the frames traveling over the LAN or between sites. The capture files you take during the replication tests also provide insight on the intrasite and intersite replication mechanisms and are useful for replication troubleshooting. If you encounter unexpected replication problems and need technical assistance from Microsoft or an independent product support person, you'll probably be asked to supply a replication *NetMon trace*, which is a synonym for a Network Monitor capture file.

When you stop or pause NetMon capture, you can view detailed information on the type and content of each frame and its packets in the Capture window. The most interesting frame types involved in the replication process are LDAP (Lightweight Directory Access Protocol), TCP (Transmission Control Protocol), MSRPC (Microsoft Remote Procedure Call), and DNS. Periodic DNS replication of records for AD-integrated DNS zones occurs independently of operations on objects that appear in Active Directory Users and Computers. The ability to filter a frame type, such as LDAP, enables you or a technical service person to perform a detailed analysis of AD-specific traffic when troubleshooting replication problems.

VIEWING THE FRAME LIST AND FRAME CONTENT DETAIL

To examine the payload of typical frames transported during the immediately previous capture, perform this drill:

1. Click the toolbar's Stop/View Capture or View Capture button to open the Capture window.

> **Tip from RJ**
>
> To view a capture previously saved as a .cap file, choose File, Open and load the capture file.

2. Scroll to one of the LDAP Protocol0p: SearchRequest (3) frames (see Figure 24.19).

Figure 24.19
A small part of the Network Monitor capture buffer is shown for the domain reconstruction operation performed in the text.

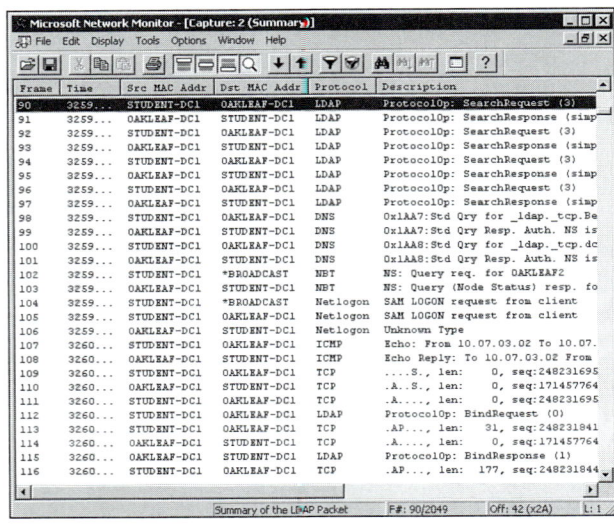

3. Double-click the frame row to divide the Capture window into Summary (top), Detail (middle), and Hex (bottom) panes.

The Summary panel displays a subset of the list shown in Figure 24.19. The Detail panel lets you examine each frame element. When you select a frame element, the Hex panel highlights the hexadecimal value of the element's bytes.

4. Double-click the parent nodes (plus signs) to expand the Detail display to include child items and nodes. Figure 24.20 illustrates most of the elements required to conduct an LDAP search for the OAKLEAF2 domain. OAKLEAF2 is the downlevel (NetBIOS) name for oakleaf.edu.

Figure 24.20
Individual frames are shown from an LDAP search with an Equality Match filter for a DnsDomain object named OAKLEAF2.

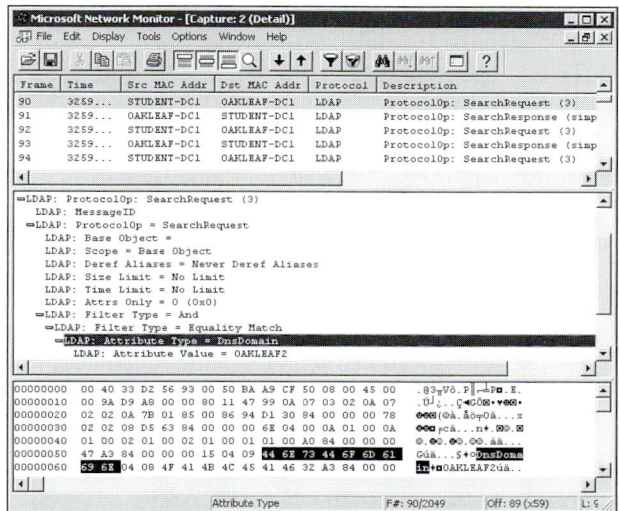

→ To review LDAP searches and filters, **see** "Searching for AD Objects with LDAP," **p. 135**.

5. Click the next (SearchResponse) row in the Summary pane, and expand the + nodes in the Detail pane. The Result Code = Success item indicates that the search operation found the OAKLEAF2 domain entry (see Figure 24.21). Success is defined by a value of 0x0 (hexadecimal 0) in the returned frame; a nonzero value represents a search failure.

Figure 24.21
This search response frame is the result of the search request frame shown in Figure 24.20.

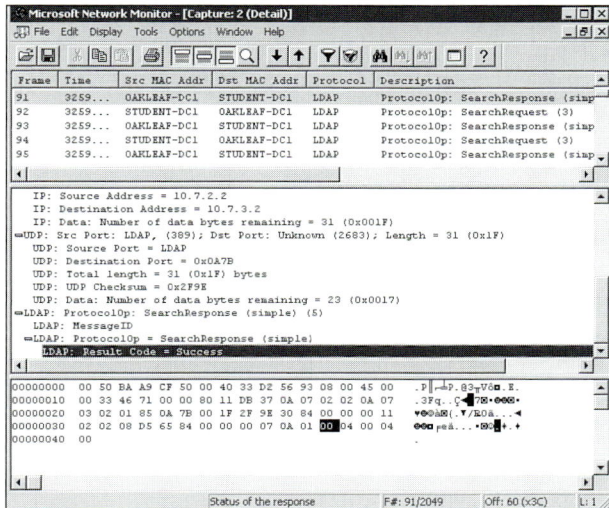

Notice the IP: Source Address (10.7.2.2 for oakleaf-dc1) and IP: Destination Address (10.7.3.2 for student-dc1) at the top of the Detail pane. The IP items in the Detail pane show the IP header information. LDAP operations take advantage of the lightweight User Datagram Protocol (UDP) to improve transmission efficiency.

6. Double-click the selected frame in the Summary pane to return to the original Capture window.

APPLYING A FRAME TYPE FILTER

If you're interested only in examining frames of a specific protocol, you can make your life easier by applying a filter. To filter for LDAP frames only, do this:

1. Click the Edit Display Filter button (left funnel icon) to open the Display Filter Dialog.
2. Double-click the Protocol==Any item to open the Expression dialog with the Protocol page active.
3. Click Disable All to remove all protocols from the Enabled Protocols list, and then scroll to and double-click the LDAP protocol in the Disabled Protocols list to enable it (see Figure 24.22).

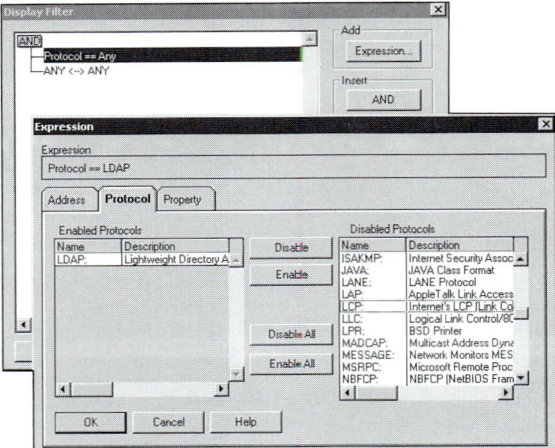

Figure 24.22
The Expression dialog of the Display Filter window shows an expression defined to display only LDAP protocol frames.

4. Click OK twice to return to the Capture window, which now displays only rows for the LDAP protocol (see Figure 24.23). The Toggle Display Filter button—to the right of the Edit Display Filter button—has a funnel icon overlaid with an international stop symbol. If the Toggle Display Filter button is depressed, click it to apply the filter; this button alternately applies and removes the filter.

Analyzing NetMon Replication Capture Files 1009

Figure 24.23
The Network Monitor capture buffer display is shown after the filter defined in Figure 24.22 was applied. Only LDAP frames appear.

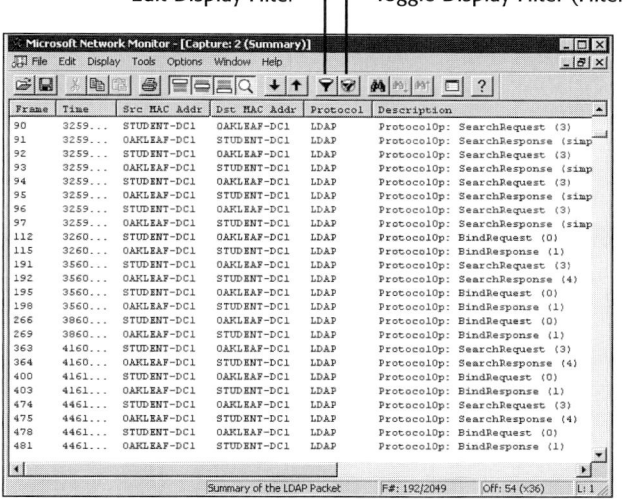

You can further narrow the filter result set by requiring a match to a particular LDAP attribute value for replication analysis. To list only frames that contain the `subschemaSubentry` attribute, which is associated with replicating the AD Schema, do this:

1. Click the Edit Display Filter button (left funnel icon) to open Display Filter Dialog.
2. Double-click Protocol==LDAP to open the Expression dialog, and click the Property tab.
3. Scroll in the Protocol Property List to LDAP, expand the node, and select Attribute Type. Accept the default Contains relation and select the ASCII option, which enables you to type characters instead of hex values in the Value text box.
4. Type **subschemaSubentry** in the Value text box (see Figure 24.24).

Figure 24.24
This example shows the Expression dialog when you specify a frame filter by LDAP Attribute Type with the value specified in the Value box.

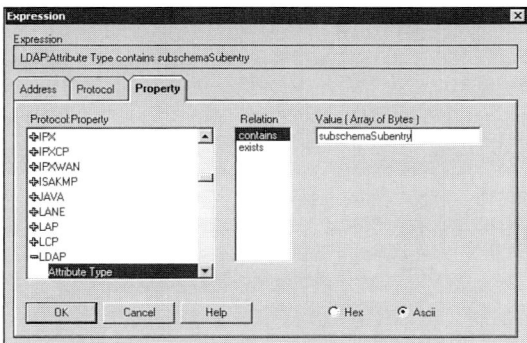

PART
IV
CH
24

5. Click OK twice to apply the more restrictive filter, and then double-click one of the members of the filtered list. Figure 24.25 shows the expansion of one of the SearchResponse frames that includes a value for the subschemaSubentry attribute.

Figure 24.25
An example shows part of the frame payload for a search response to a request for Schema-related attribute values.

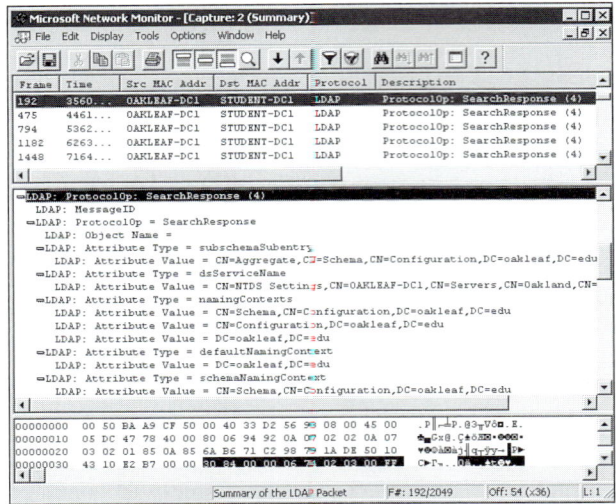

6. Click the toolbar's Toggle Display Filter button (refer to Figure 24.23) to remove the filter and display entries for all frames.

The ability to filter frames by protocol or by LDAP attribute value makes NetMon a powerful analytical tool for learning about and troubleshooting intrasite and intersite replication. The search results shown in Figure 24.25 provide the full LDAP path for replication-related attributes. For example, dsServiceName specifies the full LDAP path of the NTDS Settings you apply in Active Directory Sites and Services, including the server, container, and site names. The defaultNamingContext and schemaNamingContext attributes return the name of the domain with the server that's responsible for Domain Naming Master and Schema Master flexible single-master operations (FSMO) for the forest.

Tip from
RJ

Choose File, Print to print the parts of your filtered NetMon trace that contain the LDAP paths to replication attributes, such as schemaNamingContext. The General page of NetMon's Print dialog includes a Print Range frame that enables you to specify a range of frames. Make sure to restrict printing to a specific frame range. If you don't, you might end up printing several hundred more pages than you want.

The NetMon page of the Print dialog enables you to specify several options. The most important default option to deselect is Print Hex data; you seldom (if ever) need to include hex data when printing NetMon captures.

Using the Active Directory Replication Monitor Support Tool

The Support Tools' Active Directory Replication Monitor (ReplMon) is a Visual Basic 6.0 application (`Replmon.exe`) that enables you to test and monitor replication operations between sites. Creating Microsoft Management Console (MMC) snap-ins with Visual Basic 6.0 requires the MMC Snap-In Designer, which Microsoft released in January 2000, so ReplMon's developer designed the application to emulate MMC features. ReplMon uses the Active Directory Service Interfaces (ADSI) 2.5 and RPC intersite communication to gather its replication information. ReplMon's primary purpose is to report replication status, but its supplemental features also can deliver very detailed information on your DCs that's not easily obtainable with other Support Tools.

You can run ReplMon on any DC in any site and monitor replication connectivity to all other sites. You also can force immediate replication between sites for testing and troubleshooting. You must have at least Domain Admins privileges to run ReplMon.

> **Note**
> ReplMon doesn't have its own HTML Help file; ReplMon documentation is an element of the Network Management Tools topic of the Windows 2000 Support Tools help file.

Setting Up Replication Monitor

Follow these steps to initialize ReplMon for monitoring multiple sites with the sample site topology described in the preceding sections:

1. Choose Programs, Windows 2000 Support Tools, Tools Help to launch the Windows 2000 Server Tools help file.
2. Click the R button, and then click the `Replmon.exe` link to display the first page of the ReplMon help file.
3. Click the Run Active Directory Replication Monitor Now link to execute `Replmon.exe` and open its main form, which is divided into two panes.
4. Right-click the Monitored Servers item in the left pane, and choose Add Monitored Server to open the Add Monitored Server Wizard's first dialog.
5. Select the Search the Directory for the Name of the Server to Add option, and wait for the Wizard to identify the initial root domain (`oakleaf.edu` for this example).
6. If you run ReplMon on a DC other than the initial root domain DC and aren't logged on with valid Domain Admins credentials for the initial root domain, mark the Use Alternate Credentials to Get Site List check box and click Change to open the Enter Credentials dialog. Type your Enterprise or Domain Admins user name and password for the initial root domain, and click OK.
7. Click Next to display the second Wizard dialog. In the Sites list, expand the site node to display its servers. Select the bridgehead server you want to monitor (see Figure 24.26) and click Finish to close the dialog and add the server to the Monitored Servers node of the main form.

Figure 24.26
The Add Server to Monitor dialog enables you to specify a server to monitor with the Active Directory Replication Monitor.

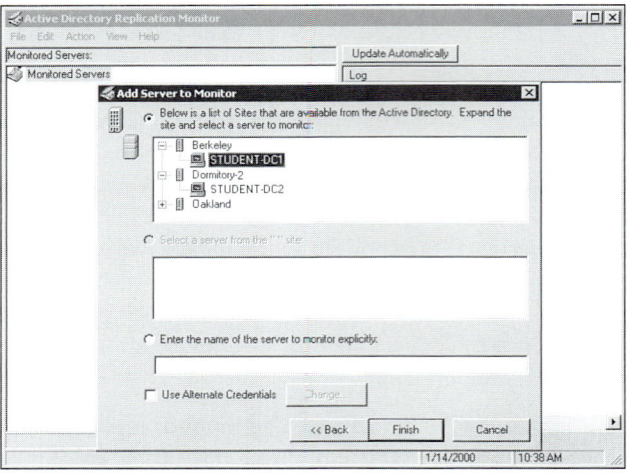

> **Note**
>
> In a site with only a single DC, the DC automatically becomes a bridgehead server. To specify a DC as a bridgehead server in a site with multiple DCs, launch Active Directory Sites and Services, right-click the DC's node, and choose Properties to open the ServerName Properties dialog's Server page. Select IP in the Transports Available for Inter-Site Data Transfer, and click Add to add IP to The Server Is a Preferred Bridgehead Server for the Following Transports list. Do the same for the SNMP transport, and click OK to close the dialog.

8. After ReplMon has gathered the required information from the selected server, expand the naming context nodes for each AD partition (see Figure 24.27). It might take a minute or two for a server in a remote site with a slow link to respond to the request. A monitor is the icon for the selected server; direct replication partners use an icon with a server box having a diagonal link to the left.

Figure 24.27
The Active Directory Replication Monitor shows the replication connections for the four Active Directory partitions of the OAKLEAF-DC1 server.

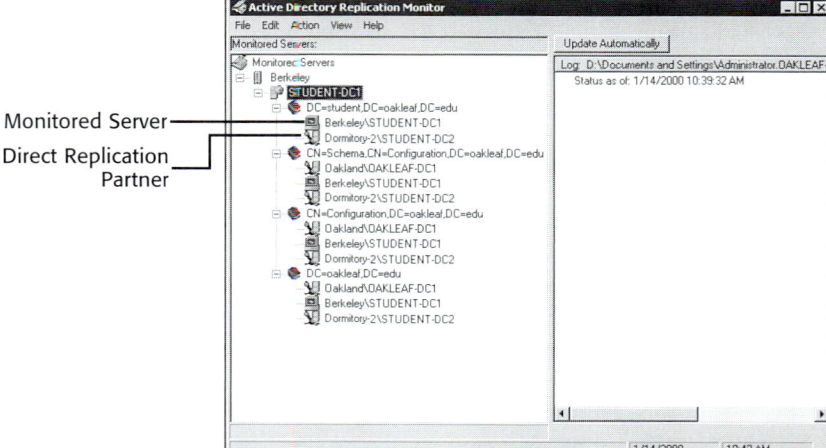

9. Repeat steps 4 through 7 for the remaining sites and servers you want to monitor—Dormitory-2/STUDENT-DC2 and Oakland/OAKLEAF-DC1 for this example.
10. Choose View, Options to open the Active Directory Replication Monitor Options dialog's General page. Mark the options you want to add; options apply to all monitored servers. Figure 24.28 shows the options most commonly selected for a production environment.

Figure 24.28
The General tab of the properties page for the Active Directory Replication Monitor Options dialog enables you to configure display and notification options as well as logging.

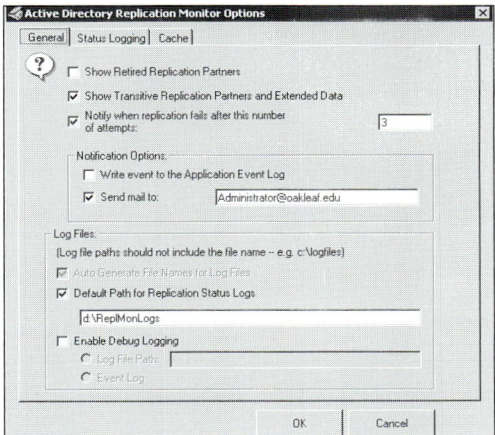

Note

Notification of replication problems by sending an email message to the Administrator mailbox after three failures prevents spurious notices that occur because of short-term site connection problems. The default location for ReplMon log files is `d:\Documents and Settings\LogonID\MyDocuments`, so it's a good practice to specify a dedicated folder for these files, which can grow very large. Check the "Troubleshooting with Active Directory Replication Monitor" topic of the ReplMon section of the Support Tools Help file for a detailed description of ReplMon options.

11. Click the Options dialog's Status Logging tab. For this example, mark the Group Policy Objects and Performance Statistics check boxes. To add network and replication performance counters to ReplMon's logs, click Add and type a backslash (\), the name of the object, another backslash, and the name of the counter you want to monitor (see Figure 24.29). Click OK twice to close the input box and the Options dialog.

Tip from
RJ

Don't mark the Status Logging page's Display Changed Attributes when Replication Occurs unless you want to troubleshoot a replication problem with a specific attribute value. Marking this check box creates extremely large log files when adding new AD objects, such as user accounts.

It's a good idea to occasionally clear attribute values that ReplMon stores in its local cache when you run ReplMon for an extended period. Once every day or two, click the Cache tab, and then click the Reset button to refresh the cache.

Figure 24.29
The Status Logging tab of the Active Directory Replication Monitor Options properties page enables you to configure monitoring of Group Policy Objects and Performance Statistics.

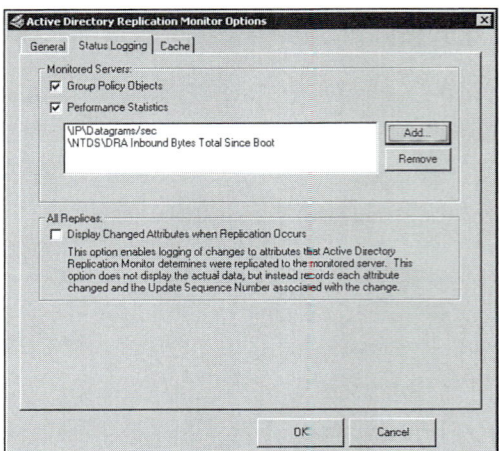

12. Choose File, Save Monitored List As to save your monitor setup to an appropriately named .ini file in \Program Files\Support Tools.

Tip from

RJ

Create a desktop shortcut to Replmon.exe to avoid the circuitous route through the Support Tools help file.

When you close and restart ReplMon, choose File, Open Script to load the .ini file you saved. It may take five minutes or more to start ReplMon if your remote sites have a slow connection. Even in a 3-site test network, opening ReplMon with the .ini file takes a couple of minutes when you have large log files.

Tip from

RJ

To clear the log files for a specific server, right-click the server node, choose Clear Logs, and click OK when asked to confirm log deletion. To remove all log files, close ReplMon and erase the .log files in the folder you specified in the General Page of the Options dialog. Restarting ReplMon generates new, empty log files.

MONITORING REPLICATION

You can run *ad hoc* replication checks or monitor replication at fixed intervals. ReplMon also enables you to check the replication properties of your servers and offers a graphic display of replication topology. To start the monitoring process and check ReplMon's other features, do this:

1. Press F5 or choose View, Refresh to perform a single replication test. The actions ReplMon performs during the refresh cycle flash in the status bar at the bottom of the left pane.

    The right window displays status reports in ascending time order for the selected server. Figure 24.30 shows two status reports for the student-dc1 DC in the Berkeley site. The caption at the top of the right pane shows the filename for the DC's .log file.

USING THE ACTIVE DIRECTORY REPLICATION MONITOR SUPPORT TOOL | 1015

Figure 24.30
Two successive status reports for the STUDENT-DC1 server in the Berkeley site are shown in the right pane of the window.

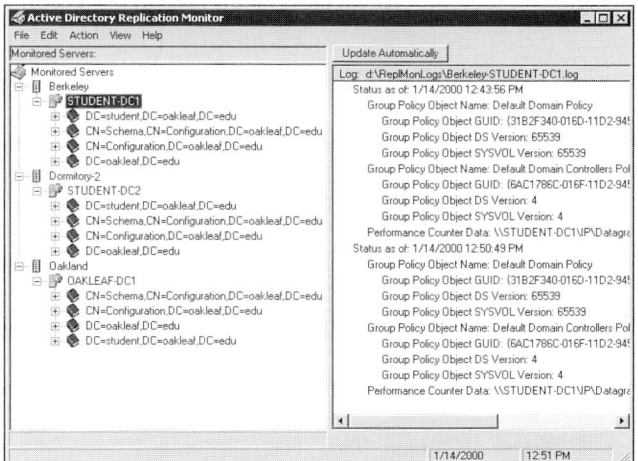

2. To monitor replication periodically, click the Update Automatically toggle button to open a message box that enables you to set the test interval in minutes. Type the test interval, which should be longer than your chosen intersite replication interval, in the text box and click OK. Use 15 minutes when you're testing replication, but set 4 or 6 hours as the interval for production operations.

   During periodic replication, the Update Automatically button changes its caption to Cancel Auto Update. Click the button to halt periodic tests.

3. To view a list of most of the other features offered by ReplMon, right-click a server node to open a context menu shown in Figure 24.31. Menu items that start with Show lead to dialogs that display additional information about the selected DC or all bridgehead servers for the domain.

Figure 24.31
The context menu displays the options available when you right-click a server in the left pane of the Active Directory Replication Monitor.

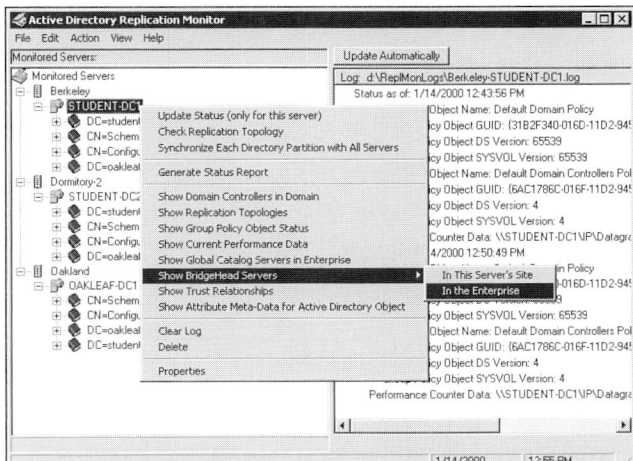

PART
IV
CH
24

4. Choose Action, Server, Generate Status Report to create a detailed .log file for the selected server. Type a name for the file in the Save As dialog and click OK to open the Report Options dialog (see Figure 24.32). Accept the default report components and click OK to generate the .log file.

Figure 24.32
The Report Options page enables you to configure optional data, which will be output in server status reports.

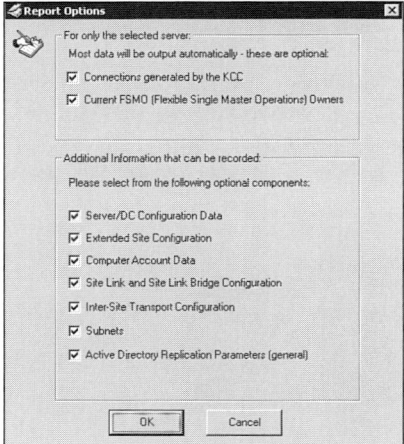

5. Click OK when the Report Complete message appears, and then open your .log file in Notepad. Figure 24.33 shows the first few lines of the file, which is several hundred lines long.

Figure 24.33
The first part of a detailed status report for a server opens in Windows Notepad.

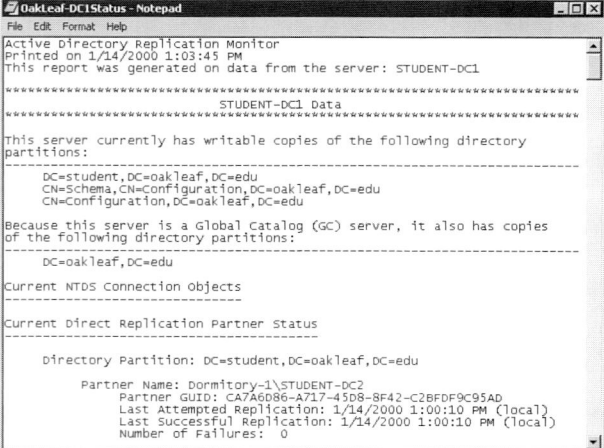

The Status report includes information returned by LDAP queries and reads important server Registry settings. Scroll to the Configuration (Registry) section of the report to review server configuration data stored in the selected DC's Registry.

Tip from
RJ

> Generate a status report for all bridgehead servers immediately after you set up your initial replication topology and confirm its operability. An initial status report for each server in a known-good replication environment serves as the basis for future troubleshooting operations. Generate a new status report for each server after every change you make to your production replication topology. If you encounter replication problems, you can compare the new status report with the archived initial copies.

6. Right-click the server node and choose Properties to open a tabbed Server Properties dialog for the selected DC (this may take a minute or two if you're connecting to a server over a slow link). Click the Server Flags tab to display the roles of the selected server and the AD services it runs in the Properties list (see Figure 24.34). If the DC doesn't support a role or run a service, an X replaces the check mark.

Figure 24.34
The Server Flags page of the Server Properties dialog marks roles that the server performs or does not perform with a check mark or an X, respectively.

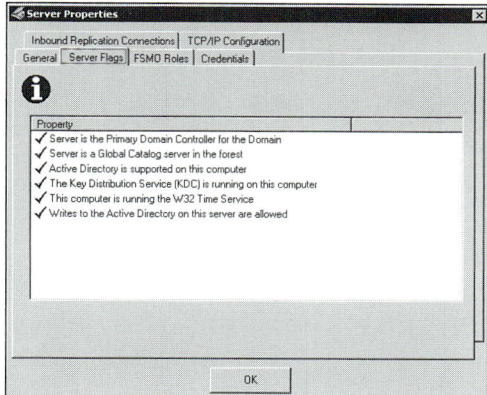

7. Click the FSMO Roles tab to list the DCs that perform FSMO roles for the oakleaf.edu or student.oakleaf.edu domains. Figure 24.35 shows the DCs that perform the FSMO roles for student.oakleaf.edu. Click the Query buttons to check connectivity to each FSMO server.

Figure 24.35
The FSMO Roles page of the Server Properties dialog displays and tests connectivity to the servers performing FSMO roles for the selected server.

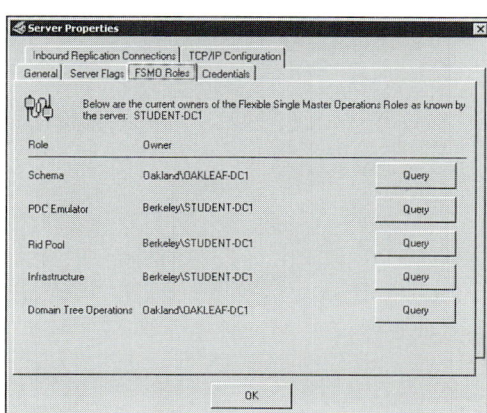

8. Click the Inbound Replication Connections tab to display a list of connections and the reason that the KCC automatically generated the connection. Figure 24.36 shows automatically generated and administrator-generated connections for the oakleaf-dc1 server.

Figure 24.36
The Inbound Replication Connections page of the Server Properties dialog shows the connections to the selected server and the reasons for their generation by the KCC.

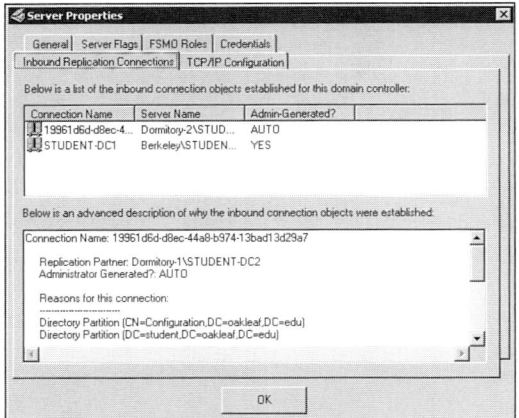

   9. To compare individual attribute values between servers, right-click a server node, and choose Show Attribute Meta-Data for Active Directory Object to open the Specify Credentials to be Used dialog. Click OK to use your current credentials, and open the View Meta-Data for Object input box.

   10. Type in the text box the full LDAP path of the object, `CN=Schema,CN=Configuration,DC=oakleaf,DC=edu` for this example, and click OK to open the Display Property Meta-Data for Object dialog (see Figure 24.37). The list displays all the object's attribute names, the local Update Sequence Number (USN), the name of the DC that was the last source of the value (Originating Server), the USN of the source attribute value (USN on Orig. Server), the version count, and the last time the value was written to the local server.

Figure 24.37
The Display Property Meta-Data for Object page displays the attribute status and source for the Schema namespace of the `oakleaf.edu` domain.

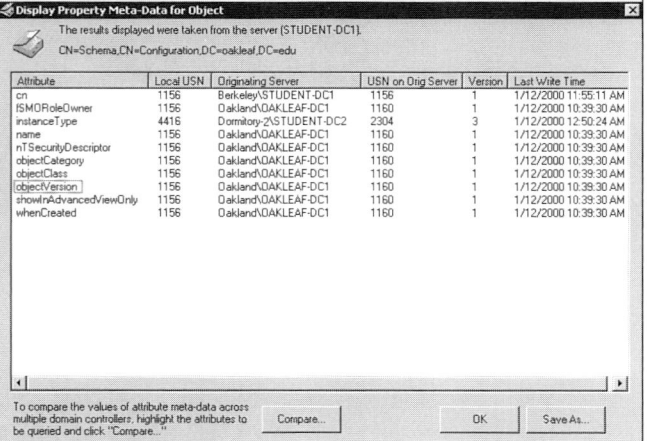

Using the Active Directory Replication Monitor Support Tool 1019

> **Note**
>
> AD uses 64-bit USNs to determine the currency of its attribute data for replication. Each DC increments by one the USN of an attribute when altering its value. All DCs maintain a copy of the USN value for each attribute, and replication of the value occurs only if another DC detects that the source USN value is greater than the current local USN value. Use of USNs minimizes replication traffic by updating only attribute values that have changed since the last successful replication.

11. In the list, select the attributes whose values you want to compare with those on other servers, and click Compare to open the Compare Attribute Data dialog. Select the Search all domain controllers in forest option to return comparisons from each DC in all sites.

12. Click Run Compare to generate the data, which may take a minute or two, depending on the intersite connection speed. Click OK to acknowledge the comparison-completed message. Figure 24.38 shows the result of comparing the status of every schema attribute on all DCs in the 3-DC sample enterprise.

Figure 24.38
The Compare Attribute Data page shows the attribute status and source for the Schema namespace of the `oakleaf.edu` domain.

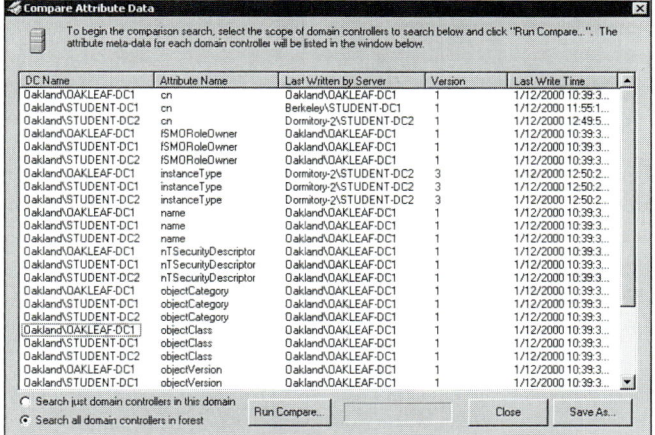

Running comparison tests on namespace attribute data is a very useful aid to troubleshooting intermittent replication failures, especially when the failures occur only within a single namespace.

ReplMon is an indispensable tool for network administrators managing many remote sites. You can expect independent software vendors (ISVs) to integrate AD site and replication management snap-ins into their general-purpose network administration tools for Windows 2000. In the meantime, ReplMon probably will handle most of your replication monitoring and troubleshooting needs.

> **Note**
>
> The Support Tools include a command-line Replication Administrator (`Repladin.exe`), which offers some of the features of ReplMon.

Troubleshooting

Replication Topology Problems

Replication Error 1511 Appears in Event Viewer's Directory Services Log

Event ID 1311 from the Knowledge Consistency Checker (see Figure 24.39) indicates that the remote bridgehead DC is down, the communication link has failed, or an NTDS connection is missing between the remote and local sites when you attempted to create a replication connection.

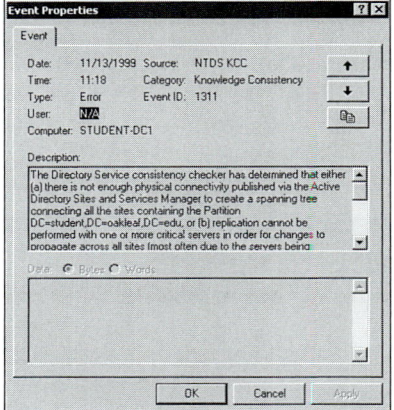

Figure 24.39
Event ID 1311, shown in the Event Viewer, indicates a replication failure between the local and remote site.

The full text of Event ID 1311's error message is as follows:

> The Directory Service consistency checker has determined that either (a) there is not enough physical connectivity published via the Active Directory Sites and Services Manager to create a spanning tree connecting all the sites containing the Partition DC=student,DC=oakleaf,DC=edu, or (b) replication cannot be performed with one or more critical servers in order for changes to propagate across all sites (most often due to the servers being unreachable).
>
> For (a), please use the Active Directory Sites and Services Manager to do one of the following:
>
> 1. Publish sufficient site connectivity information such that the system can infer a route by which this Partition can reach this site. This option is preferred.
>
> 2. Add an ntdsConnection object to a Domain Controller that contains the Partition DC=student,DC=oakleaf,DC=edu in this site from a Domain Controller that contains the same Partition in another site.
>
> For (b), please see previous events logged by the NTDS KCC source that identify the servers that could not be contacted.

You can eliminate the first two potential problems—which relate to unreachable servers—by pinging the remote server, first with its IP address and then by its fully qualified name, such as student-dc2.student.oakleaf.edu. Pinging the fully qualified name verifies that DNS is operational on the replication source. DNS also must function correctly on the remote site for replication to succeed.

The first step in resolving replication problems with a newly created site or connection is to reboot the DCs that share the connection. Rebooting the servers probably solves more than half of these types of errors by restarting the KCC, which (re)creates missing connections. If rebooting doesn't work, use ReplMon to recheck your replication topology. If all else fails, move your servers back to the initial site, delete the remote sites, and re-create your original topology, checking Event Log at each step. Make sure to wait a few minutes between each operation for the AD configuration to stabilize.

REPLICATION CONNECTIVITY PROBLEMS

Replication Warning 1566 Appears in Event Viewer's Directory Services Log

Event ID 1566 (see Figure 24.40) indicates that the remote bridgehead DC is down or the communication link to the remote site has failed after you successfully created the connection. Ping the server to check connectivity. If the ping succeeds, attempt to connect to the remote server with Active Directory Users and Computers. If this connection succeeds, the remote DC probably has a replication configuration problem. Rebooting the remote server usually solves the problem.

Figure 24.40
Event ID 1566, shown in the Event Viewer, indicates a replication failure due to a server that is unavailable.

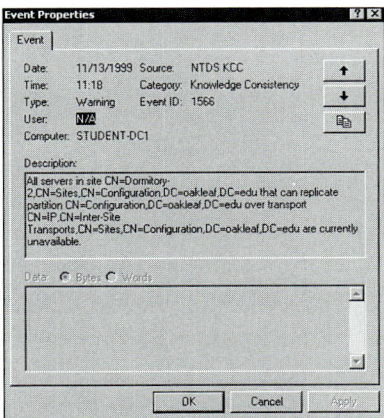

MCSE Corner: Communicating with Remote Sites and Domains

Intersite communication is important with distributed Active Directory topologies. The Directory Services exams 70-217, "Implementing and Administering a Microsoft Windows 2000 Directory Services Infrastructure," and 70-219, "Designing a Microsoft Windows 2000 Directory Services Infrastructure," both focus on large-scale distributed topologies, and both test intersite replication in different ways. For each exam you should have a grasp of the theory behind Active Directory site replication, such as what events occur when changes are made to the directory in one site connected to another site via a replication connector.

70-217 Implementing and Administering a Microsoft Windows 2000 Directory Services Infrastructure

You need to be familiar with the process for creating sites and site links for this exam. Be comfortable using the Active Directory Sites and Services administration tool to create new sites and configure site links and replication.

You also should be able to troubleshoot site replication services, including troubleshooting failed replication and optimizing replication. You need to be able to determine the cause of replication failure, either connectivity-related or otherwise. As for optimization, be able to locate replication performance bottlenecks and make topology changes to alleviate those problems. This would include using both the network monitor tool and the Active Directory replication monitor tool.

70-219 Designing a Microsoft Windows 2000 Directory Services Infrastructure

For this exam, you are required to be able to design an Active Directory site replication strategy. This capability is included as part of a larger capability of designing a complete Active Directory topology, including the definition of sites and site boundaries, introduced in Chapter 3, "Introducing the Active Directory and LDAP," and covered more in Chapter 4, "Optimizing Your Active Directory Topology." On this exam you likely will be given details about a fictitious network environment and be asked to design a site topology including intersite replication. It is important to understand the concepts learned in the first couple of sections of this chapter, including analyzing intersite replication requirements and choosing an intersite replication method.

CHAPTER 25

MANAGING REMOTE ACCESS AND ROUTING SERVICES

In this chapter

Getting Acquainted with Windows 2000's Remote Access Features   1024

Providing Basic Dial-In Network Access to Remote Clients   1025

Configuring a Production RAS Server   1037

Establishing Group Policies for DUN Clients   1048

Integrating Windows NT 4.0 RAS Servers   1050

Configuring Downlevel DUN Clients   1051

Taking Advantage of Network Address Translation (NAT)   1056

Troubleshooting   1071

MCSE Corner: Managing Remote Access and Routing Services   1072

Getting Acquainted with Windows 2000's Remote Access Features

Remote access over the switched telephone network—commonly called Dial-Up Networking (DUN)—is the most common method for mobile and telecommuting users to gain access to corporate networks. Windows for Workgroups 3.11 and all 32-bit Windows operating systems offer DUN capabilities. Before the Internet gained its overwhelming popularity, most Windows DUN clients connected to Windows NT-based networks with the simple Network BIOS Extended User Interface (NetBEUI) protocol. Firms running NetWare required clients to use Novell's IPX/SPX protocol, and clients connecting to UNIX servers used TCP/IP. Fortunately, the ubiquity of the Internet has all but eliminated NetBEUI and IPX/SPX for DUN, and almost all road warriors and telecommuters now use only TCP/IP.

All versions of Windows NT Server provide basic Remote Access Service (RAS) that can handle most organization's DUN requirements. RAS configurations range from a few occasional dial-in users who share one or two internal server modems up to large modem banks that support hundreds of simultaneous inbound connections. Many organizations have adopted Integrated Services Digital Network (ISDN) dial-up connections to increase users' data rates from the nominal 40kbps throughput of 56kbps modems to ISDN's 112kbps or 128kbps for the standard pair of bearer (B) channels. Because of its cost, ISDN has lost market share to various implementations of Digital Subscriber Line (DSL) services and Internet-based Virtual Private Networks (VPNs). VPNs are the subject of Chapter 26, "Setting Up a Virtual Private Network."

→ For a comparison between ISDN and DSL **see** "Choosing an Intersite Communication Method," **p. 987**.

> **Tip from**
> *RJ*
>
> Set up and test RAS, even if you intend to use a VPN as your primary means of connecting remote users or branch offices. RAS is required for most VPNs, and setting up RAS helps you develop client connectivity scenarios for later VPN implementations.

All versions of Windows NT Server provide support for DUN. Microsoft added a few new features to Windows NT Server 4.0's DUN capabilities by providing a no-charge Routing and Remote Access Service (RRAS) add-on. RRAS added the following DUN-related features to Windows NT 4.0 Server:

- Point-to-Point Tunneling Protocol (PPTP) for secure communication over VPNs
- Client authentication protocols—Password Authentication Protocol (PAP), Challenge Handshake Authentication Protocol (CHAP), and Microsoft's version of CHAP (MS-CHAP)
- Remote Authentication Dial-In User Service (RADIUS) support for organizations having RADIUS servers in place.

RRAS's primary emphasis, however, was on software-based routing with *multihomed* servers having two network adapters installed. Sections later in this chapter cover routing and Windows 2000's new Network Address Translation (NAT) features.

> **Note**
> Upgrading a Windows NT 4.0 RAS member server or Primary Domain Controller (PDC), with or without RRAS installed, to Windows 2000 preserves your existing DUN settings.

Windows 2000 adds the following features that you can use to establish or enhance existing remote access services:

- A new wizard for setting up your DUN server
- Integration of DUN user settings in Active Directory (AD)
- Group Policies for managing groups of DUN users
- A RADIUS server integrated with the Internet Authentication Service (IAS)
- Phone Book Services (PBS) and the Connection Manager Administration Kit (CMAK) to publish DUN telephone numbers.
- New Quality of Service (QoS) features, such as Integrated Services over Slow Links (ISSLOW).

> **Note**
> The Windows NT 4.0 Option Pack added Internet Connection Services for RAS, which included version 1.0 of the CMAK, Connection Point Services (CPS), and IAS. Windows NT uses the RADIUS protocol to connect a third-party RADIUS server to the Security Accounts Manager (SAM) database.

Providing Basic Dial-In Network Access to Remote Clients

Providing users with dial-in access to corporate networks is one of the most common responsibilities of network administrators. Although VPNs—which can dramatically reduce telecommunications costs—are becoming more popular, conventional dial-up access by clients to servers is adequate for many organizations. 56kbps (V.90) modems provide an average downstream (server-to-client) data rate of about 40kbps and an upstream (client-to-server) data rate of 33.6kbps. V.90 data rates are adequate for custom Web-based and well-designed client/server applications, such as database lookup and simple data entry. Working with large documents or downloading multi-MB roaming user profiles, however, is likely to tax the patience of modem-connected DUN users.

RAS Hardware and Telephone Requirements

The simplest and lowest-cost RAS server configuration consists of one or two internal V.90 modems, each of which connects to a dedicated telephone line. The modems are set to autoanswer incoming calls, but office workers can use the dedicated lines to dial out. Many small businesses—real estate agents, professional service organizations, consultants, and the like—find such a configuration well suited for light-duty DUN. You can install Plug and Play ISA modems in the two ISA slots—one of which usually is shared with a PCI slot—commonly provided by low-end servers. Windows 2000 Server reliably autodetects popular Plug and Play V.90 modems, such as those made by 3Com and Boca Research.

Tip from *RJ*	If you have older, non–Plug and Play ISA modems that use jumpers to assign their input/output (I/O) address and interrupt level (IRQ), replace them with current V.90 ISA or PCI modems. Windows 2000 Server and Professional usually fail to detect old modems, and fixed I/O and IRQ assignments might conflict with other adapters. If your server has ISA slots, purchase ISA modems; save the PCI slots for network and other adapter cards that benefit from PCI's faster bus data rate.

Tip from *RJ*	If you're purchasing new internal modems for DUN servers and desktop clients, buy identical models. Purchase PC card modems from the manufacturer that supplies the desktop PCs for laptops that don't have built-in modems. Having the same brand of modem at both ends of the connection provides the best assurance of reliability connectivity at the highest speed the modems and telephone lines support.

Larger organizations, whose DUN infrastructure predates the Internet and the development of VPN technology, have existing banks or racks of external modems connected to multiport serial cards. Multiport PCI serial cards—such as those made by Digi International (http://www.digiboard.com)—offer 4, 8, or 16 RS232-C ports that connect to external modems. You also can purchase multiport PCI cards with 4 or 8 built-in V.90 modems, at a cost of $300 to $400 per port.

Tip from *RJ*	Before upgrading a Windows NT 4.0 RAS server with a multiport serial or multiline modem adapter to Windows 2000 Server, make sure that the adapter is on the Windows 2000 Hardware Qualification List (HQL). You can search the HQL at http://www.microsoft.com/windows2000/upgrade/compat/search/Default.asp. After selecting Hardware Devices, try the Adapters category first—Digi International's product appears in the Adapters category—and then Communications.

When you install more than two modems, it's a common practice to connect them to telephone *hunt groups*. A hunt group consists of multiple lines assigned to a single telephone number; if the first line in the hunt group is busy, the hunt group assigns the next inbound call to the second line in the group, and so on.

> **Note**
>
> The hardware recommendations of this section apply, in general, to the current crop of ISDN adapters that emulate conventional modems. Windows 2000 treats external ISDN adapters as modems and internal ISDN adapters as network adapters. ISDN adapters, which are beyond the scope of this chapter, require Windows 2000-compliant drivers and have more complex configuration requirements than analog modems.

A Domain Controller easily can handle one or two simultaneous V.90 DUN connections in addition to its DC responsibilities. If you use multiport serial or multiline modem adapters, it's good practice to devote a lightly loaded member server to RAS communications. The member RAS server doesn't need a fast CPU or a large amount of RAM. Windows 2000 Server minimums—a 133MHz-or-faster Pentium CPU and 128MB of RAM—are sufficient for a midsize RAS server with 8–32 simultaneous V.90 connections.

Installing Windows 2000 RRAS

If you didn't install RRAS on a server during the initial setup phase, use the Add/Remove Windows Components feature of Control Panel's Add/Remove Programs tool to add the RRAS components from the distribution CD-ROM or a network installation share.

> **Tip from**
> *RJ*
>
> Install, set up, and test DHCP on a server in the subnet for the DUN clients before setting up RRAS. Although Windows 2000 RRAS enables you to manually assign a block of IP addresses to dial-up clients, using AD-integrated DHCP to assign addresses to DUN clients is *much* better practice.

→ To review setting up DHCP on the server, **see** "Configuring DHCP with the DHCP Snap-In," **p. 590**.

After installing your modem(s) or multiport adapter, verify initial operation by establishing a dial-up connection to the Internet, if you haven't done so already. Connecting to your Internet Service Provider (ISP) also checks your phone line.

Using the Phone and Modem Tool to Verify Modem Property Values

Control Panel's Phone and Modem tool is your first line of defense against initial and future modem problems. The Phone and Modem tool enables you to run diagnostic tests on a modem, add a modem that Windows 2000 didn't detect during setup or rebooting after you installed it, or remove a modem from service. The Phone and Modem tool also is useful for diagnosing Windows 2000 Professional DUN client modem problems. Windows 9x and NT Control Panels have a Modems tool with similar diagnostic capabilities.

To check a modem's properties and run a quick diagnostic test, do the following:

1. Launch Control Panel's Phone and Modem tool to open the Phone and Modem Options dialog, click the Modems page, and verify that each modem installed appears in the list and displays the correct product identification and COM port. If your server has

built-in serial ports, the first modem usually installs as COM3, the second as COM4, and so on. Plug and Play handles I/O address and IRQ assignments.

2. Select the modem to test in the list, and click Properties to open the General page of the *ModemName* Properties dialog.

3. Set the Speaker Volume control to off, if your modem has a speaker, unless you want to listen for inbound connections for diagnostic purposes; click the Diagnostics tab.

4. In the Diagnostics page, click the Query Modem button to send a complete set of the Hayes AT (attention) diagnostic/information (ATI) commands to the modem. Few, if any, modems respond to every AT diagnostic command in the query; scroll through the list to check the modem's response to some common ATI commands (see Figure 25.1).

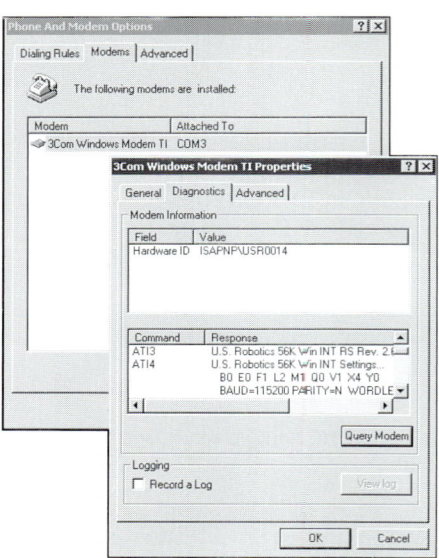

Figure 25.1
Use the Query Modem function of the Diagnostics page of the modem's properties sheet to run a diagnostic test on each modem installed in your RAS server.

Tip from
RJ

Don't panic if you receive a "Can't connect to modem" or similar message the first time you click the Query Modem button. Clicking Query Modem again usually returns the appropriate response, unless your modem actually is defective.

---

5. Click the Advanced tab and Change Default Preferences button to open the *ModemName* Default Preferences dialog, which displays the standard settings for all standard, current-manufacture modems (see Figure 25.2). The Advanced page enables you to change modem hardware settings. You seldom, if ever, need to alter default modem preferences. Click OK to close the *ModemName* Default Preferences dialog.

Providing Basic Dial-In Network Access to Remote Clients

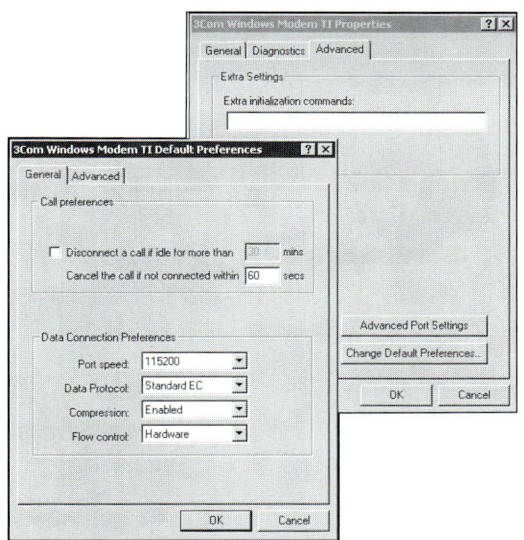

Figure 25.2
The General page of the *ModemName* Default Preferences dialog displays the standard set of initial connection settings employed by all V.90 analog modems.

6. Click the Advanced Port Settings button to view the sliders for the First-In, First-Out (FIFO) buffer settings of modems that comply with National Semiconductor's 16550 Universal Asynchronous Receiver/Transmitter (UART) specification. All modems manufactured since the early 1990s are 16550-compliant. Click OK to close the dialog.
7. Close all dialogs and Control Panel.

Setting Up Routing and Remote Access Services for DUN

If you upgrade a Windows NT 4.0 RAS server, setup automatically configures your RAS server with the properties of the original RAS configuration. In an upgrade scenario, you can skip to the "Testing the RAS Server with a Windows 2000 DUN Client" section. Otherwise, establish basic RAS configuration for initial testing with DUN clients. After you confirm basic RAS/DUN connectivity, add local RAS server policies, user profiles, and RAS Group Policies.

To set up and initially configure a new RAS server installation, do the following:

1. Choose Start, Programs, Administrative Tools, Routing and Remote Access to launch the Routing and Remote Access snap-in (`Rasmgmt.msc`). The console opens with the local computer node (oakleaf-dc1 for this chapter) with a down-pointing red arrow that indicates that the RAS Server isn't enabled (see Figure 25.3).

Figure 25.3
When you launch the Routing and Remote Access console, you're requested to perform an initial configuration of RRAS.

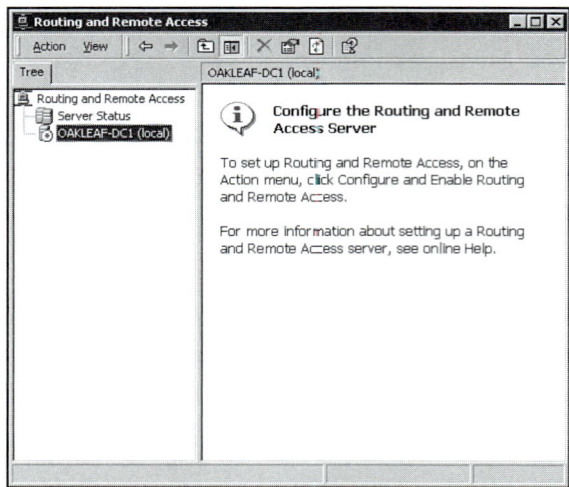

Tip from
RJ

You also can configure RRAS from the Configure Your Server dialog, but working from the Start menu is quicker.

2. Open the Action menu or right-click the server node, and choose Configure and Enable Routing and Remote Access to open the Welcome dialog of the Routing and Remote Access Server Setup Wizard. Click OK to continue.

3. In the Common Configurations dialog, select the Remote Access Server option (see Figure 25.4) and click Next.

Caution

Don't even *think* about selecting the Internet Connection Sharing (ICS) option, now or later. Installing ICS destroys your existing IP configuration and TCP/IP services.

Figure 25.4
Select Remote Access Server to provide initial, basic RAS services to DUN clients.

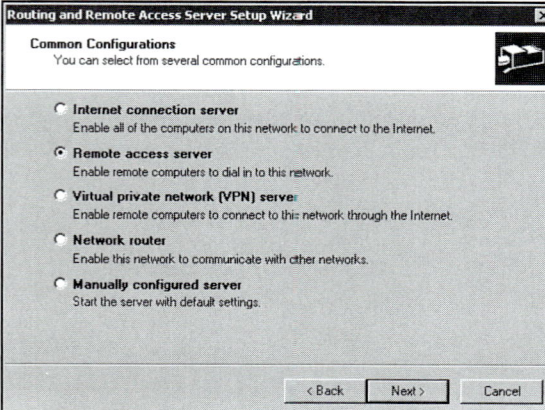

→ To learn how to prevent users from experimenting with ICS and, as a result, killing their computer's ability to connect to the network, **see** "Establishing Group Policies for DUN Clients," **p. 1048**.

4. In the Remote Access Protocols dialog, the Protocols list contains only Windows 2000's default TCP/IP protocol. If you've previously installed other protocols—such as NetBEUI or IPX/SPX—click Add to install either or both, if you have a compelling reason to provide these protocols to support downlevel clients. Click Next.

5. In the IP Address Assignment Dialog, accept the default Automatically option to use the DHCP server that handles the clients subnet to assign IP addresses. Click Next.

6. In the Managing Multiple Remote Access Servers dialog, accept the No, I Don't Want to Set Up This Server to Use RADIUS Now option and click Next.

→ To configure a RADIUS server, **see** "Using RADIUS Authentication and Accounting," **p. 1044**.

7. In the Completing the Routing and Remote Access Server Setup Wizard dialog, click Finish to dismiss the Wizard.

8. Click OK in the message box that says you must configure the DHCP Relay Agent with the address of your DHCP server. Two additional messages indicate that the RRAS service is starting.

> **Note**
> Disregard the advice about the DHCP Relay Agent if your DHCP server is on the same subnet as the RRAS server. The DHCP Relay Agent is required only if you install RRAS on a member server—or, less likely, a DC—that's on a subnet other than that of the DHCP Service.

9. Expand the server node, which now sports a green, upward-pointing arrow, and click the Ports node to display the list of RAS devices. Entries for modem(s) appear after the default set of 10 WAN Miniport drivers for PPTP connections and VPNs. Double-click the entry for your first modem to display its Port Status dialog (see Figure 25.5).

Figure 25.5
The Port Status dialog for a RAS modem displays the Listening condition while the modem is idle.

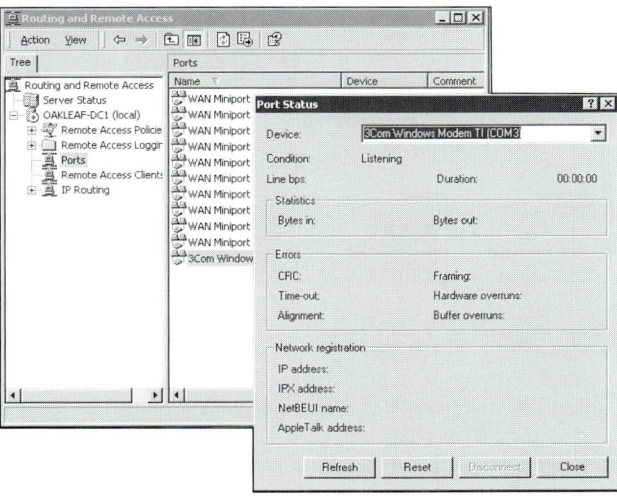

TESTING THE RAS SERVER WITH A WINDOWS 2000 DUN CLIENT

On the client side, Windows 2000's basic DUN features don't differ greatly from those of Windows NT or 9x. The primary differences between Windows 2000 Professional and downlevel DUN clients are minor changes to the procedures for setting up a new DUN connection. RAS administrators need a full understanding of what users experience when connected to your network by a modem. Thus, you should perform an initial test of DUN client connectivity with Windows 2000 Professional. Configuring a new DUN client also enables you to gain familiarity with the client-side configuration elements that your Windows 2000 users might alter if you don't restrict their access to DUN property dialogs.

To perform an initial DUN test of your new RAS server with a workstation running Windows 2000 Professional and connected to the network, do the following:

1. Verify that the modem autoanswers by using a conventional telephone handset to dial the number. The modem should answer after about two rings.

2. Launch Active Directory Users and Computers to dial in and enable your test account (Administrator, for this example); double-click the account to display its properties dialog.

3. Click the Dial-In tab and select the Allow Access option (see Figure 25.6); click OK to close the dialog.

Figure 25.6
You must enable dial-in access for the DUN test user account before the server can accept your inbound call.

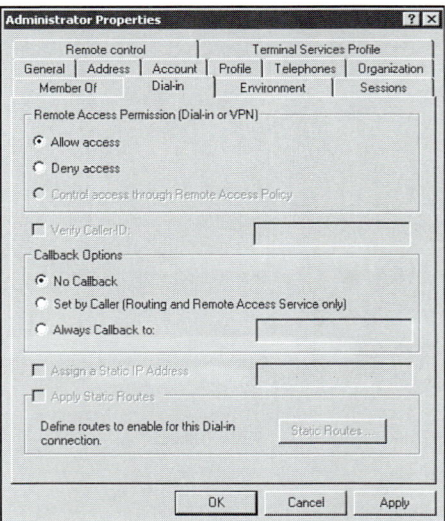

Note

The Control Access Through Remote Access Policy option for user accounts is disabled in a mixed-mode domain. If you select the Allow Access option for your DUN users in a mixed-mode domain and then later change the domain to native mode and want to apply RAS server policies to users, you must manually change the remote access permissions for each DUN user to Control Access Through Remote Access Policy.

Providing Basic Dial-In Network Access to Remote Clients | 1033

→ For more information on remote access policy, **see** "Setting Local RAS Server Policies," **p. 1038**.

4. On the workstation, right-click My Network Places, select Properties, and double-click Make New Connection to start the Network Connection Wizard. Click Next to bypass the first Wizard dialog.
5. In the Network Connection Type dialog, accept the default Dial-Up to Private Network option and click Next.
6. In the Phone Number to Dial dialog, type the local telephone number in the text box and click Next.
7. In the Connection Availability dialog, select the Only for Myself option and click Next.
8. In the Completing the Network Connection Wizard dialog, type a name for the connection in the text box, optionally mark the Add a Shortcut to My Desktop check box, and click Finish to dismiss the Wizard and open the Connect *ConnectionName* dialog.
9. In the Connect *ConnectionName* dialog, accept or type your logon ID and password in the text boxes, mark the Save Password check box, and click Dial to initiate the connection to the server (see Figure 25.7). If you have accurately typed your logon ID and password and the username passes authentication, you are ready to move to step 11. Otherwise, follow step 10.

Figure 25.7
Type the logon ID and password for the test user account to which you granted dial-in access (refer to Figure 25.6) and click Dial to make the connection.

10. If you mistype your logon ID or password, or the username is ambiguous (each DC for a domain has a local Administrator account), the dialog shown in Figure 25.8 opens as a result of authentication failure. Correct the incorrect entry, type the downlevel domain name, or both; mark the Save Password check box and click OK to retry the authentication process.

PART
IV
CH
25

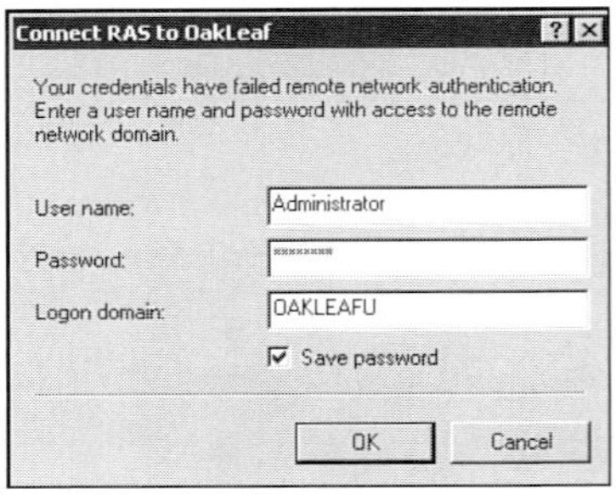

Figure 25.8
This dialog opens if you type an incorrect logon ID or password, or your logon ID requires a domain name to resolve logon ID ambiguity.

11. After a pair of messages indicates successful authentication and logon to the network, the Connection Complete dialog opens; mark the Do Not Show This Message Again check box and click OK to connect to the network by DUN.

At this point, the workstation is connected to the network by RAS, and DUN provides the same connectivity to network resources as a direct LAN connection. The connection speed, of course, is slower by several orders of magnitude. If the test workstation has a direct network connection, RAS takes over browsing and all other network-based activities until you hang up the connection. At that point, network connectivity resumes through your LAN adapter.

To configure the connections properties, follow these steps:

1. Right-click the dial-up connection icon at the right of the Task Bar's tray, and choose Status to open the General page of the *ConnectionName* Status dialog (see Figure 25.9).

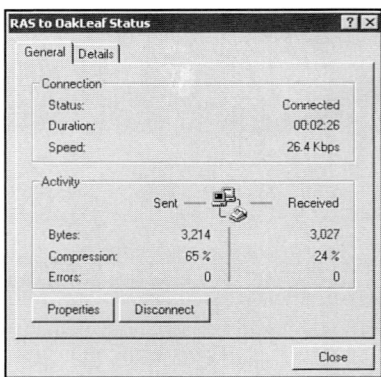

Figure 25.9
The General page displays the status, duration, and speed of the connection, plus the number of bytes, compression ratio, and errors in the upstream (sent) and downstream (received) directions.

2. Click the Details tab to view additional properties of the DUN connection and the IP addresses that RRAS and DHCP have assigned to the client and RAS server (see Figure 25.10).

Figure 25.10
The Details page of the *ConnectionName* Properties dialog shows additional, dynamic property values for the connection.

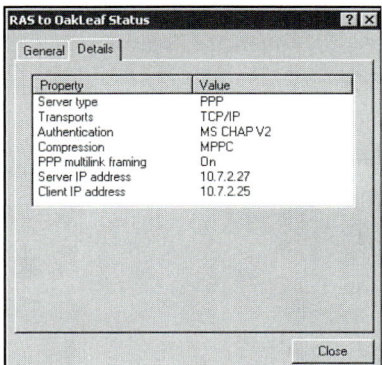

Note

In addition to the client IP address (10.7.2.25), the server has consumed an additional RAS address (10.7.2.27) from the DHCP scope for the subnet. The client and server automatically negotiate a secure authentication method that both participants support—MS-CHAP version 2 in this instance. PPP multilink framing, which supports multiple simultaneous connections between DUN clients and RAS servers, is set by default—even if the client and server have only a single modem.

3. Click the General tab, and then click Properties to open the Properties dialog for the workstation's DUN client.
4. Mark the Include Windows Logon Domain to include the downlevel domain name with your test logon ID. If you want to connect automatically, omitting the Connect *ConnectionName* dialog, clear the Prompt for Phone Number check box. Optionally, mark the Redial If Line Is Dropped check box (see Figure 25.11).

Figure 25.11
You specify client-side dialing and redialing options in the Options page of the *ConnectionName* Properties dialog.

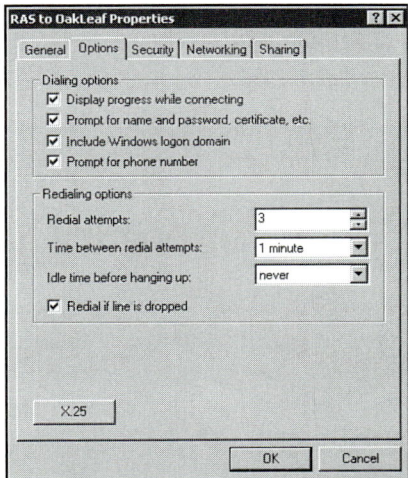

5. Click the Security tab and select Require Secured Password in the Validate My Identity as Follows list to force use of a secure authentication protocol. Optionally, mark the Automatically Use My Windows Logon Name and Password (and Domain if Any) check box (see Figure 25.12).

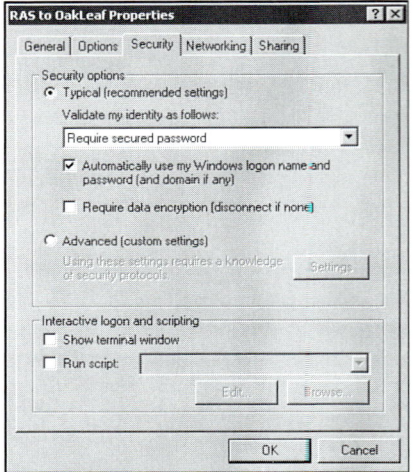

Figure 25.12
Increase the security level of the authentication protocol from the client side in the Security page of the *ConnectionName* Properties dialog.

6. Click the Networking tab to view the type of RAS server (PPP) for the connection and the networking components available to the connection. If the defaults are satisfactory, click OK twice to close all dialogs.

> **Note**
> By default, only Internet Protocol (TCP/IP) and Client for Microsoft Networks are enabled as networking components available to the RAS connection. You can add File and Print Sharing for Microsoft Networks if you want, but it's uncommon for clients to share their files and printers over a DUN connection.

When you've completed the configuration, you might want to check the status of the connection. With the connection open, return to the RAS server and check the status of the connection in the Port Status dialog you opened in step 9 of the preceding section (refer to Figure 25.5). To update the Port Status statistics, click the Refresh button. You can hang up on the client by clicking the Disconnect button, in which case the client redials the server—if you marked the Redial If Line Is Dropped check box in step 4 of the preceding procedure.

To check the RAS server's use of DHCP-assigned IP addresses, choose DHCP from the Administrative Tools menu to open the DHCP manager console, expand the RAS server node, and click Address Leases. The oakleaf-dc1 RAS server has received a total of 10 IP address leases from the scope's pool of 237 IP addresses to assign to itself and dial-in clients (see Figure 25.13). Disconnect from the network by right-clicking the DUN icon in the task bar tray and choosing Disconnect.

Figure 25.13
Setting up a RAS server automatically assigns 10 DHCP IP address leases to DUN clients.

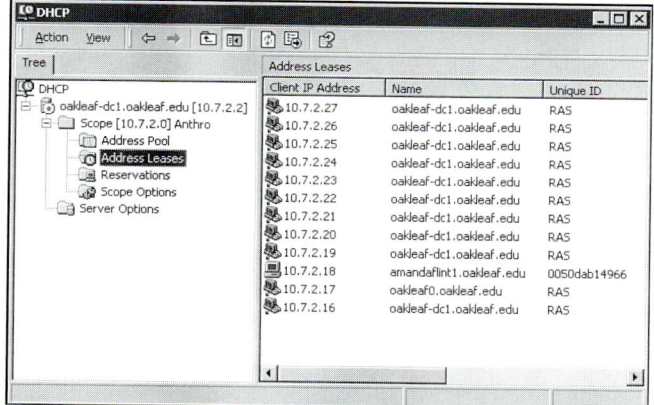

The preceding example is based on a workstation having an active network connection. To test DUN logon operations, do the following:

1. Log off from the workstation and disconnect the workstation from the LAN by unplugging the network cable.
2. In the logon dialog, type your user ID and password, mark the Log On Using Dial-Up Connection check box, and click OK to open the Network and Dial-Up Connections dialog.
3. Select the DUN connection to the server in the Choose a Network Connection list, and click Dial to open the Connect *ConnectionName* dialog.
4. If you didn't specify an automated connection in step 5 of the preceding procedure, the Connect *ConnectionName* dialog requires you to type your password.
5. Click Dial to connect to the network.
6. Disconnect the DUN session and reconnect the workstation to the LAN.

Going through an initial RAS and DUN setup, configuration, and test process provides the baseline you need to validate the choices you make when configuring the production RAS/DUN setup.

Configuring a Production RAS Server

After you've tested your initial RAS/DUN installation for basic connectivity, you set local server policies, set profiles for DUN users, and, optionally, replace the default Windows authentication and accounting with RADIUS authentication and accounting by Windows 2000's IAS.

CHAPTER 25 MANAGING REMOTE ACCESS AND ROUTING SERVICES

Tip from
RJ

> If you intend to set up a RADIUS server to handle user authentication and accounting, skip to the "Using RADIUS Authentication and Accounting" section and then apply RAS server policies and user profiles to the IAS server. When you change to a RADIUS server, you lose the local RAS server policies and user policies you set in the Routing and Remote Access snap-in.

SETTING LOCAL RAS SERVER POLICIES

Local RAS server policies apply to all DUN clients and, for Windows 2000 clients, override RAS-related Group Policies. As expected, you add and edit local RAS server policies in the Routing and Remote Access snap-in. In a native-mode domain, you must have at least one local policy in effect, or no user can connect to the server.

Caution

> Don't alter local RAS server policies or profiles in a mixed-mode domain. RAS Server Policies are disabled in mixed-mode domains, so you can't test the policies you set from a client. Setting policies without testing them can lead to unexpected—and undesirable—results when you change users' DUN permissions to use RAS policies in a native-mode domain.

Tip from
RJ

> Reboot your RAS server after changing the domain from mixed to native mode. If you don't reboot your server, setting the Control Access Through Remote Access Policy option for dial-in user accounts isn't persistent. If you specify this option and then close and reopen the *UserName* Properties sheet, DUN permission for the user reverts to Deny Access. After rebooting, the Control Access Through Remote Access Policy option persists. Microsoft might address this reboot issue in a future Service Pack (SP).

To view the single default policy for RAS servers and, optionally, add other DUN user constraints, do the following:

1. Launch the Routing and Remote Access snap-in (if necessary), expand the local server node, and click Remote Access Policies to display the single default Allow Access if Dial-In Permission Is Enabled policy.

2. Double-click the policy item in the right pane to open the policy's properties dialog. The Specify Conditions to Match List has a single default Day-And-Time Restriction (24-hour-per-day, 7-day-per-week connection permission). The default option is Deny Remote Access Permission if the condition matches. With RAS server policies in effect, this setting denies access at all times, so select the Grant Remote Access Permission.

3. To restrict users' remote access to specific days of the week or time of day, select the Data-And-Time Restriction criterion and click Edit to open the Time of Day Constraints dialog. Select the days or times to deny access (see Figure 25.14) and click OK to close the dialog.

Figure 25.14
You can use local RAS server policies to restrict all users' DUN access by time of day, day of week, or both.

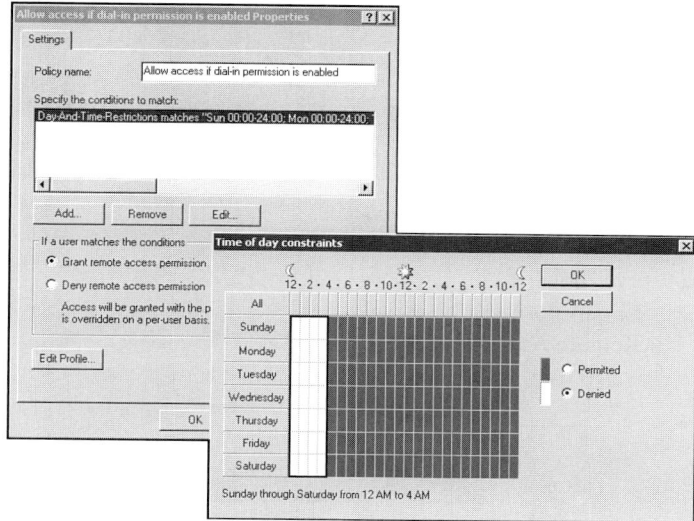

4. Click Add to open the Select Attribute dialog to add additional restrictions (constraints) to the policy.
5. Select an attribute from the list (see Figure 25.15) and click the Add button to open the dialog for the attribute. The Windows-Groups attribute, which isn't a standard RADIUS attribute, is the most useful RAS constraint in the list, so select this attribute and click Add to open the Groups dialog.

Figure 25.15
The Select Attribute dialog offers a choice of 12 RADIUS attributes and one proprietary Microsoft attribute for use as local RAS server policy constraints.

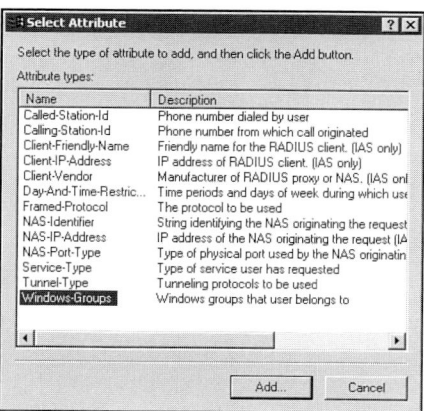

6. Click Add in the Groups dialog to open the Select Groups dialog where you can elect to restrict DUN to specific Security Groups; double-click the group(s) to add (see Figure 25.16).

Figure 25.16
You restrict DUN access to members of specific Security Groups with the Groups and Select Groups dialogs.

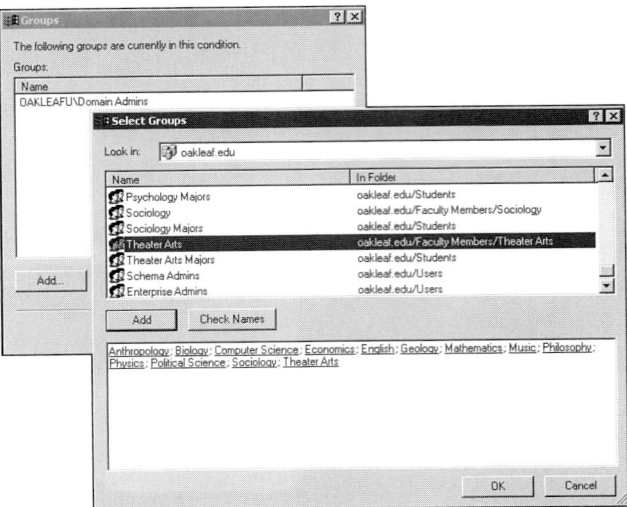

7. Click OK to close the Select Groups dialog and return to the Groups dialog. The new groups appear in the Groups list and form the second constraint of the default RAS server policy (see Figure 25.17).

Figure 25.17
When you select the Security Groups for DUN access, the Windows-Groups constraint contains a list of groups prefaced by their downlevel domain names.

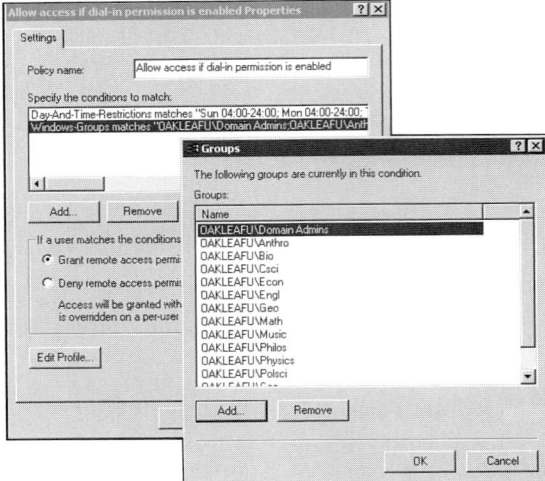

8. Click OK twice to close the two dialogs.

Each constraint you add to the local RAS server policy is evaluated in the order that you add the constraint. In Figure 25.17, the server first tests the Day-and-Time constraint and then the Windows-Groups constraint. If the attempted connection matches both criteria, the DUN user obtains a connection. Otherwise, the user sees a "not authorized" message and DUN hangs up.

> **Tip from**
> *RJ*
>
> Check each constraint you add with a DUN test client before adding another constraint. You might find multiple constraints have logical conflicts that prevent any DUN client from connecting.

You can add additional policies, which the RAS server evaluates in the order of addition. A single policy is sufficient for almost all RAS servers. To add another policy, do the following:

1. In the Routing and Remote Access snap-in, right-click the Remote Access Policies node and choose New Remote Access Policy to open the Policy Name dialog of a pseudowizard.

> **Note**
>
> A *pseudowizard* is a wizard that Microsoft didn't have time to bring to full wizard status before releasing Windows 2000 Server. The New Remote Access Policy doesn't have Welcome or Completing dialogs.

2. Type a meaningful name for the policy in the text box and click Next.
3. In the Conditions dialog, click Add to open the Select Attribute dialog. Select the attribute(s) to add with the appropriate matching criteria and then click Add to open the Groups dialog.
4. Click Add to open the Select Groups dialog. Select the group(s) to add, click OK twice to return to the Conditions dialog, and then click Next.
5. In the Permissions dialog, select the Grant or Deny Access option for the new policy and click Next.
6. In the User Profile dialog, click Finish to add the new RAS server policy. User profiles are the subject of the next section.

SETTING DUN USER PROFILES

Each RAS server policy you add has a user profile in which you can set other useful restrictive properties that apply to all DUN users connecting to the server. User profiles have settings for additional dial-in constraints, IP address settings, authentication methods, encryption, and other connection properties. The user profile settings you make apply in addition to local RAS server policies. By default, local policies have no user profile property values set. The RAS server stores user profile properties with local RAS server policies in a Jet database—\Winnt\System32\Ias\Ias.mdb.

> **Tip from**
> *RJ*
>
> If you have multiple policies, set the user profile on the first (default) policy and no other. Creating user profiles in more than one policy might create conflicts and prevent DUN user access.

To create a user profile within the default local RAS policy, do the following:

1. In the Routing and Remote Access snap-in, right-click the Remote Access Policies node and double-click the first (default) policy entry to open its properties dialog.
2. Click the Edit Profile button to open the Edit Dial-In Profile dialog with the Dial-In Constraints page active.
3. Type reasonable values in the Disconnect If Idle For and Restrict Maximum Session [Length] To spin boxes. Setting these two properties is important if you have more regular DUN users than server modems.

Note

The Restrict Access to the Following Days and Times check box and text box duplicate the default local RAS server policy's Day-And-Time constraint, so don't add the constraint in the user profile.

4. If you want to restrict dial-up use to a particular set of communication media, mark the Restrict Dial-In Media check box to enable the list, and then mark the check boxes of the types of connections permitted (see Figure 25.18).

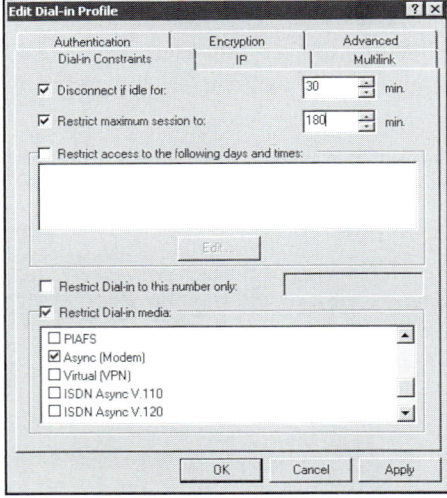

Figure 25.18
The Dial-In Constraints page of the Edit Dial-In Profile dialog enables you to drop idle user connections, limit connection duration, and, optionally, restrict the type of DUN connection.

Tip from
RJ

Specify permitted media to increase the security level of your server if, for example, users connect only via ISDN or VPN. In this case, you can prevent hackers using conventional modems from attempting to connect to your network by clearing the Async (Modem) check box, if it's marked.

5. Click Apply, check the connection with your DUN test client, and then click the Authentication tab.

6. In the Authentication page, you can add Extensible Authentication Protocol (EAP) if your client has a Smart Card reader; otherwise, don't mark this check box. MS-CHAP v2 authentication for Windows 2000 and 98 clients and MS-CHAP for Windows 95–and–earlier clients are the default authentication protocols (see Figure 25.19).

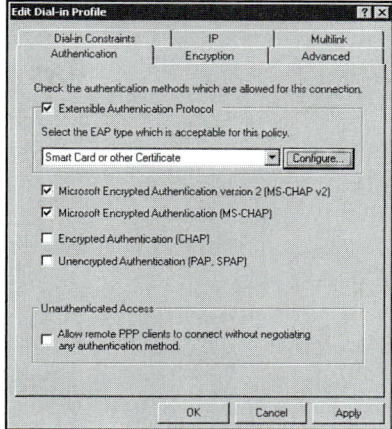

Figure 25.19
You specify permitted authentication methods in the Authentication page of the Edit Dial-In Profile dialog.

Caution

Don't enable Encrypted Authentication (CHAP) or Unencrypted Authentication (PAP, SPAP) unless it's absolutely necessary to support existing RAS hardware (SPAP for older Shiva equipment, for example) or special DUN clients. *Never* permit Unauthenticated Access to a server on your network.

7. Click Apply, run a check by logging on with your test DUN client, and then click the Encryption tab.

8. In the Encryption page, clear the No Encryption check box if you want to encrypt data sent over the dial-up connection with the Microsoft Point-to-Point Encryption (MPPE) algorithm (see Figure 25.20).

Note

Your server must support Basic (40-bit) encryption for Windows 3.x and 95 clients if you are to be able to encrypt data using MPPE. Windows 98 and 2000 clients use Strong (56-bit) encryption by default.

Figure 25.20
Clear the No Encryption check box, and leave the Basic and Strong encryption check boxes marked to require MPPE encryption of all DUN sessions.

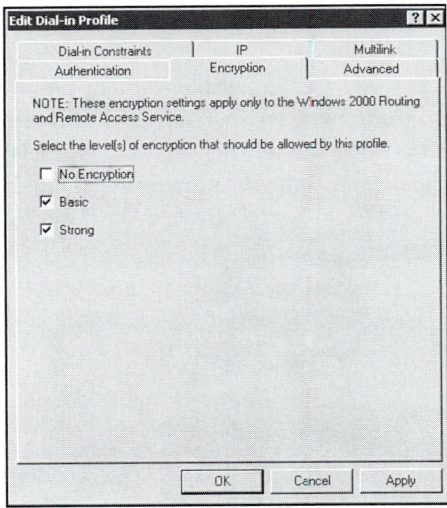

> **Note**
>
> Installing 128-bit encryption for your U.S. or Canadian server adds a Strongest (128-bit) check box to the Encryption page. Windows 2000 clients must be upgraded to 128-bit encryption to take advantage of the Strongest option.
>
> Most administrators consider dial-up connections over the switched telephone network to be reasonably secure. However, it's possible for wiretappers to intercept RAS/DUN communications. Requiring encryption also provides some—but not much—additional security against unauthorized access to your network by dial-in intruders.

→ To review encryption basics, **see** "Understanding Public Key Encryption," **p. 486**.

9. Click Apply and check connectivity with your test client(s). When you require encrypted client connections, be sure to test connectivity with each of the operating systems in use by your DUN clients.

10. Review the IP, Multilink, and Advanced pages, if you want, but you seldom need to change the default values of these pages to provide ordinary production-grade RAS services. Click OK twice to close the dialogs.

USING RADIUS AUTHENTICATION AND ACCOUNTING

If you have only a single RAS server, the default Windows authentication and account is likely to satisfy your requirements. If you have two or more RAS servers, however, it's better practice to use a single database for RAS server policies. Microsoft's IAS-based RADIUS server enables you to centralize RAS authentication and accounting in a single Jet database on a RADIUS server. RADIUS is an Internet standard, and Windows 2000 gives you the option of using third-party RADIUS servers. IAS, which is satisfactory for almost any RAS/DUN installation, is dependent on Internet Information Server (IIS) 5.0, and requires installation of IAS. Microsoft's IAS implementation of RADIUS also supports Windows NT 4.0 RAS servers.

> **Note**
> Windows 2000 Server setup installs IIS 5.0 and IAS by default. If you didn't install both components, use the Add/Remove Windows Components tool to install them from the distribution CD-ROM. IIS 5.0 is a primary component; you install IAS as a subcomponent of the Network Services component.

You can install IAS on one of your RAS servers or on a separate member server. RADIUS refers to RAS servers as *clients* or *NAS servers*. When the NAS server receives an authentication request from a DUN client, the NAS server sends an *authentication query* using the RADIUS protocol to the IAS server. IAS then requests Kerberos authentication of the client from AD. If the client obtains a Kerberos ticket, IAS notifies the RADIUS server, which in turn notifies the NAS server to permit the DUN client to log on to the network.

Microsoft made Windows 2000's IAS/RADIUS setup quick and easy. To configure IAS as a RADIUS server on another member server—oakleaf-ps1 for this example—do the following:

1. Choose Internet Authentication Service from the Administrative Tools menu to launch the Internet Authentication Service (Ias.msc) snap-in on the member server.

2. Right-click the Internet Authentication Service (Local) node, and choose Properties to open the properties sheet for the server with the Service page active.

3. Type a descriptive name for the RADIUS server in the text box and accept the default logging options.

> **Note**
> You don't need to add settings to the Realms page for ordinary RAS connections, unless your users connect through a service provider that adds a realm name to the user's logon ID.

4. Click the RADIUS tab. Delete the second set of ports, 1645 and 1646 (and their comma separators) from the two text boxes, as shown in Figure 25.21 (IAS uses TCP/IP ports 1812 for authentication and 1813 for accounting).

Figure 25.21
Specify only the standard IAS TCP/IP ports for RADIUS authentication (1812) and accounting (1813), by removing entries for ports 1645 and 1646.

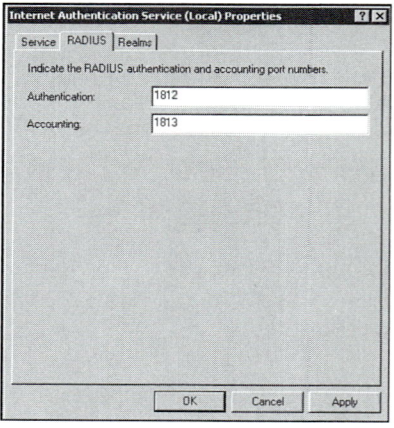

5. Click OK to save the changes, and acknowledge the message that asks you to start and stop the IAS service. If the service is running—indicated by the red Stop the IAS Service icon on the toolbar—click Stop. Click the green Start the IAS Service icon.

6. Right-click the Internet Authentication Service (Local) node, and choose Register Service in Active Directory to register the RADIUS service with AD and enable access to AD user account attributes.

7. Click OK to dismiss the two messages that deal with access to AD user attributes or that indicate IAS is already registered in AD.

> **Caution**
>
> If you don't register the IAS/RADIUS service with AD, your RAS server won't be able to find a RADIUS server when you reconfigure the RAS server to use RADIUS authentication and accounting.

8. Right-click the Clients node and choose New Client to open the Name and Protocol dialog of the Add Client pseudowizard for your first RAS server.

9. Type a short name for the server, accept the RADIUS protocol selection (see Figure 25.22), and click Next.

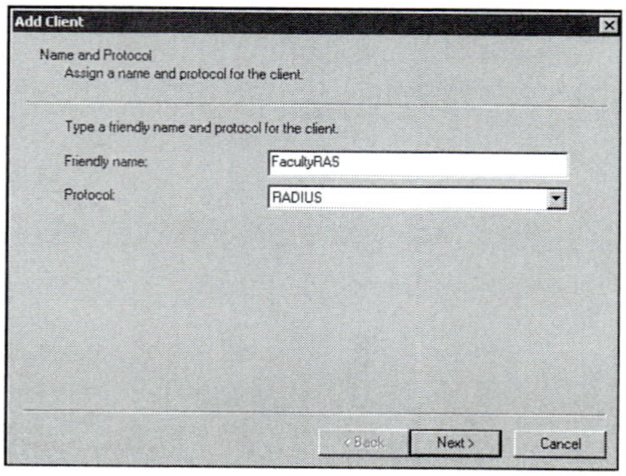

Figure 25.22
Specify a short name for your RAS server, which RADIUS considers to be a client. The name you type isn't used by IAS or RAS.

10. In the Client Information dialog, type the IP address of the RAS server and accept the default RADIUS Standard as the Client-Vendor selection.

11. Type and confirm a server password in the Shared Secret and Confirm Shared Secret text boxes (see Figure 25.23); click Finish to add the RAS server.

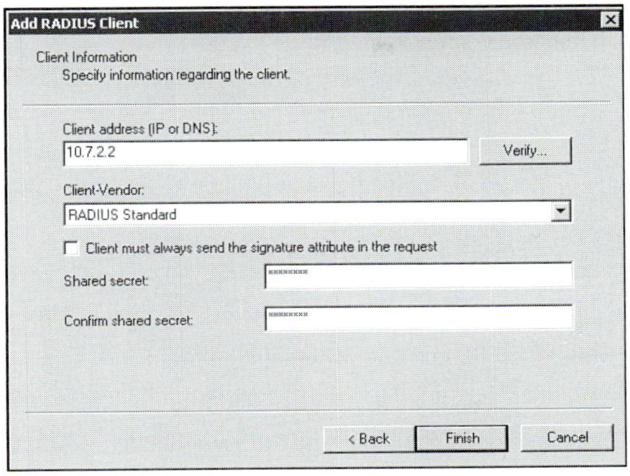

Figure 25.23
Set the RAS server IP address, protocol, and password in the IAS server's Client Information dialog.

12. Double-click the default Allow Access If Dial-In Access is Enabled policy item to open its properties dialog. Select the Grant Remote Access Permission option and click OK to close the dialog.

> **Caution**
> If your domain runs in native mode, and you don't change the default Deny Remote Access Permission option, DUN clients can't connect to the RAS server.

13. On the RAS server, launch the Routing and Remote Access console if it's not open.

14. Right-click the server node, choose Properties to open the *ServerName* (local) Properties dialog, and click the Security tab.

15. In the Security page, choose RADIUS Authentication in the Authentication Provider list and click Configure to open the Radius Authentication dialog.

16. Click Add to open the Add RADIUS Server dialog; type the *computer name* (not the "friendly" descriptive name you added in step 3) in the Server Name dialog.

17. Accept the default Time-Out, Initial Score, and Port values; click Change to open the Change Secret dialog.

18. Type and confirm the password (shared secret) you specified for the RADIUS client in step 10 (see Figure 25.24). Click OK three times to return to the *ServerName* (local) Properties dialog.

19. Acknowledge the message advising that you must start and stop the RAS server for the new settings to take effect.

Figure 25.24
Specify the RADIUS server name and type and confirm the password for the RADIUS client in the Add RADIUS Server and Change Secret dialogs.

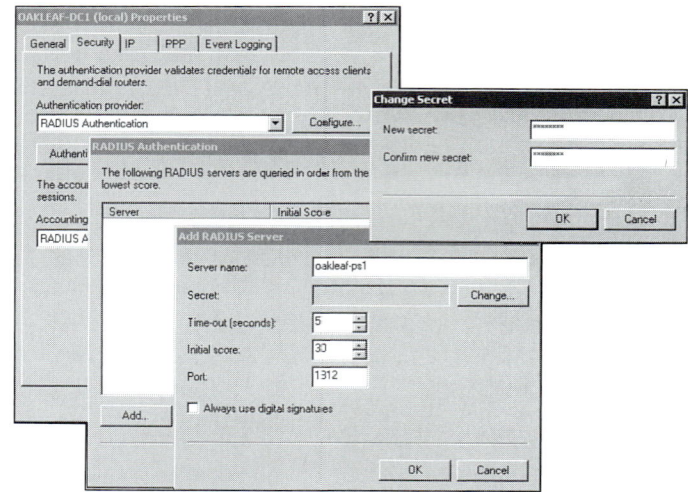

20. Select RADIUS Accounting in the Accounting Provider list, click Configure to open the RADIUS Accounting dialog, and repeat steps 16 through 19.

21. If your RAS server is running, right-click the server node and choose All Tasks, Stop to stop the RAS service.

22. Right-click the node again and choose All Tasks, Start to restart the service with authentication and accounting provided by your RADIUS/IAS server.

When you've finished this procedure, use your test DUN clients to verify RAS connectivity with RADIUS authentication. You might notice that client-side authentication takes a slightly longer time with RADIUS substituted for Windows authentication.

When you change to RADIUS authentication, you lose any local RAS server policies in effect. Changing to a RADIUS server removes the Remote Access Policies and Remote Access Logging nodes from the RAS server's tree view pane. You view, add, and modify RAS policies in the Internet Authentication Service snap-in on the RADIUS/IAS server. Return to the earlier "Setting Local RAS Server Policies" section to set RAS server policies and the "Setting DUN User Profiles" section to establish user profiles.

Establishing Group Policies for DUN Clients

If users can change DUN property settings, there's a good chance that—sooner or later—users will unintentionally disable their DUN client and request your assistance in regaining network connectivity. Fortunately, Windows 2000 Server provides an extensive list of Group Policy options to lock down users' ability to change their DUN settings. Unfortunately, Group Policies apply only to Windows 2000 DUN clients. Users of Windows 9x can change their DUN settings at will, as can the Administrator of Windows NT clients.

It's a common practice to apply DUN Group Policies to clients at the site or organizational unit (OU) level. If you have multiple domains, applying a site-level policy at the RAS server location causes all DUN clients (except Domain and Enterprise Admins) to share the same DUN policy, regardless of their domain or OU. Setting a DUN Group Policy at the OU level enables you to selectively restrict settings changes by sets of DUN users, such as salespersons. The other advantage of OU-level DUN policies is that restrictions at the OU level override any settings made at the domain or site level.

You specify Group Policies for DUN clients in the Network and Dialup Connections node of the User Configuration Administrative Templates. Most of the Group Policies in this node apply to DUN, but the policies are useful only after installing DUN on each client.

→ For a Group Policies refresher course, **see** "Understanding Windows 2000's Group Policies," **p. 618**.

To restrict the DUN options for users in an AD container, launch Active Directory Users and Computers and then follow these steps:

1. Right-click the container to which to apply the DUN policies (the Faculty Members OU for this example) and choose Properties to open the *ContainerName* Properties dialog.

2. Click the Group Policy tab and click New to add a new Group Policy. Press F2 and give the policy a meaningful name, such as **Faculty Members DUN Policies**.

3. With the new policy selected, click Edit to open the Group Policy Editor. Expand the User Configuration, Administrative Templates, Network node and click Network and Dial-Up Connections to display the list of available policies (see Figure 25.25).

Figure 25.25
The User Configuration, Administrative Templates, Network, Network and Dial-Up Connections node displays Group Policy options for DUN clients.

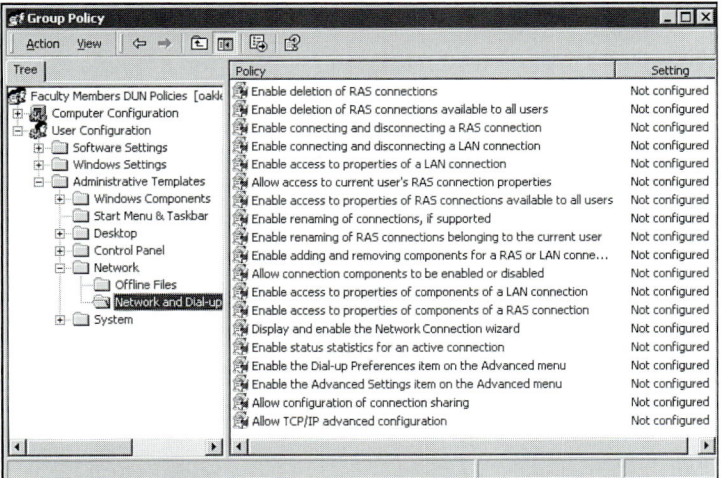

4. Double-click the Group Policy option you want to configure to open the Policy page of its properties dialog. The first option you should disable on every client is the Allow Configuration of Connection Sharing; click the Disabled radio button and then Click OK.

> **Tip from**
> *RJ*
>
> This chapter covers disabling ICS, because ICS is related to RAS and NAT. It's probably a better policy to disable ICS at the site or domain level than at the OU level. Disabling ICS at the OU level, however, overrides Not Configured or accidentally Enabled settings at higher levels in the Group Policy. Considering the importance of preventing users from enabling ICS, you might want to disable this option at *all* Group Policy levels.

5. Click the Explain tab to read a lengthy explanation of the consequences of enabling or disabling a Group Policy option, and then close the *OptionName* Properties dialog.

The names of Group Policy options applicable to RAS are reasonably self-explanatory, and most of the Explain pages tell you more than you might want to know about the consequences of setting the selected option. Thus, this chapter doesn't include a laundry list of the options and their descriptions.

Integrating Windows NT 4.0 RAS Servers

It's a common Windows NT 4.0 practice to use member servers—rather than PDCs or BDCs—as RAS servers. Windows 2000 native-mode domains accommodate Windows NT 4.0 member servers—but not BDCs—continuing their RAS duties as members of the domain. Following are the more important issues you face when mixing Windows NT and 2000 RAS Servers in a domain:

- During AD installation, you must select the Permissions Compatible with Pre-Windows 2000 Servers option in the Permissions dialog when you use `Dcpromo.exe` to install AD on the domain's DC(s).

- If your Windows NT RAS servers run on BDCs in a Windows 2000 domain, you can accommodate current and added DUN users, but you can't change the domain to native mode. BDC RAS servers use the local SAM database to authenticate DUN user accounts. In mixed mode, changes you make to user and computer accounts replicate to BDCs. Changes you make to user accounts after moving from mixed to native mode don't propagate to the BDC. As noted earlier in the chapter, you can't take advantage of Windows 2000 local RAS server policies or user profiles in mixed-mode domains.

- If Windows NT RAS runs on member servers, the member servers must have AD access for user authentication, including RAS-related attribute values. Providing Windows NT 4.0 member servers read access to AD isn't easy.

To accommodate Windows NT RAS member servers in a mixed- or native-mode domain, do the following:

1. Upgrade the member server to SP4 or higher to enable the server to read AD attribute values.

2. Add Global Security Groups for DUN users to the Builtin Pre-Windows 2000 Compatible Access Domain Local group. If you don't have an appropriate Global group structure for DUN users, add the Domain Users group.

3. Add the member server's computer account to the RAS and IAS Servers Domain Local group of the Users container. Members of the RAS and IAS Servers group have read access to AD.

Tip from
RJ

After making each change to the status of Windows NT member or BDC RAS servers, add a new test DUN user account with Active Directory Users and Computers, and log on with the new user account credentials to the RAS server. There's no substitute for step-by-step testing of each change you make to a RAS server.

Configuring Downlevel DUN Clients

If you upgrade a Windows NT 4.0 RAS server to Windows 2000 and don't make significant alterations of the local RAS server policies or user profiles, the upgrade doesn't affect existing Windows NT and 9x DUN clients. If you're building a new RAS/DUN infrastructure, you must provide DUN connectivity to your existing clients—usually a mix of PCs running Windows 9x and Windows NT 4.0 Workstation.

→ For instructions on setting up Windows 2000 Professional DUN clients, **see** "Testing the RAS Server with a Windows 2000 DUN Client," **p. 1032**.

 If you encounter problems connecting DUN clients, see the "RAS Connectivity Problems" topic of the "Troubleshooting" section near the end of the chapter.

Windows NT 4.0 Workstation Clients

The process of setting up a Windows NT 4.0 workstation to provide DUN connectivity is similar to that for Windows 2000 Professional clients. The following procedure assumes that the client PC has the TCP/IP protocol and a modem installed.

To set up the Windows NT 4.0 client for a DUN connection to your RAS server having Windows or RADIUS authentication and accounting, do the following:

1. Double-click My Computer, double-click the Dial-Up Networking node to open the Dial-Up Networking dialog, and click New to start the New Phonebook Entry Wizard.

2. Type a name for the DUN Phonebook entry in the text box and mark the I Know All About Phone Book Entries check box, even if you don't (see Figure 25.26). Click Finish to open the Basic page of the New Phonebook Entry properties dialog.

Figure 25.26
You specify the name of the connection in the first page of the New Phonebook Entry Wizard. Marking the check box bypasses the remaining Wizard pages.

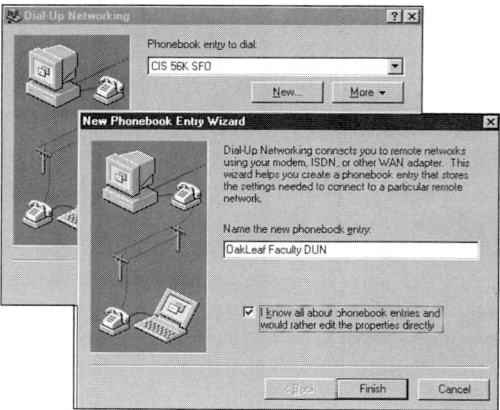

3. In the Basic page, complete the Phone Number text box—including an area code, if necessary—and accept the other default values (see Figure 25.27). Click the Server tab.

Figure 25.27
Type the phone number of the RAS server in the Basic page. If the client has more than one modem or dial-up adapter, select the modem in the Dial Using list.

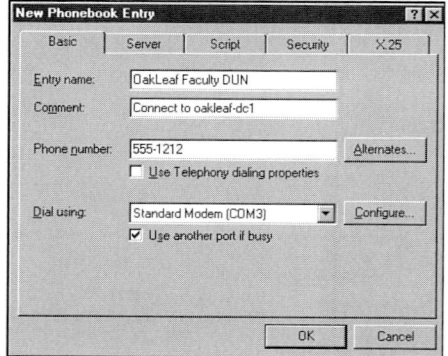

4. In the Server page, accept the default PPP, Windows NT, Windows 95 Plus, Internet entry in the Dial-Up Server Type list; mark the TCP/IP check box and clear the IPX/SPX Compatible and NetBEUI check boxes, if they're marked. Accept the Enable Software Compression and Enable PPP LCP Extensions options.

5. Click TCP/IP Settings to open the PPP TCP/IP Settings dialog, and verify that the connection uses DHCP for the IP, DNS, and WINS addresses (see Figure 25.28). Accept the Use IP Header Compression and Use Default Gateway on Remote Network options, click OK to close the PPP TCP/IP Settings dialog, and click the Security tab of the New Phonebook Entry dialog.

Configuring Downlevel DUN Clients 1053

Figure 25.28
The default settings in the Server page of the New Phonebook Entry and PPP TCP/IP Settings dialog are satisfactory for most Windows NT 4.0 DUN clients.

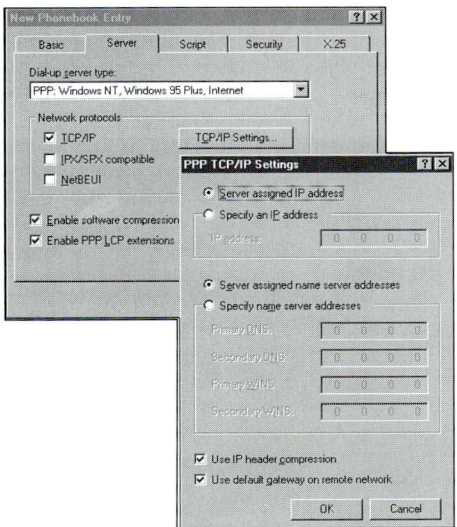

6. In the Security page, select the Accept Only Microsoft Encrypted Authentication to assure that the client uses MS-CHAP. Mark the Use Current Username and Password check box to provide automatic sign-on to the RAS server (see Figure 25.29). If you want to increase DUN data security, mark the Require Data Encryption check box to apply the MPPE encryption algorithm.

Figure 25.29
You specify client-side authentication and encryption properties in the Security page.

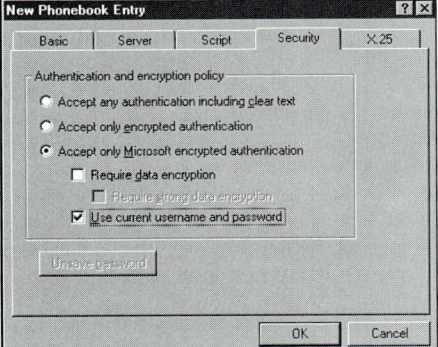

> **Note**
> The security settings you apply in the RAS server's user profiles override those you set on the client. It's a good security practice, however, to also add these settings on the DUN client. Doing so assures the proper level of authentication and, optionally, encrypted communication if there's a problem with the RAS server user profile for the connection.

Part **IV**
Ch **25**

7. Click OK; the New Phonebook Entry dialog closes and the Dial-Up Networking dialog opens (see Figure 25.30). Click the Dial button to test the DUN connection to the RAS server with the user account you used to log on to the workstation.

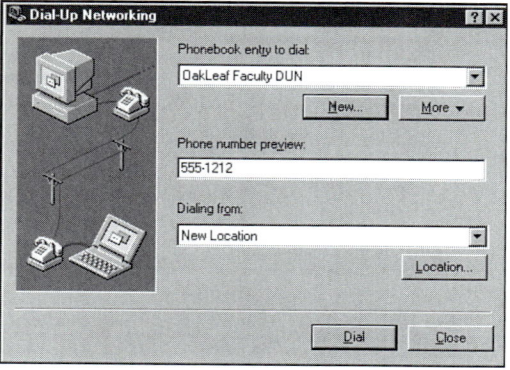

Figure 25.30
The Dial-Up Networking dialog opens when you complete the New Phonebook Entry dialog or when you double-click the Dial-Up Networking node of My Computer.

Tip from
RJ

Add a Desktop shortcut to the Dial-Up Networking node on each workstation. Users appreciate quick access to DUN connections.

Users logging on to a disconnected workstation mark the Logon Using Dial-Up Networking check box, which opens the Dial-Up Networking dialog for logon. Users with multiple DUN connections—such as a direct-dial connection to an ISP—select the connection to use in the Phone Book Entry To Dial list. Clicking the Dial button opens the Connect to *ConnectionName* dialog with the user's User Name, Password, and Domain text boxes completed. Clicking OK initiates the DUN connection.

Note

Dial-up users without a server-stored Windows NT user profile generate a new local profile for the DUN connection derived from the Default User profile. In this case, all prior user-specific settings and preferences are lost.

To alter the properties of a DUN phone book entry, select the entry in the Entry To Dial list, click More, and choose Edit Entry and Modem Properties in the context menu to open the Edit Phonebook Entry dialog, which is identical to the New Phonebook Entry dialog.

Windows 9x Clients

Setting up DUN for Windows 9x clients is a process similar to that used for Windows NT and 2000 clients. The primary difference is in the user interface for creating a new connection or modifying an existing one. The Dial-Up Networking node of My Computer contains an entry for each DUN connection. Like the preceding Windows NT example, this section's procedure assumes that the client PC has a modem installed.

Do the following to set up a DUN connection for a Windows 98 client:

1. Open My Computer, double-click Dial-Up Networking, and double-click Make New Connection to open the Make a New Connection dialog.

2. Type a name for the connection in the text box and select the modem or other dial-up adapter in the Select a Device list (see Figure 25.31). Click Next.

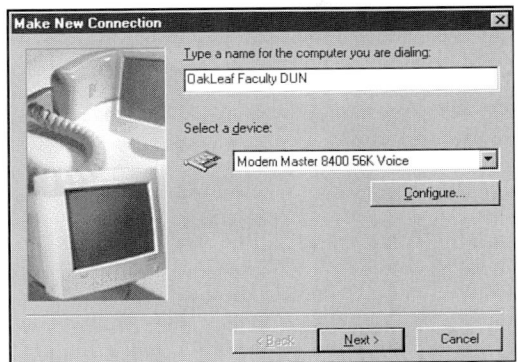

Figure 25.31
Specify the connection name, area code, and phone number for the RAS server in Windows 98's first Make New Connection dialog.

3. Select the Area Code for the connection, type the telephone number, and accept the default Country or Region Code setting. Click Next, click Finish to create the new connection, and close the dialog.

4. In the Dial-Up Networking window, right-click the new connection entry and choose Properties to open the *ConnectionName* properties dialog. The General page displays the settings you specified in steps 2 and 3.

5. Click the Server Types tab, which offers options similar to those of the Server and Security pages of Windows NT's New Phonebook Entry dialog. In addition to the default Log On To Network and Enable Software Compression settings, mark the Require Encrypted Password and, optionally, Require Data Encryption check boxes.

6. Clear the NetBEUI and IPX/SPX check boxes, if they're marked (see Figure 25.32). The default TCP/IP settings for DHCP appear in the TCP/IP Settings dialog, which is almost identical to Windows NT's PPP TCP/IP Settings dialog (refer to Figure 25.28). Click OK to close the *ConnectionName* dialog; the Dial-Up Connections window opens.

Figure 25.32
Set the security and network protocols properties of the new connection in the Server Types page of the *ConnectionName* dialog.

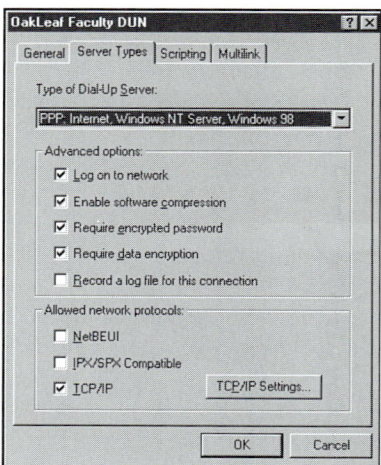

7. Double-click the new connection to open the Connect To dialog with the username you used to log on to Windows 98. Type the password for the user account and mark the Save Password check box. Click Connect to initiate the DUN connection.

Creating a DUN connection for Windows 95 clients is almost identical to the process for creating a Windows 98 client connection.

Tip from
RJ

Before setting up DUN on a client running Windows 95, make sure to obtain the latest DUN update for the operating system from Microsoft Product Support. Go to www.microsoft.com; choose Support, Knowledge Base; select the Specific Article ID option; and type **Q191494** in the My Question Is text box to read the "Dial-Up Networking 1.3 Upgrade Available" article. Article Q191540, "VPN Update for Windows 98 and Dial-Up Networking 1.3," describes a subsequent update (Vpnupd.exe) for the Windows 95 VPN client support in the Dial-Up Networking 1.3 Upgrade.

Taking Advantage of Network Address Translation (NAT)

NAT is a new feature of Windows 2000 Server that's primarily intended to enable a single connection to the public Internet to serve multiple network clients on an organization's private LAN. If you have a limited number of IP addresses assigned to your organization by your ISP, you use one or a few of these scarce addresses to provide clients with Internet connections over a T-1 or other dedicated connection. Smaller organizations or branch offices can take advantage of a single, low-cost DSL or cable modem connection to the ISP. DSL and cable modem connections require an additional network adapter in the server using NAT. Small-office/home-office (SOHO) users can share a consumer-grade cable modem connection or even a single dial-up modem connection to the Internet.

> **Note**
>
> SOHO users of Windows 2000 Professional can use ICS to share a single Internet connection among workgroup members. As noted earlier in the chapter, ICS isn't a recommended approach for Windows 2000 Server–based networks in organizations having more than about 10 or so PC clients. Thus, ICS is outside the scope of this chapter.

Reduced cost is one of the primary advantages of using NAT to provide clients with Internet connectivity. Cost reduction results from eliminating the need to equip LAN users with modems for dial-up connections to an ISP, or obtain ISP accounts for individual users, or both. Further, NAT minimizes consumption of your public IP addresses for Internet access by LAN clients. It's a common practice for small- to moderate-size firms to make the transition to NAT soon after upgrading a Windows NT 4.0 domain to Windows 2000 and AD.

UNDERSTANDING NAT PORT TRANSLATION

NAT uses a process called *port translation* to direct packets to the public Internet from clients on a private LAN and vice versa. When the server detects a client request to connect to a domain—such as oakmusic.com—that doesn't have an entry in the domain's DNS service, the request is redirected by the NAT service to the ISP's DNS server, which resolves the public IP address (209.249.8.35). For a connection to http://www.oakmusic.com, NAT sends packets to 209.249.8.35 on TCP port 80, but designates a random TCP port to intercept the TCP/IP reply from the oakmusic.com site. NAT associates the random TCP port with the private IP address—typically 10.x.x.x—of the client that initiated the request. When the reply is received, NAT checks the port number and forwards the packets to the private IP address—usually assigned by DHCP—of the requesting client with the original HTTP TCP port (80).

→ For a refresher course on TCP ports, **see** "TCP Ports and Processes," **p. 87**.

Figure 25.33 illustrates the NAT Internet routing process with either a demand-dial connection or a persistent DSL or cable modem connection to the ISP and the Internet. The figure shows the NAT and DNS services running on the same server; the AD-integrated Dynamic DNS (DDNS) service can run on any server in the domain. DDNS provides internal network address lookup and Internet domain name resolution.

Figure 25.33
The NAT server/router assigns random TCP port numbers to clients to identify TCP or UDP Internet reply packets and forward them to the destination client.

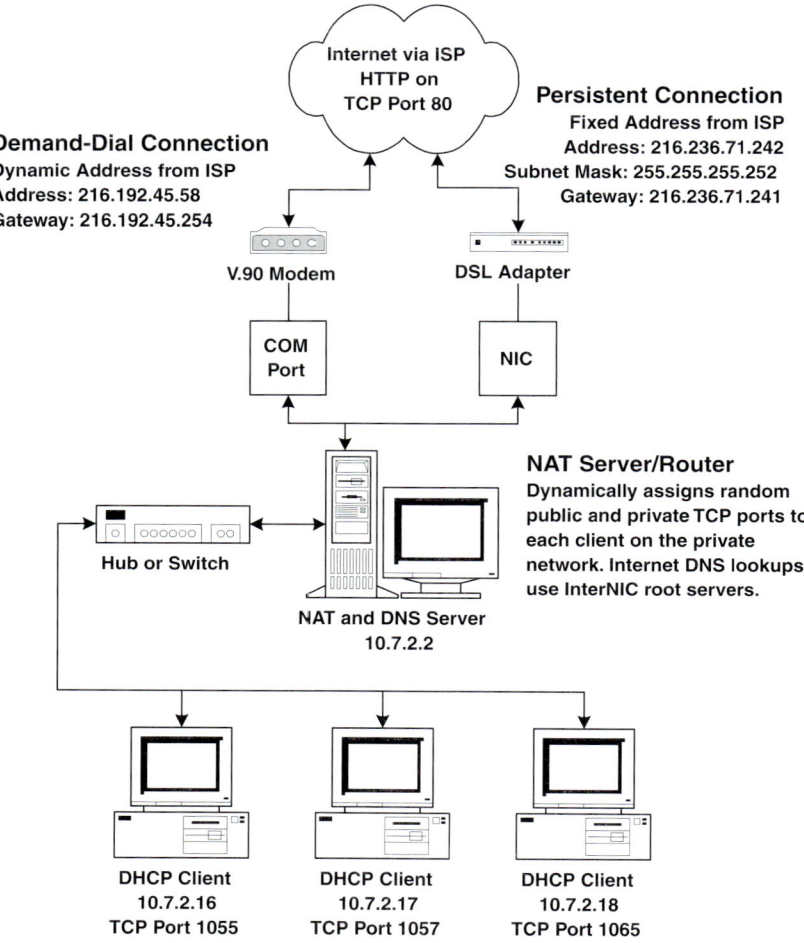

> **Note**
>
> NAT requires installation of Routing and Remote Access service, preferably on a member server, not a DC. If you haven't already done so, use the Add/Remove Windows Components feature of Control Panel's Add/Remove Programs tool to install RRAS on a server before proceeding with the sections that follow. You can use the RAS server for NAT or set up NAT on a separate member server or DC.

Configuring NAT for Connecting Clients to the Internet

Following are the basic steps in configuring a NAT router to share a full-time or demand-dial Internet connection with multiple Windows clients on a single subnet:

1. Run **route print** in the Command Prompt window to verify that you haven't previously specified a default gateway address for the NAT server. A preexisting default gateway address disables NAT routing to clients.

> **Note**
>
> If Route Print displays a `0.0.0.0, 0.0.0.0` entry in the routing list, the network adapter has a default gateway entry. To remove the entry, open the properties dialog for the Local Area Connection, select Internet Protocol (TCP/IP), and click Properties to open the General page of the Internet Protocol (TCP/IP) Properties dialog. Delete the entire IP address in the Default Gateway text box.

2. Use the Configure and Enable Routing and Remote Access Setup Wizard to add the required interfaces to the RRAS server.
3. If you require a demand-dial connection for an analog or ISDN modem, use the Demand Dial Interface Wizard to configure the demand-dial interface.
4. Configure the DNS server for the subnet to use *Root Hints* for Internet name resolution. Root Hints are 13 DNS entries for InterNIC root servers—`a.root-servers.net` through `m.root-servers.net`. If your DNS server is a root server, you must demote it to a nonroot server to install Root Hints.
5. Configure DHCP to specify the IP address of your NAT server as the default gateway (003 Router option) for clients, and then renew each client IP address lease.
6. If you have clients with fixed IP addresses, specify the IP address of the NAT server as the default gateway. However, if the DNS client isn't set up on fixed-address PCs, enable and configure DNS.

> **Note**
>
> Windows 2000's online help states that network clients must use DHCP to accommodate NAT. Tests of Windows 9x, NT, and 2000 clients with fixed IP addresses, a designated DNS server and default gateway, demonstrate that using DHCP isn't necessary.

SETTING UP NAT FOR A DEMAND-DIAL MODEM CONNECTION

If you don't have a high-speed connection to the Internet with a fixed public IP address, you can use NAT and a V.90 modem connection to handle a few—preferably fewer than three or four—simultaneous Internet client connections. When you have a high-speed connection, it's easy to change the external network connection from a modem to a network adapter. The example that follows starts with RRAS installed but not configured. Running RAS and demand-dial NAT on the same server isn't a common practice, but it is possible if you have two or more modems installed.

> **Note**
>
> Review your ISP's connection agreement or fair-use policy to determine whether the ISP prohibits use of NAT routers. If this is the case, you might be able to negotiate permission to connect via a NAT router at a surcharge; the surcharge often is based on the maximum number of connected users. Another alternative is to change your ISP to a firm that permits NAT routing.

To set up NAT for a modem connection to your ISP, do the following:

1. Right-click the server node, and choose Configure and Enable Routing and Remote Access to open the Routing and Remote Access Server Setup Wizard's Welcome dialog. Click Next.

2. In the Common Configurations dialog, accept the default Internet Connection Server. (ICS stands for Internet Connection *Sharing*, not Internet Connection *Server*.) Click Next.

3. In the Internet Connection Server Setup dialog, select the Set Up a Router with the Network Address Translation (NAT) Routing Protocol option (see Figure 25.34). Click Next.

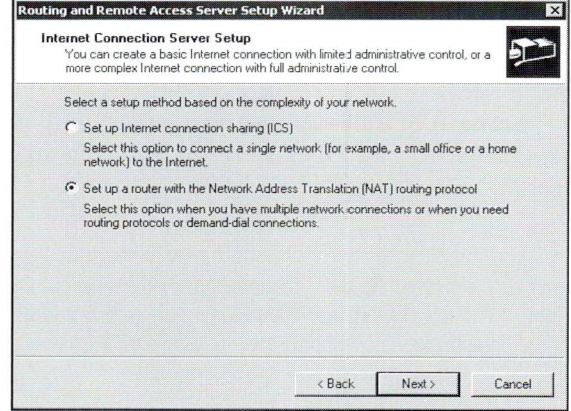

Figure 25.34
Be careful *not* to accept the default option, Set Up Internet Connection Sharing, in this dialog, or your server/router will be transformed into a mini-DHCP server.

> **Caution**
>
> Be sure not to accept the default option, Set Up Internet Connection Sharing (ICS). If you do, the NAT server/router becomes a mini-DHCP server for your network and changes all client addresses to 192.168.0.x. Microsoft should have made the NAT option the default for Windows 2000 Server.

4. In the Internet Connection dialog, select the Create a New Demand-Dial Internet Connection option (see Figure 25.35) and click Next.

Figure 25.35
Select the Create a New Demand-Dial Internet Connection option in the Internet Connection dialog for an analog or ISDN modem. You need a second network adapter (or a full-time ISDN connection/adapter) for the Use the Selected Internet Connection option.

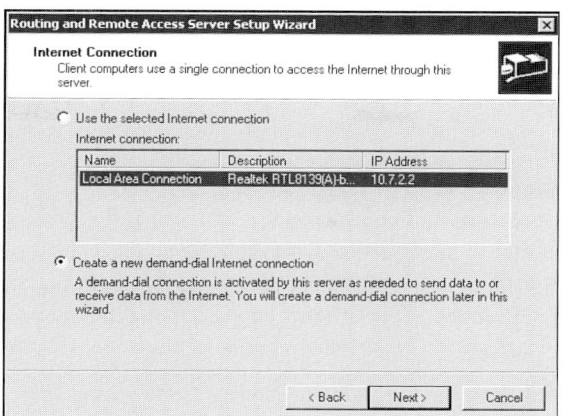

5. In the Reviewing Changes dialog, verify your prior selections and click Next. The Routing and Remote Access Service starts, and the Welcome dialog of the Demand Dial Interface Wizard opens. Click Next.
6. In the Interface Name dialog, type a descriptive name in the text box and click Next.
7. In the Connection Type dialog, accept the default Connect Using a Modem, ISDN Adapter, or Other Physical Device option and click Next.
8. In the Phone Number dialog, type the telephone number of your ISP, including the dialing prefix and area code, if required, and click Next.
9. In the Protocols and Security Dialog, accept the default Route IP Packets on This Interface option. If your ISP requires a logon script, mark the Use Scripting to Complete the Connection with the Remote Router (CompuServe requires a logon script, `Cis.scp`), as shown in Figure 39.36. The remaining options are for dialing in to the server, which isn't a common configuration. Click Next.

Figure 25.36
The Route IP Packets on This Interface check box is marked by default. Mark the Use Scripting to Complete the Connection with the Remote Router if your ISP requires a logon script.

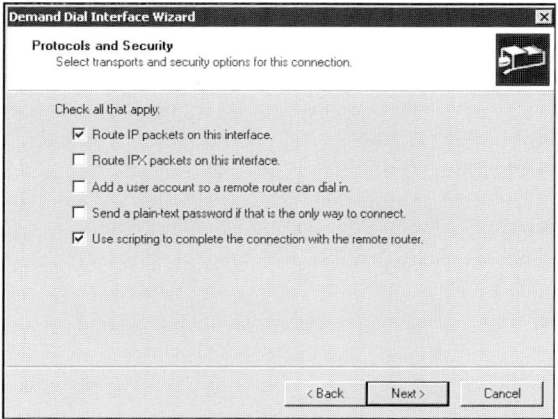

10. If you marked the Use Scripting check box, in the Router Scripting dialog, mark the Run Script check box. Standard Windows 2000 scripts are located in the \Winnt\ System32\Ras folder. If your ISP requires a custom script, add the script to the folder. Click Browse to list the scripts in the ...\Ras folder, and double-click the script you want to use. Click Next.

11. In the Dial Out Credentials dialog, type the User Name for your Internet connection, skip the Domain text box, and complete the Password and Confirm Password text boxes. Click Next and then Finish to dismiss the Demand Dial Interface Wizard.

12. In the Completing the Routing and Remote Access Server Setup Wizard, optionally check the Display Help About NAT When I Close This Wizard check box and click Finish to dismiss the Wizard.

13. In the Routing and Remote Access snap-in, click the Routing Interfaces node to display the LAN and Demand-Dial Interfaces list. To test your demand-dial connection, right-click the *NATInterfaceName* and choose Connect to open the Internet Connection message box. When the server connects to the ISP, the Internet Connection message box closes, and the Connection Status changes from Connecting to Connected.

14. Launch the Command Prompt window and ping a few Internet sites by IP address and domain name. When you ping an Internet site by domain name, such as oakmusic.com, the server uses your ISP's DNS server(s) to resolve the IP address.

15. At the command prompt, type **route print** to display the routing map with entries for the NAT router (see Figure 25.37).

Figure 25.37
The route print command displays all current routes for the NAT server. Addresses on the 216.192. 45.0 network are assigned to the demand-dial interface by your ISP (CompuServe for this example).

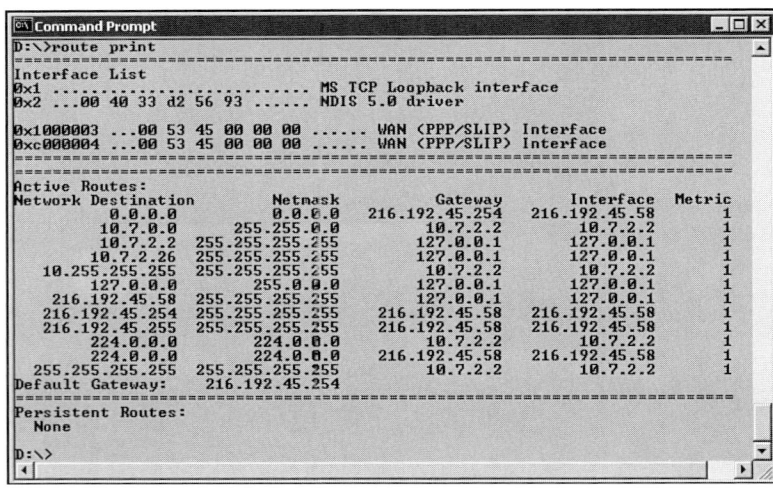

The first set of IP addresses below Network Destination and Netmask in Figure 25.37 designates the default gateway of the server (0.0.0.0, 0.0.0.0), which points to the ISP's gateway (216.192.45.254) for the dynamic IP address that the ISP assigns to the server (216.192.45.58). The list includes other routes for the ISP's 216.192.45.0 network. For example, All 10.7.x.x addresses are routes for the internal (private) network.

 If you can't ping public Internet sites by IP address and domain name, see the "NAT Demand-Dial Connection Problems" topic of the "Troubleshooting" section near the end of this chapter.

Note
The dynamic IP address assigned to the NAT server by your ISP appears as an additional Host (A) record in the DNS snap-in's list of hosts.

ADDING ROUTE HINTS TO THE CLIENTS' DNS SERVER

Network clients are required to use a domain DNS server for internal *and* external name resolution. The fact that you can resolve Internet domain names to addresses when working at the NAT router/server isn't indicative of clients' ability to resolve them. For demand-dial connections, your DNS server must have Root Hints for InterNIC root servers added; Root Hints enable clients to query the root servers for public domain name resolution.

The first AD-integrated DDNS server you create when installing the first DC is the root server for the domain. You can't add Root Hints to a root server. If the DNS snap-in displays a node identified by a single period immediately under the NAT server name, the DNS server is a root server. Demoting a root server doesn't have a significant effect on your DNS server(s).

To demote a root server and add Root Hints, or verify that Root Hints are installed on your DNS server, do the following:

1. Launch the DNS snap-in from the Administrative Tools menu and expand the *NATServerName* node.

2. If the root server node (.) is present, select it, press delete, and acknowledge the warning message that the node will be deleted from DNS and AD. If the root server node isn't present, go to step 4.

3. Open the Command Prompt window, type **net stop dns** to stop the DNS service, and then type **net start dns** to restart it. You must restart DNS to remove the root node immediately. Close the Command Prompt window.

4. Right-click the *NATServerName* node, choose Properties to open the *NATServerName* Properties dialog, and click Root Hints to verify that the 13 names and IP addresses of InterNIC root servers appear in the list (see Figure 25.38).

5. Close the properties dialog and the DNS snap-in.

Figure 25.38
Root Hints added to the DNS server provide DNS name resolution for public Internet sites.

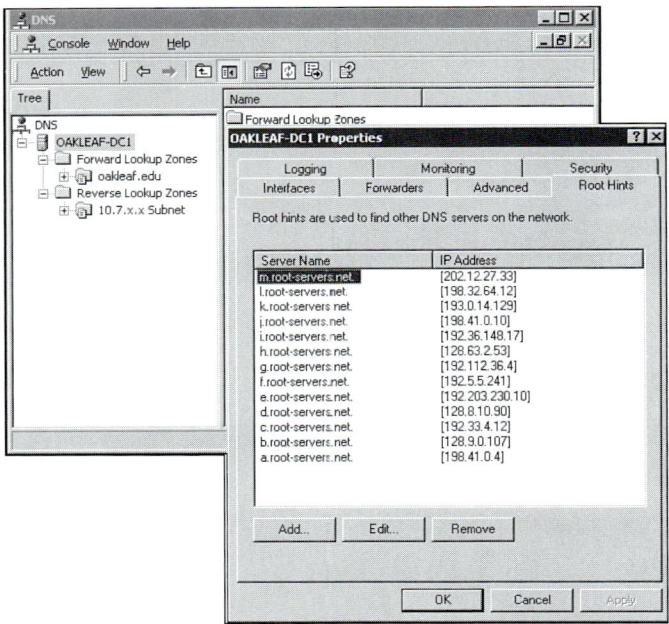

You can't test whether Root Hints are working at the NAT server; you must set up a network client PC to perform the final test of your NAT router.

Adding the NAT Server as a Gateway for Clients

You must update the DHCP options for the scope(s) of your DHCP clients by adding the IP address of your NAT server as a client gateway. If the client is unable to resolve a host to an IP address on its own subnet, it passes the request to each gateway in the order of the list supplied by DHCP. If the client doesn't use DHCP, the request is made to a set of fixed entries in the Gateway page of the client's TCP/IP Properties dialog.

→ For more information on setting DHCP scope options, **see** "Specifying DHCP Options," **p. 593**.

To add the NAT server's IP address as a gateway to DHCP, do the following:

1. Launch the DHCP snap-in from the Administrative Tools menu and expand the scope for your NAT subnet.

2. Double-click the Scope Options node to open the Scope Options dialog. Mark the 003 Router option's check box to display the Data Entry frame, if you haven't added a gateway entry previously.

3. Type the IP address of your NAT server in the IP Address text box and click Add to add it to the address list (see Figure 25.39).

4. Close the Scope Options dialog and the DHCP snap-in.

TAKING ADVANTAGE OF NETWORK ADDRESS TRANSLATION (NAT) | 1065

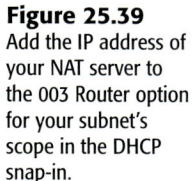

Figure 25.39
Add the IP address of your NAT server to the 003 Router option for your subnet's scope in the DHCP snap-in.

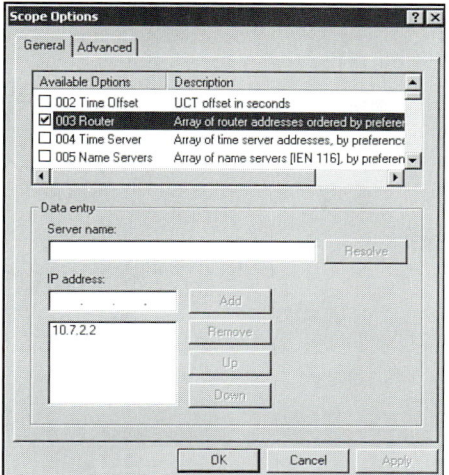

To enable DHCP clients to gain access to the NAT router prior to scheduled lease renewal, go to each client, launch the Command Prompt or MS-DOS Prompt window, and type **ipconfig /renew** to renew the lease immediately. Non-DHCP clients require you to manually add an entry for the NAT Server in the Gateway page of the TCP/IP Properties dialog for the network adapter.

TESTING CLIENT CONNECTIONS TO THE INTERNET

After renewing the lease to a test DHCP client, launch Internet Explorer (IE) on the client to test your NAT router. Verify that the client's Dial-Up Settings option is set to Never Dial a Connection or, if the client has a modem installed, Dial Whenever a Network Connection Is Not Present. If your demand-dial connection has timed out, it's likely to take a minute or so to re-establish the connection to your ISP.

 If your test client can't open a public Web site, see the "NAT Client Connection Problems" topic of the "Troubleshooting" section near the end of the chapter.

FINE-TUNING DEMAND-DIAL PROPERTIES

The default properties of the demand-dial connection are adequate for initial testing, but you should alter two property values to make demand-dialing more reliable. This is especially important if your ISP has an insufficient number of inbound phone lines and modems to support its customer base.

To add alternate ISP telephone numbers and provide for redialing on a busy signal, do the following:

1. In the Routing and Remote Access snap-in, click the Routing Interfaces node, right-click the demand-dial interface name in the list pane, and choose Properties to open the General page of the *InterfaceName* properties dialog.

PART
IV
CH
25

2. Click Alternates to open the Numbers and Addresses dialog, type an alternate inbound number for your ISP in the New Phone Number or Address text box, and click Add to add the number to the Phone Number or Addresses list.

3. Repeat step 2 for each inbound ISP phone number to try. To change the dialing sequence, select an entry and click Up or Down to move the entry.

4. Mark the Move Successful Number or Address to the Top of the List on Connection check box to dial the last number that connected (see Figure 25.40); click OK to close the dialog.

Figure 25.40
Add alternate inbound telephone numbers for your ISP in the Numbers and Addresses dialog for the demand-dial interface.

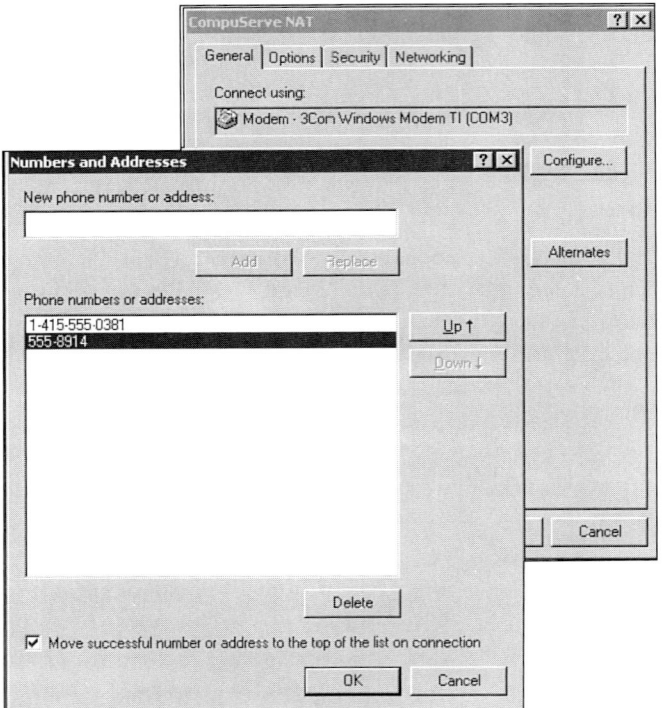

5. Click the Options tab to alter connection and dialing properties. You can extend the allowable idle time by selecting a larger value in the Idle Time Before Hanging Up list. Change the 0 default value in the Redial Attempts text box to 5 or more, and change the value in the Average Redial Intervals to 30 seconds or less (see Figure 25.41).

Taking Advantage of Network Address Translation (NAT) | 1067

Figure 25.41
Set the allowable idle time, number of redial attempts, and redial interval in the Options page of the demand-dial interface properties dialog.

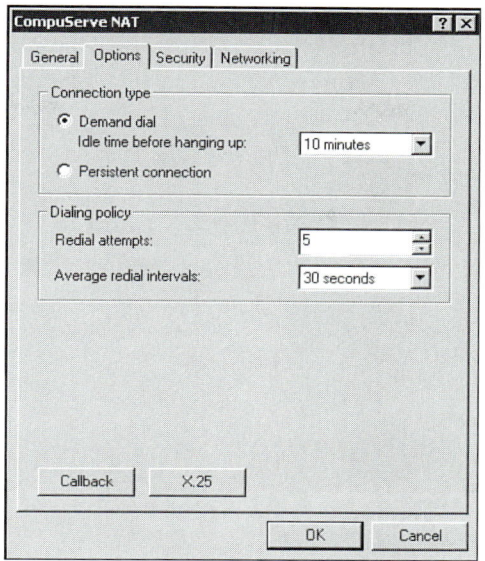

6. Explore the Security and Networking pages of the properties dialog and then click OK to close it.

The default property values in the Security and Networking pages of the *ConnectionName* Properties dialog are satisfactory for almost any demand-dial connection.

> **Tip from**
> *RJ*
>
> Limit the days and times that your demand-dial connection is available by right-clicking the connection name and choosing Dial-Out Hours to open the dialog of the same name. This dialog is identical to the Time of Day Constraints dialog for a RAS server (refer to Figure 25.14).

Configuring NAT with a DSL or Cable Modem Connection

DSL routers and cable modems connect to an additional 10BASE-T or 10/100BASE-T network adapter installed in the server running NAT. Cable-TV distribution to commercial buildings is relatively uncommon, so most organizations must use DSL to provide low-cost Internet connectivity to network clients. Asymmetric DSL (ADSL) provides higher downstream (from the Internet) than upstream (to the Internet) data rates, because downloading Web pages and other content generates most of the traffic. Consider higher-priced Symmetric DSL (SDSL) service if you intend to use your DSL connection for intersite AD replication, virtual private networking, or other uses in which a relatively similar amount of traffic flows in each direction.

Part **IV**
Ch **25**

As with a demand-dial Internet connection, you can install NAT on a DC or member server. If you expect more than about 50 users to connect to the Internet simultaneously or you use DSL or cable service for your VPNs, running NAT on a dedicated or lightly loaded member server is recommended. On a DC, address translation must compete with AD for server resources.

> **Note**
>
> If you use a member server as an Internet connection server, you must configure DNS on the server. Member servers don't run AD, so AD-integrated Dynamic DNS (DDNS) isn't an option. If you haven't set up DNS on the member server, create a new secondary DNS forward lookup zone that points to your DC's AD-integrated DNS server. The AD-integrated DNS server must have Root Hints installed, as described in the earlier "Adding Route Hints to the Clients' DNS Server" section. Failure to install Root Hints prevents clients from resolving Internet hostnames to public IP addresses. It's a good practice to add the IP address of the AD-integrated DNS server to the Root Hints list of the secondary DNS server.

→ For instructions on setting up a secondary DNS forward lookup zone, **see** "Establishing Secondary DNS Zones," **p. 381**.

The process of configuring NAT with a DSL connection to the Internet is much simpler than the demand-dial example described in the preceding sections. The procedure of this section uses a member server (`oakleaf-ps1.cakleaf.edu`) as the Internet connection server. The DSL modem is connected to a 10/100BASE-T autosensing network adapter, and must be connected to the Internet through your ISP before you configure NAT. Table 25.1 lists the network configuration parameters for the NAT server of this example.

TABLE 25.1   LAN PARAMETERS, IP ADDRESSES, AND SUBNET MASK VALUES FOR A TYPICAL DSL-BASED NAT SERVER

Local Area Connection Parameter	Address or Mask Value
NAT server private IP address	10.7.2.7
NAT server private subnet mask	255.255.255.0
NAT server public IP address	216.236.71.242
NAT server public subnet mask	255.255.255.252 (/30)
DSL provider gateway (router) address	216.236.071.241
DSL provider primary DNS server	205.214.45.10
DSL provider secondary DNS server	205.214.51.16

To configure RRAS for NAT routing of a DSL connection to the Internet, do the following:

1. Launch the Routing and Remote Access snap-in on the server in which you installed the network card for the DSL router.

2. Right-click the *ServerName* node or open the Action menu, and select Configure and Enable Routing and Remote Access to start the Routing and Remote Access Service Setup Wizard. Click Next to Bypass the Welcome dialog.

3. In the Common Configurations dialog, accept the default Internet Connection Server option and click Next.

4. In the Internet Connection Server Setup dialog, select the Set Up a Router with the Network Address Translation (NAT) Protocol option and click Next.

5. In the Internet Connection dialog, select the network adapter, usually Local Area Connection 2, that connected to the DSL router or cable modem (see Figure 25.42).

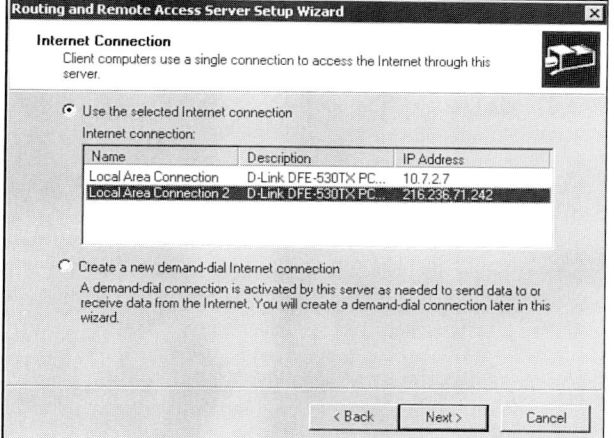

Figure 25.42
The network adapter connected to a DSL router or cable modem is the Internet connection you specify in the fourth Routing and Remote Access Service Setup Wizard dialog.

6. Click Finish to dismiss the Wizard. RRAS automatically starts and initializes.

7. Expand the Routing Interfaces node to display the four interfaces for an Internet connection server—Loopback, Local Area Connection (the private network), Local Area Connection 2 (the Internet), and Internal. Each of the interfaces should display Enabled in the Status column and Connected in the Connection State column.

8. Expand the IP Routing node and click its General subnode to display IP addresses and traffic counters for three of the four interfaces in the right pane; the Internal interface doesn't have an IP address.

9. Click the Network Address Translation (NAT) node to display the number of client mappings (Total Mappings) for Local Area Connection 2, which remains 0 until you connect LAN clients to the Internet with the NAT router.

10. Right-click My Network Places, choose Properties to open the Network and Dial-Up Connections window, right-click Local Area Connection 2 (or the name you assigned to the Internet connection), and choose Properties to open the General page of the *ConnectionName* Properties dialog.

11. In the Components Checked Are Used in This Connection list, clear the Client for Microsoft Networks and File and Printer Sharing for Microsoft Networks check boxes. Click OK to close the dialog, and close the Network and Dial-Up Connections window.

> **Caution**
>
> Binding File and Printer Sharing for Microsoft Networks to the network adapter connected to the cable modem or DSL router exposes your internal network to malicious hacker attacks. Unlike dial-up connections, which disable the Client for Microsoft Networks and File and Printer Sharing for Microsoft Networks by default, these components are enabled by default for network adapters. Hackers might gain access to network file shares and even disable your entire network if File and Printer Sharing for Microsoft Networks is enabled on a cable modem or DSL connection.

> **Tip from**
> *RJ*
>
> The Gibson Research Corporation Web site (http://grc.com) is a good source for information on protecting your network from hacker attacks. The Shields Up pages explain the susceptibility of computers running Windows Networking to attack by Trojan horse programs or viruses, such as the Windows Share Virus reported by the federal National Infrastructure Protection Center (NIPC) on April 1, 2000 (http://www.nipc.gov/nipc/advis00-038.htm). The Gibson site has a test program that evaluates the susceptibility of your NAT server—and thus your network—to NetBIOS over TCP/IP (NBT) attacks. Another test program tests the ability of hackers to scan your server for open TCP ports that are susceptible to unauthorized entry to your private network.

Leave the Routing and Remote Access Service snap-in open with the NAT node active during initial testing with clients.

Configuring Clients for DSL-Based NAT

The earlier "Adding the NAT Server as a Gateway for Clients" and "Testing Client Connections to the Internet" sections describe how to configure clients to take advantage of either demand-dial or DSL Internet connectivity with NAT. The following list recaps configuration requirements for Windows 2000, NT, and 9x clients:

- You must add the NAT server's public IP address (10.7.2.7 for this example) to the 003 Router (default gateway) and 006 DNS Servers list of scope- or server-level DHCP options. If you don't add the NAT server's DNS address, clients can't resolve public domain names but can connect to sites by typing their IP address in the browser's Address text box.

- You must run **ipconfig /release** and **ipconfig /renew** on each DHCP client to effect the preceding IP address additions or changes. You can run Winipcfg.exe and click Release All and Renew All on Windows 9x clients.

- For clients with fixed IP addresses, add the NAT server's public IP address to the Installed Gateways and DNS Server Search Order lists of the client's TCP/IP Properties dialog.

As clients connect with NAT to the Internet, the number of client mappings for the Local Area Connection 2 in the Routing and Remote Access Service snap-in increases rapidly. You must press F5 to refresh the Routing and Remote Access Service snap-in to obtain a current value for the number of addresses mapped, which varies with the clients' Internet browsing activity.

TROUBLESHOOTING

RAS CONNECTIVITY PROBLEMS

No clients can connect to the RAS server.

The most probable cause of total inability to connect to the RAS server is a modem or phone line failure. Use a telephone handset and dial the RAS server; if the server doesn't answer, check your modem and phone line with a dial-up client connection to your ISP or another RAS server.

After changing to a native-mode domain, failure of all users to connect is likely to be caused by failing to change the default Deny Remote Access Permission option of the local RAS server policy. DUN clients can't connect to the RAS server unless you set the Allow Remote Access Permission option.

→ To review local RAS server policies, **see** "Setting Local RAS Server Policies," **p. 1038**.

NAT DEMAND-DIAL CONNECTION PROBLEMS

The server fails to connect to the ISP.

The most probable cause of a failure when attempting a manual connection to your ISP is an error in the username, password, or telephone number entry when you set these properties in the Demand Dial Interface Wizard. Verify the username and reset your password by selecting the Routing Interfaces node, right-clicking the demand-dial connection, and choosing User Credentials to open the User Credentials dialog. Check the phone number being dialed by right-clicking the demand-dial connection and choosing properties to open the General page of the *ConnectionName* Properties dialog.

If the preceding steps don't solve the problem, create a new Dial-Up to the Internet connection in the My Network Connections' Network and Dial-Up Connections window. Use the telephone number and credentials of the demand-dial connection and test a conventional DUN connection to the Internet.

NAT CLIENT CONNECTION PROBLEMS

Clients can't open Web pages.

Try opening a Web page by typing its IP address—for example, `http://209.249.8.35`—in the text box. If the page opens, DNS isn't resolving public domain names. Verify that the Root Hint's page of the DNS *ServerName* Properties dialog contains the 13 InterNIC root server names and addresses. If the page doesn't open, run `ipconfig /all` or `Winipcfg.exe` on the client to verify that the address of the NAT server appears as a gateway. If the gateway is missing, renew the lease with `ipconfig /renew` or `Winipcfg`.

Clients with modems installed can't connect to the router.

Most users of IE with a modem and ISP account set their Dial-Up Settings to Always Dial My Default Connection. In IE, choose Tools, Internet Options to open the Internet Options dialog, and click the Connections tab. Select the Never Dial a Connection option for networked desktop PCs or Dial Whenever a Network Connection Isn't Present option for mobile users who also connect to the network.

MCSE Corner: Managing Remote Access and Routing Services

Remote Access is an important part of a Windows 2000 Server implementation and is tested on several exams. The base exam, 70-215, as well as exam 70-216, "Implementing and Administering a Microsoft Windows 2000 Network Infrastructure"; 70-220, "Designing Security for a Microsoft Windows 2000 Network"; and 70-221, "Designing a Microsoft Windows 2000 Network Infrastructure" test your knowledge of RRAS.

70-215 Installing, Configuring, and Administering Microsoft Windows 2000 Server

This exam tests your ability to install and configure the Remote Access Service (RAS) on a Microsoft Windows 2000 Server. There probably will be a question or two on RAS on this exam, and possibly a scenario or case study–type question. Keep in mind the importance placed on troubleshooting by Microsoft on these newer MCP exams. You should be familiar with installing RAS. You should also be able to enable user accounts to use Remote Access, and configure RAS for inbound connections. Being able to troubleshoot RAS is a very important concept to know for the exam. You should also be able to monitor RAS using the administrative tools.

70-216 Implementing and Administering a Microsoft 2000 Network Infrastructure

This exam tests your ability to work with RAS, but it is focused more to an enterprise-type environment with many locations and users. You should be familiar with configuring inbound connections with RAS, and with assigning IP addresses to clients using DHCP. It is also vital to know troubleshooting and monitoring RAS for this exam.

Installing and configuring Network Address Translation (NAT) is also covered on this exam. You should understand how to install NAT and configure NAT interfaces and properties to allow a shared connection to the Internet. You should also thoroughly understand the steps to troubleshooting NAT. The final important item to be familiar with is demand-dial routing using a modem connection and the steps to enabling and configuring this feature.

70-220 DESIGNING SECURITY FOR A MICROSOFT WINDOWS 2000 NETWORK

For this exam, you should be familiar with the authentication and encryption methods discussed in this chapter. You will be required to decide what type of authentication scheme to use, given information about the environment. This exam tests your ability to analyze the technical and business requirements of an organization and make recommendations based on those.

70-221 DESIGNING A MICROSOFT WINDOWS 2000 NETWORK INFRASTRUCTURE

To pass this exam, you are expected to have the ability to design a solution using the Windows 2000 Routing and Remote Access Service (RRAS), given the technical and business requirements of a company. You should also be able to integrate the RADIUS authentication method with the Remote Access Service. You should be able to look at the distribution of users and resources in the organization and determine the best points for the remote access servers. You should also be able to design an Internet access solution, of which NAT is one of the potential components. You should have an idea of when NAT would be the best solution for sharing an Internet connection.

CHAPTER 26

SETTING UP A VIRTUAL PRIVATE NETWORK

In this chapter

Securing Wide Area Communication over the Internet   1076

Setting Up a PPTP VPN Server   1079

Configuring Windows 2000 Dial-In PPTP Clients   1082

Setting Up Windows 9x VPN Clients   1088

Enabling Windows NT 4.0 PPTP Clients   1092

Securing the Internet Connection with PPTP Filters and Policies   1094

Configuring an L2TP VPN Server   1097

Troubleshooting   1101

MCSE Corner: Setting Up a Virtual Private Network   1103

Securing Wide Area Communication over the Internet

Wide Area Networks (WANs) traditionally have used dedicated (leased) T-1 lines, switched frame relay connections, or shared satellite transponders to interconnect geographically dispersed LANs. As the speed and reliability of the Internet backbone improved in the late 1990s, it became clear that replacing leased WAN links with data exchange via the Internet could lead to substantial cost savings. It was equally clear, however, that confidential information could easily be intercepted—and thus compromised—if the data transmitted wasn't encrypted during its travel over the public Internet. Thus, data encryption became the key to establishing Virtual Private Networks (VPNs)—secure, point-to-point Internet connections.

→ For a review of common WAN telecommunication options, **see** "Choosing an Intersite Communication Method," **p. 987**.

Initial VPN implementations involved specialized service providers who supplied complete, end-to-end VPN solutions—called value-added networks (VANs)—for medium- and large-size organizations. Most service providers installed expensive hardware encryption systems to the provider's network at each end of the VAN connection. The setup and monthly costs of service-provider VPNs were less than the traditional, long-distance WAN interconnects they replaced, but were still prohibitively costly for most small firms.

The combination of low-cost, high-speed Digital Subscriber Line (DSL) and cable modem connections to the Internet and the VPN features of Windows 2000 Server make it practical for any organization to set up its own VPN. DSL usually is *much* less costly than a T-1 connection to the Internet. The primary application for VPNs today is to provide a secure communication link for dial-in users, who connect through a local ISP to the Routing and Remote Access Service (RRAS) running on your server. You also can use a VPN for the server-to-server connection between Active Directory (AD) sites. VPNs between business partners are gaining importance as Internet-based business-to-business (B2B) e-commerce becomes a common method for conducting commercial transactions.

> **Note**
> The dial-up VPN examples of this chapter use a Windows 2000 member server with a DSL connection to the Internet and the required permanent IP address assigned by the DSL Internet Service Provider (ISP). A dial-up connection between a VPN server and an ISP isn't practical for a VPN, because the ISP's DHCP server almost always assigns a different IP address to the VPN server each time you connect. Server-to-server connections, which are beyond the scope of this chapter, require a separate DSL line for each VPN server.

Windows 2000 VPN Protocols

A VPN communication protocol must provide at least the following capabilities:

- Authentication to identify the VPN user or computer and, optionally, provide usage auditing and accounting services—Conventional Windows remote access authentication— Microsoft Challenge Handshake Authentication Protocol (MS-CHAP)—or certificate-based methods provide secure authentication.

- IP address assignment on the local private network for remote computers connecting through the public Internet—In most cases, Dynamic Host Control Protocol (DHCP) automatically provides local IP address assignment.
- Encryption to prevent unauthorized third parties from intercepting and analyzing the data transmitted over the Internet—The VPN protocol you choose determines the type of encryption used at both ends of the connection.
- Encryption key management to establish the type and strength of the data encryption method.

Most VPN protocols accommodate IP, Novell IPX, and NetBEUI traffic. This chapter covers only IP-based VPNs using TCP/IP.

Windows 2000 supports the following two VPN protocols:

- *Point-to-Point Tunneling Protocol* (PPTP) is an Internet standard (RFC 2637) that uses Microsoft Point-to-Point Encryption (MPPE) to encrypt data with the Rivest-Shamir-Adleman (RSA) RC4 cipher. MPPE uses a single, shared private key to provide conventional encryption. The default key length is 40 bits (basic); 56-bit (strong) and 128-bit (strongest) key lengths are optional. Authentication requires MS-CHAP version 1 or 2. Windows 2000, NT, and 9x support PPTP, which is the simpler of the two protocols to set up. PPTP also can encrypt Novell IPX and NetBEUI packets for Internet transmission. Downlevel clients or servers must use PPTP to connect to Windows 2000 Server's built-in VPN services.

→ For a basic description of encryption methods, **see** "Cryptography and Key-Based Encryption," **p. 486**.

- *Layer 2 Tunneling Protocol* (L2TP) combines PPTP and Layer 2 Forwarding (L2F) into an Internet standard (RFC 2661). L2TP is intended to operate over IP, X.25, frame relay, or Asynchronous Transfer Mode (ATM) network. L2TP over IP, which is the only current L2TP implementation, uses Internet Protocol Security (IPSec) to encrypt IP packets. Windows 2000's L2TP implementation supports the Extended Authentication Protocol (EAP), which supports newer authentication methods, such as Smart Cards. Currently, only Windows 2000 clients and servers support L2TP.

→ For a review of the IPSec encryption process, **see** "IP Security (IPSec) in Windows 2000," **p. 489**.

PPTP and L2TP are called *Layer 2 protocols*, because they operate at the second (Data Link) layer of the Open Systems Interconnection (OSI) Reference Model and use PPP frames to exchange data between dial-up clients and VPN servers. IPSec is a Layer 3 (network) protocol that operates at the packet level.

> **Note**
>
> When you upgrade a Windows NT 4.0 server with the Routing and Remote Access Services add-on installed and the PPTP VPN service configured, upgrading to Windows 2000 preserves all PPTP settings.

Understanding the Tunneling Process

PPTP and L2TP, as their names suggest, use tunneling methods to transport encrypted data over the Internet. Conceptually, a tunnel is akin to an underwater pipeline that delivers IP packets from one end point to another end point through an ocean of Internet traffic. The computers at each end point of a tunnel perform the following operations:

1. Mutually agree to create a tunnel.
2. Negotiate a set of parameters that determine IP addresses for each end of the tunnel and set common authentication, encryption, and compression methods.
3. Maintain the tunnel during the communication session.
4. Close the tunnel when the session terminates, either intentionally or by a hardware or software failure at either end point.

PPTP requires two PPP connections, one to establish and maintain the tunnel, called the *control channel* (TCP port 1723) and the other for sending and receiving data, called the *tunnel channel* (TCP protocol 47). Encrypted data flowing through an Internet tunnel—called the *payload*—is encapsulated with a *tunnel data transfer protocol header* added by the tunnel client. PPTP uses generic route encapsulation (GRE), which supports encryption, compression, or both. The tunnel server strips that header from the encapsulated data, decrypts the payload, and forwards it to the specified host or service running on the private network. The reverse process occurs when the tunnel server returns data to the tunnel client.

Tunnels come in two types: voluntary and compulsory. When a client, such as a user with a dial-up Internet connection, requests a VPN connection, the dial-up client is the tunnel client and the RRAS server is the tunnel server. Special VPN servers—called front-end processors (FEPs) for PPTP or L2TP Access Concentrators (LACs)—can create compulsory tunnels to which clients must connect. Windows 2000 VPNs provide voluntary tunnels; VANs commonly use compulsory tunnels for dedicated VPNs. Figure 26.1 illustrates a voluntary-tunnel PPTP VPN between a dial-up client and a DSL-connected Windows 2000 VPN server running RRAS.

SETTING UP A PPTP VPN SERVER | 1079

Figure 26.1
Data is encrypted at the remote tunnel client, travels via PPP to the remote dial-up ISP, is routed over the Internet, and connects to the multihomed VPN server via a DSL modem. Decryption occurs during routing from the public `216.236.71.242` address to the private `10.7.2.0` network.

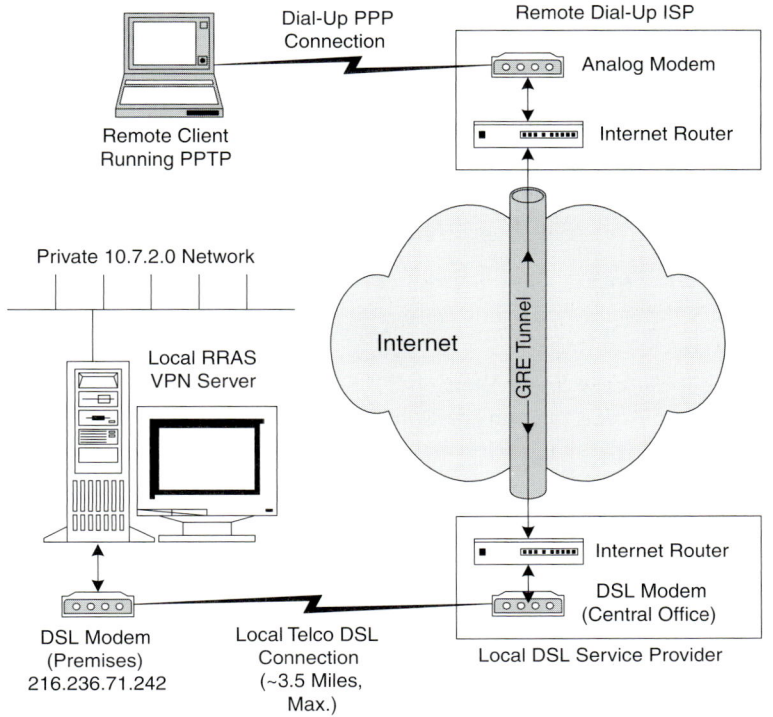

> **Note**
> PPTP dominates the Windows VPN universe, because it's available for all 32-bit Windows operating systems and provides a level of security that's acceptable for most organizations, other than financial institutions and many federal agencies. L2TP is a recent VPN entrant, and its use isn't widespread. L2TP provides a higher degree of authentication and encryption security through the use of Public Key Infrastructure (PKI) certificates.

PART
IV
CH
26

SETTING UP A PPTP VPN SERVER

Installing RRAS on a member server or DC and configuring the server as a VPN tunnel server automatically establishes a set of PPTP and L2TP ports. PPTP is the simpler of the two Windows 2000 VPN protocols to set up and manage. Most Windows 2000 network administrators must support downlevel clients, so it's a common practice to set up PPTP first, and then configure L2TP for Windows 2000 clients. The procedure that follows assumes that you've installed RRAS, but have not yet configured and enabled RRAS on the server, and have an operational DHCP server on your network segment. Installing a tunnel server requires that the RRAS server have a persistent—not a dial-up—connection to the Internet and a permanent, public IP address assigned by your ISP.

→ For instructions on adding RRAS to a server, **see** "Installing Windows 2000 RRAS," **p. 1027**.

> **Caution**
>
> You can't run VPN routing and Network Address Translation (NAT) for an Internet connection server on the same computer. If your RRAS server is configured to use NAT, you must disable the server by right-clicking the *ServerName* node in the Routing and Remote Access snap-in and choosing Disable Routing and Remote Access. Disabling RRAS permanently removes your NAT configuration.

To set up a VPN server from scratch, do the following:

1. Choose Programs, Administrative Tools, Routing and Remote Access to open the snap-in of the same name. The right pane displays a Configure the Routing and Remote Access Server page.

2. Right-click the *ServerName* node, and choose Configure and Enable Routing and Remote Access to open the Routing and Remote Access Server Setup Wizard. Click Next to bypass the Welcome dialog.

3. In the Common Configurations dialog, select the Virtual Private Network (VPN Server) option and click Next.

4. In the Remote Client Protocols dialog, verify that TCP/IP appears in the Protocols list. Accept the default Yes, All of the Available Protocols Are on This List option, and click Next.

> **Note**
>
> If you want to enable remote clients to communicate with IPX or NetBEUI, you must exit the Wizard, add the missing network protocols to the server, and start again at step 2. Using IPX or NetBEUI protocols on a VPN is beyond the scope of this book.

5. In the Internet Connection dialog, select the network adapter that connected to the router/modem with a connection to the Internet. This example uses a DSL modem with a public 216.236.71.242 IP address (see Figure 26.2). Click Next.

Figure 26.2
Select the network adapter connected to your Internet router/modem in the Routing and Remote Access Server Setup Wizard's Internet Connection dialog.

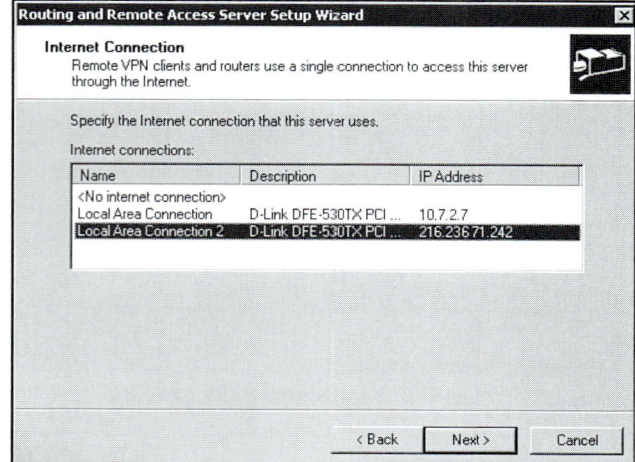

→ For the IP configuration of the DSL network adapter used in this chapter's examples, **see** "Configuring NAT with a DSL or Cable Modem Connection," **p. 1067**.

6. In the IP Address Assignment dialog, accept the Automatically option to use your subnet's DHCP server to allocate IP address leases to the server and each dial-in client. Click Next.

> **Tip from**
> *RJ*
>
> Verify that your DHCP scope has a sufficient number of available IP addresses to accommodate the number of simultaneous VPN clients you must handle.

7. In the Managing Multiple Remote Access Servers dialog, accept the No, I Don't Want to Set Up This Server to Use RADIUS Now option. You can change from Windows to RADIUS authentication and accounting later, if you want. Click Next and Finish to dismiss the Wizard.

→ For instructions on setting up and using a RADIUS server, **see** "Using RADIUS Authentication and Accounting," **p. 1044**.

8. Click OK to close the message that instructs you to set up the DHCP Relay Agent. You need the DHCP Relay Agent only if your network's DHCP server is on another subnet.

RRAS starts and completes its initial VPN configuration at this point. Expand the nodes to display all the items added, and click the Ports node to display a list of the server's VPN ports. Using the Wizard to configure VPN automatically adds 128 PPTP and 128 L2TP ports to the server (see Figure 26.3), and enables inbound and outbound demand-dial connections for the ports.

Figure 26.3
Using the Routing and Remote Access Server Setup Wizard to configure VPN automatically adds 128 PPTP and 128 L2TP ports to the server.

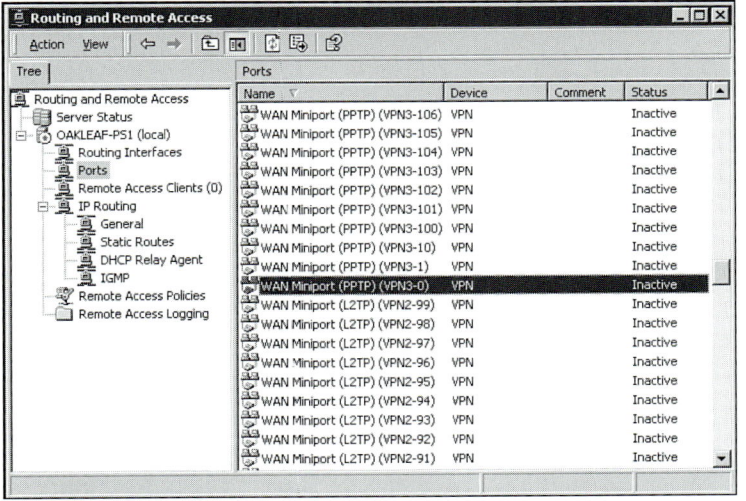

If you want to reduce the number of VPN ports or disable demand-dial VPN, do the following:

1. Right-click the Ports node, and choose Properties to open the Ports Properties dialog.
2. Select the WAN Miniport (PPTP) device, and click Configure to open the Configure Device—WAN Miniport (PPTP) dialog.
3. Clear the Demand-Dial Routing Connections (Inbound and Outbound) check box, unless you want to support direct user dial-up VPN to modem(s) installed on the server.

→ For an explanation of demand-dial RAS, **see** "Providing Basic Dial-Up Network Access to Remote Clients," **p. 1025**.

4. Type a reasonable number of simultaneous PPTP connections for a test configuration in the Maximum Ports text box (see Figure 26.4).
5. Repeat steps 2 through 4 for the L2TP device, and then click OK to close both dialogs.

Figure 26.4
Disable demand-dial routing, unless you intend to provide this service, and specify 10 or 20 maximum ports for each VPN protocol.

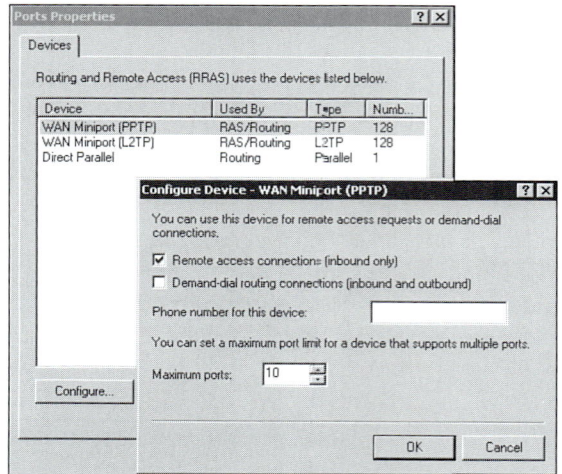

CONFIGURING WINDOWS 2000 DIAL-IN PPTP CLIENTS

One of this book's guiding principals for network administrators is to test with typical clients what you configure on servers. Setting up PPTP tunnel clients to connect to the VPN server by a dial-up ISP connection is considerably more complex than initial server setup. The procedure differs for each client operating system. As expected, Windows 2000 clients are the easiest to configure for basic PPTP communication.

Windows 2000 delivers Microsoft's first integrated "Dial-up and Connect to the VPN" feature. Windows 9x and NT require users to first connect to their local ISP to establish an Internet connection, and then manually initiate the VPN connection. Configuring the connection, however, is a two-step process—first you create the connection to the remote ISP, and then you configure the VPN parameters.

Configuring the ISP Dial-Up Connection

To configure a modem-equipped test client running Windows 2000 Professional for the first phase of the dial-up PPTP VPN connection to the server, do the following:

1. Right-click My Network Places, and choose Properties to open the Network and Dial-Up Connections Window.

2. Double-click the Make New Connection icon to start the Network Connection Wizard.

3. If you haven't previously configured the test client's modem, the Location Information dialog opens. Select your Country/Region in the list, type your area code in the text box, click OK to open the Phone and Modem Options, and click OK to accept the default My Location selection and close the dialog.

4. Click Next to bypass the Wizard's welcome dialog, accept the default Dial-Up to Private Network option, and click Next.

5. In the Phone Number to Dial dialog, mark the Use Dialing Rules check box to enable the Area Code text box, and then type the dial-up ISP's area code and telephone number in the two text boxes (see Figure 26.5). Click Next.

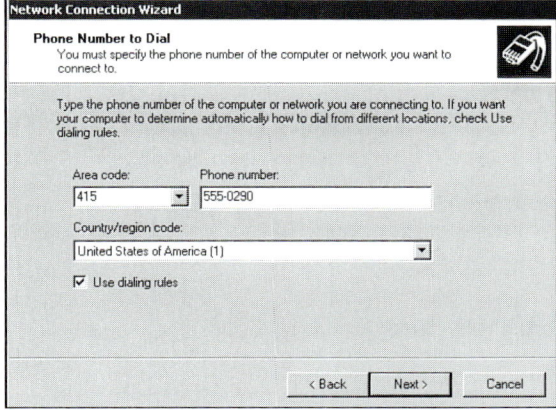

Figure 26.5
Marking the Use Dialing Rules check box lets Windows determine whether the ISP dial string requires a 1 + area code prefix. Alternatively, clear the check box and type the entire phone number in the text box.

6. In the Connection Availability dialog, accept the default All Users option if you want to give any user the right to run Dial-Up Networking (DUN) to log on to the network. Click Next.

7. In the Completing the Network Connection Wizard, rename the connection to a meaningful name, mark the Add a Shortcut to My Desktop check box, and click Finish to dismiss the Wizard and open the Connect *ConnectionName* dialog.

8. Type your dial-up user ID in the User Name text box, add your password, mark the Save Password check box, and click Properties to open the *ConnectionName* properties dialog.

9. Click the Options tab, and mark or clear the check boxes to enable the dialing options you want (see Figure 26.6).

Figure 26.6
The first phase of adding the dial-up VPN connection is to set dialing, logon, and network parameters for the modem connection to the remote ISP.

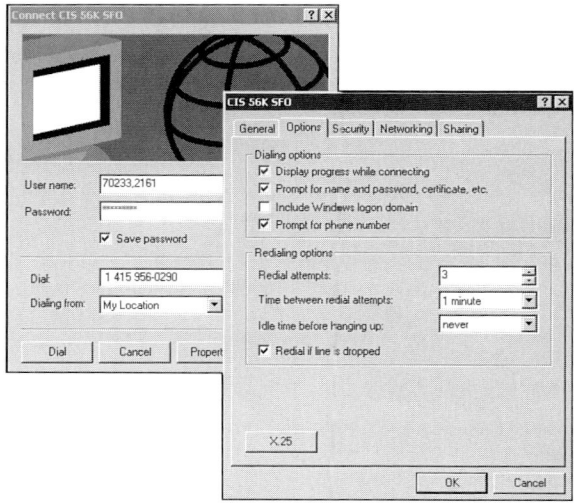

10. If your ISP requires use of a logon script, such as Cis.scp for CompuServe, click the Security tab, mark the Run Script check box, and click Browse to display a list of scripts in the client's \Winnt\System32\Ras folder. Double-click the appropriate script to add it to the combo list. Most ISPs require unsecured (clear-text) passwords.

11. Click the Networking tab, verify that the File and Printer Sharing for Microsoft Networks check box is clear, and clear the Client for Microsoft Networks check box.

12. If your dial-up ISP issues permanent IP addresses or requires that you specify DNS server addresses, select the Internet Protocol (TCP/IP) item in the Components list, and click Properties to open the Internet Protocol (TCP/IP) Properties dialog. Mark the necessary options and add the required IP addresses to the text boxes (see Figure 26.7).

Figure 26.7
Removing unneeded components from the dial-up connection improves security. Some ISPs, such as CompuServe, require that you specify their DNS server addresses.

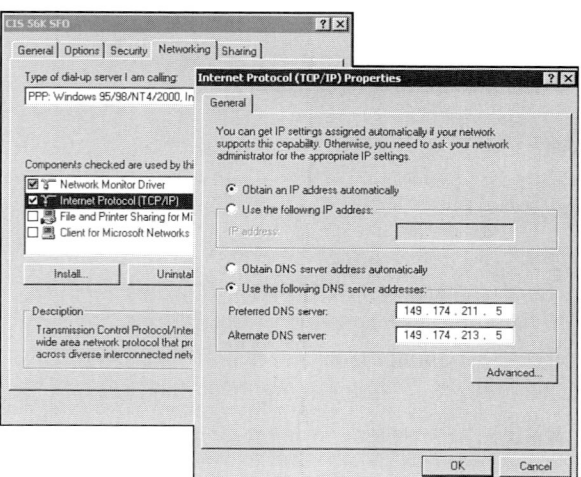

CONFIGURING WINDOWS 2000 DIAL-IN PPTP CLIENTS | 1085

13. Click OK to close the properties dialog and return to the Connect *ConnectionName* dialog. Click Dial to test your connection to the local ISP.

14. When the Connection Complete dialog opens, mark the Do Not Display This Message Again check box and click OK.

15. Right-click the *ConnectionName* icon and choose Disconnect to drop the connection to the ISP.

> **Note**
>
> The Save Password feature of the Connect *ConnectionName* dialog doesn't work in the release version (build 2195) of Windows 2000 Professional or Server. You must re-enter your password each time you establish a dial-up connection.

SETTING UP AND TESTING THE WINDOWS 2000 VPN CONNECTION

The process of configuring Windows 2000 clients for PPTP or L2TP connections is quite similar; you need to change only one network property value—Type of VPN Server I Am Calling—from Automatic to PPTP. Specifying PPTP as the server type eliminates the protocol negotiation step.

To configure the PPTP VPN connection, do the following:

1. In the Dial-Up and Network Connections dialog, double-click the Make New Connection icon to start the Network Connection Wizard a second time. Click Next to bypass the Welcome dialog.

2. In the Connection Type dialog, select the Connect to a Private Network Through the Internet option and click Next.

3. In the Public Network dialog, accept the default Automatically Dial the Initial Connection option, which defaults to the first ISP dial-up connection you've defined. Accept or select a different connection in the list and click Next.

4. In the Destination Address dialog's text box, type the IP address assigned to the VPN network adapter of the server (see Figure 26.8). Click Next.

Figure 26.8
Unless your VPN server's IP address has a registered domain name, use the server's IP address to specify the tunnel server.

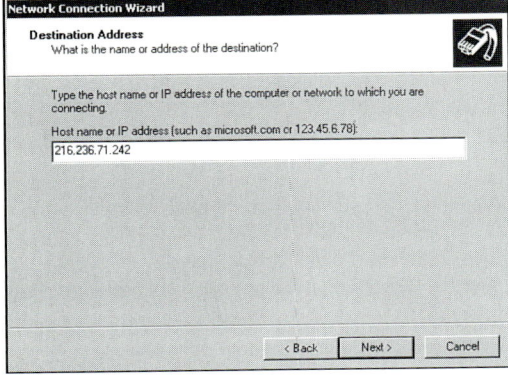

PART
IV
CH
26

5. In the Connection Availability dialog, again accept the default All Users option so you can use the VPN connection to log on to the network. Click Next.

6. In the Completing the Network Connection Wizard dialog, rename the connection, and click Finish to dismiss the Wizard. In this case, adding a desktop shortcut for the connection is the default.

7. In the Connect *VPNConnectionName* dialog, accept or type your user ID, type your password, and click Properties to open the *VPNConnectionName* properties dialog.

8. Click the Options tab, mark the Include Windows Logon Domain and Re-Dial if Line Is Dropped check boxes.

9. Click the Security tab and mark the Automatically Use My Windows Logon Name and Password (and Domain, if Any) check box. If you want to specify a different login ID, password, or domain each time you connect to a VPN, clear the check box.

10. Click the Networking tab, select Point to Point Tunneling Protocol (PPTP) in the Type of VPN Server I Am Calling list, and clear the File and Printer Sharing for Microsoft Networks check box (see Figure 26.9).

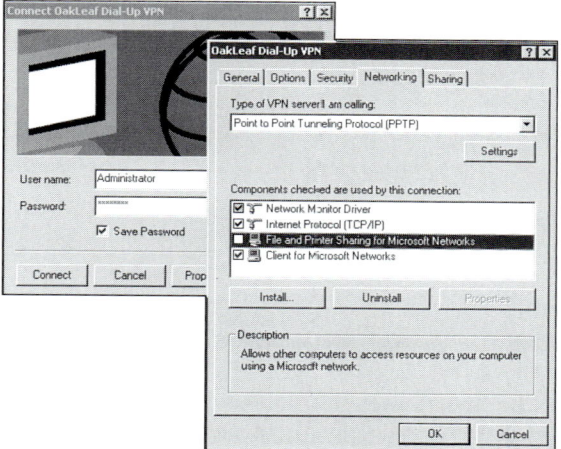

Figure 26.9
You must select Point to Point Tunneling Protocol (PPTP)—not Automatic—before you fully set up the L2TP protocol. If you accept the Automatic default, the VPN connection fails.

11. Click OK to close the properties dialog and return to the Connect *VPNConnectionName* dialog. Click Dial to dial the ISP and automatically establish the VPN tunnel. In the Initial Connection dialog, mark the Do Not Display This Reminder Again check box, and click Yes to continue.

Tip from
RJ

Verify that you can browse computers and their shares for which the test account you use has permissions. Even if the test client is connected to the network, browsing and other networking operations use the VPN tunnel. You can verify this by watching the traffic flow on the two dial-up connections in the taskbar's tray as you browse the private network.

CONFIGURING WINDOWS 2000 DIAL-IN PPTP CLIENTS   1087

12. Right-click the ISP *ConnectionName* icon, and choose Disconnect to drop the connection and close the VPN tunnel. Disconnecting with the *VPNConnectionName* icon doesn't drop the connection to the ISP.

 If you have a problem establishing the Windows 2000 client's PPTP tunnel, see the "Windows 2000 PPTP Connection Problems" topic in the "Troubleshooting" section at the end of this chapter.

TESTING DOMAIN LOGON WITH THE VPN CONNECTION

The final step in testing your Windows 2000 PPTP VPN is to verify that clients can log on to the private network with the VPN connection. Do the following to test remote VPN logon:

1. Disconnect the test client from the network by removing its network cable.
2. Choose Start, Shutdown, Log Off *UserName*, and then press Ctrl+Alt+Delete to display the Log On to Windows dialog.
3. Change your logon ID, if you want, type your password, and mark the Log On Using Dial-Up Connection check box.
4. Click OK to open the Network and Dial-Up Connections dialog, select the *VPNConnectionName* in the Choose a Network Connection list, and click Dial to start the connection process.
5. In the Connect *ConnectionName* dialog, replace the default values with the logon ID and password for the client's ISP connection, and click Dial. After connecting to the ISP, VPN authentication fails because the logon process substitutes your ISP logon ID and password for the network logon ID and password.
6. In the Connect *VPNConnectionName* dialog, retype your network logon ID and password, and add the domain name. Click OK to retry authentication and connect.

Note Look for Microsoft to correct with a service release or patch the failure to use in the *VPNConnectionName* dialog the logon credentials you provided in the Log on To Windows dialog.

7. Right-click the *VPNConnectionName* icon, and choose Status to open the General page of the *VPNConnectionName* Status dialog, which displays connection activity and the percentage compression for sent and received packets (see Figure 26.10, bottom).
8. Click the Details page to display properties of the PPTP connection (see Figure 26.10, top).

Note The local network's DHCP server leases the Server IP Address and Client IP Address values shown in Figure 26.10. The server (oakleaf-ps1) used for the examples of this chapter has a fixed IP address of 10.7.2.7. The tunnel server uses its second IP address (10.7.2.28) only for PPTP operations.

9. Close the Status dialog, and disconnect the dial-up connection to the ISP, which terminates the VPN tunnel. Click Cancel when the automatic reconnect message appears.

PART
IV
CH
26

Figure 26.10
The General page of the *VPNConnection-Name* Status dialog displays the number of outbound and inbound bytes, and the percentage of packet compression in both directions. The Details page lists property values for the VPN connection.

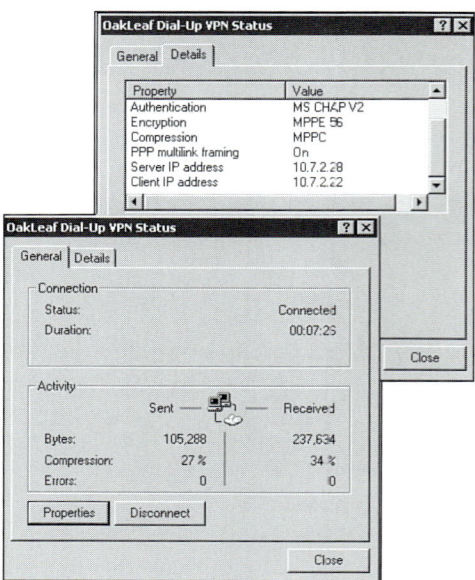

If the test client has a large user profile, it might take several minutes to log on with a 56kbps modem connection. The logon time increases—compared with a direct modem connection to the server—by about 20% or more. The added overhead of the tunnel headers and other PPTP baggage reduces the typical 40kbps data rate of a 56kbps modem to about 33kbps, which your users with analog modem connections are likely to notice. Microsoft Point-to-Point Compression (MPPC) improves the data rate, but conventional data compression—typically 15% to 20% for sent packets and 3% to 5% for received packets—also occurs over nonsecure dial-up connections.

Setting Up Windows 9x VPN Clients

Windows 98 Second Edition includes a PPTP VPN client that's fully compatible with Windows 2000's PPTP implementation, as well as that of Windows NT 4.0 with Service Pack 4 and the RRAS add-on installed. Earlier versions of Windows 9x need the following upgrades and updates:

- Windows 95, including the OEM Service Release (OSR) 2 version, requires the Dial-Up Networking 1.3 Performance and Security upgrade and Microsoft Virtual Private Networking update, which are available at http://www.microsoft.com/windows95/downloads/. You must install Dial-Up Networking 1.3 before installing the VPN update. The update replaces MS-CHAP V1 with MS-CHAP V2 authentication.

- Windows 98 (version 4.10.1998, with or without Service Pack 1) requires the Microsoft Virtual Private Network update, which you can download from http://www.microsoft.com/windows98/downloads/corporate.asp. This update isn't required for clients running Windows 98 SE.

> **Note**
> Additional information on the upgrade and update is available in the "VPN Update for Windows 98 and Dial-Up Networking 1.3" Microsoft Knowledge Base article Q191540.

Establishing a VPN connection with Windows 9x is a two-step process. You establish an independent DUN connection to the client's ISP, and then open a second DUN connection that uses the Dial-Up Adapter #2 (VPN) component that bridges the two connections. The following procedure assumes that the client currently has a functioning dial-up ISP connection, so you add only a new VPN DUN entry in this case. The example uses Windows 98 SE; adding a VPN DUN entry with Windows 95 is quite similar.

Before starting the client VPN setup procedure, verify that VPN is installed on the computer. Right-click Network Neighborhood, and choose Properties to open the Network dialog. Verify that the three required components and one binding—Dial-Up Adapter, Dial-Up Adapter #2 (VPN Support), Microsoft Virtual Private Networking Adapter, and NDISWAN -> Microsoft Virtual Private Networking Adapter—appear in the components list (see Figure 26.11).

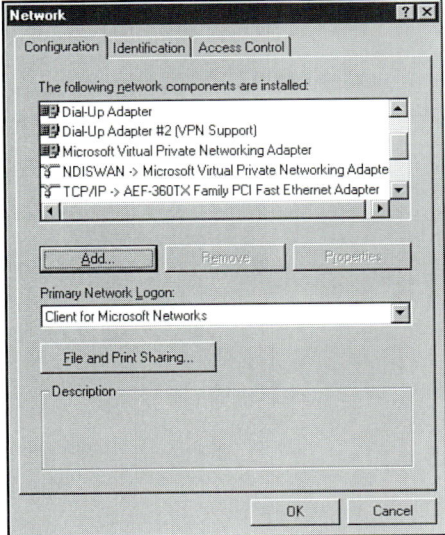

Figure 26.11
Dial-Up Adapter and the three following entries in the Network components list are required to support dial-up PPTP connections.

Configuring a Windows 98 PPTP Tunnel Client

To add a Windows 98 PPTP DUN client connection to your Windows 2000 VPN server, do the following:

1. In My Computer or Explorer, open Dial-Up Networking, and double-click Make New Connection to open the Make New Connection wizard.

2. Replace My Connection with a descriptive connection name, and select Microsoft VPN Adapter in the Select a Device list. Click Next.

3. In the second dialog, type the public IP address of your server (216.236.71.242 for this example) in the text box, and click Next and Finish to add the new connection.

4. Right-click the newly added connection, and choose Properties to open the *VPNConnectionName* Properties dialog.

5. Mark the Require Encrypted Password and Require Data Encryption check boxes, and clear the NetBEUI and IPX/SPX Compatible check boxes unless you need to support one of these protocols (see Figure 26.12). The Log on to Network and Enable Software Compression options are enabled by default. Click OK to close the dialog.

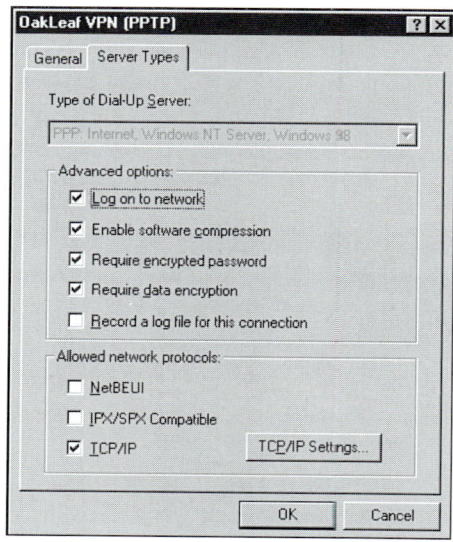

Figure 26.12
Add the Require Encrypted Password and Require Data Encryption options and remove unneeded protocol support in the VPN connection's Network dialog.

The default TCP/IP properties for the VPN connection use DHCP to assign a network address and the IP address of DNS server(s), so you don't need to alter the settings.

TESTING THE WINDOWS 98 PPTP CONNECTION

To test the new PPTP connection, do the following:

1. Open the DUN connection to the ISP, and wait for the connection to complete.

2. Double-click the VPN connection to open the Connect To dialog.

3. Type your username and password in the text boxes, mark the Save Password check box, and click Connect to open the PPTP tunnel.

4. Right-click the VPN connection and choose Properties to open the Connected To *VPNConnectionName* dialog, which displays only basic information on traffic and protocols in use (see Figure 26.13).

Figure 26.13
Windows 98's properties dialog for a VPN connection provides limited information about the connection. Microsoft Mutual Challenge Handshake Authentication is the full name of MS-CHAP V2.

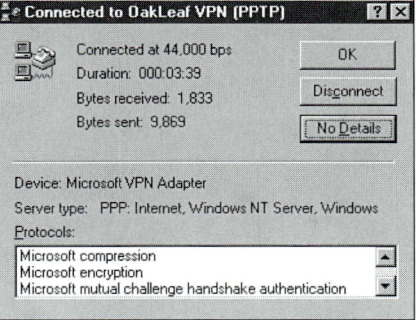

5. To check the IP addresses the PPTP server assigns to the client, run Winipcfg.exe and select the PPP Adapter for the VPN (see Figure 26.14). You can determine the correct PPP Adapter by the presence of your private network's IP addresses in the Ethernet Adapter frame.

Figure 26.14
Winipcfg's dialog for the VPN's PPP Adapter displays the DHCP-assigned IP address of the client on the private network.

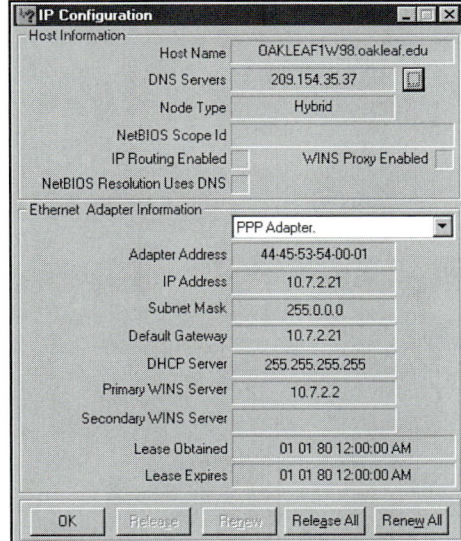

If your test client is connected directly to the network, VPN operations take precedence over wired connections. You can verify that the client is using the modem connection by the slow speed of the server browsing in Network Neighborhood and by watching the connection icons in the taskbar tray.

| **Tip from** RJ | Add desktop shortcuts for the ISP and VPN connections. Windows 9x doesn't offer Windows 2000's option to automatically add desktop shortcuts for DUN connections. |

Tip from
RJ

Don't bother trying to connect to the Internet with your ISP connection while a VPN connection is active. The ISP connection is dedicated to PPTP operations while the tunnel is active. Close the VPN connection to return the ISP connection to its normal Internet connectivity functions.

 If you encounter a problem with establishing the Windows 9x client's PPTP tunnel, see the "Windows 9x PPTP Connection Problems" topic in the "Troubleshooting" section at the end of this chapter.

ENABLING WINDOWS NT 4.0 PPTP CLIENTS

Windows NT Workstation 4.0 clients connect to VPNs in a manner similar to that for Windows 9x. Windows NT requires separate phone book entries for the connection to the client's ISP and the VPN server. Remote Access Service (RAS) and the PPTP protocol must be installed on clients to enable VPN operation. Like the preceding section, it's assumed that the test client already has a phone book entry for the DUN connection to the client's ISP.

ADDING THE PPTP PROTOCOL

If you haven't installed PPTP protocol on the client, do the following:

1. Right-click Network Neighborhood, choose properties to open the Network properties dialog, and click the Protocols tab.

2. Click Add to open the Select Network Protocol dialog, select Point to Point Tunneling Protocol in the Network Protocol list (see Figure 26.15), and click OK to copy the required files from the Windows NT Workstation distribution CD-ROM or a network share.

Figure 26.15
Begin the addition of the PPTP protocol in the Select Network Protocol dialog.

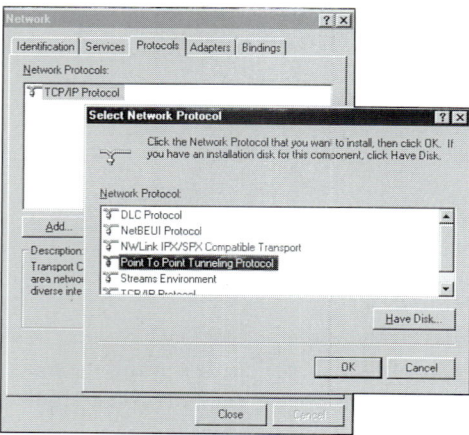

3. In the PPTP configuration dialog, select a reasonable number, such as 3 to 5 in the Number of Virtual Private Networks spin box, and click OK.

4. Click OK to confirm the message that you must configure the PPTP ports, and open the Remote Access Setup dialog.

5. Click Add to open the Add RAS Device dialog, and select the first VPN you added—VPN1-RASPPTPM—in the RAS Capable Devices list (see Figure 26.16). Click OK to close the dialog, click Cancel to close the RAS Server TCP/IP Configuration dialog, and add the VPN1 port to the RAS Setup list. Repeat this step if you want to add more VPN ports now.

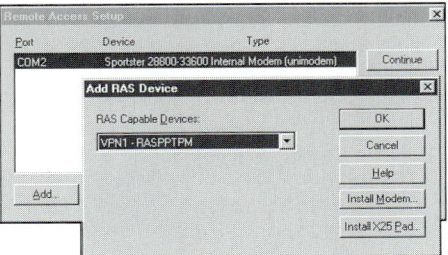

Figure 26.16
You add the first VPN RAS device to the RAS Setup list in the Add RAS Device dialog.

6. Select each VPN port in sequence, click Configure to open the Configure Port Usage dialog, and select the Dial Out Only option (see Figure 26.17). Click OK to close the dialog, and click Continue to return to the Network dialog.

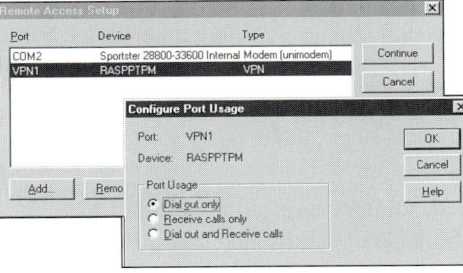

Figure 26.17
Select the Dial Out Only option for the PPTP connection.

7. Click Close to close the Network dialog and add the PPTP bindings. Restart the client when requested by the message.

8. Apply the latest service pack to bring the PPTP protocol up to date. SP4+ is required to provide MS-CHAP V2 authentication.

Adding and Testing the Phonebook Entry for the First VPN

To create the VPN1 connection, do the following:

1. Open Dial-Up Connections in My Computer or Explorer, and double-click Add New Connection to open the Dial-Up Networking dialog.

2. Click New to open the New Phonebook Entry dialog, and replace the MyDial-upServer Entry Name with a descriptive name.

3. Select RASPPTPM (VPN1) in the Dial Using list, and type the server's public IP address in the Phone Number text box (see Figure 26.18). Click OK to add the new entry, which uses DHCP to assign the client's IP address for the tunnel.

Figure 26.18
Selecting one of the VPN ports in the Dial Using list and substituting the IP address of the VPN tunnel server configures Windows NT Workstation for dial-in.

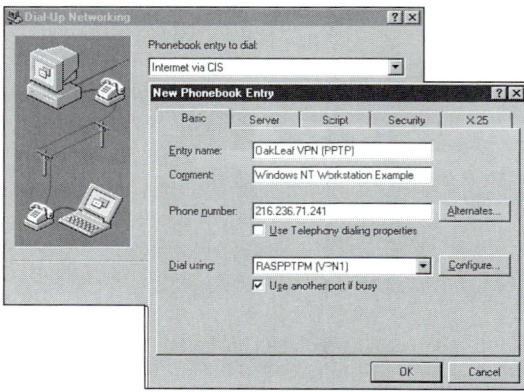

4. Select the connection to the client's ISP in the Phonebook Entry to Dial list, click Dial, and wait until the connection is established.

5. Reopen the Dial Up Networking dialog, select the *VPNConnectionName* entry in the Phone Book Entry to Dial list, and click Dial to open the Connect To *VPNConnectionName* dialog.

6. In the Connect To dialog, accept or change the client logon ID, type the password, accept or change the domain name, and click OK to establish the PPTP connection.

When the tunnel is established, run **ipconfig /all** if you want to check the IP addresses assigned by DHCP to the PPTP client. Verify that you can browse shares on the domain's server(s), and then disconnect to terminate the VPN tunnel.

SECURING THE INTERNET CONNECTION WITH PPTP FILTERS AND POLICIES

When you configure RRAS as a VPN server, the Routing and Remote Access Server Setup Wizard adds a default set of input and output TCP filters for PPTP and L2TP VPNs. The PPTP filters restrict the VPN server to receiving and sending only PPTP control and tunnel channel data. The L2TP filters restrict UDP traffic to User Datagram Protocol (UDP) ports 500 and 1701. The two sets of filters create a simple firewall between the private network and the public Internet. The default filters also enable the server to act as an on-demand PPTP tunnel client that connects to other PPTP servers.

Securing the Internet Connection with PPTP Filters and Policies   1095

Tip from
RJ

Online help's "Set PPTP Input Filters" and "Set PPTP Output Filters" topics state that you must manually configure the filters and add IP Address and Subnet Mask property values for each filter. Unless you have special routing requirements, the default filter properties suffice.

To view and optionally configure input and output filters to enable PPTP traffic only through the interface to the Internet adapter, do the following:

1. In the Routing and Remote Access Service snap-in, click the *ServerName*, IP Routing, General node to display the four standard routing interfaces in the right pane.

2. Right-click the interface for the network adapter that connects to the Internet, usually Local Area Connection 2, and choose Properties to open the General Page of the *ConnectionName* Properties dialog (see Figure 26.19).

Figure 26.19
The General Page of the *ConnectionName* Properties dialog for the network adapter dedicated to the server's Internet connection allows you to input and output packet filters.

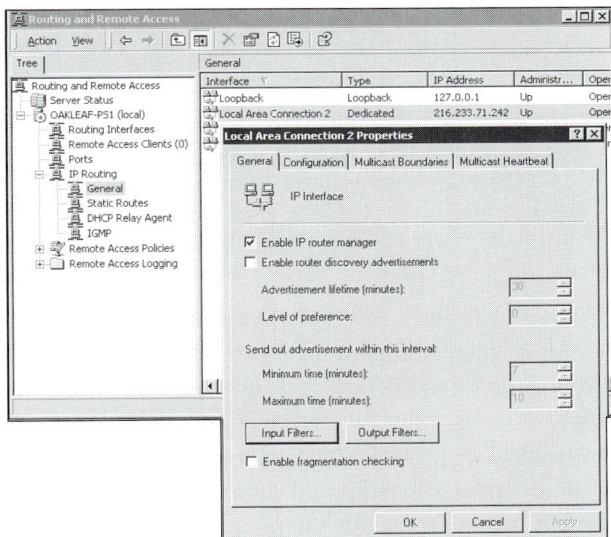

3. Click the Input Filters button to open the Input Filters dialog, which displays the default set of three PPTP and two L2TP input filters. Scroll to the right to display the Protocol, Source Port or Type, and Destination Port or Type for each of the filters (see Figure 26.20).

Figure 26.20
The default set of PPTP and L2TP Input Filters added by the Routing and Remote Access Server Setup Wizard.

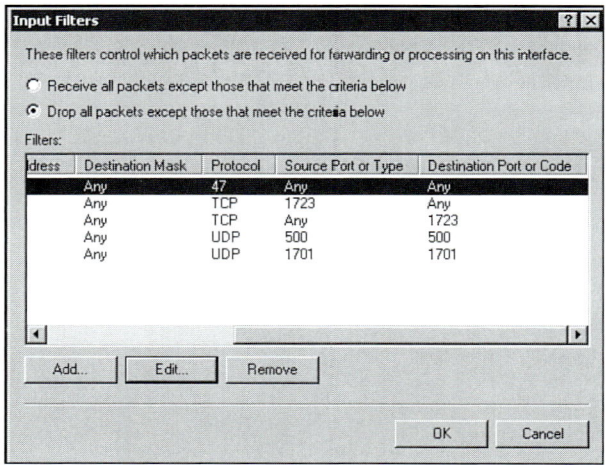

Tip from
RJ

The default Drop All Packets Except Those That Meet the Criteria Below option is the most important setting in the Input and Output Filters dialogs. You can test the filters by temporarily selecting the Receive All Packets Except Those That Meet the Criteria option and attempting a client PPTP connection. If you selected Automatic in the Networking page of the *VPNConnectionName* Properties dialog, the client attempts to make an L2TP connection and fails with a "missing certificate" message. If you specified Point-to-Point Tunneling Protocol (PPTP), you will receive a "There was no answer" message.

4. Select one of the PPTP filters and click Edit to open the Edit IP Filter dialog, which is empty except for an entry in the Protocol list, Source Port, Destination Port, and—for one PPTP filter—the Protocol Name text box. An empty or 0 field results in the Any entries that appear in the Input Filters dialog. Close the dialog.

5. If you don't intend to set up an L2TP VPN on the server, select each of the UDP protocol entries in the Input Filters list and click Remove. It's good security policy to remove any VPN protocols you don't need.

6. Optionally, repeat steps 3 through 5 for the Output filters.

Initializing RRAS adds a default Remote Access Policy named Allow Access if Dial-in Permission Is Enabled, which grants 7-day, 24-hour access to any user having the permission. If you want to restrict access to members of a particular group and require a particular VPN protocol, you can edit the default policy or add another policy. Local RAS policies apply only when your Windows 2000 domain runs in native mode. For example, you can restrict VPN access to a special Global group, such as VPNUsers. You also can specify the types of tunneling protocols that your server accepts. Specifying particular tunneling protocols in a local RAS policy, however, overlaps the responsibility of filters.

→ To review editing and adding Remote Access Policies, **see** "Setting Local RAS Server Policies," **p. 1038**.

Configuring an L2TP VPN Server

Tip from
RJ

Remember to add the Domain Admins group when specifying the Windows-Group attribute. Members of the Domain Admins group need VPN rights for test and administrative activities.

Configuring an L2TP VPN Server

Setting up an L2TP VPN server is more complex than configuring a PPTP server because of the need to establish Security Associations (SAs) between the VPN server and client computers. An SA is similar to the terms and conditions of a contract; both computers must agree to a set of security parameters, which include the computer's IP address, authentication method, and tunnel type. PPTP depends only on the user's logon credentials; L2TP adds computer authentication for added security. L2TP computer authentication depends on computer certificates. For this reason, L2TP currently is used more commonly for server-to-server VPNs than for client dial-up applications.

Note

The default set of L2TP input and output filters added by the Routing and Remote Access Server Setup Wizard is adequate for conventional dial-up L2TP VPN. You don't need to change the default filter settings.

Providing Servers and Clients with Computer Certificates

Before you implement an L2TP VPN, your network must have an Enterprise Root Certificate Authority (CA) and be set to automatically issue certificates to each computer on the network. If you already have an Enterprise Root CA that issues certificates for the Encrypting File System (EFS) or other secure activities, implementing L2TP is relatively simple. If you don't have an existing Enterprise Root CA, you must install and configure Certificate Services on a DC—preferably a DC serving the VPN server's domain.

Caution

The DC that you choose to make the Enterprise Root CA server can't be demoted to a member server, which means that you can't rename it or change its domain. Make sure that the DC you choose for initial installation of Certificate Server, often the Primary Domain Controller (PDC) Emulator for the domain, is properly configured and fully operational before proceeding. The Enterprise Root CA server's system partition should run on a RAID 1 mirror set to assure continued operation in the event of a disk drive failure.

→ For instructions on how to install and configure an Enterprise Root DC, **see** "Establishing and Managing Certificate Authority Servers," **p. 506**.

When your certificate server is running, you can specify automatic issuance of certificates for computers in the domain. The following example uses the default Microsoft Base Cryptographic Provider and the Secure Hash Algorithm (SHA) 1, with a key length of 1024 bits.

> **Tip from**
> *RJ*
>
> If your Windows 2000 VPN test client isn't connected to the local network, restore the LAN connection before starting the following procedure so the client obtains a certificate during the next logon or policy refresh interval.

To begin issuing computer certificates, do the following:

1. Choose Programs, Administrative Tools, Active Directory Users and Computers to launch the snap-in.
2. Right-click the *DomainName* node, choose Properties to open the *DomainName* Properties dialog, and click the Group Policy tab.
3. Select Default Domain Policy in the Group Policy Object Links list and click Edit to open the Group Policy Editor.
4. Expand the Computer Configuration, Windows Settings, Security Settings, and Public Key Policies nodes, right-click the Automatic Certificate Request Settings node, and choose New to open the Automatic Security Request Setup Wizard. Click OK to bypass the Welcome dialog.
5. In the Certificate Template dialog's list, select Computer (see Figure 26.21). Click Next.

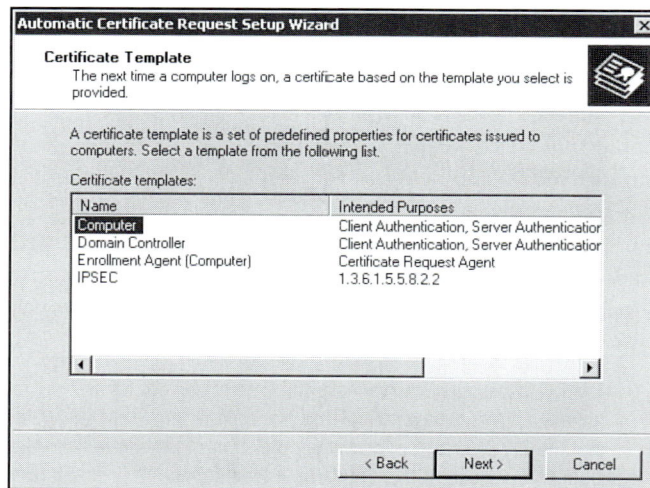

Figure 26.21
The Automatic Certificate Request Setup Wizard's Certificate Template dialog allows you to choose from several templates. The Computer template is used to issue certificates for L2TP.

6. In the Certification Authority dialog, select the CA to issue the machine certificates—usually the Enterprise CA (see Figure 26.22).

Figure 26.22
If you have more than one certificate authority, you can select the appropriate authority from the list. Smaller organizations usually have only an Enterprise Root CA.

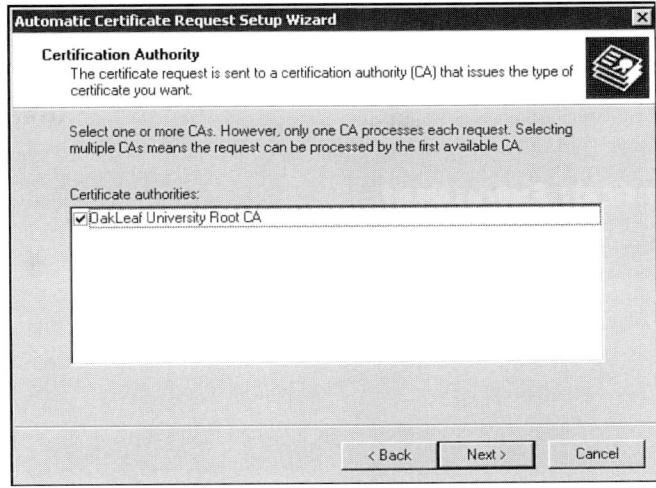

7. Click Next to review your selections, and then click Finish to dismiss the Wizard and add a Computer item to the Automatic Certificate Request list.
8. To verify the certificate, right-click the Computer item in the list and choose Properties to open the Computer Properties dialog (see Figure 26.23).

Figure 26.23
The Automatic Certificate Request node displays a list of templates for auto-enrolling computers. The Computer Properties dialog displays the certificate type, purpose, and name of the CA.

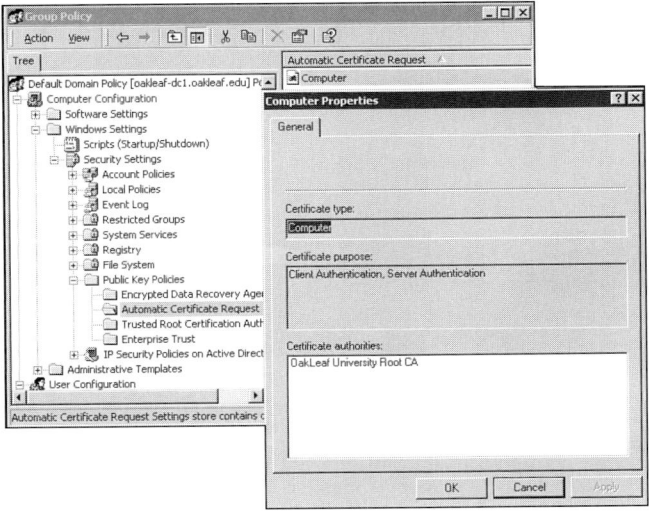

9. Click OK to close the dialog, close the Group Policy Editor, and click OK to close the *DomainName* Properties dialog.
10. Install a certificate on each server you don't want to reboot by opening the Command Prompt and typing **secedit /refreshpolicy machine_policy**. Otherwise, the CA server

issues a computer certificate at the Group Policy refresh interval or the next time each computer in the domain logs on to the network.

11. Log on to the LAN with the test client to obtain a certificate for use with the L2TP connection, and then disconnect the client from the LAN to verify L2TP connectivity.

Verifying Certificate Enrollment

To verify certificate enrollment of the Windows 2000 servers and clients on your network, do the following:

1. Choose Start, Run, and type **certsrv.msc** in the Open dialog. Click OK to open the Certificate Authority snap-in.

2. Expand the *RootCAName* node and click Issued Certificates to display a list of the computer certificates for enrolled computers on the LAN.

Tip from
RJ

To revoke an issued certificate, right-click the certificate in the list, choose Revoke, and confirm the revocation.

---

3. Double-click one of the entries in the list to open the Certificate properties dialog, and click the Details tab to display the full set of certificate properties (see Figure 26.24).

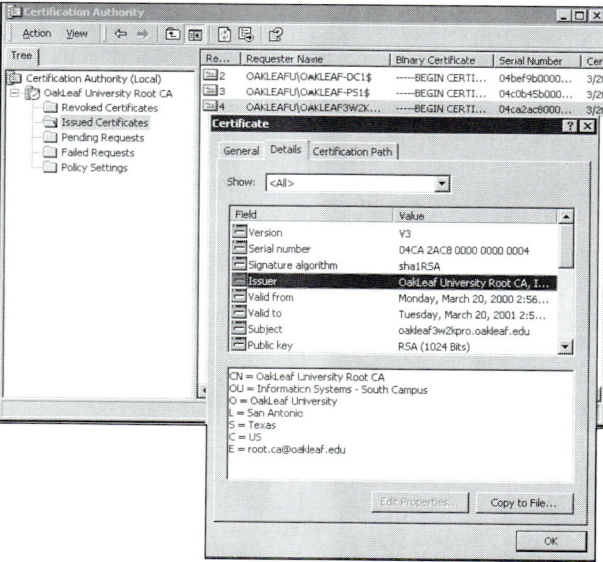

Figure 26.24
The Certificate properties dialog displays detailed information on each computer certificate issued by Windows 2000's Certificate Services.

4. If you want to save a copy of the certificate in one of the standard X.509 or other common formats, click Copy to File to start the Certificate Export Wizard. Follow the Wizard's instructions to create a .cer or .p7b file for the certificate.

TROUBLESHOOTING 1101

Requiring client certificates complicates provision of L2TP dial-up VPN services, but the added security provided by the L2TP over the IPSec tunnel compensates for the added setup effort. There's no significant performance difference between PPTP and L2TP. If you decided to standardize on L2TP VPNs for Windows 2000 clients, consider providing the PPTP service as a backup.

Tip from
RJ

If you have mobile users who can't physically connect to the LAN or connect via PPTP to receive their certificates, export a .cer file for each such user's computer to a disk. Mail the disk to the user and include instructions for importing a certificate. In Windows 2000 Professional's online help, search for "certificate" in the index to obtain the details for importing a certificate with the Import Certificate Wizard.

TESTING A WINDOWS 2000 VPN CLIENT

After the client obtains a valid computer certificate, setting up a dial-up L2TP connection on the client is quite similar to the process for setting up a dial-up PPTP connection. To test a Windows 2000 Professional client's L2TP VPN connectivity, do the following:

1. Follow steps 1 through 9 of the "Setting Up and Testing the VPN Connection" section earlier in this chapter. Use the dial-up connection to the ISP you created for the PPTP VPN for the L2TP connection.

2. In step 10, click the Networking tab, select Layer-2 Tunneling Protocol (L2TP) in the Type of VPN Server I Am Calling list, and clear the File and Printer Sharing for Microsoft Networks check box.

3. Continue with steps 11 and 12.

4. Verify the ability of the client to log on the network by following the procedure described in the earlier section "Testing Domain Logon with the VPN Connection," but using your new L2TP connection.

5. If you want to use less-secure PPTP as a backup VPN protocol, right-click your L2TP connection, choose Properties, click the Networking tab, Select Automatic in the Type of VPN Server I Am Calling list, click OK, and repeat step 4.

L2TP is the default protocol when you specify Automatic as the VPN server type. If the client can't connect with L2TP, a second attempt is made with PPTP.

 If you encounter a problem establishing the client's L2TP tunnel, see the "Windows 2000 L2TP Connection Problems" topic in the next section.

TROUBLESHOOTING

WINDOWS 2000 PPTP CONNECTION PROBLEMS

The client connects to the Internet, but fails to authenticate with the VPN server with a "no certificate" message.

The most probable cause of this problem is that the client has specified L2TP as the VPN protocol in the Networking page of the connection properties dialog, and you haven't configured L2TP on the VPN server. Occasionally, using the Automatic setting also fails. If you support only PPTP, clients should specify Point to Point Tunneling Protocol (PPTP) in the Type of VPN Server I Am Calling list.

WINDOWS 9X PPTP CONNECTION PROBLEMS

When you attempt to open a VPN connection to the server, the following error message occurs: "The Microsoft Dial Up adapter is in use or not responding properly. Disconnect other connections and then try again. If this problem persists, shut down and restart your computer. Error 645."

The most common cause of this message is a missing Dial-Up Adapter #2 (VPN Support) component in the installed components list of the Configuration page of the Network properties dialog. If the Dial-Up Adapter #2 component is missing, you must remove and reinstall Virtual Private Networking. To add the missing component to a Windows 98 computer, do the following:

1. Launch Control Panels' Add/Remove Programs tool to open the Add/Remove Programs Properties dialog.
2. Click the Windows Components tab, select Communications in the Components list, and click Details to open the Communications dialog.
3. Clear the Virtual Private Networking check box at the bottom of the Components list, click OK twice to close the two dialogs, and reboot your computer when requested.
4. Repeat steps 1 through 3, but mark the Virtual Private Networking check box to reinstall the components. You must have the Windows 98 distribution CD-ROM or a connection to a network share with the setup files to add the required components.
5. Verify that Dial-Up Adapter #2 (VPN Support) appears in the components list of the Configuration page of the Network properties dialog.

For clients running Windows 95, remove and reinstall the Dial-Up Networking 1.3 Upgrade.

An "Access Denied" error message appears when attempting to open a VPN connection to the domain.

This error occurs if you must specify a domain name to open a DUN connection to your ISP. Windows 9x VPN supports only a single domain name entry. Few ISPs require a domain name for logon, so this problem occurs infrequently. To get around this problem, open Control Panel's Network tool and change the client's Primary Network Logon setting to Windows Logon, and then make the VPN connection.

WINDOWS 2000 L2TP CONNECTION PROBLEMS

The client connects to the ISP, but receives a "no certificate" message when attempting to create the L2TP tunnel.

The client hasn't received its certificate or its certificate has expired or been revoked. Verify in the Certificate Authority snap-in that the client has obtained a certificate. If no certified clients can connect with the L2TP server, you have a problem with the server certificate.

MCSE Corner: Setting Up a Virtual Private Network

There are four exams that cover the Windows 2000 VPN features: 70-215, "Installing, Configuring, and Administering Microsoft Windows 2000 Server"; 70-216, "Implementing and Administering a Microsoft Windows 2000 Network Infrastructure"; 70-220, "Designing Security for a Microsoft Windows 2000 Network"; and 70-221, "Designing a Microsoft Windows 2000 Network Infrastructure."

70-215 Installing, Configuring, and Administering Microsoft Windows 2000 Server

For exam 70-215, you should be able to install, configure, and troubleshoot a VPN server under Windows 2000. Important concepts to be familiar with are the basics of VPNs—such as how tunneling works—the protocols that are involved (PPTP and L2TP over IPSec), and what VPN protocols supply (Authentication, Addressing, Encryption, Key Management). You should know the steps to installing the software to create a functional VPN and configuring the VPN to allow connections. You should also know the steps to troubleshooting the different kinds of connections.

70-216 Implementing and Administering a Microsoft Windows 2000 Network Infrastructure

For exam 70-216, as with 70-215, you need to be able to configure an L2TP over IPSec VPN on a Windows 2000 Server. This exam is geared toward larger implementations, such as multiple sites with many users, whereas exam 70-215 is based around a single-server implementation. You should have a thorough knowledge of VPN concepts and a good grasp of installing and configuring VPNs, including automatic enrollment for client and server computer certificates.

70-220 Designing Security for a Microsoft Windows 2000 Network

The important skill for exam 70-220 is to be able to know when a VPN is the best method of forming a network connection in terms of security. You should be able to take an environment, assess the parameters of that environment—such as the number of users, number of offices, and so forth—and be able to provide secure remote access solutions, using VPNs when necessary. You also need to be able to design security for those remote access solutions, so you should understand authentication and encryption as they relate to VPNs.

70-221   Designing a Microsoft Windows 2000 Network Infrastructure

For exam 70-221, understand where it is best to use a VPN solution and how a VPN is best implemented. You should be able to take factors, such as the number of users in an organization and how they are distributed, into account and use that information to come up with the most efficient design to provide the required services. The exam will most likely present you with a hypothetical environment to analyze and require you to answer questions based on that analysis. A general technical overview of the service provided by a VPN is important to this exam.

CHAPTER 27

ADMINISTERING INTERNET INFORMATION SERVER 5.0

In this chapter

Assessing the Role of Internet Information Server 5.0   1106

Upgrading to or Installing IIS 5.0   1106

Adding a Test Web Site as a Virtual Directory   1115

Assigning a Conventional URL to the Default Web Site   1118

Adding a New Virtual Site with a Host Header Record   1119

Reading Web Server Log Files   1123

Setting Up the Default FTP Site   1125

Adding a Newsgroup to the Default NNTP Virtual Server   1128

Configuring the Default SMTP Virtual Server   1133

Troubleshooting   1134

MCSE Corner: Administering Internet Information Server 5.0   1136

Assessing the Role of Internet Information Server 5.0

Internet Information Server (IIS) 4.0, included with the Windows NT 4.0 Option Pack, has proven itself as a reliable and scalable World Wide Web and File Transfer Protocol (FTP) server. In a continuing effort to increase IIS's share of the Web server business, Microsoft added a multitude of new features to successive versions of IIS. The following list describes IIS 5.0's primary services and their most important new features:

- World Wide Web (HTTP) service for intranets and the Internet—IIS 5.0 adds Web Distributed Authoring and Versioning (WebDAV) and Web folders for collaborative generation and editing of documents stored on a Web server. IIS 5.0 simplifies the creation of multiple Web sites—called *virtual sites*—on a single server. IIS 5.0 also supports the eXtensible Markup Language (XML), which promises to become the foundation for business-to-business (B2B) e-commerce and other data-intensive Web operations.

- FTP service for delivering files to clients—IIS 5.0 adds *FTP restart* to enable a client that loses its connection when downloading a file to reconnect and resume transfer of only the missing part of the file.

- Network News Transfer Protocol (NNTP) service for establishing Usenet-like newsgroups—A newsgroup is a database containing user-contributed messages concerning a specified topic. Message threads organize individual contributions into a hierarchy of initial postings of subtopic messages and replies from users. Clients need a newsreader—such as Microsoft Outlook or Outlook Express—to read NNTP content.

- Simple Mail Transfer Protocol (SMTP) service for handling outbound email—IIS 5.0's implementation of SMTP is intended primarily for delivering email messages generated by Web-based forms. IIS 5.0 doesn't include a Post Office Protocol 3 (POP3) or Internet Mail Access Protocol (IMAP) server for storing and delivering inbound mail, so IIS 5.0 doesn't qualify as a full-fledged email server.

→ For more detailed descriptions of the new features of IIS 5.0, **see** "Internet Information Server 5.0," **p. 44**.

IIS 5.0 delivers all the functions needed to establish a high-performance Web-based intranet for organizations ranging in size from small companies to multinational corporations with hundreds of thousands of employees and business-partner users. IIS 5.0 also is suited for running public Web sites on the Internet, but this chapter concentrates on the administration of IIS 5.0 in a private intranet scenario.

Upgrading to or Installing IIS 5.0

You can upgrade your existing Web site to IIS 5.0 without migrating your Windows NT network to Windows 2000 Server, if IIS 3+ runs on a member server. Several market research organizations report that upgrading large intranet Web sites probably will be the primary initial market for Windows 2000 Server and Advanced server. Although IIS 5.0's security system integrates fully with AD, IIS 5.0 also respects Windows NT 4.0's NTLM security.

When you upgrade a Windows NT 4.0 server running IIS 4.0 or earlier to Windows 2000, Setup automatically updates existing Web and other IIS 4.0 services to IIS 5.0. The upgrade process is transparent; the only change you're likely to notice is a 20%-or-better increase in performance on sites with heavy traffic. Setup automatically adds the SMTP service to the server, unless you specify otherwise. If you want to add Windows 2000 Server's NNTP service, after upgrading use the Add/Remove Windows Components feature of Control Panel's Add/Remove Software tool to install NNTP, as described in the next section.

Tip from
RJ

If your existing Web server has less than 128MB of RAM, you might observe a slowdown in site performance, especially when clients initially connect to the site. 256MB of RAM is a good starting point for a production Web server with more than 50 simultaneous users.

If you don't intend to use FTP and SMTP services, remove them with the Add/Remove Windows Components tool. FTP and SMTP services don't consume much disk space or server resources, but running services you don't need isn't a good administrative practice.

INSTALLING OR MODIFYING THE INSTALLATION OF IIS 5.0

Running a clean installation of Windows 2000 Server or Advanced Server automatically installs the Web, FTP, and SMTP services. Installing NNTP is an option you can select during Setup's network installation phase; you also can prevent installation of any or all default IIS 5.0 services during the initial setup operation.

Tip from
RJ

Unless you have only two Windows 2000 servers, which act as primary and backup domain controllers (DCs), install IIS 5.0's Web, FTP, and other services on a member server. The Active Directory (AD) running on DCs consumes a substantial amount of server resources that otherwise could be devoted to IIS 5.0. The same advice applies to other applications, such as SQL Server and Exchange Server, that have substantial server resource requirements and heavy network traffic.

 For a detailed description of a clean Windows 2000 server installation, **see** "Installing Windows 2000 on a New Server," **p. 384**.

If you didn't install IIS 5.0 during server setup or need to add a missing IIS service, do the following:

1. Launch Control Panels' Add/Remove Programs tool, and click the Add/Remove Windows Components button to open the Windows Components Wizard's dialog.

2. Select Internet Information Services (IIS) in the Components list, and click Details to open the Internet Information Services (IIS) dialog.

3. In the Subcomponents of Internet Information Services (IIS) list, mark or clear the check boxes of the services and features you want to install or remove, respectively (see Figure 27.1). Click OK to begin installing or removing the components.

Figure 27.1
Add or remove IIS 5.0 features or services in the Windows Components Wizard's Subcomponents of Internet Information Services (IIS) dialog.

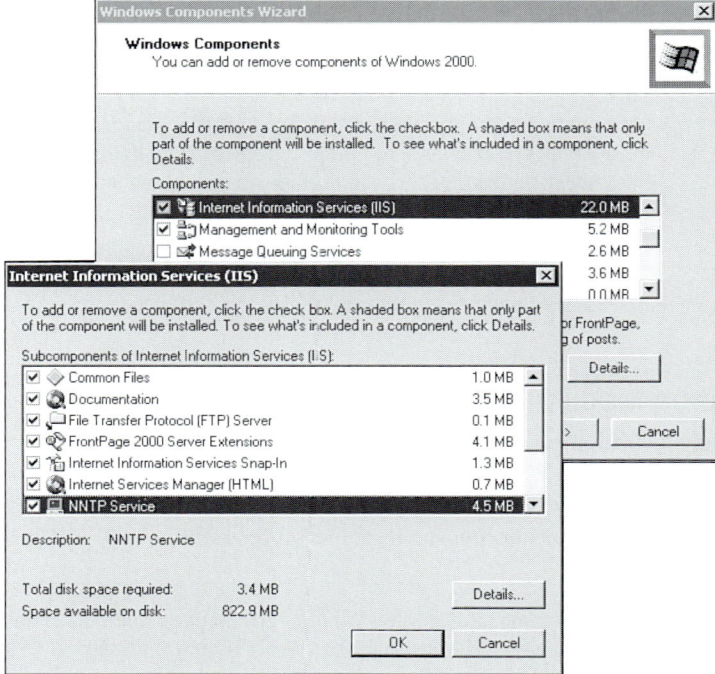

4. If you added a service in the preceding step, insert the Windows 2000 Server distribution CD-ROM or connect to a network share with the installation files when requested.
5. Click Finish when installation completes and close the Wizard dialogs.

Reviewing the Default IIS 5.0 Installation

Installing IIS 5.0 adds the Internet Information Services snap-in (`iis.msc` in `\Winnt\System32\Inetsrv`) and a Web-based administrative tool (in `\Winnt\System32\Inetsrv\Iisadmin`). To open the IIS snap-in, choose Programs, Administrative Tools, Internet Services Manager. Expand the Default Web Site node to display the entire site structure in the tree-view pane, including the NNTP and SMTP virtual servers used in later examples of this chapter, and some of the files that IIS 5.0 setup installs in the list pane (see Figure 27.2).

Figure 27.2
The Default Web Site node contains a standard set of folders and files on which you can base a new Web site.

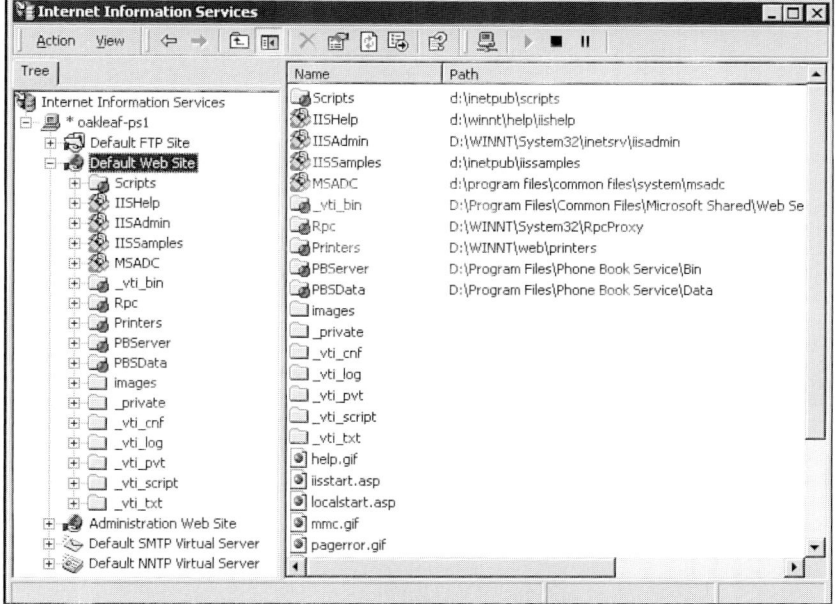

Following are brief descriptions of the important folders and files of the Default Web Site:

- Scripts holds Common Gateway Interface (CGI) and other scripts that aren't embedded as JScript or VBScript in ASP files. The default Scripts folder is empty.

- IISHelp, IISAdmin, IISamples, and MSDAC are virtual directories with pointers to help files for IIS 5.0, the Web-based administration application, some sample scripts, and the Microsoft Data Access Components, respectively. Only the IISHelp and IISAdmin virtual directories have readable content.

- _vti, _bin, _private, and all other folders with the _vti prefix are added by the FrontPage Extensions for IIS 5.0. The _vti prefix is an abbreviation for Vermeer Technologies, Inc., a firm that Microsoft acquired to obtain the original technology for the FrontPage Web site design application.

- Rpc, Printers, PBServer, and PBSData are folders for the Remote Procedure Call (RPC) proxy, Web-based printing, and the Phone Book services of the Connection Manager Administration Kit (CMAK), respectively.

- images is an empty folder for storing commonly used .gif and .jpg images that you don't include in content-related subfolders.

Sections later in the chapter cover Default FTP Site, Administrative Web Site, Default SMTP Virtual Server, and Default NNTP Virtual Server.

Setting Master IIS Properties

Each virtual Web site and virtual directory on the server inherits property values from the values you set in the *ServerName* Properties dialog and its child dialogs. To establish baseline properties for all Web sites on your server, do the following:

1. Right-click the * *ServerName* node, and choose Properties to open the default Internet Information Services page of the * *ServerName* Properties dialog. You can restrict the maximum network bandwidth devoted to IIS by marking the Enable Bandwidth Throttling check box and typing the maximum data rate of IIS in kbps in the Maximum Network Use text box. For a 100BASE-T network, start with values between 5,000kbps and 10,000Kbps.

> **Note**
> You also can change or add associations between registered Multipurpose Internet Mail Extensions (MIME) types and file extensions by clicking the Edit button of the Computer MIME Map to open the File Types dialog. Windows 2000 has the latest version of registered file types, so you probably won't need to edit or add to the existing list.

2. With WWW Service selected in the Master Properties list, click Edit to open the WWW Service Master Properties for *ServerName* dialog.

3. If you want to limit the maximum number of simultaneous connections, select the Limited To option and type the number of connections in the text box. You also can lower the Connection Timeout value, which defaults to 900 seconds. When you restrict the number of connections, 300 seconds or less is a more appropriate timeout.

4. Clear the HTTP Keep-Alives Enabled setting if you want clients to reconnect to the server each time they open a new page.

> **Tip from**
> *RJ*
> If your site has only a few hundred users or you have a high-performance Web server, accept the default HTTP Keep-Alives Enabled setting to improve users' browsing experience. HTTP Keep-Alives decrease server performance by maintaining all client connections for the Connection Timeout duration you specified in step 2.

5. Accept the default Enable Logging choice if you want to track usage of the entire site; otherwise, clear the check box. The Active Log Format list's default W3C Extended Log Format is the most common choice (see Figure 27.3). Click Properties to set the log time period—the default is daily—and the fields to include or omit from the log files.

Figure 27.3
You can limit the number of simultaneous connections, change connection timeouts, disable persistent Web server connections, and alter default logging properties in the Web Site page of the Master Properties dialog.

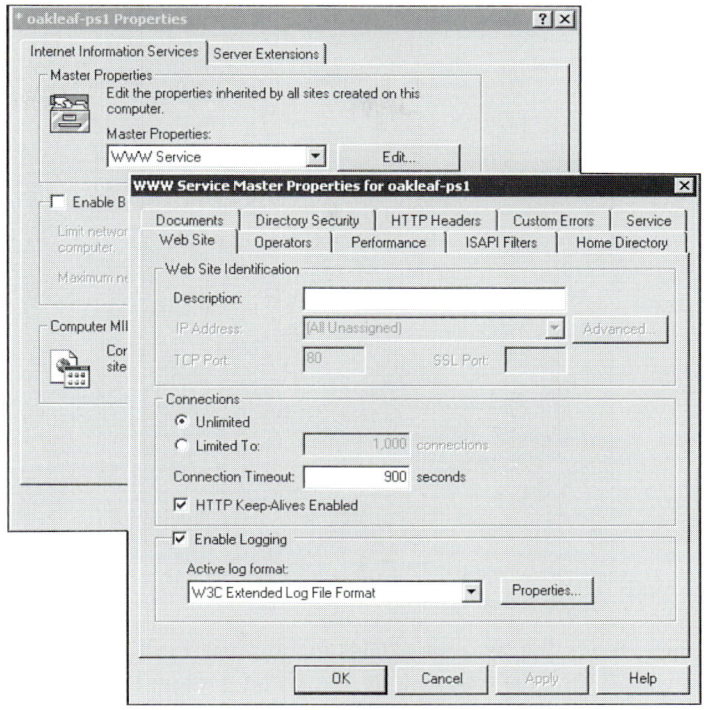

6. Click the Operators tab, and click Add to open the Select Users and Groups dialog to add administrative accounts from your domain to the Web site operators group.

7. Select or type the names of groups you want to have Operators privileges for the Web server, and click Check Names to verify your typing or selections. Click OK to close the dialog and add the groups to the Operators list.

Tip from
RJ

Adding Enterprise Admins and Domain Admins to the Operators group is an important step when you run IIS 5.0 on a member server. Member servers have only local security groups by default. Alternatively, you can add Enterprise Admins and Domain Admins to the local Administrators group.

---

8. Click the Performance tab and set the Performance Tuning Slider to the maximum number of hits (page views) you expect your production site to receive, if you cleared the HTTP Keep-Alives Enabled check box in step 4. Otherwise, set the Slider to the maximum number of daily connections.

9. If your site runs out-of-process applications, such as CGI scripts, leave the Enable Process Throttling check box marked, and change the default Maximum CPU Use value, if necessary (see Figure 27.4). If you don't mark the Enforce Limits check box, exceeding the Maximum CPU Use value only adds an event to the log.

Figure 27.4
Set the Performance Tuning slider to the estimated number of hits (page views) or connections per day you expect your server to support. You also can restrict the percentage of CPU resources devoted to out-of-process applications.

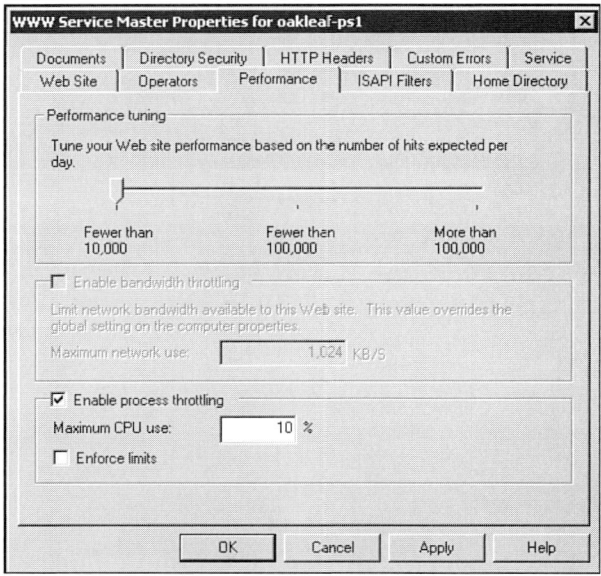

10. To increase the default security level for all sites, click the Directory Security tab, and then click Edit in the Anonymous Access and Authentication Protocol frame to open the Authentication Methods dialog.

11. Clear the Anonymous Access check box and accept the default Integrated Windows Authentication option (see Figure 27.5).

Figure 27.5
Clear the Anonymous Access check box; Anonymous Access is appropriate for public Internet sites, but not for private intranets. Integrated Windows Authentication requires all users to be authenticated by a Windows 2000 or NT domain.

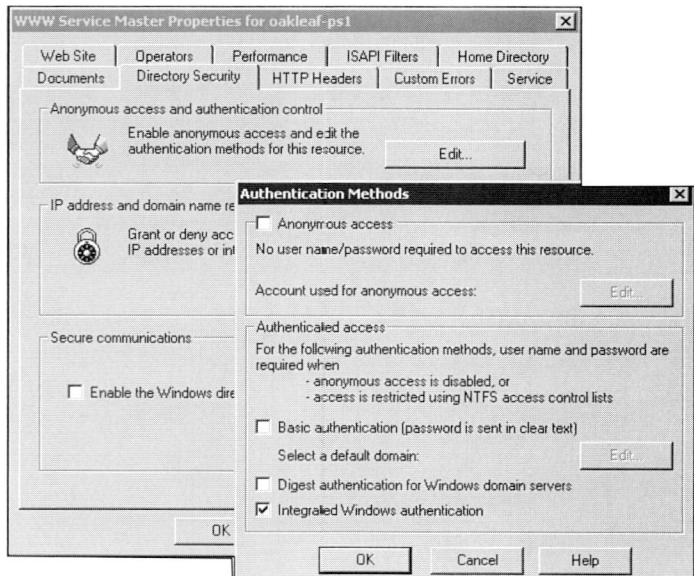

UPGRADING TO OR INSTALLING IIS 5.0 | 1113

12. For better security, limit the IP address of users who can log on to the site by clicking Edit in the IP Address and Domain Name Restrictions frame to open the eponymous dialog. Select the Denied Access option.

13. Click Add to open the Grant Access On dialog, and then mark the Group of Computers option and complete the Network ID and Subnet Mask text boxes for the subnet (see Figure 27.6); click OK to add the network to the Access list of the IP Address and Domain Name Restrictions dialog. Repeat this step for each subnet whose members are allowed access to your Web sites.

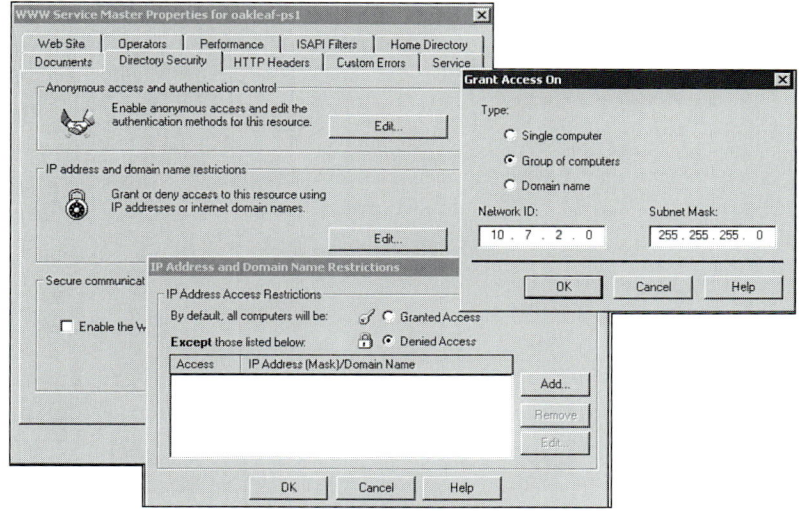

Figure 27.6
Restricting logon to users with computer accounts in specified subnets tightens Web site security.

Tip from
RJ

Don't select the Domain Name option in the Grant Access On dialog. Specifying the domain name requires a reverse lookup operation on the domain's DNS server each time a user connects. Reverse DNS lookups are slower than forward lookups and require a significant amount of DC resources.

14. Click OK to close the IP Address and Domain Name Restrictions dialog, and click OK again to close the WWW Service Master Properties for *ServerName* dialog and save your changes.

15. If the changes you made in the preceding steps conflict with existing settings for virtual sites or directories, the Inheritance Overrides dialog opens. To apply the new settings to all subordinate sites and directories, called *child nodes*, click Select All (see Figure 27.7); click OK.

PART
IV
CH
27

Figure 27.7
Click Select All to apply changes you make at the Service Master level to the current properties of lower-level sites and directories.

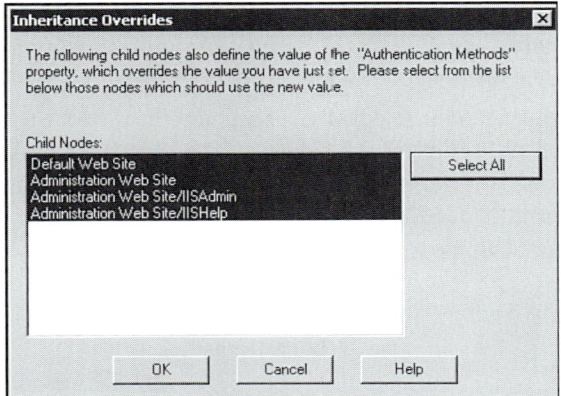

You can override the changes you make in the pages of the WWW Service Master Properties for *ServerName* dialog in similar properties dialogs for child nodes. Properties dialog pages that aren't covered in the preceding steps are discussed in sections later in this chapter.

Connecting to IIS 5.0 from Client Browsers

After you've set default server properties for the Web site, verify the settings from any client on a listed subnet running Internet Explorer (IE) 4.0 or later. Follow these steps to perform an initial Web site test and confirm that only members of the Operators group can administer the site with the Web-based administrative tool:

1. Log on to the client with an administrative account in your domain, launch IE on the client, type the Web server name in the address bar, and press Enter to open the Default Web Site's "Under Construction" page. IE automatically adds the http:// prefix and / suffix to the address for you.

> **Note**
> The Iisstart.asp file generates the "Under Construction" page. Iisstart.asp is one of the default page names specified in the Documents page of the properties dialog for most default virtual sites and directories.

2. Add an **IISHelp/** suffix to the server address to open the default page of the online help for IIS 5.0. Expand the nodes of the Contents frame to display the individual help pages.

3. Replace the IISHelp/ suffix with **IISAdmin/** to open the Web-based administrative tool for IIS 5.0. Click OK to acknowledge the warning that the administrative connection to the server isn't secure. Figure 27.8 shows the opening page of the Web-based tool. This page displays only the virtual folders for the Default Web Site, which include an entry for a Web-shared printer (BrotherLaser).

Figure 27.8
The Web-based IIS 5.0 administrative tool's default page lists only virtual folders and Web-shared printers.

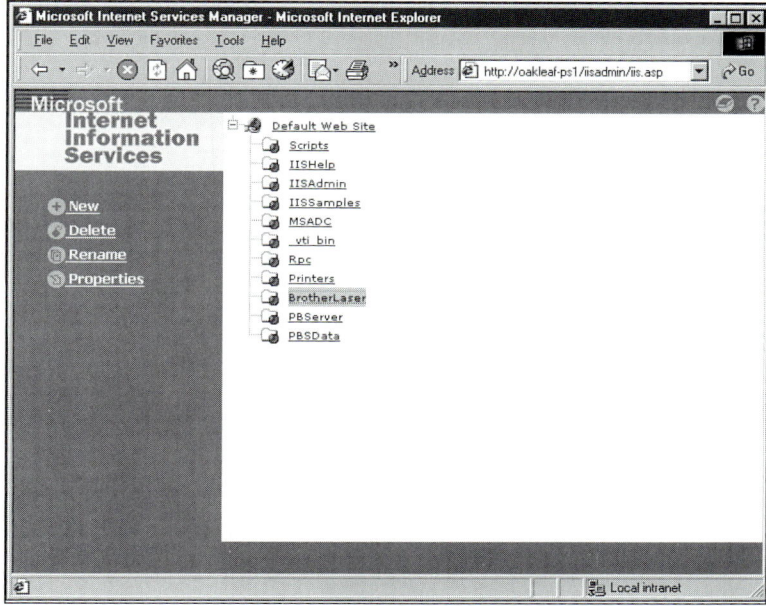

Tip from	
RJ	Use the Internet Information Services snap-in for Web site management whenever possible. IIS 4.0's Web-based administrative tool menu choice is missing from Windows 2000's Programs\Administrative Tools menu (with good reason). The snap-in and its properties dialogs are much more detailed and accessible than the Web-based tool's graphically challenged HTML equivalents.

4. Log off the client and log on with a Domain User account to test security of the IISAdmin virtual directory. Launch IE and type `http://servername/iisadmin/` in the address bar. After a few seconds, an Enter Network Password dialog opens, demonstrating that only members of the Operators group—local Administrators, Enterprise Admins, and Domain Admins for this example—can access the Web-based administrative tool.

Optionally, perform additional tests to check Web site security, such as attempting to log on from a client on another subnet that isn't listed in the Domain Names.

 If clients encounter problems connecting to the network Web site, see the "Web Server Problems" topic of the "Troubleshooting" section at the end of the chapter.

ADDING A TEST WEB SITE AS A VIRTUAL DIRECTORY

If you have existing Web content, you can test the performance of IIS 5.0 by adding to the default Web site a virtual directory that points to the source files for the existing site. You don't need a production site for the test; for instance, you can use the staging files for a public site. The following example uses the local (staging) copy of the FrontPage 98 files for the public `oakmusic.com` site that's hosted by OakLeaf Music's ISP.

> **Tip from**
> *RJ*
>
> If you don't have existing HTML content to use in this example, but you have Microsoft Word or another application that can save documents in HTML format, create a new folder and save an HTML file as `Default.htm` in the folder.

To add a test site to the default Web site, do the following:

1. In the Internet Information Services snap-in, right-click the Default Web Site node, and choose New, Virtual Directory to open the Virtual Directory Creation Wizard. Click Next to bypass the Welcome dialog.

2. In the Virtual Directory Alias dialog, type a descriptive name—**OakMusic** for this example—in the text box, and click Next.

3. In the Web Site Content Directory dialog, click Browse and navigate the network to the folder that contains the content for the virtual directory (see Figure 27.9). Click OK to add the path to the Directory text box, and click Next.

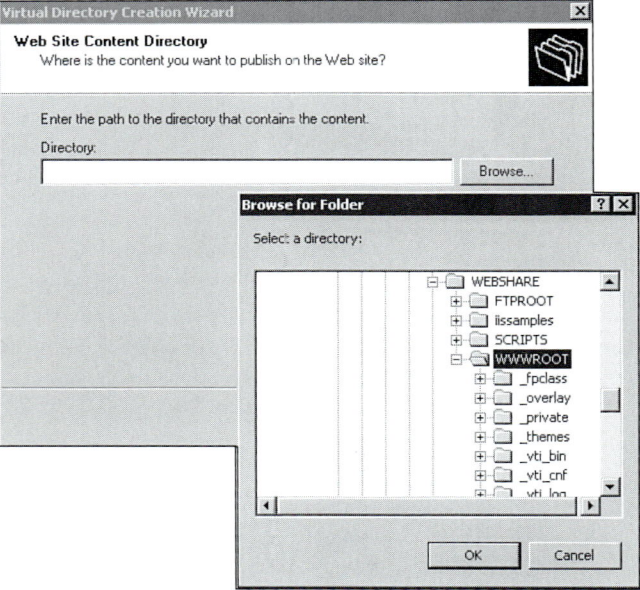

Figure 27.9
Browse the network for the folder that contains the content and related files for the new virtual directory.

4. In the User Name and Password, browse for or type (in **DOMAIN*UserName*** format) your administrative user account in the User Name text box and add your password. Click Next to open the Confirm Password dialog, type your password again, and click OK.

Adding a Test Web Site as a Virtual Directory 1117

Tip from
Don't type your user principal name (`UserName@domain.ext`) in the User Name text box. Substituting a UPN for the downlevel user name syntax results in an error when you complete the Wizard and add the virtual directory to the Default Web site.

5. In the Access Permission dialog, accept the default Read and Run Scripts (such as ASP) options, unless you need to grant users permission to execute Internet Service API (ISAPI) applications or CGI scripts for the site. Click Next and then Finish to dismiss the Wizard and add the new virtual directory to the Default Web Site (see Figure 27.10).

Figure 27.10
The Internet Information Services snap-in displays the new virtual directory and its subfolders.

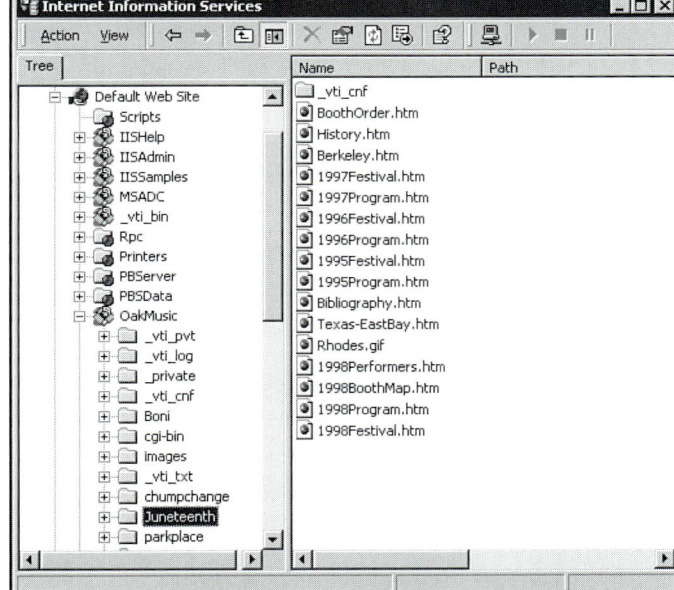

6. Launch IE on a test client, type `http://servername/alias/` in the address bar, and verify that you can navigate the added virtual directory.

Tip from
Relax the security restrictions in the Directory Security page of the *DirectoryName* Properties dialog when you publish a set of public Web pages on your intranet site. Anonymous logon and granting access to all computers is appropriate for public pages. The security settings you make at the directory level override the settings in the Master Properties dialog.

PART
IV
CH
27

Assigning a Conventional URL to the Default Web Site

You can instruct users to type **http://***servername* to open the default document of the Web site, but most folks expect to use conventional URLs, such as **http://www.***whatever***.com**, to access sites. To conform the address of your intranet site to the Internet URL standard, you need to add a DNS forward lookup entry for the site.

→ For the basics of DNS forward lookup zones, **see** "Taking Advantage of Windows 2000 Server's DNS Service," **p. 82**.

To specify an Internet URL for an intranet site, using the Default Web Site as an example, do the following:

1. On the primary DNS server for your network, launch the DNS snap-in, right-click the Forward Lookup Zones node; choose New Zone to open the New Zone Wizard, and click Next to bypass the Welcome dialog.

2. In the Zone Type dialog, accept the default Standard Primary option, because this is a temporary DNS entry that you delete after completion of the test. Click Next.

3. In the Zone Name dialog, type the URL for the Default Web Site; **www.oakmusic.com** is used for this example. Click Next.

4. In the Zone File dialog, accept the defaults to create a new zone file named by appending **.dns** to the URL. Click Next and Finish to add the zone and dismiss the Wizard.

5. Right-click your new forward lookup zone entry, and choose New Alias to open the New Resource Record dialog for an Alias (CNAME) record.

6. Type the fully qualified domain name of the Web server in the text box—**oakleaf-ps1.oakleaf.edu** for this example (see Figure 27.11). Alternatively, click Browse to open the Browse dialog, double-click the first entry in the browse list until the list of hosts appears, select your Web server, and click OK.

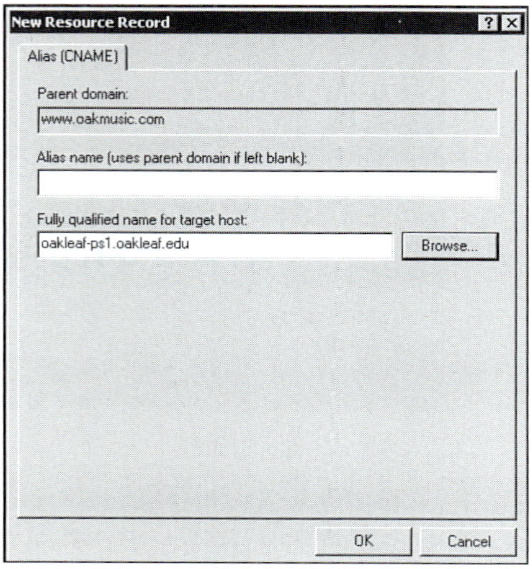

Figure 27.11
Create an Alias (CNAME) record for the Web server in the new forward lookup zone named by the site's URL.

7. Click OK to close the New Resource Record dialog and add the Alias to the site's forward lookup zone (see Figure 27.12).

Figure 27.12
The Web site's forward lookup zone has Start of Authority (SOA), Name Server (NS), and Alias (CNAME) records.

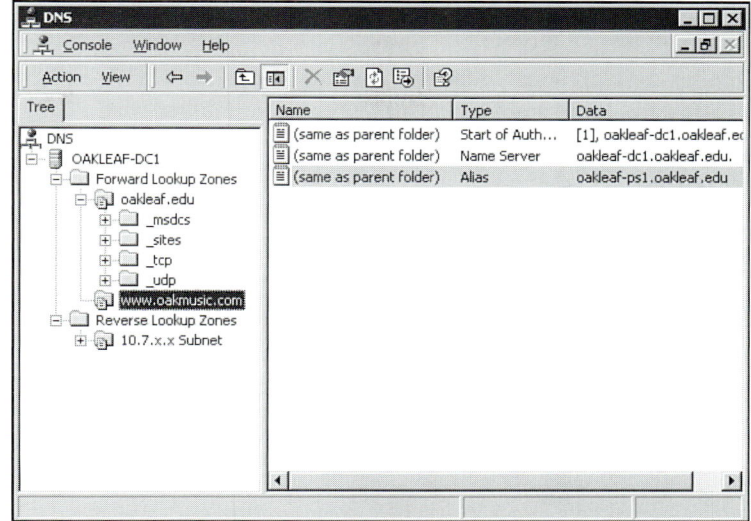

8. On a test client, log in with a domain user account, launch IE, and type the URL for the Default Web Site in the Address bar. The site is secure, so the Enter Network Password Dialog opens.

9. Type the logon ID, password, and domain name of the user; mark the Save This Password in Your Password List check box, and click OK to open the site's default document.

> **Note**
> The Enter Network Password dialog opens for a secure Web site when users connect by a DNS Alias record, because the Web server doesn't authenticate the user when establishing the connection. When you use the `http://servername` address, the server authenticates the user prior to making the connection. If you permit anonymous logon to the site, the Enter Network Password dialog doesn't appear.

Adding a New Virtual Site with a Host Header Record

As mentioned at the beginning of the chapter, IIS 5.0 supports multiple virtual sites on the same server. Connecting to the Default Web Site is straightforward, but connecting to a second (or third) site on the server requires a method by which the user can specify the desired site in his or her browser. Following are your alternatives for specifying a site based on the URL that the user types:

- Multiple server IP addresses—You can install additional network adapters with individual IP addresses or assign multiple IP addresses to a single network adapter. In this case, you must add a DNS forward lookup zone and a Host record—not an Alias (CNAME) record—with the adapter's IP address for each site's URL. When you create the new site, you specify the site's IP address during the virtual site setup process.

- Different TCP port numbers—The default port for HTTP is 80; you can specify different sites by assigning them a different port number, such as 8001. Users must append the port number after the URL for the default Web site, as in http://www.oakmusic.com:8001. You add a DNS forward lookup zone and Alias (CNAME) record, and specify the port number during the setup process. Most users are likely to forget to add the colon (:) and port number.

→ To review how TCP ports work, **see** "TCP Ports and Processes," **p. 87**.

- Host Header Records—A host header record—also called a *host header name*—delivers the host name of the desired Web site in the HTTP header the browser sends to the Web server. Current versions of all commercial browsers support host headers. IIS 5.0 looks up the host name in a local list of host header records and directs the request to the virtual site with the requested name. You add a DNS forward lookup zone and Alias (CNAME) record, and add the host header name when you define the new site.

Until the advent of host header records, multiple IP addresses were the most common method of directing users to one of several sites hosted on the same Web server. Prior to IIS 5.0, using host header records involved a rather complex process, but many commercial Web sites adopted this approach. IIS 5.0 greatly simplifies the use of host header records for multiple virtual sites.

To add a new virtual Web site with a host header record—www.musicvideo.com for this example—from existing HTML content, do the following:

1. On Web server, launch the Internet Information Services snap-in, if necessary; right-click the * *ServerName* node, and choose New, Site to start the Web Site Creation Wizard. Click Next to bypass the Welcome dialog.

2. In the Web Site Description dialog's text box, type a brief description of the site. Click Next.

3. In the IP Address and Port Settings dialog, accept the default (All Unassigned) IP address value and 80 as the TCP port. Type the URL for the new virtual site in the Host Header for This Site text box (see Figure 27.13). Click Next.

ADDING A NEW VIRTUAL SITE WITH A HOST HEADER RECORD | 1121

Figure 27.13
The value of the host header record is the complete URL for the new virtual site.

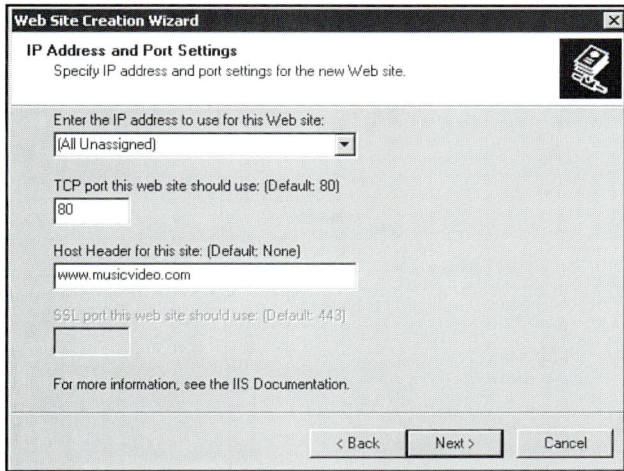

> **Note**
> If you choose the multiple IP address option for multiple virtual sites, you select a preassigned IP address in the Enter the IP Address to Use for This Web Site list. For the different TCP port number option, you designate an unassigned port—usually in the range of 8001 to 65535—in the TCP Port This Web Site Should Use text box.

4. In the Web Site Home Directory dialog, click Browse, and then navigate to and select the folder that contains the content for the new Web site (see Figure 27.14). Click OK to close the Browse dialog and add your selection to the Path text box.

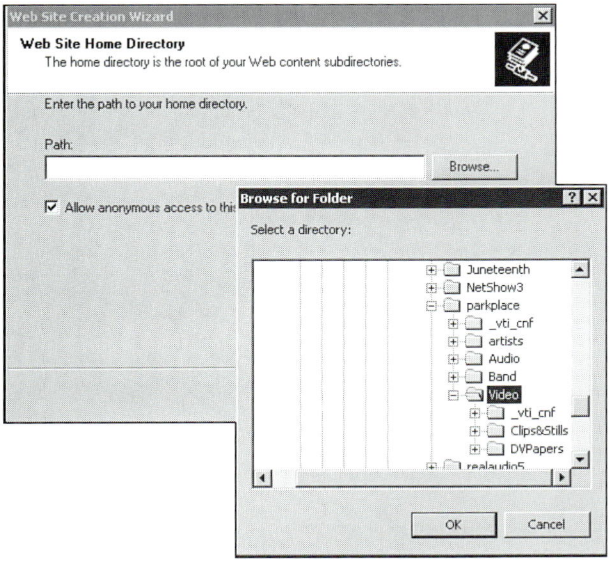

Figure 27.14
Specify the folder that contains the source files for the new virtual Web site.

PART
IV

CH
27

> **Note**
>
> For this example, the content is a deeply nested subfolder (Video) of the FrontPage staging files for the public www.oakmusic.com Web site. Specifying a new virtual site for a particular area of a large intranet Web site is a common practice. You can view the content used for this example by visiting www.oakmusic.com and clicking the Park Place Music Video link.

5. If the new site needs to be secure, clear the Allow Anonymous Access to This Web Site check box; otherwise, accept the default for anonymous access. Click Next.

6. If the Web Site Security Credentials dialog opens, type your administrative logon ID and password. Click Next and confirm the password.

7. In the Web Site Permissions dialog, accept the default Read and Run Scripts options, unless you need to grant users additional permissions.

8. Click Next and Finish to add the new virtual site and dismiss the Wizard. The new site appears, as shown in Figure 27.15.

Figure 27.15
The new Show Me Music Video virtual site contains links to source files that describe the production of a 35mm music video and a documentary about the filming.

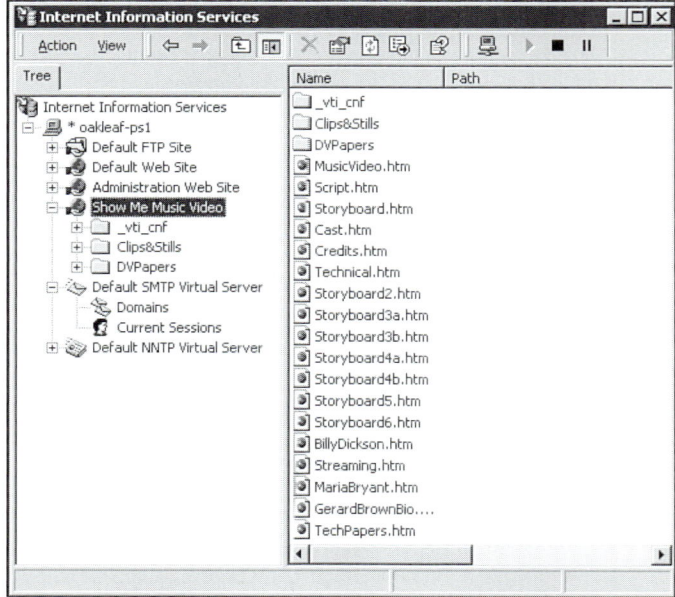

9. Add a DNS forward lookup zone and Alias (CNAME) resource record for the URL you added in step 3, as described in the preceding "Assigning a Conventional URL to the Default Web Site" section.

Reading Web Server Log Files

> **Note**
> If you're using a subsection of an existing site as the source for your new virtual site, the root folder (Video for this example) needs a `Default.htm` or `Default.asp` file that opens when users connect to the virtual site. Alternatively, you can specify the primary navigation page of the subsite (`MusicVideo.htm` for this example) as the default document.

10. To specify a custom default document for a subsite, right-click the new site's node, choose Properties to open the *SiteName* Properties dialog, and click the Documents tab.

11. Click Add to open the New Default Document Dialog, type the name of the custom default document (**MusicVideo.htm**), and click OK to add the entry to the bottom of the list. Select the new entry and click the up-arrow button to move the custom default document to the top of the list. Click OK to close the dialog and add the new default document for the site.

12. At a test client, type the URL you specified in steps 3 and 9 to verify that the host header name works. You specified anonymous access in step 5, so the Enter Network Password dialog doesn't open for this site. If you're using production content, test navigation within the new virtual site.

 If clients display errors when attempting to open the virtual Web site, see the "Web Server Problems" topic of the "Troubleshooting" section at the end of the chapter.

> **Tip from**
> *RJ*
> Images won't appear in pages linked from a subsite if the graphics files are stored in the `...\images` folder of the primary site. The subfolder used to create a virtual site must contain the images or have its own subfolder—Clips&Stills for this example—that contains the required graphics files (refer to Figure 27.15).

Reading Web Server Log Files

Web site activity logging is turned on by default, unless you specifically set logging off in the Master Properties dialog or the properties dialog for a specific site. The default location for Web server log files is `\Winnt\System32\Logfiles\W3C`*n*, where *n* is a sequence number for the server's individual Web sites. The Default Web Site log files are in ...\W3SVC1, the Administrative Web Site logs are in ...\W3SVC2, and the virtual Web sites you add put their logs in ...\W3SVC3 and higher. Individual log files are named ex*YYMMDD*.log, where ex is an abbreviation for (W3C) Extended, *YY* is the last two digits of the year, *MM* is the month, and *DD* is the day the file was created. By default, IE 5.0 creates a new log every day.

→ To change activity logging settings, **see** "Setting Master IIS Properties," **p. 1110**.

To view a log file, navigate to the directory that contains the file(s) in which you're interested. Double-click one of the log files to display its contents in Notepad (see Figure 27.16). The first four lines of the log file have a pound sign (#) as a prefix to indicate that the lines contain comments. The `#Fields` line consists of a space-separated list of the names of the log's fields. The remaining lines in the log consist of space-separated field values; hyphens replace missing values. IIS 5.0 adds an entry for each page viewed by the user and each graphics file opened by the page. A Web site with heavy traffic easily can generate multi-megabyte log files in a few hours.

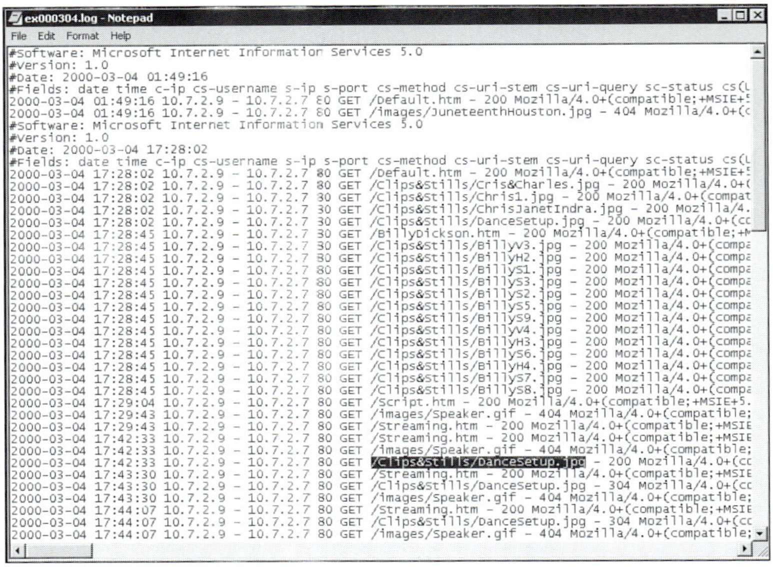

```
ex000304.log - Notepad
File Edit Format Help
#Software: Microsoft Internet Information Services 5.0
#Version: 1.0
#Date: 2000-03-04 01:49:16
#Fields: date time c-ip cs-username s-ip s-port cs-method cs-uri-stem cs-uri-query sc-status cs(U
2000-03-04 01:49:16 10.7.2.9 - 10.7.2.7 80 GET /Default.htm - 200 Mozilla/4.0+(compatible;+MSIE+5
2000-03-04 01:49:16 10.7.2.9 - 10.7.2.7 80 GET /images/JuneteenthHouston.jpg - 404 Mozilla/4.0+(c
#Software: Microsoft Internet Information Services 5.0
#Version: 1.0
#Date: 2000-03-04 17:28:02
#Fields: date time c-ip cs-username s-ip s-port cs-method cs-uri-stem cs-uri-query sc-status cs(U
2000-03-04 17:28:02 10.7.2.9 - 10.7.2.7 80 GET /Default.htm - 200 Mozilla/4.0+(compatible;+MSIE+5
2000-03-04 17:28:02 10.7.2.9 - 10.7.2.7 80 GET /Clips&Stills/Cris&Charles.jpg - 200 Mozilla/4.0+(
2000-03-04 17:28:02 10.7.2.9 - 10.7.2.7 80 GET /Clips&Stills/Chris1.jpg - 200 Mozilla/4.0+(compat
2000-03-04 17:28:02 10.7.2.9 - 10.7.2.7 80 GET /Clips&Stills/ChrisJanetIndra.jpg - 200 Mozilla/4.
2000-03-04 17:28:02 10.7.2.9 - 10.7.2.7 80 GET /Clips&Stills/DanceSetup.jpg - 200 Mozilla/4.0+(cc
2000-03-04 17:28:45 10.7.2.9 - 10.7.2.7 80 GET /BillyDickson.htm - 200 Mozilla/4.0+(compatible;+M
2000-03-04 17:28:45 10.7.2.9 - 10.7.2.7 80 GET /Clips&Stills/BillyV3.jpg - 200 Mozilla/4.0+(compa
2000-03-04 17:28:45 10.7.2.9 - 10.7.2.7 80 GET /Clips&Stills/BillyH2.jpg - 200 Mozilla/4.0+(compa
2000-03-04 17:28:45 10.7.2.9 - 10.7.2.7 80 GET /Clips&Stills/BillyS1.jpg - 200 Mozilla/4.0+(compa
2000-03-04 17:28:45 10.7.2.9 - 10.7.2.7 80 GET /Clips&Stills/BillyS3.jpg - 200 Mozilla/4.0+(compa
2000-03-04 17:28:45 10.7.2.9 - 10.7.2.7 80 GET /Clips&Stills/BillyS2.jpg - 200 Mozilla/4.0+(compa
2000-03-04 17:28:45 10.7.2.9 - 10.7.2.7 80 GET /Clips&Stills/BillyS5.jpg - 200 Mozilla/4.0+(compa
2000-03-04 17:28:45 10.7.2.9 - 10.7.2.7 80 GET /Clips&Stills/BillyS9.jpg - 200 Mozilla/4.0+(compa
2000-03-04 17:28:45 10.7.2.9 - 10.7.2.7 80 GET /Clips&Stills/BillyV4.jpg - 200 Mozilla/4.0+(compa
2000-03-04 17:28:45 10.7.2.9 - 10.7.2.7 80 GET /Clips&Stills/BillyH3.jpg - 200 Mozilla/4.0+(compa
2000-03-04 17:28:45 10.7.2.9 - 10.7.2.7 80 GET /Clips&Stills/BillyS6.jpg - 200 Mozilla/4.0+(compa
2000-03-04 17:28:45 10.7.2.9 - 10.7.2.7 80 GET /Clips&Stills/BillyH4.jpg - 200 Mozilla/4.0+(compa
2000-03-04 17:28:45 10.7.2.9 - 10.7.2.7 80 GET /Clips&Stills/BillyS7.jpg - 200 Mozilla/4.0+(compa
2000-03-04 17:28:45 10.7.2.9 - 10.7.2.7 80 GET /Clips&Stills/BillyS8.jpg - 200 Mozilla/4.0+(compa
2000-03-04 17:29:04 10.7.2.9 - 10.7.2.7 80 GET /Script.htm - 200 Mozilla/4.0+(compatible;+MSIE+5.
2000-03-04 17:29:43 10.7.2.9 - 10.7.2.7 80 GET /images/Speaker.gif - 404 Mozilla/4.0+(compatible;
2000-03-04 17:29:43 10.7.2.9 - 10.7.2.7 80 GET /Streaming.htm - 200 Mozilla/4.0+(compatible;+MSIE
2000-03-04 17:42:33 10.7.2.9 - 10.7.2.7 80 GET /Streaming.htm - 200 Mozilla/4.0+(compatible;+MSIE
2000-03-04 17:42:33 10.7.2.9 - 10.7.2.7 80 GET /images/Speaker.gif - 404 Mozilla/4.0+(compatible;
2000-03-04 17:42:33 10.7.2.9 - 10.7.2.7 80 GET /Clips&Stills/DanceSetup.jpg - 200 Mozilla/4.0+(cc
2000-03-04 17:43:30 10.7.2.9 - 10.7.2.7 80 GET /Streaming.htm - 200 Mozilla/4.0+(compatible;+MSIE
2000-03-04 17:43:30 10.7.2.9 - 10.7.2.7 80 GET /Clips&Stills/DanceSetup.jpg - 304 Mozilla/4.0+(cc
2000-03-04 17:43:30 10.7.2.9 - 10.7.2.7 80 GET /images/Speaker.gif - 404 Mozilla/4.0+(compatible;
2000-03-04 17:44:07 10.7.2.9 - 10.7.2.7 80 GET /Streaming.htm - 200 Mozilla/4.0+(compatible;+MSIE
2000-03-04 17:44:07 10.7.2.9 - 10.7.2.7 80 GET /Clips&Stills/DanceSetup.jpg - 304 Mozilla/4.0+(cc
2000-03-04 17:44:07 10.7.2.9 - 10.7.2.7 80 GET /images/Speaker.gif - 404 Mozilla/4.0+(compatible;
```

Figure 27.16
The default W3C Extended Log File Format is the most common format for collecting activity data for private and public Web sites.

Tip from *RJ*

Unless you need to log access to your intranet Web site for accounting or other administrative purposes, save disk space by disabling logging. To disable logging of all sites, clear the Enable Logging check box of the server's Master Properties dialog's Web Site page. You can selectively enable or disable activity logging of individual virtual sites on the server.

The first two fields are the date in YYYY-MM-DD format and the time in 24-hour HH:MM format. The remaining fields are the IIS 5.0 defaults or the fields you specify in the Extended Properties page of the Extended Logging Properties dialog. You open this dialog by clicking Properties on the Web Site page of the *SiteName* Properties dialog (see Figure 27.17).

Note

If you scroll to the bottom of the Extended Logging Options list, you encounter a Process Accounting heading and cleared check box with a set of default entries below the heading. Marking the Process Accounting check box and one or more of the subordinate check boxes adds Job Object counter data for Web server CPU usage to the log. For a brief description of this new Windows 2000's feature, search online help for "job objects."

SETTING UP THE DEFAULT FTP SITE | 1125

Figure 27.17
You can alter the fields included in the W3C Extended Log File Format file for a site in the Extended Properties page of the Extended Logging Properties dialog.

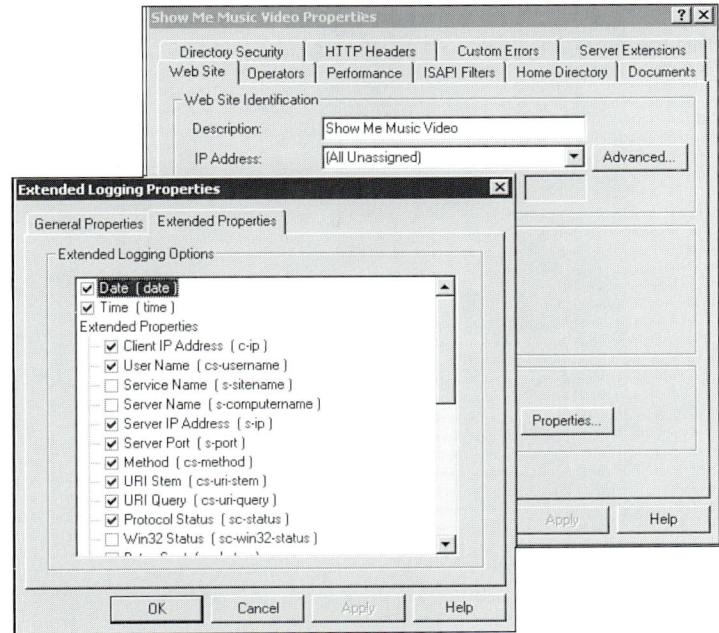

SETTING UP THE DEFAULT FTP SITE

Setting up the Default FTP Site and adding folders and files for downloading by users is much simpler than configuring Web sites. You can specify default FTP property settings for the server by right-clicking the *ServerName* node, choosing Properties, selecting FTP Settings in the Master Properties list, and clicking Edit. The example of this section sets FTP properties for the Default FTP Site.

> **Note**
> Most of the steps of the following procedure parallel those for setting the Master properties for the Web server. Thus, the instructions for configuring the FTP site are abbreviated.

→ For more detailed instructions for configuring IIS 5.0 site properties, **see** "Setting Master IIS Properties," **p. 1110**.

To set up and test IIS 5.0's Default FTP site, do the following:

1. In the Internet Information Services snap-in, right-click the Default FTP Site node, and choose Properties to open the FTP Site page of the Default FTP Site Properties dialog.

2. You can change the administrative name of the site, specify the maximum number of simultaneous connections, adjust the connection timeout period, and enable or disable logging (see Figure 27.18). Alternatively, accept the default values if you want only to test the FTP service.

PART
IV
CH
27

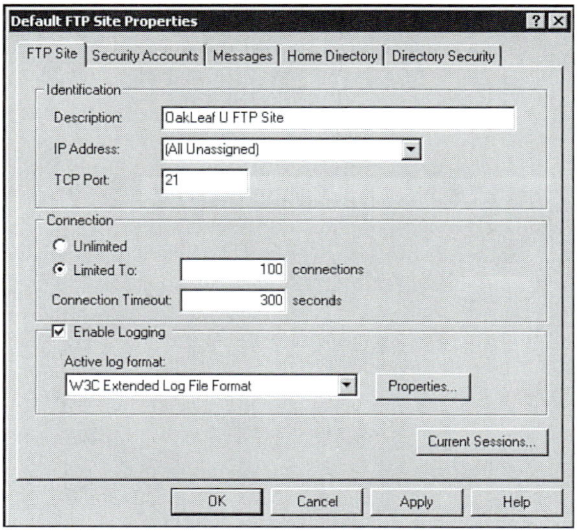

Figure 27.18
Set site identification, connection, and logging properties in the FTP Site page of the Default FTP Site Properties dialog.

3. Click the Security Accounts tab; click Add, and add the Enterprise Admins and Domain Admins groups to the FTP Site Operators list (see Figure 27.19).

> **Caution**
>
> In most cases, you should not clear the Anonymous Access check box in the Security Accounts sheet of the FTP properties dialog. Requiring a password for access to your FTP site can compromise users' security, because the passwords travel across the network in clear text and are therefore vulnerable to detection by hackers. Most FTP sites allow Anonymous Access.

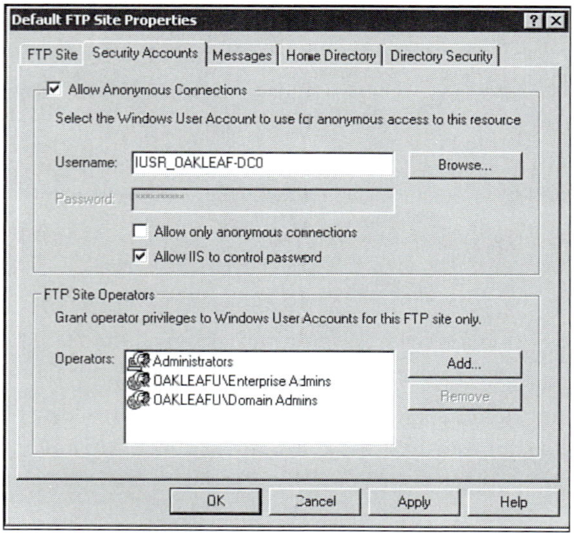

Figure 27.19
Always add members of the Enterprise Admins and Domain Admins groups as Operators for all Web, FTP, NNTP, and SMTP sites.

4. If you want to increase the security of your FTP site, click the Directory Security tab, mark the Denied Access option, and then add the network IP address and subnet mask for each subnet whose clients you want to be able to connect to the FTP site (see Figure 27.20).

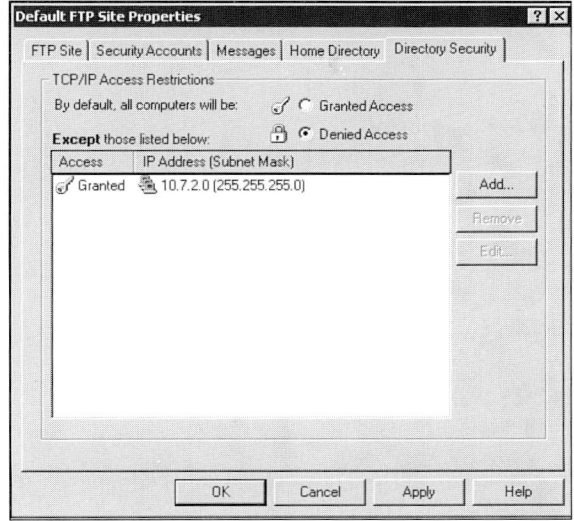

Figure 27.20
You can restrict connections to the FTP site by granting access only to clients having specified subnet addresses.

5. Unless you want to add a welcome message for the FTP site or change the default FTP home folder from \Inetpub\Ftproot, click OK to close the dialog and save your changes.
6. Add subfolders to the \Inetpub\Ftproot folder and copy a few files to the folders to test clients' ability to navigate the subfolders and download files.
7. Launch IE on a test client and type **ftp://servername/** in the address bar to connect to the FTP site. Verify in IE's status panel at the bottom of the window that you're logged on as User: Anonymous.
8. Navigate to one of the test files to download—Adsi25.msi in the \Inetpub\Ftproot\ADSI25 Download folder for this example—and double-click the file to download it to the client (see Figure 27.21).

Figure 27.21
Internet Explorer enables you to download files from a network FTP site by typing `ftp://servername/` in the address bar and navigating to the subfolder that contains the files.

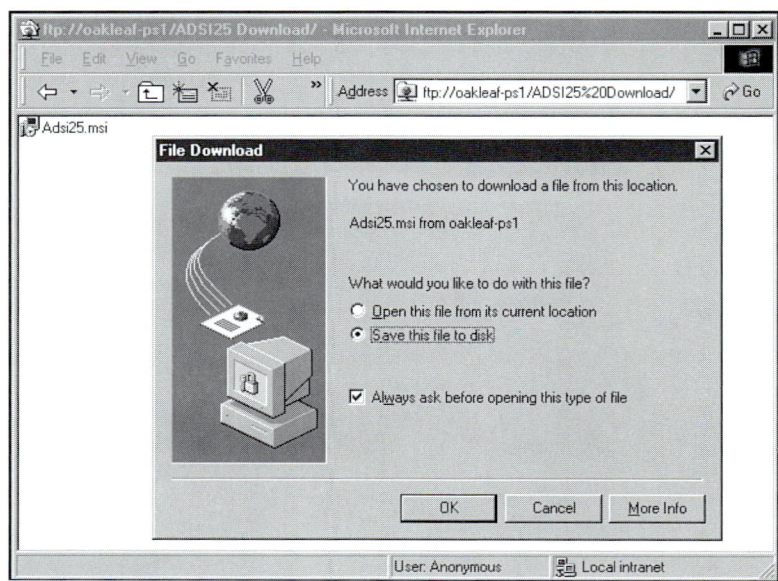

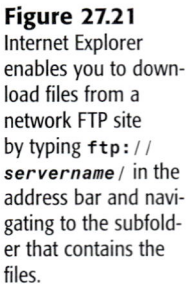 *If clients have problems with the FTP site, see the "FTP Server Problems" topic of the "Troubleshooting" section at the end of the chapter.*

Adding a Newsgroup to the Default NNTP Virtual Server

Like the Default FTP Server, it's easy to modify the properties of the Default NNTP Server to set up one or more newsgroups for participation by intranet users. Users must have a newsgroup reader—typically Microsoft Outlook or Outlook Express—to establish a newsgroup account, read messages, and post messages. The Default NNTP Server has several control newsgroups for control messages that synchronize newsgroup content between servers. If you have only a single NNTP server, you can safely delete the control newsgroups.

Setting the Properties of the Default NNTP Virtual Server

To set the properties of the Default NNTP Server, do the following:

1. In the Internet Information Services snap-in, right-click the Default NNTP Server node and choose Properties to open the General page of the site properties dialog.

2. Optionally, rename the server and click Connection to open the Connection dialog, which enables you to limit the number of connections and set the default timeout value. It's uncommon to log newsgroup servers. Figure 27.22 illustrates the basic newsgroup properties for this example.

Figure 27.22
Specify the administrative name of the newsgroup server and set connection and timeout limits in the General page of the server's properties dialog.

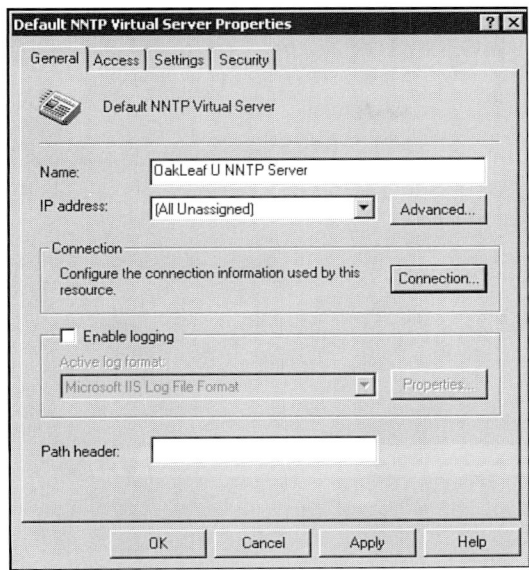

3. Click the Access tab, and click Authentication to open the Authentication Methods dialog. Clear the Allow Anonymous and Basic Authentication check boxes, and accept the remaining default Windows Security Package option (see Figure 27.23). Private newsgroups usually don't allow anonymous logon, and Basic Authentication exposes clear text passwords sent across the network. Click OK to close the Authentication Methods dialog.

Figure 27.23
Increase security for all newsgroups on the server by clearing the Allow Anonymous and Basic Authentication check boxes.

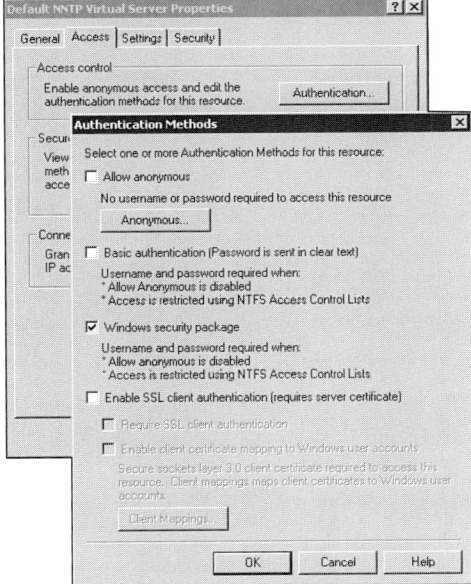

4. If you want to limit connections to clients with IP addresses in specific subnets, click Connection to open the Connection dialog, and add the network ID and subnet mask for each subnet.

5. Click the Settings tab. Change the default Limit Post Size and Limit Connection Size to more reasonable values, such as 100KB per message and 1MB per session. Limits apply to the message and its attachments, if any.

6. If your NNTP server is a standalone newsgroup server, clear the Allow Feed Posting (from other NNTP servers), Allow Servers to Pull News Articles from This Server, and Allow Control Messages check boxes. If the newsgroup isn't moderated, you can leave the SMTP Server for Moderated Groups and Default Moderator Domain text boxes empty. Replace the default entry in the Administrator EMail Account text box (see Figure 27.24).

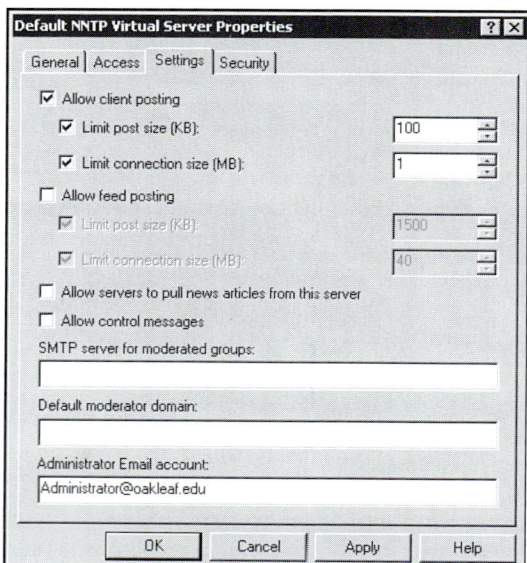

Figure 27.24
The options specified in this Settings page apply to standalone NNTP servers.

7. Click OK to close the Default NNTP Virtual Server dialog and save your changes.
8. Click the Newsgroups node and delete the four default newsgroups in the list pane if your NNTP server runs in standalone mode.

ADDING THE FIRST NEWSGROUP

To add a new newsgroup to the renamed NNTP server, perform this quick drill:

1. Right-click the Newsgroups node, and choose New Newsgroup to start the New Newsgroup Wizard.

ADDING A NEWSGROUP TO THE DEFAULT NNTP VIRTUAL SERVER | 1131

2. Type a short name for the newsgroup—**OakNews** for this example—in the Welcome dialog and click Next.

3. Complete the Description and Pretty Name text boxes. The Pretty Name appears only for newsreaders that support the LIST PRETTYNAME instruction. Click Finish to dismiss the pseudowizard.

After deleting the four default control newsgroups and adding the new newsgroup, the Newsgroups node and list appears, as shown in Figure 27.25.

Figure 27.25
The Newsgroups node displays the new OakNews newsgroups. You also can set Expiration Policies for the site and change the location of the Virtual Directories that store messages.

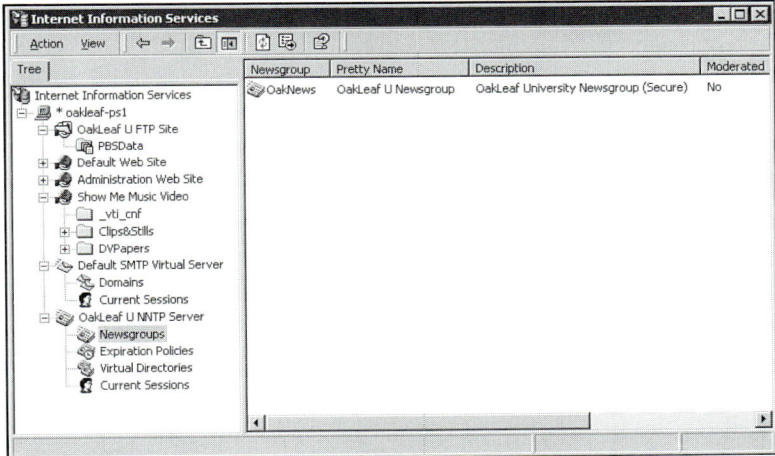

ESTABLISHING A NEWSGROUP ACCOUNT AND ADDING MESSAGES

Microsoft's free Outlook Express application, which installs in conjunction with IE 5+, is the standard newsreader application for many Windows 9x, NT, and 2000 users. This example assumes that you've already configured Outlook Express for email or newsgroup reading. To create an NNTP server newsgroup account and post a message on the new newsgroup, do the following:

1. On a test client, choose Programs, Outlook Express to launch the application. Choose Tools, Accounts to open the Internet Accounts dialog and click Add, News to start the Internet Connection Wizard.

2. In the Name dialog, type the name of a domain user test account, such as **Gary Almgren**, in the Display Name text box and click Next.

3. In the Internet News Email Address dialog, type the user's email address—**Gary.Almgren@oakleaf.edu** for this example. Click Next.

4. In the Internet News Server Name dialog, type the server name (**oakleaf-ps1**) in the News (NNTP) Server text box, and mark the My News Server Requires Me to Log On check box (see Figure 27.26). Users must log on because anonymous access isn't permitted. Click Next.

PART
IV
CH
27

Figure 27.26
Only the server name is required to specify an NNTP server in the same domain as the user's account. Marking the My News Server Requires Me to Log On check box leads to an authentication dialog.

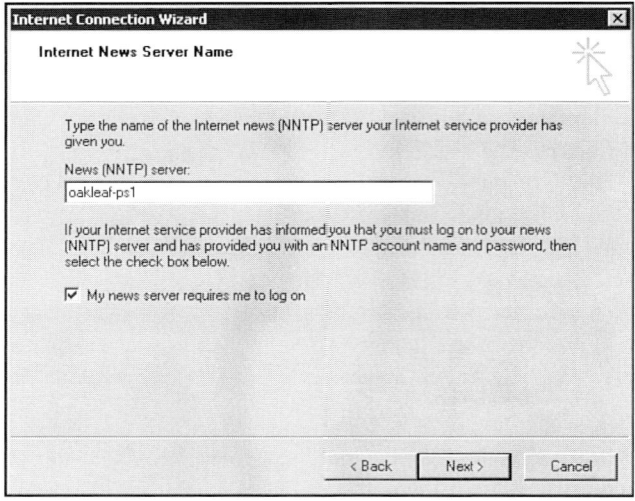

5. In the Internet News Server Logon dialog, type the test user's logon ID and password, and mark the Remember Password and Log on Using Secure Password Authentication (SPA) check box. SPA is necessary because you cleared the Basic Authentication check box in step 3 of the preceding section. Click Next and Finish to complete the account and get rid of the Wizard.

6. In the News page of the Internet Accounts dialog, double-click the entry for the new account to open the *ServerName* Properties dialog. Click the Connection tab, mark the Always Connect to This Account Using check box, and select Local Area Network in the list.

7. Click OK to close the dialog and display a message asking whether you'd like to download a list of newsgroups from the server. Click Yes to download the newsgroup list to the Newsgroup Subscriptions dialog.

8. Double-click the new newsgroup name to which to subscribe, indicated by an icon added to the left of the name (see Figure 27.27). Click Go To to open the empty newsgroup.

Figure 27.27
After setting up the newsgroup server account for the test user and downloading the list of newsgroup(s), double-click the name(s) of the newsgroups to which you want the user to subscribe.

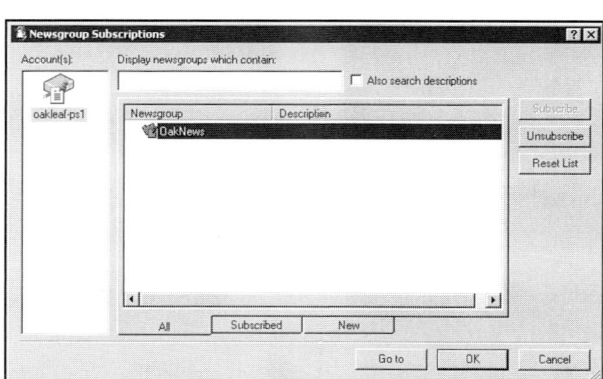

9. Click New Post to open the message posting window, type a message description in the Subject line, and compose a message in the text box. Click Send to post the message and close the window. Acknowledge the message box that states that the message might not appear immediately.

10. Press F5 to refresh Outlook Express's window and display the message you added.

 If clients display error messages when attempting to connect to the NNTP site, see the "NNTP Server Problems" topic of the "Troubleshooting" section at the end of the chapter.

The sample newsgroup you created in the preceding sections is very broadbrush. Most NNTP servers provide a large number of newsgroups categorized by user interest or organizational function. Creating a set of newsgroups that parallel your AD organizational unit (OU) structure is a logical initial approach. For instance, a university might establish official (moderated) newsgroups for each academic department, and then add unmoderated newsgroups covering sports, campus activities, and the like.

Configuring the Default SMTP Virtual Server

IIS 5.0's SMTP service is intended primarily for sites using FrontPage as a Web authoring tool, running moderated newsgroups with the NNTP service, or both. The FrontPage Extensions need SMTP to handle `mailto` operations. The NNTP service uses SMTP to mail messages to the moderator of a newsgroup for review prior to posting.

The process of configuring SMTP services is similar to setting up NNTP services, so this section concentrates on setting property values that are unique to SMTP. Following are the settings you make in the six pages of the Default SMTP Virtual Server Properties dialog:

- General page—The General page is identical to that for the NNTP server. You can change the administrative name of the server, set connection limit and timeout values, and enable or disable logging.

- Access page—Specify Access Control properties in the same manner as for the NNTP server. The Access page has an additional feature, Relay Control, that enables you to restrict receipt of messages to those from specified subnets or domains.

- Messages page—This page sets property values similar to those on the NNTP Settings page. You can limit the size of a single message, the number and size of all messages for a single user session, and the number of recipients for any message. Most of the default values are too large for normal FrontPage or NNTP use; Figure 27.28 illustrates more appropriate values. The minimum value of the Limit Number of Recipients per Message To property is 100.

    If SMTP can't send a message to the designated recipient, the service generates a Non-Delivery Report (NDR). Type the email address of the person to receive NDRs in the Send Copy of Non-Delivery Report To text box. If SMTP can't send the NDR, it moves the undeliverable message to the designated Badmail Directory.

Figure 27.28
Reduce the default limits for message size and number in the Messages page of the Default SMTP Virtual Server Properties dialog.

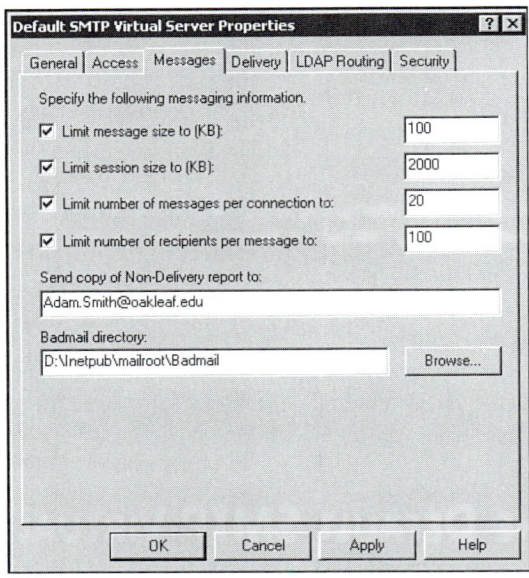

- Delivery page—This page sets time intervals for retry operations on outgoing mail, and notification and expiration operations on local and outgoing mail. The default values are satisfactory as a starting point for your SMTP services.

- LDAP Routing page—The SMTP service can use AD, Site Server, or Exchange 2000 LDAP routing for message delivery. This feature is disabled by default, and LDAP mail routing is beyond the scope of this chapter.

- Security page—This page is identical to the Security page of the NNTP properties dialog. Add the Enterprise Admins and Domain Admins groups to the local Operators group.

The SMTP service stores outgoing messages as .eml (email) files in the \Inetpub\Mailroot\Pickup folder. Messages that can't be delivered immediately move to the ...\Queue folder for deferred delivery. It's a good administrative practice to periodically check the ...\Queue and ...\Badmail folders to check for outgoing mail problems. The ...\Drop folder stores incoming mail files that you can read with Notepad or any other text file viewer.

Troubleshooting

Web Server Problems

Users can't connect to the default or any other network Web site.

The most common cause of this problem is users with modem-equipped clients—especially laptops—having set their browser connection preferences to dial-out only. In IE 5+, choose Tools, Internet Options; click the Connections tab and verify that the user has set the correct option in the Dial-Up Settings frame. Select Never Dial a Connection for PCs permanently connected to the network or Dial Whenever a Network Connection Is Not Present for mobile users who alternate between network and modem-based connections. Selecting Always Dial My Default Connection prevents the client from connecting via the LAN.

Another cause of downlevel clients' inability to connect to the intranet Web server is a DNS problem. If users can connect by specifying the Web site's IP address—for example, http://10.7.2.7/—DNS name resolution is the problem. Use Winipcfg.exe or Ipconfig.exe to verify that the client's DNS server address setting is correct. If you've made changes to DNS server IP addresses recently, run **ipconfig /release** and **ipconfig /renew** or use **Winipcfg** on a DHCP client to update its IP configuration.

*Users can connect to the default Web site with the conventional http://*servername *address, but can't connect to the default or a virtual site with an http://www.*sitename.ext/ *address.*

You have a problem with the DNS forward lookup zone you created for the default or virtual Web site. In the DNS snap-in on the DSN server or at a workstation with the Administrative Tools installed, check the Alias (CNAME) resource record for the www.sitename.ext forward lookup zone for the domain. Verify that the alias specifies the fully qualified domain name (FQDN) of the Web server.

If the DNS forward lookup zone entries for a virtual Web site appear to be correct, compare the entry for the host header record with the name of the forward lookup zone. In the Internet Information Services snap-in, click the * ServerName node to display the list of servers on the site. The Host Header Name column of the list pane displays all host header records for virtual Web sites.

FTP SERVER PROBLEMS

Users can't upload files to the FTP site.

Uploading files to the FTP site requires use of the command-line Ftp.exe application that's included with Windows 9x, NT, and 2000, or a graphical FTP client, such as FTP Explorer. FTP Explorer (available from http://www.ftpx.com) is a shareware application that commercial users must license after a 30-day trial period.

You must enable Write privileges for the FTP folder in the Home Directory page of the *SiteName* Properties dialog. If you permit anonymous logons to the FTP site, any user can upload *and* delete files in the FTP folder. It's a very uncommon practice to grant write privileges to anonymous FTP users.

NNTP SERVER PROBLEMS

Users receive Can't connect to server and Logon error messages when attempting to download names of newsgroups from the NNTP server.

The most common cause of this problem is failure to mark the Log on Using Secure Password Authentication (SPA) check box in the Internet Connection Wizard's Internet News Server Logon dialog. Clients need SPA if you don't permit Basic Authentication.

Other sources of these errors are incorrect or incomplete designation of the NNTP server's name, or a bad user logon ID or password.

MCSE Corner: Administering Internet Information Server 5.0

Virtually all Windows 2000 networks run Internet, intranet, or both services. For this reason, Internet Information Server (IIS) 5.0 is covered on the base Windows 2000 server exam, 70-215, "Installing, Configuring, and Administering Windows 2000 Server." It's likely that there will be a future IIS 5.0 exam to replace the current exam, 70-087, "Implementing and Supporting Microsoft Internet Information Server 4.0."

For exam 70-215, you must be familiar with setting access controls to Web sites and published files. There are two important parts of this chapter to study for the exam. First, you need to be familiar with configuring access to Web sites. You should have an understanding of how file permissions affect Web site permissions and how directory security in IIS works, including anonymous access and Windows authentication. You should also know how to limit access based on client IP address. The second important element is troubleshooting IIS 5.0. You must know the steps to take when the site access controls are not functioning as expected.

PART V

ADVANCED MANAGEMENT AND ENTERPRISE SYSTEMS

28 Managing Transaction and Messaging Services   1139

29 Deploying Windows Terminal Services   1195

30 Clustering with Windows 2000 Advanced Server   1227

CHAPTER 28

MANAGING TRANSACTION AND MESSAGING SERVICES

In this chapter

Understanding the Role of Windows 2000 Application Servers   1140

Bonding Components with COM and Its Derivatives   1145

Brokering Objects and Processing Transactions   1147

Exploring the Windows 2000 Component Services Tool   1150

Understanding COM+'s Role-Based Security   1153

Installing COM+ Applications   1156

Installing the Sample Bank Application and Creating a File DSN   1171

Administering the Distributed Transaction Coordinator   1178

Upgrading or Installing Message Queuing Services   1180

Managing Message Queuing Services   1187

Troubleshooting   1192

MCSE Corner: Exam Question Types Part II   1193

Understanding the Role of Windows 2000 Application Servers

Servers that run back-end services such as databases, messaging systems, intranets, and Web sites traditionally are known as *application servers*. Novell NetWare gained its early lead in the network operating system market as a file- and printer-sharing server. Windows NT's greatest initial success came as an application server running SQL Server, Exchange Server, and other Microsoft BackOffice applications—often in a mixed Novell and Microsoft environment. Smaller firms commonly run SQL Server, Exchange, and Internet Information Server (IIS) on a single server—the original BackOffice bundle approach. As small firms grow into large organizations, network administrators move each back-end application onto one or more dedicated servers to support the added load of more users and new back-end applications. It's a common practice to install application servers as member servers in Windows NT resource domains. This approach reserves user and computer account administration to Windows NT Primary Domain Controllers (PDCs). Member servers don't incur the overhead of client authentication traffic to and from PDCs and Backup Domain Controllers (BDCs). Thus member servers can devote all their resources to running applications. The primary problem with Windows NT resource domains is the complexity of the non-transitive trusts administrators must establish between the resource and other domains.

→ For more information on Windows NT non-transitive trusts, **see** "Administering Domains and Trusts," **p. 105**.

In a conventional domain reconstruction scenario, application servers in Windows NT resource domains become member servers in Windows 2000 domains. You can place member servers in a new child domain—such as `resource.domain.com`—or in an Organizational Unit (OU) of the parent domain. In either case, you can delegate administration of the application servers to others. Active Directory (AD) automatically creates transitive trusts with all other domains in the domain tree, so you don't need to manually create trusts.

→ For instruction on how to upgrade Windows NT servers in resource domains to Windows 2000 child domains, **see** "Upgrading Resource Domains," **p. 392**.

Windows 2000 member servers avoid consuming the hefty resource requirements of AD, devoting all their RAM and disk drives to running Windows 2000 and applications. Windows 2000-enhanced applications, such as Exchange 2000, SQL Server 7.5, Commerce Server 4.0, and, to a lesser extent, IIS 5.0, however, require AD to implement their full feature set. Application servers running transaction and messaging services don't require installation of AD.

Purpose-Built Application Servers

Application servers suddenly became a hot topic in 1999, fueled by the promise of Internet e-commerce riches. By the end of that year, more that 50 seasoned hardware/software vendors and startup firms offered purpose-built application servers. Clusters of specialty application servers use load-balancing software to run high-volume intranets or, more commonly,

Internet sites. The most common use of purpose-built application servers, however, is serving as an intermediary between back-end relational database management systems (RDBMSs)—SQL Server, IBM DB2, Oracle, Informix, and the like—and Web sites or clients. A typical example of the intermediary role is IBM's original Payment Server (now called WebSphere Payment Manager), which includes IBM's Net Commerce server software, to handle multiple e-commerce payment methods. WebSphere is a Java-based application server intended primarily to connect Web servers with back-end DB2 databases.

This chapter refers to specialty application servers as *app servers* to distinguish them from traditional application servers—conventional Windows NT/2000 and UNIX boxes running heavy-duty database, email, and Web servers. App servers often come with dedicated developer tools, such as IBM's VisualAge for Java, and include a set of services to enable object-oriented programming (OOP) and communication between programmable objects, called *components*. Enterprise JavaBeans is one approach to developing general-purpose, interoperable components that run on an app server. The app servers discussed in this chapter are Windows 2000 member servers running COM+ component services and Microsoft Message Queue Services.

> **Note**
> This chapter is intended for Windows 2000 administrators, not component developers. Administrators must have an understanding of component architecture to deploy, manage, and troubleshoot componentized applications on Windows 2000 servers and, in many cases, clients.

THREE-TIER COMPONENT ARCHITECTURE

It's highly probable that every reader of this book is familiar with the concept of three-tier application architecture—the successor to the two-tier client/server design. Three-tier architecture—with Windows 2000 running on each tier—is the foundation for Windows Distributed interNet Architecture (DNA) 2000. The `www.microsoft.com/dna/` page provides links to several resources that describe the latest marketing slogan for Web-based distributed applications.

→ If you're up-to-date on COM, multitier architecture, and MTS 2.0, **see** "Exploring the Windows 2000 Component Services Tool," **p. 1150**.

For the sake of completeness, following are the definitions of the services that define the three tiers:

- *Data services* maintain durable information on magnetic media—typically fixed disks and tapes—or on optical discs. A common synonym for durable is persistent, and back-end is a common substitute for data services. Relational, object, and message databases are the most common information stores, but directories are destined to play a much more important role as organizations adopt Windows 2000 Server and AD. Depending on your point of view, data services are the top or bottom tier. Database administrators consider data services to be the highest level of the hierarchy, whereas Web developers and Webmasters place them at the bottom.

- *Business services*, also called *business rules*, represent the middle tier. Business services are collections of interoperable components, often called business objects, that enforce organizational practices, such as obtaining authorization for credit card purchases prior to entering an order, billing the card holder upon shipping the order, and collecting sales taxes, if applicable. A goal for middle-tier components is reusability, the ability to mix and match standard components for use by multiple data sources and client applications. Information transiting the business services tier is ephemeral—that is, not persistent. In most cases, business services are transactional; operations that don't pass muster at the business services layer are rejected and aren't passed to the data services layer.

- *Presentation services*, also called *client services* during the early days of three-tier design, enable the end user to interact with the business services layer. Before the browser age, presentation services were the province of custom Windows client applications created with Visual Basic, Access, C++, Delphi, or some other Windows front-end development tool. Each user needs a copy of the client application on his or her PC to access the other two tiers. A Web server becomes the presentation layer for browser-based applications. Microsoft Active Server Pages (ASP), for example, connect to the business services layer and send and receive browser-agnostic HTML code to and from Internet Explorer (IE) or Netscape Navigator running on the client. Every end user is presumed to have an HTML-compliant browser. Browsers capable of handling the current permutations and combinations of Extensible Markup Language (XML) tags aren't yet omnipresent.

> **Note**
>
> Component-based architectures aren't limited to three tiers, although three is the most common number of layers. Many developers use the term n-*tier*, which implies more than three tiers, for projects that have multiple layers of business service components. Browser-based applications can be considered four-tier—data services, business services, Web services, and presentation services (the browser). Some authors, however, include Web servers in a middle tier called *application services*.

The two-tier client/server architecture usually incorporates business logic in the client (presentation) tier. Clients connect directly to back-end data services—usually an RDBMS—by one or more application programming interfaces (APIs), such as Microsoft's original Open Database Connectivity (ODBC) API. If the structure of the database changes, developers must rewrite the entire client front end and redistribute the revised version to all users. In contrast, three-tier developers need only change the data-related elements of the middle-tier, which resides on one or a few application servers, to accommodate database schema changes. The changes are transparent to clients that connect to the middle-tier components. Similarly, if business rules—such as sales tax calculation or collection methods—change, only the middle tier need be altered.

Understanding the Role of Windows 2000 Application Servers 1143

Tip from
RJ

> Don't confuse *n*-tier architecture with the thin-client/fat-client controversy. Removing business rules from client applications reduces their obesity, but doesn't make them sylph-like. You still need 32-bit Windows whatever on the desktop and, for many browser-based applications, IE or Netscape Navigator/Communicator. By no stretch of the imagination can the Windows 2000 Professional and IE 5.0 combination qualify as a thin client.
>
> Thin-client architecture, which minimizes client resource requirements, relies on a fast network connection to fat servers with vast resources. Windows Terminal Services, the subject of Chapter 29, "Deploying Windows Terminal Services," is an example of technology that supports relatively thin clients. Network computers (NCs)—championed by Oracle's Larry Ellison—are another thin-client approach. The latest, but not necessarily the greatest, incarnation of the NC doesn't have a fixed disk, but loads the client operating system—and whatever additional applications fit into the NC's limited RAM—from a built-in CD-ROM. The thinnest traditional client is a dumb terminal connected to a UNIX box or mainframe. Other truly thin-client contenders are the new breeds of cellular telephones and digital wristwatches that display email and Web content.

The primary purpose of app servers is to host middle-tier business service components. Figure 28.1 illustrates the *n*-tier architecture of a large-scale Internet-based e-commerce system using Windows 2000 technologies. SQL Server 7+ runs on a two-node cluster under Windows 2000 Advanced Server to provide the durable store for customer transaction data. ActiveX Data Objects (ADO) provide the connection between the data and business services layers. Business service components run under Windows 2000 AppCenter Server on multiple app servers with Component Load Balancing (CLB). Multiple Windows 2000 servers run Internet Information Server (IIS) 5.0 with Network Load Balancing (NLB) to provide scalable, high-availability presentation services to multiple PC clients with compatible browsers. Distributed COM (DCOM) connects the business and presentation services layers.

→ For a brief description of CLB and NLB, **see** "Delivering Scalability," **p. 304**.

One of the characteristics that distinguishes app servers for hosting business service components from conventional application servers running RDBMSs and Web servers is the app server's minimal fixed-disk storage requirement. Most app servers use local disk drives only to store the server operating system, built-in or add-on component management services, images of the business service component software, and the paging file. High-performance app servers run all instances of their components in RAM to eliminate the performance hit of writing to and reading from the paging file. Thus a mirror set of 4GB or 9GB drives usually proves adequate for an app server. Most purpose-built app servers are rack-mounted and have a small form factor—often 3.5 inches or less in height.

Note

> Many app server vendors—Sun Microsystems and IBM, for example—deliver a standardized hardware package bundled with an operating system, component management services, and software development tools. Microsoft doesn't sell server hardware, so its app server offering is a combination of Windows 2000 Server or AppCenter Server with the Visual Studio 6+ suite of Internet development (Visual InterDev) and component programming tools (Visual Basic, Visual C++, and Visual J(ava)++). Microsoft hadn't finalized the specifications for AppCenter Server when this book was written.

PART
V
CH
28

Figure 28.1
The architecture shown here is appropriate for a very high traffic Windows 2000–based Web site using COM components.

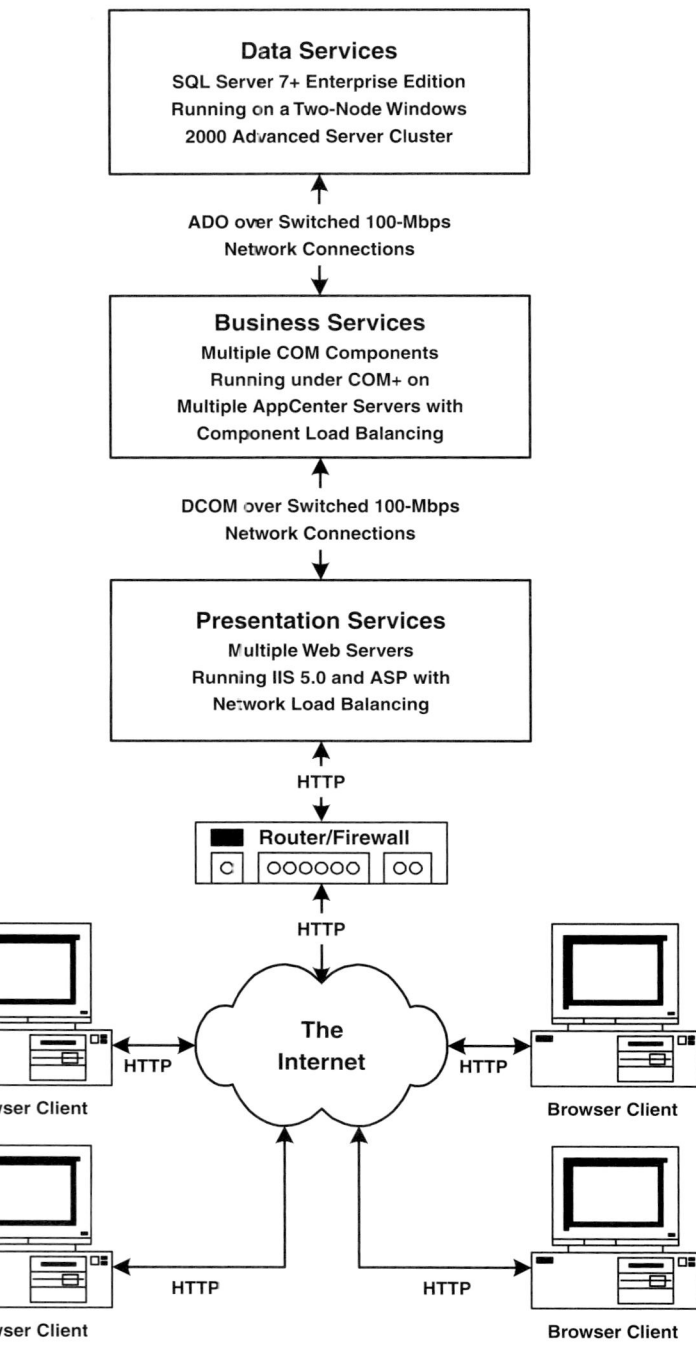

Bonding Components with COM and Its Derivatives

Microsoft's brand of glue that bonds the components and tiers is the Component Object Model (COM)—a derivative of the Object Linking and Embedding (OLE) technology of 1991's Windows 3.1 and some earlier versions of Microsoft Office components. COM is a specification that defines how objects communicate through a set of predefined interfaces. COM has been ported to several UNIX flavors, but COM remains primarily a Windows-based technology. The Common Request Broker Architecture (CORBA), which claims to be an "open" specification, is the favorite of UNIX vendors. JavaBeans is a specification for writing reusable components with the platform-neutral Java programming language. Despite the increasing competition, COM and its descendants continue to be the most widely used component architecture because of Windows' ubiquity.

Since COM's formal introduction in 1993, Microsoft has added many new and useful features based on the original COM specification. Following are some of the most important of these COM-based technologies, in approximate chronological sequence:

- *Automation* (formerly OLE Automation) is a wrapper over COM that permits developers to use languages other than C++ to create reusable COM components. Visual Basic, including Visual Basic for Applications (VBA) and its Visual Basic Script (VBScript) subset, is the most popular language for writing components. You also can write COM components with Microsoft's and others' implementation of Java and C++, but using Visual Basic or VBScript is easier and quicker for most programmers.

- *ActiveX* is Microsoft's trademark for lightweight automation components, with or without visible elements, and enabling technologies that are optimized for intranet and Internet applications. ActiveX components are scriptable—meaning that you can write VBScript or JavaScript (now officially ECMAScript) code to manipulate ActiveX objects. ActiveX Controls and ActiveX Database Objects (ADO) are commonly used ActiveX implementations. ADO 2.5 is included with Windows 2000.

- *Distributed COM* (DCOM, formerly Network OLE) is the 1996 Microsoft specification that permits COM objects to communicate over a network connection via remote procedure calls (RPCs). 32-bit DCOM is included with Windows 98, NT 4.0, and 2000, and a DCOM upgrade is available for Windows 95. DCOM is essential for implementing three-tier applications.

- *Distributed Transaction Coordinator* (DTC) originally was a DCOM-enabled add-on to Microsoft SQL Server 6.0. Windows 2000 Server automatically installs DTC, which manages transactions across multiple databases. Transaction processing is one of the subjects of the "Brokering Objects and Processing Transactions" section that follows.

- *Active Server Pages* (ASP), introduced with IIS 2.0, is a server-based Web technology that generates browser-agnostic HTML pages from a combination of conventional HTML code, optional graphic images, and VBScript or JavaScript code. ASP uses ADO to connect directly to back-end databases or DCOM to communicate with business service components.

- *Microsoft Transaction Server* (MTS, originally code-named Viper) is middleware for creating scalable, *n*-tier applications. Middleware is loosely defined as software to provide location, communication, conversion, translation, and security services for middle-tier components. DCOM, DTC, and ADO provide MTS's underpinnings. Microsoft includes MTS 2.0 and DTC in the no-charge Windows NT 4.0 Option Pack. Windows 2000 subsumes MTS 2.0 into COM+ 1.0.

- *Microsoft Message Queue Server* (MSMQ) 1.0 is an add-on to Windows NT 4.0+ that provides asynchronous communication between components or applications. The sending application places messages in a queue and the receiving application removes them for processing. MSMQ's messaging system is similar to AD's intersite communication method—if the message's destination computer is down or its network connection is broken, the message stays in the source queue until the destination computer can process it. MSMQ is transaction-enabled for integration with MTS. COM+ lets you designate components as message-enabled for use with Windows 2000's MSMQ 2.0.

→ For the details of setting up MSMQ 2.0 or upgrading from version 1.0 to 2.0, **see** "Upgrading or Installing Message Queuing Services," **p. 1180**.

- *COM+* (COM Plus) is the Windows 2000 successor to MTS 2.0. COM+ is a runtime environment for components and provides a number of services for managing the creation (and destruction) of instances of components. When a presentation service (client) uses a DCOM RPC to a business service component, COM+ allocates an in-memory image (instance) of the component to the client. If there are no free instances in the pool of the particular component requested by the client, COM+ creates an additional instance. When the component instance completes its work on behalf of the client, it is returned to the pool or removed from memory. Instantiating components is only one of COM+'s services; the remainder are discussed in the sections that follow.

Tip from
RJ

> Before you upgrade any server running MTS 2.0 components, launch the MTS Explorer and make a checklist of the property settings for each custom package and its components. If you have a large number of packages and components, use an Excel worksheet to save property values. Alternatively, use a screen-capture application to save in a consistent sequence bitmap files of each property page for packages and components.
>
> Use MTS's Transaction List to verify that there are no in-doubt transactions prior to upgrading from Windows NT 4.0 to Windows 2000 Server on machines running MTS 2.0 and DTC. If in-doubt transactions are present, resolve them manually before proceeding with the upgrade.

ActiveX, DCOM, ASP, and DTC/MTS currently are the most widely used of Microsoft's COM-based technologies. MSMQ remains a niche component environment for developers who must deal with non-real-time transactions or whose network infrastructure is subject to repeated interruptions. The fact that Windows 2000 Server's Setup program doesn't install MSMQ by default is further evidence of today's limited deployment of message-based transaction processing in mainstream *n*-tier applications. COM+'s Queued Components feature, which makes it easier to write components that execute asynchronously, will expand use of the MSMQ infrastructure in 2000 and beyond, especially in e-commerce applications.

Tip from
RJ

You can learn more about COM+ from Microsoft's COM+ Resource Kit and Windows 2000 Developer's Readiness Kit. Microsoft distributed the COM+ Resource Kit, consisting of two CD-ROMs, at Tech*Ed 99 in Dallas, Texas. The `http://www.microsoft.com/com/resources/compluscd/default.asp` page contains links to the entire content of the COM+ Resource Kit. The Windows 2000 Developer's Readiness Kit CD-ROM includes most of the COM+ Resource Kit's content. If you have Visual Studio 6.0 Professional or Enterprise editions, order the no-charge (except shipping and sales tax) Readiness Kit from `http://msdn.microsoft.com/vstudio/prodinfo/datasheet/winkit.asp`.

BROKERING OBJECTS AND PROCESSING TRANSACTIONS

Until developers rewrite their components to take full advantage of new COM+ features, Windows 2000 administrators must continue to deploy and support legacy MTS 2.0-based components. Fortunately, Windows 2000 Server and COM+ handle MTS 2.0 components without requiring rewriting and recompiling the components. Microsoft provides cursory references to COM+'s capabilities in the help file for the Component Services administrative tool, also called the Component Services snap-in (Comexp.msc). Component Services snap-in's help file (Comexp.chm) includes only the basic information you need to administer COM+ applications. If you're responsible for assuring that existing MTS components run properly after upgrading from Windows NT 4.0 to Windows 2000 Server, you need a basic understanding of MTS and the services it provides.

Note

Make sure you have a fall-back scenario in place before upgrading Windows NT servers running MTS 2.0 to Windows 2000. Upgrading servers running MTS 2.0 with properly written components is transparent. If developers have broken the MTS rules for component code, however, it's likely that the components will exhibit unexpected behavior when running under COM+. You also might need to have developers make minor modifications to client applications written in Visual Basic or VJ++.

Plan to duplicate your Windows NT application servers, test the duplicates in a simulated production environment, run and test Windows 2000 upgrades, and then bring the upgraded servers into production.

→ For examples of typical VJ++ client-side problems with COM+ applications, **see** "Testing the Components and File DSN with the Sample Bank Client," **p. 1176**.

MTS is a combination object broker and transaction processor that runs as a service under Windows NT 4.0 and as part of the operating system under Windows 2000. Following are simplified definitions of basic MTS terms:

PART
V
CH
28

- *Objects*, in MTS terms, are ActiveX (COM) dynamic link libraries (DLLs) that incorporate MTS-specific code. Classical programmable objects exhibit attributes defined by property values and behavior specified by methods. MTS-compliant objects (components) don't expose properties; they rely entirely on method calls to communicate with clients and other components. To activate an MTS object, the client or another component calls one of its methods. Most MTS components have multiple methods, such as `Component.AddRecord`, `Component.UpdateRecord`, `Component.DeleteRecord`, and the like.

- *Object brokers*, also called object request brokers (ORBs), provide a means by which clients and objects locate other objects over a network connection. ORBs maintain a catalog of objects and their locations on remote servers. MTS stores its catalog in the Windows NT Registry; COM+'s catalog is a separate set of registration files in the \Winnt\Registration folder. MTS uses a client proxy to specify the server on which the components reside. Exporting an MTS package creates an executable file to generate the proxy on the client. COM+ uses IntelliMirror, AD's Class Store, and the Microsoft Installer to generate the application proxy and install the client-side application, if required, automatically.

- *Transactions* define a series of actions that must execute as a group. If each action of the group executes properly, the transaction commits and modifies durable information—typically in one or more databases. If any action fails, the transaction aborts and any changes to durable information are rolled back to their values prior to start of transaction execution. A typical transaction is withdrawal of funds from an ATM—if the bank can't debit the database record for your account, due either to a computer failure or lack of funds, the ATM aborts the transaction and refuses to deliver the cash.

- *Transaction processors* (TPs), also called transaction monitors (TMs), originally were developed to handle very large numbers of simultaneous transactions against mainframe databases. IBM's Customer Information Control System (CICS) is one of the most widely used TPs. TPs also handle transactions that span two or more databases by a process called *two-phase commit*. Two-phase commit assures that updates to each database succeed, or the transaction aborts and restores both databases to their original stage. Both MTS and COM+, in conjunction with DTC, provide TP services; COM+ provides improved scalability by implementing object pooling and, with Windows 2000 AppCenter Server, CLB.

> **Note**
> If you're a component programmer, you're probably acquainted with an MTS-defined property called `CanBePooled`. Setting `CanBePooled = True` (or `False`) has no effect in MTS 2.0-hosted components, because MTS 2.0 doesn't support pooled components. `CanBePooled` works with COM+.

Microsoft designed MTS and COM+ primarily to handle transaction-oriented applications typified by airline reservation systems, stock trading, and Internet-based retail commerce. Figure 28.2 illustrates the relationship of the elements of an MTS or COM+ TP system for Internet or intranet and conventional Win32 clients. The DTC connects MTS or COM+ components to multiple databases and platforms.

BROKERING OBJECTS AND PROCESSING TRANSACTIONS | 1149

Figure 28.2
This data flow diagram shows the components of an MTS 2.0– or COM+ 1.0–based transaction processing system for databases on mainframe, UNIX, or Windows NT/2000 systems.

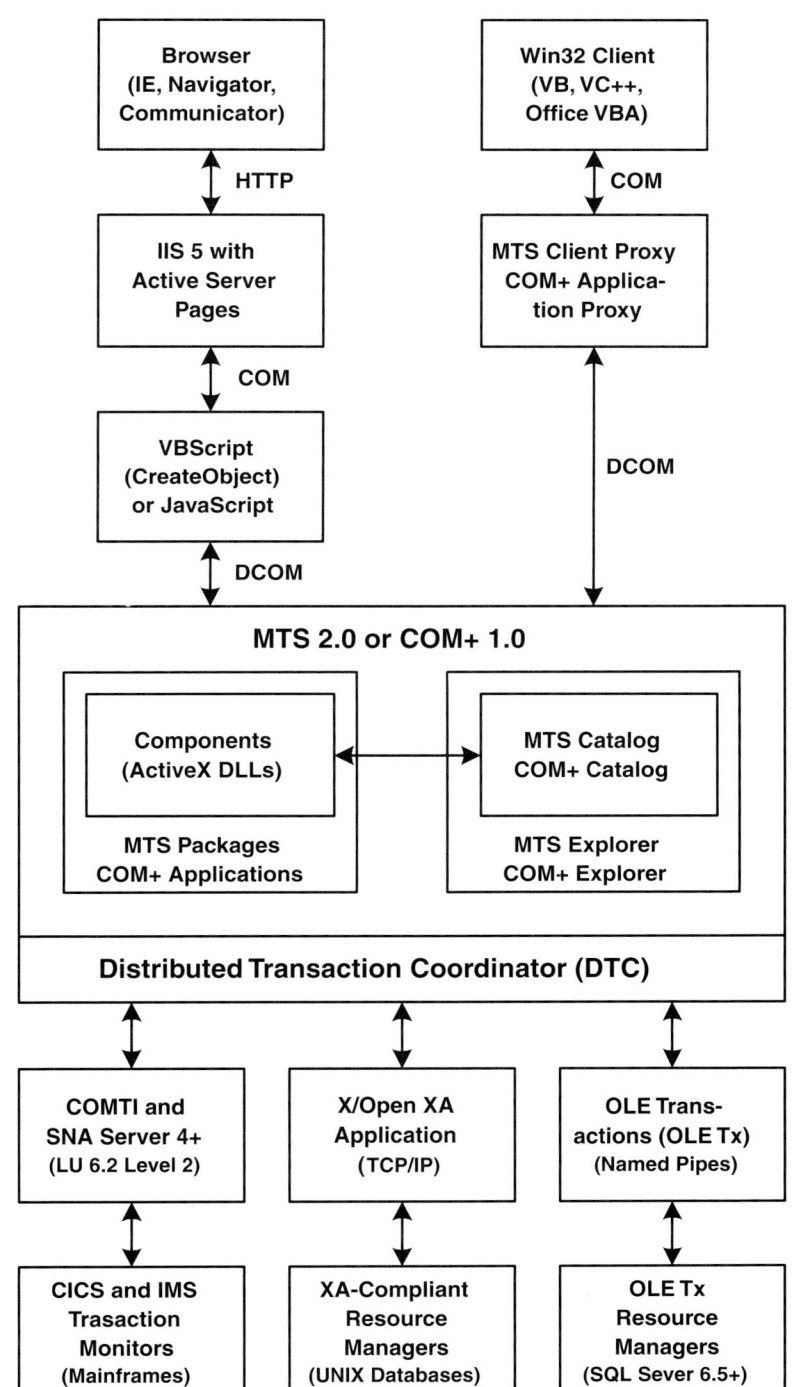

It isn't necessary to use the transaction processing features of MTS and COM+. The Visual C++ version of MTS 2.0's Sample Bank application uses transactions to credit and debit accounts, but the Tic-Tac-Toe application doesn't need to maintain transactional integrity. Sample Bank preserves its state in Account and Receipt tables that the `Bank.CreateTable` object adds to the SQL Server pubs database. Tic-Tac-Toe uses MTS 2.0's Shared Property Manager to preserve the state of the game between player actions.

Stateful Versus Stateless Components

Statefulness is an important consideration when writing MTS and COM+ components. Stateful components store property values and often must exist for the duration of a client session. The memory consumption of multiple instances of stateful components causes major application scalability problems. Stateless components, on the other hand, don't preserve values between successive method calls. When a client calls a stateless component, the component performs its work, returns information to the client, and disconnects. Conventional HTML pages are a good example of statelessness; clients connect to the Web server, download the page, and immediately disconnect from the server.

To take advantage of the efficiency of stateless components and still preserve transient property values locally, MTS uses the Shared Property Manager (SPM). Microsoft intended the In-Memory Database (IMDB) to substitute for the SPM, but IMDB disappeared from COM+ after Windows 2000 Server Release Candidate 2 (RC-2). COM+ applications that need to store transient values must continue to use the SPM until Microsoft releases a successor to the ill-fated IMDB.

> **Tip from**
> *RJ*
>
> Fawcette Technical Publications' *Visual Basic Programmer's Journal* Web site (http://www.vbpj.com) offers many technical articles on MTS programming with Visual Basic.

Exploring the Windows 2000 Component Services Tool

Windows 2000 Server automatically installs the Component Services administrative tool during the setup process. Setup also adds a basic collection of support applications for COM+ and IIS 5.0. The Component Services snap-in's feature set is similar to that of MTS 2.0 Explorer, but access to some elements has changed, and property sheets for components offer many new property value settings.

> **Note**
>
> As mentioned earlier, MTS 2.0 includes two complete sample packages, Sample Bank and Tic-Tac-Toe, with client front ends. COM+ doesn't provide sample applications, and upgrading MTS 2.0 to COM+ only upgrades custom MTS packages, not the samples. The Sample Bank and Tic-Tac-Toe applications disappear from the COM+ Explorer after an upgrade. You must install at least one custom MTS or COM+ application to test your COM+ 1.0 installation and evaluate its new services.

Exploring the Windows 2000 Component Services Tool 1151

→ For instructions on how to install the Tic-Tac-Toe and Sample Bank clients under COM+ 1.0, **see** "Installing and Testing the Tic-Tac-Toe MTS 2.0 Sample Application," **p. 1158** and "Installing the Sample Bank Application and Creating a File DSN," **p. 1171**.

To launch the Component Services snap-in and test its basic functions, do the following:

1. Choose Programs, Administrative Tools, Component Services to open the Component Services console, which displays Component Services, Event Viewer (Local), and Services (Local) nodes.

2. Expand the Component Services, Computers, My Computer, COM+ Applications, System Application, Components nodes. Icons for the four COM+ system application components appear in the left and right panes (see Figure 28.3).

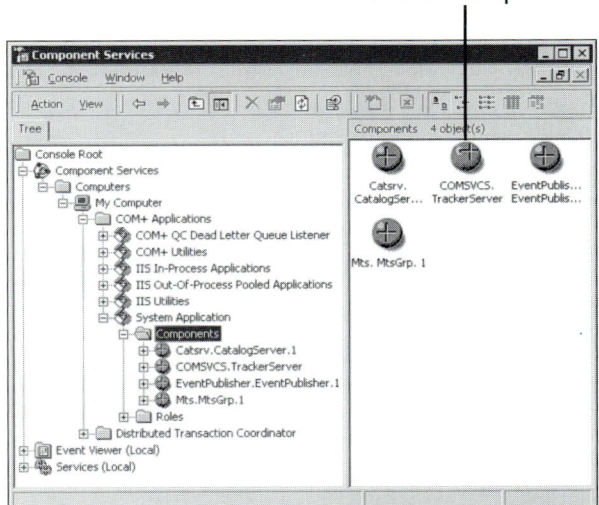

Figure 28.3
The COM+ components shown in the right pane (and under the selected components container in the left pane) provide services for all COM+ applications you install.

COM+ activates the COMSVCS.TrackerServer component during system startup; a rotating icon in the right pane indicates component activation.

3. Right-click one of the component icons in either pane and choose Properties to open the tabbed Properties dialog for the component (see Figure 28.4).

PART
V
CH
28

Figure 28.4
The General page of the COMSVCS.Tracker-Server properties sheet shows a description of the component, the filename of the library containing the component, and a pair of globally unique IDs (GUIDs) for the component.

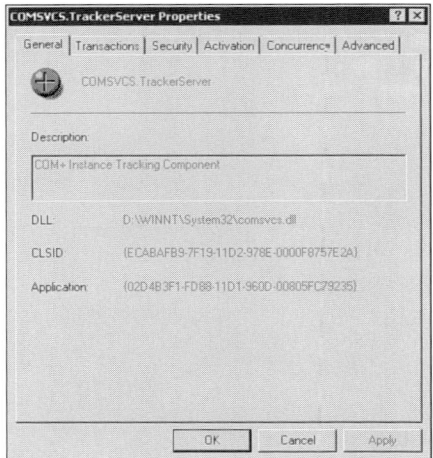

All property values for default COM+ components and all but Security properties for default COM+ applications are read-only. You can set property values for COM+ components you install or custom MTS components you upgrade when you install Windows 2000 Server.

4. Expand the COMSVCS.TrackerServer, Interfaces, IGetAppData, Methods node to display the component's methods (see Figure 28.5).

Figure 28.5
The right pane of the Component Services snap-in shows the five methods of the COMSVCS.Tracker-Server component that implement the functions of that component.

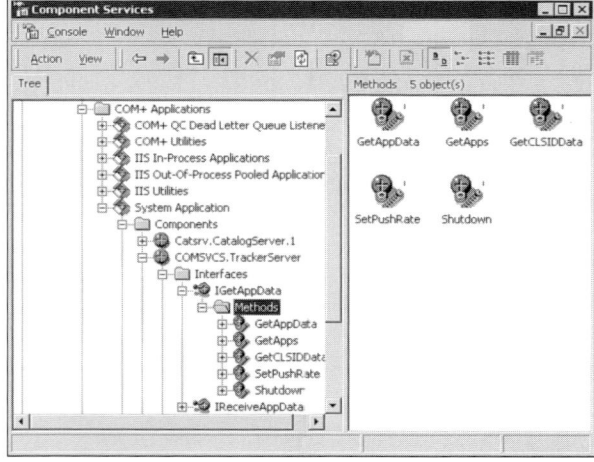

Each component has a set of one or more methods. Unlike MTS 2.0, COM+ lets you assign security roles at the method level; MTS 2.0 restricts role-based security to packages and components. Role-based security is one of the subjects of the next section.

5. Expand the Distributed Transaction Coordinator node and click the Transaction Statistics node. Figure 28.6 shows statistics after running many transaction tests with MTS 2.0 sample components.

Figure 28.6
The transaction statistics for the Distributed Transaction Coordinator are shown in the right pane of the Component Services snap-in after running about 24,000 transactions.

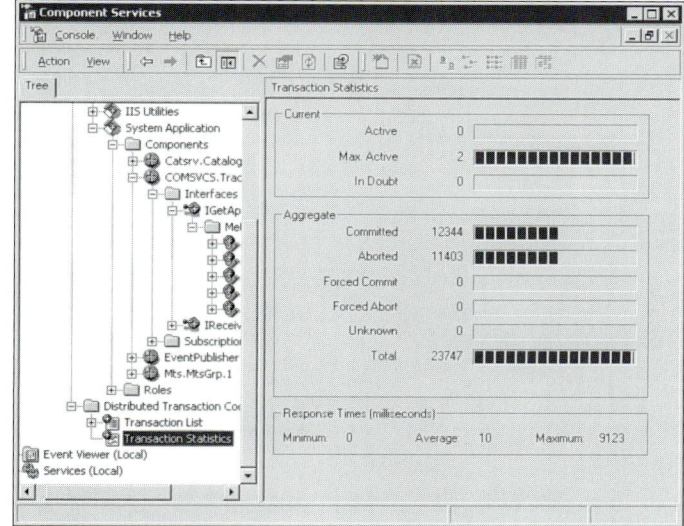

Transaction statistics are useful for troubleshooting problems with COM+ applications. For example, the almost equal number of committed and aborted transactions shown in Figure 28.6 usually indicates concurrency conflicts in a back-end database.

The Distributed Transaction Coordinator's Transaction List node displays in-doubt transactions that have neither committed nor aborted. The Transaction Statistics pane includes a value for the number of in-doubt transactions. In-doubt transactions usually are the result of a network communication failure between computers participating in the transaction. You must manually resolve in-doubt transactions that appear in the list. When resolving in-doubt transactions, you often need to check the associated database record(s) to verify transactional consistency. Verifying that an in-doubt transaction hasn't caused errors in the database isn't an easy process.

The remaining two Component Services nodes—Event Viewer (Local) and Services (Local)—expedite access to the Event Viewer and Services consoles, respectively.

Understanding COM+'s Role-Based Security

COM+, like MTS 2.0, uses role-based security. Roles are similar to global security groups—but you can add both global and local groups to roles. COM+ roles are similar to SQL Server 7.0's predefined Server Roles, but you can define your own COM+ roles for most applications. Most of the pre-installed components have a default set of roles assigned, and custom COM+ components often have a set of predefined roles. Components check security by calling the `IsUserInRole("RoleName")` method for a role specified by `RoleName`. You must add a `RoleName` role for the component if the developer has enabled security, and then add groups or users to the role.

You examine roles by expanding the Roles node for the application, then expanding its subnodes. Figure 28.7 shows the predefined roles for the System Application component and the default local groups assigned to the roles. By default, the Everyone group is the only user member of the Any Application, Reader, and Server Application roles.

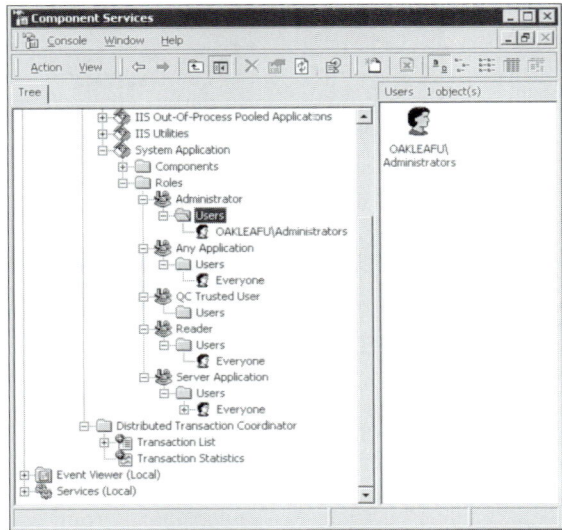

Figure 28.7
The left pane of the Component Services snap-in shows the predefined roles for the System Application COM+ application that establishes administrative security and assigns default groups as users in roles.

Adding Groups to the Administrators Role

One of the most important first steps in administering COM+ is to establish administrative security for the COM+ System Application. By default, the local Administrator account is the only user having administrative rights for the COM+ System Application, which include the rights to add, modify, and delete custom components. You can't add new roles to the System Application, but several other default applications let you add custom roles. If your app server is a member server in a domain—the most common configuration—you add Domain Admins to the Administrators, Users container. If you've upgraded a Windows NT 4.0 PDC or are a member server in a Windows NT 4.0 domain having a local or global MTS Administrators group, you also add this group to the Administrators role.

To add new groups or users to a role—in this case MTS Administrators—do this:

1. Right-click the Administrators, Users node and choose New, User to open the Select Users or Groups dialog.

2. Select the domain of the Domain Admins group to add in the Look In list, select Domain Admins in the Name list, and click Add to add the group to users in the role.
3. Upgrading a Windows NT PDC having MTS 2.0 installed in the domain retains the MTS Administrators group. Select the domain of the MTS Administrators group; if it's present, select the group in the Name list; and click Add (see Figure 28.8).

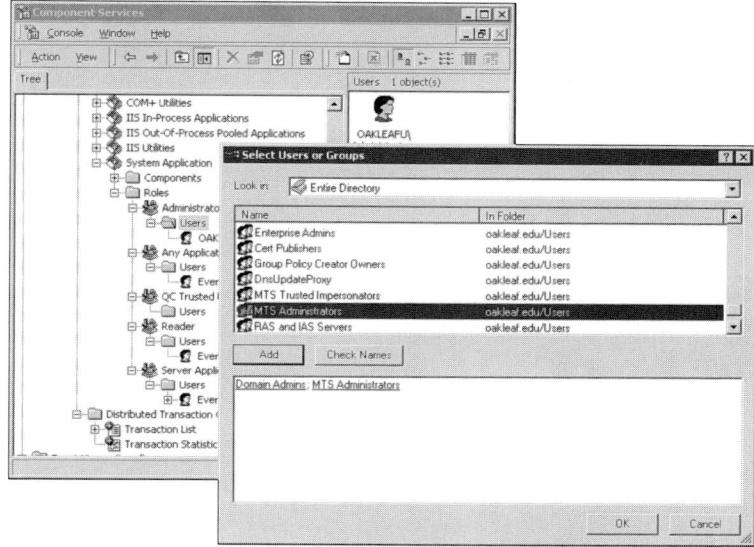

Figure 28.8
The Select Users and Groups dialog is used to add groups to the Administrators role of the COM+ System Application.

4. Click OK to add the additional Global or Domain Local groups to the Users container of the role (see Figure 28.9).

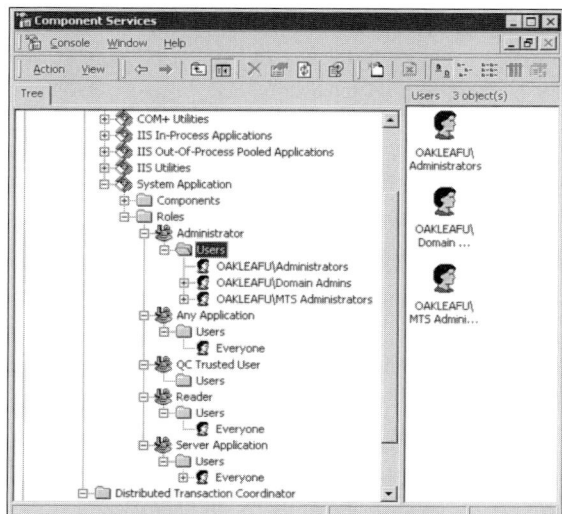

Figure 28.9
The right pane of the Component Services snap-in is shown after adding the Domain Admins and MTS Administrators groups from the OAKLEAFU domain to the Users container of the Administrators role for the COM+ System Application.

Tip from
RJ

When you upgrade a server running MTS 2.0, verify that the System Application's role includes the Domain Local Administrators group and other Global groups in the package's original roles. MTS 2.0 doesn't automatically add the local Administrators group to the role for its System package, which is equivalent to COM+ System Application.

ADDING AND DELETING ROLES

You can add roles to those predefined applications, such as IIS In-Process Applications, that permit new roles. To add a role to In-Process Applications, follow this drill:

1. Expand the In-Process Applications node, right-click the Roles node, and choose New, Role to open the Role dialog.
2. Type the name of the role in the text box, and click OK to add it.
3. Add groups (or users) appropriate to the role as described in the preceding section.

If you want to add a role but not implement security at this point, add the Everyone group to the role. To delete a role, right-click the role, choose Delete, and confirm removal of the role.

INSTALLING COM+ APPLICATIONS

The Component Services snap-in offers two methods for creating new COM+ applications—installing and importing. In most cases, installing is the preferred method because it registers the ActiveX DLL(s) for the application during the installation process. Importing assumes that entries for the DLLs were added to the Registry previously. You install COM+ applications by one of the two following methods:

- Running the Microsoft Installer (.msi) file you or the component developer generated for a server application.
- Creating a new COM+ application and importing the ActiveX DLL(s) for the server.

In either case, you must be prepared to set the properties of the application and its components to ensure that the application runs as expected. If the application connects to an RDBMS, you also must set up a data source specification—often called a data source name or DSN—that identifies the RDBMS on the network, provides logon credentials, specifies the type of driver for the connection, and points to the appropriate database.

UNDERSTANDING COM+ PROPERTIES

COM+ components don't expose internal property values to clients or other objects, but they do have external properties that control how COM+ creates instances of the component and which users have access to applications, components, and their methods. Creating a new COM+ application requires that you set several property values for the application, and, optionally, its individual components and component methods. Setting application, component, and method properties in properties dialogs is called *declarative programming*.

Developers can use code in the components to set many of these properties, but letting the COM+ administrator set operational properties usually is the better approach. Some properties that require Run As a Service privileges, such as the local account under which the component runs, must be set by the COM+ administrator.

The component developer is responsible for providing recommended COM+ property values for his or her component. As a COM+ administrator, however, you're usually responsible for installing the component on one or more servers, establishing security, and dealing with other site- and computer-specific properties.

Following are the most common categories of declarative properties you add when installing a new COM+ application, classified by their properties dialog page:

- *Security* specifies at the application level whether access authorization is required to use the application, the level of security of the access check, and the level of authentication security required.

    At the component and method levels, you specify the roles permitted to activate the component and its methods, respectively. If you don't specify required roles for components that call the `IsCallerInRole()` method, these components return an error message when called by a client or another object.

- *Identity* specifies the account under which the application runs. The default is Interactive User, which requires a user with Administrators privileges to be logged on to the server. Your applications won't allow users or other components to connect without the required logon, which leads to serious problems after app servers in server closets or remote locations reboot. The Identity page only appears at the application level.

Tip from
RJ

> Specify the account to replace Interactive User before you set any other property values. The account you specify must have Log On As a Service rights.

- *Activation* at the application level specifies whether the application is of the Library or Server type. Server applications, the default type, run in their own process; Library applications run in the process of the component that activates (creates) the application. Unless the component's developer tells you to install the application as a Library, accept the default Server type.

    At the component level, the Activation page lets you specify object pooling, add a constructor string, enable Just-in-Time (JIT) activation, and enable COM+'s loosely coupled events and statistics. The next section includes brief descriptions of these features in conjunction with installing sample applications.

- *Queuing* lets you specify at the application level if the component is intended for use with MSMQ. If so, you can specify whether the application listens for messages from MSMQ. Queued Components (QCs) have special coding requirements related to in/out and out parameters, so the component developer specifies the MSMQ-related property values.

- *Advanced* lets you specify at the application level how long until an idle process shuts down, permissions for deletions and modifications, debugging operations, whether the application uses a Compensating Resource Manager (CRM), and if the component is to support 3-Gigabyte Tuning (3GT or 3GB).

  At the component level, Advanced lets you type the name of a Queuing Exception Class, if the component developer has provided the class.

- *Transaction* properties determine if the components of the application use transactions. You set transaction properties on individual components, so the transaction page only appears at the component level.

- *Concurrency* lets you specify synchronization support at the component level, if your components require or support synchronization. Accept the default choice, which is based on your component's code and other property values, unless instructed to do otherwise by the developer.

In the case of MTS 2.0 packages upgraded to COM+ applications by installing Windows 2000 Server, start by accepting the property values that appear in the pages of the properties dialog for each application and its components. After you verify the applications behave as expected, you can tune the application and its components to take advantage of new COM+ features.

→ For examples of COM+ property dialogs and pages, **see** "Inspecting Application and Component Properties," **p. 1162**.

INSTALLING AND TESTING THE TIC-TAC-TOE MTS 2.0 SAMPLE APPLICATION

As noted earlier in the chapter, installing COM+ doesn't include sample applications, nor does it upgrade MTS 2.0's two sample applications to COM+. Microsoft's reluctance to supply or upgrade these early samples might be that they aren't optimized for COM+. It's important, however, that you gain proficiency with the COM+ component installation process by installing and testing one or two sample components.

> **Note**
> To obtain the sample application components, you must have access to an MTS 2.0 installation on Windows NT Server 4.0. Alternatively, install a copy of the Windows NT Server Option Pack 4.0 on a Windows NT Server with Service Pack 3+.

The MTS 2.0 Tic-Tac-Toe package consists of a Visual Basic 5.0 client application (Tclient.exe) and a Visual C++ ActiveX DLL (Tserver.dll). Windows 2000's Setup installs the required Visual Basic runtime file (Msvbvm50.dll) for Tclient.exe and the Visual Basic 6.0 runtime (Msvbvm60.dll) in \Winnt\System32.

To install the DLL as a COM+ application and test its operation with Tclient.exe, do the following:

1. Create a \Program Files\MTS Clients folder on your Windows 2000 Server. Alternatively, you can use the empty \Program Files\ComPlus Applications folder to hold the Tclient.exe file.

2. Copy Tserver.dll from \Program Files\Mts\Samples\Packages to \Program Files\ COMPlus Applications and Tclient.exe from \Program Files\Mts to \Program Files\MTS Clients.

3. If it's not running, open the Component Services snap-in; right-click the COM+ Applications node; choose New, Application to start the COM Application Install Wizard. Click Next to bypass the Welcome dialog.

4. In the Install or Create a New Application dialog, click the Create an Empty Application button, and click Next.

5. In the Create an Empty Application dialog, type the name of the application, **Tic-Tac-Toe** for this example. The application name must match exactly the MTS package name. Accept the default Server Application option, and click Next.

6. In the Set Application Identity dialog, select the This User option, and type or browse for the account under which the application runs. If you haven't added a COMPlusAdmin account, which must be a member of the Administrators local group of a member server, select the local Administrator account. Either account you use must have Log On As a Service privilege. Add and confirm the account password (see Figure 28.10).

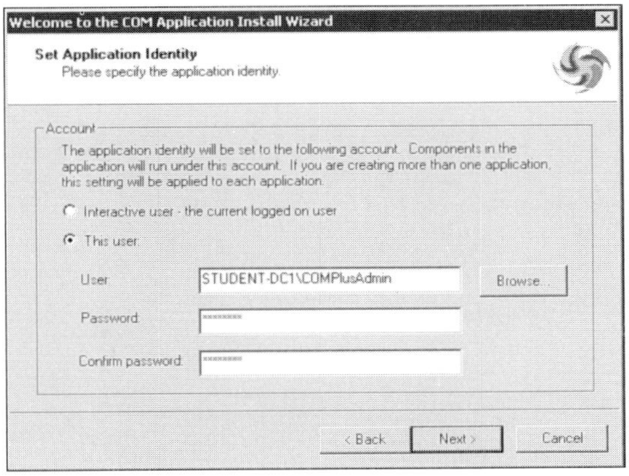

Figure 28.10
The COM Application Install Wizard requires you to specify an account with the Log On As a Service privilege under which the application components run.

7. Click Next and then select Finish to add the empty Tic-Tac-Toe application to COM+ Applications. The Components and Roles nodes of the application are empty at this point.

8. Right-click the Components node, and choose New, Component to open the first dialog of the COM Component Install Wizard. Click Next to bypass the first dialog.

9. In the Import or Install a Component dialog, click the Install New Component(s) button (see Figure 28.11). The other two options aren't applicable at this point. Click Next.

Figure 28.11
From the COM Application Install Wizard, you can choose whether to install new components or install components that are already registered.

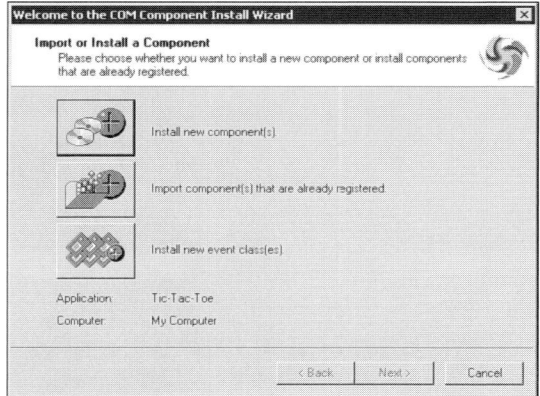

10. In the Install New Components dialog, click Add to open the Select Files to Install dialog. Navigate to the \Program Files\COMPlus Applications folder and double-click Tserver.dll to add it to the Files to Install list (see Figure 28.12). Click Next and Finish to add the components.

Figure 28.12
You must specify the components to install in the COM Application Install Wizard. The Tclient.dll ActiveX file is shown with its two components, Computer and Human.

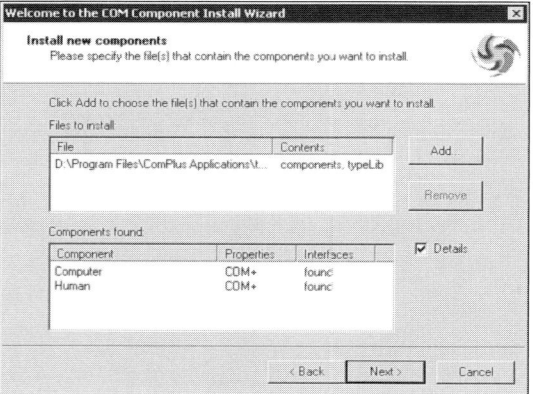

If the Contents column of the Files to Install list doesn't include both components and typeLib (type library) entries, or if the Details check box is marked and the Components Found list is empty, you haven't selected the right DLL.

11. Expand the Components node of the Tic-Tac-Toe application and its subnodes to display the methods for both components (see Figure 28.13). Tic-Tac-Toe lets you (the IHuman interface) play against the computer (IComputer) or another instance of IHuman.

INSTALLING COM+ APPLICATIONS | 1161

Figure 28.13
The Tic-Tac-Toe COM+ application and the interfaces and methods contained under the tServer.Computer and tServer.Human components are shown in the left pane of the Component Services snap-in.

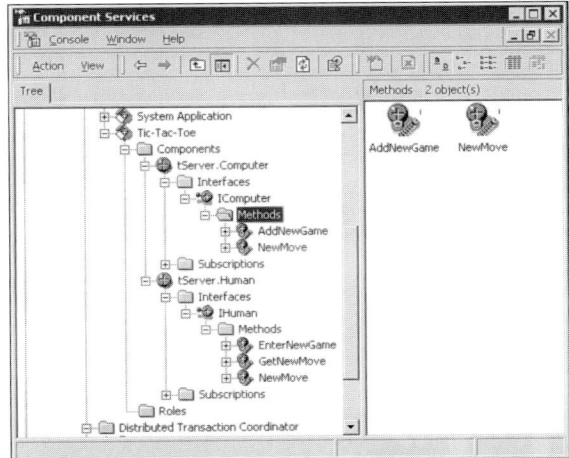

12. Launch the Tclient.exe client, click Play Against the Computer, and match your skill against the developer's code (see Figure 28.14). You can tie or lose—but not win—with the Hard option selected. As mentioned earlier in the chapter, the server components use COM+'s SPM to store game state between plays.

Figure 28.14
The Tic-Tac-Toe COM+ application is shown running, playing a game against the computer.

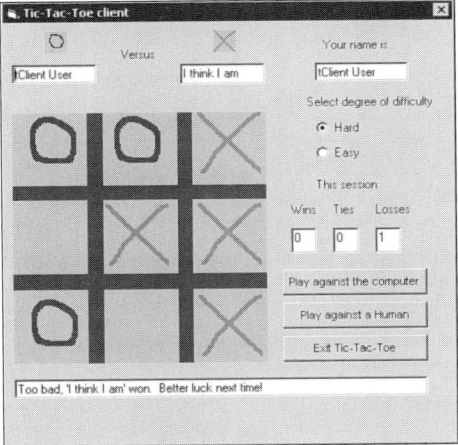

13. Start a new game, click Play Against a Human, and open another instance of Tclient.exe to play against yourself (see Figure 28.15). Alternatively, another player on a networked computer can open an instance of the local Tclient.exe and play against you.

PART
V
CH
28

Figure 28.15
Two instances of the Tic-Tac-Toe COM+ application are shown running on the same computer concurrently.

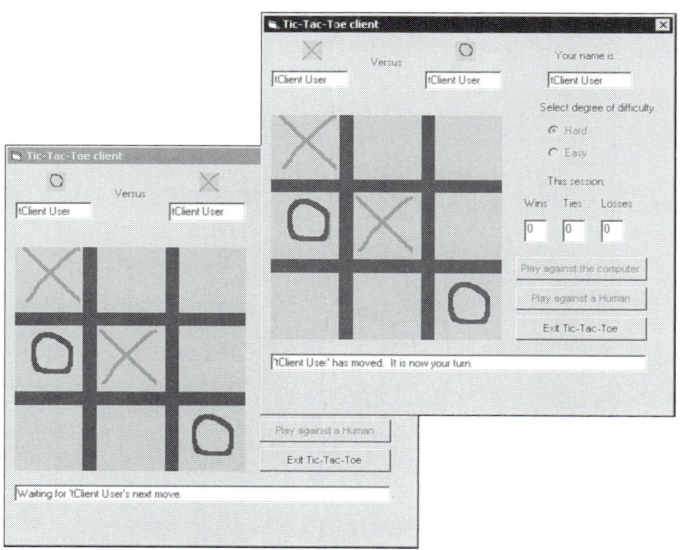

INSPECTING APPLICATION AND COMPONENT PROPERTIES

The COM Application Install Wizard sets the most important property of the application, the identity of the account under which the application runs. The COM Component Install Wizard generates components with default property settings, which are adequate for learning COM+ basics. When you install a production component, however, you must be prepared to set the component's properties in the Component Services snap-in.

> **Tip from**
> *RJ*
>
> When you install a custom COM+ application, the component developer ordinarily provides a checklist of settings for the components. If you're upgrading MTS 2.0 components, get a new COM+ properties checklist from the developer; otherwise, use the MTS 2.0 checklist you created from the property pages of the MTS package and components, in accordance with the tip in the preceding "Bonding Components with COM and Its Derivatives" section. Using the previous MTS 2.0 settings for COM+ applications and components works in almost all cases. COM+'s application and component property pages, illustrated by the figures that follow, are very similar to those of MTS 2.0.

To inspect and alter the properties of a COM+ application and its components, using Tic-Tac-Toe as an example, run this drill:

1. Right-click the Tic-Tac-Toe application, and choose Properties to open the General page of the Tic-Tac-Toe Properties dialog. The page displays the Application ID, a 32-character globally unique ID (GUID) generated when you created the empty application. Type a description for the application if you want.

2. Click the Security tab to display the default security properties (see Figure 28.16). Accept the defaults—no Access Checks for This Application, Perform Access Checks at

the Process and Component Level, Packet-Level Authentication, and Impersonate Impersonation Level—until after you test the component on a remote computer. If you mark the Enforce Access Checks for This Application check box, you encounter Access Denied errors with default client DCOM security settings.

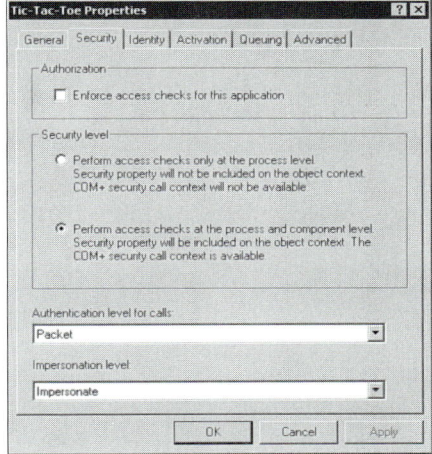

Figure 28.16
The Security tab of the Tic-Tac-Toe Properties dialog shows the default settings as configured by the COM Application Installation Wizard.

Tip from
RJ

Select Connect authentication if you plan to install clients on Windows 9x computers. Windows 9x clients have limited DCOM security capability, and can't participate in Call or Packet authentication levels.

3. Click the Identity tab to display the account under which the application runs. You can change the account to any other user account that has Run As a Service privileges on the app server.

4. Click the Activation tab. You can change the application type to Library, but Tserver.dll isn't designed to be a library application.

5. Click the Queuing tab. Tic-Tac-Toe isn't a good candidate for a queued application, so leave the Queued check box clear. You ordinarily use QCs for components that must communicate over unreliable wide-area networks.

6. Click the Advanced tab to set the time until the idle application shuts down (see Figure 28.17). The default three minutes is suited for a simple component; it's a common practice to set a longer time period for complex, non-pooled components that are heavy hitters during the startup process. Accept the default values for the remainder of the properties, and click OK to save your settings, if you made any changes. Otherwise, click Cancel.

Figure 28.17
The default settings of the Advanced page of the Tic-Tac-Toe Properties dialog allow you to set permission, debugging, and other options.

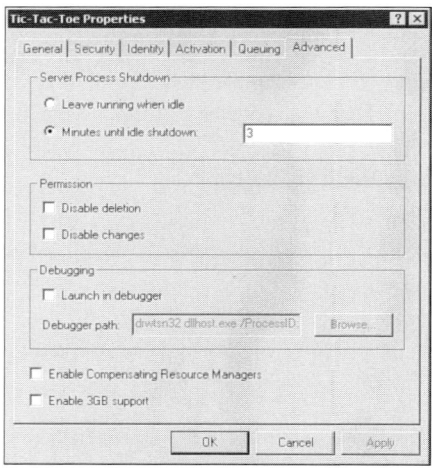

7. Right-click the tServer.Computer component to display the General page of its properties dialog. The Description text box displays the class description added by the component developer. Labels display the path to the ActiveX DLL, the GUID for the Class ID (CLSID) of the component, and the application's GUID. The CLSID identifies the Registry entries for the component and its interfaces. Your GUID and CLSID will differ.

8. Click the Transactions tab. Neither of Tic-Tac-Toe's two components supports transactions (see Figure 28.18). If the developer specifies transactions, either the Required or Requires New option usually appears selected. In some cases, you may be requested to specify the level of transaction support.

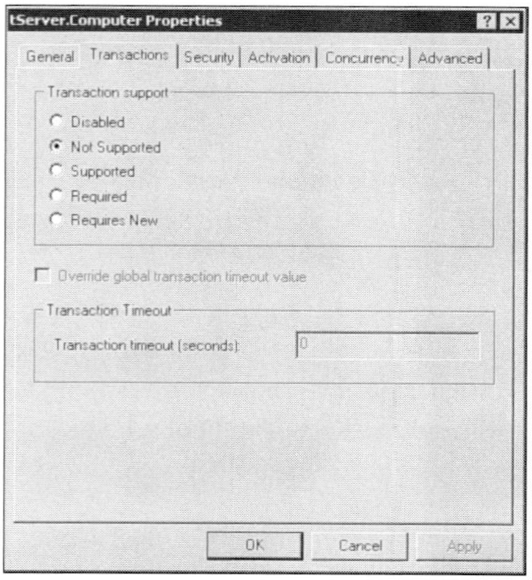

Figure 28.18
The Transactions page of the tServer.Computer component Properties component allows you to configure the level of transaction support.

INSTALLING COM+ APPLICATIONS 1165

9. Click the Security tab to display security settings at the component level. Figure 28.19 shows the Enforce Component Level Access Checks property enabled and two added roles—Ordinary Players (Domain Users) and Power Players (Domain Admins). By default, access checks aren't enforced, and no roles appear in the Name list.

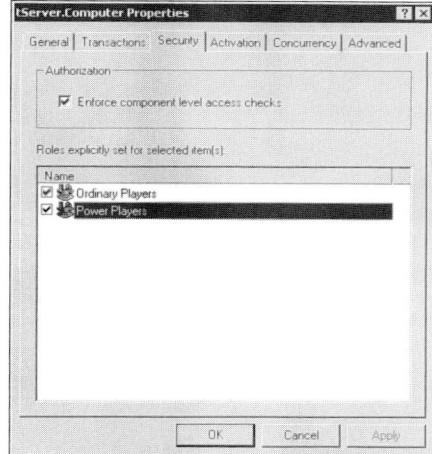

Figure 28.19
The Security page of the tServer.Computer Properties dialog shows the two roles whose members may activate the component.

10. Click the Activation tab (see Figure 28.20). Object pooling isn't needed for components as simple as tServer.Computer and tServer.Human. Object pooling is beneficial, however, for complex components—especially those that connect to databases. The component developer ordinarily recommends the Minimum Pool Size, Maximum Pool Size, and Creation Timeout values. Construction strings are a new COM+ feature that lets you pass custom parameters, such as the path to a DSN, to components. Just In Time (JIT) Activation is a MTS 2.0 feature that conserves server resources by activating the component only when the client executes one of its methods.

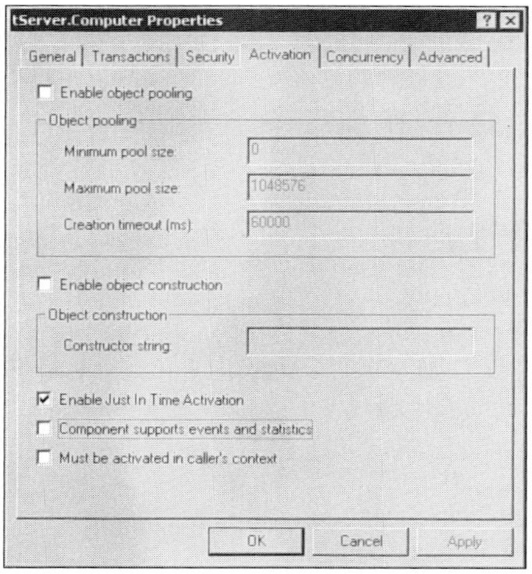

Figure 28.20
The Activation page of the tServer.Computer Properties dialog shows only Just In Time Activation enabled.

PART
V
CH
28

11. Click the Concurrency tab to display synchronization and threading properties. JIT component activation requires synchronization support, so Disabled, Not Supported, and Supported options are disabled. The Threading Model property is determined by the component developer, so its value is read-only.

12. Click the Advanced tab. If the component is a QC, and the component developer has written a class (component) for handling queuing exceptions (errors), type the name of the class in the text box.

Component developers can automate the setting of COM+ application and component properties with a VBScript or JavaScript file that runs under the Windows Scripting Host (WSH). It's very uncommon, however, to find a component developer willing to spend the time and effort to write and test such scripts.

INSTALLING THE TIC-TAC-TOE CLIENT ON REMOTE WORKSTATIONS

The two instances of Tclient.exe communicate with Tserver.dll's components by local procedure calls, not RPCs over DCOM. To run Tic-Tac-Toe on a remote workstation you must export a client .msi (Microsoft Installer) file. Client .msi files serve the same purpose as the client .exe files that MTS 2.0 exports to create a DCOM proxy stub for the components on the remote workstation. Unfortunately, the Export Wizard doesn't offer to let you package the client application .exe in the .msi file, which would eliminate the need to provide both the client and DCOM setup executables. The target workstation must have the Windows Installer application to use .msi files.

To use the COM Application Export Wizard to create a client proxy package, and install the client and proxy from the remote computer, do the following:

1. Right-click the application, Tic-Tac-Toe for this example, and choose Export to start the wizard. Click Next to bypass the first dialog.

2. In the Application Export Information dialog, select the Application Proxy option, click Browse to open the Export Application to File dialog, and navigate to the \Program Files\COM Applications folder. Type the name of the package, **Tic-Tac-Toe**, and click OK to return to the wizard dialog (see Figure 28.21).

Figure 28.21
You use the COM Application Export Wizard to create a client export package (.msi) file for the Tic-Tac-Toe application.

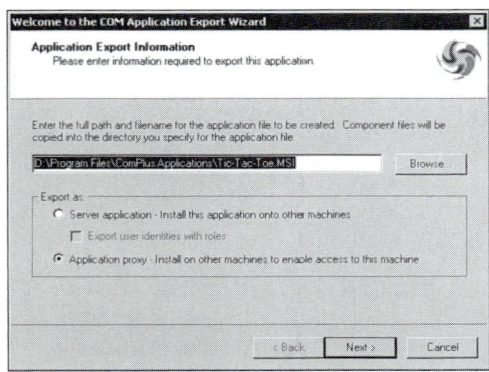

INSTALLING COM+ APPLICATIONS | 1167

3. Click Next and then Finish to create the .msi file and an associated .msi.cab compressed cabinet file for Web-based distribution (see Figure 28.22).

Figure 28.22
Windows Explorer shows the two files created by the COM Application Export Wizard, Tic-Tac-Toe.msi and Tic-Tac-Toe.msi.cab.

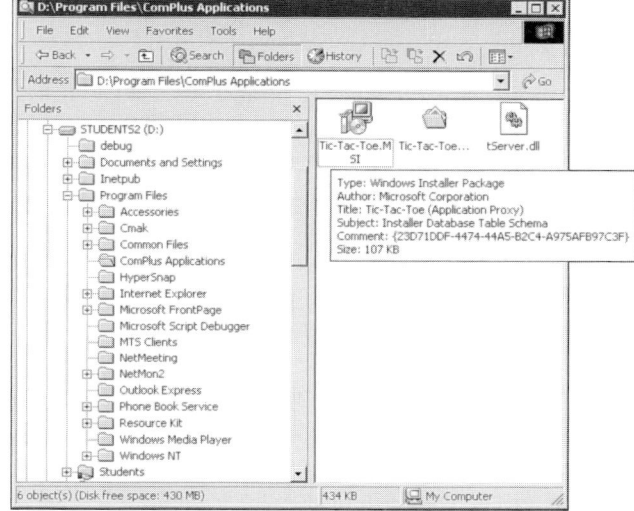

4. Share the ComPlus Applications folder and, if you used it, the MTS Clients folder.
5. Copy Tclient.exe from the app server to the \Program Files\ComPlus Applications folder of a remote computer running Windows 2000 Professional or Server.
6. Run Tic-Tac-Toe.msi from the remote app server, or copy it to \Program Files\ComPlus Applications and run it locally on the workstation. Running the .msi file creates in the \Program Files\ComPlus Applications folder a subfolder named for the component's GUID, {23D71DDF-4474-44A5-B2C4-A975FB97C3F} (see Figure 28.23). The GUID of the component you create will differ. The subfolder contains a copy of Tserver.dll, which contains the type library for component registration.

Figure 28.23
When you run the Tic-Tac-Toe.msi file, the installer creates a directory—named after the GUID of the COM component—that contains a copy of the tServer.DLL file.

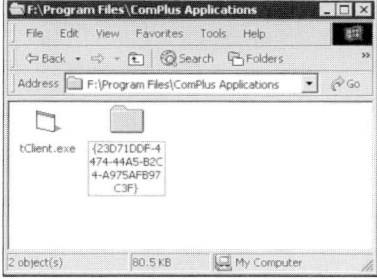

PART
V
CH
28

You can use IntelliMirror's Application Installation Service to create a package that automatically installs the client and the proxy on a single or multiple computers.

→ For more information on IntelliMirror's Application Installation Service, **see** "Using the Application Installation Service," **p. 846**.

SETTING CLIENT DCOM PROPERTIES

You use the Distributed COM Configuration Properties dialog to set up DCOM for the workstations (base clients) that run COM+ applications. Setup for Windows 2000 Professional and Server editions, Windows NT 4.0 Workstation and Server, and Windows 98 installs the Dcomcnfg.exe utility. Windows 95 predates DCOM, but OEM Service Releases (OSRs) 1, 2, 2.1, and 2.5 install version 1.2 of Dcom95.exe, the Windows 95 version of Dcomcnfg.exe. Version 1.3 adds support for Visual Basic 6.0, variant variables that contain user-defined data structures, and other improvements. If you have Windows 95 clients without Dcom95.exe or that run a version earlier than 1.3, download version 1.3 from http://www.microsoft.com/com/dcom/dcom95/dcom1_3.asp.

Client-side DCOM is enabled by default by Windows 2000 and NT, but not by Windows 95—after installing Dcom95.exe—or Windows 98. Running DCOM on Windows 9x requires connecting to the Windows 2000 domain and setting user-level security. You receive an error message if you attempt to start Dcomcnfg.exe with share-level security in effect. As noted earlier, Windows 9x DCOM clients offer only limited security options. Otherwise, setting up client-side DCOM is almost identical for all four operating systems.

> **Note**
>
> If your app server runs COM+ components that connect to other components running on remote app servers, including Windows NT 4.0 servers, run Dcomcnfg and set the default properties to suit the applications' requirements. In most cases, you can set the same Dcomcnfg property values as those for other app servers running MTS 2.0 or COM+. For new distributed applications, the distributed component developer should provide you with a settings list for default Dcomcnfg properties and application properties.

To set up DCOM on a Windows 2000 Professional workstation, do the following:

1. Run Dcomcnfg.exe on the remote computer to open the General page of the Distributed COM Configuration Properties dialog (see Figure 28.24). References to every DCOM application proxy installed on the client appear in the Applications list.

INSTALLING COM+ APPLICATIONS | 1169

Figure 28.24
The Applications page of the Distributed COM Configuration Properties (Dcomcnfg.exe) utility shows the client proxy for the Tic-Tac-Toe application selected.

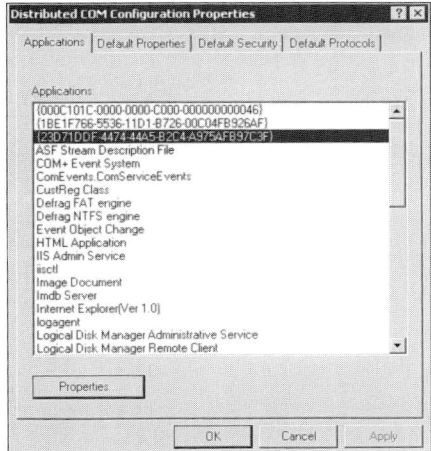

2. Double-click the item in the list with the same GUID as that for the client proxy you just installed, {23D71DDF-4474-44A5-B2C4-A975FB97C3F} for this example, to open the General page of the application's properties sheet (see Figure 28.25).

Figure 28.25
The General page of the properties dialog for the Tic-Tac-Toe DCOM client proxy shows the application name, type, and Authentication Level.

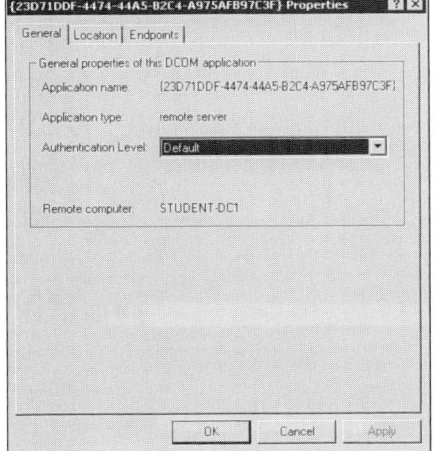

The Default Authentication Level selection works for most applications that don't have access checking enabled. For secure applications, set the Authentication Level to a value equal to or higher than that required by the application and its components.

3. Click the Location tab if you want the client to use components on a computer other than that specified by the client .msi file (see Figure 28.26). If you aren't running AppCenter Server with component load balancing, you might need to specify a different app server to balance the component load across two or more servers.

PART
V
CH
28

Figure 28.26
Use the Location page of the Properties dialog for the Tic-Tac-Toe DCOM client proxy to set the NetBIOS name of the server that hosts the DCOM component.

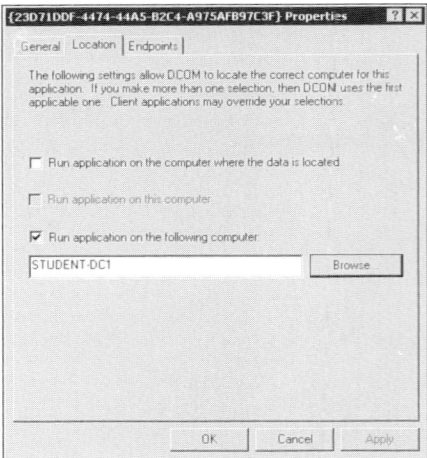

Type the NetBIOS name of the alternate app server computer in the text box, or browse for the computer name. Only when dictated by the component developer should you enable any check box except the default—Run Application on the Following Computer.

4. Click the Endpoints page and click Add to display in the Protocol Sequence list the protocols that the DCOM client can use to contact the app server for the COM+ application. The Windows 2000 default is Connection-oriented TCP/IP, but several other protocols are available, and you can specify static or dynamic endpoints (see Figure 28.27). Click OK to save any changes you made or Cancel to make sure you don't accidentally change a property value.

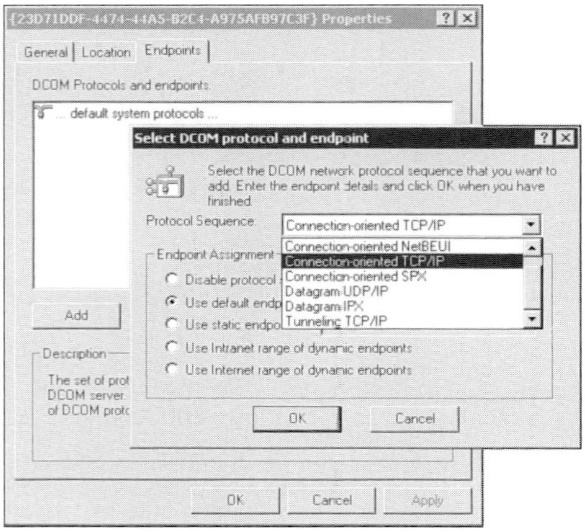

Figure 28.27
The DCOM Endpoint Properties dialog enables you to choose the DCOM protocol sequence and endpoint details for the DCOM client proxy.

RPC endpoints specify a transport—such as TCP/IP, NetBIOS, or named pipes—and port on which applications listen for calls. For named pipes over TCP/IP, the endpoint is a TCP/IP port number and the name of a pipe. You set the TCP/IP port number or range of port numbers in the Default Protocols page of Dcomcnfg. You might need to specify a port number or range to communicate with the app server through a firewall. Click Add to open the Properties for COM Internet Services, and click Add again to open the Add Port Range dialog. Type the port number or range (see Figure 28.28), and click OK twice to return to Dcomcnfg's dialog.

Figure 28.28
By specifying a range of ports for the DCOM client communication, you can enable communication through a firewall or other packet filter.

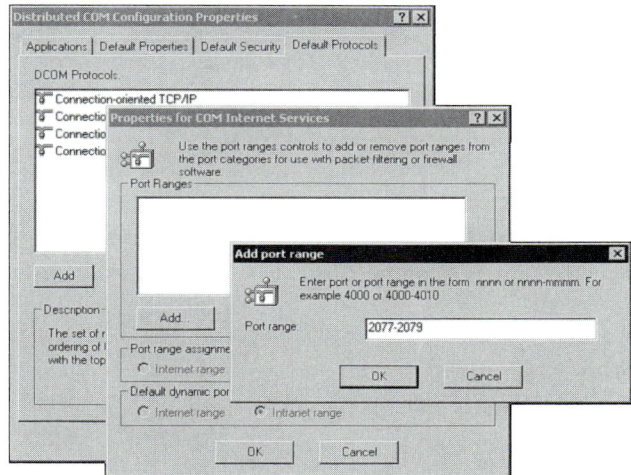

For more information on RPC endpoints related to DCOM, visit http://msdn.microsoft.com/library/psdk/midl/mi-laref_4sqc.htm. If your custom DCOM application requires other than the default endpoint properties, the component developer is responsible for providing you the proper settings.

 If COM+ front ends on client PCs can't connect to a component because of security problems, see the first of the "Security-Related Problems" topics in the "Troubleshooting" section near the end of the chapter.

INSTALLING THE SAMPLE BANK APPLICATION AND CREATING A FILE DSN

The majority of component applications that Windows 2000 administrators are requested to install involve connections between client front ends and back-end databases. The Sample Bank MTS package is an example of a typical middle-tier business service layer that executes database transactions. As mentioned in the "Exploring the Windows 2000 Component Services Tool" section earlier in the chapter, installing Windows NT 4.0 Option Pack also sets up the Sample Bank application.

Sample Bank requires network access to the SQL Server 6.5+ or Microsoft Data Engine (MSDE) 1.0+ pubs sample database, and you must create a File DSN to specify the name of the server on which SQL Server or MSDE is running and the pubs data source. Establishing ODBC data sources—in the form of User, System, or File DSNs—usually is a database administrator (DBA) responsibility, but network administrators often are called upon to perform the duty. Installing the Sample Bank application provides you a preview of the typical steps you take when setting up any middle-tier COM+ or MTS 2.0 component that's designed to manage database transactions.

> **Note**
>
> MSDE 1.0 is the desktop or small workgroup version of SQL Server 7.0 that's included with Microsoft Office Professional and Premium versions. MSDE 1.0 also is a no-charge add-on for Visual Studio 6.0 Professional and Enterprise editions. If you have a Professional or Enterprise Visual Studio, Visual Basic, Visual C++, Visual InterDev, Visual J++, or Visual FoxPro 6.0 license, you can order MSDE 1.0 on a CD-ROM at http://msdn.microsoft.com/vstudio/msde/order.asp.

The Sample Bank application consists of a single Visual Basic 5.0 client, Vbbank.exe, and three ActiveX DLLs—Vbacct.dll (Visual Basic), Vcacct.dll (Visual C++), and Vjacct.dll (Visual J++). The client lets you choose between components written in each of the three languages supported by Microsoft Visual Studio 5+.

If you have network access to SQL Server 6.5+, preferably a development installation of SQL Server 7.0 or 2000, the following sections demonstrate how to install the three components, create a File DSN, run the Vbbank.exe client, and export client and server Microsoft Installer packages.

Installing the Sample Bank Components

Installation of Sample Bank follows the same basic steps as those for Tic-Tac-Toe. Do the following to install the Sample Bank MTS 2.0 package as a COM+ application:

1. Copy Vbbank.exe and the three ActiveX DLLs to the ComPlus Applications folder of your app server.
2. Create an empty application named Sample Bank, and then add the three component DLLs to the application. Your new application appears in the Component Services snap-in as shown in Figure 28.29. Components without a .VC or .VJ extension are written in Visual Basic 5.0.

INSTALLING THE SAMPLE BANK APPLICATION AND CREATING A FILE DSN | 1173

Figure 28.29
The Component Services snap-in shows the Visual Basic, Visual C++ (.VC,) and Visual J++ (.VJ) components of the MTS 2.0 Sample Bank Application.

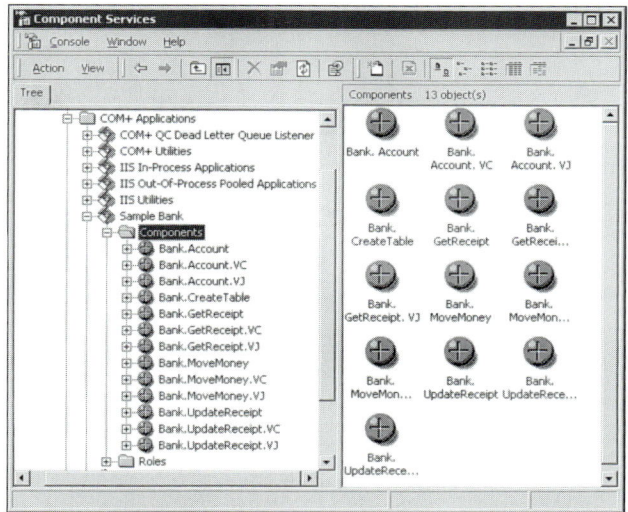

> **Note**
> ADO 2.5+ and COM-based OLE DB data providers are the preferred methods for connecting to RDBMSs that support these technologies. Microsoft supplies native OLE DB providers for Jet (Access), SQL Server, DB2, and Oracle databases, plus an OLE DB Provider for ODBC Drivers, which was called Kagera during its development. (Component developers continue to refer to this provider as Kagera.) Sample Bank uses Kagera and ADO to connect to SQL Server. The native OLE DB provider for SQL Server offers slightly better performance than Kagera.

CREATING A FILE DSN

You use Windows 2000's Data Sources (ODBC) administrative tool to create new ODBC data sources. Windows NT and Windows 9x use Control Panel tools—ODBC Data Sources and ODBC Data Sources (32bit), respectively—for creating and modifying DSNs.

To create the MTSSamples.dsn required by the Sample Bank components, do the following:

1. Choose Administrative Tools, Data Sources (ODBC) to open the ODBC Data Source Administrator; click the File DSN tab; and click Add to open the drivers selection dialog of the Create a New Data Source Wizard. The default location for ODBC File DSNs is \Program Files\Common Files\ODBC\Data Sources.

2. Scroll to the bottom of the Name list, and select the SQL Server driver (see Figure 28.30). Click Next to open the second wizard dialog.

PART
V
CH
28

Figure 28.30
In the Create New Data Source dialog, you must choose the driver to use for the new DSN, SQL Server in this case.

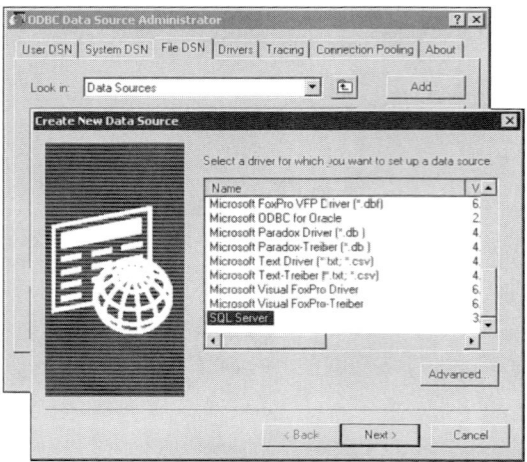

3. Type the name of the File DSN in the text box. The file name must be **MTSSamples** for the Sample Bank application. The wizard adds the .dsn extension.

4. Click Next, review the specification for MTSSamples.dsn, and click Finish to begin setting SQL Server parameters.

5. In the first Create a New Data Source to SQL Server dialog, type an optional description, and select in the Server list the NetBIOS name of the computer running SQL Server (see Figure 28.31). If the server's running on the computer you're using, select (local). Click Next.

Figure 28.31
This step in the Create New Data Source dialog requires you to choose the SQL Server to connect to and, optionally, enter a description for the DSN.

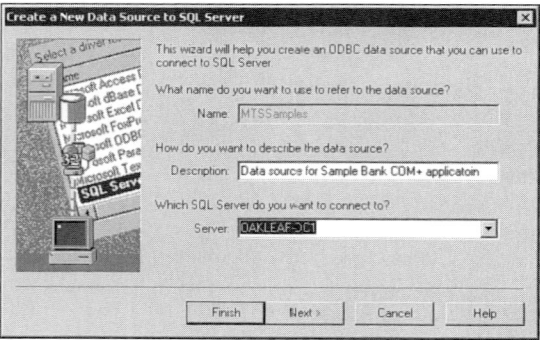

6. Select the With SQL Server Authentication option, and type your SQL Server login ID and password—**sa** and an empty password for an unsecured server (see Figure 28.32). Alternatively, if the server is installed with Windows NT authentication, select the With Windows NT Authentication option. Click Next.

INSTALLING THE SAMPLE BANK APPLICATION AND CREATING A FILE DSN | 1175

Figure 28.32
The next step in the Create New Data Source is to specify the authentication type and login information for the database.

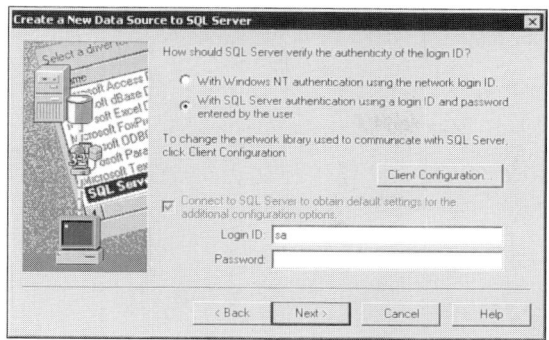

Clicking Client Configuration opens the Add Network Library Configuration dialog that lets you select one of several connection-based network protocols (endpoints). The default is named pipes, but you can select the TCP/IP or Multiprotocol option if your server is configured to use these protocols.

7. Mark the Change the Default Database To check box and select pubs from the list (see Figure 28.33). Accept the remaining defaults, and click Next.

Figure 28.33
The Create a New Data Source dialog requires you to specify the default database on the server to which to connect, and the ANSI character options.

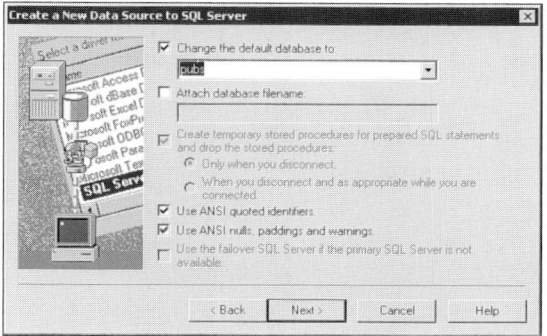

The Attach Database Filename option lets you specify a particular SQL Server 7+ database file (*Filename*.mdf). If you choose this option, you type the name of the database (usually *Filename*) in the Change the Default Database To box.

8. Accept the defaults in the language and logs dialog, and click Finish.
9. In the SQL Server Setup dialog, review the File DSN property values (see Figure 28.34).

PART
V
CH
28

Figure 28.34
The SQL Server Setup dialog presents you with a summary of the information collected and allows you to either test the new data source or accept the information as-is.

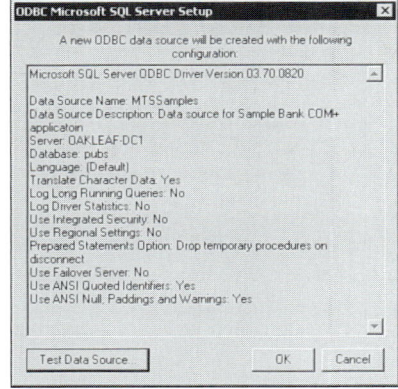

10. Click Test Data Source to verify your connection to the pubs database, which returns a Test Completed Successfully! message if SQL Server/MSDE is started and the DSN property values you entered are correct. Click OK twice to close the dialogs, save MTSSamples.dsn, dismiss the wizard, and close the ODBC Data Source Administrator.

Testing the Components and File DSN with the Sample Bank Client

To use Vbbank.exe to test your work in the prior two sections, do the following:

1. Launch Vbbank.exe, accept all default options, and click Submit. After the few seconds required to instantiate the components and make the initial connection to the pubs database, a confirmation of a MoveMoney operation appears in the Results text box (see Figure 28.35).

Figure 28.35
The Sample Bank application shows the result of its default operation, adding one dollar to account 1.

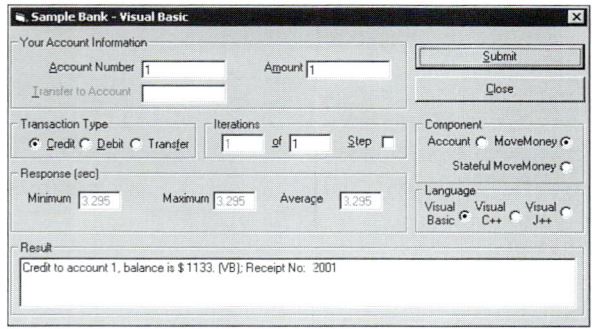

The MoveMoney operation, which simply credits an account by executing the Bank.MoveMoney component, isn't a transaction, because the operation doesn't debit another account. The times shown in the Response frame are typical for the initial Submit operation. Successive operations occur much faster, because the application's components remain in memory for the three-minute duration you specified in the Advanced page of the applications properties dialog (refer to Figure 28.17).

2. Select the Transfer option in the Transaction Type frame, type **2** in the Transfer to Account text box, type **100** in the Amount text box, and select the Visual C++ option in the Language frame. A transfer between accounts qualifies as a transaction, and the Visual C++ components have the transactions `Required` property value set.

3. Arrange the Component Services snap-in and Sample Bank windows so you can observe the component cue ball icons while the transaction executes. Click Submit and observe the simulated rotation of the Bank.Account.VC and Bank.MoveMoney.VC icons during component activation (see Figure 28.36).

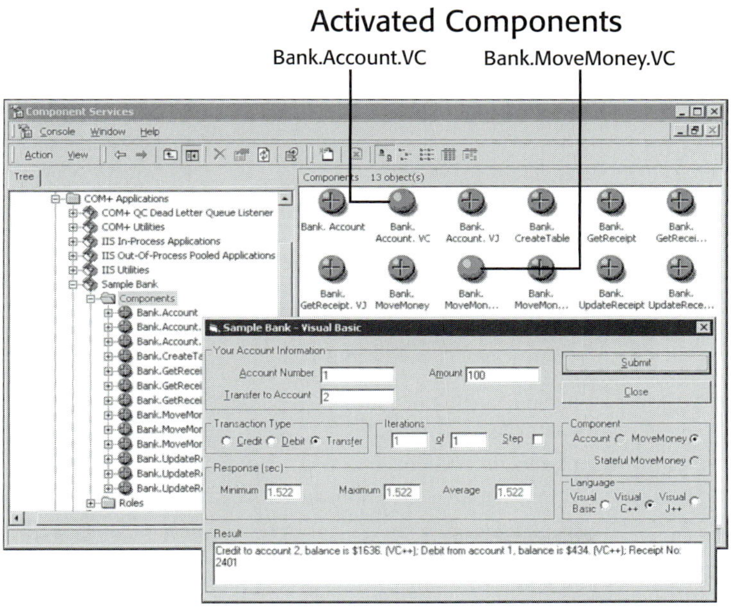

Figure 28.36
The Component Services snap-in in the background shows the Bank.Account.VC and the Bank.MoveMoney.VC components activated while executing a Transfer transaction.

You might need to let a couple of minutes expire from the last operation to observe the component icon rotation. When the components are loaded into memory, execution of the transaction requires only about 0.1 second.

Changing the programming language option lets you compare speed of execution of components written in Visual Basic and Visual C++. The Visual J++ component throws an OLE DB for ODBC Drivers "Can't have multiple recordsets" error when run under Windows 2000.

Exporting Sample Bank Client and Server Installer Packages

Exporting the client proxy to a SampleBankProxy.msi file follows the same procedure as that for the Tic-Tac-Toe proxy in the preceding "Installing the Tic-Tac-Toe Client on Remote Workstations" section. After you install the client proxy and copy Vbbank.exe to the remote workstation, run the Vbbank client to check DCOM performance across the network. The default client DCOM property settings for Tic-Tac-Toe are satisfactory for Sample Bank.

If you want to balance the Sample Bank component load across multiple app servers, you create a server application package, and then run the SampleBankApp.msi on other app servers. Balancing the load requires that you specify the alternate location in the Location page of the client's DCOM properties sheet for the application (refer to Figure 28.26) or create client proxy .msi files on the alternate app server. Server application .msi files are the successor to MTS 2.0 package (.pak) files.

To export a server application package for Sample Bank and install the COM+ application on another app server, do the following:

1. Right-click the Sample Bank application node, and choose Export to start the COM Application Export Wizard. Click Next to bypass the Welcome dialog.

2. In the Application Export Information dialog, type the filename—**SampleBankApp.msi** for this example—in the text box, and accept the default Server Application option.

3. Click Next; wait for the wizard to create the SampleBankApp.msi file; and then click Finish to dismiss the wizard.

4. On another app server, navigate to the SampleBankApp.msi file in the original server's \Program Files\ComPlus Applications folder, and double-click SampleBankApp.msi to install the application and its components. Installation of the Microsoft Installer package takes only a few seconds.

5. Close the Component Services snap-in if it's open, and launch it to verify installation of the Sample Bank application and its components. Pressing F5 or choosing Action, Refresh in an open instance of Component Services snap-in doesn't display the newly added application.

You can test the second installation of the Sample Bank application by changing the server NetBIOS name in the Location page of the Sample Bank property dialog to the name of the second app server.

 If DCOM front ends on your PC clients begin slowing down as you add more users of a component, see the "Performance-Related Problems" topic in the "Troubleshooting" section near the end of the chapter.

Administering the Distributed Transaction Coordinator

Installing Windows 2000 Server automatically adds the DTC service and sets its properties for automatic startup during the boot process. The DTC comes into play with QCs and when your components require connections to an XA-compliant transaction manager, use COM TI and Microsoft SNA Server to connect to CICS, or connect to multiple databases that participate in a single transaction.

ADMINISTERING THE DISTRIBUTED TRANSACTION COORDINATOR | 1179

The default DTC properties are adequate for most DTC operations, but you might need to verify or alter the default values. If you do, run this drill:

1. Choose Administrative Tools, Computer Management to open the Computer Management snap-in, expand the Services and Applications node, and click Services to display the list of Windows 2000 services in the right pane.

2. Right-click the Distributed Transaction Coordinator item, and choose Properties to open DTC's tabbed properties dialog for the local computer with the General page active (see Figure 28.37).

Figure 28.37
The General page of the DTC Properties dialog for the local computer shows the Description, Startup Type, and status of the DTC service.

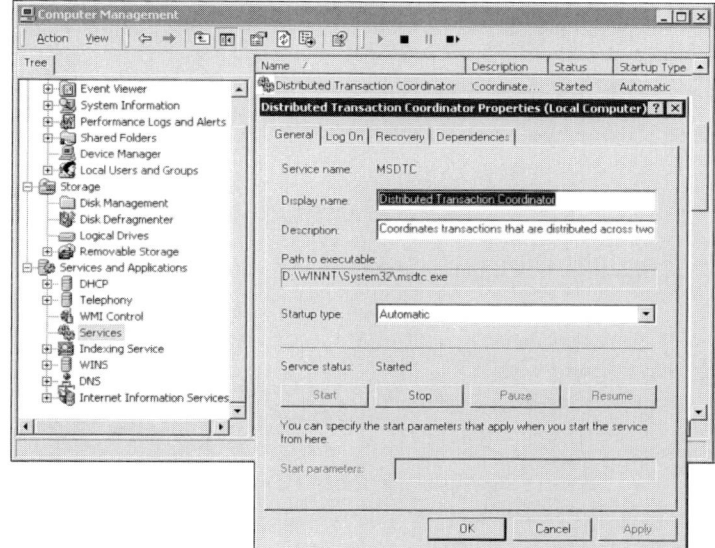

3. If you or someone else has changed the default Startup Type value, and you need DTC for QCs or other custom components, choose Automatic from the Startup Type list, and click Start to start the DTC service.

4. A software vendor or component developer may request that you change settings on the Recovery page. By default, no action occurs on the first, second, third, or subsequent DTC failures; All failures, however, add entries to the Application event log. Figure 28.38 shows a common set of responses to DTC failures.

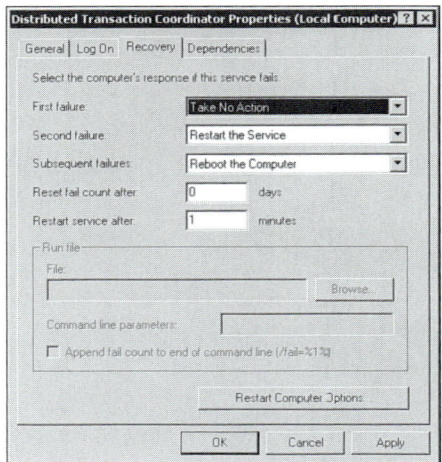

Figure 28.38
The Recovery page of the DTC Properties dialog for the local computer shows some possible options that occur upon failure of the DTC service. The defaults are to take no action for the First, Second, and subsequent failures.

Accepting the default Reset Fail Count After value of 0 days results in the fail count never resetting. You can specify a longer Restart Service After period if requested, but one minute usually is adequate.

The LogOn page specifies the account under which the DTS service runs; the default is the Local System account with Allow Service to Interact with Desktop permission. It's an uncommon practice to change the account.

The Dependencies page displays the processes on which DTC depends—Remote Procedure Call (RPC) and Security Accounts Manager. If either of these two services fail, DTC won't start. If Security Accounts Manager doesn't start, all other services that depend on a logon fail, too. The only service that's dependent on the DTC is Message Queuing (MSMQ); an entry appears for Message Queuing Services in the dependent services list only if you've installed or upgraded MSMQ.

Upgrading or Installing Message Queuing Services

Regardless of whether you upgrade a Windows NT 4.0 server with MSMQ 1.0 installed, which is the most likely scenario for most Windows 2000 administrators, or install MSMQ 2.0 from scratch, you must perform a few administrative actions. MSMQ's network topology is quite similar to that of AD—for example, you locate one or more MSMQ server(s) in the equivalent of AD sites.

Upgrading from MSMQ 1.0 to 2.0

If MSMQ 1.0 is installed on a Windows NT 4.0 Server that you're upgrading to Windows 2000, Setup's Report System Compatibility dialog indicates that Microsoft Message

Queuing Services are not compatible with Windows 2000. Select the entry in the list and click Details. The Compatibility Details message advises you to run the Windows 2000 "Migration Utility" after Setup completes, but there is no "Migration Utility" option in the Windows 2000 Configure Your Server function.

→ For a review of upgrading the initial Windows NT 4.0 PDC to Windows 2000 and installing AD as the initial root domain controller, **see** "Upgrading a Windows NT 4.0 Production Server," **p. 352**.

MSMQ 1.0 requires a local or network connection to SQL Server 6.5+ to store the MQIS (Message Queue Information Store) database for the Primary Enterprise Controller (PEC). The first installation of MSMQ 1.0 under Windows NT 4.0 Server must be a PEC in order to add MSMQ clients and additional MSMQ servers to the system. MSMQ 2.0 uses the AD database for the MQIS, so the PEC computer, even if it's a member server in a resource domain, must have AD installed as a domain controller (DC) to permit the upgrade. All Primary Site Controllers also must be promoted to DCs.

> **Caution**
>
> You must upgrade the MSMQ 1.0 PEC before upgrading any other MSMQ servers. The PEC you upgrade *must* become the initial root domain for your AD installation. After you upgrade the PEC, upgrade the Backup Site Controllers (BSCs) in each site. Finally, upgrade the Primary Site Controllers (PSCs) in each site. Each PSC also must be a Global Catalog (GC) server. Failure to observe this upgrade sequence results in the inability of MSMQ 2.0 to communicate across sites.
>
> If you use secure communications between site controllers, you must export the Windows NT server certificate before upgrading. For additional important information on the upgrade sequence and other restrictions, refer to the "Upgrade Requirements and Considerations for Message Queuing" topic in the online help for the Message Queuing Upgrade Wizard.
>
> Immediately before upgrading the PEC, manually force synchronization between the PEC and all PSCs and BSCs in the enterprise. Failure to synchronize all servers is likely to result in MSMQ "dead letters"—messages that can't reach their destination.

> **Tip from**
> *RJ*
>
> Before you upgrade MSMQ 1.0, launch Active Directory Sites and Services, and rename the default-first-site-name node to the name of your MSMQ 1.0 PEC site. Otherwise, two sites appear below the Sites node.

After you complete the upgrade of your PEC computer to the initial root domain controller of your new Windows 2000 forest, do the following to migrate MSMQ from version 1.0 to 2.0:

1. Click the Finish Setup link in the Windows 2000 Configure Your Server dialog to open the Add/Remove Programs dialog (see Figure 28.39).

Figure 28.39
Use the Add/Remove Programs dialog to upgrade a Windows NT 4.0 installation of MSMQ 1.0 to Windows 2000 MSMQ 2.0.

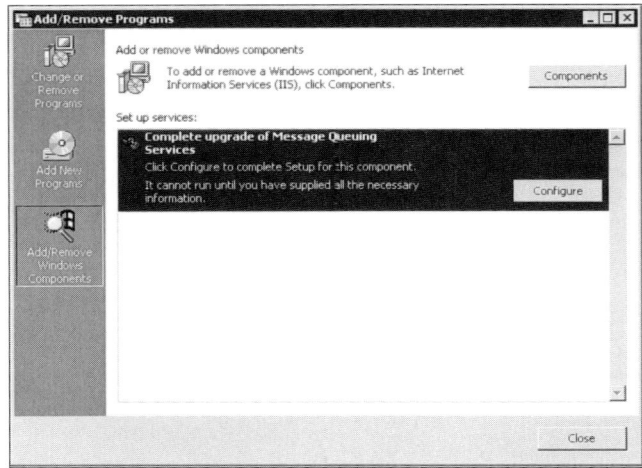

2. Click Configure in the Complete Upgrade of Message Queuing Services item to start the Message Queuing Upgrade Wizard.

3. Click Help to open the Wizard's online help file, expand the Message Queuing link, click the Checklists item, and then the Checklist: Upgrade for MSMQ 1.0 Controller Servers link. Thoroughly read the checklist topics before proceeding. You can cancel the upgrade process in any wizard dialog prior to upgrading the MQIS database to AD.

4. Close the online help file, and click Next to bypass the Welcome dialog.

5. In the Message Queuing Upgrade Logging dialog, select the level of detail for the upgrade log file. The default option is Error(s) only. Select the Trace, Warnings, and Errors or All Events option to ensure that the Mqmig.log file includes sufficient information to repair any damage that occurs during upgrade (see Figure 28.40). Click Next.

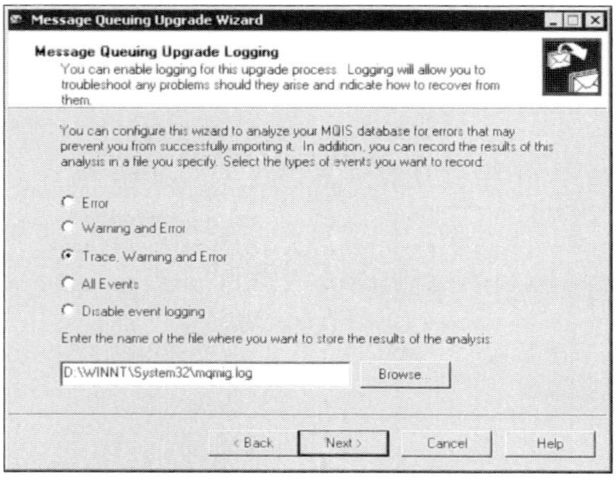

Figure 28.40
The Message Queuing Upgrade Wizard enables you to specify the level of detail in the MSMQ upgrade log file that's used for troubleshooting migration problems.

6. In the Pre-Upgrade Step: Analyze MQIS Database for Errors dialog, accept the Scan Database default (see Figure 28.41), and click Next to have the wizard perform a test of the MQIS database. If the database is inconsistent or has other errors, the wizard appends entries to Mqmig.log. Click Next.

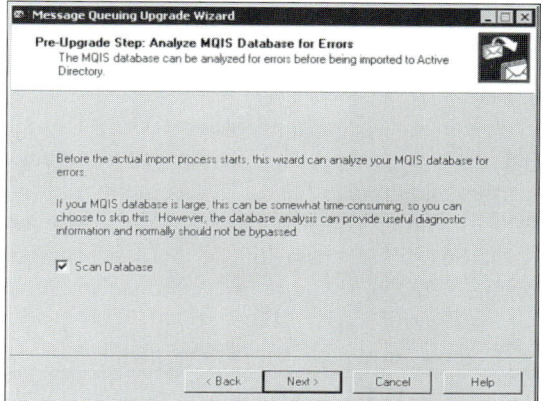

Figure 28.41
The Pre-Upgrade Step of the Message Queuing Upgrade Wizard gives you the option of scanning the MQIS database for errors, and is the second-to-last chance to stop the process before making irreversible changes to MSMQ 1.0.

7. In the Ready to Import the MQIS Database dialog, the View Log File button is enabled if the wizard discovers database errors. If errors occur, read the log file before proceeding.

> **Caution**
> If there are any significant errors in the log file at this point, click Cancel and resolve the errors. You probably need help from the developer of message-enabled components to determine the severity of the errors and how to resolve them, if resolution is possible. Rerun the Message Queuing Upgrade Wizard when you're sure that the errors have been resolved or won't interfere with an orderly upgrade.

8. Click Next to start the database import process. The length of time the Importing the MQIS Database dialog remains open depends on the complexity of your site topology and the number of message queues for the components installed on your app servers (including this server).

9. In the last wizard dialog, click Review Log to open Mqmig.log in Notepad. The log that results from upgrading an active MSMQ 1.0 PEC might have a few hundred—or thousand—lines. Print the log for later reference if you encounter MSMQ problems; developers of the QCs you upgrade are likely to request a copy of the Mqmig.log.

Installing an MSMQ 2.0 Server

If you didn't specify installation of Message Queuing Services during a new Windows 2000 Server installation, or you upgraded a Windows NT 4.0 Server without MSMQ 1.0, use the Windows Components feature of Control Panel's Add/Remove Programs tool to install

MSMQ. Windows 2000 Setup doesn't install MSMQ 2.0 by default because you must promote the new server to AD before installing the first MSMQ 2.0 server.

> **Tip from**
> *RJ*
>
> Read the online help file for MSMQ 2.0—Msmq.chm in the \Winnt\Help folder—before installing the first MSMQ server. Windows 2000 Setup installs the online help files for MSMQ 2.0. Msmq.chm's "Install Message Queuing" topic contains additional information you should read before installing MSMQ on a production server.

The first MSMQ 2.0 server you add—the equivalent of MSMQ 1.0's PEC—must reside on a Windows 2000 DC, but not necessarily the initial root domain controller. However, if you need interoperability between Windows NT 4.0 MSMQ clients and servers you add after installing the MSMQ 2.0 PEC for a forest, you must install the PEC on the PDC emulator for the domain—usually the first server in the domain that you promote to AD. You also must weaken security during the AD promotion process to permit Windows NT 4.0 MSMQ clients to interoperate with MSMQ 2.0.

> **Note**
>
> MSMQ 2.0 doesn't designate servers as PECs, PSCs, and BSCs. Like DCs, MSMQ 2.0 treats all servers as equals, but—like the initial root domain controller—the first MSMQ server you install is more equal than the others. The first MSMQ server is the equivalent of AD's PDC emulator; the first MSMQ server you install provides connectivity between Windows 2000 and Windows NT PSCs and BSCs.

To install MSMQ 2.0 from scratch on the initial root domain DC, follow these steps:

1. Launch Control Panel's Add/Remove Programs tool, click Windows Components, and mark the Message Queuing Services check box in the components list.

2. Insert the distribution CD-ROM for your server version, and click OK to start the installation process.

3. In the Message Queuing Type dialog, accept the only Message Queuing Server option, and don't mark the Enable Routing check box (see Figure 28.42). Microsoft recommends that you don't install message routing on domain controllers, which are presumed to remain online at all times. Click Next.

4. In the Windows NT 4.0 Message Queuing Clients dialog, mark the Yes, Weaken the Permissions option if you intend to support Windows NT 4.0 messaging clients (see Figure 28.43). A messaging client is a computer running a client application that connects to COM+ components with message queues rather than by DCOM RPCs. Otherwise, accept the default No, Do Not Change the Permissions option. Click Next to install MSMQ 2.0, which requires a few minutes.

UPGRADING OR INSTALLING MESSAGE QUEUING SERVICES | 1185

Figure 28.42
This dialog of the Windows Components Wizard allows you to select the type of MSMQ software to install (server or client) with the default selections shown.

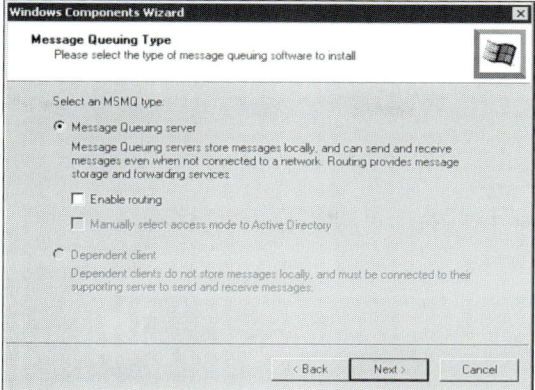

Figure 28.43
The Windows NT 4.0 Message Queuing Clients dialog of the Windows Components Wizard allows you to weaken the security of an MSMQ 2.0 installation to accommodate Windows NT 4.0 MSMQ 1.0 clients.

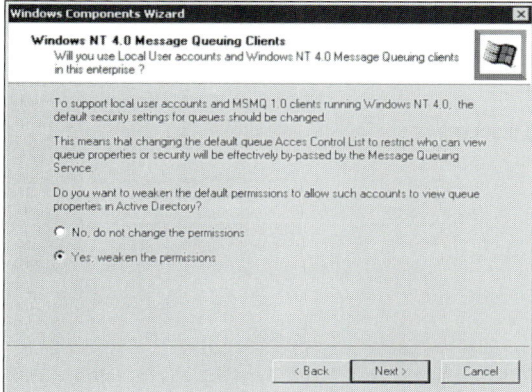

5. Click Finish to dismiss the wizard and close the Add/Remove Programs tool.

INSTALLING AN MSMQ 2.0 CLIENT FOR WINDOWS 2000 PROFESSIONAL

Workstations that use messaging to communicate with MSMQ 2.0 server components require installation of the MSMQ 2.0 client. To install the client components on computers running Windows 2000 Professional, do the following:

1. Launch Control Panel's Add/Remove Programs tool, click Windows Components, and mark the Message Queuing Services check box in the components list.

PART
V
CH
28

2. Insert the distribution CD-ROM for your server version, and click OK to start the installation process.

3. In the Message Queuing Type dialog, accept the default Independent Client option, unless the workstation has a permanent, reliable network connection and you don't want to provide local message storing capability. Mark the Manually Select Access Mode to Active Directory check box if you want to specify a particular server hosting MSMQ 2.0 (see Figure 28.44). Click Next.

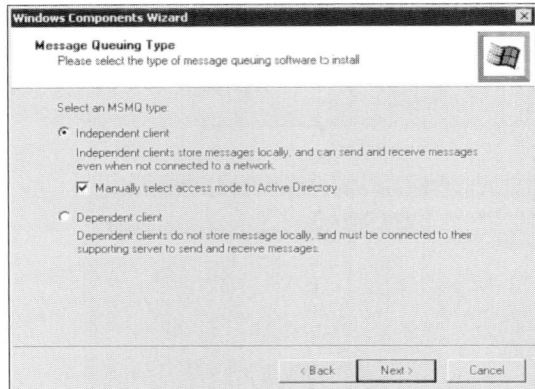

Figure 28.44
Use the Message Queuing Type dialog to specify whether MSMQ clients are independent (use resources on the local machine) or dependent (use server resources).

4. If you marked the Manually Select Access Mode to Active Directory check box, the Message Queuing Server dialog opens. Accept the default Message Queuing Will Access a Directory Service, and type the name of the DC hosting MSMQ 2.0 (see Figure 28.45). If your client has applications that connect to MSMQ 1.0 servers, mark the Authenticate MSMQ 1.0 Controller check box. Click Next to start the client installation process.

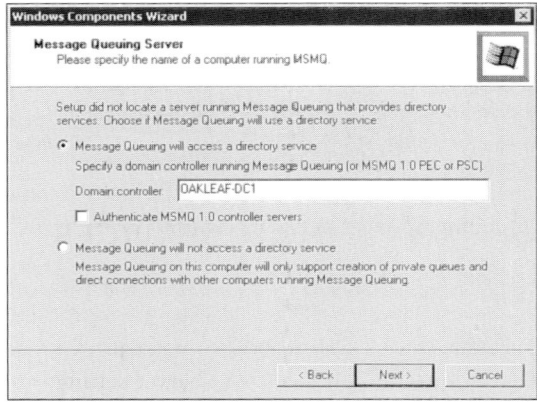

Figure 28.45
When performing a client install, you must specify the AD enabled server running an MSMQ server, and check the Authenticate MSMQ 1.0 Controller Servers if the client uses applications that access MSMQ 1.0 servers.

MANAGING MESSAGE QUEUING SERVICES | 1187

5. Click Next to run the MSMQ 2.0 client installation process, click Finish to dismiss the wizard, and close the Add/Remove Programs tool.

INSTALLING MSMQ 2.0 ON MEMBER SERVERS

Member app servers that don't have AD installed offer you the option of installing MSMQ 2.0 in the server or client configuration. When you start the installation process, the initial Message Queuing Type dialog enables the Message Queuing Server and Dependent Client options, and offers two check boxes to let you Enable Routing and Manually Select Access Mode to Active Directory. When installing MSMQ 2.0 on an app server, accept the default Message Queuing Server option, and mark the Enable Routing check box (see Figure 28.46). When you click Next, the wizard connects to the closest AD-enabled MSMQ server, and commences the MSMQ 2.0 installation process.

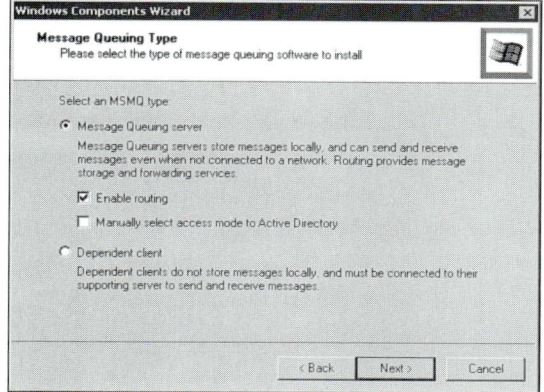

Figure 28.46
The Message Queuing Type dialog on a member server (non-Domain Controller) allows you to install either an MSMQ server or client.

Note

If the Windows Components Wizard can't find an AD-enabled MSMQ server, the second wizard dialog opens (refer to Figure 28.45). If you type the name of a server to which your app server can't connect, the installation process starts, but terminates with an error message. In this case, run My Computer, Properties, demote the app server to a workgroup server, then reconnect the server to the domain with the AD-enabled MSMQ server. You only need to reboot the app server once—after respecifying its domain name.

MANAGING MESSAGE QUEUING SERVICES

You manage MSMQ 2.0 servers primarily with the Active Directory Sites and Services snap-in. You must have MSMQ 2.0 installed at multiple sites—or at least on multiple computers—to enable most administrative options. In most cases, the developer responsible for writing QCs supplies you recommended MSMQ Server settings and topology. As an administrator, you need to know where and how to set the MSMQ property settings the developer gives you.

PART
V
CH
28

> **Note**
>
> If you intend to manage servers running MSMQ 2.0 from a workstation running Windows 2000 Professional, you must install the Server Administrative Tools, which include the Active Directory Sites and Services snap-in.

For a brief introduction to MSMQ administrative operations, do the following:

1. Open the Active Directory Sites and Services snap-in, and choose View, Show Services Node to alter the contents of the left pane to display services.

2. Expand the Services node, right-click MsmqServices, and choose Properties to open the MsmqServices Properties dialog. The General page (see Figure 28.47) lets you specify message lifetime in the network; MSMQ occasionally uses the term *network* as a synonym for site. 90 days is the default; you can specify message lifetime in days, hours, or minutes. The Object and Security pages are similar to those for most other AD objects.

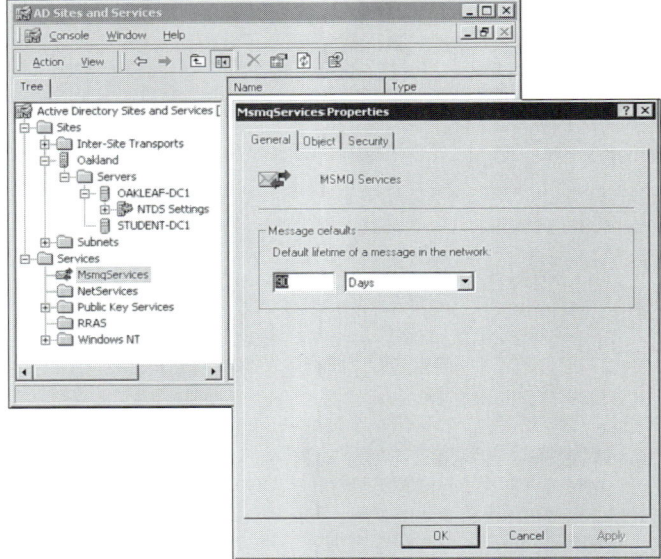

Figure 28.47
The General page of the MsmqServices Properties sheet—accessed from the Active Directory Sites and Services snap-in—enables you to specify the default lifetime for a message on the network.

3. MSMQ Settings don't appear in the left pane's tree view, but clicking the server name displays an MSMQ Settings entry in the right pane if MSMQ 2.0 is installed. You probably won't have to change the properties of MSMQ Settings under normal circumstances.

4. You can define MSMQ foreign sites by right-clicking the MsmqServices node, and choosing New Foreign Site. Type the name of the site—**Berkeley** for this example—in the text box, and click OK. You don't need to have an MSMQ server operational in the site in order to define it, nor does the site need to exist. Adding a new MSMQ foreign

MANAGING MESSAGE QUEUING SERVICES | 1189

site is the equivalent of adding a new AD site. You must close and reopen the Active Directory Sites and Services snap-in for the new site to appear; pressing F5 or choosing Action, Refresh doesn't work.

→ For more information on Windows 2000's intersite communication features, **see** "Analyzing Intersite Replication Requirements and Administration," **p. 984**.

5. If you add a sample foreign site, right-click MsmqServices, and choose New Foreign Computer. Select the foreign site name from the list and type the name of the computer running or to be set up to run MSMQ 2.0—**student-dc1** for this example.

6. Right-click MsmqServices again, and choose New, MSMQ Routing link to open the Routing Link dialog. Figure 28.48 illustrates adding a second routing link between the Oakland and Berkeley sites. An incredibly long object ID in the right pane represents the previously added routing link.

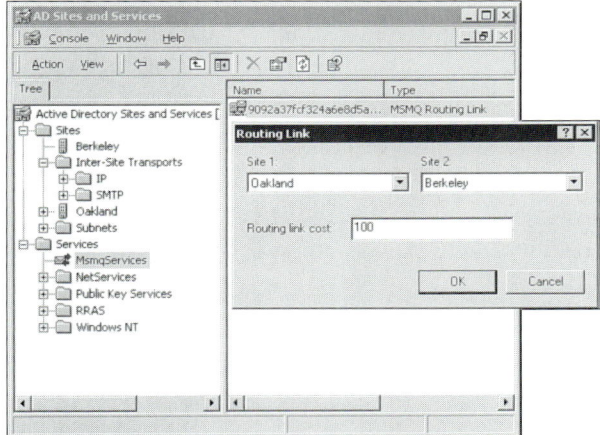

Figure 28.48
From the Active Directory Sites and Services snap-in, you can add a dedicated MSMQ 2.0 routing link to a remote site.

7. Right-click the routing link to open its properties dialog, and click the Site Gates tab. For each routing link with a foreign site, you must specify a site gate that is responsible for handling messages between sites. Select the MSMQ server in the Site Servers list, and click Add to add the selected server to the Site Gates list (see Figure 28.49).

PART
V
CH
28

Figure 28.49
The Site Gates page of the properties sheet for the newly created MSMQ 2.0 link allows you to specify the Site Gates server for a foreign site.

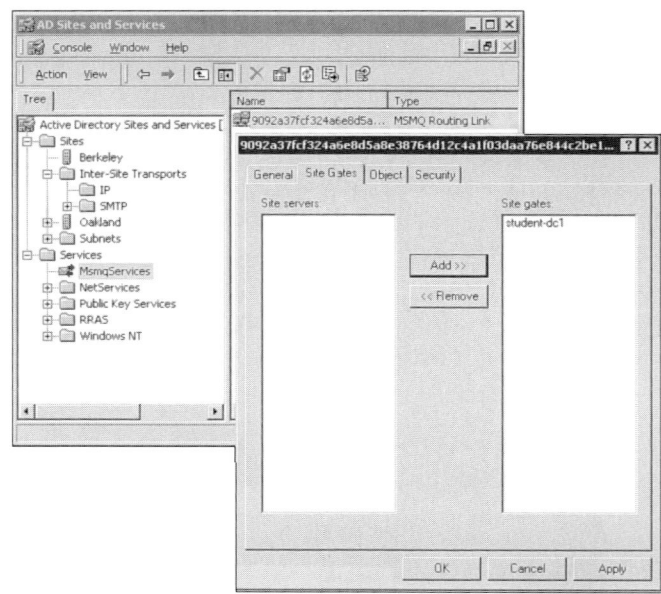

MSMQ routing links use the DEFAULTIPSITELINK transport by default. It's possible—but not common—to use the Simple Mail Transport Protocol (SMTP) as the message transport.

The other MSMQ 2.0 administrative application is Control Panel's Message Queuing tool that sets the drives and folders for local MSMQ files and establishes certificate-based security for communication between clients and servers. To check out the Message Queuing tool, do this:

1. Launch Control Panel's Message Queuing tool to display its General page (see Figure 28.50). You can specify location of message files, message logs, and transaction logs on different drives to gain a nominal increase in performance.

Figure 28.50
The General page of the Message Queuing tool enables you to configure the storage locations for local MSMQ files.

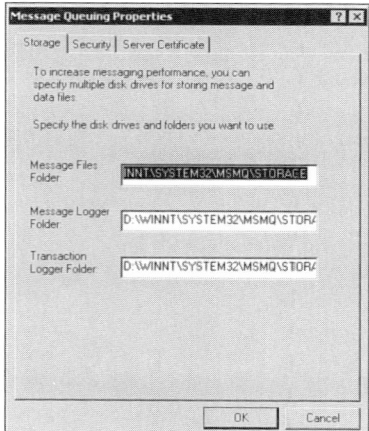

2. Click the Security tab to specify user certificates for messages and server certificates for authentication (see Figure 28.51). The Security page lets you add, view, and remove AD user certificates for messages, implement certificate-based secure communication channels between message servers, and renew certificates and cryptographic keys.

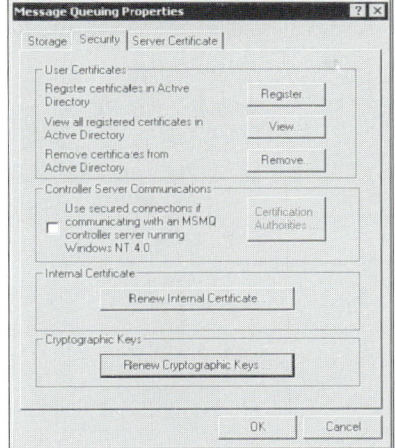

Figure 28.51
The Security page of the Message Queuing tool is used to configure certificate-based user and server identities for MSMQ security purposes.

→ For the basics of Windows 2000's Certificate Services, **see** "Working with User Certificates," **p. 512**.

3. Click Register to open the Personal Certificates dialog that lists user certificates registered by AD. By default, certificates for the local Administrator account of remote computers appear in the list.

4. Select one of the certificates and click View Certificate to display a typical user certificate (see Figure 28.52) for the MSMQ app server added in the preceding "Installing MSMQ 2.0 on Member Servers" section. The first certificate in the list is for the MSMQ client workstation added in the earlier "Installing an MSMQ 2.0 Client for Windows 2000 Professional" section. By default, the term of the certificate is eight years from the date you register it in the Security page. Click OK twice to close the dialogs.

Figure 28.52
Clicking the register button in the Security page of the Message Queuing Properties tool allows you to register a certificate, in this case for the Administrator account of the student-dc1 application server running MSMQ 2.0 server.

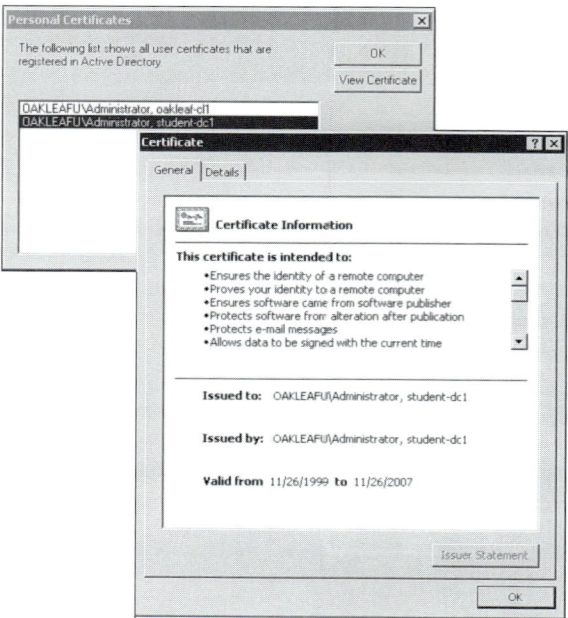

5. Click the Server Certificate tab and the Select a Certificate for Server Authentication button to open the Select Server Certificate for Message Queuing dialog. The list includes all certificates valid for the local MSMQ 2.0 server. Double-click a certificate item to close the dialog, and then click OK to close the Message Queuing Properties dialog and save your changes.

 If the Application event log fills with MSMQ security errors when testing a new QC or during production use of a QC, see the second item in the "Security-Related Problems" topic in the following "Troubleshooting" section.

TROUBLESHOOTING

SECURITY-RELATED PROBLEMS

Clients throw "Access Denied" or similar errors when attempting to instantiate a COM+ application.

The most common problem that causes these errors is the client's authentication level being set lower than that of the COM+ application. For a quick determination if this is the problem, temporarily clear the Enforce Access Checks for This Application check box on the Security page of the server's applications property dialog (refer to Figure 28.16). Test client access, and then adjust either the authentication level of the component or the DCOM proxy to match.

Message queuing throws security errors in the Application event log.

Problems with certificates are the most common cause of MSMQ security errors and warnings. For instance, clicking the Renew Internal Certificate or Renew Cryptographic Keys button of the Message Queuing Properties dialog's Security page results in in-process messages being rejected by computers that expected the prior certificate or cryptographic key.

Performance-Related Problems

Bottlenecks on app servers appear to result in poor-to-unacceptable component response.

Network congestion, inadequate server resources, and a variety of other impediments can result in a severe performance hit on applications and Web sites that depend on COM+ components. The Windows DNA Performance Kit, available at http://www.microsoft.com/Com/resources/WinDNAperf.asp, includes a Web Driver application that emulates a large number of clients connecting to IIS 4+—and PerfCol for monitoring a large number of performance counters on multiple computers. The Windows DNA Performance Kit also provides a "test harness" that aids in learning app server tuning techniques and developing your own performance testing applications. The kit includes an HTML Help file that contains a wealth of information on app server performance testing and optimization.

MCSE Corner: Exam Question Types Part II

Some of the MCSE exam question types were covered in Chapter 13, including multiple choice, choose all that apply, and select and place. In this chapter, the case study, scenario, and simulation question types are explained.

Case Study

The case study presents the examinee with a large amount of information. The information is usually arranged in a tabbed page format, with an "All" tab that displays all of the contained information in one tab. The case study can also contain exhibits such as charts and pictures. You are first given a chance to look through the information in the case study and exhibits, and then are presented with questions (usually several) pertaining to the case study information. These questions can be multiple choice or choose all that apply. You may also be presented other question types, like arranging answers in categories and lists. You should watch for answers that are "distracters" or answers that look like they are right but which, with careful examination, are actually wrong. You can go to the case study or exhibit screens at any time by clicking a button.

Scenario

A scenario question is an older question type similar to the case study in that it provides a hypothetical environment you must be able to analyze. They differ in that there is much less information provided with the scenario. There is also only one question to answer instead of several.

In a scenario question, you are given four pieces of information to be analyzed. First is a scenario outlining the hypothetical environment. Next are required outcomes and optional outcomes. Last is a proposed solution. You must be able to determine what the proposed solution provides. The options are usually neither the required nor optional outcomes, the required outcome only, the required outcome and one of the optional outcomes, or the required outcome and more than one of the optional outcomes. Here is an example:

Scenario: You live in a house. The wall is dirty. You don't like what color the wall is.

Required Outcome: Make the wall clean.

Optional Outcomes: Change the color of the wall; make the room larger.

Proposed Solution: Get some cleaning solution and a sponge. Use this to clean the wall.

The answer in this case would be that the proposed solution provides the required outcome but none of the optional outcomes.

SIMULATION

The simulation question is simply a simulated environment that you must work through to answer a question. The testing computer will simulate a system and require you to perform a given operation, such as install a protocol or configure a Web server. To pass these questions you must be able to perform the required actions in a real-world environment.

CHAPTER **29**

DEPLOYING WINDOWS TERMINAL SERVICES

In this chapter

Understanding Windows NT 4.0, Terminal Server Edition   1196

Comparing Windows 2000 Terminal Services with Windows NT 4.0, Terminal Server Edition   1198

Installing Windows 2000 Terminal Services Server   1199

Using Terminal Services' Configuration Snap-In   1205

Using Terminal Services Manager   1211

Licensing Terminal Services   1214

Installing and Deploying the Terminal Services Client   1217

Troubleshooting   1224

MCSE Corner: Deploying Windows Terminal Services   1225

Understanding Windows NT 4.0, Terminal Server Edition

To gain a thorough knowledge of Windows 2000 Terminal Services, you don't have to look far from its predecessor—Windows NT 4.0, Terminal Server Edition (TSE). In truth, Windows 2000 Terminal Services is only a minor departure from TSE. The basic architecture, tools, and operability still endure in this latest incarnation. If you, however, don't have any experience with Terminal Server 4.0, there's no need to worry. This section highlights some of the major concepts of the Windows "thin-client" architecture and the Windows NT 4.0, Terminal Server Edition. For those of you who already have a detailed working knowledge of TSE, you can skip to "Comparing Windows 2000 Terminal Services with Windows NT 4.0, Terminal Server Edition," later in this chapter.

Terminology

The many terms associated with the Terminal Services discussion can be confusing. So before you delve into this chapter, here's a list of the terms and abbreviations used to refer to both Terminal products:

- *Windows NT 4.0, Terminal Server Edition* is the predecessor to Windows 2000 Terminal Services. It is also referred to as Terminal Server 4.0 or simply TSE.
- *Windows 2000 Terminal Services* is the remote access product integrated in the Windows 2000 operating system. It is also referred to as Terminal Services or TS. A server running Terminal Services is called a Windows 2000 Terminal Server or simply Terminal Server.
- *Terminal Server Client 4.0* refers to the client shipped with Windows NT 4.0, Terminal Server Edition.
- *Terminal Services Client* refers to the client shipped with Windows 2000.

Windows NT 4.0 Server Versus Windows NT 4.0, Terminal Server Edition

Terminal Server 4.0 was the first attempt by Microsoft to provide the same server-based application processing that mainframe and UNIX systems have always offered. It was not simply an add-on to the existing Windows NT 4.0 operating system, but a new architecture developed to allow the true sharing of computer resources among a large number of users. To better understand how TSE operates, it's important to understand the architectural differences between it and Windows NT 4.0 Server.

As with many network operating systems, the plain version of Windows NT 4.0 Server allows only one interactive session at a time. There are file sharing, printer pooling, Web hosting, ftp services, and other features that allow individuals to share the resources of a Windows NT 4.0 server, but there is only one interactive session allowed to log in to the server console. This means that the normal computer user cannot run Microsoft Office or any other application solely from the server; the client workstation also has to share in the processing.

At a technically detailed glance, Windows NT 4.0 Server is incapable of allowing more than one interactive session because Windows NT assigns only one session ID (Session ID 0) to all processes started by the individual logged into the console. Every process started by Session ID 0 is then allotted 2GB of virtual memory addressing for execution. In addition, Windows NT 4.0 starts only one instance of the Windows subsystem that is responsible for the display, keyboard, and mouse drivers. As you can see, Windows NT 4.0 Server at its core is incapable of handling multiple users.

In contrast, TSE was built from the ground up with a different architecture. Instead of a single session ID for every process, TSE assigns a unique session ID to every user logged in. Because every user must have a separate memory space for his or her processes, each user session is allocated its own memory space called the *sessionspace*. Each process within the sessionspace is then allotted Windows NT's standard 2GB of virtual memory address space. TSE also starts a separate instance of the Windows subsystem responsible for the display, keyboard, and mouse drivers for each user session.

Remote Desktop Protocol (RDP)

In order to communicate and segregate the many different types of data needed for Terminal Server 4.0, a new, more extensible protocol was needed. Microsoft developed the Remote Desktop Protocol (RDP) to answer this need. RDP is an extension of the T-120 protocol standard, and although it's currently only used for thin-client communication, RDP could eventually have other uses in multimedia and broadband communications. RDP can create separate virtual channels for transporting different types of traffic such as encrypted data, application data, and licensing data—all simultaneously. (In fact, RDP allows 64,000 separate channels to transmit these types of data.) RDP is also extensible in the fact that it was written to work independently of the transport layer. Although it currently works over only TCP/IP, future releases of RDP could be used to communicate over IPX, NetBIOS, or a variety of other network transport protocols.

In the context of TSE, RDP provides the key communication engine that communicates the keyboard, mouse, and display data to the client. And despite the potential of this protocol, it currently uses only one virtual channel and transmits only via TCP/IP for Terminal Server 4.0 communication.

Tip from
RJ

> If you need greater flexibility across platforms or protocols, you may be interested in Citrix's Metaframe add-on for Windows NT 4.0 Server, Terminal Server Edition. This add-on provides support for the ICA (Independent Client Architecture) client. The ICA client is optimized to communicate using only 10kbps and supports a variety of protocols, such as IPX, SPX, and NetBIOS. Citrix has also developed the ICA client for a variety of platforms, such as UNIX, Linux, and Windows 3.1. The Metaframe server offers a variety of administrative tools to help administrators manage client sessions. To learn more about Metaframe and other Citrix products, visit the company's Web site at http://www.citrix.com.

Comparing Windows 2000 Terminal Services with Windows NT 4.0, Terminal Server Edition

Much is shared between TSE and its latest incarnation, Windows 2000 Terminal Services, but there are several new features and a few tools have actually been removed. The biggest difference between Terminal Server 4.0 and Windows 2000 Terminal Services lies in the fact that Terminal Services is integrated into the Windows 2000 operating system. Instead of being a separate flavor of the Windows operating system, Terminal Services offers added functionality to the base Win2000 OS. The obvious benefit of this change is that you no longer have to maintain separate Service Packs and hot fixes from other Windows 2000 servers in your environment. TSE requires separate Service Packs because, in reality, it lives as a different operating system. Terminal Services skirts that problem by running as an add-on to Windows 2000.

Terminal Services also has added another layer of functionality by allowing two different operating modes. The Application Server mode mimics the functionality of TSE by serving applications to remote clients. There is not much difference between TSE and a Windows 2000 server running Terminal Services except in the area of licensing (more on Terminal Services licensing later in this chapter). The other mode, Remote Administration mode, adds the biggest bang for network administrators. Terminal Services in Remote Administration mode allows two administrators to initiate remote sessions for management and administrative purposes. The two connections don't require licenses, so this mode provides a great built-in solution for remote administration of your Windows 2000 server. In addition, the Remote Administration Mode has very low overhead, so it can be added to any Win2000 server in your environment.

Although this feature is reserved only for the Windows 2000 Advanced and Data Center servers, Network Load Balancing (NLB) is a powerful new addition. NLB allows administrators to group servers in a cluster of up to 32 servers. The cluster can then distribute IP traffic evenly among the servers. This feature is not reserved for Terminal Services; however, it can be implemented as an effective way to evenly distribute Terminal Services Client sessions.

Tip from
RJ

With Terminal Server 4.0, there are two other ways to simulate network load balancing. Citrix offers network load balancing via its add-on Metaframe. For more information on Metaframe, visit Citrix's Web site at http://www.citrix.com. The other method involves using DNS in a round-robin fashion. In this scenario, servers are grouped under one DNS entry. When clients attempt to connect to the DNS entry, IP addresses are served out in a pseudo-random order, thus distributing clients among servers. The DNS round-robin method also can be used for Windows 2000 Terminal servers.

As mentioned earlier, the licensing architecture for Windows 2000 Terminal Services is much stricter than its predecessor's. This time around you must buy Microsoft License Packs (or MLPs) to load on a Windows 2000 Terminal Services License Server. When clients attempt to start a Terminal Services session, the Terminal server searches for an available license from the Terminal Services License Server. If none are available, a client cannot initiate a session. However, Microsoft does offer one large carrot to Terminal Services customers: All versions of the Windows 2000 operating system include a valid Terminal Services license. The MLPs are necessary only for operating systems other than Windows 2000.

There are some other minor changes that make Terminal Services a more robust product. For instance, Microsoft has included a Terminal Server User group that adds the same sort of functionality as the Authenticated Users group. This allows you to set specific permissions for users that connect as clients. Terminal Services also includes the capability of optimizing process scheduling for Windows 2000 Professional or for the Windows 2000 server products. In TSE, the processing scheduling could only emulate the processing of Windows NT 4.0 Workstation. With Terminal Services, you can optimize processing to act as a server.

> **Note**
> Although Terminal Services is now integrated with Windows 2000, there is still currently no support for Active Directory. Future releases will undoubtedly address this shortcoming.

There are only a few things that have been removed in the transition from Terminal Server 4.0 to Terminal Services. Most of these changes are minor. For instance, User Properties for Netware users has been removed. This change should not affect much in the manner of administration.

The most notable change is the absence of a few command-line tools. Here's a list of the tools that are no longer offered:

- `Qobject`—Used to query information on TS objects
- `Peruser`—Used by administrators to set file associations on a per-user basis instead of globally for all users
- `Migrate`—Used to migrate Netware users to Citrix Winframe servers
- `Arevfix`—An obscure utility, used to fix problems with older versions of Advanced Revelation on Citrix Winframe servers

Installing Windows 2000 Terminal Services Server

The Terminal server is the hub of the Terminal Services architecture. It does all the back-end processing to allow application serving or simple remote administration. It is important to plan the implementation of the Terminal server carefully. This section is meant to help with your planning by detailing the hardware requirements, installation procedures, and administrative issues associated with Windows 2000 Terminal Services server.

Installation Considerations

Regarding hardware requirements and, thus, server planning, everything depends on the mode in which you decide to run Terminal Services. In a nutshell, Remote Administration mode offers administrators the ability to remotely administer their servers. It does not serve out applications to the general public and is not built for that purpose. Instead, it runs as a background process that is meant to be as unobtrusive as possible. So for a Terminal server running in Remote Administration mode, simply follow the guidelines outlined for Windows 2000 server.

→ For Windows 2000 Server hardware requirements, **see** "Upgrading Existing Servers for Windows 2000," **p. 313**.

Here are some of the benefits of the Remote Administration mode:

- Remote Administration mode does not require additional licensing, so you don't have to set up the TS License Server or buy any additional Microsoft License Packs (MLPs). This feature, however, does have one drawback in that only two administrators can initiate sessions simultaneously. This may not be much of a factor in smaller server environments; however, large IS organizations may find this a bit limiting.

- Because Terminal Services operating in the Remote Administration mode is not serving out applications, the impact on the server is minimal. This allows you to install Terminal Services for remote administration of servers that might not otherwise have enough resources to run a third-party remote administration program. The biggest reason for the reduced overhead lies in how Terminal Services handles serving applications. A Terminal server in Application Server mode must allocate server resources differently. It must ensure that applications that normally could not run in multiuser mode have the resources to do so under Terminal Services. Overall, Remote Administration mode reduces Terminal Services to a bare-bones service creating the smallest footprint possible.

- For those Windows NT 4.0 administrators that have to administer several different domains, you know how cumbersome it is to authenticate to each necessary domain. You have to log off in your current context and log in again to the proper domain. With Terminal Services, that problem is virtually nonexistent. You can now remain logged into your primary domain, initiate a TS session to a server in another domain or forest, and remotely administer servers in that domain. This is not a highly trumpeted feature of Terminal Services, but if you have multiple domains or forests, this feature will undoubtedly be worthwhile.

If you are installing Terminal Services in Application Server mode to mimic the functionality of Windows NT 4.0, Terminal Server Edition, the hardware requirements are more stringent than the Remote Administration mode. At the time this book went to press, Microsoft had not published the additional hardware requirements for running Terminal Services. However, the hardware requirements for Terminal Server 4.0 are still good guidelines for capacity planning. Keeping in mind that your environment may have unique needs and requirements, here are the general guidelines that Microsoft advised for Terminal Server 4.0:

- Processor—15–45 users per Pentium-class processor
- RAM—4–12MB of RAM per user
- Network bandwidth—2–6kbps per user

Tip from
RJ

> To review the underlying logic behind the hardware requirements for Windows NT 4.0, Terminal Server Edition, download the "Windows NT Server 4.0, Terminal Server Edition Capacity Planning Guide" from `http://www.microsoft.com/NTServer/terminalserver/deployment/capacplan/tscapacity.asp`.

In addition to the modes and hardware requirements, keep these points in mind as you plan for Terminal Services in the Application Server mode:

- As with most resource-intensive applications, you should install Terminal Services in Application Mode on standalone servers. The added overhead of domain controller services can adversely affect application serving.
- For the same reason, you should not install TS in Application Mode on any server already running resource-intensive applications, such as Microsoft Exchange, Microsoft SQL server, and so on.
- You also need to install a license server within 90 days of your Terminal Services installation. Refer to the section "Licensing Terminal Services" later in this chapter for more information.

Tip from
RJ

> Citrix Metaframe will also be designed to work with Windows 2000 Terminal Services. There are many features that this add-on can offer. You can find more information on Metaframe interoperability with Terminal Services from Citrix's Web site at `http://www.citrix.com`.

Performing the Installation

If you recall the steps you performed during the setup of your Windows 2000 server, you had several choices in the Windows components you wanted to install, as shown in Figure 29.1. Certificate Services, IIS, Remote Installation services, Script Debugger, Terminal Services Licensing, Windows Media Services, and other components are listed. Fortunately, Terminal Services happens to be one of those optional components.

Figure 29.1
The Windows Components Wizard is used to install Terminal Services either upon the initial installation of Windows 2000, or any time later.

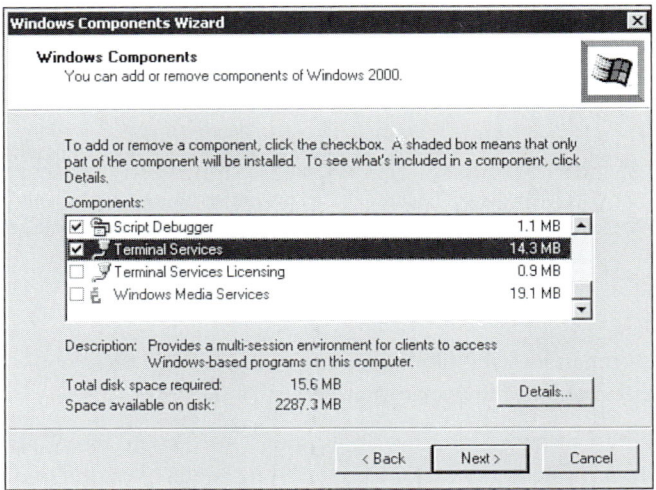

To install the Terminal Services component, mark the check box labeled Terminal Services and click Next to continue the installation. After the Windows setup continues, you are prompted with another dialog asking for the Terminal Services mode, as shown in Figure 29.2. According to the features and your needs, select the appropriate mode and then click Next. The Windows setup continues to set up Terminal Services and any other components you select. That's all you do to ensure that Terminal Services is installed.

→ For complete instructions on setting up Windows 2000 Server, **see** "Installing Windows 2000 on a New Server," **p. 384**.

Figure 29.2
During the Terminal Services setup process, select the mode in which Terminal Services will run, either the limited Remote administration mode or the full Application server mode.

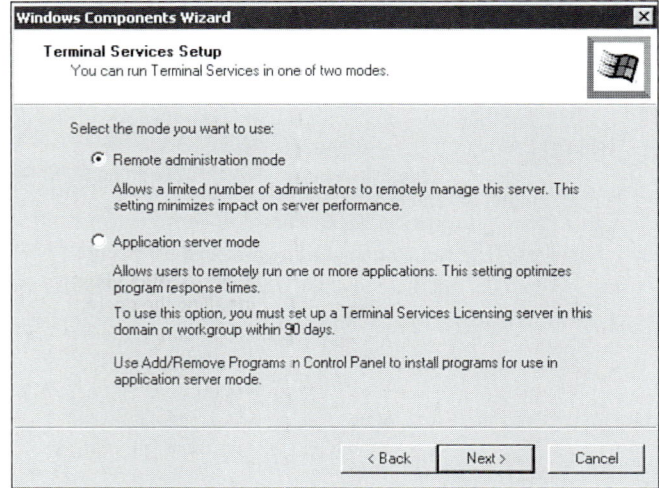

If you've already installed your Windows 2000 server and don't have a desire to repeat the setup, Microsoft has you in mind. To install Terminal Services after the Windows 2000 setup has completed, follow these steps:

1. Launch Control Panel.
2. From Control Panel, double-click the Add/Remove Programs icon.
3. In the left pane, select Add/Remove Windows Components. This brings up the Windows Components dialog.
4. Select Terminal Services and then click Next to begin the installation.
5. You're prompted with the Terminal Services Setup dialog (refer to Figure 29.2); select the appropriate mode and click Next.
6. After the installation is complete, click Finish. You're then prompted to reboot your server.

Whether you installed Terminal Services during the Windows 2000 setup or through the Control Panel, there is one administrative task left to ensure that the necessary clients can initiate TS sessions. You must ensure that anyone who needs to start a TS session has the right to log on locally to the server running Terminal Services. In Windows NT 4.0, Terminal Server Edition, the installation process automatically gave the group Everyone the Logon Locally right. In Windows 2000 Terminal Services, this must be set manually by modifying the domain policy. After you've granted rights to the necessary groups or users, Terminal Services is ready to go.

→ For complete instructions on modifying a domain policy, **see** "Using the Group Policy Snap-in to Edit Group Policy Objects," **p. 622**.

UPGRADING FROM WINDOWS NT 4.0, TERMINAL SERVER EDITION

Previous chapters within this book outlined the migration from Windows NT 4.0 to Windows 2000 Server. The following section outlines processes and pitfalls associated with upgrading from Windows NT 4.0, Terminal Server Edition, to Windows 2000 Server running Terminal Services.

→ For more information on upgrading Windows NT 4.0 Server to Windows 2000 Server, **see** "Upgrading Windows NT 4.0 Production Server," **p. 352**.

Caution

> As with any new operating system (especially network operating systems), the safest migration method is not to upgrade at all. By installing the operating system from scratch, you eliminate any possibility that the previous operating system might cause problems. That, however, is not always a realistic server installation plan for many organizations. Very often monetary or time restrictions force administrators to upgrade the operating system in-place on an existing machine. In this situation, have two backups of the current server before you begin. If your upgrade fails, the time you save with backups more than pays for the backup effort.

If you're upgrading from Terminal Server 4.0 to the Windows 2000 server, Microsoft has designed the upgrade path to be painless. The first thing you must do (besides having two current backups on hand) is install Terminal Server 4.0 Service Pack 4. Service Pack 4 has additional features and tools necessary for a successful migration. When you've completed the SP4 installation and rebooted your system, simply follow the upgrade path outlined previously for upgrading to Windows 2000 server. You don't even need to reinstall the applications that were previously installed on your TSE server.

If, however, you plan to upgrade from Terminal Server 4.0 with Metaframe installed or from any other operating systems, keep these upgrade requirements in mind:

- If you upgrade from any Windows NT operating system other than Windows NT 4.0, Terminal Server Edition and plan to run Terminal Services in Application Server mode, you have to uninstall all applications and reinstall them after the Windows 2000 upgrade. This effectively changes the applications from running in single-user mode to allowing them to be served via Terminal Services. This step is, of course, unnecessary for Terminal Services running in Remote Administration mode.

- If you are upgrading from Terminal Server 4.0 with Citrix Metaframe installed, you have to uninstall Metaframe. Windows 2000 cannot effectively upgrade a server with Metaframe installed. Unfortunately, after the upgrade, all Citrix ICA clients installed in your environment no longer work. So for now, you have to upgrade the clients to Win2000 Terminal Services clients.

- If you're currently running Citrix Winframe, you're out of luck. There's currently no upgrade path to Windows 2000 server.

Installing Applications

After completing the setup of Terminal Services in Application Server mode, you'll want to begin serving applications to your user community. With TS, the application installation process requires a little extra work. Terminal Services has two modes—Install mode and Execute mode. As the name implies, Install mode allows the installation of applications. While Terminal Services is in Install mode, registry modifications are captured, file installation is monitored, and shortcuts are written to the All Users menu. This mode is critical to application serving because it actively monitors an application's installation process and ensures that all users have the proper settings and files to execute the newly installed application.

For normal application serving, however, Terminal Services runs in Execute mode. This mode ensures that all users receive their own copy of registry settings, the %systemroot% folder, and necessary files to run installed applications. Execute mode creates the necessary illusion of a single Windows interface so that multiple users can have their own copy of critical Windows settings. Follow these steps to install an application:

1. From a Command Prompt, run the following command: **CHANGE USER / INSTALL**. You will receive a "User session is ready to install applications" message. If you forget this step, Terminal Services notifies you with the error message shown in Figure 29.3.

USING TERMINAL SERVICES' CONFIGURATION SNAP-IN   1205

PART
V
CH
29

> **Note**
> You can also switch to Install mode by using the Add/Remove Programs applet in the Control Panel.

Figure 29.3
An error message is displayed if you attempt to install an application when Terminal Services is running in Execute mode.

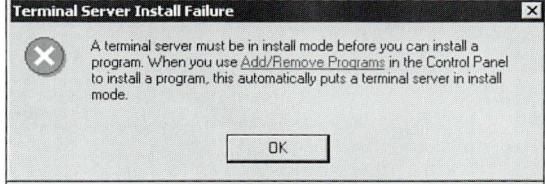

2. Run the application's setup program. You may be required to reboot the server. If so, you can skip the next step. The server automatically restarts in Execute mode.

3. If the application setup program does not require a reboot, from a command prompt, you have to run the following command: **CHANGE USER /EXECUTE**. This returns a "User session is ready to execute applications" message.

> **Tip from**
> *RJ*
> If you're unsure which mode Terminal Services is currently in, simply use the command **CHANGE USER /QUERY**. This command displays the current TS installation mode.

USING TERMINAL SERVICES' CONFIGURATION SNAP-IN

The Terminal Services connection is the communication link that allows clients to connect to the Terminal server. When you installed Terminal Services, it automatically configured a TCP/IP connection by default. The Terminal Services Configuration snap-in, shown in Figure 29.4, is used to modify this default connection, add a new one, or remove any unneeded connections. Although you don't use this snap-in on a regular basis, Terminal Services Configuration is important in the initial configuration of Terminal Services.

> **Note**
> Any settings that are modified within this snap-in are global and apply to all clients.

Figure 29.4
The Terminal Services Configuration snap-in is used to configure global Terminal Services settings and connections.

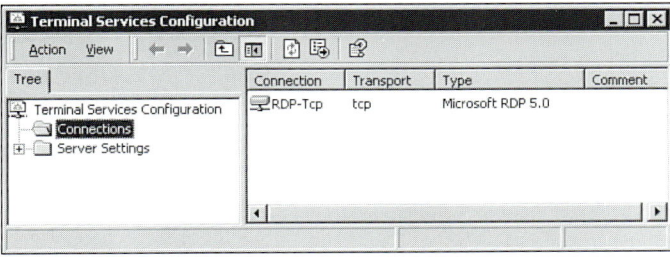

Adding a New Terminal Services Connection

A Terminal Services connection is simply a defined set of behaviors that applies to a network adapter. Only one connection can be defined for any given network adapter. You can see in Figure 29.4 that there is only one connection listed: RDP-TCP. This connection is set up by default during the installation of Terminal Services. In many environments, the default connection is the only one necessary; however, defining additional connections can give Terminal Services added functionality. For example, if you wanted administrators to use a separate, dedicated network connection, you could define the default adapter for the general user community and a second adapter for network administrators only. To add a new connection:

1. Select Connections in the left pane.
2. Click the Action menu and select Create New Connection.
3. From the Create New Connection Wizard Welcome screen, click Next.
4. Select Microsoft RDP 5.0 as the connection type and click Next.
5. Select the encryption level that you want this connection to employ. Click Next to continue. (Don't worry if you're uncertain about this setting; you can change it when you configure the connection, as explained in the following section.)
6. Remote Control allows a client to share a session with another user. The user has to have Full Control access to use this feature, so it's usually reserved for administrators. Select the remote control policy you'd like to apply to this connection and click Next. (The Remote Control feature is explained in more detail later in the following section.)
7. Type a descriptive name for this connection, choose TCP for the transport protocol, and type any comments you'd like to associate to this connection. Click Next to continue.
8. Select the network adapter to use for this connection. Only one network adapter can be used for each connection. You also have the ability to limit the number of connections to this adapter. This setting can be helpful if you have a slower network card speed. Click Next.
9. Click Finish to complete the addition of the new connection.

Modifying Connection Properties

To modify the properties of a connection, right-click on the connection and choose Properties to open the connection's RDP-Tcp properties sheet. The General page's main function is to allow the administrator to modify the encryption settings of the communication between the server and client (see Figure 29.5).

Figure 29.5
You can enter optional comments and set the encryption level for the connection on the General page of the RDP-Tcp Properties dialog.

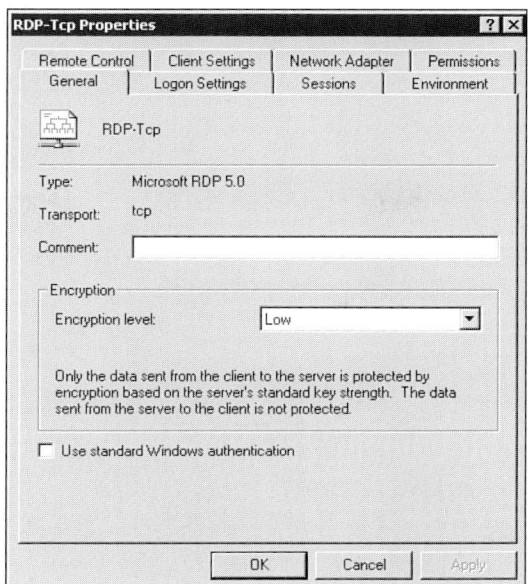

Following is a brief description of each setting:

- Low provides 56-bit encryption for Windows 2000 TS clients and 40-bit encryption for Windows NT 4.0 TSE clients. This security setting consumes the least amount of resources because only the data sent from the client to the server is encrypted.

- Medium provides the same type of encryption as the Low setting; however, data sent both to *and* from the server is encrypted. This setting requires more resources from the client and the server.

- High provides 128-bit encryption for U.S. and Canadian Terminal Services users. This setting also requires additional resources to encrypt and decrypt the data transmitted.

The Logon Settings page allows you to supply a common username and password for every client session. In other words, every user who initiates a connection to the Terminal Server will use one set of login credentials. Because each user is not required to authenticate with a user account and password, there is a greater potential for unauthorized or even malicious use of Terminal Services. In addition, administrators are unable to determine which users have actually initiated client sessions, because all users will appear under a common username. So although this can be a convenient feature, use common user credentials only when absolutely necessary.

The Sessions page allows you to free up Terminal Services licenses and resources in an efficient manner. You have a variety of options to end or simply disconnect client sessions after a specified amount of time. For instance, the settings shown in Figure 29.6 ensure that active users are never forced off, and idle users are disconnected only after thirty minutes;

if the user session stays disconnected for one hour, the session is ended. Setting the time limits becomes critical if you are running Terminal Services in Application Server mode and have a limited number of client licenses. These settings can also free up precious resources on an overloaded server.

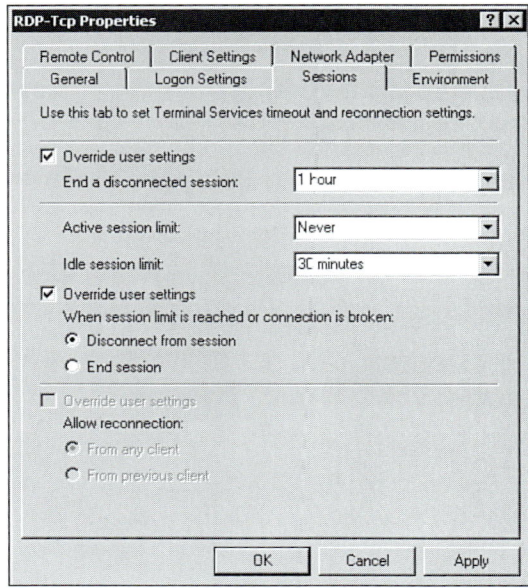

Figure 29.6
The Sessions page of the RDP-Tcp Properties dialog is used to set session timeouts for idle clients.

> **Note**
> The Allow Reconnection setting applies only to Citrix ICA clients.

If you'd like all your clients to run a specified program every time they start a session, you can set that application on the Environment page. For example, you may want every user to start Internet Explorer to view the corporate intranet Web page. Disable Wallpaper is another important setting on this page. To reduce network traffic, check this option to eliminate the constant redraws of a bitmap wallpaper file.

An important new feature added to Terminal Services is the capability of remotely controlling another user's Terminal Services session, as shown in Figure 29.7. For example, administrators receive calls when users run into problems within a session. Remote Control gives these administrators the ability to view and/or interact with the users' session and—you hope—fix the users' problems. If you do not want administrators (or any other users) to take control of a client session, you can set up Remote Control so that the administrator cannot interact with the session, but simply can view the session activities. The Remote Control page allows you to set this option, enable remote control and set the properties associated.

Figure 29.7
The Remote Control page of the RDP-Tcp Properties dialog allows the configuration of the remote controlling of client workstations.

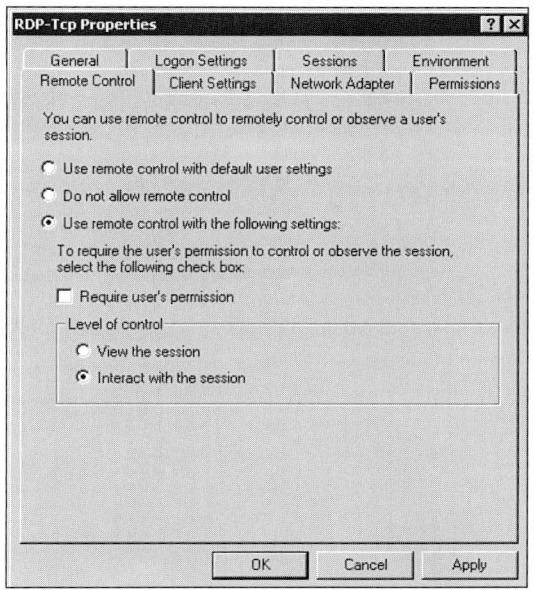

The Client Settings page enables you to override any settings of the TS clients. In some situations, this may be beneficial. For a more detailed discussion of the client features, refer to the section "Deploying the Terminal Services Client," later in this chapter.

The Network Adapter page allows you to assign the connection to a specific network adapter. You can also limit the number of clients that can connect using this Terminal Services connection.

The Permission page, shown in Figure 29.8, offers granularity in determining what actions users are allowed to perform while in the Terminal Services session. Here's a short explanation of the permission settings:

- Full Control—Reserve this permission only for the server's administrators. This allows all actions to be performed regarding Terminal Services. This setting is required to allow a user to remotely control another Terminal Service client session.

- User Access—This should be the typical setting for most of your users. It allows them to log on, log off, disconnect, and reconnect to a disconnected session.

- Guest Access—You may want to use this setting for users that need to access TS for only one application. With this permission, users can only log on and log off. They cannot disconnect sessions or use any other advanced features.

Figure 29.8
The Permissions page of the RDP-Tcp Properties dialog is used to configure the users who have administrative, user, and guest access to the Terminal Services server.

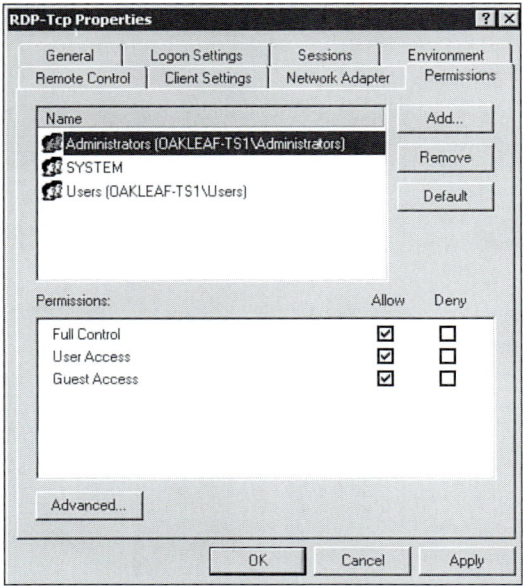

Using the Server Settings Folder

The Terminal Services Configuration snap-in also contains the Server Settings folder. Click Server Settings to view individual server properties, as shown in Figure 29.9. There are only a few settings under this folder, but they are important to the configuration of Terminal Services. Here's quick guide to each setting:

- Terminal Server Mode—This displays which mode Terminal Services is currently running in; to change the mode, you must use Add/Remove Programs in the Control Panel.

- Delete Temporary Folders on Exit—Each user, by default, has his or her own temporary folder created under the system's Temp folder. The user's folder is named with the user's session ID and assigned to the environmental variable TEMP. By default, the system removes these folders when the user session is ended. If you have programs that need the users' temporary folders to endure, you can change the setting here.

- Use Temporary Folders Per Session—By default, this option is enabled. You can disable the use of user temporary folders and have everyone use the system's Temp folder.

- Internet Connector Licensing—Internet Connector licenses are purchased separately as an add-on to Terminal Services. Connector licenses enable Internet users to connect to your Terminal server and run Windows applications via a Web browser. Microsoft offers this option more for demonstration purposes than as a viable client solution. Using this client, companies do not have to rewrite Windows software to demonstrate their software via the Web. Use this setting to enable this add-on.

- Active Desktop—Terminal Services is compatible with the Active Desktop feature of Internet Explorer. This setting enables or disables the running of the Active Desktop on

TS clients. You'll want to consider whether this is a necessary option, because Active Desktop does send more screen data to and from the client.

Figure 29.9
The Server Settings in the right pane of the Terminal Services snap-in are used to configure client settings for the Terminal Server.

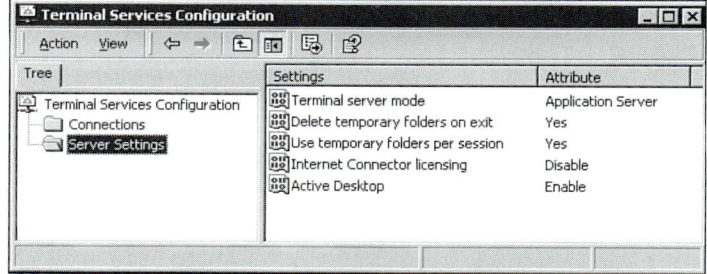

USING TERMINAL SERVICES MANAGER

The Terminal Services Manager is the most frequently used administration tool. To start this utility, click Terminal Services Manager from the Administrative Tools Start Menu folder. You can use it to manage Terminal servers in trusted domains and perform a variety of administrative tasks. You can also monitor users, sessions, and running applications. When a client connects to a particular Terminal server, the user, session information, and list of used processes appears within the Processes page of the Terminal Services Manager window. In Figure 29.10, for example, the Processes page of Terminal Services Manager displays all the processes that Student1 is currently running in the sample OAKLEAF-TS connection. This information can be very helpful in terminating a hung process or clearing processes from a session that ended abnormally.

Figure 29.10
The Terminal Services Manager tool's right pane shows the currently running processes for the user selected in the left pane (Student1).

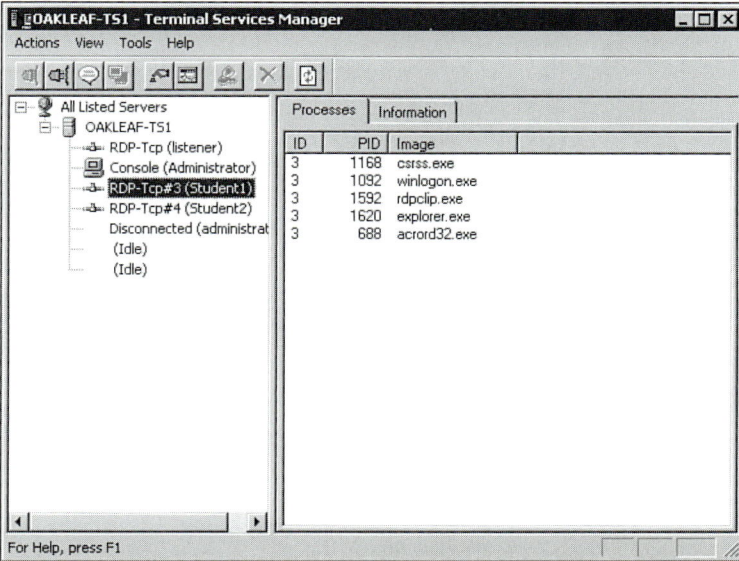

The Terminal Services Manager Information page displays all the client's information, such as login name, computer name, client version, IP address, and a variety of other useful information (see Figure 29.11).

Figure 29.11
The Terminal Services Manager's right pane shows the session information for the user selected in the left pane.

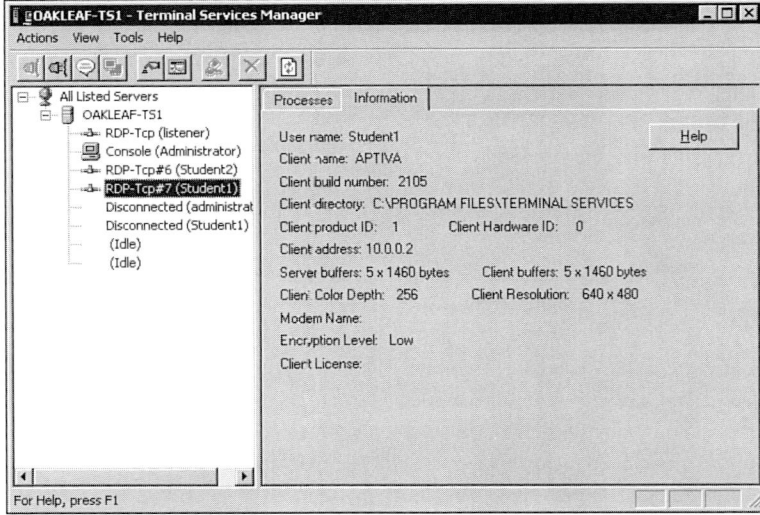

You can also display all users, sessions, or processes by clicking the Terminal Server name in the Terminal Services Manager's left pane. For example, you can sort all the currently running processes by username and determine all instances of a particular process, as shown in Figure 29.12.

Figure 29.12
By selecting the Terminal Server in the left pane of the Terminal Services Manager, you can view all of the processes running on the server in the right pane.

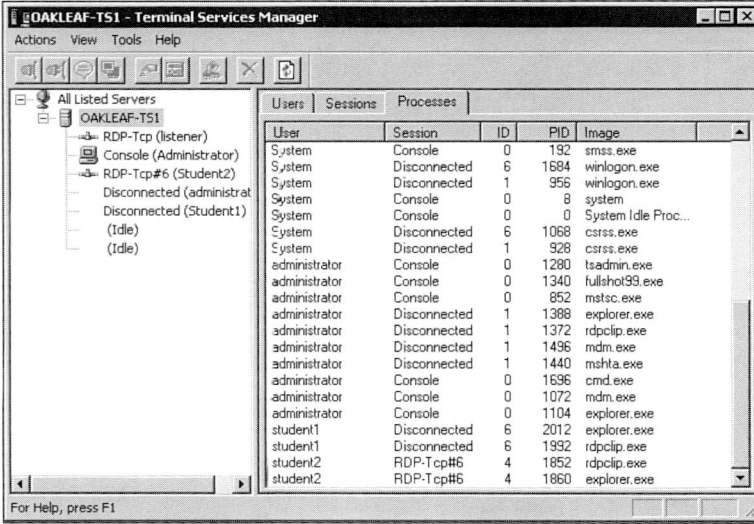

USING TERMINAL SERVICES MANAGER | 1213

The Sessions tab shows the status of all client sessions; by clicking the Users tab, you can see a list of all users that are currently logged in. Right-click a username to produce a context menu with options for modifying the user's session, as shown in Figure 29.13.

Figure 29.13
Right-clicking a user from within the Terminal Services Manager brings up the Session Action menu from which you can perform actions such as disconnecting the user and sending messages.

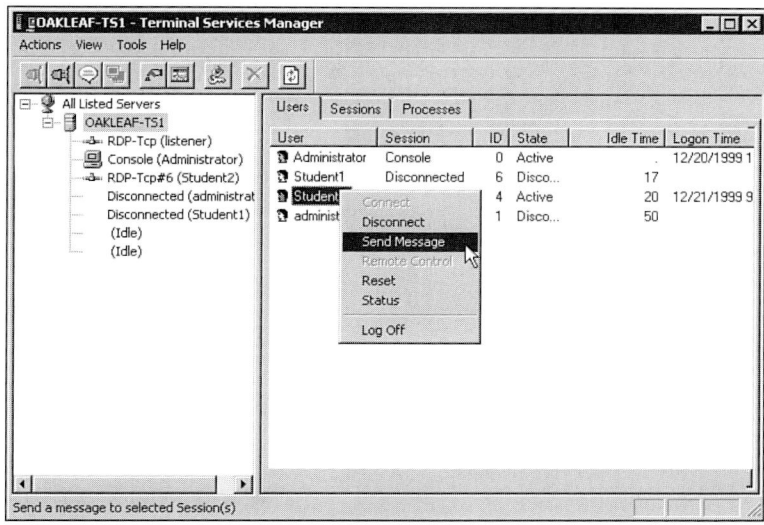

You can invoke most Terminal Services Manager commands from the command line. Here's a list of commands, as well as a short description of each:

- Change logon—Allows administrators to temporarily disable client sessions on the Terminal Server.
- Change port—Allows you to add, modify, or delete COM port mappings. This command is mostly used for MS-DOS application compatibility.
- Change user—As mentioned previously in this chapter, this command switches application modes to allow administrators to install new applications.
- Cprofile—Cleans up wasted space in a user profile or removes user-specific file associations.
- Flattemp—Enables or disables user-specific temporary folders. Instead, all users share the system's Temp folder.
- Logoff—Terminates a user session.
- Msg—Sends a message to user(s).
- Query Process—Displays specific information about processes currently running.
- Query Session—Displays specific information about sessions currently running.
- Query Termserver—Displays all the Terminal servers on the network.
- Query User—Displays specific information about the users currently logged on.

- Register—Administrators can use this command to register special programs to run in a global context.
- Reset Session—Deletes a session from the Terminal server.
- Shadow—Allows remote control of another Terminal Services session. As mentioned previously, Remote Control allows a user to control another user's session without actually controlling the mouse or keyboard.
- Tscon—Connects to Terminal server and initiates a client session. This command acts like the Terminal Services Client.
- Tsdiscon—Disconnects from a Terminal server session.
- Tskill—Kills a process.
- Tsprof—Copies the user configuration from one user to another.
- Tsshutdn—Allows an administrator to shut down or reboot a Terminal server.

 To overcome problems running applications when Terminal Services is running in Remote Administration mode, see "Terminal Server Application Compatibility," in the Troubleshooting section at the end of this chapter.

LICENSING TERMINAL SERVICES

If you deploy Windows 2000 Terminal Services in Application Server mode, you must use the Licensing Terminal Services tool.

> **Note**
> If you plan to use only the Remote Administration mode, you can skip this section and move on to "Installing and Deploying the Terminal Services Client."

Microsoft has taken a bold step with Terminal Services licensing. As with all software products, tracking licenses can be the bane of an administrator's existence. There are third-party utilities to track licensing through "software metering"; however, most solutions produce a good deal of network traffic and are obtrusive to the users. The Terminal Services solution is a great resource for network administrators.

The entire solution revolves around the Terminal Services License Server (License Server). When a Windows 2000 Terminal Server first starts, it locates all License Servers within its site. (Thereafter, the Terminal Server refreshes its list at a variety of intervals depending on the situation.) Initially, no License Server is required for a Terminal Services Client to connect to the Terminal Server. However, after ninety days, a License Server is mandatory for any clients to connect. This 90-day grace period begins when the first client connects to the server. After a License Server is installed, the Terminal Server queries the nearest License Server to request a license or validate any existing client license. When the license is issued or verified, the License Server issues a certificate for clients to finally connect to the Terminal Server.

Luckily, for clients that are running Windows 2000, no additional licenses are necessary, because a Terminal Services license is included in every Windows 2000 operating system license. For other operating systems, however, you must purchase Terminal Services Client Access Licenses (CALs). Microsoft sells these licenses in Microsoft License Packs (MLPs), and they must be installed on the License Server. When the licenses are installed, Microsoft License Key Clearinghouse must digitally certify them. This organization is the certificate authority (CA) and must be contacted each time licenses are installed to receive the proper digital certificates.

INSTALLING TERMINAL SERVICES LICENSE SERVER

The process of installing the License Server is very similar to the process of installing Terminal Services. It's important to note that the License Server can be installed on any Windows 2000 server; however, it can be started only on a standalone server or a domain controller. It cannot be started on a domain member server.

To install the License Server, follow these steps:

1. Launch the Control Panel.
2. From the Control Panel, double-click Add/Remove Programs.
3. From the left pane, select Add/Remove Windows Components. This opens the Windows Components dialog.
4. Select Terminal Services Licensing and then choose Next to begin the installation.
5. In the Terminal Services Setup screen, select the Application Server mode and click Next.
6. The Terminal Services Licensing Setup dialog appears (see Figure 29.14). In most cases, you keep the default settings in this screen. The Your Entire Enterprise option is designed to have the License Server serve licensing for the entire site; the Your Domain or Workgroup option serves licensing for only a specific domain or workgroup. The path listed is where the License Server will store the licenses. Click Next to begin the installation process.

Figure 29.14
The Terminal Services Licensing Setup dialog requires you to specify the role of the server and the location of the license database before configuring the server as a License Server.

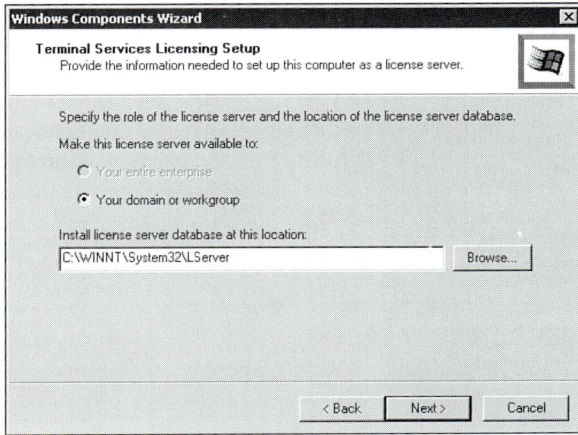

7. After the installation is complete, click Finish.
8. To activate the License Server, an administrator must open Terminal Services Licensing from the Administrative Tools folder. This tool then searches for available License Servers.
9. To activate the License Server, right-click on the appropriate server and select Activate Server, as shown in Figure 29.15, to start the Licensing Wizard.

Figure 29.15
You must right-click the server and select Activate Server to make the server active.

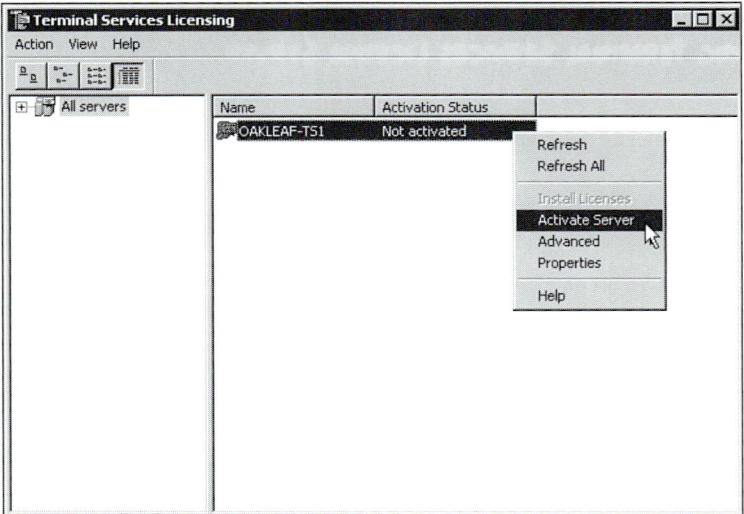

10. In the Welcome dialog, click Next. The Connection Method dialog asks for a connection method. Choose one of the following:
    - The Internet or fax method if you have an Internet connection or a modem setup
    - The World Wide Web method to manually enter the necessary information via a Web page
    - The Telephone method to manually give information to a customer service representative

    Then choose Next.
11. The Connection Wizard walks you through the necessary steps to license your Terminal Server. Be sure to fill out all information completely and accurately, because Microsoft uses this information to send you the necessary activation codes.

 If you encounter problems during Licensing Services installation, see the "Licensing Services" information in the Troubleshooting section at the end of this chapter.

Installing and Deploying the Terminal Services Client

The Windows 2000 client comes in three architectural flavors: 16-bit version for Intel platforms, 32-bit version for Intel platforms, and 32-bit version for Alpha platforms. Users can use two different clients to connect to the Windows 2000 Terminal server: the Windows 2000 Terminal Services Client and the Terminal Server 4.0 client.

Tip from
RJ

> Terminal Server 4.0 clients use RDP version 4.0, and Windows 2000 clients use RDP 5.0. RDP 5.0 has various improvements; however, the biggest benefit is that it reduces network traffic approximately 30–40% over RDP 4.0. This fact may entice administrators to switch clients to ease traffic on overburdened LANs.

What's New in the Terminal Services Client?

Although Terminal Services is not a large departure from NT 4.0, Terminal Server Edition, the Terminal Services Client has several new features and benefits:

- Printer redirection to print to a local printer—This capability allows a client to connect to a Terminal server, run applications on the Terminal server, and print any output to a printer attached to the local computer. For example, from OakLab1, Student1 initiates a TS connection to OAKLEAF-TS. Within this session, she writes a five-page film review in MS Word. While running MS Word within the client session, she simply prints the document. The TS client then redirects the print job to the default printer as defined by OakLab1. This feature can also be disabled from within the Terminal Services Configuration so that all print jobs go to a printer physically attached to the Terminal server. LPT and COM ports can also be mapped to facilitate printing from MS-DOS and older Windows applications.

- Clipboard redirection—This feature allows users to cut and paste data from the local computer to the Terminal Services Client session and vice versa.

- 32 Virtual channels—Virtual channels provide a mechanism to allow the Terminal server to gain access to the client's local computer resources. For example, the printer and Clipboard redirection features use virtual channels to communicate effectively to the local computer. Microsoft also offers an SDK to allow developers to make use of custom virtual channels for their own purposes. Two channels are reserved for the core communication by RDP; however, 30 other channels are available for other functions.

- Session Remote Control—In the initial release of Windows 2000 Terminal Services, only two clients can share the same TS session. This enables a single administrator to remotely control a user's client session.

- Client-side bitmap caching—This feature allows the client to store bitmaps that are viewed within the client session. This improves the performance of the session. These bitmaps are stored under the client folder's Cache subfolder. The default size is 10MB. This cache is freed upon the end of the session.

- Data encryption—The Windows 2000 Terminal Services Client has been enhanced from 40-bit encryption to 56-bit encryption. This provides greater security and ensures that malicious users cannot "eavesdrop" on client sessions. A 128-bit Terminal Services Client version is still available for North American customers.
- Multilingual User Interface (MUI)—This user interface allows clients to display the client session in different languages.

Hardware Requirements

The Terminal Services Client is compatible with the following operating systems: Windows for Workgroups 3.11, Windows 95, Windows 98, Windows NT, and Windows 2000. You can also install the Terminal Server 4.0 client on Windows CE and gain connectivity to the Windows 2000 Terminal server.

The hardware requirements for the Terminal Services client are unchanged from the Terminal Server 4.0 client:

- VGA display with 640×480 resolution with 16 colors
- Mouse and keyboard
- Microsoft TCP/IP
- 8MB RAM recommended for Windows for Workgroups 3.11 clients
- 16MB RAM recommended for Windows 95 and 98
- Windows NT 3.51, Windows NT 4.0, and Windows 2000 clients require no additional hardware above the operating system base hardware requirements

Installing the Terminal Services Client

The installation process for the Terminal Services Client is straightforward and simple. Follow these steps to install the Terminal Services client:

1. Run the Setup.exe designed for your particular operating system (the different executables are covered in more detail later in this section); the client installation Wizard opens.
2. Click Continue when presented with the Welcome dialog.
3. Fill in your pertinent Name and Organization information and click OK. Verify that the information is correct; click OK. The License Agreement dialog appears.
4. Click I Agree on the License Agreement dialog; the Terminal Services Client Setup dialog appears, as shown in Figure 29.16.
5. Verify the destination of the Terminal Services Client files, and then click the large button to start the installation.

INSTALLING AND DEPLOYING THE TERMINAL SERVICES CLIENT 1219

Figure 29.16
The Terminal Services client installation begins when you click the large button in this dialog.

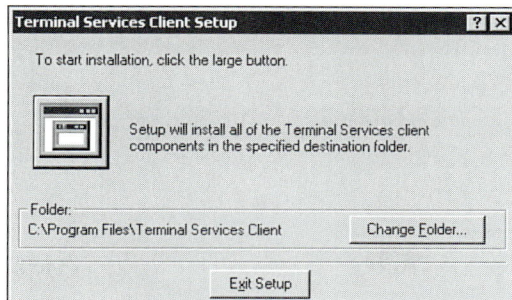

PART
V
CH
29

6. If you're installing the Terminal Services Client on a computer running Windows NT 4.0 or Windows 2000, you have two additional options for installation, as shown in Figure 29.17. By clicking Yes, the installation makes the Terminal Services client icons available to all users that log on to your workstation or server. By clicking No, the installation makes the icons available to only the current user.

Figure 29.17
Determine whether Terminal Services client icons will be available to all users or just the current user.

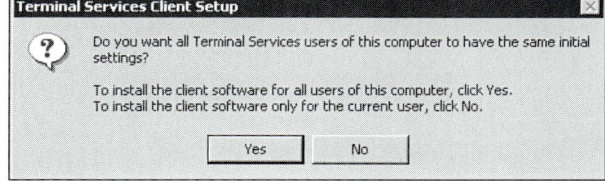

7. The installation process then checks for necessary disk space and copies all necessary files to the destination computer. After the installation completes, click OK to finish the setup process.

DEPLOYING THE TERMINAL SERVICES CLIENT

Although the Terminal Services Client installation process is straightforward, deploying the client to the workstations in your environment takes more planning. Fortunately, Microsoft offers several features to help administrators make the deployment easier.

For starters, Microsoft has included the Terminal Services Client Creator, which is installed during the setup of Terminal Services. This tool creates floppy disks for the installation of the client. However, the Client Creator can only create floppy disk copies of the client installation files, so many administrators may find this method too laborious for a general distribution method. Follow these steps to create the disk set:

1. From the Start Menu's Administrative Tools folder, click Terminal Services Client Creator. This opens the Client Creator utility.

2. Select the type of operating system where you plan on installing the Terminal Services Client. Note the number of disks that are required for installation, as shown in Figure 29.18.

3. Select the destination drive and then click OK. Follow the instructions to finish the creation of the installation set.

Figure 29.18
The Terminal Services Client Creator is used to create Terminal Services client installation disks to install the client on various types of workstations.

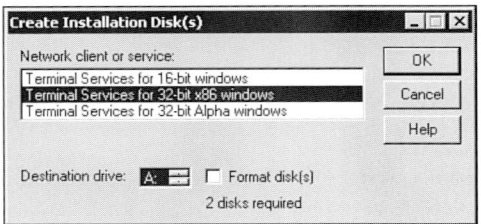

Because the Terminal Services Client Creator might not suit your needs, the Windows 2000 Terminal Server also stores the client setup files under the `\Winnt\System32\Client\Tsclient` folder. Each set of setup files is stored under its own hardware-specific folder—Win16 for Windows 3.11 For Workgroups, Win32 for 9x/NT clients, and Win32a for Alpha clients. Simply run `Setup.exe` in the `Disk1` subfolder to begin the installation. This method is also offered to enable you to create floppies by copying the `Disk1` folder to one floppy, `Disk2` to the next, and so forth. Again, many administrators may find this method too laborious for a general distribution method.

For a more automated distribution method, there's a subfolder under `\Winnt\System32\Client\Tsclient` named `Net` that stores all installation files in one client-specific folder to run from the network. Again, there are Win16, Win32, and Win32a subdirectories from which to select your specific hardware. Simply run `Setup.exe` to begin the installation.

Terminal Services also offers several command-line options when installing the Terminal Service Client. From any of the previously mentioned deployment methods, run **Setup.exe** with one of the following command-line options to help automate the client installation:

- **/Q**—During installation, the user sees the default setup background, a quick message stating that installation is beginning, and a copy gauge showing the status of the file copy operation. After the installation has completed, an exit dialog appears. The user must click OK to finish setup.

- **/Q1**—During installation, the user sees only a quick message stating that installation is beginning, the setup background, and a copy gauge showing the status of the file copy operation. The user is never required to interact with the installation process.

- **/QT**—During installation, the user sees no installation status and is not required to interact with any dialog boxes. The installation process suppresses all user interfaces.

INSTALLING AND DEPLOYING THE TERMINAL SERVICES CLIENT | 1221

SETTING UP TERMINAL SERVICES CONNECTIONS

After you have the Terminal Services Client installed on the appropriate workstations, you'll have to set up a new connection to the Terminal Server. This connection holds the default settings used to begin each client session. To set up a client connection, follow these steps:

1. Launch the Client Connection Manager, as shown in Figure 29.19.

Figure 29.19
The Client Connection Manager is used to configure the client to connect to a Terminal Server. The preconfigured settings are displayed.

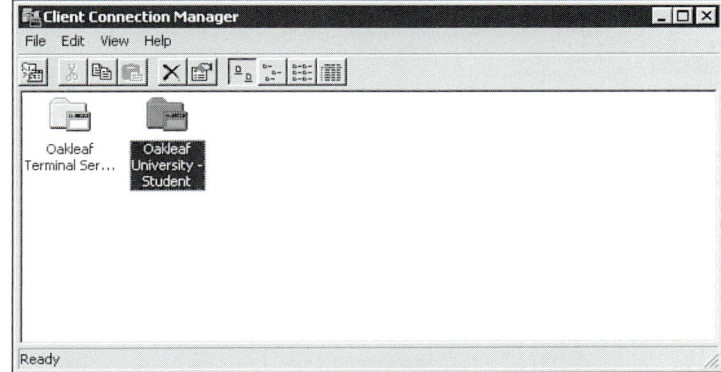

2. From the File menu, select New Connection; the Client Connection Manager Wizard opens.
3. On the Welcome screen, click Next to open the Create a Connection dialog.
4. In the Connection Name text box, enter a descriptive title for the connection, and then enter the server name or IP address of the Terminal server in the Server Name or IP Address text box (see Figure 29.20); click Next to continue.

Figure 29.20
The Client Connection Manager Wizard requires you to specify a connection name and the resolvable name or IP address of the server.

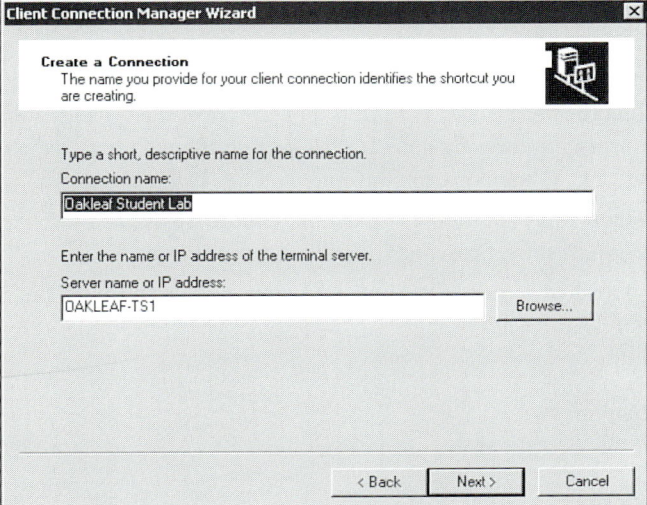

5. The Automatic Logon dialog allows you to enter the user, domain, and password to automatically log in every time you start a connection to the Terminal server. Choose this option only if it fits within the security regulations of your environment; click Next to continue.

6. In the Screen Options dialog, shown in Figure 29.21, select the screen resolution and window status; click Next to continue.

Figure 29.21
The Screen Options window of the Client Connection Manager wizard is used to set the screen area and specify whether the client comes up in a window or full-screen mode.

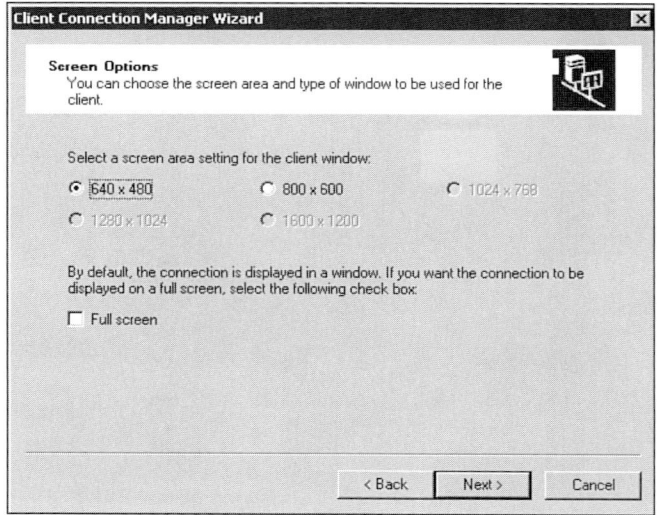

7. The Connection Properties dialog allows you set two options that can help speed up the connection communication speed. Data compression allows a type of burst communication for use over modems or slow network connections. Bitmap caching ensures that bitmaps are not continually sent during the communication of the session. Click Next to continue.

8. The Starting a Program dialog enables you to specify a program to open automatically every time the connection is started. For instance, the settings shown in Figure 29.22 start Internet Explorer by default; that session then is restricted to running Internet Explorer only. Click Next to continue.

9. On the Icon and Program group dialog, choose the icon you'd like to use and the program group to store the icon. Click Next to continue.

10. On the Finished screen, click Finish to complete the setup of the connection.

Figure 29.22
Starting a program every time a Terminal Services session starts restricts the session to running only that program.

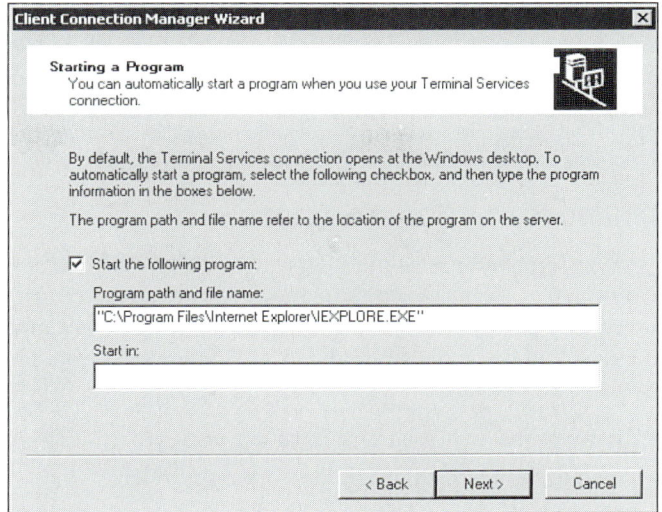

To open the connection, simply double-click on the icon within the Client Connection Manager or select the icon from the Start Menu.

Setting Up a Default Connection

Most network administrators want to set up a default connection for all users within their environment—especially if the Terminal Services Client is being deployed automatically from the login script. Microsoft has provided a method to do just this. Follow these steps to create a default connection:

1. Follow the steps listed previously to create a new connection from the Client Connection Manager.
2. When the connection setup is complete, highlight in the left tree pane of the Client Connection Manager the connection you'd like to distribute to all users, and then select File, Export, as seen in Figure 29.23.

Figure 29.23
Exporting client session settings is essential to setting up a default connection.

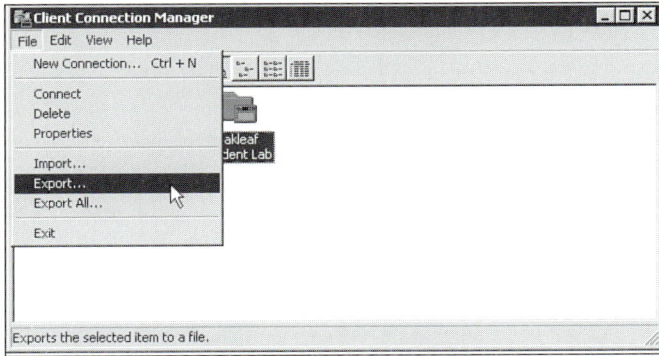

3. You are prompted for a filename and location to save these settings. Save this file to the installation folder you've prepared for the users as a file with a .CNS extension. During the client installation, this CNS file is copied to all users automatically.

> To resolve problems you encounter with the Terminal Services Client installation, see "Client Problems" in the Troubleshooting section at the end of this chapter.

HOT-KEY COMBINATIONS FOR CLIENT SESSIONS

Because many key combinations cannot effectively interact with a client session, Microsoft has provided alternative means to access these missed functions. For example, if you want to perform a screen capture of the desktop within the TS client, you cannot simply hit the Print Screen key. If you do, you capture the local Windows desktop. Here are the hot-key combinations available to clients:

- Alt+Pg+Up cycles through programs from left to right.
- Alt+Pg+Down cycles through programs from right to left.
- Alt+Insert cycles through programs in the order in which they were started.
- Alt+Home opens the Start menu.
- Alt+Del displays the Windows pop-up menu from the active window.
- Ctrl+Alt+End brings up the Windows 2000 Security dialog. This allows you to log off, reboot, shut down the server, and so on.
- Ctrl+Alt+Break toggles the Terminal Services Client window between normal and full-screen modes.
- Ctrl+Asterisk (× on the numeric keypad) ends a remote control session.
- Ctrl+Alt+Minus (– on the numeric keypad) places a snapshot of the active windows within the TS client window on the Clipboard (the same as pressing Alt+Print Screen on the local computer).
- Ctrl+Alt+Plus (+ on the numeric keypad) places a snapshot of all contents within the TS client window on the Clipboard (the same as pressing Print Screen on the local computer).

TROUBLESHOOTING

CLIENT PROBLEMS

The Terminal Services Client receives the error message `The local policy of this system does not permit you to logon interactively.`

As in Windows NT 4.0, this error refers to the fact that the prospective user does not have the right to Logon Locally from the local policy or the default domain Group Policy. If an individual or a group of users encounters this error, simply modify the domain or local policy to extend this right to the appropriate users.

User settings are being overwritten or saved improperly.

If your environment uses roaming profiles, this presents an awkward situation for clients. For instance, the settings that they save for the Terminal Services connection may overwrite the settings that are normally saved for the roaming profile. The best way to fix this problem is to avoid using roaming profiles. The second best solution is to implement a profile for the local computer and a separate profile for Terminal Services. You can implement a Terminal Services profile through the normal user administration tools.

Terminal Server Application Compatibility

The Terminal server is installed in Remote Administration mode, but it has problems running certain applications.

If two administrators simultaneously try to access the same application on a Terminal server running in Remote Administration mode, they encounter the same errors as if an application were installed in Execute mode on a Terminal server running in Application Server mode. Only one administrator at a time can run this particular application, or the Terminal server has to be switched to run in Application Server mode.

Licensing Services

During License Server installation, the message `PID is missing or corrupt` *is encountered.*

The Windows 2000 Product ID was missing or corrupted during the installation of Windows 2000. Because the License Server ID is built on this PID, this creates a snowball effect. The only remediation possible is to reinstall Windows 2000.

License Wizard cannot install certificates.

There are a variety of possible causes for this problem; however, two causes are most likely. First, the Wizard is being run by a user without Administrator rights on the Terminal server. Second, there are no certificates or the License Wizard cannot open the database housing the certificates. In the latter case, ensure that the `pstore` process is running.

MCSE Corner: Deploying Windows Terminal Services

Windows Terminal Services is an integrated part of Windows 2000 Server. Understanding the function and administration of Terminal Services is important for any of the Windows 2000 MCP exams. Your ability to work with Terminal Services is examined in 70-215, "Installing, Configuring and Administering Windows 2000 Server," and 70-220, "Designing Security for a Microsoft Windows 2000 Network."

70-215 Installing, Configuring, and Administering Microsoft Windows 2000 Server

You must have an understanding of the terminology and the operation of Terminal Services and the Remote Desktop Protocol (RDP) for exam 70-215. Although not directly tested, they help you better understand the questions asked about Terminal Services.

Going into this exam, you should be comfortable performing a complete install of Terminal Services. You must also be able to use the configuration tool for Terminal Services and the Terminal Services Manager to configure and monitor Terminal Services. You should be able to use the configuration tool to add Terminal Services connections and modify connection properties. This chapter explains how to perform all these operations.

The exam also tests your ability to configure Terminal Services for application sharing and to install and configure applications for use with Terminal Services. Remember the focus on troubleshooting of these newer exams and be ready to answer questions about troubleshooting Terminal Services and shared applications.

You also need to familiarize yourself with remotely administering servers using Terminal Services. You should be able to configure the servers for Terminal Services administration, install and configure the Terminal Services client, and set up a connection to enable server administration.

70-220 Designing Security for a Microsoft Windows 2000 Network

For exam 70-220, you are required to know how to design Terminal Services security. You should have an understanding of the function of Terminal Services and RDP, and how the security between client and server works. You must be able to work within a set of given parameters to ensure that the Terminal Services implementation you establish is secure.

CHAPTER 30

CLUSTERING WITH WINDOWS 2000 ADVANCED SERVER

In this chapter

Introducing Cluster Technology and Terminology   1228

Using Clustering to Improve Service Availability   1229

Understanding the Elements of Cluster Services   1231

Installing and Configuring the Cluster Service   1234

Installing Applications in a Cluster Environment   1238

Using Cluster Administrator   1243

Troubleshooting   1251

MCSE Corner: Registering for an Exam, What to Expect, and Testing Innovations   1252

Introducing Cluster Technology and Terminology

A *cluster* is a group of independent computers and external fixed-disk subsystems—redundant arrays of independent disks (RAID) systems—that usually appear on the network as a single system identified by one computer name. The clustered system also can provide multiple system images, known as *virtual servers*, to a network, client, or application.

A cluster can have many NetBIOS names, TCP/IP hostnames, and multiple IP addresses; each machine in the cluster must also have its own name. The cluster itself may be named "cluster," but it also can be named "sales," because it holds the sales data for your company, or "hr," because it holds your human resources files. In this case the names "sales" and "hr" are virtual servers. Each virtual server must have a name, an IP address, and one or more *resources* (disk partitions, file shares, applications, and so forth). Grouping resources into virtual servers makes it easier to fail the entire group to another node in the cluster or move all necessary resources to another cluster during upgrade or expansion.

Clusters can be configured in one of two ways: active/active or active/passive. As the titles suggest, an *active/active* cluster scenario has two or more server computers actively serving applications and resources to the network. In an *active/passive* cluster scenario, the passive server sits in standby mode, waiting for something on the primary node to fail. The passive server doesn't supply any network resources while the active server is online.

The idea behind clustering servers is to dramatically increase the availability of networked services and applications. Windows 2000 Cluster Service is supported on Windows 2000 Advanced Server and Windows 2000 DataCenter Server.

A *node* is defined as an individual server computer in a cluster. Advanced Server currently supports two-node clustering; DataCenter Server supports four-node clustering. If a node in a cluster fails, Cluster Service detects the failure and transfers ownership of the failed cluster resource(s) to another node.

To perform this wizardry, Cluster Service requires very specific hardware and network configurations.

Tip from
RJ

The standard practice is to purchase the combination of servers and RAID subsystems as a complete clustering solution from a single vendor. Verify that the hardware you intend to use for a Windows 2000 clustering environment is included on both Microsoft's Hardware Compatibility List (HCL) and the equipment manufacturer's HCL. You can find Microsoft's HCL for Windows 2000 Cluster Service and Windows 2000 DataCenter Cluster Service at www.microsoft.com/hcl. Search All Products of the Cluster/RAID System type.

Using Clustering to Improve Service Availability

The primary goal of a cluster is increasing the availability of a particular service. Critical Web and database services commonly use clustering to provide high availability. There is a great deal of confusion about the terminology associated with high-availability networks. Following are generally accepted industry definitions for availability:

- *High availability* defines a system having 99.9% percent available uptime or better (62.2 or fewer minutes per month downtime).
- *Fault-tolerant availability* delivers 99.99% uptime (6.2 or fewer minutes per month downtime).
- *Fault-resilient availability* is defined as 99.999% uptime (sometimes called *five nines*, 0.62 or fewer minutes per month downtime).

A correctly configured Windows NT 4.0 Server averages 99.5% availability, which implies about 3.6 hours per month of downtime. Cluster Service uptimes depend on the computer/RAID system components you choose and your network topology. For example, Stratus Computer (http://www.stratus.com/) claimed in mid-April, 2000, that its Stratus ftServer products deliver 99.999% (*five-nines*) hardware availability to Windows 2000. Hardware availability figures, however, must be combined with software reliability data to produce an overall system reliability value. It wouldn't be surprising to find vendors willing to commit to 99.99% overall availability with Windows 2000 Advanced or DataCenter Server and five-nines hardware.

→ For a more extensive discussion of availability issues, **see** "Maximizing Availability," **p. 298**.

Redundancy, although often confused with availability, is a separate issue. *Redundant* components—such as multiple power supplies in a server and hot-spare drives in a RAID subsystem—often are used in high-availability systems, but high-availability systems are not inherently redundant. Redundant high-availability systems can be created with exponentially increasing costs. Stratus uses redundancy to achieve five-nines hardware availability.

Figure 30.1 shows an example of a Windows 2000 DataCenter Server high-availability cluster with four nodes. Figure 30.2 shows the same cluster configured for redundancy. The switch, hub, and fibre switch in Figure 30.1 are all single points of failure that could jeopardize the entire cluster. In Figure 30.2, there is no single point of failure except the shared-disk array. Most manufacturers build redundant systems into their disk arrays so that there is no single point of failure inside drive enclosures. This means that there is no single point of failure throughout the entire system shown in Figure 30.2. Building a redundant architecture dramatically increases hardware cost.

Figure 30.1
This four-node high-availability cluster provides at least 99.9% uptime. There are several single points of failure in the hubs and routers.

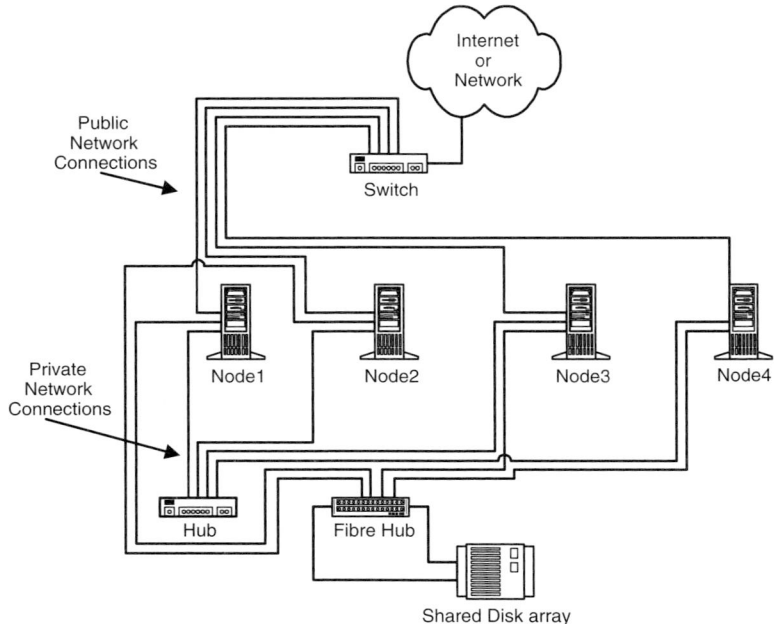

Figure 30.2
This four-node high-availability, redundant cluster provides 99.99% uptime, contains no single point of failure, and costs approximately 75% more than the cluster shown in Figure 30.1.

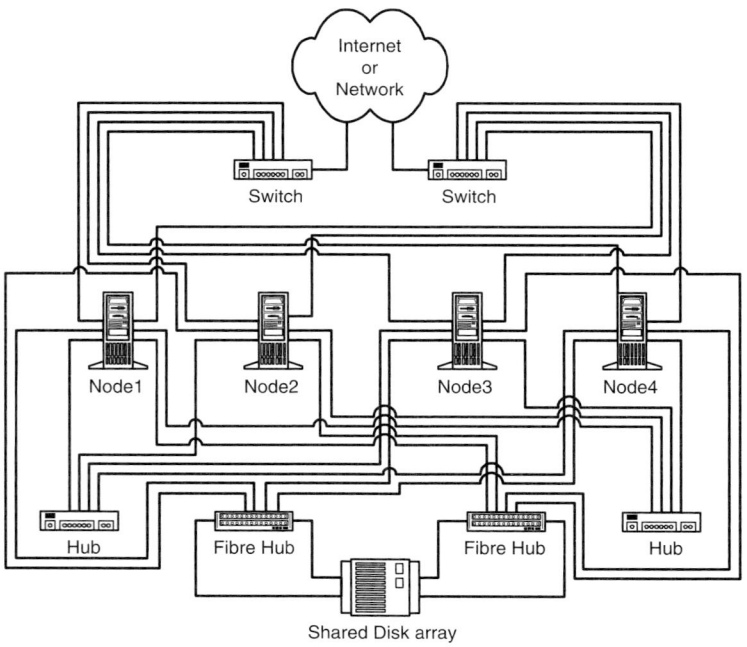

Understanding the Elements of Cluster Services

There are numerous configurations for a clustered network, as noted previously, but there are certain elements present in all cluster configurations. These elements are

- *Server computers (nodes)*—The machines running the operating system, Cluster Service, and server application
- *Shared-disk subsystem*—Contains all data that is shared by the nodes of the cluster
- *Heartbeat connection*—Connects the nodes to each other, so the nodes can communicate status

> **Note**
> Microsoft calls the heartbeat connection a *private network connection*. In this book, the term *private network connection* describes a network that uses private IP addresses, such as 10.x.x.x.
>
> Microsoft calls the LAN connection a *public network connection*. This book uses *public network connection* to describe a connection to the Internet that uses IP addresses assigned by InterNIC.

- *LAN connection*—Connects the nodes to the LAN or Internet so that users can connect to the clustered resources
- *Resources*—All files, services, disk partitions, and other elements needed to provide the desired cluster functionality

The following sections discuss each of these cluster elements in detail.

Cluster Servers

In theory, any server that's compatible with Windows 2000 is compatible with Windows 2000 Cluster Service. That is to say, the service will install on the server; actually getting the hardware to function properly in a clustered environment is a different matter. Microsoft supports only clusters that are *wholly* comprised of components on their HCL, and the components on Microsoft's HCL are almost invariably "matched sets" from vendors.

Generally, the server computer components most critical to cluster compatibility are the host bus adapter (HBA)—SCSI or Fibre Channel—and the shared bus array.

An array may have a shared bus, but that doesn't mean a controller supports the shared bus. Conversely, just because an HBA or RAID controller supports a shared bus doesn't mean the array has a shared bus. Both must be present for clustering.

The Shared-Disk Subsystem

The two basic types of disk subsystems are available for use as shared bus arrays in a clustered environment:

- *Dumb arrays* consist of a box of disks controlled by array controllers located in each server. The array controllers contain and manage all RAID configuration data for the array. Dumb arrays often are called *just a bunch of disks*, or JBOD.
- *Smart arrays* contain the array controllers locally and connect to the servers via HBAs, which off-load RAID processing from the server to the array, improving performance.

To keep application data consistent between nodes of the cluster, the nodes must use the same disk resources on the shared-disk subsystem. There are two models for dealing with how the nodes connect to the disk resources on the disk subsystem; *shared-nothing* and *shared-everything*. In a shared-nothing model, only one node is able to use (own) a disk resource at a given time. In a shared-everything model, all nodes can access all disk resources all the time. The shared-everything model requires a lot of file-locking information to be transferred between nodes along with the other heartbeat information. The shared-nothing model simplifies the process by giving ownership of the disk resource to one node, and only that node can access the disk resource. If the owner node fails, the disk resource ownership is transferred to another node (failed over). Microsoft Cluster Service uses a shared-nothing model to control disk resources.

To support clustering, the disk arrays need to be configured with a Quorum disk. The Quorum disk maintains state information on each node in the cluster and plays a critical role in failing over resources. Because of this pivotal role, and the desire for maximum availability, the Quorum disk should be mirrored across two physical disks. You should not place other applications on the same physical disk(s) as your Quorum disk.

Tip from
RJ

Microsoft recommends a disk of no less than 500MB for this task, but it's a better practice to use a 1GB (minimum) partition of a mirror set as the quorum disk. The remaining free space of the array can be partitioned for use by the application running on the cluster.

THE HEARTBEAT CONNECTION

Physically, the heartbeat connection in a cluster environment is some form of network connectivity between nodes. This connectivity can be in the form of an Ethernet crossover cable connected to a network adapter card (NIC) on each node or a standard Ethernet connection to a hub or switch, as long as the nodes are able to communicate.

Nodes in a cluster use the heartbeat connection to retrieve and disseminate information about the cluster's current operational state and that of the resources, services, and applications owned by each node of the cluster. A node in the cluster is able to recognize a failure in a resource service or application served by another node in the cluster due to failure of heartbeat communication from the failed node.

To prevent inadvertent failovers due to lost heartbeat packets, it's often desirable to have multiple network connections available for heartbeat communications. Windows 2000 simplifies this process in the Cluster Service installation wizard by prompting you to enter secondary network paths.

UNDERSTANDING THE ELEMENTS OF CLUSTER SERVICES | 1233

Tip from
RJ

> If you intend to use multiple networks for heartbeat communications, be sure to properly outfit your server with enough NICs to support each path. Dual-port NICs can save you valuable expansion slots.

THE LAN CONNECTION

The LAN connection is the network interface through which clients access the applications, services, or other resources on the cluster. A client is defined as any user or computer that accesses resources on your cluster.

Tip from
RJ

> It isn't a recommended practice in a production environment, but it's possible to use the LAN connection for heartbeat communications. Doing so increases traffic on the LAN and slightly decreases costs by reducing the number of NICs necessary for the installation. In a testing environment this may be a consideration. You must realize that this compromises the security of your cluster's private node-to-node communications and increases the traffic on the LAN.

PART
V

CH
30

CLUSTER RESOURCES

The term *resources* is used often when discussing clustering and cluster services. A resource is any item necessary to provide a service to the end users. That is a very vague definition but these examples should help clarify it. A resource can be a *disk resource*—a physical disk or disk partition that the applications or users must be able to access. A resource can be a server application—such as Microsoft Exchange. A resource also can be an IP address, as in the case of Internet Information Server (IIS), where an IP address is assigned to each Web site on a server. The name of a computer can be a resource if that name is necessary for users to access functions on the cluster.

Because resources can be any item, it's impossible to list every possible resource. Understanding that a resource is one—and only one—item is the key to understanding how resources are used. Resources are combined into functional groups, and the groups are treated by the cluster service as complete units. When a resource fails on one node of a cluster, the complete group is failed to another node of the cluster.

For example, the resources necessary for a shared folder on a file server are a server name (this can be a virtual server name), an IP address, a share name, and a disk resource (the disk or partition where the files reside). These are grouped. If any one of these resources (such as a disk partition) fails, the entire group fails, because the service (in this case, a file share) would not be available to the users.

Installing and Configuring the Cluster Service

Before installing the Cluster Service you must complete all the following steps:

1. Ensure that you have a detailed connection diagram of the cluster you intend to build.
2. Connect all cabling according to your connection diagram.
3. Install the Windows 2000 Advanced Server or DataCenter Server operating system on one node of the cluster.
4. Install any vendor-supplied software necessary to control your shared-disk subsystem on your functional node.
5. Use the vendor-supplied software to create a mirrored disk set on the shared-disk subsystem; this is your Quorum disk.
6. Use the vendor-supplied software to configure the remainder of your shared-disk subsystem for the applications to be served by your cluster. It's best to separate each application onto its own logical partition (you may segregate them onto their own physical partitions if you want, but it's not essential). The partitions (drives) are used when you set up resource groups for the applications for failover purposes. Separate partitions allow individual applications to fail over separately.
7. Install the Windows 2000 Advanced Server or DataCenter Server operating system on the remaining node(s) of your cluster.
8. Install any vendor-supplied software necessary to control your shared-disk subsystem on all nodes of the cluster.
9. Ensure that all nodes of the cluster can communicate with the shared-disk subsystem by using the vendor-supplied software.
10. Verify that all nodes of the cluster can communicate with other computers on the network and can communicate with each other.

Preinstallation Checklist

Before you begin the installation, complete the following checklist to avoid many common problems encountered during installation:

- Consider again the issues of scalability if projected network traffic was underestimated and actual traffic overburdens your cluster.
- Make sure that all servers that act as cluster nodes have at least two NICs (or at least one dual-port NIC).
- Check that all NICs' link lights are lit. This gives a degree of certainty that the cables are connected and functioning properly. Cabling a cluster can be a daunting task, so you may want to check the cabling against your diagram again.
- Ensure that all servers that act as cluster nodes can see the shared disks that participate in the cluster.

- Double-check that all servers participating in the cluster build have either Windows 2000 Advanced Server or Windows 2000 DataCenter Server.
- Be sure that you have your Windows 2000 Advanced Server or Windows 2000 DataCenter CD-ROM, or access to these files on a system drive or network share.
- Decide which external disk resources will be used by your cluster. Use your SAN administration software to determine which disk resources are available.

> **Caution**
>
> Most clusters use all external disk resources. As the IT community continues to move toward Storage Area Network (SAN) environments, this configuration becomes increasingly critical. In a SAN environment, disk storage subsystems can be used by multiple clusters. You must carefully select only the disk resources available for ownership by your cluster, and be sure that they are not in use by another cluster.

INSTALLING CLUSTER SERVICE

Installing the Cluster Service component is a quick process. The installation occupies only 0.8MB of disk space on your system partition, and the server does not need to be rebooted to proceed. To install cluster services on your Windows 2000 Advanced Server or DataCenter Server, follow these steps for each node of your cluster:

1. Select Add/Remove Windows Components from the Add/Remove Programs Control Panel applet and click the Cluster Service check box; click Next to install the service.
2. After installing the Cluster Service component a Welcome dialog tells you to close any open programs before proceeding with Cluster Service configuration. Click Next to continue.
3. The next dialog warns that your hardware must be compatible with Microsoft's HCL for Cluster Service; select I Understand, and click Next to proceed.

> **Note**
>
> Whether you're creating a new cluster or adding a new node to a cluster, the setup and configuration steps are nearly identical. Therefore, they are covered simultaneously with the differences highlighted in applicable steps.

4. The Create or Join a Cluster dialog asks you to indicate whether you're creating a new cluster or adding to an existing cluster (see Figure 30.3); make the appropriate selection and click Next.

Figure 30.3
Select whether this is the first node in the cluster or you're joining a node to an existing cluster.

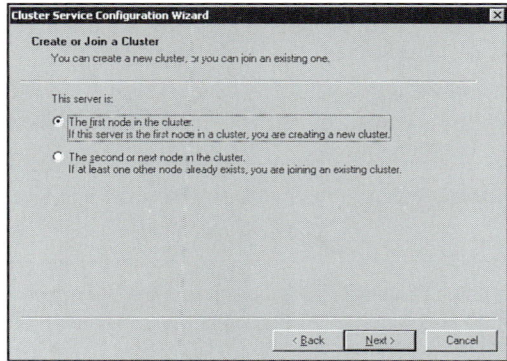

5. Type the name of the cluster in the Cluster Name dialog.

   If you're creating a new cluster, type the name of the cluster and click Next.

   If you're adding a node to an existing cluster, a browse dialog opens and lets you select the appropriate cluster; click Next.

Tip from
RJ

Cluster names don't support special characters—except hyphens—and are limited to 63 characters. Best practice dictates limiting names to 15 characters for cross-platform and backward compatibility.

---

6. In the Select an Account dialog, use the Domain drop-down list to select an Administrative account for the Cluster Service (this is the domain to which your cluster nodes are bound). Type the username and password of your administrative account (see Figure 30.4); click Next.

   If you're adding a new node to an existing cluster, skip to step 9. If this is the first node in your cluster continue with steps 7 and 8.

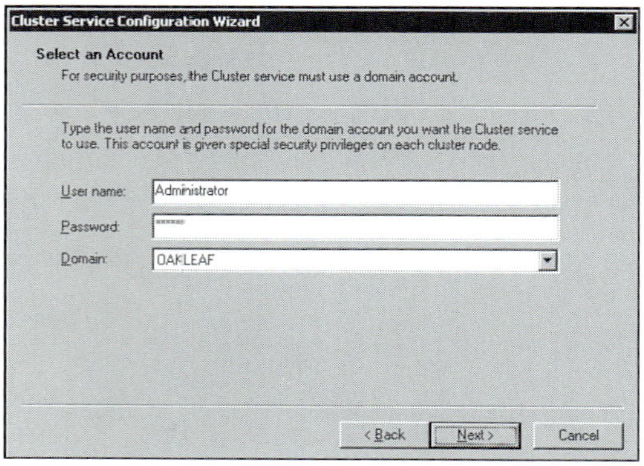

Figure 30.4
Type your administrator username and password. Be sure this is a domain administrative account, preferably a specially made service account.

INSTALLING AND CONFIGURING THE CLUSTER SERVICE | 1237

Tip from
RJ

Don't use the Administrator account for the Cluster Service, but instead use a service account created specifically for this purpose. This allows you to change passwords on your administrative account without adversely affecting (killing) the cluster.

7. In the Add or Remove Managed Disks dialog, use the Add and Remove buttons to configure the Managed Disks list to contain only those disks to be used by your cluster (see Figure 30.5); click Next.

Figure 30.5
Select the disk resources this cluster utilizes. Unless you're in a SAN environment, your cluster ordinarily uses all disk resources.

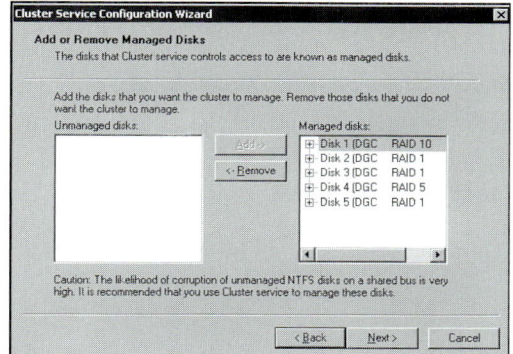

8. In the Cluster File Storage dialog, use the Disks drop-down list to select the Quorum disk (the disk partition to store the shared checkpoint and log files for your cluster); click Next.

9. In the Network Connections dialog, type the name of the network to be used by the node you're configuring. Make sure the Enable This Network For Cluster Use check box is marked, and then make a selection in the list below it to specify whether the interface is public, private, or both (see Figure 30.6); click Next.

Another dialog opens for each of your network connections. Repeat step 9 for each network connection, and then proceed to step 10.

Figure 30.6
Specify whether your interfaces are public (LAN), private (heartbeat), or both.

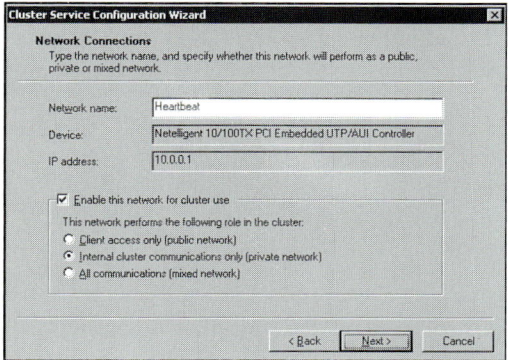

PART
V
CH
30

> **Note**
>
> Using a network interface for both private and public communications isn't recommended. Doing so compromises overall security of the cluster and increases traffic on the public network.

10. In the IP Address text box of the Cluster IP Address dialog, type the IP address you intend to use for remotely administering the cluster (see Figure 30.7). This address *cannot* be the same as any node in the cluster. You don't need to do anything with the network option in this dialog; any changes to the network options can be done in the Cluster Server Administrator. Click Next.

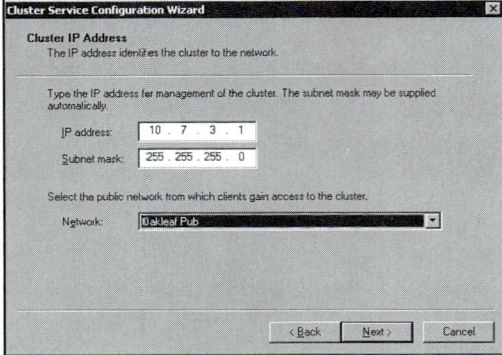

Figure 30.7
The cluster must have an IP address for itself in addition to the IP addresses for each node.

This node of the cluster is done. If you intend to install more nodes on this cluster, you must install Microsoft Cluster Service on each node by repeating the preceding steps.

 If you encounter problems installing the Cluster Service, see the "Cluster Service Installation Problems" topic of the "Troubleshooting" section at the end of the chapter.

INSTALLING APPLICATIONS IN A CLUSTER ENVIRONMENT

All applications installed in a cluster environment should be set up as *virtual servers*. As explained earlier, a virtual server is a computer name and IP address that can be moved from node to node in a cluster. By setting up an application in a virtual server, the entire application—complete with the computer name that the application is running on and its IP address—can be moved to another node in case of failure.

After it's created, a virtual server can be grouped with other resources that are failed over when the virtual server is failed over. Failing over the entire group in this manner ensures that all the components necessary for an application are available when the resource group comes online on another node.

Microsoft uses the shared-nothing cluster model in Windows NT 4.0 and Windows 2000, so 99% of all out-of-the-box software operates properly on clusters in Windows 2000. A few types of applications, including tape backup software and network monitoring software, need to be *cluster-aware applications*. Cluster-aware applications know they are operating on a cluster and take special actions to accommodate the cluster and perform their tasks. You don't need to purchase cluster-aware software for everything; it's only for applications that must access and be aware of clustered servers on a physical level, not just the virtual level.

For example, if your tape backup application needs to know that your data resides on drive K of your server, the application needs to be cluster-aware, because drive K might change from server to server (node to node) within your cluster. If, however, your application is content to know that its data is on a certain share on your server, it does not need to be cluster-aware. Even when the share moves from one node to another, the share name and server name remain the same; thus, the data is still available. The server name remains the same because it's a virtual server. Virtual server names can move from node to node along with other resources.

If you intend to run multiple instances of a database from two or more nodes on your cluster, your database software must be cluster-aware. SQL Server Enterprise Edition and Oracle Parallel Server are examples of cluster-aware database systems. Because of the nature of Web servers (including IIS 5.0), they fall into the 99% that run correctly out of the box. Only your software vendor can tell you whether its application is cluster-aware.

You must set up the virtual server for your application before you use the vendor's software to install the service on the server. This means that before you install IIS on a node of your cluster (for example, Node-A), you must first set up a virtual server for it. The virtual server has a name (for example, IIS) and an IP address. After the virtual server is established, you administer all IIS resources on your cluster through the machine name IIS, not the machine name Node-A (which is your node's machine name).

All applications and services that are to fail over must be installed on all nodes on which you want them to run or to fail over. For example, if you want to run Exchange 2000 Server Enterprise Edition on one node of your cluster and have it fail to another node, Exchange 2000 Server must be installed on both of those nodes. Some software applications allow both nodes to operate simultaneously (for example, Microsoft SQL Server and Exchange 2000 Server), and some require that the second node be inactive until failover occurs (for example, Exchange Server 5+). Contact your software vendor to find out whether you can operate both nodes simultaneously in an active/active configuration for your software.

 If you encounter problems installing applications on the server, see the "Troubleshooting Application Installation" topic of the "Troubleshooting" section at the end of this chapter.

Setting Up a Virtual Server for Shared Folders

On your existing servers, you most likely have shared folders, and you might want to share critical folders on your cluster servers as well. You use the Cluster Administrator snap-in to set up shared folders. The Cluster Administrator displays all servers in your cluster and also displays the cluster's groups, resources, and configuration settings. You'll learn more about Cluster Administrator later in the section "Using Cluster Administrator."

To set up a virtual server for shared folders on your cluster follow these steps:

1. Choose Cluster Administrator from the Administrative Tools menu to open the snap-in. Right-click the cluster item in the navigation tree (see Figure 30.8), and choose Configure Application from the context menu to open the Cluster Application Wizard. Click Next to bypass the Welcome dialog.

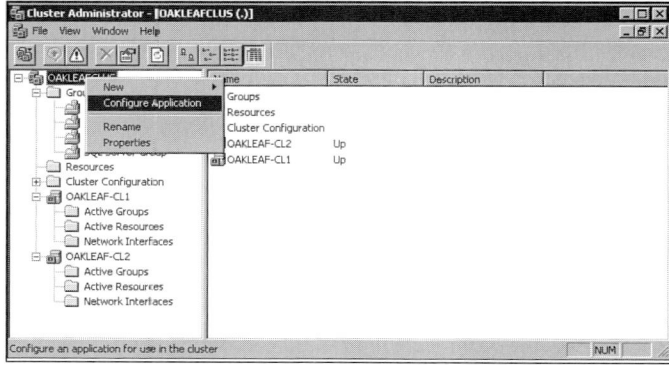

Figure 30.8
The Configure Application command starts the Cluster Application Wizard in which you set up shared folders on your cluster.

2. In the Select or Create a Virtual Server dialog, select Create a new Virtual Server (see Figure 30.9). Click Next.

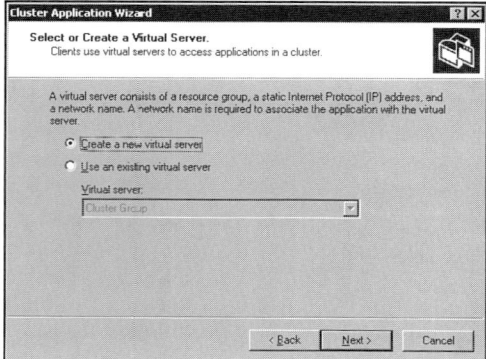

Figure 30.9
Select Create a New Virtual Server to create a virtual server for shared folders.

3. In the Resource Group Name Dialog, type a descriptive name for the Virtual Server resource group; you also can type a description of the resource that is accessible to administrators only. Click Next.

4. In the Virtual Server Access Information dialog, assign a name and an IP address to the virtual server (see Figure 30.10). This IP address must be unique on your network and accessible to your network clients. Clients use this name and IP address to access your virtual server resources. Click Next.

INSTALLING APPLICATIONS IN A CLUSTER ENVIRONMENT | 1241

Figure 30.10
The virtual server needs its own IP address, which is different from the cluster IP address and the IP addresses of the nodes.

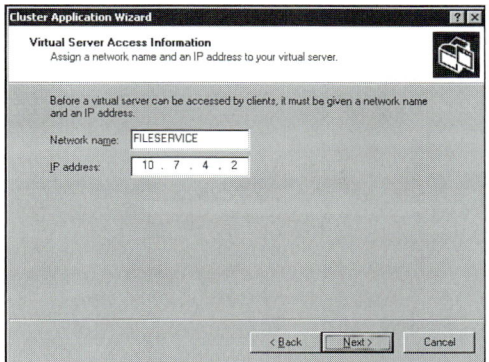

PART
V
CH
30

5. In the Enter Subnet Mask dialog, type the subnet mask that corresponds to your network and choose a public network from the Network drop-down list (see Figure 30.11). Click OK to return to the Virtual Server Access Information dialog, and then click Next. You have now provided all the required properties for the virtual server.

Figure 30.11
Enter the subnet mask for your virtual server. This is the subnet mask of your LAN. An invalid subnet mask can cause communication failure.

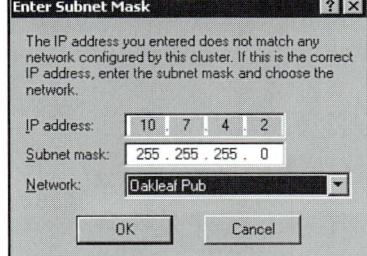

Caution

Do not use an existing IP address from one of the servers in your cluster for the virtual server IP address.

6. In the Advanced Properties dialog, you can view and set advanced virtual server properties. To view advanced settings, make a selection in the Categories list and click the Advanced Properties button. You'll learn more about these properties later in this chapter. For now, click Next to close this dialog and finish creating the virtual server.

7. The Create Application Cluster Resource dialog prompts you to create a cluster resource to manage the application. Click Yes, Create a Cluster Resource for My Application Now, and then click Next.

8. The Application Resource Type dialog prompts you to define a resource type; in the Resource Type drop-down list, choose one of the predefined selections—for this example, File Share (see Figure 30.12). Click Next.

Figure 30.12
Select the correct type of resource for the application or service that this virtual server hosts.

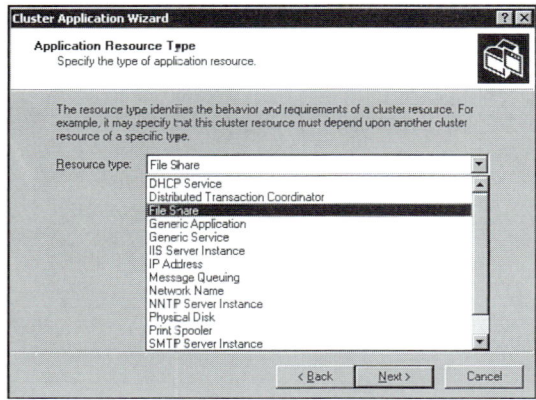

9. In the Application Resource Name and Description dialog, type the name by which the application will be managed within the cluster. For this example, type the name **Fileshare** in the Name textbox. You have the option of entering a brief description of the application. Click Next to create the File Share application resource.

10. The File Share Parameters dialog prompts you to define the shared directory this resource will serve. Type a share name and path applicable to your cluster and, if you choose, provide a brief descriptive comment to help identify the resource. In the User Limit area, set the maximum number of users that can access the resource at any one time (see Figure 30.13). Click Next.

Figure 30.13
The Parameters page is specific to the resource type that you selected. This figure shows the Parameters page for a resource type of FILESHARE. A resource type of IP Address displays a Parameters page that prompts for an IP address; a Network Name resource type has a Parameters page that prompts for the name.

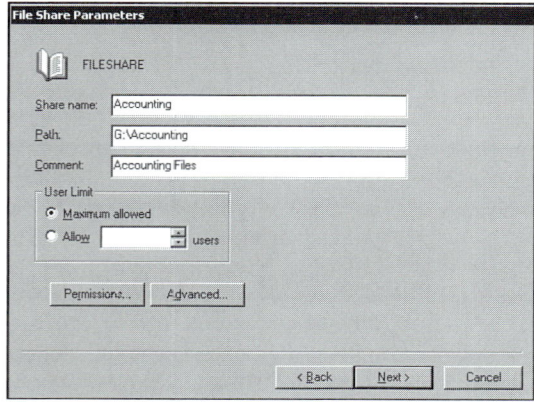

Note
In most cases, you don't need to limit the number of users. You might need to limit the number of users if a software license restricts usage to a specific number of users or if you have a highly secure area to which you want to grant access to only one user at a time.

11. A verification dialog opens, allowing you to check your settings and back up to modify them if necessary. Click Finish to install the resource on the cluster.

At this point, you have set up a file share resource on your cluster. File sharing is a native service of Windows 2000, so you don't need to run installation software. To install cluster-aware applications (such as the Enterprise editions of Exchange 2000 Server or SQL Server 7+), follow the instructions provided by the software vendor. Each clustered application requires a virtual server and its own application-specific resources.

Using Cluster Administrator

Cluster Administrator is a standard Microsoft Management Console (MMC) snap-in, as shown in Figure 30.14. The left pane contains a tree of cluster objects. Each cluster object contains a series of folder icons that house groups, resources, and cluster configuration settings, in addition to cluster nodes.

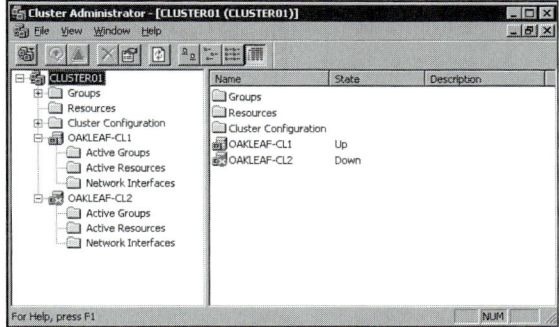

Figure 30.14
The Cluster Administrator provides access to all configuration settings of the cluster and indicates status of all resources, resource groups, and cluster nodes.

Status indicators and entries in the right pane of the Cluster Administrator let you know when a resource, resource group, or cluster node is online, offline, or failed. *Up* indicates that the item is online and functioning properly. *Offline* indicates that the item was taken offline by an administrator for maintenance or troubleshooting purposes. (The resource won't fail over to another node in Offline mode.) *Down* indicates that the item has failed. If the item is a resource or resource group, the cluster attempts to move the failed item to another node. If the item still fails on the other node, it remains in a Down state. If the item functions properly on the other node, the item returns to an Up state on the new node.

Working with Resource Groups

A resource group is defined as a collection of resources, such as disk drives, network cards, applications, application databases, and IP addresses that are managed by Cluster Service as a single logical unit. Every newly created cluster contains a default cluster group. This group has three resources: an IP address, a name, and a physical (Quorum) disk. As you learned in previous sections of this chapter, you can create other groups during application installation via the Cluster Application Installation (CAI) Wizard, or through the Cluster Administrator snap-in.

When creating groups, it's important that you include all resources that an individual application, service, or resource needs to function properly. During a failover scenario, entire groups—rather than individual resources within those groups—fail over between nodes. The resources are available only as a complete group, so you can be assured that if the group fails over to another node, it carries with it all resources that are necessary to provide functionality for a particular service or application.

When you create a resource group, you're given the option of designating a Preferred Owner for the group. The Preferred Owner is a node that is the default server for the group and all of its resources. If the Preferred Owner fails, another node takes ownership of the group's resources. When the Preferred Owner node again becomes available, it fails the resources of the group back to itself. This arrangement allows active/active scenarios and a crude form of load balancing between cluster nodes.

> **Note**
>
> There are only two scenarios in which you might want to use preferred owners. If you're running an active/active cluster, specify a preferred owner for each application's resource group. If you have an unbalanced active/passive cluster where the active node is significantly more powerful than the passive node and the passive node is used only in case of failure, specify the preferred owner as the more powerful node.

To create a resource group, do the following:

1. In the Cluster Administrator tool, right-click the *Clustername*/Groups listing, select New, and select Group to open the New Group dialog.
2. Type the name of the resource group in the Name textbox of the New Group dialog, as shown in Figure 30.15. It's a common practice to use the virtual server name for the resource group name so the groups are easily identifiable in the Cluster Administrator. Click Next.

Figure 30.15
Use the virtual server name to name your new resource group so you can identify the group in Cluster Administrator. You can add a short description of the group, too, if necessary.

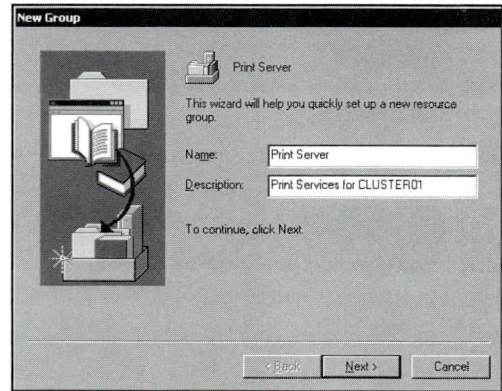

3. In the Preferred Owners dialog's Available Nodes, you can select one or more preferred owners for the group and arrange his or her priority in the list. Click Finish to create the group.

With the group created, you now need to assign resources to it. If you set up your group earlier using the CAI Wizard, it makes creating resources for the group much easier. If you did not set up your group with the Wizard, you must create your resources manually.

Assigning Resources

As stated earlier, resources are essential items necessary for a given application or service to function properly. Resources can be hostnames, IP addresses, physical disks, shared directories, applications, services, and application databases.

All resources managed by your cluster appear in the Cluster Administrator's Resources folder, regardless of whether they are members of a resource group. All resources that are members of a resource group also appear in the Groups folder. The resources and resource groups also appear inside the folder for the node that is currently managing them (if any).

When assigning resources to resource groups, you're prompted for *dependencies*. Dependencies are any items required for the resource to function correctly. For example, a network name (server name) requires an IP address or it will not function; a file share requires a disk resource on which the files reside (a network name for the users to access it) and the network name requires an IP address. It isn't practical to list the dependencies for every possible resource, but logic and common sense should put you on the right track.

To create a resource and assign it to the group you created in the preceding section, do the following:

1. Right-click the Resources folder in the Cluster Administrator window, and then select New, Resource to open the New Resource dialog.
2. Type the resource name in the Name textbox, and (optionally) a resource description. Use the Resource Type and Group drop-down lists to define the resource type and identify to which resource group it belongs (see Figure 30.16). Click Next.

Figure 30.16
You must give your resource a name, type, and group. The description is optional. Mark the Run This Resource in a Separate Resource Monitor check box if you want to profile the individual resource in PerfMon.

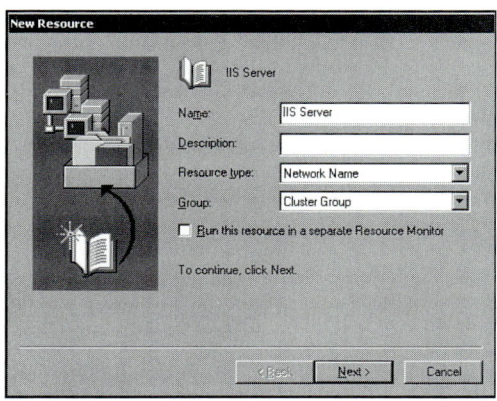

> **Note**
>
> Marking the Run This Resource in a Separate Resource Monitor check box consumes system resources. Don't mark this check box unless the resource *must* be monitored separately from other cluster resources.

3. Delete from the Possible Owners list in the Possible Owners dialog, shown in Figure 30.17, the name of any nodes in your cluster that are incapable of serving this resource (by default, all nodes are possible owners). Click Next.

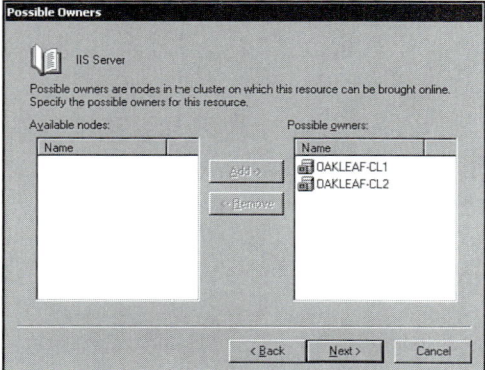

Figure 30.17
If there is a node that cannot host the resource, remove that node from the possible owners.

4. In the Dependencies dialog, list any resources upon which the new resource is dependent. Select those resources from the Available Resources list, and use the Add button to place them in the Resource Dependencies list (see Figure 30.18). Click Next.

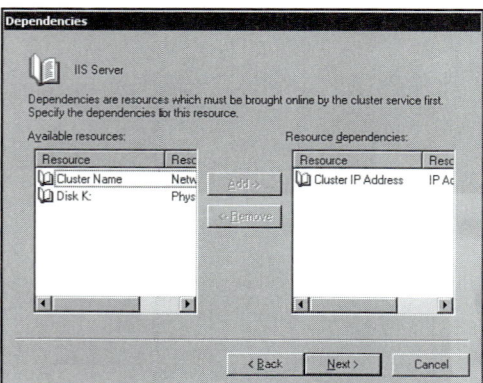

Figure 30.18
Select all resources on which this resource is dependent. For example, a Shared Directory resource is dependent upon a Physical Disk resource, a Cluster Name resource requires an IP Address resource, and so on.

5. In the *Resource type* Parameters dialog, enter the specific parameters associated with the resource type you have selected. For example, if you have selected an IP Address resource type, you're prompted for that IP address. When you've entered the appropriate parameters, click Finish.

You now see the newly created resources in Cluster Administrator under the Resources heading. Initially, the resources are offline and identified with a yellow triangle (see Figure 30.19).

Figure 30.19
Here you see the newly created resources IIS Server Name and IIS Server IP Address in the Cluster Administrator. Note that the resources are offline when newly created.

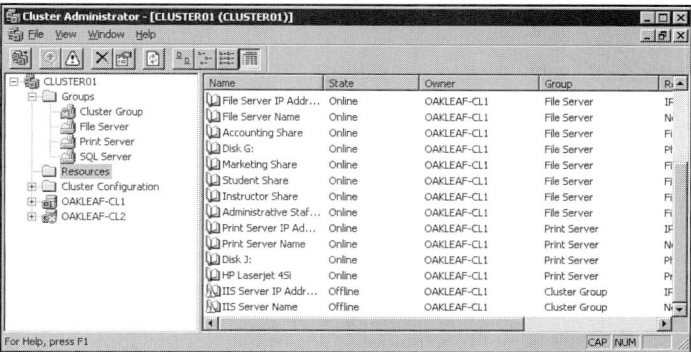

It's very rare to change resource group affiliations, but it may be desirable in an instance such as changing the function of a cluster. For example, if you were no longer running IIS on your cluster but were installing SQL Server on it, you might want to change the disk resources from the old IIS group to the SQL Server group rather than recreate the disk resources.

To change the group affiliation for a resource, right-click the resource name, choose Change Group, and choose the name of the new group with which you want it affiliated (see Figure 30.20).

Figure 30.20
Here, you see the administrator moving the resources IIS Server Name and IIS Server IP Address to the IIS Server group.

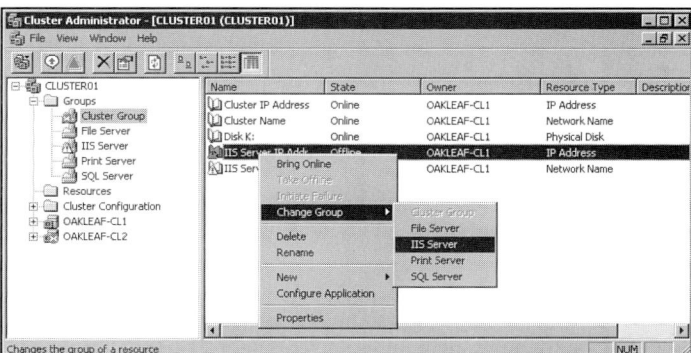

To bring a resource online, right-click the name of that resource in the Cluster Administrator and choose Bring Online. The resource name might appear in several places in the Cluster Administrator: the groups folder, the resources folder, or under the node controlling the resource. You can right-click the name in any location; all instances of the name refer to the same resource and offer the same menu choices.

Working with Cluster Nodes

Cluster nodes are listed in the left pane of the Cluster Administrator window. Each node contains three folder icons: Active Groups, Active Resources, and Network Interfaces.

Working within the Cluster Administrator, you can bring entire nodes, specific groups, specific resources, or specific network interfaces online or offline. You can also fail these items between nodes. You often take items offline or fail them to another node during maintenance operations. Use the following techniques to work with cluster nodes in Cluster Administrator:

- To bring a node online, right-click the node name in the left pane of Cluster Administrator, and choose Start Cluster Service, as shown in Figure 30.21.

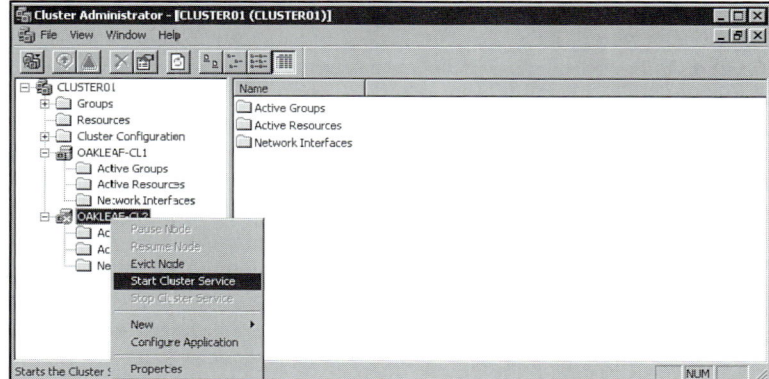

Figure 30.21
Here, you see the administrator bringing node OAKLEAF-CL2 online.

- To bring a resource or group online, right-click the resource or group name and choose Bring Online.
- To take a node, resource, or group offline, right-click its name and choose Take Offline.
- To fail a group to another node in a cluster, right-click its name and choose Move. In a cluster with more than two nodes, you're presented with a list of nodes to which to fail the group.

> **Note**
> Failing to another node means that the resource is stopped on the current node and started on the node to which you select to fail. This is different from taking the resource or group offline. Offline items are stopped, but they are not started on another node; they remain stopped until brought online manually.

> **Caution**
> To preserve quorum disk stability, stop the cluster service on a node before taking it offline.

USING CLUSTER ADMINISTRATOR | 1249

RESOURCE GROUP FAILOVER AND FAILBACK

A resource group can fail to another node a predetermined number of times over a given period of time. These failover parameters exist so that if a node fails, comes back online, fails again, and continues in this cycle, that node can be isolated and repaired. The default failover threshold for a group is 10 failovers in a 6-hour period. Other resources have different default failover thresholds tailored to the specific functions they perform.

The failover threshold settings are located in the group's Failover Property page, which you access by right-clicking on the group name, choosing Properties, and then clicking the Failover tab (see Figure 30.22.)

PART
V
CH
30

Figure 30.22
These are the default settings for group failover properties. You ordinarily don't need to change the failover parameter values.

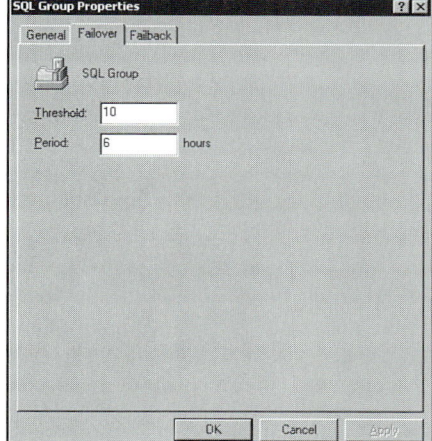

The default setting of 10 failovers in a 6-hour period is generally acceptable for these settings. If you're experiencing more than 10 failovers in 6 hours, you have a hardware or software problem that needs to be resolved, rather than settings that need to be adjusted.

The Failback property page allows you to prevent or define failbacks. Failback is the action of returning a resource or group to its primary node after it has failed over to another node. If failbacks are allowed, you must decide whether the failback should occur immediately or at predetermined times.

Tip from
RJ

The time setting on the Failback property page of the Group Properties dialog uses the hours value of the 24-hour clock. So if you want the group to fail back between 11:00 p.m. and midnight, set the hours to 23 and 0.

Setting Advanced Properties of Resources

The advanced properties sheet of a resource can be accessed by right-clicking on the resource name and choosing Properties and then selecting the Advanced tab. From the Advanced Properties sheet you can control precisely how you want a resource to act in case of failure and how the cluster node will determine that the resource has failed. The Advanced Properties sheet is shown in Figure 30.23.

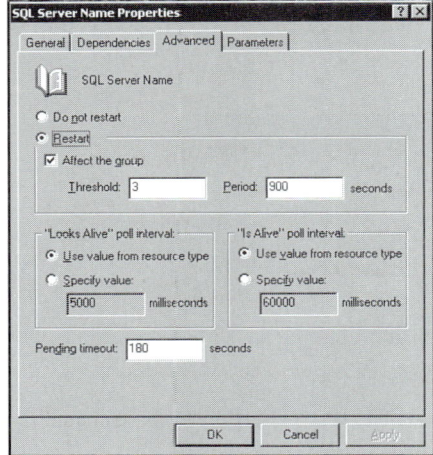

Figure 30.23
These are the default settings for a resource as seen in the Advanced properties page.

Most cluster resources attempt to restart on failure, rather than fail over to another node. If the restart is unsuccessful, they initiate a failover. In the Advanced Properties page for a resource you can enable or disable the restart function.

The Restart Threshold setting of the Advanced Properties page of a resource is similar to the Failover Threshold. The Restart Threshold defines how many restarts should be attempted before initiating failover between nodes. You can select to have the restart affect the entire resource group, which will attempt to restart every resource in the group, or affect only the individual resource in question. By default, the entire group restarts.

The *ResourceName* Properties dialog's Advanced Property page also allows you to specify a Looks Alive Poll Interval and an Is Alive Poll Interval. A Looks Alive poll tells other nodes on the cluster that this resource appears to be available, but in fact might not be available (it could be hung). The Is Alive poll attempts to use the resource and sends the result to the other nodes on the cluster. The Is Alive poll attempts to use the resource, so it's more likely to detect a failure. The Is Alive poll uses substantial bandwidth, memory, and CPU time. In order to save on bandwidth, memory, and CPU time of all nodes, the Is Alive poll is set to a time far less frequent than the Looks Alive poll.

The Use Value from Resource Type setting uses the default polling interval values for the selected resource type. It's seldom necessary to change these settings. The default values for the resource type are defined by the resource type that you selected in the Application Installation Wizard; the default values can't be viewed or changed.

> **Tip from**
> *RJ*
>
> If the servers in your cluster are not identical, verify that all servers are able to support the resources (applications or services) that will be failed between nodes. Preconfigured cluster systems use identical servers for each node, which is the recommended practice.

TROUBLESHOOTING

CLUSTER SERVICE INSTALLATION PROBLEMS

The Cluster Service is not available as an optional Windows component.

Check to be sure you're running Windows 2000 Advanced Server or Windows 2000 DataCenter Server. The Cluster Service component is not available on standard Windows 2000 Server installations.

The Quorum disk icon isn't present on all servers in the cluster.

Failure to detect the Quorum disk usually is caused by hardware limitations or failure. Check to be sure your array controllers, host bus adapters (HBAs), and array enclosures are on the Windows 2000 Cluster Service HCL at http://www.microsoft.com/hcl/.

The physical disks don't appear on both nodes of the cluster.

Failure to recognize physical disks most commonly occurs as a result of RAID controller issues. Check to be sure your array controllers, host bus adapters (HBAs), and array enclosures are on the Windows 2000 Cluster Service HCL at http://www.microsoft.com/hcl/.

The Cluster Service component won't install on my Windows 2000 Advanced Server or Windows 2000 DataCenter Server.

Check to be sure the build version of the CD-ROM or installation server share that you use as the source of components is the same as, or later than, your Windows 2000 Advanced Server or Windows 2000 DataCenter Server build on the cluster computers.

Attempts to install Cluster Service on my Windows 2000 Advanced Server or DataCenter Server throws an "unauthorized" error.

You must have Administrative privileges to install Cluster Service on a system.

TROUBLESHOOTING APPLICATION INSTALLATION

Application won't install on a Windows 2000 cluster.

Many applications, such as remote control software, don't work on clusters. Check with the publisher of the application for the availability of cluster-aware versions or issues associated with cluster installations.

MCSE Corner: Registering for an Exam, What to Expect, and Testing Innovations

This final MCSE corner gives you information on how to register for an MCSE exam, and what to expect when you arrive at the testing center.

Registering for an Exam

Exams must be taken at a Sylvan Prometric or Virtual University Enterprises (VUE) testing center and registration is done directly. Contact Sylvan Prometric at 800-755-EXAM within the U.S. or Canada, or online at http://www.2test.com. VUE is located at http://www.vue.com/ms. The MCSE exams cost $100 for each attempt.

What to Expect

The testing center consists of one room (or several) containing a few testing stations, usually three. The testing room is monitored by CCTV to prevent cheating. The only thing you are allowed to take into the testing room is a pencil and paper provided by the testing center. You may not take cell phones, pagers, calculators, or PDAs into the testing room, so practice doing your binary math on paper!

Testing Innovations

Until recently, one of the problems with the MCSE exam track was the fact that almost anyone could go to a "brain-dump" Web site and memorize the questions and answers, and then take the test and pass. This led to a large number of "paper MCSEs" with no real world experience, which soured some employers from hiring based on the MCSE. Microsoft is attempting to change that with their new series of exams.

First of all, the new exams have a heavy focus on troubleshooting. Much troubleshooting skill is intuitive and cannot be learned from any book, so this makes the exam much more difficult for those without experience. Some of the questions are not knowledge-based questions, but rather experience-based questions, which require some work with the respective product to know the answer.

The other innovation used to protect the integrity of the exams is adaptive testing, as discussed in the Chapter 10 MCSE Corner. These exams are much better at testing the actual skill of the examinee. The exams also change questions using a question pool to avoid the brain-dump–type memorization, and research is underway to track the questions that an examinee has received during previous testing sessions. This prevents an examinee from passing an exam solely by memorizing the questions during the first or second failed attempt.

PART VI

APPENDIXES

A Installing and Using the ADS125 Active Directory Application   1255

B Glossary   1287

APPENDIX A

Installing and Using the ADSI25 Active Directory Application

ADSI25 Application Description

The ADSI25 application (ADSI25.exe and ADSI25.vbp) is a Visual Basic 6.0 application intended for the following basic purposes:

- Adding a large number of groups, user and computer accounts, and shared folders in a consistent manner to Windows NT 4.0 and Windows 2000 domains for evaluating the behavior and capabilities of Active Directory (AD) and its administrative tools.

- Providing a sufficient number of groups and accounts to demonstrate the upgrade process from Windows NT 4.0 Server to Windows 2000 Server in a real-world environment. The group and account structures are suited to simulating in-place upgrades and domain restructure with the Active Directory Migration Tool (ADMT) or Clone Principal scripts.

- Adding all common attribute values to user accounts to test AD's search (LDAP query) and filter capabilities.

- Demonstrating VBA coding techniques for adding, deleting, and querying AD objects with the LDAP OLE DB provider; adding and deleting users and groups in Windows NT 4.0 domains with the WinNT provider; and adding Exchange Server 5.5+ mailboxes with the LDAP provider under Windows NT 4.0.

ADSI25 runs under Windows NT 4.0 Server or Workstation and Windows 2000 Professional, Server, Advanced Server, or Datacenter Server. ADSI25 won't run under Windows 9x.

> **Caution**
>
> Don't run ADSI25 in a production Windows NT 4.0 or Windows 2000 domain. ADSI25 is intended solely for test and evaluation purposes on a standalone network. Although ADSI25 has a Remove All button to delete objects it adds to the Windows NT SAM and Windows 2000's Active Directory databases, unexpected problems might result in loss of production objects or corruption of Registry and AD database files. See the disclaimer in the "User License" section near the end of this appendix.

ADSI25 creates Windows NT User, Computer, and Computer objects and Windows 2000 User, Computer, Group, and organizationalUnit (OU) objects for OakLeaf University, a fictional four-year institution with a single campus in a Texas city. If you have Exchange Server 5.5+ running under Windows NT 4.0 Server, ADSI25 optionally creates mailboxes for each user. Mailboxes contain employee and student attribute values that Windows NT 4.0 User objects don't accommodate.

> **Note**
>
> Employee and student names were created by scrambling data from a telephone directory database. Thus, you'll find odd first- and last-name relationships, such as Wen-Yu Schwartzkopf. Any resemblance between the names, addresses, and telephone numbers of OakLeaf U employees and students, and those of real persons (living or dead) is purely coincidental. Most city names for employee residences don't correspond to names of actual Texas cities. Some Windows 2000 attribute data, such as officeLocation and telephoneNumber, is derived from the EmployeeID field.

FEATURE SET

In a Windows NT domain, ADSI25 offers the following features:

- Displays all user and group accounts in the domain, plus group membership in high-performance list boxes
- Creates up to about 27,500 staff, faculty, and student groups, and user and computer accounts
- Allows adding student user and computer accounts to a second, trusted domain
- Adds mailboxes with users' personal data to Exchange Server 5.5+
- Adds and deletes individual users

In a Windows 2000 domain, ADSI25 augments the Windows NT features with the following:

- Adds personal attributes to employee and student accounts
- Adds business-related attributes, such as office location and office telephone number for employee accounts
- Adds manager and direct reports to faculty accounts
- Assigns to student accounts faculty advisors from the student's major department
- Adds managedBy and other custom attribute values to computer accounts

The added attribute values let you test AD's LDAP query functions to find specific users and computers. You must add all employees to AD before you can add manager, direct reports, and managedBy attribute values.

Data Source

A Jet 4.0 (Access 2000) database, Oakleaf.mdb, provides the information for creating security groups, organization units, and user accounts. Figure A.1 shows the Relationships window of Access 2000 displaying the fields of and relationships between the 10 tables of Oakleaf.mdb.

Figure A.1
The Relationships window of Access 2000 shows the tables contained within the Oakleaf.mdb database and their relationships to one another.

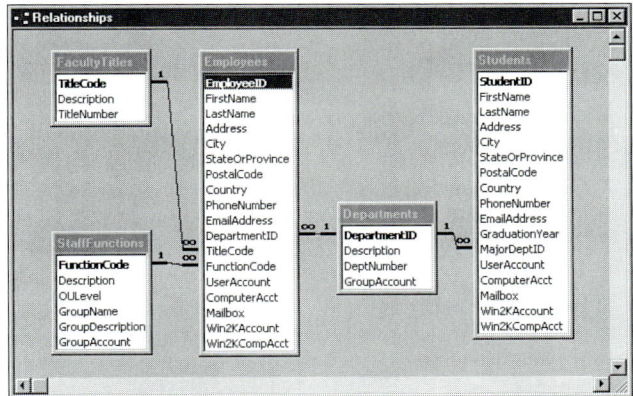

ADSI25 uses the following tables to create Windows NT and 2000 User and Group objects, and attribute values for objects:

- *StaffFunctions* is a list of 10 administrative departments—Recruiters, Registrars, and the like—plus the three primary group and account divisions—Faculty, Non-Faculty Staff, and Students.
- *Departments* is a list of the 15 academic departments of Oakleaf U, plus Non-Faculty Staff.
- *Employees* contains data for 2,275 staff and faculty members, including names, home addresses, home telephone numbers, email IDs, department IDs, and title or function codes.
- *FacultyTitles* is a list of 10 titles—Dean, Department Chairperson, Professor, Teaching Assistant, and so on—for teaching staff.
- *Students* contains name, home address, home telephone number, email address, graduation year, and major subject data for 25,344 students.

ADSI25 uses email addresses to create user account names; there are no duplicate email addresses in the database. User accounts are added in random order by sorting on the PhoneNumber field.

> **Note:** Oakleaf.mdb is derived from the Beckwith.mdb Jet 3.5 database created by Steven Gray and Rick Lievano for *Roger Jennings' Database Workshop: Microsoft Transaction Server 2.0* (Sams Publishing, ISBN 0-672-31130-5), and incorporated in *Database Developers Guide with Visual Basic 6* (Sams Publishing, ISBN 0-672-31063-5) and *Special Edition Using Access 2000* (Que Corporation, ISBN 0-7897-1606-2).

The following ANSI SQL-92 statements create the ActiveX Data Object (ADO) 2.1 Recordsets for employees and students:

```
SELECT Employees.EmployeeID, Employees.FirstName, Employees.LastName,
       Employees.Address, Employees.City, Employees.StateOrProvince,
       Employees.PostalCode, Employees.Country, Employees.PhoneNumber,
       Employees.EmailAddress, FacultyTitles.Description,
       Departments.DepartmentID, Departments.Description,
       StaffFunctions.Description, StaffFunctions.GroupName,
       StaffFunctions.FunctionCode, Employees.UserAccount,
       Employees.Mailbox, Employees.Win2KAccount, Employees.Win2KCompAcct
  FROM StaffFunctions RIGHT JOIN (FacultyTitles
       RIGHT JOIN (Departments RIGHT JOIN Employees
           ON Departments.DepartmentID = Employees.DepartmentID)
           ON FacultyTitles.TitleCode = Employees.TitleCode)
           ON StaffFunctions.FunctionCode = Employees.FunctionCode
  ORDER BY Employees.PhoneNumber

SELECT Students.StudentID, Students.FirstName, Students.LastName,
       Students.Address, Students.City, Students.StateOrProvince,
       Students.PostalCode, Students.Country, Students.PhoneNumber,
       Students.EmailAddress, Students.GraduationYear,
       Departments.DepartmentID, Departments.Description AS Major,
       Students.UserAccount, Students.Mailbox, Students.Win2KAccount,
       Students.Win2KCompAcct
  FROM Departments INNER JOIN Students
           ON Departments.DepartmentID = Students.MajorDeptID
  ORDER BY Students.PhoneNumber"
```

Installation Prerequisites

Prerequisites for installing ADSI25 depend on the operating system in use. Running ADSI25's Setup.exe installs the Visual Basic executable file (ADSI25.exe), other required runtime files, the project file (ADSI25.vbp), and form and module files.

If you want to explore or modify the source code for ADSI25, you must have Visual Basic 6.0 with SP3+ installed on the workstation or server on which you install ADSI25.

Creating Test Shares

Before installing ADSI25 under Windows 2000 or Windows NT, create and share the following two folders on the domain controller(s):

- An Employees folder shared as *ComputerName*\Employees.

- A Students folder shared as *ComputerName*\Students. If you use separate domains for employees and students, the shared Students folder should be located on the PDC or DC for the student domain.

Alternatively, you can use a single share, such as *ComputerName*\OakLeaf for both employees and students. Separate shares on the two DCs or PDCs are required when you specify individual domains for employees and students.

Initially, accept the default share permissions for the Everyone group. The share(s) must exist before you run ADSI25 for the first time. If ADSI25 can't access the share(s), you receive an error message when you click OK in the startup (ADSI25: Create Users, Groups, and Computers) dialog.

> **Caution**
>
> ADSI25 requires 0-length, non-complex passwords to operate correctly under Windows 2000 or NT. If you don't allow 0-length passwords, ADSI25 throws an error when you attempt to add user accounts. If you specify complex passwords, adding accounts is very slow and users receive null (empty) passwords, which you must create when logging on with an ADSI25-generated account. In Windows 2000, check the Computer Configuration\Windows Settings\Security Settings\Account Policies\Password Policy node of the Default Domain Policy. Set Minimum Password Length to 0 characters and set Passwords Must Meet Complexity Requirements to Disabled.

→ For more information on setting password policy, **see** "Enforcing Computer Security Policies," **p. 625**.

Installation on a Windows 2000 DC or Workstation

Installing Windows 2000 Professional or Server creates the required data access and Active Directory infrastructure for running ADSI25. You must have a Windows 2000 test domain operational to run ADSI25 with the OLE DB `LDAP://` provider.

Following are the default Windows 2000 domain and server names used in the examples of this book:

- Root domain: `oakleaf.edu`. The downlevel domain name is OAKLEAFU.
- Site name: Oakland.
- Initial DC name: `oakleaf-dc1.oakleaf.edu`. The downlevel name is \\OAKLEAFU\OAKLEAF-DC1.
- Second DC name: `oakleaf-dc2.oakleaf.edu`. The downlevel name is \\OAKLEAFU\OAKLEAF-DC2.
- Child domain name (for students): `student.oakleaf.edu`. The downlevel name is STUDENT.
- Child DC name (for students): `student-dc1.student.oakleaf.edu`.

You can run ADSI25 with one or two domains and use any domain name(s) you like, including those of your existing test domains. If you want to clear old AD entries from your

Windows 2000 test installation and, optionally, use the preceding names for your domains and DCs, run Dcpromo.exe, demote all DCs to standalone servers, and use the Active Director Installation Wizard to re-create the domain(s).

→ For details on using Dcpromo.exe, **see** "Administering Domains and Trusts," **p. 105**.

Following are the basic Windows 2000 Professional or Workstation requirements for running ADSI25:

- A minimum of 96MB of RAM is required to run ADSI25 with acceptable performance; 128MB of RAM is recommended. Pentium II or later computers running at 300+MHz are recommended for performance testing.

  The timing data shown in the figures of this appendix is for a 300MHz Pentium II workstation with Ultra-DMA/33 EIDE drives connected by a 100Mbps 100BaseTx network to 300MHz Pentium II servers having Ultra-wide SCSI drives (Seagate 4.3GB and 9GB Barracudas).

- Installing ADSI25 requires about 10MB of free disk space; Oakleaf.mdb alone occupies 5MB.

- Substantial free disk space is required for expansion of AD's files. Each user account consumes about 16KB of disk space; adding all 27,500 users requires about 500MB. If you have more than one DC, each DC must have sufficient free disk space to accommodate the new AD objects. (New objects replicate between DCs within a site every five minutes or so.)

- You must log on to Windows 2000 as a member of the Domain Admins or Enterprise Admins Global group to add AD objects.

- If you want to add student accounts in other than the default (OAKLEAFU) domain, you must create the domain prior to running ADSI25 with a second domain specified. The students domain can be a child of the employees domain or in another domain tree. Both domains must be located in the same forest.

INSTALLATION ON A WINDOWS NT 4.0 WORKSTATION OR SERVER

Running ADSI25 under Windows NT 4.0 involves considerably more preparation than running the application on a Windows 2000 domain controller (DC). Windows NT mode is intended primarily for creating large numbers of Windows NT groups and user accounts prior to upgrading a PDC to Windows 2000. You can, however, run ADSI25 under Windows NT and create user and computer accounts, OUs, and other AD objects on one or two Windows 2000 DC(s).

Note

When running under Windows NT 4.0, ADSI25 uses the `IADsOpenDSObject` method to manipulate Windows 2000 AD objects. `IADsOpenDSObject` requires passing your user name (Administrator@oakleaf.edu for this example) and password with each AD operation. When you run ADSI25 on a Windows 2000 DC, the code executes the simpler `GetObject` method, which uses your logon credentials to access AD objects.

Following are the default Windows NT domain and server names used in many of the examples of this book:

- Primary domain: OAKLEAFNT
- Primary PDC: OAKLEAF-PDC
- Secondary (students) domain: STUDENTNT
- Secondary PDC: STUDENT-PDC

Following are the system and software requirements for running ADSI25 on a Windows NT 4.0 Workstation or Server:

- Windows NT 4.0 SP4+ is required for ADSI25 installation. A minimum of 64MB of RAM is required to run ADSI25 with acceptable performance; 128MB of RAM is recommended. Each user/computer account requires about 1KB of disk space on PDCs and BDCs; adding all 27,500 users consumes 30MB.

    If you add optional mailboxes, each user mailbox consumes another 2KB on the drive that stores the Exchange Server directory.

- You must install Active Directory Interfaces (ADSI) 2.5+ prior to running ADSI25. The version of ADSI 2.5 for Windows NT (Ads_nt.exe) that was current when this book was written is included in the \Seuw2ks\ADSI25 folder of the accompanying CD-ROM. You can obtain the latest version of ADSI at http://www.microsoft.com/windows/server/Technical/directory/adsilinks.asp. It's recommended that you run the ADSI 2.5 Setup program before running ADSI25's Setup.exe. ADSI files install in your \Winnt\System32 folder.

- Microsoft Data Access Components (MDAC) 2.1+, which include the Jet 4.0 OLE DB data provider (Jolt), are required for ADSI25 operation. ADSI25's Setup program installs MDAC 2.1, if your computer doesn't have a later version of MDAC installed. MDAC components are located in the \Program Files\Common Files\System\Ado and \Program Files\Common Files\System\OLE DB folders.

- Installing ADSI25 requires between 15MB and 25MB of free disk space, depending on the other components—such as ADSI 2.5 and MDAC 2.1—you must add to support ADSI25.

- To add entries to Windows 2000's AD from a Windows NT computer, a Windows 2000 DC must be located on the same or an accessible subnet. Windows NT 4.0 and Windows 2000 domains of different names coexist on the same subnet. This book's examples use the OAKLEAF (oakleaf.com) Windows NT 4.0 domain and the OAKLEAFU (downlevel name for oakleaf.edu) Windows 2000 domain.

- If you intend to run ADSI25 to create Windows NT accounts, you must have sufficient free space in your server's Registry file to accommodate a large number of SAM database entries. 10,000 users increase the base Registry size to about 24MB. 64MB of free space is sufficient for 27,500 users. Windows 2000 uses AD to store account information, so you need not be concerned with Registry size on the Windows 2000 DC.

To increase available space in the Registry, open Control Panel's System tool, click the Performance tab of the System Properties dialog, click Change to open the Virtual Memory dialog, and set the Maximum Registry Size to 64MB. You must reboot the server for the change to become effective. If you have BDCs, you also must increase the Registry size on each BDC.

- You must be a member of the Windows NT Domain Admins group to run ADSI25 from a remote computer. To view and add users, groups, and OUs to a Windows 2000 domain controller (DC), you must be a member of the Domain Admins Global group and provide your logon credentials for the Windows 2000 domain(s). The default Windows 2000 username is Administrator.

- Register Adsecurity.dll after running ADSI25's Setup program, which installs Adsecurity.dll (from the ADSI 2.5 Software Development Kit (SDK) in the d:\ADSI25 folder). Adssecurity.dll is required to add mailboxes to Exchange Server 5.5+.

    Choose Start, Run, type **regsvr32 *d*:\ADSI25\Adsecurity.dll** in the Open text box, where *d* is the drive on which you installed ADSI25, and click OK. The "DllRegisterServer in Adssecurity.dll succeeded" message confirms proper registration. You only need to register Adssecurity.dll if you intend to add Exchange Server mailboxes.

- Exchange Server 5.5+ running under Windows NT 4.0 Server is required for optional addition of Exchange mailboxes. You must have Exchange Server administrator privileges and provide your administrator account name, password, and other Exchange-specific settings to add mailboxes. You receive an error if you attempt to add mailboxes for users without Exchange Server 5.5+ running.

Running the ADSI25 Setup Program

The \Seuw2ks\ADSI25 folder of the accompanying CD-ROM includes the following setup files:

- ADSI25.msi, a self-contained Microsoft Installer package that installs all files required for ADSI25 under Windows 2000 Server or Professional. You can't use ADSI25.msi to install the application under Windows NT 4.0, because it doesn't include all the necessary files required for Windows NT 4.0.

- Setup.exe and ADSI25.cab created by the Visual Studio 6.0 Package and Deployment Wizard. Setup.exe is intended for installation of ADSI25 under Windows NT 4.0. If you encounter problems using ADSI25.msi, you can use Setup.exe to install ADSI25 under Windows 2000.

The following two sections describe the ADSI25 installation process for Windows 2000 and NT.

ADSI25.MSI for Windows 2000

The Microsoft Visual Studio Installer from the Windows 2000 Developer's Readiness Kit was used to create ADSI25.msi. The installation process is identical to that for most other

Windows 2000 services and applications. Do the following to install ADSI25 under Windows 2000:

1. Double-click ADSI25.msi in the \Seuw2ks\ADSI25 folder of the accompanying CD-ROM to start the Installer and open the splash screen with the Windows 2000-only message. Click Next.
2. In the Welcome to the ADSI25 Setup Wizard dialog, click Next.
3. In the Select Installation Folder dialog, accept the default folder, d:\Program Files\ADSI25, or click Browse to specify a different location. Click Next.
4. In the Confirm Installation dialog, click Next to start the setup process.
5. Review the text in the ADSI25 Information dialog for the latest installation notes. Click Next.
6. In the Installation Complete dialog, click Close to dismiss the Setup Wizard.

Setup adds a Shortcut to ADSI25 to your Desktop, and an ADSI25 for Active Directory choice to your Start menu. The Visual Studio Installer version used to create ADSI25.msi doesn't add menu choices to the Start, Programs menu.

SETUP.EXE FOR WINDOWS NT 4.0

The setup program for ADSI25 running under Windows NT 4.0 SP4+ (or Windows 2000) is typical for Visual Studio applications that use the Package and Deployment Wizard. Do the following to install ADSI25.exe, and its support and source files:

1. If you're installing under Windows NT 4.0, double-click Ads_nt.exe in the \Seuw2ks\ADSI25 folder on the accompanying CD-ROM to install the ADSI 2.5 extensions, if you haven't done so already.
2. Double-click Setup.exe in the \Seuw2ks\ADSI25 folder to copy the initial installation files.
3. When the ADSI25 Version 1.0 Setup dialog appears, close all running applications (other than Setup.exe) and click OK to continue.
4. In the second Setup dialog, accept the default installation folder, C:\Program Files\ADSI25, or click Change Directory to change the installation location (see Figure A.2).

Figure A.2
Click Change Directory if you want to select a target installation directory other than the default.

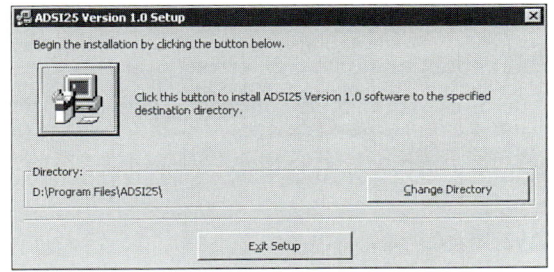

5. Click OK if asked if you want to create the directory.
6. Click the large button to begin the install process. Setup installs MDAC 2.1, if necessary, and then expands the ADSI25 files from the .cab file.

Note Depending on the service pack or software installed on your computer, Setup might open a message stating that "some system files are out of date on your system." If you receive this message, click OK, and then click Yes when asked if you want to reboot your computer. Run ADSI25's Setup program again.

Caution If Version Conflict messages that state "A file being copied is not newer than the version currently on your system" appear during the installation process, click Yes in each instance to keep the file on your system.

7. When Setup completes, click OK, and then click OK again to reboot your computer, if requested.

Note If you install ADSI25 with Setup.exe under Windows 2000 or under Windows NT with a later version of MDAC already present, the MDAC version included in the ADSI25.cab file won't overwrite the existing files.

If you dual-boot Windows NT and Windows 2000 on the computer, install a separate copy of ADSI25 for each operating system.

Files Added by Setup

Setup adds the following files to your \Program Files\ADSI25 folder:

- ADSI25.exe, the executable file for the program
- Oakleaf (Clear).mdb, which the program renames to Oakleaf.mdb when run for the first time
- Source code files with .frm, .frx, and .bas extensions; a Visual Basic project file, ADSI25.vbp; and .txt files to populate the help dialogs
- Ad25test.txt, a short text file that's renamed and copied into each share subfolder
- Read1st.txt, a text file with brief installation instructions
- Readme25.doc, a Microsoft Word 98 file containing illustrated installation and operating instructions
- CompAcct.txt, a list of the LDAP attributes for typical computer account entries created with ADSI25

- LDAP_Props.txt, a list of the mandatory and optional LDAP attributes for container, user, organizationalUnit, computer, and volume (published file share) objects
- RecipProperties.txt, a list of the LDAP attributes for Exchange recipient (mailbox) objects

Running ADSI25

ADSI25's Setup program adds a Program Files choice and ADSI25.msi adds a Start menu choice for ADSI25. Launch ADSI25.exe from Start, [Programs,] ADSI25 for Active Directory. On startup, ADSI25 detects the operating system. The appearance of the opening form depends on whether you run ADSI25 under Windows 2000 or Windows NT 4.0.

Tip from
RJ

If you have less than 128MB of RAM, shut down other running applications and nonessential services before starting ADSI25. Doing so increases the amount of available RAM for caching AD entries and the large Recordset objects that ADSI25 creates.

Running ADSI25 Under Windows 2000

Figure A.3 shows ADSI25's opening form (frmStart) under Windows 2000 Professional or Server. ADSI25 is intended to run on a Windows 2000 DC. If you run ADSI under Windows 2000 Professional, you must map the root folder of the server drive on which to install shared folders for employees and students to a local logical drive letter. The Windows NT 4.0 option for using the WinNT OLE DB provider is disabled when you run ADSI25 under Windows 2000.

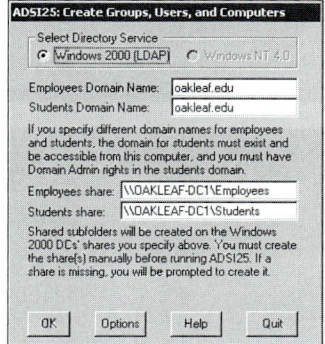

Figure A.3
ADSI25's startup dialog under Windows 2000 displays default values for Windows 2000 domain names and server shares.

To continue your first test of ADSI25, do the following:

1. Type the Windows 2000 domain name for employee and student users in the two Domain Name text boxes.

    It's recommended that you use the same domain for both employees and students for initial testing.

→ For detailed instruction on the use of separate employee and student domains, **see** "Adding Students to a Different Domain," **p. 1279**.

2. Click Options to open the ADSI25 Options form (see Figure A.4).

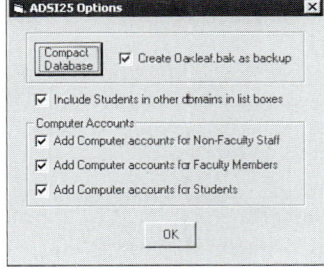

Figure A.4
The ADSI Options form (frmOptions) is used to compact the Oakleaf.mdb database and to set options for which accounts will be created by the application.

3. Click Compact Database with the Create Oakleaf.bak As Backup check box marked to create a safety backup of the database.

   Compact Database uses the Jet Replication Objects (JRO) `JetEngine.CompactDatabase` method. Compacting Oakleaf.bak takes about 30 seconds.

4. Accept the default settings to create computer accounts for all users, and click OK to return to the startup dialog.

5. If you want to add students to a separate domain at this point, type the full domain name in the Students Domain Name text box, and click OK to display the Students Domain Credentials frame.

   Type the name of the domain controller on which to install the students' shares in the Windows 2000 DC and change the Drive for Student Shares value to the logical drive mapped to the root folder of the students' DC (see Figure A.5). Type your admin username and password for the students domain, if the students domain is in a different forest.

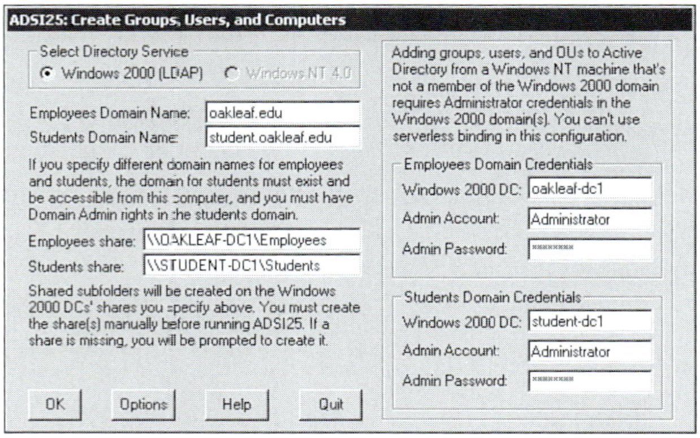

Figure A.5
The ADSI25: Create Groups, Users, and Computers dialog allows you to specify a separate domain for student accounts and shared folders. It also allows you to enter credentials when the local machine is Windows NT 4.0 and not a member of the target Windows 2000 Domain.

6. Click OK to open ADSI25's main form (frmGroupsUsers), which displays the default set of groups and users created by Windows 2000 Server's setup, plus any groups and users you've added to the domain. The list boxes display the full LDAP path to the user, including the LDAP:// provider prefix.

 If you encounter error message(s) when you click OK, see the "Startup Problems" topic in the "Troubleshooting" section at the end of this appendix.

7. Click an item in the Groups list box to display group members in the lower Users In Selected Group list, and click the Administrator user to display your default group membership in the Selected User's Groups list (see Figure A.6).

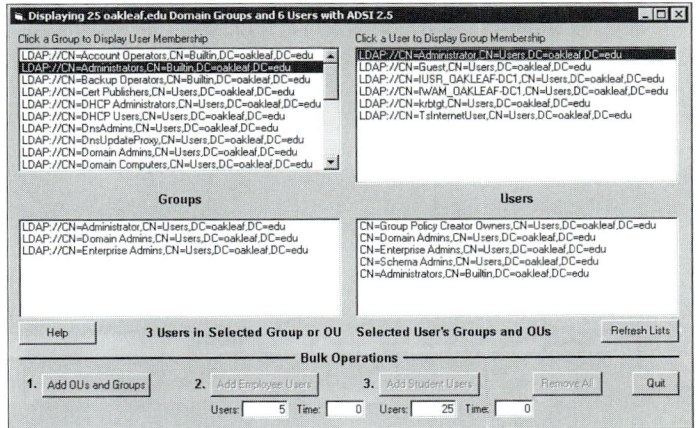

Figure A.6
ADSI25's main form displays default groups and users created by Windows 2000 Server's Setup program before the ADSI25 utility is run to create the batch of new groups and users.

8. Click Add OUs and Groups to create the 72 groups for staff, faculty, and student accounts. Adding the required groups and OUs enables the Add Employee Users and Add Student Users buttons.

9. Scroll through the Groups and OUs list to examine the added security groups (CN=*GroupName*) and OUs (OU=*OrganizationalUnitName*).

10. Click Add Employee Users to add five employees. After a few seconds, five (the default) employee accounts appear in the Users list. Click Add Employee Users again to demonstrate the faster addition of new AD objects after caching occurs.

11. Click the Groups and OUs list's OU=Computer Science item to display its single member, and double-click the User list's CN=Craig A Gieger item to display the first eight attribute names and values for his account (see Figure A.7).

Computer NetBIOS Name isn't a user attribute; code generates the value. You must alter the AD schema to add an AD attribute for the computer account ID.

Figure A.7
The lower-left list box shows the users contained in the group or OU selected in the upper left, while the lower right shows the attributes for the user selected in the upper right.

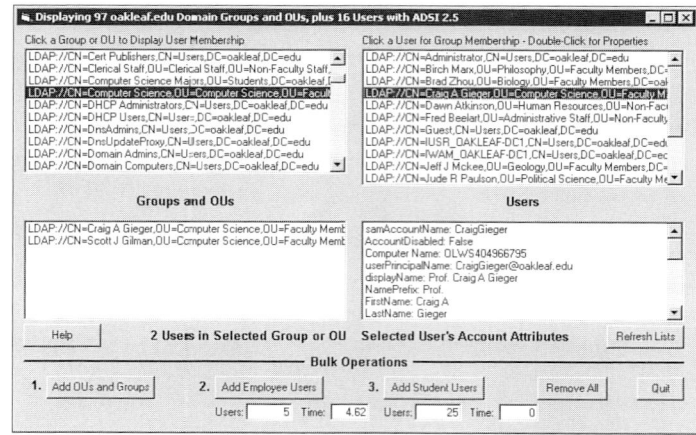

12. Click the CN=Faculty Members item in the Groups and OUs list to display membership of the security group, which consists of all faculty members.

13. Scroll the Selected User's Groups and OUs list to display addition User object attributes and values (see Figure A.8).

Figure A.8
The lower-left box shows the members of the Faculty Members security group selected in the upper left, while the lower-right box shows attributes for a user selected in the upper right.

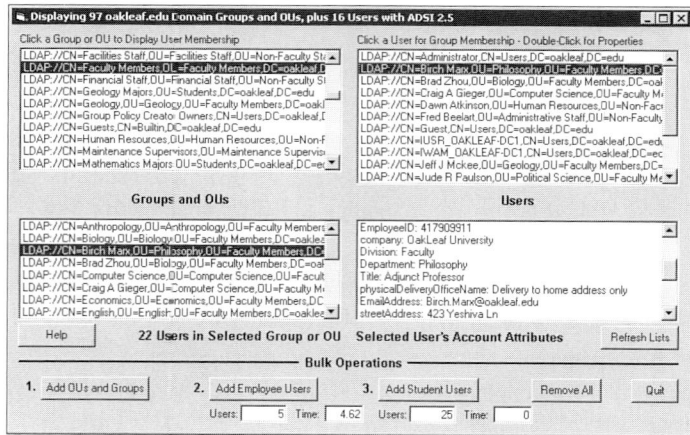

14. Launch Explorer and verify that the Employees folder you shared on the specified drive has \Faculty and \Staff subfolders, and that each of the subfolders contains additional folders (see Figure A.9). Also verify that the shared Students folder contains subfolders.

Figure A.9
Windows Explorer shows the \\Shared\Employees\Faculty subfolder that contains a text file (faculty.txt) which is created upon the opening of the ADSI25 utility's main dialog.

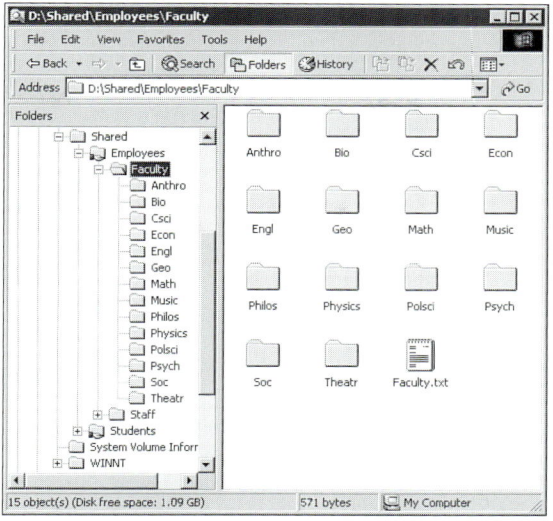

⚠ If group and user items don't appear in the main form's list, see the "Operational (Main Form) Problems" topic of the "Troubleshooting" section at the end of this appendix.

Note ADSI25 assigns "password" as the `password` attribute value to all user accounts.

ADDING ALL EMPLOYEE ACCOUNTS

Some features of ADSI25 aren't operable until you add all employee users to AD. To complete addition of staff and faculty members, do the following:

1. Type **2500** (or any number equal to or greater than the total number of employee user accounts) in the Users text box under Add Employee Users to add the remaining 2,270 employee accounts. A progress bar displays the task completion percentage.

    ADSI25 adds user accounts at a rate of about two per second.

2. After ADSI25 adds all employee accounts, the message box shown in Figure A.10 opens. Click Yes to add `manager` and `directReports` attribute values for faculty members.

    Each Department Chairperson reports to a Dean, and faculty members (except Teaching Assistants) report to their Department Chairperson. ADSI25 randomly assigns Teaching Assistants as direct reports of department professors.

Figure A.10
Once all of the employees have been added to AD, this message box requires you to specify whether or not to add the manager and directReports attributes to the newly created user accouns.

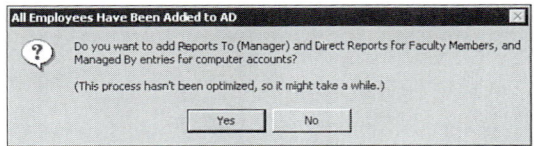

3. After a few minutes, the message box shown in Figure A.11 opens. Click Yes to add the `managedBy` attribute values to employee and student computer accounts.

Figure A.11
This message box allows you to specify whether or not to add the `managedBy` attribute to the newly created computer accounts in AD.

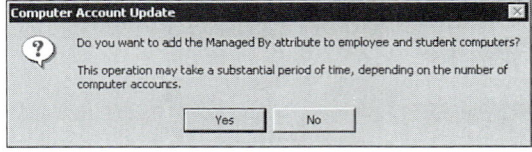

> **Note**
> If you elect to bypass attribution addition after adding all employees, you can add the attribute values later by clicking Add Employee Users. ADSI25 detects that all employee accounts are added and displays the message box shown in Figure A.10.

4. Double-click the `CN=Gary Almgren` entry in the Users list and scroll the attributes in the Selected User's Groups and OUs list to the `manager` attribute (see Figure A.12).

Gary Almgren is the Anthropology Department Chairperson and Greg Allen is the Dean of the Anthropology department. The multivalued `directReports` property (a `Variant` array) includes all professors and lecturers in the department.

Figure A.12
In the lower-right box you can see the values of the `manager` and `directReports` attributes for the Anthropology Department Chairperson.

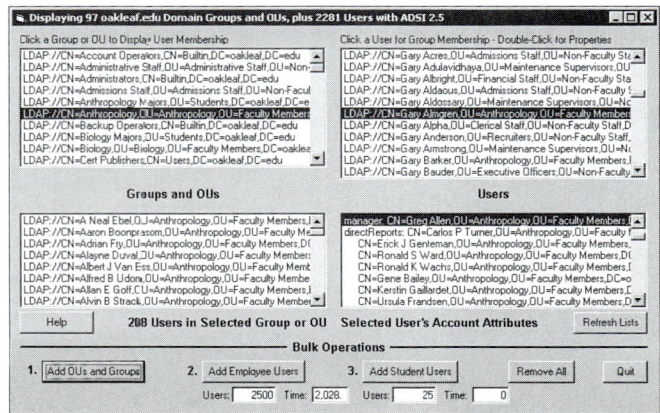

5. To verify that the attribute values added by ADSI25 appear in the appropriate pages and fields of the *Username* Properties sheet, launch the Active Directory Users and Computers snap-in, expand the nodes, and find the User entry for Gary Almgren (see Figure A.13).

Figure A.13
The Active Directory Users and Computers snap-in displays the accounts created by the ADSI25 utility.

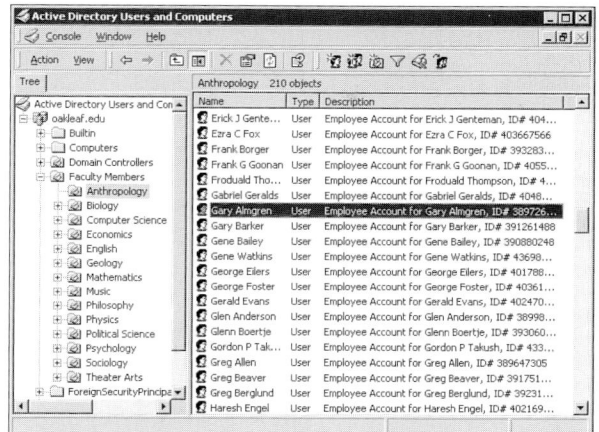

6. Double-click the Gary Almgren item to open the General page of the Gary Almgren Properties dialog (see Figure A.14, left).
7. Click the Address tab to display home address information (see Figure A.14, right).

Figure A.14
In the General (left) and Address (right) pages of the Properties dialog for a selected user, you can see 13 of the attributes added by the ADSI25 utility.

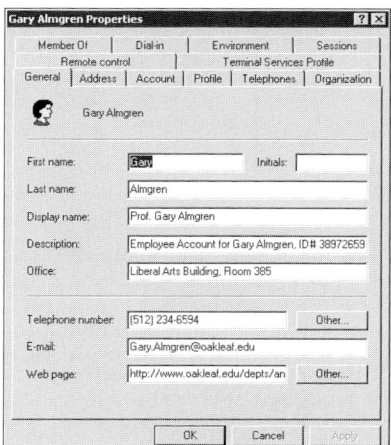 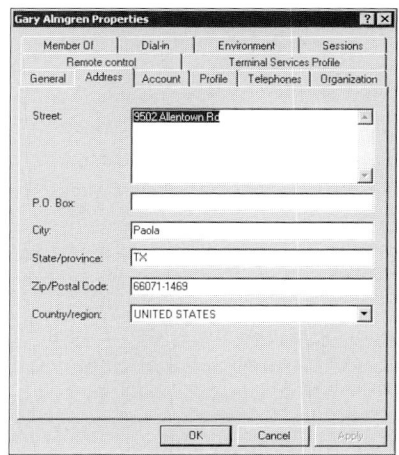

8. Click the Account (see Figure A.15, left), Organization (see Figure A.15, right), Member Of (see Figure A.16, left), and Telephones (see Figure A.16, right) tabs to display more user object attributes added by ADSI25.

Figure A.15
The Account (left) and Organization (right) pages of the Properties dialog for the user show 10 more of the attributes automatically added by ADSI25.

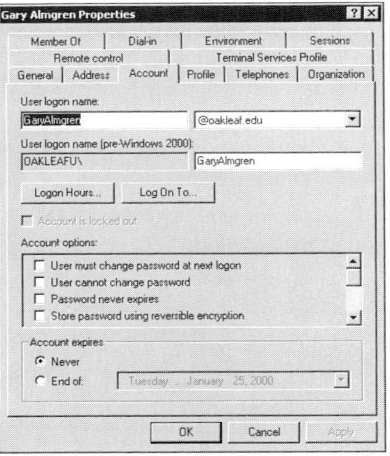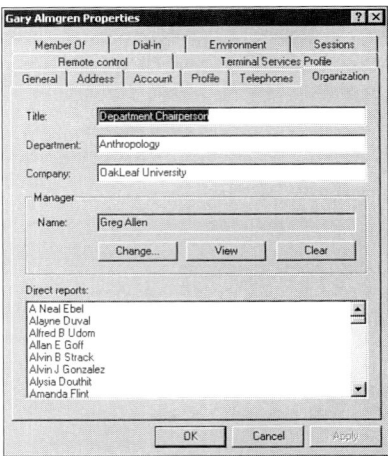

The Organization page displays the Manager and Direct Reports added in step 3. You can view the Greg Allen Properties dialog by clicking View, but double-clicking Direct Reports items doesn't open the individual's *UserName* Properties sheet.

Figure A.16
The Member Of (left) and Telephones (right) pages show the last two of the 25 attributes added to a `user` account created by ADSI25.

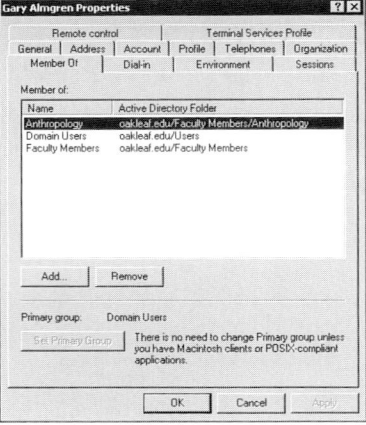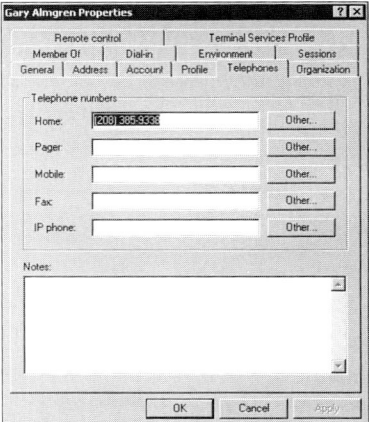

9. Close the Gary Almgren Properties dialog, and double-click the Computers node to display a list of employee Computer objects, which have an OLWS (OakLeaf WorkStation) prefix followed by a nine-digit ID number.

    Computer accounts are added to the downlevel Computers group, rather than the users' OUs, to avoid mixing computers and users in OU lists. Computer accounts are disabled, but you can multiselect all the accounts, right-click the selection, and choose Enable from the context menu to enable the selected accounts.

10. Scroll to and double-click the Gary Almgren entry to display the General page of the OLWS389726594 Properties sheet (see Figure A.17, left). Computer accounts appear in Last Name alphabetical order.

11. Click the Operating System (see Figure A.17, right), Member Of (see Figure A.18, left), and Managed By (see Figure A.18, right) tabs to view the other Computer attribute values that ADSI25 adds. When the computer connects to the network, it automatically replaces the Operating System attribute values. The Managed By attribute value specifies the responsible help-desk person for the computer.

Figure A.17
The General (left) and Operating System (right) pages for a selected computer account show the first seven `computer` object attribute values added by ADSI25.

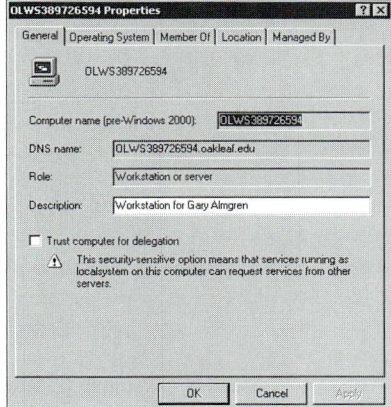
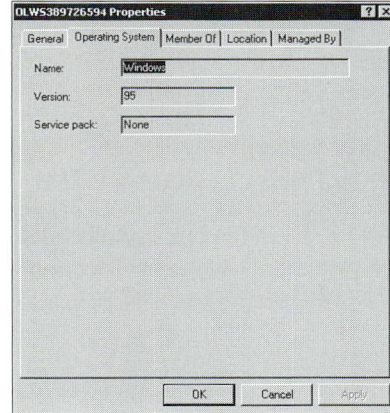

Figure A.18
Member Of (left) and Managed By (right) pages for the OakLeaf U computer show the last seven attribute values created automatically.

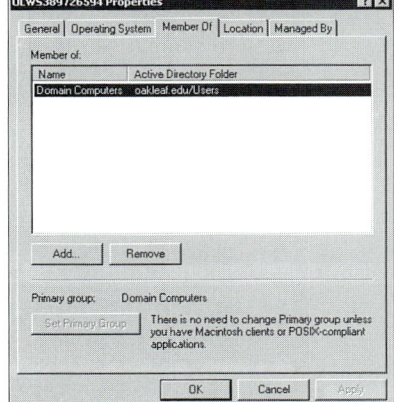
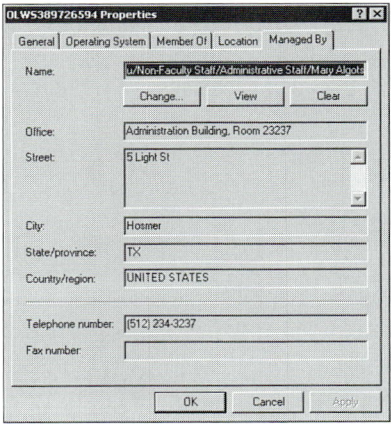

Note

Correlating LDAP attribute names and *UserName* Properties dialog text box captions, for the most part, is a guessing game. When this book was written, Microsoft hadn't published a list of dialog property name captions and their LDAP attribute name counterparts.

It's clear from the property pages shown in the preceding five figures that manually entering detail information for user and computer accounts would be a time-consuming and very costly process. ADSI 2.5's primary value is the ability to write relatively simple directory-enabled applications to transfer data to AD from directories having OLE DB LDAP providers or from a human-resources database, such as Oakleaf.mdb.

Adding Student Accounts

The primary purpose of student accounts is to increase the number of directory objects for AD performance testing. Student accounts have attribute values similar to those for employees, but the Students OU categorizes students by graduation year—Freshmen, Sophomores, Juniors, and Seniors—for ease of reclassification. Students also are members of department security groups, such as Anthropology Majors and Computer Science Majors. ADSI25 assigns student manager attribute values by random selection of assistant, associate, or full professors from the student's major department.

To add student accounts to AD, do the following:

1. Type the number of students you want to add in the Users text box under the Add Student Users button.

2. Click Add Student Users to start the addition process. You might have to manually shorten some student account names to 20 characters or less because Windows NT limits logon ID values to a maximum of 20 characters.

   ADSI25 automatically drops the trailing surname of persons with long account names and hyphenated last names, which handles most of the long-name problems.

3. If you've added all employee accounts to AD, you receive a message similar to that shown in Figure A.11 after adding each group of student accounts. Click OK to assign a help-desk person to enable and manage each student's computer account.

Figure A.19 shows the first eight members of the Biology Majors Security Group and eight attributes of a student user object. The (2003) following Biology is the student's graduation year. ADSI25 assigns students to OUs based on graduation year.

Figure A.19
The lower-left box of the ADSI25 utility shows the members of the Biology Majors Security Group selected in the upper left, while the attributes for the user selected in the upper-right box are shown in the lower right.

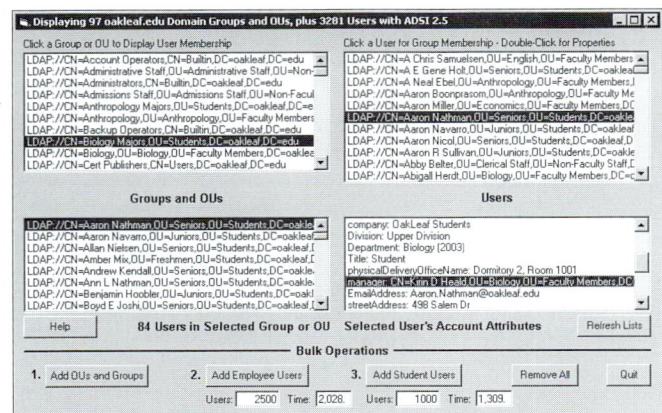

As you increase the number of student accounts, it takes longer to load the Users list. Adding a total of 10,000 users to AD causes ADSI25 to take a few minutes to load or reload its lists. There is little difference between the list load time on a DC and on a remote workstation if the network has light traffic.

By default, AD only loads the first 2,000 list entries; you receive a message from Active Directory Users and Computers if the list you're opening has more than 2,000 items. Increase the size of the lists by following the message box's instructions; doing so slows Active Directory Users and Computers performance.

RUNNING ADSI25 UNDER WINDOWS NT

ADSI has the following two operating modes when running under Windows NT 4.0:

- *Windows NT 4.0* directory mode, the default, creates user and group accounts, and shared folders on a Windows NT 4.0 PDC or BDC. This mode offers the option of creating Exchange Server 5.5+ mailboxes to store attribute values not available with the WinNT OLE DB provider.
- *Windows 2000 (LDAP)* mode duplicates the operation of ADSI25 under Windows 2000. The only difference is the need to supply logon credentials for the Windows 2000 domain(s). You can't create mailboxes in this mode.

To launch ADSI25 under Windows NT 4.0 Workstation or Server, follow the same procedure as for Windows 2000.

USING WINDOWS NT 4.0 MODE

To add groups and accounts to a Windows NT 4.0 PDC, do the following:

1. Accept the default Windows NT 4.0 option, type the name of the employees and students domain(s) in the two text boxes, and type the share names (see Figure A.20). You use your Administrator logon credentials to add accounts to the Windows NT domain(s).

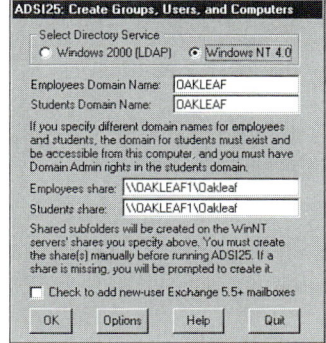

Figure A.20
The initial dialog of the ADSI25 utility shows the default entries for domain names and folder shares under Windows NT 4.0.

Unless you consider it important to test separate domains for employees and students, or you want to create two Windows NT domains for in-place upgrades, use the same domain for both.

2. If you want to add Exchange Servermailboxes for user accounts, mark the Check to Add New-User Exchange 5.5+ Mailboxes check box. The startup dialog expands as shown in Figure A.21.

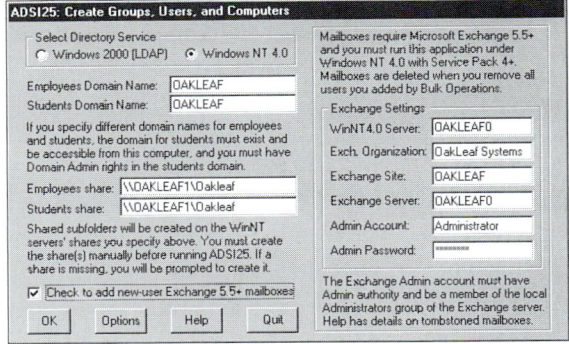

Figure A.21
Under Windows NT 4.0, ADSI25 can be used to create Exchange 5.5+ mailboxes for each of the created users. The information required for this operation is entered in the right side of this dialog.

Note

If you don't want to add mailboxes at this point, you can do so later by marking the Check to Add New-User Exchange 5.5+ Mailboxes check box and clicking the Test Mailboxes button on ADSI25's main form. Test Mailboxes checks users' accounts for mailbox flags, and then gives you the option to add the missing mailboxes.

3. Replace the default text box entries in the Exchange Settings frame with settings for your test Exchange Server installation.

4. Click OK to close the startup dialog and open ADSI25's main form, which displays Windows NT 4.0 default groups and users, plus any groups and users you or applications, such as Microsoft Transaction Server, have added.

5. Add as many employee and student users as you want, following the procedure in the earlier "Running ADSI25 Under Windows 2000" and "Adding Student Accounts" sections. Figure A.22 shows ADSI25's main form after adding several hundred employee and student accounts. You can add or delete groups and users in Windows NT 4.0 mode, but not in Windows 2000 (LDAP) mode.

As is the case for Windows 2000's AD, adding more users decreases the performance of ADSI25 and the SAM database. Unlike AD, Windows NT 4.0's User Manager for Domains loads all user accounts and Server Manager loads all computer accounts, regardless of the number of accounts.

Figure A.22
The main form of ADSI25 is shown after creating users and groups on a Windows NT 4.0 computer.

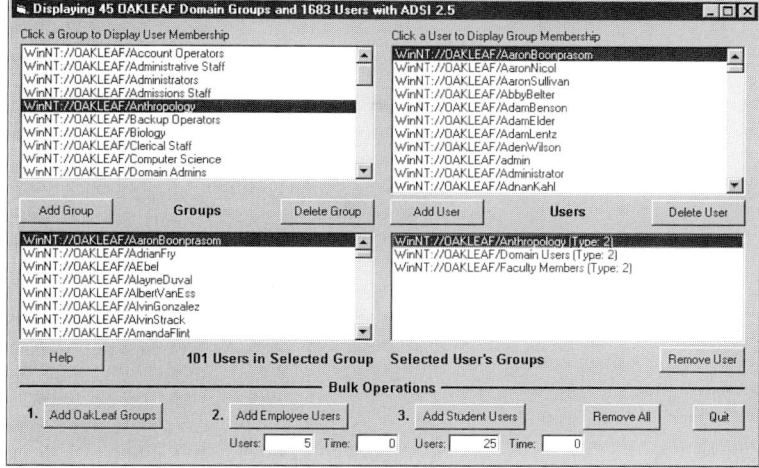

6. Launch User Manager for Domains, and double-click an employee or student account item to display account properties (see Figure A.23).

Figure A.23
Double-clicking an account item in the Windows NT 4.0 User Manager for Domains tool produces that user's account properties created using ADSI25.

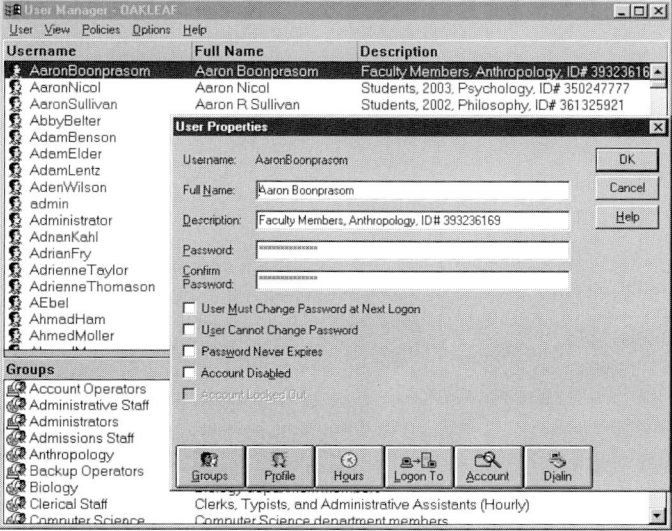

7. Launch Server Manager to verify addition of computer accounts for users (see Figure A.24). You can't see or set the properties of a computer by double-clicking its list entry unless it's connected to the network.

Figure A.24
Server Manager displays the employee computer accounts added by ADSI25. Double-click a computer entry to display the ComputerName Properties dialog for an added computer.

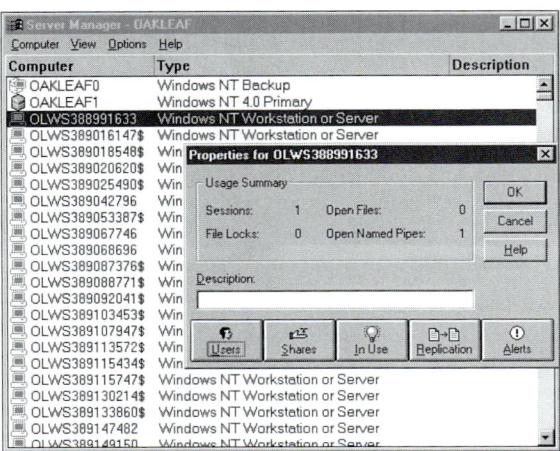

User accounts with mailboxes add to Windows NT 4.0 Server at about the same rate—two per second—as to a Windows 2000 DC. With a similar number of user and computer accounts, however, Windows NT 4.0's User Manager and Server Manager offer much faster display of and access to accounts than Windows 2000's Dsa.msc.

Note

It takes more than an hour to remove 10,000 user and computer accounts and Exchange Server mailboxes from a Windows NT 4.0 PDC with the test configuration for ADSI25 described in the "Installation on a Windows 2000 DC" section earlier in this appendix. Exchange Server 5.5+ marks mailboxes as removed but doesn't delete the user mailbox until the tombstone period expires. You can't create a new mailbox for the user until Exchange Server finally deletes user mailboxes.

You set the Tombstone Interval on the General page of Exchange Server Administrator's *Sitename*, Configuration, DS Site Configuration Properties sheet. The minimum Tombstone Interval is two days, and the value you set must be at least three times the Garbage Collection Interval (in hours).

USING WINDOWS 2000 (LDAP) MODE

Running ADSI25 on a Windows NT 4.0 server or workstation is very similar to that described in the preceding "Running ADSI25 Under Windows 2000" section. The primary difference is that you must specify the Windows 2000 DC NetBIOS name(s), and supply a valid administrator logon name and password for the Windows 2000 domain(s), as shown in Figure A.25.

ADDING STUDENTS TO A DIFFERENT DOMAIN | 1279

Figure A.25
When displaying or creating objects in a Windows 2000 Active Directory from a Windows NT 4.0 computer, you must provide administrator credentials and DC server names.

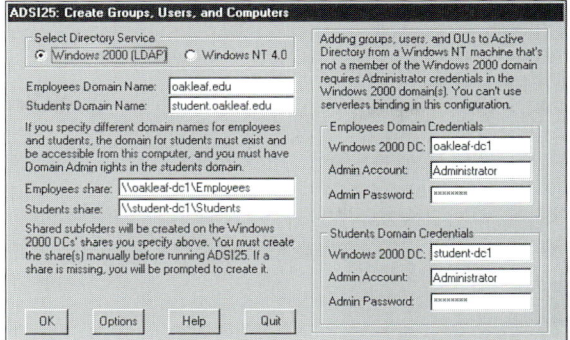

The only significant difference in the appearance of ADSI25's main form is the addition of the DC's NetBIOS name between the `LDAP://` and `CN=` elements of the list items (see Figure A.26).

Figure A.26
The main form of ASDI25 shows Windows 2000 DC server names (oakleaf-dc1 and student-dc1) added under Windows NT 4.0 to the full LDAP path for AD objects.

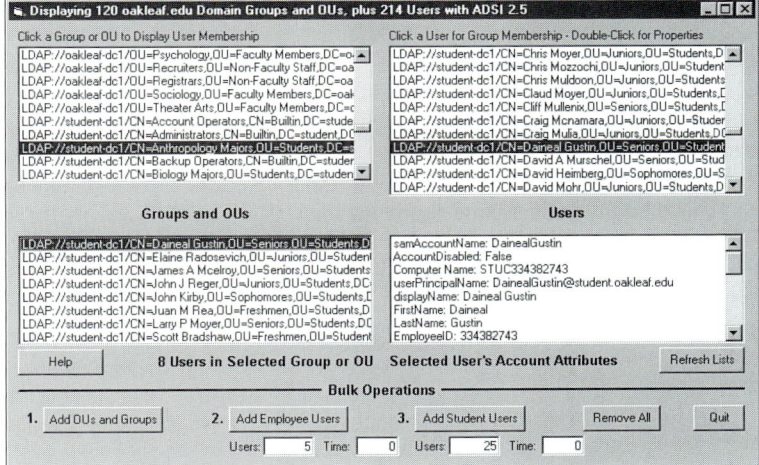

ADDING STUDENTS TO A DIFFERENT DOMAIN

ADSI25 lets you specify a different domain for student user and computer accounts, and security groups. Under Windows 2000, adding a second domain lets you experiment with child domains. Creating a second Windows NT domain for students lets you test the Windows 2000 upgrade process with multiple Windows NT domains.

→ For a review of the process of adding a child domain, **see** "Adding a Sample Child Domain," **p. 160**.

If you specify different domains for employees and students, you must do the following:

1. Create the new AD or Windows NT domain for student users before running ADSI25. If you're creating a new Windows 2000 child domain, allow at least 15 minutes for replication of AD attributes between the new child domain and the parent domain.

2. Add a Students share on the DC or PDC for the students domain.

3. If you haven't previously run ADSI25 in single-domain mode, add an Employees share on the DC or PDC for the employees domain.

4. If you've created employee or student accounts in a single domain, run ADSI25, and click Remove All to delete the user and computer accounts, OUs, and security groups you added previously. Close and reopen ADSI25.

It's a good practice to delete and re-create all ADSI25 objects before changing the configuration of your test servers.

Adding Student Accounts to a Windows 2000 Child Domain

After you create the student user domain as a child domain (`student.oakleaf.edu` for this book's examples) of the parent employees domain (`oakleaf.edu`), log on as a member of the Domain Admins group of the parent domain. Windows 2000 automatically creates a two-way, non-transitive trust between parent (`oakleaf.edu`) and child (`student.oakleaf.edu`) domains.

After logging on to the Windows 2000 server or workstation running ADSI25, do the following to add accounts in the two domains:

1. Launch ADSI25 and add the child domain's prefix (**student.** for this example) to the entry in the Students Domain Name text box.

2. Type the new path for the Students share (see Figure A.27).

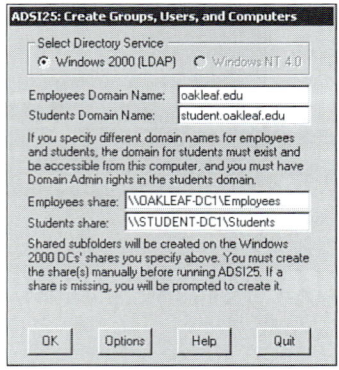

Figure A.27
The initial ADSI25 dialog shows entries for domain names and mapped drives that will create user accounts in two domains.

3. Click OK to display the Employees and Students Domain Credentials frames, and type the NetBIOS name of the DC, and your Domain Admins logon ID and password for each domain (see Figure A.28).

Figure A.28
You need to specify the name of the Domain Controller for the child domain and administrator logon credentials for both domains in order to create accounts in multiple domains.

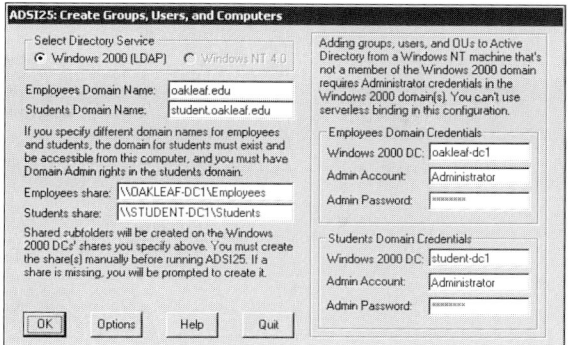

4. Click OK to close the opening dialog and display the main form.
5. Click Add OUs and Groups to create the new set of AD objects in the parent and child domains.
6. Specify the number of employee accounts you want to add to the parent domain in the left Users text box, and then click Add Employee Users.
7. Specify the number of student accounts you want to add to the child domain in the right Users text box, and then click Add Student Users.
8. Scroll toward the end of the Groups and OUs list to display the OUs for the student child domain, and click one of the OUs to display its membership.
9. Scroll down the Users list box and click one of the student items to display group membership in the Selected User's Groups and OUs list (see Figure A.29).

Figure A.29
Clicking a student name in the upper-right box of ADSI25 shows the student's membership in an OU in the child domain in the lower right.

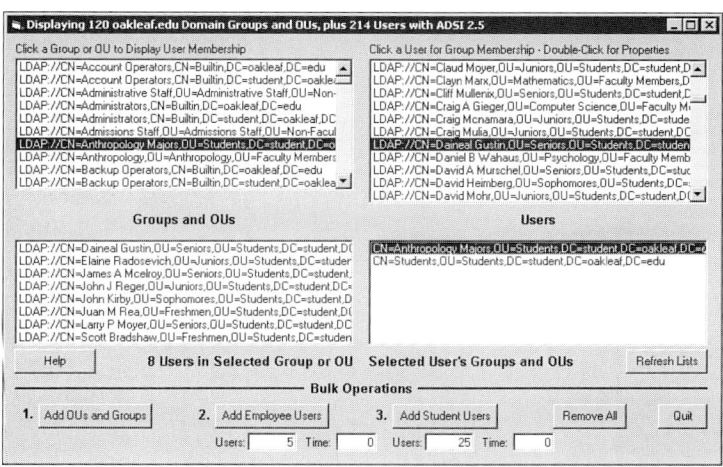

10. Double-click a student item in the Users list to display student properties (see Figure A.30). Scroll the list to verify that the user's email address points to the child domain.

Figure A.30
Double-click a student name in the upper right to see the attributes of the student that resides in the child domain in the lower-right box.

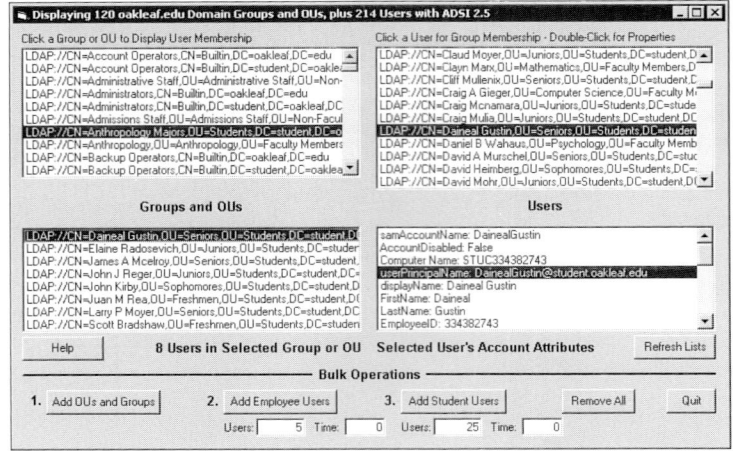

To verify that student OUs and Security Groups are added correctly to the child domain, do the following:

1. Launch the Active Directory Users and Computers snap-in, right-click the Active Directory Users and Computers node, and choose Connect to Domain to open the Connect to Domain dialog.

2. Add the child domain prefix to the parent domain name in the domain text box (see Figure A.31). Click OK to change the console's domain.

Figure A.31
The Connect To Domain dialog in Active Directory Users and Computers is used to connect to a domain other than the local one, in this case the `student.oakleaf.edu` child domain.

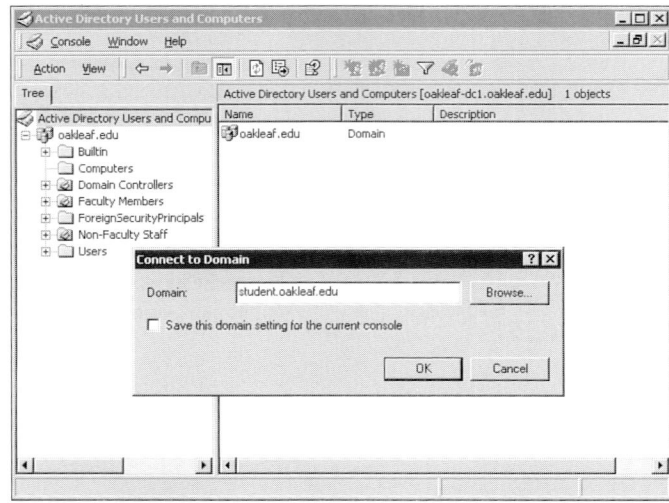

3. Expand the Students OU to display the four second-level class OUs and verify that the user accounts added correctly (see Figure A.32).

Figure A.32
The left pane of the Active Directory Users and Computers snap-in shows the Students OU with the child OUs corresponding to year. The right pane shows some of the user accounts in the Students/Freshmen OU.

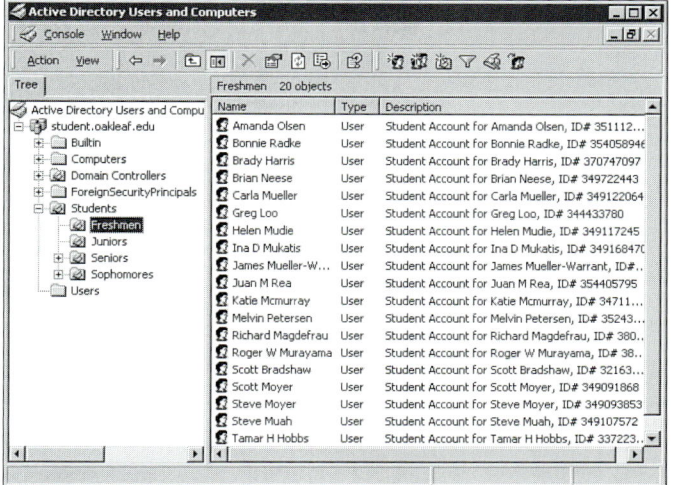

Adding Student Accounts to a Second Windows NT Domain

Creating separate domains for employees and students (OAKLEAFNT and STUDENT-NT for this example) lets you test multiple in-place upgrades to Windows 2000, and create a representative parent and child domain structure. You don't need to create non-transitive trusts between the two domains if you have the same logon ID (Administrator) and password in both Windows NT domains.

To run ADSI25 in Windows NT directory mode and create user, group, and computer accounts in the two domains, do the following:

1. After creating the two domains, add the Employees share to the primary domain (OAKLEAFNT), and the Students share to the secondary domain (STUDENTNT).

2. Install Ads_nt.exe, and then run ADSI25's Setup Program on the PDC of the primary domain (OAKLEAF-PDC for this example).

→ To review the setup process for ADSI25 on a Windows NT PDC, **see** "Installation on a Windows NT 4.0 DC or Workstation," **p. 1259**.

3. Run ADSI25 for Active Directory to open the startup form. Type the employees and students domain names and the UNC names of the two shares in the text boxes (see Figure A.33).

Figure A.33
The initial dialog for ADSI25 shows the domain and folder share entries required when adding users to two separate domains under Windows NT 4.0.

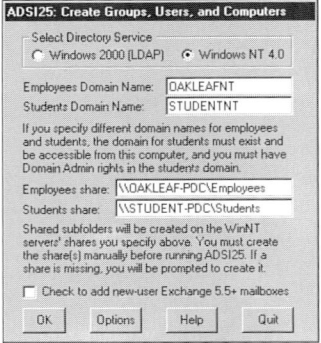

4. Click OK to open the main form, which displays Windows NT 4.0 default groups and accounts in both domains (see Figure A.34).

Figure A.34
The main form of ADSI25 shows the default users and groups for both specified domains before any accounts or groups are added.

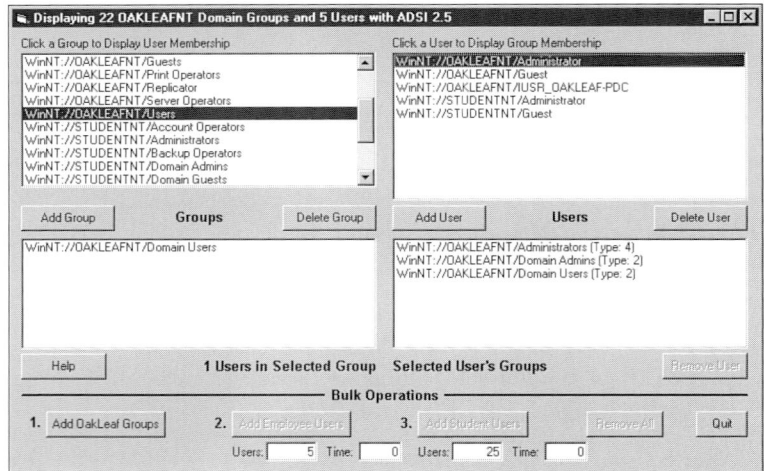

5. Click Add Groups and Users to add the ADSI25 group structure and create the Employees and Students subfolders.
6. Add a few hundred employee and student accounts to test the account addition process. Figure A.35 shows the first eight user accounts in the Anthropology Majors global group and the group membership of one of the group's students.

Figure A.35
The main form of ADSI25 now shows the newly added users and groups for both specified Windows NT 4.0 domains.

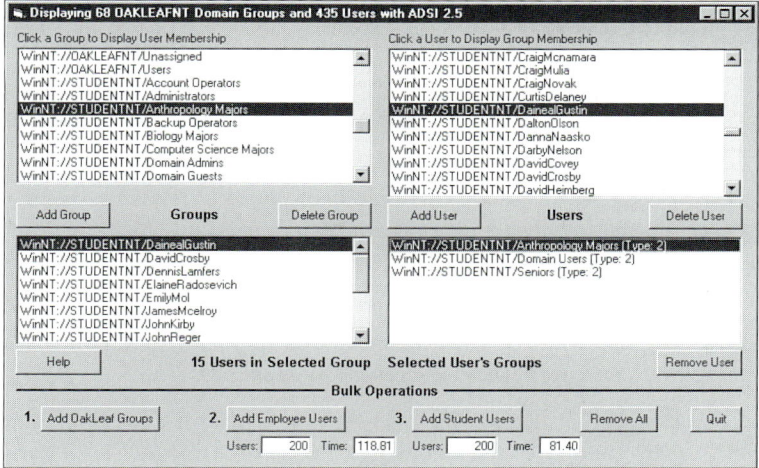

REMOVING ADSI25 FROM YOUR SYSTEM

Use Control Panel's Add/Remove Programs tool to uninstall ADSI25. Removing ADSI25 with the Microsoft Installer or Visual Studio Setup program doesn't remove Oakleaf.mdb or the \Program Files\ADSI25 folder, because running ADSI25 the first time renames the original Oakleaf (Clear).mdb to Oakleaf.mdb.

Note
You must reboot your computer before uninstalling ADSI25 from a Windows 2000 computer. Windows 2000 sometimes retains a lock on the ADSI25.exe file after you close the application. This problem doesn't occur when running ADSI25.exe under Windows NT 4.0.

USER LICENSE

The ADSI25 software and other software included on the CD-ROM that accompanies this book are licensed by the copyright owner, Roger Jennings, as-is, without warranty of any kind, either expressed or implied, including but not limited to the implied warranties of merchantability and fitness for a particular purpose. Neither the author, publisher, nor its dealers or distributors assumes any liability for any alleged or actual damages arising from the use of this program. (Some states do not allow for the exclusion of implied warranties, so the exclusion might not apply to you.)

You may use any elements of the ADSI25 source code for any purpose you want, including writing commercial programs for resale. You may not distribute the ADSI25.exe file included on the accompanying CD-ROM or compiled from the source code, nor are you allowed to distribute the ADSI25 source code in its entirety.

Troubleshooting

Startup Problems

Clicking OK in the startup dialog opens an "Employees (or Students) Share (\\ComputerName\ShareName) has not been created or is not accessible" message.

You didn't create the required shared folder(s) prior to running ADSI25 for the first time. Just creating the folder(s) on the machine running ADSI25 isn't sufficient; you must share the folder(s) to enable the ADSI25 startup program to detect them. Use My Computer or Explorer to verify that the required folder(s) are shared.

If the UNC share name(s) you type in the startup dialog doesn't match the name of the computer or share, or both, you receive the same message.

You also receive this message in a two-domain or parent-child domain environment if ADSI25 can't connect to the secondary or child domain. ADSI25's startup program tests share access before performing other tests. Use My Network Places to verify existence and correct naming of the share.

In any of the preceding cases, after correcting the share problem or typographic errors in the domain name or share name text boxes, click OK to open the main form.

When using Windows NT 4.0's Windows 2000 (LDAP) mode, clicking OK in the startup dialog opens an "Invalid credentials for Employees (or Students) domain" message.

You must provide a valid Domain Admins or Enterprise Admins logon ID and password in the credentials (right) pane of the startup dialog. If you specify two domains, you must provide the logon credentials for each domain, even if you use an Enterprise Admins logon ID and password for the primary (employees) domain.

Operational (Main Form) Problems

Lists of the main form are empty.

The domain name(s) you typed in the startup dialog don't correspond to the actual domain names. Use downlevel (NetBIOS) names for Windows NT domain names, and fully qualified domain names (FQDNs) for Windows 2000 domains.

If you're running ADSI25 on a workstation, the test for server shares only verifies network connectivity to the specified servers, rather than the Windows PDC or Windows 2000 PDC emulator DC.

Lists of the main form don't include groups or users from a secondary or child domain.

There is a mismatch between the name you typed for the student domain and the actual domain name. ADSI25 doesn't perform error checking on access to the students' domain.

APPENDIX B

GLOSSARY

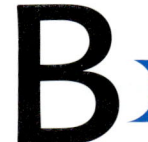

10BaseT, 100BaseT   The most common network cabling method for Ethernet, which handles traffic at a speed of up to 10Mbps (10BaseT) or 100Mbps (100BaseT). 10BaseT uses pairs of unshielded twisted conductors to connect a network interface card (NIC) and an Ethernet hub. 10Base2 (thin Ethernet, or *thinnet*) uses coaxial cable connections between computers and doesn't require a hub. Thin Ethernet is more commonly employed in Europe than in North America. 100BaseT, also called fast Ethernet, is a newer medium that supports up to 100Mbps on 10BaseT Category 5 (shielded twisted pair) cabling. Gigabit Ethernet (1000BaseT) supports speeds of up to 1000Mbps. See *Ethernet*, *hub*, *NIC*, *STP*, and *UTP*.

Access Control Entry (ACE)   An item in a (Discretionary) Access Control List that grants to user or group accounts specific permissions for access to an object, such as a file, folder, or share. Typical Windows 2000 folder permissions include Full Control, Write, Read (only), List Folder Contents, Execute, and combinations of permissions, such as Modify (Read, Write, and Delete) and Read & Execute. System Access Control Lists (SACLs) contain ACEs to specify which security-related events are audited for success, failure, or both. See *Access Control List* and *System Access Control List*.

Access Control List (ACL)   Part of Windows 2000's security description that controls access to a Windows 2000 object, such as a file. The owner of an object can change Access Control Entries (ACEs) in the list to grant or revoke permissions (access rights) of users or groups for the object. ACLs also are called DACLs, Discretionary Access Control Lists. See *Access Control Entry* and *System Access Control List*.

access token   A Windows 2000 object that identifies a logged-on (authenticated) user. The access token contains the user's security ID (SID), the groups to which the user belongs, and other security information. See *SID*.

activation   An ActiveX and Microsoft Transaction Server (MTS) term meaning to place an object in a running state, which includes binding the object, or to invoke a method of the object. See *MTS*.

Active Directory   See *AD*.

Active Directory Service Interface(s)   See *ADSI*.

ActiveX   A family of Microsoft object technologies, formerly called *OLE*, based on the Common Object Model (COM), serving as one of the foundations of Microsoft's Internet products. See *COM* and *DCOM*.

ActiveX control   An insertable COM object (component) that usually provides user interface components and can fire events. ActiveX controls are lightweight versions of OLE Controls (OCXs).

ActiveX Data Objects   See *ADO*.

AD   An abbreviation for *Active Directory*, the directory service used by Windows 2000. AD is a hierarchical, distributed database (derived from the Microsoft Exchange Server database) that contains information on all enterprise resources, regardless of the domain in which they're located. See *resource*.

address   The binary value, usually displayed and written in hexadecimal format, of a particular location in your computer's RAM. Address commonly is used to refer to an Ethernet network adapter card's unique identification code, called a MAC address. See *MAC*.

Address Resolution Protocol   See *ARP*.

address space   Memory allocated to an application by the operating system. See *virtual address space*.

ADO   The abbreviation for *ActiveX Data Objects*, a library of COM and Automation objects for providing 32-bit Windows applications access to flat, relational, or hierarchical tabular data through `Recordset` objects created with OLE DB data providers. LDAP queries return records to ADO `Recordsets`. ADO is the replacement for Data Access Objects (DAO) introduced by early versions of Microsoft Access. Windows 2000 installs ADO version 2.1. See *Automation*, *COM*, *MDAC*, *OLE DB*, and `Recordset`.

ADSI   The abbreviation for *Active Directory Service Interface(s)*, which provides a COM-based communication layer for reading and updating Active Directory and other directory services, such as NetWare Directory Services (NDS) and Windows NT's SAM (Service Account Manager) database. Windows 2000 Server installs ADSI 2.5, which also is available as a Software Development Kit (SDK). See *AD*, *NDS*, and *SAM*.

aggregate object   An ActiveX and OLE term that refers to an object class that contains one or more member objects of another class.

alert   In Windows 2000, a message sent between two simultaneously executing threads that results in an asynchronous procedure call (APC) executed by the receiving thread. Also means a message indicating abnormal operation of a Windows 2000 process.

ANSI   An abbreviation for the *American National Standards Institute*. In the Windows context, ANSI refers to the ANSI character set. Windows 9x and Windows 2000 include both ANSI (suffix A) and Unicode (suffix W) versions of Windows API functions. See *ASCII* and *Unicode*.

API   An abbreviation for *application program interface*. Generically, a method by which a program can obtain access to or modify the operating system. See *DLL*.

ARP   The IETF abbreviation for *Address Resolution Protocol*, which matches IP addresses to the Medium Access Control (MAC) address assigned to network interface cards (NICs), and vice versa. See *MAC*.

ASCII   Abbreviation for *American Standard Code for Information Interchange*. A set of standard numerical values for printable, control, and special characters used by PCs and most other computers. Other commonly used codes for character sets are ANSI (used by Windows 3.1+), Unicode (used by Windows 9x and Windows 2000), and EBCDIC (Extended Binary-Coded Decimal Interchange Code, used by IBM for mainframe computers). See *Unicode*.

asymmetric multiprocessing   A multiprocessing technique in which individual processors are dedicated to particular tasks, such as running the operating system or performing user requests. See *SMP*.

asynchronous   A process that can occur at any time, regardless of the status of the operating system or applications that are running. An example is Windows 2000's asynchronous procedure call (APC).

asynchronous I/O   Input/output operations in which an application issues an I/O request to a device, and then continues operation while the device transfers data. Asynchronous I/O greatly speeds fixed-disk file operations. See *synchronous I/O*.

attribute   A property of a class, having a name and a value. `Description` is an attribute of many Active Directory (AD) classes. See *class* and *property*.

auditing   Windows 2000's capability to record and report security-related events, such as accessing, creating, or deleting files.

authentication   The process of verifying (validating) a user's logon ID and password, usually used to provide access to network resources. Windows 2000 uses Kerberos authentication. See *Kerberos*.

Automation   An ActiveX term that refers to a means of manipulating another application's objects by the use of a programming language, most commonly Visual Basic Scripting Edition (VBScript or VBS) and Visual Basic for Applications (VBA), a programming language. VBS is very closely related to VBA. See *script*, *VBS*, and *WSH*.

Automation controller   An ActiveX-compliant Windows application with an application programming (macro) language, such as VBA, that can reference and manipulate objects exposed by ActiveX components and Automation servers. *Automation controller* replaces the term *OLE Automation client*.

Automation server   Technically, any Windows application that supports Automation operations by exposing a set of objects for manipulation by Automation client applications. In ActiveX terminology, ActiveX components are Automation servers. See *Automation*.

autoplay   A feature of Windows 9x's and Windows 2000's CD-ROM file system (CDFS) that automatically executes a program on the CD-ROM when the disk is inserted into the CD-ROM drive.

back end   In client/server database systems, the database server (usually a relational database management system, RDBMS). Back end now commonly is used to describe any server-based service that connects to a client application or browser. For example, Internet Information Server 5.0 is Windows 2000's back end for Web, FTP, SMPT, and NNTP services delivered to clients' browsers. See *front end*.

background   In multitasking computer operations, a running application or process that isn't visible onscreen and isn't receiving user-generated input, such as keystrokes or mouse clicks. User-generated requests, such as opening files and connecting to shares can run in the background.

basic disk   A single physical disk that contains one or more primary partitions and optional extended DOS partitions, each of which is identified by a drive letter to define a basic volume. Basic disks and volumes are the Windows 2000 equivalent of Windows NT 4.0's disks and volumes. Windows 2000 permits a basic disk to have up to four primary partitions, each of which can host a single operating system to permit multi-booting. Dynamic disks, which aren't compatible with Windows NT's NTFS 4.0, offer additional features, such as dynamic volumes that can be expanded after their creation. See *dynamic disk* and *NTFS*.

BDC   An abbreviation for *Backup Domain Controller*, a Windows NT server that provides an alternative source of authentication for network users. Account and group information from a Primary Domain Controller (PDC) is replicated periodically to each BDC in the domain. Windows 2000 replaces BDCs and PDCs with domain controllers (DCs). See *DC, PDC, and PDC emulator*.

BRI   An abbreviation for *Basic Rate Interface*, the standard ISDN service for business and residential Internet connections. Most BRIs have two 64kbps B (bearer) channels and one 16kbps D (data) channel, providing a maximum bandwidth of 128kbps. See *ISDN* and *PRI*.

bridge   An active network device used to divide a network into mutually isolated segments while maintaining the whole as a single network. Bridges operate at the data-link layer of the OSI Reference Model. See *OSI*.

buffer   An area in memory of a designated size (number of bytes or characters) reserved, typically by an application, to hold a portion of a file or the value of a variable.

business rules   A set of rules for entering data in a database that are specific to an enterprise's methods of conducting its operations. Business rules are in addition to rules for maintaining the domain and referential integrity of tables in a database. Business rules most commonly are implemented in a three-tier client/server database environment. See *three-tier*.

CAB An acronym for Cabinet file that contains multiple, related compressed files that commonly are used to install applications, services, drivers, and the like for Windows operating systems and applications. For example, most Windows 2000 printer drivers are stored in a 51MB Driver.cab file; specific driver files are extracted from the CAB file when you install a supported printer. CAB files are similar to ZIP archive files.

cache A block of memory reserved by hardware, an application, or a service for temporary storage. Caches usually store data from disk files in memory to make access to the data faster. By default, Windows 2000 caches all disk read and write operations.

cache manager A component of Windows 2000's I/O system that uses the virtual memory (VM) manager to create temporary storage in the paging file to speed disk I/O operations. See *VM*.

CAT An abbreviation for the category of 10/100BaseT Ethernet cabling. CAT-5 (shielded twisted pair, STP) cabling has become the standard for both 10BaseT and 100BaseT connections. See *10BaseT, 100BaseT,* and *STP*.

CDFS The 32-bit protected-mode *Compact Disc file system* used by Windows 2000 and 9x. CDFS complies with ISO 9660's level two standards for long file and folder names. Windows 2000 also supports the Universal Disk Format (UDF), which complies with ISO 13346, for read-only DVD-ROM data.

channel A dedicated communication connection between a transmitting and a receiving device. Channel is also used to identify an I/O port in mini- and mainframe computers.

CISC *Complex instruction set computer*, a microprocessor whose internal instructions often involve many individual execution steps and thus many clock cycles. The Intel 80x86 processors are the most common CISC devices. See *RISC*.

class The definition of a particular type of object. Active Directory (AD) class definitions are stored in its Schema. The most common Active Directory object classes are User, Computer, and Group. See *instance* and *schema*.

class identifier See *CLSID*.

Class Store A feature of Active Directory (AD) that specifies the location of networked application components. The Class Store doesn't extend the AD schema with additional object classes. Instead, Class Store is an additional AD namespace that stores pointers to custom-programmed COM and COM+ objects. See *COM, COM+,* and *schema*.

client The device or application that receives data from or manipulates a server device or application. The data may be in the form of a file received from a network file server, or an object created from an ActiveX component or OLE server. See *Automation controller*.

CLSID An identification tag that's associated with an ActiveX or OLE 2.0 object created by a specific component or server. CLSID values appear in the Registry and must be unique for each type of object that the server can create. See *Registry*.

clustering   A server architecture that emulates multiprocessing by interconnecting two or more individual computers in order to share the application processing load. Windows 2000 Advanced Server and Datacenter Server support clustering.

CN   The LDAP common name (display name) for a directory object, such as CN=Gary Almgren, the CN for a user. See *DN* and *LDAP*.

collection   A group of objects of the same class that are contained within another object. Collections are named as the plural of their object class.

COM   An acronym for *Component Object Model*, the name of Microsoft's design strategy to implement OLE 2+ and ActiveX. Distributed COM (DCOM) allows networked and cross-platform implementation of ActiveX and OLE 2+ operations and Automation. See *Automation* and *DCOM*.

COM+   An extension to Microsoft Distributed Component Object Model (DCOM), which incorporates Microsoft Transaction Server (MTS), Microsoft Message Queue Server (MSMQ), and an in-memory database (IMDB) as runtime components. COM+ (pronounced "comm plus"), which also provides component load-balancing and event services, is part of Microsoft's Windows Distributed interNet Architecture (Windows DNA). See *COM*, *DCOM*, *MDAC*, *MTS*, *MSMQ*, and *Windows DNA*.

common name   See *CN*.

Component Object Model   See *COM*.

Component Services   The Windows 2000 name for Microsoft Transaction Server (MTS) as a COM+ component. See *COM+* and *MTS*.

concurrent application   An application capable of simultaneous execution in multiple address spaces. Windows 2000 uses threads of execution to support concurrent applications.

console   A character-based interface to an operating system. Windows 2000 uses the Command Prompt tool as the console. Microsoft Management Console (MMC) snap-ins also are called consoles. See *MMC* and *snap-in*.

container   In Active Directory (AD), a construct that holds groups of similar objects and, optionally, other containers. You can nest AD object containers to any depth you want. Some of the Windows 2000 default containers created during AD installation don't permit nesting.

context switching   The process of saving an executing thread or process and transferring control to another thread or process. Windows 2000's context switching, one of the major bottlenecks in COM operations, is substantially faster than in Windows NT 4.0.

control   A synonym for a visible dialog or window object, such as include labels, text boxes, lists, combo lists, option buttons, and command buttons.

control object   In Windows 2000, an object that controls system tasks, such as asynchronous and deferred procedure calls.

crossover (cable)   A 10/100BaseT cable with the transmit and receive conductors reversed on one of its RJ-45 plugs. A crossover cable permits interconnecting two network interface cards (NICs) without the use of a hub or switch. Crossover cables sometimes are used to connect an expansion port of a hub to another hub. See *hub*, *straight-through*, and *switch*.

datagram   A variable-length IP packet with a maximum size of 65,535 octets (bytes), the maximum number of octets that a 16-bit number can specify. Datagrams consist of a variable-length header with a minimum size of 20 octets followed by data (often called *payload*.) See *octet*.

DC   The abbreviation for a Windows 2000 Domain Controller, which takes the place of Windows NT's Primary and Backup Domain Controllers (PDCs and BDCs, respectively).

DC (LDAP)   The abbreviation for *domain component*, an element of an LDAP distinguished name in Active Directory. DCs consist of the second- and first-level domain names in left-to-right sequence, for example `DC=oakleaf,DC=edu` for the `oakleaf.edu` domain. See *DN* and *LDAP*.

DCOM   An acronym for *Distributed Component Object Model* that allows communication and manipulation of objects over a network connection. Windows NT 4.0 was the first Microsoft operating system to support DCOM (formerly called NetworkOLE). See *COM*.

DDNS   The abbreviation for *Dynamic Domain Name Service*, a feature of Windows 2000 Server that integrates DNS with Active Directory to dynamically update DNS records. See *DNS*.

default   A value assigned or an option chosen when no value is specified by the user or assigned by a program statement.

delegation   The process of assigning administrative authority for an organizational unit (OU) to persons or groups that aren't members of the Domain Admins group. Domain Admins have administrative authority for the entire domain and subdomains, if present. Delegation allows Domain Admins to assign a particular set of administrative privileges at any level in the OU hierarchy. See *OU*.

departmental networks   Networks having 25 or fewer servers and less than 500 clients. Departmental networks traditionally have been the primary market for Windows NT Server. See *enterprise networks*.

device   A computer system component that can send or receive data, such as a keyboard, display, printer, disk drive, or modem. Windows 2000 uses device drivers to create device objects that connect applications to devices.

Dfs   Microsoft's abbreviation for the *Distributed File System*, a Windows 2000 service for linking file shares on multiple servers under a single share name. Replication of Dfs file shares provides load balancing and automatic fail-over to replicated shares if a primary file server is unavailable.

DHCP Abbreviation for *Dynamic Host Configuration Protocol*, an Internet standard protocol that allows IP addresses to be pooled and assigned as needed to clients. Windows 2000 includes DHCP manager, an MMC snap-in (Dhcp.msc). See *IP* and *IP address*.

disk mirroring Creating on two or more physical disk drives exact duplicates of a disk volume to make files accessible in case of failure of one drive of the mirror set. See *RAID*.

disk striping Distributing the data for a single logical disk volume across two or more physical disk drives. Simple disk striping (RAID 0) provides faster I/O operation. Disk striping with parity (RAID 5) provides faster I/O and protection from failure of a physical disk in a stripe set. See *RAID*.

dispatcher A Windows 2000 operating system component that schedules the execution of application threads.

distinguished name See *DN*.

DLC An abbreviation for *Data Link Control*, a Windows 2000 protocol used to communicate with mainframes and older networked laser printers.

DLL An abbreviation for *dynamic link library*, a file containing a collection of Windows functions designed to perform a specific class of operations. Most DLLs carry the DLL extension, but some Windows DLLs, such as Gdi32.exe, use the EXE extension. Functions within DLLs are called (invoked) by applications as necessary to perform the desired operation.

DN The LDAP abbreviation for *distinguished name*. DNs constitute the namespace of the directory, and must be unique within the scope of the directory. The scope of most LDAP directories is the entire Internet. The DN consists of a left-to-right expression of the directory hierarchy. A typical Active Directory DN representation is CN=Gary Almgren, OU=Anthropology,OU=Faculty Members,DC=oakleaf,DC=edu. See *CN*, *DC (LDAP)*, and *OU*.

DNS The abbreviation for *Domain Name Service*, an Internet standard for translating friendly names, such as www.oakmusic.com into Internet Protocol (IP) addresses, such as 209.249.8.35.

DNS (Windows) An abbreviation for Microsoft's *Digital Nervous System*, a slogan introduced by Bill Gates at the first annual Microsoft CEO Summit Conference held in Seattle on May 8, 1997. The idea behind Microsoft's DNS (not the Internet's DNS) is that remaining competitive in the "digital age" requires firms to adopt a new information technology mindset.

domain In Windows 2000, a group of networked workstations and servers that share a common DNS domain name, such as oakleaf.edu, and run within a particular security boundary. In Windows NT 4.0, a group of workstations and servers that share a common Security Accounts Manager (SAM) database and allow a user to log on to any resource in the domain with a single user ID and password.

domain component See *DC (LDAP)*.

Domain Controller   See *DC*.

domain integrity   The process of assuring that values added to fields of a table comply with a set of rules for reasonableness and other constraints. See *business rules* and *three-tier*.

Domain Local group   See *Security Groups*.

Domain Name System   See *DDNS* and *DNS*.

dynamic disk   A new feature of Windows 2000, implemented by the Disk Management feature, that permits multiple physical disks to be combined into a single dynamic volume identified by a drive letter. You can increase the capacity of a dynamic volume by adding more physical disks, volume mount points, and reparse points, and taking advantage of link tracking. See *basic disk*, *link tracking*, *reparse points*, and *volume mount points*.

Dynamic Domain Name Service   See *DDNS*.

dynamic link library   See *DLL*.

enterprise networks   Networks having 50 or more servers and more than 1,000 clients. UNIX is the predominate operating system for enterprise networks. Microsoft designed Windows 2000 and Active Directory to gain a substantial share of the enterprise network market. See *departmental networks*.

entry   In LDAP terminology, a record that holds information about a particular instance of a directory object class—usually a real-world entity. An entry consists of one or more named attributes, which have a type and one or more values. The *attribute type* has a *syntax* that specifies the storage format of values. See *attribute* and *LDAP*.

environment   A combination of the computer hardware, operating system, and user interface. A complete statement of an environment follows: a Pentium PCI-bus computer with 64MB of RAM, a Wide and Fast SCSI host adapter, SVGA display adapter, sound card, and two-button mouse, using the Windows 2000 Professional operating system.

environmental subsystem   In Windows 2000, the four sets of APIs that support Win32, MS-DOS, POSIX, and OS/2 applications.

ESE   The abbreviation for *Extensible Storage Engine*, the database used to store Active Directory information. ESE is based on the special Jet database used by Microsoft Exchange Server. See *Jet*.

Ethernet   A networking medium that was developed at the Xerox Palo Alto Research Center (PARC) in the 1970s; was improved by Xerox, Intel, and Digital; and is now the most popular network medium and cabling method for LANs. The IEEE 802.3 specification for Ethernet is the most common implementation. See *10BaseT*, *100BaseT*, and *IEEE*.

exception   An error, such as division by zero, detected by hardware or by the operating system. Fatal exceptions halt execution of an application and, in a few circumstances, kill the operating system. Proper exception handling within an application or script can gracefully handle all but fatal exceptions.

executable Code, usually in the form of a disk file, that can be run by the operating system in use to perform a particular set of functions. Executable files in Windows carry the extension EXE and may obtain assistance from dynamic link libraries (DLLs) in performing their tasks.

executive In Windows 2000, the components of the operating system that run in the kernel (ring 0) and handle interprocess communication, interrupt requests, and object security. Graphics operations have been moved from user mode to kernel mode in Windows 2000 to speed performance. See *kernel mode* and *user mode*.

Extensible Storage Engine See *ESE*.

extranet A connection between two or more private intranets that grants a specified set of users in one organization access to particular resources on another organization's intranet. The interconnection most commonly is via the public Internet using a Virtual Private Network (VPN). See *VPN*.

fail-over A fault-tolerant clustering architecture in which two servers share a common set of fault-tolerant fixed disk drives. In the event of failure of one of the servers, the other transparently assumes all server processing operations. See *clustering* and *fault tolerance*.

FAT An acronym for *file allocation table*, the disk file system used by MS-DOS, Windows 9x, and (optionally) Windows 2000. Windows NT is compatible with the 16-bit FAT system, but not the optional 32-bit FAT (FAT32) for Windows 9x. See *HPFS* and *NTFS*.

fault tolerance A computer system's capability to maintain operability, despite failure of a major hardware component such as a power supply, microprocessor, or fixed-disk drive. Fault tolerance requires redundant hardware and modifications to the operating system. Windows 2000 Server includes fault tolerance for a failed disk drive by disk mirroring (RAID 1) or disk striping with parity (RAID 5). Clustering provides fault tolerance for individual computers. See *clustering* and *RAID*.

fiber A lightweight thread, introduced in Windows NT 4.0, that makes it easier for developers to optimize scheduling within multithreaded applications. See *thread*.

File and Print Services for NetWare See *FPNW*.

firewall A method of keeping a private network secure from intrusion by unauthorized users or accepting traffic that uses particular network protocols. Firewalls can be implemented by dedicated filtering hardware, software proxy servers to isolate private (internal) networks from the public Internet; software packet filters that block traffic based on IP addresses or TCP port numbers, Network Address Translation (NAT); or any combination of these methods. See *NAT* and *proxy server*.

foreground In multitasking operations, the application or procedure that's visible and to which user-generated input is directed. In Windows, the application that has the focus is in the foreground.

forest   A set of one or more domain trees that don't share a contiguous Domain Name System (DNS) namespace with other domain trees. If you have `oakleaf.edu` and `oakmusic.com` as domains, a separate forest is required for each domain. A forest shares a common `Schema` object. See *DNS* and *tree*.

FPNW   The abbreviation for *File and Print Services for NetWare*, a Windows 2000 service that permits Windows 2000 Server to appear as a file and print server for NetWare clients.

front end   When used with database management systems, an application, a window, or a set of windows by which the user may access and view database records, as well as add to or edit them. Front end commonly is used to describe the client application for any client/server system. For example, Microsoft Outlook is the front end for Microsoft Exchange Server. See *back end*.

function   A subprogram called from within an expression in which a value is computed and returned to the program that called it through its name. Functions are classified as internal to the application language when their names are keywords.

gateway   A hardware device or software program used to translate between incompatible protocols. A gateway can function at any one layer (usually the Application layer) of the OSI Reference Model or at several layers simultaneously. For example, a gateway is used to translate between mail systems, such as SNMP and MHS. (Internet terminology uses the term *gateway* in place of *router*.)

Gateway Services for NetWare   See *GSNW*.

global   Pertaining to an entire entity, such as a Windows 2000 domain or a collection of trusted/trusting domains. Windows 2000 distinguishes Global groups from Domain Local groups; Domain Local groups have permissions only for objects in the domain in which they are created; Global groups have permissions within a domain tree. See *tree*.

Global group (Windows 2000)   See *Security Groups*.

global group (Windows NT)   A group whose members can be assigned permissions for objects shared on any server within a Windows NT domain or a trusting domain. See *local group* and *Security Groups*.

GPO   The abbreviation for *Group Policy Object*, an Active Directory (AD) object that stores a collection of policies that apply at the site, domain, or organizational unit level. See *Group Policy* and *policy*.

group   A collection of network or database users with common permissions for particular objects, such as shared files or database tables. See also *permissions* and *Security Groups*.

Group Policy   A Windows 2000 method of applying a set of customizable rules, called policies, to user and computer accounts that are members of a particular Security Group. See *GPO*, *policy*, and *Security Groups*.

Group Policy Object   See *GPO*.

GSNW The abbreviation for *Gateway Services for NetWare*, a Windows 2000 service that permits Windows clients to access NetWare directories through a Windows 2000 server. The Windows 2000 server connects to the NetWare server and reshares the directory as a conventional Windows 2000 folder share.

HAL An acronym for *hardware abstraction layer*, a Windows 2000 DLL that links specific computer hardware implementations with the Windows 2000 kernel. Windows 2000 includes HALs for 80x86 and Alpha hardware platforms.

handle An unsigned long (32-bit) integer assigned by Windows 2000 or Windows 9x to uniquely identify an instance (occurrence) of an object, such as a file or a window.

host A UNIX term for any computer connected to a TCP/IP network. Windows 2000 and this book distinguish client and server hosts.

HPFS An abbreviation for the *High-Performance File System* used by OS/2 and (optionally) Windows NT 3.x. Windows 2000 doesn't support HPFS but can connect via a network to files on HPFS volumes of Windows NT 3.x PCs.

HTML An abbreviation for *Hypertext Markup Language*, a variant of SGML (Standardized General Markup Language), a page-description language for creating files that can be formatted and displayed by World Wide Web browsers.

hub A concentrator that joins multiple clients by means of a single link to the rest of the LAN. A hub has several ports to which clients are connected directly, and one or more ports that can be used to connect the hub to the backbone or to other active network components. A hub functions as a multiport repeater; signals received on any port are immediately retransmitted to all other ports of the hub. Hubs function at the physical layer of the OSI Reference Model.

I/O manager A component of the Windows 2000 executive that handles all input/output (I/O) requests.

idle In Windows, the condition or state in which both Windows and the application have processed all pending messages in the queue from user- or hardware-initiated events and are waiting for the next event to occur. In Windows 2000 multiprocessing, one idle thread exists for each processor.

IEEE The official abbreviation for the *Institute of Electrical and Electronic Engineers*, a professional association that establishes and maintains many industry-standard specifications, such as the IEEE 1394 High-Performance Serial Bus, more commonly referred to by Apple Computer's FireWire trademark. IEEE 802.3 is the Ethernet specification. See *Ethernet*.

IETF The official abbreviation for the *Internet Engineering Task Force*, which is responsible for setting standards for Internet protocols and other Internet-related specifications. Standards appear in the form of serially numbered Requests for Comments (RFCs).

impersonation In Windows 2000, the capability of a thread in one process to assume the security identity of another process. Impersonation is employed by a named pipe to acquire and use the security ID of the service requester.

index For arrays and collections, the position of the particular element with respect to others, usually beginning with 0 (arrays) or 1 (collections) as the first element. When used with database files or tables, *index* refers to a lookup table, usually in the form of a file or component of a file, that relates the value of a field in the indexed file to its record or page number and location in the page (if pages are used).

initial root domain The domain from which Active Directory creates all other domains. The first Windows 2000 DC you install (either in a new network or by upgrading a Windows NT PDC) creates the initial root domain of the forest. The initial root domain contains the configuration and schema for the entire forest. Even if your network has only one domain, it has a forest with an initial root domain. See *forest*.

initialize In programming, setting all variables to their default values and resetting the point of execution to the first executable line of code.

in-process A term applied to Automation servers, also called *Automation DLLs*, that operate within the same process space (memory allocation) of the Automation controller manipulating the server. In-process servers commonly are called *InProc servers*. See *out-of-process*.

installable file system In Windows 2000, the capability to load a file system (such as NTFS, CDFS, FAT, or UDF) dynamically, depending on the format of the file to be opened.

instance A specific representation of an object class, such as a particular user or computer. Also a term used by Windows to describe the temporal existence of a loaded application or one or more of its windows. See *class*.

instantiate The process of creating an instance of an object in memory.

interface A noun describing a connection between two dissimilar devices or COM objects, such as Automation clients and servers. A common phrase is *user interface*, meaning the "connection" between the display-keyboard combination and the user. Use of *interface* as a verb is jargon.

interrupt An asynchronous message, usually issued by an I/O device, requesting the service of an operating system's or device driver's interrupt handler.

intranet A private network that uses Internet protocols and common Internet applications (such as Web browsers) to emulate the public Internet. Intranets on LANs and high-speed WANs provide increased privacy and improved performance compared with today's Internet.

IP An abbreviation for *Internet Protocol*, the basic network transmission protocol of the Internet.

IP address The 32-bit hexadecimal address of a host, gateway, or router on an IP network. For convenience, IP addresses are specified as the decimal value of the four address bytes, separated by periods, as in 124.33.15.1. Addresses are classified as types A, B, and C, depending on the subnet mask applied. See *subnet mask*.

IPSec The abbreviation for *Internet Protocol Security*, Windows 2000's certificate-based cryptographic system for ensuring the security of TCP/IP network communication. See *L2TP*.

IPv6 The official IETF abbreviation for *Internet Protocol version 6*, also called *IP Next Generation Protocol* (IPNg). One of the primary motives for adopting IPv6 is the need for a vastly increased number of IP addresses to support low-cost portable Internet appliances, high-priced interactive Digital TV (DTV) sets and settop boxes, and other devices needing a unique, publicly known network address.

IPX/SPX Abbreviation for *Internetwork Packet Exchange/Sequenced Packet Exchange*, the transport protocol of Novell NetWare, supported by Windows 2000's NWLink service. See *NWLink*.

ISDN An abbreviation for *Integrated Services Digital Network*, a switched telephone service that provides mid-band digital communication capabilities used for Internet connections and for remote access to LANs, as well as voice communication. Windows 2000 has built-in support for ISDN modems, more properly called *network terminators*. See *BRI* and *PRI*.

item The name given to one of the elements contained in a list box or drop-down list, or the list component of a combo box.

Jet Originally an acronym for Joint Engine Technology, an indexed sequential access method (ISAM) database introduced by Microsoft Access 1.0. Conventional Access databases are the relational "red" version. Active Directory, Exchange Server, and several Windows 2000 services use the hierarchical "blue" version, now called the Extensible Storage Engine (ESE). See *ADO*, *ESE*, and *OLE DB*.

Kerberos In Greek mythology, a three-headed dog that guarded the gates of Hades. In Windows 2000, a secure method for authenticating a request by a user, application, or service for access to Windows 2000 domains, systems, and services. Kerberos was developed by the Massachusetts Institute of Technology's Athena Project and modified by Microsoft for use by Windows 2000. Kerberos authentication, which also is used by some UNIX systems, provides the requester with a time-limited ticket that grants access to services provided by one or more servers. Once the ticket is obtained, the requester's password no longer travels over the network. When the ticket expires, Kerberos supplies a new ticket.

kernel mode The mode in which the Windows 2000 system runs, providing the operating system with access to system memory and other hardware devices.

key A collection of one or more Registry values (properties) that relate to a single object.

L2TP The abbreviation for the *Layer 2 Tunneling Protocol* introduced in Windows 2000. L2TP is a combination of the Point-to-Point Tunneling Protocol (PPTP) and Cisco Systems' Layer 2 Forwarding (L2F) protocol. L2TP uses IP Security (IPSec) to create L2TP over IPSec Virtual Private Networks (VPNs). See *IPSec*, *PPTP*, and *VPN*.

LAN An acronym for *local area network*. A LAN is a system comprising multiple computers that are physically interconnected through network adapter cards and cabling. See *WAN*.

launch   To start a Windows application.

Layer 2 Tunneling Protocol   See *L2TP*.

LDAP   The official IETF abbreviation for *Lightweight Directory Access Protocol*, an Internet-standard directory derived from the heavyweight X.500 directory. LDAP runs on TCP/IP, which eliminates the session and presentation overhead of the OSI networking model. LDAP delivers most of the capabilities of X.500, but consumes less than 10% of the resources required to support the heavyweight protocol. LDAP version 3, a proposed standard when this book was written, is the sole means of reading and writing Active Directory objects. See *AD* and *X.500*.

library   A collection of functions, compiled as a group and accessible to applications by calling the function name, together with any required arguments. DLLs are one type of library; those used by compilers to provide built-in functions are another type. See *API* and *DLL*.

Lightweight Directory Access Protocol   See *LDAP*.

link tracking   A feature of the Windows 2000 NTFS 5.0 file system's dynamic disks that lets client applications track links to file system objects when the objects have been moved. Link tracking adds a unique and permanent object identifier (OID) that refers to the file system object, wherever it's located. See *dynamic disk*.

linked object   A source document in a compound document that's included by reference to a file that contains the object's data, rather than by embedding the source document in the compound document.

local area network   See *LAN*.

local group   A Windows NT security group for granting user permissions for a particular computer. Windows 2000 Domain Controllers don't support local users and groups, but they provide a set of Builtin groups to accommodate upgrading Windows NT Server's local groups. See *Security Groups*.

locale   The environment for an operating system or application, usually based on a specific language or a dialect of a language. Windows 2000 uses the National Language Support (NLS) API to provide localization.

logical   The manifestation of physical devices in software, including operating systems. For example, a logical disk drive may consist of a part of the space on a single disk drive or, using Windows 2000's capability of spanning drives, space on multiple disk drives.

logon   The process by which Windows 2000 detects an attempt by a user to gain access to the operating system. Successful completion of the logon process authenticates the user.

loose consistency   The term that describes the currency of data among Active Directory Domain Controllers (DCs). Replication between DCs isn't immediate, especially over WAN links, so Microsoft describes AD database copies as having loose consistency. All copies of the AD database ultimately become identical, a process called convergence. See *DC* and *multimaster replication*.

LRPC   An abbreviation for *Lightweight Remote Procedure Call* used for communication between ActiveX controllers (OLE clients) and ActiveX components (OLE servers) residing on a single computer. See *remote procedure call (RPC)*.

MAC   An acronym for *Media Access Control*, the globally unique hardware address of an Ethernet network interface card.

machine language   Program code in the form of instructions that have meaning to and can be acted on by the computer hardware and operating system used. Object files compiled from source code are in machine language, as are executable files that consist of object files linked with library files. Windows 2000 is individually compiled for the machine language of each platform that uses a different processor.

map   To translate a physical memory address to a virtual memory (VM) address, or vice versa. Map also refers to the process of translating one or more IP addresses to another IP address. See *VM*.

MAPI   Acronym for the Windows *Messaging API* originally created by Microsoft for use with Microsoft Mail, which implements Simple MAPI. Microsoft Exchange Client and Server implement MAPI 1.0+ (also called Extended or Enhanced MAPI).

MDAC   An acronym for *Microsoft Data Access Components*, a collection of OLE DB data providers and ActiveX Data Objects (COM components) that supply applications and services with connectivity to databases, such as SQL Server, Oracle, and Jet. Windows 2000 Professional and all Server versions install MDAC 2.5. A newer version, MDAC 2.6, is required for and installed by SQL Server 2000. See *ADO*, *Automation*, *COM*, and *OLE DB*.

member server   A server that's a member of a domain, but not a Windows 2000 Domain Controller (DC), or a Windows NT PDC or BDC. See *BDC*, *DC*, and *PDC*.

MIB   An acronym for *Management Information Base*, a set of attributes for active network components, including servers, used by SNMP. Windows 2000 provides MIBs for server shares, sessions, and users, plus DHCP and WINS data. See *SNMP*.

Microsoft Management Console   See *MMC*.

Microsoft Transaction Server   See *MTS*.

middle tier   A logical entity that connects a data services layer to a presentation layer. In Windows, the middle tier usually is a COM or Automation component. See *Automation*, *COM*, and *three-tier*.

mirroring   See *disk mirroring*.

MISF   An abbreviation for *Microsoft Internet Security Framework*, a set of high-level security services that rely on CryptoAPI 2.0 functions to provide certificate- and password-based authentication. MISF also incorporates secure channel communication using SSL (Secure Sockets Layer) 2.0 and 3.0, plus PCT (Personal Communications Technology), SET (Secure Electronic Transactions) for credit-card purchases, and the Microsoft Certificate Server for issuing authentication certificates.

MMC An abbreviation for *Microsoft Management Console*, an application that hosts Windows 2000 and some Windows NT administrative tools, called *snap-ins*, to create MMC *consoles*, which may contain multiple snap-ins in a *console tree*. The administrative tools for Windows 2000 Server run as MMC consoles. See *snap-in*.

MSDSS The abbreviation for *Microsoft Directory Synchronization Services*, also called *DirSync*. MSDSS is a component of the Microsoft Services for NetWare add-on for Windows 2000 Server that provides two-way synchronization with NetWare Directory Services (NDS). See *NDS*.

MSFMU The abbreviation for *Microsoft File Migration Utility*, also called *DirSync*. MSFMU is another component of the Microsoft Services for NetWare that's designed to simplify a one-way migration of files from NetWare servers to Windows 2000 servers.

MSFU See *SFU*.

MSMQ The abbreviation for *Microsoft Message Queue Server*, a component of COM+ that uses asynchronous messaging for communication with middle-tier components. Use of messaging techniques permits transactions over unreliable communication links. If the link is down or a process in the transaction is busy, transactions are queued for completion when the link returns to service or the process becomes available. See *COM+*, *middle tier*, and *three-tier*.

MTS The abbreviation for *Microsoft Transaction Server*, a component-based transaction monitor (TM) and object request broker (ORB) for developing, deploying, and managing the middle tier of component-based applications. Microsoft added MTS 2.0 to Windows NT with the Windows NT 4.0 Option Pack. MTS now is part of COM+. See *COM+*, *middle tier*, and *three-tier*.

multicast An alternative IP mode, which lets a host transmit packets to multiple hosts that intercept packets within the Class D address range as a multicast stream. Receiving hosts must know in advance the address assigned to a multicast stream. Multicasting is used most commonly for broadcasting streaming media over private intranets. See *host* and *unicast*.

multimaster replication The replication process used by Active Directory to synchronize the content of AD databases between domain controllers (DCs) within a site and at remote locations. Multimaster means that updates to an Active Directory database copy on any computer ultimately propagate to all DCs. The replication process is similar to that for Exchange Server's directory. See *Active Directory* and *DC*.

multiprocessing The capability of a computer with two or more CPUs to allocate tasks (threads) to a specific CPU. See *SMP*.

multitasking The capability of a computer with a single CPU to simulate the processing of more than one task at a time. Multitasking is effective when one (or more) of the applications spends most of its time in an idle state, waiting for a user-initiated event such as a keystroke or mouse click.

multithreaded   An application that contains more than one thread of execution; a task or set of tasks that executes semi-independently of other task(s).

multiuser   Concurrent use of a single computer by more than one user, usually through the use of remote terminals. UNIX is inherently a multiuser operating system. *Multiuser* is often used as a term to describe an application that allows multiple users to view and update a single shared file, such as a Microsoft Access MDB file. Microsoft Terminal Services, included with Windows 2000, implements a multiuser environment for computers running the Terminal Services Client.

named pipes   A method of interprocess communication, originally developed for OS/2, that provides a secure channel for network communication.

namespace   A set of rules for assigning consistent names to objects. The Domain Name System (DNS), a set of Internet standards, provides a well-accepted namespace for computers within a hierarchically structured domain. See *DNS*.

NAT   An acronym for Network Address Translation, which lets an organization use a single Internet connection to provide Internet connectivity to multiple users on a private intranet. NAT uses TCP or UDP port translation to direct incoming IP traffic to a specific host computer and to hide internal network addresses from the outside world. Windows 2000's Routing and Remote Access Services (RRAS) supports NAT. See *RRAS*.

NBF   An abbreviation for *NetBEUI Frame*, the transport packet structure used by NetBEUI.

NCBS   An abbreviation for *Network Control Block Session*, a NetBIOS connection using the NetBEUI Frame protocol. Clients issue an NCB CALL and the destination server returns an NCB LISTEN to establish the session.

NDIS   An acronym for Microsoft's *Network Driver Interface Specification* for writing device drivers for network interface cards (NICs) that work with Windows 3.x, Windows 9x, and Windows 2000.

NDS   The abbreviation for *NetWare Directory Services*, Novell's counterpart to Microsoft's Active Directory. NDS 5.0+ provides features similar to AD and has at least a two-year head start on AD.

NetBEUI   An acronym for *NetBIOS Extended User Interface*, the transport protocol of Microsoft Networking. NetBEUI isn't a routable network, so its popularity is declining in comparison with TCP/IP.

NetBIOS   An acronym for *Network Basic Input/Output System*, the original network API for MS-DOS and the foundation for NetBEUI.

NetWare Directory Services   See *NDS*.

Network Address Translation   See *NAT*.

NFS   An abbreviation for *Network File System*, a file format and set of drivers created by Sun Microsystems Incorporated that allows DOS/Windows and UNIX applications to share files on disk drives running under UNIX. NFS relies on remote procedure calls (RPCs) for communication between clients and servers.

NIC   An acronym for *network interface card*, a plug-in adapter card that provides the physical connection to the network. The most common NICs support 10BaseT network media; 100BaseT NICs, which are 10 times faster, are gaining acceptance in Windows 2000 networks.

NT   An abbreviation for *New Technology* used first by Windows NT and upgraded for Windows 2000. Windows NT is a registered trademark of Microsoft Corporation, so the full name of the operating system, *Windows NT*, is used in this book.

NTFS   An abbreviation for *New Technology File System*, Windows NT's and 2000's replacement for the DOS FAT (File Allocation Table) and OS/2's HPFS (High-Performance File System). Windows 2000's NTFS version 5.0 offers many advantages over other file systems, including improved security and the ability to reconstruct files in the event of hardware failures. Windows 3.1+ and Windows 9x can access files stored on NTFS volumes via a network connection but can't open NTFS files directly. See *basic disk* and *dynamic disk*.

NWLink   Microsoft's implementation of the Novell NetWare IPX/SPX protocol for Windows 2000 Server and Professional. See *IPX/SPX*.

object   In programming, an element that combines data (properties) and behavior (methods) in a single container of code. Objects inherit their properties and methods from the classes above them in the hierarchy and can modify the properties and methods to suit their own purposes.

object library   A file with the extension .olb that contains information on the objects, properties, and methods exposed by an .exe or .exe file of the same filename that supports COM or Automation.

object manager   A Windows 2000 executive component that manages operating system resources. In Windows 2000, all system resources are objects.

object permissions   Permissions granted by the network administrator for users to access shared Windows 2000 objects. Object permissions also may be granted to users through group membership.

octet   A synonym for an eight-bit byte.

ODBC   An abbreviation for the Microsoft *Open Database Connectivity* API, a set of functions that provide access to client-server RDBMSs, desktop database files, text files, and Excel worksheet files through ODBC drivers. Windows 2000 and Windows 9x use 32-bit ODBC drivers. ODBC most commonly is used to connect to client/server databases, such as Microsoft SQL Server.

OLE DB   A Microsoft specification for data providers and service providers for flat, relational, and tabular data. Windows 2000 installs several OLE DB providers, including providers for LDAP, WinNT, SQL Server, and Jet, data sources. See *ActiveX*, *ADO*, Jet, and *LDAP*.

organizational unit   See *OU*.

OSI   The abbreviation for *Open System Interconnection*, the model for standard levels of networking functions and the services performed at each level. The seven-level OSI standard is defined by the International Standards Organization (ISO).

OU   The LDAP abbreviation for *organizational unit*, a named container of users and other objects. OUs provide the mechanism for dividing Windows 2000 domains into logical administrative groups.

out-of-process   An (OLE) Automation server in the form of an executable (.exe) file that operates in its own process space (memory allocation) and uses LRPCs (lightweight remote procedure calls) to communicate with the Automation client. The term *OutOfProc* often is used as shorthand for out-of-process.

page   A block of contiguous virtual memory (VM) addresses that Windows 2000 moves between physical RAM and a disk (paging) file as needed to support network operations and applications. Paging is used when physical RAM can't store the required data. See *VM*.

page fault   An event that occurs when a thread refers to an invalid (out-of-date) VM page. The VM manager must refresh the page from the page file. See *VM*.

paged pool   System memory that can be paged to Windows 2000's Pagefile.sys paging file. The non-paged pool must reside in RAM and can't be paged to disk.

parameter   The equivalent of an argument but associated with the procedure that receives the value of an argument from the calling function. The terms *parameter* and *argument*, however, are often used interchangeably.

PDC   An abbreviation for *Primary Domain Controller*, the Windows NT server in a domain that's responsible for maintaining user and group accounts for a domain. Primary and Backup Domain Controllers authenticate domain users during the logon process. Windows 2000 replaces BDCs and PDCs with domain controllers (DCs). See *BDC*, *DC*, and *logon*.

PDC emulator   A Windows 2000 Domain Controller (DC) that substitutes for a Windows 4.0 Primary Domain Controller (PDC) in a Windows 2000 mixed-mode domain. The PDC emulator is responsible for updating Windows NT 4.0 Backup Domain Controllers (BDCs) with user and computer accounts and other changes that originate on Windows 2000 DCs. By default, the first DC you install in a forest is the PDC emulator. See *BDC*, *DC*, *forest*, and *PDC*.

permissions   Authority given by a system or network administrator to perform operations, usually over a network, on protected resources, such as folders or files.

persistent object   An object that's stored in the form of a file or an element of a file, rather than only in memory.

policy   In Windows 2000, a set of rules that govern the operations of networked clients and servers. Policies for computers running Windows 2000 are enforced by Group Policy Objects (GPOs), and Domain, Domain Controller, and Local Security Policies. See *GPO* and *Group Policy*.

port   A connection to an external hardware device, such as a modem (serial port) or a printer (parallel port). In Windows 2000, a communications channel object for local procedure calls. In TCP and UDP, an address assigned to a particular application, such as TCP port 80 for Hypertext Transfer Protocol (HTTP), the TCP/IP communication protocol of the World Wide Web. See *TCP/IP* and *UDP*.

PPP   An abbreviation for *Point-to-Point Protocol*, the most common Internet protocol for connection to TCP/IP networks via conventional and ISDN modems. See *SLIP*.

PPTP   An abbreviation for *Point-to-Point Tunneling Protocol*, a Microsoft-sponsored protocol, included with Windows 2000, that uses encryption to assure privacy of communication over the Internet. See *L2TP* and *VPN*.

preemptive multitasking   The multitasking process used by Windows 2000 and Windows 9x in which the operating system assures that all active threads have the opportunity to execute. Preemptive multitasking prevents a single thread from monopolizing a processor.

PRI   An abbreviation for *Primary Rate Interface*, an ISDN service for high-speed communication. PRI has 23 64kbps B (bearer) channels and one 64kbps D (data) channel, which may be used as independent channels or bonded to provide bandwidths higher than 64kbps. See *BRI* and *ISDN*.

properties dialog   A dialog used to set the value(s) of properties of an object, such as an ActiveX control or an operating system component. Choosing Properties from a context menu opens a properties dialog, sometimes called a properties sheet. The tabbed elements of a properties sheet are called *property pages*.

property   One of the two principal characteristics of objects (the other is methods). Properties define the manifestation of the object—for example, its appearance. Properties may be defined for an object or for the class of objects to which the particular object belongs, in which case they are said to be inheritable. Active Directory substitutes the term *attribute* for *property*. See *attribute*.

protected subsystem   A process that operates in a block of virtual memory that's not shared with other processes. Windows 2000's protected subsystems prevent an errant process from killing the entire operating system.

protocol   A description of the method by which networked computers communicate. Windows 2000 allows the simultaneous use of multiple network protocols, including TCP/IP, NetBEUI, and IPX/SPX.

protocol stack Network protocol software that implements a specific protocol, such as TCP/IP.

proxy server A server that isolates connections between two networks, such as a private intranet and the public Internet. The proxy server prevents unauthorized access via the Internet to a private intranet, usually by performing IP address and TCP port translation. Proxy servers often provide Web page caching (proxy cache) to speed delivery of frequently accessed Web content by storing it locally. See *firewall* and *NAT*.

quadlet A 32-bit unit of data (double word) treated as a unit. A quadlet contains four octets. See *octet*.

query A request for information about a set of objects. In LDAP terminology, an LDAP client transmits a protocol request that describes the desired operation on the LDAP server. A query can request information about an object (read) or modify the object's property values. The server processes the query and returns an asynchronous response to the client. LDAP requires each client request to receive a response from the server, but not necessarily in the order of the client's requests. See *LDAP*.

RAID An acronym for *redundant array of inexpensive disks*, a method of connecting multiple disk drives to a single controller card to achieve faster data throughput, data storage redundancy for fault tolerance, or both. See *disk mirroring*, *disk striping*, and *fault tolerance*.

raising exceptions A process by which the operating system transfers control to a block of software (exception handler) when an error or unexpected condition occurs. Windows 2000's exception handler adds items to the event log. See *exception*.

RAS The abbreviation for Remote Access Service, an element of Windows 2000's (and NT's) Routing and Remote Access Service (RRAS). RAS provides dial-in and dial-out services using the plain old telephone system (POTS) and ISDN lines. Windows 2000's RAS supports secure communication with L2TP over IPSec and PPTP virtual private networks (VPNs). See *IPSec*, *ISDN*, *L2TP*, *PPTP*, *RRAS*, and *VPN*.

Recordset An ActiveX Data Object (ADO) that defines a memory image of or pointer to tabular data, such as a database table or query result set. The MDAC OLE DB provider for LDAP enables a query written in SQL or the LDAP query dialect to return a read-only `Recordset`. Conventional ADO database code can manipulate the resulting `Recordset`. See *ADO*, *LDAP*, and *MDAC*.

redirector Software that intercepts requests for remotely provided services, such as files in server shares, and sends the requests to the appropriate computer on the network.

Registry A database that contains information required for the operation of Windows 2000 and Windows 9x, plus applications installed under Windows 2000 and Windows 9x. The Windows Registry takes the place of Windows 3.1+'s REG.DAT, WIN.INI, and SYSTEM.INI files, plus *PROFILE*.INI files installed by Windows 3.1 applications. The Registry also includes user information, such as user IDs, encrypted passwords, and permissions. Windows 2000 and Windows 9x include RegEdit.exe for editing the Registry. The Windows 2000 and Windows 9x Registries differ in structure, and thus are incompatible.

Remote Access Service   See *RAS*.

Remote Automation Object   An out-of-process (OLE) Automation server, usually called an RAO, that resides on a server and is accessible to RAO-compliant applications that connect to the server. RAOs comprise the middle tier of three-tier client/server database applications. See *business rules* and *three-tier*.

Remote Installation Service   See *RIS*.

remote procedure call (RPC)   An interprocess communication method that allows an application to run specific parts of the application on more than one computer in a distributed computing environment. Windows 2000's DCOM uses RPCs for network communication between COM objects.

reparse points   A feature of the Windows 2000 NTFS 5.0 file system's dynamic disks used primarily to support removable storage. A reparse point on a disk drive contains user-specified information that points to the actual location of the folder or file, which might be on a CD-ROM or tape storage. See *dynamic disk*.

replication   The process of duplicating server shares and database objects (usually tables) in more than one location, including a method of periodically rationalizing (synchronizing) updates to the objects. See *multimaster replication*.

resolver   A program that executes DNS queries against one or more DNS servers. Most queries seek the IP address for a domain name; *reverse lookup* returns the domain name for a specified IP address. The Windows TCP/IP implementation (called a *TCP/IP stack*) includes a DNS resolver utility. See *DNS*.

resource   A physical entity, such as a computer, printer, or user, or a logical entity, such as a Windows 2000 service, user policy, or file folder.

resource record   Host file records that are stored in the DNS database. Resource records map IP addresses to domain names and vice-versa. See *host* and *DNS*.

RFC   The official abbreviation for *Request for Comments*, the mechanism by which the Internet Engineering Task Force establishes Internet standards. See *IETF*.

RIS   An abbreviation for Windows 2000's *Remote Installation Service*, which provides automatic installation of Windows 2000 Professional on networked clients.

RISC   An acronym for *Reduced Instruction Set Computer*, a processor that uses a simplified set of internal operating instructions to speed execution. The only RISC processor currently supported by Windows 2000 is Compact's Alpha. See *CISC*.

router   An active network component that connects one network or subnet(work) to another network or subnet. Routers operate at the network layer of the OSI and work with packets that include logical addressing information. See *subnet*.

Routing and Remote Access Service   See *RRAS*.

RRAS   The abbreviation for *Routing and Remote Access Service*, a primary component of Windows 2000 Server. RRAS enables a Windows 2000 DC or member server to be used as dial-in remote access server, Virtual Private Network (VPN) server, Network Address Translation (NAT) server, or software router. See *RAS*.

SAM   An acronym for *Security Accounts Manager*, a Windows NT subsystem that maintains a database of user account names and passwords for authentication. Windows 2000 uses Active Directory to store user accounts and passwords.

scalable   The property of a multiprocessing computer that defines the extent to which the addition of more processors increases aggregate computing capability.

schema   The Active Directory (AD) object class that contains a full description of each AD object class, including a list of the object's properties (called *attributes*) and the location of the class in the AD hierarchy. The common term for a collection of descriptions of database objects, the schema, is *metadata*, data about data. The AD Schema is *extensible*; that is, you can define your own object classes and add the definitions to the Schema object. See *attribute*.

script   In 32-bit Windows operating systems, a sequence of programming instructions that are capable of being executed by the Windows Scripting Host (WSH) included with (or added to) Windows 9x, NT, and 2000. WSH supports Visual Basic Scripting Edition (VBScript or VBS), JavaScript (also called ECMAScript), Perl, and other common scripting languages. Scripting lets system administrators automate many routine administrative tasks, including manipulating Active Directory objects. Visual Basic Applications Edition (Visual Basic for Applications or VBA) is a programming, not a scripting language. See *Automation*, *VBS*, and *WSH*.

security boundary   A means of establishing different security policies, such as password length, uniqueness, and duration, for domain resources. Active Directory domains are security boundaries.

Security Groups   A Windows 2000 term for its three types of groups—Universal, Global, and Domain Local. Global and Domain Local groups correspond to Windows NT's global group. Members of Global groups can access shared objects within an entire domain tree; members of Domain Local groups are restricted to objects within a single domain. Global groups can contain Domain Local groups and, in a native-mode domain, can nest other Global groups. Members of Universal groups, which can contain Global and Domain Local groups, can have forest-wide permissions. Universal groups exist only in native-mode domains. See *global group* and *local group*.

server   A computer on a LAN that provides services or resources to client computers by sharing its resources. Servers may be dedicated, in which case they share their resources but don't use them themselves, except in performing administrative tasks. Servers in client/server databases are ordinarily dedicated to making database resources available to client computers. Servers may also be used to run applications for users, in which case the server is called an *application server*. Peer-to-peer or workgroup servers, such as servers created by using PCs running Windows 2000 Professional to share disk folders, are another class of server.

SFU   The abbreviation for Windows Services for UNIX, a suite of applications and tools for integrating Windows 2000 (and NT) with several UNIX flavors. SFU 2.0, which Microsoft released in May, 2000, includes a Client, Server, and Gateway for NFS (Network File System), which permits Windows 2000 clients to access UNIX file system objects, and vice-versa. Server for NIS (Network Information System) lets a Windows 2000 Domain Controller act as the primary NIS server for managing UNIX accounts within a NIS domain.

shared application memory   Memory that's allocated between processes involved in a lightweight remote procedure call (LRPC). See *LRPC*.

shortcut key   A key combination that provides access to a menu choice, macro, or other function of the application in lieu of selection with the mouse.

SID   An acronym for *security ID*, a numeric value that most commonly identifies a logged-on user who has been authenticated by Windows. A SID identifies the user within groups and in Access Control Entries (ACEs) by means of an access token. See *Access Control Entry*, *Access Control List*, and *access token*.

site   Groups of computers having high-speed (10Mbps or greater) network connectivity, usually within an IP subnet. Sites define replication boundaries and can include computers in one or more domains. A Windows 2000 site is analogous to an Exchange Server site. See *subnet*.

SLIP   An abbreviation for *Serial Line Interface Protocol*, the first common method of connecting via a modem to TCP/IP networks, now less widely used. See *PPP*.

SMB   An abbreviation for *Server Message Block*, a networking protocol used by NetBEUI to implement Microsoft Networking.

SMP   An abbreviation for *symmetric multiprocessing*, implemented in Windows, which distributes tasks among CPUs using a load-sharing methodology. Applications must be multi-threaded to take advantage of SMP. See *asymmetric multiprocessing*.

snap-in   An individual management tool that is or can be added to a Microsoft Management Console (MMC) console tree. Dsa.mmc is the name of the Active Directory Users and Computers administrative tool. See *MMC*.

SNMP   An abbreviation for *Simple Network Management Protocol*, an Internet standard that defines methods for remotely managing active network components such as hubs, routers, and bridges.

SNTP   An abbreviation for *Simple Network Time Protocol*, an Internet standard that defines methods for synchronizing the system time on Windows 2000 domain controllers with a time reference, such as the U.S. Naval Observatory.

socket   A bidirectional connection between computers running TCP/IP applications. Windows 2000 uses the Windows Sockets (Winsock) API. See *Winsock*.

stack   See *protocol stack*.

standalone server   A Windows 2000 server that's not a member of a Windows 2000 or NT domain. See *member server*.

STP   The abbreviation for shielded twisted pair, a type of telephone cable that consists of multiple pairs of copper conductors twisted around one another and wrapped with a sheath of metal foil or fine copper wires. Category 5 cables for 10/100BaseT network connections use STP. See *UTP*.

straight-through (cable)   A standard 10/100BaseT cable with the transmit and receive conductors connected to the same pins on each RJ-45 connector. Straight-through cables typically connect network interface cards (NICs) to hubs and switches. See *crossover*, *hub*, and *switch*.

stripe set   See *disk striping* and *fault tolerance*.

subnet   A collection of contiguous IP addresses that, together with a subnet mask, define an isolated group of hosts. Routers interconnect subnets. See *host*, *IP address*, and *router*.

subnet mask   A local bit mask (set of flags) that specifies which bits of the IP address specify a particular IP network or a host within a subnetwork. An IP address of `128.66.12.1` with a subnet mask of `255.255.255.0` specifies host 1 (usually a router) on subnet `128.66.12.0`. The subnet mask determines the maximum number of hosts on a subnet.

switch   An alternative to a hub for connecting multiple hosts (clients, servers, routers, and the like) to a network. Hubs share network bandwidth (nominally 10Mbps or 100Mpbs) between all connected hosts. A switch creates independent connections for traffic between hosts, greatly increasing the bandwidth available to each host. Switches, which are somewhat more costly than hubs, are rapidly replacing hubs in networks with more than three or four hosts. See *hub* and *host*.

synchronous I/O   An input/output method in which the process that issues an I/O request waits for the requested process to complete before returning control to the application or operating system. See *asynchronous I/O*.

System Access Control List (SACL)   Part of Windows 2000's security system that contains Access Control Entries (ACEs) to specify which security-related events, such as failed user logons, are audited. Audit events appear in Event Viewer's Security list. See *Access Control Entry* and *Access Control List*.

system administrator   The individual(s) responsible for the administrative functions for all applications on a LAN or users of a UNIX cluster or network, usually including supervision of all databases on servers attached to the LAN. If the system administrator's (SA's) responsibility is limited to databases, the term *database administrator* (DBA) is ordinarily assigned.

system databases   Databases that control access to databases on a server or across a LAN. Microsoft SQL Server has three system databases: the master database, which controls user databases; tempdb, which holds temporary tables; and model, which is used as the skeleton to create new user databases. Any database that's not a user database is a system database.

T-1   The most common moderate-speed telecommunications connection between LANs to create a WAN. Dedicated T-1 lines provide 1.544Mbps of bandwidth. T-1 lines also are the most common method of connecting servers to the Internet.

table   A database object consisting of a collection of rows (records) divided into columns (fields) that contain data or null values. A table is treated as a database object.

TCP/IP   Abbreviation for *Transport Control Protocol/Internetwork Protocol*, the networking protocol of the Internet, UNIX networks, and the preferred protocol for Windows 2000 networks. TCP/IP is a routable network that supports subnetworks. See *IP*.

TDI   An abbreviation for *Transport Driver Interface*, used by Windows 2000 to implement multiple network protocols by using various network interface cards.

TFTP   An abbreviation for *Trivial File Transfer Protocol*, used by Windows 2000 to implement its Remote Installation Service (RIS). See *RIS*.

thread   A part of a process, such as an executing application, that can run as an object or an entity. Threads of execution are the basis of Windows 2000's symmetrical multiprocessing capability. See *multiprocessing* and *SMP*.

three-tier   An application architecture that separates the presentation service layer (user interface) from the data service layer (usually a client/server database, such as Microsoft SQL Server) with an intervening layer, usually a COM, COM+, or Automation component for Windows applications, to enforce business rules and transfer data between the presentation and data service layers. See *Automation*, *COM*, *COM+*, and *middle tier*.

time stamp   The date and time data attributes applied to a disk file when created or edited.

toggle   A property of an object, such as a check box, that alternates its state when clicked with the mouse or activated by a shortcut key combination.

Token Ring   A network medium developed by IBM in which each computer in the ring passes a token, which carries network messages, to the adjacent computer. Token Ring provides each computer on the ring with guaranteed capability to transmit at regular intervals; Ethernet doesn't provide such a guarantee. Token Ring is specified by the IEEE-802.5 standard. See *Ethernet*.

transaction   A group of processing steps that are treated as a single activity to perform a desired result. A transaction might entail all the steps necessary to modify the values in or add records to each table involved when a new invoice is created. RDBMSs that are capable of transaction processing usually include the capability to cancel the transaction by a `ROLLBACK` instruction or to cause it to become a permanent part of the tables with the `COMMIT` or `COMMIT TRANSACTION` statement. See *MTS*.

trap   Windows 2000's method of intercepting an event (such as an interrupt request or an unexpected result) that occurs during execution of a thread.

tree   A set of domains sharing a contiguous Domain Name System (DNS) namespace. For example, `oakleaf.edu`, `faculty.oakleaf.edu`, and `students.oakleaf.edu` domains have contiguous DNS namespaces, so these domains are members of a single domain tree. See *DNS* and *forest*.

trust   In Windows 2000 domain terminology, a relationship between domain controllers in which users who are members of the trusted domain can access services on another trusting domain without the need to log on to the trusting domain.

UDP   The IETF abbreviation for *User Datagram Protocol*, a simplified version of TCP that doesn't confirm packet receipt or retransmit missing packets, so UDP is classified as an *unreliable protocol*. Windows Media, RealAudio, RealVideo, and all other popular Internet-based streaming media formats commonly use UDP for delivery. See *TCP/IP*.

UNC   An abbreviation for *Unified Naming Convention*, the method of identifying the location of files on a remote server. UNC names begin with \\. Windows 2000 and Windows 9x support UNC.

unicast   The conventional IP mode, which specifies that packets flow from one host (a server) to a single specified host (the client). Unicasting is the most common mode for communication over the Internet. See *host* and *multicast*.

Unicode   A replacement for the 7-bit or 8-bit ASCII and ANSI representations of characters with a 16-bit model that allows a wider variety of characters to be used. Unicode is especially useful for representing the written characters of Asian languages. Windows 2000 and Windows 98 support Unicode.

Universal group   See Security Groups.

UNIX   Registered trademark of a multiuser operating system, now administered by the Open Systems Foundation (OSF). Extensions and modifications of UNIX include Linux, DEC Ultrix, SCO UNIX, IBM AIX, and similar products.

UPS   An abbreviation for *uninterruptible power supply*, a device used to power a computer in the event of a primary power outage.

User Datagram Protocol   See *UDP*.

user mode   The processor mode used by Windows 2000 to run applications launched by users. Threads running in user mode are restricted to calling system services. See *kernel mode*.

UTP   An abbreviation for *unshielded twisted pair*, the type of cabling originally used to implement 10BaseT network media. Shielded twisted pair (STP) now is used for both 10BaseT and 100BaseT connections. See *STP*.

VBS   The abbreviation for Visual Basic Scripting Edition (also called VBScript), one of the scripting languages supported by the Windows Scripting Host (WSH). See *script*.

VDM   Abbreviation for *virtual DOS machine*, a Windows 2000 protected subsystem for running DOS applications in a console window.

virtual address space   The range of unique virtual memory addresses allocated to the threads of a single Windows 2000 process. See *VM*.

VM   Abbreviation for *virtual memory*, a method of mapping a combination of RAM and images of RAM stored in a paging file to provide an address space larger than that available from the RAM installed in the computer.

VM manager   The Windows 2000 executive service that loads memory images stored in a paging file on demand, as well as saves memory images in the paging file when no longer needed by a thread.

volume mount points   A feature of the Windows 2000 NTFS 5.0 file system's dynamic disks that permits an entire disk volume (similar to a basic disk's partition) to be accessed as (mounted to) a folder, rather than as a drive specified by a logical drive letter. See *dynamic disk*.

VPN   An abbreviation for *Virtual Private Network*, a means of establishing secure communication channels on the Internet using various forms of encryption. See *L2TP* and *PPTP*.

WAN   An acronym for *wide area network*. A WAN is a system for connecting multiple computers in different geographical locations by switched telephone network or leased data lines; by optical or other long-distance cabling; or by infrared, radio, or satellite links. See *LAN*.

WDM   An abbreviation of *Windows Driver Model*, a 32-bit architecture for creating device drivers that run under both Windows 2000 and Windows 98.

Win32   An API for running 32-bit Windows applications under Windows 2000 and Windows 9x. The Win32 APIs of Windows 2000 and Windows 9x vary.

Win32S   A subset of the Win32 API designed to add limited 32-bit capabilities to Windows 3.1+. Very few applications have been written to the Win32S API, which appears to have become obsolete.

Windows DNA   The abbreviation for *Windows Distributed interNet Applications (Architecture)*, which defines the integration of Web and client/server application development models with COM and COM+ components. Windows DNA is the implementation element of Windows DNS. See *COM*, *COM+*, and *DNS (Windows)*.

Windows Scripting Host   See *WSH*.

WINS   An acronym for *Windows Internet Naming Service*, a proprietary Microsoft application that maps easily remembered Windows machine names to the corresponding IP addresses.

Winsock   An abbreviation for *Windows Sockets*, a networking API for implementing Windows applications that use TCP/IP, such as FTP and Telnet. See *socket*.

working set   The set of active virtual memory pages for a process stored in RAM at a given instant.

workstation   A client computer on a LAN or WAN that is used to run applications and is connected to a server from which it obtains data shared with other computers. *Workstation* is also used to describe a high-priced PC that uses a high-performance microprocessor and proprietary architecture to create what some call an "open" system. In Windows parlance, a workstation is a computer running Windows NT Workstation or Windows 2000 Professional.

WOSA   Acronym for *Windows Open Services Architecture*, which was the original foundation for such APIs as ODBC, MAPI, and TAPI. Microsoft also developed special vertical-market WOSA APIs for banking, financial, and other industries in the mid- to late-1990s. Microsoft now is in the process of replacing the WOSA APIs with Internet-capable or COM versions under the umbrella of Windows Distributed interNet Applications Architecture (Windows DNA) and Next Generation Windows Services (NGWS). For example, OLE DB is the COM-based replacement for the Open Database Connectivity (ODBC) API. See *OLE DB*.

WOW   An acronym for *Windows on Win32*, a subsystem of Windows NT and Windows 2000 that allows 16-bit Windows applications to run in protected memory spaces called *virtual DOS machines*. See *VDM*.

WSH   The abbreviation for *Windows Scripting Host*, a 32-bit Microsoft scripting engine that's included with or added (by Internet Explorer) to Windows 9x, Windows NT, and Windows 2000. WHS is capable of hosting several common scripting languages. The most common Windows 2000 application for WSH, which comes in command-line (Cscript.exe) and Windows (Wscript.exe) versions, is automating server administrative tasks. See *script*.

X.500   An International Telecommunications Union (ITU) standard for directories, which is based on the International Standards Organization (ISO) Open Standards Interconnection (OSI) networking model. ITU-T Rec(ommendation) X.500, "The Directory: Overview of Concepts, Models, and Service," 1993, is the official reference to the X.500 standard in Internet Engineering Task Force (IETF) documents. X.500 has a complex structure that's not well adapted to the Internet and consumes an excessive amount of computer resources for PC-based directory operations. See *IETF* and *LDAP*.

zone   An administrative subdivision of a DNS domain. See *DNS*.

zone file   A collection of resource records for the DNS zones for which the server is authoritative. Only one DNS server, plus a designated alternate in some cases, is authoritative for a domain. Changes to resource records of the authoritative DNS server ultimately propagate through the DNS server hierarchy to secondary DNS servers that hold a copy of the primary server's information. Secondary servers provide DNS lookup load sharing. See *DNS* and *zone*.

INDEX

Symbols

70-215 exam (MCSE), 334, 1072, 1103, 1226
70-215 exam (MCSE), 720, 855, 917
70-216 exam (MCSE), 91, 335, 615, 1072, 1103
70-217 exam (MCSE), 91, 335, 544, 855, 888
70-219 exam (MCSE), 335
70-220 exam (MCSE), 336, 888, 1073, 1103
70-221 exam (MCSE), 336, 616
70-222 exam (MCSE), 337

A

Access Control Entry. *See* ACE
Access Control List. *See* ACL
Access Permissions dialog, 1117
accessing Macintosh
 permissions, 810
 remotely, 815
accounting RAS servers, 1045-1047
accounts
 administrative, exempting, 651
 ADSI25, 1269-1275, 1283
 client computers, creating, 762-763
 clients, properties, 876
 computer
  creating, 764-765
  migrating, 248-253
 domain users, 208
  local groups, 876
 Macintosh, 807-813
 migrating, 211-220, 399
 newsgroups, 1131-1132
 Security Groups, adding, 648-649
 updating, 253-254
 users, 654
  applying System Policies, 665-668
  GPOs, 655, 657
ACE (Access Control Entry), 426
acknowledgement numbers, 88
ACL (Access Control List), 479
activating
 COM+ applications, 1157
 DHCP scopes, 597-599
Active Directory, promoting PDC, 363-366
Active Directory Computers and Users tool (OUs), 132
Active Directory Domains and Trusts snap-in, 34, 106, 170
Active Directory Installation Wizard, 98, 100-105, 163, 206, 231, 364, 378, 388-389
 troubleshooting, 190
 upgrading Windows NT, 359
Active Directory Installation Wizard Summary dialog, 103
Active Directory Migration Tool (ADMT), 535
 wizards, 32
Active Directory Migration Tool node, 399
Active Directory Migration Tool. *See* ADMT
Active Directory Object Type dialog, 227
Active Directory Schema Manager snap-in, 36
Active Directory Service Interface. *See* ASDI
Active Directory Services Interfaces. *See* ASDI
Active Directory Sites and Services snap-in, 35, 113, 178
 nodes, 113-114
Active Directory Upgrade Wizard, 394
Active Directory Users and Computers snap-in, 33, 133, 173-174, 540, 648
 Query feature, 136-137
Active Directory. *See* AD
Active Migration Tool, 31
Active Server Pages. *See* ASP
active/active clusters, 1228
 active/passive clusters, 1228
ActiveX, 1145
AD (Active Directory), 23, 94-95, 539
 administering, 109-111
 administrating, 33
  snap-ins, 33
 ADSI25 application, 1255-1264
 ASDI, 96
 attributes, 95
 child domains, adding, 160-166, 172
 class properties, viewing, 128
 clients, confirming connections, 211
 computers, 115-120
 configuring, 104
  on upgraded servers, 206-211
 contact objects, 152
 containers, 95
  computer accounts, 210
  domain user accounts, 208
  groups, 210
 database, specifying location, 101
 DDNS, 83

AD (Active Directory)

directories, 95
  integrating, 153-154
directory databases, 95
distributed directory, 96
distribution group, 152
domains, 99
  child, 158, 181-184
  OakLeaf University topology example, 155
  OUs, 157
  parent-child model, 158
  planning, 148-149
  single, 155-158
downlevel, 96
email, integrating, 151-152
enterprise-scale, 187
ESE, 95
establishing non-transitive trusts, 107-111
forests, 24-25
FRS, viewing entries, 718
FSMOs
  Domain naming master, 150
  infrastructure master, 150
  PDC emulator, 150
  relative ID, 150
  Schema master, 150
functional, 621
GC (global catalog), 95
  testing traffic, 1003-1004
geographic, 621
GPOs, linking, 638-640
Group Policies, 623-624
groups, 115-120
  adding, 118-120
hardware requirements, 984
installing, 96-97, 164, 166, 172
  Active Directory Installation Wizard, 98, 100-101, 103-105
  NetBIOS, 100
  troubleshooting, 190
migration tool, 30, 231
Migration tool. See ADMT
namespaces, 105
  viewing, 126
Network Monitor, 997-999
objects, 95
  assigning values, 129
  searching for, 135
OUs, 95
  creating, 132
pre-creating computer accounts, 763
printers, troubleshooting, 755
query feature, 136-137
removing, 97
replicating intersite, 984-986
replication, 96
Replication Monitor, 1011-1014
Replication Monitor Support tool, 1011
restoring files, 975
Schema, 23, 95
Schema Manager, 124-125, 128
services
  configuring, 992-997
  viewing, 113
shared printers, 745-746
Shared System Volume (Sysvol), 97
shares, publishing, 701-703
single-tree directories, designing, 154
sites, 96
  configuring, 992-997
  connecting, 996-997
  viewing, 113
size, 153
structures, 621
synchronous operations, 986
transitive trusts, 106
trees, 24-25
trusts, 105
upgrading, 30
  verifying, 208, 367-368
users, 115-118, 120
  adding, 118, 120
  Security Groups, 648
Users and Computers tool, 212-220

AdapterName Properties dialog, 770, CD7
adapters, networks, 767, 769-770
  changing, 774
Add a File or Folder dialog, 626-628
Add a Group Policy Object Link dialog, 639-640
Add asf File dialog, CD69
Add Computer dialog, 668, 670
Add Counters dialog, 893
Add DNS Server dialog, 276
Add Exclusion dialog, 601
Add Exclusions dialog, 592
Add Host dialog, 575
Add in the Groups dialog, 1039
Add Mirror dialog, 439
Add Monitored Server Wizard, 1011-1014
Add Network Protocol dialog, 816
Add New Drive Letter or Path dialog, 428
Add New Quota Entry dialog, 846
Add New Replica dialog, 717
Add or Remove Managed Disks dialog, 1237
Add Port dialog, 729
Add Printer Wizard, 728-730, 735, 747, 783, 801
Add RAS Device dialog, 1093
Add Recovery Agent Wizard, 503
Add Server To Monitor dialog, 1012
Add Standalone Snap-in dialog, 513
Add Standard Port Wizard, 729
Add Static Mappings dialog, 273
Add Student Users button, 1001, 1003
Add Trusted Domain dialog, 390
Add Users dialog, 665
Add Users, Contacts, Computers, or Groups dialog, 648
Add WINS Server dialog, 274
Add/Remove Snap-in dialog, 513
adding
  accounts, ADSI25 application, 1269-1275
  backup DHCP server, 271-272
  baseline traffic, 897-898
  BDCs to domains, 382
  child domains (AD), 160-166, 172
  clients, Windows 98, 1089
  counters to SysMon, 892-893
  DCs, 380
    remote sites, 380-381
  fixed DNS and WINS addresses to servers, 282-283

ANALYZING   1319

groups, 118
   to AD, 118, 120
   to child domains, 173
   to roles, 1154, 1156
network printers, 783-784
newsgroups to NNTP servers, 1128-1132
on-demand publishing points, CD35-CD36
OUs to child domains, 173
programs, DC, 361-362
roles, 1156
secondary DNS server, 281
secondary zones (DNS), 381
Security Group accounts, 648-649
TCP/IP to NetBEUI servers, 263
Terminal Services connections, 1206, 1210
tools to DC, 361-362
users
   to AD, 118, 120
   Add-Users test, 1001, 1003
   ADSI25, 1279-1283
   to child domains, 173
   GPOs, 655, 657
   groups, 292
VPN phonebook entries, 1093
Windows 9x clients, 780, 782-784

Additional Drivers dialog, 736

Address Database dialog, 999

Address Information dialog, 912

Address Resolution Protocol. *See* **ARP**

addresses (IP), 64
allocating, 66
assigning, 64
changing, 71-72
notation, 65
restricting, 65-66
unicasting, 65

administering AD
domains, 105, 188
Windows NT domains from Windows 2000, 111, 115-118, 120

administrating
AD, 33
   snap-ins, 33
child domains, 172
domains from child DCs, 172
media devices, Physical Location folder, 445-446
OU, 223-229
sites, 985-986

Administrative Templates (Group Policies), 629-630
properties, 629-630

Administrator (Windows Media), CD19-CD20
installing, CD19-CD20

Administrator Credentials dialog, 394

administrators
account, exempting, 651
delegating (GPOs), 653
exempting from GPOs, 650-652

ADMT (Active Directory Migration Tool), 232, 535, 625
features, 255
installing, 233-234, 236
prerequisites, 232
restructuring domains, 398-400
Service Account Migration Wizard, 253
summary reports, 246-247
troubleshooting migrating users, 257

ADSI (Active Directory Service Interfaces), 140, 707
25 program, window, 142
programming directory-enabled applications, 140
VBA, 141

ADSI25 application, 1255-1256, 1258-1264
creating shares, 683-685
data source, 1257-1258
Departments table, 1257
employee accounts, 1269-1274
Employees table, 1257
FacultyTitles, 1257
features, 1256
installing PDC, 200-211
LDAP, 1278
migrating accounts, 213
prerequisites, 1258-1264
removing, 1285
running, 1265-1275
Server Manager, 1277
setup program, 1262-1264
StaffFunctions table, 1257
startup, troubleshooting, 1286
student accounts, 1274-1275
Students table, 1257
test shares, 1258
testing AD traffic, 1000-1001
troubleshooting setup, 256
user license, 1285
users, students, 1279-1283
Windows NT, 1275-1278

ADSI25 Options dialog, 1001

ADSI25 Setup Wizard, 1263

ADSI25 Setup Wizard dialog, 1263

ADSP (AppleTalk Data Stream Protocol), 794

Advanced Attributes dialog, 429, 492, 949

Advanced Server, 21
specifications, 22

Advanced Streaming Format dialog, CD46

Advanced Streaming Format properties dialog, CD72

Advanced TCP/IP Settings dialog, 387, 498, 772

advantages, domain restructuring, 349

AFP (AppleTalk File Protocol), 794

AlertName Properties dialog, 908

alerts, 905-907
PerfMon, 891
remote servers, 905-907
setting on counter logs, 908, 910
asymmetric key, 487
symmetric key, 486

AliasName Properties dialog, 699

allocating IP addresses, 66

allocation unit. *See* **clusters**

Allow Shutdown from Authentication dialoges, 629

alt files, Registry, 461

altering
cluster size, 926
graphs, 894

alternate volumes, 708

Analysis Report dialog, 935

analyzing
disk caching, 938-939
Network Monitor replication capture files, 1005-1007

APP SERVERS

app servers, 676
three-tier application architecture, 1141-1143

AppCenter Server, 22
specifications, 22

AppleTalk, 792
accounts, 807-813
ELAP, 793
EtherTalk, 793
File Services, 803-807
installing, 796
interoperability, 46
LAP, 793
LocalTalk, 792
nodes, 797
non-routed, 795
numbering, 794-795
print services, 799-803
protocol, 793-794
routers, seed, 797
routing, 795
configuring, 796-803
TokenTalk, 793
troubleshooting, 823
zones, 794-795

AppleTalk Data Stream Protocol. *See* **ADSP**

AppleTalk File Protocol. *See* **AFP**

Application Export Information dialog, 1178

Application Installation Service, 846-847
Group Policy Editor, 848-849
setting up, 848-851
testing software, 851-852
troubleshooting, 854

Application Installer Service, 847-848

application pools, creating, 444

Application Resource Name and Description dialog, 1242

Application Resource Type dialog, 1241

Application Server mode (Terminal Services), 1200-1201

applications, 56
ADSI25, 1255-1264
Backup, 965-969
cluster-aware, 1239
directory-enabled, programming (ADSI), 140
inspecting properties, 1162-1165

installing
cluster environments, 1238-1239
COM+, 1156-1161
remote workstations, 1166-1168
NetTraffic, 897-898, 916
samples (MTS), testing, 1158-1159
Terminal Services, 1204

applying
frame filters, 1008-1010
Group Policies (IntelliMirror), 830-831
LDAP filters, 138
Security Settings templates (GPOs), 636-637

approving CA certificate requests (MMC snap-in), 510-511

architecture
EFS, 491
three-tier, 1141-1143
data services, 1141

architectures, domain, 24-25

archive bit, 948-949

ARP (Address Resolution Protocol), 605
IP addresses, matching, 76

ASDI (Active Directory Service Interface), 96
AD, 96

asf files, CD59
encoding from avi, CD62, CD64
publishing, ODP, CD65
WMT ASF indexer, CD51-CD54

ASF redirector, CD5

ASP (Active Server Pages), 1145

ASR, 920

assessing network requirements, 758

assigning
hierarchical folder permissions, 686-688
hierarchical share permissions, 686-688
Internet domain names, 81
IP addresses, 64, 586
DHCP, 587-588
RAS server, 1036
OUs, 157

resources (clusters), 1245-1247
URLs to Web sites, 1118-1119

associating domain names with IP addresses, 79

asx files, CD5
linking to wax files, CD66-CD67
multicasting, CD75
writing, CD65-CD67

asymmetric key algorithms, 487

Asynchronous Transfer Mode. *See* **ATM**

ATM (Asynchronous Transfer Mode), 43, 988

attribute names, Three UserName Properties dialog pages, 131

AttributeName dialog, 655

attributes (AD), 95

audio
broadcasting, CD3
illustrated, CD5
illustrated files, CD55-CD58
streaming, 53, CD2-CD3
EMMS, CD2
encoding, CD46-CD48
programs, CD5
software, CD12-CD15
stations, CD5
wma files, CD5
WMT, CD2, CD15, CD17
troubleshooting quality, CD86

Audio codec (WMT), CD47-CD48
installing, CD47-CD48

authenticating RAS servers, 1037-1038, 1045-1047

authentication (File Services), Macintosh, 805-807

authentication (LDAP), 124

Authentication Methods dialog, 1112, 1129

authentication query, 1045

authorizing computer account creation, 764-765

Automatic Logon dialog, 1222

automatic rebuild, 437

automating
backup operations, 976-977
TCP/IP settings with DHCP, 267-270

automation, 1145
Available AppleTalk Printing Devices dialog, 800
avi files, CD59-CD61
    encoding to asf, CD62, CD64

B

backbones (networks), 43
backing up
    BDC, 379-380
    PDC, 345
    Registry, 476
Backup and Recovery Tools, 48
Backup application, 965-969
    Registry, 476
Backup Database command (Mappings menu), 273
Backup Directory dialog, 273
Backup Domain Controllers. See BDCs
Backup Operators group, 680
Backup Progress dialog, 969
backup routines
    archive bit, 948-949
    automating, 976-977
    choosing, 954-956
    copy, 950
    daily copy, 953
    differential, 952
    ensuring integrity, 957-958
    full, 949
        running, 965-969
    incremental, 951
    normal, 949
    organizing tape rotation methods, 959-964
    planning, 959
    remote servers, 970
    restoring from, 971, 973-975
    System State, 953
    System Volume Information, 954
    troubleshooting, 978
backup servers, adding DHCP, 271-272
Backup Wizard, 965
backups, servers, 300-302
balancing drive workload, 936
bandwidth, CD6-CD8
    cable modems, CD7-CD8
    DSL, CD7-CD8
    latency, CD6
    limiting, CD34
    streaming media, CD6
        intranets, CD10
BDCs (Backup Domain Controllers), 645-647
    adding to domains, 382
    backup services, 379-380
    testing, 376-380
    upgrading, 266-267, 376, 379-380
        to DC, 377-378
        to PDC, 198-200
    upgrading domains, 346
BINL (Boot Information Negotiation Layer), 860
BIOS
    Boot Load Order, 860
    administrators from GPOs, 650-652
    inheritance (Group Policy), 620
bonding components with COM, 1145-1146
boot disks, RIS, 872-878
Boot Information Negotiation Layer. See BINL
booting Registry, 468
BOOTP protocol, 587
breaking mirror volumes (RAID 1), 440
broadcasting, CD3
    multicasting, editing, CD44-CD46
    unicast, CD76-CD77
broadcasts (NetBIOS), 605
    encoding, CD75-CD77
    Internet, CD9
    multicast, CD36-CD39, CD41
    multicasting stations, CD42-CD46
    programs, CD38-CD39, CD41
    stations, CD42-CD46
    streaming, CD75-CD77
    troubleshooting connections, CD87
brokering objects, 1147
brokers, 1148
Browse for Printer dialog, 783
browsers, clients connecting to IIS, 1114-1115
browsing networks, 915
browstat status command-line tool, 915
built-in groups, 116
    placing, 116
bus, SCSI, 327
business services, 1142
buttons
    Edit Display Filter, 1008-1010
    Start Leaking, 941

C

CA (Certificate Authority), 488, 1097-1098, 1100
    Certificate Services, 508-509
    choosing type, 507
    CSP (cryptographic service provider), 507
    entering information, 508
    Enterprise, 489
    Enterprise Root, 1097-1098, 1100
    establishing, 506
    installing, 506
    Intermediate, 488
    Issuing, 488
    managing, 506
    MMC snap-in, 510
        revoking certificates, 512
        viewing information, 510-511
    options, 507
    root, 488
    Standalone, 489
    subordinate, 488
    troubleshooting, 516
cable modem connections
    bandwidth, CD7-CD8
    NAT, 1067, 1069-1070
cache, increasing memory (servers), 303-304
caching
    Automatic Caching for Documents, 837
    Automatic Caching for Programs, 837
    disks, 938-939
    Manual Caching for Documents, 836
Caching Settings dialog, 836
Capture Source dialog, CD77

capturing video content, On-Demand Producer, CD58-CD61
CATs (computer adaptive tests), 482
cells, Registry, 459-460
certificates (DRA), exporting, 504-505
Certification Authority dialog, 1098
   Certificate Authorities, 487
Certificate Authority Tape dialog, 508
Certificate Authority. *See* CA
Certificate dialog, 511
certificate enrollment, verifying, 1100
Certificate Export Wizard, 505, 1100
Certificate Friendly Name and Description dialog, 514
Certificate properties dialog, 1100
Certificate Revocation dialog, 512
Certificate Services, 489
   installing, 508-509
Certificate snap-in configuration dialog, 513
Certificate Template dialog, 514
certificates, 511-512. *See also* CA
   requesting, 513-514
   revoking, 512
Certificates snap-in, 513-514
Challenge Handshake Authentication Protocol. *See* CHAP
Change Drive Letter and Paths dialog, 427
change journals, NTFS, 426
Change Mode button, 397
Change Secret dialog, 1047
Change Zone Type dialog, 369
changing
   child domain attributes, 170
   cluster size, Format.exe, 927-928
   domain models, 187-188
   files, paging size, 942-943

IP addresses, 71-72
network adapters, 774
packages, 849, 851-852
Registry values, 457-459
CHAP (Challenge Handshake Authentication Protocol), 1024
chapter 1 MCSE corner, 60
chapter 2 MCSE corner, 91
chapter 3 MCSE corner, 144
chapter 4 MCSE corner, 191
chapter 5 MCSE corner, 257
chapter 6 MCSE corner, 295
chapter 7 MCSE corner, 334
chapter 8 MCSE corner, 410
chapter 9 MCSE corner, 452
chapter 10 MCSE corner, 482
chapter 11 MCSE corner, 516
chapter 12 MSCE corner, 544
chapter 13 MCSE corner, 581
chapter 14 MCSE corner, 615
chapter 15 MCSE corner, 673
chapter 16 MCSE corner, 720
chapter 17 MCSE corner, 756
chapter 18 MCSE corner, 789
chapter 19 MCSE corner, 825
chapter 20 MCSE corner, 855
chapter 21 MCSE corner, 888
chapter 22 MCSE corner, 917
chapter 24 MCSE corner, 1022
chapter 25 MCSE corner, 1072
chapter 26 MCSE corner, 1103
chapter 27 MCSE corner, 1136
chapter 28 MCSE corner, 1193
chapter 29 MCSE corner, 1226
chapter 30 MCSE corner, 1252
Check Server Wizard, 869
checking
   disks, Chkdsk, 450
   modem properties, 1027-1028
checklists, RIS, 860-862

Child Domain Installation dialog, 394
child domains
   adding (AD), 160-166, 172
   administrating, 172
      other domains, 172
   attributes, 170
   creating, 158
      Dcpromo, 161-166
      troubleshooting, 190
   DNS zones, setting up, 166-169
   failed promotion, 396
   groups, 173
   moving to new sites, 177-178, 181
   OUs, 173
   recovering, 396
   security, Domain Security Policy Console, 182-185
   security policies, 181-184
   users, 173
Chkdsk tool, 448-450
Choose User dialog, 661
choosing
   Active Directory Migration Tool wizards, 32
   backup routine, 954-956
   CA
      options, 507
      types, 507
   intersite communication, 987-988
   IP addresses, NetBEUI, 262-265
   NICs, 762
   RAID, servers, 325
cipher command, 494-495
ciphertext, 486-487
   CIW (Client Installation Wizard), 861, 873
   Group Policy, 881
   main menu, 881
CIW Login dialog, 880
Class A addresses (IP), 64
Class B addresses (IP), 64-68
Class C addresses (IP), 64-69
Class D addresses (IP), 64
Class E addresses (IP), 64
class properties (AD), viewing, 128
classifying
   RAID, 329
   SCSI, 326-327

COM+ (Component Object Model) 1323

className Properties dialog, 128

cleaning
  disks, Disk Cleanup tool, 450
  group accounts, 287
  user accounts, 287

clearing Event Viewer, 389-392

Client (Terminal Services), 1217-1223

Client Connection Manager, 1221

Client Connection Manager Wizard, 1221

Client Information dialog, 1047

client installation disks, 821-822

Client Installation Wizard. *See* CIW

Client option (IPSec), 498

clients
  accounts
    creating, 762-763
    properties, 876
  booting, troubleshooting, 887
  command-line FTP, 562
  confirming connections, 211
  connecting to IIS, 1114-1115
  DHCP, 587
    verifying settings, 780-783
  downlevel, specifying user profiles, 658-660
  DUN, 1048-1049
  eliminating NetBEUI reliance, 287
  GUID, 861
  installing TCP/IP, 284
  IP addresses, specifying fixed, 772, 774
  Macintosh, 803
    authentication, 806-807
    interacting with, 807-813
    monitoring, 814
    permissions, 810
  migrating
    to DHCP, 284-285
    to DNS, 284-285
    to WINS, 284-285
  networking, 765-766
  NFS, 572-573
  NICs, 761-762
  PPTP
    Windows 98, 1089
    Windows NT, 1092-1093
  preparing migration, 759-760
  remote, dial-in, 1025
  RIS
    network adapter, 860
    PXE boot ROM, 860
    requirements, 862-863
  shared printers, connecting, 742-744
  Telnet, 546
  UUID, 861
  VPN, 1088-1089
    testing, 1101
  WfW, 819
  Windows 98, 780-783
  Windows NT
    connecting, 775-777
    installing, 776-777
    network properties, 777-780
  X Window, 556

clients, Telnet, 550

Cluster Administrator, 1243
  nodes, 1248
  resource groups, 1244
  resources, 1245-1247

Cluster Administrator, virtual servers, 1239-1242

Cluster File Storage dialog, 1237

Cluster Name dialog, 1236

Cluster Service, installing, 1234
  checklist, 1234-1238

cluster-aware applications, 1239

clustering servers, 300-302

clusters, 1228-1229, 1231
  active/active, 1228
  active/passive, 1228
  altering size, 926
  applications
    cluster-aware, 1239
    installing, 1238-1239
    troubleshooting, 1251
  changing size, Format.exe, 927-928
  Cluster Administrator, 1243-1244
  determining size, PerfMon, 928-931
  fault-resilient availability, 1229
  fault-tolerant availability, 1229
  heartbeat connections, 1231-1232
  high availability, 1229
  installing troubleshooting, 1251
  LAN connections, 1233
  nodes, 1228, 1231, 1248
  NTFS, 424
  private network connections, 1231
  public network connections, 1231
  Quorum disks, 1232
  redundant components, 1229
  resource groups, 1244
    failbacks, 1249
    failover, 1249
  resources, 1231-1233
    assigning, 1245-1247
  sectors, 927
  server performance, 304
  servers, 1231
  shared-disk subsystems, 1231
  shared-everything model, 1232
  shared-nothing model, 1232
  virtual servers, 1238-1239
    shared folders, 1239-1242

Codecs (coder-decoders), CD5

COM Application Export Wizard, 1166-1168, 1178

COM Application Install Wizard, 1159-1162

COM Plus. *See* COM+

COM+ (Component Object Model), 307, 1148
  ActiveX, 1145
  applications, 1156-1161
    inspecting properties, 1162-1165
  ASP, 1145
  automation, 1145
  bonding components, 1145-1146
  brokering, 1147
  Component Services tool, 1151
  components
    inspecting properties, 1162-1165
    stateful, 1150
    stateless, 1150
  DCOM, 1145
  DTC, 1145
  features, 1145
  load balancing, 307
  MSMQ, 1146
  MTS, 1146-1147
  performance troubleshooting, 1193
  Plus, 1146

COM+ (COMPONENT OBJECT MODEL)

properties, 1157-1158
  queuing, 1157
  transaction, 1158
remote workstations,
  1166-1168
roles, 1156
Sample Bank application,
  1172-1178
sample packages, testing,
  1158-1159
security, 1154, 1156
  role-based, 1154-1156
  troubleshooting, 1192
transactions, 1147

**command-line, Telnet,
547-548**

command-line FTP clients, 562

**command-lines (UNIX), FTP,
561-562**

commands
cipher, 494-495
Console menu, Save As, 125
DNS menu
  New Server, 276, 281
  New Zone, 276
groups, 292
Mappings menu
  Backup Database, 273
  Static Mappings, 273
New menu, Resource, 1245
Registry menu, Import
  Registry File, 476
Scope menu, Create, 268
Server menu, Replication
  Partners, 274
Telnet, 550
Terminal Services Manager,
  1213-1214

**Common Configuration dialog,
602, 1030, 1080**

**common home folder shares,
670-672**

**Common Request Broker
Architecture.** *See* **CORBA**

common shares, 676-677

communicating
DHCP
  clients, 587
  servers, 587
frame relay, 988
intersite, 986-987
remote, 52
sites, choosing method,
  987-988
TCP/IP, 86

comparing
NetWare to Windows 2000,
  522
TCP/IP and IPX/SPX, 521
TSE with Terminal Services,
  1198-1199
upgrades and installations,
  760-761
  complete-trust model, 393

**completing software installs,
851-852**

**Completing the Computer
Migration Wizard dialog, 252**

**Completing the Network
Connection Wizard dialog,
1033**

**Completing the Reporting
Wizard dialog, 247**

Component Object Model. *See* **COM+**

**Component Services snap-in,
1150-1152**
launching, 1151

components, 1151
bonding with COM,
  1145-1146
COM+, 1157-1158
Queued, 56
RIS checklist, 860-862
Sample Bank application,
  1176-1177
stateful, 1150
stateless, 1150

**compressing files (NTFS),
428-429**

**Computer Account Migration
Wizard, 399**

computer accounts
AD, 210
containers, 763
creating
  clients, 762-763
  delegating authority,
    764-765
migrating, 248-253

computer adaptive tests. *See* **CATs**

**Computer Migration Wizard,
32, 248-253**

**Computer Name dialog, 199,
776**

**Computer Security Settings
(Group Policies), options,
626**

**Computer Selection dialog,
248**

**computer settings (Group
Policies), 618**
security, 619

**ComputerName Properties
dialog, 496**

computers
AD, 115-118, 120
inspecting Registries, 478
migrating, 399
System Policies, 668-670

**concurrency, COM+ applica-
tions, 1158**

**conditioning systems, servers,
308-311**

Conditions dialog, 1041

**configuration files, stations,
CD42-CD46**

**Configuration Manager
(Registry), 455-456, 462**

**Configuration snap-in
(Terminal Services),
1205-1206, 1210**

**Configure DHCP Option
dialog, 592**

Configure DNS dialog, 389

Configure Gateway dialog, 533

**Configure Your Server dialog,
97**

configuring
AD, 104
  sites, 992-997
AppleTalk routing, 796-803
Certificates snap-in, 513
clients, networking, 765-766
clusters, Cluster
  Administrator, 1243
DDNS, 83
Dfs, troubleshooting, 720
DHCP, 590-591
  options, 270
DUN clients
  downlevel, 1051-1052
hardware profiles, 471-472
IAS/RADIUS, 1045
Indexing Service, 704-705
IPSec, 498
L2TP servers, 1097-1100
mapping servers, UNIX,
  566-567
media devices, Physical
  Location folder, 445-446
modems, PPTP dial-up
  connections, 1083, 1085

NAT, 1058-1059
  with cable modem connections, 1067-1070
  with DSL connections, 1067-1070
Network Monitor, 997-999
NFS, UNIX, 569
NFS clients, 572-573
Offline Files, 837-839
PerfMon, 896
physical devices, 446
PPTP connections, 1085-1087
printers
  network-attached, 728-731
  server properties, 739-741
  server-connected, 732-734
  shared, 735-738
  workstation-owned, 732-734
RAS, 1029-1031, 1037-1038
resources (clusters), 1250
RIS, 866-868
  servers, 868-871
  for testing, 866
servers
  Disk Management snap-in, 418-424
  for encryption, 495
SMTP server, 1133-1134
Synchronization Manager, 841-844
Telnet, 553
  on Windows 2000, 554-555
Windows 98 clients, 780-783
WINS, 606-607

Configuring Active Directory dialog, 104

Configuring Components dialog, 865

Confirm Password dialog, 1116

confirming client connections, 211

Connect to Domain dialog, 638

connecting
  AppleTalk, printers, 799
  clients
    to IIS, 1114-1115
    NAT, 1058-1059
    to shared printers, 742-744
    Windows NT, 775-777
  Internet
    demand-dial, 1065
    NAT, 1059-1063
  IPX, troubleshooting, 542

Macintosh clients
  File Services, 803-807
  to printers, 803
multicast asx files, CD75
PPTP, 1085-1087
printers to networks, 783-784
replications, troubleshooting, 1021
sites
  DSL, 988
  manually, 996-997
  T-1 lines, 987
UNIX NFS servers, 575-576
Windows Media Administrator, CD19-CD20

Connection Availability dialog, 1033, 1083, 1086

Connection Description dialog, 550

Connection Type dialog, 1061, 1085

ConnectionName dialog, 1033, 1083

ConnectionName Properties dialog, 498, 796, 1035, 1095

ConnectionName Status dialog, 1034

connections
  heartbeat (clusters). *See* private network connection
  LAN, 1231
  private network, 1231
  public network, 1231
  Terminal Services, 1206, 1210, 1221
    modifying, 1206-1207, 1209
  VPN, 1085-1087

connectivity (IPs), testing, 266-267

Console menu, Save As command, 125

contact objects (AD), 152

contacts, 130

ContainerName Properties dialog, 640-641, 643

containers, 763
  AD, 95

contents rules, 123

control bits, 88

control channel, 1078

Control Panel
  Phone and Modem tool, 1027-1028
  Registry, 458

Control subkey (Registry), 470
  subkeys, 470

controlling temperature, server closets, 310-311

copy backups, 950

Copy Profile dialog, 471

Copy To dialog, 661

copying hardware profiles, 471

Copying Installation Files dialoges, 355

CORBA (Common Request Broker Architecture), 1145

corporate installation image, Remote Installation Preparation Wizard, 882-883, 886

corrupted Registry, 468

counter logs (PerfMon), 891
  recording traffic, 902-904
  setting alerts, 908, 910
  testing, 906-907
  troubleshooting, 917
  viewing data, 906-907

counters, adding to SysMon, 892-893

Counters dialog, 892-893

Create a Connection dialog, 1221

Create a New Dfs Link dialog, 713

Create a New Station dialog, CD37-CD39, CD41, CD68

Create a Tree or Child Domain dialog, 388

Create a Virtual Server dialog, 1240

Create an Empty Application dialog, 1159

Create Application Cluster Resource dialog, 1241

Create command (Scope menu), 268

Create Custom Filter option, 213

Create New Connection Wizard, 1206

Create New Data Source dialog, 1174

Create New Media Pool properties dialog, 444

Create New Object (User) dialog, 118

Create New Object dialog, 132
Create or Join a Cluster dialog, 1235
Create or Join Forest dialog, 99, 206, 364, 388
Create Scope dialog, 268
Create Shared Folder dialog, 808-809
Create Tree or Child dialog, 99
Create Tree or Child Domain dialog, 162, 364
Create Volume Wizard, 419, 437
creating
   application pool, 444
   boot disks (RIS), 872-878
   clients, computer accounts, 762-763
   computer accounts, delegating authority, 764-765
   containers, 763
   corporate installation image, 882-883, 886
   Dfs roots, 710-712
   DHCP scopes, 591-592
   domain forests, 26
   domain trees, 26
   domains, child, 158-166, 172
   fault-tolerant replica sets, 716-718
   file DSN, 1173-1178
   folders, shared, 683-685
   GC server, 381
   GPOs, 632-633
   illustrated audio files, CD55-CD58
   logon scripts, 694-697
   membership files (groups), 291
   mirror (RAID 1) volume, 439
   NTGATEWAY groups, 532-533
   OUs, domains, 132
   primary zones, 276-278
   RAID 5, 437-438
   resource groups, 1244
   scopes, 268
   second-tier shares, 688-691
   secondary DNS server, 281
   shares, ADSI25, 683-685
   sites, 177
   stations, CD37-CD39, CD41
      multicasting, CD68-CD73
   synchronization sessions, 536-539, 541
   third-tier shares, 691-693
   user profiles, 661-663
   virtual servers, 1240
   volume sharing (Macintosh), 808-813
   volumes
      simple, 419-421
      spanned, 422-423
   Windows 2000 boot disk, 441
Creating New Zone dialog, 281
CryptoAPI (Cryptography Application Programming Interface), 487
CSP (cryptographic service provider), 507
custom filters, migrating users, 212-220

D

DACL (Discretionary Access Control List), 426
daily copy backups, 953
DAP (Directory Access Protocol), 122
dat files, Registry, 461
data
   encrypting, 486-487, 497
   Registry value entries, 464-465
   sniffing, 497
   users
      managing (IntelliMirror), 835
      Data Decryption Field. *See* DDF
data offset, 88
Data Recovery Agent. *See* DRA
Data Recovery Field. *See* DRF
data services, 1141
data sources, ADSI25 application, 1257-1258
Data Storage Location dialog, 509
data streams
   forks, 428
   NTFS, 428
Database and Log Locations dialog, 207, 378, 388
Database Security dialog, 627

databases
   AD
      sizes, 153
      specifying location, 101
   directory, 95
   GC (global catalog), 95
   MQIS, 1183
DataCenter Server, 22
   specifications, 22
datagrams
   elements, 74
   IP, 73
   structures, 73
   testing ping program, 75
Date and Time Settings dialog, 386
DC (Domain Controllers), 496. *See also* domains; PDC
   adding
      programs, 361-362
      remote sites, 380-381
      tools, 361-362
   ADSI25 application, 1259
   BDC, upgrading from, 377-378
   creating GCs, 381
   FSMO roles, 408-409
   hardware, DC, 985
   installing, 388-389
   Native mode, 220-222
   Network Monitor, setting up, 997-999
   operations master, 150-151
   PDC, 367-372
   remote sites, 987
   removing, 380
      from domains, 383
   replicating between in AD, 984-986
   restoring, 975
   security, 400-403
      template files, 401-403
   synchronous operations, 986-987
   testing, 367-372
      second, 379
DCNAME dialog, 374
DCOM (Distributed COM), 1145
   properties, 1168-1170
DDF (Data Decryption Field), 490
DDNS (Dynamic DNS), 41
   configuring, 83
   managing, 85-86

DIALOGS

decimal values
  Class B addresses, 68
  subnet masks, 68
declarative programming, 1157-1158
decoding IP, 64
decrypting files, 490, 492
  with EFS, 501, 503-504
default connections, Terminal Services, 1223
Default Domain Options dialog, 639
Default FTP Site Properties dialog, 1126
default FTP sites, 1125, 1127
Default NNTP Virtual Server dialog, 1130
Default Printer dialog, 750
default shares, 676-677
defining IntelliMirror, 828
defragmenting
  disks, 448, 933-934
  files, 934-935
delegating
  authority for computer account creation, 764-765
  GPO administration, 653
  OU administration, 223-229
Delegation of Control Wizard, 223-229, 653, 764
deleting
  roles, 1156
  users, groups, 292
  volumes, 423-424
delivering UDP, 89
Demand Dial Interface Wizard, 1061-1062
demand-dial connections
  properties, 1065
  troubleshooting, 1071
Demand-Dial Connections dialog, 602
demand-dial modem connections, NAT, 1059-1063
departmental networks, 21
Dependencies dialog, 1246
Deploy Software dialog, 849
deploying
  multicast asx files, CD75
  packages, 850
  Terminal Services Client, 1219-1223

designating WINS replication partners, 610-611
designing
  intersite replication network, 991-992
  Security Groups, 643
    example, 645-647
  single-domain models, 156-158
  single-tree directories, 154
Desktop Properties dialog, 631
Destination Address dialog, 1085
determining cluster size (PerfMon), 926, 928-931
developing
  migration plan, 194-197
    Device Manager, 316-320
  servers, 321
  troubleshooting feature, 321
Dfs (Distributed File System), 50, 415, 676-677, 708
  configuring troubleshooting, 720
  downlevel volumes, 709
  fault-tolerant shares, 716-718
  fault-tolerant volumes, 709
  File Replication service, 716-718
  hierarchy, 709
  implementing, 51
  leaf folders, 708
  mid-level junctions, 708
  PKTs, 709
  post-junction junctions, 708
  referrals, 709
  root volumes, 708
    creating, 710-712
    populating, 712-715
  shares, testing, 715-716
DHCP, 586
  automating TCP/IP settings, 267-270
  backup server, adding, 271-272
  BOOTP protocol, 587
  clients, 587
    testing Internet connections, 1065
  configuring, 270, 590-591
  features, 588
  gateways, NAT, 1064
  Global menu, 269
  hardware requirements, 985
  installing, 589-590
  IP addresses, assigning, 587-588

migrating clients, 284-285
options, 269-270, 593
properties, 600-601
Relay Agent, 601
  installing, 602-603
scopes, 268, 591-592
  activating, 597-599
  options, 593-596
  testing, 597-599
servers, 587
snap-in, 590-591
testing, 375
troubleshooting, 293, 613
verifying, 285-286
verifying settings, 780-783
viewing statistics, 600-601
Windows NT upgrades, 359-360
DHCP Manager utility, 268
DHCP Options, Global dialog, 269
Dial Out Credentials dialog, 1062
dial-in remote clients, 1025
Dial-Up and Network Connections dialog, 1085
dial-up connections
  L2TP, 1101
  PPTP, 1082, 1085-1087
    testing, 1087
Dial-Up Networking, Macintosh, 815
Dial-Up Networking dialog, 1051, 1093
dialogs
  Access Permissions, 1117
  Active Directory Installation Wizard summary, 103
  Active Directory Object, 227
  AdapterName Properties, 770, CD7
  Add a File or Folder, 626-628
  Add a Group Policy Object Link, 639-640
  Add asf File, CD69
  Add Computer, 668, 670
  Add Counters, 893
  Add DNS Server, 276
  Add Exclusion, 601
  Add Exclusions, 592
  Add Host, 575
  Add in the Groups, 1039
  Add Mirror, 439
  Add Network Protocol, 816
  Add New Drive Letter or Path, 428

Add New Quota Entry, 846
Add New Replica, 717
Add or Remove Managed Disks, 1237
Add Port, 729
Add RAS Device, 1093
Add Server To Monitor, 1012
Add Standalone Snap-in, 513
Add Static Mappings, 273
Add Trusted Domain, 390
Add Users, 665
Add Users, Contacts, Computers, or Groups, 648
Add WINS Server, 274
Add/Remove Snap-in, 513
Additional Drivers, 736
Address Database, 999
Address Information, 912
Administrator Credentials, 394
ADSI25 Options, 1001
ADSI25 Setup Wizard, 1263
Advanced Attributes, 429, 492, 949
Advanced Streaming, CD46
Advanced Streaming Format properties, CD72
Advanced TCP/IP, 772
Advanced TCP/IP Settings, 387, 498
AlertName Properties, 908
AliasName Properties, 699
Allow Shutdown Authentication, 629
Analysis Report, 935
Application Export Information, 1178
Application Resource Name and Description, 1242
Application Resource Type, 1241
AttributeName, 655
Authentication Methods, 1129
Authentications, 1112
Automatic Logon, 1222
Available AppleTalk Printing Devices, 800
Backup Directory, 273
Backup Progress, 969
Browse for Printer, 783
Caching Settings, 836
Capture Source, CD77
Certificate, 511
Certificate Authority Tape, 508
Certificate Friendly Name and Description, 514
Certificate properties, 1100

Certificate Revocation, 512
Certificate snap-in, 513
Certificate Template, 514
Certification Authority, 1098
Change Drive Letter and Paths, 427
Change Secret, 1047
Change Zone Type, 369
Child Domain Installation, 394
Choose User, 661
CIW Login, 880
className Properties, 128
Client Information, 1047
Cluster File Storage, 1237
Cluster Name, 1236
Common Configuration, 602, 1030, 1080
Completing the Computer Migration Wizard, 252
Completing the Network Connection Wizard, 1033
Completing the Reporting Wizard, 247
Computer Name, 199, 776
Computer Selection, 248
ComputerName Properties, 496
Conditions, 1041
Configure DHCP Option, 592
Configure DNS, 389
Configure Gateway, 533
Configure Your Server, 97
Configuring Active Directory, 104
Configuring Components, 865
Confirm Password, 1116
Connect to Domain, 638
Connection Availability, 1033, 1083, 1086
Connection Description, 550
Connection Type, 1085
ConnectionName, 1033, 1083
ConnectionName Properties, 498, 796, 1035, 1095
ConnectionName Status, 1034
ContainerName Properties, 640-643
Copy Profile, 471
Copy To, 661
Copying Installation Files, 355
Counters, 892-893
Create a Connection, 1221
Create a New Dfs Link, 713
Create a New Station, CD37-CD39, CD41, CD68

Create a Tree or Child Domain, 388
Create a Virtual Server, 1240
Create and Empty Application, 1159
Create Application Cluster Resource, 1241
Create New Data Source, 1174
Create New Media Pool properties, 444
Create New Object, 132
Create New Object (User), 118
Create or Join, 1235
Create or Join Forest, 99, 206, 364, 388
Create Scope, 268
Create Shared Folder, 808-809
Create Tree of Child, 99
Create Tree or Child Domain, 162, 364
Creating New Zone, 281
Data Storage Location, 509
Database and Log Locations, 207, 364, 378, 388
Database Security, 627
DCNAME, 374
Default Domain Options, 639
Default FTP Site Properties, 1126
Default NNTP Virtual Server, 1130
Default Printer, 750
Demand-Dial Connections, 602
Dependencies, 1246
Deploy Software, 849
Desktop Properties, 631
Destination Address, 1085
DHCP Options, Global, 269
Dial Out Credentials, 1062
Dial-Up and Network Connections, 1085
Dial-Up Networking, 1051, 1093
Directory Services Restore Mode, 389
Directory Services Restore Mode Administrator Password, 164
Display an Existing Dfs Root, 714
Display Filter, 1008
Distributed COM Configuration Properties, 1168, 1170
Domain Controller Type, 98, 162, 388

DIALOGS

Domain Controllers, 996
Domain Name Properties, 185
Domain Properties, 623
Domain Selection, 238, 246-247, 253
DomainName, 752, 777
DomainName Properties, 171, 500, 632
Driver File Details, 318
Driver Properties, 741
DTC Properties, 1179
Edit Alias, 697-698
Edit Dial-In Profile, 1042-1043
Edit IP Filter, 1096
Encryption Warning, 493
Enter Credentials, 1011
Enter Subnet Mask, 1241
Export Private Key, 505
Export Registry File, 476
Extended Logging Properties, 1125
File Share Parameters, 1242
File System Verification, 323-324
FileName Properties, 810
FileOrFolderName, 682
Filter Options, 139
Find Custom Search, 213
Find Shared Folders, 702
Find Users, Contacts and Groups, 136
Folder Options, 473
Folder Selection, 246
FolderName Properties, 429, 492, 680
Format Volume, 421
Friendly Descriptions and Help Text, 867
Grant Access On, 1113
Group Options, 241
Group Policy Refresh Interval for Computers Properties, 629-630
Group Selection, 240
GroupOrUser properties, 682
Groups, 1040
Hardware Profiles, 471
Identification Changes, 777
Idle Settings, 842
Import or Install a Component, 1159
Import Policy From, 636
Inheritance Overrides, 1113
Initial Settings, 866
Initial Synchronization, 538
Input Filters, 1096
Input Source, CD77

Insert Media, CD57
Install Hardware Device, 318
Install Network Component Type, 387
Install New Components, 1160
Install or Configure DNS, 364
Install or Create a New Application, 1159
Installation Complete, 1263
Installation Disk Set, 821-822
Installation File Source Location, 867
Installation Files, 355
Installation Folder, 236
Installing Components, 387
InterfaceName properties, 1065
Internet Accounts, 1132
Internet Connection, 1060, 1062-1063, 1080
Internet Information Services, 1107
Internet News Email Address, 1131
Internet News Server Logon, 1132
Internet News Server Name, 1131
Internet Protocol (TCP/IP) Properties, 498
Invalid Name, 649
IP Address and Port Settings, 1120
IP Address Array Editor, 269
IP Address Assignment, 1031, 1081
IP Address Range, 591
IP Security, 498
Items to Synchronize, 841
Lease Duration, 592
License Agreement, 1218
Local Area Connection Properties, 771
Local or Network, 560
Local or Network Printer, 800
Locate Your Printer, 750
Location and Comment, 801
LogName Properties, 902
Logon Properties, 696
Managing Conflicts During Migration, 579
Managing Multiple Remote Access Servers, 1031
Map Network Drive, 839-840
Markers, CD53
Master Properties, 1123
Message Queuing Type, 1184

Microsoft TCP/IP Connectivity, 818
Microsoft TCP/IP Properties, 264
Migration Progress, 244
Modem Dialing Information, 386
ModemName Default Preferences, 1028
ModemName Properties, 1028
Move, 219
Move Server, 178
Name the Dfs Root, 711
Name Your Printer, 801
NetBIOS Domain Name, 388
NetBIOS Name, 100
Network, 816
Network Adapter, 776
Network Connection Type, 1033
Network Connections, 1237
Network Credentials, 163, 378
Network Drivers, 817
Network Installation, 199
Network Password, 701
Network Protocols, 602
Network Settings, 766
Networking Components, 386
Networking Settings, 386
New Alert Settings, 908
New Connection, 551
New Domain Name, 100, 207, 364
New Group, 1244
New Object, 531
New Object-Computer, 763
New Object-Group, 221, 645
New Object-Printer, 743
New Object-Shared Folder, 702
New Object-Site, 993
New Object-Subnet, 180
New Object-User, 655, 657
New Phonebook Entry, 1054, 1094
New Printer Detection, 733
New Replication Partner, 611
New Reservation, 601
New Resource, 1245
New Resource Record, 1118
New Share, 533
New Zone Wizard, 84
NFS Share Permission, 572
NIS Map Selection, 577
OakLeaf Properties, 684
Offline Files, 838-839
Online Files – Add Custom Action, 839

DIALOGS

Organizational Unit, 249
Other Network File and Print Services, 802, 804
OUName Properties, 641
Output File, CD49, CD77
Output Options, CD77
Permissions, 103, 389
Personalize, 386
Phone and Modem Options, 1028
Phone Number to Dial, 1033, 1083
Policy Name, 652, 1041
PolicyName Properties, 651
Ports Properties, 1082
PPTP configuration, 1092
Print Test Page, 801
Printer Sharing, 731, 801
PrinterName, 735-738
PrinterShareName Properties, 744
Properties, 938
Protocols and Security, 1061
Public and Private Key Pair, 508
Public Network, 1085
PublishedShareName Properties, 703
Publishing Complete, CD32, CD71
Quota Entries, 845
RDP-TCP Properties, 1208
Ready to Import the MQIS Database, 1183
Ready to Publish, CD31, CD41
Regional Settings, 385
Remote Access Protocols, 1031
Remote Access Setup, 1093
Remote Boot Disk Generator, 872
Remote Installation Folder Location, 866-868
Repair Volume, 438
Replication Policy, 717
Report Selections, 247
Report System Compatibility, 205, 355
Resource Group Name, 1240
Resource type Parameters, 1246
ResourceName Properties, 1250
Restore Progress, 973
Reverse Lookup Zone, 85
Role, 1156
Schedule, 542
Scope Options, 593-596

Scope Statistics, 600
Security Policy, 183
Security Translation, 250
Select a Target Container, 241
Select an Account, 1236
Select Attribute, 1039
Select Counters, 902, 946
Select Disks, 420, 422
Select Drive, 450
Select Group, 222, 646
Select Groups, 1040
Select Installation Folder, 1263
Select Network Component Type, 771, 796
Select Network Protocol, 771, 796, 892, 1092
Select Network Service, 265
Select Publishing Method, CD31, CD41, CD70
Select Recovery Agents, 503-504
Select the Dfs Root Type, 710
Select the Printer Port, 560, 729, 800
Select User or Contact, 131
Select Users and Groups, 1111, 1155
Select Users, Computers or Groups, 836
Server Properties, 739-741, 1018
ServerName, 869, 1110
Service Account Selection, 254
Set Application Identity, 1159
Set Capture File, CD60
Setup Type, 536
Shared System Volume, 102, 207, 364, 378, 389
Show Database, 275
Signature Verification Results, 324
Software Installation Properties, 641
Source File, CD49
Specify a Program and Stream Name, CD38-CD41, CD68
Specify Format Information, CD70
Specify Stream Format Information, CD38
Specify the Dfs Root Share, 711
SQL Server Setup, 1175
Static Mappings (Local), 273
Synchronization Settings, 842

System Monitor Properties, 894
Tasks to Delegate, 225, 653
TCP/IP, 784
TCP/IP DNS Server, 282
TCP/IP Properties, 282-286
Template Security Policy Setting, 627
Template Stream Format, CD48
Templates Properties, 527
Terminal Services Licensing Setup, 1215
Terminal Services Setup, 1203
Test or Make Changes, 238
Tic-Tac-Toe Properties, 1162
Time of Day Constraints, 1038
Translate Objects, 250
Transmission, CD77
Trust Relationships, 235, 390
Unlisted or Updated Protocol, 817
User Account, 242
Username Properties, 121, 129, 656-657
Users, Computers and Groups, 684
Video Format, CD60
Virtual Memory, 942
Volume Type, 420, 423
VolumeName Properties, 811
VPNConnectionName, 1086
Web Site, 1122
Web Site Content Directory, 1116
Web Site Security Credentials, 1122
WebShareName Properties, 701
Windows 2000 Components, 386
Windows 2000 Setup Welcome, 354
Windows Components, 804, 865
Windows Installation Folder Name, 867
Windows Media Encoder, CD30
Windows NT 4.0 RAS Servers, 102
WINS Server Configuration (Local), 274
Workgroup or Computer Domain, 387
Zone File, 1118
Zone Name, 392, 1118
Zone Type, 381, 1118

differential backups, 952
Digital Subscriber Line. *See* DSL
direct connections (intranets), CD11
directories
 AD, 95
 identity management, 154
 integrating, 153-154
 meta, 153-154
 synchronizing, 534-541
  troubleshooting, 543
 UNIX, integrating, 577-579
Directory Access Protocol. *See* DAP
directory databases, AD, 95
Directory Information Tree. *See* DIT
Directory Service Client Wizard, 786
directory services, 94
Directory Services Client, Windows 9x, 786, 788
Directory Services Migration Tool, 534
Directory Services Restore Mode Administrator Password dialog, 164
Directory Services Restore Mode dialog, 389
disabled systems, recovering, 404
disabling
 EFS, 504
 hardware, servers, 320
Discretionary Access Control List. *See* DACL
Disk Cleanup tool, 448, 450
Disk Defragmenter, 448, 933-934
 Analysis Display, 935
 launching, 934
 opening, 449
 PerfMon, 935
 tuning servers, 922
Disk Management snap-in, 418-424, 437
Disk Management tools
 Chkdsk, 448, 450
 Disk Cleanup, 448, 450
disk quotas, 49, 415
 IntelliMirror, 829, 844
 setting, 845-846

disks, 416-417
 caching, 938-939
 Chkdsk, 450
 client installation, 821-822
 defragmenting, 933
 Disk Cleanup tool, 450
 Disk Quotas, 844
 dynamic, 415-417
 failure
  recovering with RAID 1, 440-441
  recovering with RAID 5, 438
 managing Disk Management snap-in, 418-424
 Quorum, 1232
 storage, organizing, 956-957
Display an Existing Dfs Root dialog, 714
Display Filter dialog, 1008
displaying NetMon data, 912, 914
distinguished name. *See* DN
Distributed COM Configuration Properties dialog, 1168, 1170
Distributed COM. *See* DCOM
distributed directory, AD, 96
Distributed File System. *See* Dfs
Distributed Transaction Coordinator. *See* DTC
distribution groups (AD), 152
DIT (Directory Information Tree), 122
 LDAP, 122
DN (distinguished name), 28, 123-124
DNA (Distributed interNet Architecture), 1141-1143
DNS (domain name system), 25, 985
 child domains, 166-169
 components, 79
 Dynamic, 83
 fixed addresses, adding to servers, 282-283
 hierarchy, 78
 migrating clients, 284-285
 name resolution, 275-276
 namespaces, 77
  FQDN, 78
 New Zone Wizard, 84
 registrars, 81
 resolver, 80
 resolving names, 77

resource records, 80
 secondary servers, adding, 281
 servers, 79
  Root Hints, 1063
 SOA tab, 86
 testing, 280, 375
 troubleshooting, 294
 verifying, 285-286
 Windows NT upgrades, 359-360
 zone files, 80
 zones, 80
  primary master name server, 80
  secondary, 381
DNS Management MMC tool, 85-86
DNS Manager, WINS lookup, 279
DNS menu
 New Server command, 276, 281
 New Zone command, 276
DNS snap-in, 83-84, 169, 396
docked profiles, 471-472
domain architecture, 24-25
Domain Controller Security snap-in, 402
Domain Controller Type dialog, 98, 162, 388
Domain Controllers dialog, 996
Domain Controllers. *See* DCs
Domain Local groups, 30
Domain Monitor Resource Kit tool, 344
domain name system. *See* DNS
Domain Properties dialog, 623
Domain Security Policy Console, 182-185
 viewing groups, 185-186
Domain Security Policy snap-in, opening, 182
Domain Selection dialog, 238, 246-247, 253
domain user accounts, 208
 adding to local groups, 876
DomainName dialog, 777
DomainName Properties dialog, 171, 185, 500, 752

DOMAINS

domains
  AD, 99
    administering, 105
  adding users, 1279-1283
  administrating from child
    DCs, 172
  administering, 188
  BDCs, adding, 382
  child
    adding, 160-166, 172
    attributes, 170
    creating, 158
    DNS zones, 166-169
    failed promotions, 396
    moving, 177-181
    security policies, 181-184
  DCs
    installing, 388-389
    removing, 383
  forests, creating, 26
  grafting objects, 154
  Group Policies, 832
    viewing, 185-186
  groups, moving, 173, 175
  Internet, 81
  Local and Global groups, 650
  migrating, testing, 230-231
  mixed mode, 397
  models, changing, 187-188
  names, ISPs, 82
  namespaces, 25
  native mode, 397
  navigating, 623-624
  OakLeaf University domain
    topology example, 155
  objects, moving, 154
  OUs, 149
    assigning, 157
    creating, 132
    moving, 173-175
  parent, 160
  parent-child model, 158
  planning, 148-149
  pruning objects, 154
  resources, 149
    upgrading, 392-395
  restructuring, 30-31, 348-349
    ADMT, 398-400
    advantages, 349
    drawbacks, 349
  restructuring test, 1005
  security, 400-403
    *Domain Security Policy
     Console, 182-185*
  security boundaries, 26
  security groups, 149, 158
  single, model, 155-158
  testing, 389-392
    second DC, 379
  trees, creating, 26
  upgrading, 343-347
    PDCs, 344
    recovering, 347-348
    sequences, 343, 345
  users, moving, 173, 175
  verifying operation, 389-392
  Windows NT, administering,
    111-120

**Domains and Trusts snap-in,
  399**

DomianName Properties dialog, 632

**dotted-decimal word notation
  (IP addresses), 65**

downlevel (AD), 96

**downlevel clients, specifying
  user profiles, 658-660**

**downlevel DUN clients,
  1051-1052**

**downlevel system policies,
  implementing, 664-668**

downlevel volumes, 709

downloading
  ODP (WMT), CD22
  WMT Rights Manager,
    CD23-CD25

**DRA (Data Recovery Agent),
  501**
  Certificate Export Wizard,
    505
  exporting certificates, 504-505
  implementing, 502-503
  private keys, 504-505

**DRF (Data Recovery Field),
  490, 501**

Driver File Details dialog, 318

Driver Properties dialog, 741

Driver Signing, 323, 769

drivers, EFS, 491

drives
  clusters, 927
  hot spare, 330
  logical, 839
  organizing, 932-933
  partitioning
    optimizing, 350-352
    RIS, 352
  properties, 937
  workload, spreading, 936

**DSL (Digital Subscriber Line),
  988**
  bandwidth, CD7-CD8
  connections, NAT, 1067-1070

**DSM snap-in, troubleshooting,
  451**

DSN, creating, 1173-1178

**DTC (Distributed Transaction
  Coordinator), 1145**
  administrating, 1178-1179

DTC Properties dialog, 1179

dumb arrays, 1232

DUN
  downlevel clients, configuring,
    1051-1052
  group policies, 1048-1049
  RAS, 1029-1031, 1041
  testing, 1032-1036
  user profiles, 1041-1043
  Windows 98, 1054

duplexing, 434

dynamic disks, 415-417
  implementing, 418-419

Dynamic DNS. *See* **DDNS**

**dynamic volume management,
  47**

E

**ECC (Error Checking and
  Correcting), 300**

Edit Alias dialog, 697-698

**Edit Dial-In Profile dialog,
  1042-1043**

**Edit Display Filter button,
  1008-1010**

Edit IP Filter dialog, 1096

editing
  Group Policy objects,
    622-623, 628
  multicast broadcast stations,
    CD44-CD46
  remote Registry, 478
  SIF, 877

**editors, Group Policies,
  695-697**

**EDRP (Encrypted Data
  Recovery Policy), 502-503**

**EFS (Encrypting File System),
  37, 415, 489-490, 678**
  Add Recovery Agent Wizard,
    503
  architecture, 491
  Certificate snap-in, 513-514
  disabling, 504
  DRA, 501-504
    implementing, 502-503

DRF, 501-504
driver, 491
EDRP, 503
FSRTL, 491
implementing, 492-496
IPSec, 497
recovering files, 501
troubleshooting, 515
Trusted for Delegation, 496
  enabling, 496-497

ELAP (Ethernet Link Access Protocols), 793

Electronic Music Management System. *See* **EMMS**

eliminating client reliance on NetBEUI, 287

EMA (Enterprise Memory Architecture), 58

email, integrating, 151-152

EMF (Enhanced Metafile Format), 725

EMMS (Electronic Music Management System), CD2

employee accounts, ADSI25, 1269-1274

emulating domain migration, 231-232

emulators, PDC, 30

enabling
clients, PPTP Windows NT, 1092-1093
hardware, servers, 320
Macintosh
  accounts, 807-813
  authentication, 806-807
NetBIOS name resolution, 272-273, 275
Offline File support, 836
performance, 905-907
Quota Management, 844-845
Trusted for Delegation, 496-497
WINS lookup, 279

encoding, CD5
avi files, to asf files, CD62, CD64
broadcasts, CD75-CD77
mp3 files, CD48-CD51
streaming media, CD46
  audio, CD46-CD48
video files, On-Demand Producer, CD58-CD61
wav files, CD48-CD51
with WMT Audio codec, CD46-CD48

Encrypted Data Recovery Policy. *See* **EDRP**

encrypting
ciphertext, 486-487
data, 486-487, 497
DDF, 490
DRF, 490
files, 490-492
  cipher command, 494-495
folders, 492
  cipher command, 494-495
plaintext, 486-487
recovery agents, 490
servers, 495-497

Encrypting File System. *See* **EFS**

encryption, 486
shared-secret, 38

Encryption Warning dialog, 493

end-node, 797

enforcing security policies (Group Policies), 625-628

Enhanced Metafile Format. *See* **EMF**

enhancing
asf files, CD51-CD54
storage
  Dfs, 415
  disk quotas, 415
  dynamic disks, 415
  EFS, 415
  filters, 415
  FRS, 415
  NTFS Change Journal, 415
  remote storage, 415
  removable media, 416
  reparse points, 415
  sparse file support, 415
  volume mount points, 415
storage management, 414
WMT, CD21

Enter Credentials dialog, 1011

Enter Subnet Mask dialog, 1241

Enterprise CAs, 489

Enterprise Memory Architecture. *See* **EMA**

enterprise networks, 21

environments
clustered, 1232, 1238-1239
NetWare, 524

ERD, recovering disabled systems, 404

Error Checking and Correcting. *See* **ECC**

errors
datagrams, testing, 75
disks, Chkdsk, 450
streaming media, trapping, CD74-CD75

ESE (Extensible Storage Engine), 95

establishing
CAs, 506
non-transitive trusts, 107-109, 111
paging file baselines, PerfMon, 944-945
Roaming User Profiles, 833-835
user profiles, 660-663

estimating replication traffic, 990

Ethernet Link Access Protocols. *See* **ELAP**

EtherTalk, 793

Event Guide (WMT), CD26-CD27
installing, CD26-CD27

Event Viewer, clearing, 389-392

examining errors (Chkdsk), 450

examples
AD configuration, 993, 995-997
adding child domains, 160-166, 172
monitoring replications, 1017
moving security groups in domains, 175
Network Monitor set up, 998-999
OakLeaf University domain topology, 155
Security Policies, 645-647
single-domain model, 155-158

exams (MCSE)
70-064, 790
70-073, 790
70-098, 790
70-210, 790
70-215, 61, 258, 295, 334, 452, 516, 673, 720, 790, 855, 917, 979, 1072, 1103, 1226
70-216, 19, 335, 516, 615, 1072, 1103
70-217, 91, 191, 335, 544, 790, 855, 888, 1022

EXAMS (MCSE)

70-219, 145, 191, 335
70-220, 336, 517, 888, 1103
70-221, 336, 616, 1073
70-222, 258, 295, 337
cost, 1252
MCSE types, 482
registering, 1252
    Execute mode (Terminal Services), 1204

exempting administrators from GPOs, 650-652

Export Private Key dialog, 505

Export Registry File dialog, 476

exporting
DRA certificates, 504-505
Sample Bank Client, 1178
Server Installer packages, 1178

Extended Logging Properties dialog, 1125

extending volume size, 421-422

extensibility, Schema, 23

Extensible Counter List, tuning servers, 925

eXtensible Markup Language. *See* XML

Extensible Storage Engine. *See* ESE

F

failbacks (resource groups), 1249

failing child domain promotions, 396

failovers (resource groups), 1249

FastLane, 535

fault tolerance, 417

fault-resilient availability (clusters), 1229

fault-tolerance volumes, 709

fault-tolerant availability (clusters), 1229

fault-tolerant shares, 716
creating, 716-718

features
ADMT, 255
ADSI25, 1256

COM, 1145
RAS, 1025

FEK (file encryption key), 490

FEPs (front-end processors), 1078

Fibre Channel RAID, 331-332

fields
AD, 95
captions for Three UserName Properties dialog pages, 131

File and Print Services for NetWare. *See* FPNW

file associations, 472

file encryption key. *See* FEK

File Replication Service. *See* FRS

file security (NTFS), 678

File Services (Macintosh), 803-807
authentication, 805-807
parameters, 804-807

File Share Parameters dialog, 1242

file system filter, 427

file system run-time library. *See* FSTRL

File System Verification dialog, 323-324

FileName Properties dialog, 810

filenames, Unicode, 428

FileOrFolderName dialog, 682

files
asf, CD51-CD54, CD59
asx, CD5, CD65-CD67
    multicasting, CD75
audio
    encoding, CD46-CD48
    illustrated, CD55-CD58
avi, CD59-CD61
    encoding, CD62, CD64
decrypting, 490-492
    with EFS, 501, 503-504
defragmenting, 934-935
DSN, 1173-1178
encoding, CD5
encrypting, 490-492
    cipher command, 494-495
indexing, 703-707
log, 1123-1124
Macintosh, 803-807, 812
    forks, 812
    sharing, 812-813

mp3, encoding, CD48-CD51
multicasting, CD68-CD73
multiple data streams, 50
NetWare, sharing with Windows, 526-529
Ntconfig.pol, 665
Offline, 836, 840-841
    setting up, 837-838
open, backup routine, 958-959
ownership, 680
paging, 941-943, 947-948
performance, improving, 947-948
permissions, 680-681
    low-level, 682
Registry, 461-464
replication capture, analyzing (Network Monitor), 1005-1007
security, 486
sharing, 676-681
    security, 678
sparse, 50, 426
streaming media, CD46
system, verifying, 323-324
templates, DCs, 401-403
wav, encoding, CD48-CD51
wax, CD65-CD67
wma, CD5

Filter Options dialog, 139

filtering
GPOs, 650, 652
options, 215

filters, 415
frame, 1008-1010
LDAP, 138
migrating users, 212-220
PPTP Internet connections, 1094-1096
troubleshooting, 144

Find Custom Search dialog, 213

Find Shared Folders dialog, 702

Find Users, Contacts and Groups dialog, 136

finding shared printers, 745-746

fixed IP addresses, clients, 772, 774

fixing disk errors (Chkdsk), 450

flat namespaces, 115-120

flexible single-master operations. *See* FSMOs

Group Policies 1335

Folder Options dialog, 473
folder security, NTFS file sharing, 678
Folder Selection dialog, 246
FolderName Properties dialog, 429, 492, 680
folders
    creating shared, 683-685
    encrypting, 492
        cipher command, 494-495
    home, 670-672
    leaf, 708
    My Documents, 852
    Offline Files, 838-839
    orphaned, 680-681
    ownership, 680
        taking, 680-681
    permissions, 680-681, 686-688
        granular, 682
    Physical Locations, 443-446
    redirecting, 852-854
    searching in AD, 702-703
    sharing
        NFS clients, 571-572
        on Intranet, 697-699, 701
forests, 24-25, 645-647
    creating, 26
    initial root domain, 26
    joining, 388
    pristine, 30-31
forks, 812
    data streams, 428
    resource (Macintosh), 812
Format Volume dialog, 421
Format.exe, changing cluster size, 927-928
FPNW (File and Print Services for NetWare), 46, 528
FQDN (fully qualified domain name), 78
frame content detail, viewing, 1006-1007
frame filters, 1008-1010
frame list, viewing, 1006-1007
frame relay (intersite communication), 988
free pools (media pools), 443
Friendly Description and Help Text dialog, 867
front-end processors. *See* FEPs
FRS (File Replication Service), 415, 676-677
    troubleshooting, 719
    viewing in AD, 718

FSMO roles, 408-409
FSMOs (flexible single-master operations), 150-151
    AD, 150-151
        Domain naming master, 150
        infrastructure master, 150
        PDC emulator, 150
        relative ID, 150
        Schema master, 150
FSTRL (file system run-time library), 491
FTP
    Internet Explorer, 563
    UNIX, 561-562
FTP servers, troubleshooting, 1135
FTP sites, setting up, 1125, 1127
full backup, running, 965-969
full LDAP path, 28
full-duplexes, 87
fully qualified domain name. *See* FQDN
functional AD topology, 621

G

Gateway Services for NetWare. *See* GSNW
gateways, 67
GC (global catalog), 25, 95, 985
    AD, 95
    testing traffic, 1003-1004
GC Server, creating, 381
GDI, 725
generating reports (ADMT), 247
streaming media broadcasts, CD12-CD15
geographical AD topology, 621
global catalog. *See* GC
global groups, 29, 650
Global groups, security, 221-222
    migrating, 220-222
Globally Unique ID. *See* GUID
GPOs (Group Policy Objects), 830
    administrators, delegating, 653

    creating, 632-633
    Delegation of Control Wizard, 653
    exempting administrators, 650-652
    filtering, 650-652
    home folders, 670
        sharing, 670-672
    importing Security Settings templates, 635-637
    linking, 638-640
    navigating, 623-624
    Registry, 454
    reorganizing, 650
    security, 625-628
        default settings, 635-637
        designing, 643, 645-647
        options, 626
        passwords, 637
    user accounts, 651, 654
        adding, 655, 657
        passwords, 655
    user profiles, establishing, 660-663
grafting objects in domains, 154
Grant Access On dialog, 1113
graphs, 894
    altering, 894
    axis, 894
    SysMon, 907
Group Account Migration Wizard, 237, 399
Group Migration Wizard, 32, 237-246
Group Options dialog, 241
Group Policies, 618. *See also* GPOs
    AD, 623-624
    AD structures, 621
    Administrative Templates, 628-630
    CIW, 881
    computer settings, 618
    default domains, 623-624
    Delegation of Control Wizard, 653
    domains, 832
    downlevel, implementing, 664-668
    DUN, 1048-1049
    editing, 622-623, 628
    Global groups, 650
    Group Policy snap-in, 622-623, 628
    hierarchy, 620

GROUP POLICIES

home folders, 670-672
   mapping, 672
   sharing, 670-671
inheritance, 620
   blocking, 620
IntelliMirror, 829-831
no exceptions, 832
OUs, 640, 833
   restricting, 640-643
policy inheritance, 620
printers, 752, 754
public keys, 626
Registry, 454, 626
RIS, 879-880
reorganizing, 650
security, 625-628
   designing, 643, 645-647
   passwords, 625
   permissions, 626-628
   populating, 643-647
   restricted groups, 626
   setting options, 626
sites, 832
System Policies, 668, 670
user accounts, 654
   adding, 655-657
User Configuration, 631
user profiles, 660
   creating, 661-663
user settings, 618-619

Group Policy Editor, installing software, 848-849

Group Policy Objects. *See* **GPOs**

Group Policy Refresh Interval for Computers Properties dialog, 629-630

Group Policy snap-in, 34, 622-624, 628-630, 641

Group security policy, 38
   Group Selection dialog, 240

GroupOrUser properties dialog, 682

groups
AD, 115-120
   adding, 118, 120
AD containers, 210
adding to roles, 1154-1156
built-in, 116
child domains, 173
cleaning accounts, 287
commands, 292
Domain Local, 30
filtering users, 212-220
global, 29
hierarchies, 28
listing commands, 292

local, domain user accounts, 876
membership files, creating, 291
migrating, testing, 237-238, 240-246
moving within domains, 173, 175
policies, viewing, 185-186
security, 29, 38, 149
   migrating, 220-222
system, 117
universal, 29
users
   adding, 292
   deleting, 292

Groups dialog, 1040

GSNW (Gateway Services for NetWare), 46, 529-531
installing, 529-530
troubleshooting, 543

GUID (Globally Unique ID), 861

H

hard-linked volumes, 418
hardware
DHCP, 985
DNS, 985
migration plans, 195
NICs, 299-300, 761-762
Plug-and-Play, troubleshooting, 333
preparing for migration, 759
RAS, 1026
requirements, 984
routers, 67, 985
SCSI, 299-300
server upgrades, 901
servers, 299-300, 315
   backups, 300-302
   disabling, 320
   enabling, 320
   MSCS, 301-302
   NICs, 299-300
   optimizing, 921
   processors, 304-305
   purchasing, 311-313
   RAID, 301, 330
   SANs, 301-302
   SCSI, 299-300
   upgrading, 313-315
streaming media requirements, CD13-CD15
telecommunication adapter, 985

Terminal Services, 1218-1223
Terminal Services requirements, 1200
WINS, 985

HARDWARE key (Registry), 470
subkeys, 470

hardware management, 315
Device Manager, 316-321

hardware profiles, 471-472
copying, 471
docked, 471-472
mobile, 471-472

Hardware Profiles dialog, 471

headers, 88
TCP, 88
   acknowledgement number, 88
   checksum, 88
   control bits, 88
   data offset, 88
   destination port, 88
   reversed field, 88
   sequence number, 88
   source port, 88
   urgent pointers, 88
   windows, 88

heartbeat connections (clusters), 1232. *See also* **private network connections**

heartbeat packets, 306

hidden shares, 677

Hierarchical Storage Management. *See* **HSM**

hierarchies
Dfs, 709
DNS, 78
Group Policies, 620
groups, 28
OUs, 29
single-domain model, 156-158
users, 28

high availability (clusters), 1229

high-level permissions, 682

history, Windows, 557

hit rate, 303-304

hives, Registry, 459-464

HKEY_CLASSES_ROOT key (Registry), 472

HKEY_CURRENT_CONFIG key (Registry), 471-472

HKEY_CURRENT_USER key (Registry), 473, 619
  subkeys, 473
HKEY_LOCAL_MACHINE root key, 466-470
HKEY_USERS key (Registry), 474
home folders, 670
  common shares, 670-672
  individual shares, 670-671
  logon scripts, 671-672
  mapping, 672
host headers
  names, 1120, 1122-1123
  records, 1120, 1122-1123
host ids
  Class B addresses, 68
  restricted, 65-66
hosts (LAN), pinging, 75
hot spare drives, 330
hot-keys, Terminal Service Clients, 1224
HSM (Hierarchical Storage Management), 48
HTML, stations, CD42-CD46
http streaming, CD5
hunt groups, 1026
HyperTerminal
  Telnet, 550-553
  Telnet client, 550-552

I

I2O (Intelligent I/O Architecture), 58
  Kernel, 58
IANA (Internet Assigned Numbers Authority), 66
IAS (Internet Authentication Service), 52
IBM, EMMS, CD2
ICANN (Internet Corporation for Assigned Names and Numbers), 66
Identification Changes dialoges, 777
identifying information (CAs), 508
identities, COM+ applications, 1157-1159
identity management, directories, 154

Idle Settings dialog, 842
IETF (Internet Engineering Task Force), 489, 497
IGMP (Internet Group Membership Protocol), 41
IIS (Internet Information Server), 44
  connecting from clients, 1114-1115
  default FTP sites, 1125-1127
  features, 44-45
  FTP servers, troubleshooting, 1135
  host headers, 1120-1123
  installing, 1106-1108
  NNTP servers, 1128-1132
    troubleshooting, 1136
  properties, 1110-1113
  SMTP server, 1133-1134
  upgrading, 1106-1107
  upgrading to 5.0, 1106-1107
  virtual sites, 1119-1123
  WebDAV, 44
  Windows Components Wizard, 1108
  XML, 45
illustrated audio files, CD5, CD55-CD58
images, SYSPREP, 885
implementing
  Dfs, 51
  downlevel system policies, 664-668
  DRA, in EFS, 502-503
  dynamic disks, 418-419
  EFS, 492, 496
  IPSec, policies, 500-501
  NTFS compression, 428-429
  Smart Cards, 40
Import or Install a Component dialog, 1159
Import Policy From dialog, 636
import pools (media pools), 443
Import Registry File command (Registry menu), 476
importing
  media pools, 444
  security settings policies (GPOs), 635-637
improvements, network printing, 725

improving
  file performance, 947-948
  performance, servers, 302-304
increasing
  L2 cache memory (servers), 303-304
  RAM, servers, 302-303
incremental backups, 951
indexing files, 703-707
Indexing Service, 704-707
  configuring, 704-705
  running, 706-707
  testing, 706-707
  troubleshooting, 719
individual home folder shares, 670-672
inheritance, Group Policies, 620
Inheritance Blocking (Group Policies), 832
Inheritance Overrides dialog, 1113
initial root domain, 26
Initial Settings dialog, 866
Initial Synchronization dialog, 538
Input Filters dialog, 1096
Input Source dialog, CD77
Insert Media dialog, CD57
inspecting
  clients TCP/IP properties, 777-780
  NICs, 777-780
Install Hardware Device Drivers dialog, 318
Install Network Component Type dialog, 387
Install New Components dialog, 1160
Install or Configure DNS dialog, 364
Install or Create a New Application dialog, 1159
Install Remove Service, tuning servers, 926
Installation Complete dialog, 1263
Installation Disk Set dialog, 821-822
Installation File Source Location dialog, 867

Installation Files dialog, 355
Installation Folder dialog, 236
installing
    AD, 96-97, 164-166, 172
        Active Directory Installation Wizard, 98-105
        NetBIOS, 100
        troubleshooting, 190
    AD administration tools, 188-189
    ADMT, 233-234, 236
    ADSI25 application, 1255-1264
    AppleTalk, 796
    Application Installation Service, 846-847
    applications
        cluster environments, 1238-1239
        COM+, 1156-1157, 1159-1161
        Sample Bank, 1172-1178
    automatically, 872-873, 875
    CA, 506
    Certificate Services, 508-509
    Cluster Service, 1234
        checklist, 1234-1238
    clusters, troubleshooting, 1251
    DCs, 388-389
    DHCP, 589-590
    DHCP Relay Agent, 602-603
    Directory Services Client
        for Windows 9x, 786, 788
    File Services (Macintosh), 803-807
    GSNW, 529-530
    IIS, 1106-1108
    Internet printing, 749-751
    IPSec, 498
    IPX, 524-525
    MSDSS, 535-536
    MSMQ, 1180-1192
    Network Monitor Driver, 892
    PDCs with ADSI25, 200-211
    PPTP protocol, 1092
    Print Services (Macintosh), 802-803
    printers
        network-attached, 727
        Plug and Play, 727
        unpublished, 747-748
    RIS, 860-862, 865
        Group Policy, 879-880
    Root Hints on DNS server, 1063
    RRAS, 1027
    sample packages, remote workstations, 1166-1168
    Schema Manager, 125, 127-128
    SFU, 565
    shared printers, 745-746
    Shared System Volume (Sysvol), 97
    software
        setting up, 848-852
        testing, 851-852
    Support Tools, 923
    TCP/IP, 284
        to NetBEUI, 263, 265
        verifying, 285
    Terminal Services, 1199-1203
        applications, 1204
    Terminal Services Client, 1217-1223
    Terminal Services License Server, 1215-1216
    User Manager (Windows NT), 112
    Windows 2000
        comparing with upgrading, 760-761
        NICs, 761-762
        professional, 766
        servers, 384-387
    Windows Installer, 847-848
    Windows NT, 776-777
    WINS, 606-607
    WMT, CD15, CD17
        Administrator, CD19-CD20
        Audio codec, CD47-CD48
        Event Guide, CD26-CD27
        Rights Manager, CD23-CD25
        Tools, CD20-CD21

Installing Components dialog, 387
Integrated Services Digital Network. *See* **ISDN**
Integrated Windows Authentication, 699
integrating
    directories and AD, 153-154
    email, 151-152
    Macintosh, 792, 796-799, 801-803
    Microsoft Exchange 2000, 59
    NetWare, 529
    UNIX, 546, 558-560
        directories, 577, 579
        printers, 558-560
    Windows 2000 into NetWare environments, 524
    Windows NT 4.0 RAS servers, 1050-1051

integrity, backup routine, 957-958
Intelligent I/O Architecture. *See* **I20**
IntelliMirror, 50, 828
    caching files, 836
    Disk Quotas, 829, 844
        setting, 845-846
    Folder Redirection, 852-854
    Group Policies, 829-831
        domains, 832
        OU, 833
    Offline Files, 829
    Roaming User Profiles, 829
        establishing, 833-835
    Synchronization, 829
    User Profiles, 833
    user settings, 829
    users
        data management, 835
        Offline Files, 836, 838-841
    Windows Installer, 829
inter-Dfs junctions, 708
interacting with Macintosh accounts, 807-813
InterfaceName properties dialog, 1065
    Intermediate CA, 488
internal IP addresses, 262-263, 265
Internet, 40, 44
    connecting
        demand-dial modem, 1059-1063
        NAT, 1058-1059
        testing clients, 1065
    domain names, assigning, 81
    PPTP connections, 1094-1096
    printing, 748-749
        installing, 749-751
        troubleshooting, 755
    security, 38
    streaming media, CD2-CD3, CD9-CD10
        broadcasts, CD9
    WANs, securing, 1076
Internet Accounts dialog, 1132
Internet Assigned Numbers Authority. *See* **IANA**
Internet Authentication Service. *See* **IAS**
Internet Connection dialog, 1060, 1062-1063, 1080

Internet Connection Wizard, 1131

Internet Engineering Task Force. *See* IETF

Internet Explorer, FTP support, 563

Internet Group Membership Protocol. *See* IGMP

Internet Information Server. *See* IIS

Internet Information Services (IIS) dialog, 1107

Internet News Email Address dialog, 1131

Internet News Server Logon dialog, 1132

Internet News Server Name dialog, 1131

Internet Print Protocol, 51

Internet Protocol (TCP/IP) Properties dialog, 498

Internet Protocol Security. *See* IPSec

interoperability, 46
   AppleTalk, 46

interprocess communication. *See* IPC

interrogation (LDAP), 124

intersite
   communicating, 986-987
   test network, designing, 991-992

intersite communication, estimating traffic, 990

Intersite Transports node (AD Sites and Services snap-in), 113

intranet
   folders, sharing, 697-699, 701
   multicasting, CD36-CD41, CD68-CD73
   printers, 750
   streaming media, CD8-CD9
      direct connections (ISP), CD11
      hardware, CD13-CD15
      planning, CD10-CD11
      software, CD11-CD15
   unicast publishing points, adding, CD28-CD32

Invalid Name dialog, 649

inverse telecine, CD22

IP, 40
   addresses
      allocating, 66
      assigning, 64
      changing, 71-72
      Class B, 68
      Class C, 69
      classes, 64
      decoding, 64
      matching with ARP, 76
      notation, 65
      restrictions, 65-66
      upstream providers, 66
   datagrams, 73-74
   next-generation protocol, 72
   routers, 67-68
   subnets, 67
   unicasting, 65

IP Address and Port Settings dialog, 1120

IP Address Array Editor dialog, 269

IP Address Assignment dialog, 1031, 1081

IP Address Range dialog, 591

IP addresses
   assigning, 586
      DHCP, 587-588
      NetBEUI, 263
   choosing NetBEUI, 262-265
   clients, specifying fixed, 772, 774
   RAS server, 1036

IP Authentication Header (IPSec), 498

IP Encapsulating Security Protocol (IPSec), 498

IP Security dialog, 498

IP Security. *See* IPSec

IPC (interprocess communication), 677

IPSec (Internet Protocol Security), 38
   configuring, 498
   encrypting data, 497
   Group Policy Editor, 500
   IETF (Internet Engineering Task Force), 497
   implementing policies, 500-501
   installing, 498
   IP Authentication Header, 498
   IP Encapsulating Security Protocol, 498
   Oakley/ISAKMP, 498
   options, 498
   policies, 499
   troubleshooting communication problems, 515

IPv6 (next-generation protocol), 73

IPX
   installing, 524-525
   troubleshooting, 542

IPX/SPX (NetWare), 521

ISDN (Integrated Services Digital Network), 988

ISPs
   dial-up connections, PPTP, 1083, 1085, 1087
   direct connections (intranets), CD11
   domain names, 82

Issuing CA, 488

Items to Synchronize dialog, 841

J

joining forests, 388

junction points, 708

junctions
   inter-Dfs, 708
   mid-level, 708
   post-junction, 708

K

KDC (Key Distribution Center), 38

Kerberos, 38
   KDC, 38, 496
   long-term key, 38
   realms, 38
   Smart Cards, 39
   tickets, 39

Kernel
   EMA, 58
   features, 58
   I2O, 58
   upgrades, 58
   WDM, 58

Key Distribution Center (KDC), 38

keys
   Registry, 466
      HARDWARE, 470

KEYS

HKEY_CLASSES_ROOT, 472
HKEY_CURRENT_USER, 473
HKEY_USERS, 474
SAM, 466
SOFTWARE, 467
SYSTEM, 467-470
Registry Editor, 463

L

L2 cache, increasing memory, 303-304
L2TP
    Access Concentrators, 1078
    certificate enrollment, 1100
    clients, testing, 1101
    connections, troubleshooting, 1103
    tunneling, 1078
    VPN servers, 1097-1100
        Enterprise Root CA, 1097-1100
LACs (L2TP Access Concentrators), 1078
LAN connections, 1231
LANs
    cluster connections, 1233
    hosts, pinging, 75
    monitoring, 890
    streaming media, CD10
LAP (Link Access Protocols), 793
latency, CD6
launching
    Component Services tool, 1151
    Disk Defragmenter, 934
    PerfMon, 892
layers, AppleTalk protocol, 793-794
LDAP (Lightweight Directory Access Protocol), 94, 122
    ADSI25, 1278
    attributes, 123
    authentication, 124
    contents rules, 123
    DIT, 122
    DN, 123-124
    filters, 138
    functions, 124
    interrogation, 124
    namespaces, 123-124
    objects, searching for, 135

    OUs, 132-133, 135
    update, 124
LDM (Logical Disk Manager), 418
leaf folders, 708
LeakyApp, 926, 941
Lease Duration dialog, 592
levels RAID, 431-436
License Agreement dialog, 1218
Licensing Terminal Services tool, 1214
    installing, 1215-1216
Licensing Wizard, 1216
Lightweight Directory Access Protocol. *See* LDAP
limiting bandwidth, streaming media, CD34
linking
    asx and wax files, CD66-CD67
    GPOs, 638-640
    shares, to populate root volumes, 712-713, 715
listing
    group commands, 292
    NIC properties, 768
    user accounts, 288-291
lists
    Control subkeys, 470
    HKEY_CURRENT_USER key subkeys, 473
    NFS differences with Windows, 576
    NFS performance parameters, 574
    server purchase recommendations, 312
    standard print monitors, 726
LMHOSTS files, 605
load balancing (servers), 305
Load Simulator, CD79-CD82
Local Area Connection, 770
Local Area Connection Properties dialog, 771
Local groups, 650
    domain user accounts, 876
Local or Network Printer dialog, 560, 800
local RAS server, 1038-1039
Local Security Authority. *See* LSA

LocalTalk, 792
Locate Your Printer dialog, 750
Location and Comment dialog, 801
log files (Web servers)
    reading, 1123-1124
    Registry, 462
logging
    Web sites, 1123-1124
    Windows Media server events, CD84-CD85
logical disk caching, 938-939
Logical Disk Manager. *See* LDM
logical drives, mapping to Offline Files, 839-840
LogName Properties dialog, 902
Logon Properties dialog, 696
logon scripts
    creating, 694-697
    home folders, 671-672
    mapping shares to drives, 694
    testing, 694-697
Logon Settings page (Terminal Services), 1207
logons, Performance Logs and Alerts service, 905
long-term key, 38
looping programs, CD74-CD75
low-level permissions
    files, 682
    folders, 682
    viewing, 682
low-virtual-memory alert, setting, 945-947
LSA (Local Security Authority), 38

M

Macintosh, 792
    accounts, 807-813
    clients
        monitoring, 814
        permissions, 810
    EtherTalk, 793
    File Services, 803-807
        authentication, 805-807
        parameters, 804-807

MICROSOFT SERVICES FOR UNIX

files, 812
   forks, 812
   sharing, 812-813
integrating, 792-803
LocalTalk, 793
networks, print services, 799, 801-803
printing, troubleshooting, 824
remote access, 815
TokenTalk, 793
volumes
   properties, 811-813
   sharing, 808-813

managing
CA, 506
DDNS, 85-86
disk configuration, 418-424
IntelliMirror, user settings, 829
memory, 940-941
MSMQ, 1187
Offline Files, 837, 840-841
printers, Internet, 750
quotas, 845-846
resources (clusters), 1245-1247
storage, 47, 416
user data
   IntelliMirror, 835
   Offline Files, 836
WINS servers, 606, 608-609

Managing Conflicts During Migration dialog, 579

Managing Multiple Remote Access Servers dialog, 1031, 1081

mandatory user profiles, 660-663
troubleshooting, 673

manually configuring AD sites, 996-997

Map Network Drive dialog, 839-840

mapping
home folders, logon scripts, 671-672
Offline Files, 839-840
shares to drives, 694

mapping servers (UNIX), 566-567

Mappings menu
Backup Database command, 273
Static Mappings command, 273

markers, video clips, CD51-CD54

Markers dialog, CD53

master domain model, 392

master file table. *See* MFT

Master Properties dialog, 1123

matching
ARP
   IP, 76
   NIC, 76
backup media capacity to disk size, 959

MCP (Microsoft Certified Professional), 60

MCSE
CATs, 482
exams. *See* exams (MCSE)
registering for exam, 1252

MCSE corner
chapter 1, 60
chapter 2, 91
chapter 3, 144
chapter 4, 191
chapter 5, 257
chapter 6, 295
chapter 7, 334
chapter 8, 410
chapter 9, 452
chapter 10, 482
chapter 11, 516
chapter 12, 544
chapter 13, 581
chapter 14, 615
chapter 15, 673
chapter 16, 720
chapter 17, 756
chapter 18, 789
chapter 19, 825
chapter 20, 855
chapter 21, 888
chapter 22, 917
chapter 24, 1022
chapter 25, 1072
chapter 26, 1103
chapter 27, 1136
chapter 28, 1193
chapter 29, 1226
chapter 30, 1252

measuring
server read and write operations size, 926-931
simulated traffic (SysMon), 898-902

media
encoding, CD5

matching backup capacity to disk size, 959
RSM, 48
streaming, 53, CD2-CD3
   ASF redirector, CD5
   bandwidth, CD6-CD8, CD34
   broadcasting, CD3
   cable modems, CD7-CD8
   encoding, CD46
   http, CD5
   illustrated, CD5
   Internet, CD9-CD10
   intranets, CD8-CD11
   latency, CD6
   multicasting, CD68-CD73
   on-demand, CD4
   programs, CD5
   publishing points, CD4
   stations, CD5
   UDP, CD5
   unicasting, CD3
   WMT, CD15, CD17

media pools, 442-443
free pools, 443
import pools, 443
importing, 444
unrecognized pools, 443

membership files (groups), creating, 291

memory, 940-941
L2 cache, increasing, 303-304
virtual, 941-944

Memory Profiling Tool, tuning servers, 924

Message Queuing Type dialog, 1184

messages, newsgroups, 1131-1132

meta-directory, 153-154

metadata, 23

MFT (master file table), 425

Microsoft Certified Professional. *See* MCP

Microsoft Cluster Service. *See* MSCS

Microsoft Excel Text Import Wizard, 288-291

Microsoft Exchange 2000, integrating, 59

Microsoft Message Queue Server. *See* MSMQ

Microsoft Services for UNIX. *See* SFU

Microsoft TCP/IP
  Connectivity Configuration
  dialog, 818
Microsoft TCP/IP Properties
  dialog, 264
Microsoft Transaction Server.
  See MTS
mid-level junctions, 708
migrating
  accounts, 399
    computer, 248-253
    filters, 212-220
    to OUs, 211-220
    Users and Computers tool,
      212-220
  ADMT, 233-236
  ADSI25, 202
  clients
    comparing upgrading with
      installing, 760-761
    to DHCP, 284-285
    to DNS, 284-285
    to WINS, 284-285
  computers, 399
  developing plans, 194-197
  domains, testing, 230-231
  emulating with Migration
    tool, 231-232
  groups, testing, 237-238,
    240-246
  planning, 342
  preparing, 759-760
  reports, 246-247
  security groups
    reorganizing, 220-222
  service accounts, 253-254
  single-domains, 198-202,
    204-206, 208, 210-211
  troubleshooting hardware, 256
  users, testing, 237-238,
    240-246
  from Windows NT, 260-261
migration
  hardware requirements, 195
  Registry, 197
  testing, 195-197
  upgrading servers, 197
Migration Progress dialog, 244
Migration tool (AD). *See*
  ADMT
mirror volumes (RAID 1)
  breaking, 440
  creating, 417439
Mission Critical Software Web
  site, 349
mixed mode, 30, 397

MMC snap-in, 512
  Certificate Authority, 510-511
  revoking certificates, 512
mobile profiles, 471-472
models
  complete-trust, 393
  domains, changing, 187-188
  master domain, 392
  multiple-master domain, 393
  parent-child, 158
Modem Dialing Information
  dialog, 386
ModemName Default
  Preferences dialog, 1028
ModemName Properties
  dialog, 1028
modems
  cable, bandwidth, CD7-CD8
  dial-up connections, 1083,
    1085
  Phone and Modem tool,
    1027-1028
  remote access, 1026
modes
  Safe, 405, 407
  Telnet, 549
modifying Terminal Services
  connections, 1206-1209
monitoring
  Macintosh clients, 814
  networks, 890
    NetMon, 911
    PerfMon, 891
  replications, 1014, 1016-1019
  Windows Media server
    events, CD84-CD85
mount points (NTFS),
  427-428
Move dialog, 219
Move Server dialog, 178
Movetree.exe Support Tool,
  187-188
moving
  child domains to new sites,
    177-181
  groups within domains, 173,
    175
  objects
    in domains, 154
    in OUs, 133, 135
  OUs within domains, 173,
    175
  users within domains, 173,
    175

Moving Pictures Experts
  Group. *See* MPEG
mp3 files, encoding,
  CD48-CD51
MPEG, 54
MQIS database, 1183
MS-DOS
  troubleshooting upgrade, 824
  upgrading, 820-822
MSCS (Microsoft Cluster
  Service), 301-302
MSDSS (Microsoft Directory
  Synchronization Services),
  534-541
  installing, 535-536
MSFMU, 534
MSMQ (Microsoft Message
  Queue Server), 1146
  installing, 1180-1192
  managing, 1187
  MQIS database, 1183
  upgrading, 1180-1192
MTBF (mean time between
  failures), 298
MTS (Microsoft Transaction
  Server), 1146-1148
  administrators, adding groups,
    1154-1156
  Component Services tool,
    1150-1152
  components
    stateful, 1150
    stateless, 1150
  object brokers, 1148
  objects, 1148
  roles, 1156
  Sample Bank application,
    1172-1178
  sample packages, 1150,
    1158-1159
  transactions, 1148
MTS 2.0 Tic-Tac-Toe pack-
  age, 1158
MTTF (mean time to failure),
  298
MTTR (mean time to repair),
  298
multicasting, CD3
  asx files, CD75
  broadcasts, CD36-CD39,
    CD41
    editing, CD44-CD46
  file-based content,
    CD68-CD73

NETWORK SETUP DIALOG 1343

stations, CD42-CD46, CD68-CD73
 troubleshooting stream problems, CD88
multihomed host, 67
multihomed NICs, 306
multimaster replication, 23
multimaster replication (AD), 984-986
multiple data streams, 50
multiple domains, migrating, 230-231
Multiple Group permissions, creating third-tier shares, 693-694
multiple-master domain model, 393
My Documents folder, redirecting, 852

N

name caching (NetBIOS), 605
name resolution, 79
 NetBIOS, enabling with WINS, 272-273, 275
 providing (DNS), 275-276
Name the Dfs Root dialog, 711
Name Your Printer dialog, 801
Named Pipes protocol, 677
names
 attributes, Three UserName Properties dialog pages, 131
 DNS, resolving, 77
namespaces (DNS), 25, 77
 AD, 105
  viewing, 126
 flat, 115-118, 120
 LDAP, 123-124
naming
 LDAP, 123-124
 value entries, 464
NAS (Network-Attached Storage), 312, 955
NAT (Network Address Translation), 52, 67, 1025
 configuring, 1058-1059
  cable modem connections, 1067, 1069-1070
  DSL connections, 1067, 1069-1070

demand-dial modem connections, 1059-1060, 1062-1063
 route print, 1059
 troubleshooting, client connection problems, 1071
native mode, 30, 397
Native mode (DCs), 220-222, 397
navigating
 domain policies, 623-624
 GPOs, 623-624
NDS (NetWare Directory Services), 94, 539
nesting Global security groups, 221-222
NetBEUI
 clients, eliminating reliance, 287
 IP addresses, choosing, 262-265
  moving to TCP/IP, 261-262
 TCP/IP
  adding, 263
  installing, 263, 265
NetBIOS
 broadcasts, 605
 installing AD, 100
 LMHOSTS, 605
 name caching, 605
 name resolution, enabling with WINS, 272-275
 resolving names to IP addresses, 604-605
 traffic, 586
 WINS, 604-605
NetBIOS Domain Name dialog, 100, 388
NETLOGON shares, 677
NetMon. *See* **Network Monitor**
NetShow, upgrading, 55
NetTraffic, 897-898
 Stop Traffic button, 898
 troubleshooting, 916
NetWare, 520
 comparing to Windows 2000, 522
 files, 528-529
  sharing with Windows, 526-527
 installing IPX, 524-525
 integrating in Windows, 529
 integrating Windows 2000, 524
 IPX/IPX, 521
 MSCE, 544

MSDSS, 535-536
MSFMU, 534
NTGATEWAY groups, 532-533
printers, 528-529
 with Windows, 526-527
security, 532-533
synchronizing directories, 534-539, 541
TCP/IP, 521
troubleshooting, 543
versions, 521
 Network Adapter dialog, 776
network adapters
 changing, 774
 RIS, 860
Network Address Translation. *See* **NAT**
Network Connection Type dialog, 1033
Network Connection Wizard, 1033, 1083-1086
Network Connections dialog, 1237
Network Credentials dialog, 163, 378
Network Drivers dialog, 817
Network Identification Wizard, 885
Network Installation dialog, 199
Network Interface Cards. *See* **NICs**
Network Load Balancing. *See* **NLB**
Network Monitor (NetMon), 997-999
 Add-Users test, 1001, 1003
 analyzing replication capture files, 1005-1007
 displaying data, 912, 914
 frame filters, 1009-1010
 starting, 911
 tuning servers, 922
Network Monitor Driver, 892
 installing, 892
network operating system. *See* **NOS**
Network Password dialog, 701
Network Protocols dialog, 602
Network Settings dialog, 766
Network Setup dialog, 816

network-attached printers, 726
  configuring, 728-731
  installing, 727

Network-Attached Storage. *See* NAS

networking, 40, 44
  clients, setting up, 765-766
  DDNS, 41
  features, 41
  IGMP, 41

Networking Components dialog, 386

Networking Settings dialog, 386

networks
  adapters, 767-770
  AppleTalk, 794-795
    non-routed, 795
  assessing requirements, 758
  backbones, 43
  browsing, 915
  departmental, 21
  designing replication test, 991-992
  enterprise, 21
  Enterprise Root CAs, 1097-1100
  integrating Macintosh, 796-803
  Macintosh, printers, 799-803
  monitoring, 890
  NetMon, 911
  printers
    adding, 783-784
    troubleshooting, 755
  printing, 724
  properties, setting, 784
  remote access, dial-in, 1025
  routers, 67
  security, 486
    encryption, 486-487
  traffic, 897-898
    graphs, 894
    recording with counter logs, 902-904
    simulating, 897-898
  troubleshooting, 788
  Windows 98, 780-783
  Windows NT, altering properties, 777-780

New Alert Settings dialog, 908

New Connection dialog, 551

New Dfs Root Wizard, 710-711

New Domain Name dialog, 100, 207, 364

New Group dialog, 1244

New menu, Resource command, 1245

New Newsgroup Wizard, 1130

New Object dialog, 531

New Object-Computer dialog, 763

New Object-Group dialog, 119, 221, 645

New Object-Printer dialog, 743

New Object-Shared Folder dialog, 702

New Object-Site dialog, 993

New Object-Subnet dialog, 180

New Object-User dialog, 655, 657

New Phonebook Entry dialog, 1054, 1094

New Phonebook Entry Wizard, 1051

New Printer Detection dialog, 733

New Replication Partner dialog, 611

New Reservation dialog, 601

New Resource dialog, 1245

New Resource Record dialog, 1118

New Scope Wizard, 379, 591-592

New Server command (DNS menu), 276, 281

New Session Wizard, 538

New Share dialog, 533

New Zone command (DNS menu), 276

New Zone Wizard, 84, 167, 257, 1118

New Zone Wizards dialog, 84

newsgroups
  messages, 1131-1132
  NNTP servers, 1128-1132
  starting accounts, 1131-1132

NFS
  clients, 572-573
  configuring, 569
  connecting, 575-576
  differences with Windows, 576
  performance parameters, 574
  sharing folders, 571-572
  sharing page, 571
  UNIX, 569

NFS Share Permission dialog, 572

NICs (Network Interface Cards), 299-300, 761-762
  ARP, matching, 76
  choosing, 762
  compatible, 762
  multihomed, 306
  properties, 767-769
    inspecting, 777-778, 780
    setting, 784
  RIS, 863
  troubleshooting, 762

NIS Map Selection dialog, 577

NLB (Network Load Balancing), 305, 1198

NNTP server
  newsgroups, 1128, 1130-1132
  troubleshooting, 1136

no exceptions policies (Group Policies), 832

No Override (Group Policies), 832

nodes, 301-302, 1228, 1248
  Active Directory Sites and Services snap-in, 113-114
  AppleTalk, 797
  clusters, 1231
  heartbeat packets, 306

non-routed AppleTalk networks, 795

non-seed routers, 795

non-transitive trusts, establishing, 107-111

normal backup routine, 949

NOS (network operating system), 676

notation IP addresses, 65

Novell's NetWare Directory Services. *See* NDS

NSI (Network Solution Inc.), 81

Nslookup utility, 280

Ntconfig.pol file, 665

NTDS settings node (AD Sites and Services snap-in), 113

NTFS, 424
  change journals, 426
  clusters, 424
    sizing, 424

compression, implementing, 428-429
data streams, 428
features, 430
file sharing security, 678
   file security, 678
   folder security, 678
   share security, 678
file system filter, 427
MFT, 425
mount points, 427-428
reparse points, 427
security, 426
   descriptors, 426
sparse files, 426
Unicode filenames, 428

NTFS Change Journal, 415

NTGATEWAY groups, creating, 532-533

numbering AppleTalk, 794-795

O

Oakleaf examples, Security Groups, 644

OakLeaf Properties dialog, 684

OakLeaf University domain topology example, 155

Oakley/ISAKMP (IPSec), 498

object request brokers. *See* **ORBs**

objects, 1148
AD, assigning values, 129
brokering, 1147
contacts, 130
Group Policies, editing, 622-623, 628
OUs, moving, 133, 135

ODP (On-Demand Producer), CD22
asf files, publishing, CD65
capturing, CD58-CD61
encoding, avi to asf, CD62, CD64
inverse telecine, CD22
wma files, publishing, CD65

Offline Files
caching methods, 836
configuring settings, 838-839
enabling support, 836
IntelliMirror, 829
mapping, 839-840
options, 837
setting up, 837-838

Synchronization Manager, 841
synchronizing, 840-841
users, IntelliMirror, 836

Offline Files dialog, 838-839

on-demand delivery, CD4

On-Demand Producer. *See* **ODP**

on-demand publishing points, CD35-CD36

Online Files – Add Custom Action dialog, 839

open files, planning backup routine, 958-959

opening
Disk Defragmenter, 449
Domain Security Policy snap-in, 182
PerfMon, 928
WINS Manager, 273

operation master, 150-151

operator requests, 443, 447
preventing, 447

optimizing
drive partitioning, 350-352
   RAID, 351
Group Policies (AD), 621
memory, 940-941
servers, 920
   hardware, 921
   server applications, 921
   system processes, 921

options
CA, 506-507
Computer Security Settings (Group Policies), 626
DHCP, 269-270
Offline Files, 838-839
packages, 849, 851-852
Quota Management, 845

ORBs (object request brokers), 1148

Organizational Unit Selection dialog, 249

organizational units. *See* **OUs**

organizing
backup routine, tape rotation methods, 959-964
disk storage, 956-957
drives, 932-933
Registry, 456

orphaned domain controllers, removing, 143

orphaned folders, 680-681

Other Network File and Print Services dialog, 802, 804

OU Group Policies, 833

OUName Properties dialog, 641

OUs (organizational units), 28, 149
AD, 95
administrating, 223-229
assigning, 157
child domains, 173
creating, domains, 132
delegating control, 228-229
Global groups, 650
GPOs, user accounts, 655
Group Policies, 640
   restricting, 640-643
hierarchies, 29
LDAP, 132-133, 135
Local groups, 650
migrating accounts, 211-220
moving objects, 133, 135
moving within domains, 173, 175
Security Groups, examples, 644

Output File dialog, CD49, CD77

Output Options dialog, CD77

ownership
files, 680
folders, 680

P

packages
changing properties, 849, 851-852
deploying, 850
viewing, 849, 851-852

paging files
establishing baselines (PerfMon), 944-945
improving performance, 947-948
size, 942-943

PAP (Password Authentication Protocol), 1024

parameters
computer settings (Group Policies), 618
File Services, Macintosh, 804-807

parent domains, adding child domains, 160

PARENT-CHILD MODEL

parent-child model, 158
partition knowledge tables. *See* PKTs
partitioning drives, 350-352
    RAID, 351
    RIS, 352
partitions, RIS servers, 864
Password Authentication Protocol. *See* PAP
passwords
    GPOs, 637
    Group Policy security, 625
    Kerberos, long-term key, 38
    troubleshooting policies, 672
    users, GPOs, 655
    virtual directory, 1116
PDC
    DHCP, testing, 375
    DNS server, setting, 276-278
    domain upgrades, recovering, 347-348
    installing ADSI25, 200-211
    programs, adding, 361-362
    promoting to Active Directory, 363-366
    tools, 361-362
    upgrading, 198-200
        verifying, 367-372
        to Windows 2000, 204-211
    upgrading domains, 345
        child domains, 396
        resource domains, 394-395
PDC emulator, 30
PerfMon, 924
    alerts, 891, 905-907
        setting, 908-910
    configuring, 896
    counter logs, 891
        recording traffic, 902-904
    determining cluster size, 926-931
    disk defragmenting, 935
    graphs, 894
    launching, 892
    monitoring networks, 891
    Network Monitor Driver, 892
    opening, 928
    paging files, establishing baselines, 944-945
    performance logs, 905-907
    SysMon, 891
    trace logs, 891
performance
    clusters, 304
    files, 947-948

networks
    SysMon, 901-902
    testing, 897-898
servers, 302-303
    hit rate, 303-304
    L2 cache, 303-304
    RAM, 302-303
    troubleshooting, 978
    upgrading, 901
streaming media, CD7-CD8
performance counters, CD82
performance logs, enabling, 905-907
Performance Logs and Alerts service, 905-907
Performance Meter, tuning servers, 925
Performance Monitor. *See* PerfMon
performance parameters (NFS), 574
Performance Tools, 924
performing
    AD replication traffic tests, 1000-1001
    replication tests, 1014
    standard installation, 766
permissions
    files, 680-681
        low-level, 682
    folders, 680-681
        assigning hierarchical, 686-688
        low-level, 682
    Group Policies, 626-628
    high-level, 682
    low-level, viewing, 682
    Macintosh clients, 810
    Multiple Group, creating third-tier shares, 693-694
    ownership, 680
    Read, creating second-tier shares, 688-691
    shares, assigning hierarchical, 686-688
    Write and Modify, creating shares, 691-693
Permissions dialog, 103, 389
Personalize Your Software dialog, 386
Phone and Modem Options dialog, 1028
Phone and Modem tool, 1027-1028

Phone Number to Dial dialog, 1033, 1083
phonebook entries, VPN, 1093
Physical Locations folder, 443-446
ping program, 75, 267
    LAN hosts, 75
PKI (Public Key Infrastructure), 37, 486-488
PKTs (partition knowledge tables), 709
placing, built-in groups, 116
plaintext, 486-487
planning
    backup routine, 956-959
        media capacity, 959
    domains, 148-149
    IP address assignments, 263
    migration, 342
    streaming media for intranets, CD10-CD11
plans, migration, 194-197
Plug and Play
    printers, 727
    troubleshooting non-plug and play, 333
Point-to-Point Tunneling Protocol. *See* PPTP
policies
    downlevel system, implementing, 664-668
    IPSec, 499-501
    passwords, troubleshooting, 672
    PPTP, 1094-1096
    RAS server, 1038-1039
    security, 400-403
policy inheritance (Group Policies), blocking, 620
Policy Name dialog, 1041
PolicyName Properties dialog, 651-652
Pool Monitor, tuning servers, 924
pooling printers, 724
populating
    Dfs root volumes by linking shares, 712-715
    Security Groups, 643
        example, 645-647
ports, 87
    registered, 87
    TCP, 87

VPN (PPTP), 1081
well-known ports, 87
Ports Properties dialog, 1082

post-junction junctions, 708

power supply, servers, 308-309

PPTP (Point-to-Point Tunneling Protocol), 1024, 1092
clients, setting up, 1088-1089
connections, troubleshooting, 1102
dial-in clients, 1082
filters, 1094-1096
policies, 1094-1096
securing Internet connections, 1094-1096
tunneling, 1078
VPN tunnel servers, 1080-1081
connecting, 1085-1087
ports, 1081
testing, 1087
Windows 98, 1089-1090
Windows NT, 1092-1093

PPTP configuration dialog, 1092

preparing
Cluster Service installation, 1234-1238
installation (RIS), 860-862
migration plans, 759-760
for Windows NT migration, 260-261

prerequisites
ADMT, 232
ADSI25, 1258-1264

presentation services, 56, 1142

preventing operator requests, 447

primary domain controllers. *See* **PDCs**

primary master name server, 80

primary zones, creating, 276-278

Print Provider, 726

Print Services, UNIX, 559

print shares, 677

Print Test Page dialog, 801

Printer Sharing dialog, 731, 801

printers, 724
adding, 783-784
configuring
network-attached, 728-731
server-connected, 732-734
workstation-owned, 732-734
GDI, 725
group policies, 752, 754
installing
network-attached, 727
Plug and Play, 727
Internet, troubleshooting, 755
intranet, 750
Macintosh, troubleshooting, 824
NetWare, sharing with Windows, 526-529
pooling, 724
Print Provider, 726
servers, 739-741
shared
AD, 745-746
connecting clients, 742-744
sharing Macintosh, 802-803
standard monitors, 726
Standard Port Monitor, 724
UNIX, integrating, 558-560
unpublished, 747-748
users, 725

PrinterShareName Properties dialog, 744

printing, 51
color, 51
Internet, 748-751
Internet Print Protocol, 51
networks, Macintosh, 799-803
shared, 725-726, 735-738
network-attached, 726
server-connected, 727
workstation-owned, 727
troubleshooting, 754
AD, 755

PrintName Properties dialog, 735-738

pristine forests, 30-31

private keys, DRA, 504-505

private network connections, 1231

Process Explode, 926

Process Resource Monitor, tuning servers, 924

Process Viewer, tuning servers, 923

processing transactions, 1147

processors, servers, 304-305

producing streaming media, CD14-CD15

production values (streaming video), CD14-CD15

profiles
hardware, 471-472
users
establishing, 660-663
specifying, 658-660

programming, directory-enabled applications (ADSI), 140

programs, CD5
adding to DC, 361-362
Load Simulator, CD79-CD80, CD82
looping, CD74-CD75
ping, 75

promoting
child domains, failure, 396
PDC to Active Directory, 363-366

properties
COM+, 1157-1158
DCOM, 1168, 1170
default shares, 676-677
DHCP, 600-601
drives, 937
DTC, 1178-1179
File Services, Macintosh, 804
IIS, setting, 1110-1113
Local Area Connection, 770
modems, 1027-1028
network adapters, 767-770
NICs, 767-769
setting, 784
packages, 849, 851-852
print servers, 739-741
volumes (Macintosh), 811-813
Windows NT networking, 777-778, 780

Properties dialog, 938

protocols
AppleTalk, 793-794
BOOTP, 587
IPv6, 73
IPX/SPX, NetWare, 521
L2TP, 1078
Named Pipes, 677
PPTP, 1078, 1080-1081, 1092
TCP/IP, NetWare, 521
Telnet, 547
VPN, 1076, 1087

Protocols and Security dialog, 1061

providing name resolution (DNS), 275-276

pruning objects in domains, 154
pseudoheader (TCP), 89
psuedowizard, 1041
Public and Private Key Pair dialog, 508
Public Key Infrastructure. *See* PKI
public keys, Group Policies, 626
public network connections, 1231
Public Network dialog, 1085
PublishedShareName Properties dialog, 703
publishing
asf files with ODP, CD65
shared printers, 743-744
shares in AD, 701-703
wma files with ODP, CD65
Publishing Complete dialog, CD32, CD71
publishing points, CD4
adding intranets, CD28-CD32
on-demand, CD35-CD36
WMT, setting up, CD28-CD32
purchasing servers, 311-313
purpose-built servers, 298
PXE boot ROM, 860

Q

Query feature (AD), 136-137
Queued components, 56
queuing
COM+ applications, 1157
managing services, 1187
MSMQ, 1180-1192
QuickStart Wizard, CD29
Quorum disks, 1232
quorum resources, 301-302
Quota Entries dialog, 845
Quota Management
options, 845
settings, 845-846
starting, 844-845
quotas, 49
setting, 845-846
viewing, 845-846

R

RADIUS (Remote Authentication Dial-In User Service), 1024
RAS, 1045-1047
server, 1037-1038
RAID (Redundant Array of Independent Disks), 301-302, 416, 430
balancing workload, 936
choosing for servers, 325
classifying, 329
Fibre Channel, 331-332
hardware controllers, 330
hot spare drives, 330
levels, 431-433, 435-436
organizing read- and write-mostly operations, 932-933
partitioning drives, 351
recovering, 437
SCSI, 325-327
software-based, 330
stacked, 434
subsystems, 330
troubleshooting, 452
RAID 0, 432-433
RAID 0/1, 434
RAID 1, 433
creating, 439
recovering system disk failure, 440-441
RAID 5, 435-436
creating, 437-438
disk failure, 438
volumes, 417
RAM, servers, 302-303, 313
RAS
configuring, 1029-1031, 1037-1038
DUN
downlevel, 1051-1052
user profiles, 1041-1043
DUN clients, 1029-1031, 1041
hardware, 1026
hunt groups, 1026
integrating Windows NT, 1050-1051
IP addresses, 1036
local server, 1038-1039
new features, 1025
RADIUS authentication, 1037-1038, 1045-1047
configuring, 1045

security, 52
setting policies, 1038-1039
telephone requirements, 1026
testing, 1032-1036
troubleshooting connectivity, 1071
RDP (Remote Desktop Protocol), 1197
RDP-TCP Properties dialog, 1208
Read permissions, creating second-tier shares, 688-691
read- and write-mostly operations, organizing drives, 932-933
read-after-write, 958
reading log files (Web servers), 1123-1124
Ready to Import the MQIS Database dialog, 1183
Ready to Publish dialog, CD31, CD41
realms (Kerberos), 38
recommendations, server purchasing, 312
recording traffic, 902-904
recovering
child domains, 396
disabled systems, 404
files with EFS, 501
RAID, 437
RAID 5, 438
Recovery Console, 407
Safe Mode, 405, 407
upgrades, 347
PDC, 347-348
recovery agents, 490
Recovery Console, 407
redirecting folders, 852-854
My Documents, 852
redirector (streaming media), CD33-CD34
Redundant Array of Independent Disks. *See* RAID
redundant components, 1229
referrals (Dfs), 709
Regedgt32.exe (Registry Editor), 455-456
Regedit.exe (Registry Editor), 455-456
Regional Settings dialog, 385
registered ports, 87

registering Schema Manager, 125-128

Registry, 454, 476. *See also* Registry Editor
ACL, 479
backing up, 476
booting, 468
  Safe Boot, 468
cells, 459-460
Configuration Manager, 455-456, 462
Control Panel, 458
corrupted, 468
features, 459
file associations, 472
files, 461-464
  alt, 461
  dat, 461
  log, 462
Group Policies, 454, 626
hardware profiles, 471-472
hives, 459-464
improvements over Windows 98, 459
information, 455
keys
  HARDWARE, 470
  HKEY_CLASSES_ROOT, 472
  HKEY_CURRENT_CONFIG, 471-472
  HKEY_CURRENT_USER, 473
  HKEY_USERS, 474
  SAM, 466
  SECURITY, 466
  SOFTWARE, 467
migration, 197
organization, 456
other computers, 478
performance, 454
root keys, 459-461, 466
  HKEY_LOCAL_MACHINE, 466-470
sav files, 461
security, 479, 481
settings, 454
  viewing, 455-456
subkeys, 459-460, 466
  Control, 470
SysInfo tool, 474
SYSTEM key, 467-470
System Summary, 474
troubleshooting, 481
user profiles, 473
value entries, 459-460, 464
  changing, 459
  data, 464-465

values, changing, 457-458
viewing organization, 459-460

Registry Editor, 455-456
keys, 463
Regedit.exe, 455-456
Regedt32.exe, 455-456
Registry menu, 476
root keys, 460-461

Registry menu, Import Registry File command, 476

Relay Agent (DHCP), 601
installing, 602-603

remote access, 1024
dial-in, 1025
Macintosh, 815

Remote Access Protocols dialog, 1031

Remote Access Setup dialog, 1093

Remote Administration mode (Terminal Services), 1200-1201

Remote Authentication Dial-In User Service. *See* RADIUS

Remote Boot Disk Generator dialog, 872

remote communication, 52
IAS, 52
RAS, 52

Remote Desktop Protocol. *See* RDP

Remote Installation Folder Location dialog, 866-868

Remote Installation Preparation Wizard (Riprep.exe), 882-886
troubleshooting, 887

Remote Installation Service. *See* RIS

Remote Installation Services Setup Wizard, 866-868

remote printers, adding, 783-784

Remote Procedure Call. *See* RPC

remote Registry, editing, 478

remote servers
alerts, 905-907
backup, 970
performance logs, 905-907

remote sites
adding DCs, 380-381, 987
connecting, 987-988
  choosing method, 987-988

remote storage, 415

Remote Storage Services. *See* RSS

remote workstations, installing sample packages, 1166-1168

removable media, 416

removable storage, 442
configuring, 446
media pools, 443
operator requests, 443, 447
Work Queue, 443, 446-447

Removable Storage Management. *See* RSM

removing
AD, 97
ADSI25, 1285
DCs, 380, 383
orphaned domain controllers, 143

reorganizing
GPOs, 650
migrated security groups, 220-222

Repair Volume dialog, 438

reparse points, 415, 427

replicating
AD, 96
  between DCs, 984-986
  testing traffic, 1000-1001
frequency, 179
monitoring, 1014, 1016-1019
multimaster, 23
troubleshooting, 1020
WINS, 610-611

replication capture files, analyzing (Network Monitor), 1005-1007

Replication Monitor, 1014
clearing log files, 1014
Support tool (AD), 1011-1014

Replication Monitor Support tool (AD), 1011

Replication Partners, 372

replication partners (WINS), 610-611

Replication Policy dialog, 717

Report Selection dialog, 247

Report System Compatibility dialog, 205, 355

Report Wizard, 246-247
Reporting Wizard, 32, 399
reports, migration, 246-247
requesting certificates, 513-514
requirements
　hardware, 759, 984
　　DHCP, 985
　　DNS, 985
　　WINS, 985
　network, 758
　RIS clients, 862-863
　RIS servers, 864
　upgrading domains, 345-347
resolvers (DNS), 80
resolving
　DNS names, 77
　NetBIOS names to IP
　　addresses (WINS), 604-605
Resource command (New menu), 1245
resource domains, upgrading, 392-394
　PDC, 394-395
resource fork (Macintosh), 812
Resource Group Name dialog, 1240
resource groups (clusters), 1244
　failbacks, 1249
　failover, 1249
Resource Record (WINS), 279
resource records (DNS), 80
Resource type Parameters dialog, 1246
ResourceName Properties dialog, 1250
resources (clusters), 1231
　advanced properties, 1250
　clusters, 1233
　　assigning, 1245-1247
　domains, 149
　　Restore Progress dialog, 973
restoring
　from backups, 971-975
　DC, 975
　servers, 920
　troubleshooting, 978
restricted groups, Group Policies, 626
restricting
　host ids, 65-66
　IP addresses, 65-66

net ids, 65-66
OU options (Group Policies), 640-643
user accounts, GPOs, 651
restructuring
　domains, 30-31, 348-349, 1005
　　ADMT, 398-400
　　advantages, 349
　　drawbacks, 349
Retry Task Wizard, 253
Reverse Lookup Zone dialog, 85
reversed field, 88
reviewing client account properties, 876
revoking
　CA certificate, 510
　certificates, 512
RID (relative ID), 150
Rights Manager (WMT), CD23-CD25
　downloading, CD23-CD25
RIPrep. *See* Remote Installation Preparation Wizard
RIS (Remote Installation Services), 352, 858, 760
　BINL (Boot Information Negotiation Layer), 860
　BIOS, Boot Load Order, 860
　boot disks, 872-873, 875-876, 878
　CIW (Client Installation Wizard), 861
　clients
　　GUID, 861
　　network adapter, 860
　　PXE boot ROM, 860
　　requirements, 862-863
　　UUID, 861
　configuring, 866-868
　　for testing, 866
　Group Policy, 879-880
　installing, 865
　　troubleshooting, 887
　partitioning drives, 352
　preparing, 860-862
　Riprep.exe, 882-886
　servers
　　configuring, 868-871
　　partitions, 864
　　requirements, 864
　SIS (Single Instance Store), 860

supported NICs, 863
TFTPD (Trivial File Transfer Protocol Daemon), 860
RMS snap-in, Work Queue, 446-447
Roaming User Profiles, 833
　establishing, 833-835
　IntelliMirror, 829
Role dialog, 1156
roles
　adding, 1156
　adding groups, 1154-1156
　COM+ security, 1154-1156
　deleting, 1156
rolling upgrades, 301
root CA, 488
Root Hints, client DNS servers, 1063
root keys (Registry), 459-461, 466
　HKEY_LOCAL_MACHINE, 466-470
root volumes, 708
　creating, 710-712
　populating, linking shares, 712-715
rotating backup tapes, 959-964
route print (NAT), 1059. *See also* gateways
　AppleTalk, 795
　hardware requirements, 985
　IPs, 67-68
　multihomed host, 67
　non-seed, 795
routing
　AppleTalk, 795
　　configuring, 796-803
　RRAS, 67
Routing and RAS. *See* RRAS
Routing and Remote Access Server Setup Wizard, 1031, 1060, 1080
Routing and Remote Access Service. *See* RRAS
Routing and Remote Access Setup Wizard, 602
RPC (Remote Procedure Call), 986-987
RRAS (Routing and Remote Access Service), 67, 1024
　installing, 1027
　NAT, 1025
　PAP, 1024

PPTP, 1024
VPN servers, PPTP, 1081
RSM (Removable Storage Management), 48, 442
  media, 48
RSM snap-in, 442-443
  configuring physical devices, 446
  operator requests, 447
RSS (Remote Storage Services), 50, 442
running
  ADSI25, 1265-1275
    Windows NT, 1275-1278
  ADSI25 setup program, 1262-1264
  ADSI25 Visual Basic application, 141
  directory synchronizations, 536-541
  Disk Cleanup tool, 450
  domain restruction test, 1005
  full backup, 965-966, 968-969
  Indexing Service, 706-707
  Recovery Console, 407
  Safe Mode, 405, 407

S

SA (security authority), 38
SACL (System Access Control List), 426
  Safe Boot options (Registry), 468
Safe Mode, 405, 407
SAM (Security Account Manager), 155
SAM key (Registry), 466
Sample Bank application
  exporting, 1178
  file DSN, 1173-1178
  installing, 1172-1178
  testing file DSN, 1176-1177
sample packages (MTS), 1150
  testing, 1158-1159
SANs (Storage Area Networks), 301-302, 955
sav files (Registry), 461
Save As command (Console menu), 125
saving PerfMon configurations, 896

scalability
  servers, 304-305
  WMT, CD78-CD80, CD82
scavenging user accounts, 288-291
Schedule dialog, 542
Scheduled Synchronization Wizard, 843-844
scheduling
  backup operations, 976-977
  Windows NT migration, 260-261
Schema, 23
  AD, 95
  snap-ins, 36
Schema Manager, 124
  AD, namespaces, 126
  installing, 125-128
  registering, 125-128
Scope menu, Create command, 268
Scope Name dialog, 591
Scope Options dialog, 593-596
Scope Statistics dialog, 600
scopes (DHCP), 591-592
  activating, 597-599
  creating, 268
  options, 593, 595-596
  testing, 597-599
scripts, logon (home folders), 671-672
scrubbing media files, CD51-CD54
SCSI, 299-300
  bus, 327
  classifying, 326-327
  RAID systems, 325-327
SDRAM (Synchronous Dynamic RAM), 300
SDS (Sun Directory Service), 94
searching
  AD objects with LDAP, 135
  folders in AD, 702-703
  users (AD), 138
second-tier shares
  creating, 688-691
  verifying, 690
secondary servers (DNS), adding, 281
secondary zones (DNS), 381
  size, 927

Secure Server option (IPSec), 498
securing
  DRA private keys, 504-505
  servers from unauthorized access, 679
  WANs over Internet, 1076
security, 36
  built-in groups, 116
  CA, 487, 507
    managing, 506
  Certificate Services, 489
  child domains, 181-184
    Domain Security Policy Console, 182-185
  COM+, 1154-1156
    applications, 1157
  computer settings, 619
  DDF, 490
  DRA private keys, 504-505
  DRF, 490
  EFS, 37, 496-497
    architecture, 491
    disabling, 504
    driver, 491
    recovering files, 501
    Trusted for Delegation, 496-497
  encrypting, 486-487
    ciphertext, 486-487
    plaintext, 486-487
    shared secret, 486
  file sharing, 678
    NTFS, 678
  files, 486
  GPOs, user accounts, 651
  Group Policies, 38, 625-628
    options, 626
    passwords, 625
  IPSec, 38, 489, 498
  Kerberos, 36-38
  NetWare, 532-533
  network, 486
  NTFS, 426
  PKI, 487-488
  policies, 400-403
  RAS, 52
  recovery agents, 490
  Registry, 479, 481
  servers
    conditioning systems, 308-311
    power supply, 308-309
    server closets, 307
    SPS, 308
  Smart Card logon, 37
Security Account Manager. *See* SAM

SECURITY AUTHORITY

security authority. *See* SA
security boundaries, 26
security descriptors, 426
Security Groups, 29, 149
    adding accounts, 648-649
    designing, 643, 645-647
    filtering GPOs, 650, 652
    hierarchies, 158
    nesting, 221-222
    populating, 643, 645-647
SECURITY key (Registry), 466
Security Policies, example, 645-647
Security Policy dialog, 183
security principal, 38
Security Settings templates, importing (GPOs), 635-637
Security Translation dialog, 250
seed routers (AppleTalk), 797
seizing FSMO roles, 408-409
Select a Target Container dialog, 241
Select an Account dialog, 1236
Select Attribute dialog, 1039
Select Counters dialog, 902, 946
Select Disks dialog, 420-422
Select Drive dialog, 450
Select Group dialog, 222, 646
Select Groups dialog, 1040
Select Installation Folder dialog, 1263
Select Network Component Type dialog, 771, 796
Select Network Protocol dialog, 771, 796, 892, 1092
Select Network Service dialog, 265
Select Publishing Method dialog, CD31, CD41, CD70
Select Recovery Agents dialog, 503-504
Select the Dfs Root Type dialog, 710
Select the Printer Port dialog, 560, 729, 800
Select User or Contact dialog, 131

Select Users and Groups dialog, 1111, 1155
Select Users, Computers or Groups dialog, 836
sequence numbers, 88
sequencing domain upgrades, 343-345
server closets, 307
    temperature control, 310-311
server computers (nodes), 1231
Server Installer packages, exporting, 1178
Server Manager, 1277
    Windows NT, 112
Server menu, Replication Partners command, 274
Server option (IPSec), 498
Server Properties dialog, 739-741, 1018
Server Settings folder (Terminal Services), 1210
server-connected printers, 727
    configuring, 732-734
ServerName dialog, 1110
ServerName Properties dialog, 869
servers, 21, 298
    applications, 921, 1141
    backup routines, 948
        archive bit, 948-949
        choosing, 954-956
        copy, 950
        daily copy, 953
        differential, 952
        incremental, 951
        integrity, 957-958
        System State, 953
        System Volume Information, 954
    backup routing, 920
    backups, 300-302
    budgeting, 311-313
    clustering, 300-302, 1231
    COM, 307
    departmental networks, 21
    DHCP, 587
        adding backup, 271-272
    DNS, 79
        secondary, 281
    Driver Signing, 323
    encrypting, 495-497
    enterprise networks, 21

Enterprise Root CA, 1097-1098, 1100
fixed DNS and WINS addresses, adding, 282-283
GC, 381
hardware
    disabling, 320
    enabling, 320
    NICs, 299-300
    processors, 304-305
    purchasing, 311-313
    SCSI, 299-300
hardware management feature, 315
    Device Manager, 316-321
hit rate, 303-304
installing Windows, 384-387
IP addresses, changing, 71-72
L2 cache, increasing, 303-304
load balancing, 305
Load Simulator, CD79-CD82
logging events, CD84-CD85
managing Disk Management snap-in, 418-424
measuring read and write operations size, 926-931
media, CD10-CD11
MSMQ, 1184-1192
NAS, 312
NetBEUI-only, 263
NFS (UNIX), connecting, 575-576
NICs, multihomed, 306
NLB, 305
NNTP, 1128-1136
nodes, 301-302
    heartbeat packets, 306
optimizing, 920
    hardware, 921
    server applications, 921
    system processes, 921
performance, 302-303
    clusters, 304
    L2 cache, 303-304
    RAM, 302-303
    troubleshooting, 978
primary master name server, 80
print, 739-741
purchasing recommendations, 312
quorum resources, 301-302
RAID, 330
    choosing, 325
    classifying, 329
    Fibre Channel, 331-332
    software-based, 330
RAM, 313

RAS, 1029-1031, 1050-1051
  configuring, 1037-1038
  testing, 1032-1036
remote backups, 970
requirements (RIS), 864
restoring, 920, 971, 973-975
RIS
  configuring, 868-869, 871
  partitions, 864
rolling upgrades, 301
scalability, 304-305
  SMP, 304-305
SCSI, 325-327
  bus, 327
securing from unauthorized access, 679
security, 307
  conditioning systems, 308-311
  physical, 307
  SPS, 308
simulating load (unicasting), CD78-CD80, CD82
SMTP, 1133-1134
system files, verifying, 323-324
Telnet, 547, 554-555
tuning, 921
  Disk Defragmenter, 922
  Extensible Counter List, 925
  Install Remove Service, 926
  Memory Profiling Tool, 924
  Network Monitor, 922
  Performance Meter, 925
  Performance Monitor, 924
  Pool Monitor, 924
  Process Explode, 926
  Process Resource Monitor, 924
  Process Viewer, 923
  Support Tools, 923
  Task List Viewer, 924
  Task Manager, 921
UNIX, mapping, 566-567
upgrading, 313-315
  ADs, 206, 208, 210-211
  Windows NT 4.0 production, 352-360, 373-375
upgrading hardware, 901
UPS, 308-309
versions, 21
  Advanced Server, 21
  AppCenter, 22
  DataCenter Server, 22
  Server, 21
  specifications, 22
virtual, 1238-1239

VPN, 1085-1087, 1094-1096
  L2TP, 1097-1100
  PPTP, 1080-1081
WINS, 606, 608-609
X Window, 556-557

Servers node (AD Sites and Services snap-in), 113

Service Account Migration Wizard, 253-254, 399

Service Account Selection dialog, 254

service accounts, migrating, 253-254

services (AD)
  configuring, 992-997
  viewing, 113

sessions (Macintosh File Services), 805

Set Application Identity dialog, 1159

Set Capture File dialog, CD60

Set Filtering Options button, 215

setting
  alerts on counter logs, 908, 910
  disk quotas, 844-846
  drive properties, 937
  Group Policy (RIS), 879-880
  home folders, 670-672
  IIS, properties, 1110-1113
  Local Area Connection properties, 770
  low-virtual-memory alert, 945-947
  NIC properties, 784
  passwords, Group Policies, 625
  PDC DNS server, 276-278
  permissions, Group Policies, 626-628
  properties
    DCOM, 1168-1170
    DTC, 1178-1179
  RAS server policies, 1038-1039
  replication frequency, 179
  scope options, 593-596
  second-tier shares, 689
  security
    child domains, 181-184
    DCs, 400-403
    domains, 400-403
    Group Policies, 625-628
  user profiles, DUN, 1041-1043

setting up
  client networking, 765-766
  clients, VPN, 1088-1089
  default FTP sites, 1125-1127
  DNS zones for child domains, 166-169
  Network Monitor, 997-999
  Offline Files, 837-838
  PPTP VPN servers, 1080-1081
  Replication Monitor, 1011-1014
  software installs, 848-849, 851-852
  virtual servers, clusters, 1239-1242
  WMT unicast publishing points, CD28-CD32

settings
  Application Installer Service, 847-848
  MSMQ, 1188
  TCP/IP, automating, 267-270
  virtual memory, 943-944

setup files, obtaining, 816-819

Setup Type dialog, 536

SFU (Microsoft Services for UNIX), 564-565
  installing, 565
  UNIX, 564-565

shared folders
  creating, 683-685
  virtual servers, 1239-1242

shared printers, 726
  AD, 745-746
  configuring, 735-738
  connecting clients, 742-744
  network-attached, 726
  server-connected printers, 727
  workstation-owned, 727

shared secret, 486

Shared System Volume (Sysvol), installing, 97

Shared System Volume dialog, 102, 207, 364, 378, 389

shared-disk subsystems (clusters), 1231
  dumb arrays, 1232
  smart arrays, 1232

shared-everything model (clusters), 1232

shared-nothing model (clusters), 1232

shared-secret encryption, 38

SHARES

shares
  common, 676-677
  creating
    ADSI25, 683-685
    second-tier, 688-691
    third-tier, 691-694
  Dfs, testing, 715-716
  fault-tolerant, 716-718
  hidden, 677
  Integrated Windows Authentication, 699
  linking to populate Dfs roots, 712-713, 715
  Macintosh. *See* volumes
  mapping to drives, 694
  NETLOGON, 677
  permissions, 686-688
  print, 677
  publishing in AD, 701-703
  security, 678
  system roots, 677
  SYSVOL, 677
  verifying, 690

sharing
  files, 676-677, 680-681
    Macintosh, 812-813
    with NetWare, 526-529
    security, 678
  folders
    NFS clients, 571-572
    on intranet, 697-699, 701
  home folders, 670-672
  printers, 725-726
    Macintosh, 802-803
    with NetWare, 526-529
  volumes (Macintosh), 808-813

shell namespace, 659-660

shortcuts, Terminal Service Clients, 1224

Show Database dialog, 275

SIF (setup information file), 877
  editing, 877

Signature Verification Results dialog, 324

simple volumes, 417
  creating, 419-421

simulating
  server load, unicasting, CD78-CD80, CD82
  traffic, 897-898
    measuring (SysMon), 898-902

Single Instance Store. *See* SIS

single-domains
  migrating, 198-202, 204-206, 208, 210-211
  model, 155-158

single-master operations, 150-151

single-servers, 299-300
  performance, 302-303
  single-tree directories, designing, 154

SIS (Single Instance Store), 860

sites
  AD, 96
    configuring, 992-997
    connecting, 996-997
    example configuration, 993-997
    viewing, 113
  administrating, 985-986
  child domains, moving to, 177-181
  communicating
    choosing method, 987-988
    estimating traffic, 990
  connecting
    DSL, 988
    frame relay, 988
    T-1 lines, 987
  creating, 177
  Group Policy, 832
  subnets, 180
  synchronous operations, 986
  Web. *See* Web sites

sizing
  AD databases, 153
  paging files, 941
  servers, 920
  volume, 421-422

Small Computer System Interface. *See* SCSI

smart arrays, 1232

Smart Card logon, 37-39
  implementing, 40

SMP (symmetrical multiprocessing), 304-305

SMTP server
  configuring, 1133-1134
  NDR, 1134

snap-ins
  Active Directory Domains and Trusts, 34, 106, 170
  Active Directory Schema Manager, 36
  Active Directory Sites and Services, 35, 113, 178
  Active Directory Users and Computers, 33, 133, 173-174, 540
  AD administrating, 33
  AD administrative for Windows 2000, 188-189
  Backup and Recovery, 48
  Certificates, 513
  Component Services, 1150-1152
  Configuration (Terminal Services), 1205-1206, 1210
  DC, 361-362
  DHCP, 590-591
  Disk Defragmenter, 922
  Disk Management, 418-419, 448, 450
  DNS, 84, 169, 396
  DNS Management MMC, 85-86
  Domain Controller Security, 402
  Domain Monitor Resource Kit, 344
  Domain Security Policy, 182
  Domains and Trusts, 399
  Extensible Counter List, 925
  Group Policy, 34, 622-624, 628-630, 641
  Install Remove Service, 926
  LeakyApp, 926
  Licensing Terminal Services, 1214-1216
  migration (AD), 30-31, 231-232
  MMC, Certificate Authority, 510
  Movetree.exe Support, 187-188
  Network Monitor, 922
  Performance, 924
  Performance Meter, 925
  Performance Monitor, 924
  Phone and Modem, 1027-1028
  Pool Monitor, 924
  Process Explode, 926
  Process Viewer, 923
  Replication Monitor Support, 1011-1014
  RSM, 442-443
  Schema Manager, 124, 127
  servers, tuning, 921
  Support, 923
  SysInfo, 474
  System Monitor, 930, 940
  System Performance Monitor, 922
  Task Manager, 921

STREAMING MEDIA 1355

Users and Computers, 212-220
WINS, 607
WMT, CD20-CD21
sniffing data, 497
SOA tab (Start of Authority), 86
sockets, 87
soft-linked volumes, 418
software
installing
Application Installation Service, 848-852
completing, 851-852
setting up, 848-852
testing, 851-852
packages, 849-852
RAID, 330
streaming media, CD11-CD15
Software Installation Properties dialog, 641
SOFTWARE key (Registry), 467
software packages. *See* packages
Source File dialog, CD49
source port, TCP header, 88
spanned volumes, 417
creating, 422-423
sparse file support, 415
sparse files, 50, 426
Specify a Program and Stream Name dialog, CD38-CD41, CD68
Specify Stream Format Information dialog, CD38, CD70
Specify the Dfs Root Share dialog, 711
specifying
AD database location, 101
DHCP options, 593
fixed IP addresses, 772, 774
group policies, printers, 752
site subnets, 180
user profiles (downlevel clients), 658-660
speed, streaming media, CD7-CD8
spreading drive workload, 936
SPS (standby power supply), 308

SQL Server Setup dialog, 1175
stacked RAID, 434
Standalone CAs, 489
standard installation, performing, 766
Standard Port Monitor, 724
standard print monitors, 726
standby power supply. *See* SPS
Start Leaking button, 941
starting
Disk Quotas, 844-845
Indexing Service, 706-707
NetMon, 911
newsgroups accounts, 1131-1132
Quota Management, 844-845
Terminal Services Manager, 1211-1213
stateful components, 1150
stateless components, 1150
Static Mappings (Local) dialog, 273
Static Mappings command (Mappings menu), 273
stations, CD5
broadcasting
editing, CD44-CD46
multicasting, CD36-CD39, CD41
configuration files, CD42-CD46
creating, CD37-CD39, CD41
HTML code, CD42-CD46
multicasting, CD42-CD46, CD68-CD73
statistics (DHCP), 600-601
Stop Traffic button, 898
storage
Backup and Recovery tool, 48
disk quotas, 49
disks, 956-957
distributed link tracking, 50
dynamic volume management, 47
IntelliMirror, 50
managing, 47
multiple data streams, 50
RSM, 48
sparse files, 50
Storage Area Networks. *See* SANs
storage management, 416
Dfs, 415
disk quotas, 415

dynamic disks, 415
EFS, 415
enhancing, 414
filters, 415
FRS, 415
NTFS Change Journal, 415
remote storage, 415
removable media, 416
reparse points, 415
sparse file support, 415
volume mount points, 415
storing information (Registry), 455
streaming media, 53, CD2-CD3
asf files, CD65
enhancing, CD51-CD54
ASF redirector, CD5
bandwidth, CD6-CD8
DSL, CD7-CD8
limiting, CD34
broadcasting, CD3
encoding, CD75-CD77
multicasting, CD36-CD39, CD41
cable modems, CD7-CD8
Codecs, CD5
EMMS, CD2
encoding, CD5, CD46, CD48-CD51
audio, CD46-CD48
http, CD5
illustrated audio files, CD5, CD55-CD58
Internet, CD9-CD10
intranets, CD8-CD9
originating content, CD11-CD15
planning, CD10-CD11
software, CD11-CD15
LANs, CD10
latency, CD6
Load Simulator, CD79-CD80, CD82
MPEG, 54
multicasting, CD3
adding streams, CD72-CD73
asx files, CD75
file-based content, CD68-CD73
NetShow, 55
on-demand, CD4
performance, CD7-CD8
programs, CD5, CD38-CD39, CD41
looping, CD74-CD75
publishing points, CD4
on-demand, CD35-CD36

1356 STREAMING MEDIA

redirector, CD33-CD34
stations, CD5
   configuration files,
     CD42-CD46
   creating, CD37-CD39,
     CD41
trapping stream errors,
   CD74-CD75
UDP streaming, CD5
unicasting, CD3,
   CD76-CD77
   simulating, CD78-CD80,
     CD82
Windows Media Audio files
   (wma), CD5
WMT, 54, CD2, CD15,
   CD17
   testing scalability,
     CD78-CD80, CD82

streams, multiple data, 50
striped volumes, 417
structures, datagrams, 73
student accounts (ADSI25), 1274-1275
student users (ADSI25), 1279-1283
subkeys
   HKEY_CURRENT_USER
     key, 473
   Registry, 459-460, 466
     Control, 470
     HARDWARE key, 470

subnet masks, 68-70
   Class B addresses, 68
   Class C addresses, 69
   decimal values, 68

subnets
   IPs, 67
   sites, 180

Subnets node (AD Sites and Services snap-in), 113
subordinate CA, 488
subsystems
   RAID, Fibre Channel,
     331-332
   shared-disks, 1231
     dumb arrays, 1232
     smart arrays, 1232

Sun Directory Service. *See* **SDS**
support
   Internet Explorer (FTP), 563
   Telnet, 547

Support Tools
   AD, Replication Monitor,
     1011-1014

installing, 923
Memory Profiling, 924
Pool Monitor, 924
Process Resource Monitor, 924
Process Viewer, 923
Task List Viewer, 924
tuning servers, 923

switching to native mode, 397
synchronizing AD databases and DCs, 23
symmetric key algorithms, 486
symmetrical multiprocessing. *See* **SMP**
Synchronization Manager, 841
   IntelliMirror, 829
   Offline Files, 841-844
   troubleshooting, 854

Synchronization Settings dialog, 842
synchronizing
   directories, 534-541
     troubleshooting, 543
   Offline Files, 840-841
   parent and child domains, 160

Synchronous Dynamic RAM. *See* **SDRAM**
synchronous operations, sites, 986
SysInfo tool (System Information tools), 474
SysMon (PerfMon), 891
   adding object counters, 892-893
   baseline data, 901-902
   graphs, 895, 907
   measuring traffic, 898-902
   simulating traffic, 898-902
   troubleshooting, 916

SYSPREP images, testing, 885
System Access Control List. *See* **SACL**
system files, verifying, 323-324
system groups, 117
System Information tools. *See* **SysInfo**
SYSTEM key (Registry), 467-470
System Monitor, 930
System Monitor graph view, 929
System Monitor Properties dialog, 894

System Monitor snap-in, 940
System Performance Monitor, tuning servers, 922
System Policies
   computers, 668, 670
   user accounts, 665-668
system processes, optimizing, 921
system roots, 677
System State, 953
   restoring, 975
System Summary (Registry), 474
System Volume Information, 954
SYSVOL shares, 677

T

T-1 lines (intersite communication), 987
taking ownership, folders, 680-681
tapes (backup), rotation methods, 959-964
Task List Viewer, tuning servers, 924
Task Manager
   tuning servers, 922
   virtual memory, settings, 943-944
Task Scheduler, automating backup routines, 976-977
Tasks to Delegate dialog, 225, 653
TCP
   congestion, 88
   headers, 88
     acknowledgement number, 88
     checksum, 88
     control bits, 88
     data offset, 88
     destination port, 88
     reversed field, 88
     sequence number, 88
     source port, 88
     urgent pointer, 88
     windows, 88
   ports, 87
   pseudoheader, 89
   windowing, 87

TCP/IP, 40
BDC, upgrading, 266-267
communicating, 86
DHCP, automating settings, 267-270
inspecting properties, 777-778, 780
installing, 284
verification, 285
moving from NetBEUI, 261-262
NetBEUI
adding, 263
installing, 263, 265
NetWare, 521
troubleshooting, 293
upgrading, 41

TCP/IP DNS Server dialog, 282

TCP/IP Port Wizard, 724

TCP/IP Properties dialog, 282-283, 784

telecince, CD22

telecommunication adapters, hardware requirements, 985

Telnet, 546
advantages, 552-553
clients, 546, 564
HyperTerminal, 550-552
command-line, 547-548
configuring Windows 2000, 553-555
disadvantages, 553
modes, 549
protocol, 547
server program, 547
servers, 554-555
support, 547
troubleshooting, 580
X Window, 556

temperatures, controlling (server closets), 310-311

template files, security (domains), 401-403

Template Security Policy Setting dialog, 627

Template Stream Format dialog, CD48

templates, Security Settings (GPOs), 635-637

Templates Properties dialog, 527

Terminal Server, 57

Terminal Services, 1196
Application Server mode, 1200-1201
applications, troubleshooting, 1225
comparing with TSE, 1198-1199
Configuration snap-in, 1205-1206, 1210
connections, 1206, 1210, 1221
default, 1223
modifying, 1206-1207, 1209
Execute mode, 1204
installing, 1199-1201, 1203
applications, 1204
Licensing tool, 1214-1216
Licensing Wizard, 1216
Logon Settings page, 1207
minimum hardware requirements, 1200
NLB, 1198
RDP, 1197
Remote Administration mode, 1200-1201
Server Settings folder, 1210
upgrading from Windows NT 4.0, 1203-1204

Terminal Services Client
deploying, 1219-1223
hardware, 1218
hot-keys, 1224
installing, 1217-1223
Troubleshooting, 1224

Terminal Services Licensing Setup dialog, 1215

Terminal Services Manager, 1211-1213
commands, 1213-1214

Terminal Services Setup dialog, 1203

test clients, SysMon, 899-902

test networks, designing, 991-992

Test or Make Changes dialog, 238

test shares (ADSI25), 1258

testing
AD traffic, 1000
restructured, 1005
Add-Users test, 1001, 1003
BDC, 376, 379-380
client Internet connections, 1065
connections, PPTP, 1090
control delegation (OUs), 228-229

counter logs, 906-907
datagrams, 75
DC, 367, 369-370, 372
Dfs shares, 715-716
DHCP, 375
DHCP scopes, 597-599
Directory Services Client, Windows 9x, 786-788
DNS, 280, 375
domains, 389-392
file DSN with Sample Bank client, 1176-1177
IIS performance, virtual directory, 1116-1117
Indexing Service, 706-707
installation, 872-873, 875
IP connectivity, 266-267
logon scripts, 694-697
migration, 195-197
hardware requirements, 195
migrations
groups, 237-246
multiple domains, 230-231
users, 237-246
network traffic, 899-902
performance, traffic simulation, 897-898
PPTP connection, 1087
RAS, 1032-1036
replication traffic, 990
replications, 1014
RIS, 866
boot disks, 872-878
sample packages (MTS), 1158-1159
software installs, 851-852
SYSPREP images, 885
traffic, GC, 1003-1004
VPN
clients, 1101
connections, 1085-1087
phonebook entries, 1093
Web sites (virtual directory), 1116-1117
WfW clients, 819
Windows NT upgrade, 358-360
WINS, 375
WMT scalability, CD78-CD82

Text Import Wizard, 288

TFTPD (Trivial File Transfer Protocol Daemon), 860

TGT (Ticket Granting Ticket), 39

third-tier shares, creating, 691-693
with Multiple Group permissions, 693-694

1358 THREE-TIER APPLICATION ARCHITECTURE

three-tier application architecture, 1141-1143
  business services, 1142
  data services, 1141
  presentation services, 1142

Tic-Tac-Toe Properties dialog, 1162

Ticket Granting Ticket. *See* TGT

tickets, Kerberos, 39

Time of Day Constraints dialog, 1038

TMs (transaction monitors). *See* TPs

TOH (Tower of Hanoi Rotation), 964

TokenTalk, 793

tools. *See* snap-ins

Tower of Hanoi Rotation. *See* TOH

TPs (transaction processors), 1148
  two-phase commit, 1148

trace logs (PerfMon), 891

tracking Registry configuration, 454

traffic
  AD replication, testing, 1000-1001
  adding users, 1001-1003
  baseline, 897-898
  GC, testing, 1003-1004
  graphs, 894
  monitoring with PerfMon, 891
  NetBIOS, 586
  recording with counter logs, 902-904
  replication, testing, 990
  simulating, 897-898
    measuring, 898-902
  testing restructured, 1005

transaction processors. *See* TPs

transactions, 1148
  processing, 1147

transferring zones, 367-372

transitive trusts, 106

Translate Objects dialog, 250

Transmission dialog, CD77

trapping stream errors, CD74-CD75

trees, 24-25, 645-647
  creating, 26
  single directories, designing, 154

Trivial File Transfer Protocol Daemon. *See* TFTPD

troubleshooting
  Active Directory installation, 190
  ADMT migrations, 257
  ADSI25
    setup, 256
    startup, 1286
  AppleTalk, 823
  Application Installation Service, 854
  audio quality, CD86
  backup routines, 978
  broadcast connections, CD87
  CA, 516
  child domain creation, 190
  client booting, 887
  cluster application installation, 1251
  cluster installation, 1251
  COM+
    performance, 1193
    security, 1192
  counter logs, 917
  custom filter problems, 144
  demand-dial connections, 1071
  Dfs configuring, 720
  DHCP, 293, 613
  directory synchronization, 543
  DNS, 294
  DSM snap-in, 451
  EFS, 515
  FRS, 719
  FTP servers, 1135
  Indexing Service, 719
  IPSec communication problems, 515
  IPX connections, 542
  L2TP connections, 1103
  Macintosh printing, 824
  mandatory user profiles, 673
  migration hardware issues, 256
  missing forward lookup zones, 90
  multicasting stream problems, CD88
  NAT client connection problems, 1071
  NetTraffic application, 916
  networks, Windows NT, 789
  NICs, 762

  NNTP server, 1136
  non-plug and play devices, 333
  password policies, 672
  PPTP connections, 1102
  printers
    Internet, 755
    networks, 755
  printing, 754
    AD, 755
  RAID implementations, 452
  RAS connectivity, 1071
  removing orphaned domain controllers, 143
  replication connectivity, 1021
  replication topology, 1020
  RIPrep, 887
  RIS installation, 887
  server performance, 978
  Synchronization Manager, 854
  SysMon, 916
  TCP/IP, 293
  Telnet, 580
  Terminal Services application compatibility, 1225
  Terminal Services Client, 1224
  UNIX printers, 581
  upgrade problems, 409-410
  video quality, CD87
  Web servers, 1135
  Windows 2000 clients, networking, 788
  WINS, 294, 614
  Wrong Registry Editor, 481

Trust Migration Wizard, 238

Trust Relationships dialog, 235, 390

Trusted for Delegation (EFS), 496
  enabling, 496-497

trusts (Windows NT), 373-375
  AD, 105
  transitive, 106

TSE (Windows NT 4.0 Terminal Server Edition), 1196. *See also* Terminal Services
  comparing with Terminal Services, 1198-1199

tuning servers, 920-921
  Disk Defragmenter, 922
  Extensible Counter List, 925
  Install Remove Service, 926
  Memory Profiling Tool, 924
  Network Monitor, 922
  Performance Meter, 925
  Performance Monitor, 924
  Pool Monitor, 924
  Process Explode, 926

Process Resource Monitor, 924
Process Viewer, 923
Support Tools, 923
System Performance Monitor, 922
Task List Viewer, 924
Task Manager, 921
tunnel channel, 1078
tunneling, 1078
two-phase commit, 1148

U

UDP, 89
UDP streaming, CD5
unattended setup cycle, 356-357
unauthorized access, preventing, 679
unicasting, CD3
broadcasting, CD76-CD77
IP addresses, 65
publishing points, CD28-CD32, CD35-CD36
intranets, CD28-CD32
simulating server load, CD78-CD80, CD82
uninstalling ADSI25, 1285
uninterruptible power supply. *See* **UPS**
Unique Sequence Number. *See* **USN**
universal groups, 29, 220-222
Universally Unique ID. *See* **UUID**
UNIX
BOOTP protocol, 587
FTP, 561-562
Internet Explorer support, 563
integrating, 546, 558-560
directories, 577, 579
printers, 558-560
Microsoft Services. *See* SFU
NFS, 569, 572-573
connecting, 575-576
sharing folders, 571-572
Print Services, 559
SFU, 564-565
Telnet, 546
troubleshooting printing, 581
users, 566-567
mapping, 566

Unlisted or Updated Protocol dialog, 817
unpublished printers, installing, 747-748
unrecognized pools (media pools), 443
update (LDAP), 124
Update Device Driver Wizard, 318
updating service accounts, 253-254
upgrading
AD, 30
verifying, 367-368
application services, 56
BDC, 266-267, 376-380
to DC, 377-378
DCs, 383
domains, 343-347
PDC, 345
recovering, 347-348
resource, 392-395
sequencing, 343-345
IIS, 44-45
incentives, 21
to IPv6, 73
issues, 21
Kernel, 58
mixed mode, 30
MS-DOS, 820-822
MSMQ, 1180-1192
native mode, 30
NetShow, 55
PDC, 198-200, 344
child domains, 396
to Windows 2000, 204-211
print services, 51
security services, 36
servers, 313-315, 901
ADs, 206, 208, 210-211
migration, 197
Windows NT 4.0 production, 352-360, 373-375
storage management, 47
streaming media, 53
TCP/IP, 41
Terminal Services, 57
Terminal Services from Windows NT 4.0, 1203-1204
troubleshooting, 409-410
Windows 2000, comparing with installing, 760-761
Windows for Workgroups, 815-819
WINS, 606-607

UPN (user principal name), 649
UPS (uninterruptible power supply), 308
servers, 309
upstream providers, 66
urgent pointers, 88
URLs, assigning, 1118-1119
User Account dialog, 242
User Configuration (Group Policies), 631
User Manager tool (Windows NT), 109-111
installing, 112
User Migration Wizard, 32
user principal name. *See* **UPN**
user profiles
DUN, 1041-1043
Registry, 473
Roaming, 833
user settings (Group Policies), 618
parameters, 619
Username Properties dialog, 121, 129, 656-657
attribute names and field captions, 131
users
accounts, 654
applying System Policies, 665-668
GPOs, 651, 655-657
migrating, 211-220
AD, 115-120
searching, 138
adding
AD, 118-120
Security Groups, 648-649
ADSI25, students, 1279-1283
child domains, 173
cleaning accounts, 287
data
managing (IntelliMirror), 835
Offline Files, 836
domain, 208
hierarchies, 28
IntelliMirror, managing settings, 829
listing, 288-291
mapping UNIX, 566
migrating, testing, 237-246
moving within domains, 173, 175

USERS

printing, 725
profiles
establishing (GPOs), 660-663
specifying, 658-660
UNIX, 566-567

Users and Computers tool, 212-220

Users, Computers and Groups dialog, 684

USN (Unique Sequence Number), 135

Usrstrat utility, 288

utilities
DHCP Manager, 268
Nslookup, 280
ping, 267
Usrstrat, 288
Windows Backup, 972
winipcfg, 286
WINS Manager, 273

UUID (Universally Unique ID), 861

V

value entries (Registry), 464
changing, 459
names, 464
Registry, 459-460

VBA (Visual Basic Applications), 140
ADSI, 141

verifying
AD upgrades, 208, 367-368
certificate enrollment, 1100
clients DHCP settings, 780-783
DHCP, 285-286
new domains, 389-392
PDC upgrades, 367-372
shares, second-tier, 690
system files, 323-324
trusts (Windows NT), 373-375
upgrades, Windows NT, 359-360
WINS, 285-286

video
asf files, CD59
avi files, CD59-CD61
encoding On-Demand Producer, CD58-CD61
illustrated audio, CD55-CD58

markers, CD51-CD54
scrubbing, CD51-CD54
streaming, 53, CD2-CD3
asf, CD51-CD54
capturing, CD58-CD61
latency, CD6
software, CD12-CD15
WMT, CD2, CD15, CD17
troubleshooting quality, CD87

Video Format dialog, CD60

viewing
AD class properties, 128
CA information (MMC snap-in), 510
counter log data, 906-907
devices, 322
DHCP statistics, 600-601
disk quotas, 844-846
frame content detail, 1006-1007
frame list, 1006-1007
FRS in AD, 718
group policies for domains, 185-186
low-level permissions, 682
namespaces, 126
NetMon data, 912, 914
packages, 849, 851-852
Registry organization, 459-460
Registry settings, 455-456
services (AD), 113
sites (AD), 113

virtual block caching, 938-939

virtual directory, Web sites, 1116-1117

virtual memory, 941
low alert, 945-947
settings, 943-944
Winmsd, 943-944

Virtual Memory dialog, 942

virtual servers, 1238-1239
creating, 1240
shared folders, 1239-1242

virtual sites
host headers, 1120-1123
IIS, 1119-1123

Visual Basic Applications. *See* VBA

volume mount points, 415

Volume Type dialog, 420, 423

VolumeName Properties dialog, 811

volumes, 416-417
alternate, 708
creating spanned, 422-423
deleting, 423-424
downlevel, 709
fault-tolerance, 709
hard-linked, 418
mirrored, 417
NTFS clusters, 424
RAID 1
breaking, 440
creating, 439
RAID-5, 417
root, 708
sharing with Macintosh clients, 808-813
simple, 417
creating, 419-421
sizing, 421-422
soft-linked, 418
spanned, 417
striped, 417

VPN protocols, 1076
connections, 1085-1087
L2TP, 1078, 1097-1098, 1100
phonebook entries, 1093
PPTP, 1078, 1094-1096
clients, 1088-1089
connections, 1087
dial-in clients, 1082-1085
servers, 1080-1081
testing clients, 1101

VPNConnectionName dialog, 1086

W

WANs
monitoring, 890
securing Internet, 1076

wav files, encoding, CD48-CD51

wax files
linking to asx files, CD66-CD67
writing, CD65-CD67

WDM (Windows Driver Model), 58

Web pages, linking asx and wax files, CD66-CD67

Web servers
log files, 1123-1124
troubleshooting, 1135

Web Site Content Directory dialog, 1116

WIZARDS 1361

Web Site Permissions dialog, 1122

Web Site Security Credentials dialog, 1122

Web sites
  FTP, 1125, 1127
  IANA, 66
  Mission Critical Software, 349
  URLs, assigning, 1118-1119
  virtual directory, 1116-1123

WebDAV (Web Distributed Authoring and Versioning), 44

WebShareName Properties dialog, 701

well-known ports, 87

WfW, upgrading, 815-819

windowing (TCP), 87

Windows 2000
  Backup application, 965-969
  comparing to NetWare, 522
  installing AD administrative tools, 188-189
  Support Tools, 923

Windows 2000 boot disks, creating, 441

Windows 2000 Components dialog, 386

Windows 2000 Components Wizard, 361-362

Windows 2000 Setup Welcome dialog, 354

Windows 98
  accommodating clients, 780-784
  clients, 780-783
  Directory Services Client, 786-788
  DUN clients, 1054
  PPTP clients, 1089
  VPN clients, 1088

Windows Backup utility, 972

Windows Components dialog, 804, 865

Windows Components Wizard, 508, 559, 802, 1108, 1202

Windows Driver Model. *See* WDM

Windows for Workgroups
  testing, 819
  upgrading, 815-819

Windows Installation Folder Name dialog, 867

Windows Installer, 847-848
  IntelliMirror, 829
  settings, 847-848

Windows Media Audio, CD5

Windows Media Encoder dialog, CD30

Windows Media Load Simulator Wizard, CD79

Windows Media Technology. *See* WMT

Windows NT
  ADSI25, 1275-1278
  altering network properties, 777-778, 780
  clients, 775-777
  domains, administering from Windows 2000, 111, 115-118, 120
  installing, 112, 776-777
  migrating, 260-261
  NetBEUI, 261-262
  networks, troubleshooting, 789
  non-transitive trusts, 109, 111
  PPTP clients, 1092-1093
  production server
    upgrading, 352-360, 373-375
  RAS servers, 1050-1051
  Terminal Services, 1196
  upgrading Terminal Services, 1203-1204
  User Manager tool, 109, 111-112

Windows NT 4.0 RAS Servers dialog, 102

Windows NT 4.0 Terminal Server Edition. *See* TSE

Windows NT Load Balancing. *See* WLBS

Windows NT production server, trusts, 373-375

winipcfg utility, 286

Winmsd, virtual memory, 943-944

WINS, 586, 604-605
  ARP, 605
  checking initial status, 607
  configuring, 606-607
  fixed addresses, adding to servers, 282-283
  hardware requirements, 985
  installing, 606-607

lookup, enabling, 279
Manager, 273
managing, 606-609
migrating clients, 284-285
NetBIOS, enabling name resolution, 272-273, 275
replicating, 610-611
Replication Partners, 372, 610-611
snap-in, 607
testing, 375
troubleshooting, 294, 614
verifying, 285-286
Windows NT upgrades, 359-360

WINS Manager, 273

WINS Resource Record, 279

WINS Server Configuration (Local) dialog, 274

wire speed, 986-987

wizards
  Active Directory Installation, 98, 100105, 163, 206, 231, 359, 364, 378, 388-389
  Active Directory Migration Tool, 32
    Group Migration, 32
    Reporting, 32
    User Migration, 32
  Active Directory Upgrade, 394
  Add Monitored Server, 1011-1014
  Add Printer, 728, 735, 747, 783, 801
  Add Recovery Agent, 503
  Add Standard Port, 729
  ADSI25 Setup, 1263
  Backup, 965
  Certificate Export, 505, 1100
  CheckServer, 869
  Client Connection Manager, 1221
  Client Installation, 861
  COM Application Export, 1166-1168, 1178
  COM Application Install, 1159, 1161-1162
  Computer Account Migration, 399
  Computer Migration, 248, 250-251, 253
  Create New Connection, 1206
  Create Volume, 419, 437
  Delegation of Control, 223-229, 653, 764
  Demand Dial Interface, 1061-1062

WIZARDS

Directory Service Client, 786
Group Account Migration, 237, 399
Group Migration, 237-238, 240-246
Internet Connection, 1131
Microsoft Excel Text Import, 288-291
Network Connection, 1033, 1083-1086
Network Identification, 885
New Dfs Root, 710
New Dfs Root Wizard, 711
New Newsgroup, 1130
New Phonebook Entry, 1051
New Scope, 379, 591-592
New Session, 538
New Zone, 167, 257, 1118
psuedo, 1041
QuickStart, CD29
Remote Installation Preparation, 882-883, 886
Remote Installation Services Setup, 866-868
Report, 246-247
Reporting, 399
Retry Task, 253
Routing and Remote Access Server Setup, 1031, 1060, 1080
Routing and Remote Access Setup, 602
Scheduled Synchronization, 843-844
Service Account Migration, 253-254, 399
TCP/IP Port Wizard, 724
Text Import, 288
Trust Migration, 238
Update Device Driver, 318
Windows 2000 Components, 361-362
Windows Components, 508, 559, 802, 1108, 1202
Windows Media Load Simulator, CD79
Write Signature and Upgrade Disk, 438

WLBS (Windows NT Load Balancing), 305
wma files, publishing with ODP, CD65
WMT (Windows Media Technology), 54, CD2
Administrator, CD15, CD17
  installing, CD19-CD20
ASF indexer, CD51-CD54
Audio codec, CD46-CD48, CD50
Audio Software Development Kit (WMASDK), CD16
enhancing, CD21
Event Guide, CD16, CD26-CD27
installing, CD15, CD17
Load Simulator, CD16
ODP, CD22
  inverse telecine, CD22
On-Demand Producer, CD16
Pay-Per-View Solution, CD16
performance counters, CD82
publishing points, CD28-CD32
Rights Manager, CD16, CD23-CD25
Server, CD15, CD17
Software Development Kit (WMSDK), CD16
testing scalability, CD78-CD80, CD82
Tools, CD16
  installing, CD20-CD21
Work Queue, 443, 446-447
Workgroup or Computer Domain dialog, 387
workstation-owned printers, 727
configuring, 732-734
workstations
DUN connectivity, 1051-1052
printing, 725-726
remote, installing sample packages, 1166-1168
shared printers, 743-744

Write and Modify permissions, creating third-tier shares, 691-693
Write Signature and Upgrade Disk Wizard, 438
writing
asx files, CD65-CD67
wax files, CD65-CD67

X

X Window, 556-557
Client, 556
display, 556
history, 557
servers, 556
XML (eXtensible Markup Language), 45, 154
IIS, 45

Y-Z

ZAW (Zero Administration Windows), 664-668
Zone File dialog, 1118
zone files (DNS), 80
Zone Name dialog, 392, 1118
Zone Type dialog, 381, 1118
zones
AppleTalk, 794-795
DNS
  child domain, 166, 172
  secondary, 381
  transfers, 80
transferring, 367-372
troubleshooting, 90

Other Related Titles

Special Edition Using Microsoft Windows 2000 Professional
By Bob Cowart and Brian Knittel
ISBN 0-7897-2125-2
$39.99 USA/
$59.95 CAN

Windows 2000 Automated Deployment Guide
By Ted Malone
ISBN 0-7897-1749-2
$39.99 USA/$59.95 CAN
Not yet available

Implementing Remote Access Services with Microsoft Windows 2000
By Marcus Goncalves
ISBN 0-7897-2138-4
$39.99 USA/$59.95 CAN
Not yet available

The Multi-Boot Configuration Handbook
By Roderick Smith
ISBN 0-7897-2283-6
$39.99 USA/$59.95 CAN

The Concise Guide to Windows 2000 Dynamic DNS
By Andy Ruth, et al.
ISBN 0-7897-2335-2
$34.99 USA/$52.95 CAN

Microsoft Windows 2000 Professional Installation and Configuration Handbook
By Jim Boyce
ISBN: 0-7897-2133-3
$39.99 USA/$59.95 CAN

Special Edition Using Microsoft Exchange Server 2000
By Kent Joshi and Software Spectrum
ISBN: 0-7897-2278-X
$49.99 USA/$74.95 CAN

Planning and Deploying Microsoft Exchange Server 2000
By Kent Joshi and Software Spectrum
ISBN: 0-7897-2279-8
$49.99 USA/$74.95 CAN
Not yet available

Microsoft Windows 2000 Registry Handbook
By Jerry Honeycutt
ISBN 0-7897-1674-7
$39.99 USA/
$59.95 CAN

Microsoft Windows 2000 Security Handbook
By Jeff Schmidt, et al.
ISBN 0-7897-1999-1
$39.99 USA/
$59.95 CAN

www.quecorp.com

All prices are subject to change.

CD-ROM Installation

Windows 98/95/NT Installation Instructions

1. Insert the CD-ROM disc into your CD-ROM drive.
2. From the Windows 98/95/NT desktop, double-click the My Computer icon.
3. Double-click the icon representing your CD-ROM drive.
4. Double-click the icon titled START.EXE to run the CD-ROM interface.

> **Note**
>
> If Windows 98/95/NT is installed on your computer and you have the AutoPlay feature enabled, the START.EXE program starts automatically whenever you insert the disc into your CD-ROM drive.

Read This Before Opening the Software

By opening this package, you are agreeing to be bound by the following agreement:

You may not copy or redistribute the entire CD-ROM as a whole. Copying and redistribution of individual software programs on the CD-ROM is governed by terms set by the licensors or individual copyright holders.

The installer and code from the author(s) are copyrighted by the publisher and the author(s).

This software is sold as-is, without warranty of any kind, either expressed or implied, including but not limited to the implied warranties of merchantability and fitness for a particular purpose. Neither the publisher nor its dealers or distributors assumes any liability for any alleged or actual damages arising from the use of this program. (Some states do not allow for the exclusion of implied warranties, so the exclusion may not apply to you.)

NOTE: This CD-ROM uses long and mixed-case filenames requiring the use of a protected-mode CD-ROM driver.